BIG ROAD
EUROPE

Contents

Travel and country information	2
Political map of Europe	3
Route planner map 1:4.5 million	**4–13**
Key to route planner map	4
Road maps 1:750,000 (parts of Scandinavia at 1:1 million and some islands at 1:2 million)	**14–199**
Key to road maps	14
Atlas symbols	15
Scandinavia	16–47
Great Britain and Ireland	48–63
Central and Western Europe	64–129
Eastern Europe	130–199
Index to place names	**200–240**

Scale 1:750,000
or 11.8 miles to 1 inch

14th edition June 2018

A05618

Published by AA Publishing (a trading name of AA Media Limited, whose registered office is Fanum House, Basing View, Basingstoke, Hampshire RG21 4EA, UK. Registered number 06112600).

ISBN: 978 0 7495 7966 1

A CIP catalogue record for this book is available from The British Library.

The contents of this atlas are believed to be correct at the time of the latest revision, it will not contain any subsequent amended, new or temporary information including diversions and traffic control or enforcement systems. The publishers cannot be held responsible or liable for any loss or damage occasioned to any person acting or refraining from action as a result of any use or reliance on material in this atlas, nor for any errors, omissions or changes in such material. This does not affect your statutory rights.

The publishers would welcome information to correct any errors or omissions and to keep this atlas up to date. Please write to the Atlas Editor, AA Publishing, The Automobile Association, Fanum House, Basing View, Basingstoke, Hampshire RG21 4EA, UK.
E-mail: *roadatlasfeedback@theaa.com*

Printed by 1010 Printing International Ltd

		+	SOS		‰				
A	112	112	112	Vignette ✓	0,5‰	✓	✓	✓	120 ÖAMTC
AL	129	127	128	×	0,1‰	×	✓	✓	+355 42 262 263 ACA
AND	110	116	118	×	0,5‰	×	×	✓	+376 80 34 00 Automòbil Club d'Andorra
B	101	112	100	×	0,5‰	×	✓	✓	+32 70 34 47 77 Touring Club Belgium
BG	166	150	160	Vignette ✓	0,5‰	✓	✓	✓	+359 2 911 46 Union of Bulgarian Motorists
BIH	122	124	123	✓	0,3‰	✓	✓	✓	+387 33 12 82 BIHAMK
BY	02	03	01	✓	0,0‰	✓	✓	✓	116 BKA
CH	112/117	112/144	112/118	Vignette ✓	0,5‰	✓	×	✓	0800 140 140 TCS
CY	112	112	112	×	0,5‰	×	✓	✓	22 31 31 31 CAA
Kıbrıs	155	112	199	×	0,0‰	×	×	✓	22 31 31 31 CAA
CZ	112	112	112	Vignette ✓	0,0‰	✓	✓	✓	12 30 ÚAMK
D	110	112	112	×	0,5‰	×	✓	✓	22 22 22 ADAC
DK	112	112	112	×	0,5‰	✓	×	✓	+45 70 13 30 40 FDM
E	112	112	112	×	0,5‰	✓	✓	✓	+34 900 11 22 22 RACE
EST	110/112	112	112	×	0,2‰	✓	✓	✓	1888 EAK
F	112/17	112/17	112/18	✓	0,5‰	×	✓	✓	0800 08 92 22 AIT
FIN	112	112	112	×	0,5‰	✓	✓	✓	0200 80 80 AL
FL	117	144	118	×	0,8‰	×	×	✓	0800 140 140 TCS
FO	112	112	112	×	0,5‰	✓	×	✓	+45 70 13 30 40 FDM
GB	112	112	112	×	0,8‰	×	×	✓	0800 82 82 82 RAC
GBZ	199	199	190	×	0,5‰	✓	×	✓	+34 900 11 22 22 RACE
GR	112/100	112/166	112/199	×	0,5‰	×	×	✓	10 400 ELPHA
H	112/107	112/104	112/105	Vignette ✓	0,0‰	✓	✓	✓	188 MAK
HR	112/192	112/94	112/93	✓	0,5‰	✓	✓	✓	+385 1 1987 HAK
I	112	112	112	✓	0,5‰	✓	✓	✓	803 116 ACI
IRL	112	112	112	×	0,5‰	×	×	✓	1800 66 77 88 AA
IS	112	112	112	×	0,5‰	✓	×	✓	+354 511 21 12 FIB
L	112/113	112	112	×	0,5‰	×	✓	✓	+352 260 00 ACL
LT	112	112	112	×	0,4‰	✓	✓	✓	1888 LAS
LV	112	112	112	×	0,5‰	✓	✓	✓	1888 LAMB
M	112	112	112	×	0,8‰	×	✓	✓	+356 21 24 22 22 RMF
MC	112	112	112	×	0,5‰	×	✓	✓	0800 08 92 22 AIT
MD	902	903	901	×	0,0‰	XI–III	✓	✓	+373 6 91 43 724 ACM
MK	192	194	193	✓	0,5‰	✓	✓	✓	196 AMSM
MNE	112	112	112	×	0,3‰	✓	✓	✓	+382 198 07 AMSCG
N	112	113	110	×	0,2‰	✓	✓	✓	08 505 NAF
NL	112	112	112	Vignette ✓	0,5‰	×	×	✓	+31 88 269 28 88 ANWB
P	112	112	112	✓	0,5‰	✓	✓	✓	707 509 510 ACP
PL	112	112	112	✓	0,2‰	×	×	✓	19637 PZM
RKS	92	94	93	×	0,5‰	✓	×	✓	+385 1 1987 HAK
RO	112	112	112	✓	0,0‰	✓ Fahrzeuge >3,5 t	✓	✓	+40 21 222 22 22 ACR
RSM	112	112	112	×	0,5‰	✓	✓	✓	803 116 ACI
RUS	02	03	01	×	0,0‰	✓	×	✓	8 800 505 08 66 AKAR
S	112	112	112	×	0,2‰	✓	✓	✓	+46 771 91 11 11 M
SK	112	112	112	✓	0,0‰	✓	✓	✓	18 124 SATC
SLO	112	112	112	Vignette ✓	0,5‰	✓	✓	✓	19 87 AMZS
SRB	92	94	93	✓	0,3‰	✓	✓	✓	1987 AMSS
TR	155	112	110	✓	0,5‰	×	×	✓	+90 212 3 47 90 45 TTOK
UA	02	03	01	×	0,0‰	✓	✓	✓	+380 9 76 68 38 30 112UA
V	112	118	115	×	0,5‰	✓	✓	✓	803 116 ACI

CANADA
Devon Island
Ellesmere
North Pole
Baffin Bay
Qaanaaq
Thule
ARCTIC OCEAN
more Laptevyh
o. Komsomolec
o. Oktjabr'skoj Revoljucii
o. Bol'ševik
p-ov Tajmyr
Resp. Saha (Jakutija)
Kalaallit Nunaat Grønland (Dan.)
Disko Ø
Qeqertarsuaq
Godhavn
Greenland Sea
Svalbard (Nor.)
Nordaustlandet
Spitsbergen
Edgeøya
Zemlja Franca-Iosifa
ova Arktičeskogo instituta
Dikson
Noril'sk
Enisej
Barents Sea
Novaja Zemlja
o. Vaigač
p-ov Jamal
Belušja Guba
Bjørnøya (Nor.)
Vorkuta
Salehard
Surgut
Pečorskoe more
o. Kolguev
Jan Mayen (Nor.)
Kirkenes
Murmansk
Resp. Komi
Pečora
Uhta
Ob'
Irtyš
Reykjavík
ÍSLAND
Norwegian Sea
Vesterålen
Lofoten
Arctic Circle
Beloe more
Arhangel'sk
Syktyvkar
Kama
R O S S I J A
EKATERINBURG
ČELJABINSK
Tobol
NORGE
SVERIGE
SUOMI FINLAND
Resp. Karelija
Luleå
Oulu
Gulf of Bothnia
Petrozavodsk
Tórshavn/Thorshavn
Føroyar/ Færøerne (Dan.)
Trondheim
PERM'
Udmurtsk. Resp.
IŽEVSK
Shetland Is.
Lerwick
Orkney Is.
Bergen
Stavanger
OSLO
Uppsala
STOCKHOLM
Tampere
Turku Åbo
Åland
HELSINKI HELSINGFORS
Gulf of Finland
Tallinn
Hiiumaa
Saaremaa
EESTI
S.-PETERBURG
Velikij Novgorod
Rybinskoe vdhr.
JAROSLAVL'
Joškar-Ola
Resp. Marij El
KAZAN'
Resp. Tatarstan
Resp. Baškortostan
UFA
Sergiev Posad
NIŽNIJ NOVGOROD
Čeboksary
Čavaš. resp.
SAMARA
Aktöbe
Ural
Rockall (U.K.)
Hebrides
ATLANTIC OCEAN
Vänern
Vättern
GÖTEBORG
Gotland
LATVIJA
RĪGA
Tver'
MOSKVA
Vladimir
RJAZAN'
Saransk
Mordovsk. Resp.
UL'JANOVSK
PENZA
UNITED KINGDOM
GLASGOW
Belfast
BAILE ÁTHA CLIATH DUBLIN
I. of Man
Liverpool
Leeds
Sheffield
BIRMINGHAM
Corcaigh
Cardiff
LONDON
ÉIRE IRELAND
North Sea
DANMARK
KØBENHAVN
Malmö
Bornholm
Öland
Baltic Sea
Klaipėda
LIETUVA (LITHUANIA)
VILNIUS
Kaliningrad
ROSSIJA
Smolensk
Tula
Orël
VORONEŽ
SARATOV
MINSK
BELARUS'
Gdańsk
Szczecin
Białystok
Brest
Homel'
NEDERLAND
AMSTERDAM
BREMEN
HAMBURG
HANNOVER
BERLIN
POLSKA
POZNAŃ
ŁÓDŹ
WARSZAWA
WROCŁAW
KYJIV
CHARKIV
UKRAJINA
1 = Adygè Respublikèm
2 = Karačaj-Čerkes Respublika
3 = Kèbèrdèi-Balkèr Respublikèm
4 = Cègat Irystony Respublikoe
5 = Galgaj Respublika
6 = Nohčijčo Respublika
7 = Samxreti Oseti
8 = Ačaris Avtonomiuri Resp.
9 = Aresp. Apsny
KAZAKSTAN
Atyrau
Astrahan'
Hal'mg-Tangč
Elista
Volga
Don
English Channel
Channel Is.
Brest
BELG.
BRÜSSEL BRUXELLES
Rotterdam
DEUTSCHLAND
DÜSSELDF.
KÖLN
LËTZEB.
LUX.
Luxembourg
FRANKFURT A.M.
LEIPZIG
DRESDEN
PRAHA
Plzeň
ČESKO
KRAKÓW
L'VIV
Vinnycja
DNIPRO
KRYVYJ RIH
DONEC'K
ZAPORIŽŽJA
Mariupol'
ROSTOV-NA-DONU
Caspian Sea
PARIS
FRANCE
STUTTGART
Strasbourg
MÜNCHEN
WIEN
Brno
SLOVENSKO
Bratislava
BUDAPEST
Debrecen
MOL-CHIŞINĂU
DOVA
ODESA
Azovskoe more
Resp. Krym
KRASNODAR
Maikop
Čerkessk
Nal'čik
Vla
Magas
Groznyj
MAH.
Dagistan Resp.
BAKI
Clermont-Ferrand
Bern
Vaduz
Zürich
LIECHT.
ÖSTERREICH
Salzburg
MAGYARORSZÁG (HUNGARY)
ROMÂNIA
Genève
SCHWEIZ SUISSE
Lyon
Ljubljana
ZAGREB
Timişoara
BUCUREŞTI
Simferopol'
Sevastopol'
Soči
Sokhumi
SAKARTVELO (GEORGIA)
TBILISI
Batumi
Zkhin
AZƏRBAYCAN
Bay of Biscay
A Coruña
Bordeaux
MILANO
TORINO
Venezia
SLOV.
HRVATSKA (CROATIA)
SRBIJA
BEOGRAD
Black Sea
Trabzon
EREVAN
HAYASTAN (ARMENIA)
TABRIZ
Santander
Montpellier
MARSEILLE
GENOVA
MONACO
SAN MARINO
Firenze
BOSNA I HERCE-GOV.
Sarajevo
Split
CRNA GORA (MONTENEGRO)
Podgorica
Prishtinë
KOSOVË
Skopje
SOFIJA
BĂLGARIJA
Plovdiv
Varna
Dunav
ĪRĀN
Porto
PORTUGAL
Valladolid
ZARAGOZA
Andorra la Vella
ANDORRA
Adriatic Sea
Dubrovnik
Tiranë
MAKEDONIJA (F.Y.R.O.M.)
Edirne
İSTANBUL
ANKARA
TÜRKİYE
ESPAÑA
MADRID
LISBOA
R. Tajo
VALÈNCIA
BARCELONA
Corse
Ajaccio
ROMA
CIVITAS VATICANA
CITTÀ DEL VATICANO
ITALIA
NAPOLI
Bari
SHQIPËRIA (ALBANIA)
Thessaloníki
Tuz G.
KONYA
ADANA
AL-MAUSIL
Balears Is.
Menorca
Mallorca
Palma
Eivissa (Ibiza)
Alacant
ELLÁDA (GREECE)
İZMİR
HALAB
AS-SŪRĪYA
BAĠDĀD
SEVILLA
MÁLAGA
Gibraltar (U.K.)
Sardegna
Cagliari
Tyrrhenian Sea
PALERMO
ATHÍNA
Aegean Sea
Kıbrıs
Lefkosia
AL-ʻIRĀQ
MEDITERRANEAN SEA
TANJA
Ceuta (Esp.)
(ORAN) WAHRĀN
Melilla (Esp.)
AL-JAZĀ'IR (ALGIER)
Constantine
Sicilia
Peloponnissos
Ródos
KÝPROS
AL-LUBNĀN (LEBANON)
BAIRŪT
DIMAŠQ
(RABAT) AR-RIBĀṬ
FĀS (FES)
TUNIS
I. di Pantelleria
Valletta
MALTA
Kriti
YISRA'EL ISRĀ'ĪL
Ram Allah
'AMMĀN
Palest. Territ.
YERUSHALAYIM
AL-URDUNN (JORDAN)
AD-DĀR-AL-BAYDA (CASABLANCA)
AL-MAGHRIB (MAROC)
MARRAKUSH
Sousse
TŪNIS (TUNISIE)
Chott El Jerid
TARĀBULUS
BANGHĀZĪ
AL-ISKANDARĪYA (ALEXANDRIA)
AL-ʻARABĪYA AS-SAʻŪDĪYA
AGĀDĪR
AL JAZĀ'IR (ALGÉRIE)
Oued Drâa
AL-QĀHIRA (CAIRO)
AL-MIṢR (EGYPT)
Asyūṭ
Red Sea
In Salah
LĪBĪYĀ
Aswān
MAKKA
ĠIDDA
MAWRĪTĀNIYA
1 : 20,000,000
0 200 400 km
0 200 miles
Taoudenni
MALI
Tamanrasset
NIGER
TCHAD
Buhairat Nasir
Bûr Sûdân (Port Sudan)
AS-SŪDĀN

1 : 4,500,000

Key map Blattübersicht Carte d'assemblage Oversigtskort

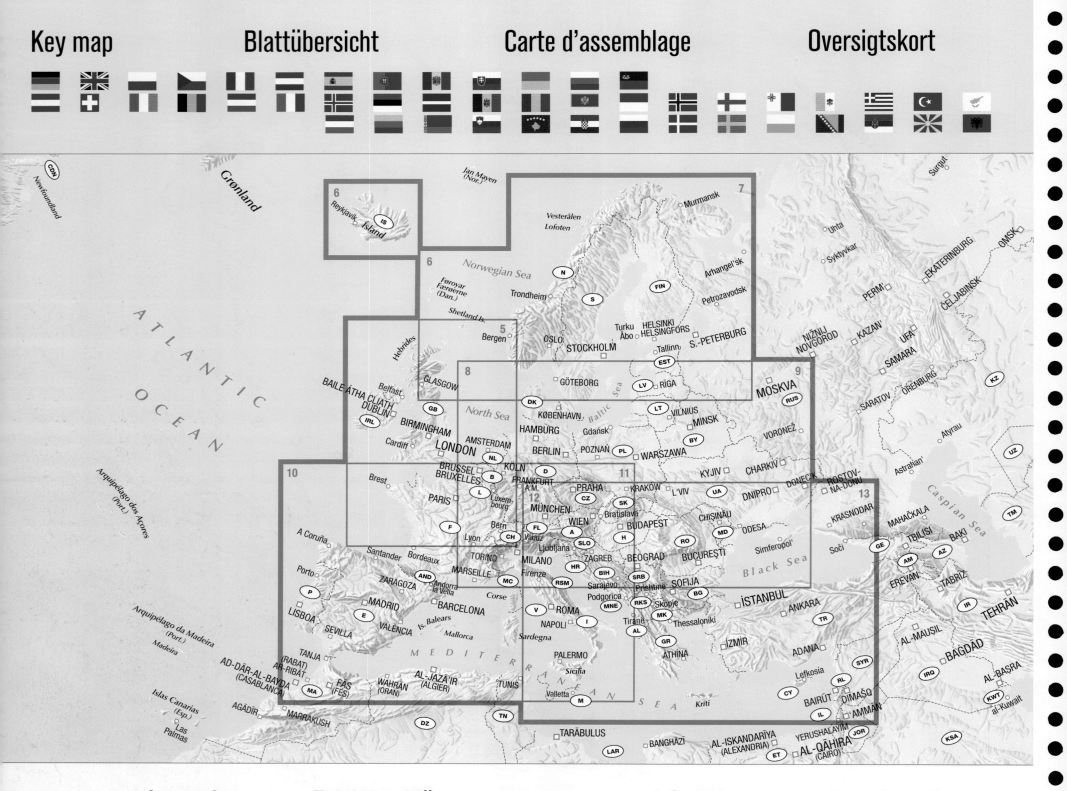

Legend   Zeichenerklärung   Légende   Tegnforklaring

	GB		D		F		DK
Motorway with junction		Autobahn mit Anschlussstelle		Autoroute avec point de jonction		Motorvej med tilkørsel	
Dual carriageway with motorway characteristics with junction		Autobahnähnliche Schnellstraße mit Anschlussstelle		Chaussée double de type autoroutier avec point de jonction		Motortrafikvej med to vejbaner med tilkørsel	
Trunk road		Fernverkehrsstraße		Route à grande circulation		Fjerntrafikvej	
Thoroughfare		Durchgangsstraße		Route de transit		Gennemfartsvej	
Main road		Hauptstraße		Route principale		Huvudled	
Connecting road		Verbindungsstraße		Route de communication		Förbindelseled	
European road number	E20	Europastraßennummer		Numéro de route européenne	E20	Europavejnummer	
Car ferry		Autofähre		Bac pour automobiles		Bilfærge	
Shipping route		Schifffahrtslinie		Ligne de navigation		Skibsrute	
Airport	✈	Verkehrsflughafen		Aéroport	✈	Lufthavn	
Capital	**BERLIN**	Hauptstadt		Capitale	**BERLIN**	Hovedstad	
National boundary		Staatsgrenze		Frontière d'Etat		Statsgrænse	
Disputed national boundary		Umstrittene Staatsgrenze		Frontière d'Etat contestée		Kontroversiel statsgrænse	
Check-point	⊖	Grenzkontrollstelle		Point de contrôle	⊖	Grænsekontrol	

1 : 4,500,000

0 50 100 150 km
0 50 100 miles

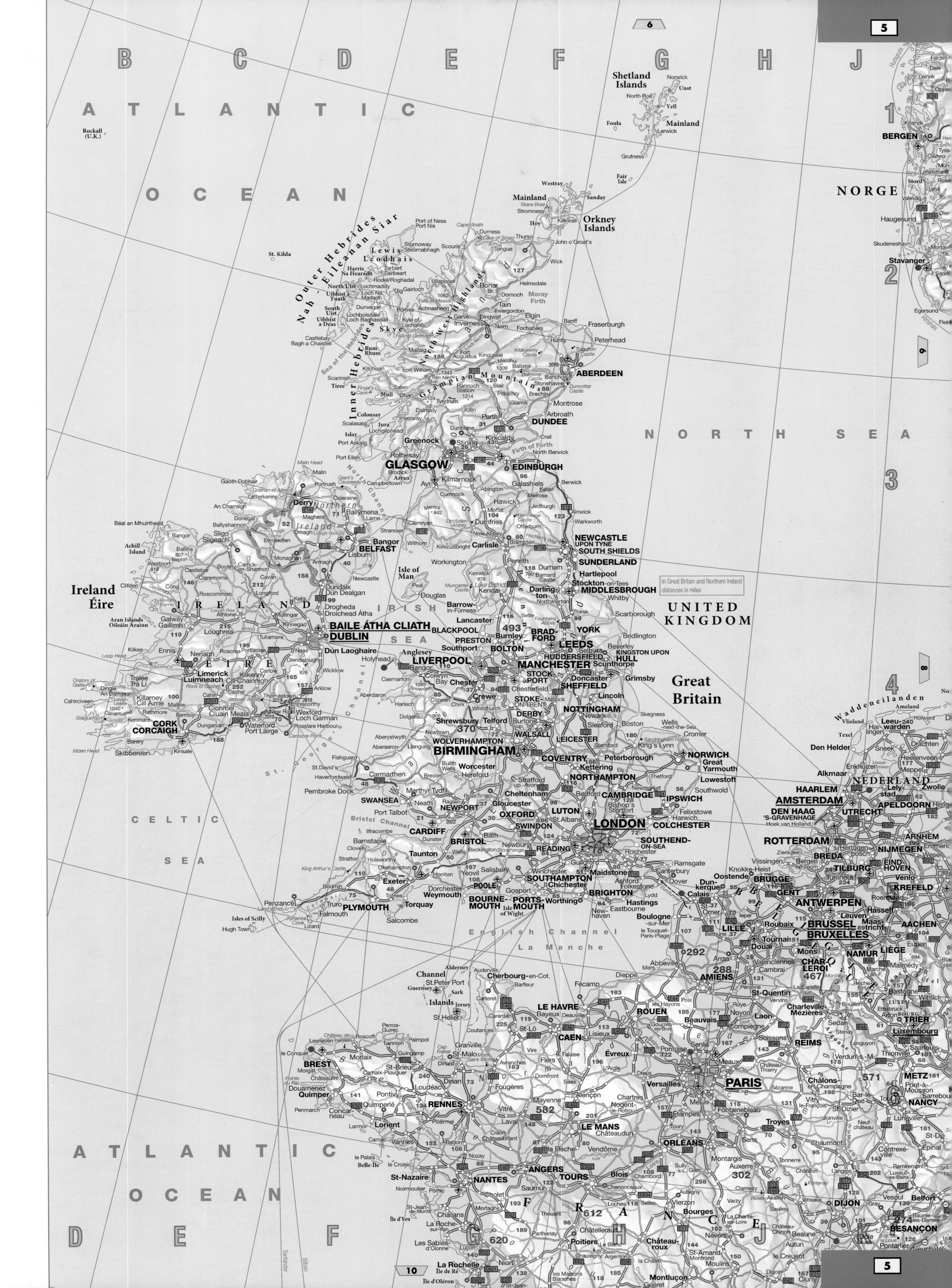
6
B C D E F G H J
ATLANTIC OCEAN
Rockall (U.K.)
Shetland Islands
Mainland
Lerwick
Fair Isle
Orkney Islands
NORGE
BERGEN
Stavanger
Haugesund
Outer Hebrides
Nah-Eileanan Siar
Lewis
Leodhais
St. Kilda
Stornoway
Harris
Skye
Inner Hebrides
North West Highlands
Grampian Mountains
Moray Firth
Inverness
Fraserburgh
Peterhead
ABERDEEN
Montrose
Arbroath
DUNDEE
Perth
Fort William
Oban
NORTH SEA
Stirling
Greenock
GLASGOW
EDINBURGH
Firth of Forth
Berwick
Ayr
Kilmarnock
Galashiels
Hawick
Dumfries
Carlisle
NEWCASTLE UPON TYNE
SOUTH SHIELDS
SUNDERLAND
Hartlepool
Stockton-on-Tees
MIDDLESBROUGH
Whitby
Scarborough
Darlington
Durham
In Great Britain and Northern Ireland distances in miles
UNITED KINGDOM
Great Britain
Northern Ireland
Derry
Coleraine
Ballymena
Larne
Omagh
Enniskillen
Bangor
BELFAST
Lisburn
Newry
Isle of Man
Douglas
Ireland Éire
IRELAND
ÉIRE
Sligo
Sligeach
Galway
Gaillimh
Athlone
Dundalk
Dún Dealgan
Drogheda
Droichead Átha
BAILE ÁTHA CLIATH
DUBLIN
Dún Laoghaire
Wicklow
Arklow
Limerick
Luimneach
Tralee
Trá Lí
Killarney
Cill Airne
Clonmel
Cluain Meala
Waterford
Port Láirge
Wexford
Loch Garman
Rosslare Harbour
CORK
CORCAIGH
Kinsale
IRISH SEA
Anglesey
Holyhead
Bangor
Caernarfon
LIVERPOOL
Chester
Crewe
Lancaster
BLACKPOOL
PRESTON
Southport
Barrow-in-Furness
Kendal
YORK
BRADFORD
LEEDS
HUDDERSFIELD
MANCHESTER
BOLTON
STOCKPORT
Beverley
KINGSTON UPON HULL
Scunthorpe
Grimsby
Doncaster
SHEFFIELD
Chesterfield
Lincoln
STOKE-ON-TRENT
DERBY
NOTTINGHAM
Newark
Skegness
Boston
King's Lynn
Cromer
NORWICH
Great Yarmouth
Lowestoft
Shrewsbury
Telford
WALSALL
WOLVERHAMPTON
BIRMINGHAM
LEICESTER
COVENTRY
Peterborough
Kettering
NORTHAMPTON
CAMBRIDGE
IPSWICH
Felixstowe
Harwich
COLCHESTER
Aberystwyth
Worcester
Hereford
Stratford-upon-Avon
Cheltenham
Gloucester
Bedford
LUTON
St. Albans
OXFORD
SWINDON
LONDON
SOUTHEND-ON-SEA
Carmarthen
Haverfordwest
Pembroke Dock
SWANSEA
NEWPORT
CARDIFF
BRISTOL
Bath
READING
Rochester
Ramsgate
Canterbury
Maidstone
Dover
Folkestone
Guildford
Salisbury
Winchester
SOUTHAMPTON
Chichester
BRIGHTON
Hastings
Eastbourne
Newhaven
Taunton
Barnstaple
Exeter
Torquay
PLYMOUTH
Truro
Falmouth
Penzance
Isles of Scilly
Bodmin
Yeovil
Dorchester
Weymouth
POOLE
BOURNEMOUTH
PORTSMOUTH
Isle of Wight
CELTIC SEA
Bristol Channel
English Channel
La Manche
Channel Islands
Guernsey
St. Peter Port
Jersey
St. Helier
Cherbourg-en-Cot.
LE HAVRE
CAEN
Rouen
ROUEN
Dieppe
Fécamp
Évreux
Beauvais
AMIENS
Abbeville
Boulogne-sur-Mer
Calais
Dunkerque
LILLE
Arras
St-Quentin
BREST
Quimper
Morlaix
St-Brieuc
St-Malo
Dinan
RENNES
Lorient
Vannes
St-Nazaire
NANTES
ANGERS
LE MANS
Alençon
Chartres
Versailles
PARIS
Meaux
Reims
Soissons
Compiègne
Laon
Charleville-Mézières
METZ
NANCY
TOURS
Blois
ORLÉANS
Vendôme
Châteaudun
Poitiers
La Rochelle
Niort
Châtellerault
Bourges
Vierzon
Nevers
Auxerre
Troyes
DIJON
Besançon
BESANÇON
Belfort
Montluçon
FRANCE
Les Sables-d'Olonne
La Roche-sur-Yon
Cholet
Saumur
Île de Ré
Île d'Oléron
Belle-Île
ATLANTIC OCEAN
D E F G H J K
10
NEDERLAND
Waddeneilanden
Den Helder
Alkmaar
HAARLEM
AMSTERDAM
DEN HAAG
'S-GRAVENHAGE
Hoek van Holland
UTRECHT
APELDOORN
ROTTERDAM
ARNHEM
NIJMEGEN
BREDA
TILBURG
EINDHOVEN
Vlissingen
BELGIQUE
BRUGGE
Oostende
GENT
ANTWERPEN
BRUSSEL
BRUXELLES
Leuven
LIÈGE
NAMUR
Mons
CHARLEROI
Tournai
AACHEN
KREFELD
Luxembourg
TRIER
1 2 3 4 5 6
9
8

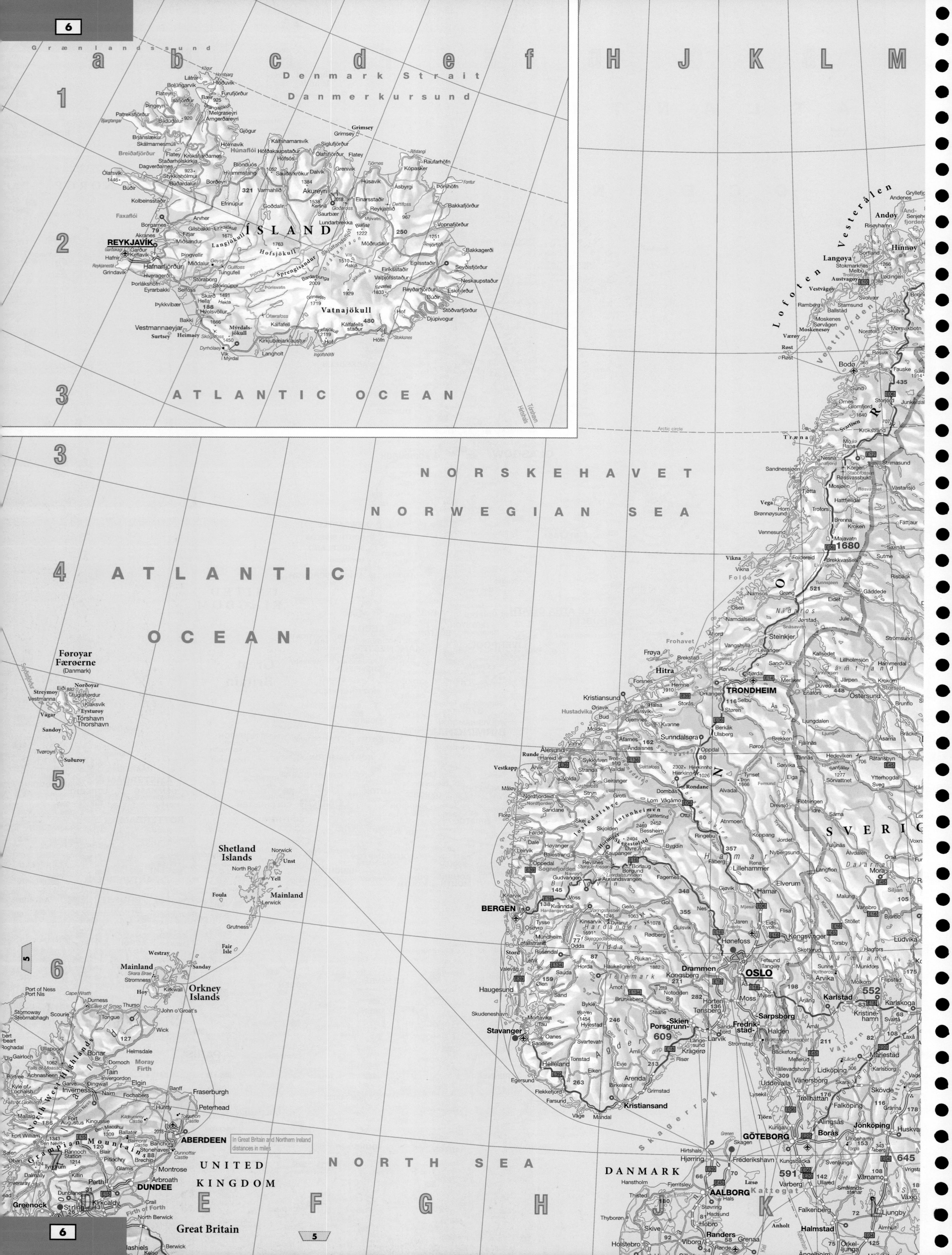
a b c d e f H J K L M
1 2 3 4 5 6 7
E F G H J K
Grænlandssund
Denmark Strait
Danmerkursund
ÍSLAND
REYKJAVÍK
Akureyri
Vatnajökull
Langjökull
Hofsjökull
Mýrdalsjökull
Grímsey
Vestmannaeyjar
ATLANTIC OCEAN
NORSKEHAVET
NORWEGIAN SEA
ATLANTIC
OCEAN
Føroyar
Færøerne
(Danmark)
Tórshavn
Thorshavn
Shetland Islands
Mainland
Lerwick
Orkney Islands
Fair Isle
Lofoten
Vesterålen
Andøy
Hinnøy
Langøya
Bodø
Arctic circle
TRONDHEIM
Kristiansund
Ålesund
Runde
Vestkapp
Jotunheimen
Hardangervidda
Sognefjorden
BERGEN
Haugesund
Stavanger
Kristiansand
Arendal
Skien
Porsgrunn
Drammen
OSLO
Lillehammer
Hamar
Fredrikstad
Sarpsborg
Skagerrak
SVERIGE
Karlstad
GÖTEBORG
Borås
Jönköping
DANMARK
AALBORG
Frederikshavn
Hirtshals
Hjørring
Kattegat
Halmstad
Randers
NORTH SEA
UNITED KINGDOM
Great Britain
ABERDEEN
DUNDEE
Inverness
Perth
Moray Firth
Grampian Mountains
North West Highlands
Firth of Forth
In Great Britain and Northern Ireland distances in miles

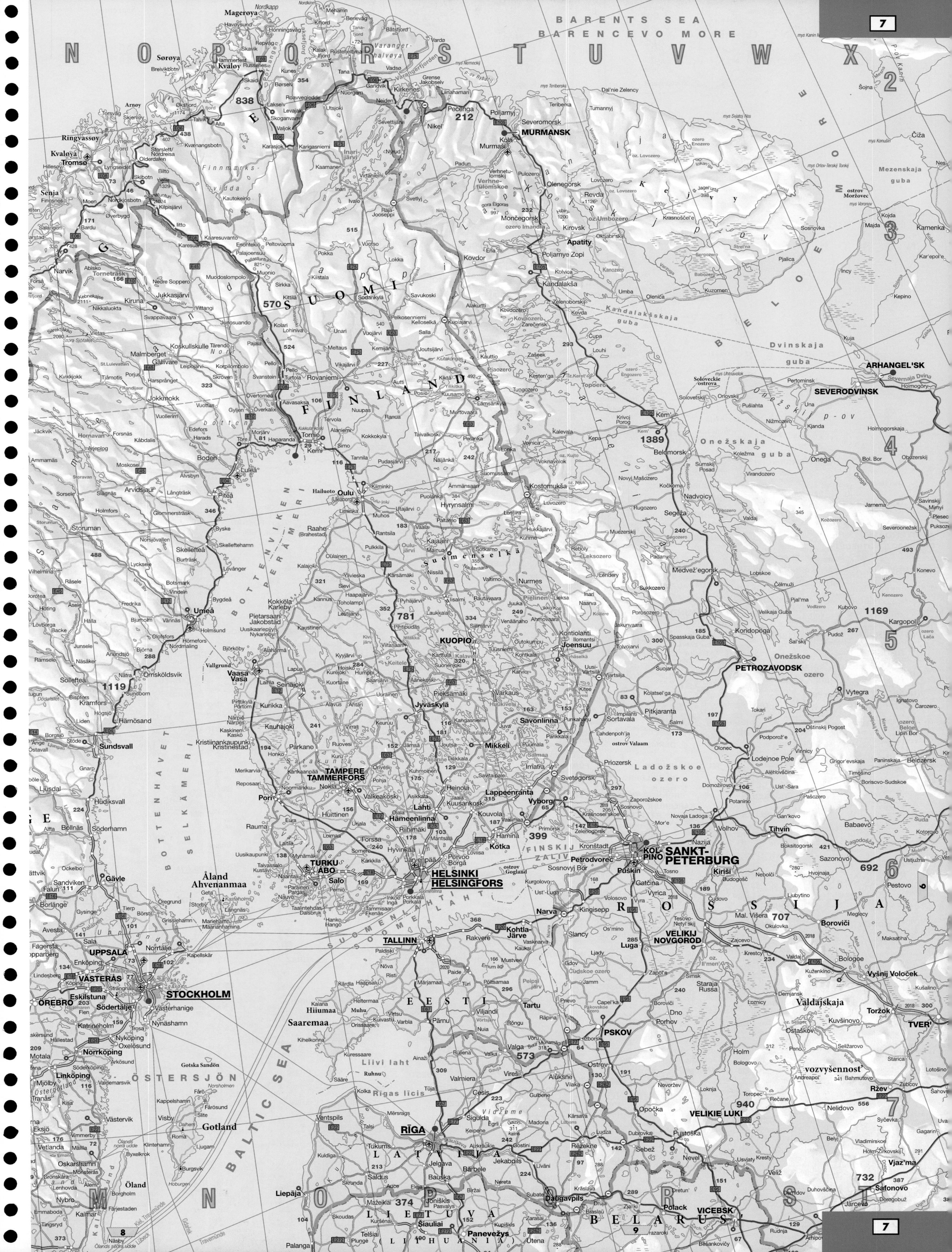
7
BARENTS SEA
BARENCEVO MORE
N O P Q R S T U V W X
2
3
4
5
6
7
Nordkapp
Magerøya
Sørøya
Hammerfest
Kvaløy
Varanger-halvøya
Vardø
Vadsø
Kirkenes
Nikel'
Pečenga
Poljarnyj
Severomorsk
MURMANSK
Kola
Murmaši
Teriberka
Dal'nie Zelency
Ringvassøy
Kvaløya
Tromsø
Senja
Finnsnes
Bardu
Narvik
Alta
Karasjok
Kautokeino
Finnmarksvidda
Inarijärvi
Ivalo
Kilpisjärvi
Kiruna
Gällivare
Jokkmokk
Boden
Luleå
Piteå
Skellefteå
Umeå
Örnsköldsvik
Härnösand
Sundsvall
Hudiksvall
Söderhamn
Gävle
Falun
Uppsala
Västerås
STOCKHOLM
Örebro
Eskilstuna
Södertälje
Nyköping
Norrköping
Linköping
Västervik
Visby
Gotland
Öland
Kalmar
Åland
Ahvenanmaa
Mariehamn
ÖSTERSJÖN
BALTIC SEA
BOTTENHAVET
SELKÄMERI
BOTTENVIKEN
PERÄMERI
SUOMI
FINLAND
Rovaniemi
Kemijärvi
Sodankylä
Tornio
Kemi
Haparanda
Oulu
Hailuoto
Raahe
Kajaani
Kuusamo
Kokkola
Karleby
Pietarsaari
Jakobstad
Vaasa
Seinäjoki
Kuopio
Joensuu
Jyväskylä
Mikkeli
Savonlinna
Pori
Rauma
Tampere
Tammerfors
Lahti
Hämeenlinna
Turku
Åbo
Salo
Helsinki
Helsingfors
Porvoo
Kotka
Hamina
Lappeenranta
Imatra
Vyborg
Kandalakša
Apatity
Kirovsk
Olenegorsk
Mončegorsk
Kovdor
Kem'
Belomorsk
Kostomukša
Segeža
Medvež'egorsk
Kondopoga
PETROZAVODSK
Onežskoe ozero
Ladožskoe ozero
Sortavala
Priozersk
SANKT-PETERBURG
Kolpino
Puškin
Petrodvorec
Kronštadt
Gatčina
Kiriši
Tihvin
Volhov
Lodejnoe Pole
Vytegra
Kargopol'
Pudož
Belozersk
ARHANGEL'SK
SEVERODVINSK
Onega
Onežskaja guba
Dvinskaja guba
Kandalakšskaja guba
BELOE MORE
Kol'skij poluostrov
Mezenskaja guba
Solovetskie ostrova
FINSKIJ ZALIV
SUOMENLAHTI
TALLINN
Kohtla-Järve
Narva
Rakvere
Paldiski
Hiiumaa
Saaremaa
Pärnu
Viljandi
Tartu
Valga
EESTI
Liivi laht
Rigas licis
RĪGA
Jelgava
Ventspils
Liepāja
Tukums
Sigulda
Valmiera
Cēsis
Daugavpils
Rēzekne
LATVIJA
LIETUVA
Šiauliai
Panevėžys
Palanga
BELARUS
Polack
VICEBSK
ROSSIJA
Kingisepp
Slancy
Luga
VELIKIJ NOVGOROD
Pskov
Ostrov
Opočka
Porhov
Dno
Staraja Russa
VELIKIE LUKI
Nevel'
Borovici
Valdaj
Valdajskaja vozvyšennost'
Vyšnij Voloček
Toržok
TVER'
Ržev
Nelidovo
Vjaz'ma
Safonovo
Jarcevo
8
9
7

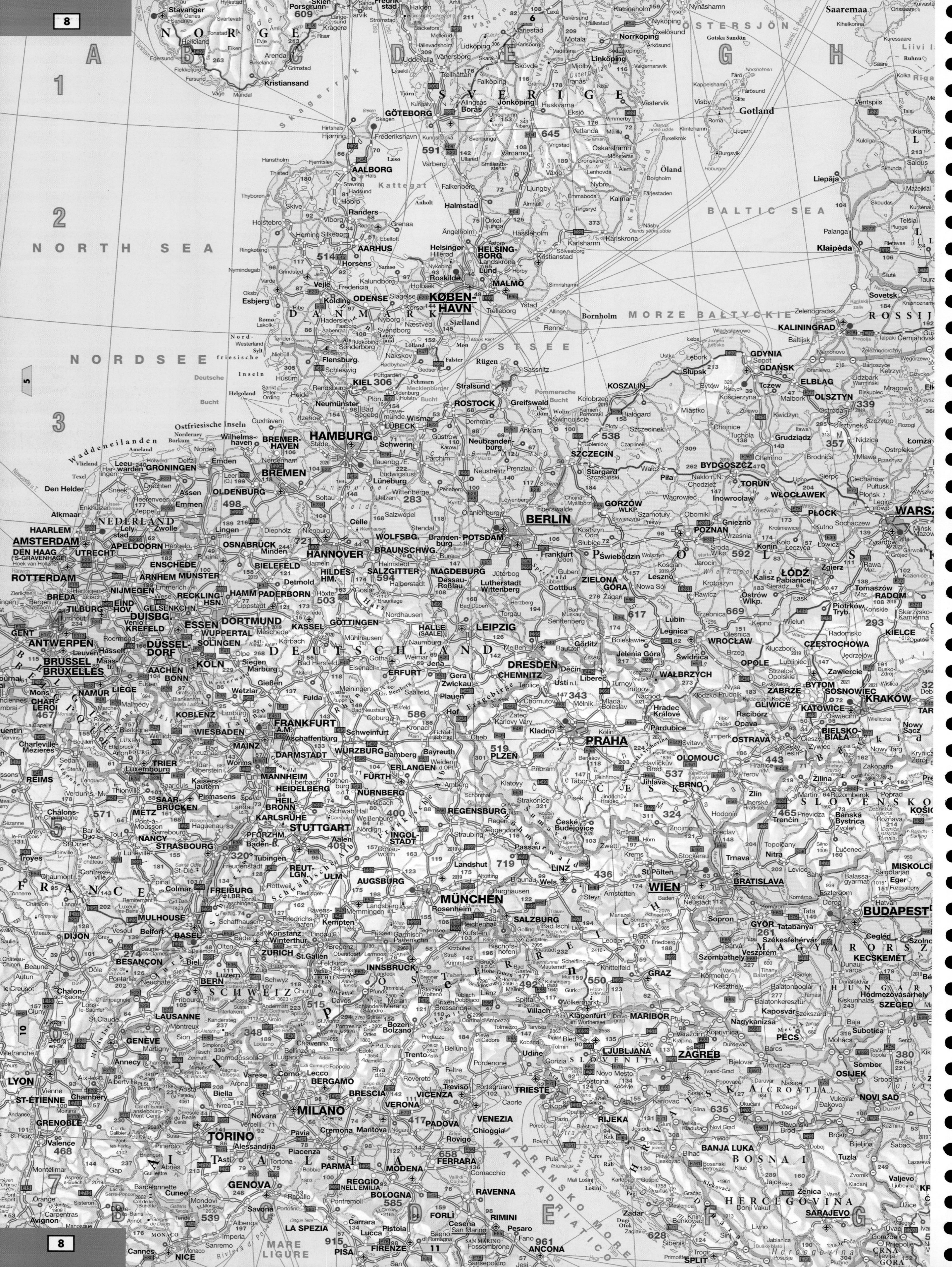
NORGE
SVERIGE
NORTH SEA
NORDSEE
BALTIC SEA
ÖSTERSJÖN
MORZE BAŁTYCKIE
OSTSEE
DANMARK
NEDERLAND
DEUTSCHLAND
POLSKA
ČESKO
SLOVENSKO
MAGYARORSZÁG
SCHWEIZ
ITALIA
FRANCE
SLOVENIJA
HRVATSKA (CROATIA)
BOSNA I HERCEGOVINA
ROSSIJA
JADRANSKO MORE
MARE ADRIATICO
MARE LIGURE
Skagerrak
Kattegat
Gotland
Öland
Bornholm
Rügen
Saaremaa
Stavanger
Kristiansand
GÖTEBORG
Jönköping
Linköping
Norrköping
Nyköping
Aalborg
AARHUS
KØBENHAVN
MALMÖ
HELSINGBORG
ODENSE
Esbjerg
KIEL
HAMBURG
BREMEN
HANNOVER
BERLIN
POTSDAM
ROSTOCK
SZCZECIN
GDAŃSK
GDYNIA
KALININGRAD
Klaipėda
Liepāja
POZNAŃ
BYDGOSZCZ
TORUŃ
ŁÓDŹ
WARSZ
WROCŁAW
KATOWICE
KRAKÓW
AMSTERDAM
ROTTERDAM
DEN HAAG ('S-GRAVENHAGE)
UTRECHT
GRONINGEN
ANTWERPEN
BRUSSEL BRUXELLES
LIÈGE
NAMUR
KÖLN
DÜSSELDORF
ESSEN
DORTMUND
DUISBG.
BONN
AACHEN
MÜNSTER
OSNABRÜCK
BIELEFELD
KASSEL
GÖTTINGEN
MAGDEBURG
LEIPZIG
HALLE (SAALE)
DRESDEN
CHEMNITZ
ERFURT
FRANKFURT
WIESBADEN
MAINZ
KOBLENZ
DARMSTADT
MANNHEIM
HEIDELBERG
KARLSRUHE
STUTTGART
NÜRNBERG
WÜRZBURG
ERLANGEN
REGENSBURG
AUGSBURG
MÜNCHEN
ULM
FREIBURG
SAARBRÜCKEN
LUXEMBOURG
METZ
NANCY
STRASBOURG
REIMS
MULHOUSE
BASEL
ZÜRICH
BERN
LUZERN
LAUSANNE
GENÈVE
BESANÇON
DIJON
LYON
GRENOBLE
ST-ÉTIENNE
TORINO
MILANO
GENOVA
BERGAMO
BRESCIA
VERONA
VICENZA
PADOVA
VENEZIA
TRIESTE
BOLOGNA
MODENA
PARMA
FERRARA
RAVENNA
RIMINI
FIRENZE
PISA
LA SPEZIA
ANCONA
NICE
INNSBRUCK
SALZBURG
LINZ
WIEN
GRAZ
KLAGENFURT
BRATISLAVA
PRAHA
PLZEŇ
BRNO
OSTRAVA
OLOMOUC
BUDAPEST
GYŐR
SZEGED
KECSKEMÉT
PÉCS
LJUBLJANA
MARIBOR
ZAGREB
RIJEKA
SPLIT
OSIJEK
NOVI SAD
BANJA LUKA
SARAJEVO
MISKOLC
KOŠICE
ŽILINA

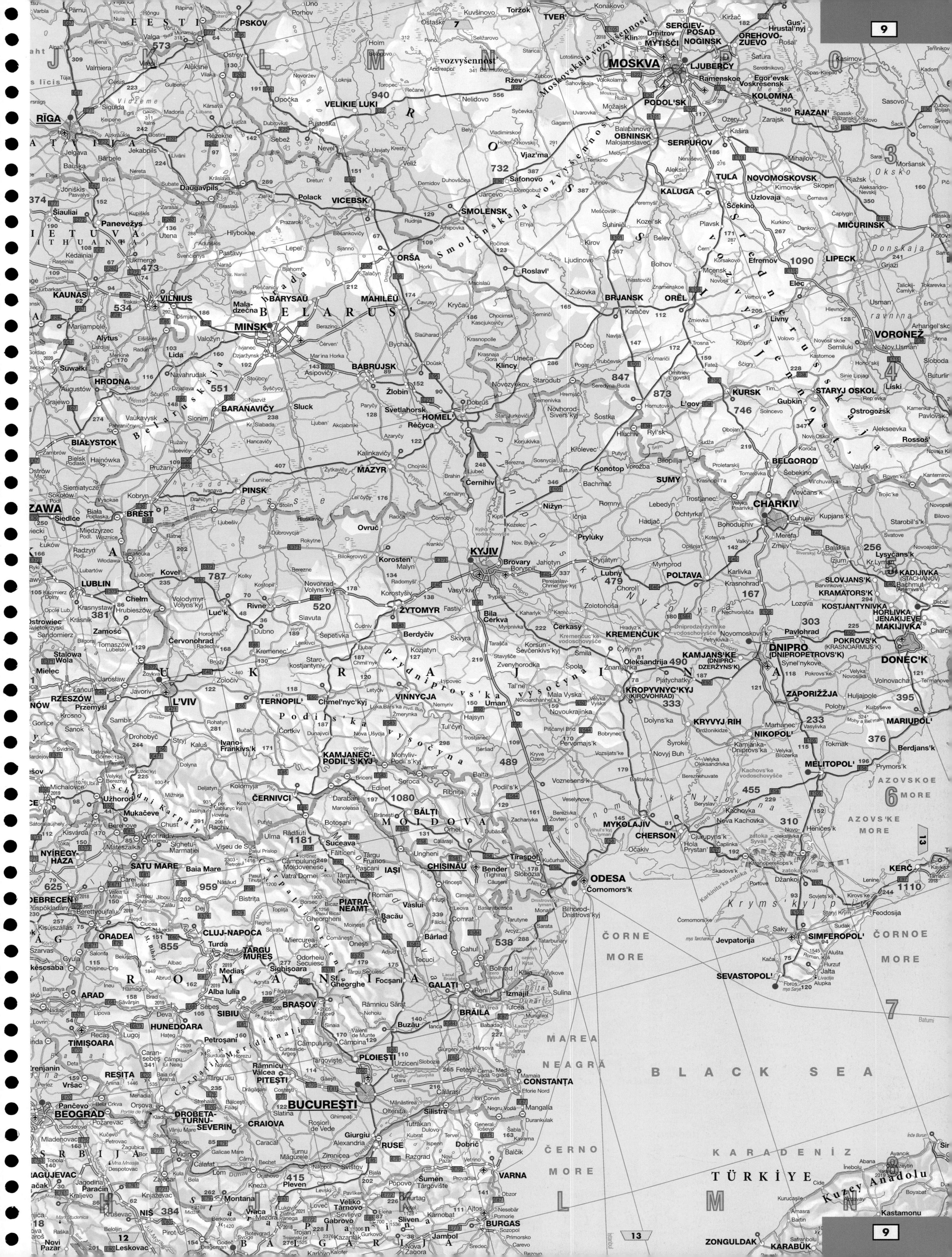

9
EESTI
PSKOV
TVER'
SERGIEV-POSAD
NOGINSK
MYTIŠČI
OREHOVO-ZUEVO
MOSKVA
LJUBERCY
PODOL'SK
KOLOMNA
RJAZAN'
RĪGA
VELIKIE LUKI
OBNINSK
SERPUHOV
TULA
NOVOMOSKOVSK
KALUGA
Vjaz'ma
Safonovo
SMOLENSK
VICEBSK
Polack
Daugavpils
Panevėžys
Šiauliai
KAUNAS
VILNIUS
ORŠA
MAHILËU
BARYSAŬ
MINSK
BELARUS'
BRJANSK
ORËL
MIČURINSK
LIPECK
VORONEŽ
KURSK
STARYJ OSKOL
BELGOROD
HRODNA
Suwałki
BABRUJSK
Žlobin
HOMEL'
Rečyca
Svetlahorsk
BARANAVIČY
Sluck
Pinsk
BIAŁYSTOK
MAZYR
Černihiv
Konotop
SUMY
CHARKIV
BREST
Ovruč
KYJIV
Brovary
Pryluky
POLTAVA
Lubny
LUBLIN
Kovel'
Luc'k
Rivne
ŽYTOMYR
Bila Cerkva
Čerkasy
KREMENČUK
DNIPRO
KAMJANS'KE
DONEC'K
L'VIV
TERNOPIL'
Chmel'nyc'kyj
VINNYCJA
Uman
KROPYVNYC'KYJ
KRYVYJ RIH
ZAPORIŽŽJA
MARIUPOL'
NIKOPOL'
MELITOPOL'
Berdjans'k
RZESZÓW
Przemyśl
Ivano-Frankivs'k
KAMJANEC'-PODIL'S'KYJ
ČERNIVCI
BĂLŢI
MOLDOVA
CHIŞINĂU
Tiraspol
ODESA
Čornomors'k
MYKOLAJIV
CHERSON
Nova Kachovka
AZOVSKOE MORE
AZOVS'KE MORE
KERČ
SIMFEROPOL'
Jevpatorija
SEVASTOPOL'
Feodosija
Jalta
ČORNE MORE
ČORNOE MORE
NYÍREGYHÁZA
SATU MARE
Baia Mare
Suceava
IAŞI
DEBRECEN
ORADEA
CLUJ-NAPOCA
TÂRGU MUREŞ
PIATRA NEAMŢ
Bacău
ARAD
TIMIŞOARA
SIBIU
BRAŞOV
GALAŢI
BRĂILA
Izmajil
Tulcea
HUNEDOARA
RESIŢA
PLOIEŞTI
PITEŞTI
Râmnicu Vâlcea
BUCUREŞTI
CONSTANŢA
MAREA NEAGRĂ
BLACK SEA
BEOGRAD
DROBETA-TURNU-SEVERIN
CRAIOVA
RUSE
Silistra
Dobrič
VARNA
Pleven
Veliko Tărnovo
Šumen
BURGAS
NIŠ
Montana
Vraca
Gabrovo
Jambol
ČERNO MORE
KARADENİZ
TÜRKİYE
Kuzey Anadolu
ZONGULDAK
KARABÜK
Kastamonu
12
13
7
9

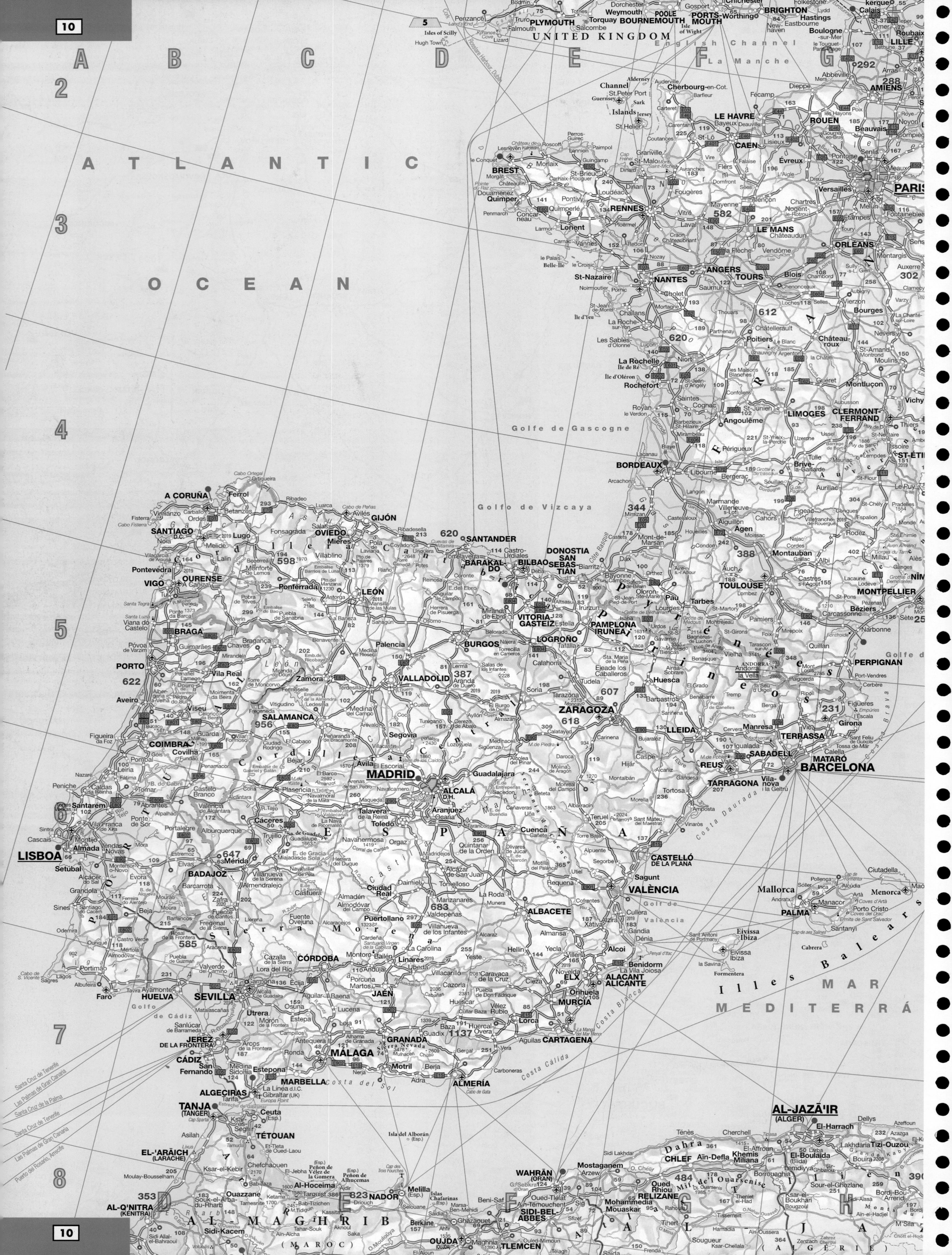

A B C D E F G
2
3
4
5
6
7
8
ATLANTIC
OCEAN
UNITED KINGDOM
English Channel
La Manche
Golfe de Gascogne
Golfo de Vizcaya
Golfo de Valencia
Costa Brava
Costa Daurada
Costa Blanca
Costa Cálida
Costa del Sol
Golfo de Cádiz
Illes Balears
MAR MEDITERRÁ
PLYMOUTH
BOURNEMOUTH
POOLE
PORTSMOUTH
BRIGHTON
Channel Islands
Cherbourg-en-Cot.
LE HAVRE
ROUEN
CAEN
AMIENS
LILLE
PARIS
BREST
Quimper
RENNES
LE MANS
ORLÉANS
NANTES
ANGERS
TOURS
Poitiers
La Rochelle
Rochefort
LIMOGES
CLERMONT-FERRAND
BORDEAUX
TOULOUSE
MONTPELLIER
PERPIGNAN
A CORUÑA
SANTIAGO
OVIEDO
GIJÓN
SANTANDER
BILBAO
DONOSTIA SAN SEBASTIÁN
VIGO
OURENSE
LEÓN
BURGOS
VITORIA GASTEIZ
PAMPLONA IRUÑEA
LOGROÑO
PORTO
BRAGA
VALLADOLID
ZARAGOZA
LLEIDA
SALAMANCA
COIMBRA
MADRID
ALCALÁ
BARCELONA
TARRAGONA
TERRASSA
SABADELL
Andorra la Vella
LISBOA
BADAJOZ
Mérida
CASTELLÓ DE LA PLANA
VALÈNCIA
ALBACETE
CÓRDOBA
SEVILLA
HUELVA
JAÉN
GRANADA
MÁLAGA
MURCIA
ALACANT ALICANTE
CARTAGENA
ALMERÍA
JEREZ DE LA FRONTERA
CÁDIZ
ALGECIRAS
MARBELLA
Gibraltar (UK)
Mallorca
PALMA
Menorca
Eivissa Ibiza
TANJA (TANGER)
Ceuta (Esp.)
TÉTOUAN
Melilla (Esp.)
NADOR
OUJDA
WAHRĀN (ORAN)
AL-JAZĀ'IR (ALGER)
AL-Q'NITRA (KENITRA)
AL-MAGHRIB (MAROC)
TLEMCEN
SIDI-BEL-ABBES
CHLEF

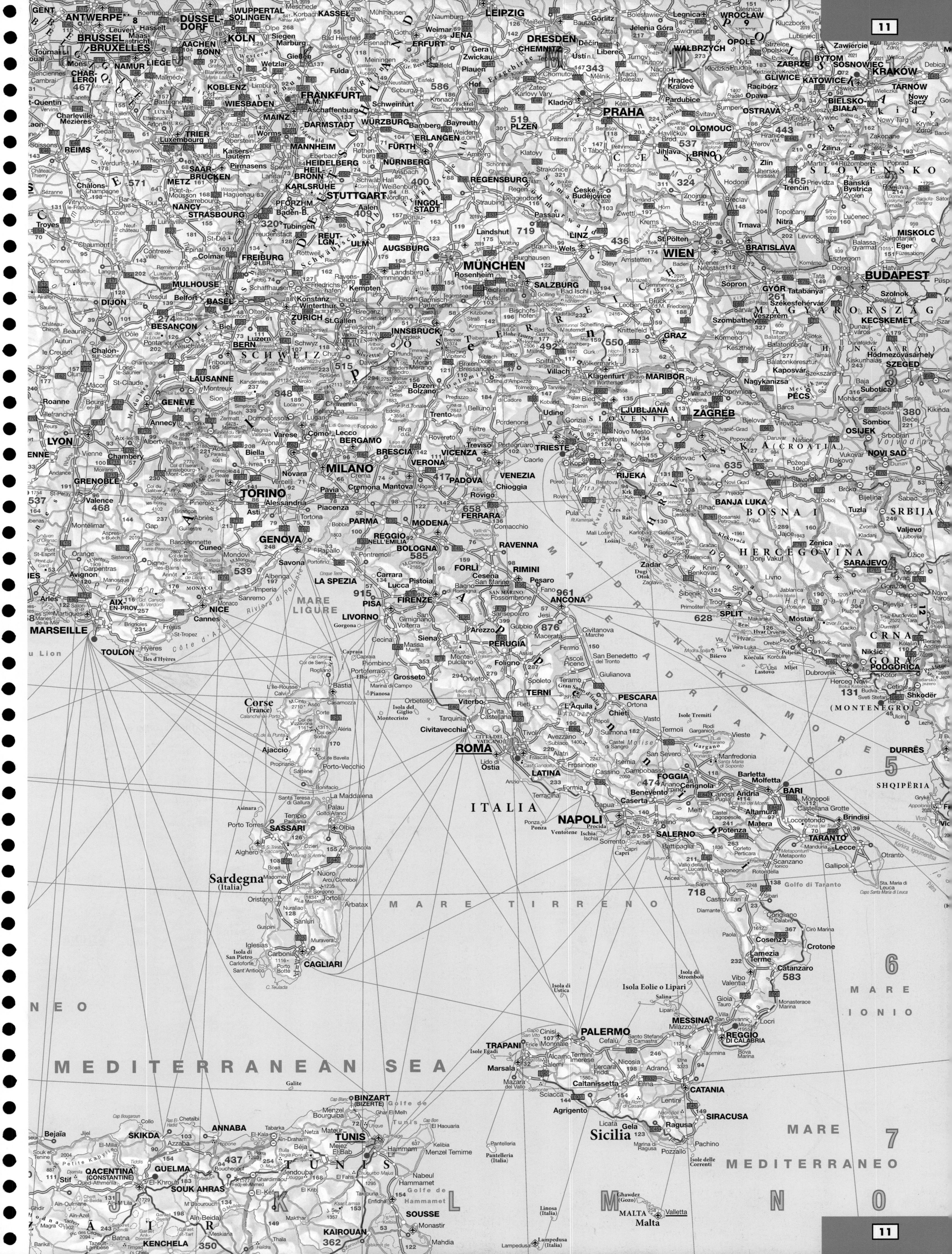
ANTWERPEN
BRUSSEL
BRUXELLES
DÜSSELDORF
KÖLN
WUPPERTAL
SOLINGEN
KASSEL
LEIPZIG
DRESDEN
CHEMNITZ
WROCŁAW
OPOLE
WAŁBRZYCH
KATOWICE
KRAKÓW
BYTOM
SOSNOWIEC
ZABRZE
GLIWICE
TARNÓW
AACHEN
BONN
LIÈGE
NAMUR
CHARLEROI
KOBLENZ
FRANKFURT A.M.
WIESBADEN
MAINZ
DARMSTADT
WÜRZBURG
ERFURT
JENA
PRAHA
PLZEŇ
OLOMOUC
OSTRAVA
BRNO
BIELSKO-BIAŁA
TRIER
LUXEMBOURG
REIMS
MANNHEIM
HEIDELBERG
HEILBRONN
KARLSRUHE
STUTTGART
NÜRNBERG
FÜRTH
ERLANGEN
REGENSBURG
INGOLSTADT
SAARBRÜCKEN
METZ
NANCY
STRASBOURG
AUGSBURG
MÜNCHEN
ULM
REUTLINGEN
LINZ
WIEN
BRATISLAVA
BUDAPEST
MISKOLC
SALZBURG
GRAZ
GYŐR
KECSKEMÉT
SZEGED
PÉCS
MULHOUSE
BASEL
FREIBURG
ZÜRICH
DIJON
BESANÇON
BERN
LAUSANNE
GENÈVE
INNSBRUCK
BOLZANO
MARIBOR
ZAGREB
LJUBLJANA
TRIESTE
LYON
GRENOBLE
TORINO
MILANO
BERGAMO
BRESCIA
VERONA
VICENZA
PADOVA
VENEZIA
GENOVA
PARMA
MODENA
BOLOGNA
FERRARA
RAVENNA
RIMINI
FIRENZE
PISA
LIVORNO
ANCONA
PERUGIA
PESCARA
ROMA
LATINA
NAPOLI
SALERNO
FOGGIA
BARI
TARANTO
BRINDISI
LECCE
MARSEILLE
TOULON
NICE
CANNES
AIX-EN-PROVENCE
AVIGNON
NOVI SAD
OSIJEK
BANJA LUKA
SARAJEVO
SPLIT
RIJEKA
PODGORICA
DURRËS
SHQIPËRIA
SLOVENSKO
MAGYARORSZÁG (HUNGARY)
SRBIJA
BOSNA I HERCEGOVINA
CRNA GORA (MONTENEGRO)
ITALIA
MARE LIGURE
MARE TIRRENO
MARE IONIO
MARE MEDITERRANEO
MEDITERRANEAN SEA
Corse (France)
Ajaccio
Bastia
Sardegna (Italia)
SASSARI
CAGLIARI
Sicilia
PALERMO
MESSINA
CATANIA
SIRACUSA
TRAPANI
REGGIO DI CALABRIA
Catanzaro
Cosenza
MALTA
Valletta
TUNIS
BINZART (BIZERTE)
SOUSSE
KAIROUAN
ANNABA
SKIKDA
QACENTINA (CONSTANTINE)
GUELMA
SOUK AHRAS
KENCHELA

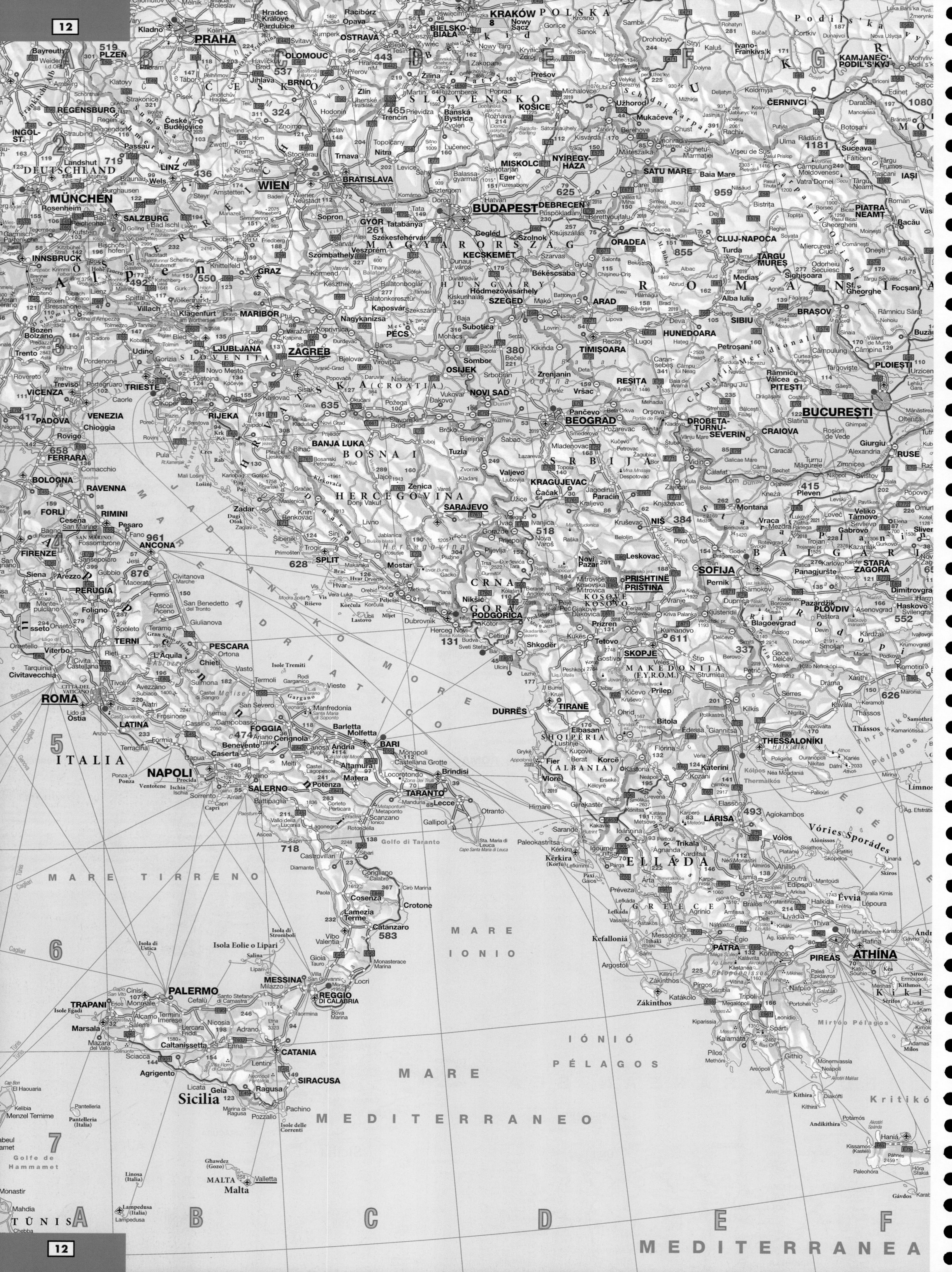
PRAHA
PLZEŇ
OLOMOUC
BRNO
OSTRAVA
KRAKÓW
POLSKA
ČESKO
REGENSBURG
INGOLST.
DEUTSCHLAND
MÜNCHEN
SALZBURG
LINZ
WIEN
BRATISLAVA
SLOVENSKO
KOŠICE
MISKOLC
NYÍREGYHÁZA
BUDAPEST
DEBRECEN
MAGYARORSZÁG
GYŐR
KECSKEMÉT
SZEGED
INNSBRUCK
GRAZ
ÖSTERREICH
MARIBOR
LJUBLJANA
SLOVENIJA
ZAGREB
HRVATSKA (CROATIA)
OSIJEK
NOVI SAD
BEOGRAD
SRBIJA
TRIESTE
RIJEKA
VENEZIA
PADOVA
VICENZA
TREVISO
FERRARA
BOLOGNA
RAVENNA
RIMINI
ANCONA
FIRENZE
PERUGIA
PESCARA
ROMA
NAPOLI
SALERNO
FOGGIA
BARI
TARANTO
Brindisi
Lecce
ITALIA
PALERMO
TRAPANI
MESSINA
REGGIO DI CALABRIA
CATANIA
SIRACUSA
Sicilia
Malta
Valletta
MARE TIRRENO
MARE IONIO
MARE MEDITERRANEO
JADRANSKO MORE
BANJA LUKA
BOSNA I HERCEGOVINA
SARAJEVO
SPLIT
CRNA GORA
PODGORICA
PRISHTINË PRIŠTINA
KOSOVO
SKOPJE
MAKEDONIJA (F.Y.R.O.M.)
TIRANË
DURRËS
SHQIPËRIA (ALBANIA)
THESSALONÍKI
ELLÁDA
GREECE
LÁRISA
PÁTRA
ATHÍNA
PIREÁS
IÓNIO PÉLAGOS
SOFIJA
PLOVDIV
BĂLGARIJA
NIŠ
KRAKUJEVAC
TIMIŞOARA
ARAD
ORADEA
CLUJ-NAPOCA
SIBIU
BRAŞOV
ROMÂNIA
BUCUREŞTI
PLOIEŞTI
CRAIOVA
PITEŞTI
IAŞI
SUCEAVA
ČERNIVCI
IVANO-FRANKIVS'K
KAMJANEC'-PODIL'S'KYJ
UŽHOROD
SATU MARE
RUSE
Pleven
STARA ZAGORA
A B C D E F G
1 2 3 4 5 6 7

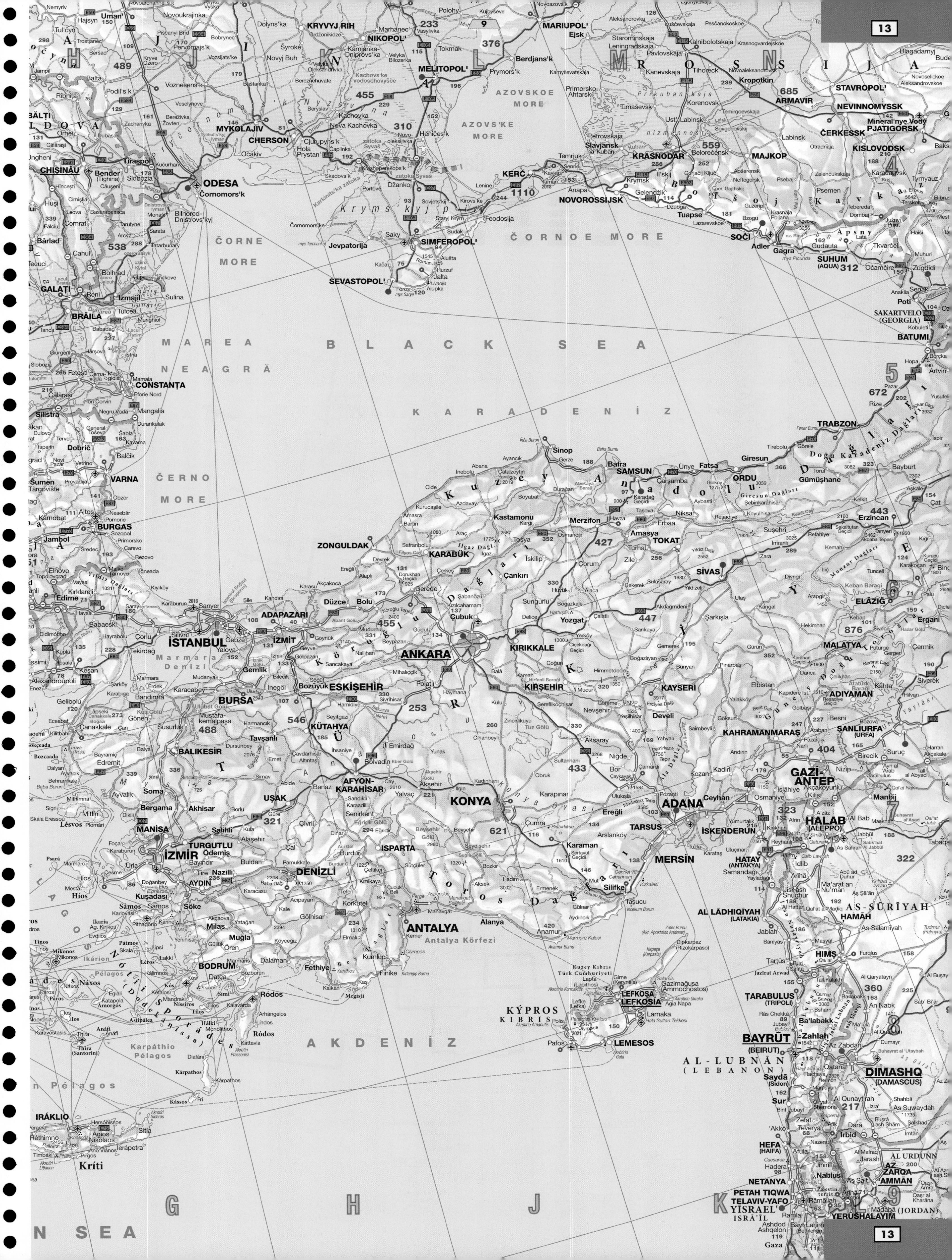
BLACK SEA
KARADENİZ
MAREA NEAGRĂ
ČERNO MORE
ČORNOE MORE
AZOVSKOE MORE
AKDENIZ
ANKARA
İSTANBUL
İZMİR
ANTALYA
KONYA
ADANA
MERSİN
BURSA
ESKİŞEHİR
SAMSUN
TRABZON
ODESA
SIMFEROPOL'
SEVASTOPOL'
KRASNODAR
NOVOROSSIJSK
CONSTANȚA
VARNA
BURGAS
LEFKOŞA LEFKOSİA
LEMESOS
BAYRŪT (BEIRUT)
DIMASHQ (DAMASCUS)
HALAB (ALEPPO)
AL-LUBNĀN (LEBANON)
AS-SŪRIYAH
AL URDUNN
YISRAEL
SAKARTVELO (GEORGIA)
KÝPROS KIBRIS
N SEA

1 : 750,000   1 : 1,000,000   1 : 2,000,000

Key map   Blattübersicht   Carte d'assemblage   Oversigtskort

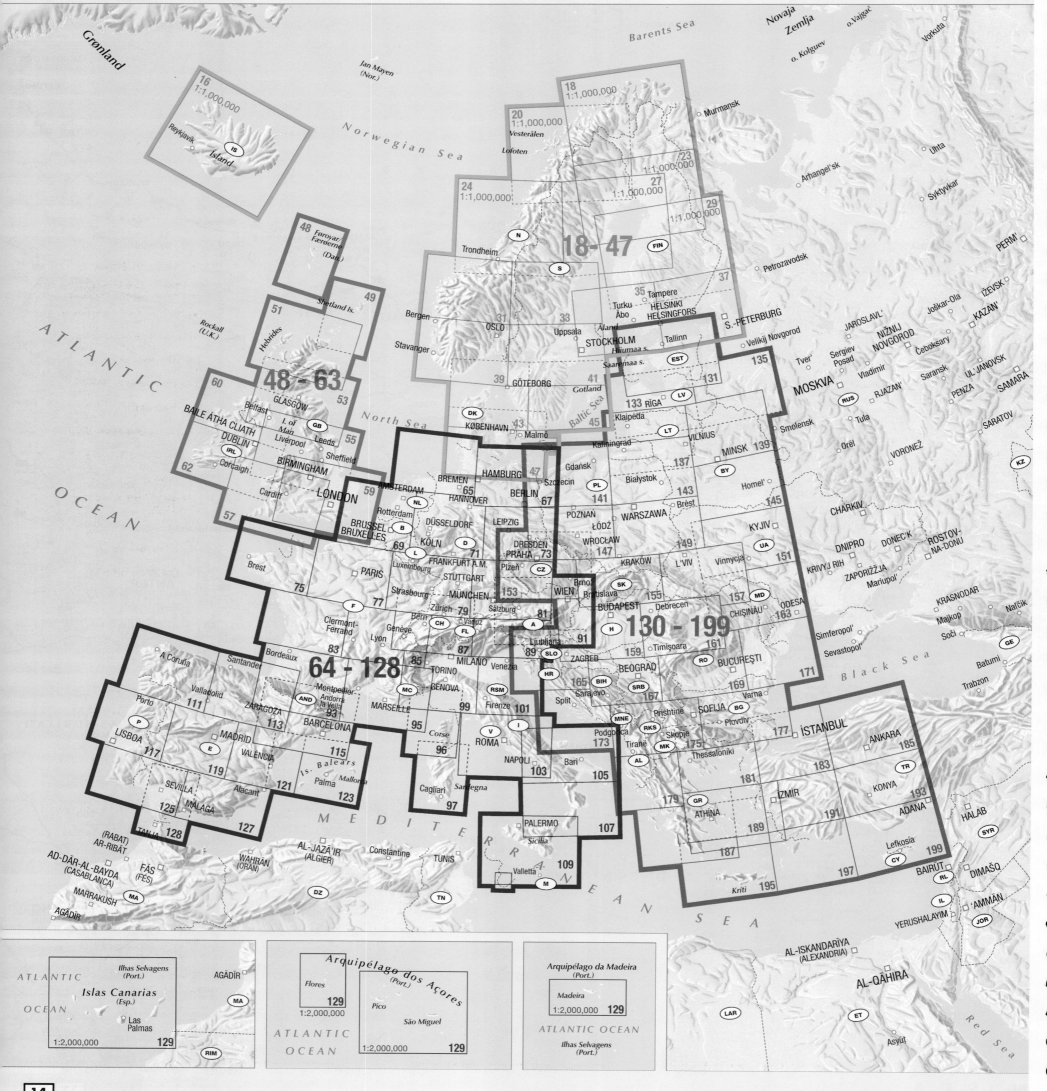

1 : 750,000   1 : 1,000,000   1 : 2,000,000

Legend   Zeichenerklärung   Légende   Tegnforklaring

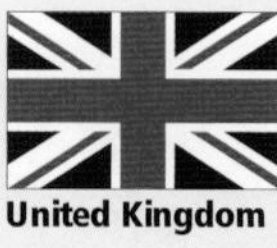

 United Kingdom
 Malta
 Deutschland
 Österreich
 Danmark

 Éire / Ireland

Liechtenstein

Schweiz / Suisse / Svizzera

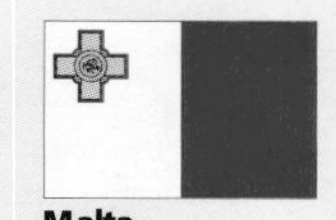

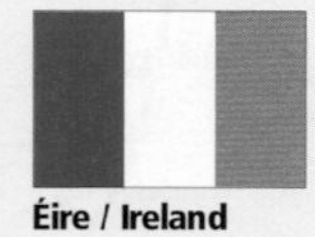

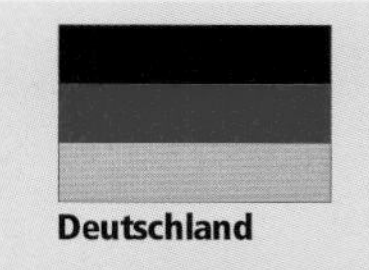

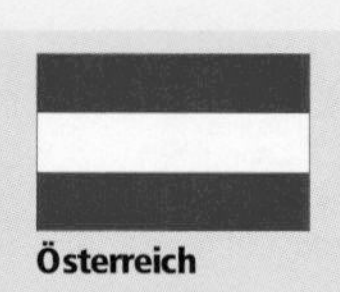

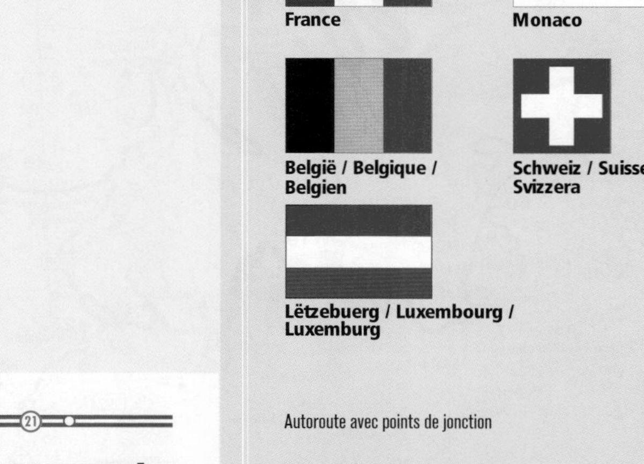

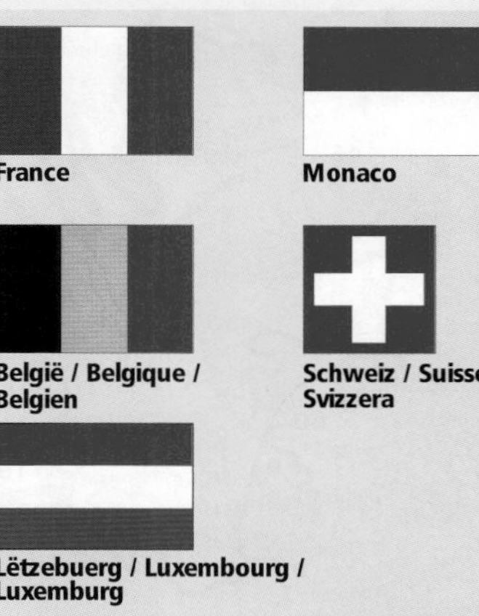

 France Monaco

Belgïe / Belgique / Belgien Schweiz / Suisse / Svizzera

Lëtzebuerg / Luxembourg / Luxemburg

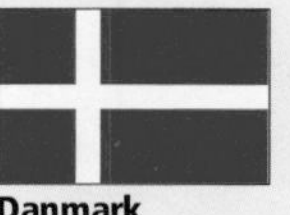

Legend	Zeichenerklärung		Légende	Tegnforklaring
Motorway with junctions	Autobahn mit Anschlussstellen		Autoroute avec points de jonction	Motorvej med tilkørsler
Tol motorway - Toll station	Autobahn mit Gebühr - Mautstelle		Autoroute à péage - Gare de péage	Afgiftsmotorvej - Vejafgiftsstation
Filling-station - Road-side restaurant - Road-side restaurant and hotel - Truckstop - Truck secure parking	Tankstelle - Raststätte - Rasthaus mit Übernachtung - Autohof - LKW -Sicherheitsparkplatz		Poste d'essence - Restaurant - Motel - Relais routier - Parking sécurisé poids lourds	Tankanlæg - Rastested - Rasteplads med overnatning - Motorvejsstation - Lastbilparkering sikkerhed
Motorway under construction - Motorway projected	Autobahn in Bau - Autobahn in Planung		Autoroute en construction - Autoroute en projet	Motorvej under opførelse - Motorvej under planlægning
Dual carriageway with motorway characteristics - under construction	Autobahnähnliche Schnellstraße - in Bau		Chaussée double de type autoroutier - en construction	Motortrafikvej med to vejbaner - under opførelse
Dual carriageway - Thoroughfare	Straße mit getrennten Fahrbahnen - Durchgangsstraße		Route à chaussées séparées - Route de transit	Vej med to vejbaner - Gennemfartsvej
Important main road - Main road - Secondary road	Wichtige Hauptstraße - Hauptstraße - Nebenstraße		Route principale importante - Route principale - Route secondaire	Vigtig hovedvej - Hovedvej - Bivej
Roads under construction	Straßen in Bau		Routes en construction	Veje under opførelse
Carriageway (use restricted) - Footpath	Fahrweg (nur bedingt befahrbar) - Fußweg		Chemin carrossable (praticabilité non assurée) - Sentier	Mindre vej (kun begrænset farbar) - Gangsti
Road closed for motor vehicles - Gradient	Straße für Kraftfahrzeuge gesperrt - Steigung		Route interdite aux véhicules à moteur - Montée	Vej spærret for motortrafik - Stigning
Pass - Closure in winter	Pass - Wintersperre		Col - Fermeture en hiver	Pas - Vinterlukning
Not recommended - closed for caravans - Car-loading terminal	Für Wohnanhänger nicht empfehlenswert - gesperrt - Autozug-Terminal		Non recommandée - interdite aux caravanes - Gare auto-train	Ikke anbefalet - forbudt for campingvogne - Autotog-terminal
Road numbers	Straßennummern		Numéros des routes	Vejnumre
Distances in km on motorways	Kilometrierung an Autobahnen		Distances en km sur autoroutes	Kilometerangivelse ved motorveje
Distances in km on other roads	Kilometrierung an übrigen Straßen		Distances en km sur autres routes	Kilometerangivelse ved øvrige veje
In Great Britain and Northern Ireland distances in miles	In Großbritannien und Nordirland Entfernungen in Meilen		En Grande-Bretagne et Irlande du Nord distances en milles	I Storbritannien og Nordirland afstænder i mils
Main line railway - Secondary line railway	Fernverkehrsbahn - Sonstige Eisenbahn		Chemin de fer: ligne à grand trafic - Chemin de fer: ligne à trafic secondaire	Jernbane med fjerntrafik - Anden jernbane
Rack-railway - Aerial cableway	Zahnradbahn - Luftseilbahn		Chemin de fer à crémaillère - Téléphérique	Tandhjulsbane - Svævebane
Car ferry - Car ferry on river	Autofähre - Autofähre an Flüssen		Bac pour automobiles - Bac fluvial pour automobiles	Bilfærge - Bilfærge på flod
Shipping route - Railway ferry	Schifffahrtslinie - Eisenbahnfähre		Ligne de navigation - Ferry-boat	Skibsrute - Jernbanefærge
Airport - Regional airport - Airfield	Verkehrsflughafen - Regionalflughafen - Flugplatz		Aéroport - Aéroport régional - Aérodrome	Lufthavn - Regional lufthavn - Flyveplads
Route with beautiful scenery - Tourist route	Landschaftlich schöne Strecke - Touristenstraße		Parcours pittoresque - Route touristique	Landskabelig smuk vejstrækning - Turistrute
Church - Monastery - Castle, palace - Mosque - Ruins	Kirche - Kloster - Burg, Schloss - Moschee - Ruinen		Église - Monastère - Château fort, château - Mosquée - Ruines	Kirke - Kloster - Borg, slot - Moské - Ruin
Archaeological excavation or ruins - Tower - Lighthouse	Ausgrabungs- oder Ruinenstätte - Turm - Leuchtturm		Site archéologique ou ruines - Tour - Phare	Udgravnings- eller ruinsted - Tårn - Fyrtårn
Monument - Cave - Waterfall - Other object	Denkmal - Höhle - Wasserfall - Sonstiges Objekt		Monument - Grotte - Cascade - Autre objet	Mindesmærke - Hule - Vandfald - Anden objekt
National park, nature park	Nationalpark, Naturpark		Parc national, parc naturel	Nationalpark, naturpark
Point of view	Aussichtspunkt		Point de vue	Udsigtspunkt
Youth hostel - Camping site	Jugendherberge - Campingplatz		Auberge de jeunesse - Terrain de camping	Vandrerhjem - Campingplads
Refuge - Isolated hotel	Berghütte - Allein stehendes Hotel		Refuge - Hôtel isolé	Bjerghytte - Enlig hotel
Prohibited area	Sperrgebiet		Zone interdite	Spærret område
National boundary - Check-point - Check-point with restrictions	Staatsgrenze - Grenzkontrollstelle - Grenzkontrollstelle mit Beschränkung		Frontière d'État - Point de contrôle - Point de contrôle avec restrictions	Statsgrænse - Grænsekontrol - Grænsekontrol med indskrænkning
Capital	Hauptstadt		Capitale	Hovedstad

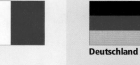

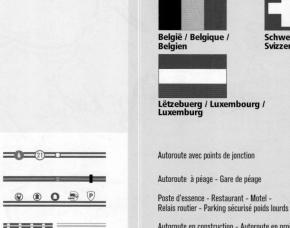

Strada del Vino

PARIS

1 : 750,000

0	10	20	30	40	50km
0		10		20	30mi

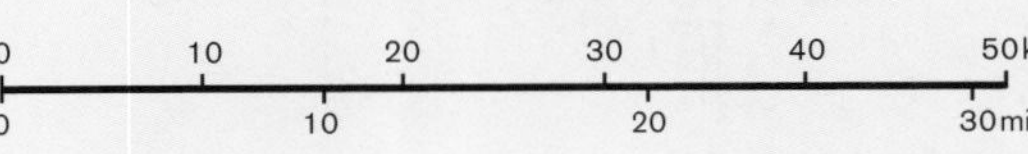

1 : 1,000,000

0	10	20	30	40	50km
0		10		20	30mi

1 : 2,000,000

0	20	40	60	80	100km
0		20		40	60mi

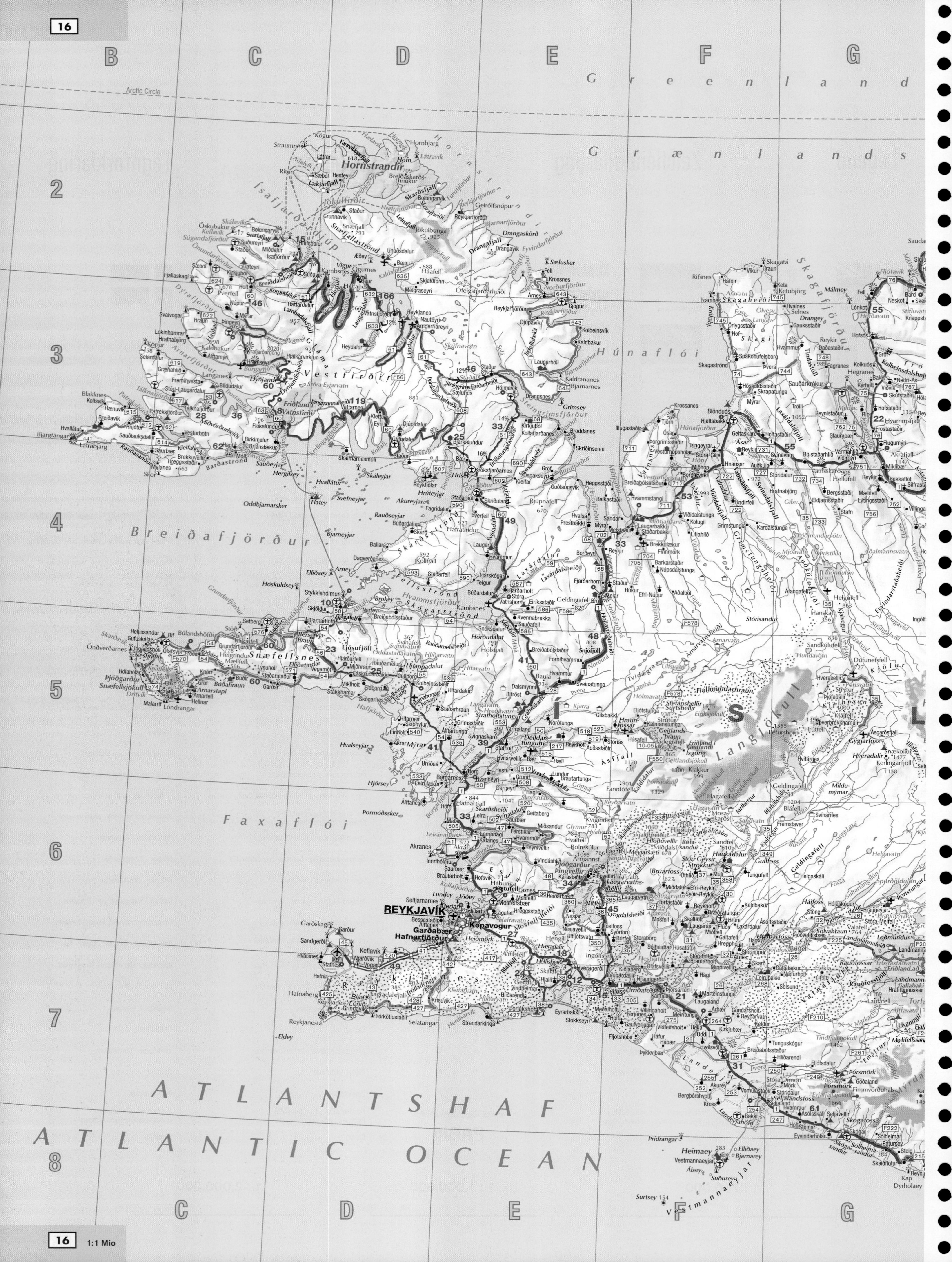
Greenland
Grænlands
Arctic Circle
Hornstrandir
Vestfirðir
Húnaflói
Breiðafjörður
Snæfellsnes
Faxaflói
REYKJAVÍK
Kópavogur
Garðabær
Hafnarfjörður
Keflavík
Langjökull
ÍSL
ATLANTSHAF
ATLANTIC OCEAN
Heimaey
Vestmannaeyjar
Surtsey

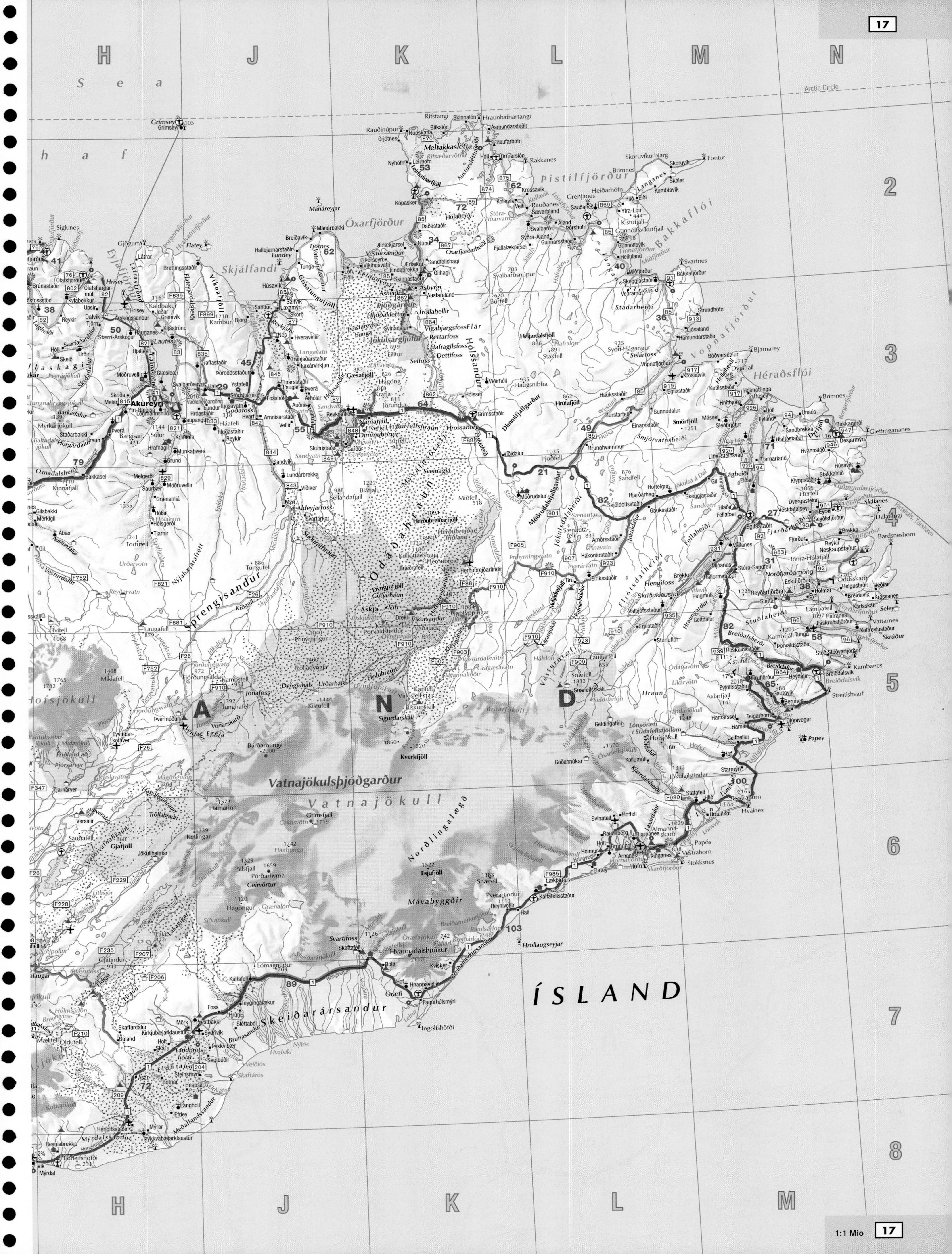
H
J
K
L
M
N
Sea
Arctic Circle
Grímsey
Rifstangi
Raufarhöfn
Melrakkaslétta
Þistilfjörður
Langanes
Bakkaflói
Öxarfjörður
Skjálfandi
Eyjafjörður
Flatey
Siglunes
Húsavík
Akureyri
Dalvík
Kópasker
Þórshöfn
Vopnafjörður
Héraðsflói
Egilsstaðir
Seyðisfjörður
Neskaupstaður
Eskifjörður
Reyðarfjörður
Fáskrúðsfjörður
Stöðvarfjörður
Breiðdalsvík
Djúpivogur
Papey
Höfn
Hvalnes
Stokksnes
Grímsstaðir
Mývatn
Reykjahlíð
Dettifoss
Ásbyrgi
Jökulsárgljúfur
Hólssandur
Ódáðahraun
Herðubreið
Askja
Dyngjufjöll
Sprengisandur
Hofsjökull
Vatnajökull
Vatnajökulsþjóðgarður
Kverkfjöll
Bárðarbunga
Grímsvötn
Hvannadalshnúkur
Öræfajökull
Skaftafell
Skeiðarársandur
Kirkjubæjarklaustur
Mýrdalssandur
Vík í Mýrdal
Ingólfshöfði
Hrollaugseyjar
Snæfell
Lónsöræfi
Kárahnjúkar
Hengifoss
ÍSLAND
A
N
D
1
2
3
4
5
6
7
8

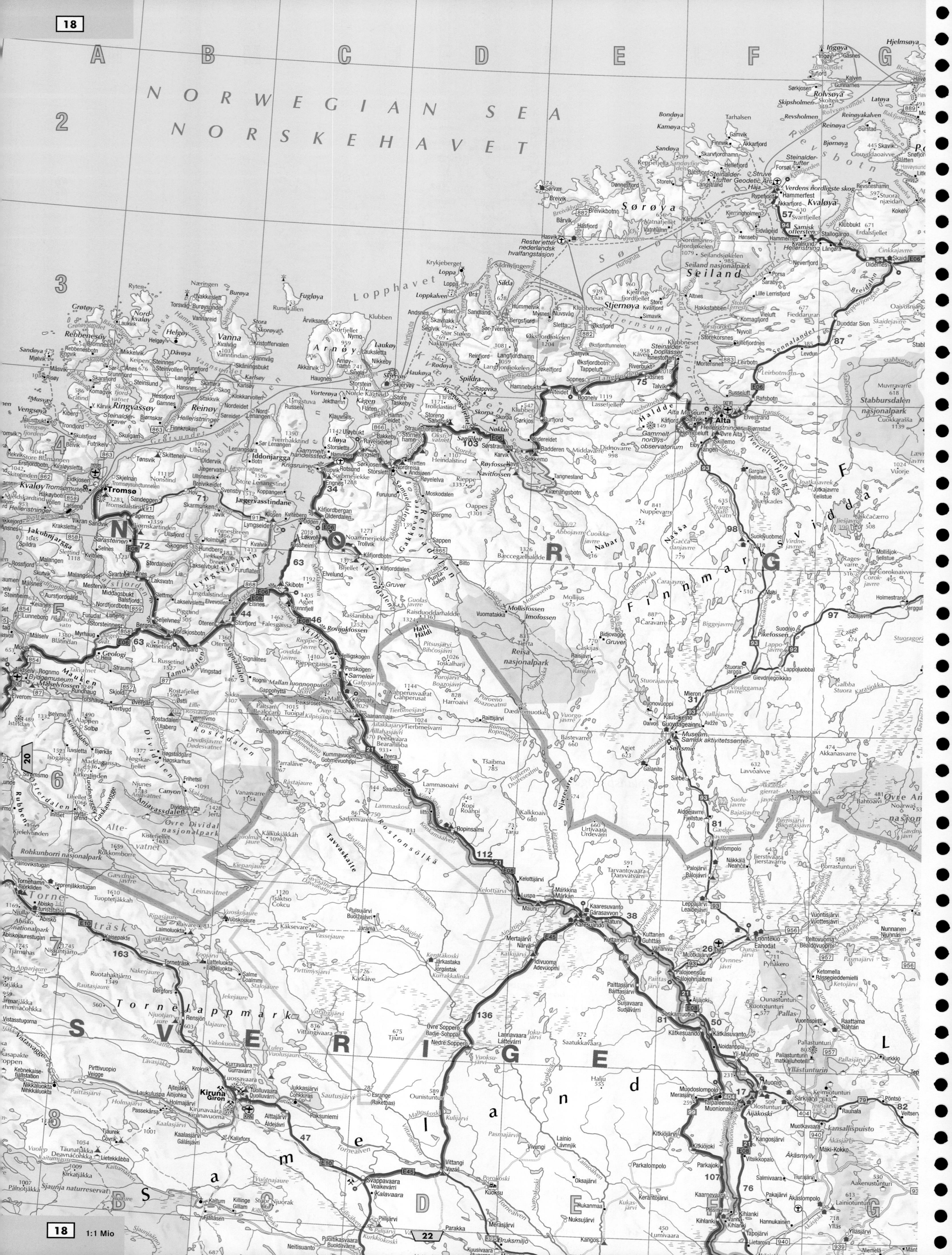
NORWEGIAN SEA
NORSKEHAVET
Sørøya
Seiland
Loppa
Arnøy
Ringvassøy
Reinøy
Vanna
Kvaløy
Tromsø
Alta
Hammerfest
Kvaløya
Stjernøya
Lopphavet
Kvænangen
Finnmarksvidda
NORGE
SVERIGE
Sameland
Tornelappmark
Reisa nasjonalpark
Stabbursdalen nasjonalpark
Øvre Dividal nasjonalpark
Rohkunborri nasjonalpark
Abisko nationalpark
Kiruna
Kautokeino
Karesuando
Muonio
Enontekiö
Skibotn
Storfjord
Nordreisa
Halti
Torneträsk
Sjaunja naturreservat
Bardufoss
Setermoen
Kilpisjärvi
Hetta

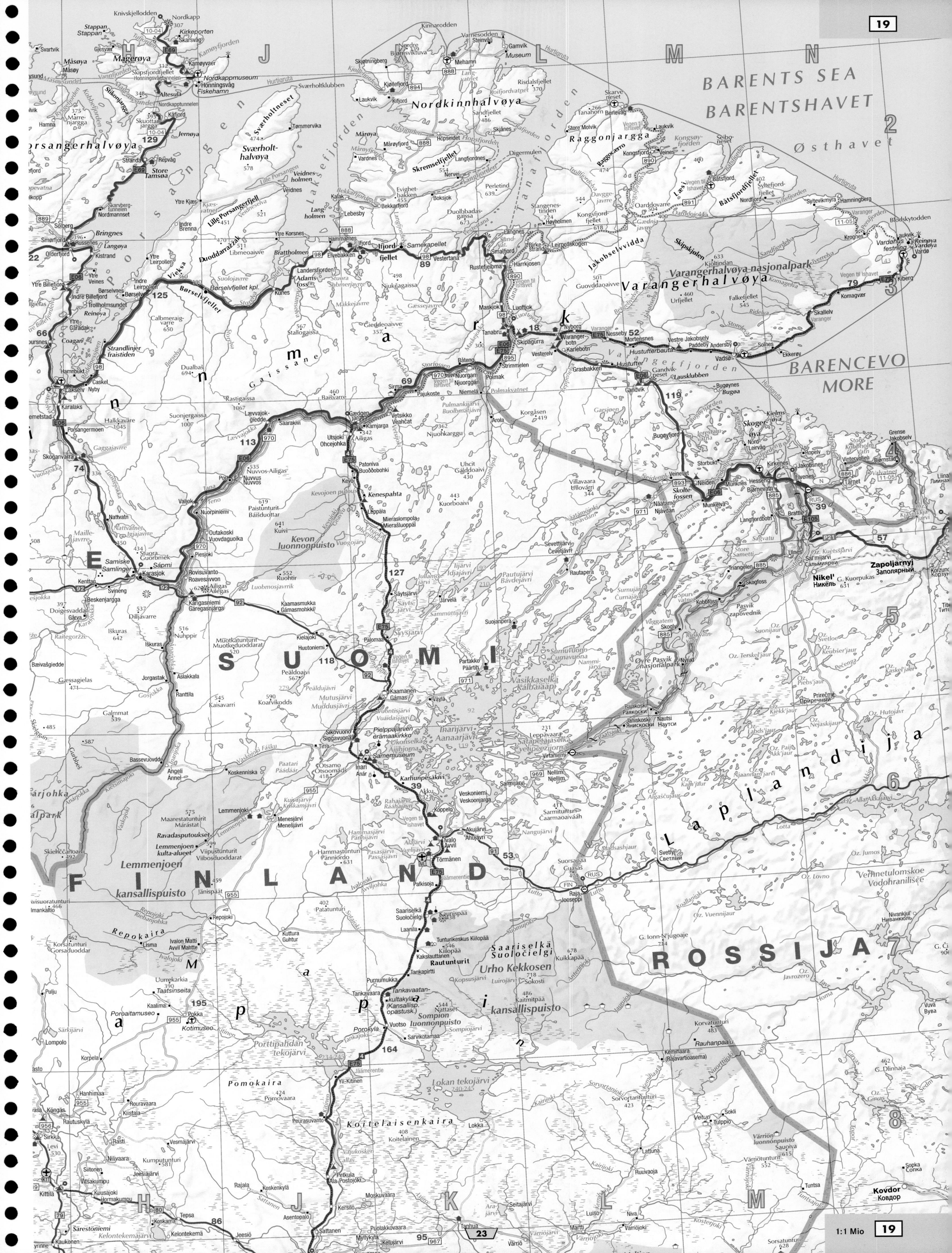
BARENTS SEA
BARENTSHAVET
Østhavet
BARENCEVO MORE
Nordkapp
Knivskjellodden
Magerøya
Honningsvåg
Nordkappmuseum
Porsangerhalvøya
Sværholt-halvøya
Nordkinnhalvøya
Mehamn
Gamvik
Kinnarodden
Raggonjargga
Berlevåg
Båtsfjord
Varangerhalvøya
Varangerhalvøya nasjonalpark
Vardø
Vadsø
Kiberg
Varangerfjorden
Kirkenes
Grense Jakobselv
Lakselv
Karasjok
Kárášjohka
Tana bru
Nesseby
Nyborg
Skipagurra
Utsjoki
Ohcejohka
Kevon luonnonpuisto
Kaamanen
Inari
Inarijärvi
Aanaarjävri
Ivalo
Saariselkä
Urho Kekkosen kansallispuisto
Lemmenjoen kansallispuisto
Sompion luonnonpuisto
Porttipahdan tekojärvi
Lokan tekojärvi
Pomokaira
Koitelaisenkaira
Vätsäri
Värriön luonnonpuisto
Övre Pasvik nasjonalpark
Pasvik zapovednik
Nikel'
Никель
Zapoljarnyj
Заполярный
Kovdor
Ковдор
Laplandija
SUOMI
FINLAND
ROSSIJA
Raja-Jooseppi
Svetlyj
Светлый
Vuotso
Kittilä
Levi
Sodankylä
Sirma
Nuorgam
Polmak
Hammerfest
Nordkinn
Bugøynes
Neiden

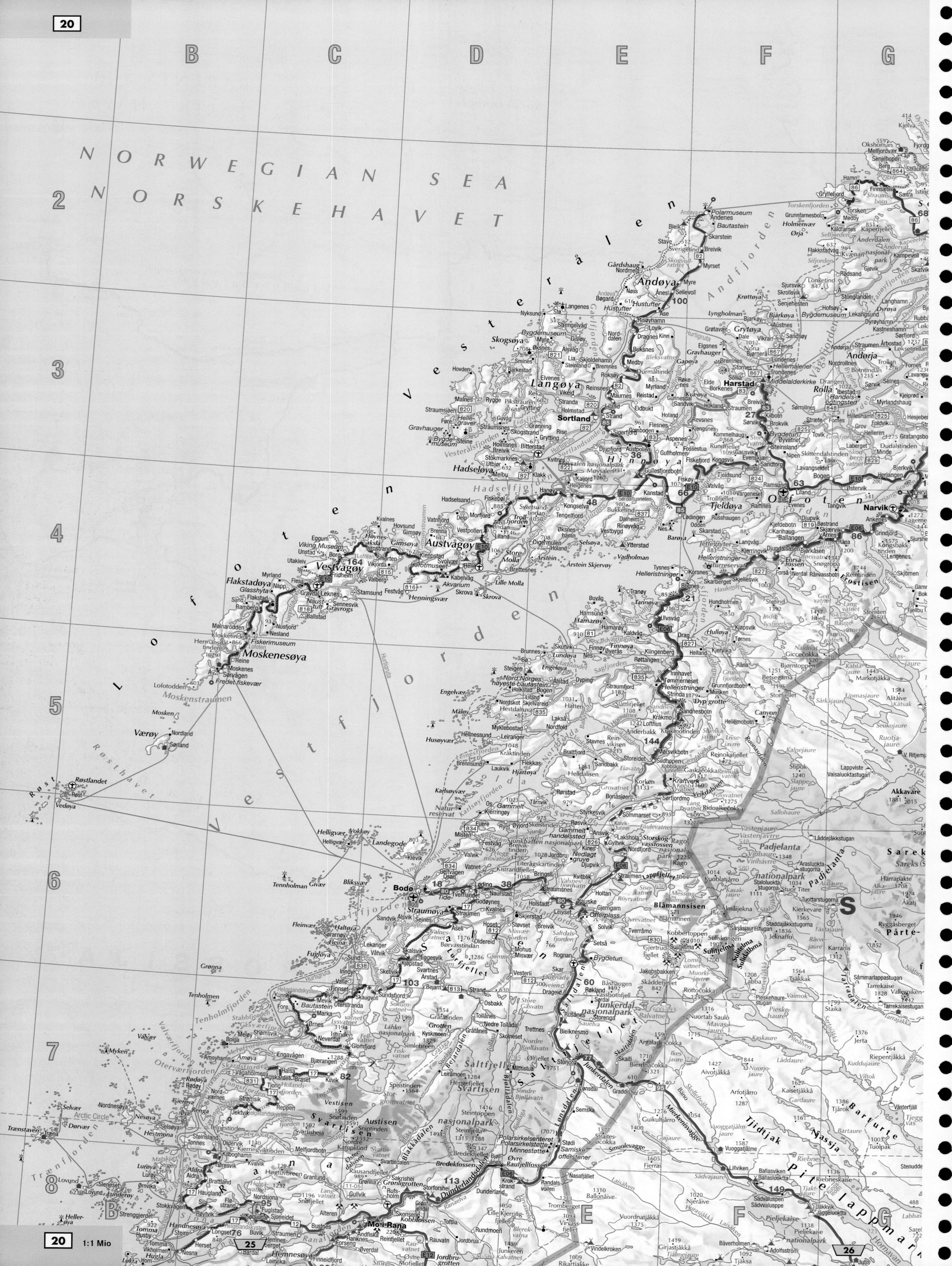
B
C
D
E
F
G
2
3
4
5
6
7
8
NORWEGIAN SEA
NORSKEHAVET
Vesterålen
Lofoten
Vestfjorden
Ofoten
Andfjorden
Andøya
Andenes
Polarmuseum
Bautastein
Skarstein
Breivik
Myrset
Bleik
Stave
Gårdshaug
Nordmela
Nøss
Hustufter
Åse
Risøyhamn
Langenes
Nyksund
Stø
Skogsøya
Bygdemuseum
Myre
Øksnes
Langøya
Sortland
Hinnøya
Harstad
Middelalderkirke
Trondenes
Hadseløya
Stokmarknes
Melbu
Hadselfjorden
Austvågøy
Svolvær
Kabelvåg
Akvarium
Henningsvær
Lofotmuseet
Vestvågøy
Leknes
Stamsund
Flakstadøya
Moskenesøya
Reine
Moskenes
Sørvågen
Fredet fiskevær
Lofotodden
Moskenstraumen
Mosken
Værøy
Nordland
Sørland
Røst
Røstlandet
Vedøya
Røsthavet
Tjeldøya
Narvik
Evenes
Ballangen
Hamarøy
Ulvsvåg
Drag
Helland
Tysfjorden
Sagfjorden
Engeløya
Steigen
Nord-Norges høyeste bautastein
Kjøpsvik
Musken
Tysfjord
Hellemobotn
Kraftverk
Sulitjelma
Blåmannsisen
Padjelanta nationalpark
Sarek
Bodø
Straumøya
Saltstraumen
Fauske
Rognan
Saltdal
Saltfjellet
Junkerdal nasjonalpark
Saltfjellet-Svartisen nasjonalpark
Svartisen
Polarsirkelsenteret
Arctic Circle
Meløy
Glomfjord
Ørnes
Gildeskål
Sandnessjøen
Lurøy
Træna
Mo i Rana
Hemnesøya
Mosjøen
Dunderlandsdalen
Ranafjorden
Storforshei
Jordbrugrotten
Grønligrotten
Krokstrand
Graddis
Lønsdalen
Kvikkjokk
Pite lappmark
Tjidtjak
Barturte
Nasja
Bardal
Korgen
E10
E06
E12
82
85
83
820
821
815
816
817
812
813
826
827
834
835
838
830
831
848
864
825
18
21
25
26
27
36
38
48
60
63
66
76
77
80
82
86
95
100
103
113
144
149
164

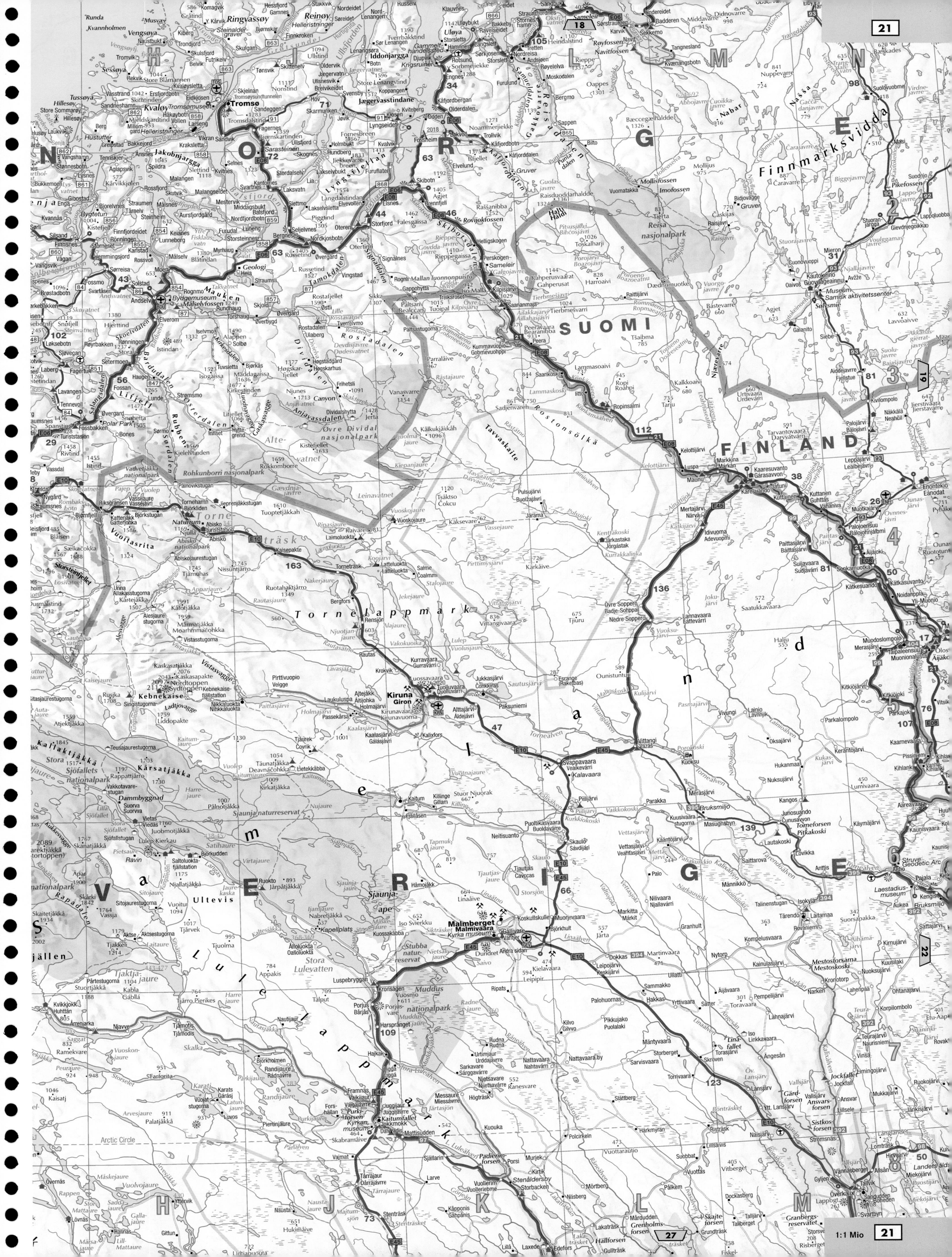

N O R G E
SUOMI
FINLAND
S V E R I G E
Finnmarksvidda
Reisa nasjonalpark
Øvre Dividal nasjonalpark
Rohkunborri nasjonalpark
Vadvetjåkka nationalpark
Abisko nationalpark
Stora Sjöfallets nationalpark
Sjaunja naturreservat
Stubba naturreservat
Muddus nationalpark
Tornelappmark
Lule lappmark
Torneträsk
Stora Lulevatten
Tromsø
Kiruna
Giron
Malmberget
Malmivaara
Gällivare
Jokkmokk
Kautokeino
Karesuando
Kaaresuvanto
Muonio
Pajala
Övertorneå
Svappavaara
Vittangi
Kilpisjärvi
Skibotn
Nordreisa
Lyngseidet
Bardufoss
Kebnekaise
Arctic Circle
Ringvassøy
Reinøy
Kvaløya
Uløya
Lyngsalpan
Reisadalen
Tamokdalen
Målselvfossen
Storsteinfjellet
Dammbyggnad
Lapporten
Struve Geodetic Arc
Laestadius-museum
1:1 Mio

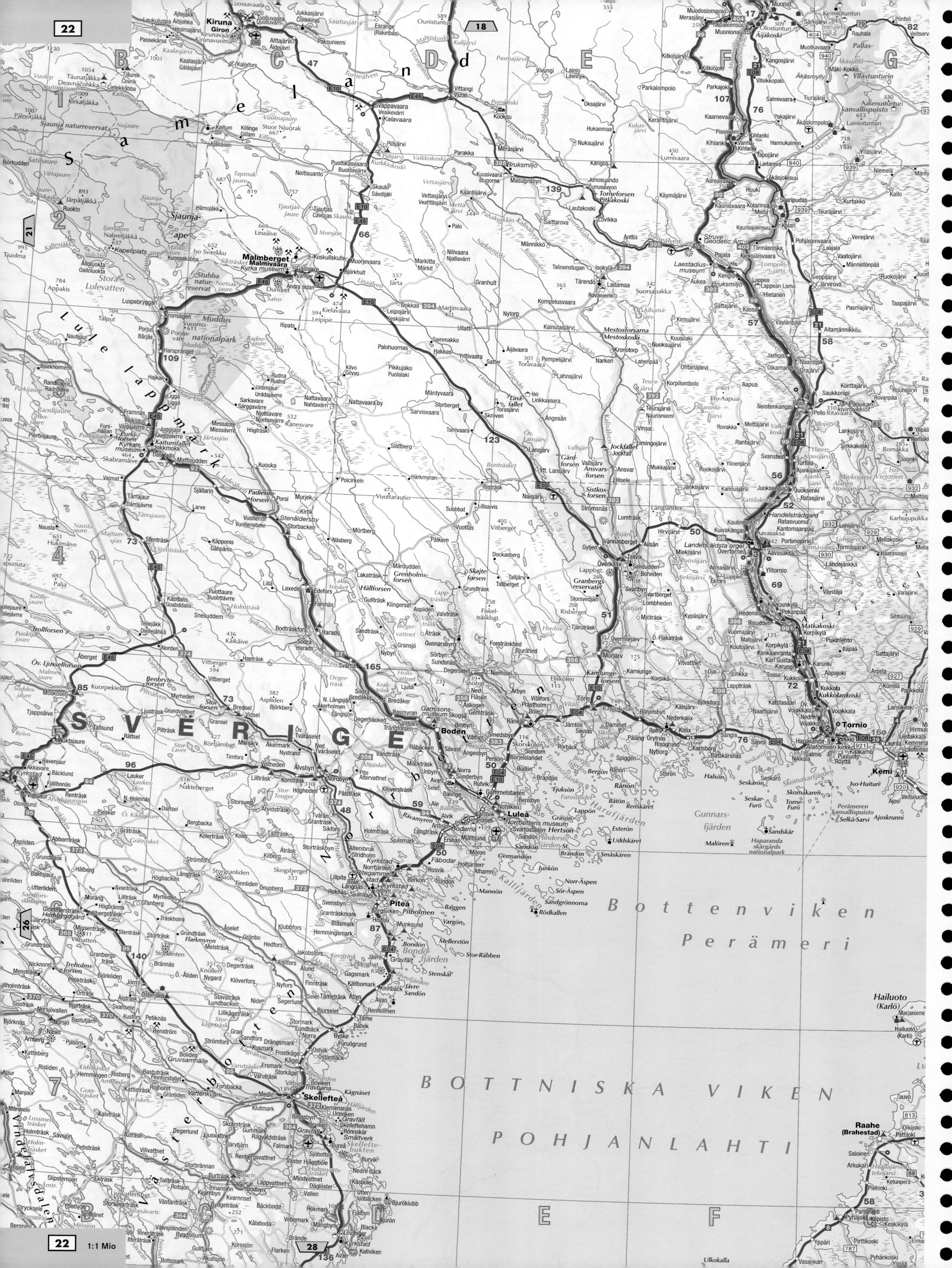
Kiruna
Giron
Svappavaara
Malmberget
Malmivaara
Gällivare
Jokkmokk
Porjus
Sameland
Lule lappmark
Muddus nationalpark
Stubba naturreservat
Sjaunja naturreservat
SVERIGE
Norrbotten
Västerbotten
Arvidsjaur
Älvsbyn
Boden
Luleå
Piteå
Skellefteå
Kalix
Haparanda
Tornio
Kemi
Övertorneå
Pajala
Kolari
Muonio
Överkalix
Haparanda skärgårds nationalpark
Bottenviken
Perämeri
BOTTNISKA VIKEN
POHJANLAHTI
Hailuoto
(Karlö)
Raahe
(Brahestad)
Vindelälvsdalen

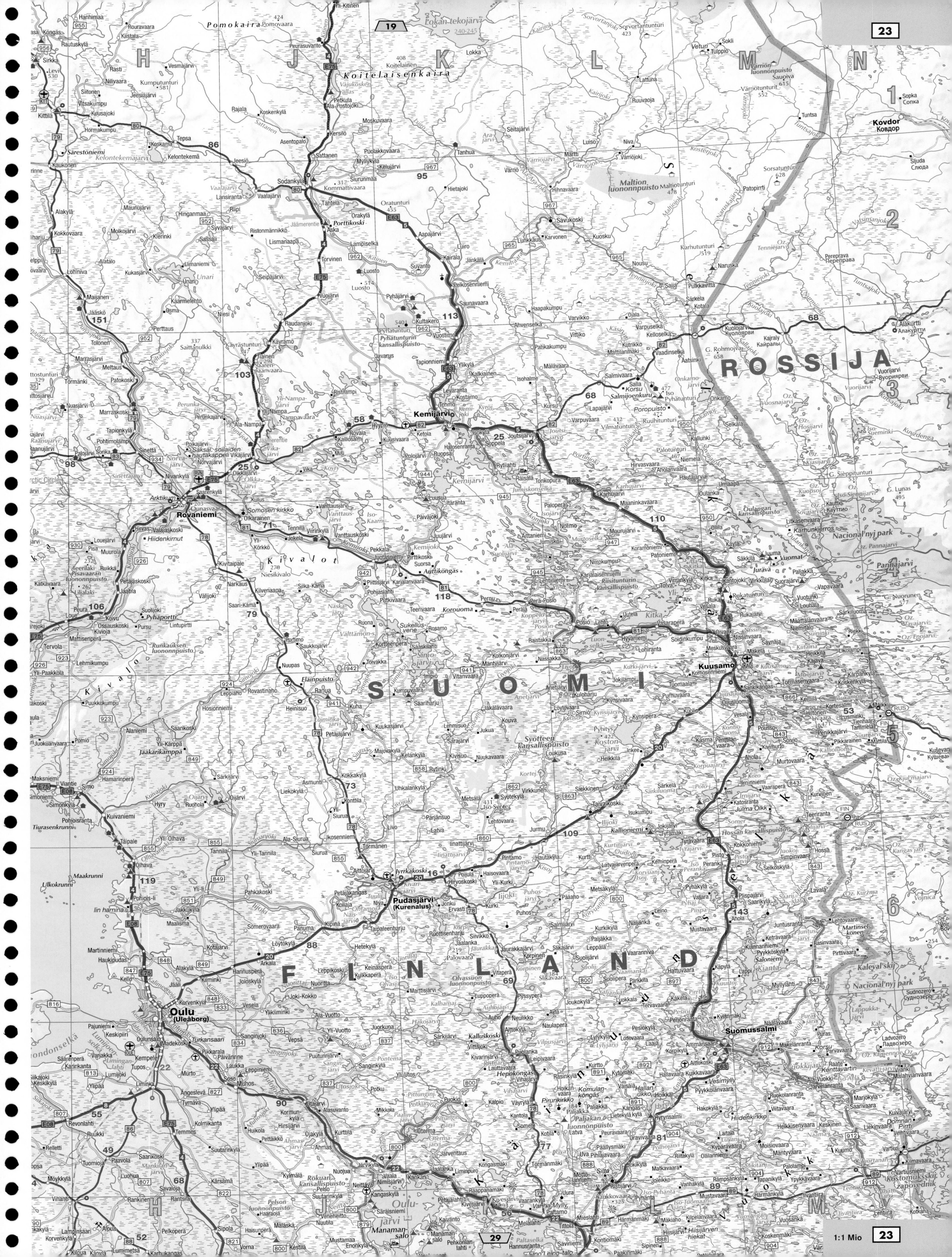
H
J
K
L
M
N
ROSSIJA
SUOMI
FINLAND
Pomokaira
Koitelaisenkaira
Kivalot
Kivalo
Sodankylä
Kittilä
Rovaniemi
Kemijärvi
Kuusamo
Pudasjärvi
(Kurenalus)
Oulu
(Uleåborg)
Suomussalmi
Kovdor
Ковдор
Maltion luonnonpuisto
Pyhätunturin kansallispuisto
Oulangan kansallispuisto
Riisitunturin kansallispuisto
Syötteen kansallispuisto
Nacional'nyj park
Kalevala
Oulujärvi
Arctic Circle
E75
E63
E8
19
29

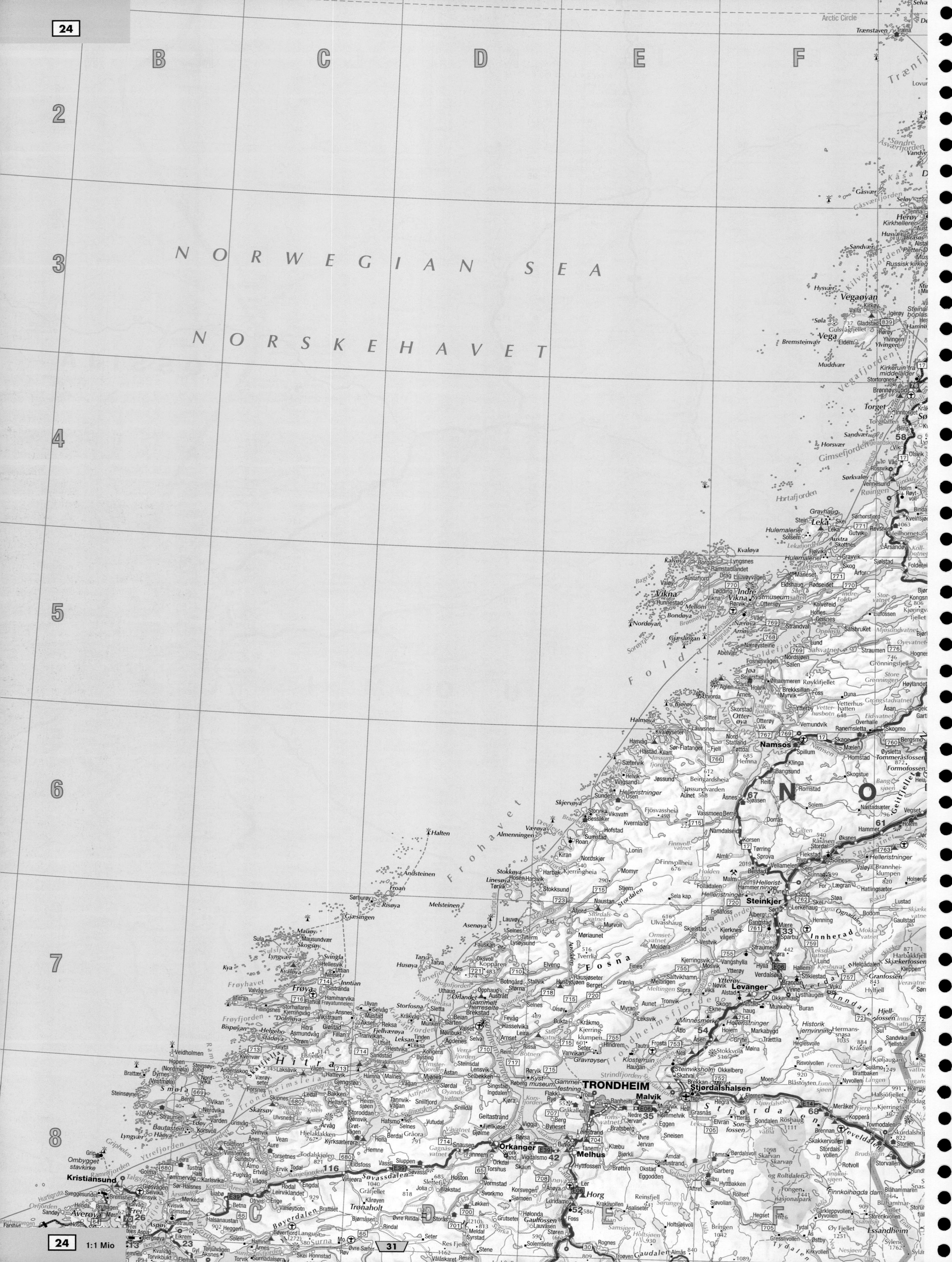
Arctic Circle
B
C
D
E
F
2
3
4
5
6
7
8
NORWEGIAN SEA
NORSKEHAVET
Trænstaven
Gåsvær
Herøy
Vegaøyan
Vega
Brønnøysund
Torget
Horsvær
Sørkvaløy
Leka
Kvaløya
Vikna
Indre Vikna
Nordøyan
Gjæslingan
Folda
Halmøya
Namsos
Skjervøya
Halten
Frohavet
Andsteinen
Froan
Sørburøy
Risøya
Melsteinen
Gjæsingen
Asenøya
Mausundvær
Kya
Frøya
Hitra
Smøla
Veidholmen
Kristiansund
Averøya
Frei
Trondheimsleia
Trondheimsfjorden
TRONDHEIM
Stjørdalshalsen
Malvik
Orkanger
Melhus
Horg
Levanger
Steinkjer
Stjørdalen
Søvassdalen
Trønaholt
Fosna
Innherad
Verdal
Snåsa
Gaulfossen
Støren
Gaudalen
Surna
Tydalen
Namsen
Rørvik
Sørvika
Kyst museum
Hellerist-ninger
Hurtigruta
E06
E14
E39
N
O

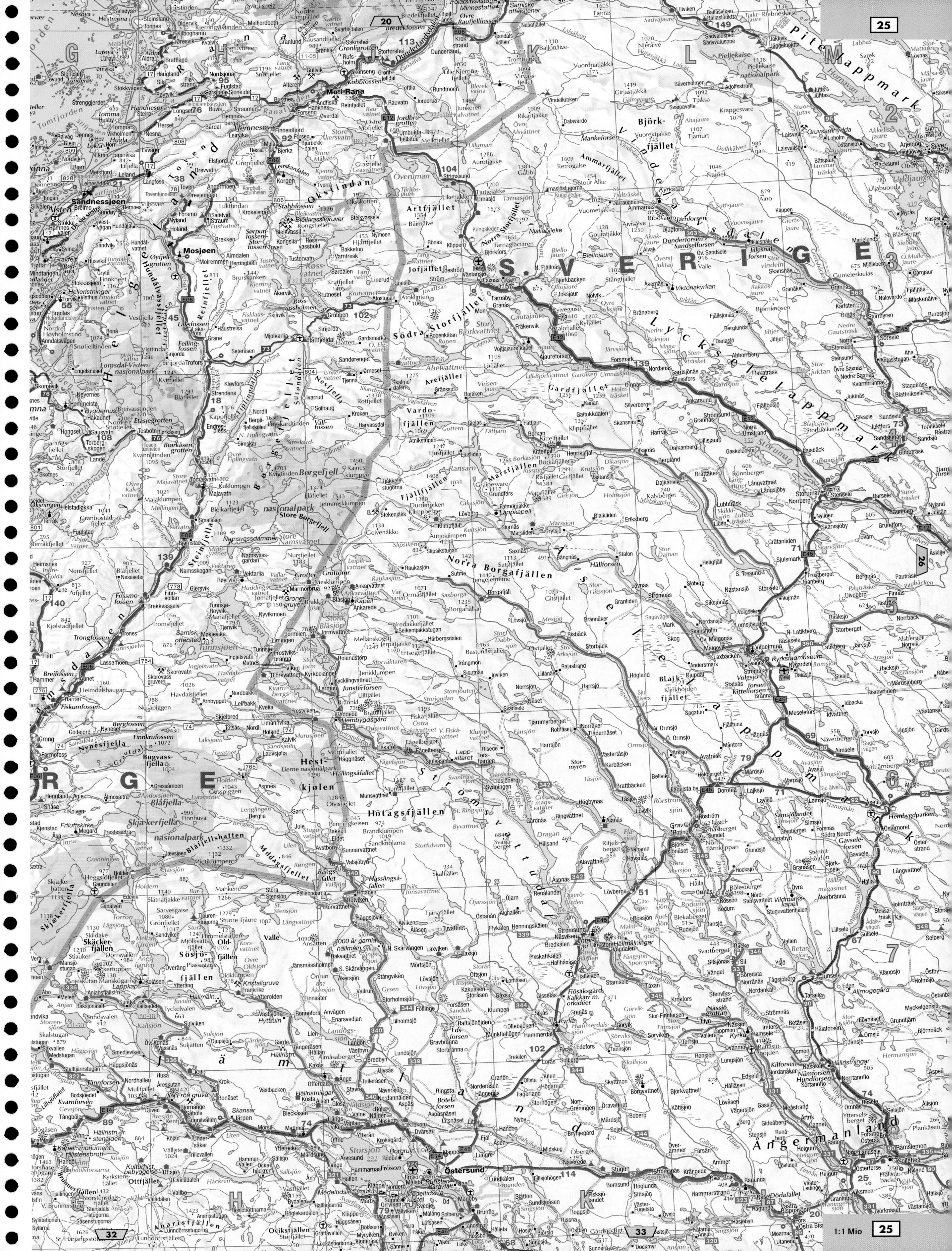
Pite lappmark
SVERIGE
Lycksele lappmark
Åsele lappmark
Ångermanland
Jämtland
Strömsvattudal
Vilhelmina
Storuman
Östersund
Mo i Rana
Mosjøen
Sandnessjøen
Okstindan
Børgefjell nasjonalpark
Store Børgefjell
Lomsdal-Visten nasjonalpark
Blåfjella-Skjækerfjella nasjonalpark
Hotagsfjällen
Norra Borgafjällen
Södra Storfjället
Vindelfjällen
Hestkjølen
Lierne nasjonalpark
1:1 Mio

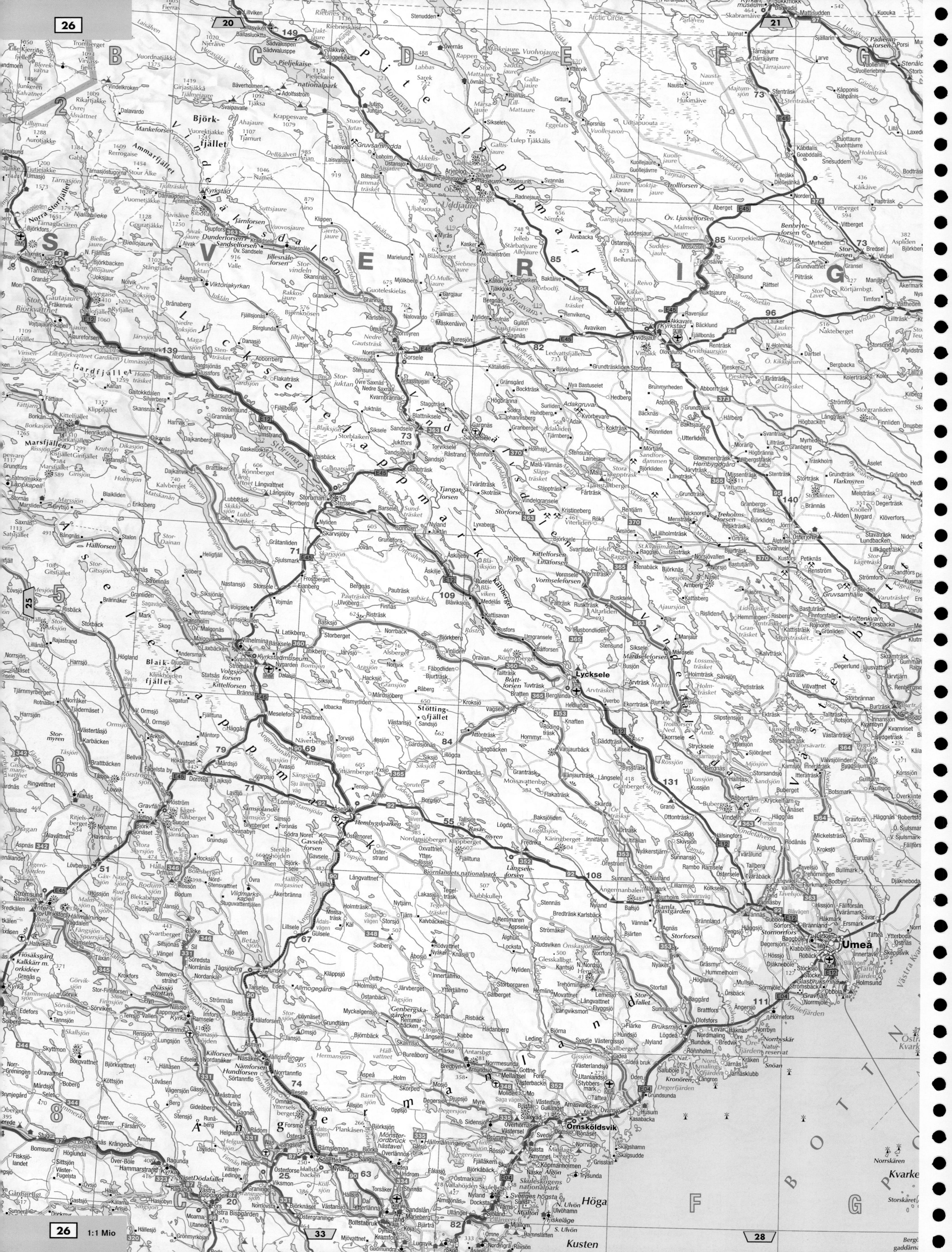
20
21
Arctic Circle
Pieljekaise nationalpark
Arjeplog
Arvidsjaur
Sorsele
Storuman
Vilhelmina
Lycksele
Umeå
Örnsköldsvik
Dorotea
Åsele
Vindeln
Vännäs
Nordmaling
Sollefteå
Kramfors
Björnlandets nationalpark
Skuleskogens nationalpark
Höga Kusten
25
33
28
S
V
E
R
I
G
B
C
D
E
F
G
2
3
5
6
7
8

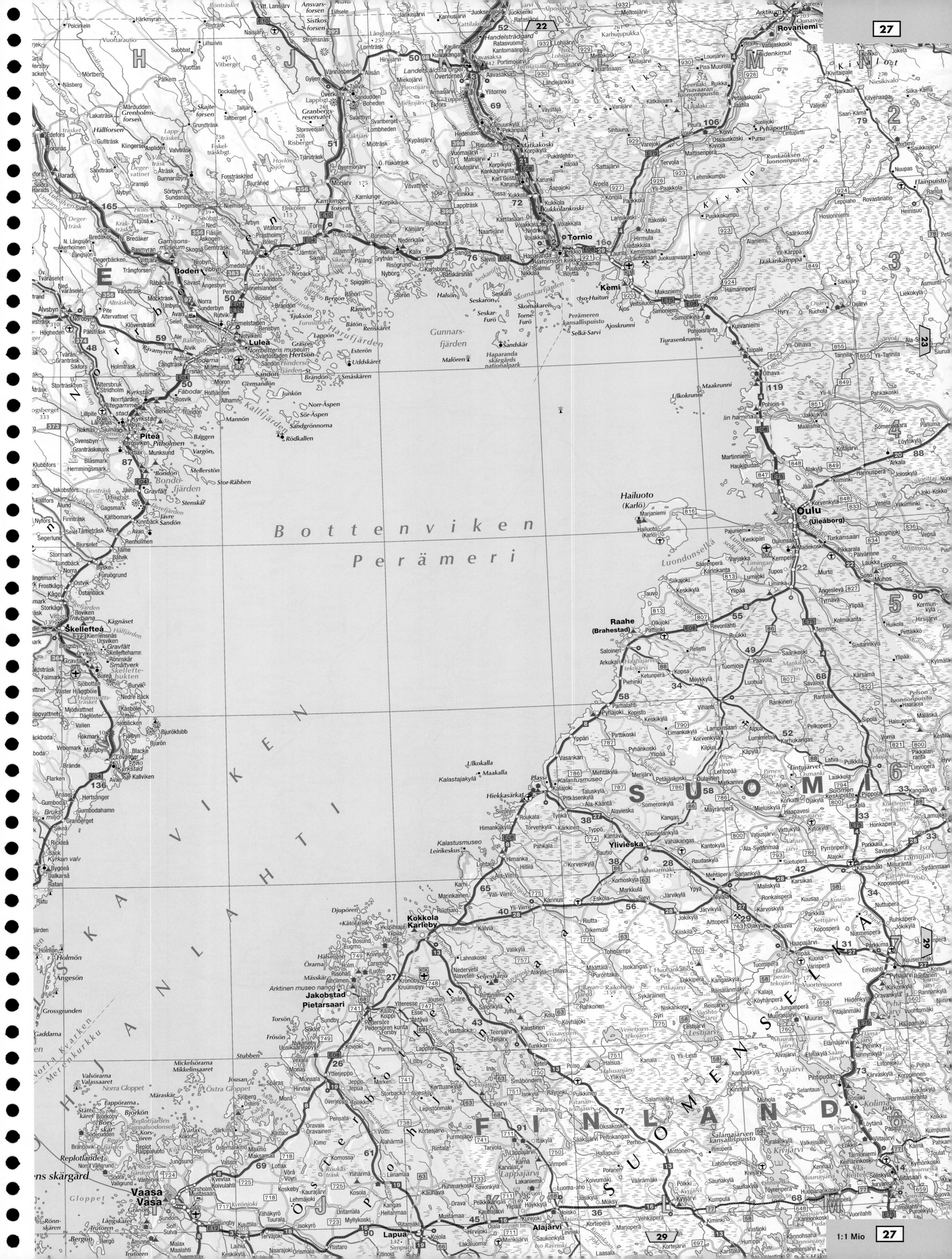
Bottenviken
Perämeri
SUOMI
FINLAND
SUOMENSELKÄ
Rovaniemi
Tornio
Haparanda
Kemi
Oulu
(Uleåborg)
Hailuoto
(Karlö)
Raahe
(Brahestad)
Ylivieska
Kokkola
Karleby
Jakobstad
Pietarsaari
Vaasa
Vasa
Lapua
Alajärvi
Luleå
Boden
Piteå
Skellefteå
Kalix
Överkalix
Haparanda skärgårds nationalpark
Norrbottens museum
Gunnarsfjärden
Kallfjärden
Holmön
Norra Kvarken
Merenkurkku
Kvarken
Lappajärvi
Nivala
Kannus
Haapajärvi
Kärsämäki
Pyhäjärvi
Kalajoki
Pyhäjoki
Oulainen
Muhos
Kempele
Ii
Simo
Keminmaa
Tervola
Ylitornio
Övertorneå
Pello
Salamajärven kansallispuisto
Runkauksen luonnonpuisto
Perämeren kansallispuisto
Arktinen museo nanoq
Kalastusmuseo
Kalastajakylä
Ulkokalla
Maakalla
Hiekkasärkät
Plassi
Pohjanmaa
Österbotten
Skellefteå bukten
Norrbotten
Kivalo
Aavasaksa
Landets äldsta orgel
Tornionlaakso
Torne älv
E4
E8
E10
E12
E75
22
23
29
1:1 Mio

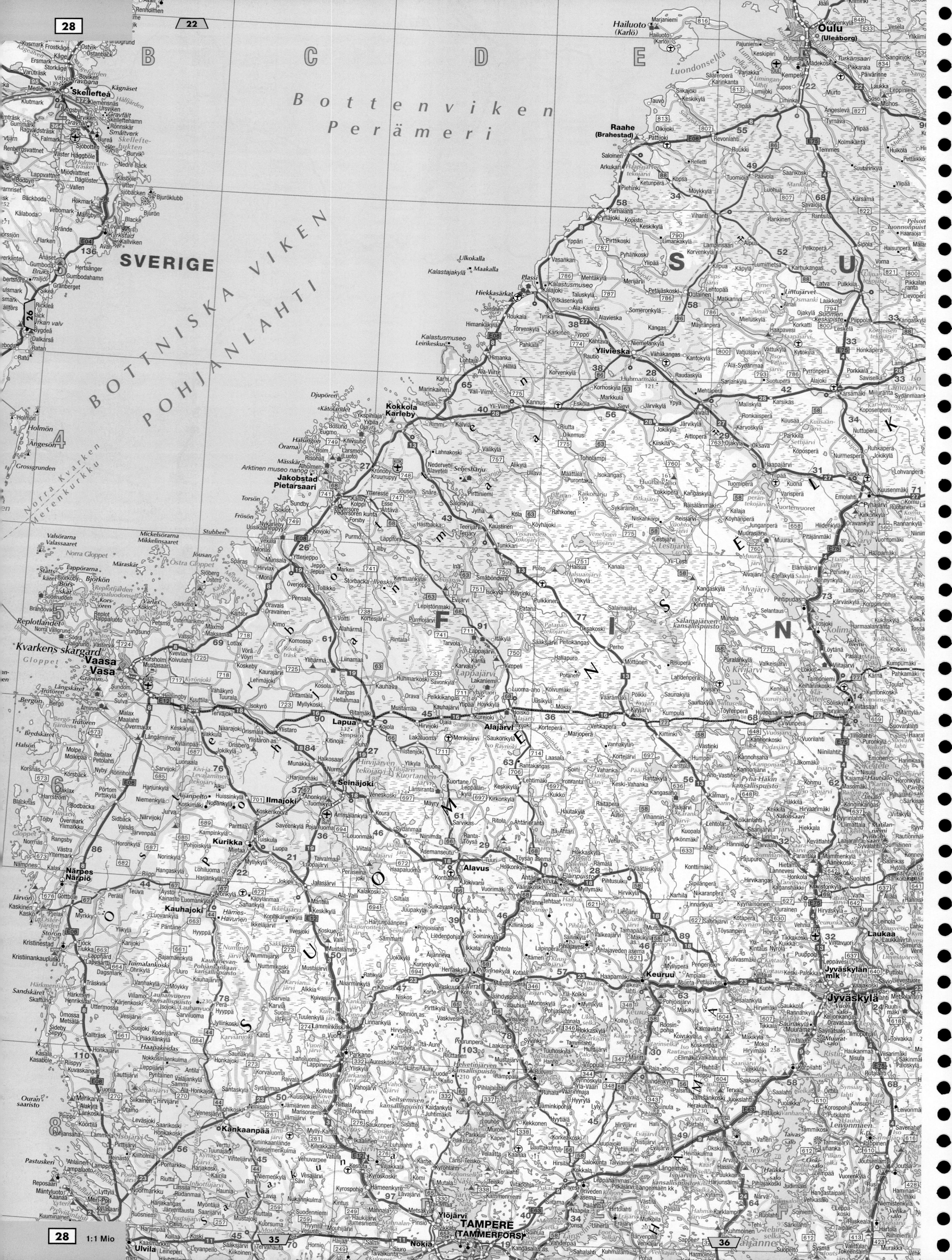
22
B
C
D
E
Bottenviken
Perämeri
SVERIGE
BOTTNISKA VIKEN
POHJANLAHTI
Norra Kvarken
Merenkurkku
Kvarkens skärgård
S
U
O
M
I
F
I
N
L
A
N
D
Skellefteå
Oulu
(Uleåborg)
Hailuoto
(Karlö)
Raahe
(Brahestad)
Ylivieska
Kokkola
Karleby
Jakobstad
Pietarsaari
Vaasa
Vasa
Lapua
Seinäjoki
Ilmajoki
Kurikka
Alajärvi
Alavus
Kauhajoki
Närpes
Närpiö
Kristinestad
Kankaanpää
Keuruu
Jyväskylä
Jyväskylän mlk
Laukaa
Tampere
(Tammerfors)
Ylöjärvi
Nokia
Ulvila
Replotlandet
Salamajärven kansallispuisto
Helvetinjärven kansallispuisto
Seitsemisen kansallispuisto
4
5
6
8
26
35
36
1:1 Mio

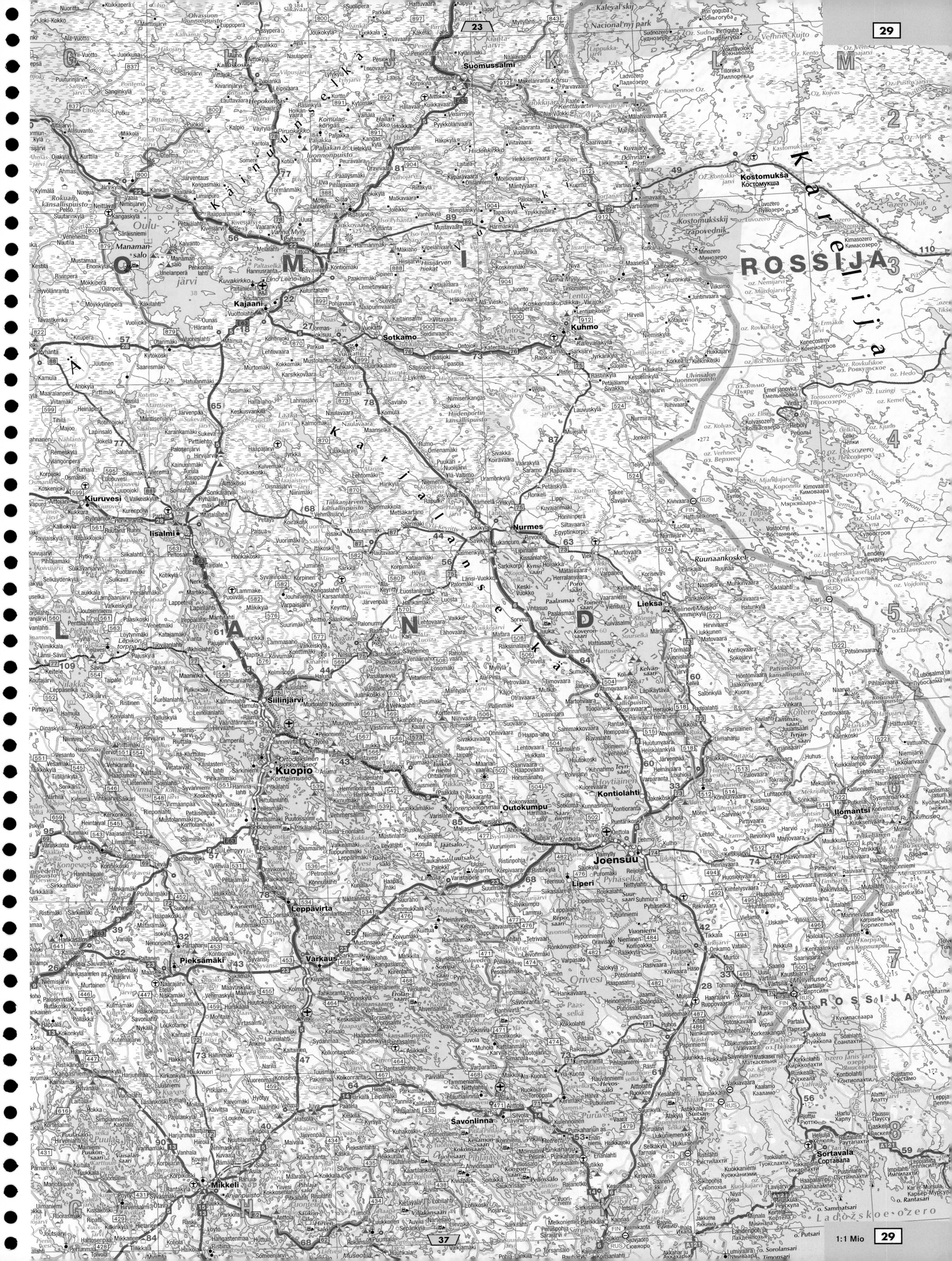
23
Kalevalʹskij Nacionalʹnyj park
Suomussalmi
Kostomukša
Костомукша
Kostomukšskij zapovednik
ROSSIJA
Karelija
Kuhmo
Sotkamo
Kajaani
Oulujärvi
Nurmes
Lieksa
Kiuruvesi
Iisalmi
Siilinjärvi
Kuopio
Outokumpu
Kontiolahti
Joensuu
Liperi
Ilomantsi
Leppävirta
Varkaus
Pieksämäki
Mikkeli
Savonlinna
Sortavala
Сортавала
Ladožskoe ozero
37
1:1 Mio

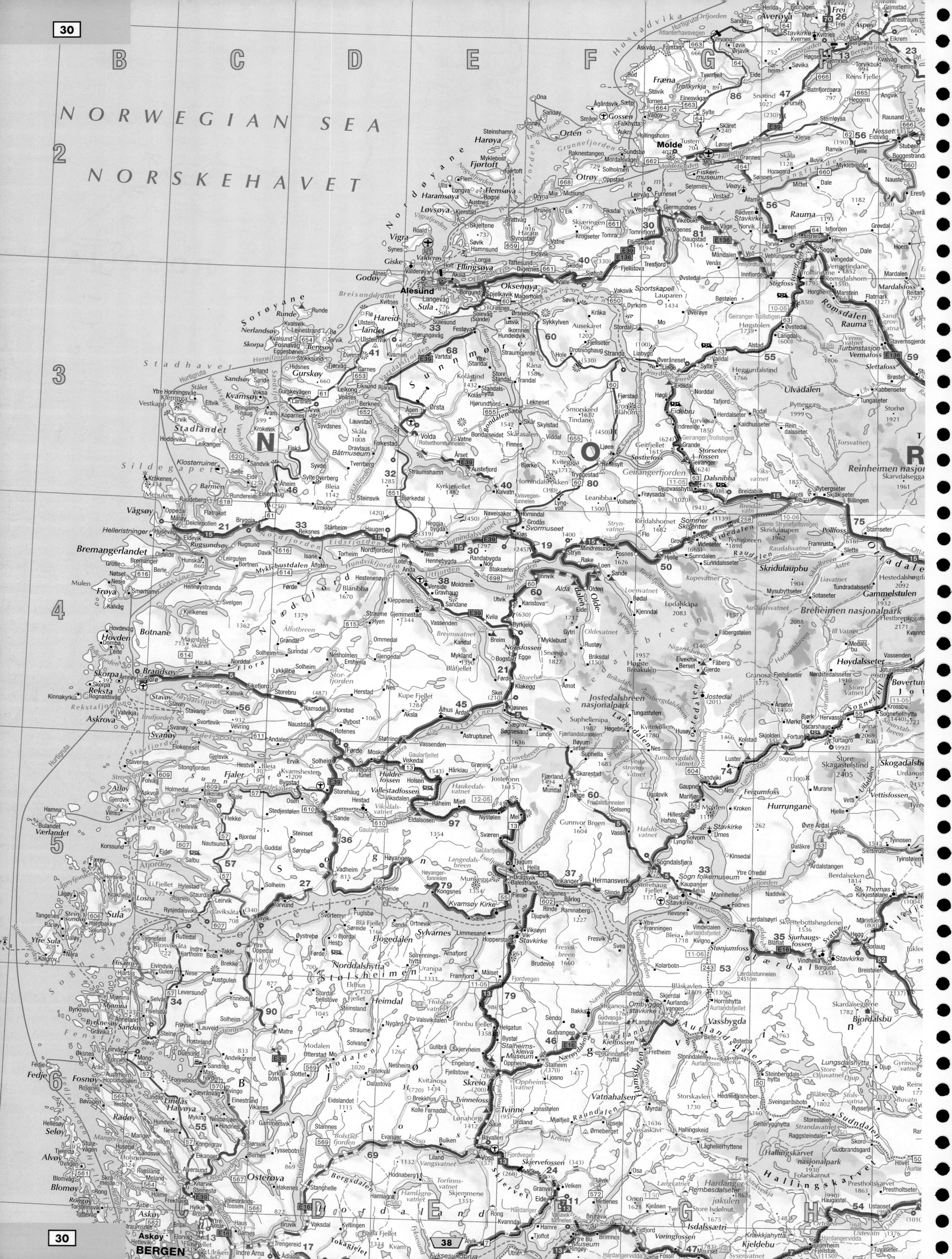
B
C
D
E
F
G
H
2
3
4
5
6
NORWEGIAN SEA
NORSKEHAVET
Molde
Ålesund
Hareidlandet
Sula
Ellingsøya
Oksenøya
Vigra
Godøy
Giske
Harøya
Fjørtoft
Flemsøya
Haramsøya
Løvsøya
Gurskøy
Kvamsøy
Sandsøy
Stadlandet
Vågsøy
Bremangerlandet
Frøya
Hovden
Botnane
Brandsøy
Reksta
Askrova
Svanøy
Atløy
Værlandet
Sula
Ytre Sula
Hisarøy
Byrknesøy
Sandøy
Fedje
Fosnøy
Lindås Halvøya
Radøy
Seløy
Alvøy
Blomøy
Askøy
Osterøya
BERGEN
Stadhavet
Nordfjord
Geirangerfjorden
Jostedalsbreen nasjonalpark
Breheimen nasjonalpark
Reinheimen nasjonalpark
Hallingskarvet nasjonalpark
Rauma
Romsdalen
Ulvådalen
Stølsheimen
Voss
Skjervet
Trollkyrkja
Trollstigen
Dalsnibba
Sognefjellet
Hardangerjøkulen
Vøringsfossen
Sogndalsfjøra
Stalheimskleiva Museum
Sunnmøre
Hurtigruta
38

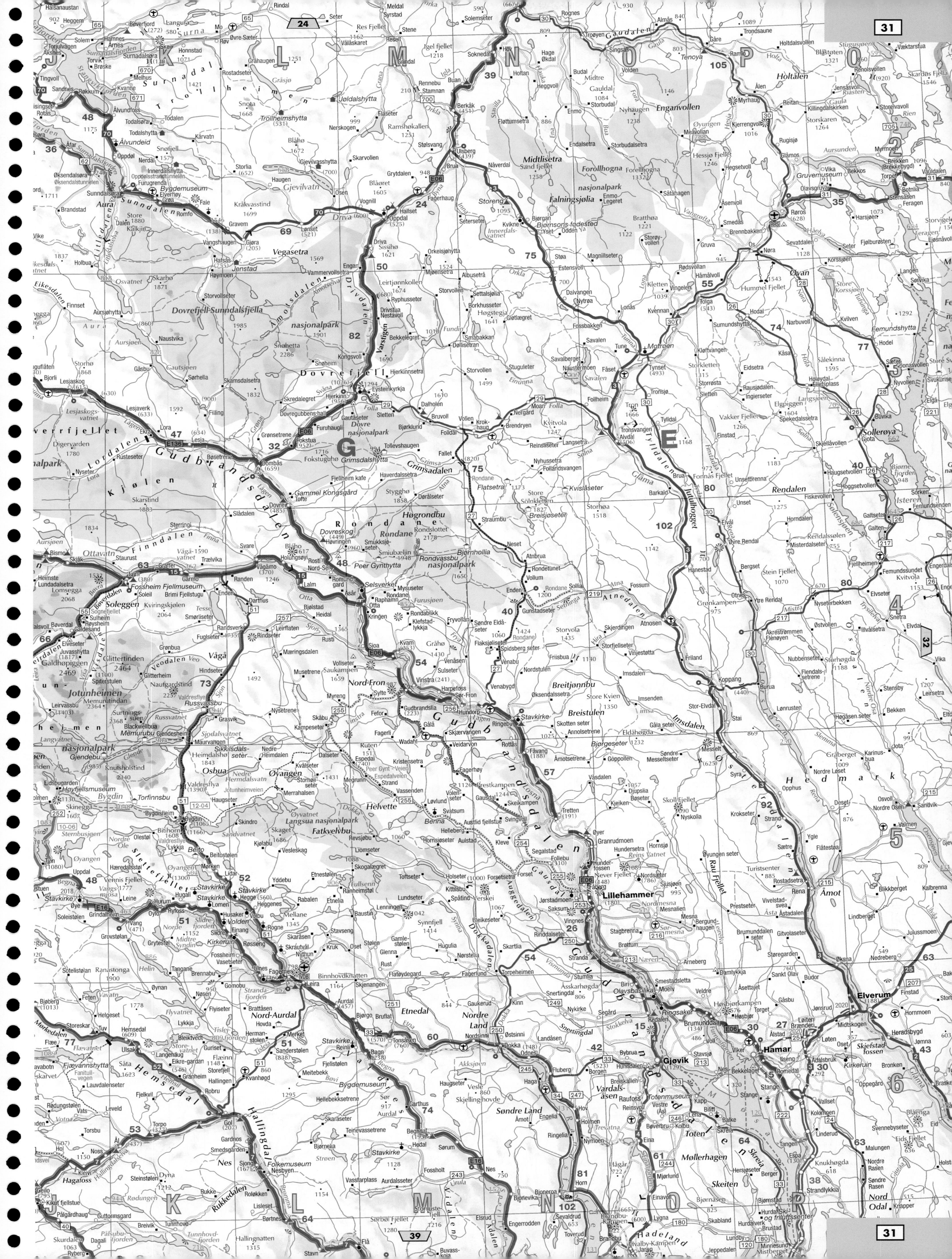
24
Surnadal
Trollheimen
Sunndalsøra
Oppdal
Dovrefjell-Sunndalsfjella nasjonalpark
Dovrefjell
Drivdalen
Midtlisetra
Forollhogna nasjonalpark
Falningsjølia
Holtålen
Røros
Tynset
Alvdal
Folldal
Dovre nasjonalpark
Grimsdalshytta
Rondane
Rondane nasjonalpark
Høgrondbu
Dombås
Dovre
Lesja
Lesjaskog
Gudbrandsdalen
Otta
Vågå
Lom
Jotunheimen
Galdhøpiggen
Glittertinden
Sjoa
Kvam
Vinstra
Nord-Fron
Ringebu
Breistulen
Imsdalen
Koppang
Rendalen
Sollerøya
Femundshytta
Hedmark
Lillehammer
Gjøvik
Hamar
Elverum
Åmot
Ringsaker
Brumunddal
Toten
Etnedal
Nordre Land
Søndre Land
Fagernes
Nord-Aurdal
Beitostølen
Valdresflya
Fatkvelvbu
Helvette
Hemsedal
Hallingdal
Gol
Nes
Ål
Hagafoss
Dokka
Biri
Moelv
Vingrom
Hadeland
Nord Odal
Møllerhagen
31

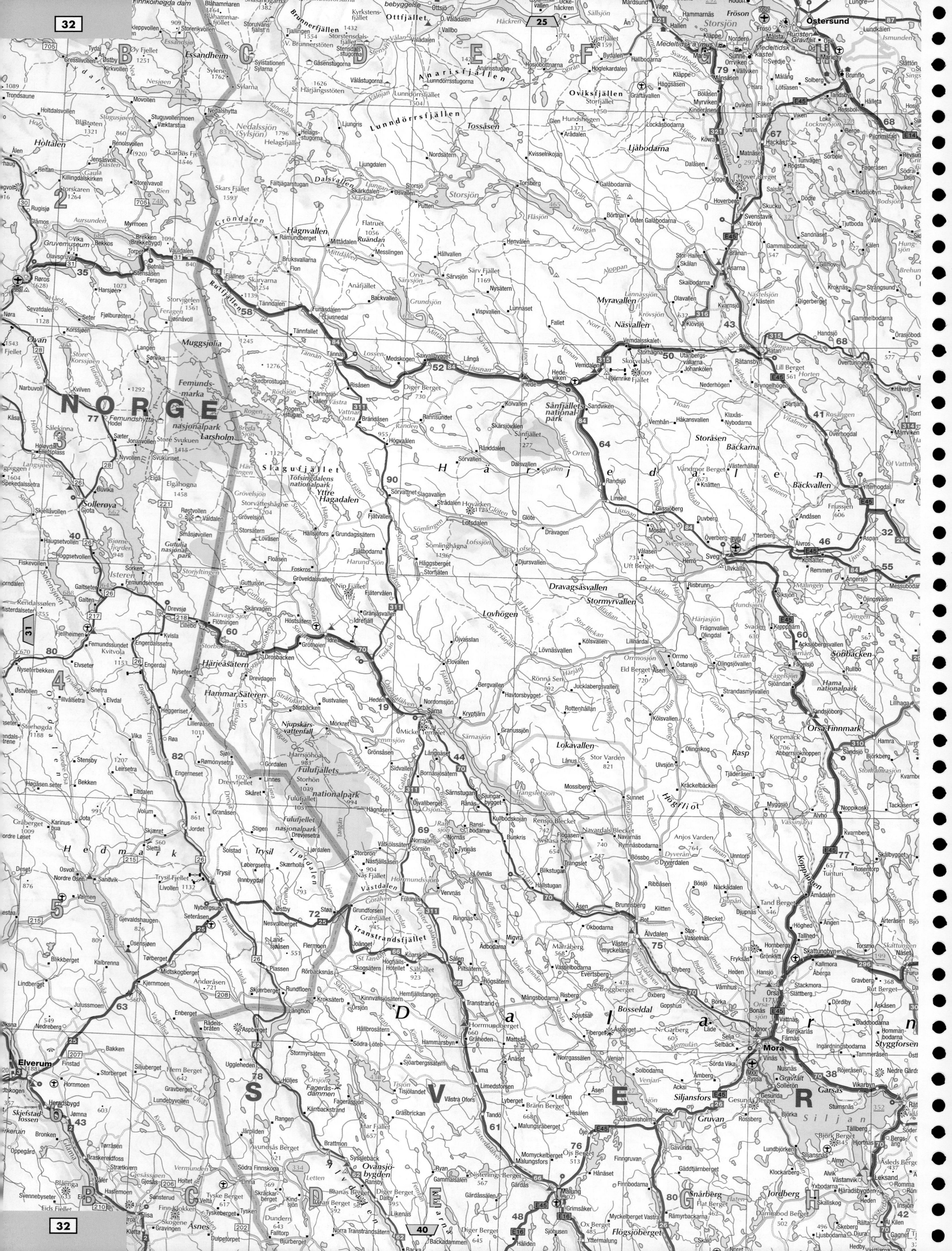

NORGE
Hedmark
SVERIGE
Härjedalen
Dalarna
Östersund
Storsjön
Frösön
Ottfjället
Anarisfjällen
Oviksfjällen
Lunndörrsfjällen
Tossåsen
Ljåbodarna
Essandheim
Sylene 1762
Nedalssjön (Sylsjön)
Holtålen
Røros
Aursunden
Grøndalen
Hågnvallen
Dalsvallen
Rutfjällen
Funäsdalen
Tännäs
Storsjö
Myravallen
Näsvallen
Vemdalen
Hede
Sånfjällets nationalpark
Femundsmarka nasjonalpark
Femundshytta
Muggsjølia
Sølekinna
Sollerøya
Isteren
Gutulia nasjonalpark
Slagufjället
Töfsingdalens nationalpark
Yttre Hagadalen
Storåsen
Bäckarna
Bäckvallen
Sveg
Hamra nationalpark
Sörbäcken
Dravagsåsvallen
Stormyrvallen
Lovhögen
Idre
Drevsjø
Härjeåsätern
Hammar Säteren
Särna
Njupskärs-vattenfall
Fulufjällets nationalpark
Fulufjellet nasjonalpark
Lokavallen
Orsa Finnmark
Rasp
Högfliot
Trysil
Ljørdalen
Transtrandsfjället
Sälen
Älvdalen
Orsa
Mora
Bosseldal
Styggforsen
Garsås
Siljan
Siljansfors
Gruvan
Elverum
Skjefstadfossen
Malung
Flögsjöberget
Snårberg
Jordberg
Leksand
Ovansjö-bygden
Fagerås-dammen
Asnes

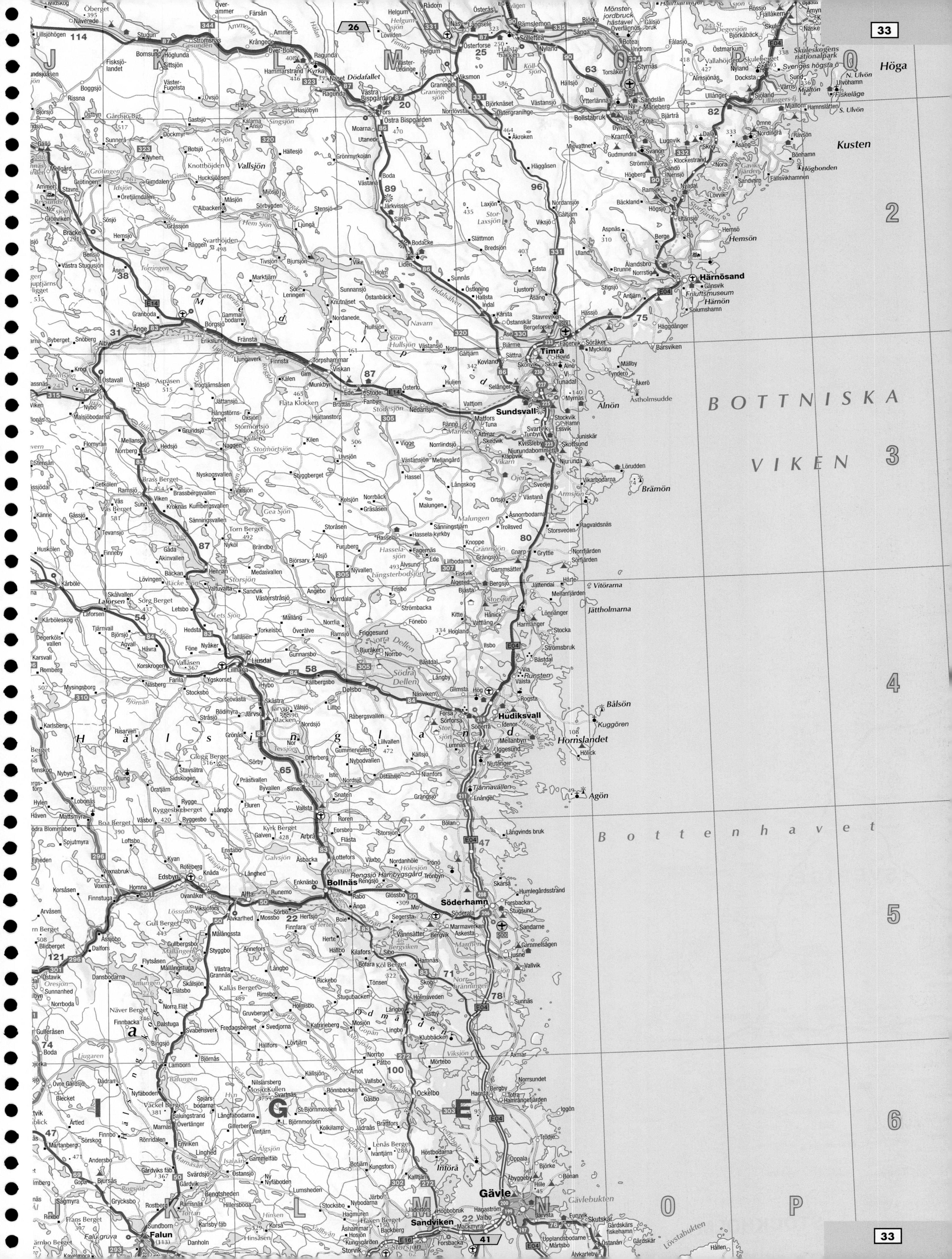
Höga
Kusten
Härnösand
Timrå
Sundsvall
Alnön
BOTTNISKA
VIKEN
Brämön
Hudiksvall
Hornslandet
Agön
Bottenhavet
Söderhamn
Bollnäs
Ljusdal
Gävle
Sandviken
Falun
Hälsingland
Gästrikland
Sollefteå
Kramfors
Ljungaverk
Fränsta
Edsbyn
Ockelbo
Delsbo
Iggesund
Järvsö
Bjästa
Njurundabommen
Medelpad
Dödafallet
Skuleskogens nationalpark
Storsjön
Indalsälven
Ljusnan
Norra Dellen
Södra Dellen
Gävlebukten
Lövstabukten

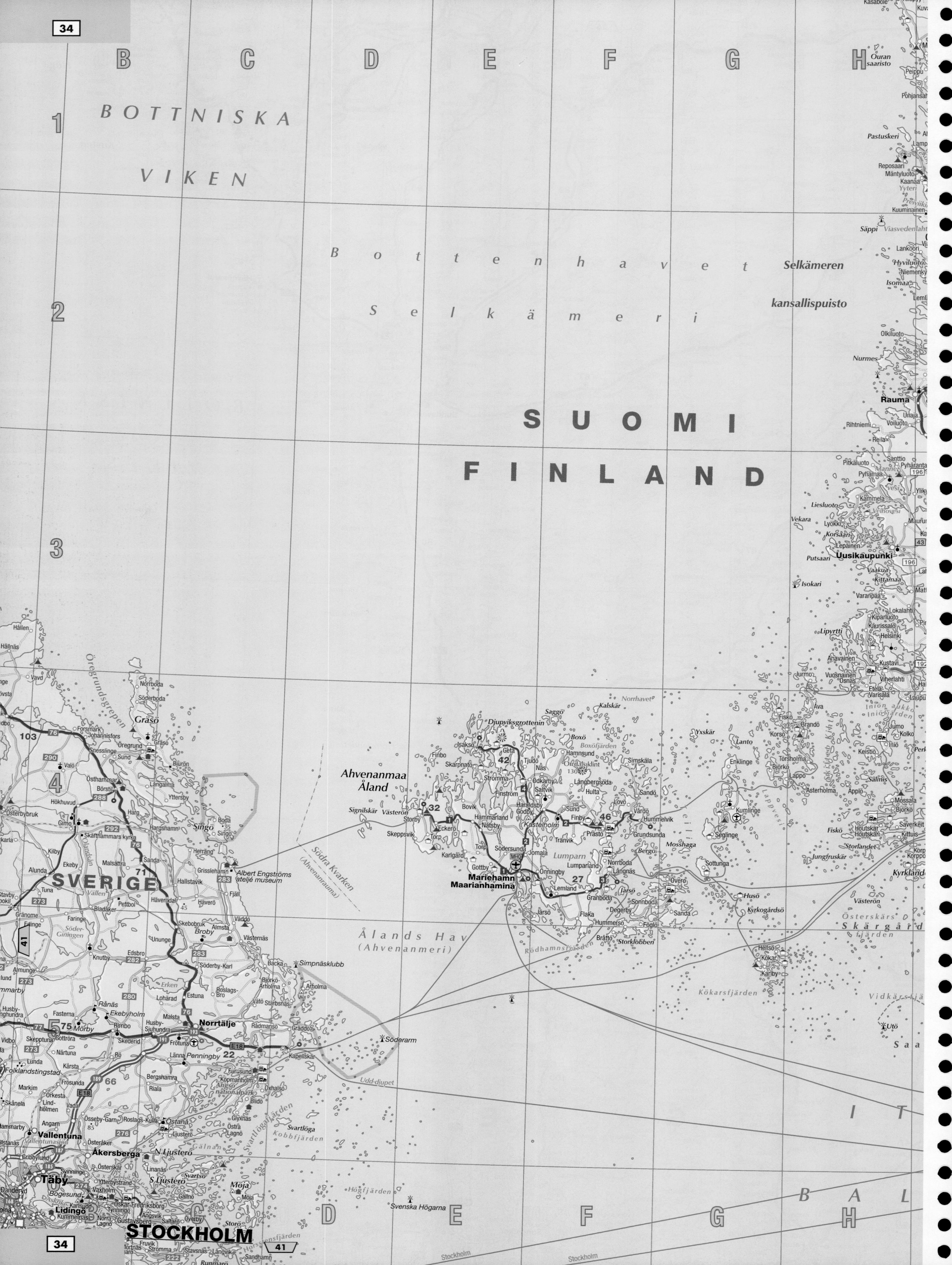
B
C
D
E
F
G
H
1
2
3
4
5
BOTTNISKA
VIKEN
Bottenhavet
Selkämeri
SUOMI
FINLAND
Selkämeren
kansallispuisto
Ahvenanmaa
Åland
Mariehamn
Maarianhamina
SVERIGE
Norrtälje
STOCKHOLM
Vallentuna
Åkersberga
Täby
Lidingö
Rauma
Uusikaupunki
Kustavi
Kyrkland
Ålands Hav
(Ahvenanmeri)
Södra Kvarken
(Ahvenanrauma)
Gräsö
Singö
Öregrundsgrepen
Östhammar
Lumparn
Kökarsfjärden
Kökar
Utö
Svenska Högarna
Söderarm
Simpnäsklubb
Möja
Ljusterö
Signilskär
Eckerö
Jomala
Lemland
Sund
Saltvik
Geta
Finström
Hammarland
Föglö
Sottunga
Kumlinge
Brändö
Vårdö
Albert Engströms ateljé museum
Udd-djupet
Stockholm
B
A
L
I
T
D
E
F
G
H

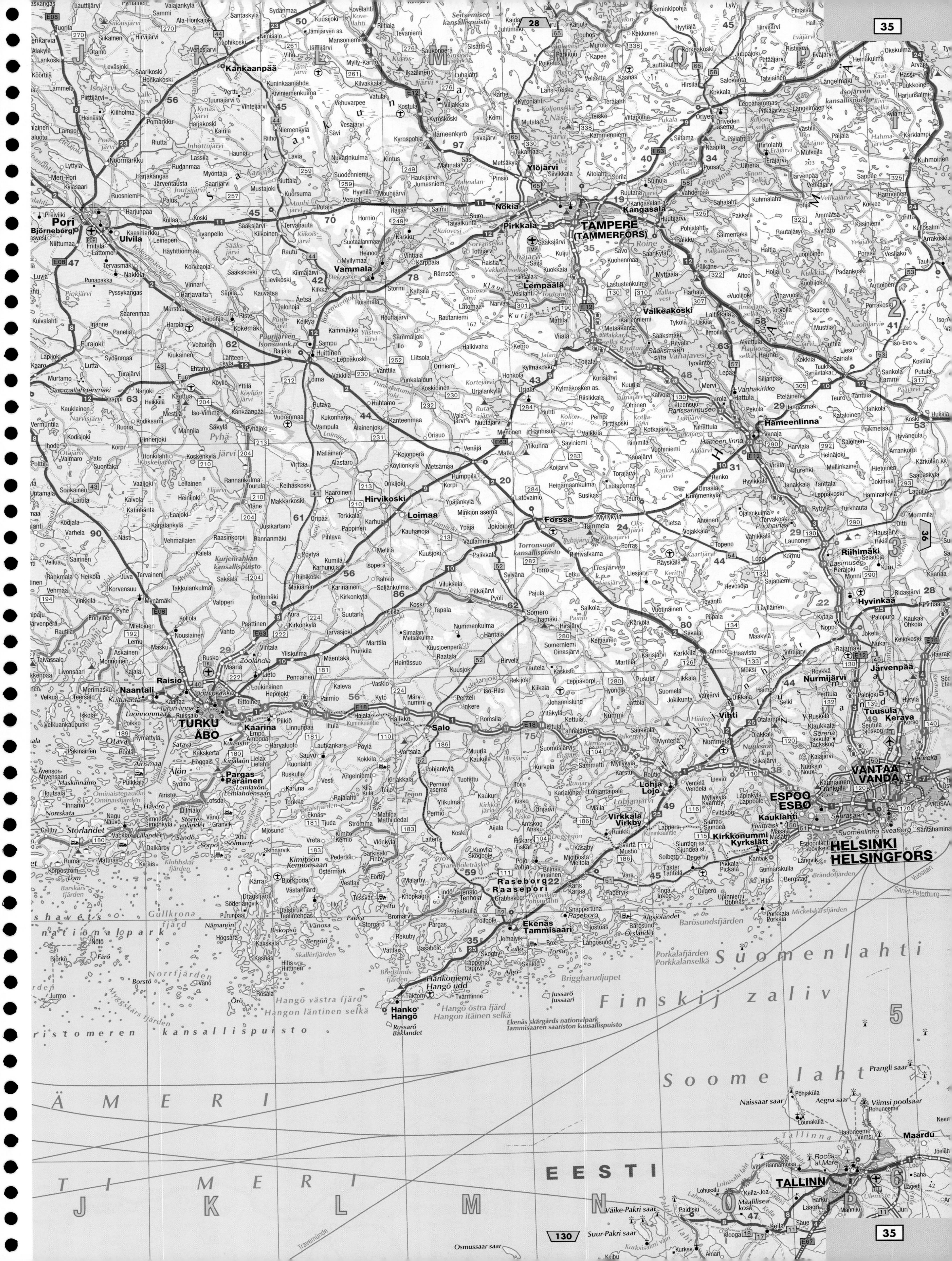
Seitsemisen kansallispuisto
Kankaanpää
Pori
Björneborg
Ulvila
Nokia
Ylöjärvi
Pirkkala
TAMPERE
(TAMMERFORS)
Kangasala
Lempäälä
Valkeakoski
Vammala
Hämeenlinna
Forssa
Torronsuon kansallispuisto
Kurjenrahkan kansallispuisto
Loimaa
Hirvikoski
Riihimäki
Hyvinkää
Järvenpää
Nurmijärvi
Tuusula
Kerava
VANTAA
VANDA
ESPOO
ESBO
Kauklahti
HELSINKI
HELSINGFORS
Kirkkonummi
Kyrkslätt
Lohja
Lojo
Virkkala
Virkby
Vihti
Salo
Raisio
Naantali
TURKU
ÅBO
Kaarina
Pargas
Parainen
Raseborg
Raasepori
Ekenäs
Tammisaari
Hanko
Hangö
Hangö västra fjärd
Hangon läntinen selkä
Hangö östra fjärd
Hangon itäinen selkä
Ekenäs skärgårds nationalpark
Tammisaaren saariston kansallispuisto
Suomenlahti
Finskij zaliv
Soome laht
EESTI
TALLINN
Maardu
Paldiski
Keila

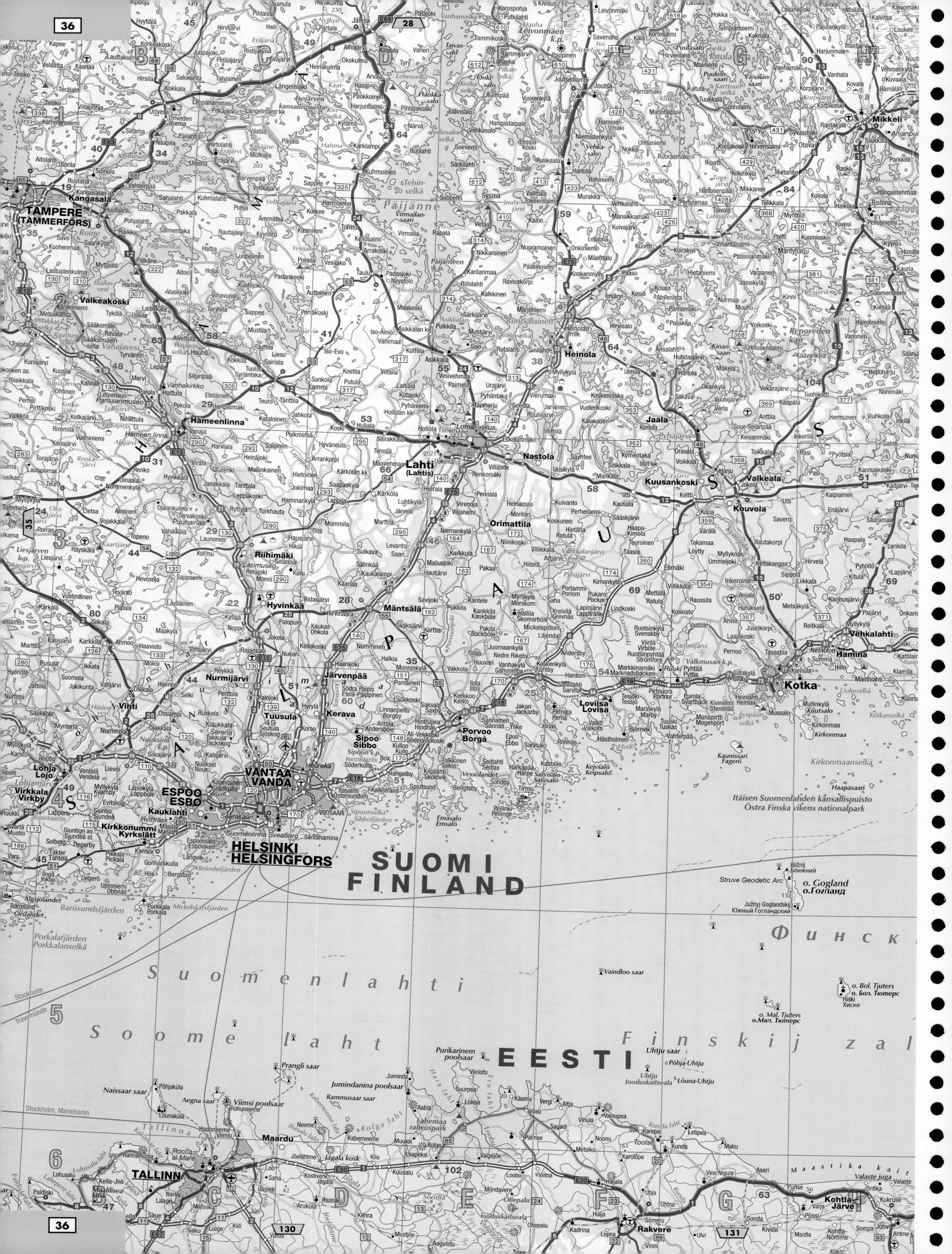
SUOMI
FINLAND
EESTI
HELSINKI
HELSINGFORS
TALLINN
TAMPERE
(TAMMERFORS)
VANTAA
VANDA
ESPOO
ESBO
Lahti
(Lahtis)
Kotka
Kouvola
Hämeenlinna
Heinola
Mikkeli
Hamina
Porvoo
Borgå
Loviisa
Lovisa
Kerava
Järvenpää
Hyvinkää
Riihimäki
Nurmijärvi
Tuusula
Mäntsälä
Orimattila
Nastola
Kuusankoski
Valkeala
Jaala
Valkeakoski
Kangasala
Lohja
Lojo
Vihti
Kirkkonummi
Kyrkslätt
Kauklahti
Sipoo
Sibbo
Maardu
Kohtla-Järve
Rakvere
Vehkalahti
Päijänne
Suomenlahti
Soome laht
Finskij zal
Финск
Itäisen Suomenlahden kansallispuisto
Östra Finska vikens nationalpark
Kirkonmaanselkä
Struve Geodetic Arc
o. Gogland
о.Гогланд
Južnyj Goglandskij
Южный Гогландский
o. Bol. Tjuters
о. Бол. Тюерс
Hiski
Хиски
o. Mal. Tjuters
о.Мал. Тюерс
Vaindloo saar
Prangli saar
Naissaar saar
Aegna saar
Viimsi poolsaar
Jumindanina poolsaar
Rammusaar saar
Purikarinem poolsaar
Uhtju saar
Lahemaa rahvuspark
Kolga laht
Tallinna laht
Kunda laht
Maastika kait
Stockholm
Travemünde
Stockholm, Mariehamn
Porkalafjärden
Porkkalanselkä
Barösundsfjärden
Mickelskärsfjärden
Brändöfjärden
Suomenlinna Sveaborg
Sipoonselkä
Sibbofjärden
Emsalo
Pellinki
Pellinge
Kaunissaari
Fagerö
Haapasaari
HÄME
PÄIJÄT-HÄME
UUSIMAA
KYMENLAAKSO
Repoveden k.p.
Leivonmäen k.p.
Päijänteen k.p.
Liesjärven k.p.
Nuuksion k.p.
Sipoon k.p.
Valkmusan k.p.

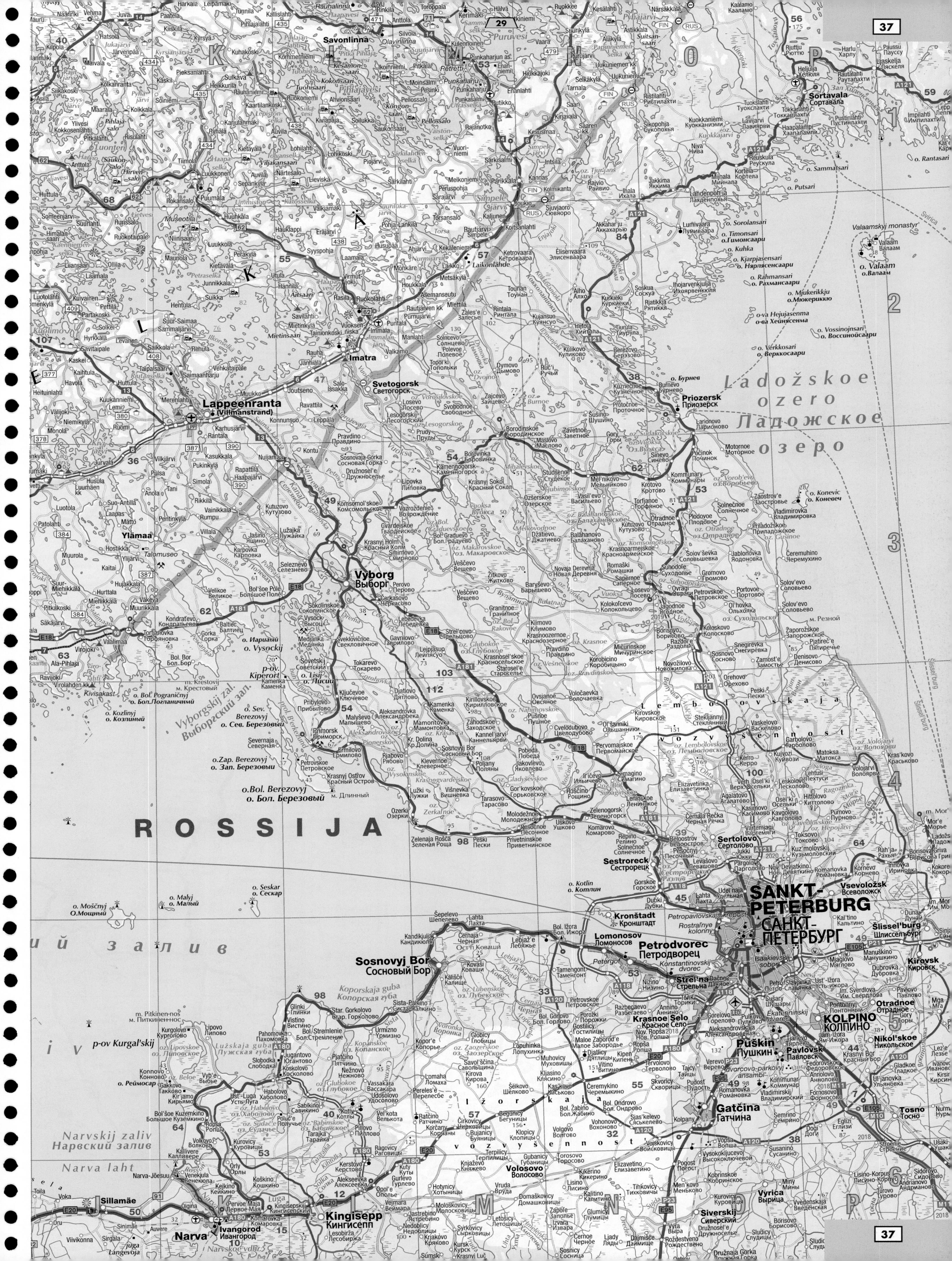
Savonlinna
Sortavala
Сортавала
Imatra
Svetogorsk
Светогорск
Lappeenranta
(Villmanstrand)
Priozersk
Приозерск
Ladožskoe
ozero
Ладожское
озеро
Valaamskij monastyr'
o. Valaam
о. Валаам
o. Konevic
о. Коневец
Vyborg
Выборг
Ylämaa
Sertolovo
Сертолово
Sestroreck
Сестрорецк
SANKT-
PETERBURG
САНКТ-
ПЕТЕРБУРГ
Vsevoložsk
Всеволожск
Šlissel'burg
Шлиссельбург
Kronštadt
Кронштадт
Lomonosov
Ломоносов
Petrodvorec
Петродворец
Sosnovyj Bor
Сосновый Бор
Krasnoe Selo
Красное Село
Puškin
Пушкин
Pavlovsk
Павловск
KOLPINO
КОЛПИНО
Otradnoe
Nikol'skoe
Никольское
Tosno
Тосно
Gatčina
Гатчина
Volosovo
Волосово
Kingisepp
Кингисепп
Ivangorod
Ивангород
Narva
Sillamäe
Siverskij
Сиверский
Vyrica
Вырица
ROSSIJA
Vyborgskij zal.
Выборгский зал.
Koporskaja guba
Копорская губа
Lužskaja guba
Лужская губа
Narvskij zaliv
Нарвский залив
Narva laht
p-ov Kurgal'skij
o. Moščnyj
О. Мощный
o. Malyj
о. Малый
o. Seskar
о. Сескар
o. Kotlin
о. Котлин
o.Bol. Berezovyj
о.Бол. Березовый
Lembolovskaja vozvyšennost'
Ižorskaja vozvyšennost'
Saimaa
FIN
RUS
E18
E20
E105
A121
A181
A180
A120

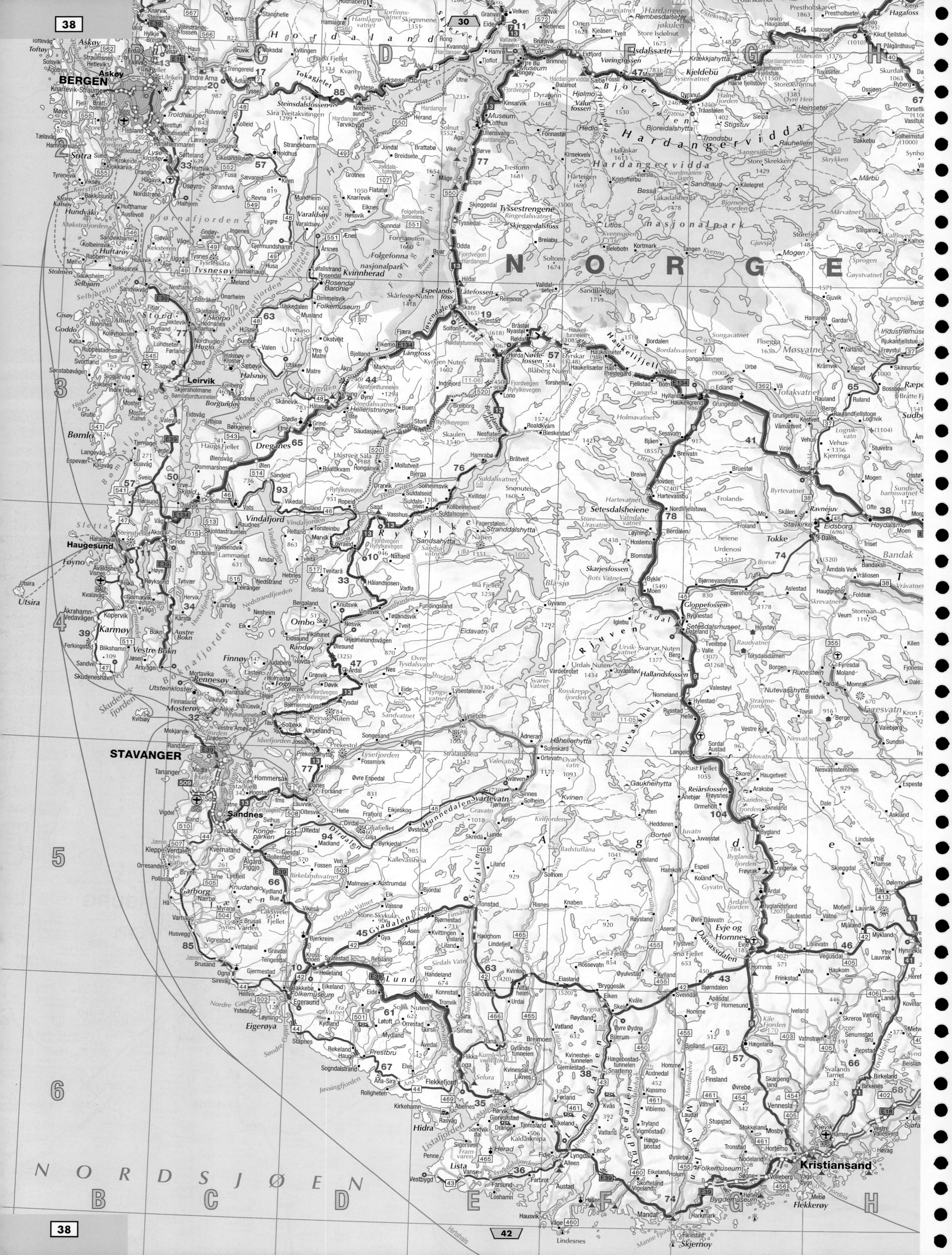
30
BERGEN
Askøy
Sotra
Hordaland
Hardangervidda
Hardangervidda nasjonalpark
Folgefonna nasjonalpark
Bjørnafjorden
Bømlo
Stord
Tysnesøy
Leirvik
Haugesund
Utsira
Karmøy
Kopervik
Skudeneshavn
Boknafjorden
Rennesøy
Finnøy
Mosterøy
STAVANGER
Sandnes
Jæren
Ryfylke
Ombo
Vindafjord
Sauda
Odda
Setesdalsheiene
Setesdal
Hardangerjøkulen
Haukelifjell
NORGE
Agder
Lysefjorden
Preikestolen
Kjerag
Gyadalen
Sirdalen
Egersund
Eigerøya
Flekkefjord
Lista
Farsund
Mandal
Lindesnes
Kristiansand
Flekkerøy
Evje og Hornnes
Byglandsfjord
Tokke
Dalen
Bandak
Totakvatnet
Møsvatnet
Skjernøy
NORDSJØEN
Hirtshals
42

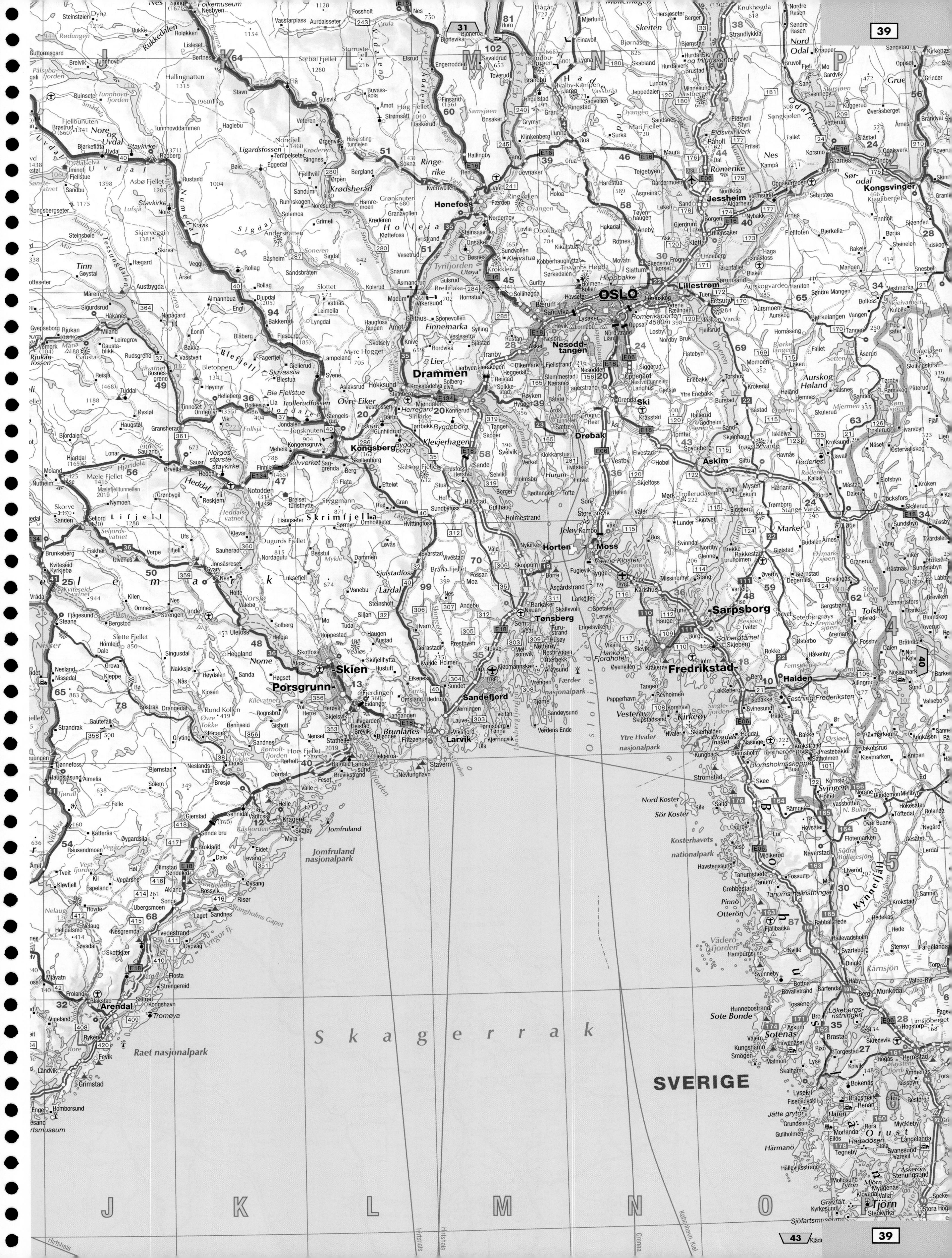

OSLO
Drammen
Hønefoss
Kongsberg
Skien
Porsgrunn
Larvik
Sandefjord
Tønsberg
Horten
Moss
Fredrikstad
Sarpsborg
Halden
Lillestrøm
Jessheim
Drøbak
Ski
Askim
Arendal
Grimstad
Notodden
Kragerø
Risør
Tvedestrand
Strömstad
Tjörn
Skagerrak
SVERIGE
Oslofjorden
Raet nasjonalpark
Jomfruland nasjonalpark
Færder nasjonalpark
Ytre Hvaler nasjonalpark
Kosterhavets nationalpark
Tyrifjorden
Numedal
Uvdal
Hallingnatten
Ringerike
Romerike
Krødsherad
Sigdal
Lifjell
Skrimfjella
Blefjell
Norges største stavkirke
Nord Koster
Sör Koster
Sotenäs
Orust
Kynnefjäll
Hirtshals
Grenaa
København, Kiel
J
K
L
M
N
O
P

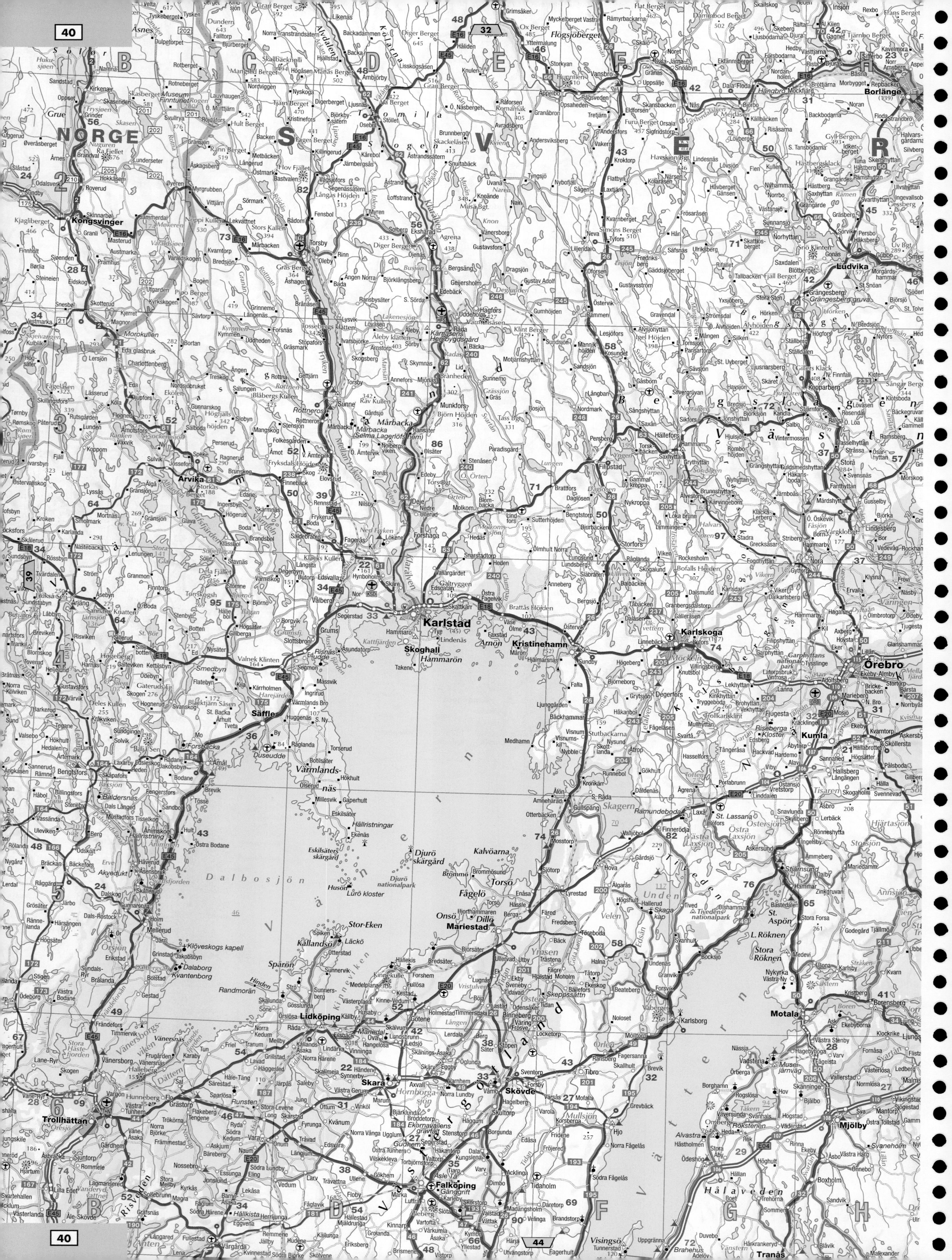
NORGE
S
V
E
R
Kongsvinger
Arvika
Säffle
Karlstad
Skoghall
Hammarön
Kristinehamn
Karlskoga
Örebro
Kumla
Borlänge
Ludvika
Lindesberg
Filipstad
Torsby
Sunne
Munkfors
Forshaga
Åmål
Mellerud
Trollhättan
Vänersborg
Lidköping
Mariestad
Skövde
Skara
Falköping
Hjo
Motala
Mjölby
Tranås
Vadstena
Askersund
Laxå
Tibro
Karlsborg
Vänern
Vättern
Dalbosjön
Värmlandsnäs
Kållandsö
Torsö
Djurö skärgård
Bergslagen
Västergötland
Dalsland
Tiveden
Hålaveden
Skagern
Unden
Viken
Fryken
E18
E20
E45
E16
E4

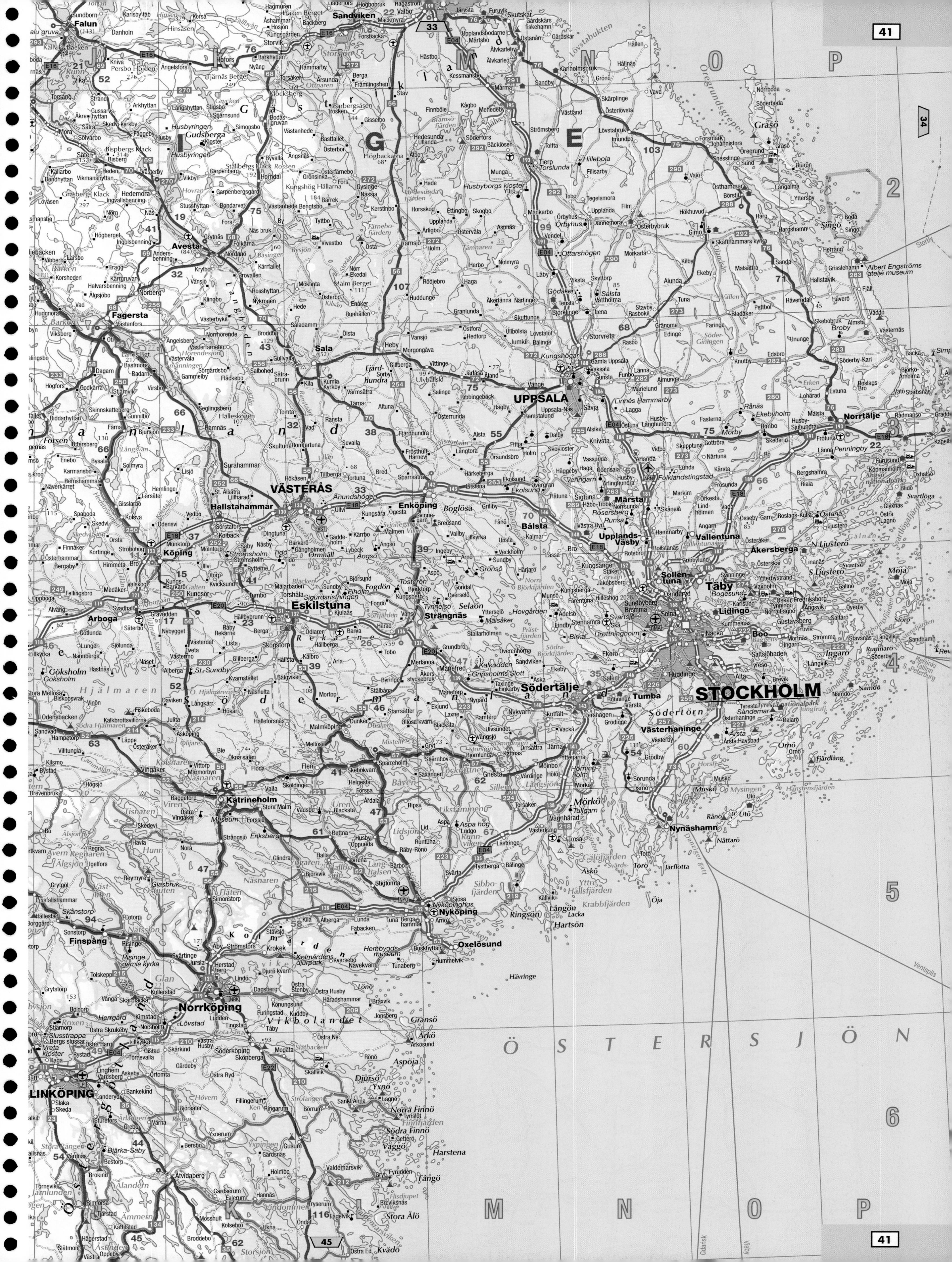
STOCKHOLM
UPPSALA
VÄSTERÅS
Eskilstuna
Norrköping
LINKÖPING
Nyköping
Södertälje
Strängnäs
Enköping
Sala
Falun
Avesta
Fagersta
Köping
Arboga
Katrineholm
Finspång
Oxelösund
Nynäshamn
Norrtälje
Sandviken
Hallstahammar
Bålsta
Märsta
Upplands-Väsby
Sollentuna
Täby
Lidingö
Vallentuna
Åkersberga
Tumba
Västerhaninge
Nacka
Solna
Sundbyberg
Huddinge
Boo
Östhammar
Gimo
Tierp
Hallstavik
Söderköping
Valdemarsvik
Åtvidaberg
Hjälmaren
Östersjön
Södermanland
Kolmården
Vikbolandet
Södertörn
Mälaren
Gräsö
Singö
Arholma
Utö
Landsort
Trosa
Gnesta
Flen
Vingåker
Kungsör
Surahammar
Hedemora
Norberg
Heby
Gävle
Älvkarleby
Skutskär
Hållnäs
Öregrund
Dannemora
Örbyhus
Mörkö
Ösmo
Sorunda
Vagnhärad
Ekolsund
Gripsholms Slott
Mariefred
Albert Engströms ateljé museum
Tyresta nationalpark
Stora Ålö
Harstena
Häradshammar
Arkösund
Gränsö

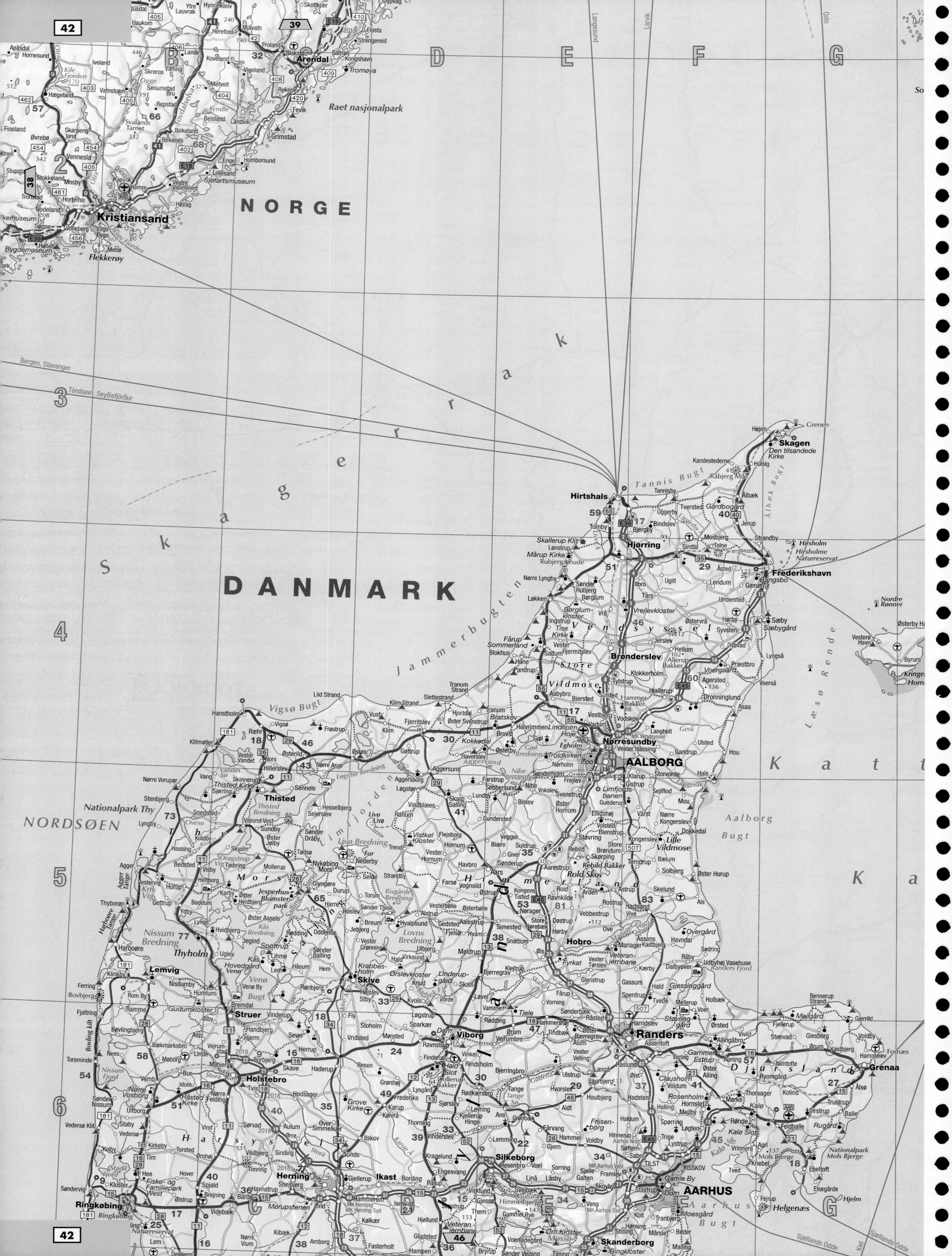

42
NORGE
Kristiansand
Arendal
Grimstad
Raet nasjonalpark
Skagerrak
DANMARK
Hirtshals
Hjørring
Skagen
Frederikshavn
Brønderslev
Nørresundby
AALBORG
Thisted
Nationalpark Thy
NORDSØEN
Jammerbugten
Vendsyssel
Himmerland
Lemvig
Struer
Skive
Viborg
Hobro
Randers
Holstebro
Herning
Ikast
Silkeborg
Grenaa
AARHUS
Skanderborg
Ringkøbing
Kattegat
Aalborg Bugt
Djursland
Aarhus Bugt
Læsø Rende
Bergen, Stavanger
Tórshavn, Seyðisfjörður
D
E
F
G
3
4
5
6
42

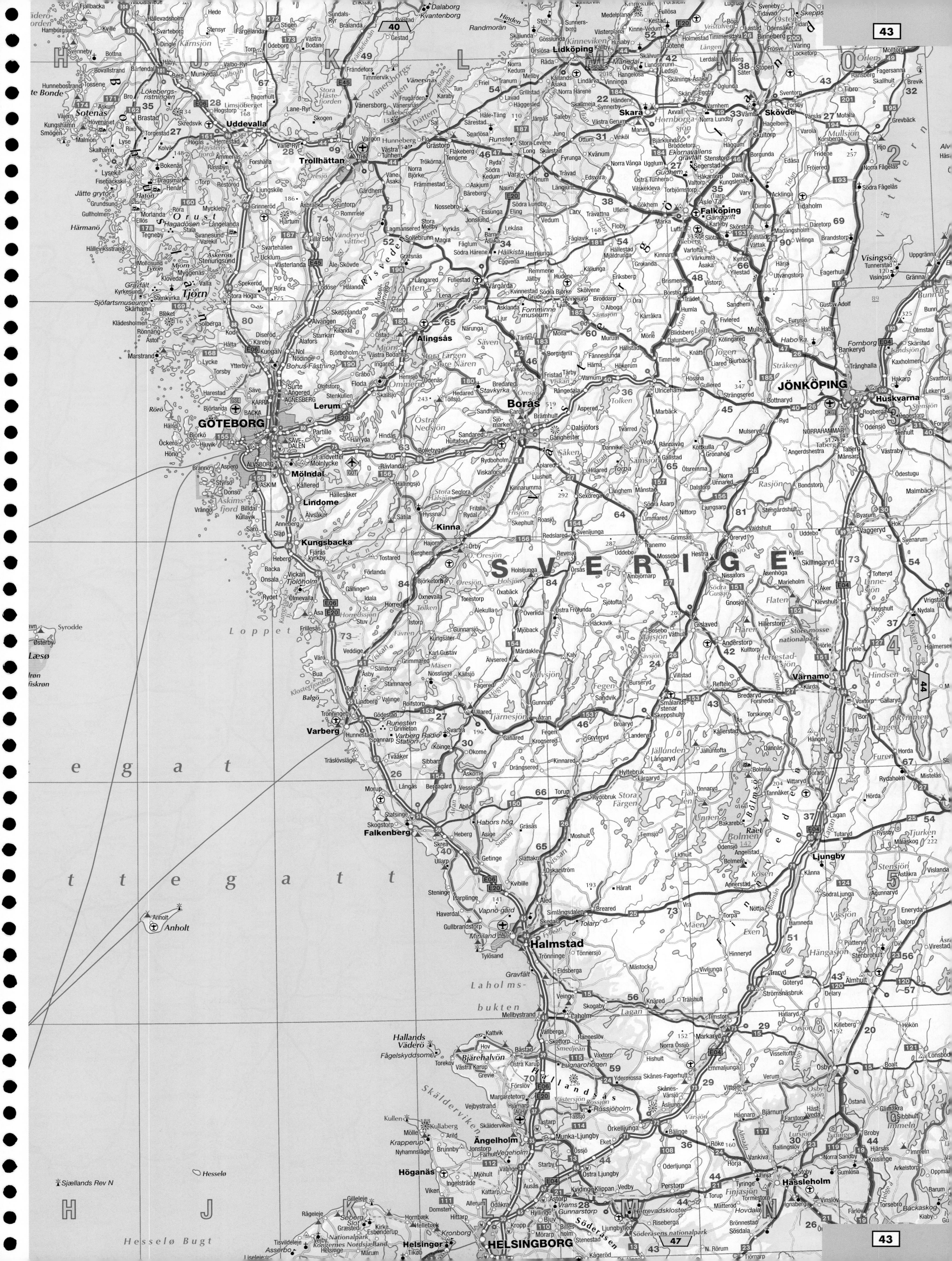

SVERIGE
GÖTEBORG
JÖNKÖPING
HELSINGBORG
Borås
Halmstad
Trollhättan
Uddevalla
Lidköping
Skara
Skövde
Falköping
Alingsås
Lerum
Mölndal
Lindome
Kungsbacka
Kinna
Varberg
Falkenberg
Ängelholm
Höganäs
Hässleholm
Ljungby
Värnamo
Gislaved
Huskvarna
Helsingør
Anholt
Læsø
Hesselø
Kattegatt
Laholmsbukten
Skälderviken
Hesselø Bugt
Orust
Tjörn
Vättern
Bolmen
Hallandsås
Söderåsen

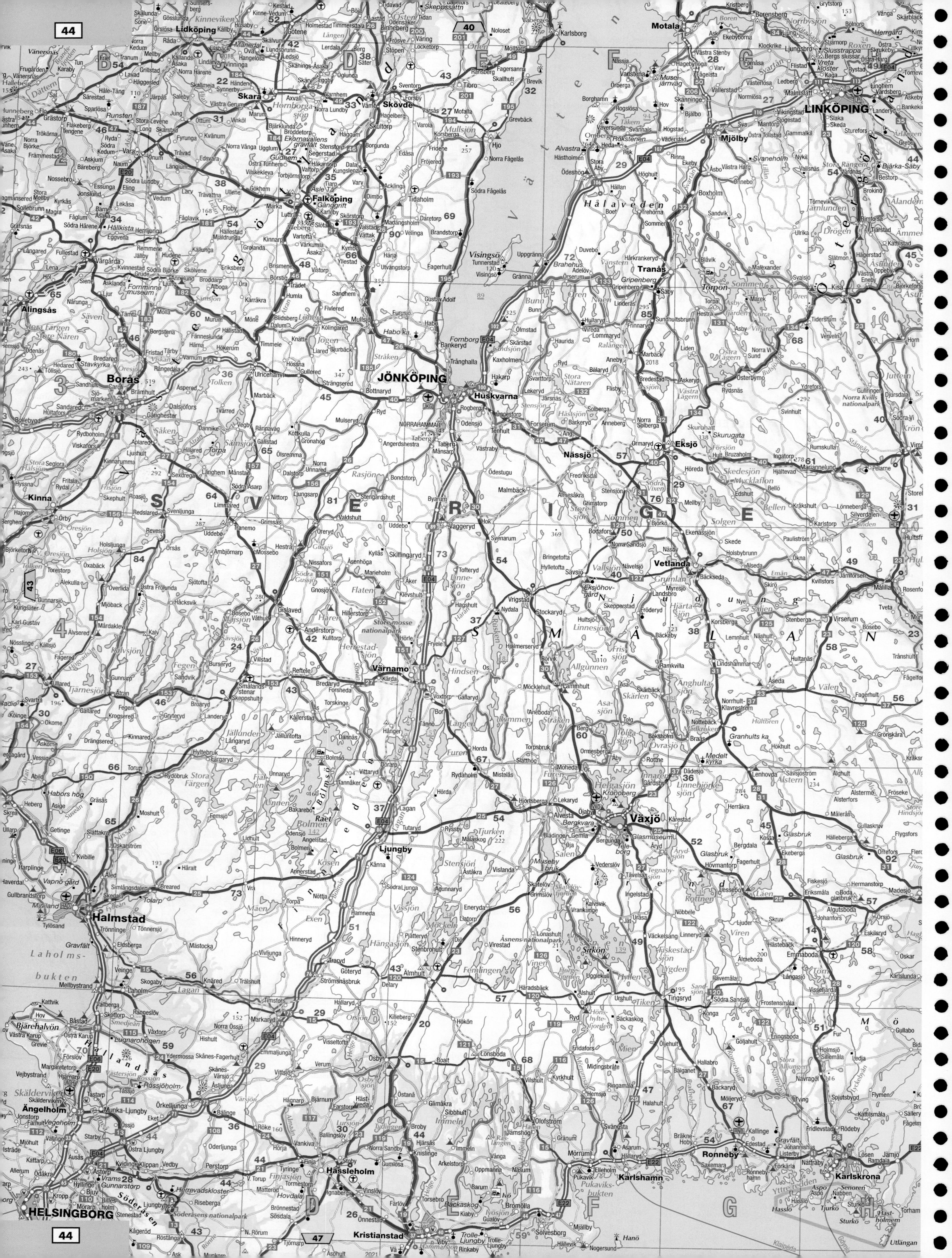

40
Lidköping
Skara
Skövde
Motala
Linköping
Mjölby
Falköping
Alingsås
Borås
Jönköping
Huskvarna
Tranås
Eksjö
Nässjö
Vetlanda
Värnamo
Ljungby
Växjö
Halmstad
Ängelholm
Hässleholm
Kristianstad
Helsingborg
Karlshamn
Ronneby
Karlskrona
Laholmsbukten
43
S V E R I G E
S M Å L A N D
47

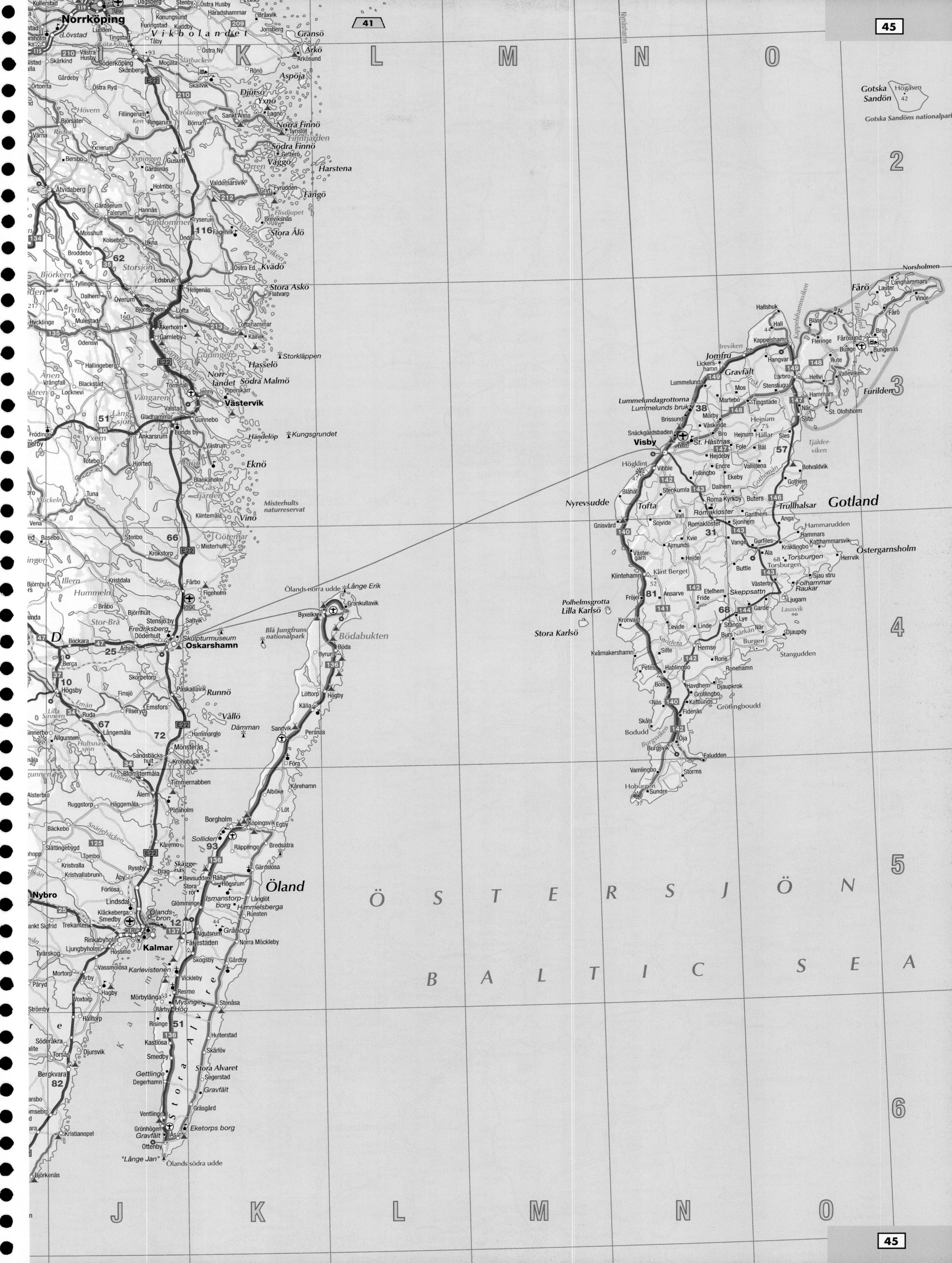
41
K
L
M
N
O
J
K
L
M
N
O
2
3
4
5
6
Norrköping
Vikbolandet
Söderköping
Arkösund
Aspöja
Djursö
Yxnö
Norra Finnö
Södra Finnö
Vaggö
Harstena
Fångö
Valdemarsvik
Stora Ålö
Kvädö
Stora Askö
Åtvidaberg
Gamleby
Storkläppen
Hasselö
Norr-landet
Södra Malmö
Västervik
Kungsgrundet
Händelöp
Eknö
Misterhults naturreservat
Vinö
Oskarshamn
Skulpturmuseum
Blå Jungfruns nationalpark
Ölands norra udde
Långe Erik
Grankullavik
Byxelkrok
Bödabukten
Böda
Byrum
Löttorp
Högby
Källa
Sandvik
Persnäs
Föra
Kårehamn
Alböke
Borgholm
Köpingsvik
Solliden
Räpplinge
Bredsätra
Gärdslösa
Öland
Runnö
Vållö
Dämman
Mönsterås
Timmernabben
Påtaholm
Kalmar
Ölandsbron
Färjestaden
Karlevistenen
Mörbylånga
Mysinge
Stenåsa
Hulterstad
Skärlöv
Stora Alvaret
Segerstad
Gräsgård
Eketorps borg
"Långe Jan"
Ölands södra udde
Nybro
Bergkvara
Kristianopel
Björkenäs
Gotska Sandön
Högåsen
Gotska Sandöns nationalpark
Norsholmen
Fårö
Lauter
Langhammars
Vinör
Hallshuk
Hall
Kappelshamn
Fleringe
Fårösund
Bunge
Bungenäs
Furilden
Jomfru
Lickershamn
Gravfält
Lummelunda
Lummelundagrottorna
Lummelunds bruk
Slite
St. Olofsholm
Visby
Snäckgårdsbaden
St. Hästnäs
Högklint
Tjäldervikken
Botvaldvik
Gothem
Nyrevsudde
Tofta
Roma Kyrkby
Romakloster
Trullhalsar
Gotland
Hammarudden
Östergarnsholm
Herrvik
Torsburgen
Klint Berget
Klintehamn
Fröjel
Polhelmsgrotta
Lilla Karlsö
Stora Karlsö
Sjau stru
Folhammar Raukar
Ljugarn
Skeppsattn
Kronvall
Hemse
Närsholmen
Djaupdy
Stangudden
Ronehamn
Grötlingbo
Grötlingboudd
Bodudd
Burgsvik
Öja
Faludden
Vamlingbo
Storms
Hoburgen
Sundre
ÖSTERSJÖN
BALTIC SEA

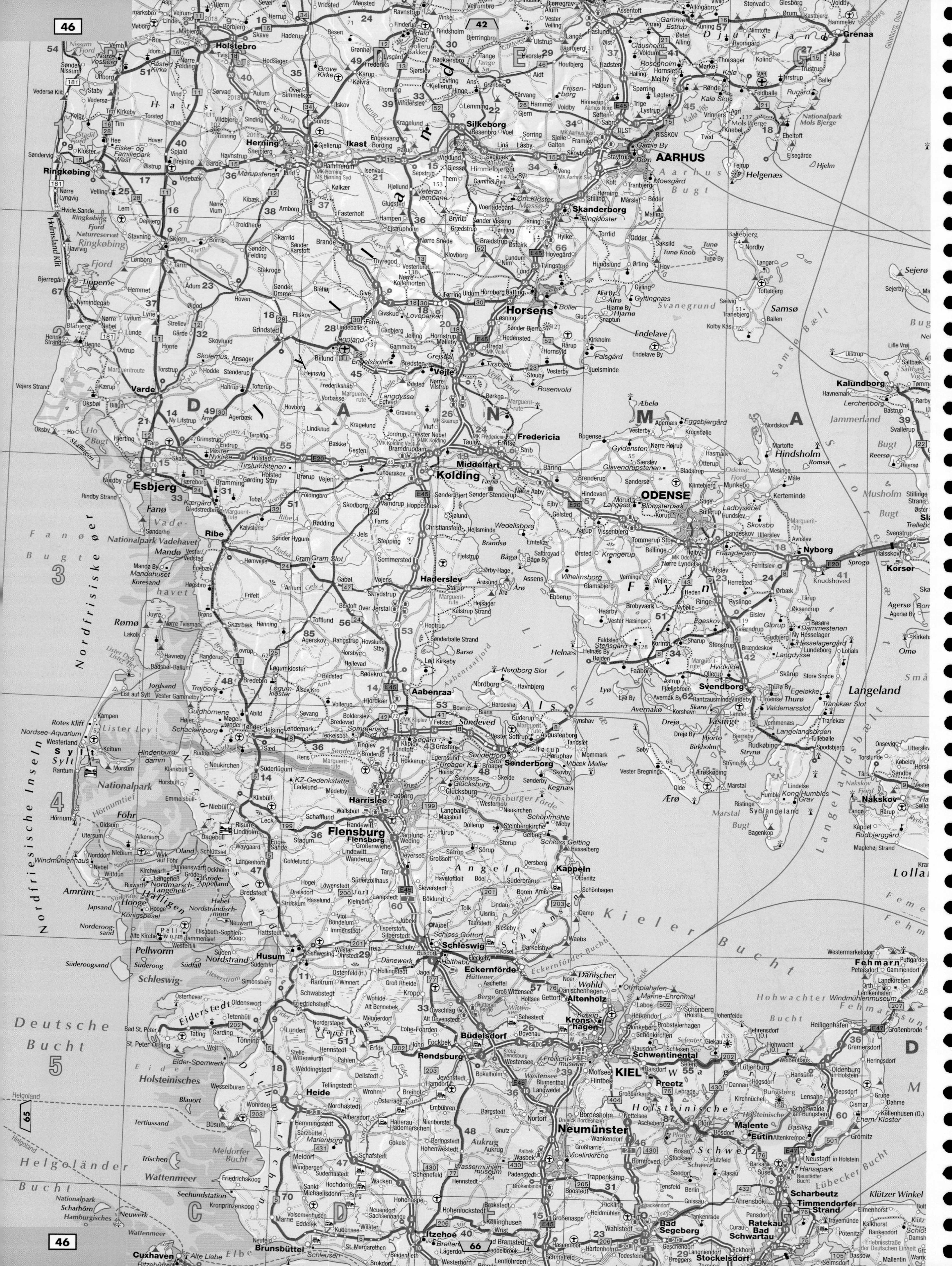
Holstebro
Herning
Ikast
Silkeborg
AARHUS
Grenaa
Ringkøbing
Skanderborg
Horsens
Vejle
Varde
Esbjerg
Kolding
Fredericia
Middelfart
ODENSE
Nyborg
Korsør
Kalundborg
Ribe
Haderslev
Aabenraa
Sønderborg
Svendborg
Langeland
Nakskov
Flensburg
Harrislee
Schleswig
Husum
Eckernförde
Kappeln
Rendsburg
Büdelsdorf
KIEL
Neumünster
Heide
Itzehoe
Brunsbüttel
Cuxhaven
Bad Segeberg
Preetz
Malente
Eutin
Fehmarn
Nationalpark Vadehavet
Nordfriesische Inseln
Nordfriesische øer
Fanø Bugt
Deutsche Bucht
Helgoländer Bucht
Kieler Bucht
Aarhus Bugt
Samsø
Fyn
Lillebælt
Storebælt
Sylt
Föhr
Amrum
Pellworm
Rømø
Fanø
Ærø
Als
Lübecker Bucht

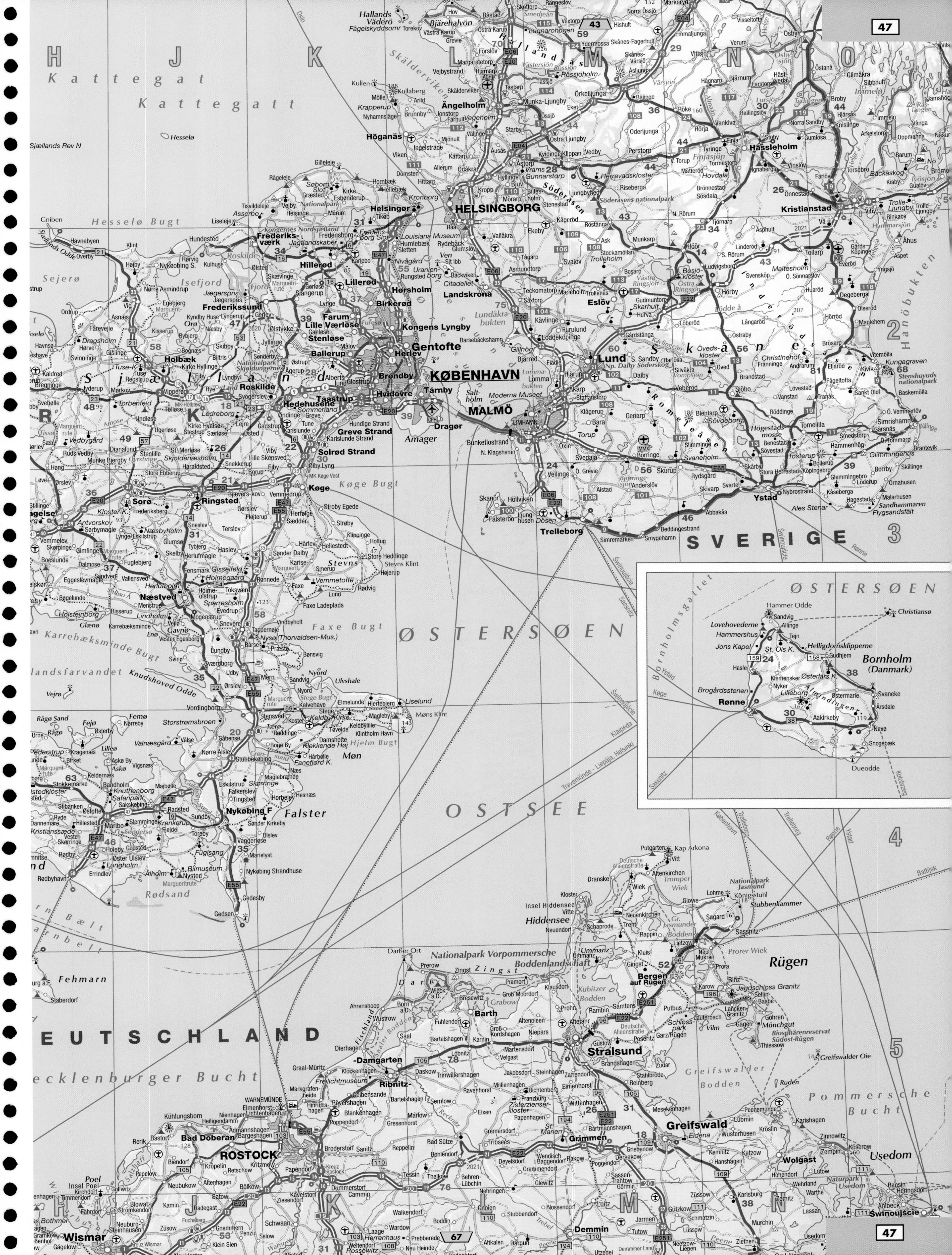
H J K L M N O
Kattegat
Kattegatt
Hesselø
Sjællands Rev N
Hesselø Bugt
Sejerø
Isefjord
Skälderviken
Hallands Väderö
Bjärehalvön
Hallandsås
Kullen
Ängelholm
Höganäs
Helsingør
HELSINGBORG
Hillerød
Frederiksværk
Frederikssund
Hørsholm
Birkerød
Farum
Kongens Lyngby
Gentofte
Ballerup
Herlev
KØBENHAVN
Brøndby
Hvidovre
Tårnby
Dragør
Amager
Landskrona
Lund
MALMÖ
Roskilde
Holbæk
Taastrup
Hedehusene
Greve Strand
Solrød Strand
Køge
Køge Bugt
Ringsted
Sorø
Næstved
Stevns
Faxe Bugt
Kristianstad
Hässleholm
Eslöv
Höör
Söderåsen
Romeleåsen
Trelleborg
Ystad
Skanör
Falsterbo
Hanöbukten
SVERIGE
Sjælland
ØSTERSØEN
Bornholm (Danmark)
Rønne
Hammer Odde
Christiansø
Nexø
Svaneke
Dueodde
Møn
Vordingborg
Nykøbing F
Falster
Rødsand
Gedser
Fehmarn
OSTSEE
DEUTSCHLAND
Mecklenburger Bucht
Rügen
Bergen auf Rügen
Sassnitz
Hiddensee
Nationalpark Vorpommersche Boddenlandschaft
Barth
Stralsund
Greifswald
Greifswalder Bodden
Pommersche Bucht
Usedom
Wolgast
Ribnitz-Damgarten
ROSTOCK
Bad Doberan
Grimmen
Demmin
Wismar
Świnoujście
1 2 3 4 5

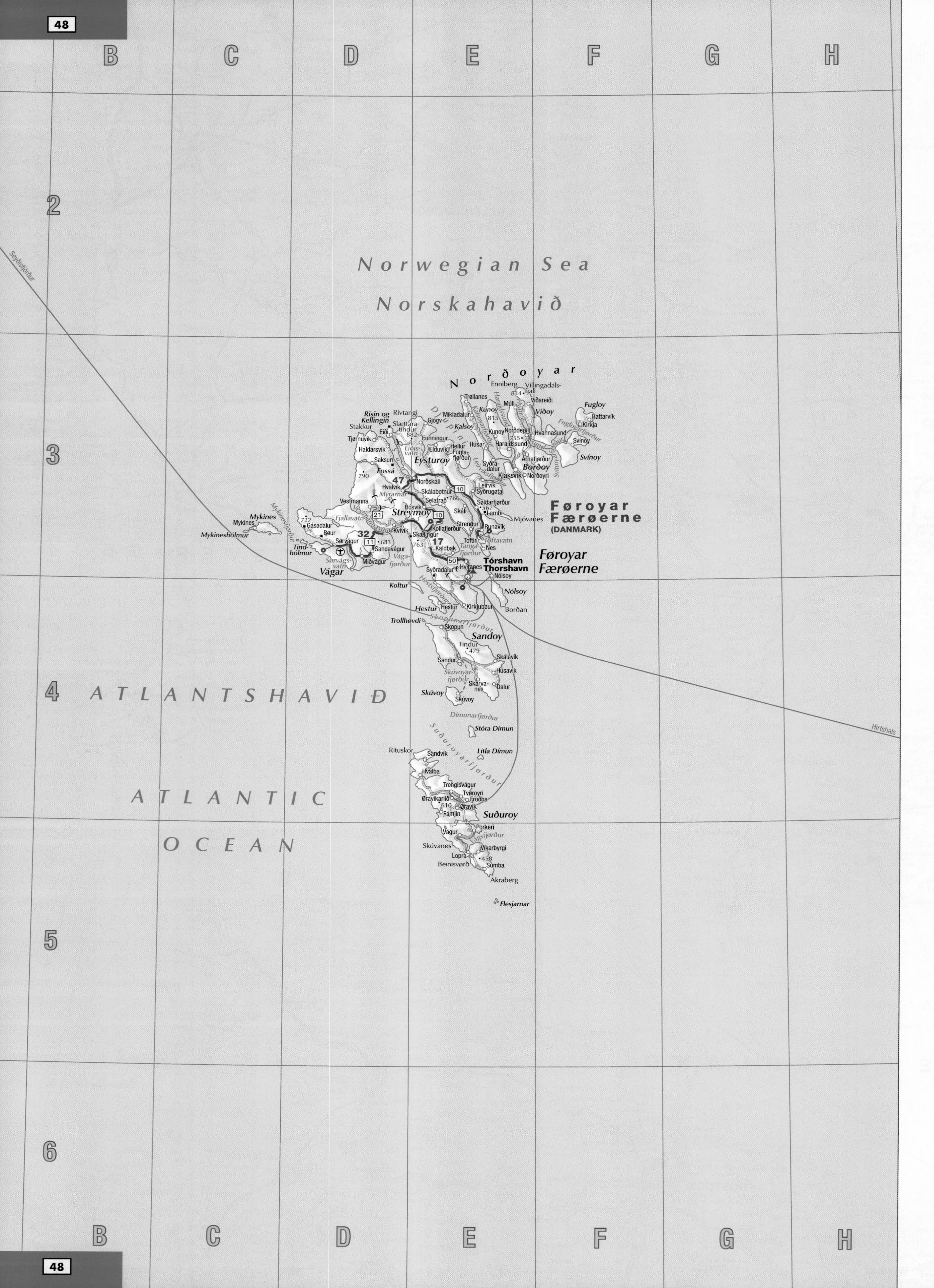

Norwegian Sea
Norskahavið

N o r ð o y a r

Enniberg Villingadals-
Trøllanes 844· fjall
Kúnoy Múli Viðareiði
Mikladalur 815 Fugloy
Risin og Rívtangi Gjógv Kalsøy Hattarvík
Kellingin Slættára- Kunoy Kirkja
Stakkur Eiði tindur Norðdepil
Tjørnuvík 882· Funningur 755· Svínoy
Haldarsvík Elduvík Húsar Hvannasund
Saksun Hellur Fugla- Svínoy
Fossá 790· **Eysturoy** fjørður Syðra- **Borðoy**
Norðskáli dalur Klaksvík Norðoyri
47 Skálabotnur Leirvík Árnafjørður
Hvalvík Selatrað 766· Syðrugøta Mjóvanes
Vestmanna Hósvík Saltangará
Streymoy Skáli Søldarfjørður **Føroyar**
Mykines Fjallavatn Norðadalur Strendur Lambi **Færøerne**
Mykines 772· Gásadalur Kvívík Kollafjørður Runavík **(DANMARK)**
Mykineshólmur Bøur **32** Skælingur Toftir
Tind- Sørvágur 683· Sandavágur 763· **17** Nes **Føroyar**
hólmur Miðvágur Kaldbak **Færøerne**
Sørvágs- **50** Hvítanes **Tórshavn**
vatn Syðradalur **Thorshavn**
Vágar Nólsoy
Koltur Nólsoy

A T L A N T S H A V I Ð

Hestur Kirkjubøur
Hestur Borðan
Trøllhøvdi Skopun
Sandoy
Tindur
·479 Skálavík
Sandur Húsavík
Skúvoyar- Skarvanes
fjørður Dalur
Skúvoy
Skúvoy
Dimunarfjørður
Stóra Dímun

A T L A N T I C
Rituskor Sandvík Litla Dímun
Sandvík
Hvalba

O C E A N
Trongisvágur
Øravíkarlíð Tvøroyri Froðba
610· Øravík
Fámjin **Suðuroy**
Vágur Porkeri
Skúvanes Víkarbyrgi
Lopra 458·
Beinisvørð Sumba
Akraberg

·Flesjarnar

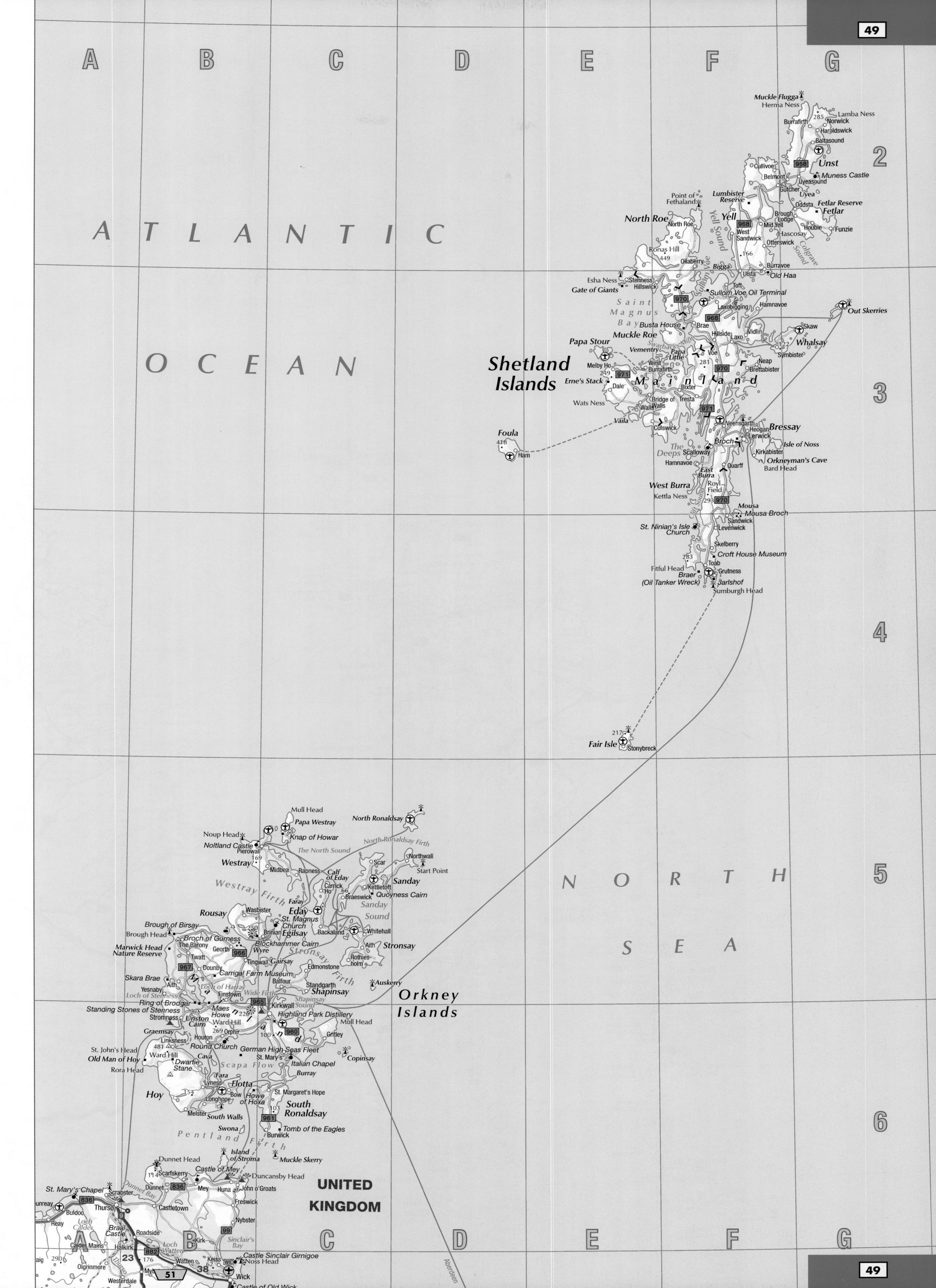

A   B   C   D   E   F   G

ATLANTIC

OCEAN

Muckle Flugga
Herma Ness
Lamba Ness
Burrafirth   285   Norwick
Haroldswick
Baltasound
968   **Unst**   Muness Castle
Cullivoe   Belmont
Point of   Lumbister   Gutcher   Uyea
Fethaland   Reserve   Uyeasound
                                                        Odsta   Fetlar Reserve
North Roe   North Roe   West   Brough   Mid Yell   Houbie   **Fetlar**
                                       Sandwick   968   Lodge   Funzie
                 Ronas Hill   Hascosay
                 449   Ollaberry   Otterswick
                                          Bigga   Burravoe
                 Esha Ness   Stenness   Ulsta   Old Haa
                 Gate of Giants Hillswick   970   Skaw
                            Saint   Sullom Voe Oil Terminal   **Out Skerries**
                 Magnus   968   Laxobigging   Hamnavoe
Shetland   **Bay**   Busta House   Brae   Hillside   Laxo   Vidlin
Islands   **Muckle Roe**   **Whalsay**
                 Papa Stour   Papa   Voe   Neap   Brettabister
                 Vementry   Little   970   Symbister
                 West   281
                 Burrafirth   **M a i n   l a n d**
                 Melby Ho 249
                 Erne's Stack   Dale'   Bixter   Veensgarth   **Bressay**
                 Wats Ness   Bridge of Tresta   971   Heogan Lerwick
                            Vaila   Walls   Cullswick   Scalloway   **Broch**   Isle of Noss
                 Foula   The   Hamnavoe   Kirkabister
                 416   Deeps   Quarff   Orkneyman's Cave
                       Ham   East   Bard Head
                                  West Burra   Burra   Royl
                                  Kettla Ness   Field
                                            29   970   Mousa
                                  St. Ninian's Isle   Sandwick   Mousa Broch
                                  Church   Levenwick
                                            Skelberry
                                  283   Croft House Museum
                 Fitful Head   Toab
                 Braer   Grutness
                 (Oil Tanker Wreck)   Jarlshof
                 Sumburgh Head

4

217   Stonybreck
Fair Isle

N O R T H

S E A

5

Mull Head
Papa Westray   North Ronaldsay
Noup Head   Knap of Howar
Noltland Castle   The North Sound   North-Ronaldsay Firth
Pierowall
Westray   169   Scar   Northwall
Midbea   Rapness   Sanday   Start Point
Westray Firth   Calf   Carrick   Sanday
           of Eday   Ho   Quoyness Cairn
Faray   Braeswick
Rousay   Wasbister   **Eday**   **Sanday**
            St. Magnus   Sound
Brough of Birsay   Church   Backaland
Brough Head   Egilsay   Whitehall
Broch of Gurness   Brinian   Aith
Marwick Head   The Barony   Wyre   **Stronsay**
Nature Reserve   Geortha   966   Rothies-
Twatt   Dounby   Edmonstone   holm
Skara Brae   Carrigal Farm Museum   Standgarth   Auskerry
Yesnaby   Aith   Balfour   **Shapinsay**
967   Loch of Harray   Standquoy
Ring of Brodgar   Finstown   Wide Firth   Shapinsay
Standing Stones of Stenness   965   Sound   Mull Head
Stromness   Ward Hill   **Kirkwall**
Graemsay   Unston   226   Highland Park Distillery
           Cairn   960   Gritley
St. John's Head   Houton   269 Orphir   Copinsay
Old Man of Hoy   Round Church   German High Seas Fleet
Rora Head   Ward Hill   St. Mary's   Italian Chapel
           Dwartie   Cava   Burray
           Stane   Scapa Flow
Hoy   Fara   Lyness   Howe
           Flotta   of Hoxa   St. Margaret's Hope
           Longhope   Bow   **South Ronaldsay**
Melster   961   Burwick
South Walls   Swona   Tomb of the Eagles
Pentland   Firth

Orkney
Islands

6

Dunnet Head
Scarfskerry   Castle of Mey
St. Mary's Chapel   Dunnet   Mey   Huna   Island of Stroma   Muckle Skerry
Scrabster   836   John o'Groats   Duncansby Head
unreay   Thurso   Castletown   Freswick
Reay   Bulldoo   Castleton   Nybster
Calder Mains   Braal   Roadside   **UNITED**
           Castle   **KINGDOM**
23   882   Kirk   Castle Sinclair Girnigoe   Noss Head
           Watten   Bay
51   38   Keiss   Wick
Westerdale   Castle of Old Wick

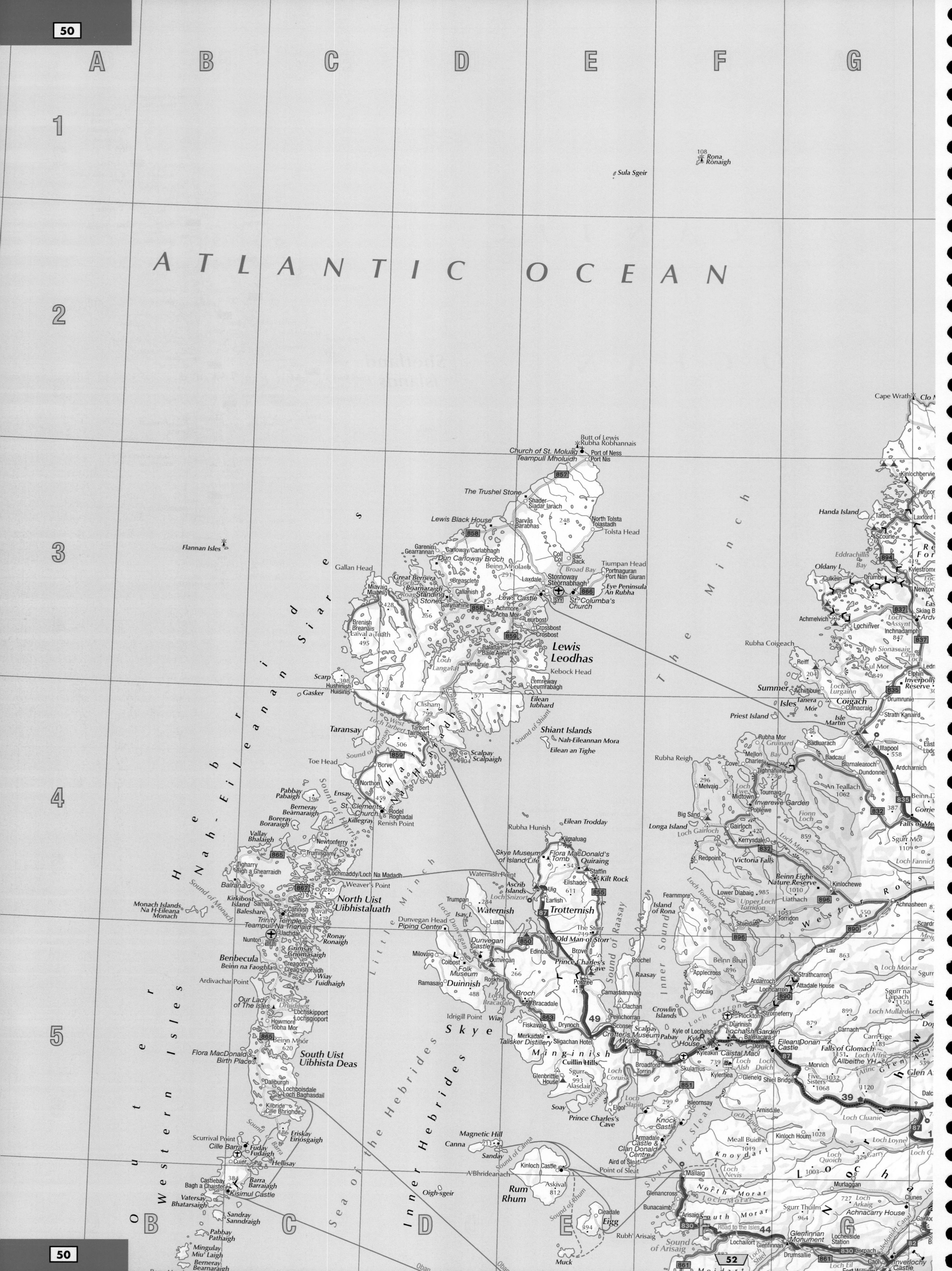
A
B
C
D
E
F
G
1
2
3
4
5
ATLANTIC OCEAN
Sula Sgeir
108
Rona
Ronaigh
Cape Wrath
Butt of Lewis
Rubha Robhannais
Church of St. Moluag
Teampull Mholuidh
Port of Ness
Port Nis
857
The Trushel Stone
Shader
Siadar Iarach
Lewis Black House
Barvas
Barabhas
248
North Tolsta
Tolastadh
Tolsta Head
858
Flannan Isles
Garenin
Gearrannan
Carloway/Carlabhagh
Dun Carloway Broch
Beinn Mholach
Coll
Back
Tiumpan Head
Portnaguran
Port Nan Giuran
Broad Bay
Gallan Head
Great Bernera
Breasclete
291
Laxdale
Stornoway
Steornabhagh
866
Eye Peninsula
An Rubha
Miavaig
Miabhig
Calanais Standing Stones
Callanish
Garynahine
Lewis Castle
St. Columba's Church
428
Achmore
Acha Mor
Leurbost
Crossbost
Brenish
Breanais
Laival a Tuath
495
859
Lewis
Leodhas
Balallan
Baile Ailein
Kintarvie
Loch Langavat
Kebock Head
Lemreway
Leumrabagh
Scarp
Hushinish
Huisinis
Gasker
Eilean Iubhard
Clisham
799
Taransay
West Loch Tarbert
Tarbert
Tairbeart
Shiant Islands
Nah-Eileannan Mora
Eilean an Tighe
Sound of Shiant
Sound of Taransay
506
Scalpay
Scalpaigh
Toe Head
Borve
Na Hearadh
Harris
Northon
Cluer
Pabbay
Pabaigh
Ensay
St. Clement's Church
459
Rodel
Roghadal
Renish Point
Berneray
Beàrnaraigh
Killegray
Boreray
Boraraigh
Sound of Harris
Vallay
Bhalaigh
865
Newtonferry
Trumisgarry
Tigharry
Tigh a Ghearraidh
Lochmaddy/Loch Na Madadh
Weaver's Point
Balranald
867
280
North Uist
Uibhistaluath
Kirkibost Island
Monach Islands
Na H-Eileana Monach
Sound of Monach
Baleshare
Trinity Temple
Teampull Na Trionaid
Uachdar
Ronay
Ronaigh
Nunton
Grimsay
Griomasaigh
Benbecula
Beinn na Faoghla
Creagorry
Creag Ghoraidh
Wiay
Fuidhaigh
Ardivachar Point
Our Lady of The Isles
Lochskipport
Loch Sgioport
Howmore
Tobha Mor
Beinn Mhor
620
Flora MacDonald's Birth Place
South Uist
Uibhista Deas
Daliburgh
Lochboisdale
Loch Baghasdail
Kilbride
Cille Bhrighde
Eriskay
Eiriosgaigh
Scurrival Point
Cille Barra
Fuday
Fudaigh
Cuier
Hellisay
Castlebay
Bagh a Chaisteil
384
Barra
Barraigh
Kisimul Castle
Vatersay
Bhatarsaigh
Sandray
Sanndraigh
Pabbay
Pathaigh
Mingulay
Miu' Laigh
Berneray
Bearnaraigh
Outer Hebrides
Western Isles
Nah-Eileanan Siar
The Minch
Little Minch
Sea of the Hebrides
Inner Hebrides
Rubha Hunish
Eilean Trodday
Kilmaluag
Skye Museum of Island Life
Flora MacDonald's Tomb
Quiraing
543
Staffin
Kilt Rock
Waternish Point
Ascrib Islands
Uig
Elishader
Loch Snizort
Earlish
611
855
Trumpan
284
Isay I.
Waternish
Trotternish
Dunvegan Head
Piping Centre
Lusta
The Storr
719
Old Man of Storr
850
Dunvegan Castle
Edinbane
Brove
Milovaig
Colbost
Folk Museum
Dunvegan
Prince Charles's Cave
266
Portree
Ramasaig
Duinnish
488
Roskhill
Loch Bracadale
Broch
Bracadale
Idrigill Point
Wiay
Skye
Fiskavaig
Drynoch
Merkadale
Talisker Distillery
Sligachan Hotel
Minginish
Cuillin Hills
Sgurr
993
Alasdair
Glenbrittle House
Loch Coruisk
Loch Scavaig
Soay
Elgol
Prince Charles's Cave
Sound of Raasay
Brochel
Raasay
Camastianavaig
Clachan
Peinchorran
Sconser
Scalpay
Crofter's Museum House
Pabay
Luib
Broadford
Torrin
Inner Sound
Fearnmore
Island of Rona
Magnetic Hill
Canna
Sanday
Sound of Canna
A'Bhrideanach
Kinloch Castle
Askival
812
Rum
Rhum
Sound of Rhum
Oigh-sgeir
Cleadale
Eigg
894
Rubh' Arisaig
Muck
Oban
Handa Island
Tarbet
Laxford
Scourie
Eddrachillis Bay
894
Oldany I.
Culkein
Drumbeg
Kylestrome
Newton
837
Achmelvich
Lochinver
Loch Assynt
Inchnadamph
847
Rubha Coigeach
Reiff
204
Achiltibuie
Cul Mor
849
Summer Isles
Tanera Mor
Coigeach
Culnacraig
Isle Martin
Elphin
Inverpolly Reserve
835
Drumrunie
Priest Island
Strath Kanaird
Rubha Mor
Gruinard Bay
Badluarach
Ullapool
558
Rubha Reigh
Cove
Mellon Charles
Tighnafiline
273
Badcaul
Blarnalearoch
Dundonnell
Ardcharnich
296
Melvaig
Loch Ewe
Tournaig
Inverewe Garden
Poolewe
An Teallach
1062
832
Big Sand
Longa Island
Loch Gairloch
Gairloch
Kerrysdale
Loch Maree
Fionn Loch
859
Redpoint
Victoria Falls
Beinn Eighe Nature Reserve
680
Kinlochewe
Loch Fannich
Sgurr Mor
1109
Loch Torridon
Lower Diabaig
985
Upper Loch Torridon
Liathach
1010
896
Torridon
1053
Achnasheen
Wester Ross
550
890
Shieldaig
Beinn Bhan
896
Lair
863
Applecross
Toscaig
Ardarroch
Lochcarron
Strathcarron
Attadale House
Loch Monar
Sgurr na Lapaich
1150
Loch Mullardoch
899
Crowlin Islands
Loch Carron
Plockton
Stromeferry
879
Kyle of Lochalsh
Duirinish
Lochalsh Garden
Balmacara
Carnach
Kyle House
Kyleakin
Caisteal Maol
739
Dornie
Eilean Donan Castle
Loch Alsh
Loch Duich
Falls of Glomach
Allbeithe YH
1151
Morvich
Five Sisters
1032
1068
Glen Affric
851
Skulamus
Kylerhea
Glenelg
Shiel Bridge
1120
39
299
Isleornsay
Arnisdale
Loch Hourn
Loch Cluanie
Knock Castle
Armadale Castle & Clan Donald Centre
Sound of Sleat
Meall Buidhe
1019
Kinloch Hourn
1028
Loch Loyne
Aird of Sleat
Point of Sleat
Knoydart
Loch Quoich
Loch Nevis
Mallaig
North Morar
Loch Morar
Glenancross
Bunacaimb
Arisaig
South Morar
Sgurr Thuilm
964
Murlaggan
Loch Arkaig
Clunes
Achnacarry House
Road to the Isles
Lochailort
Glenfinnan Monument
Glenfinnan
Loch Shiel
Locheilside Station
Drumsallie
Sound of Arisaig
861
830
44
52
Moidart
Corpach
Loch Eil
Inverlochy Castle
Caol

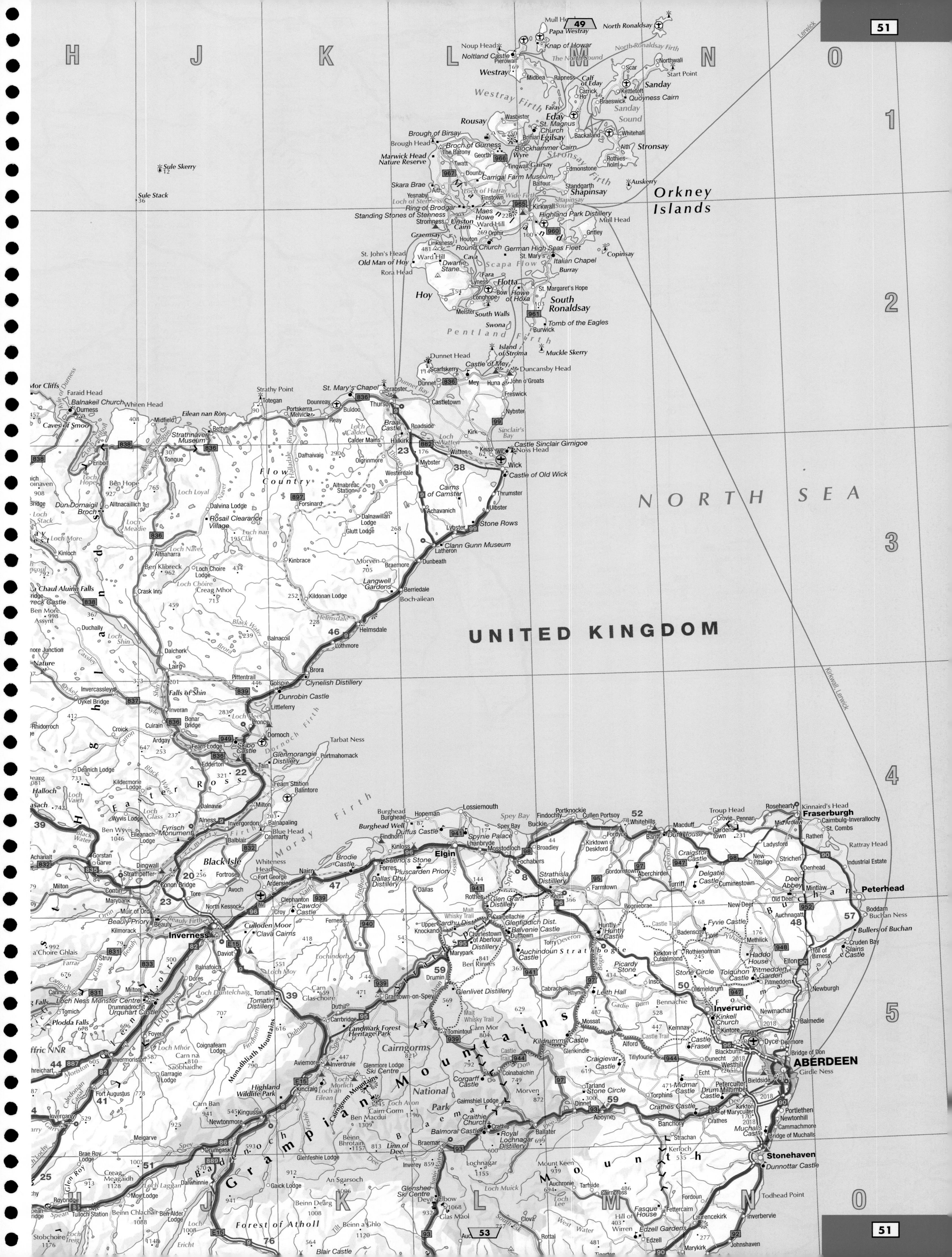

51
H
J
K
L
M
N
O
1
2
3
4
5
0
49
Mull Head
Papa Westray
North Ronaldsay
Noup Head
Noltland Castle
Pierowall
Knap of Howar
North Ronaldsay Firth
The North Sound
Westray
Midbea
Rapness
Calf of Eday
Carrick Ho
Scar
Northwall
Start Point
Sanday
Kettletoft
Braeswick
Quoyness Cairn
Westray Firth
Faray
Sanday Sound
Rousay
Wasbister
Eday
St. Magnus Church
Egilsay
Backaland
Whitehall
Stronsay
Brough of Birsay
Brough Head
Broch of Gurness
The Barony
Blackhammer Cairn
Marwick Head Nature Reserve
Georth
966
Wyre
Stronsay Firth
Aith
Rothiesholm
Twatt
Tingwall
Gairsay
967
Dounby
Corrigal Farm Museum
Edmonstone
Balfour
Auskerry
Skara Brae
Aith
Loch of Harray
Standgarth
Shapinsay
Yesnaby
Finstown
Wide Firth
Loch of Stenness
965
Kirkwall
Shapinsay Sound
Orkney Islands
Ring of Brodgar
Standing Stones of Stenness
Maes Howe
Highland Park Distillery
Stromness
Unston Cairn
Ward Hill
Mull Head
Orphir
960
Gritley
Graemsay
Houton
Linksness
Round Church
German High Seas Fleet
Copinsay
St. John's Head
Old Man of Hoy
Ward Hill
St. Mary's
Dwarfie Stane
Cava
Italian Chapel
Rora Head
Scapa Flow
Burray
Fara
Lyness
Flotta
Hoy
Bow
Longhope
Howe of Hoxa
St. Margaret's Hope
South Ronaldsay
Melsetter
South Walls
961
Swona
Tomb of the Eagles
Burwick
Pentland Firth
Island of Stroma
Muckle Skerry
Dunnet Head
Castle of Mey
Duncansby Head
Scarfskerry
Dunnet
Mey
Huna
John o'Groats
Dunnet Bay
Freswick
Mor Cliffs
Faraid Head
Balnakeil Church
Durness
Whiten Head
Strathy Point
Totegan
St. Mary's Chapel
Scrabster
Dounreay
Thurso
Castletown
Nybster
Caves of Smoo
Eilean nan Ròn
Midfield
Bettyhill
Portskerra
Melvich
Reay
Buldoo
Braal Castle
Roadside
Sinclair's Bay
Strathnaver Museum
Tongue
Loch Calder
Calder Mains
Halkirk
Loch Watten
Kirk
Keiss
Castle Sinclair Girnigoe
Noss Head
Eriboll
Dalhalvaig
Olgrinmore
Mybster
Watten
Wick
Castle of Old Wick
Flow Country
Westerdale
Ben Hope
Loch Hope
Loch Loyal
Altnabreac Station
Cairns of Camster
Thrumster
NORTH SEA
Dun Dornaigil Broch
Altnacaillich
Dalvina Lodge
Forsinard
Achavanich
Ulbster
Rosail Clearance Village
Dalnawillan Lodge
Stone Rows
Loch Meadie
Glutt Lodge
Lybster
Loch More
Loch Naver
Clann Gunn Museum
Latheron
Kinloch
Altnaharra
Kinbrace
Morven
Braemore
Dunbeath
Ben Klibreck
Loch Choire Lodge
Loch Chòire
Creag Mhor
Langwell Gardens
Berriedale
Boch-ailean
Chaul Aluinn Falls
Crask Inn
Kildonan Lodge
Ben More Assynt
UNITED KINGDOM
Duchally
Black Water
Helmsdale
Loch Shin
Balnacoil
Lothmore
Brora
Dalchork
Lairg
Pittentrail
Golspie
Clynelish Distillery
Falls of Shin
Dunrobin Castle
Invercassley
Oykel Bridge
Inveran
Littleferry
Rhidorroch
Croick
Culrain
Bonar Bridge
Loch Fleet
Dornoch
Ardgay
Fearn Lodge
Skibo Castle
Dornoch Firth
Tarbat Ness
Glenmorangie Distillery
Portmahomack
Edderton
Tain
Deanich Lodge
Kildermorie Lodge
Easter Ross
Fearn Station
Balintore
Halloch
Loch Vaich
Loch Glass
Dalnavie
Milton
Ben Wyvis
Wyvis Lodge
Alness
Invergordon
Balnapaling
Fyrisch Monument
Eileanach Lodge
Cromarty Firth
Balblair
Blue Head
Cromarty
Moray Firth
Burghead
Hopeman
Lossiemouth
Spey Bay
Findochty
Portknockie
Cullen
Portsoy
Whitehills
Troup Head
Rosehearty
Kinnaird's Head
Fraserburgh
Burghead Well
Duffus Castle
Spynie Palace
Lhanbryde
Buckie
Banff
Macduff
Duff House
Gardenstown
Pennan
Crovie
Mid Ardlaw
St. Combs
Cairnbulg-Inveralochy
Findhorn
Kinloss
Elgin
Mosstodloch
Fochabers
Broadley
Kirktown of Deskford
Fordyce
Rathen
Rattray Head
Achanalt
Gorstan
Garve
Black Isle
Whiteness Head
Sueno's Stone
Forres
Pluscarden Priory
Brodie Castle
Craigston Castle
New Pitsligo
Strichen
Industrial Estate
Strathpeffer
Dingwall
Fortrose
Fort George
Ardersier
Nairn
Dallas Dhu Distillery
Strathisla Distillery
Gordonstown
Aberchirder
Turriff
Delgatie Castle
Deer Abbey
Denhead
Mintlaw
Peterhead
Conon Bridge
Avoch
Contin
Marybank
Muir of Ord
Tore
North Kessock
Clephanton
Cawdor Castle
Croy
Dallas
Rothes
Glen Grant Distillery
Keith
Farmtown
Cuminestown
Old Deer
Boddam
Buchan Ness
Beauly Priory
Beauly
Beauly Firth
Inverness
Kilmorack
Culloden Moor
Clava Cairns
Ferness
Upper Knockando
Cardhu Dist.
Craigellachie
Glenfiddich Dist.
Balvenie Castle
Dufftown
Huntly
Huntly Castle
Bognie brae
New Deer
Auchnagatt
Fyvie Castle
Badenscoth
Fyvie
Methlick
Bullers of Buchan
Cruden Bay
Slains Castle
a'Choire Ghlais
Struy
Daviot
Lochindorb
Marypark
Charlestown of Aberlour
Aberlour Distillery
Auchindoun Castle
Strathbogie
Kirkton of Culsalmond
Rothienorman
Haddo House
Hill of Barness
Ellon
Balnafoich
Dores
Loch Moy
Ben Rinnes
Drumin
Picardy Stone
Insch
Stone Circle
Tolquhon Castle
Pitmedden Garden
Pitmedden
Newburgh
Falls
Loch Ness Monster Centre
Drumnadrochit
Urquhart Castle
Tomich
Loch Duntelchaig
Tomatin
Tomatin Distillery
Carn Glas-choire
Duthil
Grantown-on-Spey
Glenlivet Distillery
Cabrach
Rhynie
Leith Hall
Oldmeldrum
Inverurie
Kinkell Church
Kintore
Newmachar
Balmedie
Plodda Falls
Foyers
Loch Ness
Loch Mhòr
Monadhliath Mountains
Carrbridge
Landmark Forest Heritage Park
Tomintoul
Carn Mor
Mossat
Kildrummy Castle
Glenkindie
Alford
Tillyfourie
Kemnay
Bennachie
Castle Fraser
Blackburn
Dyce
Bridge of Don
ABERDEEN
Girdle Ness
Affric NNR
Invermoriston
Coignafearn Lodge
Carn na Saobhaidhe
Garragie Lodge
Cairngorms
Aviemore
Inverdruie
Glenmore Lodge Ski Centre
Colnabaichin
Corgarff Castle
Craigievar Castle
Dunecht
Echt
Westhill
Bieldside
Peterculter
Milltimber
Fort Augustus
Highland Wildlife Park
Kincraig
Loch an Eilean
Loch Morlich
Caledonian Canal
Cairngorm Mountains
National Park
Gairnshiel Lodge
Morven
Tarland
Stone Circle
Dinnet
Aboyne
Torphins
Midmar Castle
Drum Castle
Crathes Castle
Kirkton of Maryculter
Portlethen
Newtonhill
Carn Ban
Kingussie
Newtonmore
Cairn Gorm
Ben Macdui
Crathie Church
Crathie
Royal Lochnagar Distillery
Ballater
Banchory
Strachan
Muchalls Castle
Cammachmore
Bridge of Muchalls
Melgarve
Spey
Drumgask
Grampian Mountains
Badenoch
Beinn Bhrotain
Linn of Dee
Braemar
Balmoral Castle
Lochnagar
Mount Keen
Kerloch
Stonehaven
Dunnottar Castle
Glen Roy
Brae Roy Lodge
Creag Meagaidh
Glenfeshie Lodge
Inverey
Dalwhinnie
An Sgarsoch
Gaick Lodge
Auchronie
Tarfside
Mounth
Loch Lee
Fordoun
Todhead Point
Loch Laggan
Moy Lodge
Glenshee Ski Centre
Devil's Elbow
Glas Maol
Loch Muick
Cairn o' Mount
Fasque House
Fettercairn
Laurencekirk
Inverbervie
Roybridge
Tulloch Station
Beinn Chlachair
Ben Alder Lodge
Beinn Dearg
Forest of Atholl
Beinn a'Ghlo
Clova
West Water
Hill of Wirren
Edzell Gardens
Edzell
Marykirk
Johnshaven
Stobchoire
Loch Treig
Loch Ericht
Blair Castle
Rottal
South Esk
53

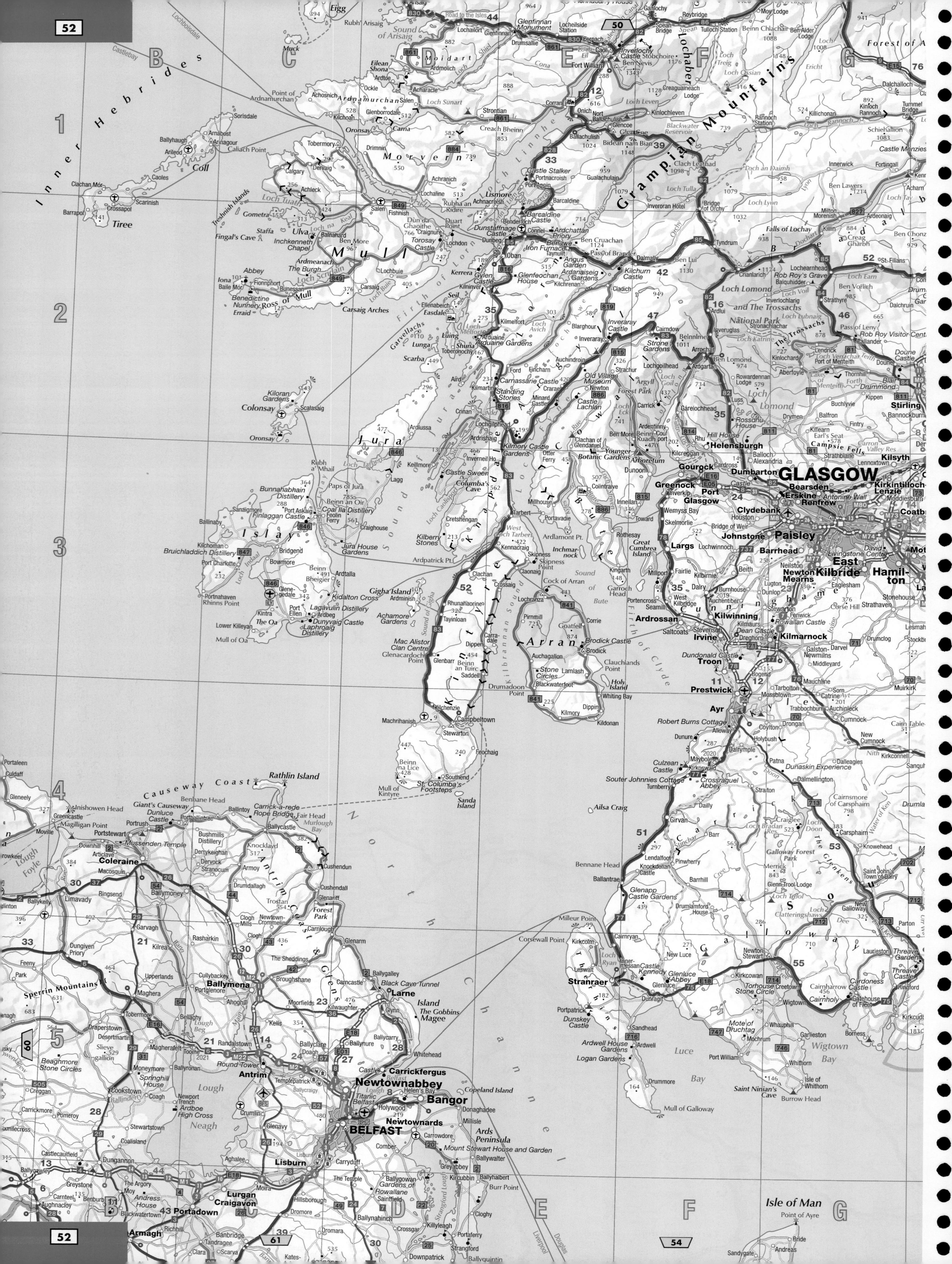
Inner Hebrides
Coll
Tiree
Mull
Ross of Mull
Iona
Staffa
Ulva
Colonsay
Oronsay
Jura
Islay
Gigha Island
Kintyre
Arran
Bute
Great Cumbrae Island
Sound of Jura
Firth of Lorn
Loch Linnhe
Firth of Clyde
Kilbrannan Sound
North Channel
Ailsa Craig
Sanda Island
Rathlin Island
Causeway Coast
Antrim Coast & Glens
Lough Neagh
Sperrin Mountains
Grampian Mountains
Lochaber
Morvern
Moidart
Ardnamurchan
Knapdale
Cowal
Argyll
Breadalbane
Loch Lomond and The Trossachs National Park
Campsie Fells
Cunninghame
Kyle
Carrick
Galloway
Wigtown Bay
Luce Bay
Mull of Galloway
Isle of Man
Fort William
Ben Nevis
Oban
Inveraray
Lochgilphead
Campbeltown
Port Ellen
Bowmore
Tobermory
Craignure
GLASGOW
Paisley
Greenock
Helensburgh
Dumbarton
Stirling
East Kilbride
Hamilton
Kilmarnock
Irvine
Ardrossan
Largs
Troon
Prestwick
Ayr
Girvan
Stranraer
Newton Stewart
BELFAST
Newtownabbey
Bangor
Newtownards
Carrickfergus
Larne
Ballymena
Antrim
Lisburn
Craigavon
Lurgan
Portadown
Armagh
Coleraine
Portrush
Portstewart
Ballymoney
Ballycastle
Limavady
Dungannon
Cookstown
Magherafelt
Ards Peninsula
Copeland Island
50
54
60
61

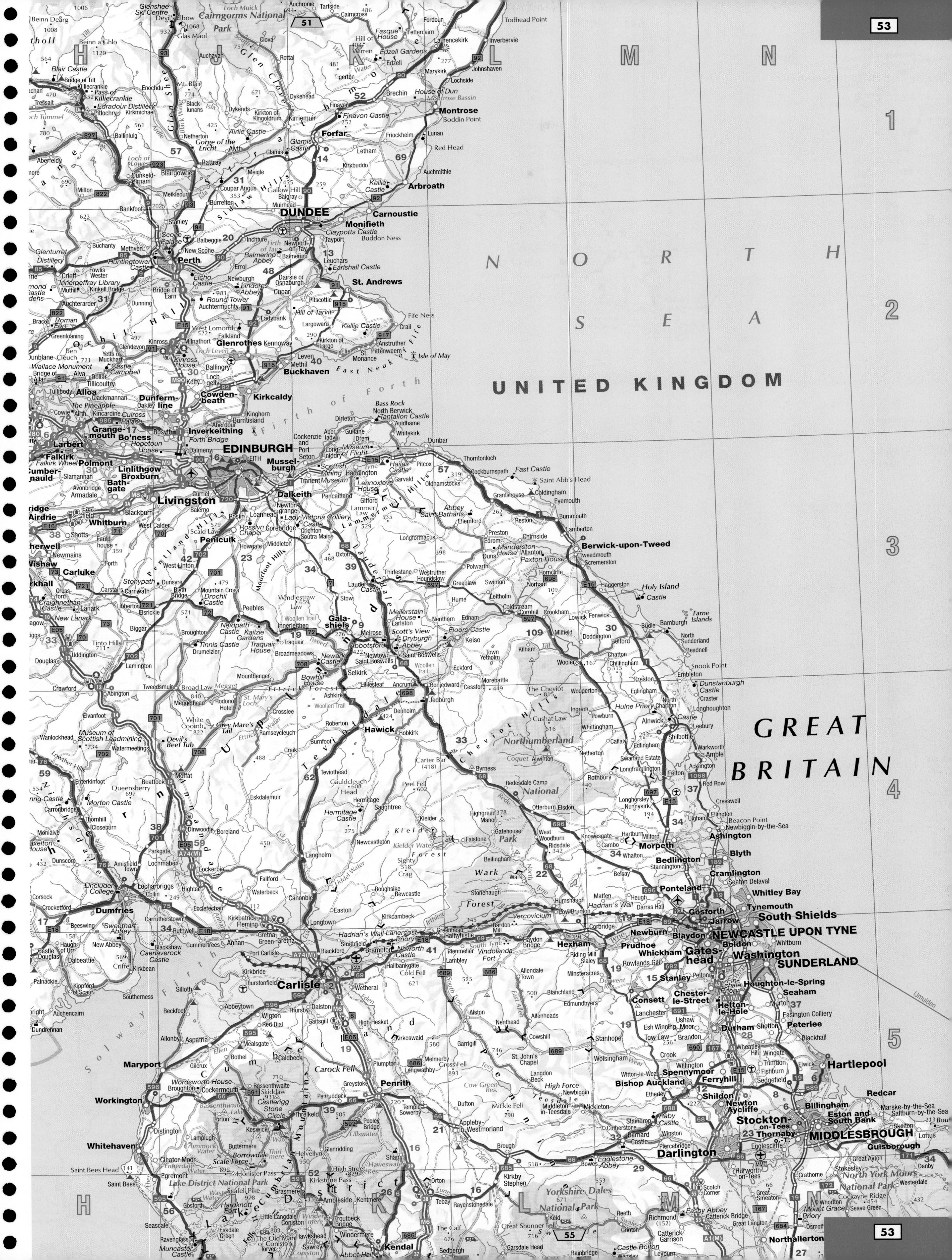

NORTH SEA
UNITED KINGDOM
GREAT BRITAIN
M
N
H
K
L
1
2
3
4
5
Cairngorms National Park
Glen Clova
Strathmore
Sidlaw Hills
Ochil Hills
Firth of Forth
East Neuk of Fife
Lammermuir Hills
Pentland Hills
Moorfoot Hills
Lauderdale
Teviotdale
Ettrick Forest
Southern Uplands
Cheviot Hills
Northumberland National Park
Kielder Forest
Wark Forest
Solway Firth
Cumbrian Mountains
Lake District National Park
North Pennines
Yorkshire Dales National Park
North York Moors National Park
Todhead Point
Montrose
Brechin
Forfar
Kirriemuir
Arbroath
Carnoustie
DUNDEE
Monifieth
Perth
St. Andrews
Fife Ness
Isle of May
Glenrothes
Kirkcaldy
Buckhaven
Dunfermline
Cowdenbeath
Alloa
Stirling
Falkirk
Grangemouth
Bo'ness
Linlithgow
Inverkeithing
North Berwick
Bass Rock
Dunbar
EDINBURGH
Musselburgh
Dalkeith
Livingston
Penicuik
Bathgate
Broxburn
Whitburn
Airdrie
Carluke
Lanark
Biggar
Peebles
Galashiels
Melrose
Kelso
Selkirk
Hawick
Jedburgh
Moffat
St. Abb's Head
Eyemouth
Berwick-upon-Tweed
Holy Island
Farne Islands
Bamburgh
Alnwick
Morpeth
Ashington
Blyth
Bedlington
Cramlington
Whitley Bay
Tynemouth
South Shields
NEWCASTLE UPON TYNE
Gateshead
Jarrow
Washington
SUNDERLAND
Houghton-le-Spring
Seaham
Chester-le-Street
Durham
Peterlee
Hartlepool
Stanley
Consett
Hexham
Spennymoor
Bishop Auckland
Ferryhill
Shildon
Newton Aycliffe
Billingham
Stockton-on-Tees
MIDDLESBROUGH
Redcar
Guisborough
Darlington
Barnard Castle
Northallerton
Richmond
Dumfries
Annan
Gretna
Carlisle
Brampton
Penrith
Keswick
Maryport
Workington
Cockermouth
Whitehaven
Egremont
Saint Bees Head
Appleby-in-Westmorland
Kirkby Stephen
Ambleside
Windermere
Kendal
Sedbergh

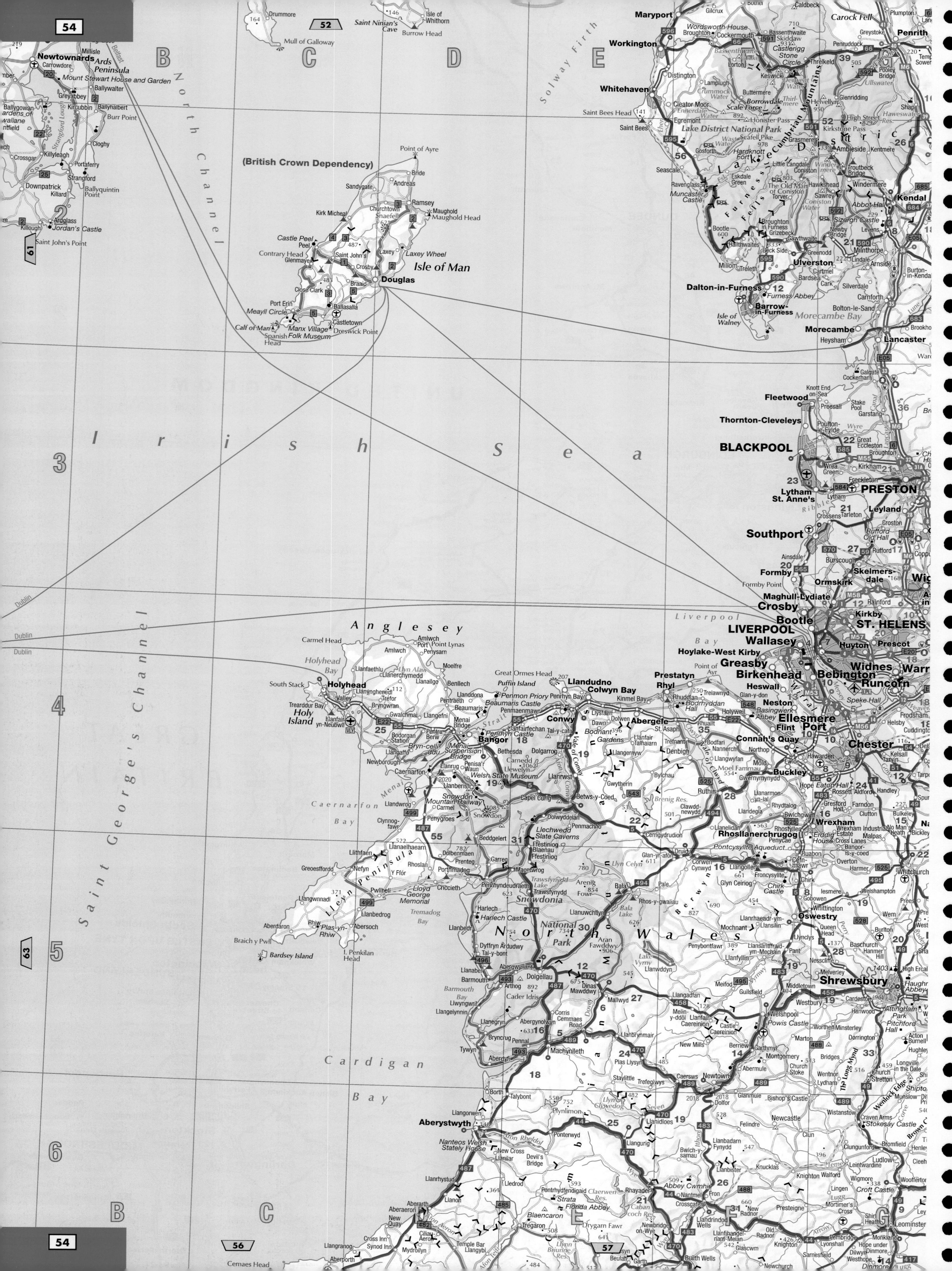

52
Drummore
Mull of Galloway
Saint Ninian's Cave
Isle of Whithorn
Burrow Head
Newtownards
Ards Peninsula
Carrowdore
Millisle
Mount Stewart House and Garden
Greyabbey
Ballywalter
Kircubbin
Ballyhalbert
Burr Point
Ballygowan
Killyleagh
Crossgar
Cloghy
Portaferry
Strangford
Downpatrick
Killard
Ballyquintin Point
Ardglass
Killough
Jordan's Castle
Saint John's Point
61
B
C
D
E
North Channel
Solway Firth
(British Crown Dependency)
Point of Ayre
Bride
Andreas
Sandygate
Ramsey
Maughold
Maughold Head
Kirk Michael
Churchtown
Snaefell
Castle Peel
Peel
Contrary Head
Glenmaye
Saint John's
Laxey
Laxey Wheel
Isle of Man
Crosby
Braaid
Douglas
Close Clark
Port Erin
Meayll Circle
Ballasalla
Castletown
Calf of Man
Spanish Head
Manx Village Folk Museum
Dreswick Point
Maryport
Workington
Whitehaven
Saint Bees Head
Saint Bees
Gilcrux
Caldbeck
Carock Fell
Penrith
Wordsworth House
Cockermouth
Bassenthwaite
Skiddaw
Castlerigg Stone Circle
Keswick
Threlkeld
Greystoke
Penruddock
Pooley Bridge
Ullswater
Distington
Lamplugh
Crummock Water
Buttermere
Borrowdale
Helvellyn
Glenridding
Cleator Moor
Ennerdale Water
Scale Force
Honister Pass
Egremont
Lake District National Park
Cumbrian Mountains
High Street
Haweswater
Shap
Kirkstone Pass
Wast Water
Scafell Pike
Grasmere
Ambleside
Kentmere
Gosforth
Hardknott Fort
Seascale
Eskdale Green
Little Langdale
Coniston
Windermere
Troutbeck Bridge
Ravenglass
Muncaster Castle
Furness Fells
The Old Man of Coniston
Torver
Hawkshead
Sawrey
Coniston Water
Kendal
Abbot Hall
Sizergh Castle
Bootle
Broughton in Furness
Grizebeck
Gawthwaite
Newby Bridge
Levens
Halthwaites
Beck Side
Greenodd
Milnthorpe
Millom
Treleth
Ulverston
Cartmel
Lindale
Arnside
Burton-in-Kendal
Dalton-in-Furness
Bardsea
Cark
Silverdale
Furness Abbey
Barrow-in-Furness
Carnforth
Isle of Walney
Morecambe Bay
Bolton-le-Sand
Morecambe
Heysham
Lancaster
Galgate
Cockerham
Knott End-on-Sea
Fleetwood
Preesall
Stake Pool
Garstang
Thornton-Cleveleys
Poulton-le-Fylde
Great Eccleston
BLACKPOOL
Wrea Green
Kirkham
Broughton
Freckleton
Lytham St. Anne's
PRESTON
Leyland
Tarleton
Crossens
Southport
Croston
Rufford Old Hall
Rufford
Burscough
Ainsdale
Formby
Formby Point
Skelmersdale
Ormskirk
Maghull-Lydiate
Crosby
Rainford
Kirkby
Bootle
ST. HELENS
LIVERPOOL
Wallasey
Prescot
Huyton
Hoylake-West Kirby
Greasby
Birkenhead
Bebington
Widnes
Runcorn
Point of Ayr
Prestatyn
Rhyl
Heswall
Speke Hall
Neston
Ellesmere Port
Flint
Connah's Quay
Chester
Irish Sea
Dublin
Saint George's Channel
Anglesey
Carmel Head
Amlwch
Amlwch Port
Point Lynas
Penysarn
Holyhead Bay
Llanfaethlu
Llyn Alaw
Llanerchymedd
Moelfre
Benllech
South Stack
Holyhead
Llanynghenedl
Valley
Trearddur Bay
Holy Island
Llanfair-yn-Neubwll
Trefor
Bryngwran
Gwalchmai
Llangefni
Llanddona
Pentraeth
Beaumaris
Beaumaris Castle
Penmon Priory
Puffin Island
Great Ormes Head
Llandudno
Colwyn Bay
Penrhyn Bay
Kinmel Bay
Abergele
Conwy
Menai Bridge
Bangor
Penrhyn Castle
Llanfairfechan
Penmaenmawr
Tal-y-cafn
Dolwen
Llysfaen
Bodnant Gardens
Llanfair Talhaiarn
Saint Asaph
Trefnant
Denbigh
Rhuallt
Bodelwyddan
Bodfari
Nannerch
Northop
Mold
Buckley
Hawarden
Bodorgan Station
Bryn-celli-ddu
Menai Suspension Bridge
Llangaffo
Newborough
Caernarfon
Llanrug
Llanberis
Bethesda
Carnedd Llewelyn
Dolgarrog
Llanrwst
Vale of Conwy
Llangernyw
Gwytherin
Moel Famau
Ruthin
Welsh Slate Museum
Snowdon Mountain Railway
Snowdon
Capel Curig
Betws-y-Coed
Dolwyddelan
Llandwrog
Caernarfon Bay
Clynnog-fawr
Penygroes
Beddgelert
Penmachno
Cerrigydrudion
Llechwedd Slate Caverns
Ffestiniog
Blaenau Ffestiniog
Llithfaen
Llanaelhaearn
Nefyn
Llyn Peninsula
Rhoslan
Dolbenmaen
Prenteg
Porthmadog
Garreg
Maentwrog
Trawsfynydd
Trawsfynydd Lake
Arenig Fawr
Llyn Celyn
Bala
Bala Lake
Criccieth
Lloyd George Memorial
Pwllheli
Llanbedrog
Abersoch
Aberdaron
Plas-yn-Rhiw
Rhiw
Braich y Pwll
Bardsey Island
Penrhyndeudraeth
Harlech
Harlech Castle
Snowdonia
Tremadog Bay
Llanbedr
Snowdonia National Park
Dyffryn Ardudwy
Tal-y-bont
Aran Fawddwy
Llanuwchllyn
Rhos-y-gwaliau
North Wales
Berwyn
Llanrhaeadr-ym-Mochnant
Penybontfawr
Llansantffraid-ym-Mechain
Llanfyllin
Lake Vyrnwy
Llanwddyn
Abergwyngregyn
Llanaber
Barmouth
Arthog
Dolgellau
Cader Idris
Dinas Mawddwy
Barmouth Bay
Llwyngwril
Llangelynnin
Mallwyd
Meifod
Guilsfield
Welshpool
Powis Castle
Llangadfan
Meifod
Cemmaes Road
Corris
Abergynolwyn
Llanegryn
Bryncrug
Pennal
Tywyn
Aberdyfi
Machynlleth
Llanbrynmair
Cardigan Bay
Carno
Caersws
Newtown
Montgomery
Berriew
Abermule
Churchstoke
Plas Llysyn
Staylittle
Trefeglwys
Borth
Talybont
Llyn Clywedog
Llanidloes
Plynlimon
Aberystwyth
Llangorwen
Nanteos Welsh Stately House
Afon Rheidol
Ponterwyd
Devil's Bridge
Llangurig
New Cross
Llanilar
Llanrhystud
Llanon
Aberarth
Aberaeron
New Quay
Llanfihangel-y-Creuddyn
Pontrhydfendigaid
Strata Florida Abbey
Claerwen Res.
Caban coch Res.
Rhayader
Blaenacaron
Tregaron
Drygarn Fawr
Llyn Brianne Res.
Cross Inn
Synod Inn
Mydroilyn
Ciliau Aeron
Temple Bar
Llangybi
Llangranog
Aberporth
Cemaes Head
Abbey Cwmhir
Nantmel
Crossgates
Llandrindod Wells
Newbridge-on-Wye
Builth Wells
Llanbister
Bwlch-y-sarnau
Llanbadarn Fynydd
Felindre
Knucklas
Knighton
New Radnor
Presteigne
Llanfihangel-nant-Melan
Glascwm
Old Radnor
Newcastle
Clun
Bishop's Castle
Clungunford
Leintwardine
Brampton Bryan
Wigmore
Croft Castle
Lingen
Mortimer's Cross
Shirl Heath
Pembridge
Lyonshall
Kington
Eardisland
Dilwyn
Weobley
Leominster
Monkland
Hope under Dinmore
Dinmore
Sarnesfield
Bromfield
Ludlow
Wistanstow
Craven Arms
Stokesay Castle
Church Stretton
Wenlock Edge
The Long Mynd
Lydham
Wentnor
Bridges
Hughley
Shipton
Longville in the Dale
Acton Burnell
Dorrington
Pitchford Hall
Attingham Park
Cardeston
Hanwood
Worthen
Minsterley
Marton
Westbury
Middletown
Shrewsbury
Haughmond Abbey
High Ercall
Melverley
Nesscliffe
Baschurch
Burlton
Queen Head
Oswestry
Whittington
Gobowen
Chirk
Chirk Castle
Glyn Ceiriog
Llangollen
Froncysyllte
Pontcysyllte Aqueduct
Ruabon
Overton
Corwen
Cynwyd
Druid
Glan-yr-afon
Llanelidan
Rhosllanerchrugog
Erddig House
Wrexham
Penycae
Bangor-is-y-coed
Cross Lanes
Malpas
No Man's Heath
Wrexham Industrial Estate
Holt
Gresford
Farndon
Clutton
Bulkeley
Tattenhall
Rossett
Aldford
Eaton Hall
Hope
Gwernymynydd
Llanarmon-yn-Iâl
Rhydtalog
Bwlchgwyn
Llandegla
Clawdd-newydd
Brenig Res.
Bylchau
Waverton
Handley
Kelsall
Tarvin
Helsby
Frodsham
Cuddington
Whitchurch
Welshampton
Harmer Hill
Hanmer
Prees
Wem
Iesmere
Llynclys
Pant
Wrexham

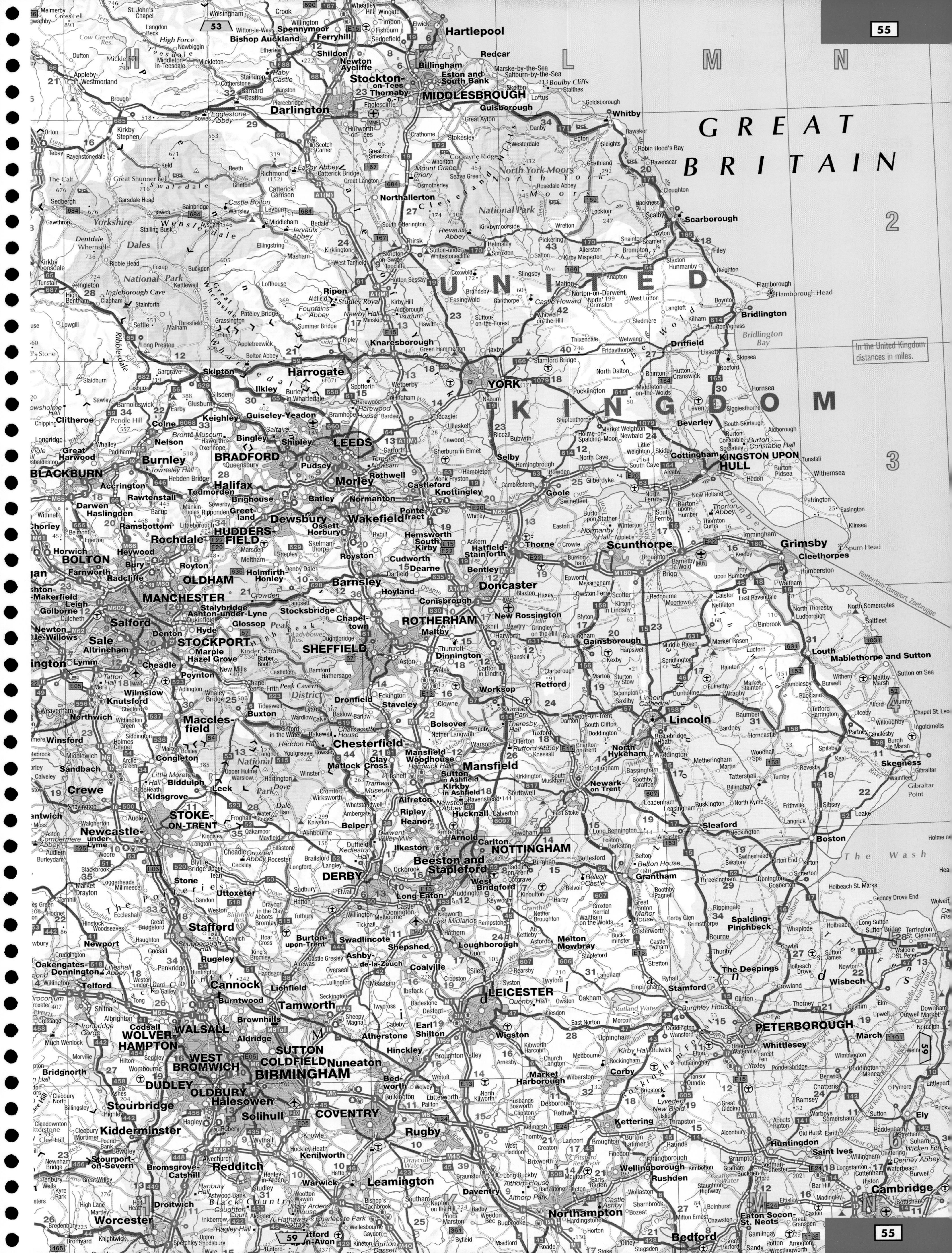
GREAT BRITAIN
UNITED KINGDOM
In the United Kingdom distances in miles.
Hartlepool
Redcar
Bishop Auckland
Stockton-on-Tees
MIDDLESBROUGH
Darlington
Guisborough
Whitby
Scarborough
Northallerton
North York Moors National Park
Yorkshire Dales National Park
Ripon
Knaresborough
Harrogate
Bridlington
Driffield
YORK
Skipton
Ilkley
Beverley
KINGSTON UPON HULL
LEEDS
BRADFORD
BLACKBURN
Burnley
Halifax
HUDDERSFIELD
Dewsbury
Wakefield
Selby
Goole
Scunthorpe
Grimsby
Cleethorpes
Rochdale
BOLTON
OLDHAM
MANCHESTER
Salford
STOCKPORT
Barnsley
Doncaster
ROTHERHAM
SHEFFIELD
Louth
Mablethorpe and Sutton
Lincoln
Macclesfield
Chesterfield
Worksop
Retford
Mansfield
Skegness
Crewe
STOKE-ON-TRENT
Newcastle-under-Lyme
Newark-on-Trent
Boston
NOTTINGHAM
DERBY
Grantham
Stafford
Loughborough
Melton Mowbray
Spalding
Peterborough
LEICESTER
Cannock
Tamworth
WALSALL
WOLVERHAMPTON
WEST BROMWICH
BIRMINGHAM
SUTTON COLDFIELD
Nuneaton
COVENTRY
Kidderminster
Redditch
Rugby
Leamington
Kettering
Huntingdon
Cambridge
Worcester
Northampton
Bedford
Wellingborough

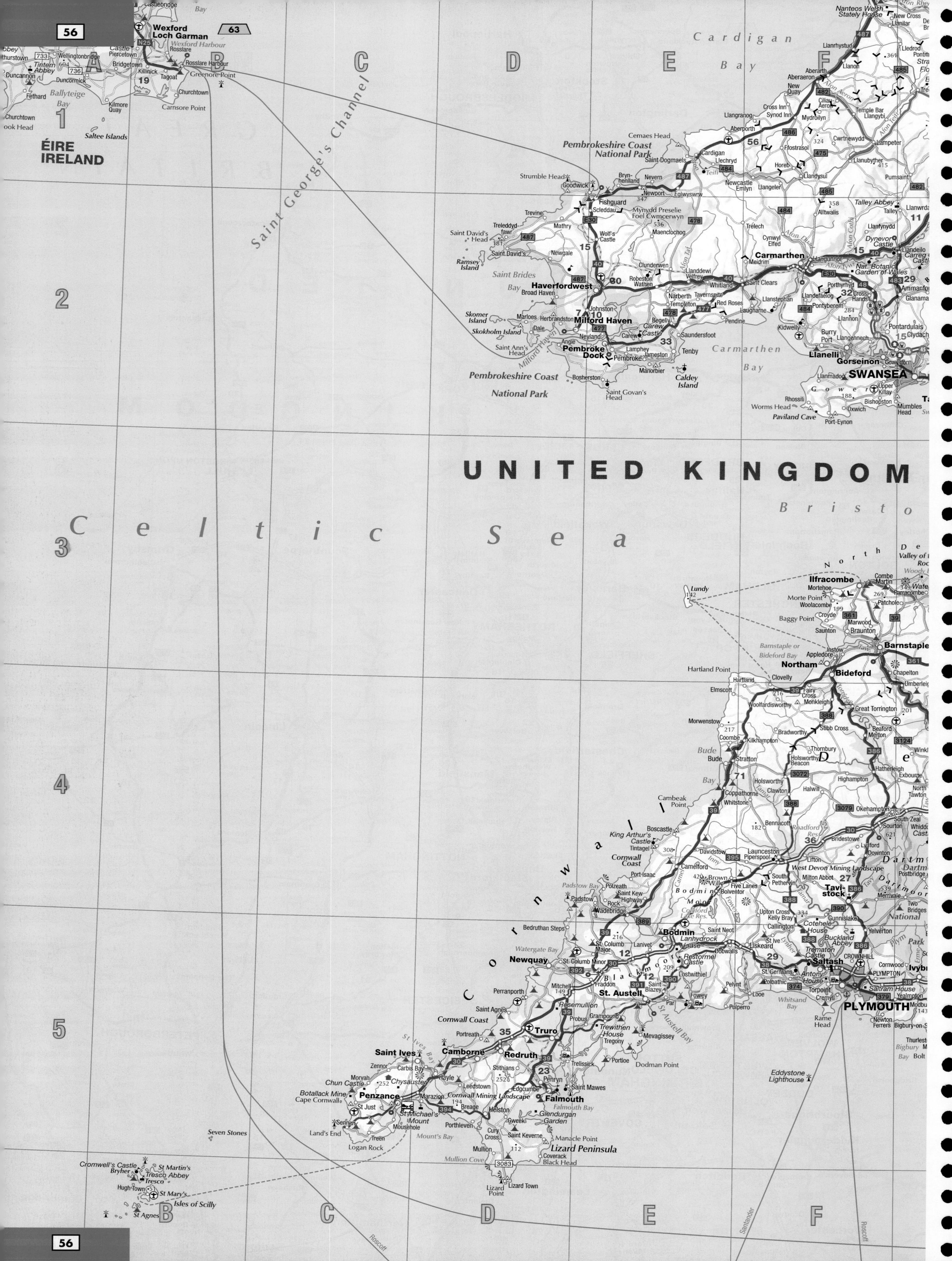
UNITED KINGDOM
Celtic Sea
ÉIRE IRELAND
Saint George's Channel
Cardigan Bay
Bristo
Wexford Loch Garman
Rosslare Harbour
Pembrokeshire Coast National Park
Fishguard
Haverfordwest
Milford Haven
Pembroke Dock
Carmarthen
Tenby
Carmarthen Bay
Llanelli
SWANSEA
Gower
Lundy
Ilfracombe
Barnstaple
Bideford
Cornwall
Bude
Launceston
Bodmin
Bodmin Moor
Newquay
St. Austell
Truro
Redruth
Camborne
Saint Ives
Penzance
Falmouth
Lizard Peninsula
Land's End
Isles of Scilly
Saltash
PLYMOUTH
Tavistock
Okehampton
Eddystone Lighthouse

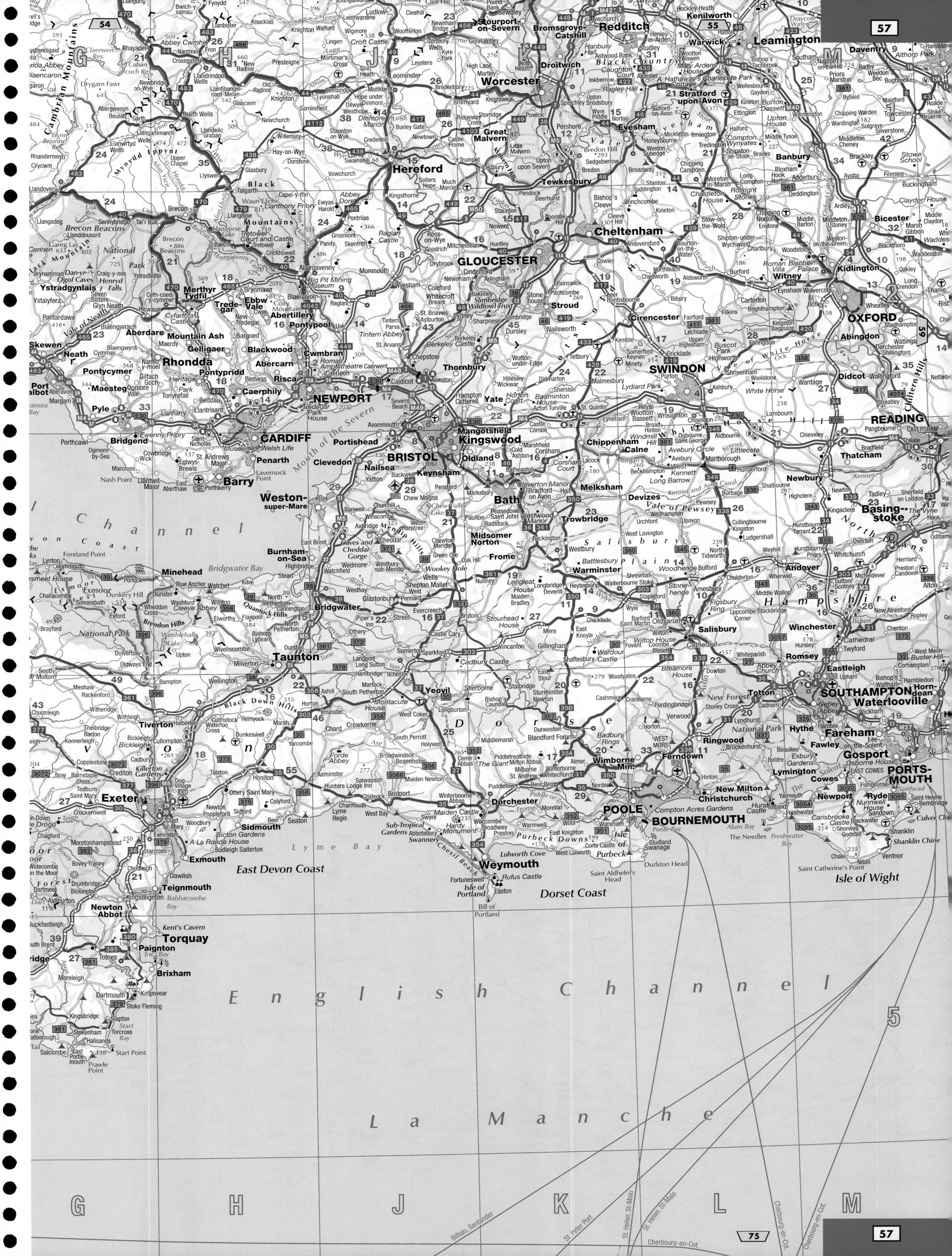
54
55
Cambrian Mountains
Rhayader
Llandrindod Wells
Builth Wells
Knighton
Ludlow
Leominster
Stourport-on-Severn
Bromsgrove
Redditch
Kenilworth
Warwick
Leamington
Daventry
Droitwich
Worcester
Stratford upon-Avon
Great Malvern
Evesham
Towcester
Hay-on-Wye
Hereford
Ledbury
Tewkesbury
Banbury
Black Mountains
Brecon
Brecon Beacons
National Park
Abergavenny
Monmouth
Ross-on-Wye
Cheltenham
GLOUCESTER
Bicester
Kidlington
Witney
OXFORD
Merthyr Tydfil
Tredegar
Ebbw Vale
Abertillery
Pontypool
Cwmbran
Aberdare
Mountain Ash
Rhondda
Neath
Skewen
Port Talbot
Maesteg
Pontypridd
Caerphilly
Blackwood
Risca
NEWPORT
Chepstow
Thornbury
Stroud
Cirencester
SWINDON
Abingdon
Didcot
Wantage
Pyle
Bridgend
CARDIFF
Penarth
Barry
Porthcawl
Portishead
Clevedon
BRISTOL
Kingswood
Keynsham
Bath
Chippenham
Calne
Marlborough
Melksham
Devizes
Trowbridge
Newbury
Thatcham
READING
Basingstoke
Weston-super-Mare
Burnham-on-Sea
Bridgwater
Minehead
Frome
Warminster
Andover
Salisbury
Winchester
Romsey
Eastleigh
SOUTHAMPTON
Waterlooville
Fareham
Gosport
PORTSMOUTH
Taunton
Tiverton
Exeter
Exmouth
Sidmouth
Yeovil
Dorchester
Weymouth
POOLE
BOURNEMOUTH
Christchurch
New Milton
Ringwood
Ferndown
Wimborne Minster
Lymington
Cowes
Newport
Ryde
Isle of Wight
Teignmouth
Newton Abbot
Torquay
Paignton
Brixham
Dartmouth
Bristol Channel
Bridgwater Bay
Mouth of the Severn
East Devon Coast
Dorset Coast
Lyme Bay
Exmoor
Salisbury Plain
Hampshire
Dorset
English Channel
La Manche
G
H
J
K
L
M
5
75

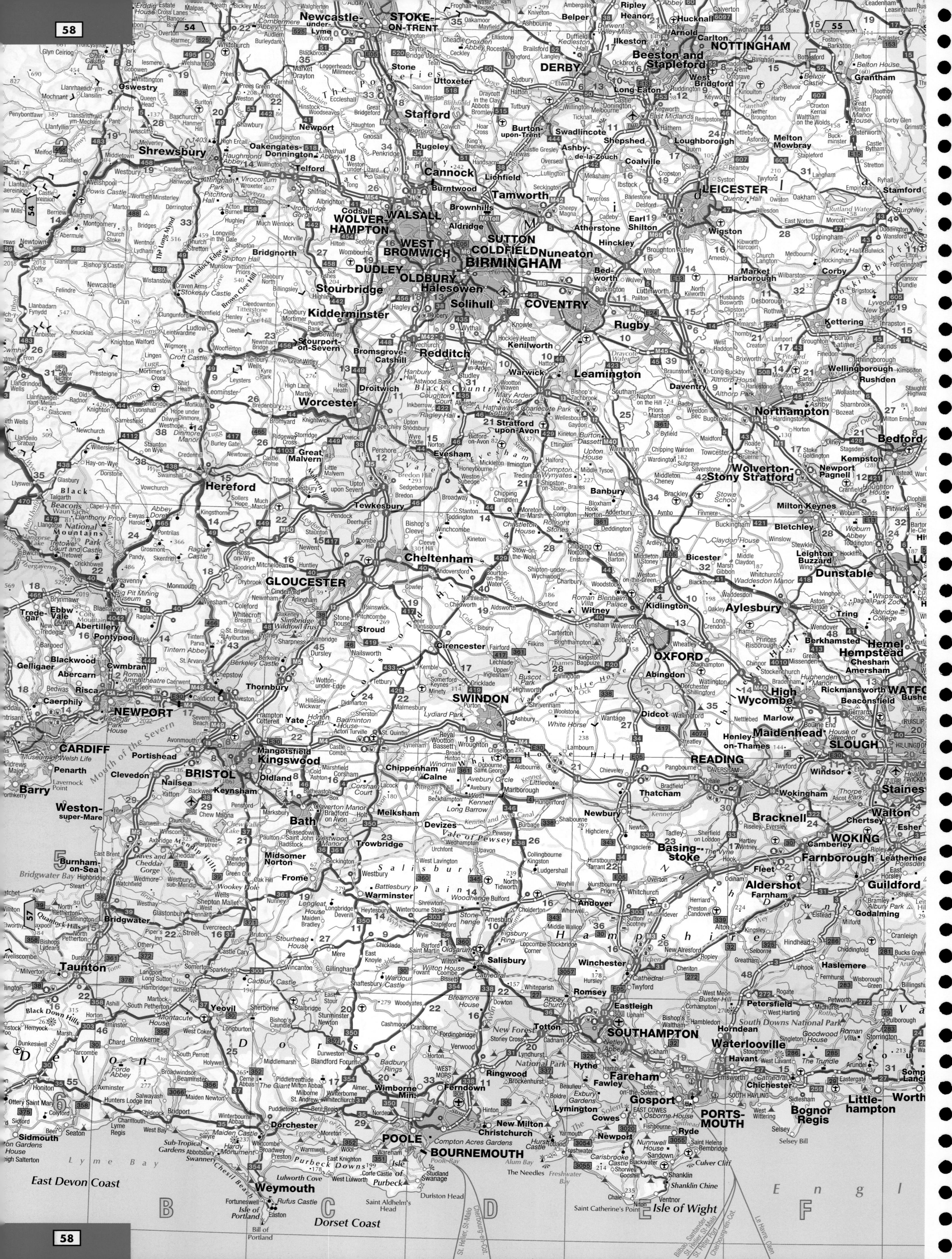

STOKE-ON-TRENT
Newcastle-under-Lyme
Ripley
Heanor
Hucknall
Arnold
Ilkeston
Beeston and Stapleford
NOTTINGHAM
Carlton
West Bridgford
DERBY
Belper
Long Eaton
Grantham
Oswestry
Shrewsbury
Stafford
Stone
Uttoxeter
Burton-upon-Trent
Swadlincote
Shepshed
Loughborough
Melton Mowbray
Oakengates-Donnington
Telford
Newport
Rugeley
Cannock
Lichfield
Tamworth
Ashby-de-la-Zouch
Coalville
LEICESTER
Wigston
Stamford
Oakham
Welshpool
Newtown
Codsall
WOLVERHAMPTON
WALSALL
Brownhills
Aldridge
SUTTON COLDFIELD
WEST BROMWICH
BIRMINGHAM
Nuneaton
Hinckley
Earl Shilton
Atherstone
Bridgnorth
DUDLEY
OLDBURY
Halesowen
Stourbridge
Solihull
COVENTRY
Bedworth
Kidderminster
Market Harborough
Corby
Kettering
Ludlow
Stourport-on-Severn
Bromsgrove-Catshill
Redditch
Rugby
Kenilworth
Warwick
Leamington
Daventry
Wellingborough
Rushden
Leominster
Droitwich
Worcester
Northampton
Stratford-upon-Avon
Bedford
Evesham
Great Malvern
Hereford
Tewkesbury
Banbury
Wolverton-Stony Stratford
Newport Pagnell
Milton Keynes
Bletchley
Cheltenham
GLOUCESTER
Bicester
Leighton Buzzard
Dunstable
Abergavenny
Monmouth
Stroud
Witney
Kidlington
Aylesbury
Tring
Hemel Hempstead
Berkhamsted
Chesham
Amersham
OXFORD
Abingdon
Ebbw Vale
Abertillery
Pontypool
Cwmbran
Caerphily
NEWPORT
Cirencester
SWINDON
Didcot
High Wycombe
Beaconsfield
Marlow
Henley-on-Thames
Maidenhead
SLOUGH
Windsor
Thornbury
Yate
Kingswood
Mangotsfield
CARDIFF
Penarth
Barry
Portishead
Clevedon
Nailsea
BRISTOL
Keynsham
Chippenham
Calne
READING
Thatcham
Newbury
Wokingham
Bracknell
Staines
Walton
Esher
Weston-super-Mare
Bath
Melksham
Devizes
Trowbridge
Frome
Midsomer Norton
Basingstoke
WOKING
Camberley
Farnborough
Fleet
Aldershot
Farnham
Guildford
Godalming
Burnham-on-Sea
Bridgwater
Warminster
Andover
Wells
Glastonbury
Taunton
Salisbury
Winchester
Haslemere
Yeovil
Romsey
Eastleigh
SOUTHAMPTON
Totton
Petersfield
Waterlooville
Havant
Chichester
Fareham
Gosport
PORTSMOUTH
Bognor Regis
Littlehampton
Ferndown
Ringwood
Wimborne Minster
Christchurch
New Milton
Lymington
POOLE
BOURNEMOUTH
Dorchester
Weymouth
Sidmouth
Swanage
Newport
Ryde
Cowes
Isle of Wight
Lyme Bay
East Devon Coast
Dorset Coast
Bristol Channel
Mouth of the Severn
Bridgwater Bay
Cotswold Hills
Chiltern Hills
North Downs
South Downs National Park
New Forest National Park
Hampshire
Dorset
Devon
Salisbury Plain
Isle of Portland
Bill of Portland
St Aldhelm's Head
The Needles
Saint Catherine's Point
Selsey Bill
English Channel

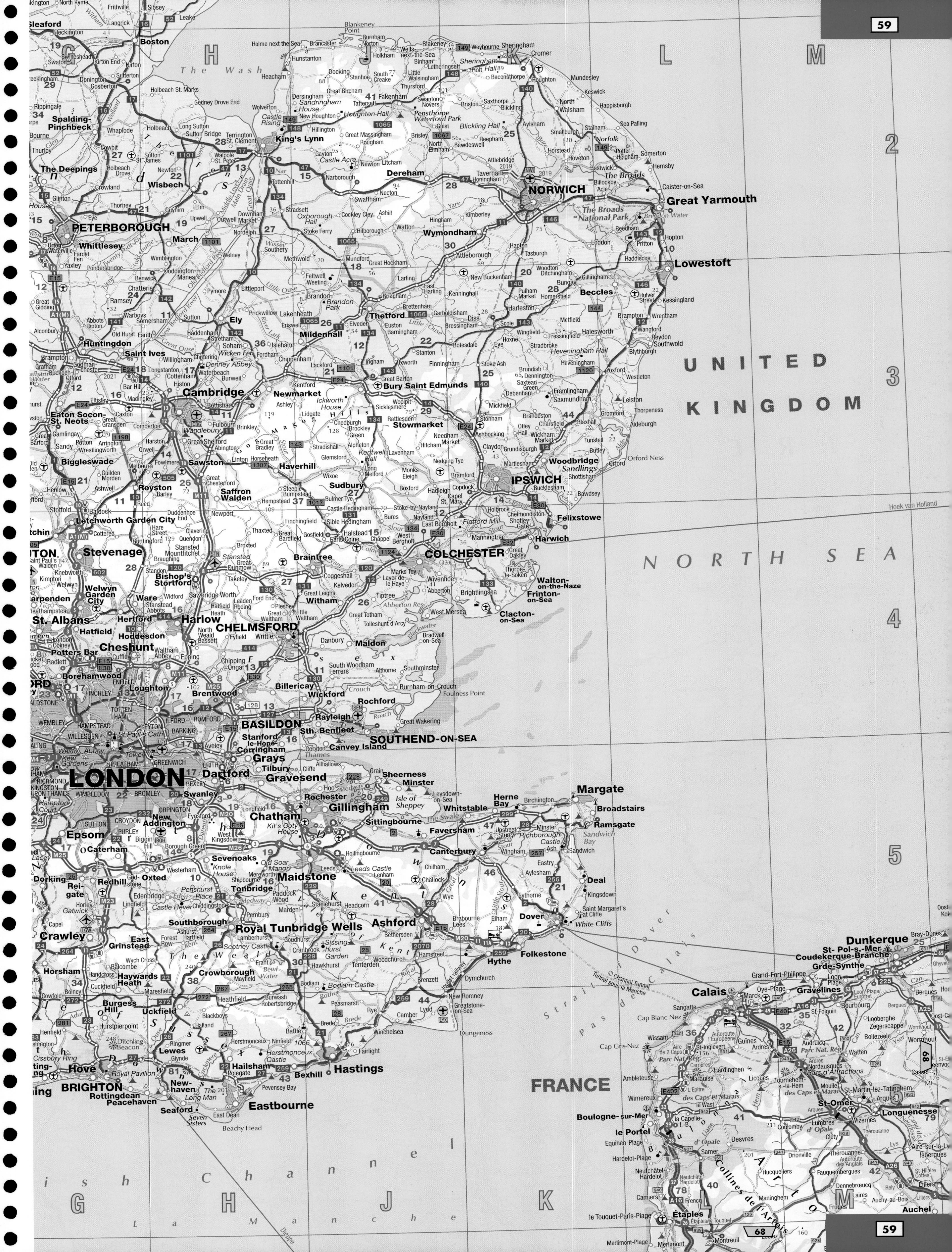

UNITED KINGDOM
NORTH SEA
FRANCE
English Channel
La Manche
The Wash
Strait of Dover
Pas de Calais
NORWICH
Great Yarmouth
Lowestoft
The Broads National Park
King's Lynn
Dereham
Wymondham
Thetford
Mildenhall
Ely
Cambridge
Newmarket
Bury Saint Edmunds
Stowmarket
Haverhill
Sudbury
IPSWICH
Felixstowe
Harwich
Woodbridge
Beccles
COLCHESTER
Braintree
Witham
Maldon
CHELMSFORD
Clacton-on-Sea
Walton-on-the-Naze
Frinton-on-Sea
Saffron Walden
Royston
Stevenage
Letchworth Garden City
Welwyn Garden City
Harlow
Hertford
Hatfield
St. Albans
Cheshunt
Bishop's Stortford
Billericay
Wickford
Rochford
Rayleigh
BASILDON
SOUTHEND-ON-SEA
Canvey Island
Grays
Tilbury
Gravesend
Dartford
LONDON
Epsom
Gillingham
Chatham
Rochester
Sittingbourne
Faversham
Whitstable
Herne Bay
Margate
Broadstairs
Ramsgate
Canterbury
Deal
Dover
Folkestone
Hythe
Ashford
Maidstone
Tonbridge
Sevenoaks
Royal Tunbridge Wells
Crowborough
Crawley
Horsham
Haywards Heath
Uckfield
Lewes
Brighton
Hove
Peacehaven
Seaford
Eastbourne
Hailsham
Bexhill
Hastings
Rye
New Romney
Dungeness
Beachy Head
PETERBOROUGH
Spalding-Pinchbeck
Boston
Sleaford
Wisbech
March
Whittlesey
Huntingdon
St Ives
Eaton Socon-St. Neots
Biggleswade
Calais
Dunkerque
Gravelines
Boulogne-sur-Mer
le Portel
Étaples
Le Touquet-Paris-Plage
St-Omer
Longuenesse
Auchel
Cap Gris-Nez
Cap Blanc Nez
Hoek van Holland
Channel Tunnel
Tunnel sous la Manche
68

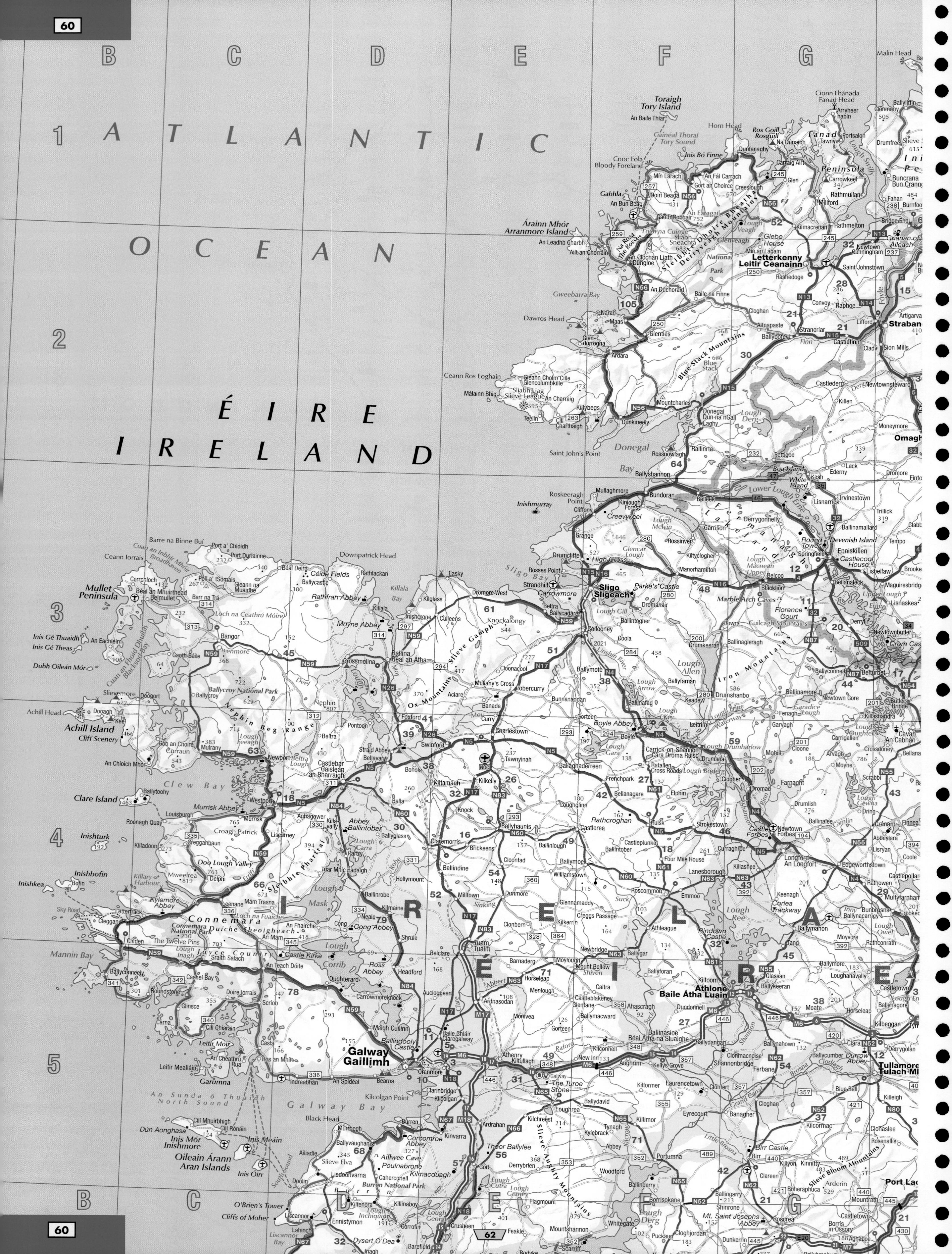
B
C
D
E
F
G
1
2
3
4
5
ATLANTIC
OCEAN
ÉIRE
IRELAND
Toraigh
Tory Island
Malin Head
Cionn Fhánada
Fanad Head
Horn Head
Ros Goill
Rosguill
Fanad
Peninsula
Inis Bó Finne
Cnoc Fola
Bloody Foreland
Gabhla
Árainn Mhór
Arranmore Island
Letterkenny
Leitir Ceanainn
Glenveagh
National Park
Derryveagh Mountains
Gweebarra Bay
Dawros Head
Ardara
Ceann Ros Eoghain
Málainn Bhig
Slieve League
Killybegs
Blue Stack Mountains
Donegal
Dún na nGall
Lough Derg
Strabane
Castlederg
Omagh
Saint John's Point
Donegal Bay
Ballyshannon
Bundoran
Lower Lough Erne
Boa Island
Irvinestown
Inishmurray
Mullaghmore
Lough Melvin
Fermanagh
Enniskillen
Devenish Island
Downpatrick Head
Céide Fields
Killala Bay
Sligo Bay
Easky
Rosses Point
Strandhill
Sligo
Sligeach
Lough Gill
Parke's Castle
Manorhamilton
Marble Arch Caves
Florence Court
Upper Lough Erne
Mullet Peninsula
Belmullet
Blacksod Bay
Inis Gé Thuaidh
Inis Gé Theas
Dubh Oileán Mór
Achill Head
Achill Island
Cliff Scenery
Ballycroy National Park
Nephin Beg Range
Nephin
Lough Conn
Ballina
Béal an Átha
Moyne Abbey
Rathfran Abbey
Ox Mountains
Slieve Gamph
Tobercurry
Ballymote
Lough Arrow
Lough Allen
Iron Mountains
Drumshanbo
Carrick-on-Shannon
Cara Droma Ruisc
Boyle Abbey
Boyle
Lough Key
Clew Bay
Clare Island
Westport
Newport
Castlebar
Caisleán an Bharraigh
Swinford
Charlestown
Kiltimagh
Knock
Claremorris
Ballyhaunis
Castlerea
Rathcroghan
Strokestown
Roscommon
Longford
An Longford
Inishturk
Croagh Patrick
Murrisk Abbey
Louisburgh
Doo Lough Valley
Killary Harbour
Inishbofin
Inishkea
Kylemore Abbey
Connemara
Connemara National Park
The Twelve Pins
Joyce Country
Clifden
Mannin Bay
Ballyconneely
Lough Mask
Cong Abbey
Lough Corrib
Ross Abbey
Oughterard
Tuam
Lough Ree
Athlone
Baile Átha Luain
Ballinasloe
Béal Átha na Sluaighe
Galway
Gaillimh
Galway Bay
Athenry
Loughrea
Slieve Aughty Mountains
Black Head
Dún Aonghasa
Inis Mór
Inishmore
Inis Meáin
Inis Oírr
Oileain Árann
Aran Islands
Slieve Elva
Ailwee Cave
Poulnabrone
Burren National Park
Kinvarra
Gort
Doolin
Lisdoonvarna
O'Brien's Tower
Cliffs of Moher
Ennistymon
Lough Derg
Portumna
Birr Castle
Slieve Bloom Mountains
Tullamore
Tulach Mhór
Port Laoise
Roscrea
Mt. Saint Josephs Abbey
Clonmacnoise
Shannonbridge
I
R
E
L
A
É
I
R
E
62

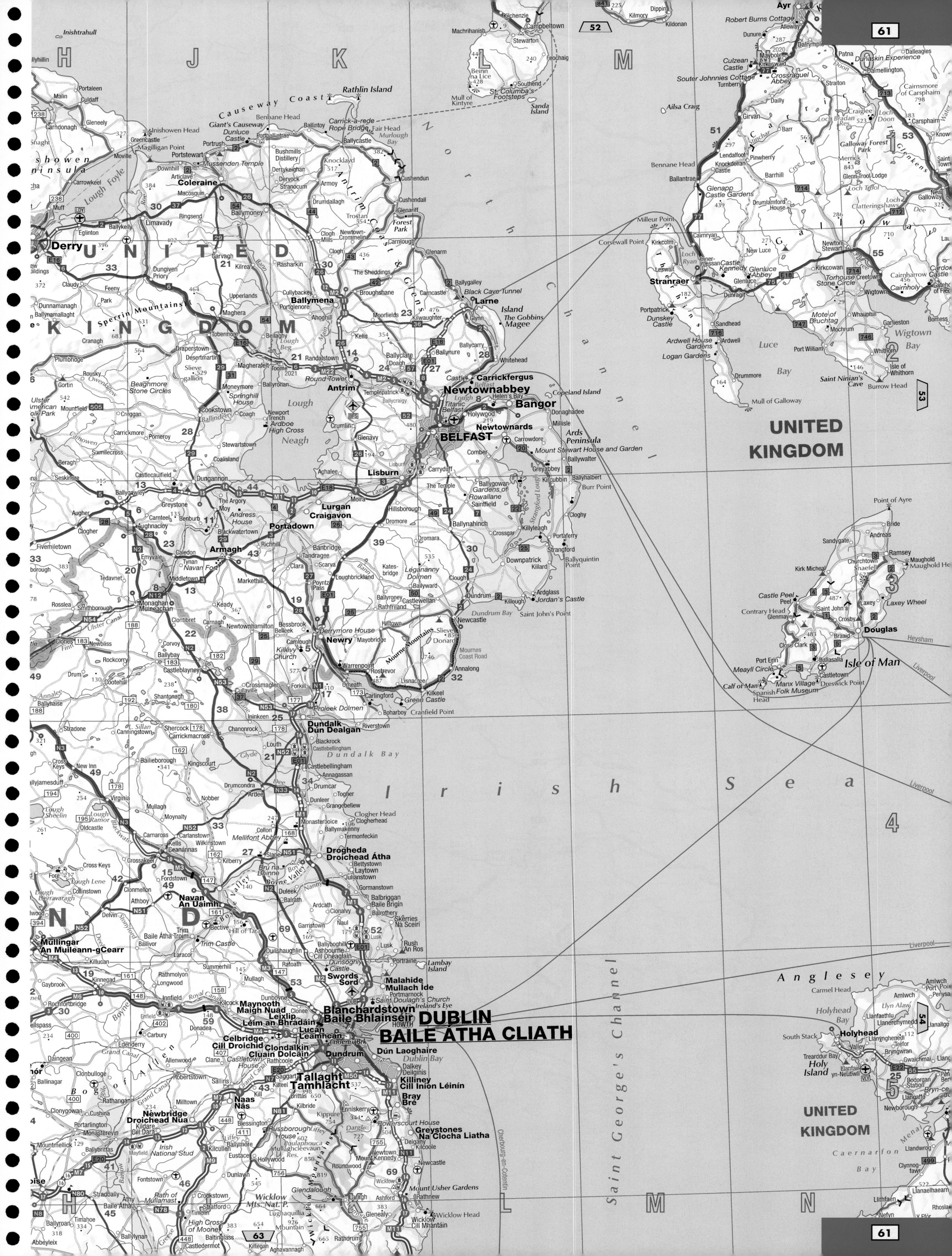
UNITED KINGDOM
UNITED KINGDOM
UNITED KINGDOM
Irish Sea
North Channel
Saint George's Channel
Causeway Coast
Antrim Coast & Glens
Inishtrahull
Rathlin Island
Giant's Causeway
Inishowen Head
Inishowen Peninsula
Lough Foyle
Malin
Culdaff
Moville
Greencastle
Magilligan Point
Portstewart
Portrush
Dunluce Castle
Bushmills Distillery
Ballintoy
Carrick-a-rede Rope Bridge
Fair Head
Murlough Bay
Benbane Head
Ballycastle
Knocklayd
Cushendun
Cushendall
Glenariff Forest Park
Mussenden Temple
Downhill
Articlave
Coleraine
Macosquin
Ballymoney
Armoy
Stranocum
Dervock
Derrykeighan
Drumdallagh
Limavady
Ringsend
Ballykelly
Eglinton
Derry
Dungiven Priory
Garvagh
Kilrea
Rasharkin
Claudy
Feeny
Park
Dunnamanagh
Ballynamallaght
Sperrin Mountains
Upperlands
Maghera
Tobermore
Cullybackey
Ballymena
Portglenore
Ahoghill
Broughshane
Carncastle
Ballygalley
Black Cave Tunnel
Larne
Island Magee
The Gobbins
Glenarm
Carnlough
Clough
Newtown-Crommelin
The Sheddings
Kilwaughter
Moorfields
Kells
Cranagh
Plumbridge
Draperstown
Desertmartin
Magherafelt
Slieve Gallion
Toome
Randalstown
Antrim
Round Tower
Ballyclare
Doagh
Ballynure
Ballycarry
Whitehead
Carrickfergus
Newtownabbey
Templepatrick
Ballycraigy
Helen's Bay
Bangor
Holywood
Titanic Belfast
BELFAST
Crumlin
Glenavy
Newtownards
Donaghadee
Millisle
Ards Peninsula
Carrowdore
Mount Stewart House and Garden
Ballywalter
Greyabbey
Copeland Island
Comber
Carryduff
Lisburn
Moneymore
Springhill House
Cookstown
Lough Neagh
Ardboe High Cross
Coagh
Newport Trench
Beaghmore Stone Circles
Gortin
Mountfield
Creggan
Carrickmore
Pomeroy
Stewartstown
Coalisland
Dungannon
Castlecaulfield
Seskinore
Beragh
Sixmilecross
Ballygawley
Augher
Clogher
Aughnacloy
Moy
The Argory
Benburb
Blackwatertown
Caledon
Armagh
Navan Fort
Tynan
Middletown
Richhill
Portadown
Lurgan
Craigavon
Moira
Hillsborough
Dromore
The Temple
Ballygowan
Gardens of Rowallane
Saintfield
Ballynahinch
Crossgar
Killyleagh
Strangford Lough
Cloghy
Portaferry
Strangford
Ballyquintin Point
Downpatrick
Killard
Ardglass
Jordan's Castle
Killough
Dundrum
Dundrum Bay
Saint John's Point
Newcastle
Slieve Donard
Mourne Mountains
Mournes Coast Road
Annalong
Kilkeel
Green Castle
Cranfield Point
Rostrevor
Warrenpoint
Newry
Mayobridge
Hilltown
Rathfriland
Castlewellan
Ballyward
Leganany Dolmen
Dromara
Banbridge
Gilford
Tandragee
Scarva
Loughbrickland
Poyntz Pass
Markethill
Keady
Newtownhamilton
Bessbrook
Derrymore House
Camlough
Killevy Church
Forkill
Crossmaglen
Cullyhanna
Omeath
Carlingford
Proleek Dolmen
Emyvale
Monaghan Muineachán
Smithborough
Rosslea
Clones
Newbliss
Ulster Canal
Rockcorry
Drum
Cootehill
Ballybay
Castleblayney
Carnagh
Clontibret
Corvoy
Shantonagh
Inniskeen
Dundalk Dún Dealgan
Riverstown
Blackrock
Castlebellingham
Dundalk Bay
Louth
Chanonrock
Carrickmacross
Shercock
Kingscourt
Baileborough
Cross Keys
New Inn
Ballyjamesduff
Virginia
Lough Ramor
Drumcondra
Ardee
Nobber
Dunleer
Grangebellew
Togher
Annagassan
Drumcar
Clogher Head
Clogherhead
Termonfeckin
Monasterboice
Collon
Mellifont Abbey
Slane
Drogheda Droichead Átha
Bettystown
Laytown
Julianstown
Gormanstown
Balbriggan Baile Brigín
Skerries Na Sceirí
Rush An Ros
Lusk
Brú na Bóinne
Boyne Valley
Duleek
Balrath
Ardcath
Naul
Garristown
Ashbourne Cill Dhéagláin
Portraine
Lambay Island
Malahide Mullach Íde
Swords Sord
Portmarnock
Saint Doulagh's Church
Ireland's Eye
HOWTH
Ratoath
Dunshaughlin
Dunsoghly Castle
Kells Ceanannas
Carlanstown
Wilkinstown
Moynalty
Mullagh
Oldcastle
Carnaross
Crossakeel
Kilberry
Fordstown
Navan An Uaimh
Athboy
Delvin
Clonmellon
Bective
Hill of Tara
Trim
Baile Átha Troim
Trim Castle
Ballivor
Laracor
Killucan
Mullingar An Muileann-gCearr
Summerhill
Rathmolyon
Longwood
Kinnegad
Enfield
Innfield
Kilcock
Maynooth Maigh Nuad
Leixlip
Léim an Bhradáin
Clonee
Dunboyne
Blanchardstown Baile Bhlainséir
DUBLIN
BAILE ÁTHA CLIATH
Lucan Leamhcán
Celbridge Cill Droichid
Clondalkin Cluain Dolcáin
Castletown House
Rathcoole
Dundrum
Dún Laoghaire
Dublin Bay
Dalkey Deilginis
Killiney Cill Iníon Léinín
Bray Brí
Tallaght Tamhlacht
Saggart
Kilteel
Brittas
Kilbride
Kippure
Enniskerry
Powerscourt House
Greystones Na Clocha Liatha
Delgany
Kilcoole
Newtown Mount Kennedy
Newcastle
Roundwood
Wicklow Mountains
Glendalough
Laragh
Ashford
Rathnew
Mount Usher Gardens
Wicklow Head
Wicklow Cill Mhantáin
Glenealy
Wicklow Mts. Nat. P.
Lugnaquilla
Rathdrum
Aghavannagh
Poulaphouca Res.
Russborough House
Blessington
Hollywood
Ballymore Eustace
Kilcullen
Naas Nás
Kill
Clane
Sallins
Prosperous
Robertstown
Carbury
Donadea
Edenderry
Allenwood
Bog of Allen
Grand Canal
Royal Canal
Newbridge Droichead Nua
Kildare Cill Dara
Irish National Stud
Monasterevin
Portarlington
Rathangan
Milltown
Clonygowan
Cushina
Mountmellick
Ballybrittas
Fontstown
Dunlavin
Crookstown
Stratford
Timolin
Rath of Mullamast
Baile Átha Í
Ballitore
High Cross of Moone
Baltinglass
Castledermot
Kiltegan
Stradbally
Timahoe
Ballyroan
Abbeyleix
Ballylynan
Daingean
Clonbullogue
Ballinagar
Rochfortbridge
Tyrrellspass
Gaybrook
Delvin
Fore
Lough Lene
Collinstown
Lough Derravaragh
Lough Sheelin
Cairnsmore of Carsphairn
Kintyre
Mull of Kintyre
Machrihanish
Campbeltown
Kilchenzie
Stewarton
Feochaig
Southend
St. Columba's Footsteps
Sanda Island
Beinn na Lice
Kilmory
Dippin
Kildonan
Ayr
Robert Burns Cottage
Alloway
Dunure
Maybole
Dalrymple
Culzean Castle
Kirkoswald
Souter Johnnies Cottage
Turnberry
Crossraguel Abbey
Patna
Dunaskin Experience
Dalleagles
Dalmellington
Straiton
Ailsa Craig
Girvan
Barr
Dailly
Carrick
Craiglee
Loch Bradan Res.
Loch Doon
Carsphairn
Galloway Forest Park
Merrick
Glentrool Lodge
Loch Trool
Lendalfoot
Pinwherry
Knockdolian Castle
Bennane Head
Ballantrae
Barrhill
Glenapp Castle Gardens
Drumlamford House
Clatteringshaws Loch
New Galloway
The Glenkens
Galloway
Milleur Point
Corsewall Point
Kirkcolm
Loch Ryan
Leswalt
Innermessan
Castle Kennedy
Glenluce Abbey
Glenluce
Stranraer
Dunragit
The Rhins
Kirkcowan
Newton Stewart
New Luce
Torhouse Stone Circle
Creetown
Cairnharrow
Cardoness Castle
Wigtown
Wigtown Bay
Whauphill
Garlieston
Mochrum
Mote of Druchtag
Portpatrick
Dunskey Castle
Sandhead
Ardwell
Ardwell House Gardens
Logan Gardens
Luce Bay
Port William
Whithorn
Isle of Whithorn
Saint Ninian's Cave
Burrow Head
Drummore
Mull of Galloway
Point of Ayre
Bride
Andreas
Sandygate
Ramsey
Maughold
Maughold Head
Kirk Michael
Churchtown
Snaefell
Castle Peel
Peel
Saint John's
Laxey
Laxey Wheel
Contrary Head
Glenmaye
Crosby
Braaid
Douglas
Close Clark
Ballasalla
Castletown
Isle of Man
Port Erin
Meayll Circle
Calf of Man
Spanish Head
Manx Village Folk Museum
Dreswick Point
Heysham
Liverpool
Liverpool
Liverpool
Cherbourg-en-Cotentin
Anglesey
Amlwch
Carmel Head
Llyn Alaw
Llanerchymedd
Llanfaethlu
Holyhead Bay
Holyhead
Holy Island
South Stack
Trearddur Bay
Valley
Llanfair-yn-Neubwll
Llangefni
Trefor
Bryngwran
Gwalchmai
Bodorgan Station
Llangadwaladr
Newborough
Caernarfon Bay
Menai
Llandwrog
Clynnog-fawr
Llithfaen
Llanaelhaearn
52
53
54
63

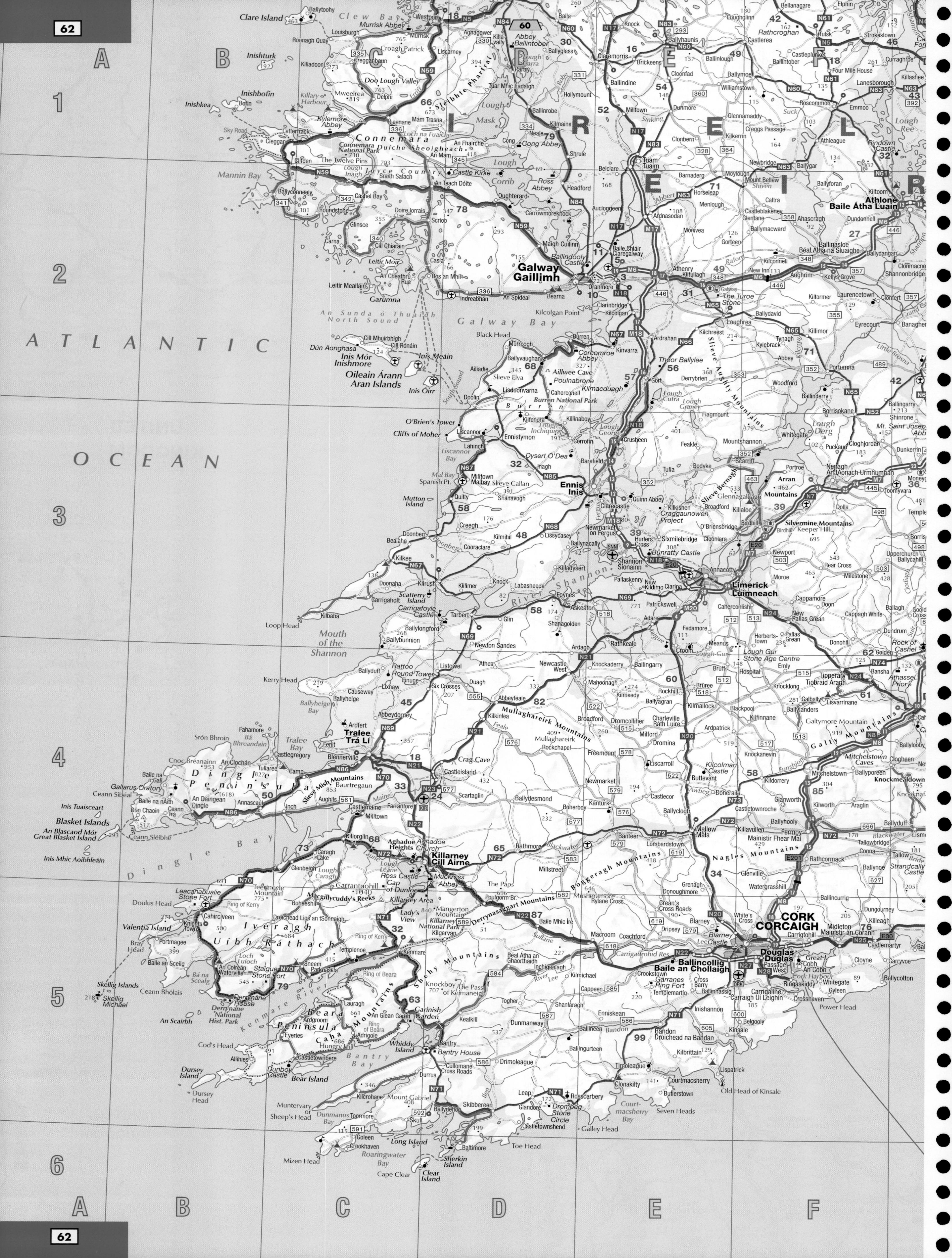
A B C D E F
1
2
3
4
5
6
ATLANTIC
OCEAN
IRELAND
EIRE
Clare Island
Clew Bay
Westport
Murrisk Abbey
Croagh Patrick
Louisburgh
Roonagh Quay
Inishturk
Killadoon
Doo Lough Valley
Delphi
Mweelrea
Inishbofin
Inishkea
Bofin
Killary Harbour
Kylemore Abbey
Leenane
Mám Trasna
Sky Road
Letterfrack
Cleggan
Clifden
Connemara
Connemara National Park
The Twelve Pins
Lough Inagh
Joyce Country
Sraith Salach
An Teach Dóite
Mannin Bay
Ballyconneely
Cashel Bay
Roundstone
Doire Iorrais
Glinsce
Carna
Cill Chiaráin
Leitir Móir
An Cheathrú Rua
Leitir Meallain
Garumna
Casla
Ros an Mhíl
Indreabhán
An Spidéal
Bearna
Scriob
Oughterard
Maigh Cuilinn
Galway
Gaillimh
Oranmore
Lough Corrib
Lough Mask
Cong
Cong Abbey
Castle Kirke
Ross Abbey
Headford
Ballinrobe
Kilmaine
Neale
Shrule
Tuar Mhic Éadaigh
Partry
Lough Carra
Abbey Ballintober
Ballyglass
Aghagower
Liscarney
Sléibhte Pharthaí
Hollymount
Claremorris
Knock
Balla
Ballyhaunis
Brickeens
Ballindine
Milltown
Sinking
Dunmore
Tuam
Belclare
Carrowmoreknock
Aucloggeen
Ballindooly Castle
Claregalway
Baile Chláir
Cloonfad
Ballinlough
Ballymoe
Williamstown
Glennamaddy
Creggs Passage
Clonbern
Kilkerrin
Moylough
Mount Bellew
Barnaderg
Horseleap
Menlough
Abbert
Ardnasodan
Monivea
Athenry
Kiltullagh
Gorteen
Raford
New Inn
Aughrim
Kellys Grove
Ballinasloe
Béal Átha na Sluaighe
Athlone
Baile Átha Luain
Castlerea
Bellanagare
Elphin
Rathcroghan
Tulsk
Strokestown
Castleplunket
Ballintober
Four Mile House
Roscommon
Lanesborough
Emmoo
Athleague
Lough Ree
Rindown Castle
Ballygar
Ballyforan
Kiltoom
Caltra
Castleblakeney
Glentane
Ahascragh
Ballymacward
Dundonnell
Kilconnell
Ballydangan
Clonmacnoise
Shannonbridge
Kiltormer
Laurencetown
Clonfert
The Turoe Stone
Loughrea
Ballydavid
Kilchreest
Killimor
Eyrecourt
Banagher
Kylebrack
Tynagh
Abbey
Portumna
Woodford
Ballinderry
Borrisokane
Shinrone
Mt. Saint Joseph Abbey
Lough Derg
Whitegate
Puckaun
Cloghjordan
Dunkerrin
Portroe
Nenagh
An tAonach Urmhumhan
Toomyvara
Arran Mountains
Dolla
Silvermine Mountains
Keeper Hill
Templederry
Borrisoleigh
Newport
Rear Cross
Upperchurch
Milestone
Moroe
Annacotty
Limerick
Luimneach
Caherconlish
Cappamore
Doon
New Pallas Green
Cappagh White
Dundrum
Rock of Cashel
Golden
Bansha
Tipperary
Tiobraid Árann
Athassel Priory
Emly
Knocklong
Galbally
Lisvarrinane
Galtymore Mountain
Galty Mountains
Ballylanders
Kilfinnane
Mitchelstown Caves
Mitchelstown
Ballyporeen
Knockmealdown
Clogheen
Kildorrery
Glanworth
Kilworth
Araglin
Fermoy
Mainistir Fhear Maí
Ballyduff
Tallowbridge
Tallow
Conna
Rathcormack
Strancally Castle
Ballynoe
Glenville
Watergrasshill
Ballincurrig
Dungourney
Midleton
Mainistir na Corann
Castlemartyr
Carrigtohill
Killeagh
Cloyne
Garryvoe
Ballycotton
Whitegate
Cobh
An Cobh
Cork Harbour
Ringaskiddy
Crosshaven
Power Head
Carrigaline
Carraigh Uí Leighin
CORK
CORCAIGH
Douglas
Passage West
Blarney
Ballincollig
Baile an Chollaigh
Crookstown
Garranes Ring Fort
Templemartin
Cross Barry
Ballinhassig
Inishannon
Belgooly
Kinsale
Old Head of Kinsale
Courtmacsherry
Butlerstown
Seven Heads
Timoleague
Clonakilty
Rosscarbery
Drombeg Stone Circle
Glandore
Leap
Castletownshend
Galley Head
Courtmacsherry Bay
Toe Head
Baltimore
Sherkin Island
Clear Island
Cape Clear
Roaringwater Bay
Skibbereen
Ballydehob
Schull
Long Island
Goleen
Crookhaven
Mizen Head
Dunmanus Bay
Toormore
Sheep's Head
Muntervary
Kilcrohane
Mount Gabriel
Durrus
Bantry
Bantry House
Bantry Bay
Whiddy Island
Drimoleague
Cullomane Cross Roads
Dunmanway
Ballineen
Bandon
Droichead na Bandan
Enniskean
Kilbrittain
Ballingurteen
Kealkill
Togher
Shehy Mountains
Béal Átha an Ghaorthaidh
Inchigeelagh
Kilmichael
Macroom
Coachford
Dripsey
Carrigadrohid Res
River Lee
Knockboy
The Pass of Keimaneigh
Kilgarvan
Kenmare
Templenoe
Sneem
Parknasilla
Ring of Kerry
Ring of Beara
Kenmare River
Beara Peninsula
Lauragh
Ardgroom
Eyeries
Caha Mountains
Hungry Hill
Adrigole
Glengarriff
Garinish Garden
Castletownbere
Bear Island
Dunboy Castle
Allihies
Dursey Island
Dursey Head
Cod's Head
An Scairbh
Derrynane House
Derrynane National Hist. Park
Staigue Stone Fort
Caherdaniel
Loch Luioch
An Coireán
Waterville
Baile an Sceilg
Ballinskelligs Bay
Ceann Bhólais
Skellig Islands
Skellig Michael
Bray Head
Portmagee
Valentia Island
Knightstown
Cahirciveen
Iveragh
Uíbh Ráthach
Doulus Head
Leacanabuaile Stone Fort
Teermoyle Mountain
Glenbeigh
Caragh Lake
Lough Caragh
Killorglin
Carrantuohill
Macgillycuddy's Reeks
Gap of Dunloe
Ross Castle
Lough Leane
Muckross Abbey
Killarney
Cill Airne
Aghadoe Heights
Aghadoe Church
Killarney Area
Lady's View
Mangerton Mountain
Killarney National Park
Derrynasaggart Mountains
The Paps
Poulgorm Br.
Baile Mhic Ire
Ballyvourney
Musheramore
Rylane Cross
Boggeragh Mountains
Millstreet
Rathmore
Ballydesmond
Boherboy
Kanturk
Banteer
Lombardstown
Mallow
Mala
Nagles Mountains
Donoughmore
Grenagh
Crean's Cross Roads
White's Cross
Ballyclogh
Castlecor
Buttevant
Kilcolman Castle
Doneraile
Castletownroche
Ballyhooly
Killavullen
Liscarroll
Newmarket
Freemount
Rockchapel
Mullaghareirk
Mullaghareirk Mountains
Dromina
Milford
Charleville
Rath Luirc
Dromcolliher
Broadford
Kilmeedy
Ballyagran
Rockhill
Kilmallock
Bruree
Bruff
Hospital
Lough Gur Stone Age Centre
Herbertstown
Pallas Grean
Meanus
Croom
Fedamore
Adare
Patrickswell
Rathkeale
Ardagh
Newcastle West
Knockaderry
Ballingarry
Mahoonagh
Abbeyfeale
Kilkinlea
Athea
Glin
Shanagolden
Askeaton
Foynes
Kildimo
Clarina
Pallaskenry
Killadysert
Labasheeda
Knock
Killimer
Kilrush
Scattery Island
Carrigaholt
Doonaha
Kilbaha
Loop Head
Kilkee
Doonbeg
Bealaha
Creegh
Cooraclare
Kilmihil
Lissycasey
Ballynacally
Newmarket on Fergus
Shannon
Sionainn
Bunratty Castle
Sixmilebridge
Hurlers Cross
Cloonlara
O'Briensbridge
Craggaunowen Project
Kilkishen
Quin Abbey
Clarecastle
Ennis
Inis
Barefield
Dysert O'Dea
Corrofin
Tulla
Bodyke
Feakle
Mountshannon
Scarriff
Slieve Bernagh
Killaloe
Birdhill
Glennagalliagh
Broadford
Flagmount
Lough Graney
Lough Cutra
Gort
Slieve Aughty Mountains
Derrybrien
Thoor Ballylee
Crusheen
Lough George
Killinaboy
Kilfenora
Lough Inchiquin
Ennistymon
Lahinch
Liscannor
Liscannor Bay
O'Brien's Tower
Cliffs of Moher
Doolin
Lisdoonvarna
Burren
Burren National Park
Caherconnell
Poulnabrone
Aillwee Cave
Kilmacduagh
Slieve Elva
Ballyvaughan
Corcomroe Abbey
Ailladie
Black Head
Murroogh
Kinvarra
Burren
Ardrahan
Kilcolgan
Clarinbridge
Kilcolgan Point
Galway Bay
Aran Islands
Oileáin Árann
Inis Mór
Inishmore
Dún Aonghasa
Cill Mhuirbhigh
Cill Rónáin
Inis Meáin
Inis Oírr
South Sound
North Sound
An Sunda ó Thuaidh
Mal Bay
Spanish Pt.
Milltown Malbay
Slieve Callan
Shanavogh
Quilty
Mutton Island
Mouth of the Shannon
River Shannon
Tarbert
Carrigafoyle Castle
Ballylongford
Ballybunnion
Newton Sandes
Listowel
Rattoo Round Tower
Finuge
Lixnaw
Six Crosses
Duagh
Ballyduff
Causeway
Ballyheige
Ballyheige Bay
Kerry Head
Abbeydorney
Ardfert
Tralee
Trá Lí
Tralee Bay
Fenit
Fahamore
Srón Bhroin
Brandon Head
Cnoc Bréanainn
An Clochán
Tullaree
Castlegregory
Camp
Blennerville
Dingle Peninsula
Slieve Mish Mountains
Baurtregaun
Gallarus Oratory
Baile na nGall
Ceann Sibéal
An Daingean
Dingle
Annascaul
Inch
Aughils
Baile an nAith
Dún Chaoin
Ceann Trá
Ceann Sléibhe
Inis Tuaisceart
Blasket Islands
An Blascaod Mór
Great Blasket Island
Inis Mhic Aoibhleáin
Dingle Bay
Castlemaine
Milltown
Farranfore
Crag Cave
Castleisland
Scartaglin
Maine
Feale
Blackwater
Bandon
Awbeg
Funshion
Maigue
Fergus
Suck
Shiven
Robe
Erriff
Sullane
Little Brosna
N5 N17 N59 N84 N60 N83 N63 N61 N6 N18 N65 N67 N66 N52 N62 N85 N68 N7 N24 N69 N20 N21 N23 N22 N71 N72 N73 N8 N25 N27 N28 N70 N86
M6 M17 M18 M7 M20 M8
E20 E30 E201
60

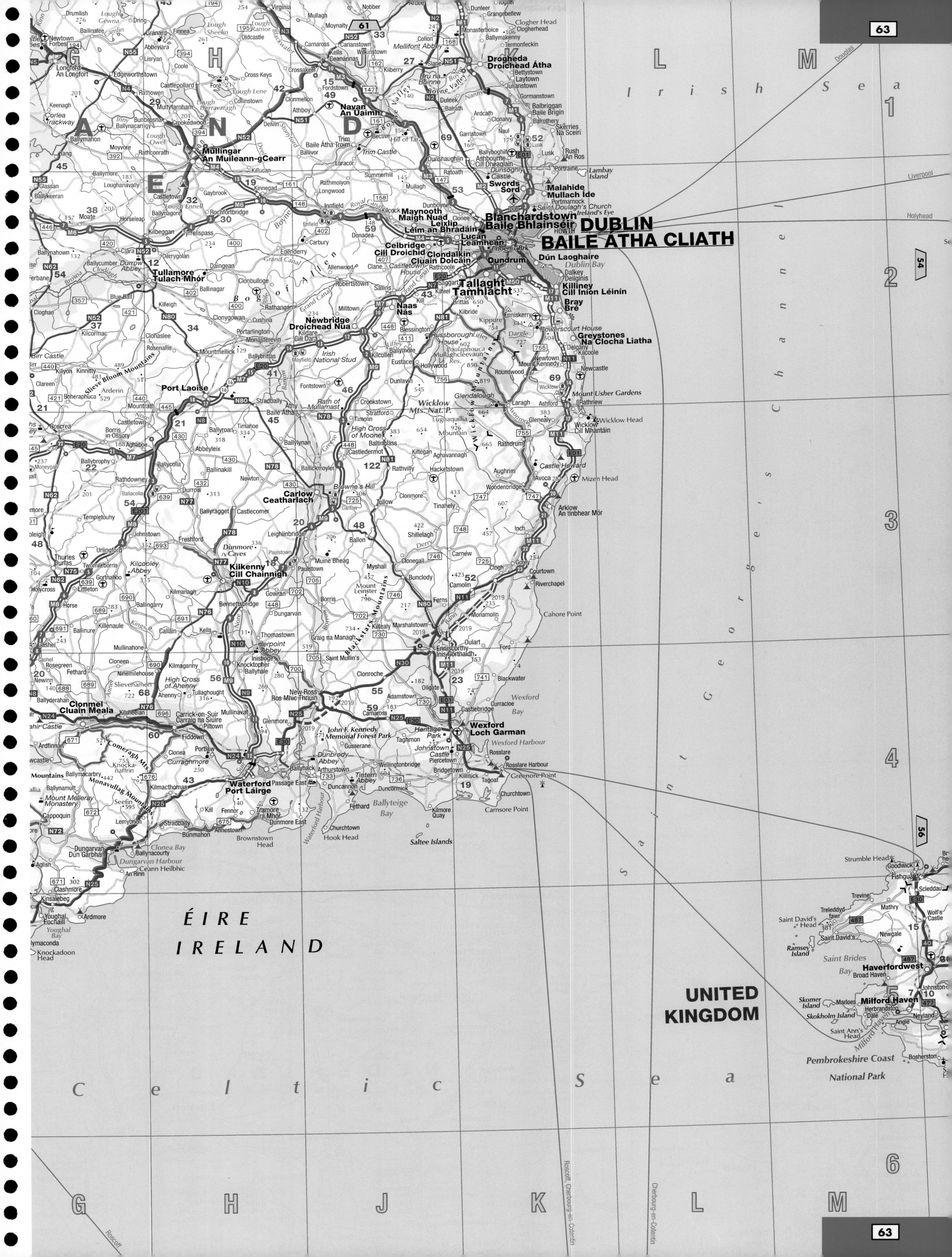
DUBLIN
BAILE ÁTHA CLIATH
Irish Sea
Saint George's Channel
Celtic Sea
ÉIRE
IRELAND
UNITED
KINGDOM
Pembrokeshire Coast
National Park
Waterford
Port Láirge
Wexford
Loch Garman
Kilkenny
Cill Chainnigh
Carlow
Ceatharlach
Port Laoise
Mullingar
An Muileann-gCearr
Drogheda
Droichead Átha
Navan
An Uaimh
Tullamore
Tulach Mhór
Clonmel
Cluain Meala
Haverfordwest
Milford Haven

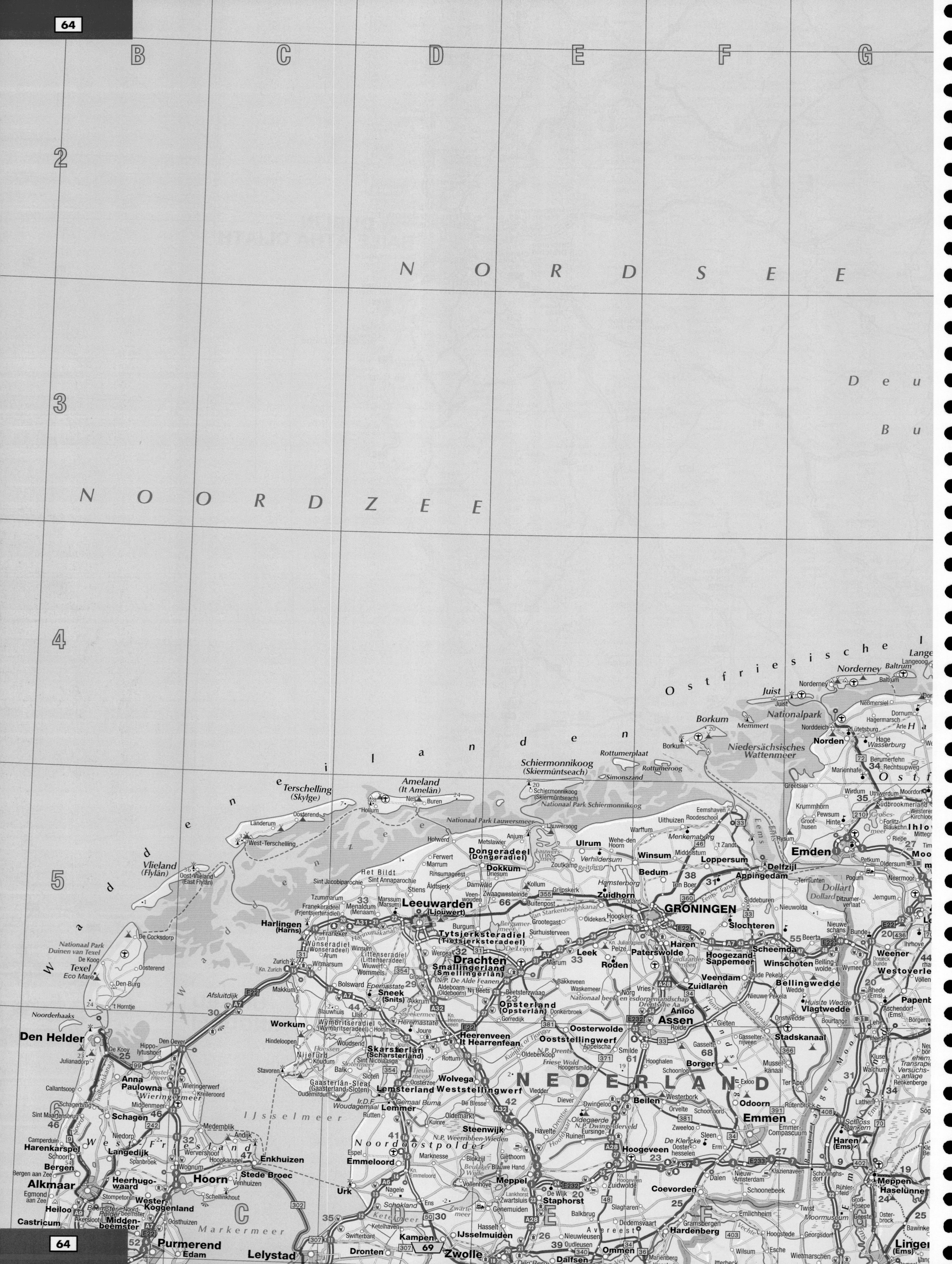
B
C
D
E
F
G
2
3
4
5
6
N O R D S E E
N O O R D Z E E
D e u
B u
O s t f r i e s i s c h e I
W a d d e n e i l a n d e n
W a d d e n z e e
Langeoog
Norderney
Baltrum
Juist
Borkum
Memmert
Nationalpark
Niedersächsisches Wattenmeer
Norden
Norddeich
Rottumerplaat
Rottumeroog
Schiermonnikoog
(Skiermûntseach)
Simonszand
Nationaal Park Schiermonnikoog
Ameland
(It Amelân)
Nes
Buren
Hollum
Terschelling
(Skylge)
West-Terschelling
Oosterend
Landerum
Vlieland
(Flylân)
Oost-Vlieland
(East Flylân)
Texel
Eco Mare
De Cocksdorp
Nationaal Park
Duinen van Texel
De Koog
Oosterend
Den Burg
't Horntje
Noorderhaaks
Den Helder
Julianadorp
De Kooy
Hippolytushoef
Den Oever
Afsluitdijk
Wieringermeer
Anna Paulowna
Callantsoog
Schagen
Sint Maartensbrug
Medemblik
Andijk
Wervershoof
Enkhuizen
Harenkarspel
Langedijk
Schoorl
Bergen
Bergen aan Zee
Alkmaar
Egmond aan Zee
Heiloo
Castricum
Heerhugowaard
Wester-Koggenland
Middenbeemster
Hoorn
Stede Broec
Purmerend
Edam
Markermeer
IJsselmeer
Lelystad
Dronten
Kampen
Zwolle
Urk
Emmeloord
Noordoostpolder
Lemmer
Lemsterland
Stavoren
Workum
Hindeloopen
Makkum
Bolsward
Sneek
(Snits)
Harlingen
(Harns)
Franeker
Leeuwarden
(Ljouwert)
Het Bildt
Dokkum
Dongeradeel
(Dongeradiel)
Nationaal Park Lauwersmeer
Lauwersoog
Tytsjerksteradiel
Drachten
Smallingerland
Heerenveen
It Hearrenfean
Skarsterlân
Wolvega
Weststellingwerf
Steenwijk
Meppel
Staphorst
Oosterwolde
Ooststellingwerf
Opsterland
Leek
Roden
Ulrum
Winsum
Bedum
Zuidhorn
GRONINGEN
Haren
Paterswolde
Zuidlaren
Assen
Anloo
Veendam
Hoogezand-Sappemeer
Slochteren
Appingedam
Delfzijl
Loppersum
Eemshaven
Scheemda
Winschoten
Bellingwedde
Vlagtwedde
Stadskanaal
Borger
Beilen
Odoorn
Emmen
Hoogeveen
Coevorden
Hardenberg
Ommen
Dalfsen
IJsselmuiden
NEDERLAND
Emden
Dollart
Krummhörn
Hinte
Weener
Westoverledingen
Papenburg
Haren
(Ems)
Meppen
Haselünne
Lingen
(Ems)
Twist
Moormuseum
Emlichheim
E22
A7
A28
A32
A6
E232
E233
A37
69

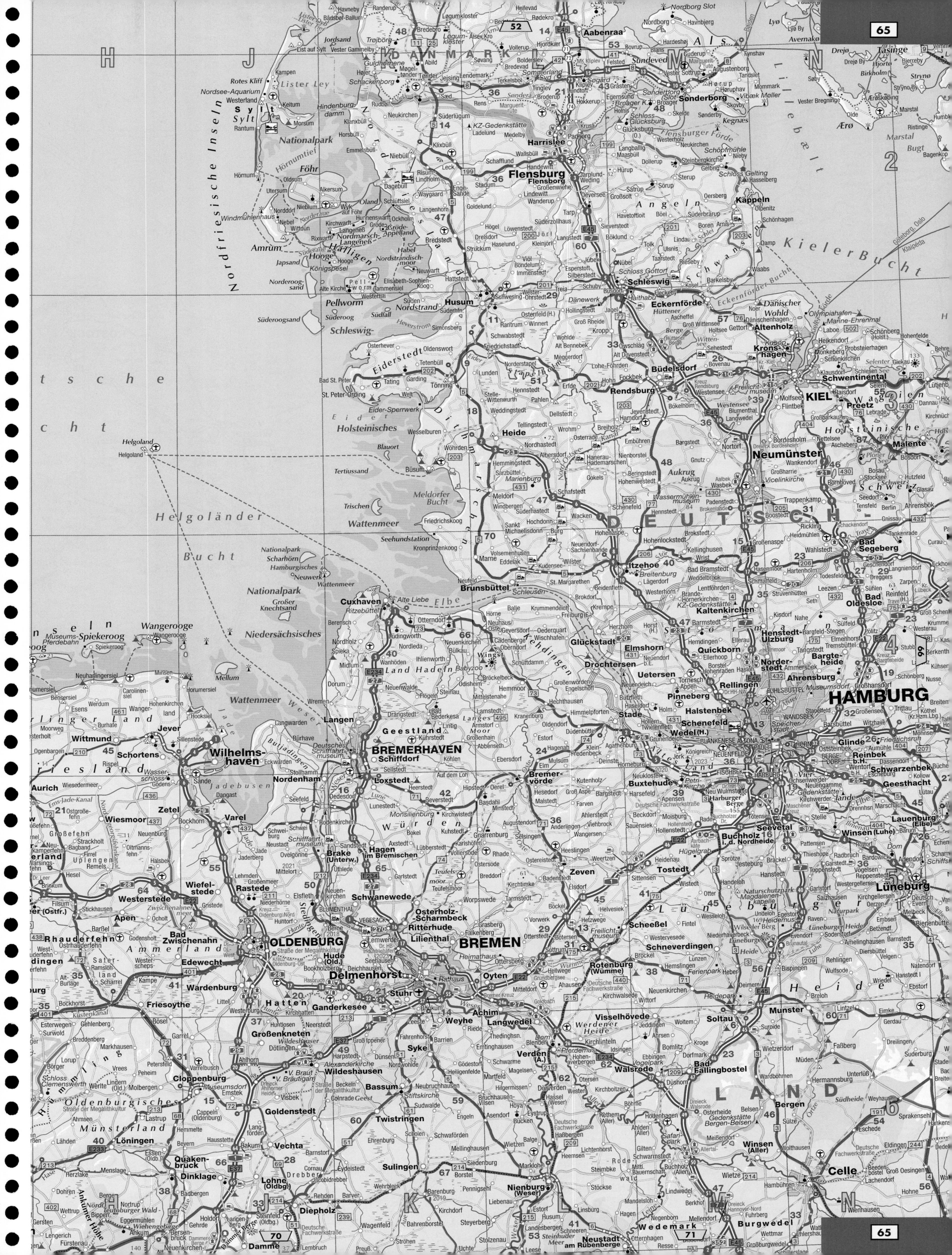
DANMARK
Aabenraa
Sønderborg
Sylt
Westerland
Nationalpark
Föhr
Amrum
Halligen
Pellworm
Husum
Flensburg
Harrislee
Schleswig
Eckernförde
Kappeln
Angeln
Kieler Bucht
Kiel
Schwentinental
Preetz
Plön
Malente
Neumünster
Rendsburg
Büdelsdorf
Heide
Tönning
Eiderstedt
Dithmarschen
Helgoland
Helgoländer Bucht
Büsum
Meldorfer Bucht
Wattenmeer
Brunsbüttel
Itzehoe
Cuxhaven
Elbe
Glückstadt
Elmshorn
Bad Segeberg
Bad Oldesloe
Kaltenkirchen
Henstedt-Ulzburg
Norderstedt
Quickborn
Ahrensburg
Pinneberg
HAMBURG
Wedel (H.)
Stade
Buxtehude
Bremervörde
Geestland
BREMERHAVEN
Schiffdorf
Nordenham
Wilhelmshaven
Jever
Wittmund
Schortens
Wangerooge
Spiekeroog
Niedersächsisches Wattenmeer
Jadebusen
Varel
Zetel
Wiesmoor
Aurich
Westerstede
Rastede
Bad Zwischenahn
Ammerland
OLDENBURG
Edewecht
Wardenburg
Delmenhorst
Ganderkesee
BREMEN
Stuhr
Achim
Oyten
Lilienthal
Osterholz-Scharmbeck
Schwanewede
Brake (Unterw.)
Hude (Old.)
Friesoythe
Cloppenburg
Löningen
Vechta
Dinklage
Quakenbrück
Lohne (Oldb.)
Diepholz
Damme
Wildeshausen
Bassum
Syke
Weyhe
Twistringen
Sulingen
Nienburg (Weser)
Verden (A.)
Rotenburg (Wümme)
Zeven
Tostedt
Buchholz i. d. Nordheide
Seevetal
Winsen (Luhe)
Lüneburg
Geesthacht
Reinbek
Glinde
Schwarzenbek
Lauenburg (Elbe)
Lüneburger Heide
Soltau
Schneverdingen
Walsrode
Bad Fallingbostel
Munster
Bergen
Celle
Winsen (Aller)
Wedemark
Burgwedel
Neustadt am Rübenberge
DEUTSCHLAND
52
70
71

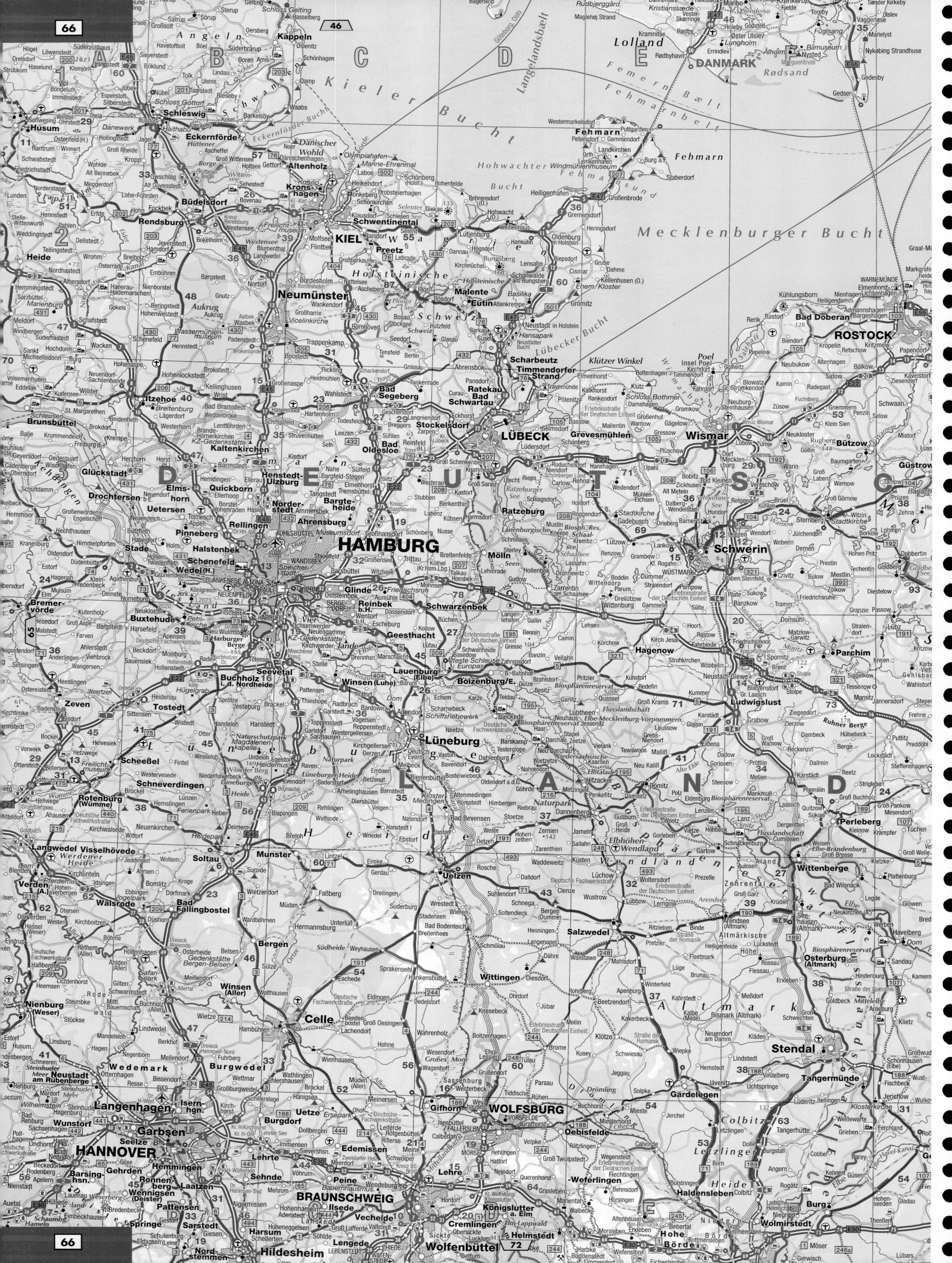

Angeln
Kieler Bucht
Langelandsbælt
Lolland
DANMARK
Femern Bælt
Fehmarnbelt
Fehmarn
Hohwachter Bucht
Mecklenburger Bucht
Lübecker Bucht
Schleswig
Husum
Eckernförde
Kappeln
Kiel
Schwentinental
Preetz
Rendsburg
Büdelsdorf
Heide
Neumünster
Plön
Malente
Eutin
Oldenburg in Holstein
Heiligenhafen
Fehmarn
Neustadt in Holstein
Scharbeutz
Timmendorfer Strand
Bad Segeberg
Itzehoe
Brunsbüttel
Glückstadt
Kaltenkirchen
Henstedt-Ulzburg
Quickborn
Elmshorn
Uetersen
Pinneberg
Norderstedt
Bargteheide
Ahrensburg
Bad Oldesloe
Stockelsdorf
Ratekau
Bad Schwartau
LÜBECK
Grevesmühlen
Wismar
Bad Doberan
ROSTOCK
Bützow
Güstrow
Ratzeburg
Mölln
Schwerin
Stade
Drochtersen
Halstenbek
Schenefeld
Wedel (H.)
Rellingen
HAMBURG
Glinde
Reinbek
Schwarzenbek
Buxtehude
Bremervörde
Geesthacht
Hagenow
Parchim
Ludwigslust
Lauenburg (Elbe)
Boizenburg/E.
Seevetal
Buchholz i. d. Nordheide
Winsen (Luhe)
Tostedt
Zeven
Lüneburg
Scheeßel
Schneverdingen
Rotenburg (Wümme)
Soltau
Munster
Uelzen
Dannenberg
Perleberg
Wittenberge
Langwedel
Visselhövede
Verden (A.)
Walsrode
Bad Fallingbostel
Bergen
Salzwedel
Wittingen
Osterburg (Altmark)
Nienburg (Weser)
Winsen (Aller)
Celle
Stendal
Tangermünde
Neustadt am Rübenberge
Burgwedel
Langenhagen
Garbsen
Gifhorn
WOLFSBURG
Gardelegen
Wunstorf
HANNOVER
Burgdorf
Uetze
Lehrte
Sehnde
Oebisfelde
Laatzen
Hemmingen
Gehrden
Barsinghausen
Wennigsen (Deister)
Pattensen
Lehre
Weferlingen
Haldensleben
Burg
BRAUNSCHWEIG
Peine
Königslutter a. Elm
Helmstedt
Sarstedt
Hildesheim
Wolfenbüttel
Wolmirstedt
Lüneburger Heide
Altmark
Wendland
Colbitz-Letzlinger Heide
Drömling

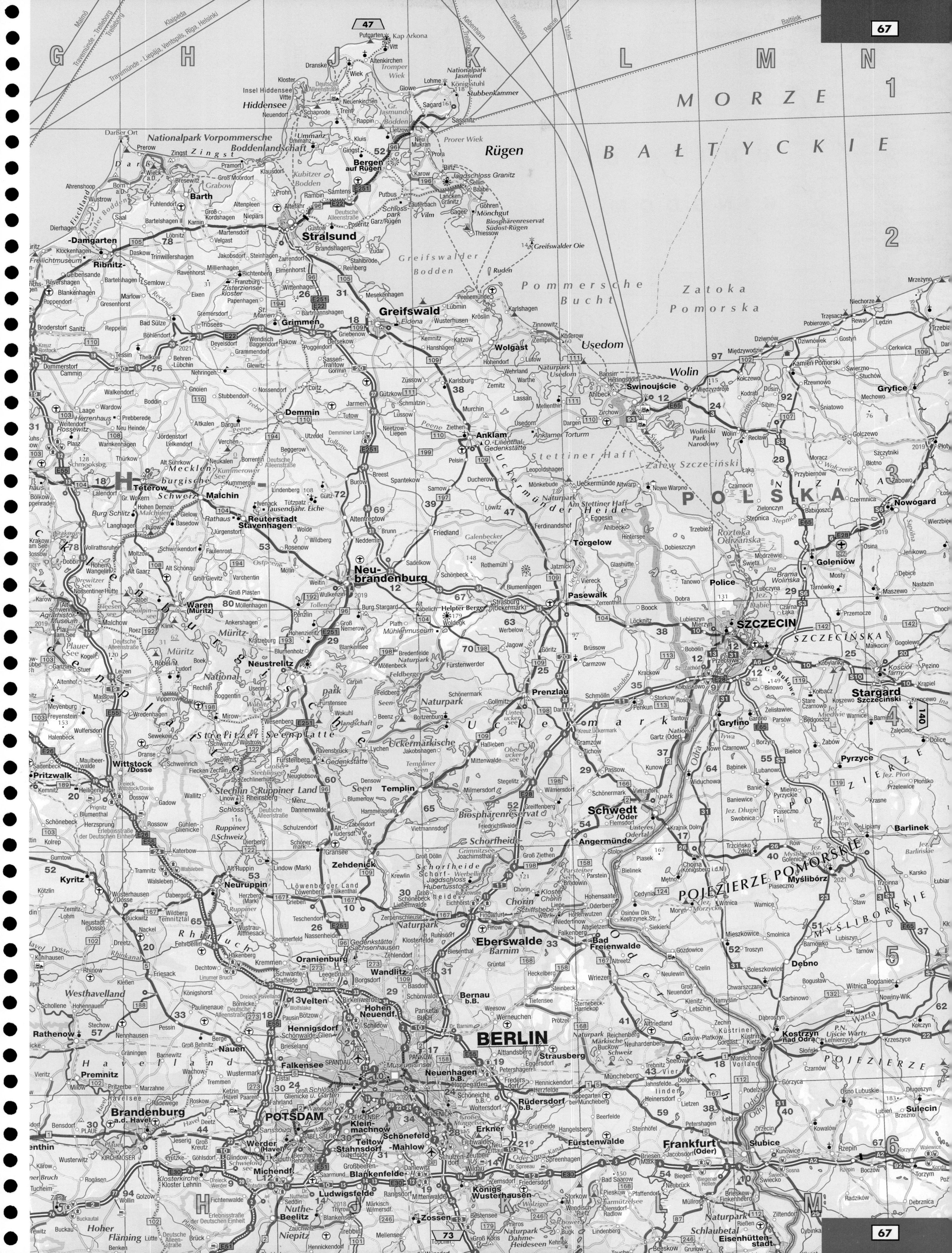
MORZE BAŁTYCKIE
Rügen
Hiddensee
Nationalpark Vorpommersche Boddenlandschaft
Nationalpark Jasmund
Kap Arkona
Stralsund
Bergen auf Rügen
Greifswalder Bodden
Greifswald
Pommersche Bucht
Zatoka Pomorska
Usedom
Wolgast
Wolin
Świnoujście
Stettiner Haff
Zalew Szczeciński
Anklam
Demmin
Ribnitz-Damgarten
Barth
Grimmen
Teterow
Malchin
Reuterstadt Stavenhagen
Neubrandenburg
Pasewalk
Torgelow
Ueckermünde
Police
SZCZECIN
Goleniów
Nowogard
Stargard Szczeciński
Gryfino
Pyrzyce
Myślibórz
Barlinek
POLSKA
Waren (Müritz)
Müritz
Neustrelitz
Prenzlau
Templin
Schwedt /Oder
Angermünde
Uckermark
Wittstock /Dosse
Pritzwalk
Kyritz
Neuruppin
Zehdenick
Oranienburg
Eberswalde
Bad Freienwalde
Bernau b.B.
Strausberg
BERLIN
Hennigsdorf
Falkensee
Nauen
Rathenow
Premnitz
Brandenburg a.d. Havel
POTSDAM
Werder (Havel)
Teltow
Ludwigsfelde
Zossen
Königs Wusterhausen
Erkner
Fürstenwalde
Frankfurt (Oder)
Słubice
Kostrzyn nad Odrą
Sulęcin
Eisenhüttenstadt
Beelitz
Michendorf
Westhavelland
Havelland
Fläming
POJEZIERZE POMORSKIE
MYŚLIBORSKIE
Schorfheide
Barnim
Oderbruch

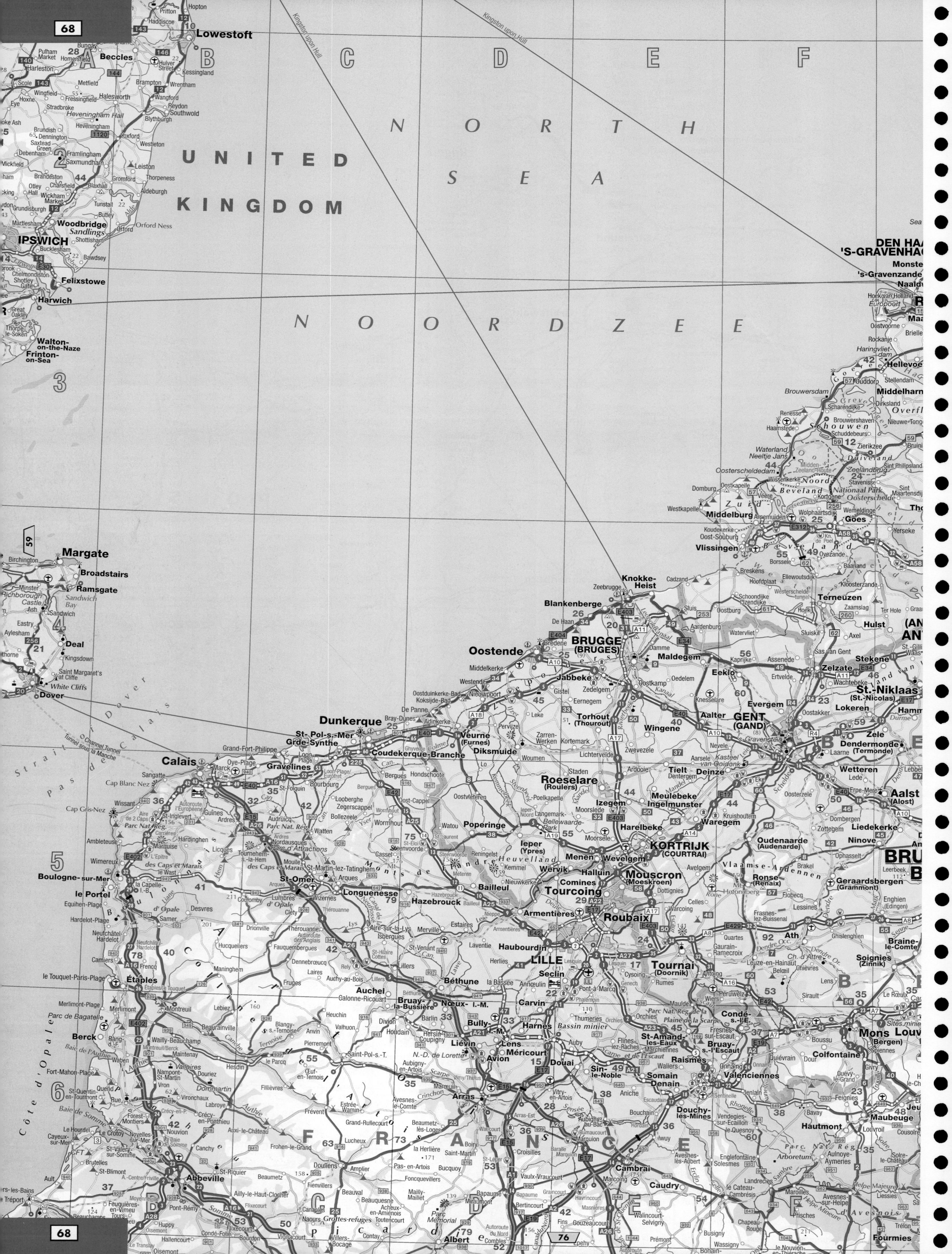

UNITED KINGDOM
NORTH SEA
NOORDZEE
Lowestoft
Beccles
Kessingland
Halesworth
Southwold
Heveningham Hall
Framlingham
Saxmundham
Leiston
Aldeburgh
Orford Ness
Woodbridge
Sandlings
IPSWICH
Felixstowe
Harwich
Walton-on-the-Naze
Frinton-on-Sea
Margate
Broadstairs
Ramsgate
Sandwich Bay
Deal
White Cliffs
Dover
Strait of Dover
Pas de Calais
Channel Tunnel
Tunnel sous la Manche
DEN HAAG
'S-GRAVENHAGE
's-Gravenzande
Hoek van Holland
Europoort
Brielle
Hellevoetsluis
Middelharnis
Brouwersdam
Schouwen
Zierikzee
Waterland Neeltje Jans
Oosterscheldedam
Nationaal Park Oosterschelde
Middelburg
Goes
Vlissingen
Terneuzen
Hulst
Knokke-Heist
Zeebrugge
Blankenberge
De Haan
BRUGGE (BRUGES)
Oostende
Middelkerke
Maldegem
Eeklo
Jabbeke
Nieuwpoort
Diksmuide
Veurne (Furnes)
De Panne
Torhout (Thourout)
Wingene
Aalter
GENT (GAND)
Evergem
Zelzate
St.-Niklaas (St.-Nicolas)
Lokeren
Dendermonde (Termonde)
Wetteren
Aalst (Alost)
Roeselare (Roulers)
Izegem
Meulebeke
Ingelmunster
Tielt
Deinze
Waregem
Harelbeke
KORTRIJK (COURTRAI)
Wevelgem
Menen
Ieper (Ypres)
Poperinge
Heuvelland
Oudenaarde (Audenarde)
Ronse (Renaix)
Geraardsbergen (Grammont)
Liedekerke
Ninove
Mouscron (Moeskroen)
Tourcoing
Roubaix
Wervik
Halluin
Comines
Armentières
Dunkerque
St-Pol-s.-Mer
Grde-Synthe
Coudekerque-Branche
Gravelines
Calais
Grand-Fort-Philippe
Sangatte
Cap Blanc Nez
Cap Gris-Nez
Wissant
Marquise
Guînes
Ardres
Bourbourg
Bergues
Hondschoote
Wormhout
Cassel
Steenvoorde
Bailleul
Hazebrouck
St-Omer
Arques
Longuenesse
Boulogne-sur-Mer
Wimereux
le Portel
Desvres
Lumbres
Aire-sur-la-Lys
Hardelot-Plage
Neufchâtel Hardelot
Camiers
Étaples
Le Touquet-Paris-Plage
Berck
Montreuil
Fruges
Béthune
Lillers
Auchel
Bruay-la-Buissière
Nœux-l.-M.
Bully-l.-M.
Liévin
Lens
Avion
Méricourt
Carvin
Harnes
Hénin-Beaumont
Douai
Sin-le-Noble
Somain
Denain
Arras
Saint-Pol-s.-T.
Hesdin
Doullens
Abbeville
St-Valery-sur-Somme
Le Crotoy
Baie de Somme
Baie de l'Authie
Côte d'Opale
Fort-Mahon-Plage
Quend
Rue
Cayeux-sur-Mer
Albert
Bapaume
Cambrai
Caudry
LILLE
Seclin
Haubourdin
Tournai (Doornik)
Ath
Braine-le-Comte
Soignies (Zinnik)
Mons (Bergen)
Colfontaine
Maubeuge
Hautmont
Valenciennes
Raismes
St-Amand-les-Eaux
Condé-s.-l'E.
Bruay-s.-l'Escaut
Douchy-les-Mines
Le Cateau-Cambrésis
Avesnes-sur-Helpe
Fourmies
FRANCE
Collines d'Artois
Picardie
Kingston upon Hull

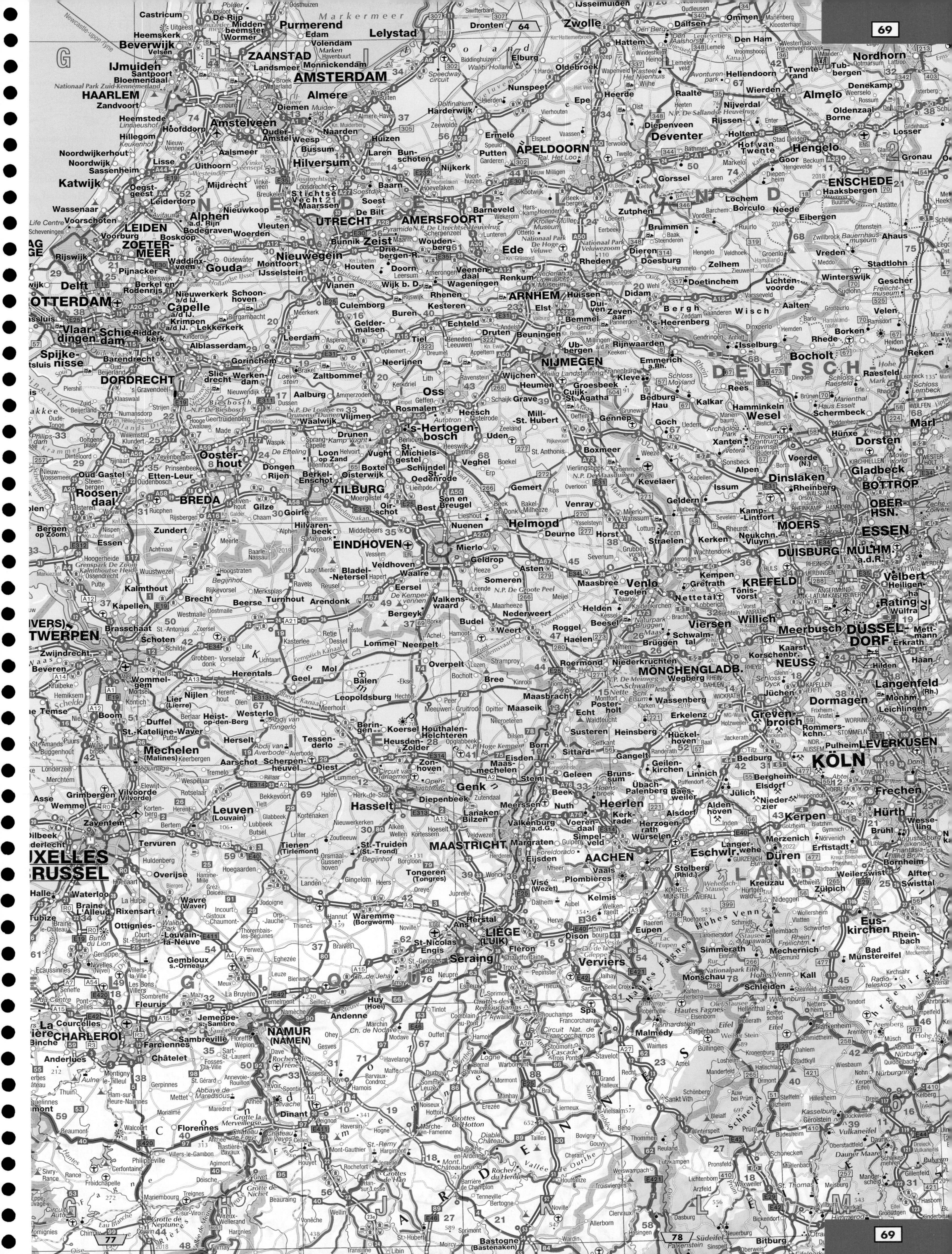
64
70
77
78
Markermeer
Purmerend
Lelystad
Dronten
Zwolle
Beverwijk
IJmuiden
ZAANSTAD
AMSTERDAM
HAARLEM
Zandvoort
Almere
Amstelveen
Hilversum
Harderwijk
APELDOORN
Deventer
Almelo
Hengelo
ENSCHEDE
Nordhorn
Katwijk
LEIDEN
Alphen a.d. Rijn
UTRECHT
AMERSFOORT
Zeist
Nieuwegein
ZOETERMEER
Gouda
Delft
ROTTERDAM
Capelle a/d IJ.
Vlaardingen
Schiedam
Spijkenisse
DORDRECHT
Ede
ARNHEM
NIJMEGEN
Doetinchem
Bocholt
Emmerich a.Rh.
Kleve
Oss
's-Hertogenbosch
Waalwijk
Oosterhout
Roosendaal
BREDA
TILBURG
EINDHOVEN
Helmond
Venlo
KREFELD
Wesel
Dorsten
Gladbeck
BOTTROP
OBER-HSN.
ESSEN
MOERS
DUISBURG
MÜLHM. a.d.R.
Velbert
Ratingen
DÜSSELDORF
Viersen
MÖNCHENGLADB.
NEUSS
Langenfeld
Dormagen
LEVERKUSEN
KÖLN
Frechen
Hürth
Kerpen
Düren
Eschwlr.
AACHEN
Heerlen
MAASTRICHT
Genk
Hasselt
Sittard
Roermond
Weert
Turnhout
Mechelen
Leuven
Tienen
ANTWERPEN
BRUXELLES BRUSSEL
Waterloo
Wavre
Charleroi
NAMUR (NAMEN)
Huy
LIÈGE (LUIK)
Seraing
Verviers
Spa
Malmédy
Eupen
Monschau
Euskirchen
Dinant
Bastogne (Bastenaken)
Bitburg
Prüm
Daun
NEDERLAND
DEUTSCHLAND
BELGIË

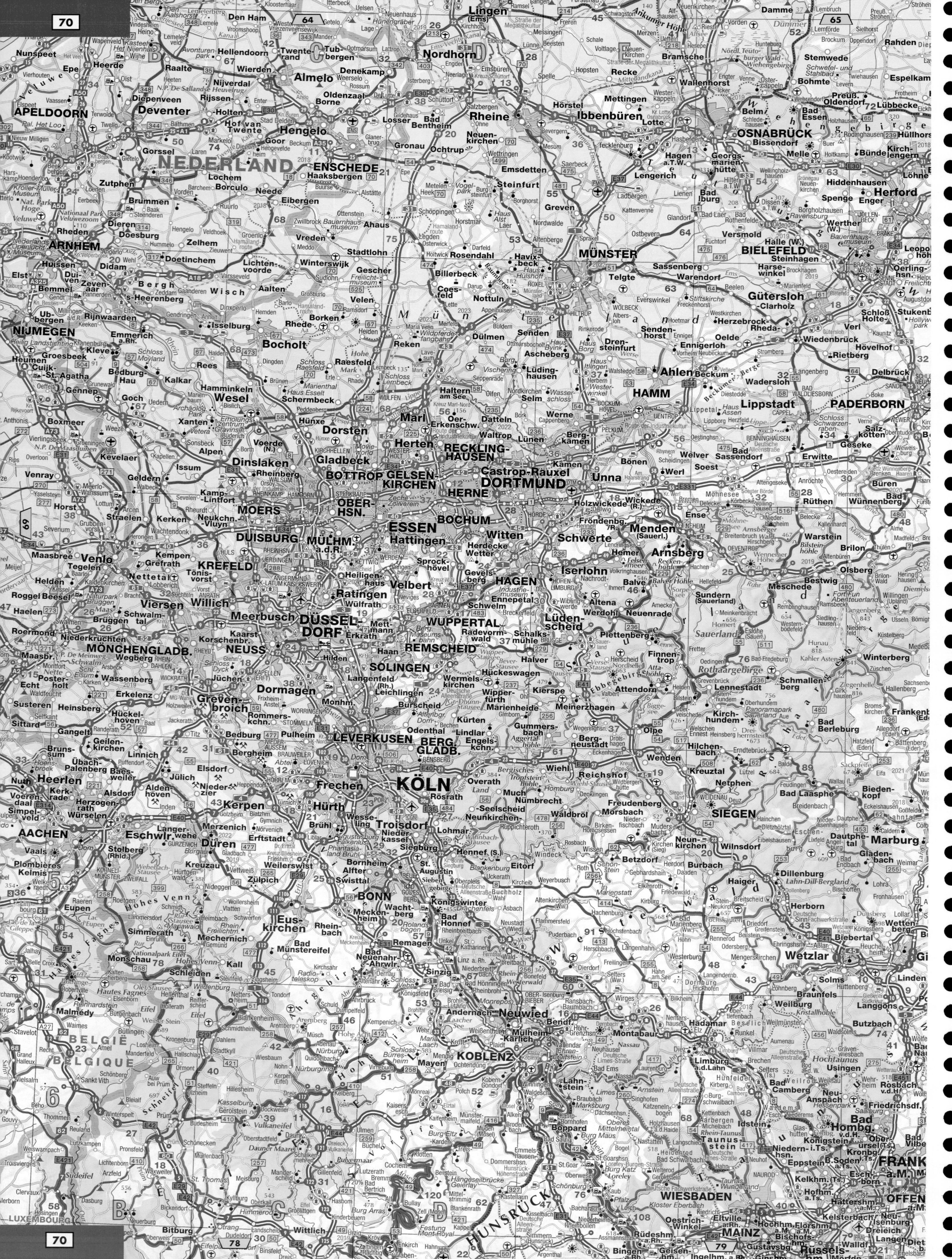

NEDERLAND
APELDOORN
Deventer
Hengelo
ENSCHEDE
Almelo
Nordhorn
Lingen (Ems)
Rheine
Ibbenbüren
OSNABRÜCK
Herford
ARNHEM
NIJMEGEN
MÜNSTER
BIELEFELD
Gütersloh
Bocholt
Wesel
HAMM
Lippstadt
PADERBORN
Dorsten
Marl
RECKLING-HAUSEN
Castrop-Rauxel
DORTMUND
Unna
GELSEN-KIRCHEN
BOTTROP
HERNE
OBER-HSN.
MOERS
ESSEN
BOCHUM
DUISBURG
MÜLHM. a.d.R.
Witten
Schwerte
HAGEN
Iserlohn
Arnsberg
Venlo
KREFELD
Velbert
Ratingen
DÜSSEL-DORF
WUPPERTAL
Lüden-scheid
MÖNCHENGLADB.
NEUSS
REMSCHEID
SOLINGEN
Dormagen
Greven-broich
LEVERKUSEN
BERG. GLADB.
KÖLN
Kerpen
Hürth
Troisdorf
SIEGEN
Heerlen
AACHEN
Düren
BONN
Marburg
Wetzlar
Neuwied
KOBLENZ
Limburg a.d.Lahn
BELGIË
BELGIQUE
LUXEMBOURG
HUNSRÜCK
WIESBADEN
MAINZ

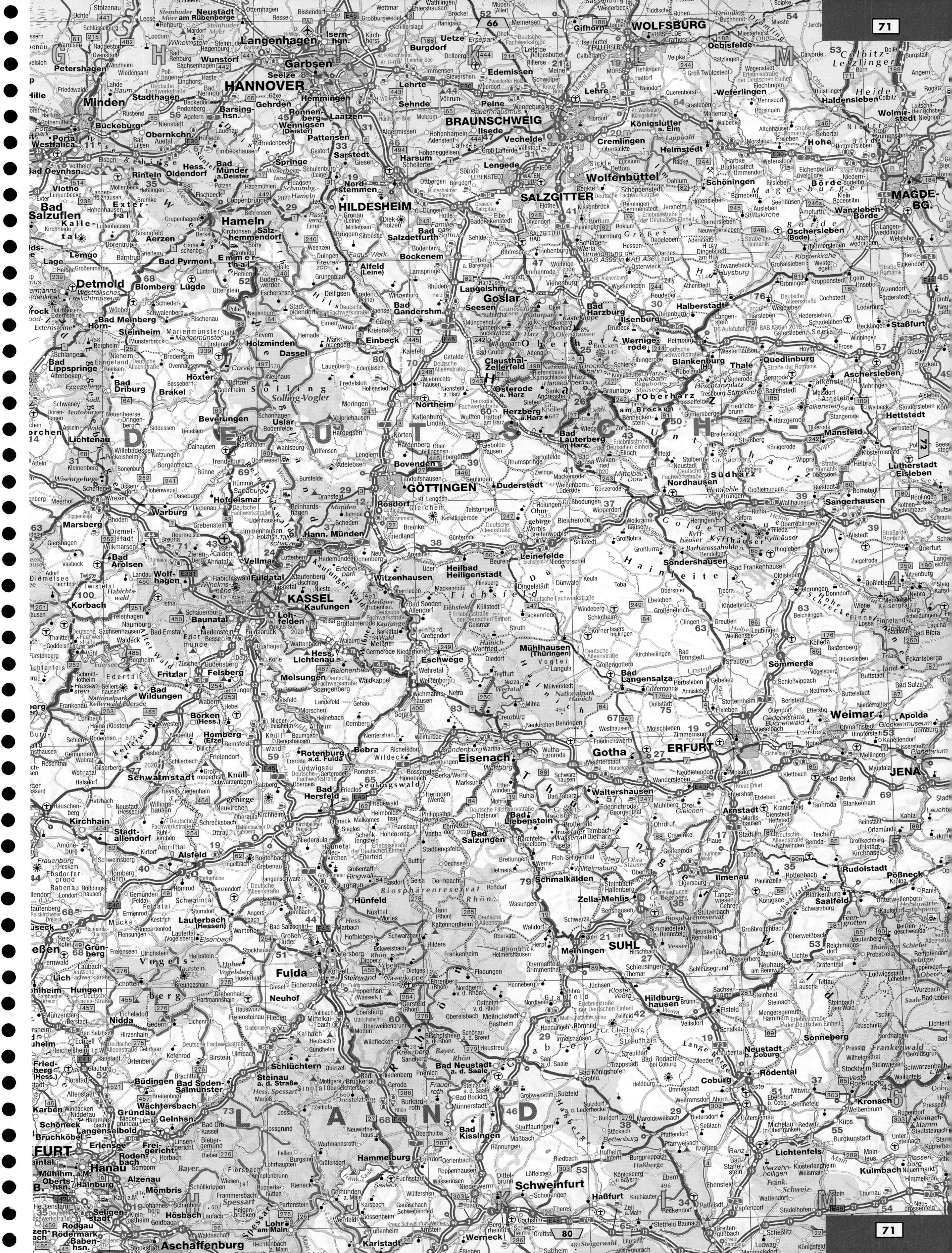
Neustadt am Rübenberge
Langenhagen
Garbsen
HANNOVER
Minden
Bückeburg
Stadthagen
Porta Westfalica
Bad Oeynhausen
Vlotho
Bad Salzuflen
Lemgo
Detmold
Horn
Rinteln
Hameln
Bad Pyrmont
Lügde
Blomberg
Wunstorf
Lehrte
Sehnde
Burgdorf
Uetze
Edemissen
Peine
BRAUNSCHWEIG
WOLFSBURG
Gifhorn
Oebisfelde
Königslutter a. Elm
Helmstedt
Schöningen
Wolfenbüttel
SALZGITTER
HILDESHEIM
Sarstedt
Pattensen
Springe
Elze
Alfeld (Leine)
Bockenem
Salzdetfurth
Goslar
Seesen
Langelsheim
Bad Harzburg
Wernigerode
Ilsenburg
Halberstadt
Blankenburg
Thale
Quedlinburg
Aschersleben
Haldensleben
MAGDEBURG
Wanzleben-Börde
Oschersleben (Bode)
Staßfurt
Einbeck
Dassel
Holzminden
Höxter
Brakel
Bad Driburg
Bad Lippspringe
Northeim
Osterode a. Harz
Herzberg a. Harz
Clausthal-Zellerfeld
Bad Lauterberg im Harz
Uslar
Beverungen
Bad Karlshafen
Bovenden
GÖTTINGEN
Duderstadt
Nordhausen
Sangerhausen
Hettstedt
Mansfeld
Lutherstadt Eisleben
Hofgeismar
Warburg
Marsberg
Bad Arolsen
Wolfhagen
Vellmar
Hann. Münden
KASSEL
Kaufungen
Lohfelden
Baunatal
Witzenhausen
Heilbad Heiligenstadt
Leinefelde
Sondershausen
Bad Frankenhausen
Korbach
Fritzlar
Bad Wildungen
Felsberg
Melsungen
Hess. Lichtenau
Eschwege
Mühlhausen (Thüringen)
Bad Langensalza
Sömmerda
Borken (Hess.)
Homberg (Efze)
Rotenburg a. d. Fulda
Bebra
Eisenach
Gotha
ERFURT
Weimar
Apolda
JENA
Schwalmstadt
Bad Hersfeld
Kirchhain
Stadtallendorf
Alsfeld
Waltershausen
Arnstadt
Bad Salzungen
Bad Liebenstein
Schmalkalden
Zella-Mehlis
Ilmenau
Rudolstadt
Saalfeld
Pößneck
Hünfeld
Lauterbach (Hessen)
Grünberg
Fulda
Meiningen
SUHL
Hildburghausen
Neuhof
Nidda
Schlüchtern
Bad Neustadt a. d. Saale
Coburg
Neustadt b. Coburg
Sonneberg
Rödental
Kronach
Büdingen
Bad Soden-Salmünster
Gelnhausen
Wächtersbach
Gründau
Langenselbold
Hanau
Alzenau
Bad Kissingen
Hammelburg
Schweinfurt
Haßfurt
Lichtenfels
Kulmbach
Aschaffenburg
Lohr am Main
Karlstadt
Werneck
Rodgau
Rödermark
D E U T S C H L A N D

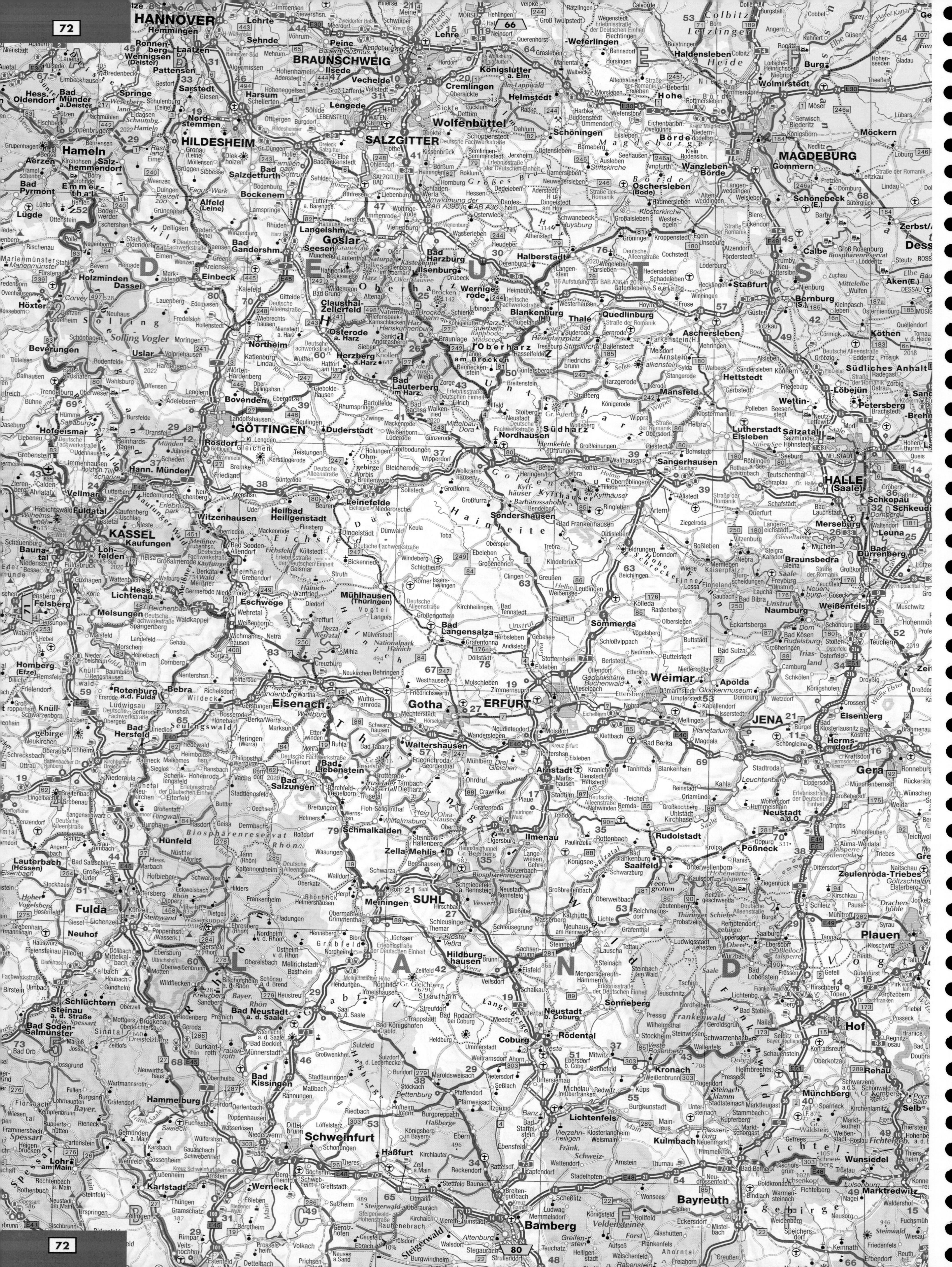
HANNOVER
BRAUNSCHWEIG
HILDESHEIM
SALZGITTER
Wolfenbüttel
MAGDEBURG
GÖTTINGEN
KASSEL
HALLE (Saale)
ERFURT
Weimar
JENA
Gera
Eisenach
Gotha
SUHL
Fulda
Plauen
Hof
Bamberg
Bayreuth
Schweinfurt
Coburg

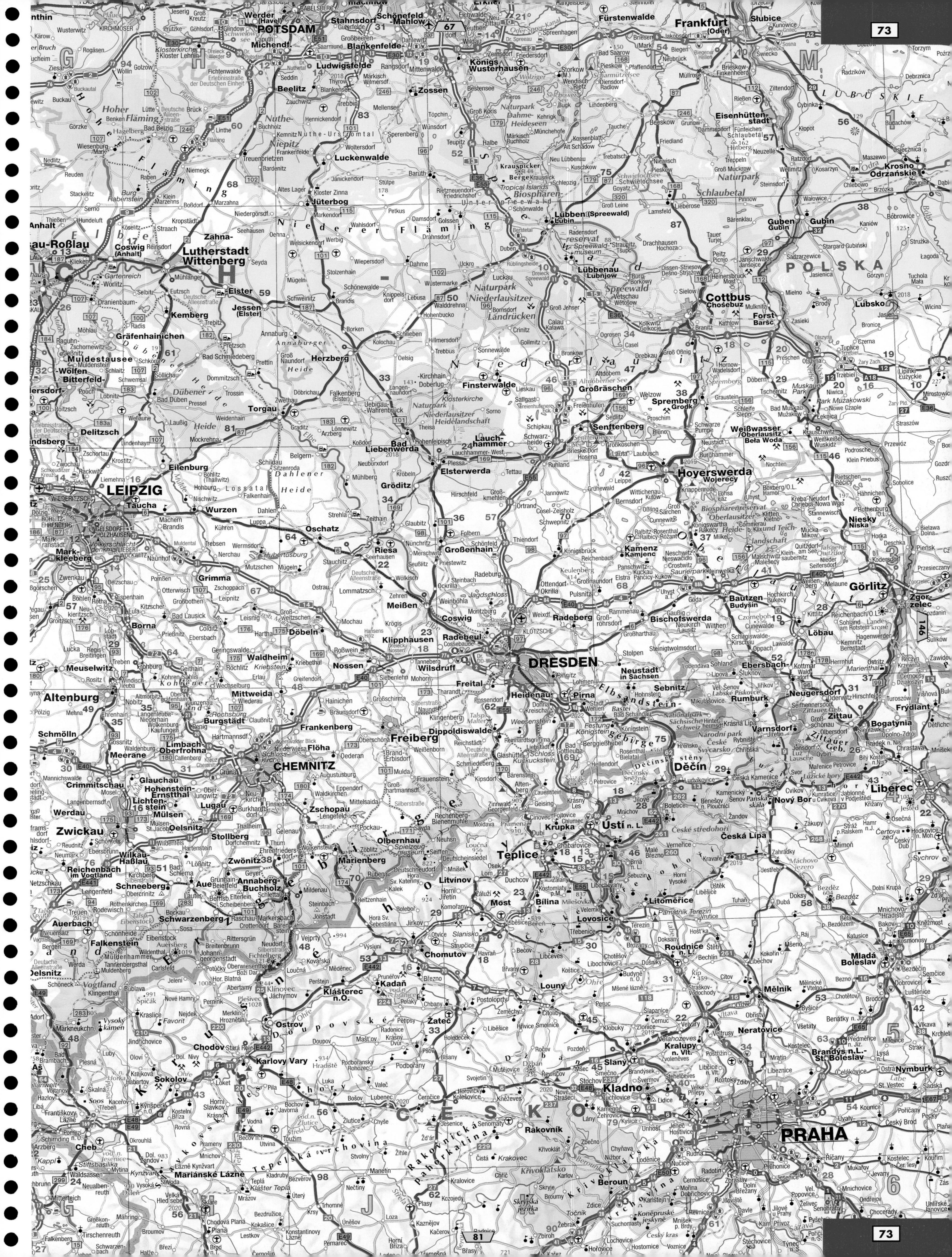

73
POTSDAM
Werder (Havel)
Stahnsdorf
Schönefeld
Michendf.
Blankenfelde
Ludwigsfelde
Königs Wusterhausen
Fürstenwalde
Frankfurt (Oder)
Słubice
Beelitz
Zossen
Eisenhüttenstadt
Luckenwalde
Krosno Odrzańskie
Jüterbog
Lübben (Spreewald)
Lübbenau
Guben
Gubin
POLSKA
LUBUSKIE
Lutherstadt Wittenberg
Coswig (Anhalt)
Kemberg
Jessen (Elster)
Herzberg
Cottbus
Chośebuz
Forst
Lubsko
Gräfenhainichen
Muldestausee
Bitterfeld-Wolfen
Finsterwalde
Großräschen
Spremberg
Torgau
Senftenberg
Weißwasser /Oberlausitz
Delitzsch
Bad Liebenwerda
Lauchhammer
Eilenburg
Elsterwerda
Hoyerswerda
LEIPZIG
Taucha
Wurzen
Gröditz
Oschatz
Riesa
Großenhain
Kamenz
Niesky
Markkleeberg
Grimma
Meißen
Coswig
Radeberg
Bischofswerda
Bautzen
Görlitz
Zgorzelec
Borna
Döbeln
Radebeul
Löbau
Meuselwitz
Waldheim
Nossen
Wilsdruff
DRESDEN
Neustadt in Sachsen
Ebersbach-
Altenburg
Mittweida
Freital
Heidenau
Pirna
Sebnitz
Neugersdorf
Frankenberg
Freiberg
Dippoldiswalde
Zittau
Bogatynia
Schmölln
Burgstädt
Flöha
Varnsdorf
Limbach-Oberfrohna
Meerane
CHEMNITZ
Děčín
Glauchau
Crimmitschau
Hohenstein-Ernstthal
Lichtenstein
Liberec
Nový Bor
Werdau
Lugau
Zschopau
Zwickau
Oelsnitz
Stollberg
Olbernhau
Ústí n. L.
Česká Lípa
Wilkau-Haßlau
Zwönitz
Marienberg
Teplice
Reichenbach im Vogtland
Schneeberg
Aue
Annaberg-Buchholz
Litvínov
Most
Bílina
Litoměřice
Lovosice
Auerbach
Schwarzenberg
Falkenstein
Chomutov
Roudnice n. L.
Mladá Boleslav
Kadaň
Klášterec n.O.
Louny
Mělník
Ostrov
Žatec
Neratovice
Chodov
Karlovy Vary
Kralupy n. Vlt.
Slaný
Sokolov
Kladno
Brandýs n.L.-St. Boleslav
Nymburk
Rakovník
PRAHA
Cheb
Mariánské Lázně
Beroun
Říčany
Č E S K O
Erzgebirge
Niederlausitz
Oberlausitz
Niederer Fläming
Spreewald
Dübener Heide
Dahlener Heide
Elbsandstein-gebirge
Dahme-Heideseen
81

62

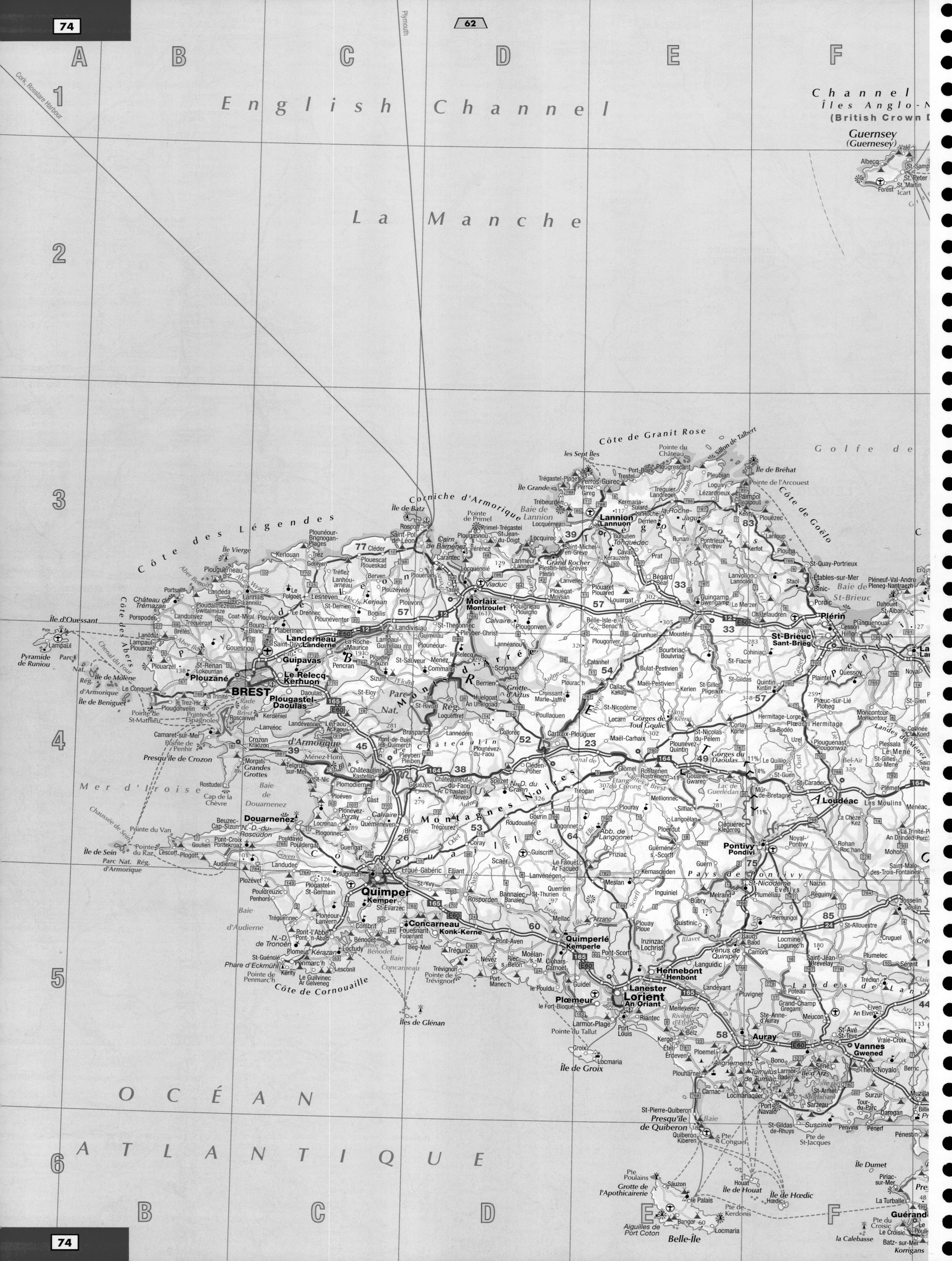
A
B
C
D
E
F
1
2
3
4
5
6
English Channel
La Manche
Channel
Îles Anglo-N
(British Crown D
Guernsey
(Guernesey)
Cork, Rosslare Harbour
Plymouth
Côte de Granit Rose
Golfe de
Côte des Légendes
Corniche d'Armorique
Côte de Goëlo
Côte des Abers
Île d'Ouessant
Pyramide de Runiou
Île de Molène
Île de Beniguet
Île Vierge
Île de Batz
Île Grande
les Sept Îles
Île de Bréhat
Pointe de l'Arcouest
Sillon de Talbert
Roscoff
Saint-Pol-de-Léon
Morlaix
Montroulet
Lannion
Lannuon
Perros-Guirec
Tréguier
Paimpol
Guingamp
Gwengamp
St-Brieuc
Sant-Brieg
Plérin
Baie de St-Brieuc
St-Quay-Portrieux
Landerneau
Landerne
BREST
Plouzané
Guipavas
Le Relecq-Kerhuon
Plougastel-Daoulas
Rade de Brest
Presqu'île de Crozon
Camaret-sur-Mer
Crozon
Morgat
Mer d'Iroise
Chaussée de Sein
Île de Sein
Pointe du Raz
Pointe du Van
Parc Nat. Rég. d'Armorique
Douarnenez
Baie de Douarnenez
Audierne
Baie d'Audierne
Quimper
Kemper
Concarneau
Konk-Kerne
Penmarc'h
Phare d'Eckmühl
Côte de Cornouaille
Îles de Glénan
Châteaulin
Carhaix-Plouguer
Monts d'Arrée
Montagnes Noires
Rostrenen
Loudéac
Pontivy
Pondivi
Pays de Pontivy
Lac de Guerlédan
Quimperlé
Kemperle
Lanester
Lorient
An Oriant
Hennebont
Henbont
Plœmeur
Port-Louis
Île de Groix
Auray
Vannes
Gwened
Golfe du Morbihan
Presqu'île de Quiberon
Quiberon
Belle-Île
Le Palais
Aiguilles de Port Coton
Grotte de l'Apothicairerie
Île de Houat
Île de Hœdic
Île Dumet
La Turballe
Guérande
Le Croisic
Batz-sur-Mer
Landes de Lanvaux
OCÉAN
ATLANTIQUE

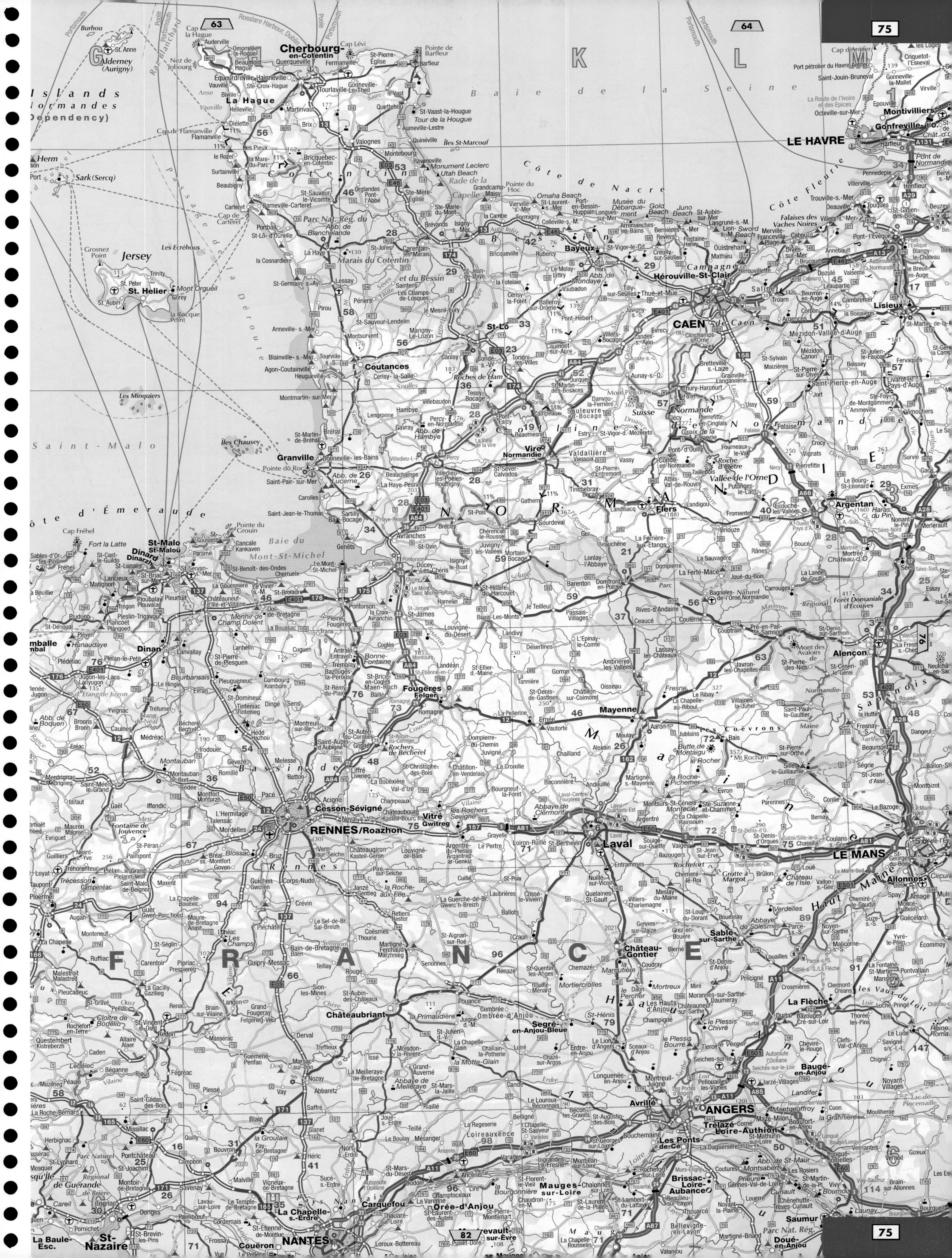
63
64
K
L
M
Cherbourg-en-Cotentin
Cap de la Hague
La Hague
Alderney (Aurigny)
Islands Normandes Dependency)
Baie de la Seine
LE HAVRE
Montivilliers
Gonfreville-l'Orcher
Herm
Sark (Sercq)
Jersey
St. Helier
Mont Orgueil
Les Minquiers
Îles Chausey
Saint-Malo
Côte d'Émeraude
Côte de Nacre
Côte Fleurie
Omaha Beach
Utah Beach
Gold Beach
Juno Beach
Sword Beach
Valognes
Coutances
St-Lô
Bayeux
CAEN
Hérouville-St-Clair
Lisieux
Honfleur
Granville
Avranches
Vire Normandie
Flers
Argentan
Falaise
Alençon
Fougères
St-Malo
Dinard
Dinan
Baie du Mont-St-Michel
Pointe du Grouin
Cap Fréhel
Mayenne
Laval
LE MANS
RENNES/Roazhon
Cesson-Sévigné
Vitré
Château-Gontier
Sablé-sur-Sarthe
La Flèche
Châteaubriant
Segré-en-Anjou-Bleue
ANGERS
Avrillé
Les Ponts-de-Cé
Saumur
Doué-en-Anjou
Carquefou
La Chapelle-s.-Erdre
NANTES
St-Nazaire
La Baule-Esc.
Redon
F R A N C E
N O R M A N D I E
Suisse Normande
Haut Maine
Marais du Cotentin
Parc Nat. Rég. du Marais du Cotentin et du Bessin
Bassin de Rennes
82
76

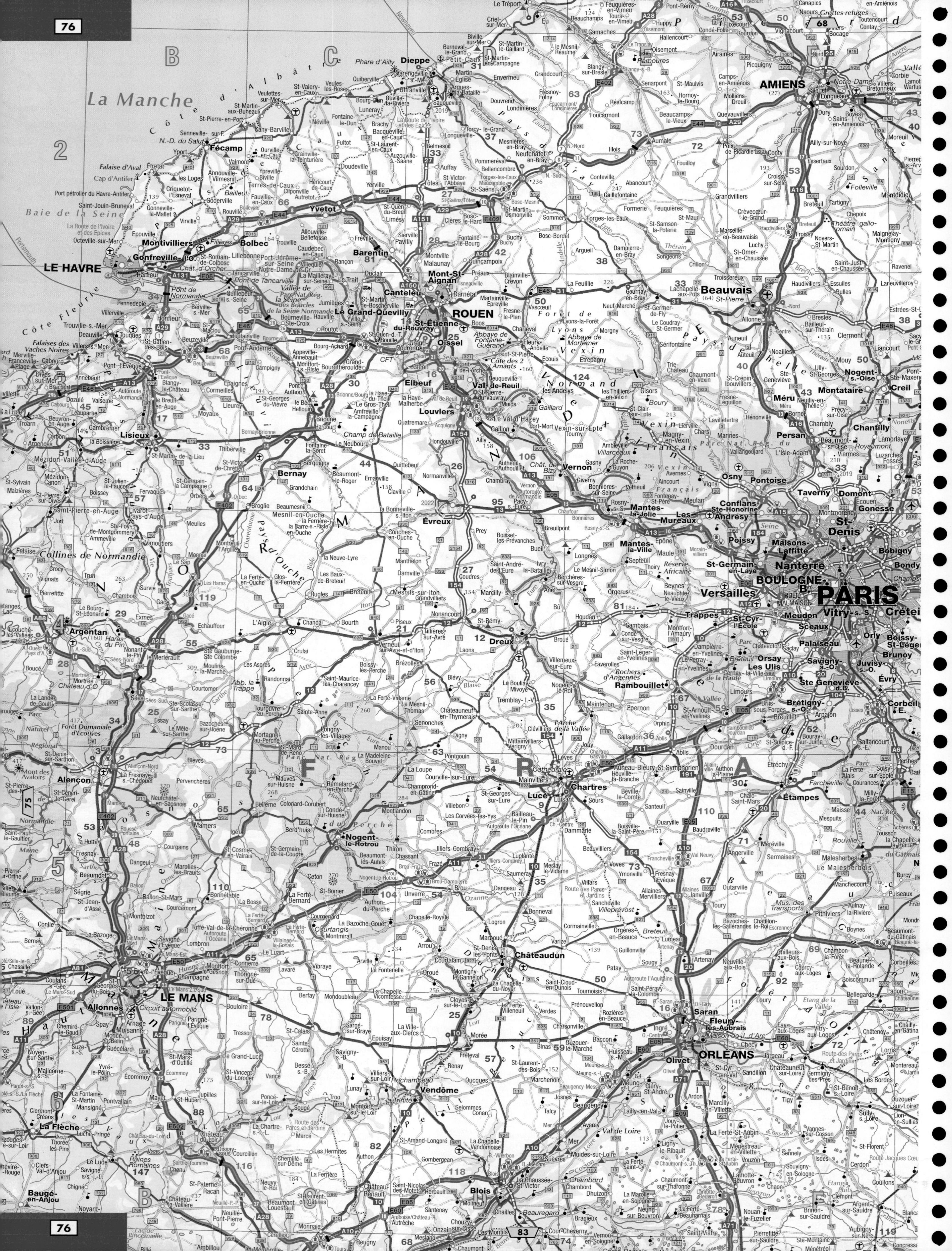
La Manche
Côte d'Albâtre
Baie de la Seine
Côte Fleurie
Collines de Normandie
Pays de Caux
Pays de Bray
Vexin Normand
Vexin Français
Pays d'Ouche
Forêt de Lyons
Dieppe
Fécamp
Yvetot
LE HAVRE
Bolbec
Montivilliers
Barentin
ROUEN
Elbeuf
Louviers
Évreux
Bernay
Lisieux
Vernon
Beauvais
AMIENS
PARIS
Versailles
Nanterre
BOULOGNE-B.
St-Denis
Pontoise
Mantes-la-Jolie
Rambouillet
Dreux
Chartres
Étampes
Argentan
Alençon
Nogent-le-Rotrou
LE MANS
Châteaudun
Vendôme
ORLÉANS
Blois
La Flèche
Montargis
Chantilly
Creil
Méru
Évry
Corbeil-E.

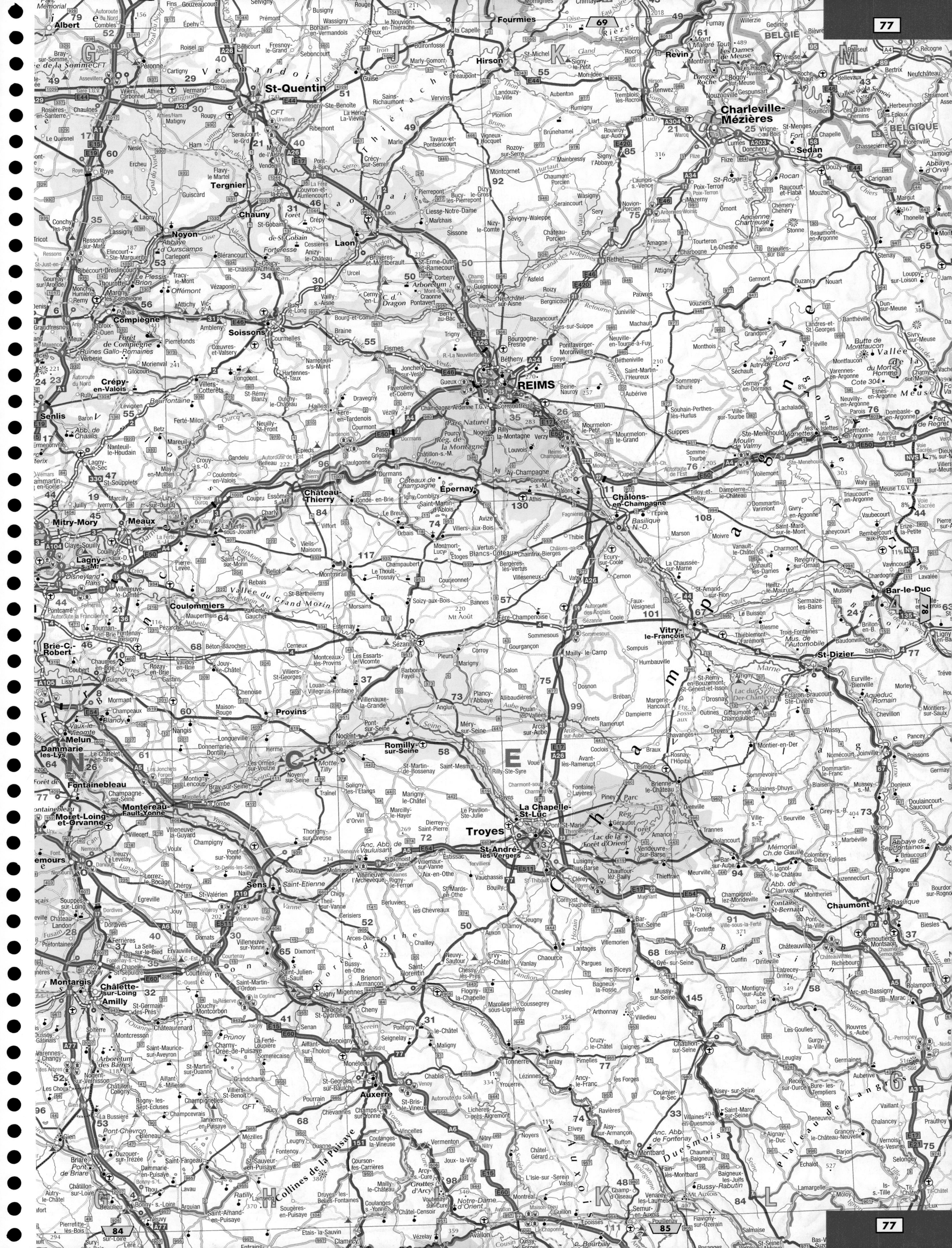

St-Quentin
Fourmies
Hirson
Revin
Charleville-Mézières
Sedan
BELGIË
BELGIQUE
Albert
Péronne
Tergnier
Chauny
Noyon
Laon
Rethel
Compiègne
Soissons
Crépy-en-Valois
Senlis
REIMS
Épernay
Château-Thierry
Meaux
Mitry-Mory
Lagny
Coulommiers
Châlons-en-Champagne
Ste-Menehould
Bar-le-Duc
Vitry-le-François
St-Dizier
Sézanne
Provins
Melun
Fontainebleau
Montereau-Fault-Yonne
Nogent-sur-Seine
Romilly-sur-Seine
Troyes
La Chapelle-St-Luc
St-André-les-Vergers
Sens
Chaumont
Montargis
Auxerre
Tonnerre
Avallon
Vermandois
Thiérache
Champagne
Argonne
Brie
Pays d'Othe
Plateau de Langres
Collines de la Puisaye
Duesmois
Vallée du Grand Morin
Lac du Der-Chantecoq
Lac de la Forêt d'Orient
69
78
84
85

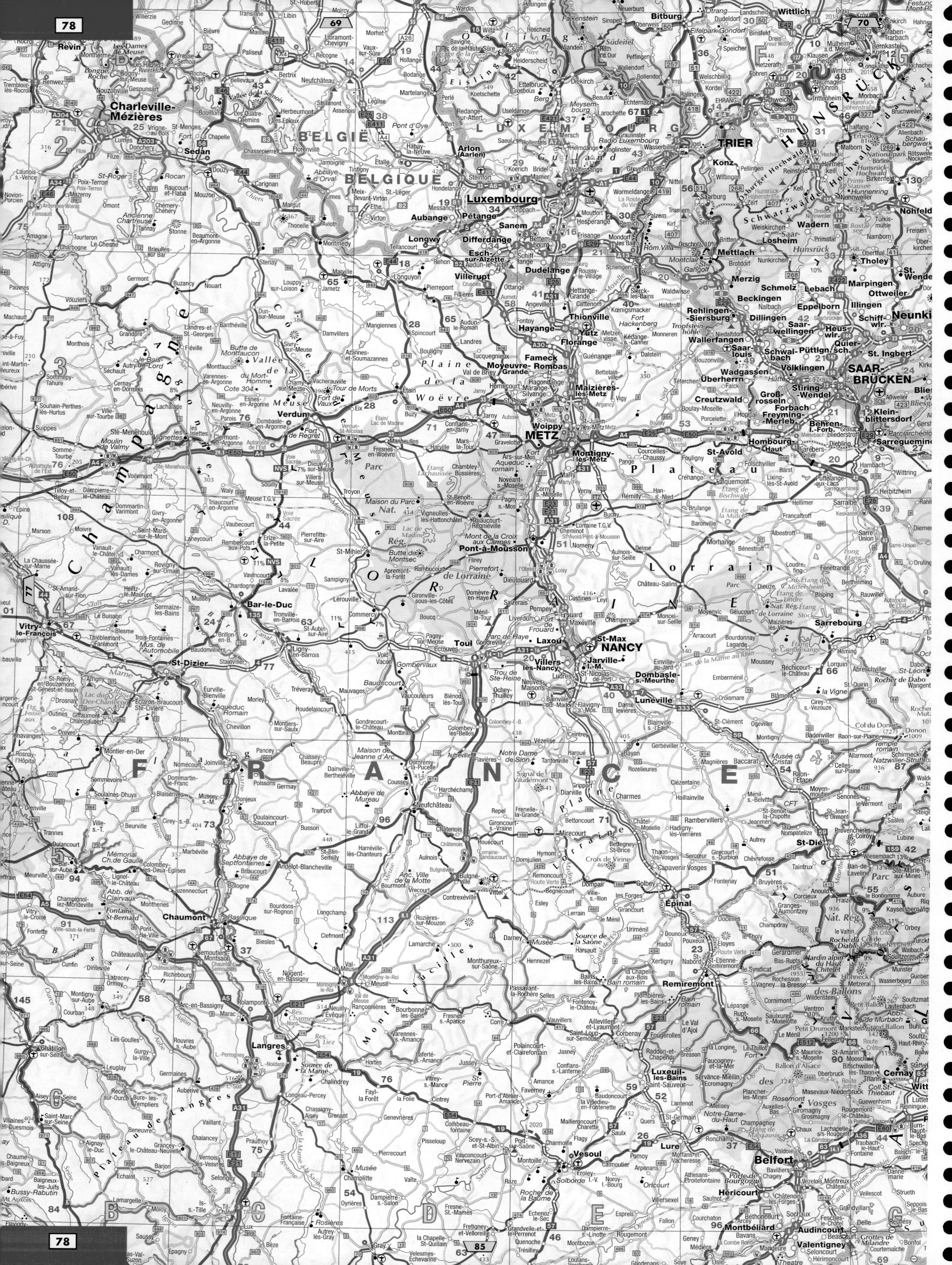
69
70
BELGIË
BELGIQUE
LUXEMBOURG
Luxembourg
HUNSRÜCK
TRIER
Wittlich
Bitburg
Charleville-Mézières
Sedan
Arlon (Aarlen)
Longwy
Esch-sur-Alzette
Dudelange
Thionville
Hayange
Merzig
Saarlouis
SAARBRÜCKEN
Völklingen
Sarreguemines
St-Avold
Forbach
METZ
Verdun
Champagne
Vallée de la Meuse
Plaine de la Woëvre
Plateau Lorrain
LORRAINE
Pont-à-Mousson
Bar-le-Duc
Vitry-le-François
St-Dizier
Toul
NANCY
Lunéville
Sarrebourg
Commercy
FRANCE
Neufchâteau
Chaumont
Épinal
St-Dié
Remiremont
Langres
Vesoul
Lure
Belfort
Montbéliard
Héricourt
Luxeuil-les-Bains
Vittel
Contrexéville
Mirecourt
Châtillon-sur-Seine
Plateau de Langres
Monts Faucilles
Vosges
85

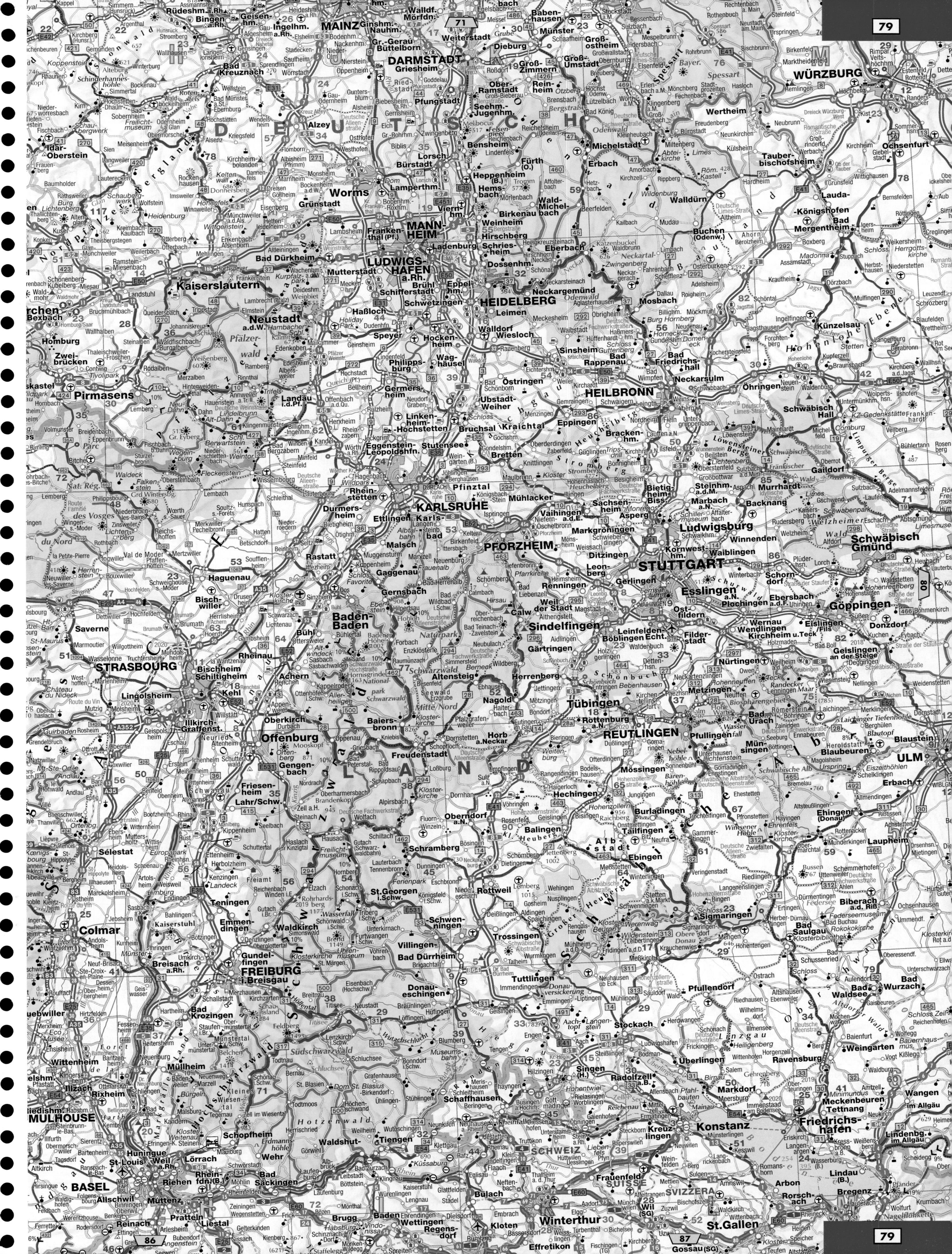
71
MAINZ
DARMSTADT
WÜRZBURG
Worms
MANN-HEIM
LUDWIGS-HAFEN a.Rh.
HEIDELBERG
Kaiserslautern
Neustadt a.d.W.
Pirmasens
Landau i.d.Pf.
HEILBRONN
KARLSRUHE
PFORZHEIM
STUTTGART
Ludwigsburg
Esslingen a.N.
Schwäbisch Gmünd
Göppingen
Baden-Baden
STRASBOURG
Offenburg
Tübingen
REUTLINGEN
ULM
Colmar
FREIBURG i.Breisgau
MULHOUSE
BASEL
Konstanz
Friedrichs-hafen
Winterthur
St.Gallen
DEUTSCHLAND
SCHWEIZ
SUISSE
SVIZZERA
80
86
87

DEUTSCHLAND

WÜRZBURG
ERLANGEN
FÜRTH
NÜRNBERG
REGENSBURG
INGOLSTADT
ULM
AUGSBURG
MÜNCHEN

Kitzingen
Ochsenfurt
Tauberbischofsheim
Bad Mergentheim
Rothenburg ob der Tauber
Ansbach
Schwabach
Crailsheim
Dinkelsbühl
Ellwangen (Jagst)
Aalen
Schwäbisch Gmünd
Schwäbisch Hall
Göppingen
Heidenheim a.d.Brenz
Nördlingen
Donauwörth
Eichstätt
Neuburg a.d.D.
Weißenburg in Bayern
Treuchtlingen
Neumarkt i.d.Opf.
Amberg
Kelheim
Freising
Landshut
Dachau
Fürstenfeldbruck
Landsberg a.L.
Memmingen
Kaufbeuren
Kempten (Allg.)
Füssen
Garmisch-Partenkirchen
Mittenwald
Bad Tölz
Starnberg
Weilheim i.OB.
Schongau
Rosenheim
Lindau (B.)
Bregenz
Dornbirn

ÖSTERREICH

Fränkische Alb
Frankenhöhe
Schwäbische Alb
Ammergebirge
Karwendelgebirge
Wettersteingebirge
Mangfallgebirge
Rofangebirge
Allgäuer Alpen
Bodensee

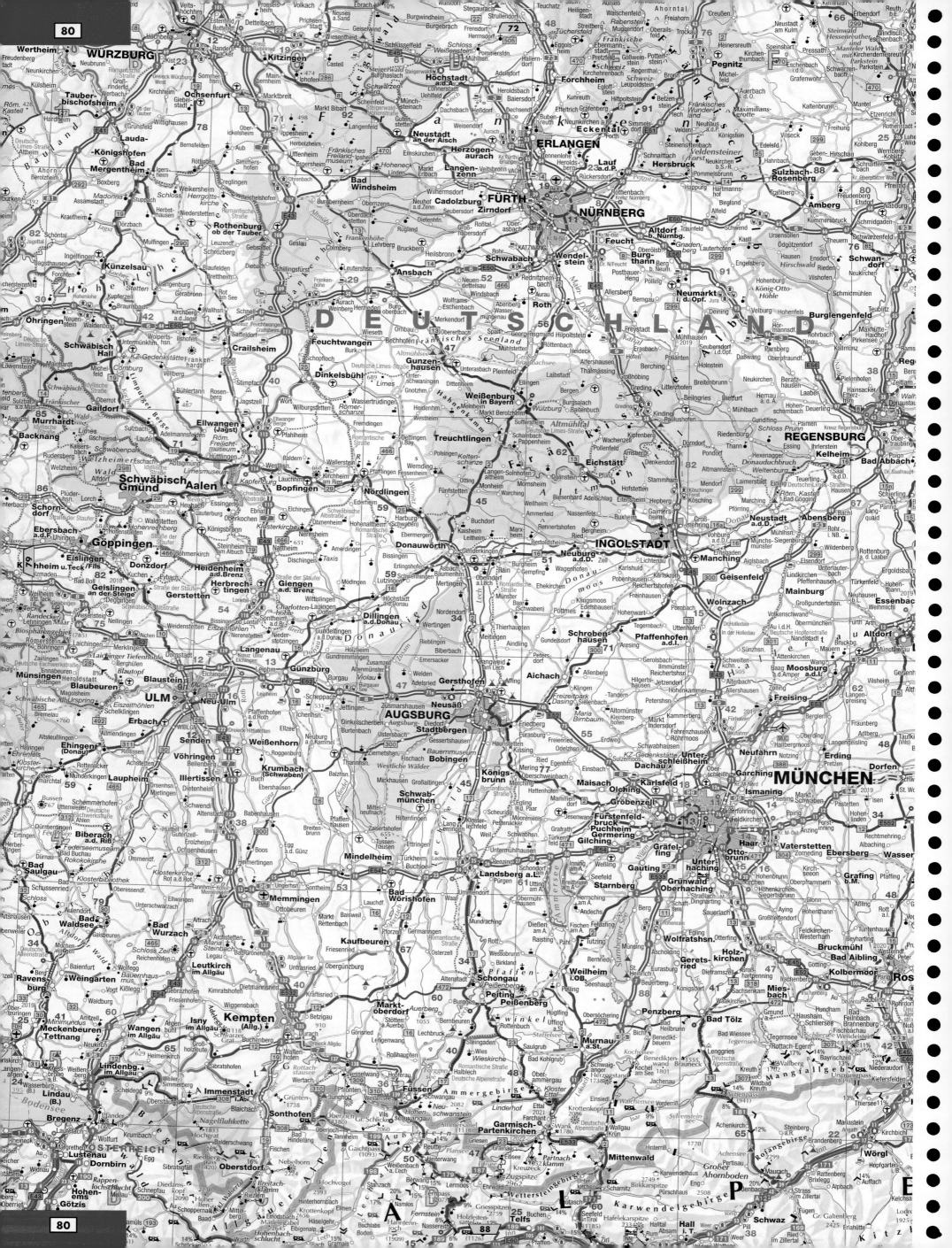

PLZEŇ
Rokycany
Příbram
Tachov
Klatovy
Domažlice
Sušice
Strakonice
Písek
Tábor
Vlašim
ČESKÉ BUDĚJOVICE
Český Krumlov
Prachatice
Vimperk
Třeboň
Weiden i.d.O.
Cham
Roding
Furth i.W.
Regen
Zwiesel
Deggendorf
Straubing
Plattling
Landau a.d.I.
Dingolfing
Landshut
Vilshofen
Passau
Osterhofen
Hauzenberg
Freyung
Schärding
Pocking
Pfarrkirchen
Eggenfelden
Vilsbiburg
Mühldorf am Inn
Waldkraiburg
Altötting
Burghausen
Braunau a.I.
Ried im Innkreis
Freistadt
LINZ
Leonding
Traun
Wels
Steyr
Amstetten
Vöcklabruck
Gmunden
Trostberg
Traunreut
Traunstein
Freilassing
SALZBURG
Bad Reichenhall
Hallein
Bad Ischl
Kufstein
Saalfelden a.S.M.
Bischofshofen
St. Johann i.P.
Ö S T E R R E I C H
Č E S K O
Böhmerwald
Bayerischer Wald
Šumava
Oberpfälzer Wald
Hausruck
Chiemgauer Alpen
Salzburger Kalkalpen
Dachsteingruppe
Totes Gebirge
Sengsengebirge
Rottenmanner Tauern
Schladminger Tauern
Kitzbüheler Alpen
Kaisergebirge
Ennstaler Alpen
Eisenerzer Alpen

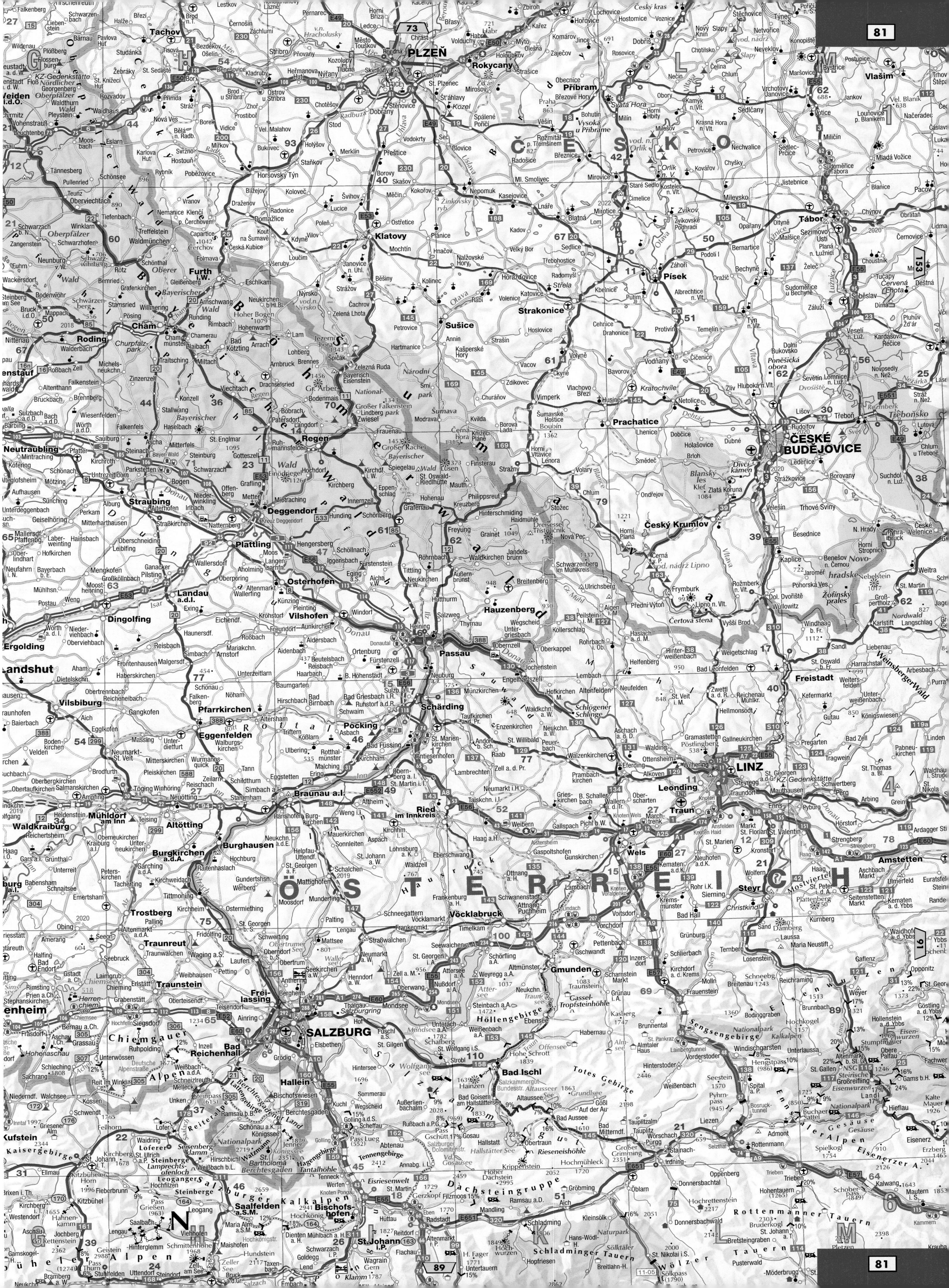

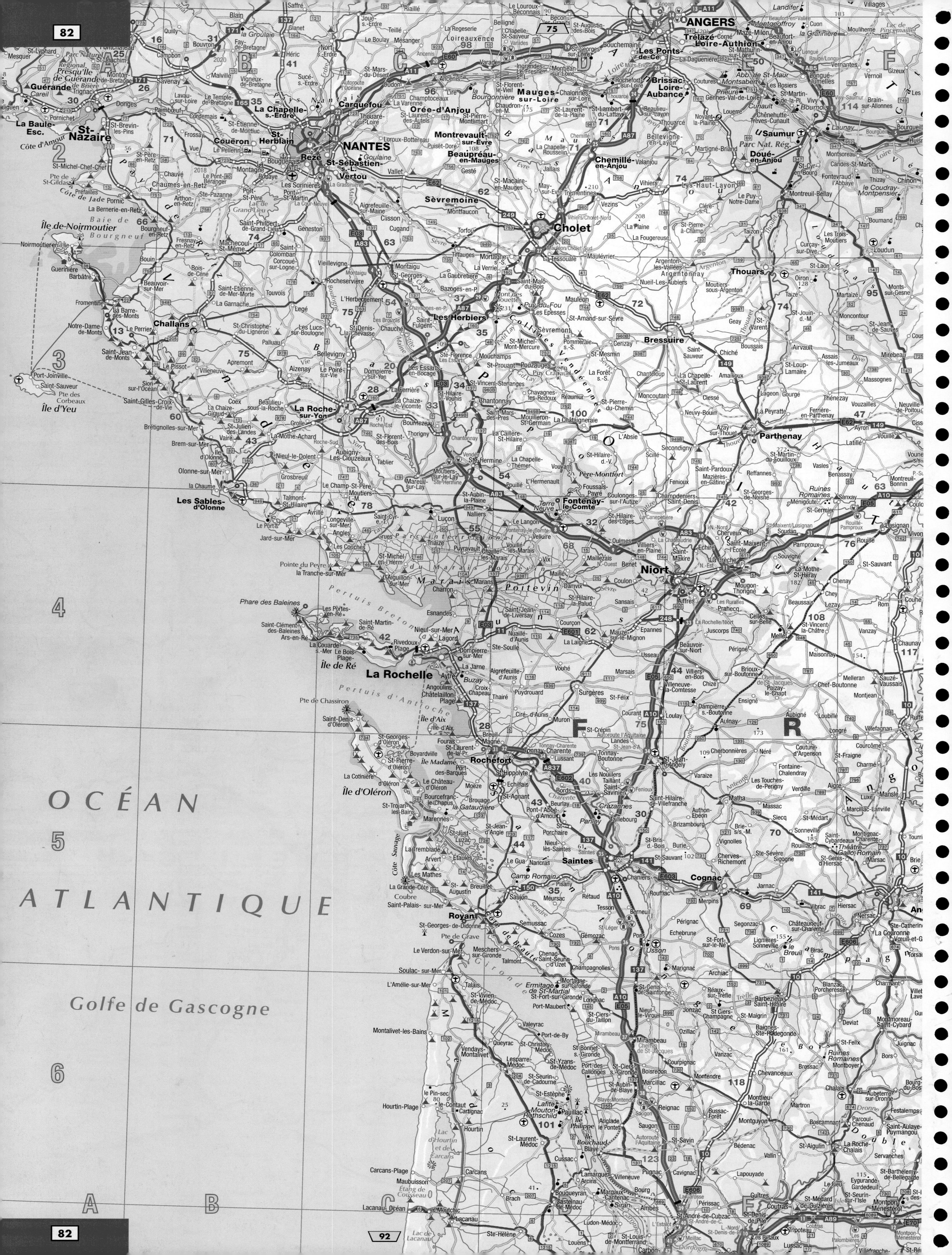
OCÉAN
ATLANTIQUE
Golfe de Gascogne
ANGERS
NANTES
St-Nazaire
La Baule-Esc.
Guérande
Rezé
St-Herblain
Carquefou
Cholet
Saumur
Doué-en-Anjou
Chemillé-en-Anjou
Thouars
Bressuire
Parthenay
Niort
La Roche-sur-Yon
Les Herbiers
Challans
Les Sables-d'Olonne
Fontenay-le-Comte
Luçon
La Rochelle
Rochefort
Saintes
Cognac
Royan
Île-de-Noirmoutier
Île d'Yeu
Île de Ré
Île d'Oléron
Pertuis Breton
Pertuis d'Antioche
Marais Poitevin
Phare des Baleines
Pte de Chassiron
Pte de Grave
Soulac-sur-Mer
Lacanau-Océan
Hourtin-Plage
Carcans-Plage
Montalivet-les-Bains
Pauillac
Blaye
Jonzac
Barbezieux-St-Hilaire
Surgères
St-Jean-d'Angély
Melle
Loudun
Sèvremoine
Montaigu
Clisson
Pornic
A
B
C
D
E
F
2
3
4
5
6
92

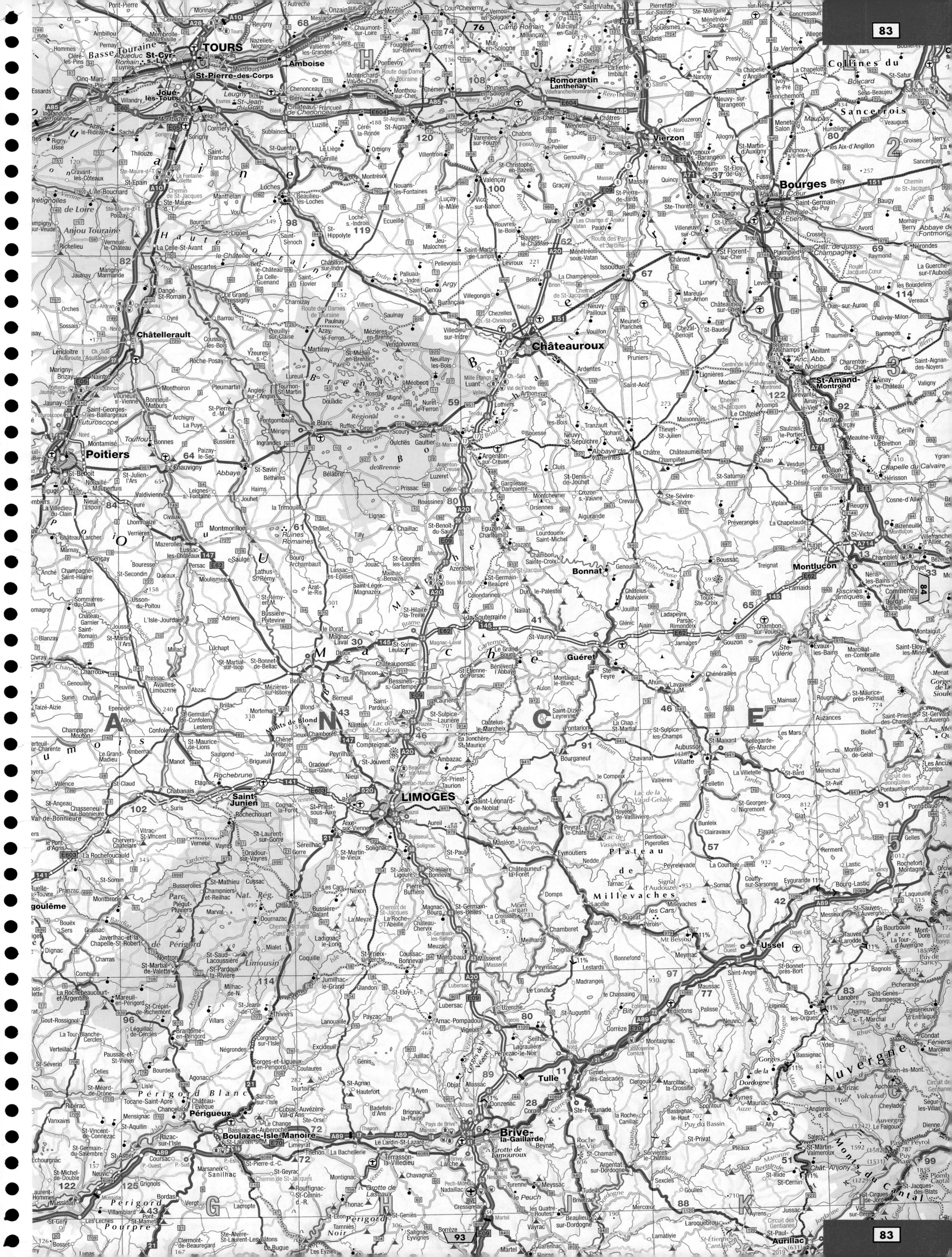
TOURS
St-Cyr-s.-L.
St-Pierre-des-Corps
Joué-lès-Tours
Amboise
Chenonceaux
Romorantin Lanthenay
Vierzon
Bourges
Sancerrois
Collines du Sancerrois
Loches
Châtellerault
Châteauroux
Issoudun
St-Amand-Montrond
Poitiers
Futuroscope
Parc Régional de la Brenne
Le Blanc
Argenton-sur-Creuse
La Châtre
Montluçon
Bellac
Guéret
La Souterraine
Aubusson
Limoges
Saint-Junien
Rochechouart
Confolens
Angoulême
Plateau de Millevaches
Ussel
Tulle
Brive-la-Gaillarde
Périgueux
Boulazac-Isle-Manoire
Périgord Blanc
Périgord Pourpre
Périgord Noir
Aurillac
Monts du Cantal
Auvergne
FRANCE

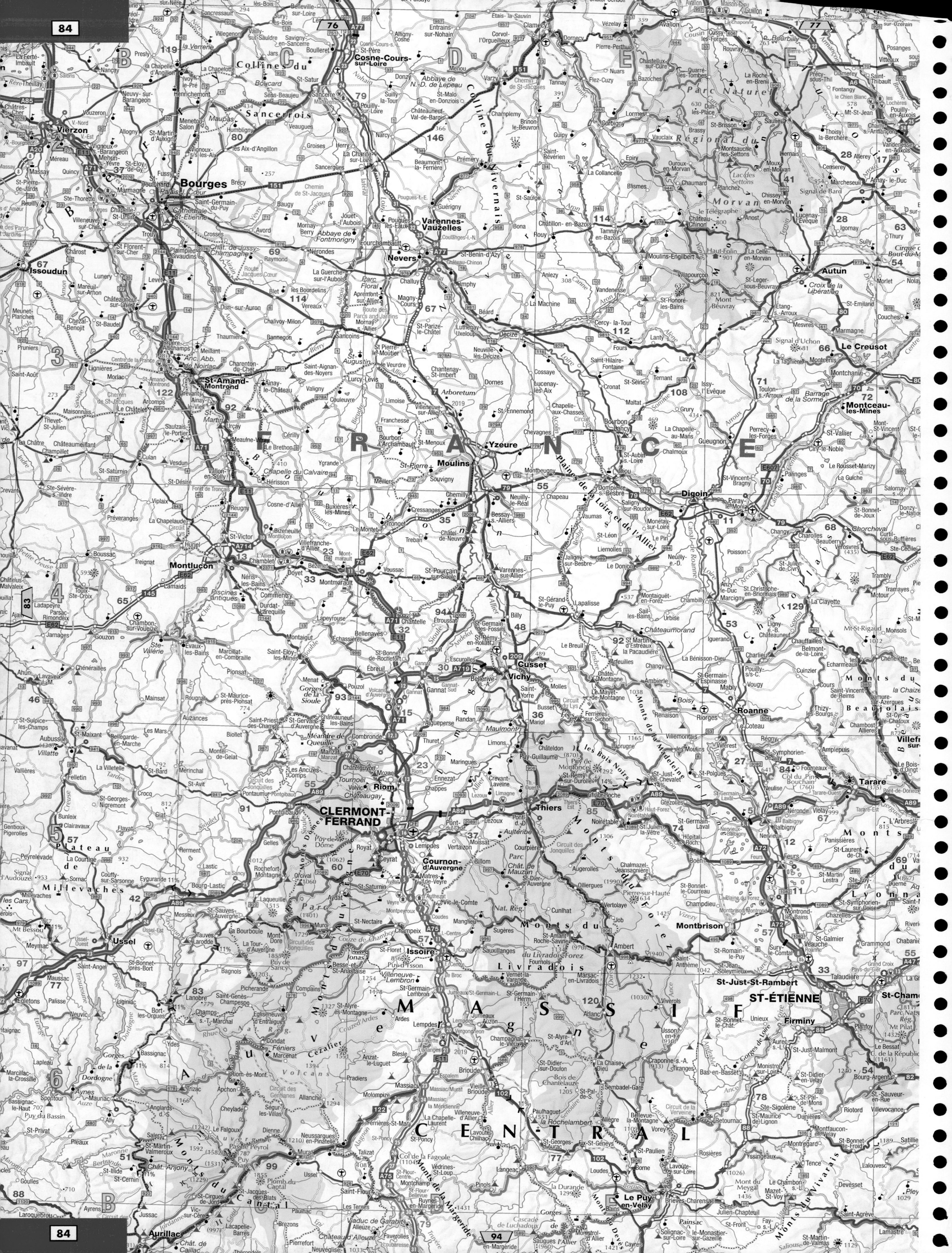
FRANCE
MASSIF CENTRAL
Bourges
Vierzon
Issoudun
Cosne-Cours-sur-Loire
Sancerre
Collines du Sancerrois
Nevers
Varennes-Vauzelles
Collines du Nivernais
Clamecy
Vézelay
Avallon
Parc Naturel Régional du Morvan
Château-Chinon
Autun
Le Creusot
Montceau-les-Mines
Decize
Moulins
Yzeure
St-Amand-Montrond
Montluçon
Digoin
Paray-le-Monial
Roanne
Vichy
Cusset
Gannat
Riom
Thiers
CLERMONT-FERRAND
Puy de Dôme
Cournon-d'Auvergne
Issoire
Ambert
Montbrison
ST-ÉTIENNE
Firminy
St-Just-St-Rambert
Tarare
Feurs
Ussel
Brioude
Le Puy-en-Velay
Aurillac
Saint-Flour
Murat
Monts du Forez
Monts de la Madeleine
Livradois
Plateau de Millevaches
Monts du Cantal
Monts de la Margeride
Monts du Vivarais
Volcans d'Auvergne
Sologne Bourbonnaise
Plaine de la Loire et de l'Allier
A71
A72
A75
A77
A89
E11
E62
E70

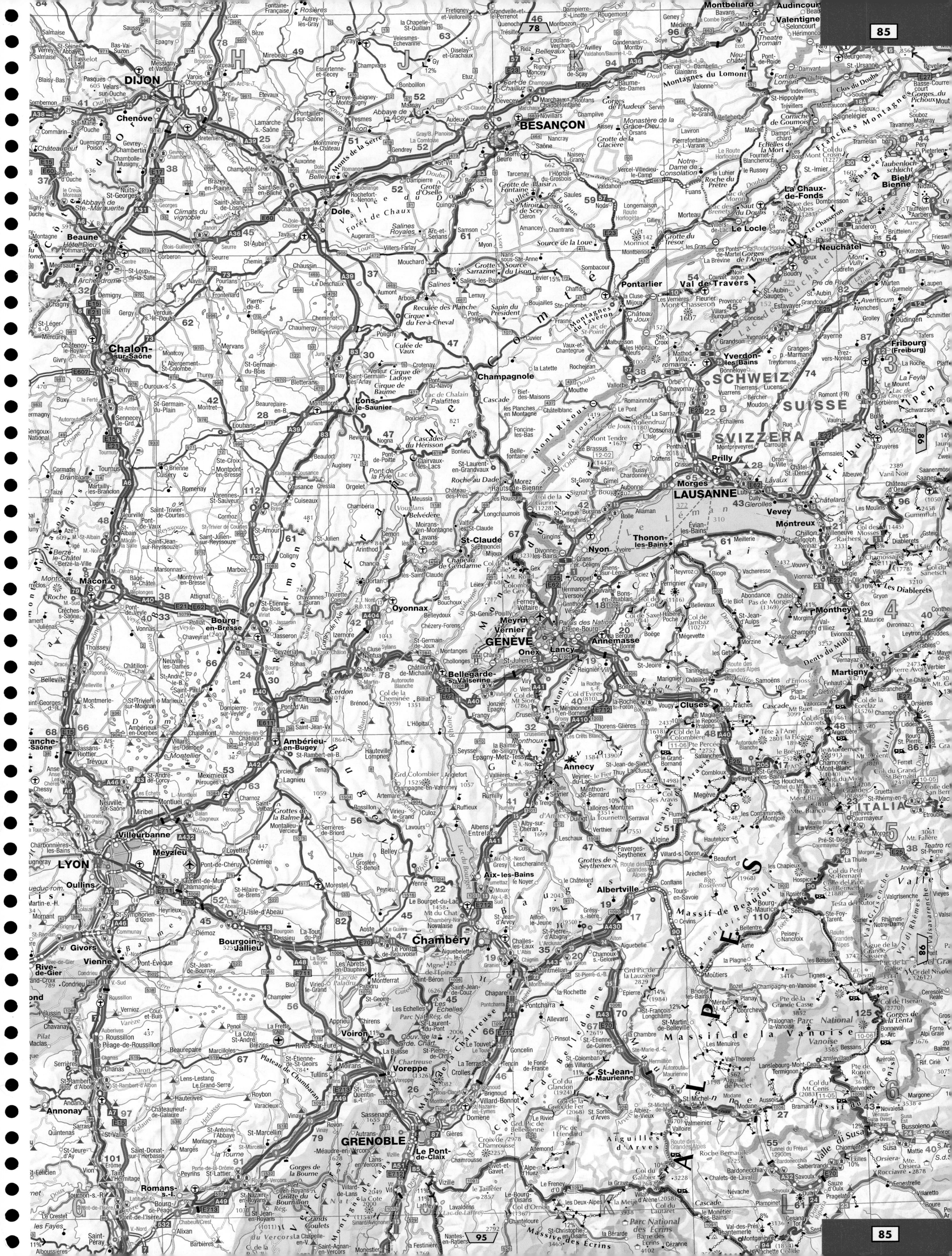
DIJON
Chenôve
Beaune
Chalon-sur-Saône
Mâcon
Villeurbanne
LYON
Meyzieu
Oullins
Givors
Vienne
Annonay
Romans-s.-I.
Bourg-en-Bresse
Ambérieu-en-Bugey
Oyonnax
Lons-le-Saunier
Champagnole
Dole
BESANÇON
Pontarlier
Val de Travers
Neuchâtel
Le Locle
La Chaux-de-Fonds
Biel/Bienne
Fribourg (Freiburg)
Yverdon-les-Bains
SCHWEIZ
SUISSE
SVIZZERA
LAUSANNE
Morges
Vevey
Montreux
Monthey
Martigny
Thonon-les-Bains
Nyon
GENÈVE
Annemasse
Meyrin
Vernier
Onex
Lancy
Bellegarde-s.-Valserine
St-Claude
Cluses
Annecy
Aix-les-Bains
Chambéry
Albertville
Bourgoin-Jallieu
Voiron
Voreppe
GRENOBLE
Le Pont-de-Claix
St-Jean-de-Maurienne
ITALIA
Massif de la Vanoise
Massif de Beaufort
Parc National des Écrins
Montbéliard
Valentigne
Audincourt

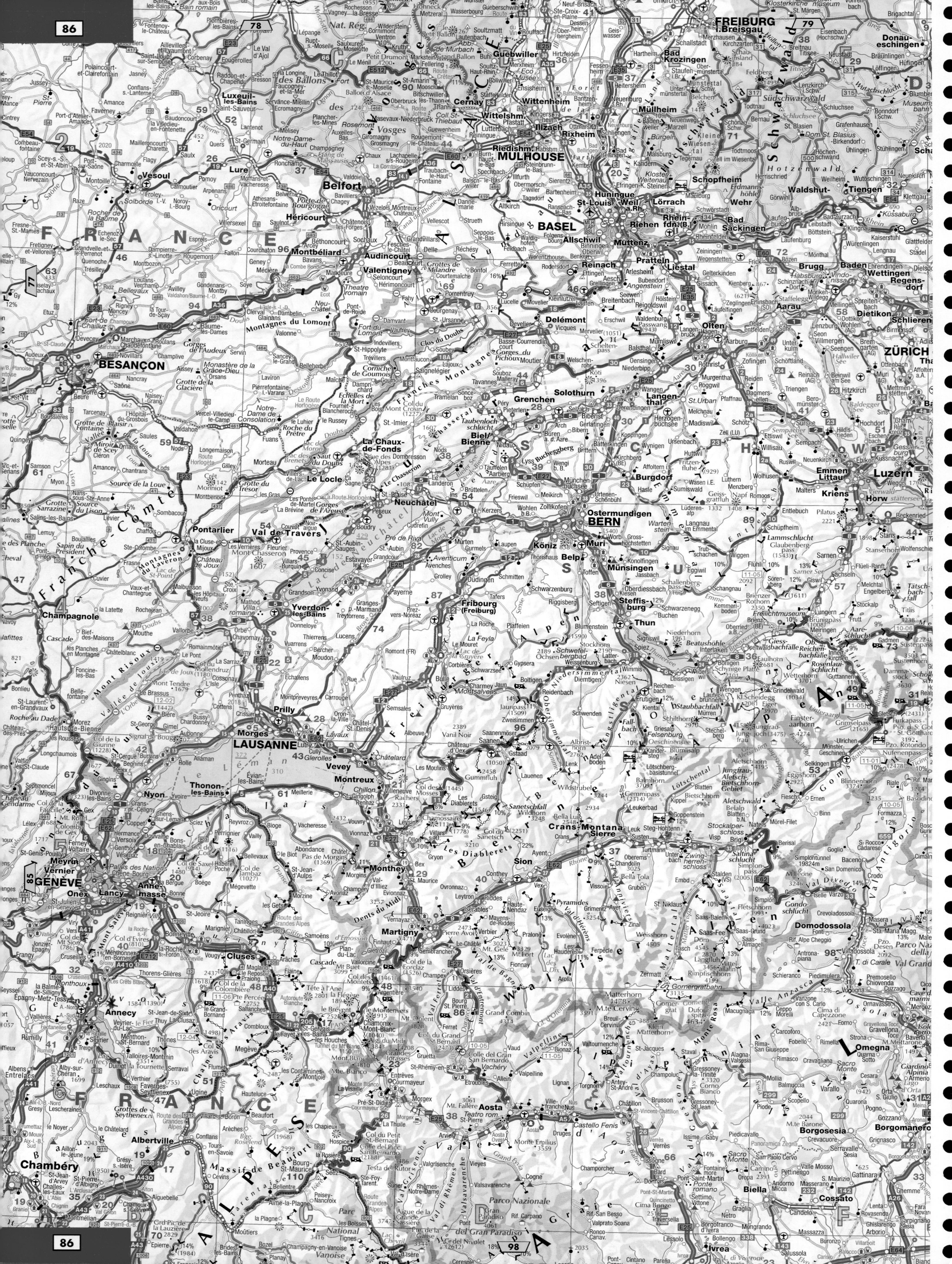
FRANCE
FREIBURG i. Breisgau
MULHOUSE
BASEL
Belfort
Montbéliard
Vesoul
BESANÇON
Franche-Comté
Delémont
Solothurn
Grenchen
Biel/Bienne
La Chaux-de-Fonds
Le Locle
Neuchâtel
Pontarlier
BERN
Thun
Fribourg (Freiburg)
Yverdon-les-Bains
LAUSANNE
Morges
Vevey
Montreux
Thonon-les-Bains
Lac Léman
Nyon
GENÈVE
Annemasse
Annecy
Chambéry
Albertville
Sion
Sierre
Crans-Montana
Martigny
Monthey
Aosta
Courmayeur
Chamonix-Mont-Blanc
Zermatt
Domodossola
Biella
Ivrea
Omegna
Borgomanero
Luzern
ZÜRICH
Aarau
Olten
Baden
Lörrach
Schopfheim
Waldshut-Tiengen
Schwarzwald
Vosges
Alsace
Jura
Alpes
Parco Nazionale del Gran Paradiso

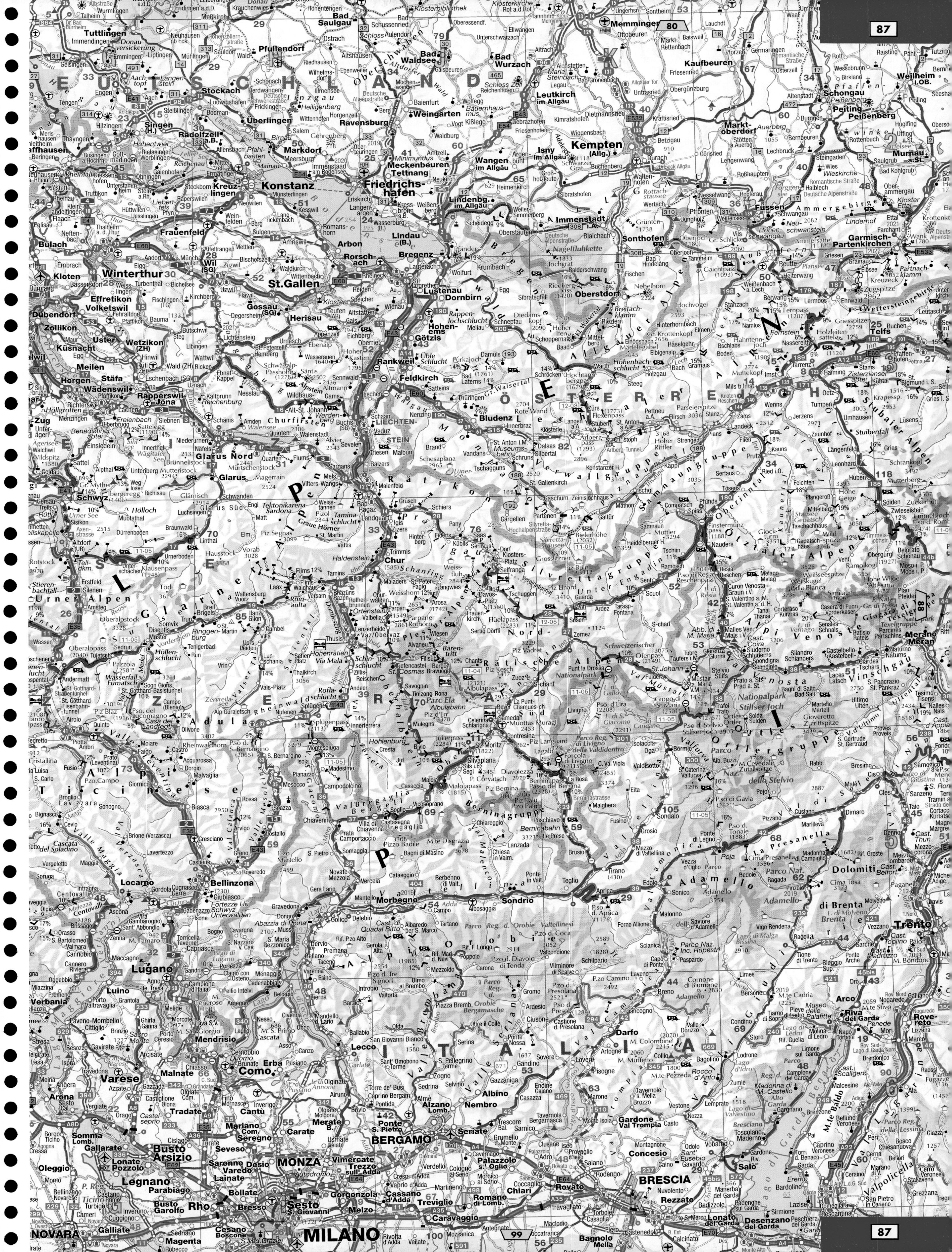
DEUTSCHLAND
ÖSTERREICH
SCHWEIZ
ITALIA
Tuttlingen
Pfullendorf
Bad Saulgau
Bad Waldsee
Bad Wurzach
Memmingen
Kaufbeuren
Schongau
Weilheim i.OB.
Stockach
Singen (H.)
Radolfzell a.B.
Überlingen
Markdorf
Ravensburg
Weingarten
Leutkirch im Allgäu
Kempten (Allg.)
Marktoberdorf
Peiting
Peißenberg
Konstanz
Kreuzlingen
Friedrichshafen
Meckenbeuren
Tettnang
Wangen im Allgäu
Isny im Allgäu
Lindenbg. im Allgäu
Immenstadt i.A.
Sonthofen
Füssen
Murnau a.St.
Garmisch-Partenkirchen
Frauenfeld
Arbon
Rorschach
Lindau (B.)
Bregenz
Oberstdorf
Winterthur
Wil (SG)
St.Gallen
Lustenau
Dornbirn
Kloten
Effretikon
Volketswil
Gossau (SG)
Herisau
Hohenems
Götzis
Dübendorf
Zollikon
Uster
Wetzikon (ZH)
Küsnacht
Meilen
Stäfa
Horgen
Wädenswil
Rapperswil-Jona
Rankweil
Feldkirch
Bludenz
Zugspitze 2962
Telfs
Imst
Landeck
Glarus Nord
Glarus
Schwyz
Altdorf (UR)
Chur
Davos
St. Moritz
Bormio
Meran Merano
Brunnen
Bellinzona
Locarno
Lugano
Mendrisio
Chiavenna
Sondrio
Morbegno
Lecco
Como
Varese
Erba
Tradate
Cantù
Mariano Comense
Seregno
Carate
Merate
Busto Arsizio
Gallarate
Legnano
Saronno
Desio
Monza
Bergamo
Seriate
Vimercate
Brescia
Rho
Sesto S. Giovanni
Milano
Novara
Magenta
Treviglio
Chiari
Rovato
Salò
Lonato del Garda
Desenzano del Garda
Riva del Garda
Rovereto
Trento
Arco
Dolomiti di Brenta
Adamello
Nationalpark Stilfser Joch
Parco Nazionale dello Stelvio
Ortlergruppe
Ötztaler Alpen
Silvrettagruppe
Rätikon
Berninagruppe
Alpi Orobie
Lago di Garda
Bodensee
Allgäuer Alpen
Lechtaler Alpen
Verwallgruppe
Samnaungruppe
Rätische Alpen
Glarner Alpen
Urner Alpen
Alpi Ticinesi
Adula
Vinschgau
Val Venosta
Valtellina
Val Camonica
Engadin
Prättigau
Schanfigg
Oberinntal
Stubaier Alpen
Ammergebirge
Wettersteingebirge
Ammersee
Forggensee
Bernina 4049
Piz Palü
M.te Disgrazia 3678
Schesaplana 2965
Säntis 2502
Tödi 3614
Albulapass
Flüelapass
Julierpass
Malojapass
Splügenpass
Ofenpass
Reschenpass
Arlbergpass
Passo dello Stelvio
Passo del Tonale
Passo d. Aprica
Valpolicella
Monte Baldo

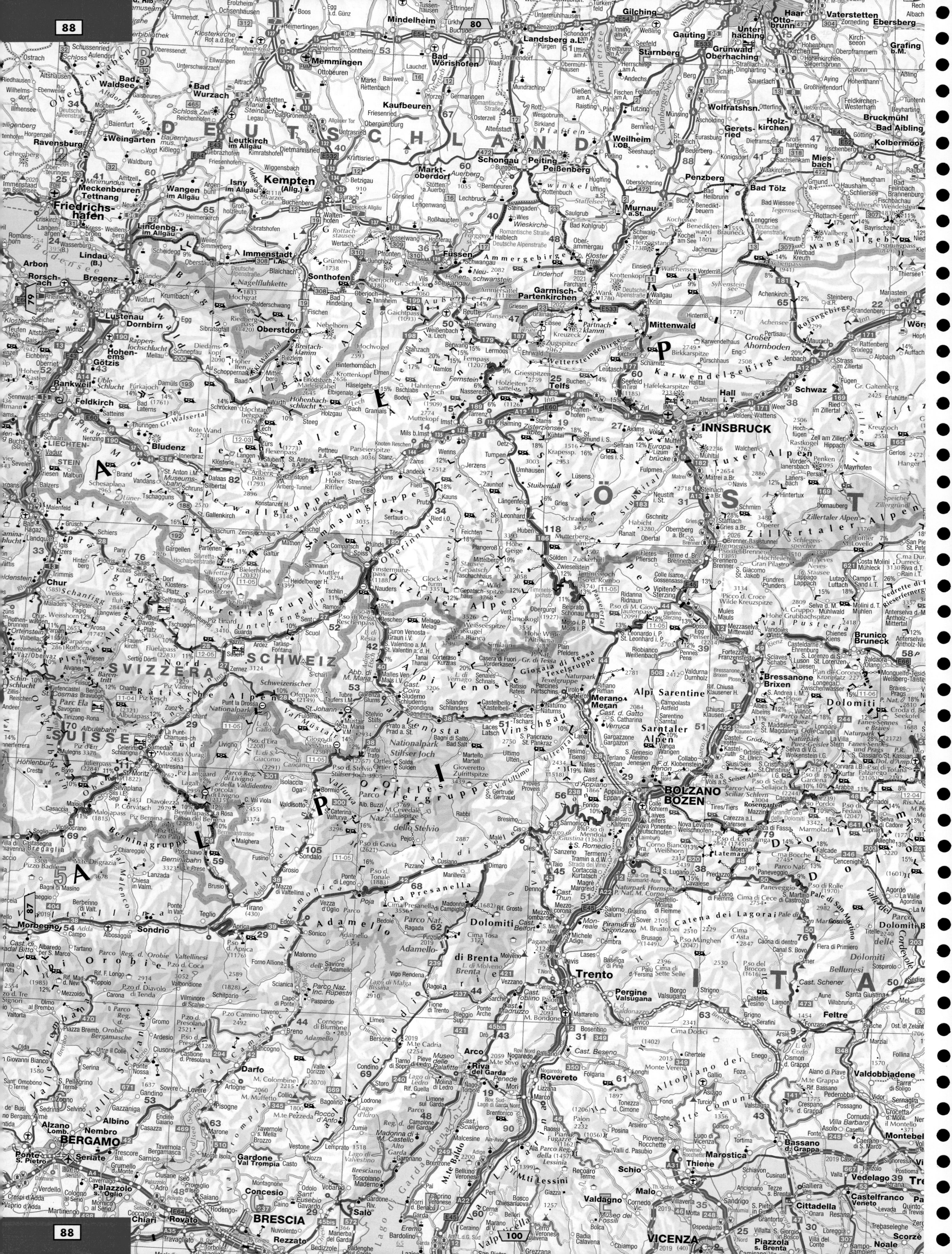
DEUTSCHLAND
ÖSTERREICH
SCHWEIZ
SVIZZERA
SUISSE
ITALIA
LIECHTENSTEIN
Memmingen
Mindelheim
Bad Wörishofen
Landsberg a.L.
Kaufbeuren
Kempten (Allg.)
Ravensburg
Friedrichshafen
Lindau (B.)
Bregenz
Dornbirn
Feldkirch
Bludenz
Chur
Schongau
Peiting
Peißenberg
Weilheim i.OB.
Starnberg
Penzberg
Bad Tölz
Garmisch-Partenkirchen
Mittenwald
Füssen
Oberstdorf
Sonthofen
Immenstadt i.A.
INNSBRUCK
Hall i.T.
Schwaz
Telfs
Landeck
Imst
Bolzano Bozen
Merano Meran
Bressanone Brixen
Brunico Bruneck
Trento
Rovereto
Riva del Garda
Bergamo
Brescia
Vicenza
Bassano d. Grappa
Feltre
Sondrio
Chiari
Valdobbiadene
Montebello
Allgäuer Alpen
Lechtaler Alpen
Ötztaler Alpen
Stubaier Alpen
Zillertaler Alpen
Karwendelgebirge
Dolomiti
Alpi Orobie
Adamello
Ortles
Schweiz
Lago di Garda
Bodensee

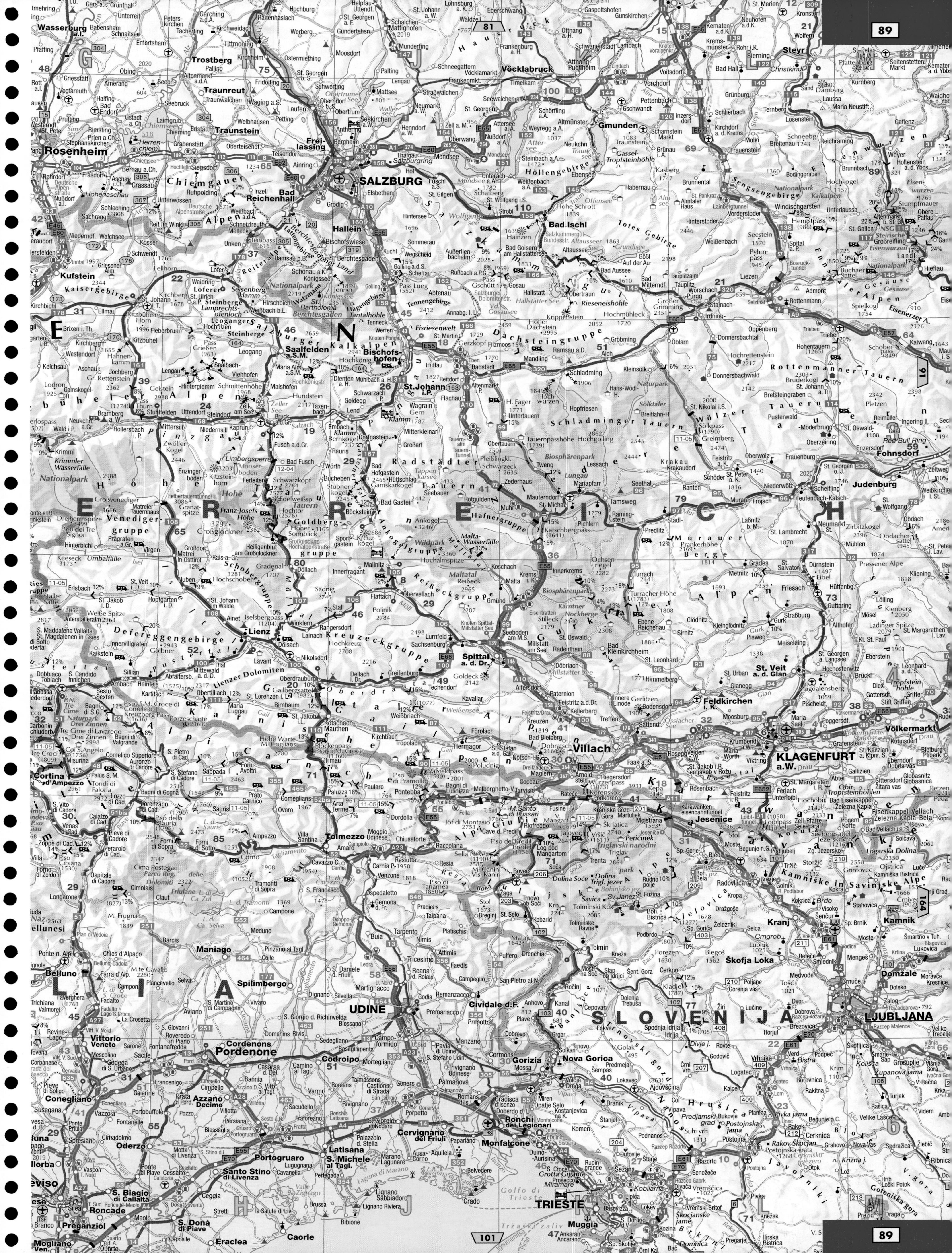

Wasserburg a.I.
Rosenheim
Trostberg
Traunreut
Traunstein
Chiemgauer Alpen
Freilassing
SALZBURG
Bad Reichenhall
Hallein
Vöcklabruck
Gmunden
Bad Ischl
Steyr
Kufstein
Kaisergebirge
Kitzbühel
Saalfelden a.St.M.
Bischofshofen
St.Johann i.P.
Zell a.See
Lienz
Spittal a.d.Dr.
Villach
KLAGENFURT a.W.
Völkermarkt
Feldkirchen i.K.
St. Veit a.d. Glan
Judenburg
Fohnsdorf
Tamsweg
Schladming
Dachsteingruppe
Hohe Tauern
Großglockner
Venedigergruppe
Nationalpark
Cortina d'Ampezzo
Tolmezzo
UDINE
Pordenone
Cordenons
Conegliano
Belluno
Spilimbergo
Maniago
Codroipo
Cervignano del Friuli
Monfalcone
TRIESTE
Muggia
Gorizia
Nova Gorica
Jesenice
Kranj
Kamnik
Škofja Loka
LJUBLJANA
Domžale
Bovec
Tolmin
Idrija
Postojna
Sežana
Latisana
Portogruaro
Caorle
Eraclea
S. Donà di Piave
Oderzo
Treviso
Mogliano Ven.
Preganziol
Roncade
Lignano Sabbiadoro
Grado
Golfo di Trieste
SLOVENIJA
Triglavski narodni park
Julijske Alpe
Karawanken
Savinjske Alpe
Kamniške Alpe
Gailtaler Alpen
Karnische Alpen
Lienzer Dolomiten
Kreuzeckgruppe
Reißeckgruppe
Ankogelgruppe
Goldberggruppe
Schobergruppe
Radstädter Tauern
Schladminger Tauern
Wölzer Tauern
Rottenmanner Tauern
Totes Gebirge
Höllengebirge
Sengsengebirge
Ennstaler Alpen
Gesäuse
Nockberge
Gurktaler Alpen
Kitzbüheler Alpen
Berchtesgadener Alpen
Tennengebirge
Hochkönig
Dolomiti

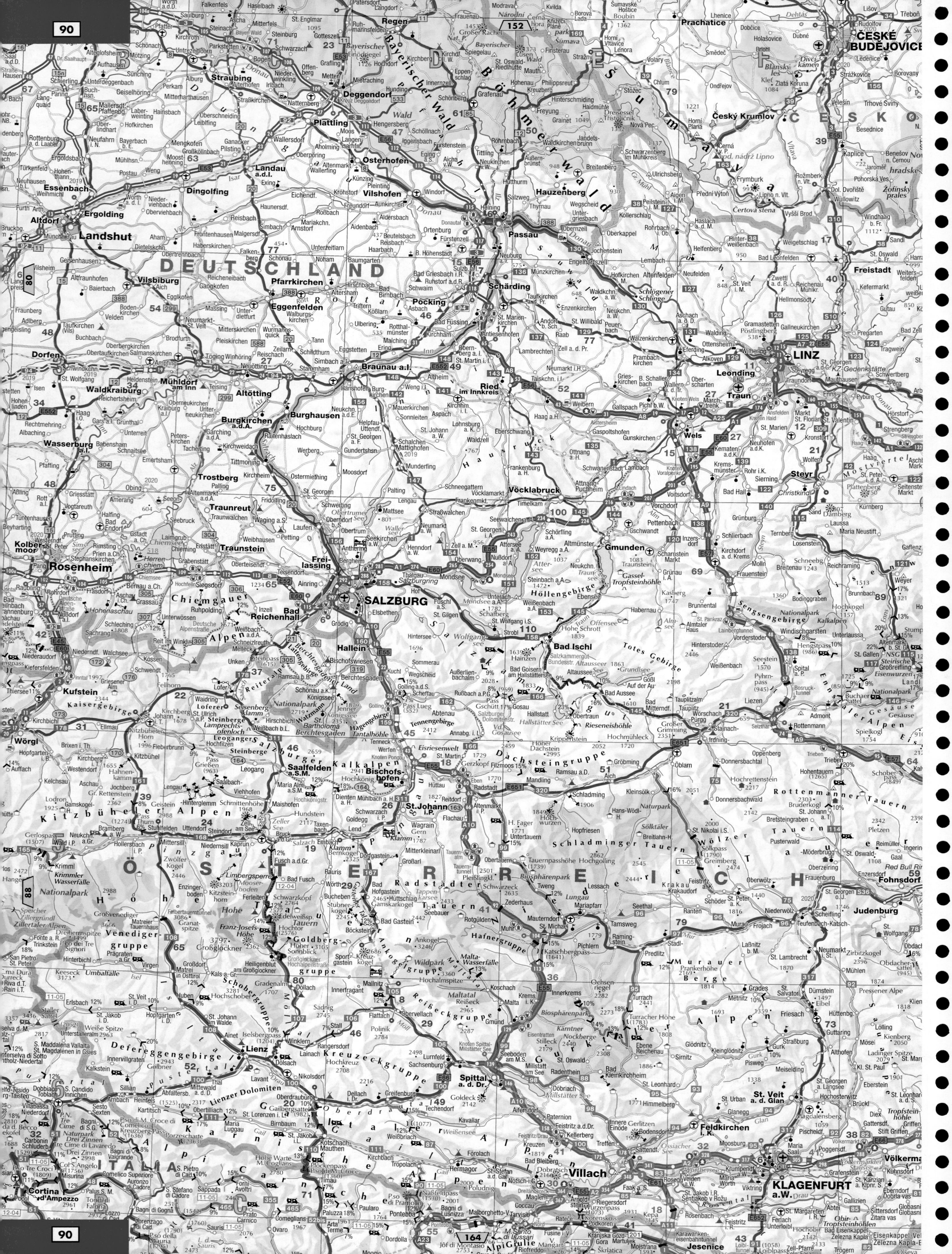
DEUTSCHLAND
ÖSTERREICH
ČESKO
ITALIA
ČESKÉ BUDĚJOVICE
Regen
Deggendorf
Straubing
Plattling
Landau a.d.I.
Dingolfing
Landshut
Ergolding
Altdorf
Essenbach
Vilsbiburg
Osterhofen
Vilshofen
Passau
Hauzenberg
Pfarrkirchen
Eggenfelden
Pocking
Schärding
Braunau a.I.
Mühldorf am Inn
Altötting
Waldkraiburg
Burghausen
Burgkirchen a.d.A.
Wasserburg a.I.
Trostberg
Traunreut
Traunstein
Rosenheim
Kolbermoor
Freilassing
SALZBURG
Bad Reichenhall
Hallein
Ried im Innkreis
Vöcklabruck
Gmunden
Bad Ischl
Wels
Traun
Leonding
LINZ
Steyr
Freistadt
Český Krumlov
Prachatice
Kufstein
Wörgl
Saalfelden a.S.M.
Bischofshofen
St. Johann i.P.
Radstadt
Schladming
Lienz
Spittal a.d. Dr.
Villach
KLAGENFURT a.W.
Feldkirchen i.K.
St. Veit a.d. Glan
Judenburg
Fohnsdorf
Cortina d'Ampezzo
Jesenice
Bayerischer Wald
Böhmerwald
Šumava
Chiemgauer Alpen
Kitzbüheler Alpen
Hohe Tauern
Radstädter Tauern
Dachsteingruppe
Totes Gebirge
Niedere Tauern
Schladminger Tauern
Wölzer Tauern
Rottenmanner Tauern
Gurktaler Alpen
Karnische Alpen
Lienzer Dolomiten
Venediger-gruppe
Glocknergruppe
Goldberg-gruppe
Ankogelgruppe
Reißeckgruppe
Kreuzeckgruppe
Schobergruppe
Defereggengebirge
Kaisergebirge
Tennengebirge
Hagengebirge
Salzburger Kalkalpen
Höllengebirge
Kalkalpen
Steinberge
Chiemsee
Attersee
Mondsee
Wolfgangsee
Traunsee
Wörthersee
Millstätter See
Ossiacher See
Donau
Inn
Salzach
Drau
Moldau
Vod. nádrž Lipno

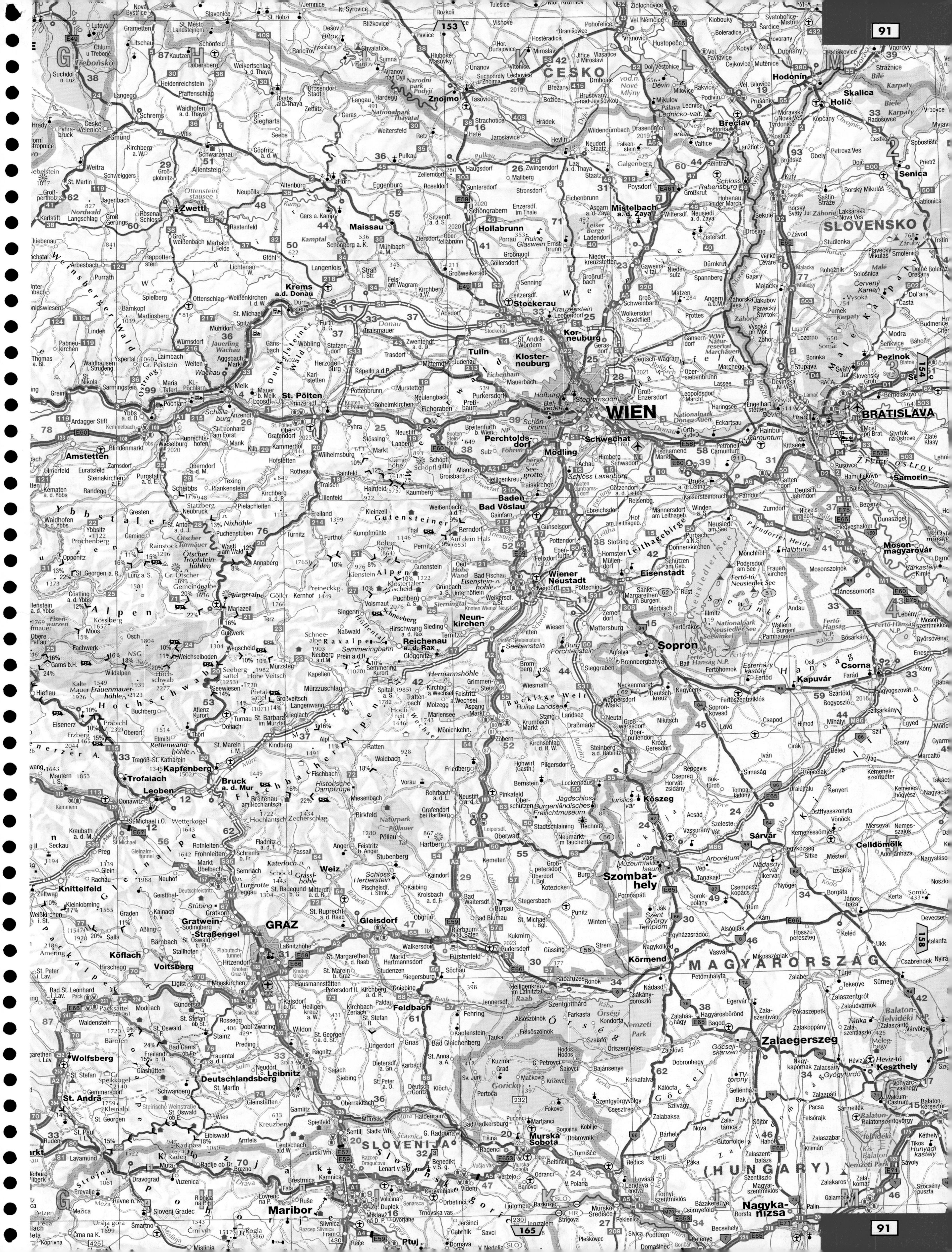
ČESKO
SLOVENSKO
MAGYARORSZÁG
(HUNGARY)
SLOVENIJA
WIEN
BRATISLAVA
GRAZ
St. Pölten
Krems a.d. Donau
Stockerau
Korneuburg
Klosterneuburg
Tulln
Zwettl
Maissau
Hollabrunn
Mistelbach a.d. Zaya
Znojmo
Hodonín
Břeclav
Skalica
Holíč
Senica
Malacky
Pezinok
Šamorín
Schwechat
Mödling
Perchtoldsdorf
Baden
Bad Vöslau
Wiener Neustadt
Neunkirchen
Eisenstadt
Sopron
Mosonmagyaróvár
Csorna
Kapuvár
Amstetten
Ybbs a.d. Donau
Melk
Mariazell
Bruck a.d. Mur
Kapfenberg
Leoben
Trofaiach
Knittelfeld
Weiz
Gleisdorf
Köflach
Voitsberg
Gratwein-Straßengel
Leibnitz
Deutschlandsberg
Wolfsberg
St. Andrä
Feldbach
Fürstenfeld
Kőszeg
Szombathely
Sárvár
Celldömölk
Körmend
Zalaegerszeg
Keszthely
Nagykanizsa
Murska Sobota
Maribor
Ptuj
Reichenau a.d. Rax
Neusiedler See
Wienerwald
Hochschwab
Kremser A.
Bucklige Welt
Weinviertel
Ottenstein-stausee
Gutensteiner Alpen
Raxalpe
Semmeringbahn
Schneeberg
Ybbstaler Alpen
Malé Karpaty
Záhorie
Orseg
Göcsej
Nationalpark Thayatal
Nationalpark Donau-Auen
E49
E59
E60
E65
E66
E57
E58
E461
E575
153
154
158
165

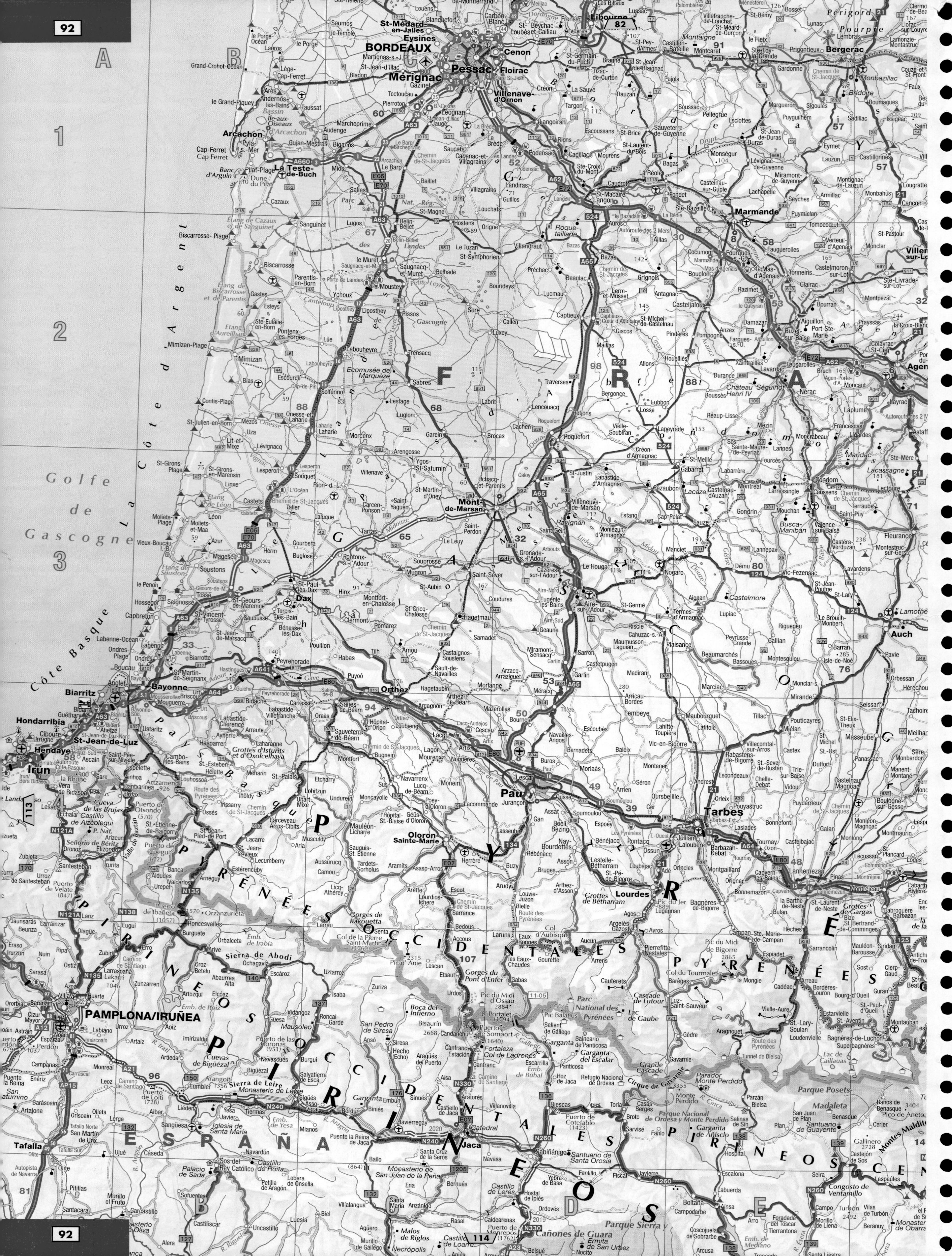

A
B
C
D
E
1
2
3
BORDEAUX
Mérignac
Pessac
Cenon
Floirac
Villenave-d'Ornon
Libourne
Bergerac
Arcachon
La Teste-de-Buch
Marmande
Agen
Golfe de Gascogne
La Côte d'Argent
Côte Basque
Mont-de-Marsan
Dax
Biarritz
Bayonne
Anglet
St-Jean-de-Luz
Hendaye
Irun
Hondarribia
Orthez
Pau
Tarbes
Lourdes
Oloron-Sainte-Marie
Auch
Lannemezan
PAMPLONA/IRUÑEA
Tafalla
Jaca
FRANCE
ESPAÑA
PYRÉNÉES
PYRÉNÉES OCCIDENTALES
PIRINEOS OCCIDENTALES
PIRINEOS
Pays Basque
Landes de Gascogne
Parc National des Pyrénées
Parque Nacional de Ordesa y Monte Perdido

Aurillac
Figeac
Cahors
Villefranche-de-Rouergue
Rodez
Millau
Moissac
Castelsarrasin
Montauban
Gaillac
Albi
Carmaux
Graulhet
TOULOUSE
Castres
Mazamet
Castelnaudary
Carcassonne
Béziers
Narbonne
Pamiers
St-Gaudens
Foix
Quillan
Rivesaltes
PERPIGNAN
ANDORRA
Causse de Gramat
Causse Comtal
Causse de Sévérac
Monts de Lacaune
Montagne Noire
Les Corbières
PYRÉNÉES ORIENTALES

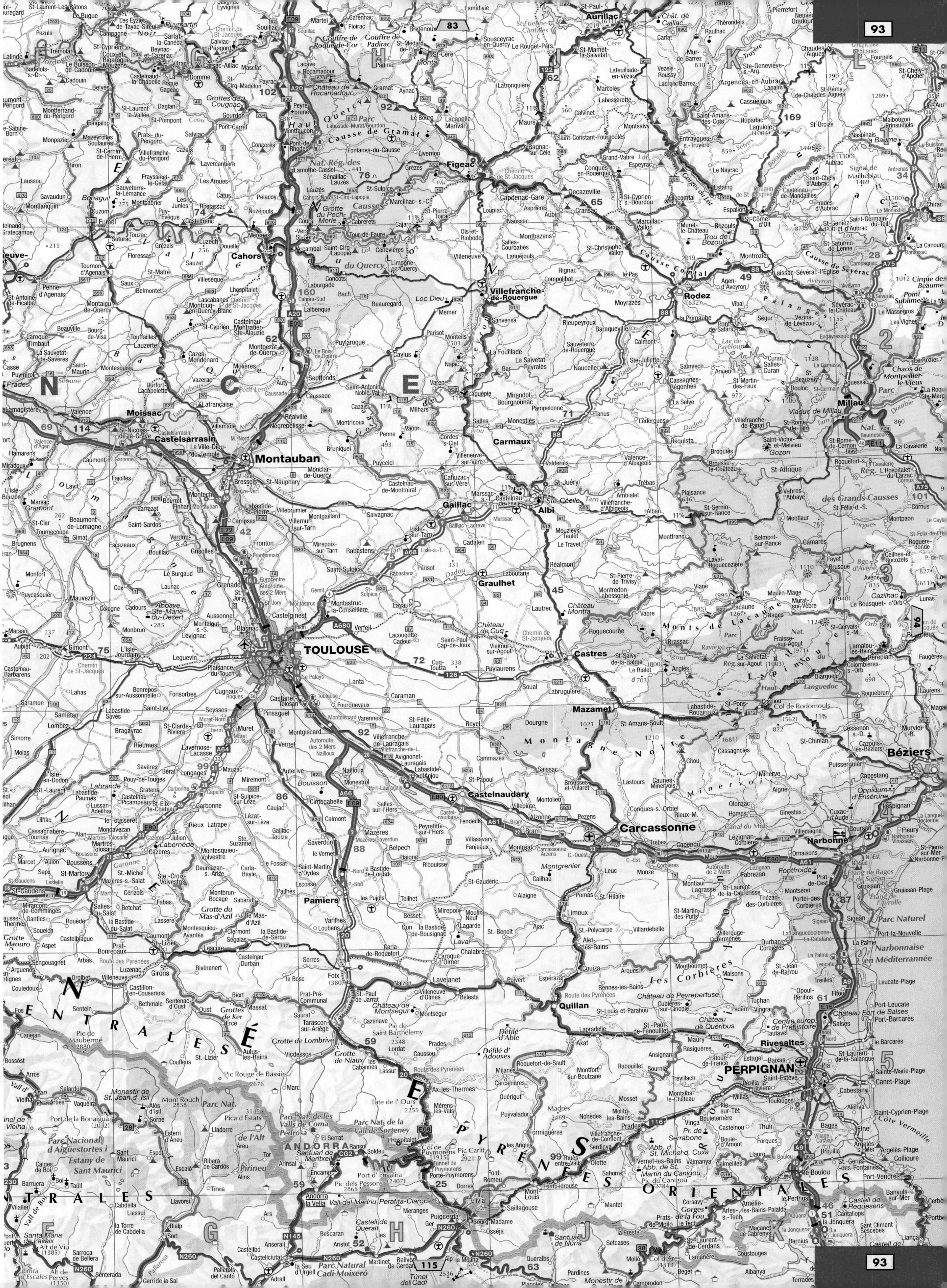

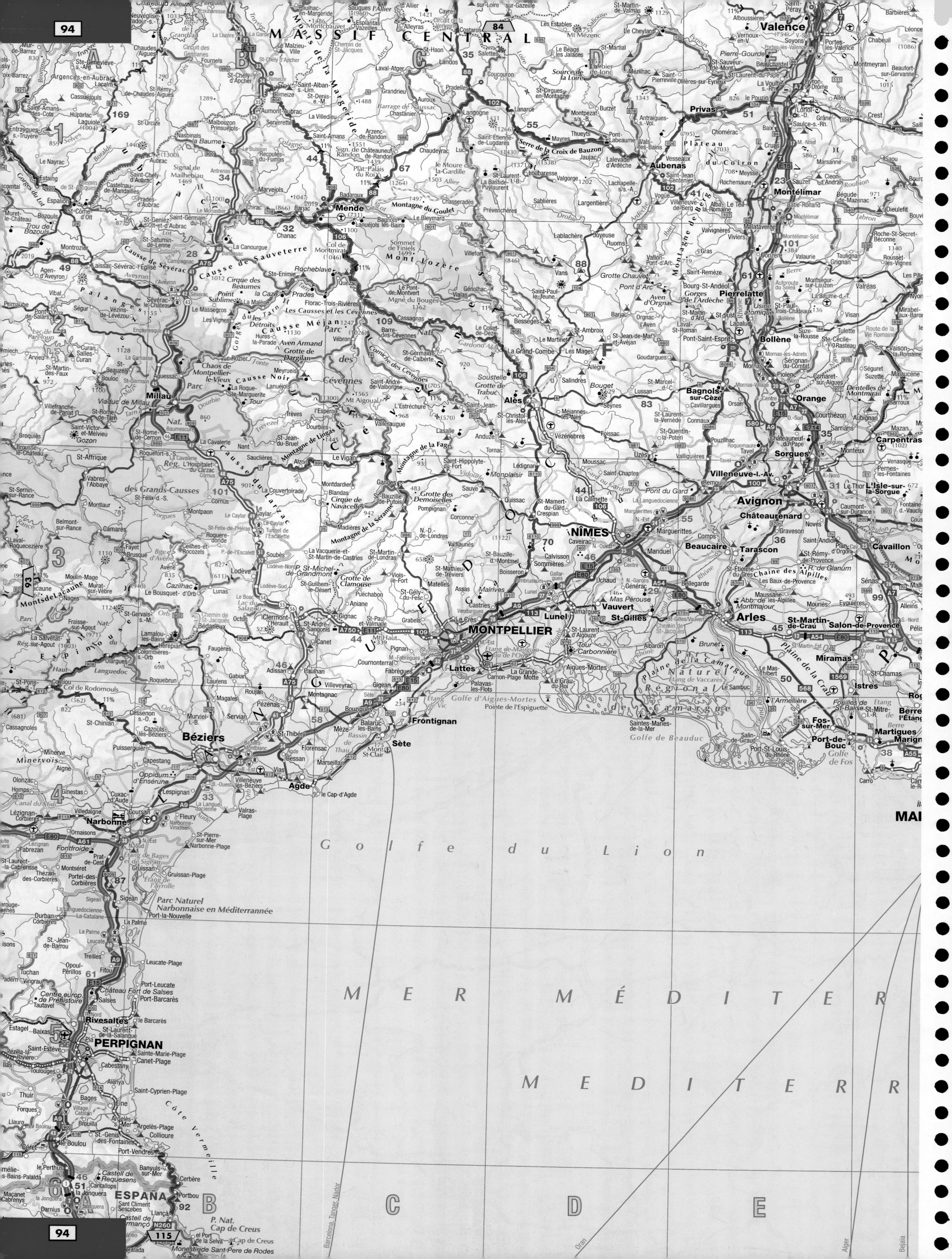
MASSIF CENTRAL
84
Valence
Privas
Aubenas
Montélimar
Mende
Millau
Alès
Bagnols-sur-Cèze
Orange
Avignon
Carpentras
Sorgues
Villeneuve-l.-Av.
NÎMES
Beaucaire
Tarascon
Cavaillon
Arles
Salon-de-Provence
Lunel
MONTPELLIER
Lattes
Sète
Frontignan
Béziers
Agde
Narbonne
PERPIGNAN
Rivesaltes
Martigues
Istres
Miramas
Golfe du Lion
MER MÉDITER
ESPAÑA
Golfe d'Aigues-Mortes
Parc Naturel Narbonnaise en Méditerranée
Côte Vermeille
115

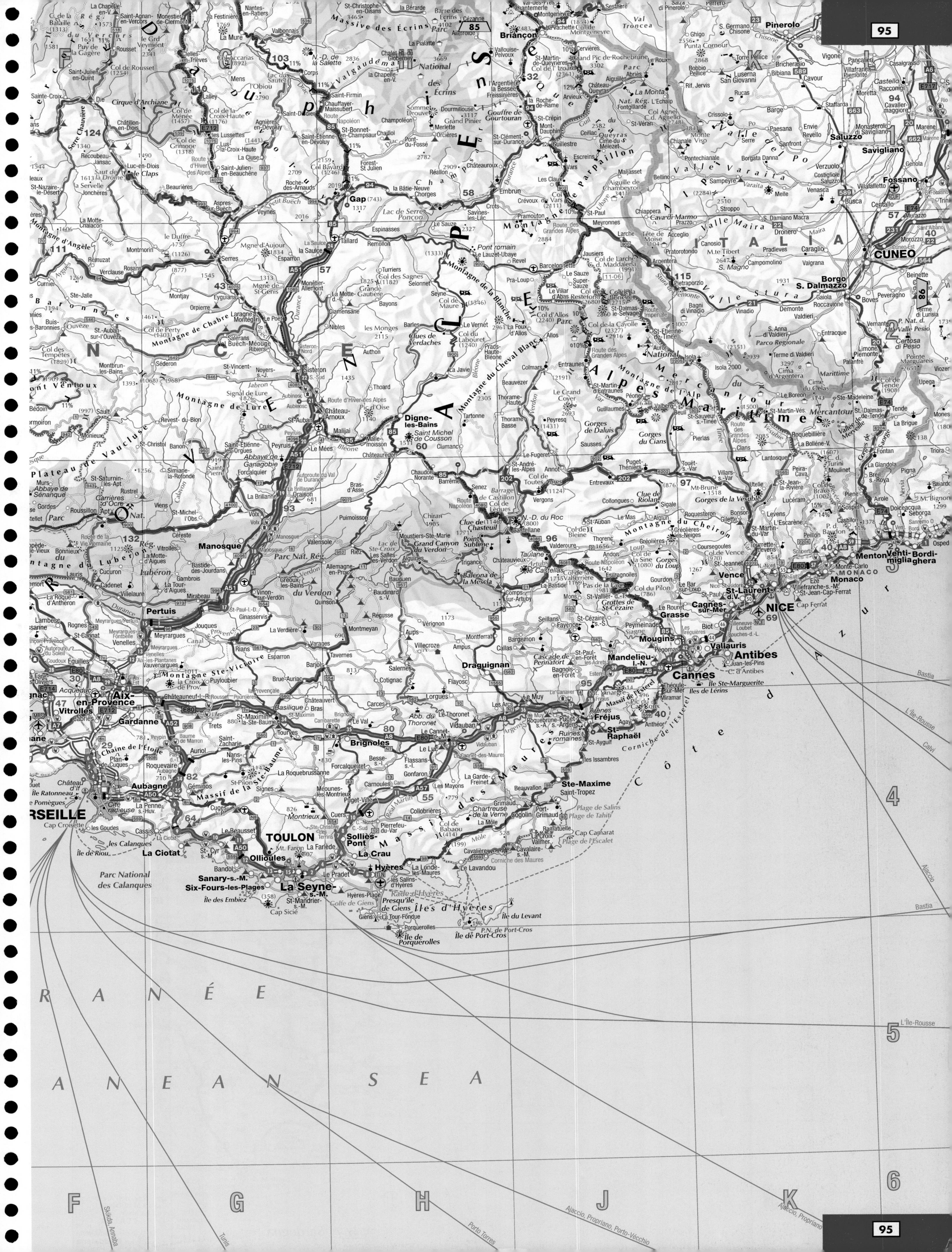
Briançon
Pinerolo
Gap
Saluzzo
Savigliano
Fossano
CUNEO
Borgo S. Dalmazzo
ITALIA
Barcelonnette
Embrun
Sisteron
Digne-les-Bains
Manosque
Pertuis
Aix-en-Provence
Vitrolles
Gardanne
Aubagne
MARSEILLE
Cassis
La Ciotat
TOULON
La Seyne-s.-M.
Hyères
La Crau
Brignoles
Draguignan
Fréjus
St-Raphaël
Ste-Maxime
Saint-Tropez
Cannes
Antibes
Grasse
Vence
NICE
Monaco
Menton
Ventimiglia
Bordighera
Mercantour
Alpes Maritimes
Parc National des Écrins
Massif des Maures
Massif de l'Esterel
Îles d'Hyères
Île de Porquerolles
Île de Port-Cros
Île du Levant
Parc National des Calanques
Côte d'Azur
Plateau de Vaucluse
Montagne de Lure
Montagne du Lubéron
Grand Canyon du Verdon
Parc Nat. Rég. du Verdon
MÉDITERRANÉE
MEDITERRANEAN SEA
Bastia
Calvi
L'Île-Rousse
Ajaccio
Ajaccio, Propriano, Porto-Vecchio
Porto Torres
Tunis
Skikda, Annaba
F
G
H
J
K
1
2
3
4
5
6

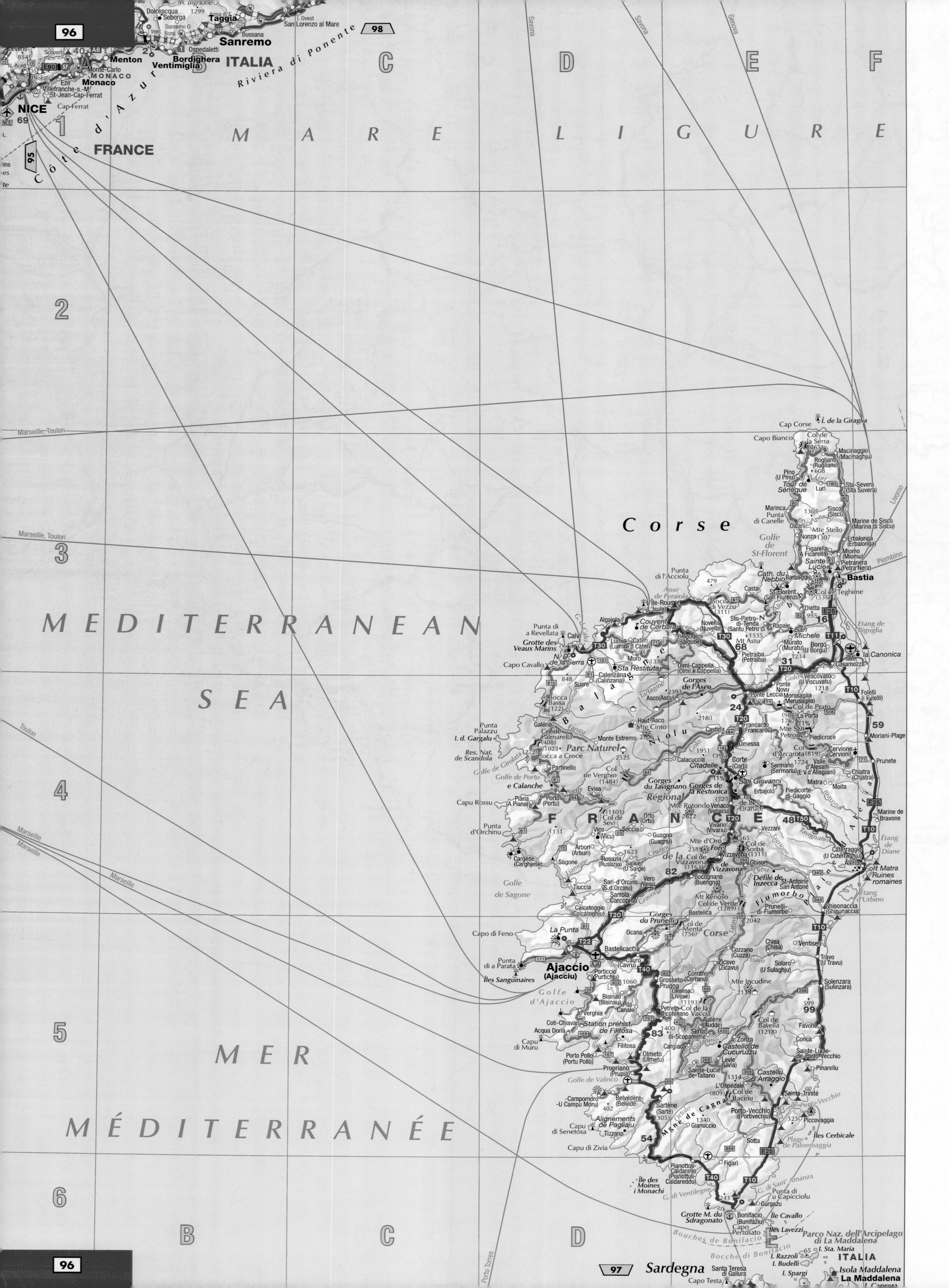

MARE LIGURE
MEDITERRANEAN SEA
MER MÉDITERRANÉE
Corse
FRANCE
ITALIA
Côte d'Azur
Riviera di Ponente
NICE
Monaco
Menton
Ventimiglia
Bordighera
Sanremo
Taggia
Villefranche-s.-M.
St-Jean-Cap-Ferrat
Cap Ferrat
Eze
Monte-Carlo
98
95
97
Marseille, Toulon
Marseille
Toulon
Savona
Genova
Livorno
Piombino
Porto Torres
Cap Corse
Capo Bianco
Bastia
Calvi
L'Île-Rousse
Corte
Ajaccio (Ajacciu)
Propriano
Sartène
Porto-Vecchio
Bonifacio
Golfe de St-Florent
Golfe de Porto
Golfe de Sagone
Golfe d'Ajaccio
Golfe de Valinco
Bouches de Bonifacio
Bocche di Bonifacio
Parc Naturel Régional de la Corse
Sardegna
Santa Teresa di Gallura
Capo Testa
Parco Naz. dell'Arcipelago di La Maddalena
La Maddalena
Îles Sanguinaires
Îles Cerbicale
Îles Lavezzi
Île Cavallo
C
D
E
F
B
1
2
3
4
5
6

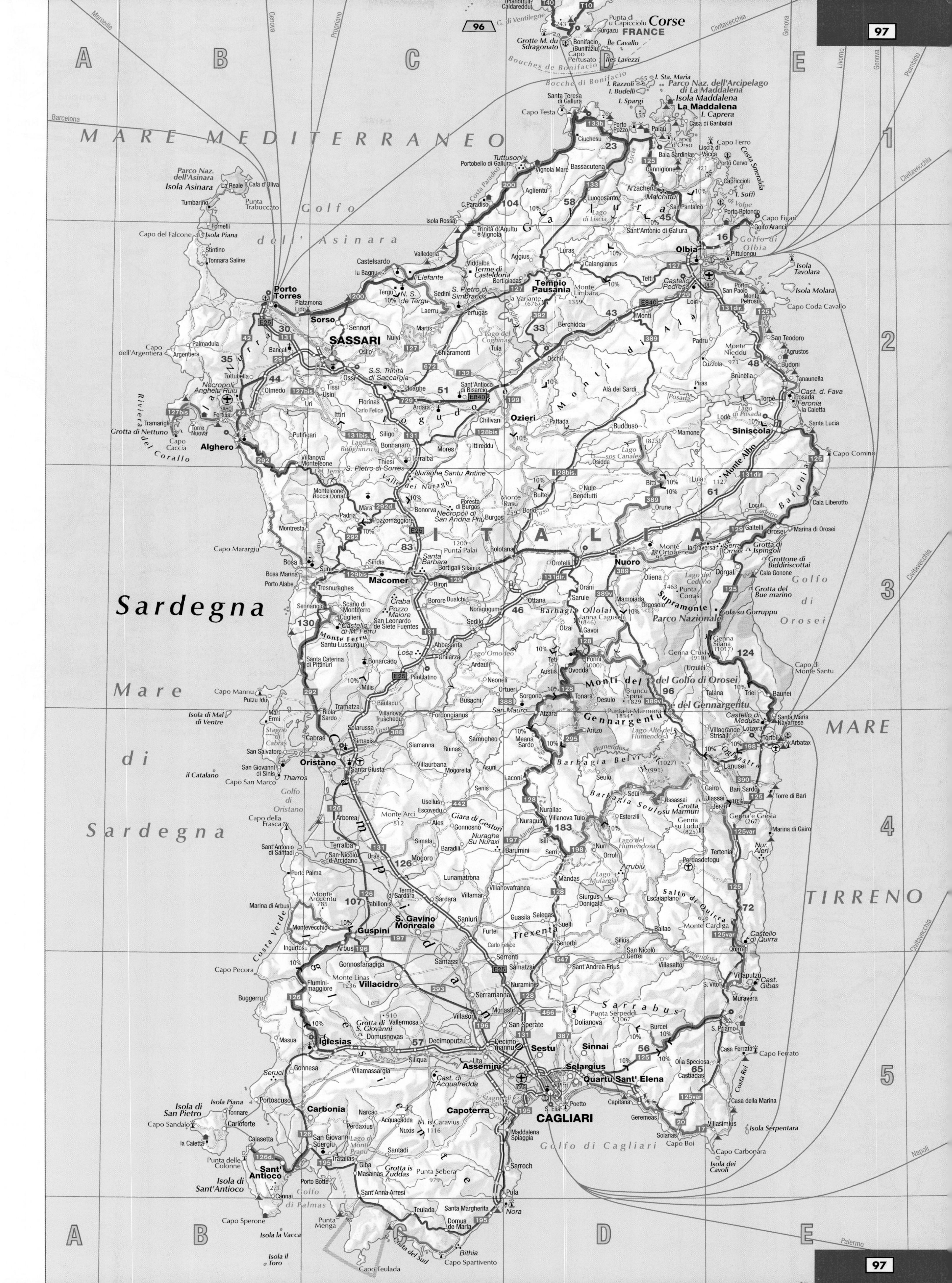
96
Corse
FRANCE
Bonifacio (Bunifaziu)
Bouches de Bonifacio
Bocche di Bonifacio
Parco Naz. dell'Arcipelago di La Maddalena
La Maddalena
Santa Teresa di Gallura
Capo Testa
MARE MEDITERRANEO
Parco Naz. dell'Asinara
Isola Asinara
Golfo dell' Asinara
Capo del Falcone
Stintino
Porto Torres
Castelsardo
Tempio Pausania
Olbia
Golfo di Olbia
Isola Tavolara
Arzachena
Palau
Porto Cervo
Costa Smeralda
Gallura
Sorso
SASSARI
Alghero
Capo Caccia
Riviera del Corallo
Capo dell'Argentiera
Logudoro
Ozieri
Monti di Alà
Siniscola
Capo Comino
Monte Albo
Baronia
Nuoro
Oliena
Orosei
Golfo di Orosei
Dorgali
Supramonte
Parco Nazionale
ITALIA
Macomer
Bosa
Capo Marargiu
Sardegna
Monte Ferru
Barbagia Ollolai
Monti del Gennargentu
Parco Nazionale del Golfo di Orosei e del Gennargentu
Barbagia Belvì
Barbagia Seulo
MARE TIRRENO
Arbatax
Tortolì
Lanusei
Ogliastra
Mare di Sardegna
Oristano
Golfo di Oristano
Capo San Marco
Campidano
Sarrabus
Trexenta
Salto di Quirra
Guspini
S. Gavino Monreale
Villacidro
Costa Verde
Iglesias
Carbonia
Isola di San Pietro
Carloforte
Isola di Sant'Antioco
Sant'Antioco
Golfo di Palmas
Capo Teulada
Costa del Sud
Capo Spartivento
CAGLIARI
Golfo di Cagliari
Quartu Sant'Elena
Assemini
Capo Carbonara
Isola dei Cavoli
Isola Serpentara
Villasimius
A
B
C
D
E
1
2
3
4
5

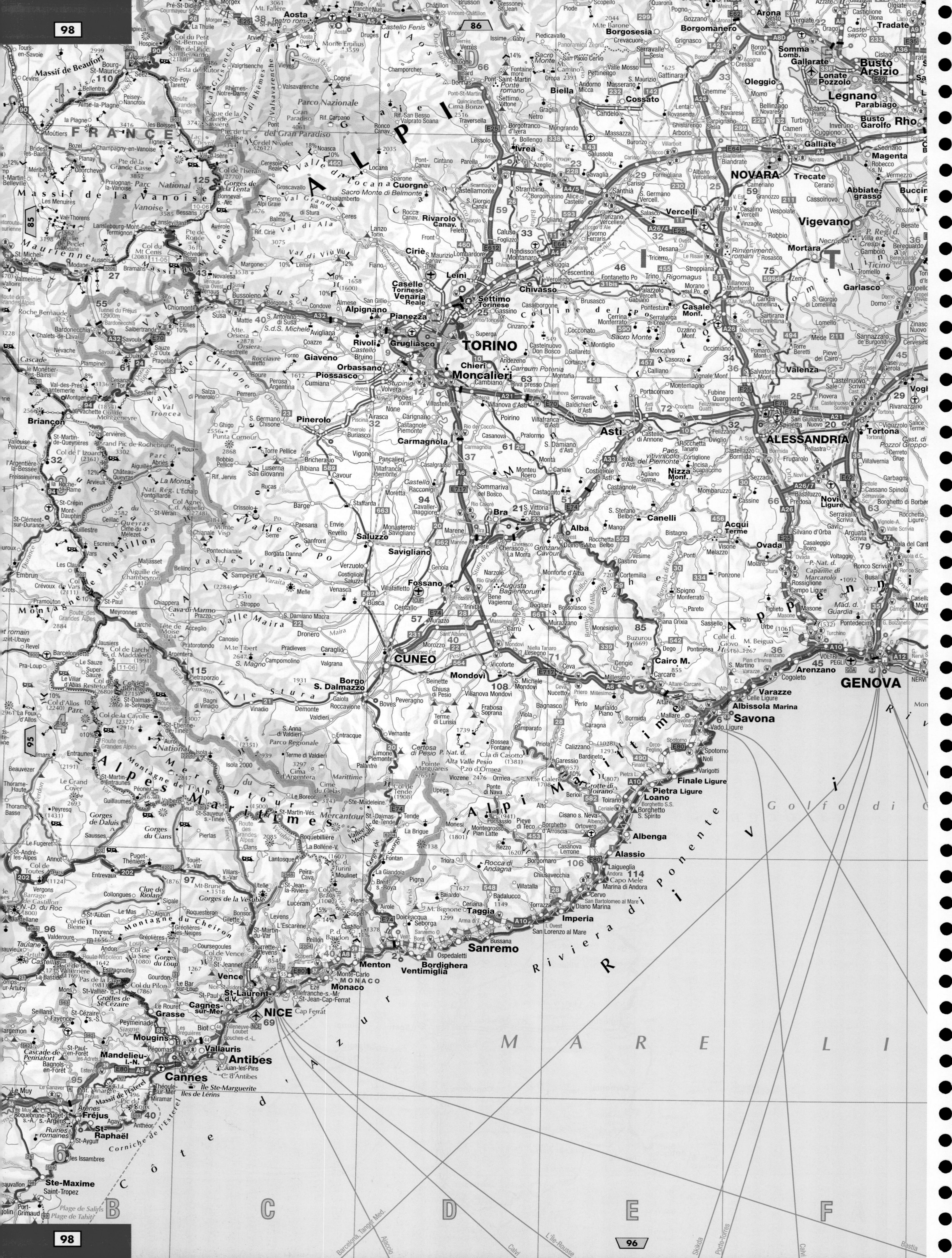
86
FRANCE
ALPI
Massif de la Vanoise
Parco Nazionale del Gran Paradiso
Aosta
Ivrea
Biella
Borgomanero
Novara
Vercelli
Legnano
Busto Arsizio
Gallarate
Vigevano
Mortara
Chivasso
Torino
Moncalieri
Pinerolo
Carmagnola
Asti
Alessandria
Casale Monf.
Valenza
Tortona
Novi Ligure
Acqui Terme
Alba
Bra
Saluzzo
Savigliano
Fossano
Cuneo
Mondovì
Ovada
Genova
Savona
Albenga
Alassio
Imperia
Sanremo
Ventimiglia
Bordighera
Menton
Monaco
Nice
Antibes
Cannes
Grasse
Fréjus
St-Raphaël
Ste-Maxime
Briançon
Alpes Maritimes
Alpi Marittime
Appennini
Riviera di Ponente
Golfo di
Côte d'Azur
MARE LI
B
C
D
E
F
1
4
6
85
95
96

87

100

Oltrepò Pavese

Liguria

Appennino Tosco-Emiliano

Alpi Apuane

Riviera di Levante

Versilia

Monti del Chianti

Colline Metallifere

Valli Grandi Veronesi

Valpolicella

Lago di Garda

MILANO

BERGAMO

BRESCIA

VERONA

VICENZA

MONZA

PAVIA

PIACENZA

CREMONA

PARMA

REGGIO NELL'EMILIA

MODENA

BOLOGNA

LA SPEZIA

LIVORNO

FIRENZE

Mar Ligure

103

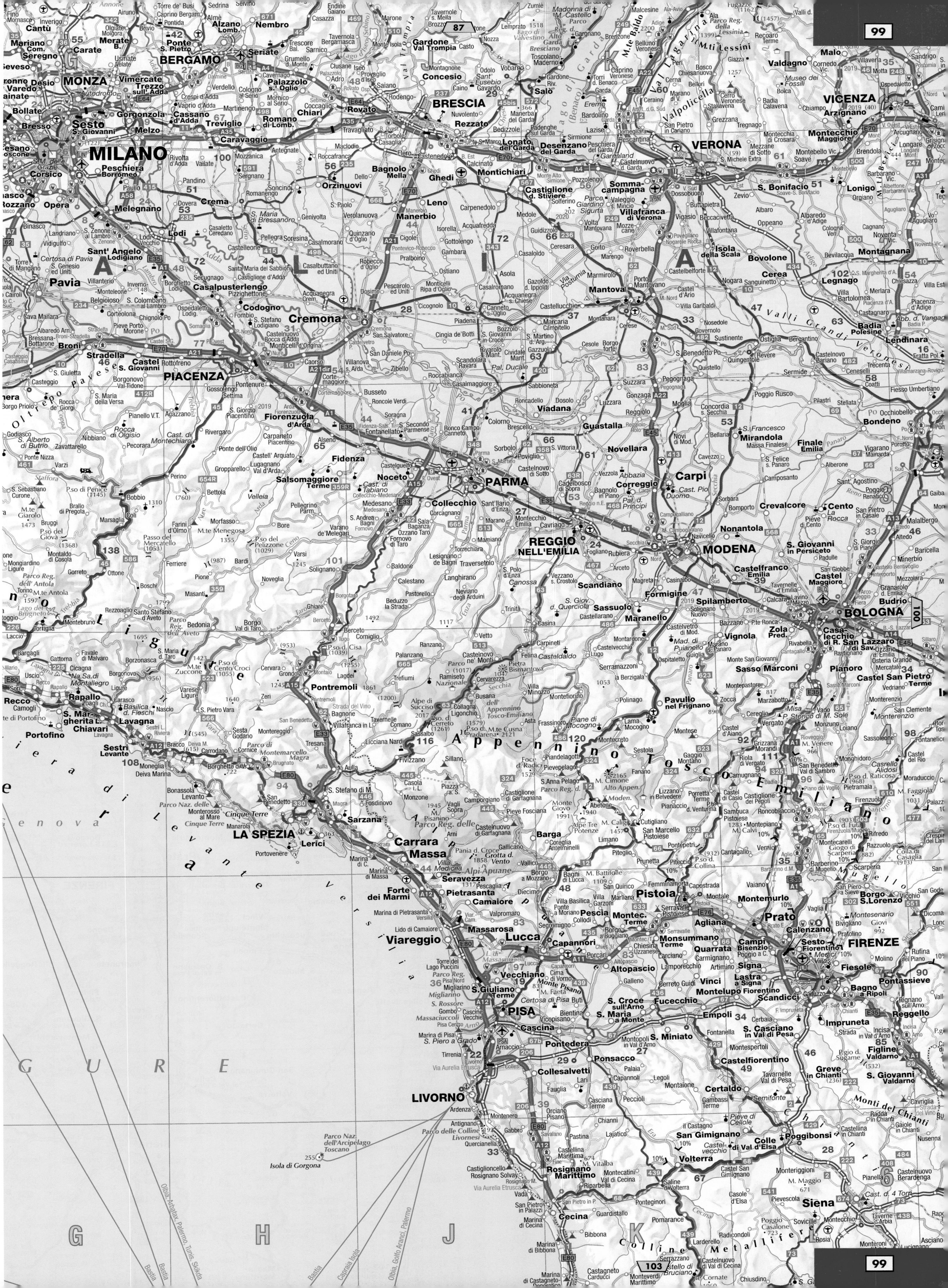

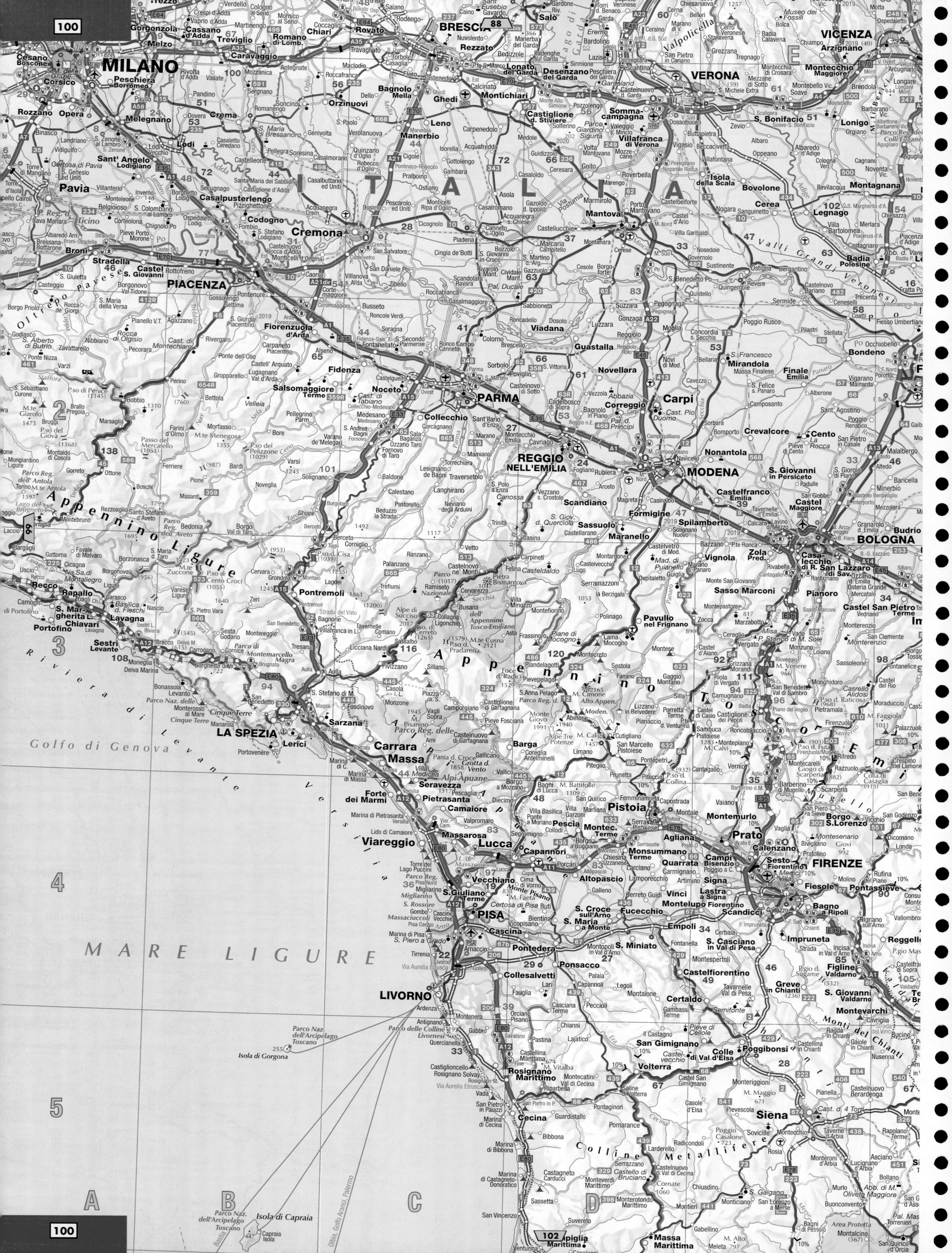
MILANO
BRESCIA
VERONA
VICENZA
Pavia
Lodi
Crema
Cremona
PIACENZA
PARMA
Mantova
Legnago
REGGIO NELL'EMILIA
MODENA
Carpi
BOLOGNA
Sassuolo
Vignola
Pistoia
Prato
FIRENZE
Lucca
PISA
LIVORNO
Viareggio
Massa
Carrara
LA SPEZIA
Sarzana
Pontremoli
Chiavari
Rapallo
Portofino
Sestri Levante
Empoli
Siena
Volterra
Poggibonsi
Cecina
Piombino
Massa Marittima
I T A L I A
Appennino Ligure
Appennino Tosco-Emiliano
Alpi Apuane
Colline Metallifere
Riviera di Levante
Versilia
Golfo di Genova
MARE LIGURE
Chianti
Isola di Gorgona
Isola di Capraia
Parco Naz. dell'Arcipelago Toscano
88
99
102
A
B
C
D
E
1
2
3
4
5

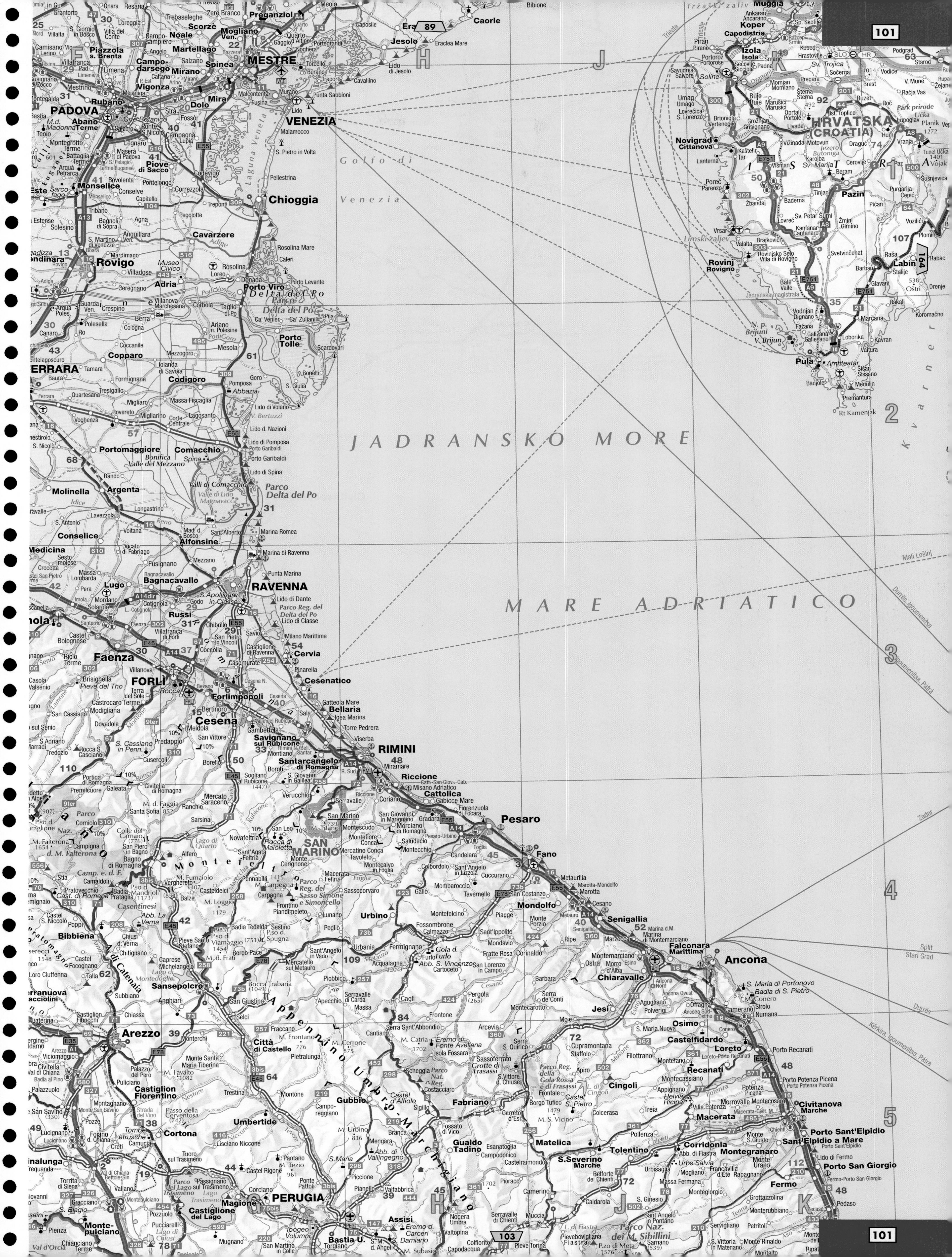
JADRANSKO MORE
MARE ADRIATICO
Golfo di Venezia
HRVATSKA (CROATIA)
SAN MARINO
Appennino Umbro-Marchigiano
Parco Delta del Po
MESTRE
VENEZIA
PADOVA
Chioggia
Rovigo
Adria
Porto Viro
Porto Tolle
FERRARA
Copparo
Codigoro
Comacchio
Portomaggiore
Argenta
Molinella
Conselice
Alfonsine
Lugo
Bagnacavallo
RAVENNA
Russi
Faenza
FORLÌ
Forlimpopoli
Cervia
Cesenatico
Cesena
Bellaria
Savignano sul Rubicone
Santarcangelo di Romagna
RIMINI
Riccione
Cattolica
Pesaro
Fano
Senigallia
Ancona
Jesi
Chiaravalle
Osimo
Loreto
Recanati
Macerata
Civitanova Marche
Porto Sant'Elpidio
Porto San Giorgio
Fermo
Tolentino
Matelica
Fabriano
Gubbio
Gualdo Tadino
Urbino
Città di Castello
Sansepolcro
Arezzo
Cortona
Castiglion Fiorentino
Umbertide
PERUGIA
Assisi
Bastia U.
Castiglione del Lago
Montepulciano
Bibbiena
Koper
Capodistria
Izola
Piran
Umag
Novigrad
Poreč
Rovinj
Pula
Pazin
Labin
Brijuni
Jesolo
Caorle
Monselice
Este
Piove di Sacco
Dolo
Mira
Mogliano Ven.
Preganziol
Noale
Mirano
Spinea
Abano Terme
Cavarzere
Mondolfo
Castelfidardo
Cingoli
S.Severino Marche
Corridonia
Montegranaro
Sant'Elpidio a Mare
Pergola
Magione
101

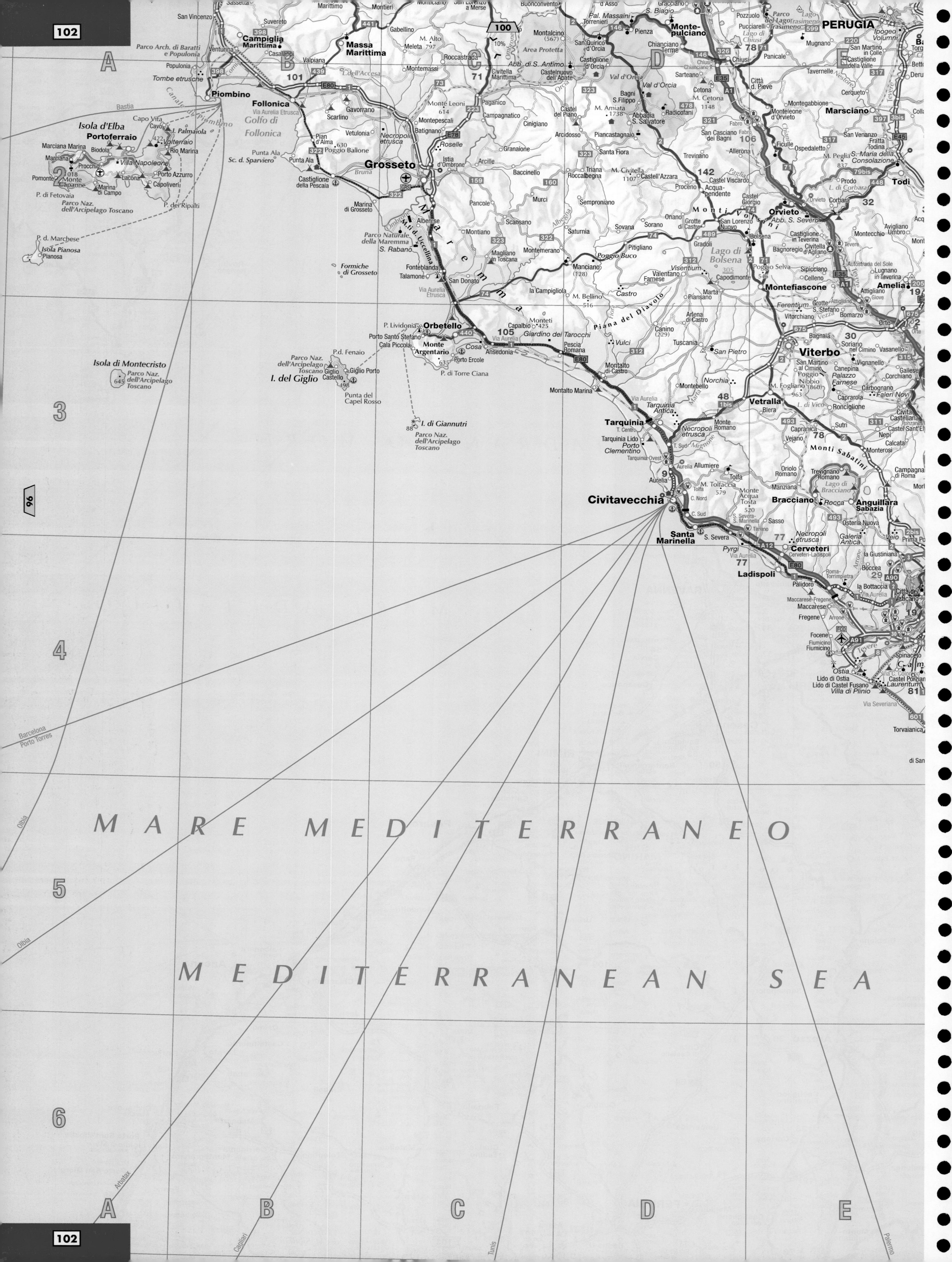
A
B
C
D
E
2
3
4
5
6
96
San Vincenzo
Suvereto
Campiglia Marittima
Massa Marittima
Parco Arch. di Baratti e Populonia
Populonia
Tombe etrusche
Piombino
Follonica
Golfo di Follonica
Bastia
Isola d'Elba
Portoferraio
Capo Vita
Cavo
I. Palmaiola
Volterraio
Rio Marina
Marciana Marina
Biodola
Procchio
Villa Napoleone
Porto Azzurro
Monte Capanne
Lacona
Capoliveri
Marina di Campo
Pomonte
P. di Fetovaia
Parco Naz. dell'Arcipelago Toscano
P. del Ripalti
P. d. Marchese
Isola Pianosa
Pianosa
Gavorrano
Scarlino
Vetulonia
Punta Ala
Sc. d. Sparviero
Castiglione della Pescaia
Grosseto
Marina di Grosseto
Roselle
Istia d'Ombrone
Montalcino
Montepulciano
Pienza
Chianciano Terme
Val d'Orcia
Abb. di S. Antimo
Castel del Piano
M. Amiata
Abbadia S. Salvatore
Radicofani
Arcidosso
Santa Fiora
Roccalbegna
Sorano
Pitigliano
Manciano
Saturnia
Scansano
Magliano in Toscana
Parco Naturale della Maremma
Alberese
Maremma
Talamone
Fonteblanda
Formiche di Grosseto
Orbetello
Monte Argentario
Porto Santo Stefano
Porto Ercole
Ansedonia
Cosa
Capalbio
Giardino dei Tarocchi
P. di Torre Ciana
Isola di Montecristo
Parco Naz. dell'Arcipelago Toscano
I. del Giglio
Giglio Porto
Giglio Castello
Punta del Capel Rosso
I. di Giannutri
Montalto di Castro
Montalto Marina
Vulci
Piana del Diavolo
Canino
Tuscania
Lago di Bolsena
Bolsena
Capodimonte
Marta
Montefiascone
Orvieto
Viterbo
Vetralla
Tarquinia
Tarquinia Lido
Porto Clementino
Allumiere
Tolfa
Civitavecchia
Santa Marinella
S. Severa
Cerveteri
Ladispoli
Bracciano
Lago di Bracciano
Anguillara Sabazia
Monti Sabatini
Fiumicino
Ostia
Lido di Ostia
Lido di Castel Fusano
Torvaianica
PERUGIA
Marsciano
Todi
Amelia
Città d. Pieve
Chiusi
Acquapendente
Monti Volsini
Fregene
Maccarese
Barcelona
Porto Torres
Olbia
Arbatax
Cagliari
Tunis
Palermo
MARE MEDITERRANEO
MEDITERRANEAN SEA

MARE ADRIATICO

ITALIA

ROMA
NAPOLI
PESCARA
Chieti
Teramo
Ascoli Piceno
L'Aquila
Terni
Foligno
Rieti
Narni
Campobasso
Isernia
Benevento
Caserta
Avellino
SALERNO
Frosinone
Latina
Cassino
Sora
Sulmona
Avezzano
Vasto
San Salvo
Lanciano
Ortona
Francavilla al Mare
Montesilvano Marina
Roseto degli Abruzzi
Giulianova
San Benedetto del Tronto
Grottammare
Martinsicuro
Pineto
Atri
Penne
Guardiagrele
Atessa
Pozzuoli
Portici
Ercolano
Torre del Greco
Torre Annunziata
Castellammare di Stabia
Sorrento
Afragola
Casoria
Aversa
Marcianise
Maddaloni
Nola
Pomigliano d'A.
Marigliano
Nocera Inferiore
Angri
Cava de' Tirreni
Aprilia
Anzio
Nettuno
Terracina
Gaeta
Formia
Fondi
Sabaudia
Pontinia
Priverno
Sezze
Cisterna di Latina
Velletri
Cori
Colleferro
Valmontone
Anagni
Alatri
Ferentino
Veroli
Isola del Liri
Ceccano
Pontecorvo
Minturno
Sessa Aurunca
Teano
Mondragone
Capua
Santa Maria Capua Vetere
Montesarchio
Cervinara
Tivoli
Guidonia
Frascati
Grottaferrata
Marino
Ciampino
Albano Laziale
Genzano di Roma
Pomezia
Ardea
Monterotondo
Mentana
Fonte Nuova
Palestrina
Zagarolo
Artena
Piedimonte Matese

Mare Adriatico

Monti della Laga
Gran Sasso d'Italia
Monti Sibillini
Monti Reatini
Monti Simbruini
Monti Ernici
Monti Lepini
Monti Ausoni
Monti Aurunci
Monti del Matese
Monti del Sannio
Monti del Frentani
Montagna della Maiella
Parco Nazionale d'Abruzzo
Parco Naz. dei M. Sibillini
Appennino Umbro-Marchigiano

Golfo di Gaeta
Golfo di Napoli
Costiera amalfitana

Isola di Ponza
Isola di Ischia
Isola di Procida
Isola di Capri
Isola Palmarola
Isola Zannone
Isola Ventotene
Isola Santo Stefano

M. Vettore 2478
Gran Sasso 2912
M. Amaro 2793
M. Velino 2486
M. Meta 2241
Corno Grande 2912

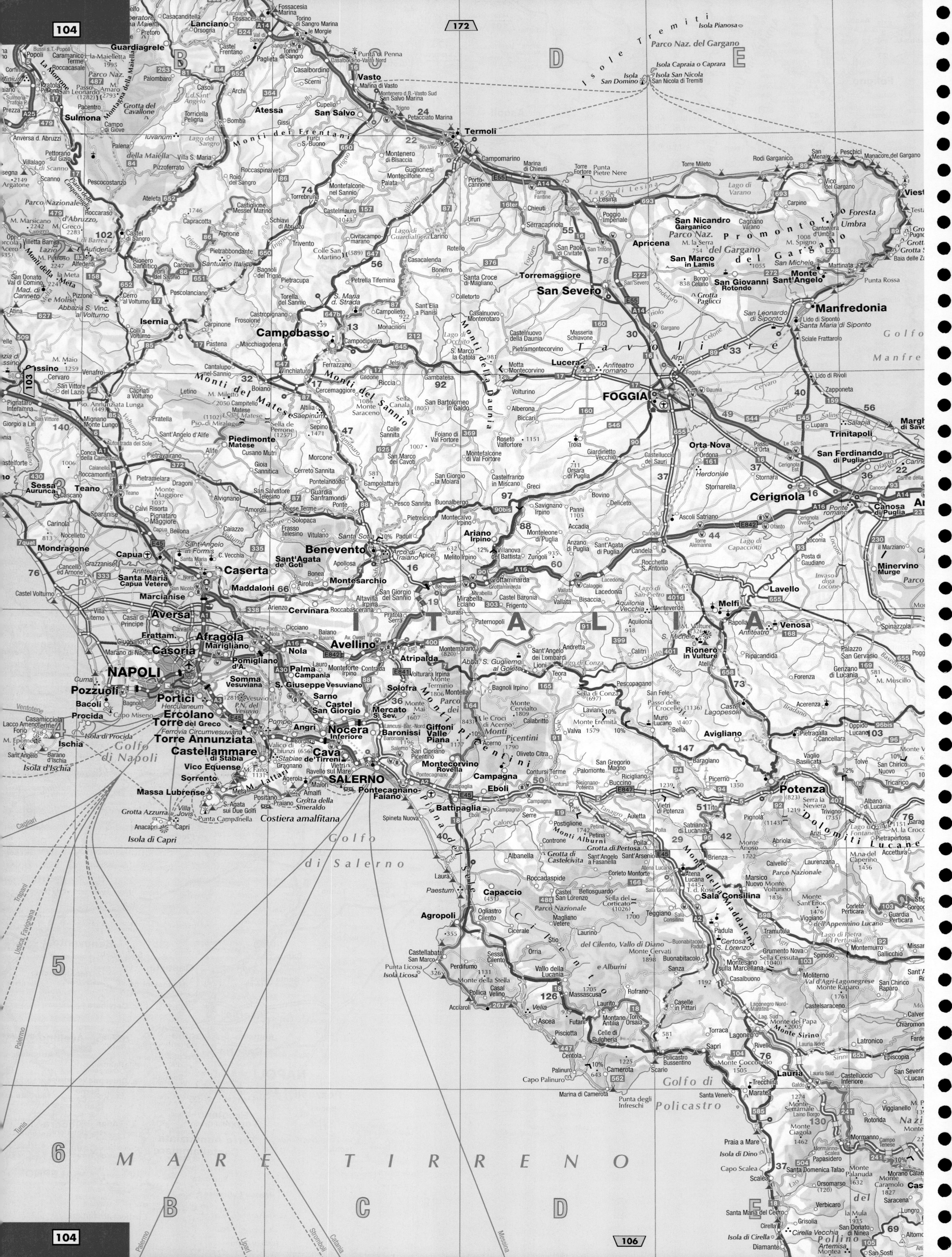
172
B
C
D
E
Isole Tremiti
Isola Pianosa
Parco Naz. del Gargano
Isola Capraia o Caprara
Isola San Domino
Isola San Nicola
San Nicola di Tremiti
Lanciano
Orsogna
Fossacesia Marina
Torino di Sangro Marina
Guardiagrele
Vasto
Marina di Vasto
San Salvo
San Salvo Marina
Atessa
Sulmona
Termoli
Campomarino
Monti dei Frentani
Lesina
Lago di Lesina
Lago di Varano
Rodi Garganico
Peschici
Vieste
Promontorio del Gargano
Foresta Umbra
Apricena
San Nicandro Garganico
San Marco in Lamis
San Giovanni Rotondo
Monte Sant'Angelo
Manfredonia
Golfo di Manfredonia
Torremaggiore
San Severo
Lucera
FOGGIA
Tavoliere
Campobasso
Isernia
Castel di Sangro
Cassino
Venafro
Monti del Matese
Monti del Sannio
Monti della Daunia
Piedimonte Matese
Teano
Sessa Aurunca
Mondragone
Capua
Caserta
Santa Maria Capua Vetere
Maddaloni
Marcianise
Aversa
Afragola
Casoria
NAPOLI
Pozzuoli
Bacoli
Procida
Portici
Ercolano
Torre del Greco
Torre Annunziata
Castellammare di Stabia
Vico Equense
Sorrento
Massa Lubrense
Ischia
Isola d'Ischia
Golfo di Napoli
Capri
Isola di Capri
Anacapri
Costiera amalfitana
Amalfi
Positano
Nocera Inferiore
Cava de' Tirreni
SALERNO
Pontecagnano-Faiano
Battipaglia
Eboli
Golfo di Salerno
Benevento
Sant'Agata de' Goti
Montesarchio
Avellino
Atripalda
Nola
Pomigliano d'Arco
Somma Vesuviana
S. Giuseppe Vesuviano
Sarno
Mercato S. Sev.
Solofra
Baronissi
Ariano Irpino
Monti Picentini
Orta Nova
Cerignola
Canosa di Puglia
Trinitapoli
San Ferdinando di Puglia
Minervino Murge
Lavello
Melfi
Venosa
Rionero in Vulture
Avigliano
Potenza
ITALIA
Agropoli
Capaccio
Paestum
Sala Consilina
Padula
Monti della Maddalena
Dolomiti Lucane
Parco Nazionale del Cilento, Vallo di Diano e Alburni
Vallo della Lucania
Sapri
Golfo di Policastro
Maratea
Lauria
Praia a Mare
Scalea
Isola di Dino
Diamante
MARE TIRRENO
5
6
106

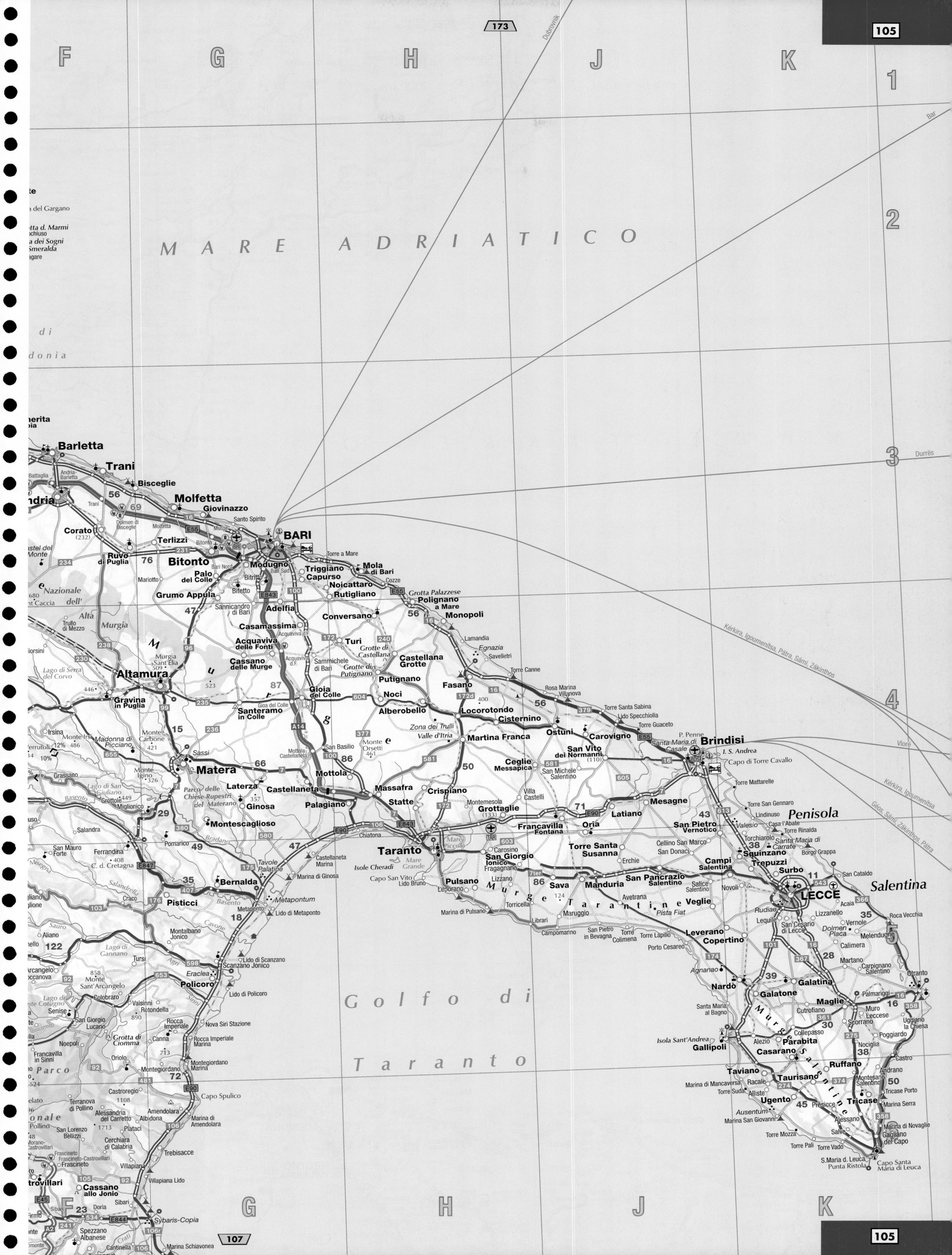

MARE ADRIATICO

F G H J K

Barletta
Trani
Biscéglie
56
Molfetta
Giovinazzo
69
Corato
(232)
Santo Spirito
Ruvo di Puglia
76
Bitonto
BARI
Terlizzi
231
Palo del Colle
Modugno
Triggiano
Torre a Mare
Mola di Bari
Grumo Appula
Capurso
Noicattaro
Cozze
47
Adelfia
Rutigliano
Grotta Palazzese
Casamassima
Conversano
56
Polignano a Mare
Acquaviva delle Fonti
172
Turi
240
Monopoli
Lamandia
Egnazia
Altamura
Cassano delle Murge
Grotte di Castellana
Castellana Grotte
Savelletri
Torre Canne
Gravina in Puglia
87
Putignano
Fasano
Rosa Marina
99
Gioia del Colle
604
Noci
172d
56
Torre Santa Sabina
15
236
Alberobello
Lido Specchiolla
379
Locorotondo
Cisternino
Torre Guaceto
Zona dei Trulli
Matera
66
Santeramo in Colle
A14
377
Valle d'Itria
Ostuni
Carovigno
E55
581
Martina Franca
San Vito dei Normanni
Brindisi
50
Céglie Messápica
San Michele Salentino
605
Mottola
86
Massafra
Crispiano
581
Villa Castelli
Statte
172
Grottaglie
71
Latiano
Mesagne
43
613
Francavilla Fontana
Oria
E90
TARANTO
603
San Giorgio Iónico
Torre Santa Susanna
Cellino San Marco
San Pietro Vernótico
Pulsano
71cr
Sava
Manduria
San Pancrazio Salentino
Campi Salentina
Squinzano
124
Trepuzzi
Surbo
11
LECCE
Murge Tarantine
Veglie
Salentina

Golfo di Taranto

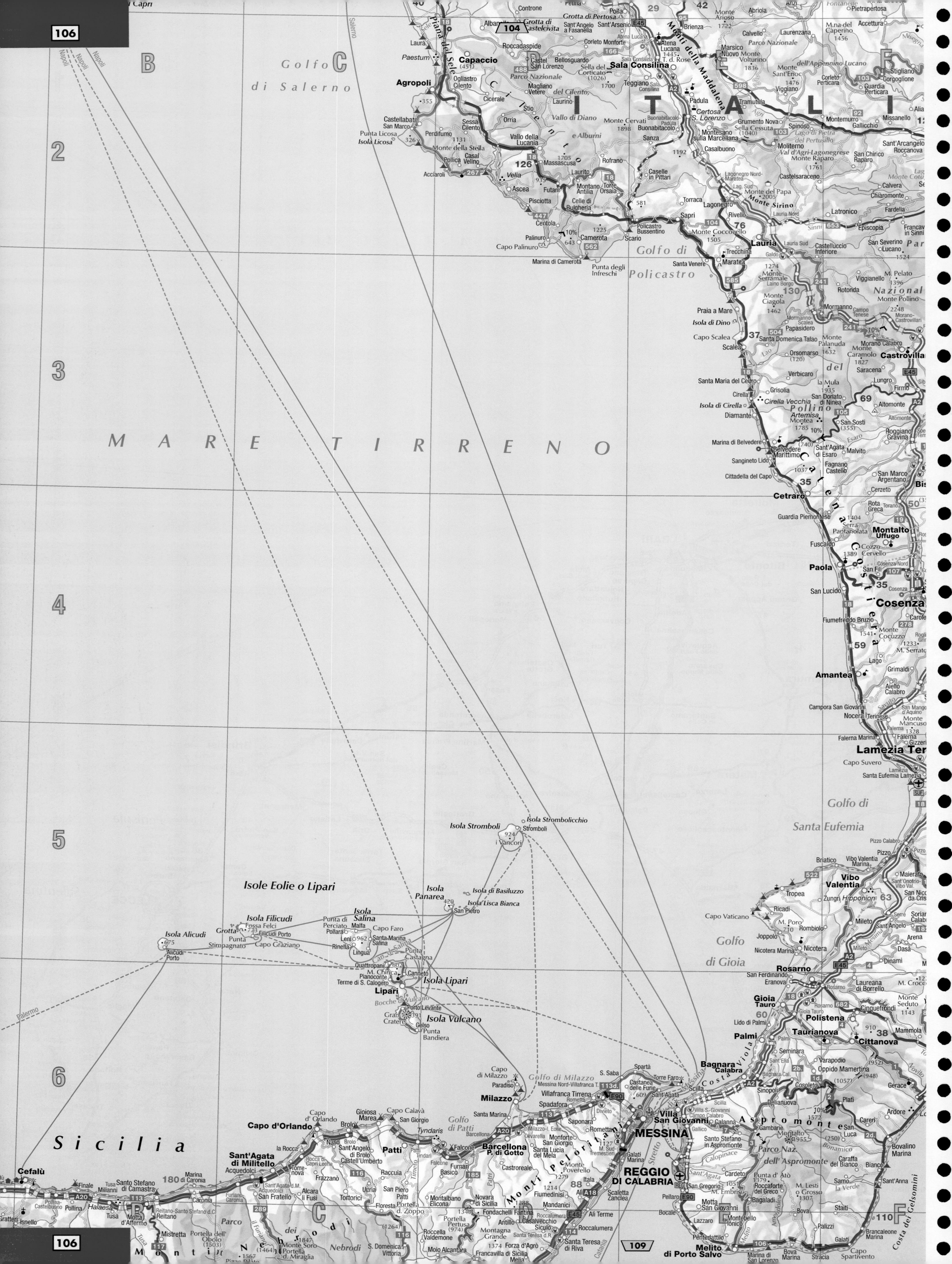

Golfo di Salerno
MARE TIRRENO
ITALIA
Sicilia
Isole Eolie o Lipari
Isola Stromboli
Isola Strombolicchio
Stromboli
Isola Panarea
Isola di Basiluzzo
Isola Lisca Bianca
San Pietro
Isola Salina
Isola Filicudi
Isola Alicudi
Alicudi Porto
Filicudi Porto
Capo Graziano
Punta Stimpagnato
Malfa
Pollara
Leni
Rinella
Lingua
Santa Marina Salina
Capo Faro
Quattropani
Pianoconte
Canneto
Terme di S. Calogero
Lipari
Isola Lipari
Bocche di Vulcano
Porto Levante
Isola Vulcano
Gelso
Punta Bandiera
Capo di Milazzo
Golfo di Milazzo
Milazzo
Golfo di Patti
Capo d'Orlando
Capo Calavà
Gioiosa Marea
Brolo
Patti
Tyndaris
Falcone
Barcellona P. di Gotto
Villafranca Tirrena
Spadafora
MESSINA
Villa San Giovanni
REGGIO DI CALABRIA
Monti Peloritani
Stretto di Messina
Torre Faro
Scilla
Bagnara Calabra
Costa Viola
Aspromonte
Parco Naz. dell' Aspromonte
Montalto
Gambarie
Santo Stefano in Aspromonte
Melito di Porto Salvo
Bova Marina
Capo Spartivento
Bovalino Marina
Bianco
Sant'Anna
Costa dei Gelsomini
Palmi
Gioia Tauro
Rosarno
Polistena
Taurianova
Cittanova
Golfo di Gioia
Nicotera
Capo Vaticano
Tropea
Vibo Valentia
Pizzo
Golfo di Santa Eufemia
Lamezia Ter
Capo Suvero
Amantea
Cosenza
Paola
Fuscaldo
Montalto Uffugo
Cetraro
Catena Costiera
Diamante
Isola di Cirella
Scalea
Capo Scalea
Isola di Dino
Praia a Mare
Maratea
Golfo di Policastro
Sapri
Lauria
Castrovillari
Pollino
Marina di Camerota
Capo Palinuro
Palinuro
Camerota
Pisciotta
Ascea
Velia
Acciaroli
Punta Licosa
Isola Licosa
Castellabate
Agropoli
Paestum
Capaccio
Cilento
Vallo di Diano
Sala Consilina
Padula
Certosa S. Lorenzo
Monti della Maddalena
Lagonegro
Monte Sirino
Cefalù
Sant'Agata di Militello
Santo Stefano di Camastra
Nebrodi
Monti Nebrodi
Mistretta
Novara di Sicilia
Taormina
104
109

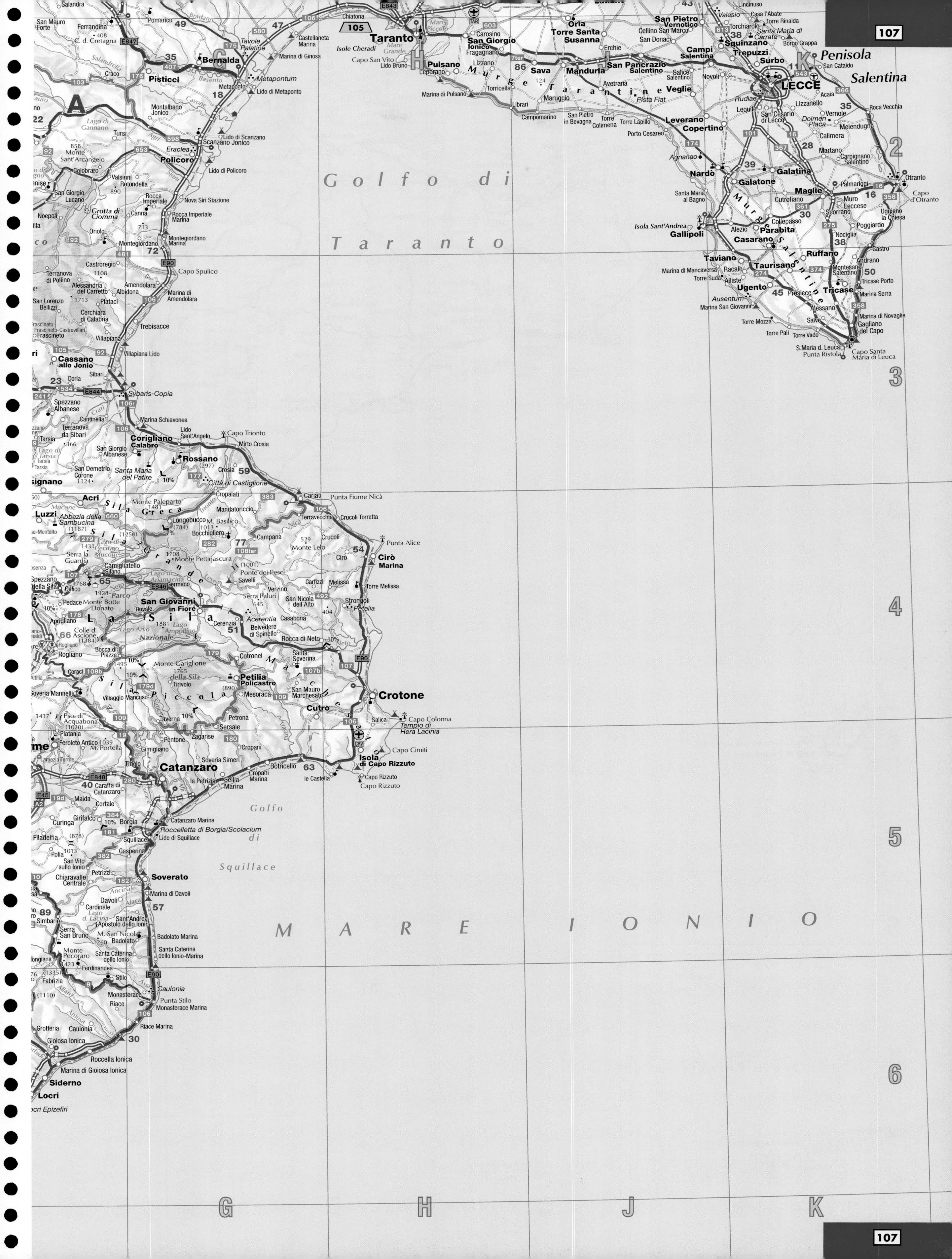

Golfo di Taranto
Golfo di Squillace
MARE IONIO
Penisola Salentina
Murge Tarantine
Murge Salentine
Sila Greca
Sila Grande
La Sila
Sila Piccola
Parco Nazionale
Taranto
Pulsano
San Giorgio Ionico
Sava
Manduria
Oria
Torre Santa Susanna
San Pancrazio Salentino
San Pietro Vernotico
Squinzano
Trepuzzi
Campi Salentina
Surbo
LECCE
Veglie
Leverano
Copertino
Nardò
Galatina
Galatone
Maglie
Otranto
Gallipoli
Parabita
Casarano
Taviano
Taurisano
Ruffano
Ugento
Tricase
Gagliano del Capo
Capo Santa Maria di Leuca
S.Maria d. Leuca
Bernalda
Pisticci
Metapontum
Policoro
Eraclea
Scanzano Jonico
Capo Spulico
Trebisacce
Villapiana Lido
Cassano allo Jonio
Sibari
Sybaris-Copia
Corigliano Calabro
Rossano
Capo Trionto
Mirto Crosia
Cariati
Punta Fiume Nicà
Crucoli Torretta
Punta Alice
Cirò Marina
Cirò
Strongoli
Crotone
Capo Colonna
Capo Cimiti
Isola di Capo Rizzuto
Capo Rizzuto
Cutro
Petilia Policastro
San Giovanni in Fiore
Acri
Luzzi
Catanzaro
Catanzaro Marina
Roccelletta di Borgia/Scolacium
Lido di Squillace
Soverato
Marina di Davoli
Badolato Marina
Santa Caterina dello Ionio-Marina
Caulonia
Punta Stilo
Monasterace Marina
Riace Marina
Roccella Ionica
Marina di Gioiosa Ionica
Siderno
Locri
Locri Epizefiri
G
H
J
K
2
3
4
5
6

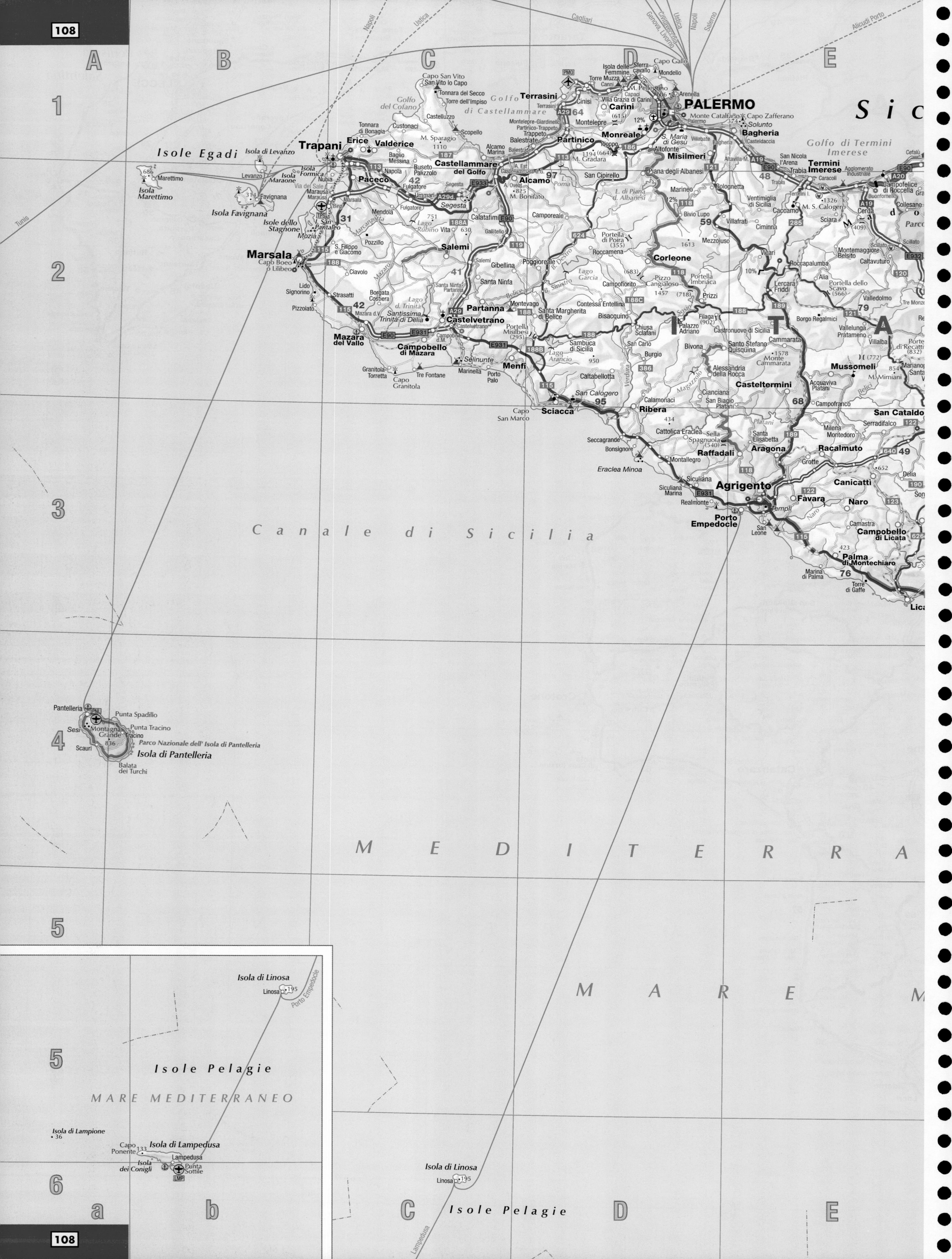
A
B
C
D
E
1
2
3
4
5
6
a
b
Isole Egadi
Isola di Levanzo
Isola Marettimo
Marettimo
Levanzo
Favignana
Isola Favignana
Isola Formica
Isola Maraone
Isole dello Stagnone
Mozia
Trapani
Erice
Valderice
Paceco
Marsala
Capo Boeo o Lilibeo
Mazara del Vallo
Campobello di Mazara
Castelvetrano
Partanna
Salemi
Alcamo
Castellammare del Golfo
Golfo di Castellammare
Golfo del Cofano
Capo San Vito
San Vito lo Capo
Terrasini
Partinico
Monreale
Carini
Cinisi
PALERMO
Bagheria
Misilmeri
Piana degli Albanesi
Corleone
Termini Imerese
Golfo di Termini Imerese
Menfi
Sciacca
Capo San Marco
Ribera
Raffadali
Aragona
Agrigento
Porto Empedocle
Favara
Canicattì
Naro
Racalmuto
Campobello di Licata
Palma di Montechiaro
Casteltermini
Mussomeli
San Cataldo
Lercara Friddi
Cammarata
Santo Stefano Quisquina
Bivona
Alessandria della Rocca
Selinunte
Eraclea Minoa
Canale di Sicilia
MEDITERRA
MARE
Sic
ITA
Pantelleria
Punta Spadillo
Punta Tracino
Montagna Grande
Parco Nazionale dell' Isola di Pantelleria
Isola di Pantelleria
Balata dei Turchi
Scauri
Sesi
Isola di Linosa
Linosa
Isole Pelagie
MARE MEDITERRANEO
Isola di Lampione
Capo Ponente
Isola di Lampedusa
Lampedusa
Isola dei Conigli
Punta Sottile
Tunis
Cagliari
Napoli
Ustica
Alicudi Porto
Porto Empedocle

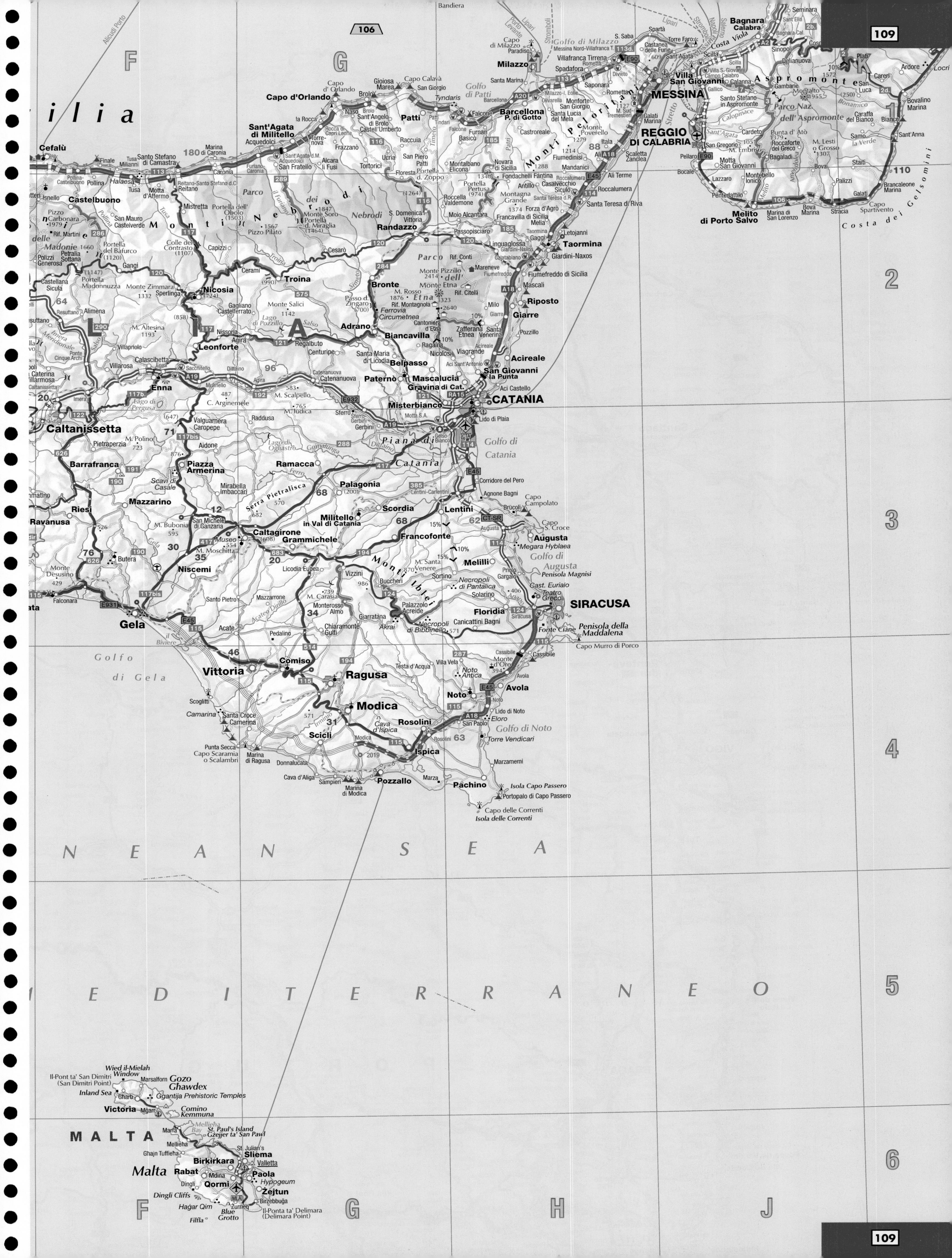
MESSINA
REGGIO DI CALABRIA
CATANIA
SIRACUSA
Ragusa
Modica
Gela
Vittoria
Caltanissetta
Enna
Taormina
Acireale
Milazzo
Capo d'Orlando
Cefalù
Nicosia
Leonforte
Piazza Armerina
Caltagirone
Noto
Pachino
Pozzallo
MALTA
Gozo
Valletta
Sliema
Birkirkara
Rabat
Qormi
Paola
Golfo di Gela
Golfo di Catania
Golfo di Noto
Golfo di Augusta
N E A N S E A
M E D I T E R R A N E O
F G H J
1 2 3 4 5 6

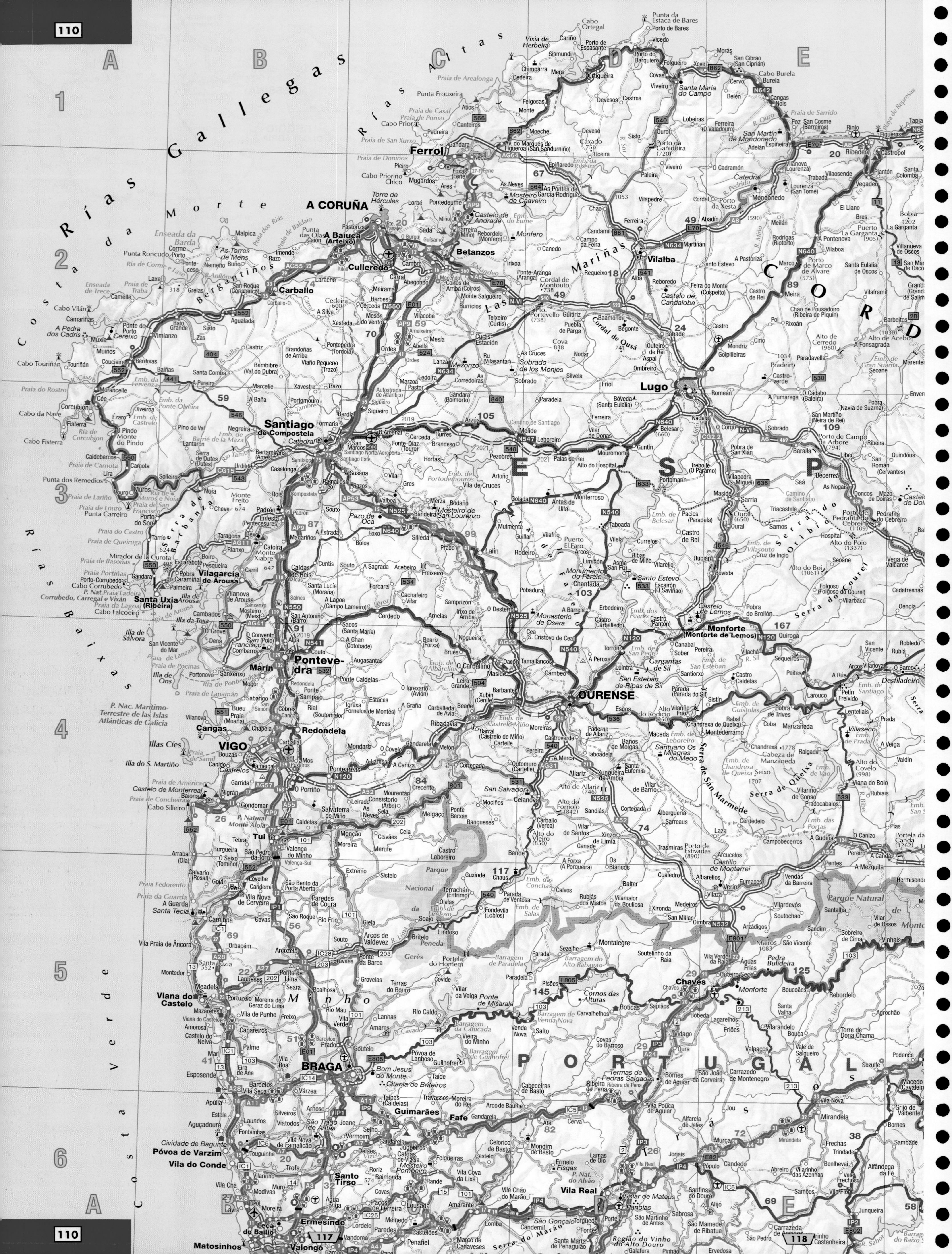

A
B
C
D
E
1
2
3
4
5
6
Rías Altas
Rías Gallegas
Costa da Morte
Rías Baixas
Costa Verde
A CORUÑA
Ferrol
Betanzos
Carballo
Culleredo
A Baiuca (Arteixo)
Santiago de Compostela
Lugo
Vilalba
Pontevedra
Vilagarcía de Arousa
Santa Uxía (Ribeira)
Marín
Redondela
VIGO
Cangas
Tui
OURENSE
Monforte (Monforte de Lemos)
Chaves
Viana do Castelo
BRAGA
Guimarães
Póvoa de Varzim
Vila do Conde
Vila Real
Matosinhos
Valongo
Ermesinde
Santo Tirso
Fafe
Cabo Ortegal
Cabo Fisterra
Cabo Touriñán
Cabo Vilán
Cabo Prior
Cabo Prioriño Chico
Cabo Silleiro
Cabo Burela
Punta da Estaca de Bares
Illas Cíes
Illa de Ons
Illa de Sálvora
P. Nac. Marítimo-Terrestre de las Islas Atlánticas de Galicia
Parque Nacional da Peneda-Gerês
Parque Natural de Montesinho
Las Mariñas
Serra do Courel
Serra de Queixa
Serra de San Mamede
Serra do Barbanza
Serra do Marão
Minho
ESPAÑA
PORTUGAL
CORDILLERA
Santa María do Campo
Castelo de Andrade
Mosteiro de Caaveiro
Castelo de Candaloba
Sobrado de los Monjes
Monasterio de Osera
Castelo de Lemos
Monumento do Farelo
Mosteiro de San Lourenzo
Pazo de Oca
Torre de Hércules
Bom Jesus do Monte
Citânia de Briteiros
Termas de Pedras Salgadas
Solar de Mateus
Região do Vinho do Alto Douro
Cornos das Alturas
117
118

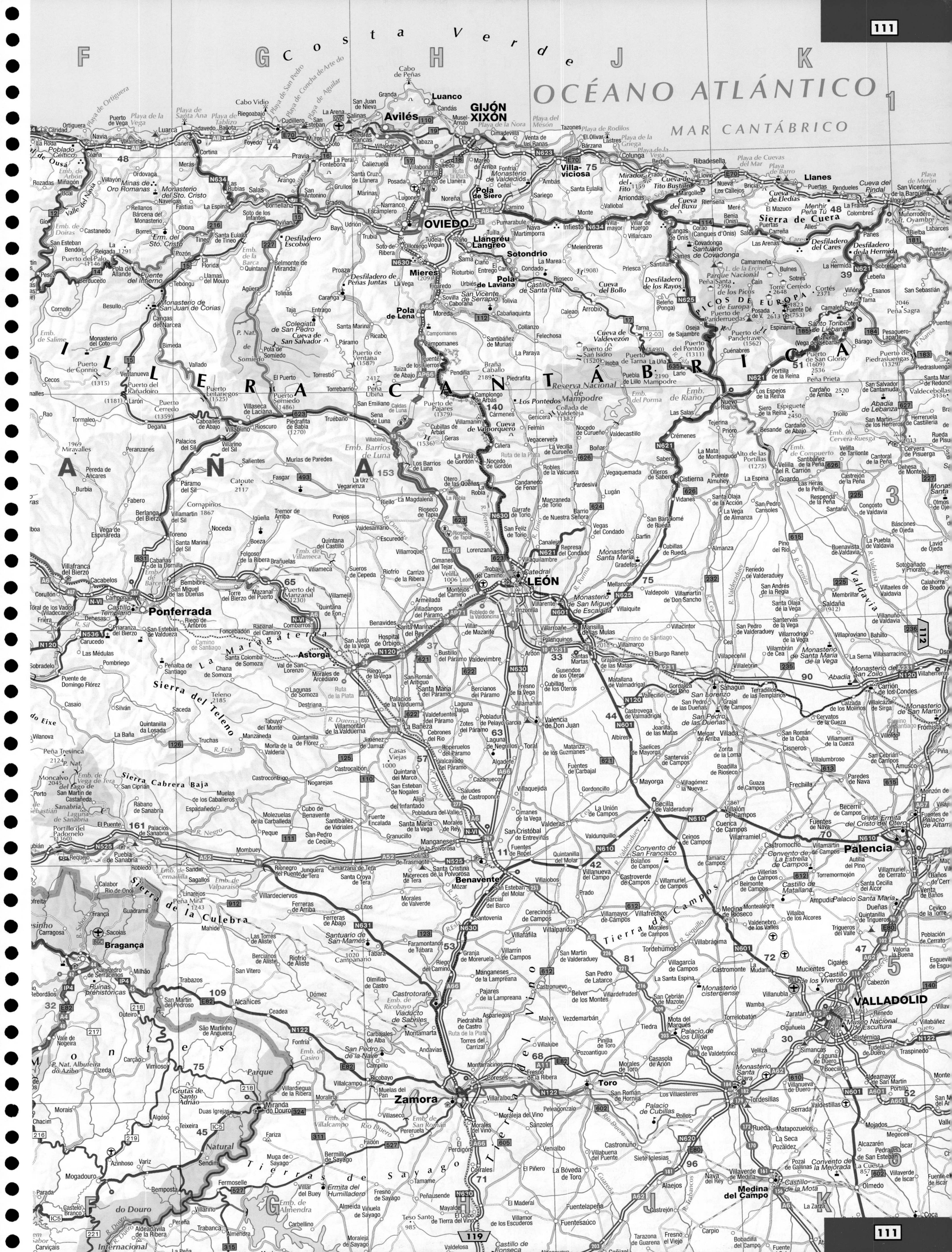
F
G
H
J
K
Costa Verde
OCÉANO ATLÁNTICO
MAR CANTÁBRICO
Cabo de Peñas
Luanco
Avilés
GIJÓN
XIXÓN
Luarca
Navia
Pravia
Villaviciosa
Ribadesella
Llanes
OVIEDO
Pola de Siero
Llangréu
Langreo
Sotrondio
Mieres
Pola de Laviana
Pola de Lena
Cangas de Onís
Covadonga
Santuario de Covadonga
Picos de Europa
Sierra de Cuera
Cangas del Narcea
Tineo
Potes
CORDILLERA CANTÁBRICA
Puerto de Pajares
Riaño
Puerto de San Glorio
Puerto de Piedrasluengas
Cervera de Pisuerga
Guardo
Cistierna
Villablino
Emb. Barrios de Luna
LA AÑA
Ponferrada
Villafranca del Bierzo
Bembibre
Astorga
La Maragatería
Sierra del Teleno
Teleno 2185
LEÓN
Catedral
Mansilla de las Mulas
Sahagún
Valencia de Don Juan
La Bañeza
Sierra Cabrera Baja
Sierra de la Culebra
Bragança
Benavente
Tierra de Campos
Tierra del Vino
Medina de Rioseco
Palencia
Carrión de los Condes
VALLADOLID
Tordesillas
Toro
Zamora
Medina del Campo
Tierras de Sayago
Miranda do Douro
Parque Natural do Douro Internacional
Montes
N-VI
A6
A66
N630
N601
N610
N620
A231
E80
E82
N122
A52
N525
119
112

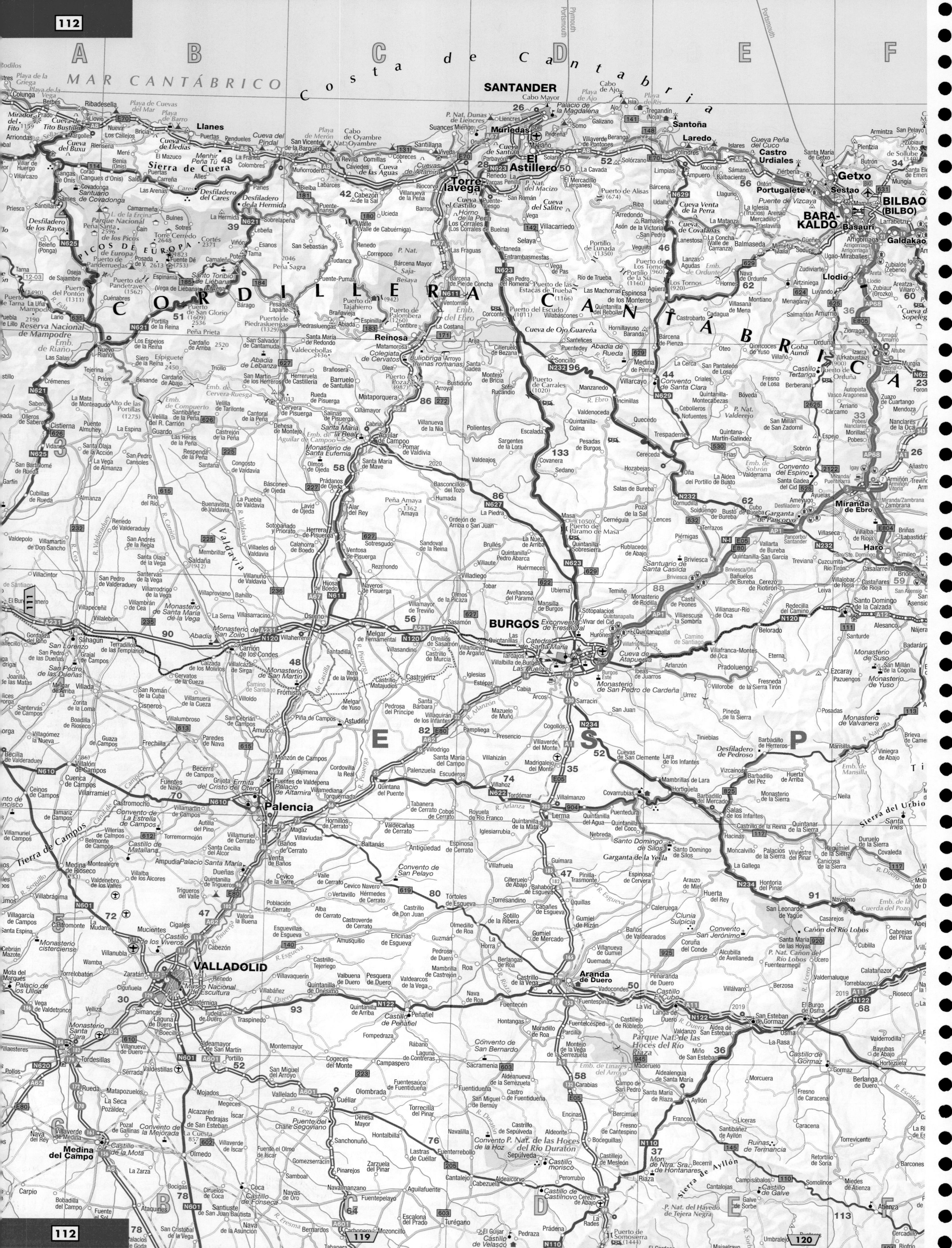
A
B
C
D
E
F
MAR CANTÁBRICO
Costa de Cantabria
SANTANDER
Cabo Mayor
Llanes
Sierra de Cuera
Muriedas
El Astillero
Torrelavega
Laredo
Santoña
Castro Urdiales
Getxo
Portugalete
Sestao
BILBAO (BILBO)
BARAKALDO
Basauri
Galdakao
Llodio
PICOS DE EUROPA
CORDILLERA CANTÁBRICA
Reinosa
Reserva Nacional de Mampodre
Emb. del Ebro
Medina de Pomar
Villarcayo
Miranda de Ebro
Haro
Briviesca
BURGOS
Catedral de Santa María
Las Huelgas
Cueva de Atapuerca
Monasterio de San Pedro de Cardeña
Aguilar de Campoo
Monasterio de Santa María la Real
Alar del Rey
Herrera de Pisuerga
Osorno
Sahagún
Carrión de los Condes
Frómista
Castrojeriz
Palencia
Dueñas
Lerma
Covarrubias
Santo Domingo de Silos
Garganta de la Yecla
Santo Domingo de la Calzada
Belorado
Pradoluengo
Medina de Rioseco
VALLADOLID
Museo Nacional de Escultura
Simancas
Tordesillas
Medina del Campo
Castillo de la Mota
Peñafiel
Castillo de Peñafiel
Aranda de Duero
P. Nat. de las Hoces del Río Duratón
Sepúlveda
Parque Nat. de las Hoces del Río Riaza
El Burgo de Osma
San Esteban de Gormaz
Cañón del Río Lobos
Ayllón
Cuéllar
Riaza
Sierra de Ayllón
Tierra de Campos
Sierra del Urbión
E
S
P
Plymouth Portsmouth
Portsmouth
111
113
119
120

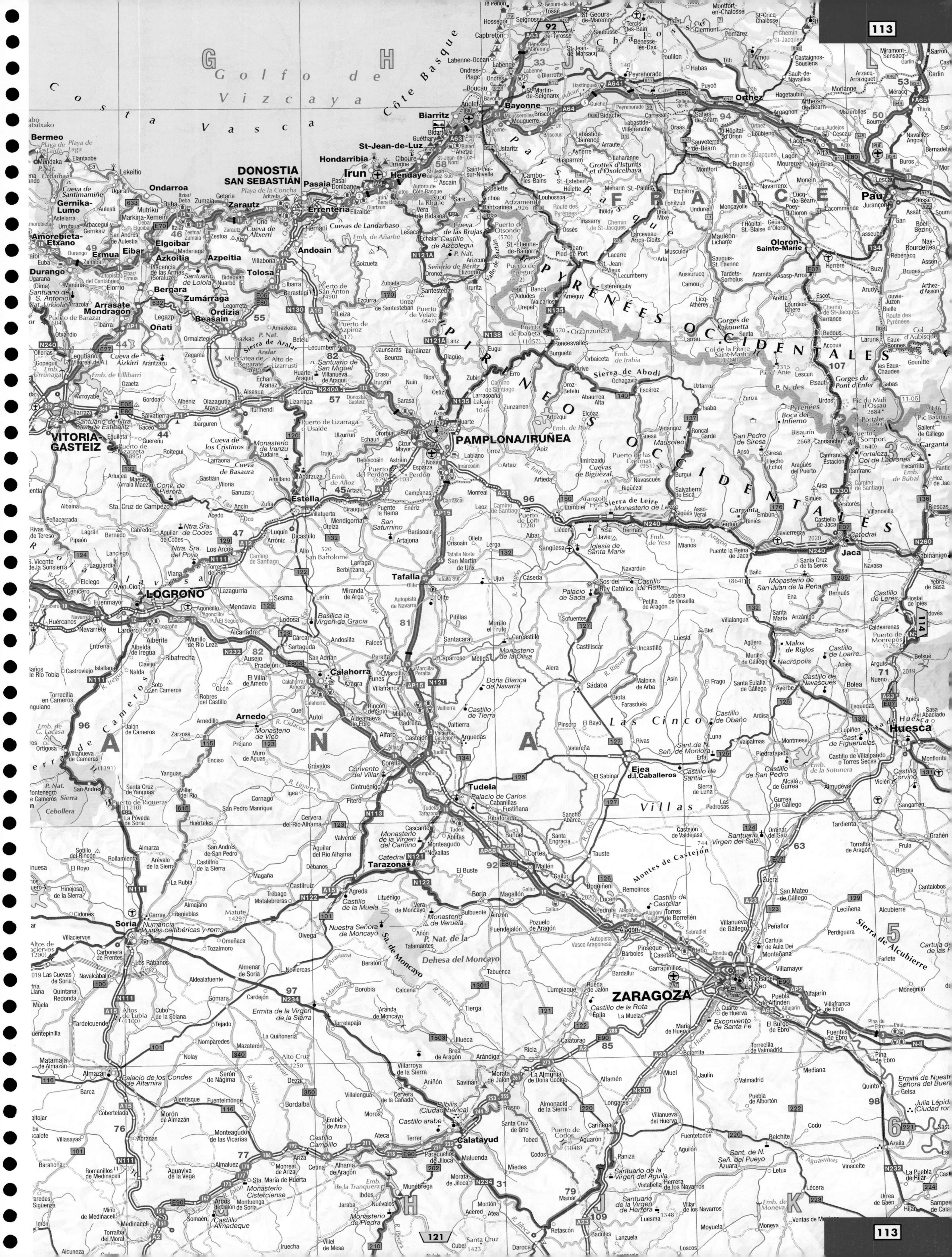
Golfo de Vizcaya
Costa Vasca
Côte Basque
Bermeo
Gernika-Lumo
Amorebieta-Etxano
Durango
Ermua
Eibar
Elgoibar
Azkoitia
Azpeitia
Zumarraga
Ordizia
Beasain
Tolosa
Ondarroa
Lekeitio
Zarautz
Getaria
Zumaia
Arrasate Mondragón
Bergara
Oñati
DONOSTIA
SAN SEBASTIÁN
Pasaia
Errenteria
Andoain
Irun
Hondarribia
Hendaye
St-Jean-de-Luz
Biarritz
Anglet
Bayonne
Capbreton
Hossegor
Labenne-Océan
Ondres-Plage
Boucau
St-Geours-de-Maremne
Peyrehorade
Orthez
Salies-de-Béarn
Sauveterre-de-Béarn
Navarrenx
Mauléon-Licharre
Oloron-Sainte-Marie
Pau
Lescar
Cambo-les-Bains
Hasparren
Espelette
St-Pée-sur-Nivelle
Ascain
Ainhoa
Sare
St-Etienne-de-Baigorry
St-Jean-Pied-de-Port
Pays Basque
FRANCE
PYRÉNÉES OCCIDENTALES
PIRINEOS OCCIDENTALES
Roncesvalles
Burguete
Orbaiceta
Sierra de Abodi
Ochagavía
Isaba
Roncal
Elizondo
Santesteban
Leitza
Lekunberri
Sierra de Aralar
Alsasua
Etxarri-Aranaz
Huarte-Araquil
VITORIA-GASTEIZ
PAMPLONA/IRUÑEA
Estella
Puente la Reina
Tafalla
Olite
Sangüesa
Lumbier
Sierra de Leire
Monasterio de Leyre
Embalse de Yesa
Jaca
Canfranc
Col du Somport
Pic du Midi d'Ossau
Sabiñánigo
Monasterio de San Juan de la Peña
Los Arcos
Viana
LOGROÑO
Navarrete
Fuenmayor
Lodosa
Calahorra
Arnedo
Alfaro
Castejón
Corella
Tudela
Cascante
Tarazona
Borja
Mallén
Alagón
Ejea d.l.Caballeros
Las Cinco Villas
Sádaba
Uncastillo
Sos del Rey Católico
Huesca
Ayerbe
Almudévar
Zuera
ZARAGOZA
Sierra de Alcubierre
Montes de Castejón
La Muela
Épila
Calatayud
Ateca
La Almunia de Doña Godina
Cariñena
Daroca
Belchite
Fuentes de Ebro
Pina de Ebro
Quinto
Soria
Numancia (Ruinas celtibéricas y rom.)
Almazán
Medinaceli
Ágreda
Olvega
Sierra de Moncayo
Dehesa del Moncayo
Monasterio de Veruela
Monasterio de Piedra
Sierra de Cameros
Sierra de la Demanda
Ariza
Alhama de Aragón
ESPAÑA

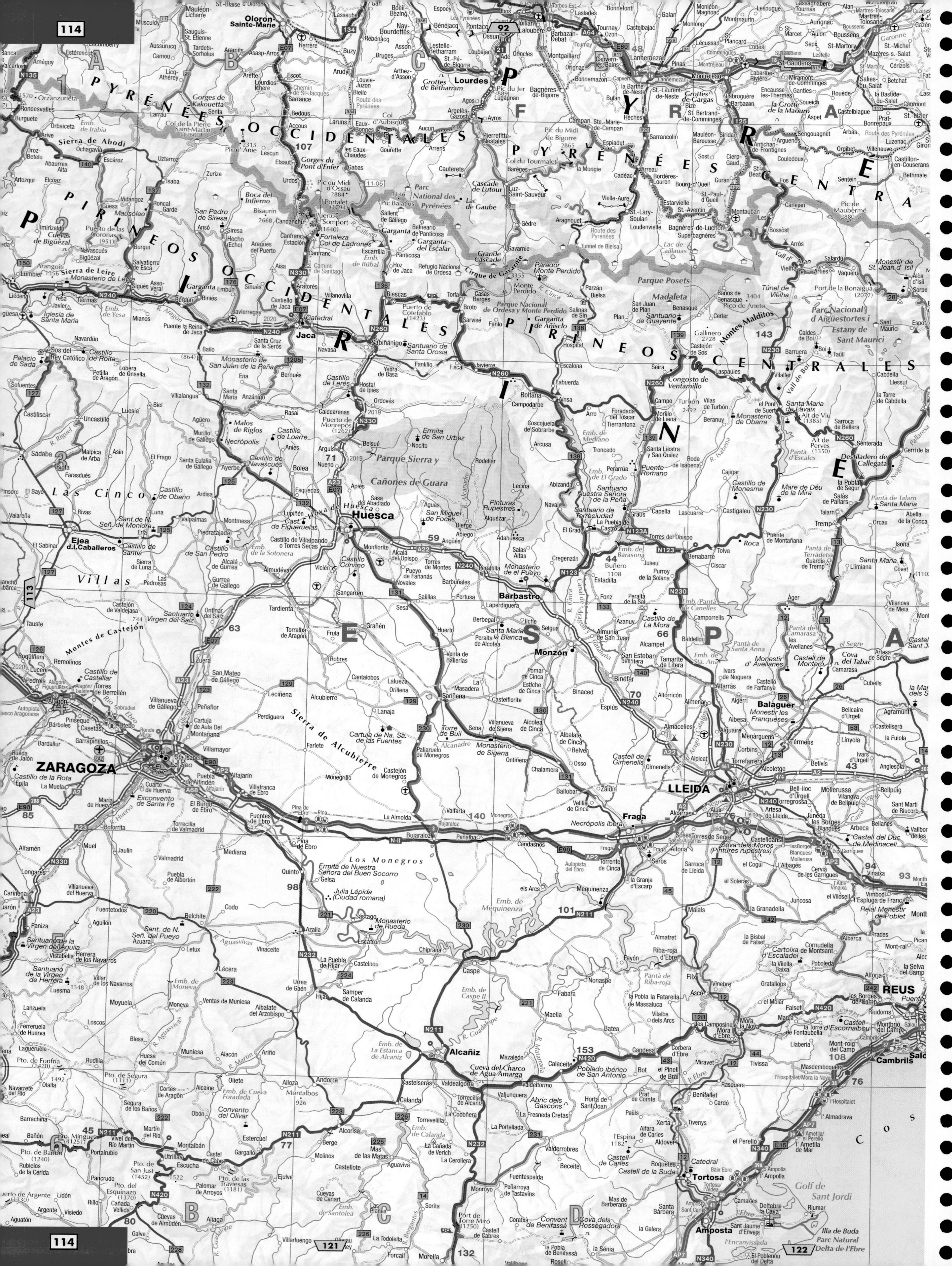
PYRÉNÉES OCCIDENTALES
PYRÉNÉES CENTRALES
PIRINEOS OCCIDENTALES
PIRINEOS CENTRALES
ESPAÑA
Oloron-Sainte-Marie
Lourdes
Bagnères-de-Bigorre
Lannemezan
St-Gaudens
Montréjeau
Bagnères-de-Luchon
Parc National des Pyrénées
Pic du Midi d'Ossau 2884
Col du Tourmalet
Cirque de Gavarnie
Monte Perdido 3355
Parque Nacional de Ordesa y Monte Perdido
Parque Posets-Madaleta
Pico de Aneto 3404
Montes Malditos
Parc Nacional d'Aigüestortes i Estany de Sant Maurici
Vielha
Jaca
Sabiñánigo
Biescas
Canfranc
Ainsa
Boltaña
Parque Sierra y Cañones de Guara
Huesca
Barbastro
Monzón
Binéfar
Tremp
Balaguer
Lleida
Fraga
Ejea d.l.Caballeros
Tauste
Montes de Castejón
ZARAGOZA
Sierra de Alcubierre
Los Monegros
Caspe
Alcañiz
Mequinenza
Emb. de Mequinenza
Flix
Mora d'Ebre
Gandesa
Tortosa
Amposta
Golf de Sant Jordi
Parc Natural Delta de l'Ebre
REUS
Cambrils
Valderrobres
Morella
Montalbán
Utrillas
Andorra
Belchite
Sierra de Abodi
Sierra de Leire
Roncesvalles
Las Cinco Villas
Monasterio de San Juan de la Peña
Monasterio de Sigena
Monasterio de Rueda
Cartuja de Aula Dei
Santuario de Torreciudad
Necrópolis ibera

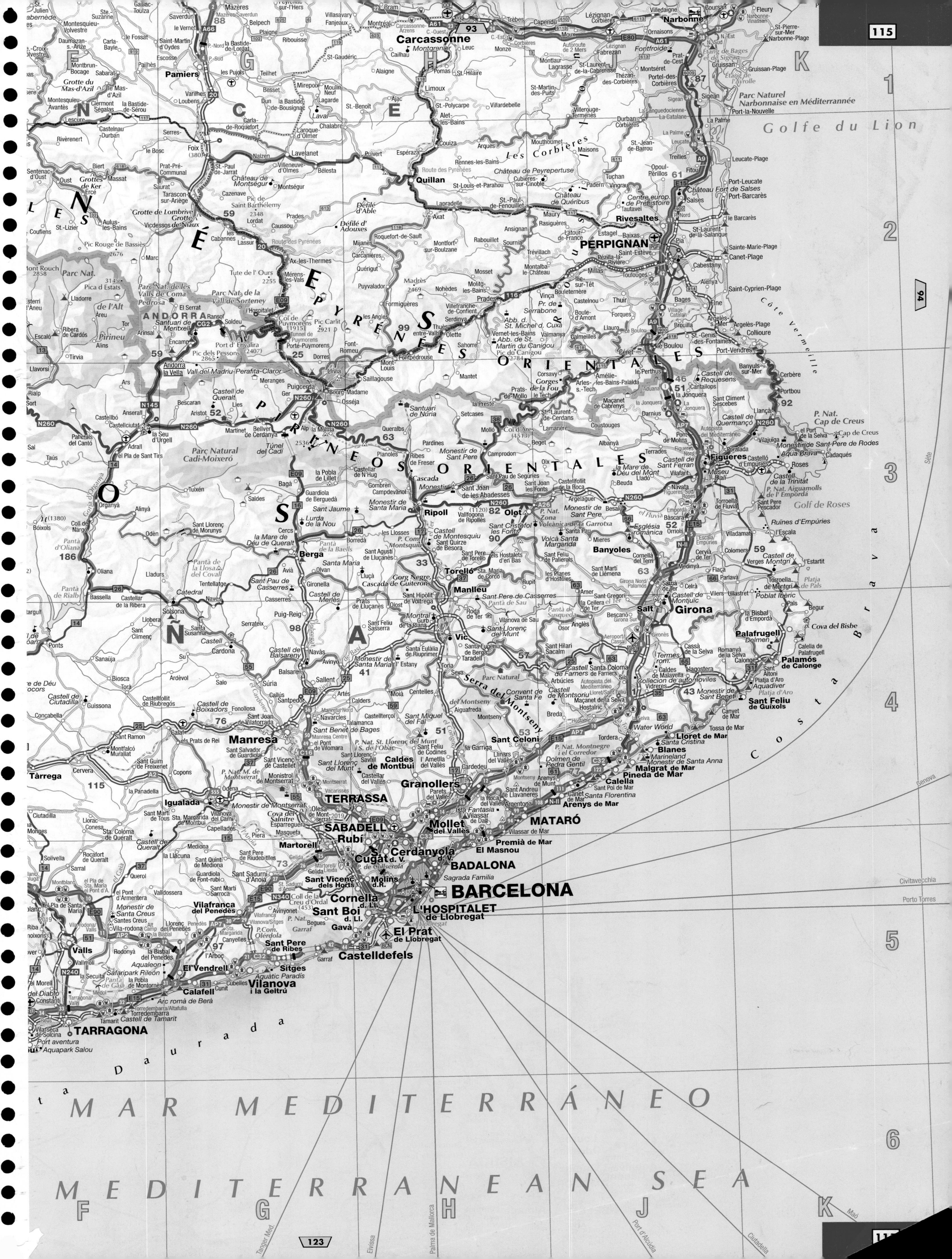

Carcassonne
Narbonne
Pamiers
Foix
Limoux
Quillan
Lavelanet
Les Corbières
Château de Peyrepertuse
Château de Montségur
Château de Quéribus
Parc Naturel Narbonnaise en Méditerranée
Golfe du Lion
Port-la-Nouvelle
Leucate-Plage
Port-Leucate
Port-Barcarès
Rivesaltes
PERPIGNAN
Canet-Plage
Saint-Cyprien-Plage
Argelès-Plage
Collioure
Port-Vendres
Banyuls-sur-Mer
Cerbère
Côte Vermeille
Prades
Font-Romeu
Mont-Louis
Bourg-Madame
Puigcerdà
Céret
Le Perthus
Amélie-les-Bains-Palalda
PYRÉNÉES ORIENTALES
PIRINEOS ORIENTALES
ANDORRA
Andorra la Vella
Encamp
Soldeu
Pas de la Casa
Parc Nat. de les Valls de Coma Pedrosa
Parc Nat. de la Vall de Sorteney
La Seu d'Urgell
Parc Natural Cadí-Moixeró
Túnel del Cadí
Organyà
Oliana
Solsona
Berga
Ripoll
Olot
Camprodon
Santuari de Núria
Figueres
Roses
Cadaqués
Llançà
Portbou
P. Nat. Cap de Creus
Golf de Roses
Castelló d'Empúries
L'Escala
Ruïnes d'Empúries
Banyoles
Girona
Torroella de Montgrí
L'Estartit
Begur
Palafrugell
Palamós
Sant Feliu de Guíxols
Lloret de Mar
Tossa de Mar
Blanes
Costa Brava
Vic
Manlleu
Torelló
Sant Celoni
Serra del Montseny
Granollers
Malgrat de Mar
Pineda de Mar
Calella
Arenys de Mar
MATARÓ
Premià de Mar
El Masnou
BADALONA
BARCELONA
Sagrada Familia
L'HOSPITALET de Llobregat
El Prat de Llobregat
Castelldefels
Sitges
Vilanova i la Geltrú
Calafell
El Vendrell
TARRAGONA
Port aventura
Aquapark Salou
Manresa
Montserrat
TERRASSA
SABADELL
Rubí
Mollet del Vallès
Cerdanyola d. V.
S. Cugat d. V.
Martorell
Igualada
Vilafranca del Penedès
Sant Boi d. Ll.
Cornellà d. Ll.
Gavà
Valls
Cervera
Tàrrega
Costa Daurada
MAR MEDITERRÁNEO
MEDITERRANEAN SEA
Génova
Civitavecchia
Porto Torres
Maó
Ciutadella
Port d'Alcúdia
Palma de Mallorca
Eivissa
Tanger Med.

93
94
123

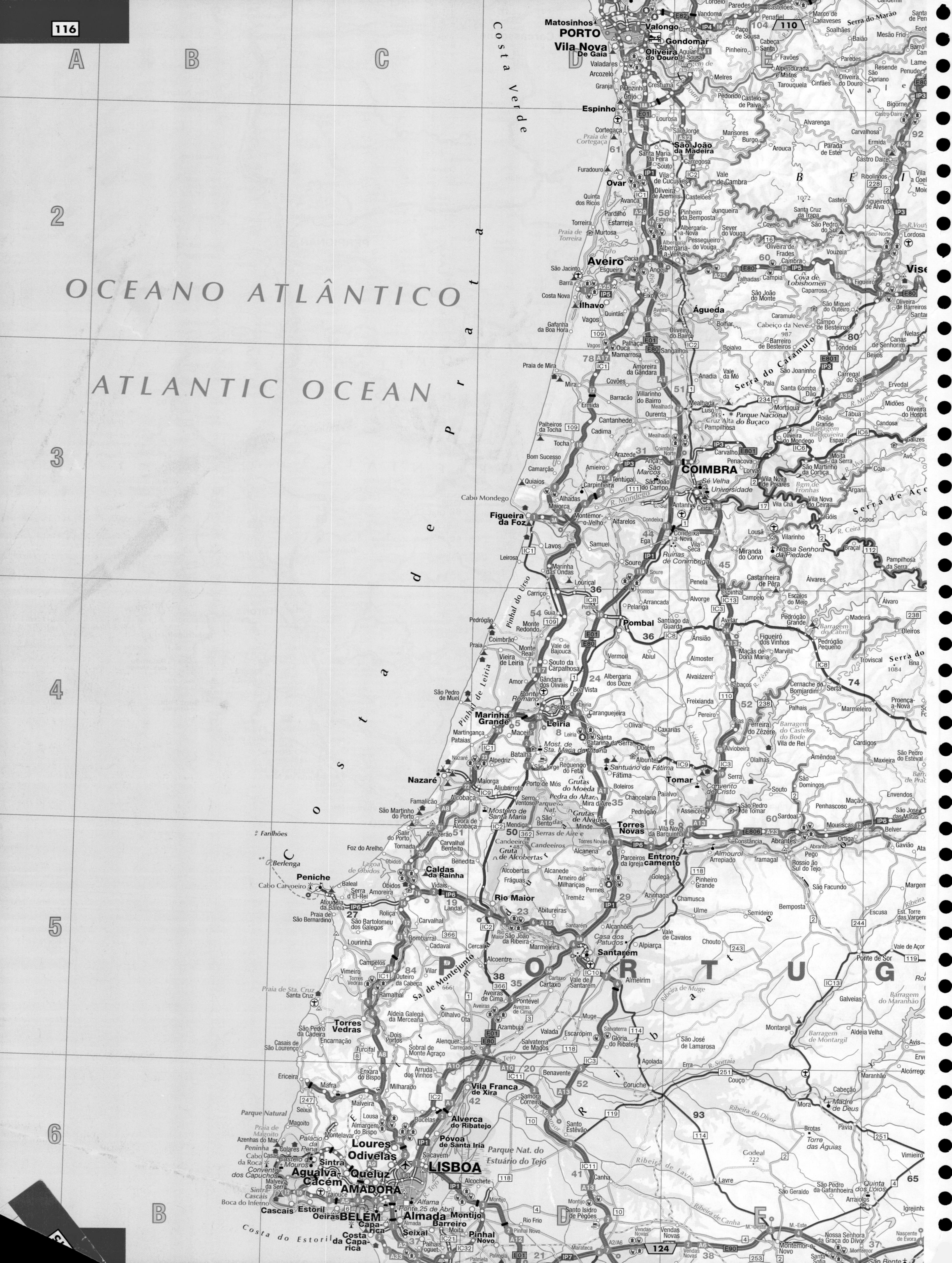

A
B
C
D
E
2
3
4
5
6
OCEANO ATLÂNTICO
ATLANTIC OCEAN
Costa Verde
Costa de Prata
Costa do Estoril
PORTUGAL
Matosinhos
PORTO
Vila Nova de Gaia
Valongo
Gondomar
Oliveira do Douro
Espinho
Cortegaça
São João da Madeira
Santa Maria da Feira
Ovar
Oliveira de Azeméis
Estarreja
Murtosa
Albergaria-a-Velha
Aveiro
Ílhavo
Vagos
Águeda
Oliveira do Bairro
Mira
Cantanhede
Mealhada
Luso
Parque Nacional do Buçaco
COIMBRA
Sé Velha
Universidade
Figueira da Foz
Cabo Mondego
Lousã
Pombal
Leiria
Marinha Grande
Pinhal de Leiria
Batalha
Fátima
Santuário de Fátima
Nazaré
Alcobaça
Tomar
Convento de Cristo
Torres Novas
Entroncamento
Abrantes
Caldas da Rainha
Óbidos
Peniche
Berlenga
Farilhões
Cabo Carvoeiro
Rio Maior
Santarém
Cartaxo
Almeirim
Azambuja
Torres Vedras
Ericeira
Mafra
Sintra
Cascais
Estoril
Oeiras
BELÉM
Amadora
Agualva-Cacém
Queluz
Loures
Odivelas
LISBOA
Almada
Barreiro
Seixal
Montijo
Alcochete
Vila Franca de Xira
Alverca do Ribatejo
Póvoa de Santa Iria
Parque Nat. do Estuário do Tejo
Benavente
Coruche
Pinhal Novo
Cabo da Roca
Serra do Caramulo
Serra de Montejunto
Serras de Aire e Candeeiros
Grutas de Alvados
Grutas da Moeda
Mosteiro de Santa Maria
Serra da Estrela
Viseu
Castelo de Paiva
Arouca
Vale de Cambra
Tondela
Vila Nova de Poiares
Penela
Ansião
Figueiró dos Vinhos
Pedrógão Grande
Sertã
Ponte de Sor
Mora
Montemor-o-Novo
Vendas Novas

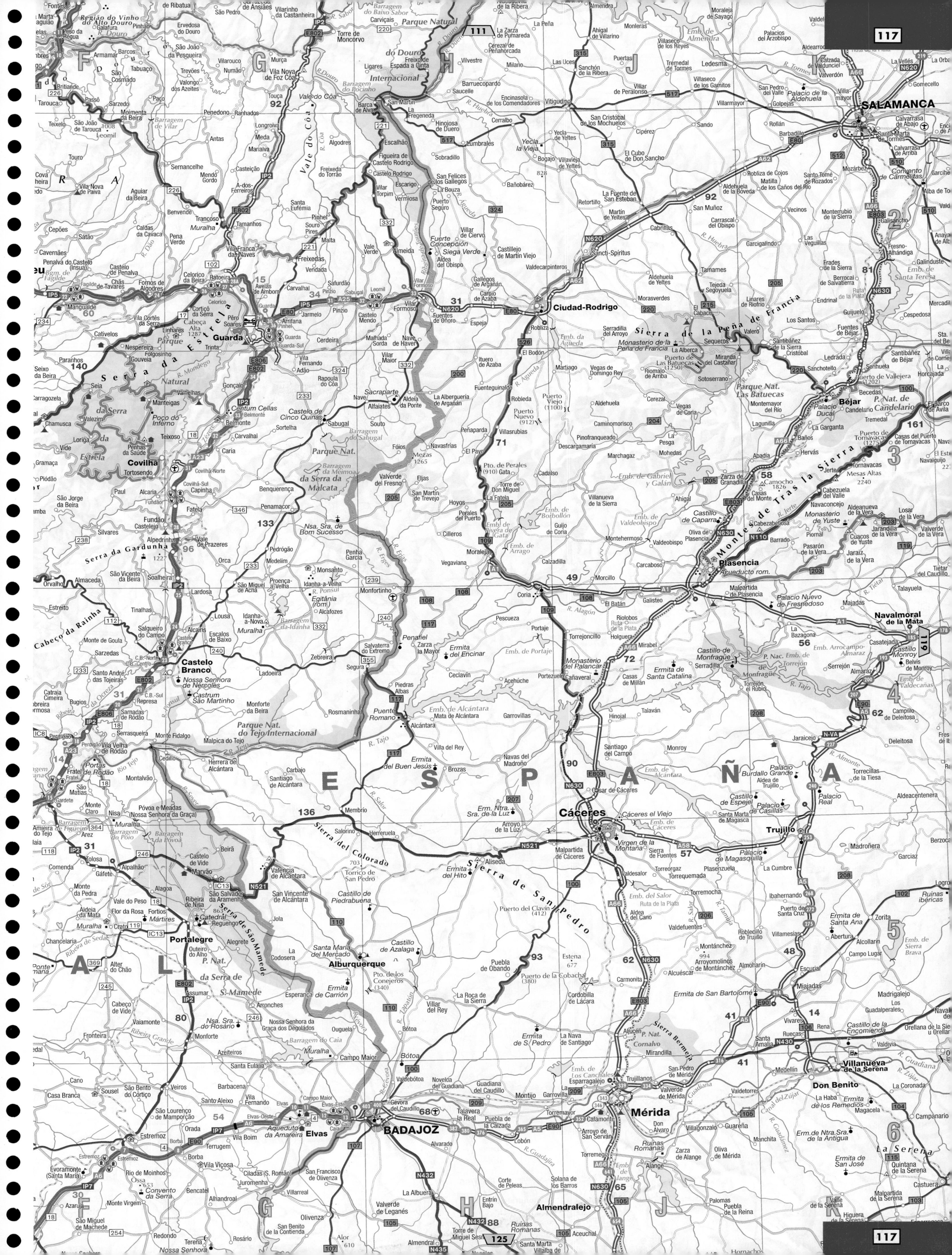

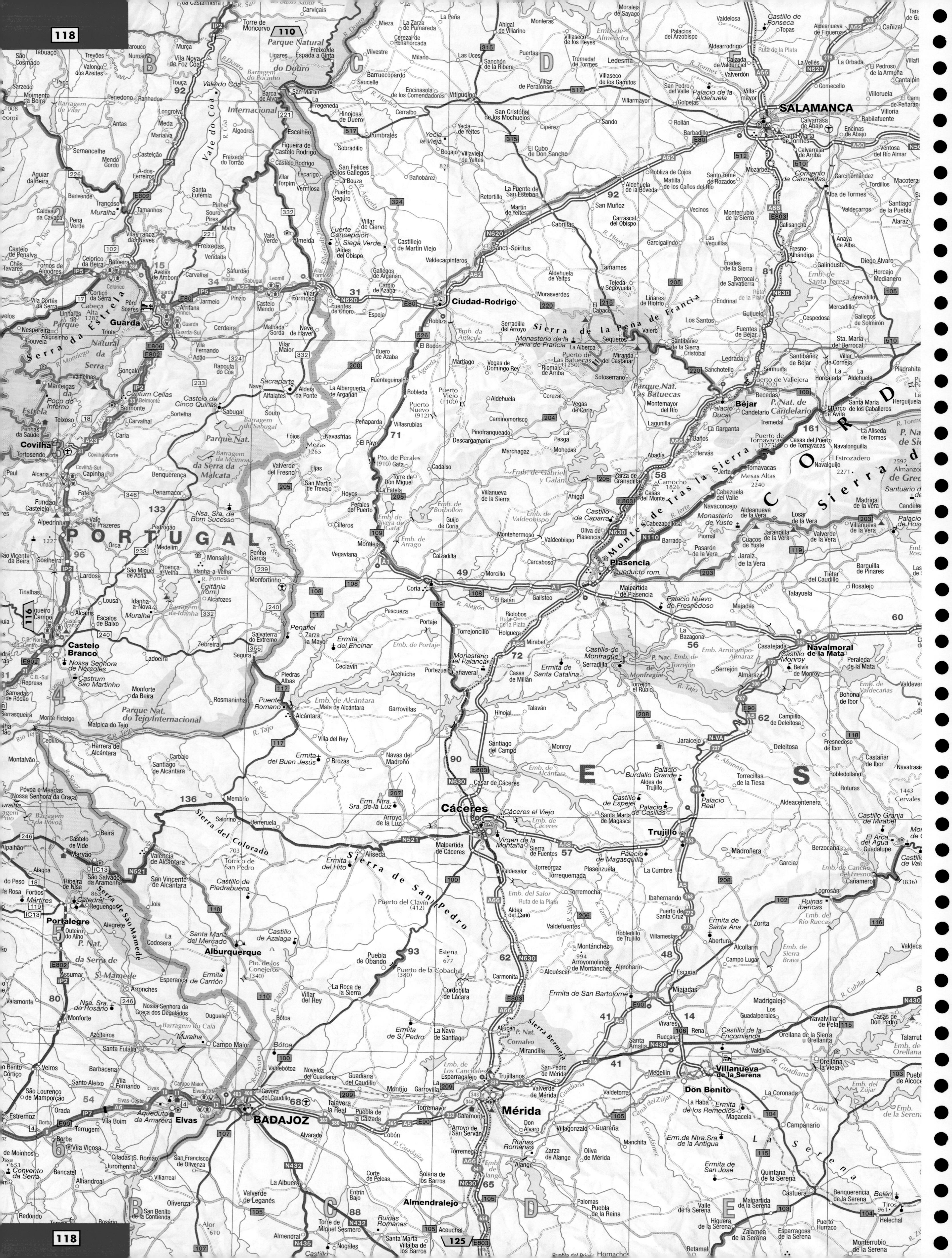
SALAMANCA
Ciudad-Rodrigo
Guarda
Covilhã
Castelo Branco
Portalegre
Elvas
BADAJOZ
Mérida
Cáceres
Trujillo
Plasencia
Béjar
Navalmoral de la Mata
Villanueva de la Serena
Don Benito
Almendralejo
Alburquerque
Miajadas
Coria
PORTUGAL
Parque Natural do Douro Internacional
Serra da Estrela
Parque Natural da Serra da Estrela
Parque Nat. da Serra da Malcata
Parque Nat. do Tejo Internacional
P. Nat. da Serra de S. Mamede
Sierra de la Peña de Francia
Parque Nat. Las Batuecas
Monte de Tras la Sierra
Sierra de Gredos
P. Nat. de Candelario
P. Nac. de Monfragüe
Sierra del Colorado
Sierra de San Pedro
Sierra Bermeja
P. Nat. Cornalvo
La Serena
Emb. de Alcántara
Emb. de Gabriel y Galán
Emb. de Valdecañas
R. Tajo
R. Guadiana
E S
C O R D

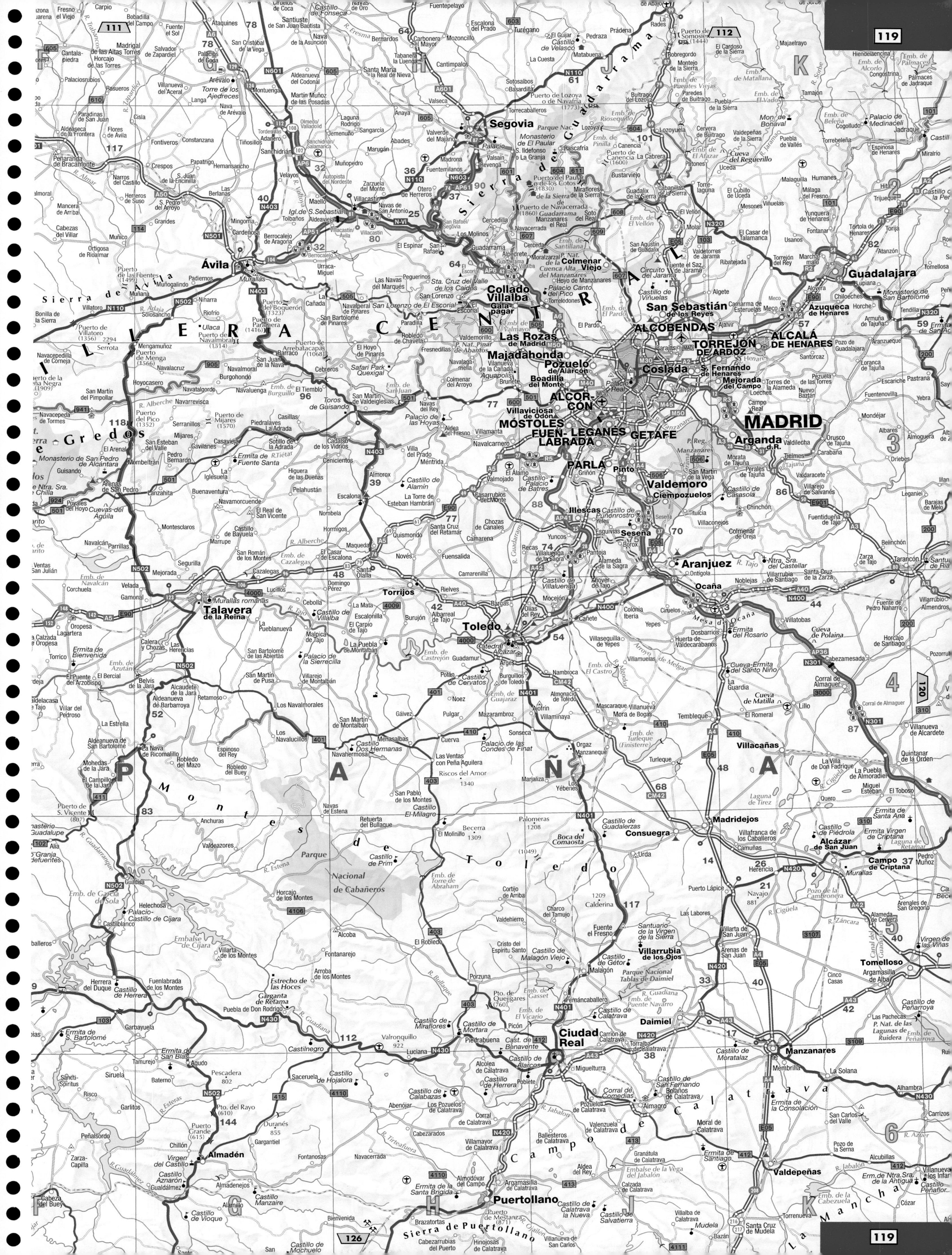
Segovia
Ávila
Sierra de Ávila
Sierra de Guadarrama
Collado Villalba
Las Rozas de Madrid
Majadahonda
Pozuelo de Alarcón
Boadilla del Monte
Alcorcón
Móstoles
Fuenlabrada
Leganés
Getafe
Parla
Pinto
Valdemoro
Ciempozuelos
Illescas
Seseña
MADRID
Alcobendas
San Sebastián de los Reyes
Torrejón de Ardoz
Coslada
Alcalá de Henares
Guadalajara
Azuqueca de Henares
Arganda
Aranjuez
Ocaña
Toledo
Torrijos
Talavera de la Reina
Sierra de Gredos
Montes de Toledo
Parque Nacional de Cabañeros
Consuegra
Madridejos
Villacañas
Alcázar de San Juan
Campo de Criptana
Tomelloso
Manzanares
Daimiel
Ciudad Real
Puertollano
Almadén
Valdepeñas
Campo de Calatrava
Sierra de Puertollano
La Mancha
Herrera del Duque
Villarrubia de los Ojos
Almagro
Miguelturra
Membrilla
La Solana

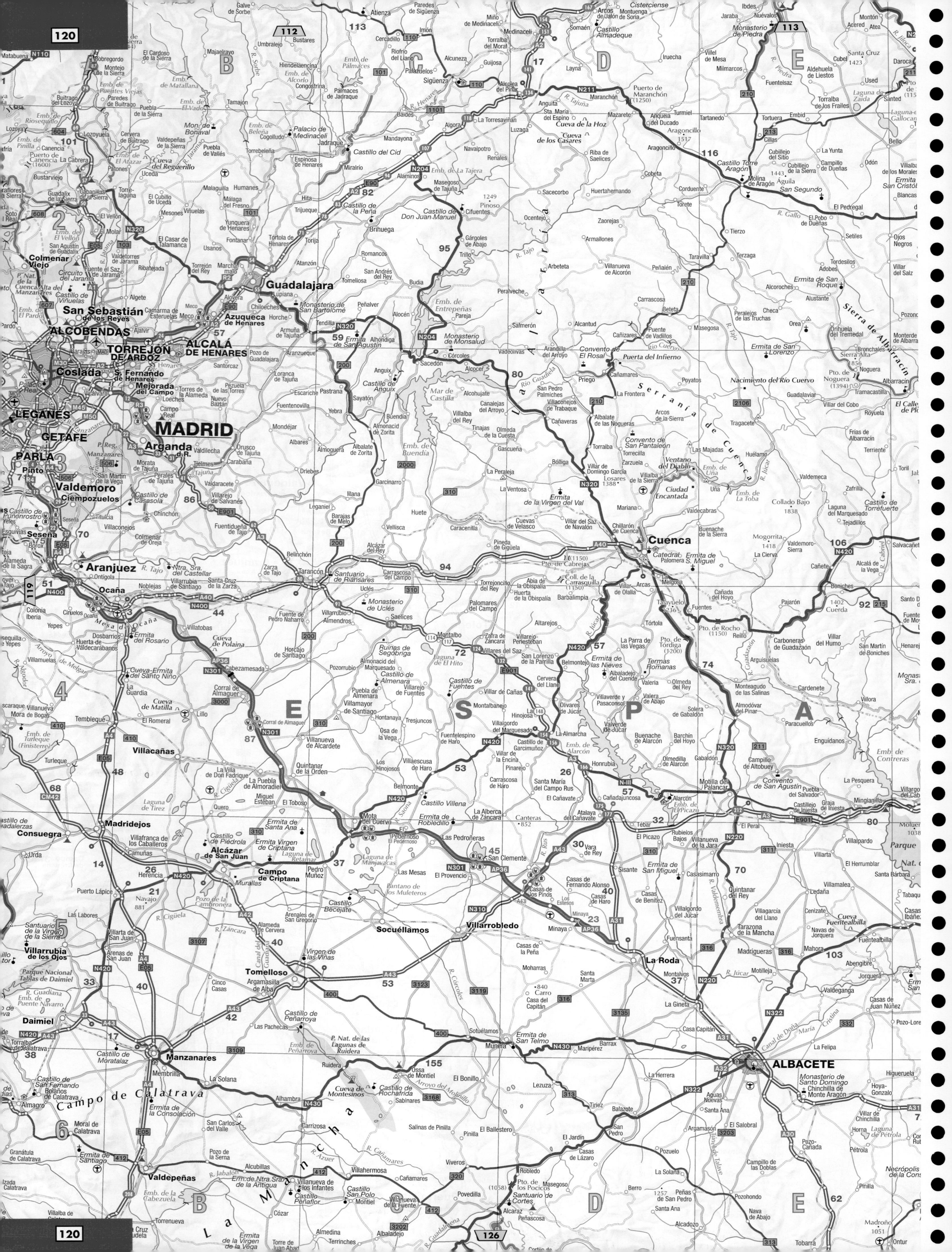
MADRID
ALCOBENDAS
San Sebastián de los Reyes
TORREJÓN DE ARDOZ
ALCALÁ DE HENARES
Coslada
LEGANÉS
GETAFE
PARLA
Pinto
Valdemoro
Ciempozuelos
Arganda
Colmenar Viejo
Aranjuez
Ocaña
Guadalajara
Azuqueca de Henares
Sigüenza
Atienza
Medinaceli
Molina de Aragón
Brihuega
Cifuentes
Sacedón
Pastrana
Huete
Tarancón
Cuenca
Ciudad Encantada
Serranía de Cuenca
Sierra de Albarracín
La Alcarria
Motilla del Palancar
Honrubia
Belmonte
Mota del Cuervo
San Clemente
Quintanar de la Orden
Madridejos
Consuegra
Villacañas
Alcázar de San Juan
Campo de Criptana
Pedro Muñoz
Las Pedroñeras
Socuéllamos
Villarrobledo
La Roda
Tomelloso
Argamasilla de Alba
Daimiel
Manzanares
Membrilla
La Solana
Villarrubia de los Ojos
Parque Nacional Tablas de Daimiel
P. Nat. de las Lagunas de Ruidera
Ruidera
Ossa de Montiel
Munera
Valdepeñas
Almagro
Campo de Calatrava
La Mancha
ALBACETE
Chinchilla de Monte Aragón
Tarazona de la Mancha
Quintanar del Rey
Madrigueras
Alcaraz
Villanueva de los Infantes
Emb. de Entrepeñas
Emb. de Buendía
Emb. de Alarcón
Emb. de Contreras
E S P A
A3
A4
A31
A40
A43
AP36
N320
N420
N301
N430
N211
N204
N322
N400
E90
E901
E05

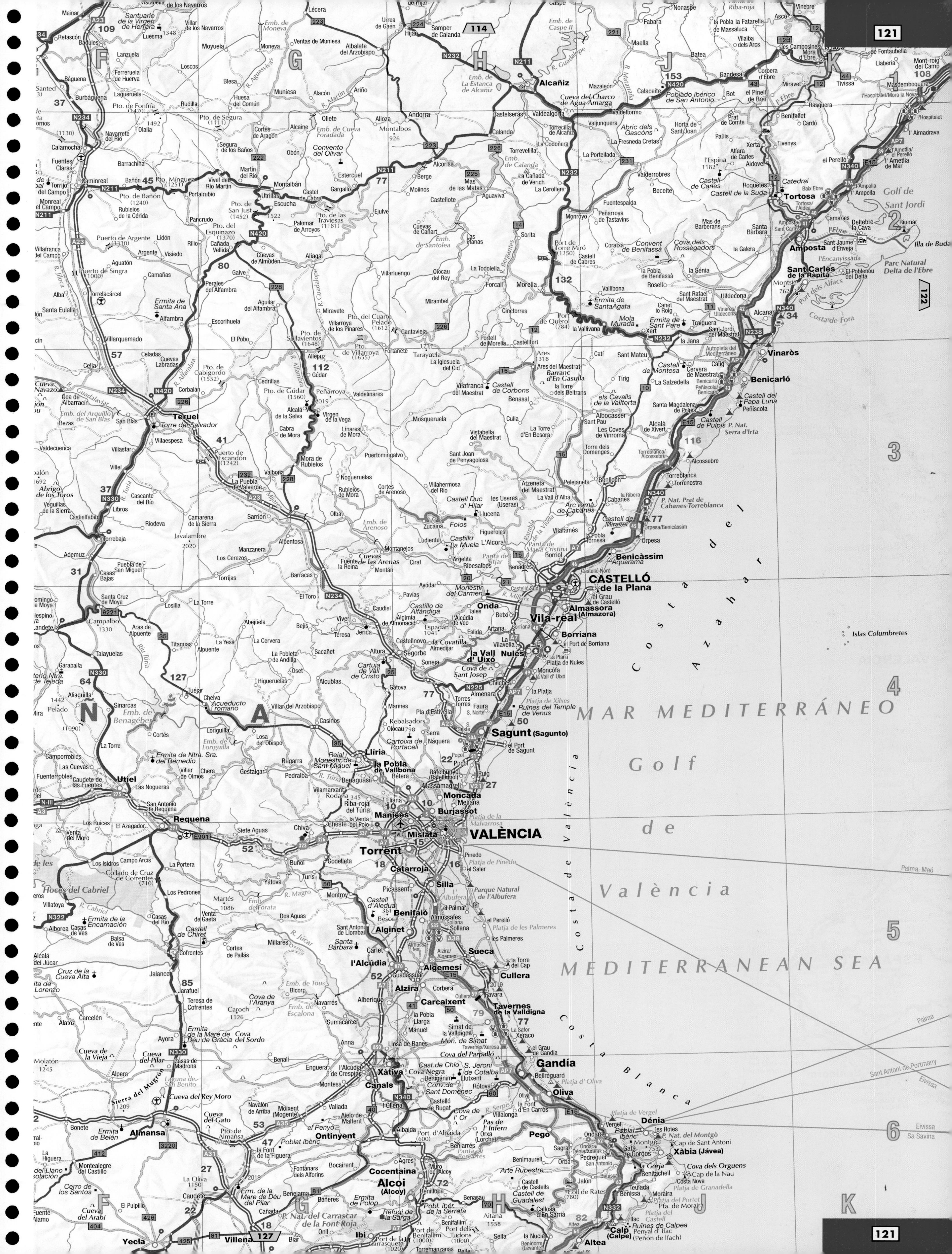
MAR MEDITERRÁNEO
Golf de València
MEDITERRANEAN SEA
Costa del Azahar
Costa de València
Costa Blanca
Golf de Sant Jordi
Parc Natural Delta de l'Ebre
Islas Columbretes
VALÈNCIA
CASTELLÓ de la Plana
Teruel
Alcañiz
Tortosa
Amposta
Vinaròs
Benicarló
Morella
Vila-real
Sagunt (Sagunto)
Torrent
Gandía
Xàtiva
Alcoi (Alcoy)
Dénia
Xàbia (Jávea)
Calp (Calpe)
Altea
Requena
Utiel
Almansa
Villena
Yecla
Ontinyent
Sueca
Cullera
Alzira
Algemesí
Oliva
Llíria
Burjassot
Manises
Mislata
Nules
Borriana
Onda
Benicàssim
Segorbe
Sant Carles de la Ràpita
Caspe
Pto. de Singra
Ermita de Santa Ana
Torre del Salvador
Cova del Sordo
Cueva del Rey Moro
Hoces del Cabriel
Palma, Maó
Palma
Sant Antoni de Portmany
Eivissa
Sa Savina
122
114
127

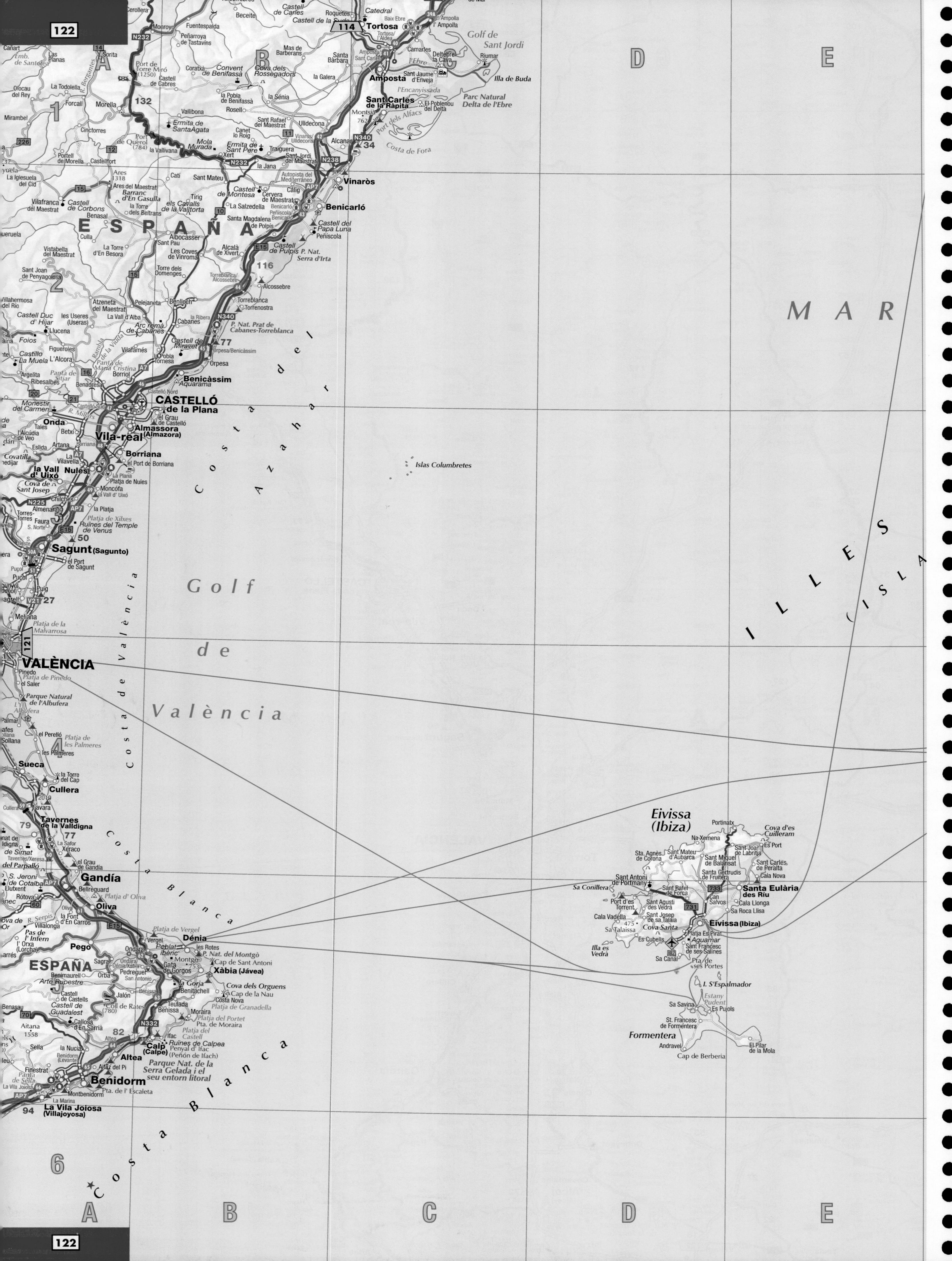
MAR
ILLES
(ISLA
Golf de València
Costa del Azahar
Costa de València
Costa Blanca
ESPAÑA
Islas Columbretes
Golf de Sant Jordi
Parc Natural Delta de l'Ebre
Illa de Buda
Costa de Fora
Tortosa
Amposta
Sant Carles de la Ràpita
Vinaròs
Benicarló
Peñíscola
Alcossebre
Torreblanca
Orpesa
Benicàssim
CASTELLÓ de la Plana
Vila-real
Almassora (Almazora)
Borriana
Nules
la Vall d' Uixó
Onda
Sagunt (Sagunto)
VALÈNCIA
Parque Natural de l'Albufera
Sueca
Cullera
Tavernes de la Valldigna
Gandía
Oliva
Pego
Dénia
Xàbia (Jávea)
Calp (Calpe)
Altea
Benidorm
La Vila Joiosa (Villajoyosa)
Morella
Sant Mateu
Eivissa (Ibiza)
Sant Antoni de Portmany
Santa Eulària des Riu
Sant Josep de sa Talaia
Eivissa (Ibiza)
Formentera
Sant Francesc de Formentera
Cap de Berberia
El Pilar de la Mola
I. S'Espalmador
Portinatx
Sant Joan de Labritja
Sant Miquel de Balansat
Illa es Vedrà
A
B
C
D
E
1
2
3
4
6

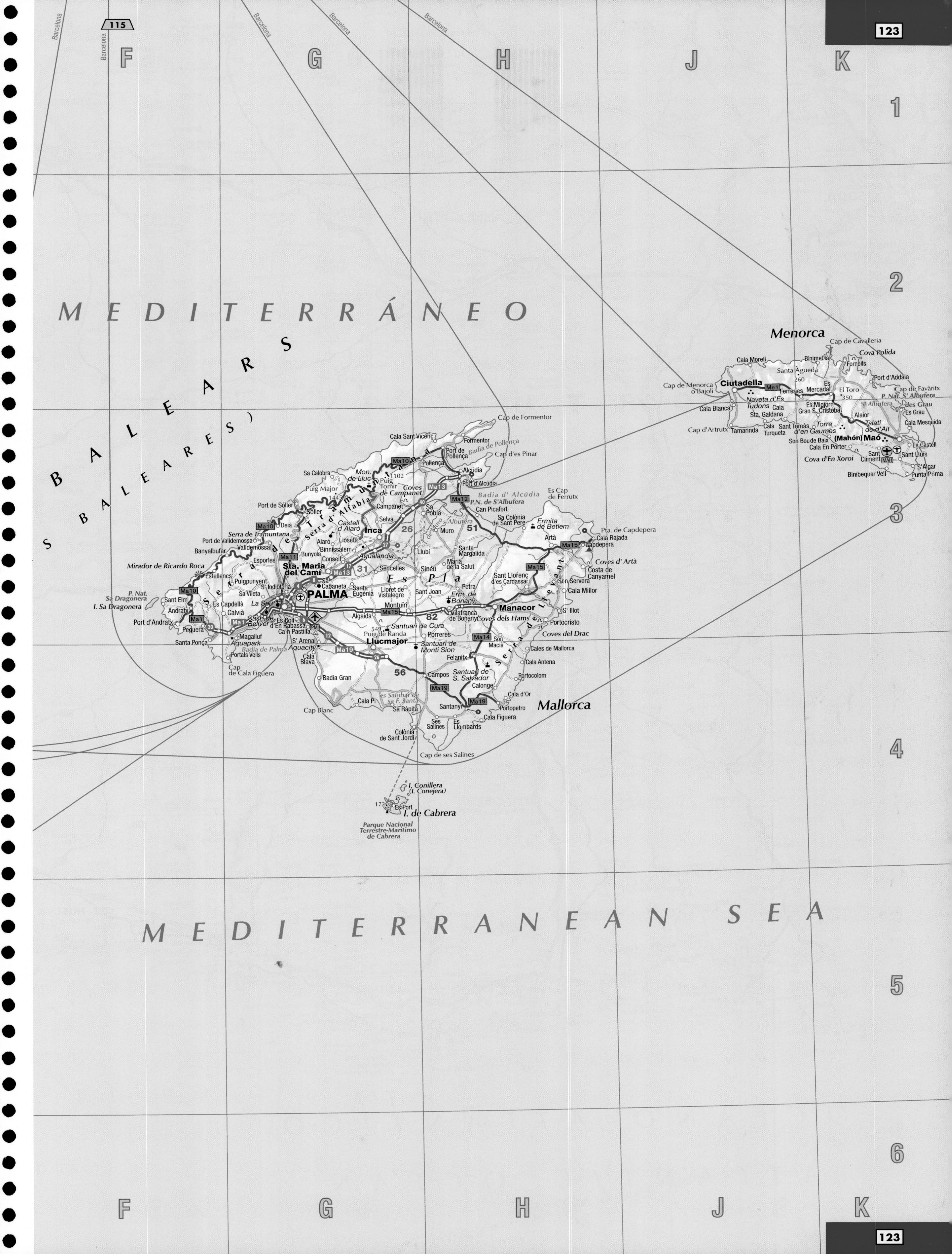

F　　　　　G　　　　　H　　　　　J　　　　　K

1

2

MEDITERRÁNEO

Menorca

B A L E A R S

(B A L E A R E S)

Cap de Cavalleria
Cova Polida
Cala Morell　Binimel·la　Fornells
Santa Agueda　　Port d'Addaia
Cap de Menorca　Ciutadella　260　Es　S'Albufera
o Bajoli　Ferreries Mercadal　El Toro　P. Nat. S'Albufera
Cala Blanca　Naveta d'Es　350　des Grau
Tudons　Cala　Gran S. Cristóbal　Alaior　Es Grau
Cap d'Artrutx　Tamarinda　Sant Tomàs　Torre　Talatí　Cala Mesquida
Son Boude Baix　d'en Gaumes　de d'Alt
Cala En Pòrter　(Mahón) Maó
Binibequer Vell　Sant　S'Algar
Cova d'En Xoroi　Climent　Sant Lluís
Punta Prima

3

Cap de Formentor
Cala Sant Vicenç　Formentor
Sa Calobra　Mon.　Port de　Badia de Pollença
de Lluc　Puig　Pollença　Cap d'es Pinar
Puig Major　Tomir　Coves　Pollença
1102　de Campanet　Alcúdia
Port de Sóller　Sóller　Ma13　Port d'Alcúdia
Deià　Campanet　Badia d'Alcúdia　Es Cap
Ma10　Castell　Selva　Sa　Ma12　P.N. de S'Albufera　de Ferrutx
Port de Valldemossa　d'Alaró　Inca　26　Pobla　Can Picafort
Banyalbufar　Alaró　Lloseta　Muro　51　Sa Colònia　Ermita　Pta. de Capdepera
Valldemossa　Binissalem　de Sant Pere　de Betlem　Cala Rajada
Mirador de Ricardo Roca　Bunyola　Aigualandia　Llubí　Artà　Ma15　Capdepera
Esporles　Consell　Santa　Coves d'Artà
Puigpunyent　Santa Maria　Ma13　Sencelles　Margalida　Costa de
P. Nat.　Estellencs　del Camí　31　Sineu　Maria　Son Servera　Canyamel
Sa Dragonera　Ma11　Sa Cabaneta　Santa　Lloret de　de la Salut　Ma15
I. Sa Dragonera　S'Indioteria　Eugènia　Vistalegre　Petra　Sant Llorenç　Cala Millor
Sant Elm　Es Capdellà　PALMA　Montuïri　Sant Joan　Erm. de　des Cardassar　S' Illot
Andratx　La Seu　Bonany
Port d'Andratx　Ma1　Calvià　Aigaida　Ma15　82　Vilafranca　Manacor　Portocristo
Peguera　Ma1　Es Coll　Puig de Randa　Porreres　de Bonany　Coves dels Hams　Coves del Drac
Magaluf　Ca'n Pastilla　Llucmajor　541　Santuari de Cura　Son　Cales de Mallorca
Santa Ponça　Aquapark　S' Arenal　Santuari de　Macià
Portals Vells　Badia de Palma　Aquacity　Ma19　Monti Sion　Felanitx　Cala Antena
Cala　Santuari de S. Salvador　Portocolom
Cap　Blava　56　Campos　Calonge
de Cala Figuera　Badia Gran　Cala d'Or
Cala Pi　Ma19　Santanyí　Portopetro
Es Salobar de　Sa Ràpita　Ma19　Mallorca
sa F. Santa　Ses　Es　Cala Figuera
Salines　Llombards
Cap Blanc　Colònia
de Sant Jordi

4

I. Conillera
(I. Conejera)
172　Es Port　I. de Cabrera
Parque Nacional
Terrestre-Marítimo
de Cabrera

MEDITERRANEAN SEA

5

6

F　　　　　G　　　　　H　　　　　J　　　　　K

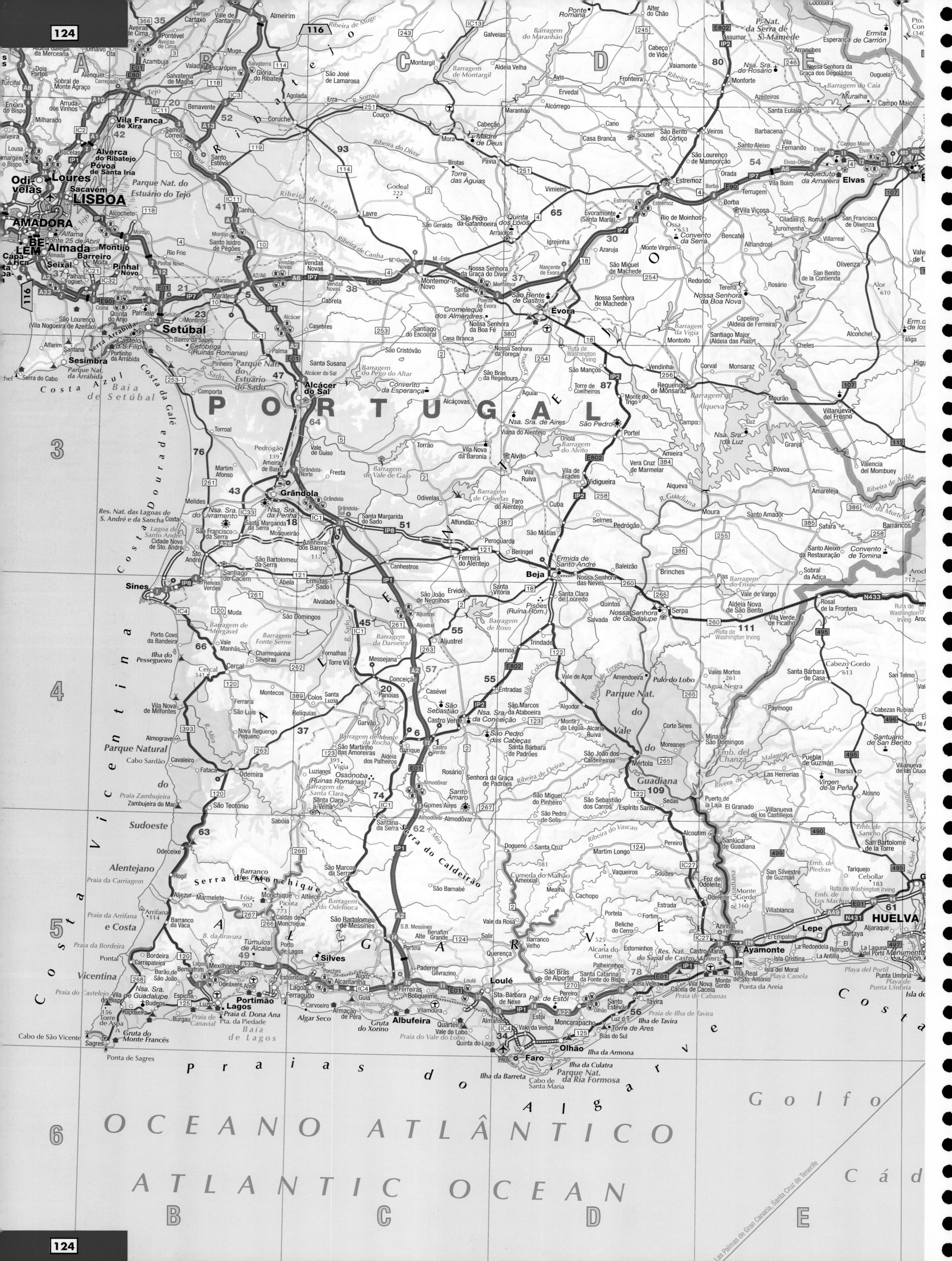
PORTUGAL
OCEANO ATLÂNTICO
ATLANTIC OCEAN
Golfo
Cád
Costa Azul
Baía de Setúbal
Costa da Galé
Costa Dourada
Costa Vicentina
Costa Vicentina
Parque Natural do Sudoeste Alentejano e Costa Vicentina
Praias do Algarve
Costa
Ribatejo
Alentejo
Algarve
Parque Nat. do Vale do Guadiana
Parque Nat. do Estuário do Tejo
Parque Nat. do Estuário do Sado
Parque Nat. da Ria Formosa
Serra de Monchique
Serra do Caldeirão
LISBOA
Loures
Odivelas
AMADORA
Almada
Barreiro
Seixal
Montijo
Sacavém
Vila Franca de Xira
Setúbal
Sesimbra
Palmela
Alcácer do Sal
Grândola
Sines
Santiago do Cacém
Évora
Estremoz
Elvas
Beja
Serpa
Moura
Mértola
Odemira
Aljustrel
Castro Verde
Almodôvar
Lagos
Portimão
Silves
Albufeira
Loulé
Faro
Olhão
Tavira
Ayamonte
HUELVA
Lepe
Sagres
Cabo de São Vicente
Ponta de Sagres
Cabo de Santa Maria
Montemor-o-Novo
Vendas Novas
Coruche
Benavente
Almeirim
Reguengos de Monsaraz
Vidigueira
Cuba
Ferreira do Alentejo
Monchique
Vila Real de Sto. António
Olivenza
A

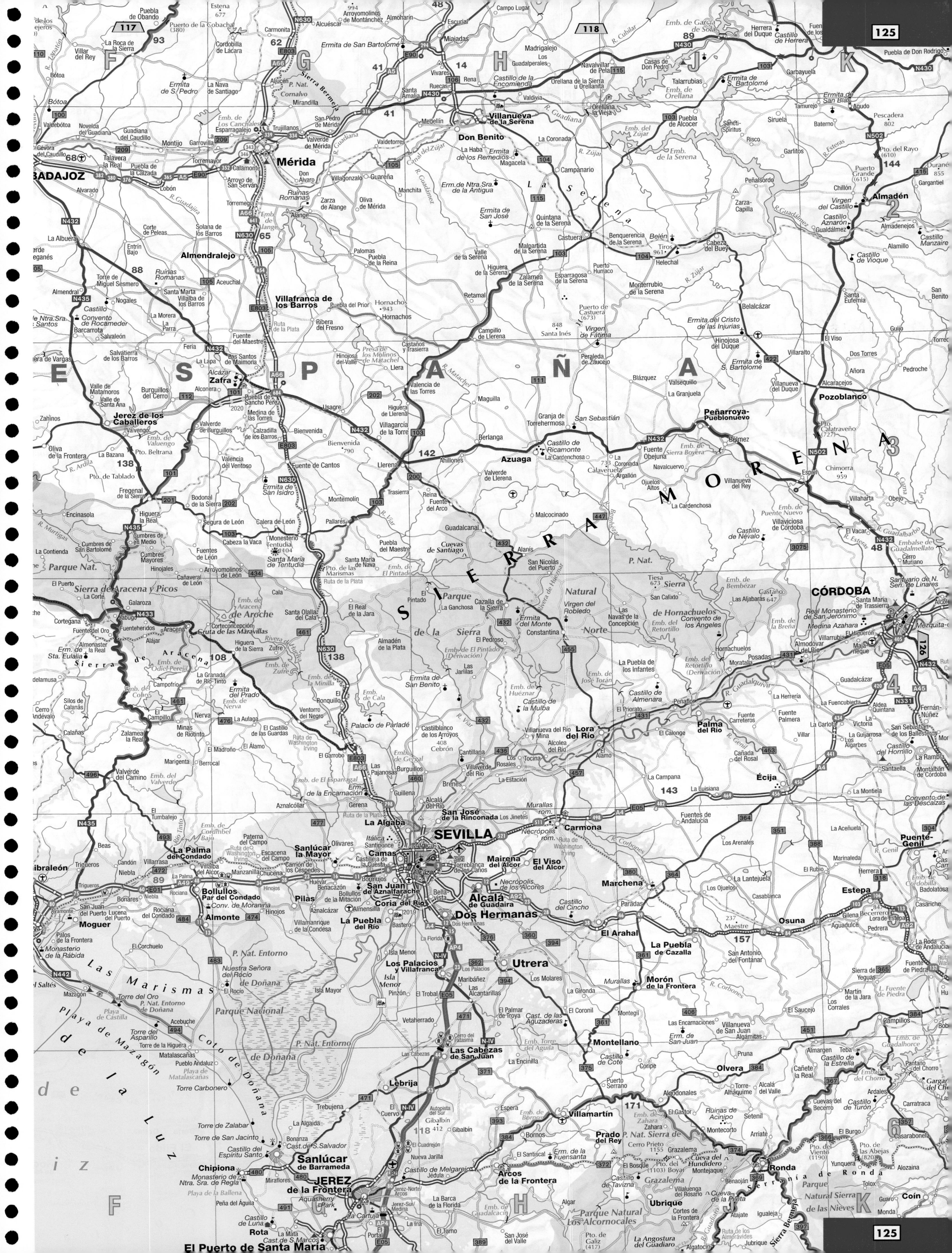

E S P A Ñ A
S I E R R A   M O R E N A
BADAJOZ
Mérida
Don Benito
Villanueva de la Serena
Almendralejo
Villafranca de los Barros
Zafra
Jerez de los Caballeros
Fregenal de la Sierra
Llerena
Azuaga
Peñarroya-Pueblonuevo
Pozoblanco
Almadén
CÓRDOBA
Lora del Río
Palma del Río
Écija
Carmona
SEVILLA
La Algaba
Camas
Sanlúcar la Mayor
Alcalá de Guadaira
Dos Hermanas
Coria del Río
La Puebla del Río
Utrera
Los Palacios y Villafranca
Marchena
El Arahal
La Puebla de Cazalla
Osuna
Estepa
Morón de la Frontera
Montellano
Las Cabezas de San Juan
Lebrija
Olvera
Villamartín
Prado del Rey
Arcos de la Frontera
Ubrique
Grazalema
Ronda
Sanlúcar de Barrameda
Chipiona
Rota
JEREZ de la Frontera
El Puerto de Santa María
Moguer
Almonte
Bollullos Par del Condado
La Palma del Condado
Parque Nacional de Doñana
Coto de Doñana
Las Marismas
Playa de Mazagón
de la Luz
Sierra de Aracena y Picos
Parque Natural Sierra de Hornachuelos
Parque Natural de la Sierra Norte
La Serena
Sierra de Grazalema
Parque Natural Los Alcornocales
Parque Natural Sierra de las Nieves
Serranía de Ronda
Río Guadalquivir
Río Guadiana
Puente-Genil
Constantina
Cazalla de la Sierra
Aracena
Castuera
Cabeza del Buey

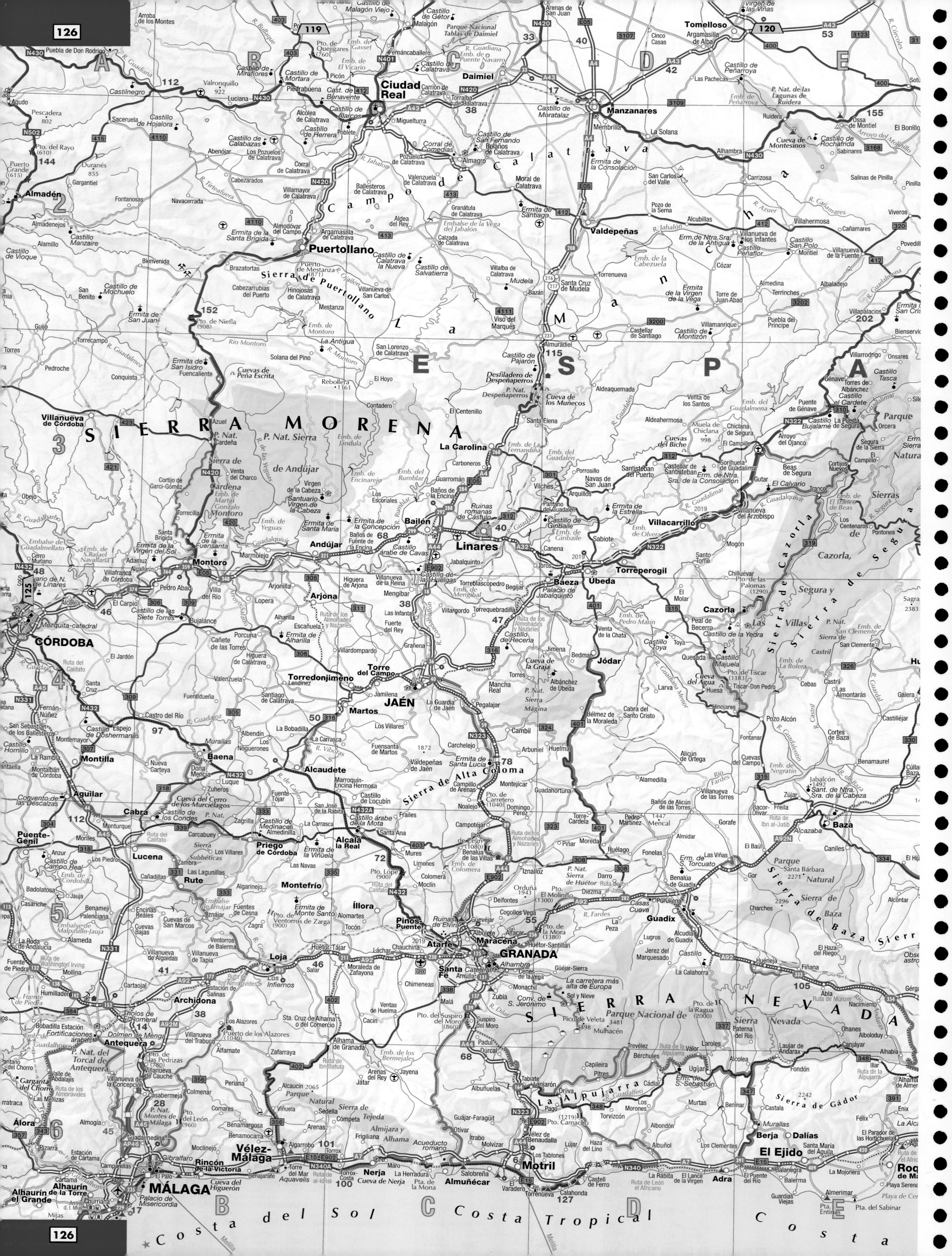

Ciudad Real
Daimiel
Tomelloso
Manzanares
Almadén
Puertollano
Valdepeñas
Campo de Calatrava
La Mancha
Sierra de Puertollano
ESPAÑA
SIERRA MORENA
P. Nat. Despeñaperros
Desfiladero de Despeñaperros
P. Nat. Sierra de Andújar
Sierra de Cardeña
La Carolina
Bailén
Linares
Andújar
Montoro
Villanueva de Córdoba
CÓRDOBA
Baeza
Úbeda
Torreperogil
Villacarrillo
Cazorla
Sierra de Cazorla
Segura y Las Villas
Sierra de Segura
Jódar
Arjona
Martos
JAÉN
Torredonjimeno
Alcaudete
Baena
Montilla
Aguilar
Cabra
Lucena
Rute
Priego de Córdoba
Alcalá la Real
Sierra de Alta Coloma
Sierra Mágina
Montefrío
Íllora
Loja
Pinos-Puente
Atarfe
Maracena
GRANADA
Santa Fe
Guadix
Baza
Huéscar
Sierra de Baza
SIERRA NEVADA
Parque Nacional de Sierra Nevada
Pico de Veleta 3398
Mulhacén 3481
La Alpujarra
Sierra de Gádor
Archidona
Antequera
P. Nat. del Torcal de Antequera
Sierra de Tejeda
Almijara y Alhama
Vélez-Málaga
Rincón de la Victoria
MÁLAGA
Nerja
Almuñécar
Salobreña
Motril
Adra
Berja
Dalías
El Ejido
Costa del Sol
Costa Tropical

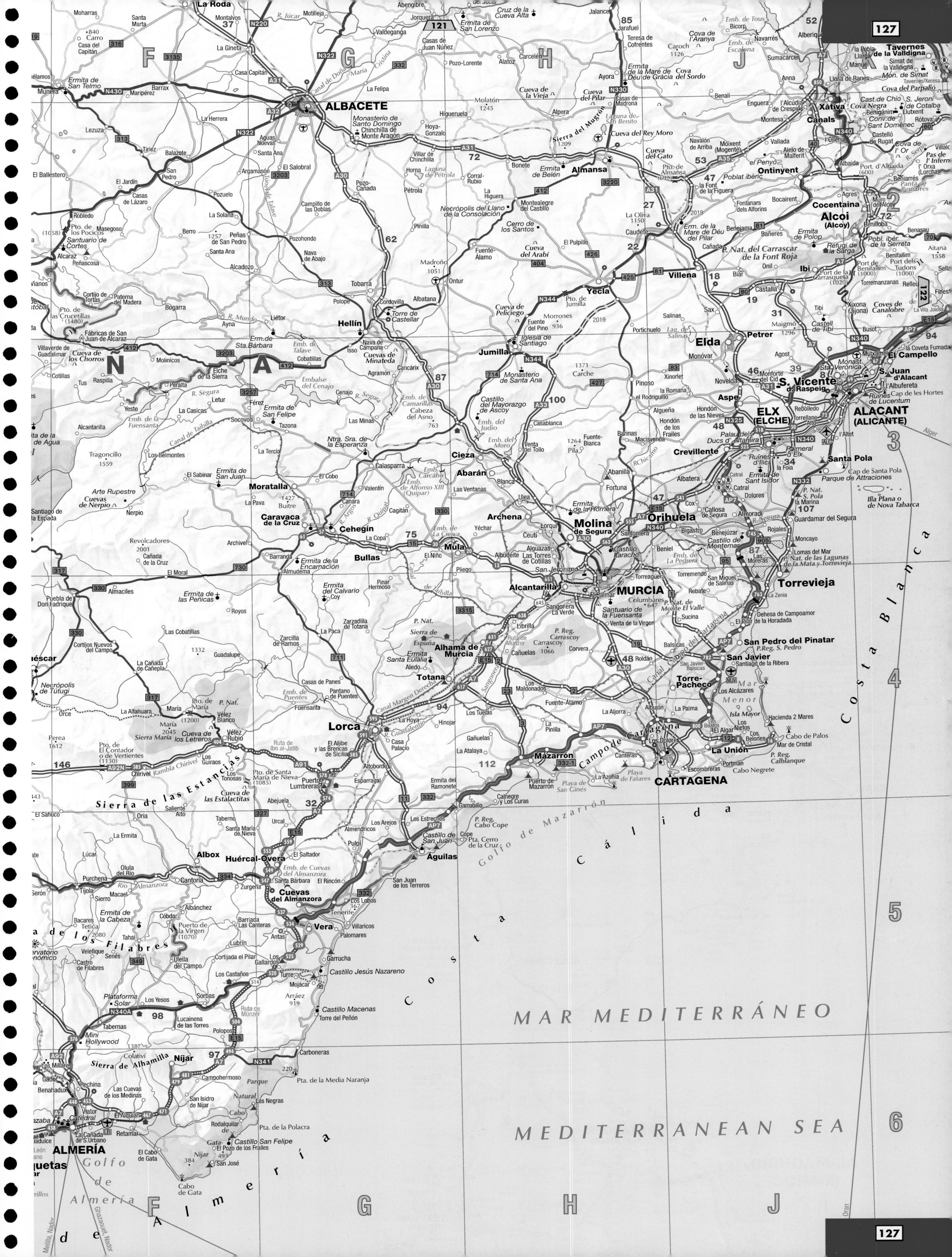
ALBACETE
La Roda
Hellín
Tobarra
Jumilla
Yecla
Almansa
Villena
Elda
Petrer
Ontinyent
Xàtiva
Canals
Alcoi (Alcoy)
Cocentaina
Ibi
El Campello
S. Vicente del Raspeig
ALACANT (ALICANTE)
ELX (ELCHE)
Santa Pola
Crevillente
Aspe
Novelda
Orihuela
Torrevieja
Guardamar del Segura
San Pedro del Pinatar
San Javier
Torre-Pacheco
La Unión
CARTAGENA
Mazarrón
Águilas
MURCIA
Molina de Segura
Alcantarilla
Archena
Cieza
Abarán
Mula
Bullas
Cehegín
Caravaca de la Cruz
Moratalla
Alhama de Murcia
Totana
Lorca
Puerto Lumbreras
Huércal-Overa
Cuevas del Almanzora
Vera
Albox
Níjar
ALMERÍA
Mini Hollywood
Plataforma Solar
Sierra de las Estancias
Sierra de Alhamilla
Sierra de los Filabres
Sierra María
Mar Menor
Cabo de Palos
Cabo de Gata
Golfo de Mazarrón
Golfo de Almería
Costa Cálida
Costa Blanca
Costa de Almería
MAR MEDITERRÁNEO
MEDITERRANEAN SEA
F G H J
2 3 4 5 6

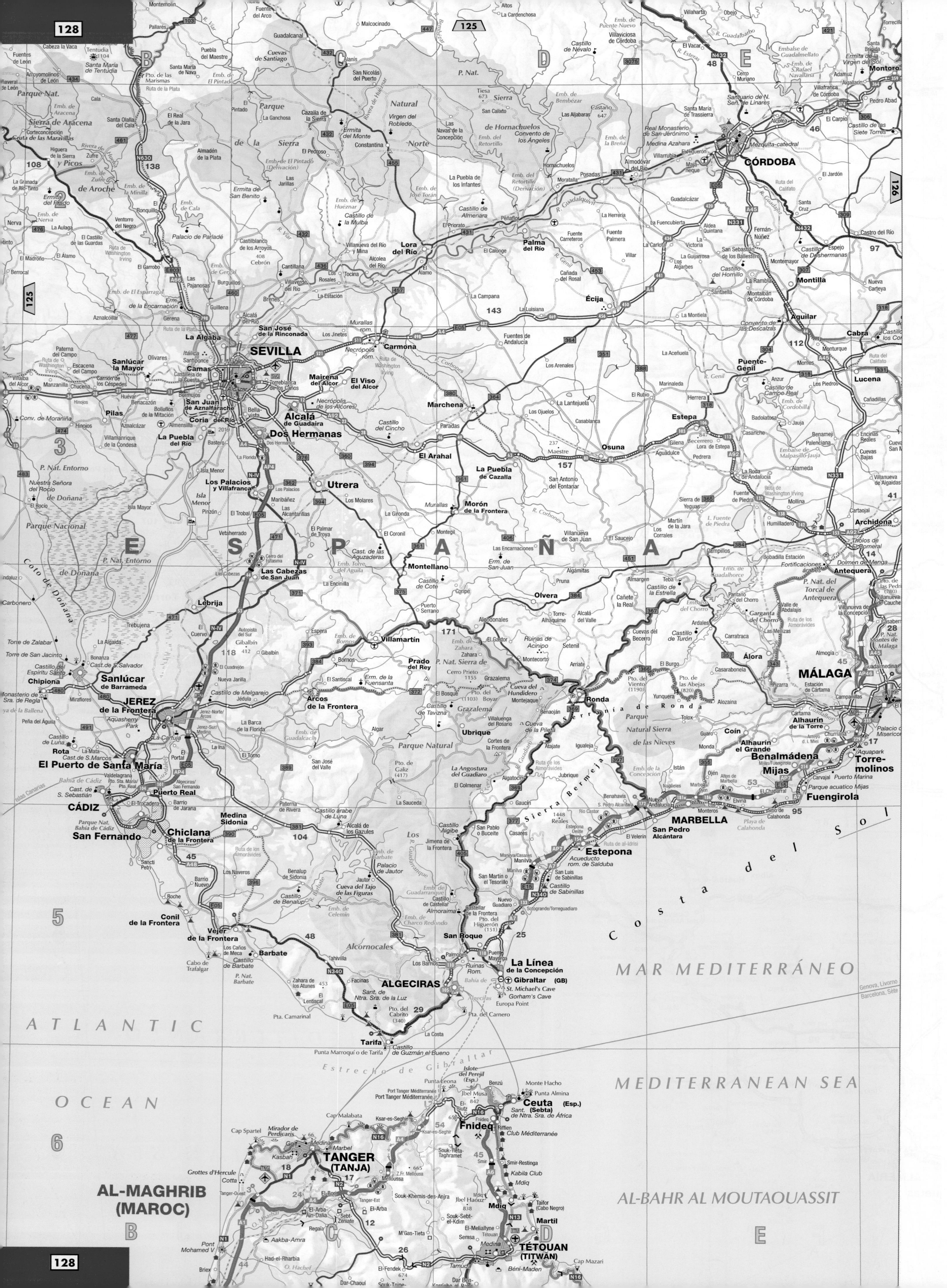
125
126
B
C
D
E
2
3
5
6
Sierra de Aracena
Gruta de las Maravillas
y Picos
de Aroche
Parque Nat.
de la Sierra
Parque Natural Sierra Norte
de Hornachuelos
Medina Azahara
CÓRDOBA
Mezquita-catedral
Lora del Río
Palma del Río
Écija
Montilla
Aguilar
Cabra
Lucena
Puente-Genil
Estepa
Osuna
Carmona
SEVILLA
La Algaba
San José de la Rinconada
Camas
Mairena del Alcor
El Viso del Alcor
Marchena
Alcalá de Guadaira
Dos Hermanas
San Juan de Aznalfarache
Coria del Río
La Puebla del Río
Sanlúcar la Mayor
Pilas
El Arahal
La Puebla de Cazalla
Utrera
Los Palacios y Villafranca
Morón de la Frontera
Parque Nacional de Doñana
Coto de Doñana
E S P A Ñ A
Las Cabezas de San Juan
Lebrija
Montellano
Olvera
Archidona
Antequera
MÁLAGA
Villamartín
Prado del Rey
P. Nat. Sierra de Grazalema
Ronda
Serranía de Ronda
Parque Natural Sierra de las Nieves
Ubrique
Arcos de la Frontera
Sanlúcar de Barrameda
Chipiona
JEREZ de la Frontera
Rota
El Puerto de Santa María
Puerto Real
CÁDIZ
San Fernando
Chiclana de la Frontera
Medina Sidonia
Conil de la Frontera
Vejer de la Frontera
Barbate
Cabo de Trafalgar
Alcornocales
ALGECIRAS
San Roque
La Línea de la Concepción
Gibraltar (GB)
Europa Point
Tarifa
Sierra Bermeja
Estepona
MARBELLA
San Pedro Alcántara
Coín
Alhaurín el Grande
Alhaurín de la Torre
Benalmádena
Mijas
Torremolinos
Fuengirola
Costa del Sol
MAR MEDITERRÁNEO
ATLANTIC
OCEAN
Estrecho de Gibraltar
MEDITERRANEAN SEA
Ceuta (Esp.)
(Sebta)
Fnideq
TANGER
(TANJA)
Cap Spartel
Cap Malabata
AL-MAGHRIB
(MAROC)
AL-BAHR AL MOUTAOUASSIT
Mdiq
Martil
TÉTOUAN
(TITWAN)
Cap Mazari

a

b

c

d

ATLANTIC

OCEAN

Lajes das Flores

A T L A N T I C

O C E A N

Ilha do Corvo • Vila do Corvo

Ponta da Barca Santa Cruz da Graciosa
Ilha Graciosa   Praia
402 Luz

Açores
(Port.)

Pta. do Albarnaz Ponta Delgada
Ilha das Flores   Santa Cruz das Flores
Fajã Grande
Lajedo   Lajes das Flores
Pta. da Terceira
Rocha Alta

Grupo Central

Lajes das Flores Can

Ilha Terceira   Biscoitos
Doze Ribeiras   1023 Praia da Vitória
Sto. António   São Sebastião
Rosais   Angra do Heroísmo
Velas 1053 Ilha de São Jorge
Cedros   Sa. do Topo
Pedro São Roque Topo
Capelo Miguel do Pico
Lombega Horta Calheta
Lajes Madalena M.d.Pico
Ilha do Faial 2351
São Mateus Lajes
Ilha do Pico do Pico
Piedade

Faial, Pico, S. Jorge

Grupo Ocidental

Terceira

2810

A r q u i p é l a g o   d o s   A ç o r e s

486

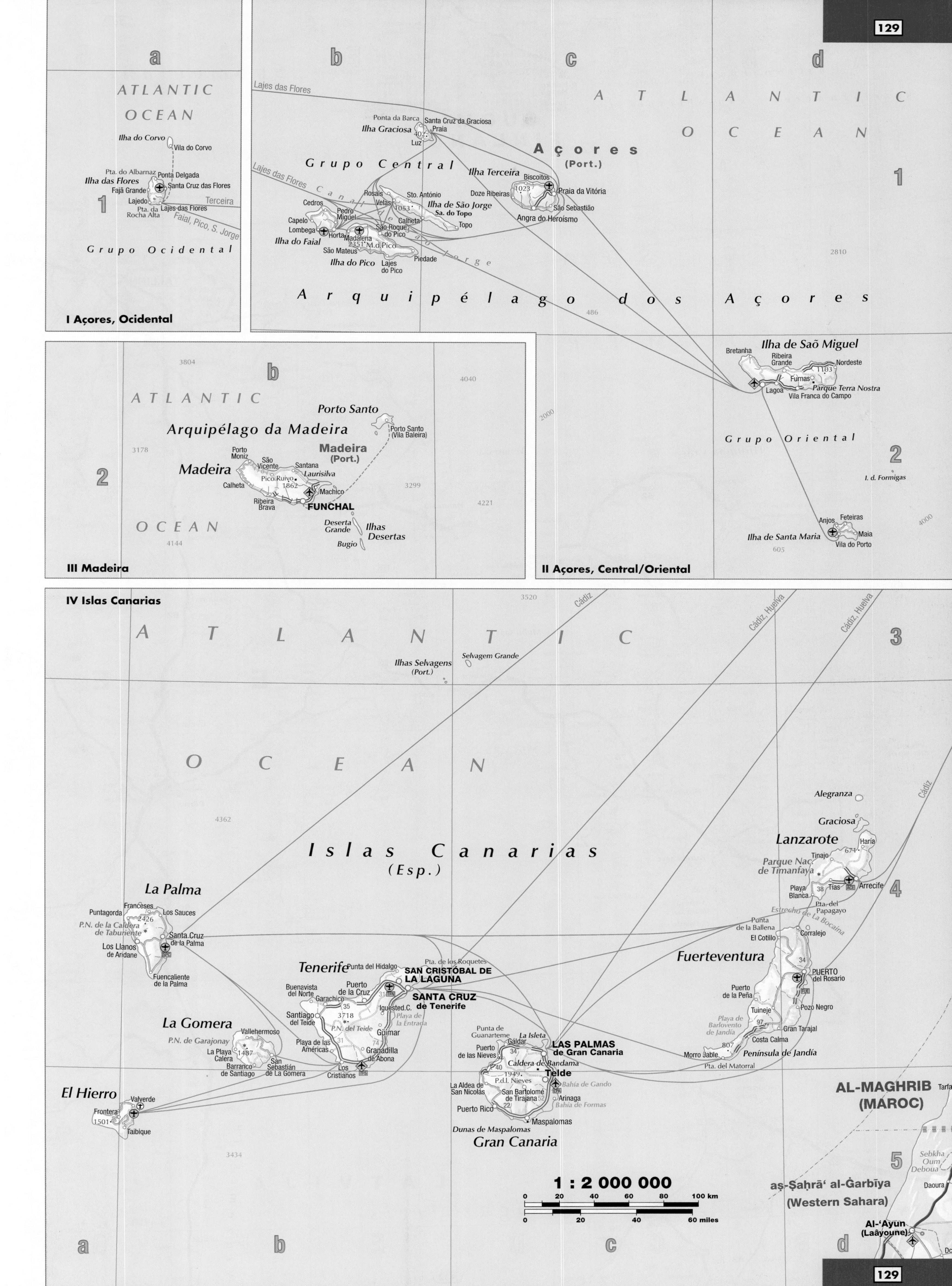

I Açores, Ocidental

3804

b

4040

ATLANTIC

Porto Santo

Arquipélago da Madeira

Porto Santo
(Vila Baleira)

Madeira
(Port.)

3178

Porto
Moniz
São
Vicente Santana
Madeira Pico Ruivo Laurisilva
2   Calheta 1862 Machico
Ribeira   **FUNCHAL**
Brava

O C E A N

Deserta
Grande   Ilhas
Desertas
Bugio

4144

4221

3299

Bretanha Ilha de Saõ Miguel
Ribeira Nordeste
Grande 1103
Furnas
Lagoa Parque Terra Nostra
Vila Franca do Campo

Grupo Oriental

2000

2

I. d. Formigas

Anjos Feteiras
Ilha de Santa Maria Maia
605 Vila do Porto

4000

III Madeira

II Açores, Central/Oriental

IV Islas Canarias

3520 Cádiz

Cádiz, Huelva

Cádiz, Huelva

3

A T L A N T I C

Ilhas Selvagens
(Port.)   Selvagem Grande

Cádiz

O C E A N

4362

I s l a s   C a n a r i a s

(Esp.)

Alegranza

Graciosa

Lanzarote   Haria

Parque Nac. Tinajo 674
de Timanfaya

La Palma

Franceses Los Sauces
Puntagorda 2426
P.N. de la Caldera
de Taburiente Santa Cruz
Los Llanos de la Palma
de Aridane
Fuencaliente
de la Palma

Playa 38 Tías Arrecife
Blanca
Pta. del
Papagayo 4
Estrecho de La Bocaina
Punta
de la Ballena Corralejo
El Cotillo

Fuerteventura 34

PUERTO
del Rosario

Tenerife Punta del Hidalgo Pta. de los Roquetes
SAN CRISTÓBAL DE
LA LAGUNA
Buenavista Puerto
del Norte de la Cruz
Garachico **SANTA CRUZ**
35 **de Tenerife**
Santiago Igueste d.C. Playa de
del Teide 3718 la Entrada
P.N. del Teide Güímar

La Gomera

P.N. de Garajonay
Vallehermoso
La Playa 1487
Calera San
Barranco Sebastián
de Santiago de La Gomera

Playa de
las Américas 31
Los
Cristianos Granadilla
de Abona

Punta de
Guanarteme La Isleta
Puerto Gáldar
de las Nieves 34
LAS PALMAS
de Gran Canaria
Caldera de Bandama
1949 **Telde**
P.d.l. Nieves
San Bartolomé Arinaga
San Nicolás de Tirajana
Puerto Rico 22

Puerto
de la Peña
Tuineje
97 Gran Tarajal
Playa de
Barlovento 807 Costa Calma
de Jandía
Morro Jable Península de Jandía
Pta. del Matorral

Bahía de Gando
Bahía de Formas

El Hierro Valverde
Frontera
1501
Taibique

Dunas de Maspalomas
Maspalomas

Gran Canaria

AL-MAGHRIB
(MAROC) Tarfa

3434

aş-Şaḥrā' al-Ġarbīya
(Western Sahara)

Sebkha
Oum
Deboua

Daoura

Al-'Ayun
(Laâyoune)

1 : 2 000 000

0   20   40   60   80   100 km

0   20   40   60 miles

a

b

c

d

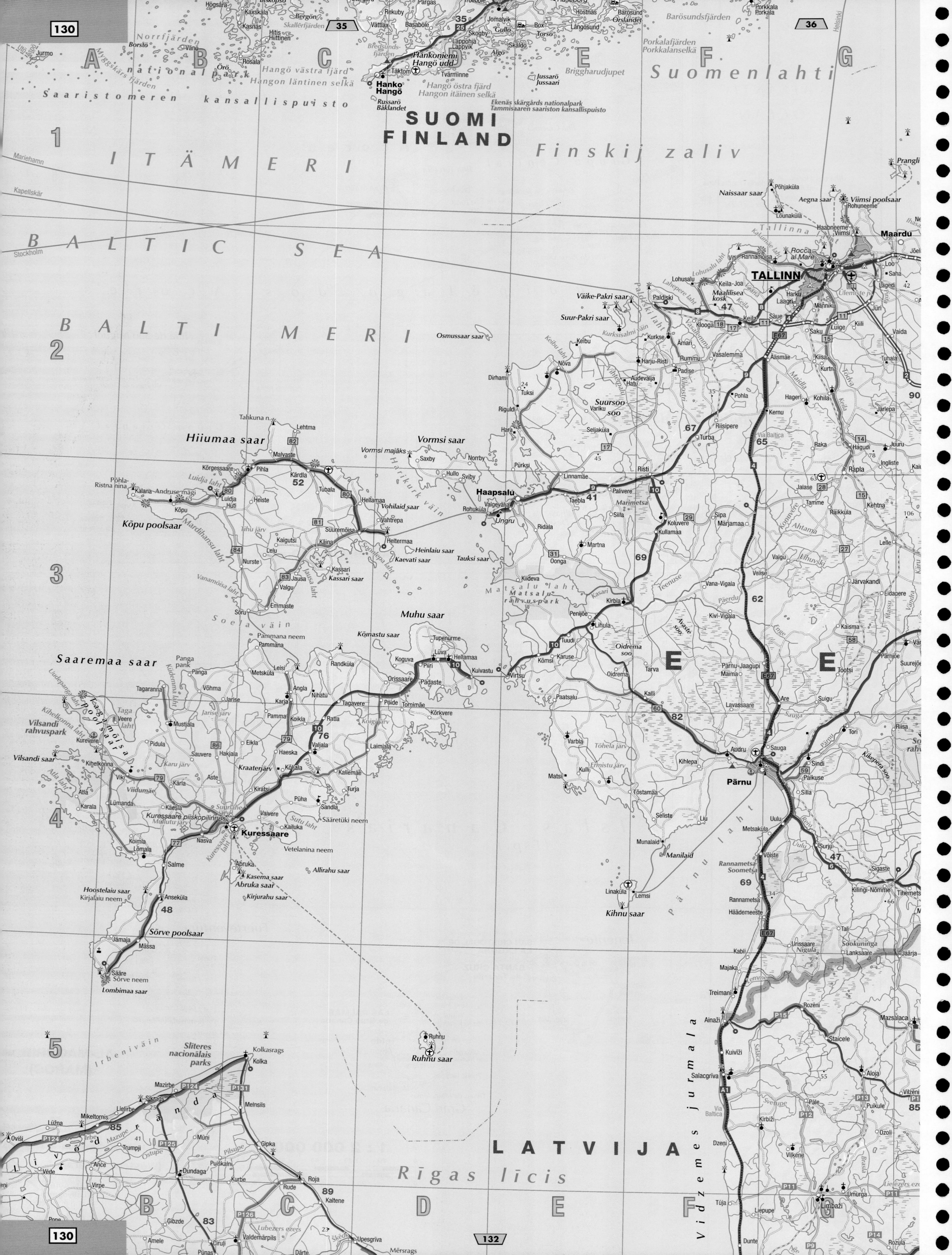

130
35
36
SUOMI
FINLAND
Finskij zaliv
Suomenlahti
ITÄMERI
BALTIC SEA
BALTI MERI
Saaristomeren kansallispuisto
Hankoniemi
Hangö udd
Hanko
Hangö
Hangö västra fjärd
Hangon läntinen selkä
Hangö östra fjärd
Hangon itäinen selkä
Ekenäs skärgårds nationalpark
Tammisaaren saariston kansallispuisto
Porkkala
Porkkalanselkä
Barösundsfjärden
Brigghardjupet
Mariehamn
Kapellskär
Stockholm
Helsinki
TALLINN
Maardu
Paldiski
Keila
Viimsi poolsaar
Aegna saar
Naissaar saar
Prangli
Väike-Pakri saar
Suur-Pakri saar
Osmussaar saar
Hiiumaa saar
Kärdla
Kõpu poolsaar
Käina
Emmaste
Vormsi saar
Haapsalu
Matsalu rahvuspark
Lihula
Virtsu
Muhu saar
Saaremaa saar
Kuressaare
Vilsandi rahvuspark
Sõrve poolsaar
Abruka saar
Kihnu saar
Ruhnu saar
Rapla
Märjamaa
Pärnu
Tootsi
Vändra
Sindi
Surju
Häädemeeste
Ainaži
Salacgrīva
Limbaži
Kolka
Slīteres nacionālais parks
Irbenivāin
Roja
Dundaga
Valdemārpils
Mērsrags
LATVIJA
Rīgas līcis
Vidzemes jurmala
Pärnu laht
E67
A
B
C
D
E
F
G
1
2
3
4
5
130
132

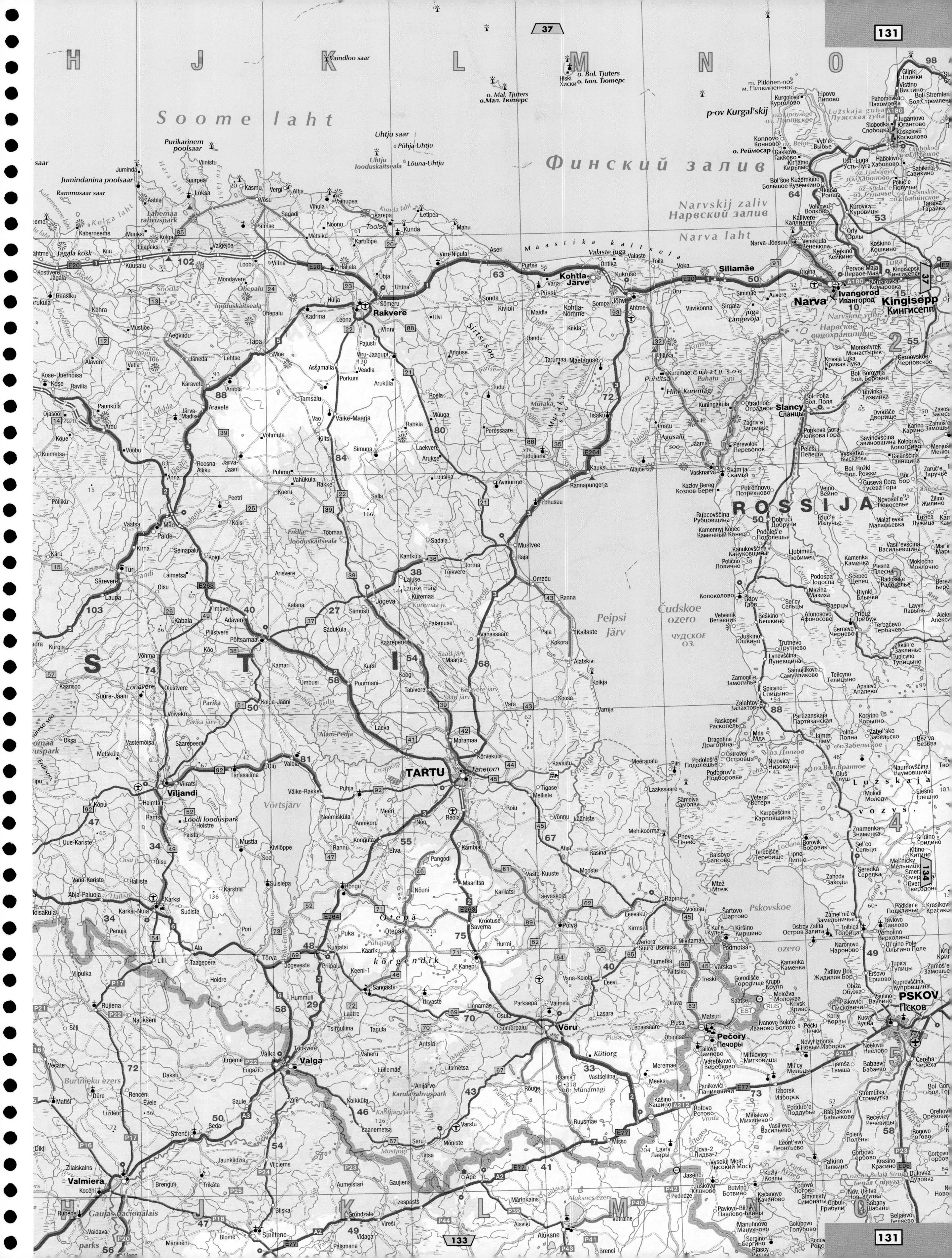
131
37
H
J
K
L
M
N
O
Soome laht
Финский залив
Narvskij zaliv
Нарвский залив
Narva laht
p-ov Kurgal'skij
Vaindloo saar
o. Bol. Tjuters
о. Бол. Тютерс
o. Mal. Tjuters
о.Мал. Тютерс
Uhtju saar
Purikarinem poolsaar
Jumindanina poolsaar
Rammusaar saar
Lahemaa rahvuspark
Rakvere
Kohtla-Järve
Sillamäe
Narva
Ivangorod
Ивангород
Kingisepp
Кингисепп
Slancy
Сланцы
ROSSIJA
Peipsi Järv
Čudskoe ozero
ЧУДСКОЕ ОЗ.
Pskovskoe ozero
Lužskaja vozvyš.
Mustvee
Jõgeva
Põltsamaa
Paide
Türi
Viljandi
TARTU
Võrtsjärv
Elva
Otepää
Põlva
Võru
Valga
Valka
Pečory
Печоры
PSKOV
Псков
Gdov
Гдов
S
T
I
Valmiera
Burtnieku ezers
Gaujas nacionalais parks
Alūksne
133
134
131

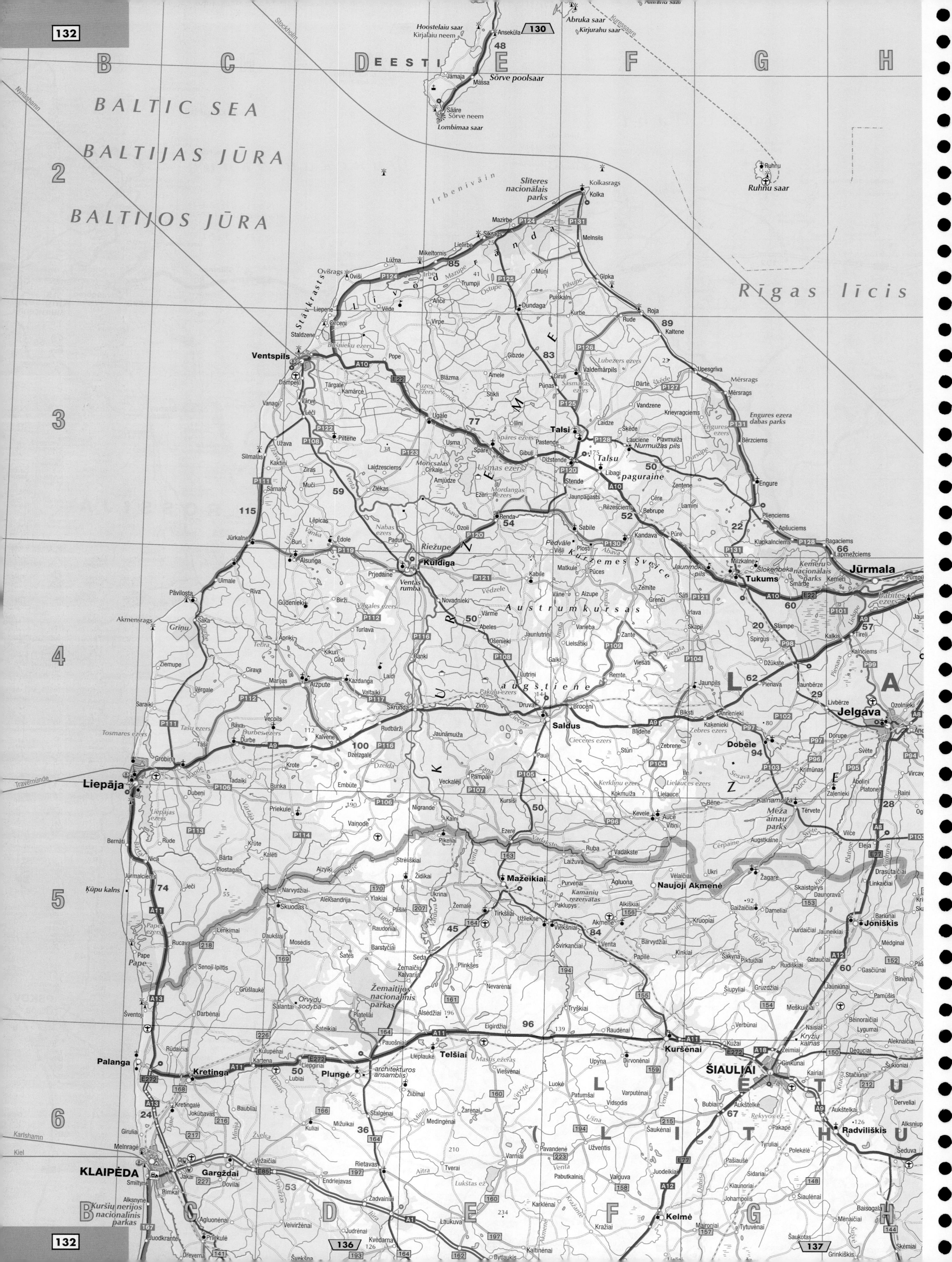
130
B
C
D EESTI
E
F
G
H
Hoostelaiu saar
Kirjalaiu neem
Anseküla
Abruka saar
Kirjurahu saar
Sõrve poolsaar
Jämaja
Mässa
Sääre
Sõrve neem
Lombimaa saar
BALTIC SEA
BALTIJAS JŪRA
BALTIJOS JŪRA
2
3
4
5
6
Ruhnu
Ruhnu saar
Irbeniväin
Slīteres nacionālais parks
Kolkasrags
Kolka
Mazirbe
Sīkrags
Lielirbe
Melnsils
Mikeltornis
Lūžņa
Ovišrags
Oviši
Mūni
Gipka
Trumpji
Pilsupe
Puiškalni
Roja
Dundaga
Kurbe
Rude
Kaltene
Līvõd rānda
Stāvkrasts
Liepene
Vēde
Ance
Circeni
Vīrpe
Staldzene
Ventspils
Pope
Ģibzde
Lubezers ezers
Upesgrīva
Dampeļi
Blāzma
Amele
Valdemārpils
Dārte
Mērsrags
Tārgale
Kamārce
Stikli
Pūņas
Vandzene
Krievragciems
Engures ezera dabas parks
Vanagi
Vārve
Ugāle
Ilīni
Talsi
Laidze
Šķēde
Lauciene
Plavmuiža
Nurmuižas pils
Bērzciems
Užava
Piltene
Usma
Spāre
Pastende
Gibuļi
Dižstende
Talsu pauguraine
Silmalas
Kaktiņi
Laidzesciems
Moricsalas
Cirkale
Amjūdze
Usmas ezers
Stende
Libagi
Engure
Ziras
Sārnate
Muči
Zlēkas
Ezēri
Mordangas ezers
Jaunpagasts
Zentene
Abava
Rēzesciems
Cēre
Bebrupe
Lamini
Plienciems
Apšuciems
Lēpicas
Nabas ezers
Ozoli
Renda
Sabile
Jūrkalne
Buri
Ēdole
Padure
Riežupe
Pēdvāle
Plosti
Kandava
Pūre
Klapkalnciems
Ragaciems
Alsunga
Kuldīga
Vīšli
Kurzemes Šveice
Jaunmoku pils
Milzkalne
Slokenbeka
Ķemeru nacionālais parks
Lapmežciems
Jūrmala
Tukums
Smārde
Ķemeri
Ulmale
Priedaine
Ventas rumba
Kabile
Matkule
Pūces
Zemīte
Sāti
Grenči
Pāvilosta
Rīva
Birži
Novadnieki
Vāne
Aizupe
Vēdzele
Austrumkursas
Babītes ezers
Gudenieki
Vilgales ezers
Vārme
Ābeles
Jaunlutriņi
Varieba
Zante
Irlava
Skapji
Slampe
Akmeņrags
Grīņu
Saka
Turlava
Ošenieki
Lielsātiki
Spirgus
Kalnciems
Kalkis
Tireli
Apriķi
Kikuri
Cildi
Ranki
Galki
Viesāti
Dzūkste
Ziemupe
Cīrava
Laidi
Lutriņi
Remte
Jaunpils
Pienava
Jaunbērze
Vērgale
Mārijas
Aizpute
Kazdanga
Valtaiki
augstiene
Livbērze
Jelgava
Ozolnieki
Saraiki
Skrunda
Zirņi
Pakuļu-ezers
Druva
Broceni
Bikšti
Annenieki
Kakenieki
Zebres ezers
Vecpils
Rāva
Durbes ezers
Kalvene
Rudbārži
Jaunāmuiža
Saldus
Blīdene
Dobele
Dorupe
Svēte
Tosmares ezers
Tāši
Durbe
Dzelzgale
Cieceres ezers
Stūri
Zebrene
Grobiņa
Krote
Dzelda
Pampāļi
Pauli
Ile
Krimūnas
Ābolini
Platone
Liepāja
Tadaiķi
Bunka
Embūte
Veckalēji
Kerkliņu ezers
Lielauces ezers
Sesava
Zaļenieki
Dubeni
Kokmuiža
Lielauce
Kalnamuiža
Liepājas ezers
Priekule
Nīgrande
Kursīši
Bēne
Meža ainau parks
Tērvete
Vaiņode
Kalni
Ezere
Keveļe
Auce
Vītiņi
Bernāti
Rude
Krūte
Kalēti
Pikeliai
Vadakstė
Ruba
Vadakste
Cerpaine
Augstkalne
Vilce
Eleja
Nīca
Bārta
Laižuva
Plostagals
Streliškiai
Židikai
Mažeikiai
Velaičiai
Ukri
Žagarė
Drąsutaičiai
Jūrmalciems
Aizviki
Purvėnai
Agluona
Naujoji Akmenė
Linkaičiai
Ķūpu kalns
Ječi
Narvydžiai
Ukrinai
Kamanų rezervatas
Skaistgirys
Daunorava
Skuodas
Aleksandrija
Ylakiai
Pašilė
Žemalė
Tirkšliai
Paklupys
Alkiškiai
Gaižaičiai
Dameliai
Lenkimai
Daukšiai
Raudonial
Užlieknė
Viekšniai
Akmenė
Kruopiai
Jurdaičiai
Jauneikiai
Joniškis
Rucava
Mosėdis
Barstyčiai
Svirkančiai
Venta
Barvydžiai
Mėdginai
Pape
Šates
Seda
Papilė
Kinkiai
Sakyna
Piktuižiai
Gataučiai
Žemaičių Kalvarija
Plinkšės
Rudiškiai
Gasčiūnai
Senoji-Ipiltis
Grūšlaukė
Žemaitijos nacionalinis parkas
Nevarėnai
Šiupyliai
Gruzdžiai
Binėnai
Šventoji
Salantai
Orvydų sodyba
Plateliai
Alsėdžiai
Tryškiai
Meškuičiai
Pamūšis
Darbėnai
Šateikiai
Eigirdžiai
Raudėnai
Verbūnai
Naisiai
Kryžių kalnas
Beinoraičiai
Lygumai
Rūdaičiai
Kulupėnai
Pauošniai
Telšiai
Kuršėnai
Kužai
Zeimiai
Dauguciai
Aleknaičiai
Palanga
Kretinga
Kartena
Lepgiriai
Lieplaukė
Masčio ežeras
Upyna
Dirvonėnai
Ginkūnai
Šukioniai
Lubiai
Plungė
architektūros ansamblis
Viešvėnai
Šiauliai
Kairiai
Stačiūnai
Kretingalė
Jokūbavas
Baubliai
Žlibinai
Luokė
Patumšai
Varputėnai
Vidsodis
Bubiai
Aukštelkė
Rėkyvos ež.
Aukštelkai
Derveliai
Stalgėnai
Medingėnai
Žarėnai
Pakapė
Alksniupiai
Girulai
Kuliai
Mižuikiai
Šaukėnai
Tyruliai
Radviliškis
Melnragė
Užventis
Pavandenė
Polekėlė
Šeduva
Karlshamn
Kiel
KLAIPĖDA
Gargždai
Vėžaičiai
Rietavas
Tverai
Varniai
Pabutkalnis
Valguva
Juodeikiai
Pašiaušė
Sidariai
Smiltynė
Jakai
Dovilai
Endriejavas
Lukštas ež.
Kiaunoriai
Johampolis
Šiaulėnai
Alksnynė
Rimkai
Žadvainiai
Karklėnai
Kelmė
Baisogala
Kuršių nerijos nacionalinis parkas
Agluonėnai
Veiviržėnai
Kražiai
Maironiai
Tytuvėnai
Mėnaičiai
Judrėnai
Kvėdarna
Laukuva
Juodkrantė
Priekulė
Šaukotas
Grinkiškis
Skėmiai
Dreverna
Švėkšna
Bytlaukis
Kaltinėnai
136
137
Rīgas līcis
LATVIJA
LIETUVA
LITHUANIA
KURZEME
Stockholm
Nynäshamn
Kuressaare
Travemünde

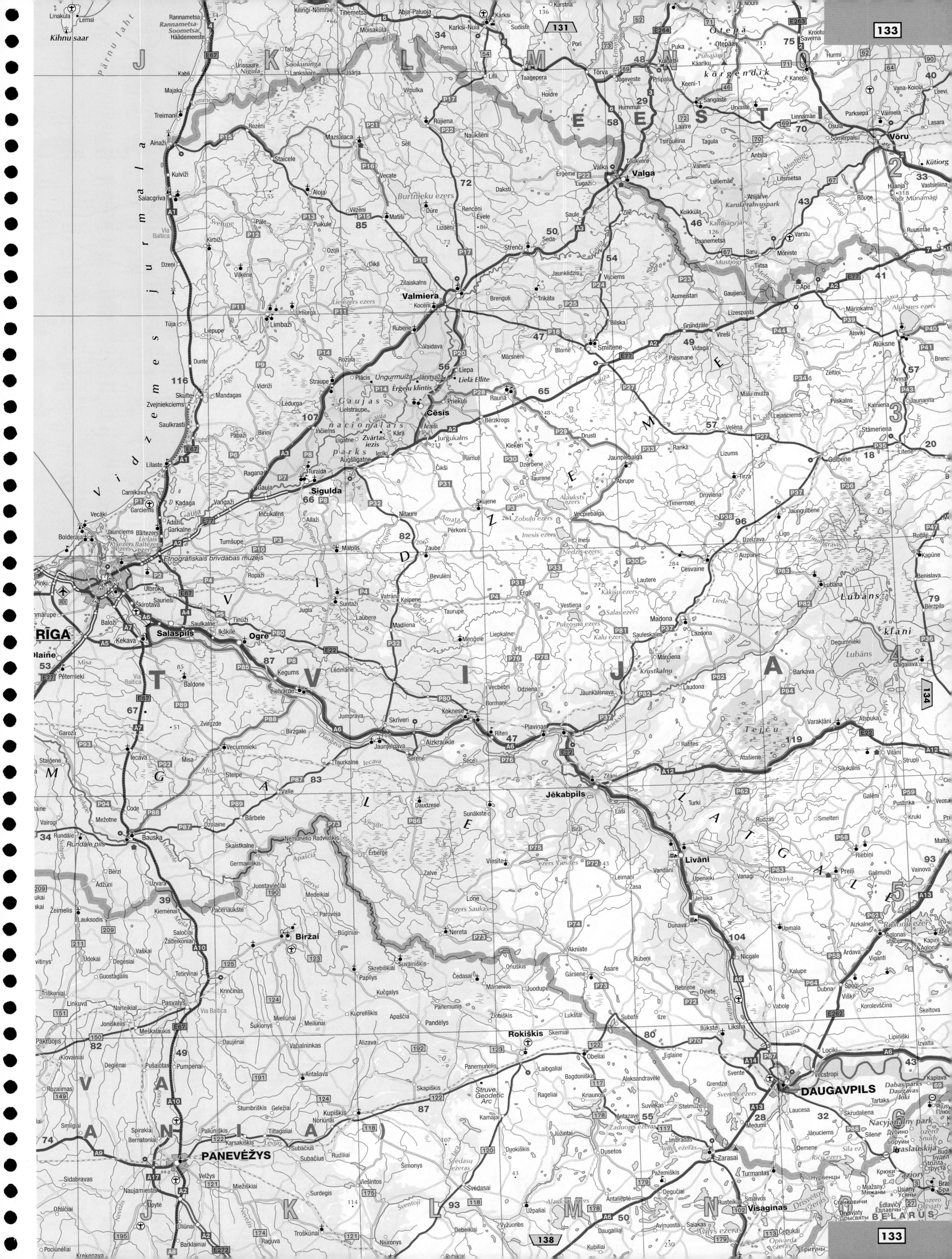

Kihnu saar
Rannametsa
Häädemeeste
Otepää
Valga
Võru
Valmiera
Cēsis
Sigulda
Gaujas nacionālais parks
Ungurmuiža
Ērgeļu klintis
Lielā Ellīte
Limbaži
Salacgrīva
Ainaži
Rūjiena
Mazsalaca
Burtnieku ezers
Smiltene
Alūksne
Gulbene
Madona
Lubāns
Ogre
Salaspils
RĪGA
Etnogrāfiskais brīvdabas muzejs
Olaine
Bauska
Rundāle pils
Jēkabpils
Līvāni
Preiļi
Aglonas
Daugavpils
Krāslava
Panevėžys
Pasvalys
Biržai
Rokiškis
Zarasai
Visaginas
Kupiškis
Struve Geodetic Arc
Vidzemes jūrmala
Pärnu laht
EESTI
LATVIJA
VIDZEME
LATGALE
ZEMGALE
LIETUVA
BELARUS
Haanja
Suur Munamägi
Karula rahvuspark
Teiču
Dabas parks Daugavas loki
Jaunjelgava
Aizkraukle
Koknese
Pļaviņas
Iecava
Vecumnieki
Kekava
Baldone
Saulkrasti
Skulte
Carnikava
Ādaži
Lielvārde
Skrīveri
Cesvaine
Varakļāni
Viļāni
Rēzekne
Ape
Strenči
Mustjõgi
131
134
138

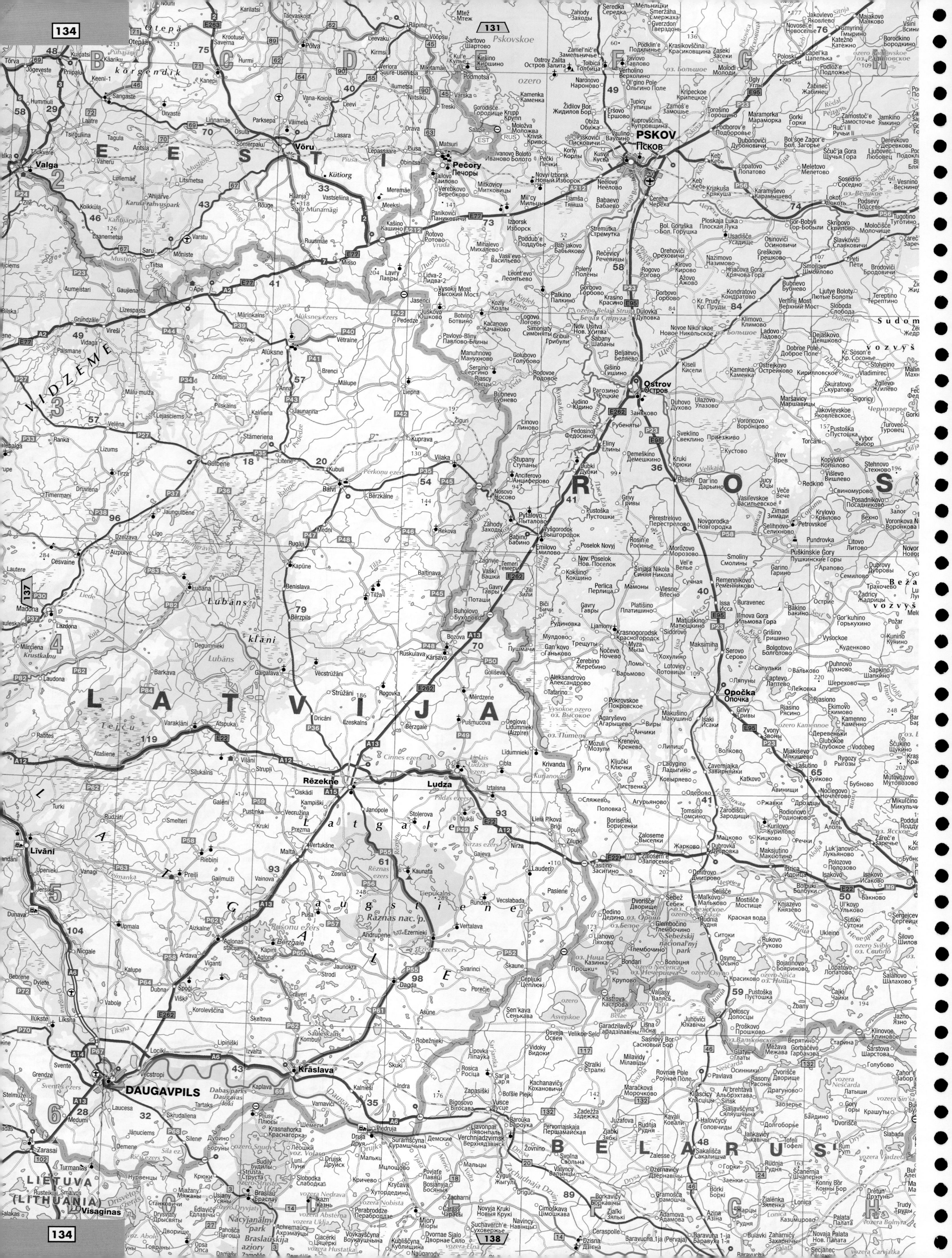
131
EESTI
Valga
Võru
Otepää
Põlva
Pečory
Печоры
PSKOV
Псков
Pskovskoe ozero
Kirsino
Izborsk
Изборск
Ostrov
Остров
Palkino
Палкино
VIDZEME
Alūksne
Gulbene
Balvi
Vilaka
Madona
Lubāns
Pytalovo
Пыталово
ROS
Opočka
Опочка
Puškinskie Gory
Пушкинские Горы
Krasnogorodsk
Красногородск
LATVIJA
Karsava
Rēzekne
Ludza
Varakļāni
Līvāni
Preiļi
Latgales augstiene
Raznas nac. p.
Aglona
Dagda
Krāslava
DAUGAVPILS
Zilupe
Sebež
Себеж
Sebežskij nacional'nyj park
Idrica
Идрица
BELARUS'
Verchnjadzvinsk
Верхнядзвінск
Braslau
Браслаў
Nacyjanalny park Braslauskija azlory
LIETUVA
(LITHUANIA)
Visaginas
Zarasai
Turmantas
E77
E262
E22
A13
A12
E95
M9
137
138

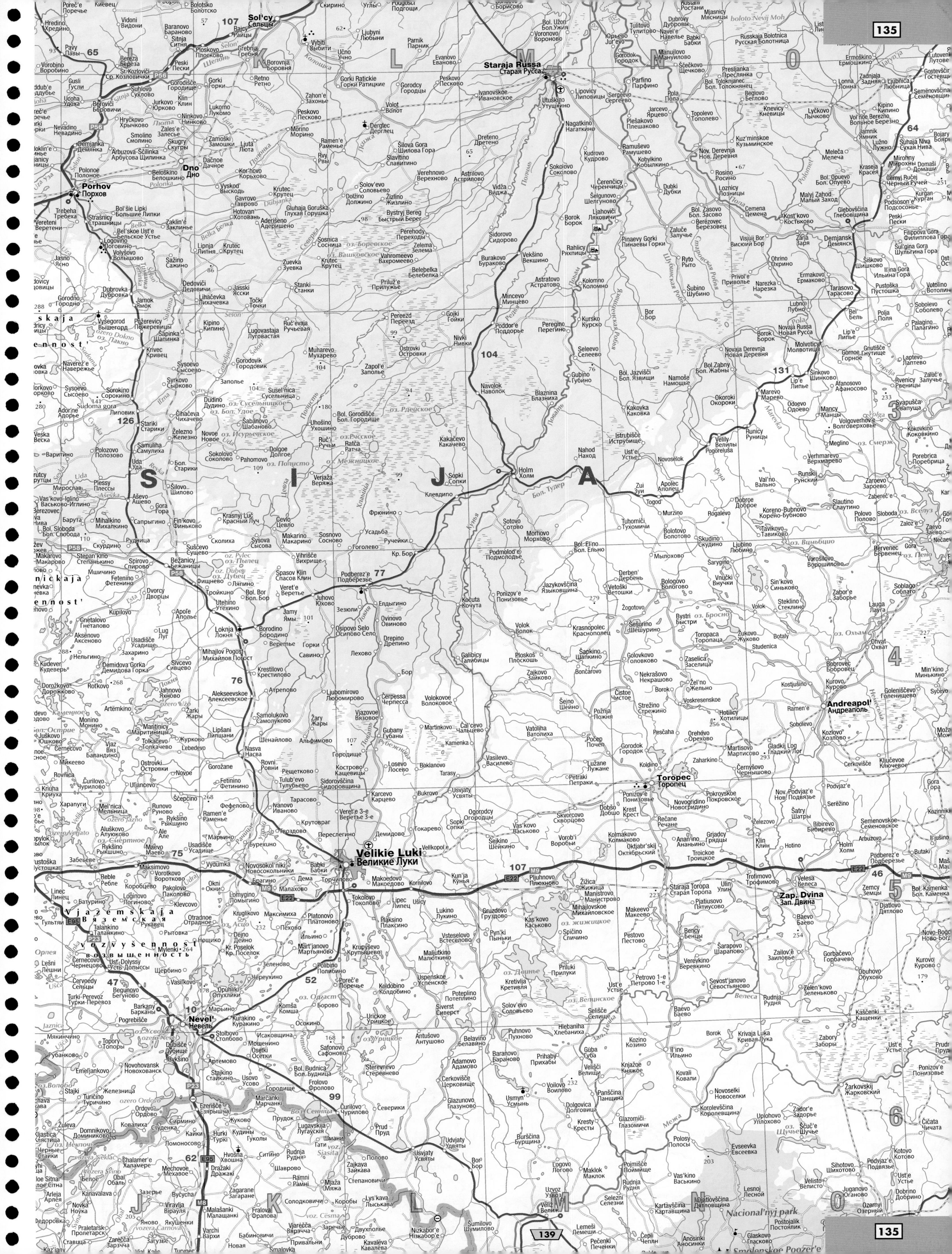
Staraja Russa
Старая Русса
Porhov
Порхов
Dno
Дно
Sol'cy
Сольцы
Demjansk
Демянск
Holm
Холм
Andreapol'
Андреаполь
Toropec
Торопец
Velikie Luki
Великие Луки
Nevel'
Невель
Zap. Dvina
Зап. Двина
Velіž
Велиж
Novosokol'niki
Новосокольники
Loknja
Локня
Bežanicy
Бежаницы
Kun'ja
Кунья
Staraja Toropa
Старая Торопа
S
I
J
A
Vjazemskaja
Вяземская
vozvyšennost'
возвышенность
Nacional'nyj park
Smolenskoe Poozer'e
E22
E95
M9
P23
P56
P58
104
107
126
131
65
76
77
52
99
75
62
47
46
64
10
139

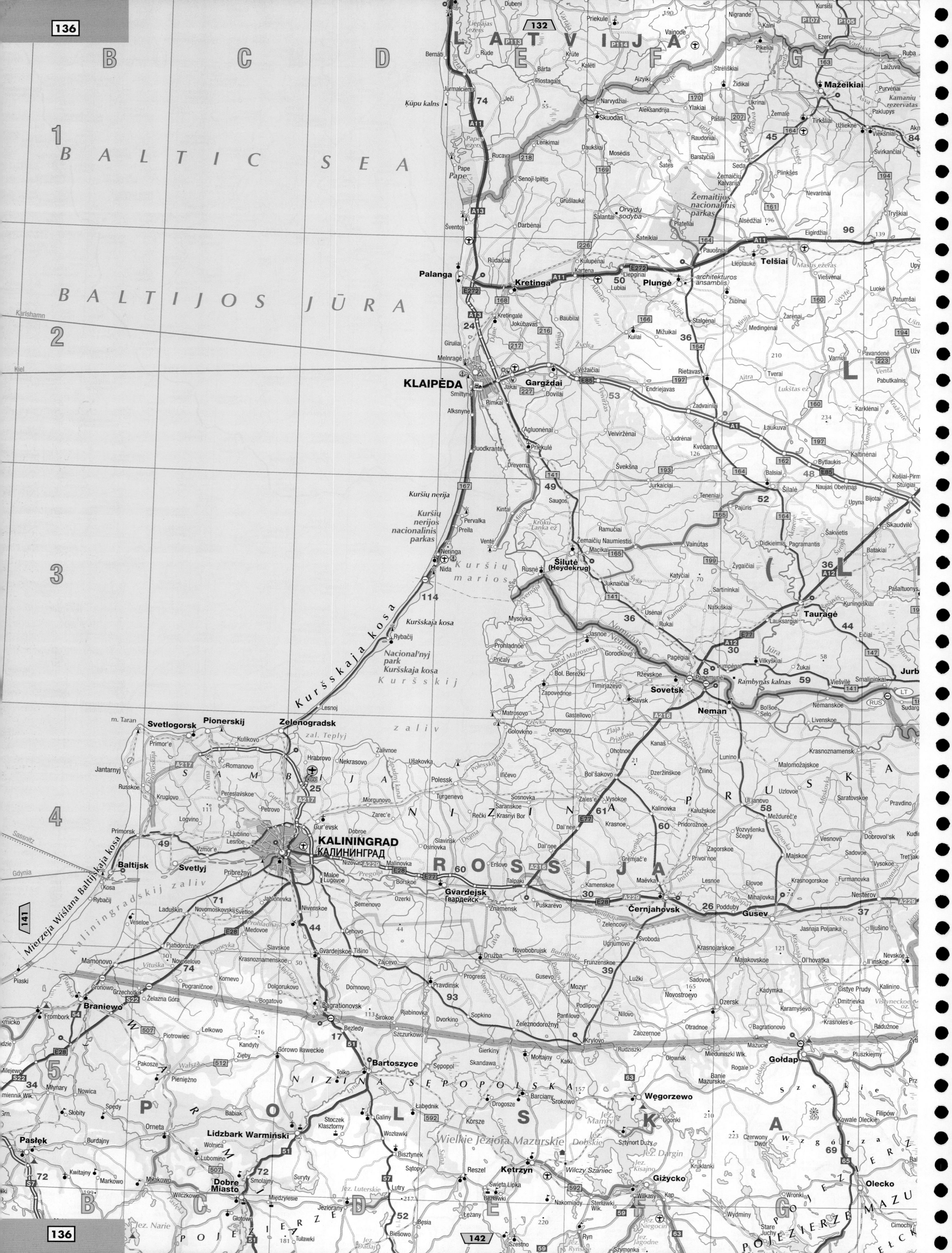

132
142
141
B
C
D
E
F
G
L
1
2
3
4
5
LATVIJA
BALTIC SEA
BALTIJOS JŪRA
KLAIPĖDA
KALININGRAD
КАЛИНИНГРАД
ROSSIJA
Liepājas ezers
Bernāti
Nīca
Jūrmalciems
Ķūpu kalns
Papes ezers
Pape
Rucava
Dubeni
Priekule
Vaiņode
Rude
Bārta
Krūte
Kalēti
Rolstagals
Aizvīķi
Streliškiai
Židikai
Mažeikiai
Narvydžiai
Aleksandrija
Ylakiai
Skuodas
Lenkimai
Daukšiai
Mosėdis
Senoji Įpiltis
Grūšlaukė
Šalantai
Orvydų sodyba
Šventoji
Darbėnai
Palanga
Kretinga
Kartena
Lubiai
Plungė
Telšiai
Žemaitijos nacionalinis parkas
Plateliai
Žemaičių Kalvarija
Seda
Šateikiai
Rūdaičiai
Kūlupėnai
Kretingalė
Jokūbavas
Baubliai
Kuliai
Mižuikai
Stalgėnai
Girulai
Melnragė
Gargždai
Smiltynė
Dovilai
Jakai
Rimkai
Alksnynė
Veiviržėnai
Endriejavas
Rietavas
Žadvainiai
Laukuva
Juodkrantė
Agluonėnai
Priekulė
Dreverna
Judrėnai
Kvėdarna
Švėkšna
Kuršių nerija
Kuršių nerijos nacionalinis parkas
Pervalka
Preila
Neringa
Nida
Ventė
Kintai
Saugos
Ramučiai
Žemaičių Naumiestis
Mačikai
Šilutė (Heydekrug)
Rusnė
Kuršių marios
Šilalė
Vainutas
Juknaičiai
Katyčiai
Tauragė
Pagėgiai
Panemunė
Rambynas kalnas
Viešvilė
Smalininkai
Jurbarkas
Kurššaja kosa
Rybačij
Nacional'nyj park Kurššaja kosa
Kurššskij zaliv
Mysovka
Jasnoe
Prohladnoe
Gorodkovo
Bol. Berežki
Sovetsk
Neman
Slavsk
Lesnoj
Zelenogradsk
Pionerskij
Svetlogorsk
m. Taran
Primor'e
Kulikovo
Jantarnyj
Romanovo
Hrabrovo
Nekrasovo
Polessk
Russkoe
Kruglovo
Pereslavskoe
Petrovo
Morgunovo
Turgenevo
Logvino
Primorsk
Baltijsk
Svetlyj
Gur'evsk
Dobroe
Slavinsk
Osinovka
Gvardejsk
Гвардейск
Talpaki
Kamenskoe
Černjahovsk
Gusev
Nesterov
Krasnoznamensk
Dobrovol'sk
Ozersk
Pravdinsk
Železnodorožnyj
Krylovo
Bagrationovsk
Mamonovo
Ladušin
Kaliningradskij zaliv
Mierzeja Wiślana Baltijskaja kosa
Braniewo
Frombork
Bartoszyce
Sępopol
Gołdap
Węgorzewo
Kętrzyn
Giżycko
Olecko
Lidzbark Warmiński
Dobre Miasto
Pasłęk
Orneta
Korsze
Reszel
Wielkie Jeziora Mazurskie
Nizina Sępopolska
Pojezierze Mazurskie
Kalinino
Ozerki
Mazurskie

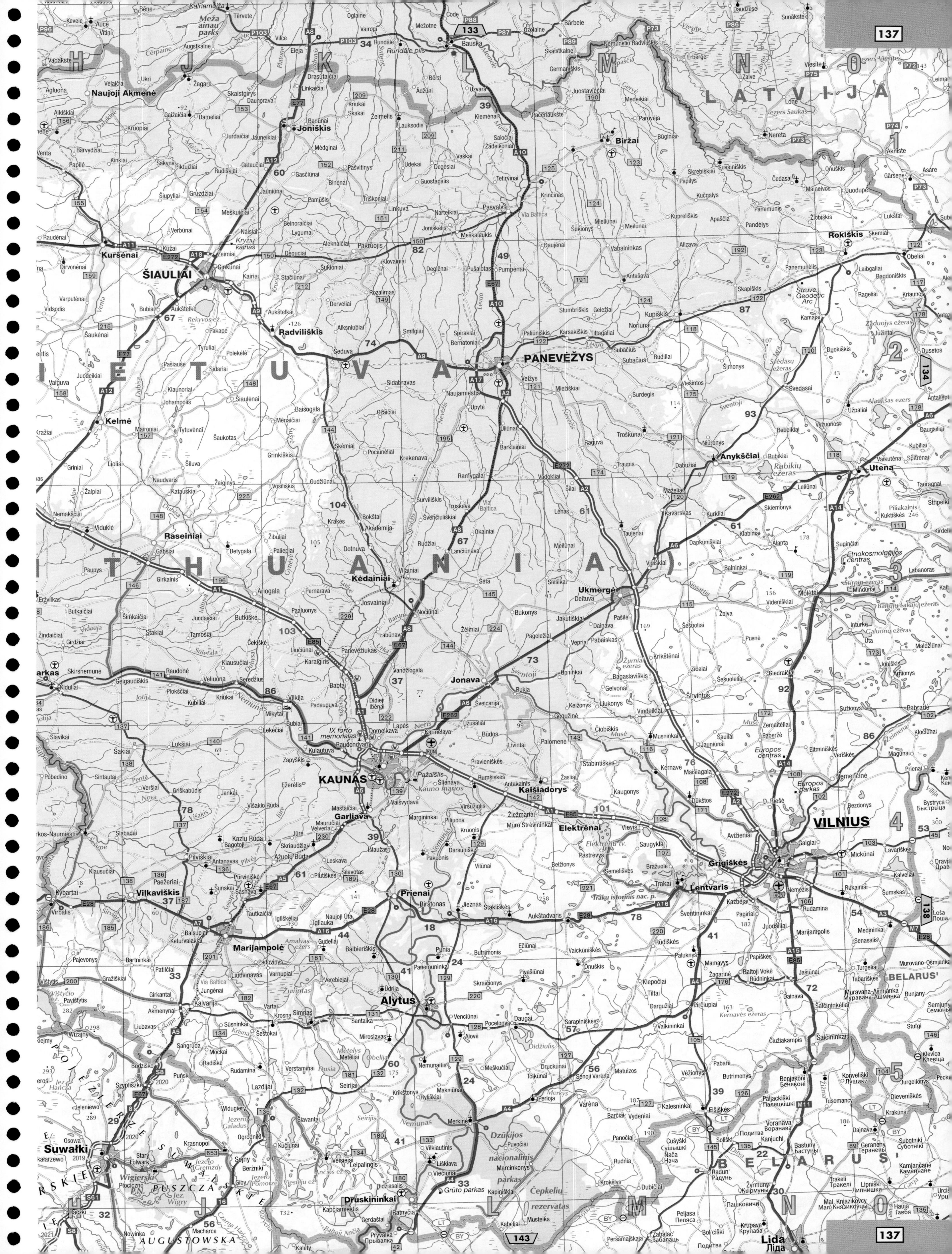

LATVIJA
LIETUVA (LITHUANIA)
BELARUS'
ŠIAULIAI
Kuršėnai
Naujoji Akmenė
Joniškis
Radviliškis
Kelmė
Raseiniai
Bauska
Rundāle pils
Pasvalys
Biržai
PANEVĖŽYS
Rokiškis
Kupiškis
Anykščiai
Utena
Kėdainiai
Ukmergė
Jonava
Molėtai
KAUNAS
Garliava
Kaišiadorys
Elektrėnai
Prienai
Vilkaviškis
Marijampolė
Kalvarija
Alytus
Lazdijai
Druskininkai
Trakai
Lentvaris
Grigiškės
VILNIUS
Nemenčinė
Varėna
Merkinė
Šalčininkai
Eišiškės
Suwałki
Sejny
Lida
Лида
Dzūkijos nacionalinis parkas
Čepkelių rezervatas
Trakų istorinis nac. p.
Kryžių kalnas
Via Baltica
Nemunas
Neris
Šventoji
Nevėžis
Dubysa
Mūša
Struve Geodetic Arc
Kauno marios
IX forto memorialas
Grūto parkas
Europos centras
AUGUSTOWSKA
POJEZIERZE SUWALSKIE
Wigierski P.N.
PUSZCZA

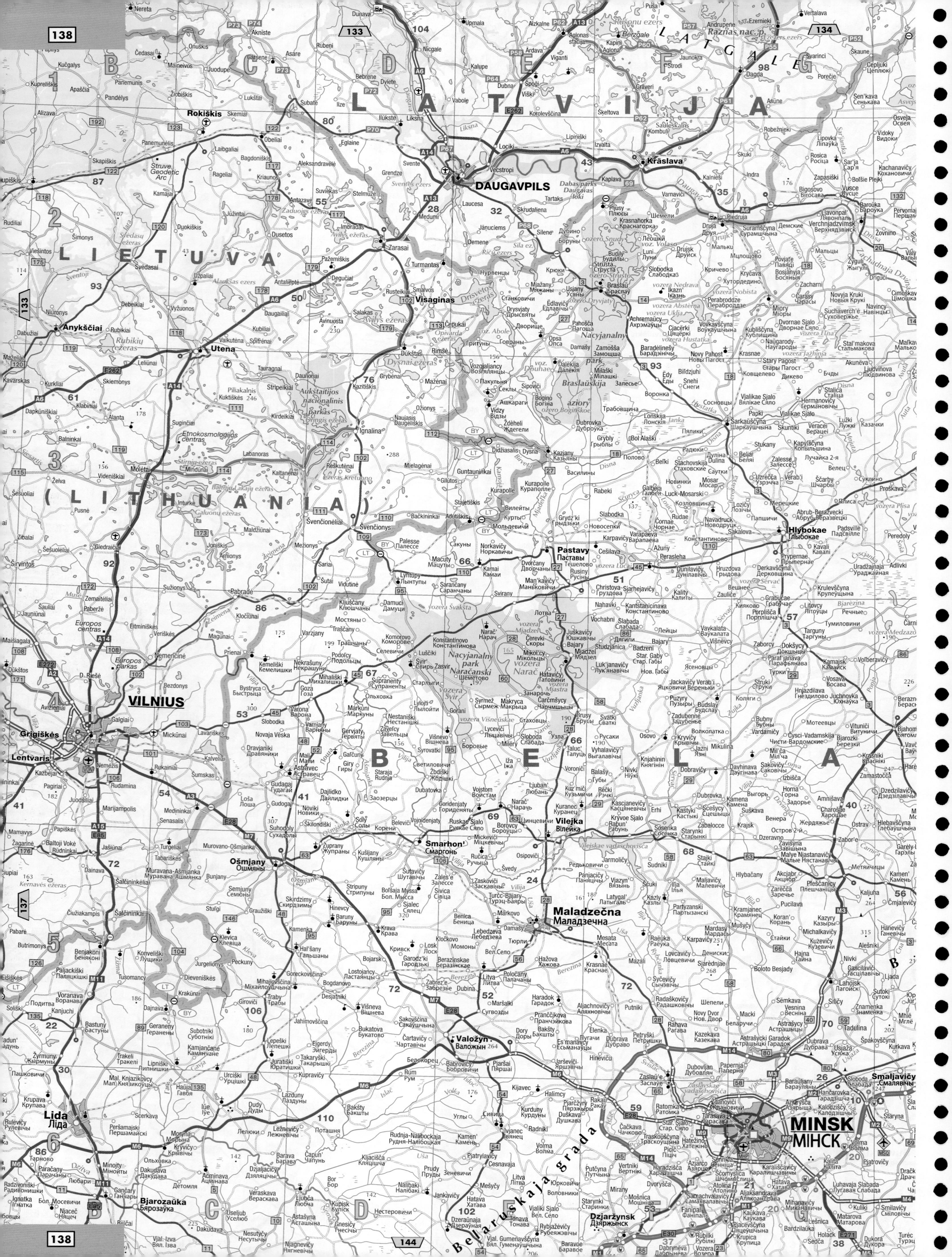

LATVIJA
LATGALE
LIETUVA
(LITHUANIA)
BELA
DAUGAVPILS
Rokiškis
Anykščiai
Utena
Visaginas
Ignalina
Zarasai
Krāslava
Braslaŭ
Браслаў
Pastavy
Пастаў
Hlybokae
Глыбокае
VILNIUS
Grigiškės
Lentvaris
Ašmjany
Ашмяны
Smarhon'
Смаргонь
Vilejka
Вілейка
Maladzečna
Маладзечна
Valožyn
Валожын
Lida
Ліда
Bjarozaŭka
Бярозаўка
Dzjaržynsk
Дзяржынск
MINSK
МІНСК
Smaljavičy
Смалявічы
Nacyjanalny park Naračanski
Nacyjanalny park Braslaŭskija azjory
Aukštaitijos nacionalinis parkas
Europos centras
Europos parkas
Struve Geodetic Arc
Belaruskaja grada
Daugava
vozera Narač
vozera Svir
Zaslaŭ
Zaslaŭskae vadashovišča
Vilejskae vadashovišča

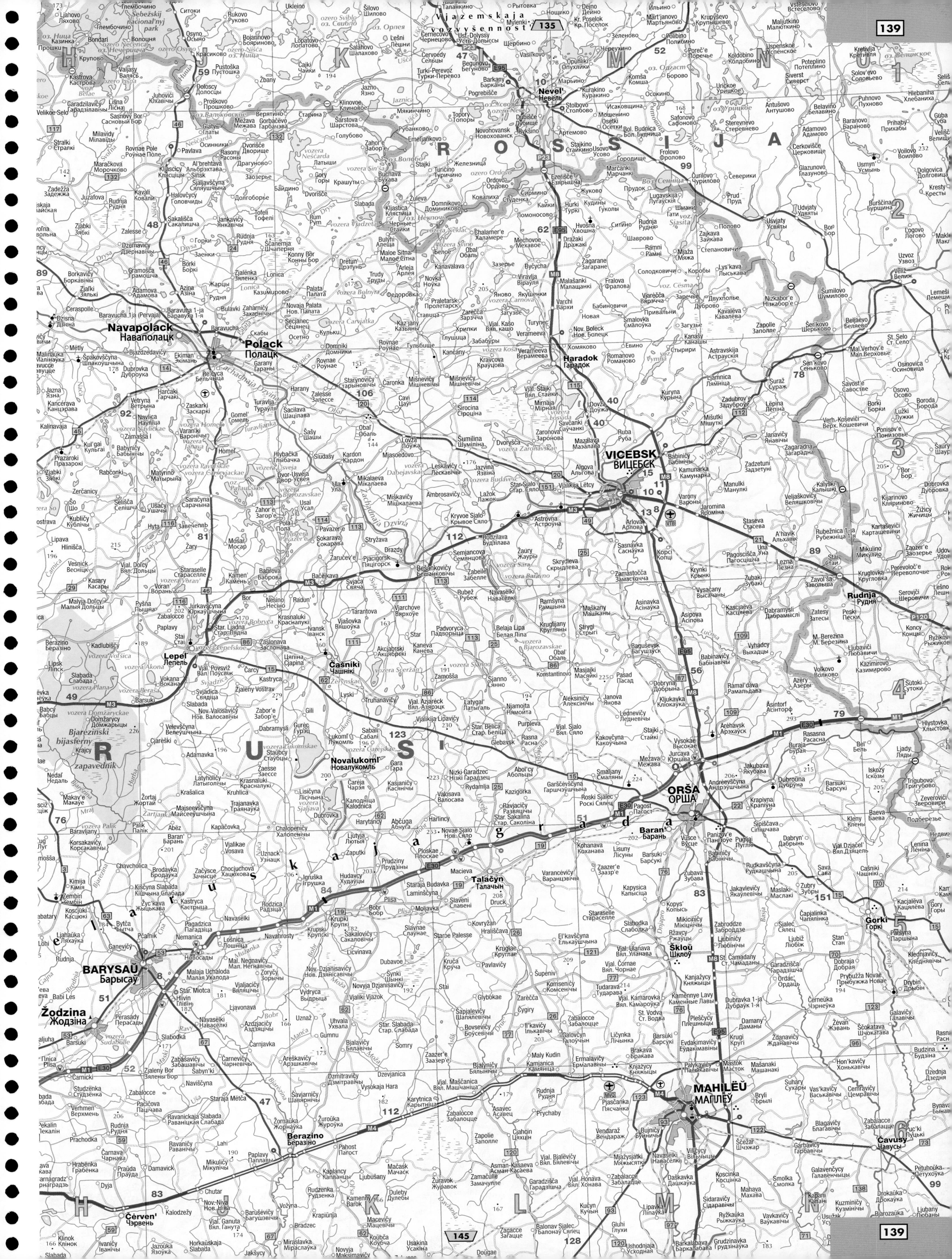
Vjazemskaja vozvyšennost'
135
ROSSIJA
Nevel'
Невель
Navapolack
Наваполацк
Polack
Полацк
Haradok
Гарадок
VICEBSK
ВИЦЕБСК
Lepel'
Лепель
Novalukoml'
Новалукомль
ORŠA
ОРША
BARYSAŬ
Барысаў
Žodzina
Жодзіна
Berazino
Беразіно
Talačyn
Талачын
Škloŭ
Шклоў
MAHILËŬ
МАГІЛЁЎ
Gorki
Горкі
Čavusy
Чавусы
Červen'
Чэрвень
Rudnja
Рудня
Bjarezinski bijasferny zapaviednik
Belaruskaja hrada
145

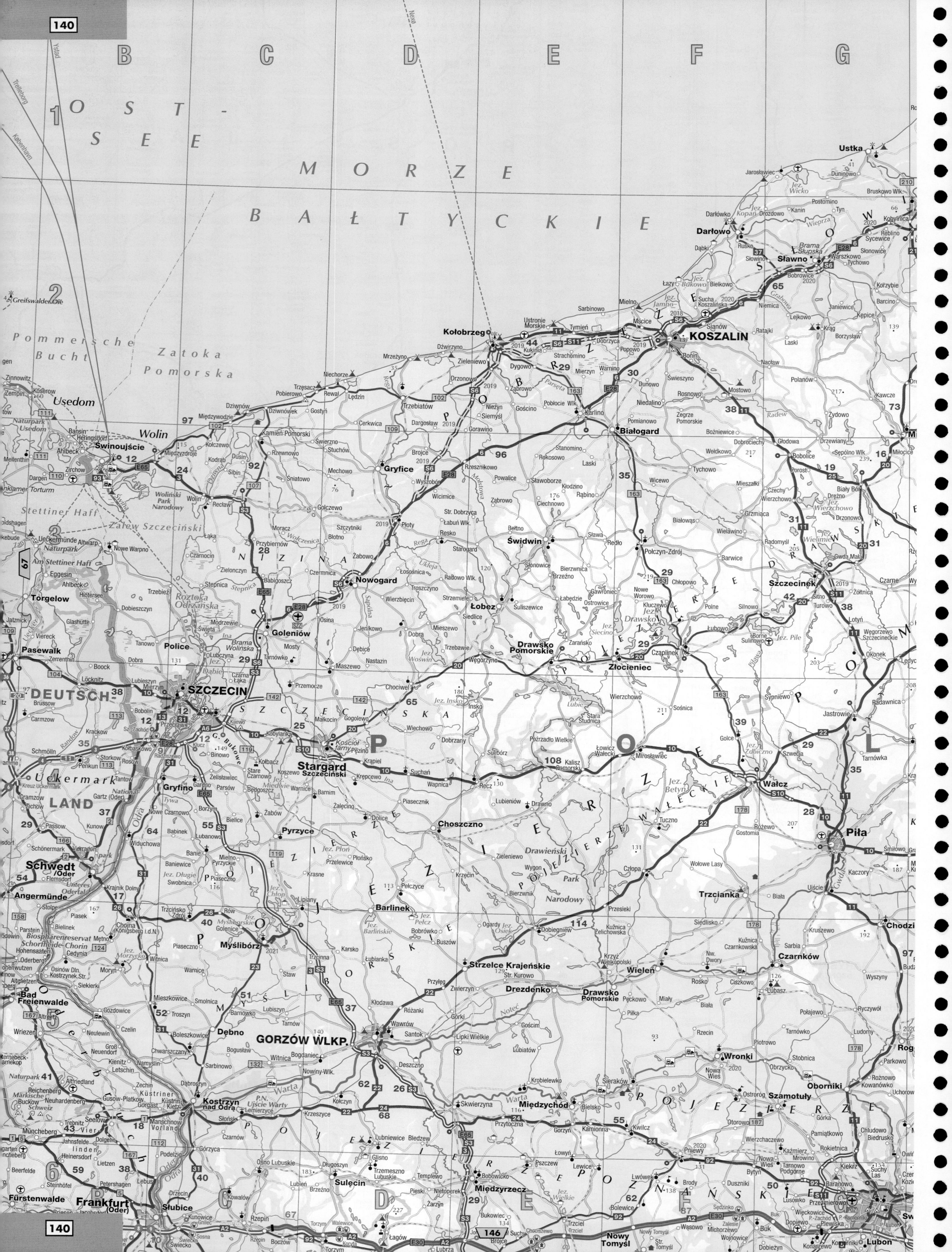
B
C
D
E
F
G
1
2
3
5
6
OST-
SEE
MORZE
BAŁTYCKIE
Pommersche
Bucht
Zatoka
Pomorska
Usedom
Wolin
Stettiner Haff
Zalew Szczeciński
Świnoujście
Międzyzdroje
Kołobrzeg
KOSZALIN
Darłowo
Sławno
Ustka
Białogard
Karlino
Gryfice
Trzebiatów
Płoty
Nowogard
Goleniów
Police
SZCZECIN
Stargard Szczeciński
Świdwin
Łobez
Drawsko Pomorskie
Złocieniec
Połczyn-Zdrój
Szczecinek
Wałcz
Piła
Choszczno
Pyrzyce
Gryfino
Myślibórz
Barlinek
Strzelce Krajeńskie
Drezdenko
GORZÓW WLKP.
Dębno
Kostrzyn nad Odrą
Słubice
Frankfurt (Oder)
Sulęcin
Międzyrzecz
Międzychód
Wronki
Szamotuły
Oborniki
Czarnków
Trzcianka
Wieleń
Nowy Tomyśl
Torgelow
Pasewalk
Schwedt /Oder
Angermünde
Bad Freienwalde
Fürstenwalde
DEUTSCHLAND
Uckermark
NIZINA
SZCZECIŃSKA
POJEZIERZE
POMORSKIE
WAŁECKIE
DRAWSKIE
MYŚLIBORSKIE
LUBUSKIE
POZNAŃSKIE
Drawieński Park Narodowy
Woliński Park Narodowy
Warta
Odra
Noteć

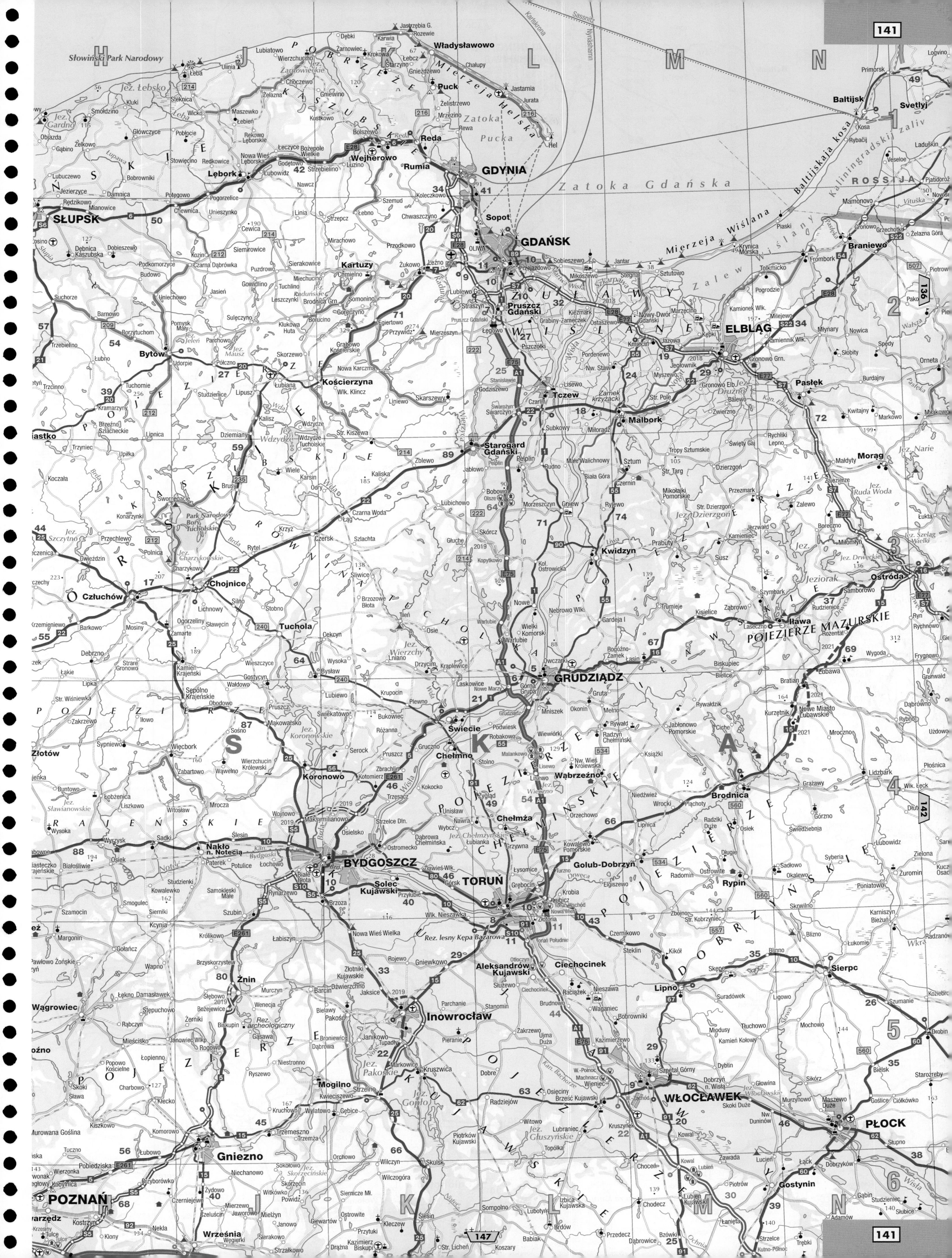

Słowiński Park Narodowy
Władysławowo
Jastrzębia G.
Rozewie
Karwia
Dębki
Lubiatowo
Żarnowiec
Krokowa
Chałupy
Jastarnia
Jurata
Hel
Mierzeja Helska
Łeba
Puck
Zatoka Pucka
Jez. Łebsko
Jez. Gardno
Smołdzino
Kluki
Choczewo
Gniewino
Reda
Wejherowo
Rumia
GDYNIA
Lębork
Zatoka Gdańska
SŁUPSK
Sopot
GDAŃSK
Kartuzy
Pruszcz Gdański
Żuławy Wiślane
Nowy Dwór Gdański
ELBLĄG
Baltijsk
Svetlyj
Baltijskaja kosa
Kaliningradskij zaliv
ROSSIJA
Mamonovo
Braniewo
Mierzeja Wiślana
Zalew Wiślany
Frombork
Tolkmicko
Bytów
Kościerzyna
Tczew
Malbork
Pasłęk
Starogard Gdański
Pelplin
Sztum
Gniew
Morąg
Kwidzyn
Prabuty
Ostróda
Iława
Pojezierze Mazurskie
Człuchów
Chojnice
Park Narodowy Bory Tucholskie
Tuchola
Bory Tucholskie
Grudziądz
Świecie
Chełmno
Wąbrzeźno
Brodnica
Nowe Miasto Lubawskie
Lubawa
Lidzbark
Złotów
Więcbork
Sępólno Krajeńskie
Koronowo
Nakło n. Notecią
BYDGOSZCZ
TORUŃ
Solec Kujawski
Chełmża
Golub-Dobrzyń
Rypin
Pojezierze Chełmińskie
Pojezierze Dobrzyńskie
Aleksandrów Kujawski
Ciechocinek
Lipno
Sierpc
Szubin
Żnin
Inowrocław
Wągrowiec
Mogilno
Kruszwica
Radziejów
WŁOCŁAWEK
PŁOCK
Gostynin
Gniezno
POZNAŃ
Września
Pojezierze Kujawskie
Jez. Gopło

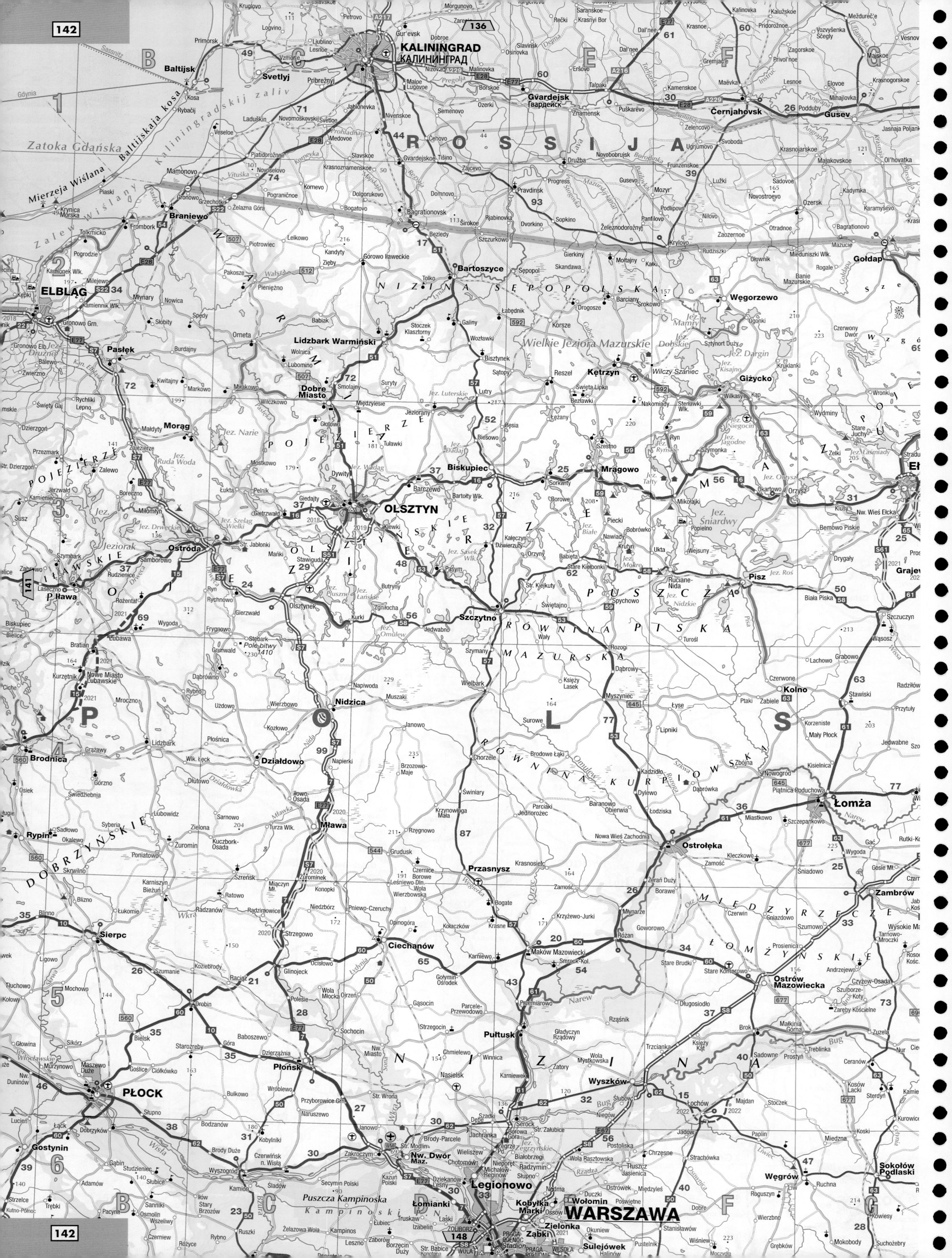
KALININGRAD
КАЛИНИНГРАД
R O S S I J A
Zatoka Gdańska
Baltijskaja kosa
Kaliningradskij zaliv
Mierzeja Wiślana
Zalew Wiślany
Baltijsk
Svetlyj
Gvardejsk
Гвардейск
Černjahovsk
Gusev
Bagrationovsk
Pravdinsk
Mamonovo
Braniewo
Frombork
ELBLĄG
Pasłęk
Bartoszyce
Lidzbark Warmiński
Dobre Miasto
Kętrzyn
Giżycko
Węgorzewo
Gołdap
Reszel
Biskupiec
Mrągowo
OLSZTYN
Ostróda
Morąg
Iława
Lubawa
Nowe Miasto Lubawskie
Brodnica
Działdowo
Nidzica
Szczytno
Pisz
Grajewo
Kolno
Łomża
Ostrołęka
Przasnysz
Mława
Ciechanów
Maków Mazowiecki
Różan
Ostrów Mazowiecka
Zambrów
Pułtusk
Wyszków
Płońsk
Sierpc
Rypin
PŁOCK
Gostynin
Nw. Dwór Maz.
Legionowo
Łomianki
Kobyłka
Marki
Wołomin
Ząbki
Zielonka
Sulejówek
WARSZAWA
Węgrów
Sokołów Podlaski
NIZINA SĘPOPOLSKA
Wielkie Jeziora Mazurskie
POJEZIERZE OLSZTYŃSKIE
POJEZIERZE IŁAWSKIE
RÓWNINA MAZURSKA
RÓWNINA PISKA
PUSZCZA PISKA
RÓWNINA KURPIOWSKA
DOBRZYŃSKIE
MIEDZYRZECZE ŁOMŻYŃSKIE
N I Z I N A
Jez. Śniardwy
Puszcza Kampinoska
Narew
Bug
Wisła
P
L
S

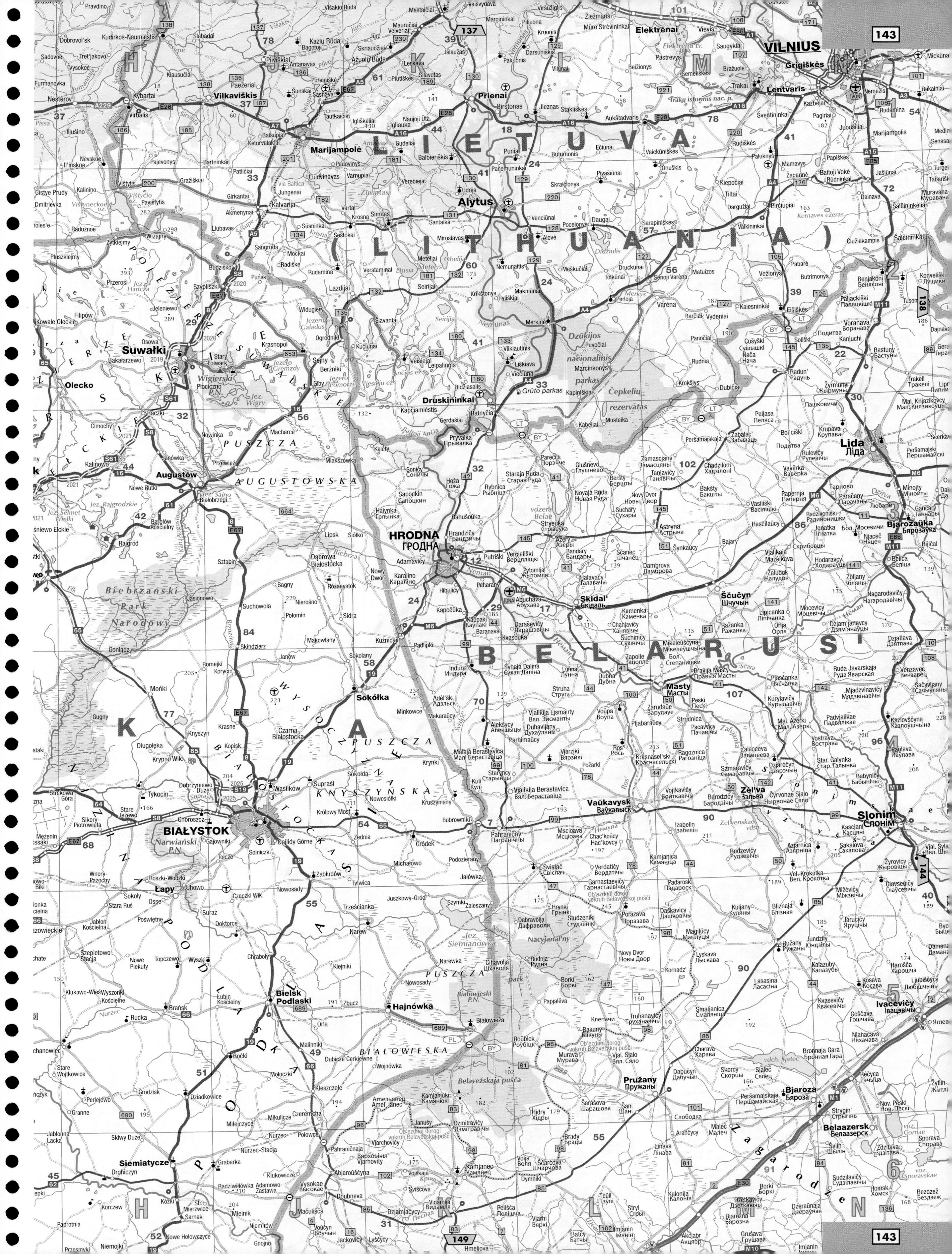

LIETUVA
(LITHUANIA)
BELARUS'
VILNIUS
Grigiškės
Lentvaris
Elektrėnai
Trakai
Vievis
Prienai
Birštonas
Marijampolė
Vilkaviškis
Kybartai
Virbalis
Kalvarija
Alytus
Lazdijai
Seirijai
Merkinė
Druskininkai
Varėna
Eišiškės
Dzūkijos nacionalinis parkas
Čepkelių rezervatas
Suwałki
Olecko
Sejny
Wigierski P.N.
Augustów
Raczki
PUSZCZA AUGUSTOWSKA
Biebrzański Park Narodowy
HRODNA
ГРОДНА
Skidal'
Скідаль
Ščučyn
Шчучын
Lida
Ліда
Masty
Масты
Vaŭkavysk
Ваўкавыск
Zel'va
Зэльва
Slonim
Слонім
Sokółka
Wasilków
BIAŁYSTOK
Narwiański P.N.
Łapy
Tykocin
PUSZCZA KNYSZYŃSKA
WYSOCZYZNA BIAŁOSTOCKA
PODLASKA
Bielsk Podlaski
Hajnówka
Białowieża
Białowieski P.N.
PUSZCZA BIAŁOWIESKA
Belavežskaja pušča
Kamjanec
Каменец
Pružany
Пружаны
Bjaroza
Бяроза
Belaazersk
Белаазерск
Ivacevičy
Івацэвічы
Siemiatycze
Drohiczyn
Zagarodze

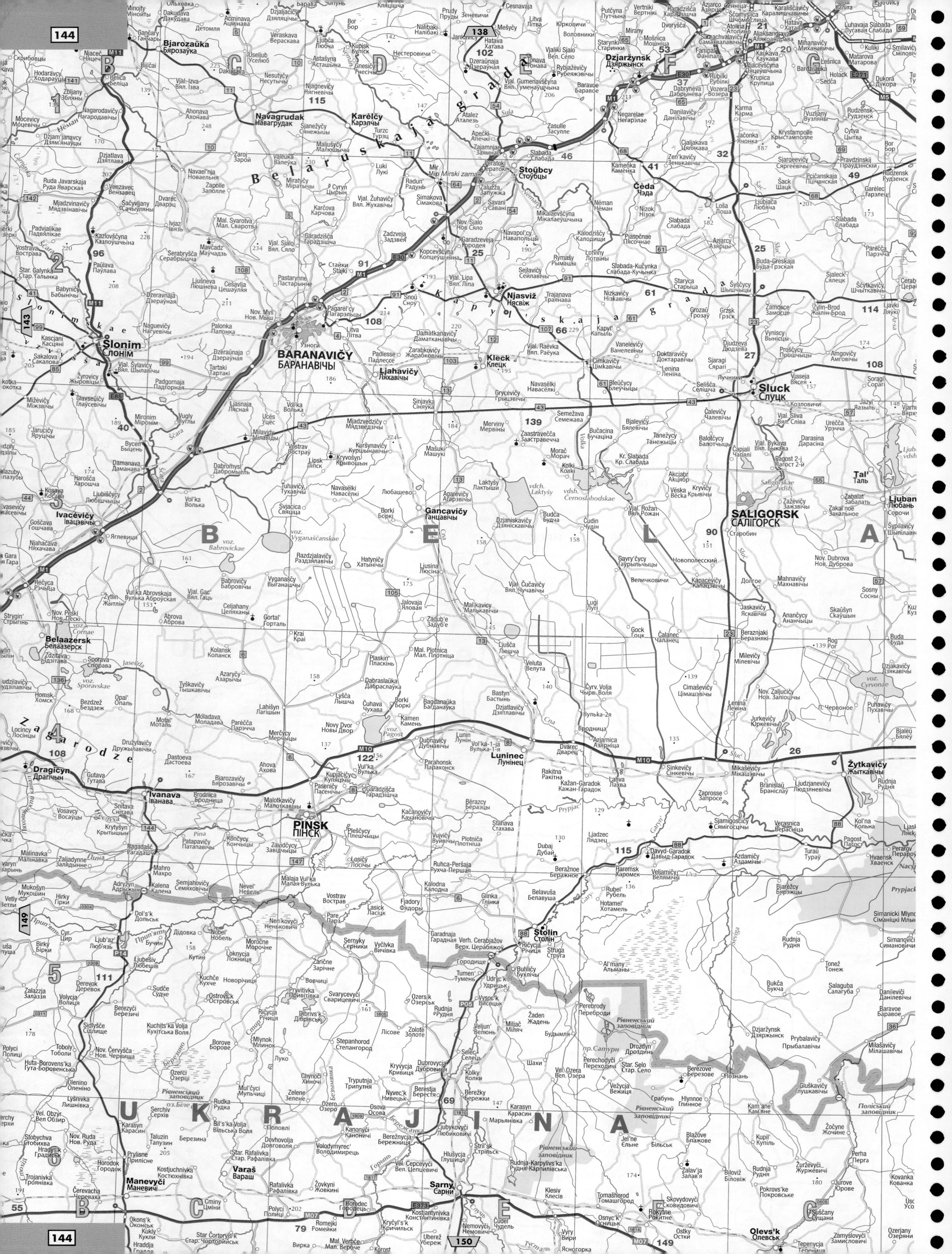
Navagrudak
Навагрудак
Karėlčy
Карэлічы
Bjarozaŭka
Бярозаўка
Dzjaržynsk
Дзяржынск
Stoŭbcy
Стоўбцы
Mir
Čėda
Чэда
Njasviž
Нясвіж
Kleck
Клецк
Ljahavičy
Ляхавічы
BARANAVIČY
БАРАНАВІЧЫ
Slonim
Слонім
Sluck
Слуцк
SALIGORSK
САЛІГОРСК
Ljuban
Любань
Gancavičy
Ганцавічы
Ivacėvičy
Івацэвічы
Belaazersk
Белаазерск
Luninec
Лунінец
Mikaševičy
Мікашэвічы
Žytkavičy
Жыткавічы
Dragičyn
Драгічын
Ivanava
Іванава
PINSK
ПІНСК
Stolin
Столін
Davyd-Gradok
Давыд-Гарадок
Sarny
Сарни
Manevyči
Маневичі
Varaš
Вараш
Rokytne
Рокитне
Olevs'k
Олевськ
Belaruskaja grada
Kapyl'skaja grada
Slonimskae vyšša
Zagarodze
B E L A
U K R A J I N A
Рівненський заповідник
Поліський заповідник
M1
M10
E30
E85
E373
M07
M11

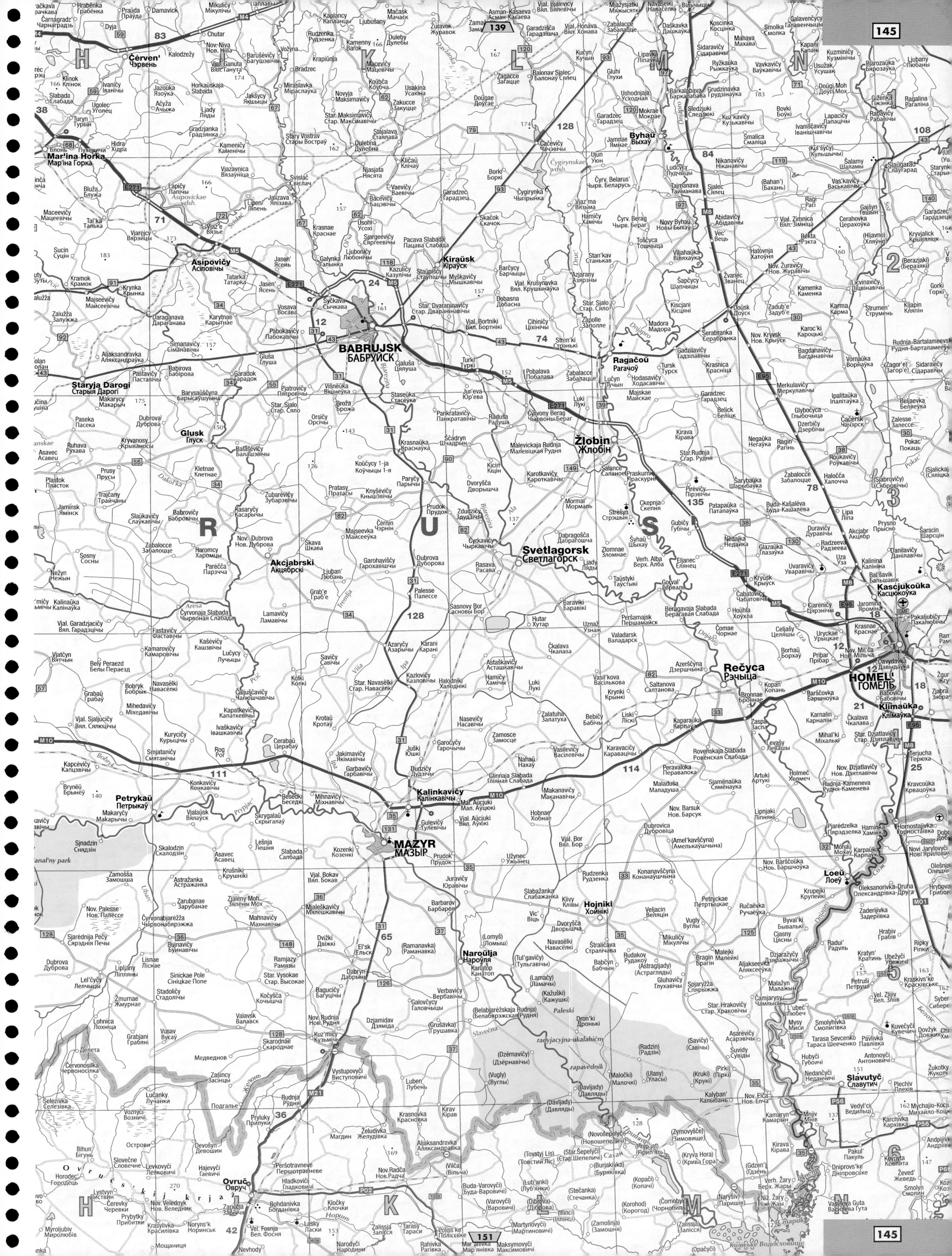
Červen'
Чэрвень
Mar'ina Horka
Мар'іна Горка
Asipovičy
Асіповічы
Kiraŭsk
Кіраўск
Byhaŭ
Быхаў
BABRUJSK
БАБРУЙСК
Ragačoŭ
Рагачоў
Staryja Darogi
Старыя Дарогі
Glusk
Глуск
Žlobin
Жлобін
Svetlagorsk
Светлагорск
Akcjabrski
Акцябрскі
Kascjukoŭka
Касцюкоўка
Rečyca
Рэчыца
HOMEL'
ГОМЕЛЬ
Klimaŭka
Клімаўка
Petrykaŭ
Петрыкаў
Kalinkavičy
Калінкавічы
MAZYR
МАЗЫР
Loeŭ
Лоеў
Hojniki
Хойнікі
Naroŭlja
Нароўля
Slavutyč
Славутич
Ovruč
Овруч
Prypjat'
Припять
Čornobyl'
Чорнобиль
Ovruc'kyj krjaž
E271
E95
M5
M10
M8
M1
M21
P56
P02
139
151
H
K
L
M
N
R
U
S
1
2
3
4
5
6

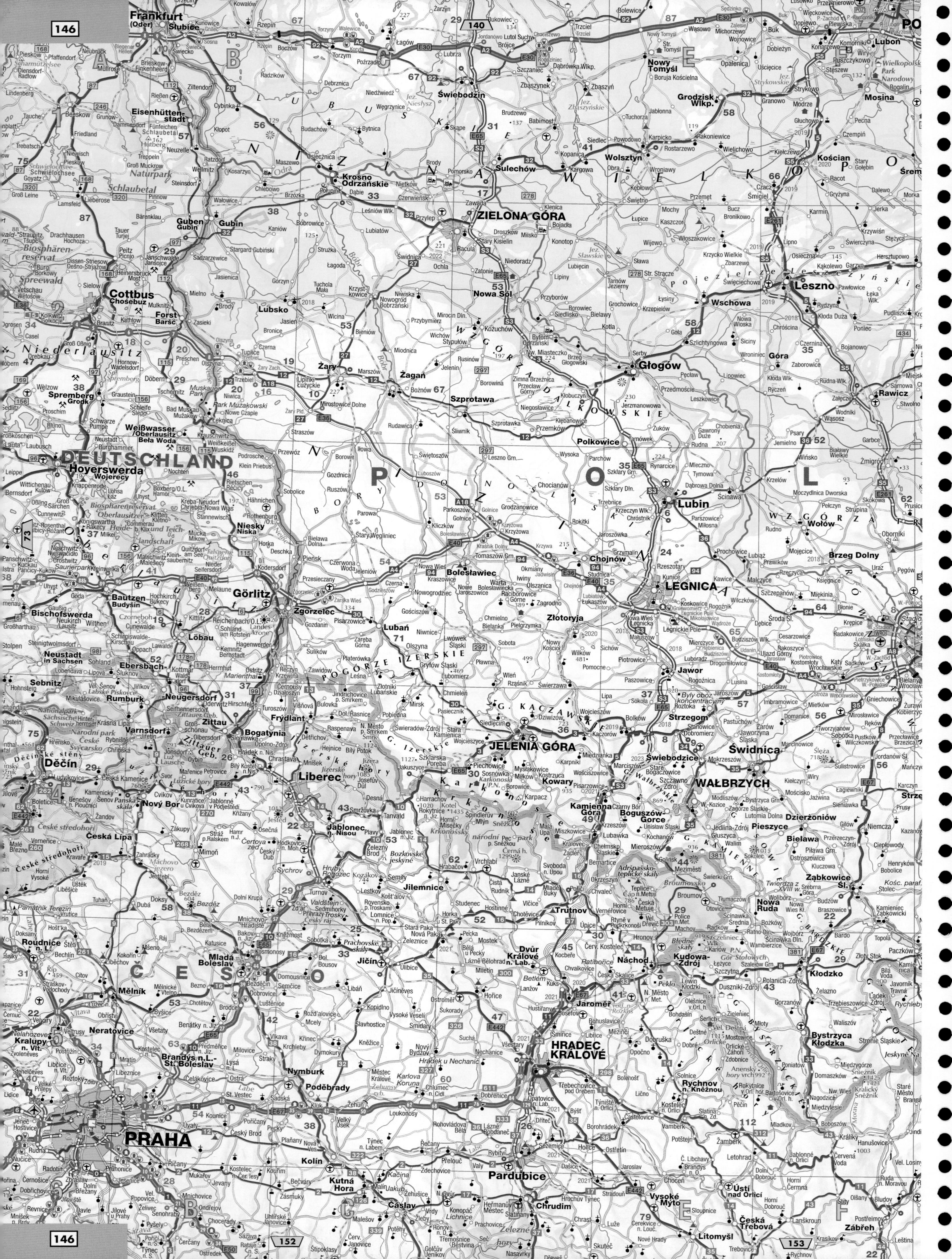

Frankfurt (Oder)
Słubice
Eisenhüttenstadt
Świebodzin
Nowy Tomyśl
Grodzisk Wlkp.
Mosina
Luboń
Sulechów
Wolsztyn
Kościan
Krosno Odrzańskie
ZIELONA GÓRA
Guben
Gubin
Cottbus
Chośebuz
Forst
Barść
Lubsko
Nowa Sól
Wschowa
Leszno
Spreewald
Niederlausitz
Żary
Żagań
Głogów
Rawicz
Spremberg
Grodk
Szprotawa
Polkowice
Weißwasser /Oberlausitz
Bela Woda
DEUTSCHLAND
Hoyerswerda
Wojerecy
Lubin
Wołów
Niesky
Niska
Chojnów
Brzeg Dolny
Bolesławiec
LEGNICA
Görlitz
Zgorzelec
Bautzen
Budyšin
Bischofswerda
Złotoryja
Lubań
Löbau
Neustadt in Sachsen
Ebersbach
Jawor
Sebnitz
Rumburk
Neugersdorf
Frýdlant
Strzegom
Varnsdorf
Zittau
Bogatynia
JELENIA GÓRA
Świdnica
Děčín
Liberec
Świebodzice
WAŁBRZYCH
Nový Bor
Jablonec n. Nisou
Kowary
Kamienna Góra
Boguszów-Gorce
Dzierżoniów
Česká Lípa
Bielawa
Pieszyce
Ząbkowice Śl.
Jilemnice
Trutnov
Nowa Ruda
Roudnice n. L.
Mladá Boleslav
Jičín
Dvůr Králové n. Lab.
Náchod
Kudowa-Zdrój
Kłodzko
Mělník
ČESKO
Neratovice
Jaroměř
Kralupy n. Vlt.
Brandýs n.L.-St. Boleslav
HRADEC KRÁLOVÉ
Bystrzyca Kłodzka
Nymburk
Poděbrady
Rychnov n. Kněžnou
PRAHA
Kolín
Pardubice
Kutná Hora
Čáslav
Chrudim
Vysoké Mýto
Ústí nad Orlicí
Česká Třebová
Litomyšl
Zábřeh
POLSKA

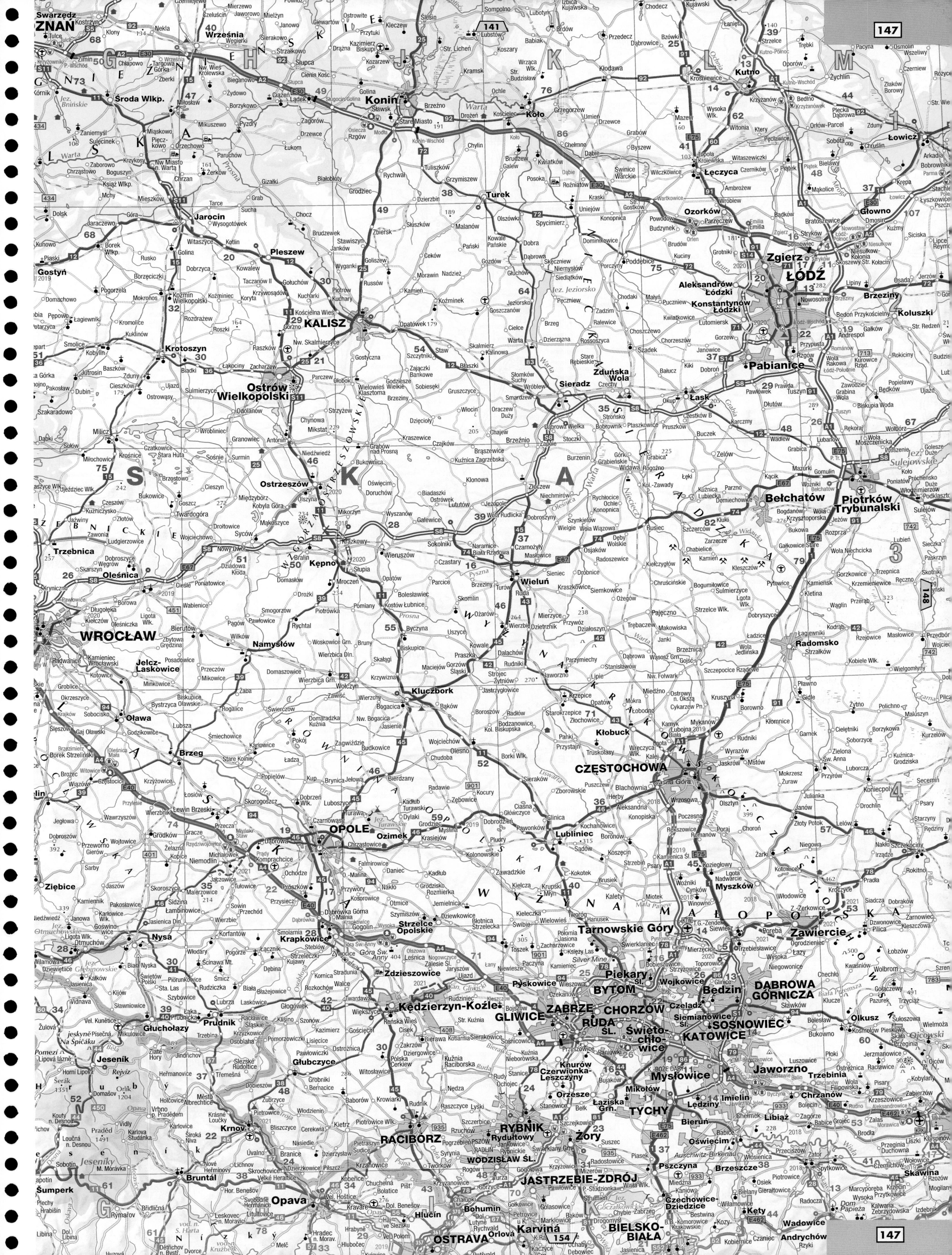

POZNAŃ
Września
Środa Wlkp.
Konin
Koło
Kutno
Łęczyca
Łowicz
Turek
Jarocin
Pleszew
Ozorków
Zgierz
ŁÓDŹ
Aleksandrów Łódzki
Konstantynów Łódzki
Brzeziny
Koluszki
Gostyń
Krotoszyn
KALISZ
Pabianice
Ostrów Wielkopolski
Sieradz
Zduńska Wola
Łask
Milicz
Ostrzeszów
Bełchatów
Piotrków Trybunalski
Trzebnica
Kępno
Wieluń
Oleśnica
WROCŁAW
Namysłów
Radomsko
Jelcz-Laskowice
Kluczbork
Oława
Brzeg
Kłobuck
CZĘSTOCHOWA
OPOLE
Ozimek
Lubliniec
Myszków
Strzelce Opolskie
Tarnowskie Góry
Zawiercie
Nysa
Krapkowice
Zdzieszowice
Piekary Śl.
BYTOM
Będzin
DĄBROWA GÓRNICZA
Kędzierzyn-Koźle
GLIWICE
ZABRZE
CHORZÓW
RUDA ŚL.
Świętochłowice
SOSNOWIEC
KATOWICE
Olkusz
Prudnik
Głuchołazy
Głubczyce
Mysłowice
Jaworzno
Chrzanów
Jeseník
Krnov
RACIBÓRZ
RYBNIK
Żory
TYCHY
Oświęcim
Šumperk
Bruntál
WODZISŁAW ŚL.
JASTRZĘBIE-ZDRÓJ
Pszczyna
Opava
Hlučín
Bohumín
Karviná
OSTRAVA
BIELSKO-BIAŁA
Kęty
Wadowice
Andrychów
Skawina

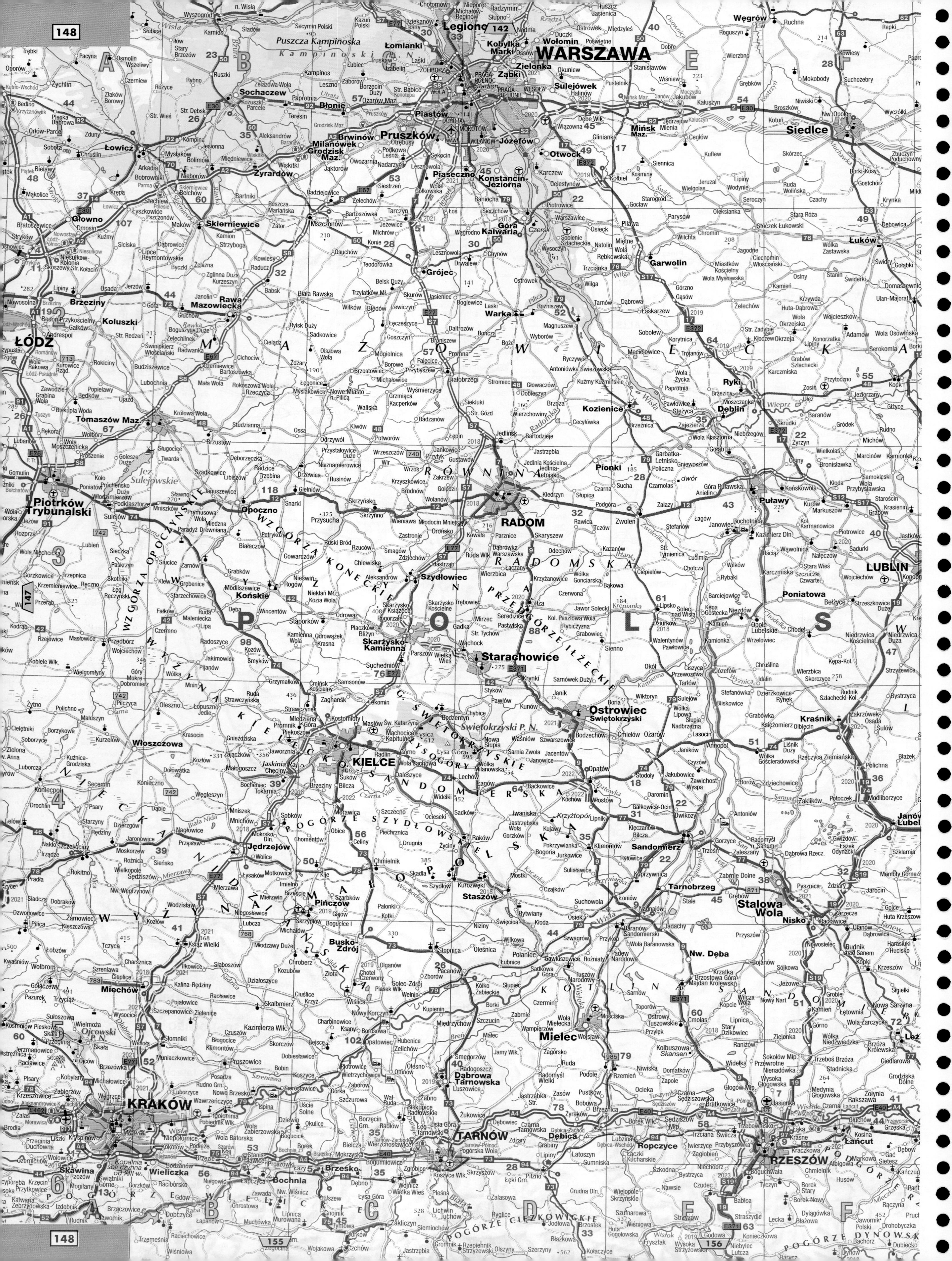
WARSZAWA
Legionowo
Łomianki
Wołomin
Zielonka
Ząbki
Sulejówek
Pruszków
Piastów
Brwinów
Milanówek
Grodzisk Maz.
Józefów
Otwock
Mińsk Maz.
Węgrów
Siedlce
Sochaczew
Błonie
Łowicz
Żyrardów
Piaseczno
Konstancin-Jeziorna
Góra Kalwaria
Skierniewice
Głowno
Brzeziny
Koluszki
ŁÓDŹ
Rawa Mazowiecka
Grójec
Warka
Garwolin
Łuków
Ryki
Dęblin
Kozienice
Puławy
Tomaszów Maz.
Piotrków Trybunalski
Opoczno
RADOM
Pionki
Zwoleń
LUBLIN
Szydłowiec
Końskie
Skarżysko-Kamienna
Starachowice
Ostrowiec Świętokrzyski
Kraśnik
Włoszczowa
KIELCE
Opatów
Sandomierz
Tarnobrzeg
Stalowa Wola
Nisko
Jędrzejów
Pińczów
Busko-Zdrój
Staszów
Nw. Dęba
Mielec
Miechów
Dąbrowa Tarnowska
KRAKÓW
TARNÓW
Dębica
Ropczyce
RZESZÓW
Łańcut
Wieliczka
Bochnia
Brzesko
Skawina
Puszcza Kampinoska
M A Z O W I E C K A
R Ó W N I N A R A D O M S K A
WZGÓRZA OPOCZYŃSKIE
WZGÓRZA KONECKIE
PRZEDGÓRZE IŁŻECKIE
G. ŚWIĘTOKRZYSKIE
ŁYSOGÓRY
W Y Ż Y N A K I E L E C K A
POGÓRZE SZYDŁOWSKIE
N I E C K A N I D Z I A Ń S K A
K O T L I N A S A N D O M I E R S K A
POGÓRZE CIĘŻKOWICKIE
POGÓRZE DYNOWSKIE
P O L S K A
155
156

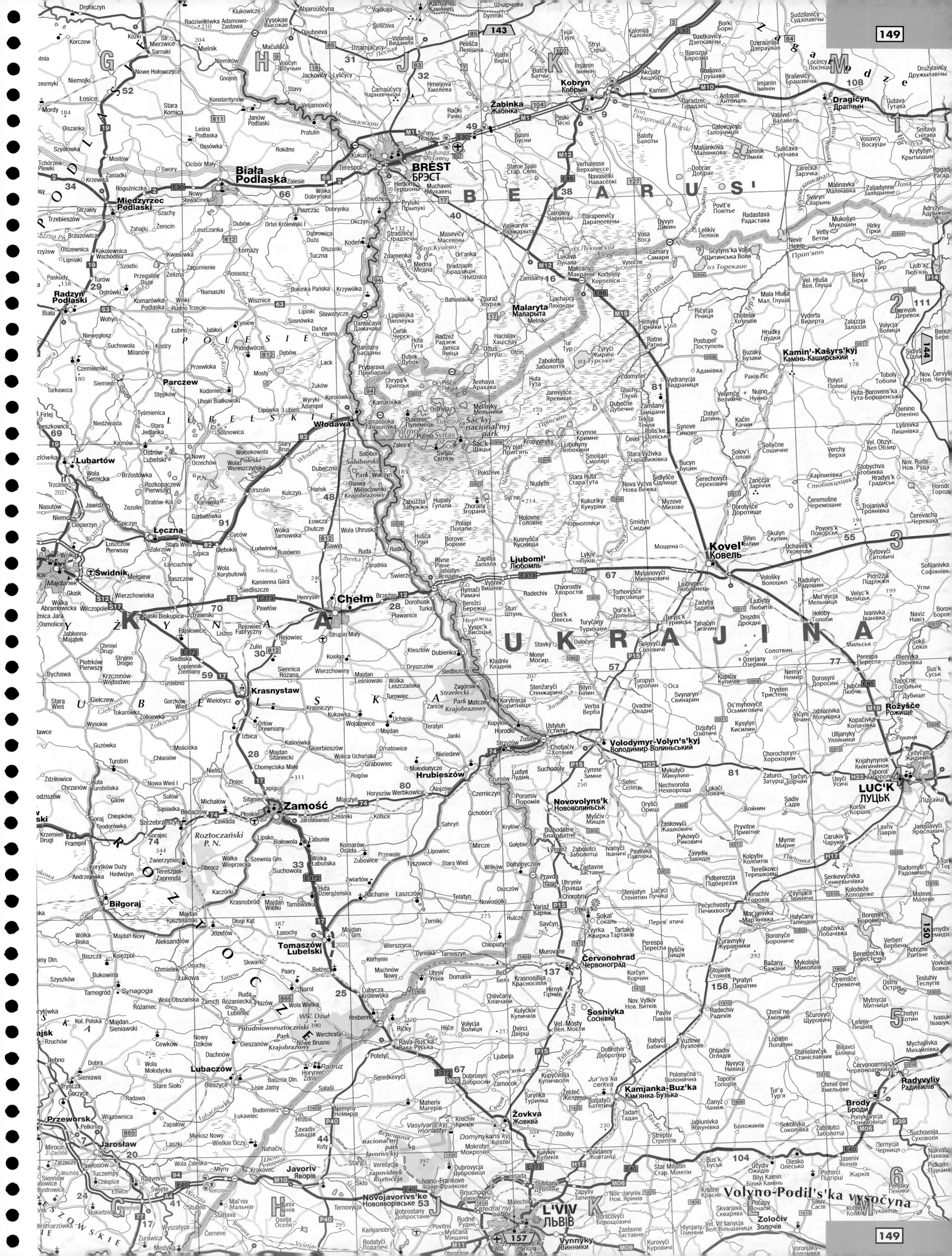
BELARUS'
UKRAJINA
POLESIE
LUBELSKIE
LUBELSKA
ROZTOCZE
PODLASIE
Volyno-Podil's'ka vysočyna
BREST
БРЭСТ
Biała Podlaska
Międzyrzec Podlaski
Radzyń Podlaski
Kobryn
Кобрын
Žabinka
Жабінка
Malaryta
Марарыта
Dragičyn
Драгічын
Kovel'
Ковель
Luc'k
Луцьк
Chełm
Włodawa
Łęczna
Lubartów
Świdnik
Krasnystaw
Zamość
Hrubieszów
Tomaszów Lubelski
Biłgoraj
Lubaczów
Jarosław
Przeworsk
Ljuboml'
Любомль
Volodymyr-Volyns'kyj
Володимир-Волинський
Novovolyns'k
Нововолинськ
Červonohrad
Червоноград
Sosnivka
Соснівка
Kamjanka-Buz'ka
Кам'янка-Бузька
Žovkva
Жовква
Javoriv
Яворів
Novojavorivs'ke
Нововолинське
L'VIV
ЛЬВІВ
Brody
Броди
Radyvyliv
Радивилів
Rožyšče
Рожище
Kamin'-Kašyrs'kyj
Камінь-Каширський
Šac'kyj nacional'nyj park
Poleski P.N.
Roztoczański P.N.
Sobiborski Park Miejscowy Krajobrazowy
Strzelecki Park Krajobrazowy
Południoworoztoczański Park Krajobrazowy
Zapovidnyk Roztoččja
Jur'ivs'ka cerkva
Vasylyans'kyj monastyr
Dominykans'kyj kostel
Katedral'nyj sobor
E30
E85
E372
E373
E40
M1
M12
M19
M07
M06
M09
M10
H17
H22
P15
143
149
144
150
157

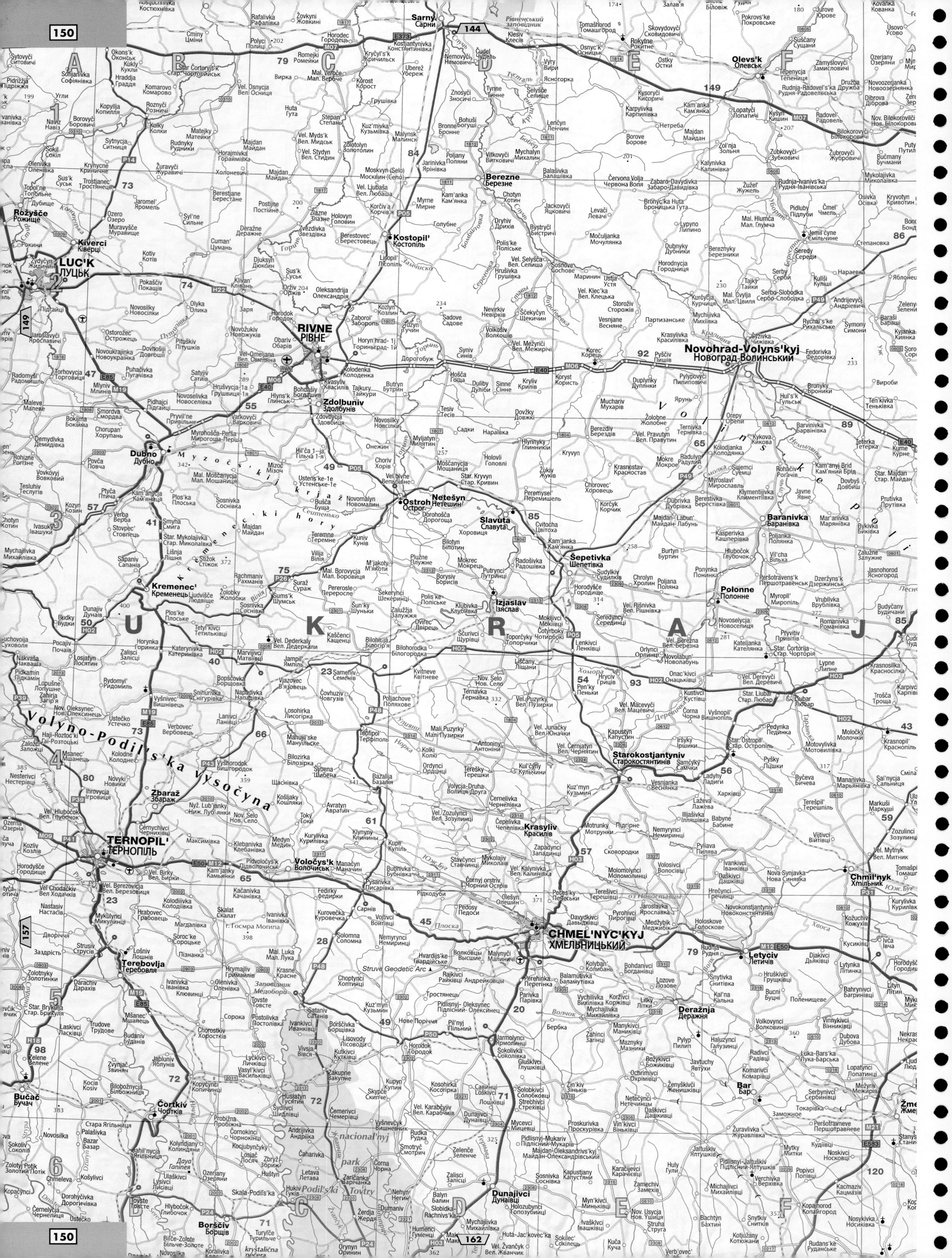
Sarny
Сарни
Olevs'k
Олевськ
LUC'K
ЛУЦЬК
Kiverci
Ківерці
Rožyšče
Рожище
Kostopil'
Костопіль
Berezne
Березне
RIVNE
РІВНЕ
Zdolbuniv
Здолбунів
Novohrad-Volyns'kyj
Новоград-Волинський
Dubno
Дубно
Ostroh
Острог
Netešyn
Нетешин
Slavuta
Славута
Šepetivka
Шепетівка
Baranivka
Баранівка
Kremenec'
Кременець
Izjaslav
Ізяслав
Polonne
Полонне
Starokostjantyniv
Старокостянтинів
Zbaraž
Збараж
TERNOPIL'
ТЕРНОПІЛЬ
Voločys'k
Волочиськ
Krasyliv
Красилів
CHMEL'NYC'KYJ
ХМЕЛЬНИЦЬКИЙ
Chmil'nyk
Хмільник
Letyčiv
Летичів
Terebovlja
Теребовля
Deražnja
Деражня
Bar
Бар
Čortkiv
Чортків
Bučač
Бучач
Dunajivci
Дунаївці
Borščiv
Борщів
Myzoc'kyj krjaž
Kremenec'ki hory
Volyno-Podil's'ka vysočyna
Volyns'ke polissja
U K R A J
Struve Geodetic Arc
Podil's'ki Tovtry
nacional'nyj park
E40
E50
E85
E373
M06
M07
M12
M19
M21
H02
H03
P05
P24
P48
P49
P50
144
149
157
162

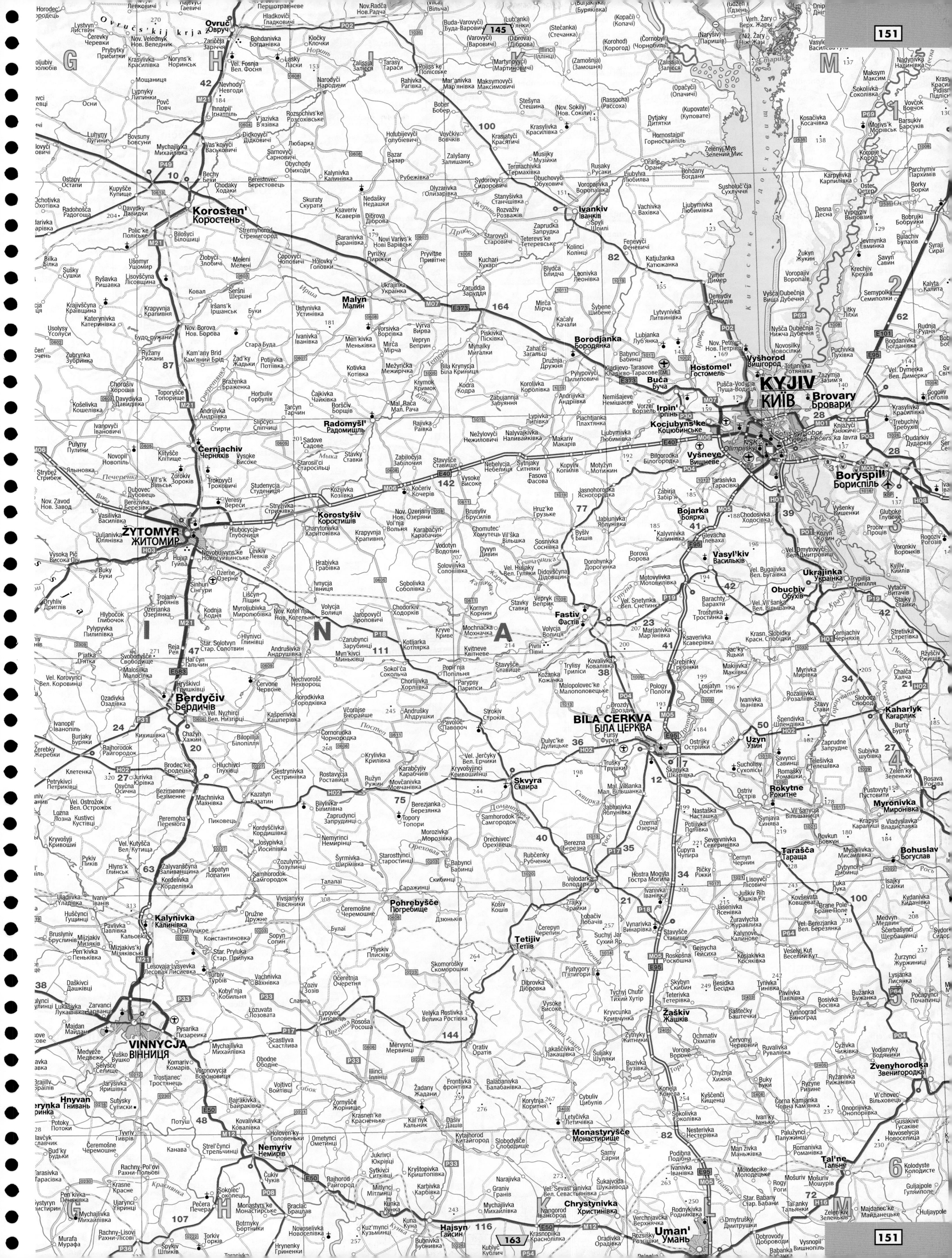
Ovruč
Овруч
Korosten'
Коростень
Malyn
Малин
Ivankiv
Іванків
Borodjanka
Бородянка
Vyšhorod
Вишгород
Hostomel'
Гостомель
KYJIV
КИЇВ
Brovary
Бровари
Irpin'
Ірпінь
Buča
Буча
Kocjubyns'ke
Коцюбинське
Vyšneve
Вишневе
Boryspil'
Бориспіль
Radomyšl'
Радомишль
Černjachiv
Черняхів
Korostyšiv
Коростишів
ŽYTOMYR
ЖИТОМИР
Fastiv
Фастів
Bojarka
Боярка
Vasyl'kiv
Васильків
Ukrajinka
Українка
Obuchiv
Обухів
Berdyčiv
Бердичів
BILA CERKVA
БІЛА ЦЕРКВА
Skvyra
Сквира
Kaharlyk
Кагарлик
Uzyn
Узин
Rokytne
Рокитне
Myronivka
Миронівка
Tarašča
Тараща
Bohuslav
Богуслав
Kalynivka
Калинівка
Pohrebyšče
Погребище
Tetijiv
Тетіїв
Žaškiv
Жашків
Zvenyhorodka
Звенигородка
VINNYCJA
ВІННИЦЯ
Hnyvan
Гнівань
Nemyriv
Немирів
Monastyryšče
Монастирище
Chrystynivka
Христинівка
Tal'ne
Тальне
Hajsyn
Гайсин
Uman'
Умань
145
163
151

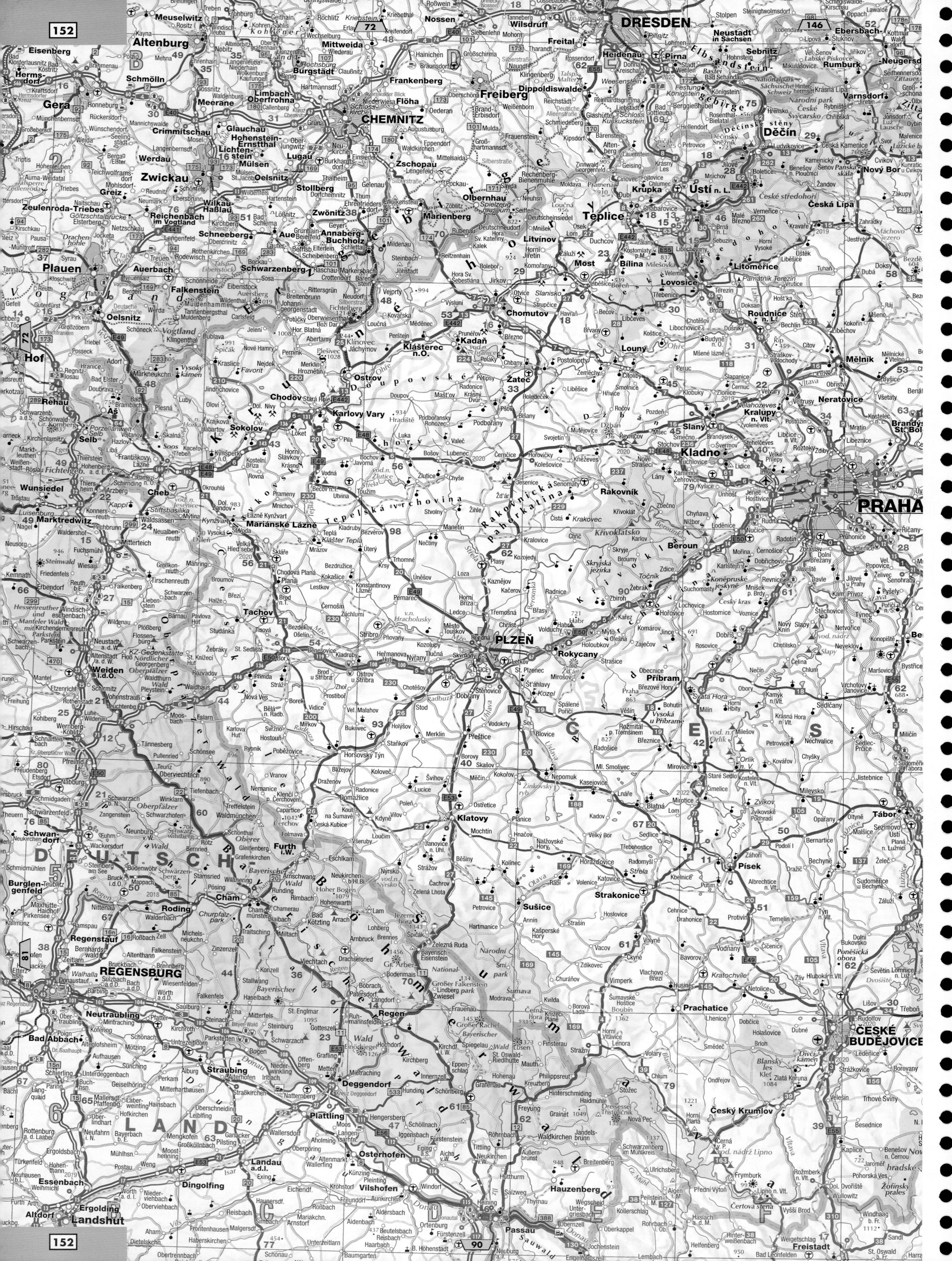

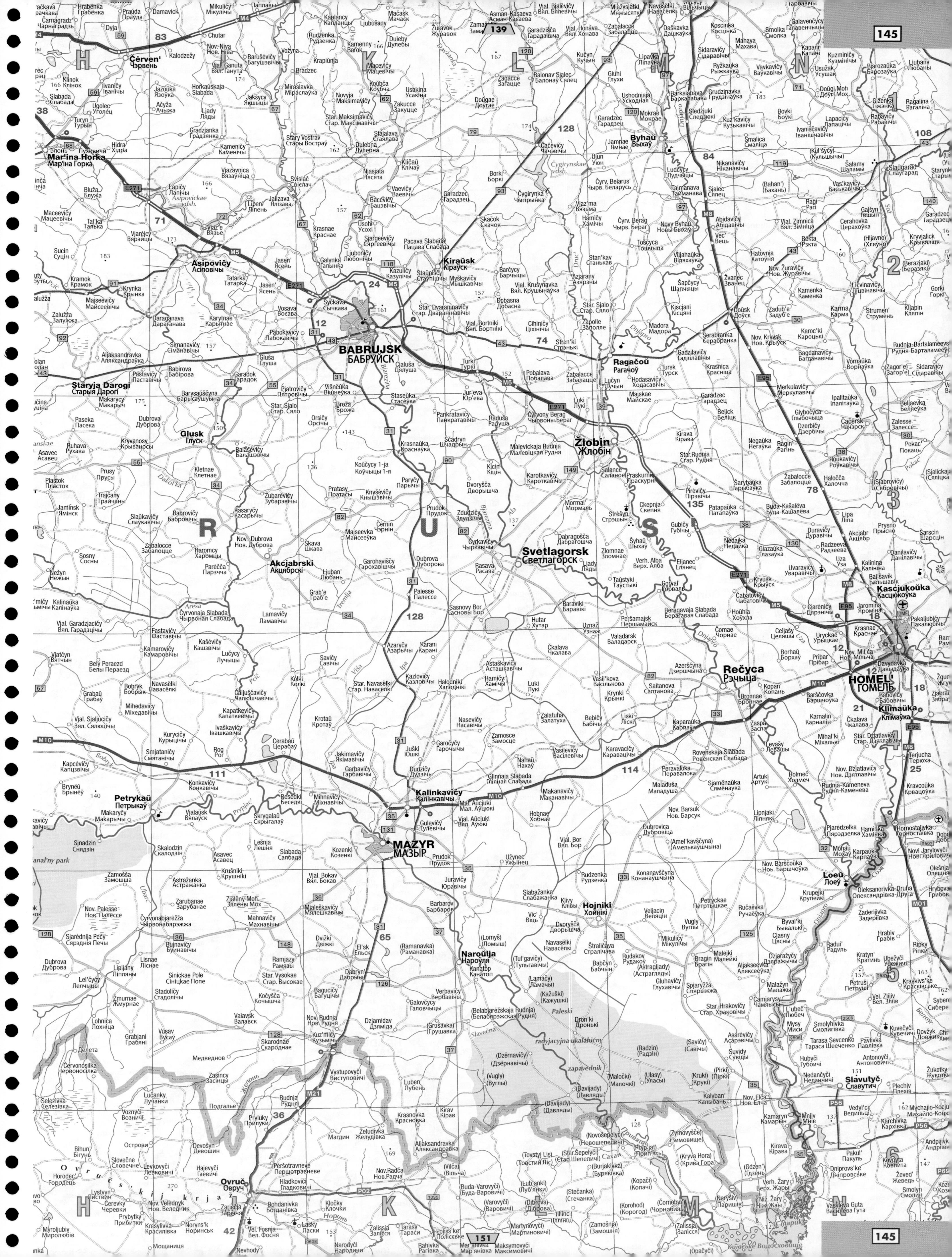

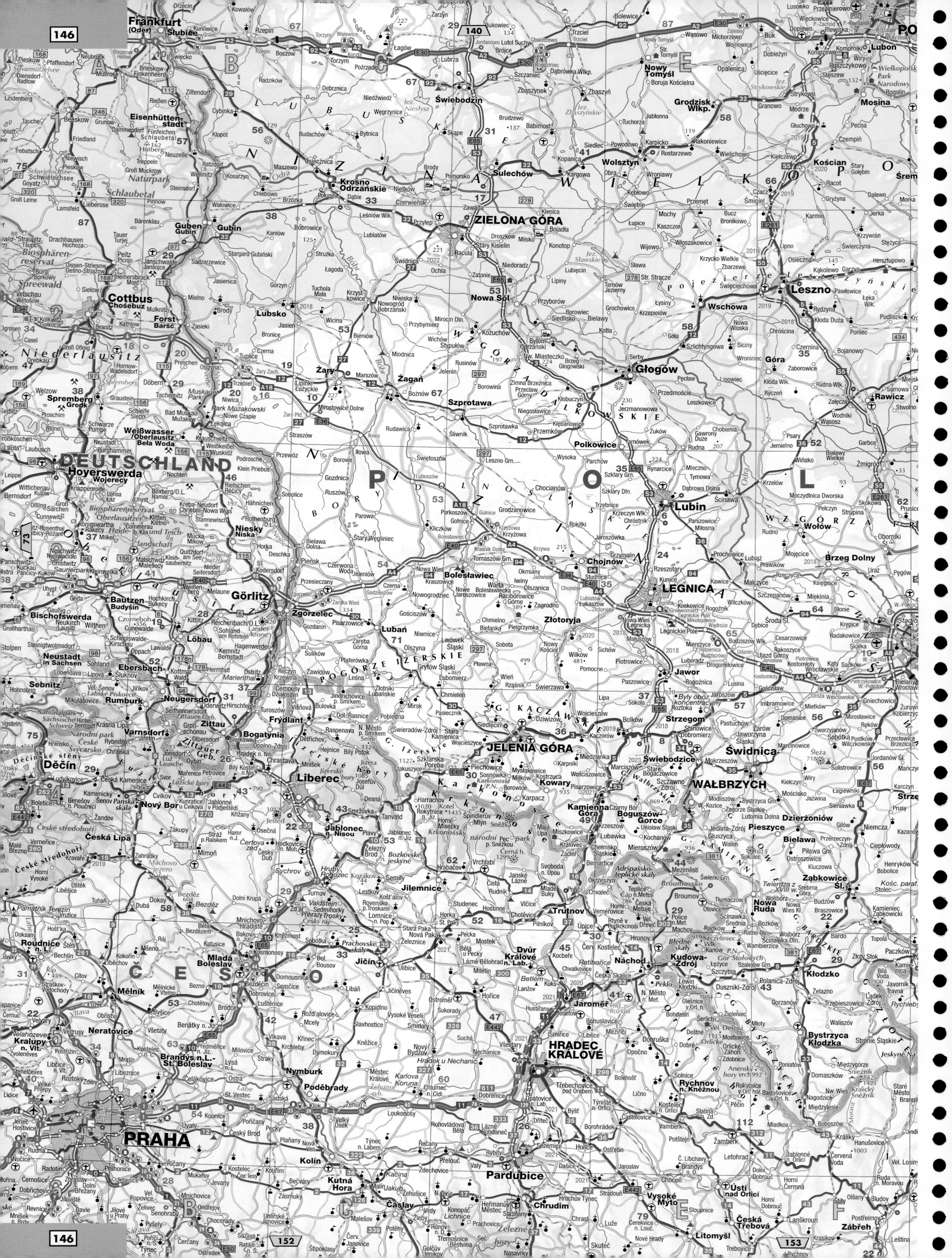
140
152
153
DEUTSCHLAND
POLSKA
ČESKO
Frankfurt (Oder)
Słubice
Eisenhüttenstadt
Cottbus
Chóśebuz
Forst
Baršć
Guben
Gubin
Spremberg
Grodk
Weißwasser /Oberlausitz
Běła Woda
Hoyerswerda
Wojerecy
Niesky
Niska
Bautzen
Budyšin
Görlitz
Zgorzelec
Löbau
Bischofswerda
Neugersdorf
Rumburk
Varnsdorf
Zittau
Bogatynia
Děčín
Česká Lípa
Nový Bor
Liberec
Jablonec n. Nisou
Mladá Boleslav
Mělník
Neratovice
Kralupy n. Vlt.
Brandýs n.L.- St. Boleslav
PRAHA
Nymburk
Poděbrady
Kolín
Kutná Hora
Čáslav
Jičín
Jilemnice
Trutnov
Dvůr Králové n. Lab.
Jaroměř
HRADEC KRÁLOVÉ
Pardubice
Chrudim
Vysoké Mýto
Litomyšl
Česká Třebová
Ústí nad Orlicí
Rychnov n. Kněžnou
Náchod
Kudowa-Zdrój
Kłodzko
Bystrzyca Kłodzka
Zábřeh
Nowa Ruda
Wałbrzych
Świdnica
Dzierżoniów
Bielawa
Ząbkowice Śl.
Świebodzice
Strzegom
Jawor
Legnica
Złotoryja
Jelenia Góra
Kamienna Góra
Kowary
Lubań
Bolesławiec
Chojnów
Lubin
Polkowice
Głogów
Wołów
Brzeg Dolny
Leszno
Wschowa
Rawicz
Kościan
Śrem
Mosina
Grodzisk Wlkp.
Nowy Tomyśl
Wolsztyn
Sulechów
Świebodzin
ZIELONA GÓRA
Krosno Odrzańskie
Nowa Sól
Lubsko
Żary
Żagań
Szprotawa
Zbąszynek
Zbąszyń
Sulęcin
Rzepin
Łagów
Lubrza
Niederlausitz
Spreewald
Oberlausitz
NIZINA WIELKOPOLSKA
BORY DOLNOŚLĄSKIE
POGÓRZE IZERSKIE
G. KACZAWSKIE
Karkonosze
Krkonoše
Góry Izerskie
G. Wałbrzyskie
G. Sowie
G. Stołowe
Orlické hory
Góry Bystrzyckie
Pojezierze Leszczyńskie
Wzgórza Dalkowskie
Wzgórza Trzebnickie
Muskauer Park
Park Mużakowski
Naturpark Schlaubetal
Biosphärenreservat Spreewald
Nationalpark Sächsische Schweiz
Národní park České Švýcarsko
Krkonošský národní park
České středohoří
Zittauer Geb.
Lužické hory
Jizerské hory
Český ráj
Sněžka
Śnieżnik
Śnieżka
Ślęża
Odra
Labe
Vltava
E30
E36
E40
E65
E67
E261
E442
A2
A4
A18
S3
S5

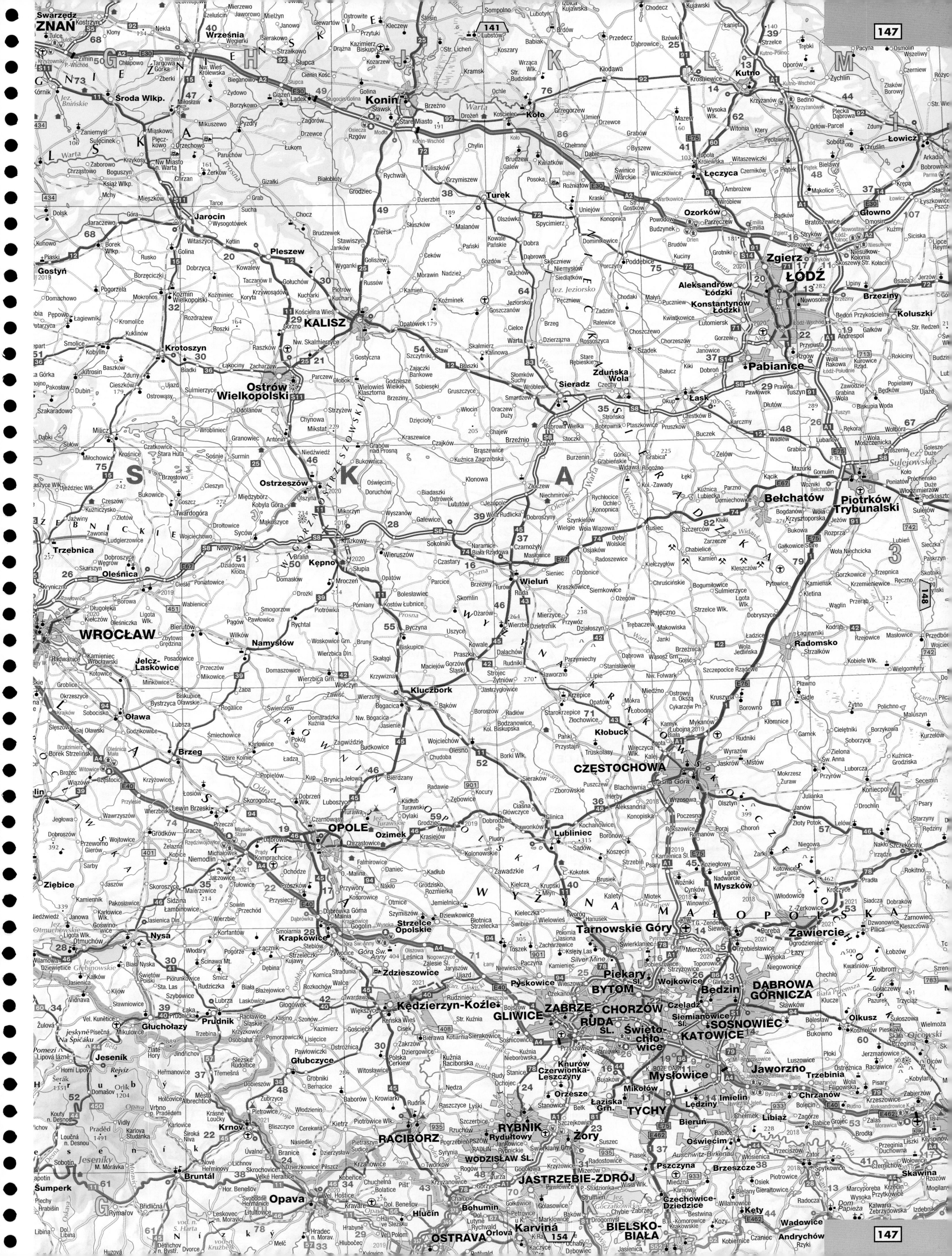

147
POZNAŃ
Września
Konin
Koło
Kutno
Łęczyca
Łowicz
Środa Wlkp.
Jarocin
Pleszew
Turek
Uniejów
Ozorków
Zgierz
ŁÓDŹ
Aleksandrów Łódzki
Konstantynów Łódzki
Brzeziny
Koluszki
Gostyń
KALISZ
Krotoszyn
Ostrów Wielkopolski
Sieradz
Zduńska Wola
Łask
Pabianice
Tuszyn
Bełchatów
Piotrków Trybunalski
Ostrzeszów
Kępno
Wieruszów
Wieluń
Trzebnica
Oleśnica
WROCŁAW
Jelcz-Laskowice
Namysłów
Oława
Brzeg
Kluczbork
Kłobuck
CZĘSTOCHOWA
Radomsko
OPOLE
Ozimek
Lubliniec
Krapkowice
Strzelce Opolskie
Tarnowskie Góry
Myszków
Zawiercie
Nysa
Prudnik
Głuchołazy
Kędzierzyn-Koźle
Zdzieszowice
GLIWICE
ZABRZE
BYTOM
Piekary Śl.
CHORZÓW
RUDA ŚL.
Świętochłowice
KATOWICE
SOSNOWIEC
Będzin
DĄBROWA GÓRNICZA
Czeladź
Olkusz
Jaworzno
Mysłowice
Tychy
Chrzanów
Głubczyce
RACIBÓRZ
RYBNIK
Żory
WODZISŁAW ŚL.
JASTRZĘBIE-ZDRÓJ
Pszczyna
Oświęcim
Brzeszcze
Kęty
Wadowice
Andrychów
BIELSKO-BIAŁA
Czechowice-Dziedzice
Jeseník
Krnov
Bruntál
Opava
Šumperk
OSTRAVA
Hlučín
Bohumín
Karviná
147

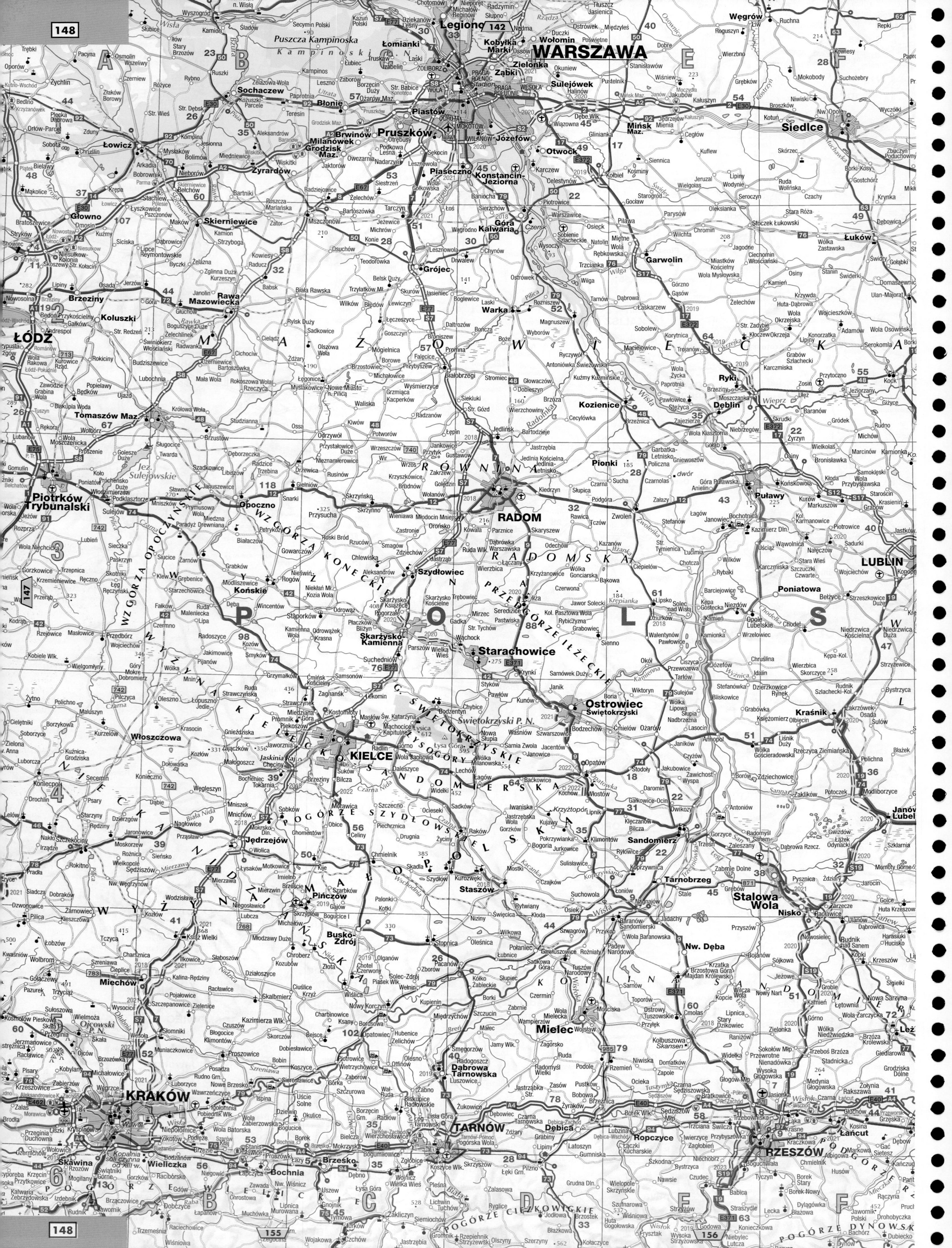
148
142
147
155
156
148
WARSZAWA
Legionowo
Łomianki
Kobyłka
Marki
Wołomin
Ząbki
Zielonka
Sulejówek
Piastów
Pruszków
Brwinów
Milanówek
Grodzisk Maz.
Józefów
Otwock
Piaseczno
Konstancin-Jeziorna
Góra Kalwaria
Grójec
Warka
Mińsk Maz.
Siedlce
Węgrów
Łuków
Garwolin
Ryki
Dęblin
Puławy
Kozienice
Pionki
RADOM
Białobrzegi
Sochaczew
Błonie
Żyrardów
Łowicz
Skierniewice
Głowno
Brzeziny
Koluszki
ŁÓDŹ
Rawa Mazowiecka
Tomaszów Maz.
Piotrków Trybunalski
Opoczno
Końskie
Szydłowiec
Skarżysko-Kamienna
Starachowice
Ostrowiec Świętokrzyski
KIELCE
Włoszczowa
Jędrzejów
Pińczów
Busko-Zdrój
Staszów
Sandomierz
Tarnobrzeg
Stalowa Wola
Nisko
Kraśnik
LUBLIN
Poniatowa
Opole Lubelskie
Nw. Dęba
Mielec
Dąbrowa Tarnowska
TARNÓW
Dębica
Ropczyce
RZESZÓW
Łańcut
Brzesko
Bochnia
Wieliczka
KRAKÓW
Skawina
Miechów
Puszcza Kampinoska
Kampinoski P. N.
Świętokrzyski P. N.
M A Z O W I E C K A
R Ó W N I N A   R A D O M S K A
P O L S
W Y Ż Y N A   K I E L E C K A
W Y Ż Y N A   N I D Z I A Ń S K A
N I E C K A   N I D Z I A Ń S K A
WZGÓRZA OPOCZYŃSKIE
WZGÓRZA KONECKIE
PRZEDGÓRZE IŁŻECKIE
G. ŚWIĘTOKRZYSKIE
ŁYSOGÓRY
S A N D O M I E R S K A
POGÓRZE SZYDŁOWSKIE
M A Ł O P O L S K A
K O T L I N A   S A N D O M I E R S K A
POGÓRZE CIĘŻKOWICKIE
POGÓRZE DYNOWSKIE
Wisła

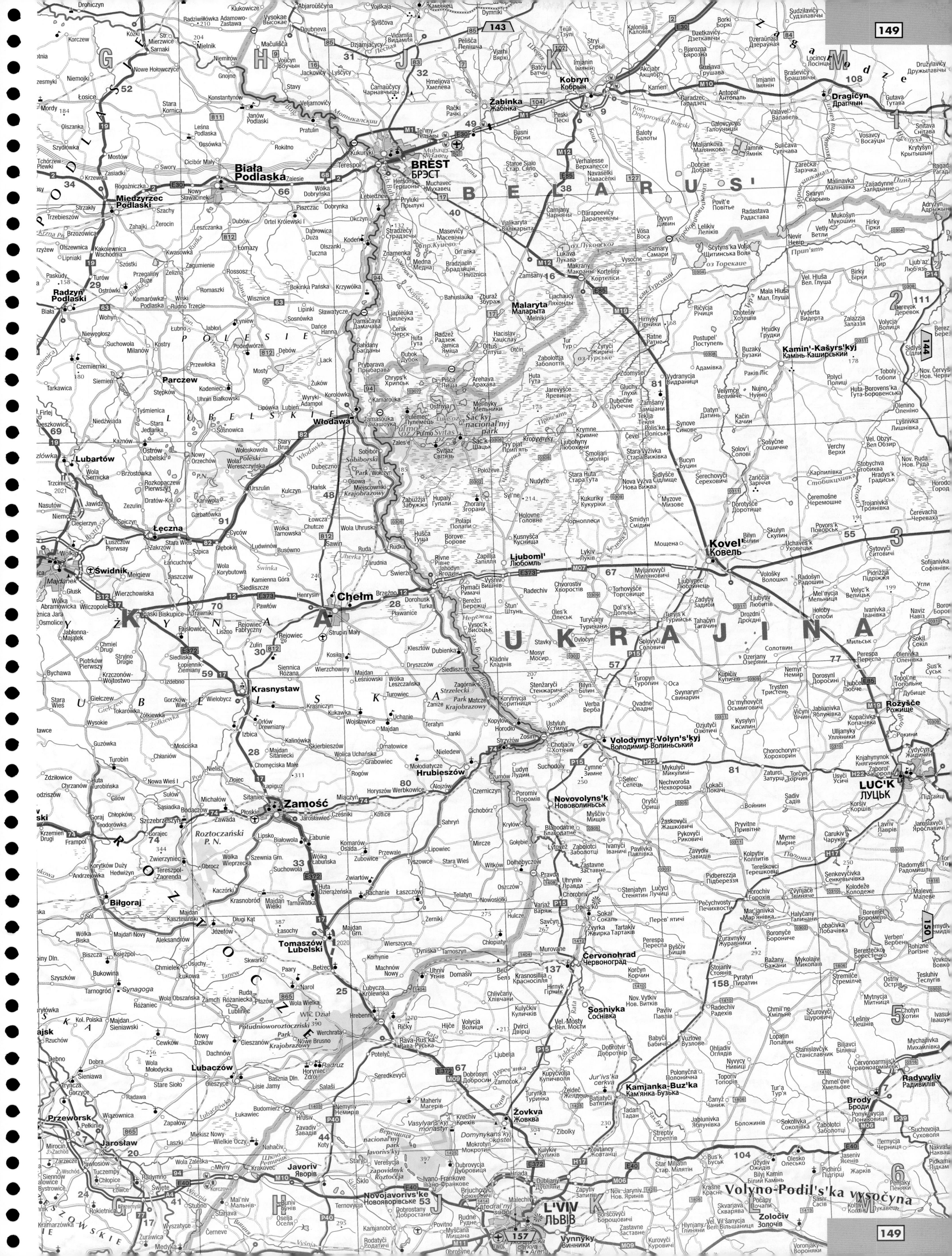
BELARUS'
UKRAJINA
PODLASKIE
LUBELSKIE
ROZTOCZE
POLESIE
Volyno-Podil's'ka vysočyna
Zagarodze
BREST
БРЭСТ
Biała Podlaska
Międzyrzec Podlaski
Radzyń Podlaski
Parczew
Włodawa
Lubartów
Łęczna
Świdnik
Chełm
Krasnystaw
Zamość
Hrubieszów
Tomaszów Lubelski
Biłgoraj
Lubaczów
Jarosław
Przeworsk
Kobryn
Кобрын
Žabinka
Жабінка
Malaryta
Маларыта
Dragičyn
Драгічын
Kamin'-Kašyrs'kyj
Камінь-Каширський
Kovel'
Ковель
Ljuboml'
Любомль
Volodymyr-Volyns'kyj
Володимир-Волинський
Novovolyns'k
Нововолинськ
Červonohrad
Червоноград
Sokal'
Сокаль
Luc'k
ЛУЦЬК
Rožyšče
Рожище
Sosnivka
Соснівка
Žovkva
Жовква
Kamjanka-Buz'ka
Кам'янка-Бузька
Javoriv
Яворів
Novojavorivs'ke
Нововорівське
L'VIV
ЛЬВІВ
Brody
Броди
Radyvyliv
Радивилів
Zoločiv
Золочів
Rava-Rus'ka
Рава-Руська
Šac'kyj nacional'nyj park
Roztoczański P. N.
Poleski P. N.
Majdanek
E30
E85
E372
E373
E40
M1
M07
M09
M10
M12
M19
P15
H22
143
144
150
157
149

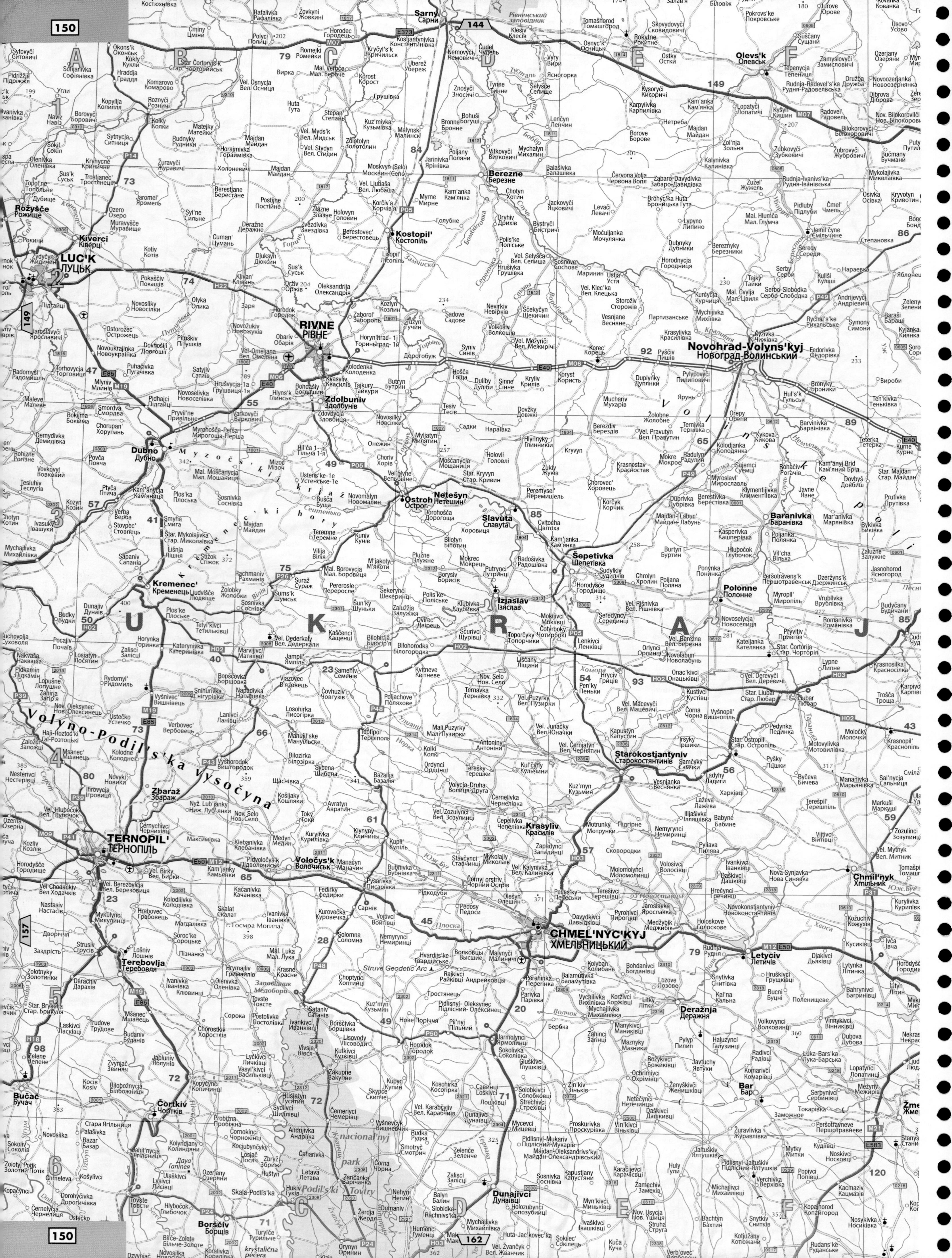

150
144
Sarny
Сарни
Rivnens'kyj zapovidnyk
Olevs'k
Олевськ
Rožyšče
Рожище
Kiverci
Ківерці
LUC'K
ЛУЦЬК
Kostopil'
Костопіль
Berezne
Березне
RIVNE
РІВНЕ
Novohrad-Volyns'kyj
Новоград-Волинський
Zdolbuniv
Здолбунів
Dubno
Дубно
Ostroh
Остроư
Netešyn
Нетешин
Slavuta
Славута
Šepetivka
Шепетівка
Baranivka
Баранівка
Kremenec'
Кременець
Izjaslav
Ізяслав
Polonne
Полонне
Myzoc'kyj krjaž
Kremenec'ki hory
Volyns'ke polissja
U K R A J
Volyno-Podil's'ka vysočyna
Starokostjantyniv
Старокостянтинів
Zbaraž
Збараж
Krasyliv
Красилів
TERNOPIL'
ТЕРНОПІЛЬ
Voločys'k
Волочиськ
Chmil'nyk
Хмільник
CHMEL'NYC'KYJ
ХМЕЛЬНИЦЬКИЙ
Letyčiv
Летичів
Terebovlja
Теребовля
Deražnja
Деражня
Bar
Бар
Čortkiv
Чортків
Bučač
Бучач
Dunajivci
Дунаївці
Borščiv
Борщів
Žmerynka
Жмеринка
Podil's'ki Tovtry
nacional'nyj park
Struve Geodetic Arc
162
149
157
150

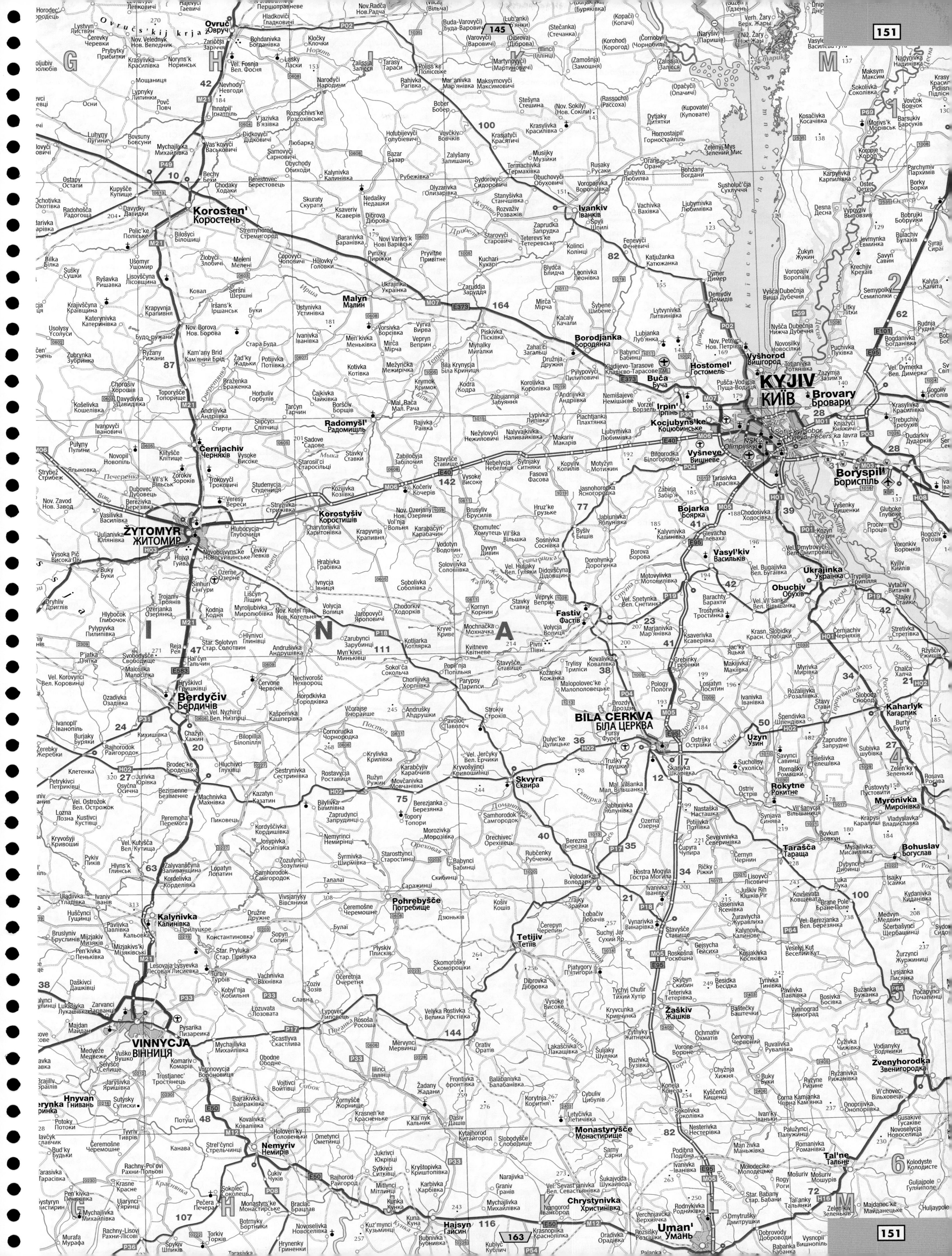

Ovruč
Овруч
Korosten'
Коростень
Malyn
Малин
Radomyšl'
Радомишль
Černjachiv
Черняхів
Korostyšiv
Коростишів
ŽYTOMYR
ЖИТОМИР
Berdyčiv
Бердичів
Ivankiv
Іванків
Borodjanka
Бородянка
Vyšhorod
Вишгород
Hostomel'
Гостомель
Buča
Буча
Irpin'
Ірпінь
KYJIV
КИЇВ
Brovary
Бровари
Boryspil'
Бориспіль
Vyšneve
Вишневе
Bojarka
Боярка
Vasyl'kiv
Васильків
Fastiv
Фастів
Obuchiv
Обухів
Ukrajinka
Українка
BILA CERKVA
БІЛА ЦЕРКВА
Uzyn
Узин
Kaharlyk
Кагарлик
Skvyra
Сквира
Rokytne
Рокитне
Myronivka
Миронівка
Tarašča
Тараща
Bohuslav
Богуслав
Tetijiv
Тетіїв
Pohrebyšče
Погребище
Kalynivka
Калинівка
VINNYCJA
ВІННИЦЯ
Hnyvan
Гнівань
Nemyriv
Немирів
Žaškiv
Жашків
Monastyryšče
Монастирище
Zvenyhorodka
Звенигородка
Tal'ne
Тальне
Chrystynivka
Христинівка
Uman'
Умань
Hajsyn
Гайсин
Kyjivs'ke vodoschovyšče
Київське водосховище
Ovruč'skij krjaž
G
H
I
K
L
M
I
N
A
1
2
3
4
5
6

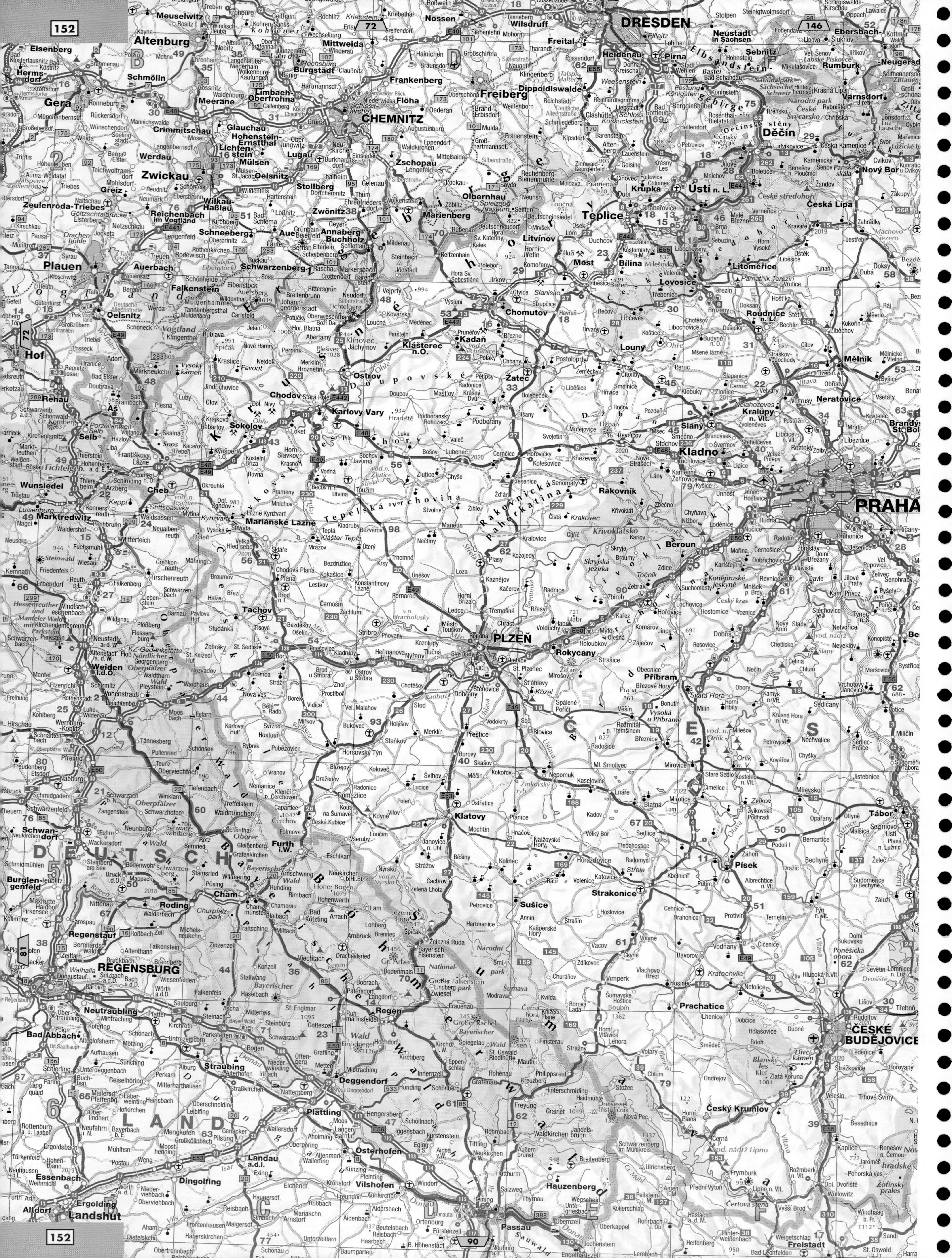

152
146
72
DRESDEN
CHEMNITZ
PRAHA
PLZEŇ
REGENSBURG
ČESKÉ BUDĚJOVICE
Altenburg
Gera
Zwickau
Plauen
Hof
Freiberg
Meißen
Děčín
Ústí n. L.
Teplice
Most
Chomutov
Karlovy Vary
Cheb
Mariánské Lázně
Sokolov
Žatec
Louny
Kladno
Rakovník
Beroun
Příbram
Rokycany
Klatovy
Domažlice
Písek
Strakonice
Tábor
Český Krumlov
Prachatice
Sušice
Cham
Deggendorf
Straubing
Passau
Landshut
Weiden i.d.O.
Amberg
Marktredwitz
Selb
Wunsiedel
Mělník
Litoměřice
Lovosice
Pirna
Heidenau
Freital
Annaberg-Buchholz
Marienberg
Olbernhau
Aue
Schneeberg
Reichenbach im Vogtland
Oelsnitz
Tachov
Stříbro
Horažďovice
Vimperk
Regen
Zwiesel
Freistadt
DEUTSCHLAND
ČESKÁ
Krušné hory
Erzgebirge
Doupovské hory
Český les
Oberpfälzer Wald
Bayerischer Wald
Šumava
Böhmerwald
Brdy
Křivoklátsko
Vogtland
Elbsandsteingebirge
České středohoří
Tepelská vrchovina
Rakovnická pahorkatina
152

POLSKA

JELENIA GÓRA

WAŁBRZYCH

Świdnica

Liberec

HRADEC KRÁLOVÉ

Pardubice

Jihlava

BRNO

OLOMOUC

SLOVENSKO

ÖSTERREICH

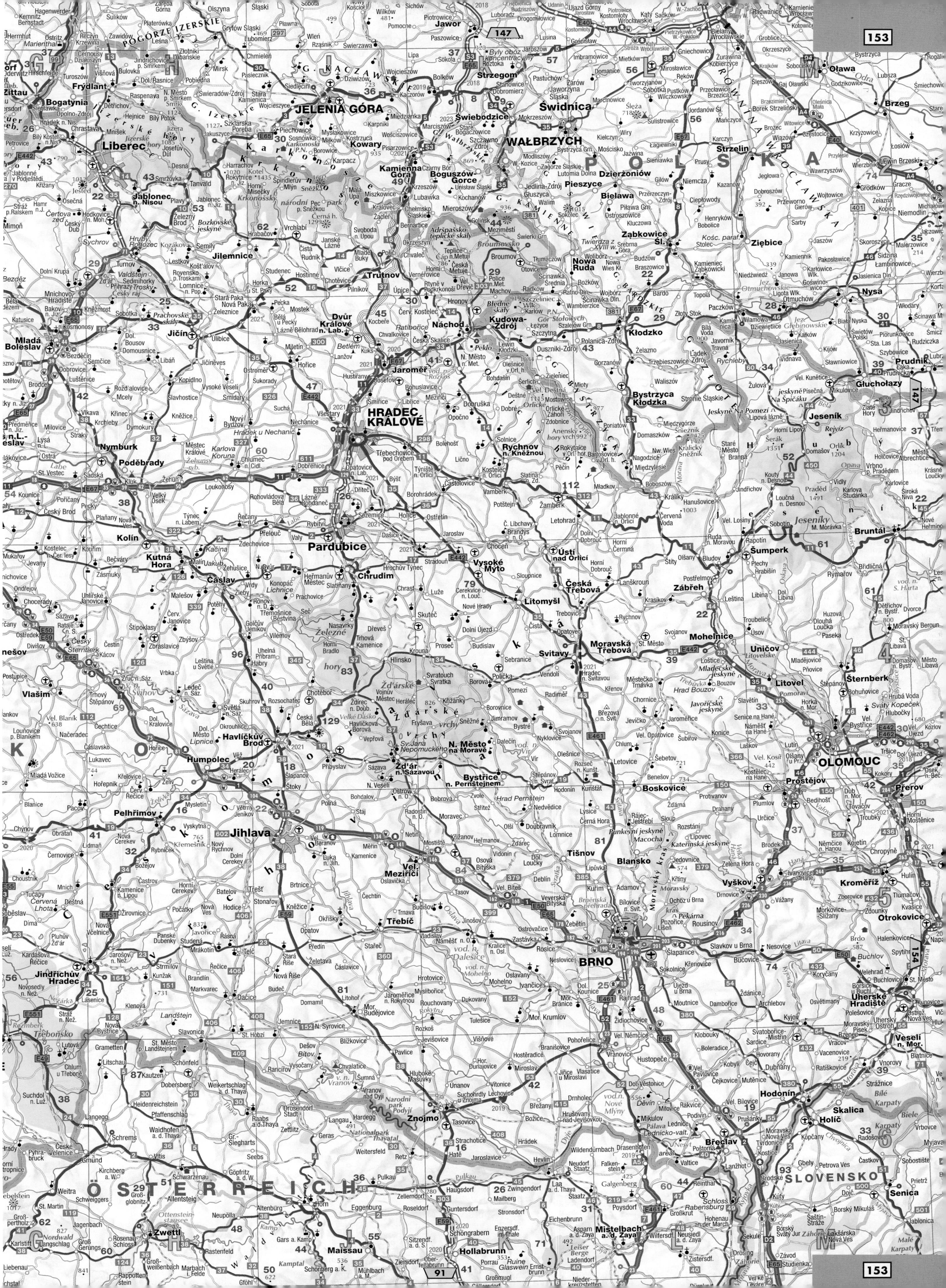

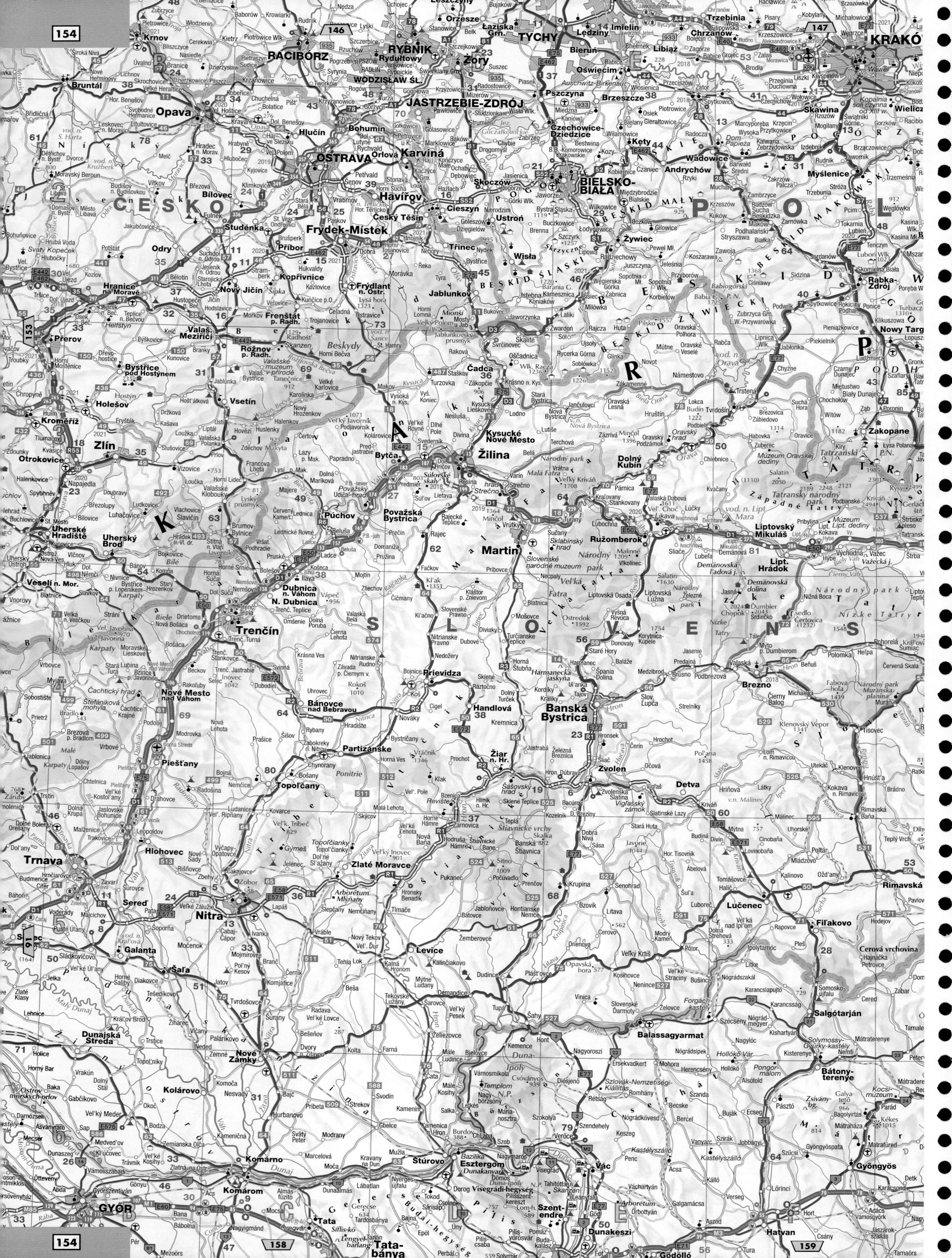

154
146
147
153
158
159
154
Krnov
RACIBÓRZ
RYBNIK
Żory
TYCHY
Chrzanów
KRAKÓW
Oświęcim
Bruntál
Opava
WODZISŁAW ŚL.
JASTRZĘBIE-ZDRÓJ
Hlučín
Bohumín
OSTRAVA
Karviná
Havířov
Český Těšín
Cieszyn
Skoczów
BIELSKO-BIAŁA
Wadowice
Andrychów
Myślenice
Bílovec
Frýdek-Místek
Příbor
Třinec
Żywiec
Kopřivnice
Nový Jičín
Frýdlant n. Ostr.
Frenštát p. Radh.
Jablunkov
Hranice na Moravě
Valaš. Meziříčí
Rožnov p. Radh.
Přerov
Bystřice pod Hostýnem
Vsetín
Holešov
Kroměříž
Zlín
Otrokovice
Uherské Hradiště
Uherský Brod
Veselí n. Mor.
Čadca
Kysucké Nové Mesto
Žilina
Bytča
Považská Bystrica
Púchov
Martin
Ružomberok
Dolný Kubín
Liptovský Mikuláš
Lipt. Hrádok
Zakopane
Nowy Targ
Rabka-Zdrój
Trenčín
Dubnica n. Váhom
N. Dubnica
Nové Mesto nad Váhom
Prievidza
Bánovce nad Bebravou
Handlová
Partizánske
Piešťany
Topoľčany
Banská Bystrica
Brezno
Žiar n. Hr.
Zvolen
Detva
Trnava
Hlohovec
Sereď
Nitra
Zlaté Moravce
Galanta
Šaľa
Levice
Lučenec
Fiľakovo
Dunajská Streda
Nové Zámky
Kolárovo
Komárno
Štúrovo
Esztergom
Komárom
GYŐR
Tata
Tatabánya
Szentendre
Vác
Dunakeszi
Balassagyarmat
Salgótarján
Bátonyterenye
Gyöngyös
Hatvan
Gödöllő
Č E S K O
P O L S K A
S L O V E N S K O

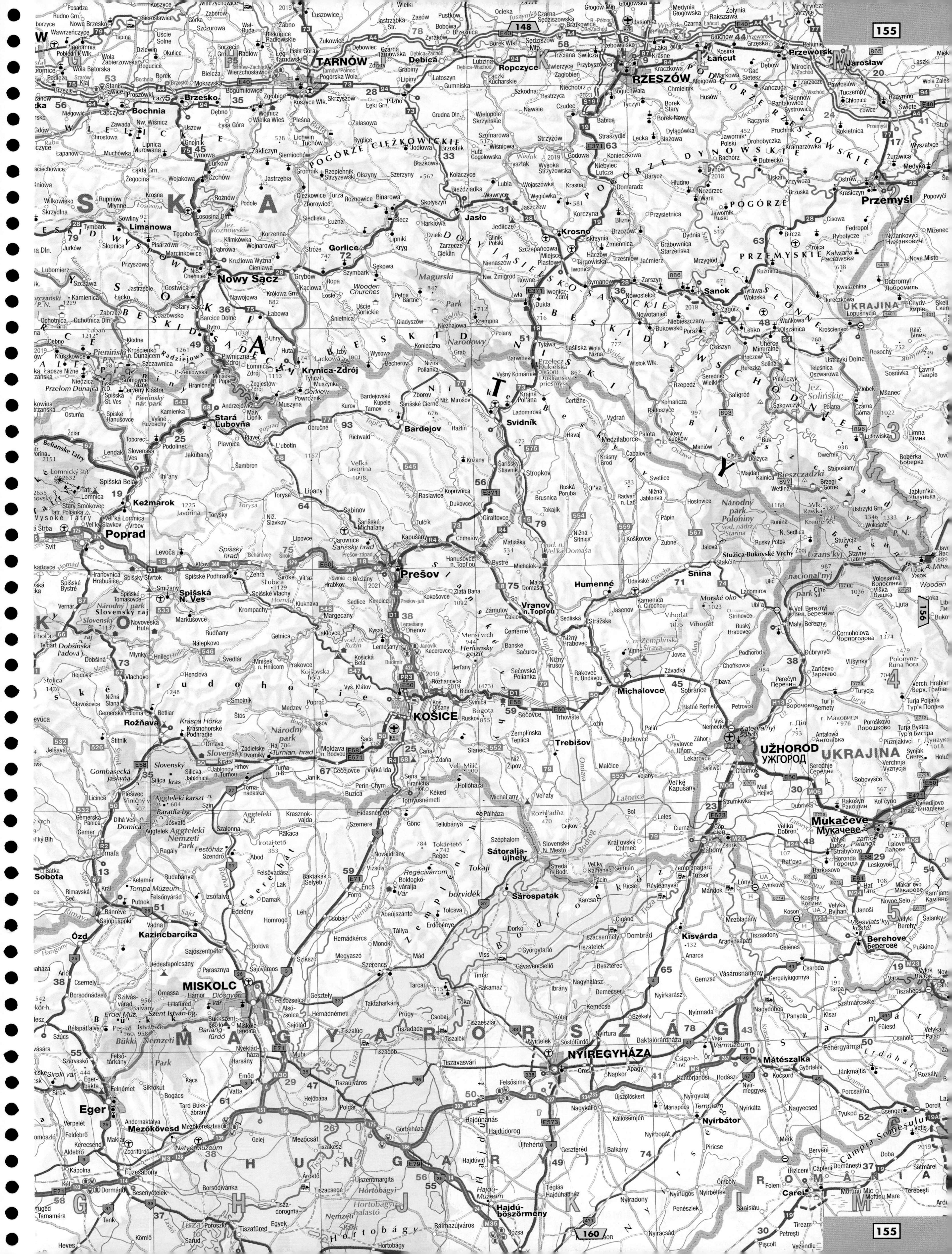

TARNÓW
Dębica
Ropczyce
RZESZÓW
Łańcut
Przeworsk
Jarosław
Bochnia
Brzesko
Limanowa
Nowy Sącz
Gorlice
Jasło
Krosno
Sanok
Przemyśl
Krynica-Zdrój
Stará Ľubovňa
Bardejov
Svidník
Humenné
Snina
Kežmarok
Poprad
Levoča
Prešov
Spišská N. Ves
Vranov n. Topľou
Michalovce
Trebišov
KOŠICE
Rožňava
UŽHOROD
УЖГОРОД
Mukačeve
Мукачеве
Berehove
Берегове
UKRAJINA
Sátoraljaújhely
Sárospatak
Kisvárda
MISKOLC
Kazincbarcika
Ózd
Eger
Mezőkövesd
NYÍREGYHÁZA
Mátészalka
Nyírbátor
Hajdúböszörmény
Carei
POGÓRZE CIĘŻKOWICKIE
POGÓRZE DYNOWSKIE
PODGÓRZE RZESZOWSKIE
BESKID SĄDECKI
BESKID NISKI
BIESZCZADY
Aggteleki Nemzeti Park
Bükki Nemzeti Park
Hortobágyi Nemzeti Park
MAGYARORSZÁG
HUNGARY
ROMÂNIA
156

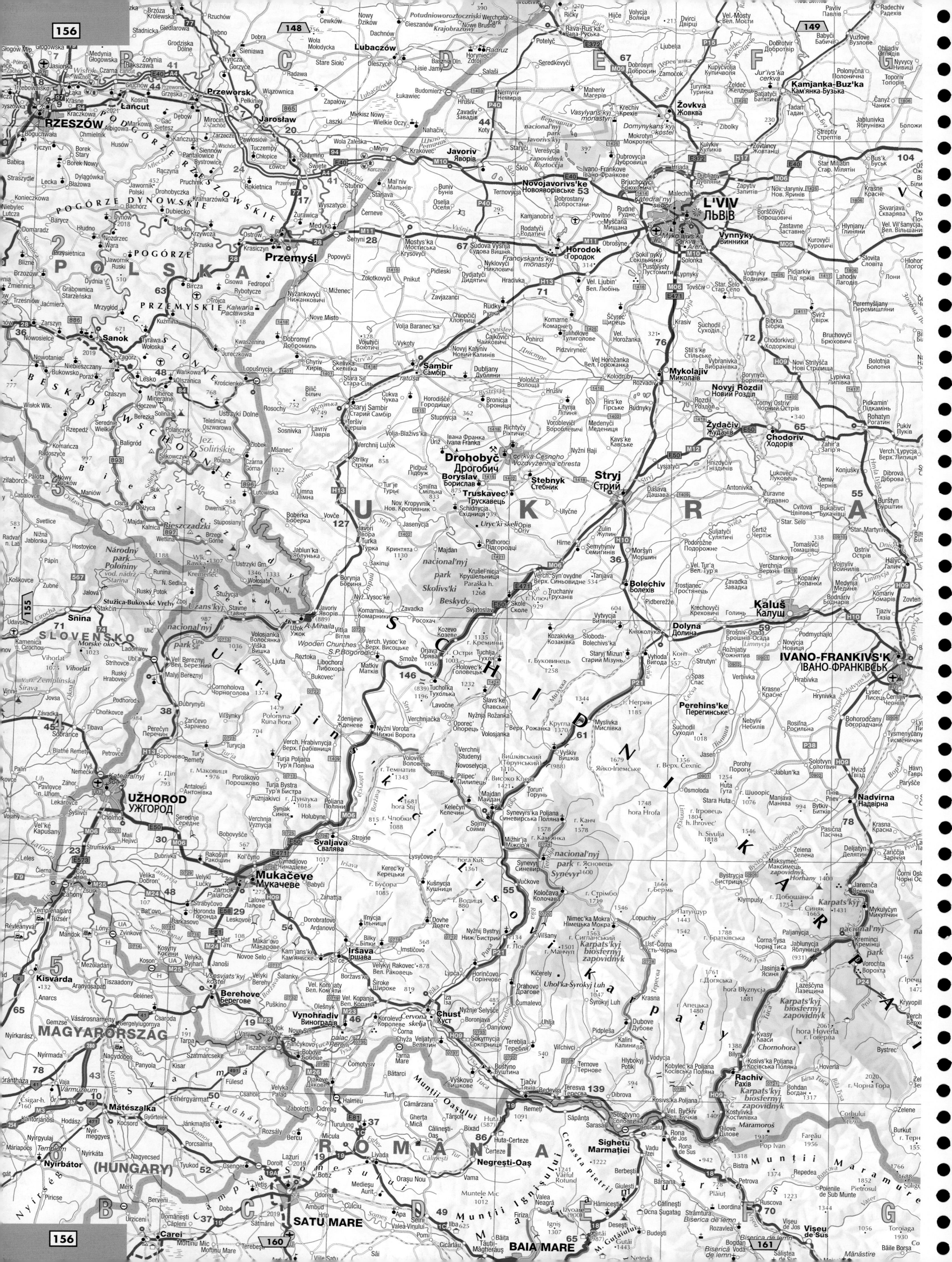
148
149
RZESZÓW
Łańcut
Przeworsk
Jarosław
Lubaczów
Przemyśl
Sanok
POLSKA
L'VIV
ЛЬВІВ
Žovkva
Жовква
Javoriv
Яворів
Horodok
Городок
Sambir
Самбір
Drohobyč
Дрогобич
Boryslav
Борислав
Truskavec'
Трускавець
Stryj
Стрий
Mykolajiv
Миколаїв
Žydačiv
Жидачів
Chodoriv
Ходорів
Kaluš
Калуш
Dolyna
Долина
IVANO-FRANKIVS'K
ІВАНО-ФРАНКІВСЬК
Nadvirna
Надвірна
UKRAJINA
SLOVENSKO
Snina
UŽHOROD
УЖГОРОД
Mukačeve
Мукачеве
Svaljava
Свалява
Berehove
Берегове
Vynohradiv
Виноградів
Chust
Хуст
Rachiv
Рахів
MAGYARORSZÁG
(HUNGARY)
Kisvárda
Mátészalka
Nyírbátor
ROMÂNIA
SATU MARE
Negreşti-Oaş
Sighetu Marmaţiei
BAIA MARE
Carei
Vişeu de Sus
155
160
161

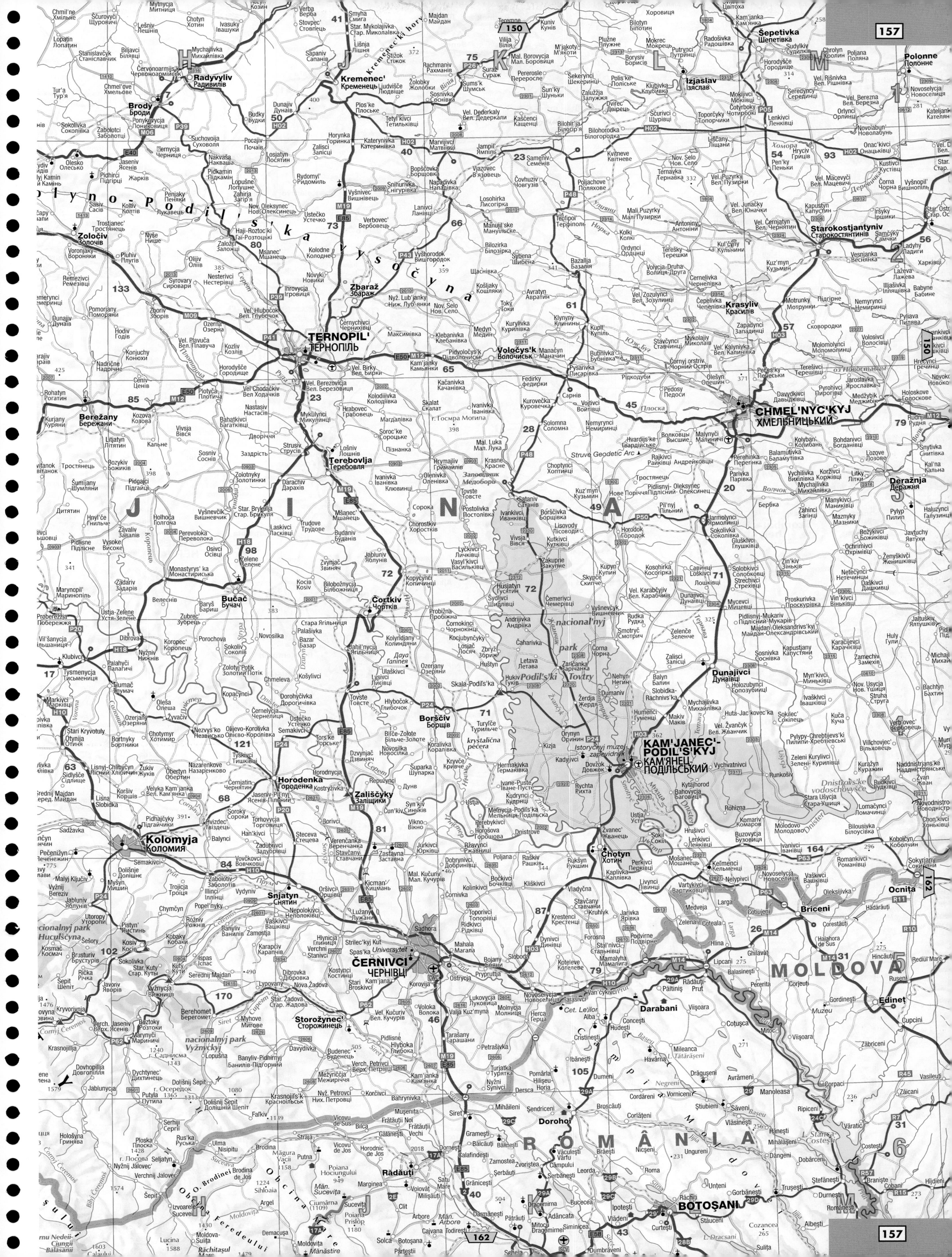
Radyvyliv
Радивилів
Kremenec'
Кременець
Brody
Броди
Izjaslav
Ізяслав
Šepetivka
Шепетівка
Polonne
Полонне
Zoločiv
Золочів
Zbaraž
Збараж
Starokostjantyniv
Старокостянтинів
TERNOPIL'
ТЕРНОПІЛЬ
Voločys'k
Волочиськ
Krasyliv
Красилів
CHMEL'NYC'KYJ
ХМЕЛЬНИЦЬКИЙ
Berežany
Бережани
Terebovlja
Теребовля
Deražnja
Деражня
J
I
N
A
Bučač
Бучач
Čortkiv
Чортків
Dunajivci
Дунаївці
Borščiv
Борщів
KAM'JANEC'-
PODIL'S'KYJ
КАМ'ЯНЕЦЬ-
ПОДІЛЬСЬКИЙ
Horodenka
Городенка
Zališčyky
Заліщики
Kolomyja
Коломия
Chotyn
Хотин
Ocniţa
Sniatyn
Снятин
Briceni
ČERNIVCI
ЧЕРНІВЦІ
MOLDOVA
Edineţ
Storožynec'
Сторожинець
Darabani
Dorohoi
ROMÂNIA
Rădăuţi
BOTOŞANI
Podil's'ka vysočyna
nacional'nyj park Podil's'ki Tovtry
nacional'nyj park Vyžnyckyj
nacional'nyj park Huculščyna
Dnistrovs'ke vodoschovyšče
162
150

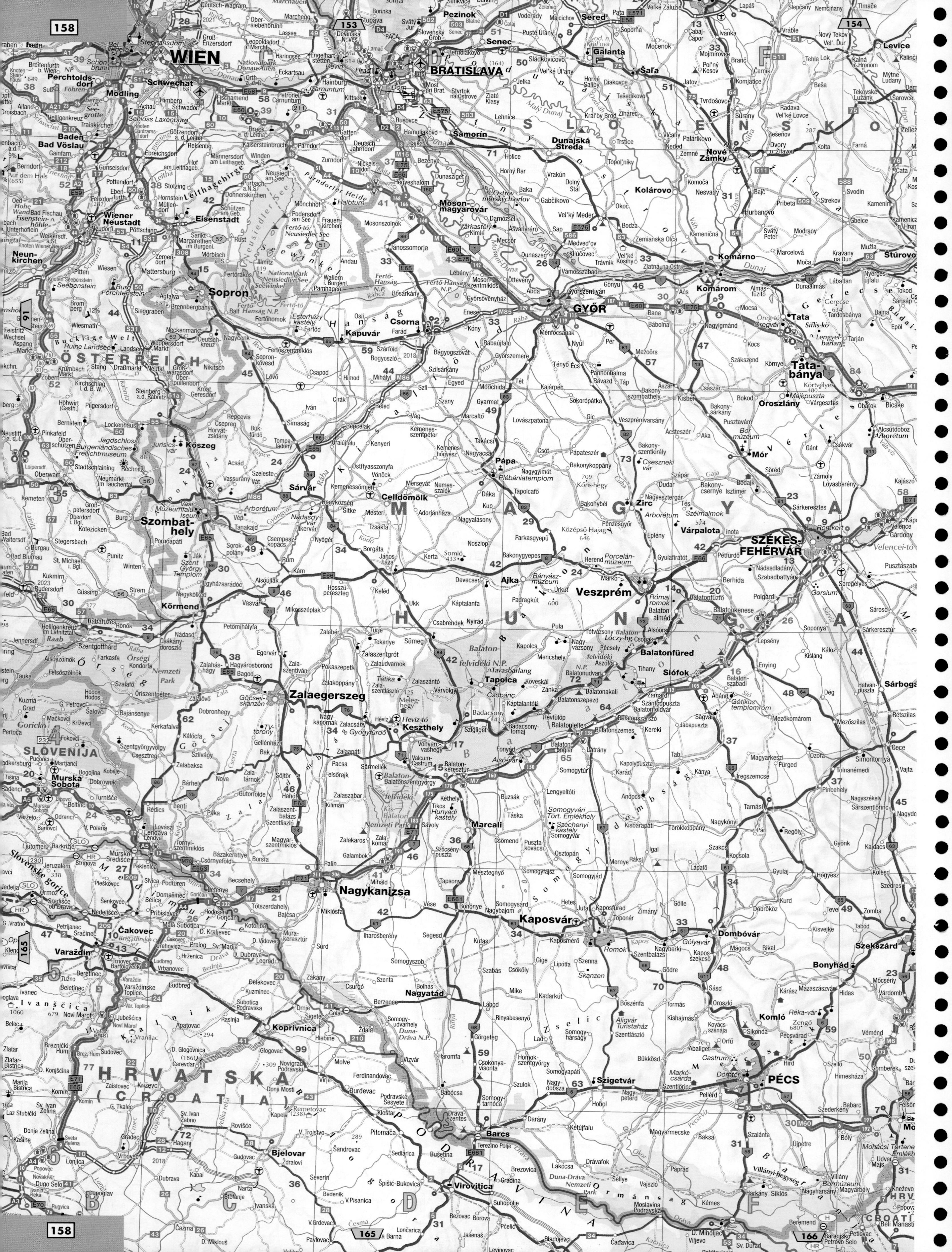

158
153
154
WIEN
BRATISLAVA
Schwechat
Mödling
Perchtoldsdorf
Baden
Bad Vöslau
Wiener Neustadt
Eisenstadt
Neunkirchen
Pezinok
Senec
Sereď
Galanta
Šaľa
Šamorín
Dunajská Streda
Nové Zámky
Kolárovo
Komárno
Štúrovo
Levice
SLOVENSKO
Mosonmagyaróvár
Sopron
Kapuvár
Csorna
GYŐR
Komárom
Tata
Tatabánya
Oroszlány
Mór
ÖSTERREICH
Kőszeg
Szombathely
Sárvár
Celldömölk
Pápa
Zirc
Várpalota
SZÉKESFEHÉRVÁR
Ajka
Veszprém
Körmend
MAGYARORSZÁG
Zalaegerszeg
Tapolca
Keszthely
Balatonfüred
Siófok
Marcali
Nagykanizsa
Kaposvár
Dombóvár
Szekszárd
Bonyhád
Komló
PÉCS
Szigetvár
Nagyatád
Barcs
SLOVENIJA
Murska Sobota
Čakovec
Varaždin
Koprivnica
HRVATSKA (CROATIA)
Bjelovar
Virovitica
158
165
166

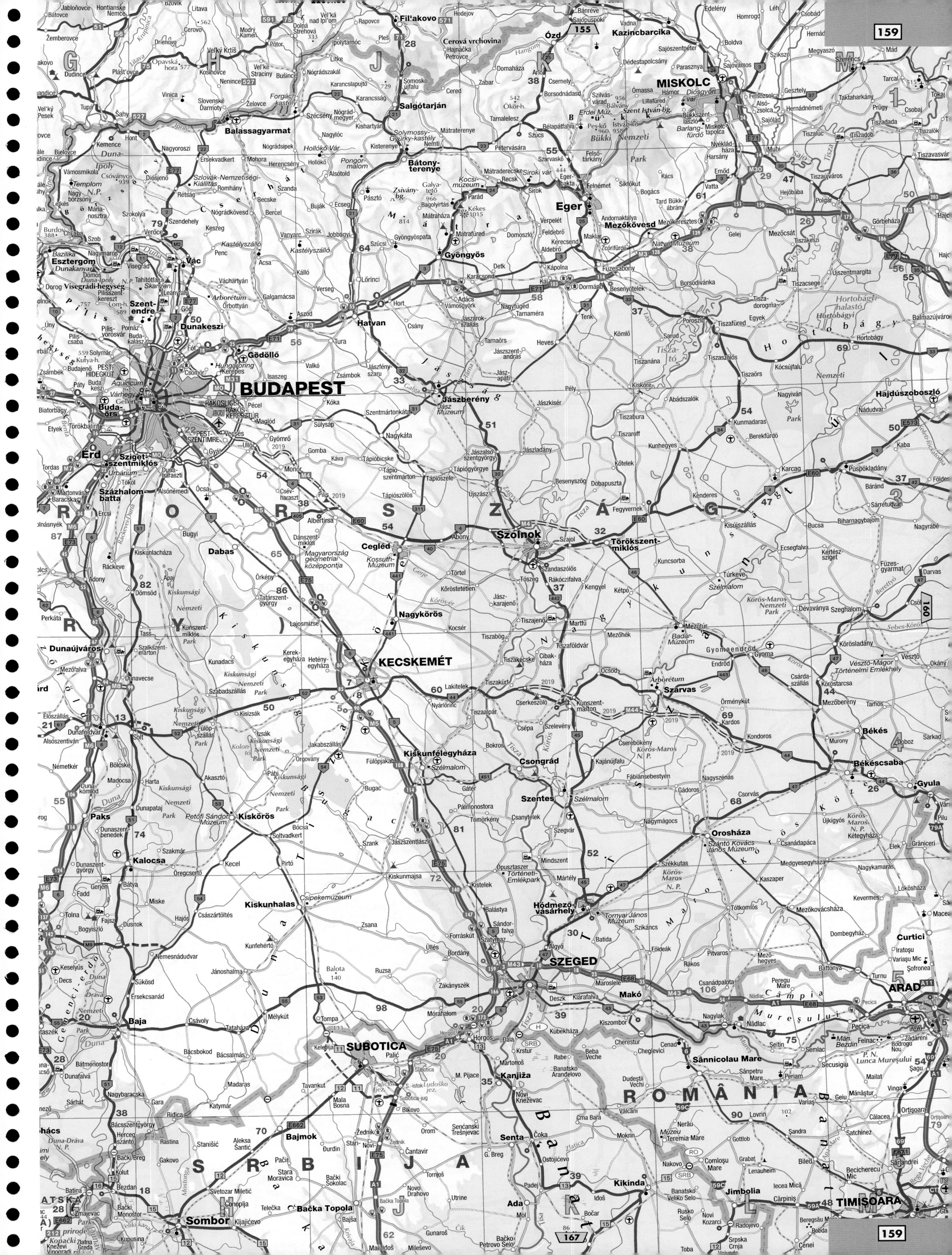
BUDAPEST
MISKOLC
Eger
Salgótarján
Balassagyarmat
Vác
Esztergom
Szentendre
Gödöllő
Hatvan
Gyöngyös
Jászberény
Szolnok
Cegléd
Kecskemét
Nagykőrös
Kiskunfélegyháza
Csongrád
Szentes
Hódmezővásárhely
SZEGED
Makó
Orosháza
Békéscsaba
Gyula
Szarvas
Mezőtúr
Karcag
Mezőkövesd
Tiszafüred
Hajdúszoboszló
Kiskunhalas
Kiskőrös
Kalocsa
Paks
Dunaújváros
Baja
Érd
Szigetszentmiklós
Százhalombatta
SUBOTICA
Sombor
Senta
Kikinda
Kanjiža
Bačka Topola
ARAD
TIMIŞOARA
Sânnicolau Mare
Jimbolia
ROMÂNIA
SRBIJA
MAGYARORSZÁG
Hortobágyi Nemzeti Park
Kiskunsági Nemzeti Park
Bükki Nemzeti Park
Körös-Maros Nemzeti Park
Duna-Ipoly N.P.
Mátra
Duna
Tisza
Körös
Maros
Banat
Bačka
155
160
167

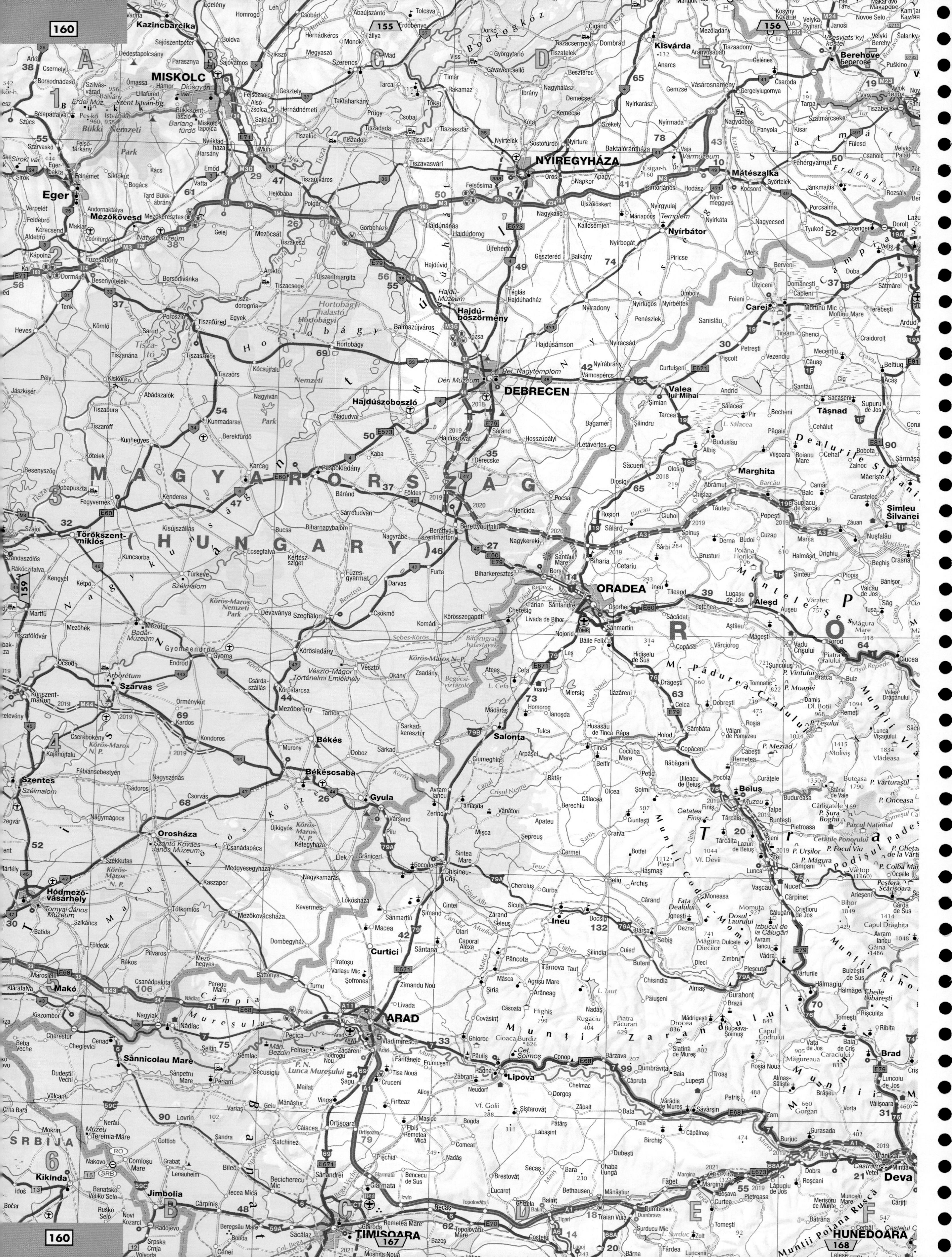

155
156
MAGYARORSZÁG
(HUNGARY)
R O
SRBIJA
MISKOLC
Kazincbarcika
Eger
Mezőkövesd
NYÍREGYHÁZA
Kisvárda
Mátészalka
Nyírbátor
Berehove
Hajdúböszörmény
DEBRECEN
Hajdúszoboszló
Carei
Valea lui Mihai
Tășnad
Marghita
Șimleu Silvaniei
ORADEA
Aleșd
Salonta
Beiuș
Törökszentmiklós
Szarvas
Szentes
Hódmezővásárhely
Makó
Orosháza
Békéscsaba
Békés
Gyula
Kikinda
Jimbolia
Sânnicolau Mare
ARAD
Curtici
Ineu
Lipova
TIMIȘOARA
Brad
Deva
HUNEDOARA
Hortobágy
Bükki Nemzeti Park
Körös-Maros Nemzeti Park
Câmpia Mureșului
Munții Zarandului
Munții Codru-Moma
Munții Pădurea Craiului
Munții Bihor
Munții Apuseni
Munții Poiana Ruscă
Munții Meseș
Dealurile Silvaniei
Câmpia Someșului
167
168
159

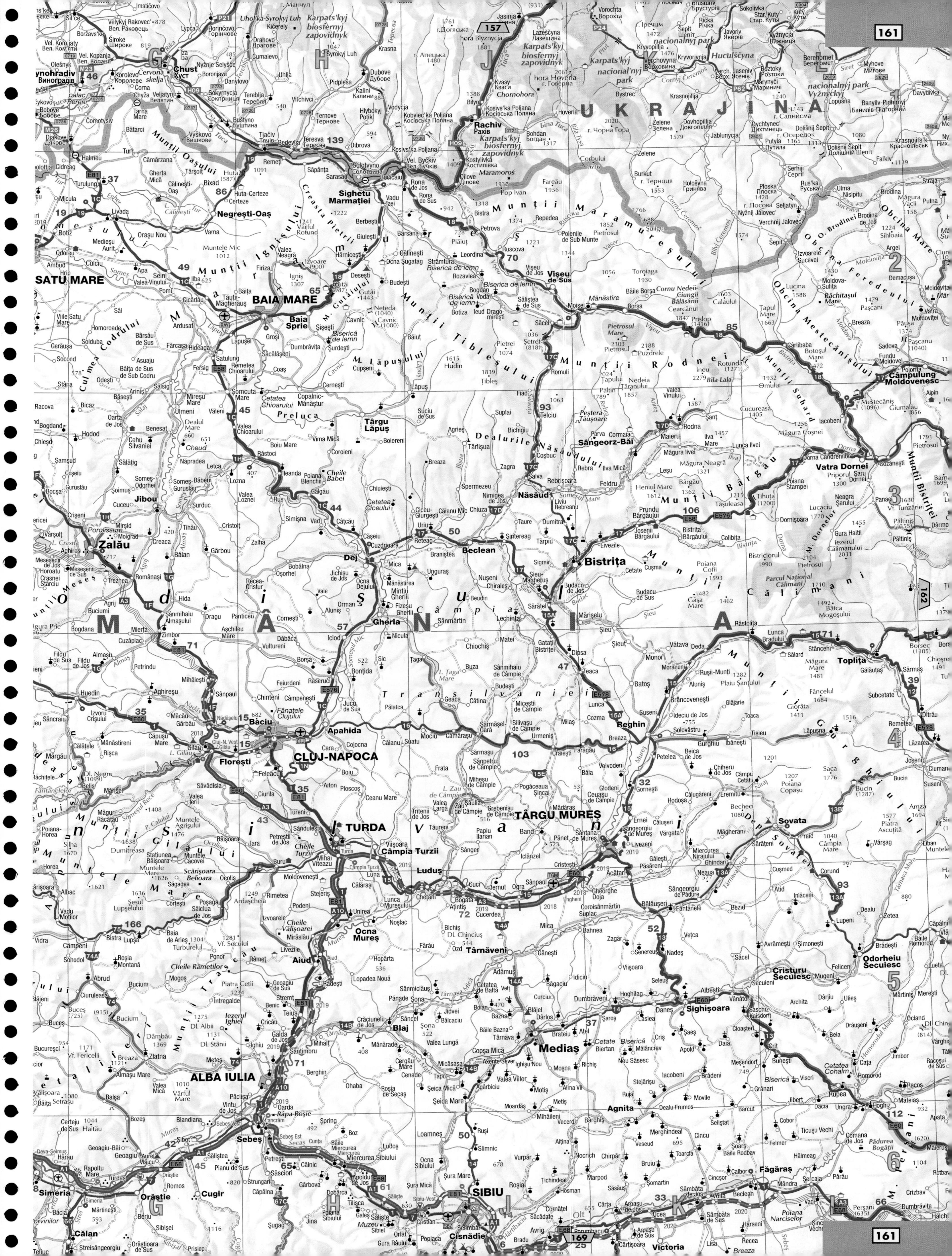
UKRAJINA
ROMÂNIA
SATU MARE
BAIA MARE
Sighetu Marmației
Negrești-Oaș
Baia Sprie
Vișeu de Sus
Câmpulung Moldovenesc
Vatra Dornei
Târgu Lăpuș
Sângeorz-Băi
Năsăud
Bistrița
Beclean
Dej
Gherla
Zalău
Jibou
Huedin
Cluj-Napoca
Florești
Apahida
Turda
Câmpia Turzii
Luduș
Târgu Mureș
Reghin
Toplița
Sovata
Odorheiu Secuiesc
Cristuru Secuiesc
Sighișoara
Mediaș
Târnăveni
Ocna Mureș
Aiud
Blaj
Alba Iulia
Sebeș
Zlatna
Orăștie
Simeria
Călan
Cugir
Sibiu
Cisnădie
Agnita
Făgăraș
Victoria
Rupea
Munții Rodnei
Munții Maramureșului
Munții Țibleșului
Munții Bârgăului
Munții Călimani
Munții Gurghiului
Munții Apuseni
Câmpia Transilvaniei
Chust Хуст
Rachiv Рахів
Vynohradiv Виноградів
Karpats'kyj biosfernyj zapovidnyk
Karpats'kyj nacional'nyj park
Vyžnyckyj nacionalnyj park
162

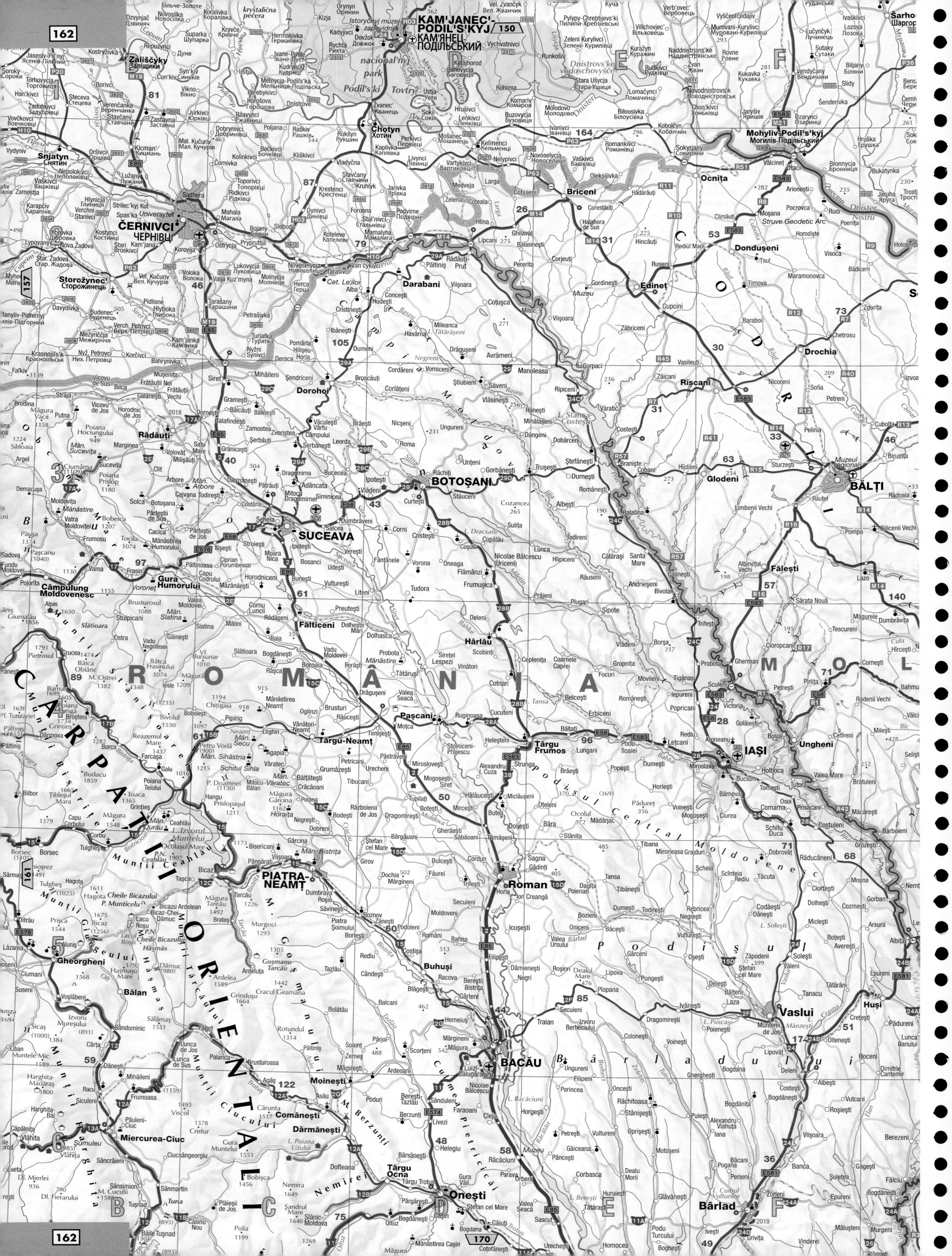

162
KAM'JANEC'-PODIL'S'KYJ
КАМ'ЯНЕЦЬ-ПОДІЛЬСЬКИЙ
150
Zališčyky
Заліщики
Chotyn
Хотин
Mohyliv-Podil's'kyj
Могилів-Подільський
Snjatyn
Снятин
ČERNIVCI
ЧЕРНІВЦІ
Storožynec'
Сторожинець
157
Briceni
Ocnița
Edineț
Dondușeni
Drochia
Rîșcani
Glodeni
BĂLȚI
Fălești
Ungheni
Darabani
Dorohoi
Rădăuți
BOTOȘANI
SUCEAVA
Gura Humorului
Câmpulung Moldovenesc
Fălticeni
Hârlău
Pașcani
Târgu-Neamț
Târgu Frumos
IAȘI
PIATRA-NEAMȚ
Roman
Buhuși
Vaslui
Huși
BACĂU
Moinești
Comănești
Dărmănești
Târgu Ocna
Onești
Bârlad
Gheorgheni
Bălan
Miercurea-Ciuc
R O M Â N I A
M O L
CARPAȚII ORIENTALI
C O D R I I
Podișul Central Moldovenesc
Podișul Bârladului
Munții Ceahlău
Munții Bistriței
Munții Stânișoarei
Munții Giurgeului
Munții Hășmaș
Munții Tarcăului
Munții Ciucului
Munții Berzunți
Munții Nemirei
Obcina Mare
Câmpia Moldovei
Podil's'ki Tovtry
nacional'nyj park
Dnistrovs'ke vodoschovyšče
Struve Geodetic Arc
161
170
162

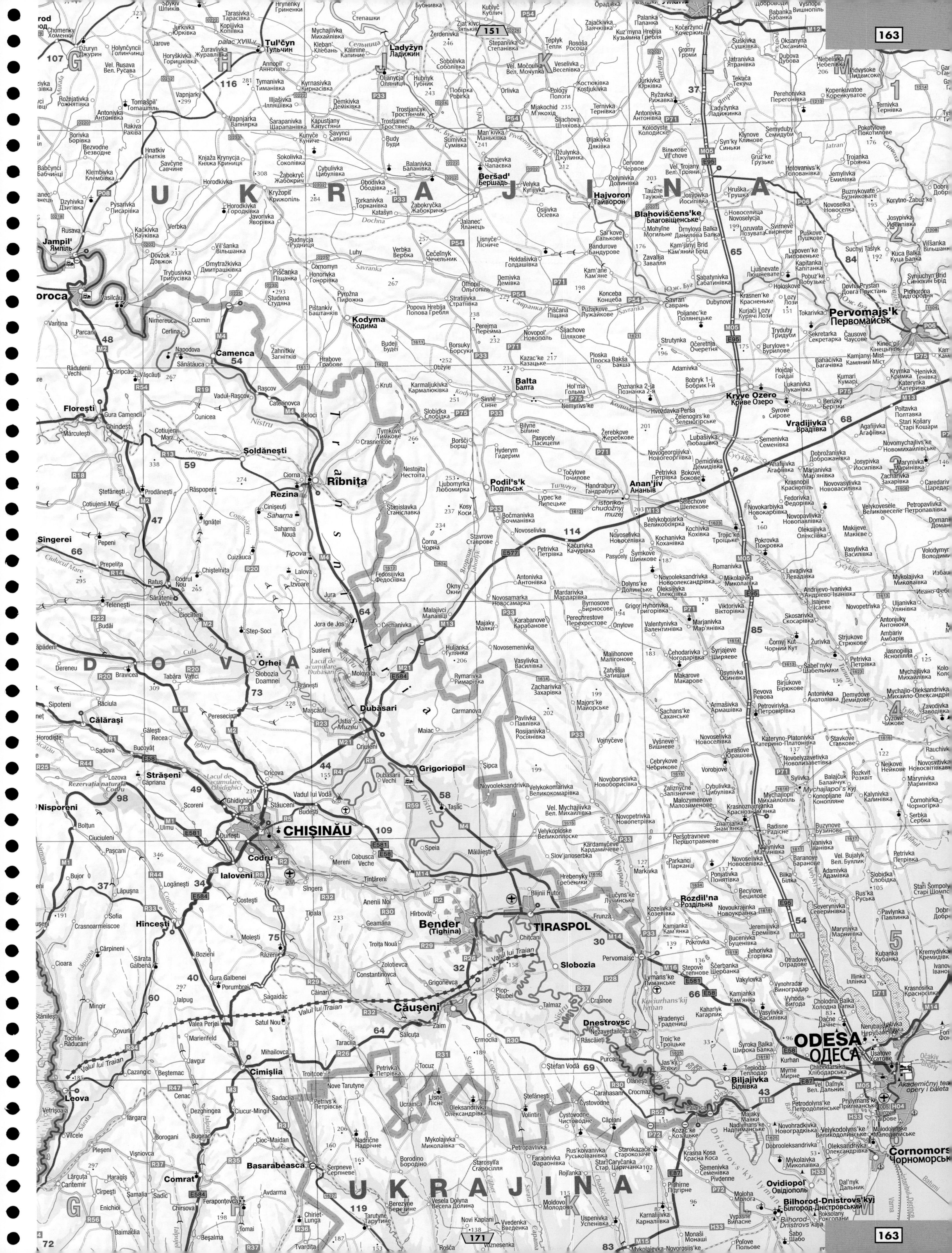
U K R A J I N A
M O L D O V A
Transnistria
UKRAJINA
CHIȘINĂU
ODESA
ОДЕСА
TIRASPOL
Bender (Tighina)
Pervomajs'k
Первомайськ
Balta
Балта
Kodyma
Кодима
Podil's'k
Подільськ
Anan'jiv
Ананьїв
Kryve Ozero
Криве Озеро
Vradijivka
Врадіївка
Rozdil'na
Роздільна
Hajvoron
Гайворон
Blahoviščens'ke
Благовіщенське
Beršad'
Бершадь
Ladyžyn
Ладижин
Tul'čyn
Тульчин
Jampil'
Ямпіль
Soroca
Camenca
Florești
Șoldănești
Rîbnița
Rezina
Orhei
Dubăsari
Grigoriopol
Călărași
Strășeni
Nisporeni
Ialoveni
Hîncești
Căușeni
Slobozia
Dnestrovsc
Cimișlia
Leova
Basarabeasca
Comrat
Biljajivka
Біляївка
Čornomorsk
Чорноморськ
Ovidiopol'
Овідіополь
Bilhorod-Dnistrovs'kyj
Білгород-Дністровський
Nistru
Valul lui Traian
E95
E577
E58
E581
E584
E87
M05
M13
M14
M15
M16
P33
P54
P71

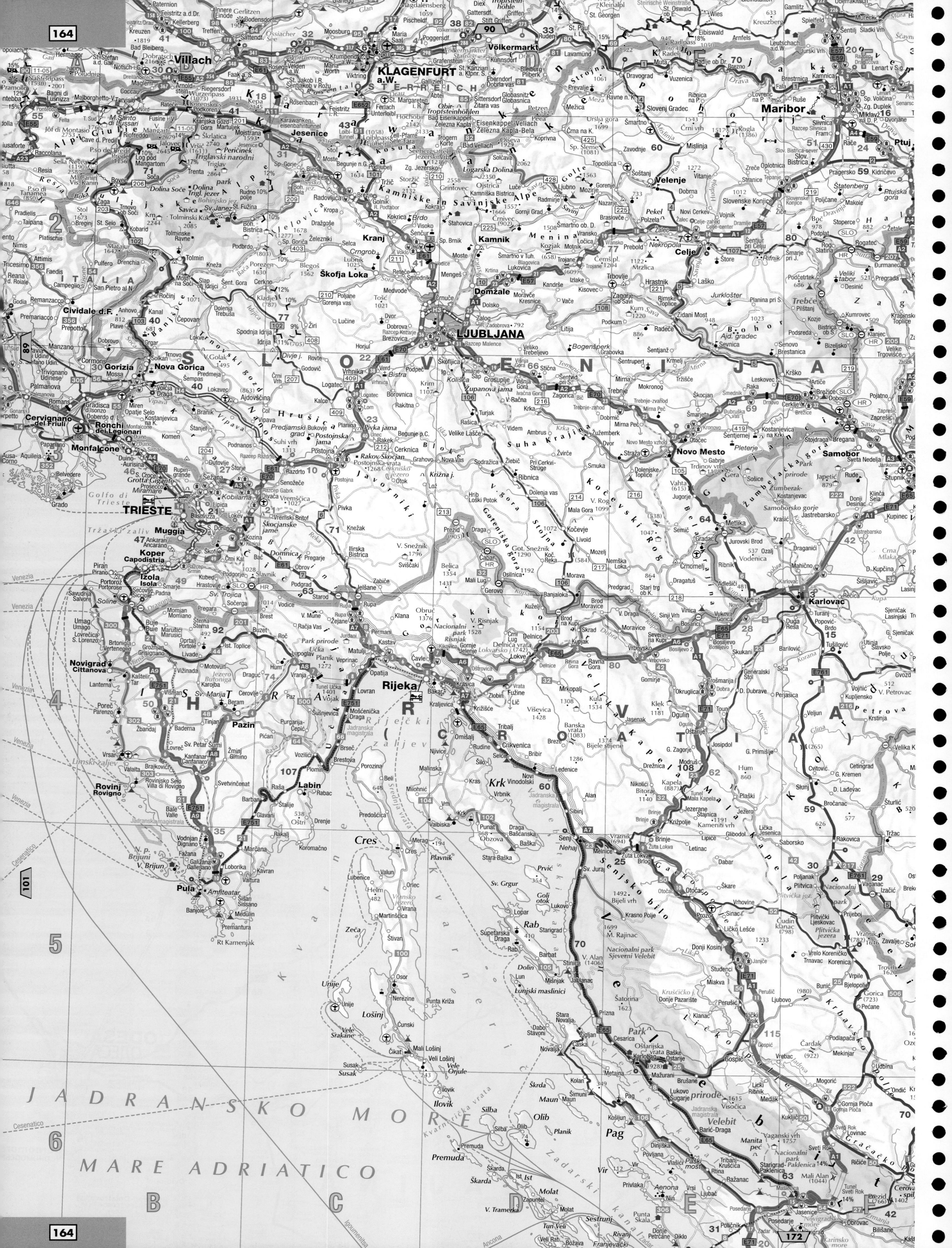

164
Villach
KLAGENFURT a.W.
Völkermarkt
ÖSTERREICH
Jesenice
Maribor
Ptuj
Velenje
Celje
Kranj
Kamnik
Škofja Loka
Domžale
LJUBLJANA
SLOVENIJA
Nova Gorica
Gorizia
Cividale d.F.
ITALIA
Cervignano del Friuli
Ronchi dei Legionari
Monfalcone
TRIESTE
Muggia
Koper Capodistria
Izola Isola
Piran Pirano
Portorož Portorose
Postojna
Novo Mesto
Krško
Samobor
Karlovac
Rijeka
Opatija
Pazin
Novigrad Cittanova
Poreč Parenzo
Rovinj Rovigno
Pula
Labin
Cres
Krk
Lošinj
Mali Lošinj
Rab
Pag
Senj
Ogulin
Gospić
Karlobag
HRVATSKA
Kvarner
Kvarnerić
JADRANSKO MORE
MARE ADRIATICO
Golfo di Trieste
Tržaški zaliv
Riječki zaljev
Velebit
Velika Kapela
Mala Kapela
Gorski kotar
Kočevski Rog
Julijske Alpe
Triglavski narodni park
Kamniško-Savinjske Alpe
Karawanken
Nacionalni park Sjeverni Velebit
Plitvička jezera
Premuda
Silba
Olib
Molat
Ist
Susak
Unije
164
172

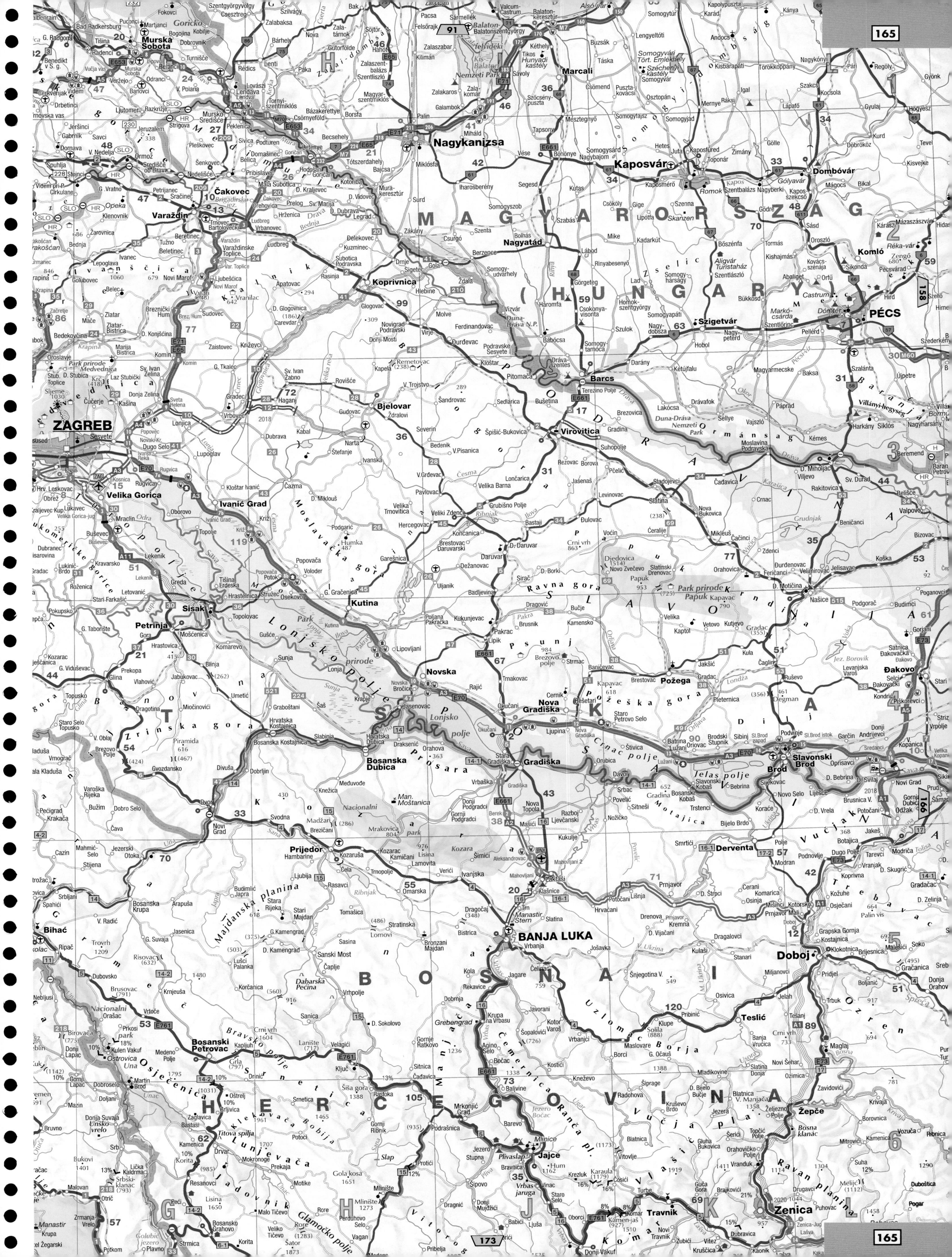

MAGYARORSZÁG
(HUNGARY)
BOSNA I HERCEGOVINA
SLAVONIJA
ZAGREB
Nagykanizsa
Kaposvár
PÉCS
Koprivnica
Bjelovar
Virovitica
Barcs
Čakovec
Varaždin
Murska Sobota
Velika Gorica
Ivanić Grad
Sisak
Petrinja
Kutina
Novska
Nova Gradiška
Požega
Slavonski Brod
Đakovo
Našice
Gradiška
Bosanska Dubica
Prijedor
BANJA LUKA
Derventa
Doboj
Teslić
Bihać
Bosanski Petrovac
Jajce
Travnik
Zenica
Žepče
Nagyatád
Szigetvár
Dombóvár
Marcali
Komló
Lonjsko polje
Moslavačka gora
Papuk
Psunj
Zrinska gora
Kozara
Vlašić

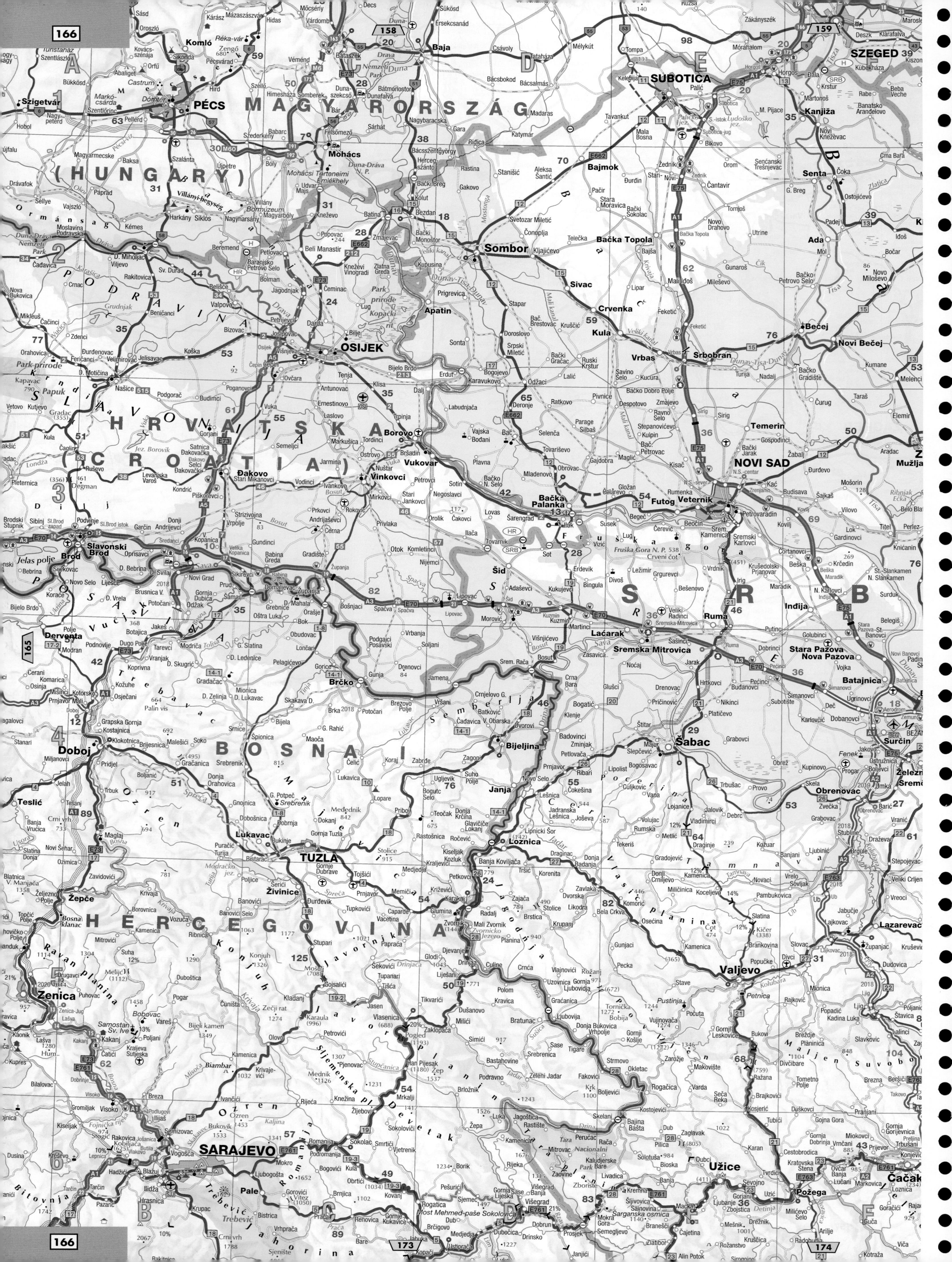
166
158
159
165
173
174
MAGYARORSZÁG
(HUNGARY)
HRVATSKA
(CROATIA)
BOSNA I HERCEGOVINA
SRBIJA
SZEGED
PÉCS
SUBOTICA
Baja
Mohács
Sombor
OSIJEK
Vukovar
Vinkovci
Đakovo
Slavonski Brod
NOVI SAD
Sremska Mitrovica
Ruma
Šabac
Valjevo
Užice
Čačak
Bijeljina
Brčko
TUZLA
Doboj
Zenica
SARAJEVO
Senta
Kanjiža
Bačka Topola
Vrbas
Kula
Apatin
Bačka Palanka
Stara Pazova
Nova Pazova
Obrenovac
Lazarevac
Požega
Loznica
Zvornik
Lukavac
Živinice
Derventa
Teslić
Kakanj
Visoko
Pale
Fruška Gora N. P.
Park prirode Kopački rit
Podravina
Sava
Drina
Dunav
Tisa
Ozren
Majevica
Jahorina
Romanija
Javor
Povlen
Maljen
Suvobor
Medvednik
Zlatibor
Tara
Nacionalni Park
166

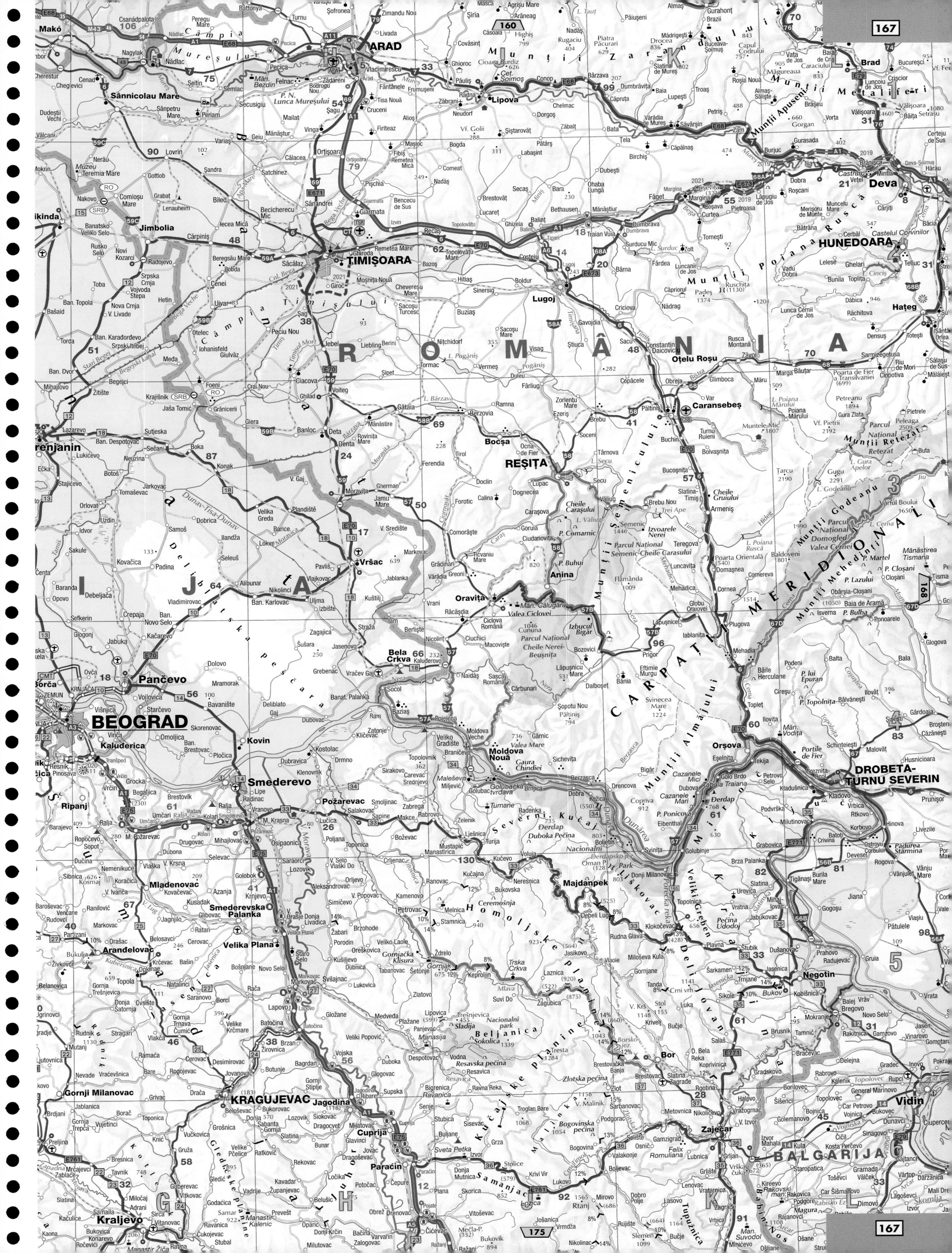

ROMÂNIA
ARAD
TIMIŞOARA
Lugoj
REŞIŢA
Caransebeş
Deva
HUNEDOARA
Haţeg
Brad
Lipova
Oţelu Roşu
Bocşa
Oraviţa
Anina
Orşova
DROBETA-TURNU SEVERIN
Vršac
Bela Crkva
Pančevo
BEOGRAD
Smederevo
Požarevac
Kovin
Zrenjanin
Jimbolia
Sânnicolau Mare
Makó
Mladenovac
Smederevska Palanka
Velika Plana
Aranđelovac
KRAGUJEVAC
Jagodina
Ćuprija
Paraćin
Kraljevo
Gornji Milanovac
Majdanpek
Bor
Zaječar
Negotin
Vidin
BALGARIJA
Munţii Zarandului
Munţii Metaliferi
Munţii Poiana Ruscă
Munţii Semenicului
Munţii Almăjului
CARPAŢII MERIDIONALI
Munţii Retezat
Munţii Godeanu
Munţii Mehedinţi
Câmpia Mureşului
Câmpia Timişului
Deliblatska peščara
Homoljske planine
Beljanica
Kučajske planine
Gledićske planine
Šumadija
Severni Kučaj
Đerdap
Dunărea
160
168
175

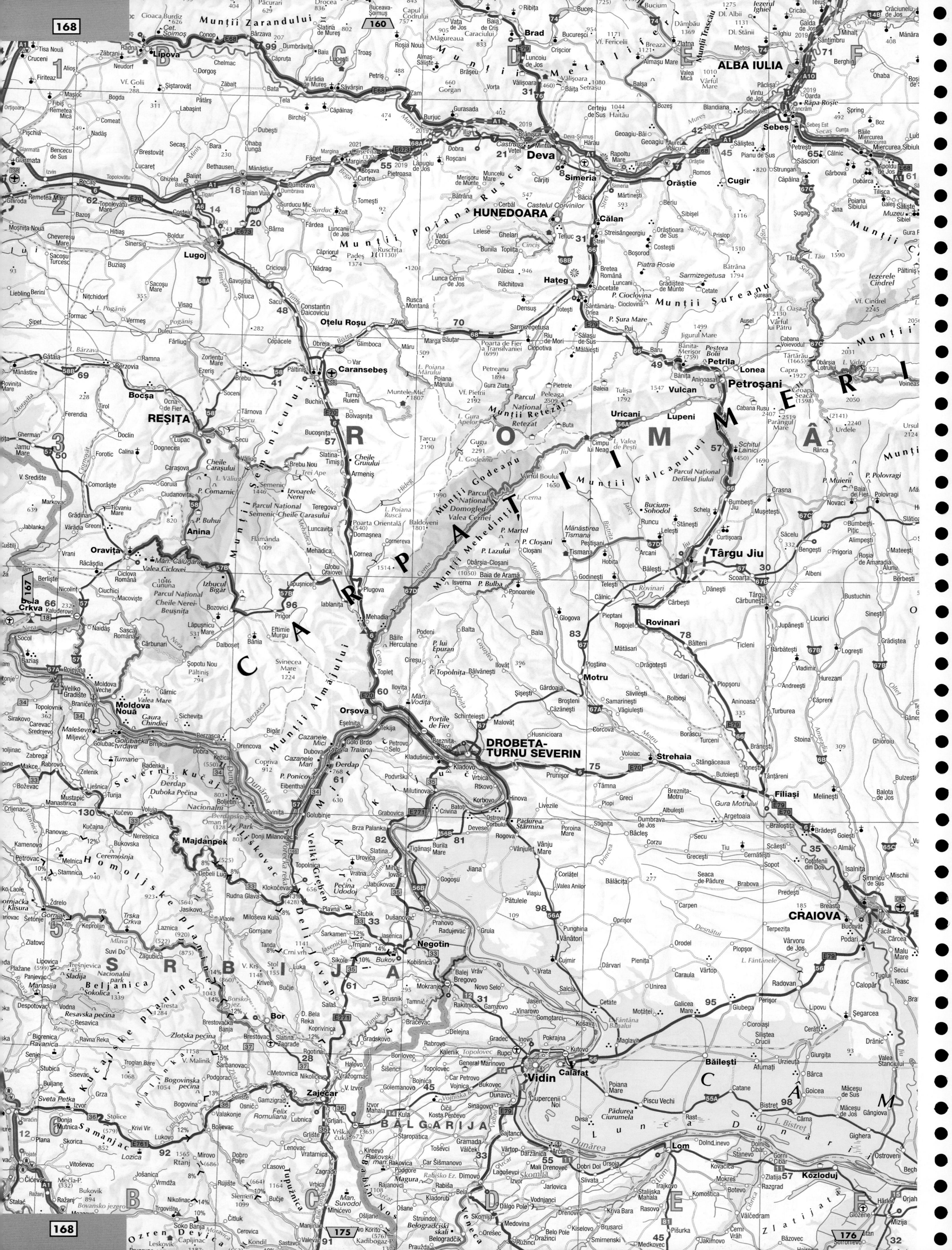
160
167
175
176
ROMÂNIA
CARPAŢII MERIDIONALI
SRBIJA
BĂLGARIJA
Munţii Zarandului
Munţii Metaliferi
Munţii Trascău
Munţii Poiana Ruscă
Munţii Şureanu
Munţii Retezat
Munţii Vâlcanului
Munţii Godeanu
Munţii Mehedinţi
Munţii Semenicului
Munţii Almăjului
Munţii Cindrel
Lunca Dunării
Dunărea
ALBA IULIA
Lipova
Brad
Deva
Simeria
Orăştie
Sebeş
Cugir
HUNEDOARA
Călan
Haţeg
Lugoj
Caransebeş
Oţelu Roşu
REŞIŢA
Bocşa
Anina
Oraviţa
Petroşani
Petrila
Lonea
Vulcan
Uricani
Lupeni
Târgu Jiu
Rovinari
Motru
Orşova
DROBETA-TURNU SEVERIN
Strehaia
Filiaşi
CRAIOVA
Băileşti
Calafat
Vidin
Lom
Kozloduj
Negotin
Majdanpek
Bor
Zaječar
Moldova Nouă
Bela Crkva
Veliko Gradište
Kladovo
Mehadia
Băile Herculane
Parcul Naţional Cheile Nerei-Beuşniţa
Parcul Naţional Semenic-Cheile Caraşului
Parcul Naţional Domogled-Valea Cernei
Parcul Naţional Defileul Jiului
Parcul Naţional Retezat
Porţile de Fier
Đerdap Nacionalni park
Homoljske planine
Kučajske planine
Beljanica
Veliki Greben
Deli Jovan
Miroč
Sarmizegetusa
Castelul Corvinilor

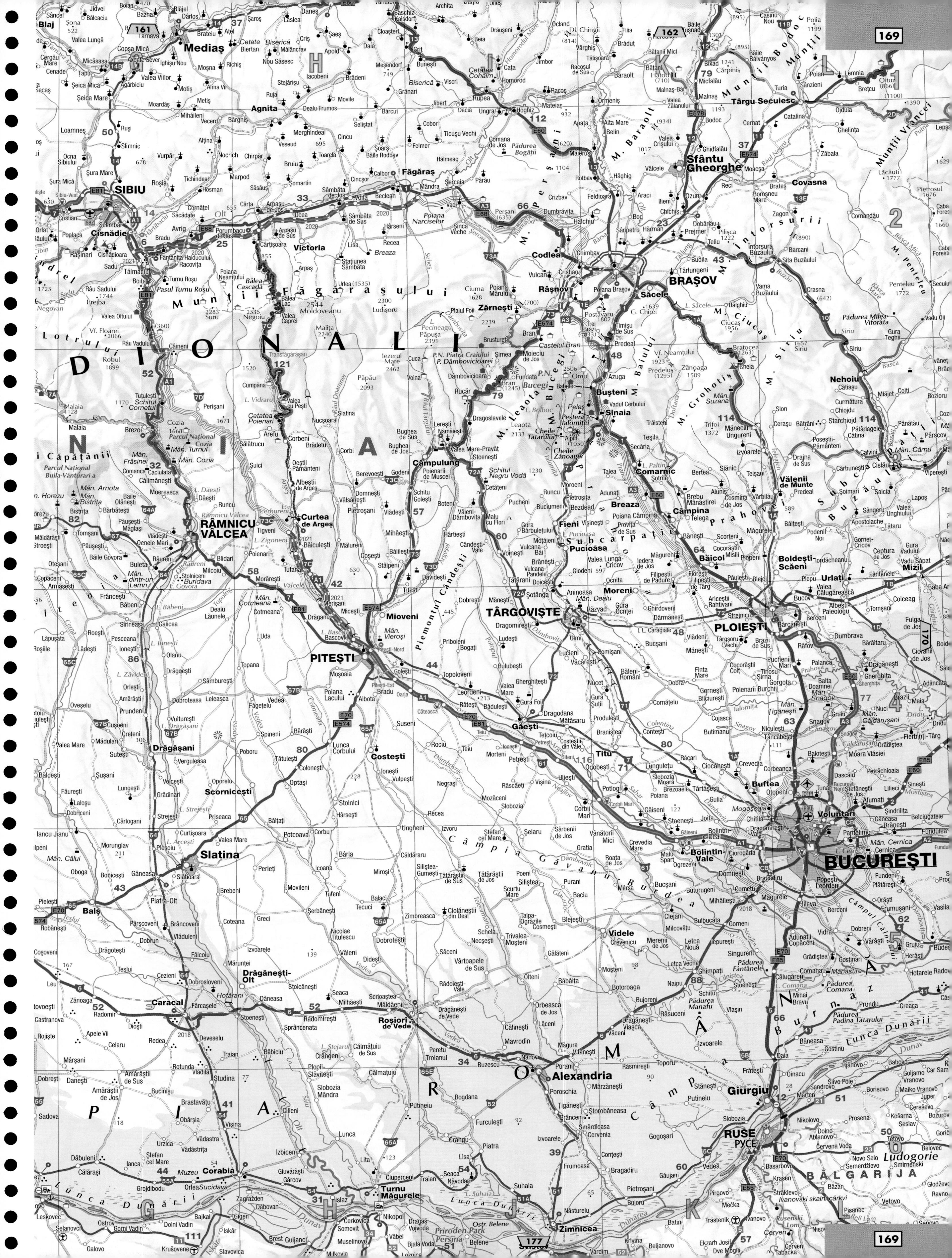
Blaj
Mediaş
Agnita
Făgăraş
SIBIU
Cisnădie
Victoria
Sfântu Gheorghe
Târgu Secuiesc
Covasna
Codlea
Râşnov
Zărneşti
BRAŞOV
Săcele
Munţii Făgăraşului
D I O N A L I
N I A
Moldoveanu 2544
Buşteni
Sinaia
Campulung
Curtea de Argeş
RÂMNICU VÂLCEA
Câmpina
Breaza
Fieni
Pucioasa
Băicoi
Boldeşti-Scăeni
Urlaţi
Mizil
Vălenii de Munte
Nehoiu
TÂRGOVIŞTE
Moreni
PLOIEŞTI
Mioveni
PITEŞTI
Costeşti
Găeşti
Titu
Drăgăşani
Scorniceşti
Slatina
Balş
Drăgăneşti-Olt
Caracal
Roşiori de Vede
Alexandria
Videle
Bolintin-Vale
Buftea
Otopeni
Voluntari
BUCUREŞTI
Giurgiu
RUSE
РУСЕ
Corabia
Turnu Măgurele
Zimnicea
Nikopol
Câmpia Găvanu-Burdea
Câmpia Burnaz
R O M Â N A
C Â M P I A
Lunca Dunării
Dunav
BĂLGARIJA
Ludogorie
Subcarpaţii
M. Baiului
M. Ciucaş
Munţii Bodoc
Munţii Vrancei
Lotrului
Parcul Naţional Cozia
P.N. Bucegi

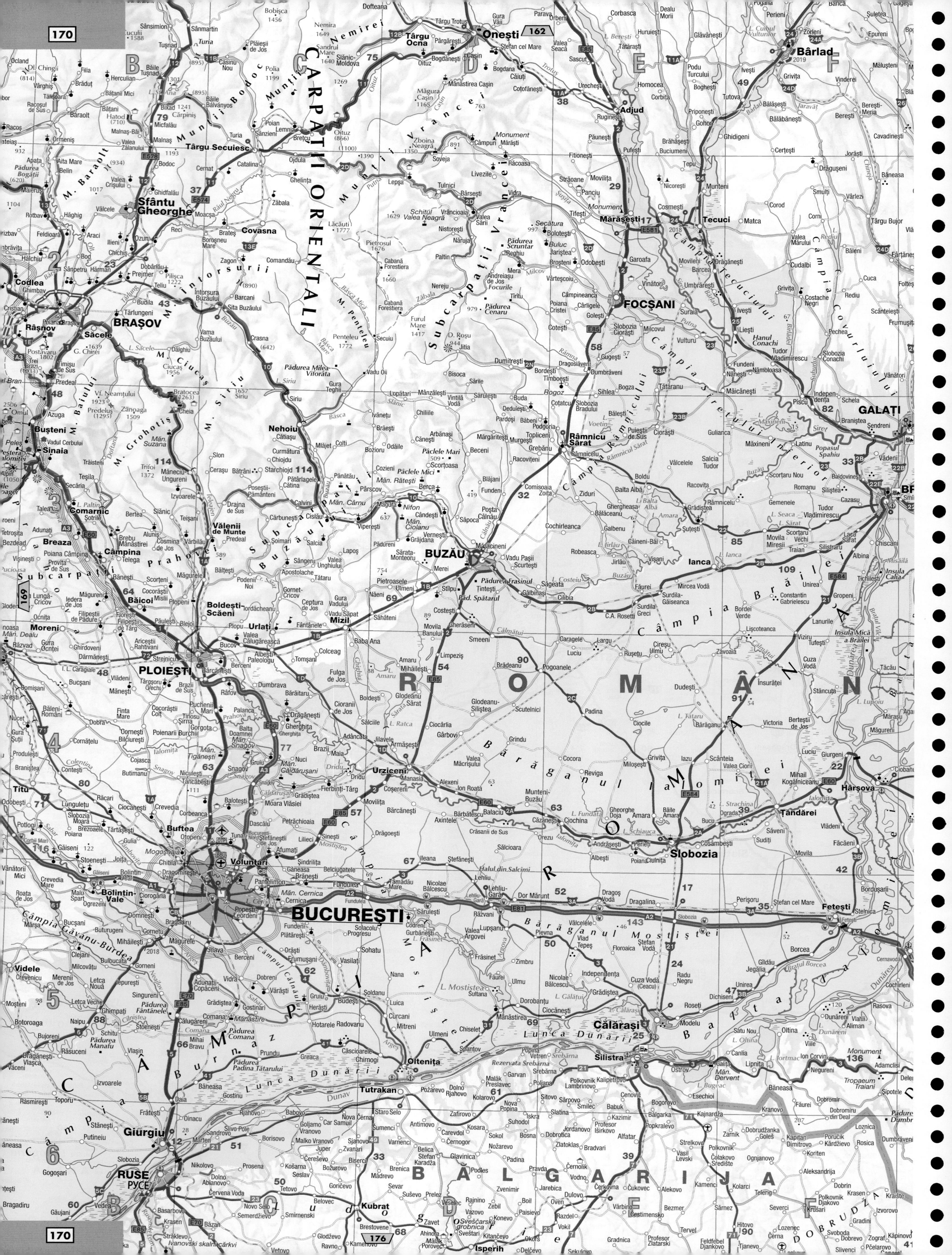

CARPAŢII ORIENTALI
Munţii Vrancei
Subcarpaţii Vrancei
Munţii Bodoc
M. Baraolt
Munţii Întorsurii
M. Ciucaş
M. Siriu
M. Penteleu
M. Grohotiş
M. Baiului
Subcarpaţii Buzăului
Subcarpaţii Prahovei
Câmpia Tecuciului
Câmpia Siretului Inferior
Câmpia Covurluiului
Câmpia Râmnicului
Câmpia Brăilei
Bărăganul Ialomiţei
Bărăganul Mostiştei
Câmpia Mostiştei
Câmpia Burnaz
Câmpia Găvanu-Burdea
Lunca Dunării
Baltă Ialomiţei
ROMÂNIA
BALGARIJA
DOBRUDŽA
Oneşti
Târgu Ocna
Bârlad
Adjud
Târgu Secuiesc
Sfântu Gheorghe
Covasna
Codlea
Râşnov
Braşov
Săcele
Mărăşeşti
Tecuci
Focşani
Galaţi
Buşteni
Sinaia
Comarnic
Breaza
Câmpina
Nehoiu
Vălenii de Munte
Râmnicu Sărat
Buzău
Băicoi
Boldeşti-Scăeni
Urlaţi
Mizil
Ploieşti
Ianca
Moreni
Urziceni
Slobozia
Ţăndărei
Hârşova
Feteşti
Buftea
Voluntari
Bolintin-Vale
BUCUREŞTI
Olteniţa
Călăraşi
Silistra
Tutrakan
Giurgiu
RUSE
РУСЕ
Kubrat
Isperih
Videle
Titu
E85
E60
E81
E70
E584
E581
E574
E578
162
169
176

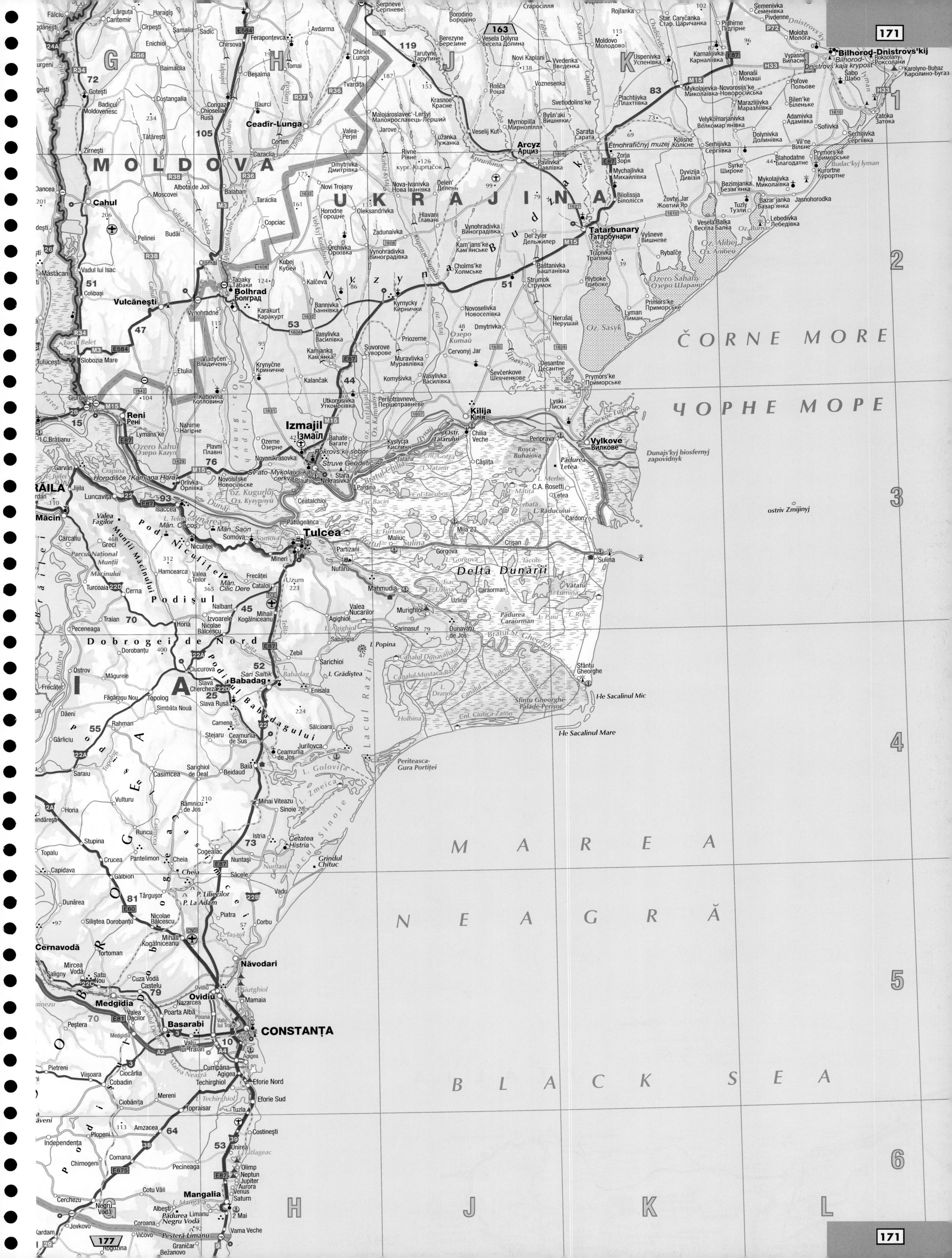
MOLDOVA
UKRAJINA
Budžak
Nyzyna
ČORNE MORE
ЧОРНЕ МОРЕ
MAREA NEAGRĂ
BLACK SEA
Delta Dunării
Dunajs'kyj biosfernyj zapovidnyk
ostriv Zmijinyj
Podişul Dobrogei de Nord
Podişul Babadagului
Munţii Măcinului
Parcul Naţional Munţii Măcinului
Bilhorod-Dnistrovs'kyj
Bilhorod-Dnistrovs'kaja krypost
Tatarbunary
Татарбунари
Arcyz
Арциз
Bolhrad
Болград
Izmajil
Ізмаїл
Reni
Рені
Kilija
Кілія
Vylkove
Вилкове
Cahul
Ceadîr-Lunga
Vulcăneşti
Giurgiuleşti
Tulcea
Sulina
Măcin
Babadag
Medgidia
Basarabi
Ovidiu
Năvodari
CONSTANŢA
Mangalia
Cernavodă
Eforie Nord
Eforie Sud
Techirghiol
Agigea
Costineşti
Olimp
Neptun
Jupiter
Aurora
Venus
Saturn
2 Mai
Vama Veche
Mamaia
Histria
Cetatea Histria
Periteasca-Gura Portiţei
Sfântu Gheorghe
Ile Sacalinul Mic
Ile Sacalinul Mare
Lacul Razim
L. Golovita
L. Zmeica
L. Sinoie
Ozero Kahul
Ozero Sasyk
Oz. Sasyk
Ozero Šahany
Oz. Alibej
Oz. Kugurluj
Oz. Jalpuh
Bratul Chilia
Bratul Sulina
Bratul Sf. Gheorghe
Pădurea Letea
Pădurea Caraorman
C.A. Rosetti
Letea
Periprava
Chilia Veche
Crişan
Caraorman
Mila 23
Maliuc
Mahmudia
Murighiol
Dunavăţu de Jos
Zatoka
Karolyno-Buhaz
Serhijivka
Lebedivka
Prymors'ke
Lyman
Strumok
Trapivka
Vyšneve
Rybal'če
Bilolissja
Sarata
Dmytrivka
Novoselivka
Suvorove
Kyslycja
Orlivka
Plavni
Kotlovina
Nahirne
Cantemir
Comrat
Taraclia
Basarabeasca
Brăila
Isaccea
Niculiţel
Somova
Mineri
Nufăru
Sarinasuf
Jurilovca
Enisala
Baia
Mihai Viteazu
Istria
Nuntaşi
Săcele
Corbu
Mihail Kogălniceanu
Poarta Albă
Valu lui Traian
Cumpăna
Tuzla
Topraisar
Amzacea
Comana
Pecineaga
Albeşti
Limanu
Negru Vodă
H
J
K
L
G
1
2
3
4
5
6
163
177
E87
E584
E81
E60
E675
M15
M3
A2
A4

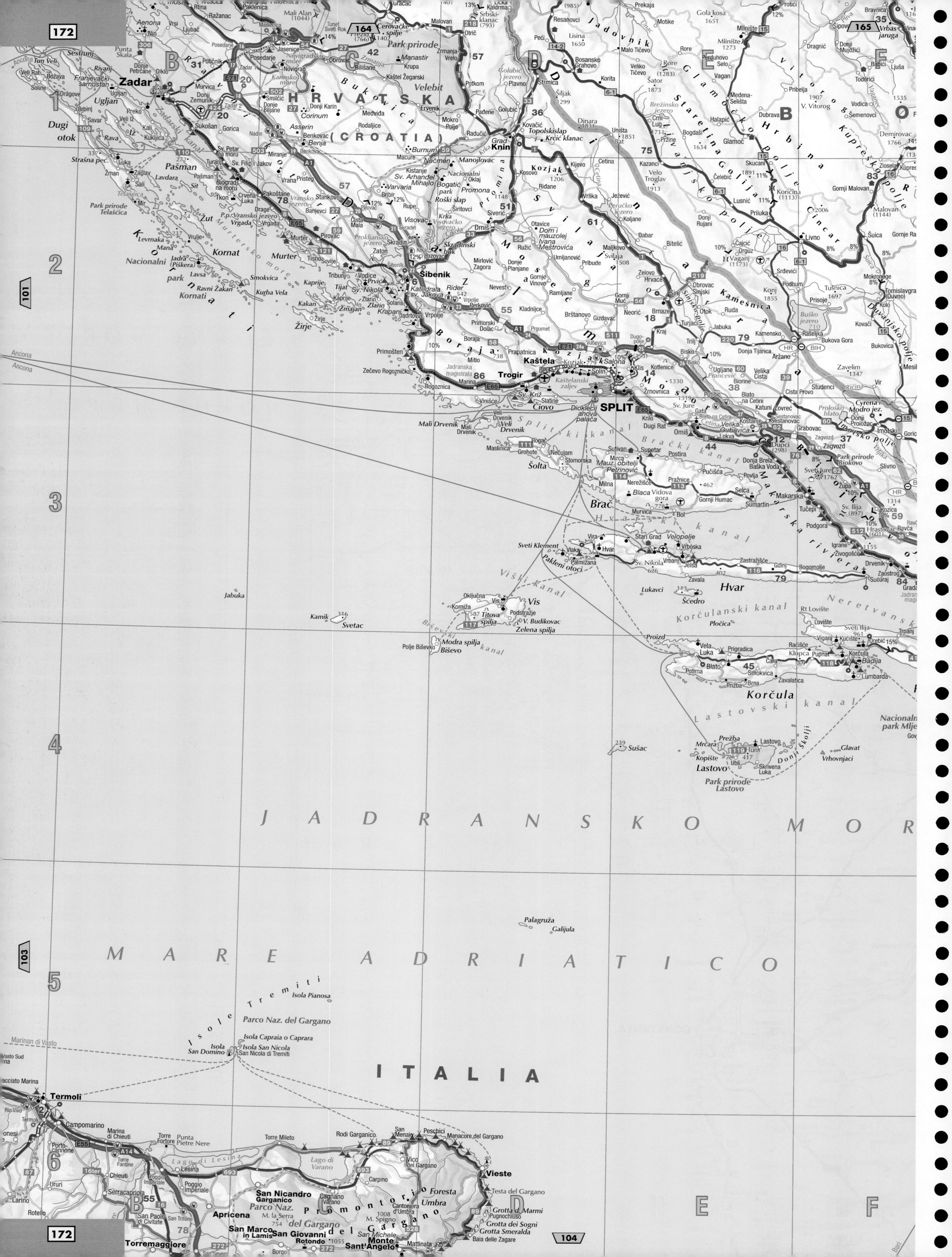
164
165
101
103
104
HRVATSKA
(CROATIA)
ITALIA
JADRANSKO MOR
MARE ADRIATICO
Zadar
Dugi otok
Ugljan
Pašman
Kornat
Nacionalni park Kornati
Park prirode Telašćica
Murter
Žirje
Šibenik
Knin
Drniš
Trogir
Kaštela
Solin
SPLIT
Omiš
Makarska
Sinj
Šolta
Brač
Hvar
Vis
Biševo
Svetac
Jabuka
Korčula
Lastovo
Park prirode Lastovo
Sušac
Palagruža
Galijula
Isole Tremiti
Isola Pianosa
Parco Naz. del Gargano
Termoli
Vieste
Apricena
Foresta Umbra
Promontorio del Gargano
Velebit
Park prirode Biokovo
Livno
Tomislavgrad (Duvno)
Buško jezero
Splitski kanal
Brački kanal
Hvarski kanal
Viški kanal
Korčulanski kanal
Lastovski kanal
Makarska rivijera
Nacionalni park Mljet

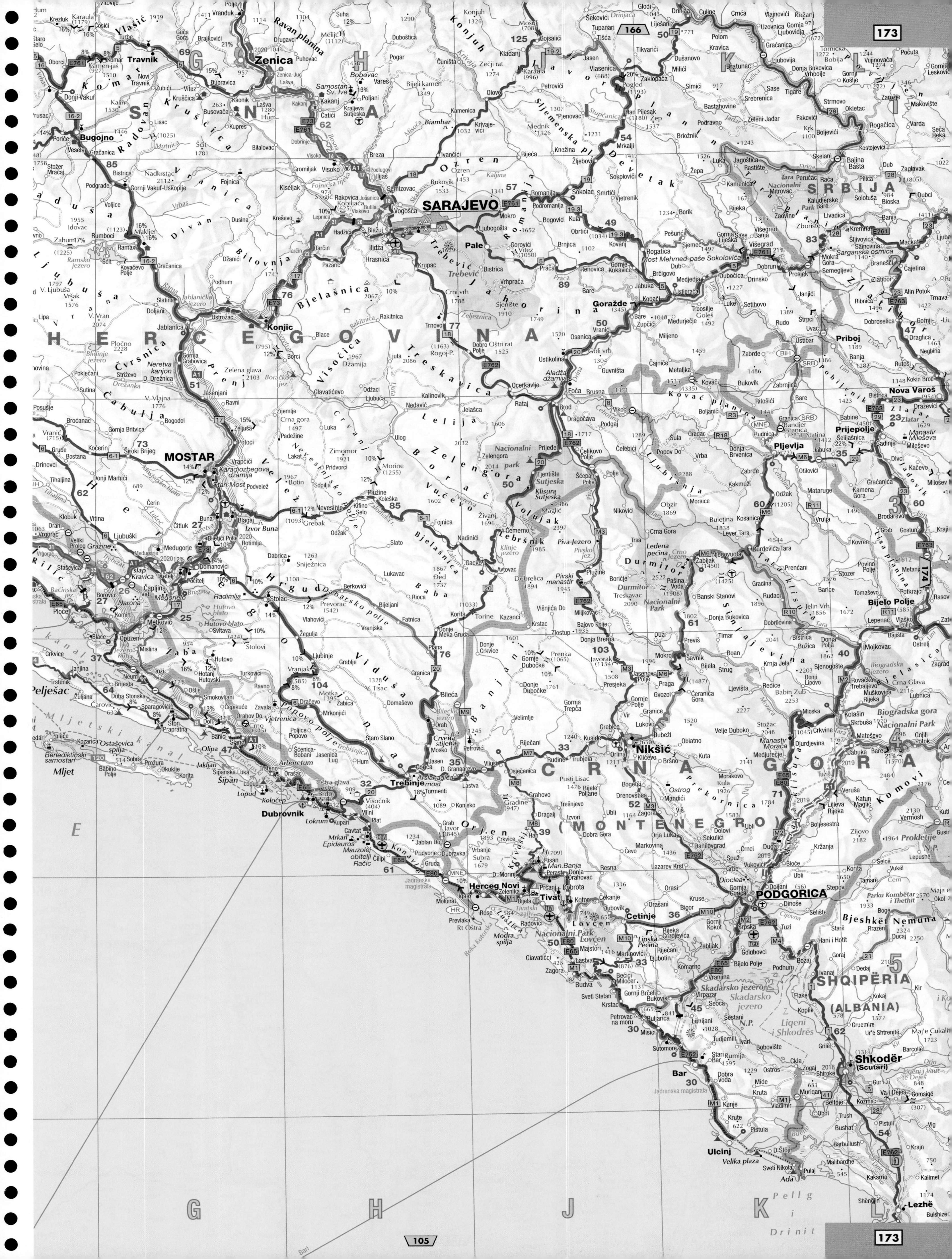

166
174
105
HERCEGOVINA
SRBIJA
CRNA GORA
(MONTENEGRO)
SHQIPËRIA
(ALBANIA)
SARAJEVO
PODGORICA
MOSTAR
Zenica
Travnik
Bugojno
Konjic
Pale
Goražde
Foča
Višegrad
Priboj
Nova Varoš
Prijepolje
Pljevlja
Bijelo Polje
Nikšić
Trebinje
Dubrovnik
Herceg Novi
Tivat
Kotor
Cetinje
Budva
Bar
Ulcinj
Shkodër
(Scutari)
Lezhë
Mljet
Pelješac
Skadarsko jezero
Durmitor
Nacionalni Park
Biogradska gora
Nacionalni Park
Nacionalni park Lovćen
Prokletije
Bjeshkët Nemuna
Velika plaza
Ada
E
G
H
J
K
L

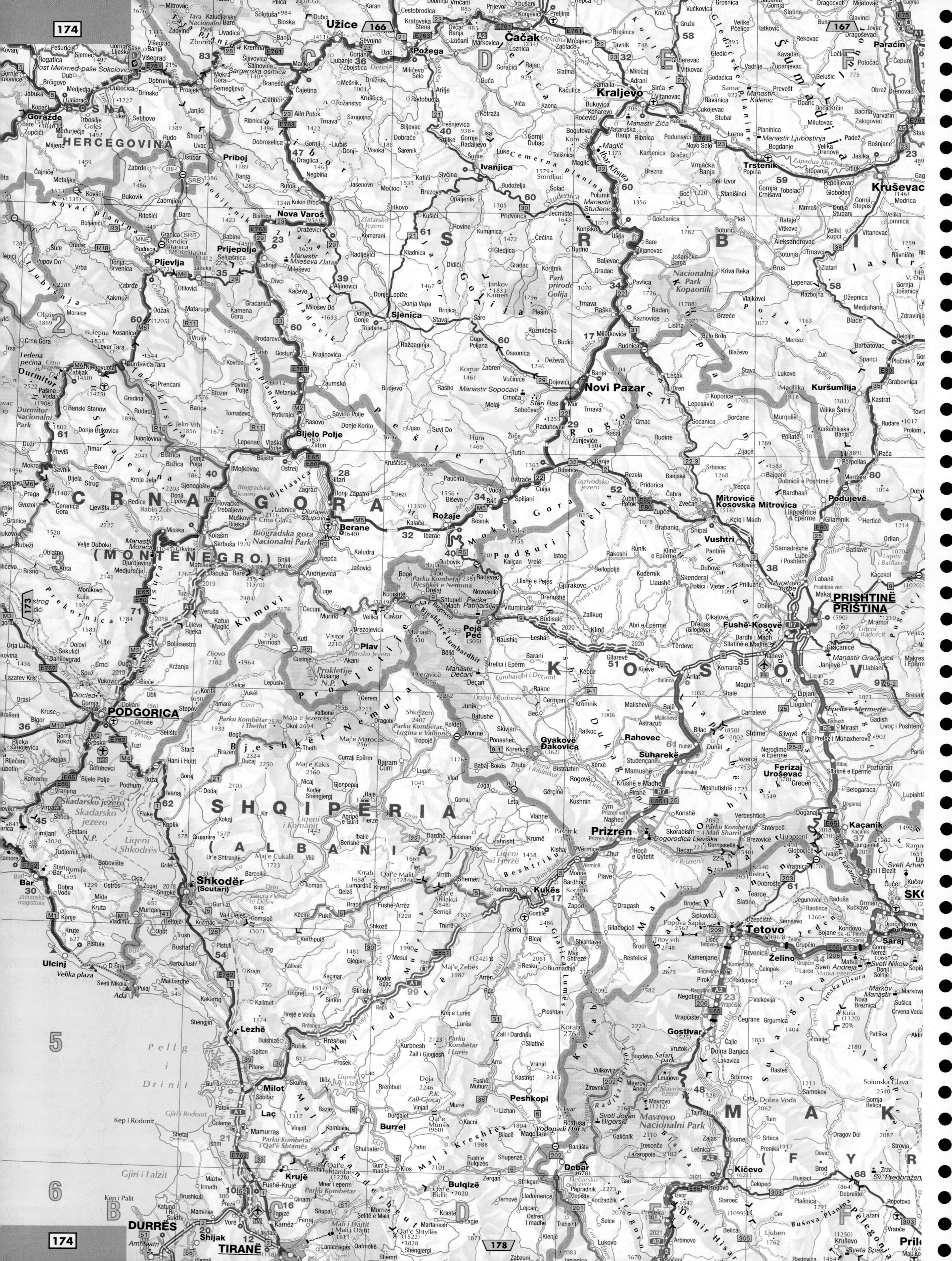

174
166
167
178
Užice
Čačak
Kraljevo
Požega
Ivanjica
Trstenik
Kruševac
Paraćin
Priboj
Nova Varoš
Prijepolje
Pljevlja
Sjenica
Novi Pazar
Raška
Bijelo Polje
Berane
Rožaje
Tutin
Kuršumlija
Podujevë
Mitrovicë
Kosovska Mitrovica
Vushtri
PRISHTINË
PRIŠTINA
Fushë-Kosovë
Pejë
Peć
Gyakovë
Đakovica
Rahovec
Suharekë
Prizren
Ferizaj
Uroševac
Kaçanik
Tetovo
Gostivar
Kičevo
Debar
Kukës
Peshkopi
Bulqizë
Burrel
Shkodër
(Scutari)
Lezhë
Laç
Krujë
Milot
DURRËS
TIRANË
Shijak
Ulcinj
Bar
PODGORICA
Plav
Kolašin
Mojkovac
Durmitor
Goražde
BOSNA I HERCEGOVINA
CRNA GORA
(MONTENEGRO)
SHQIPËRIA
(ALBANIA)
KOSOVO
SRBIJA
MAK
(F. Y. R
Skadarsko jezero
Pellg i Drinit
Prokletije
Bjeshkët e Nemuna
Mavrovo Nacionalni Park
Nacionalni Park Kopaonik
Biogradska gora Nacionalni Park
Durmitor Nacionalni Park
Manastir Studenica
Manastir Sopoćani
Manastir Dečani
Manastir Žiča
Saraj
Želino
Sveti Nikola
Velika plaza
Ada
Jadranska magistrala

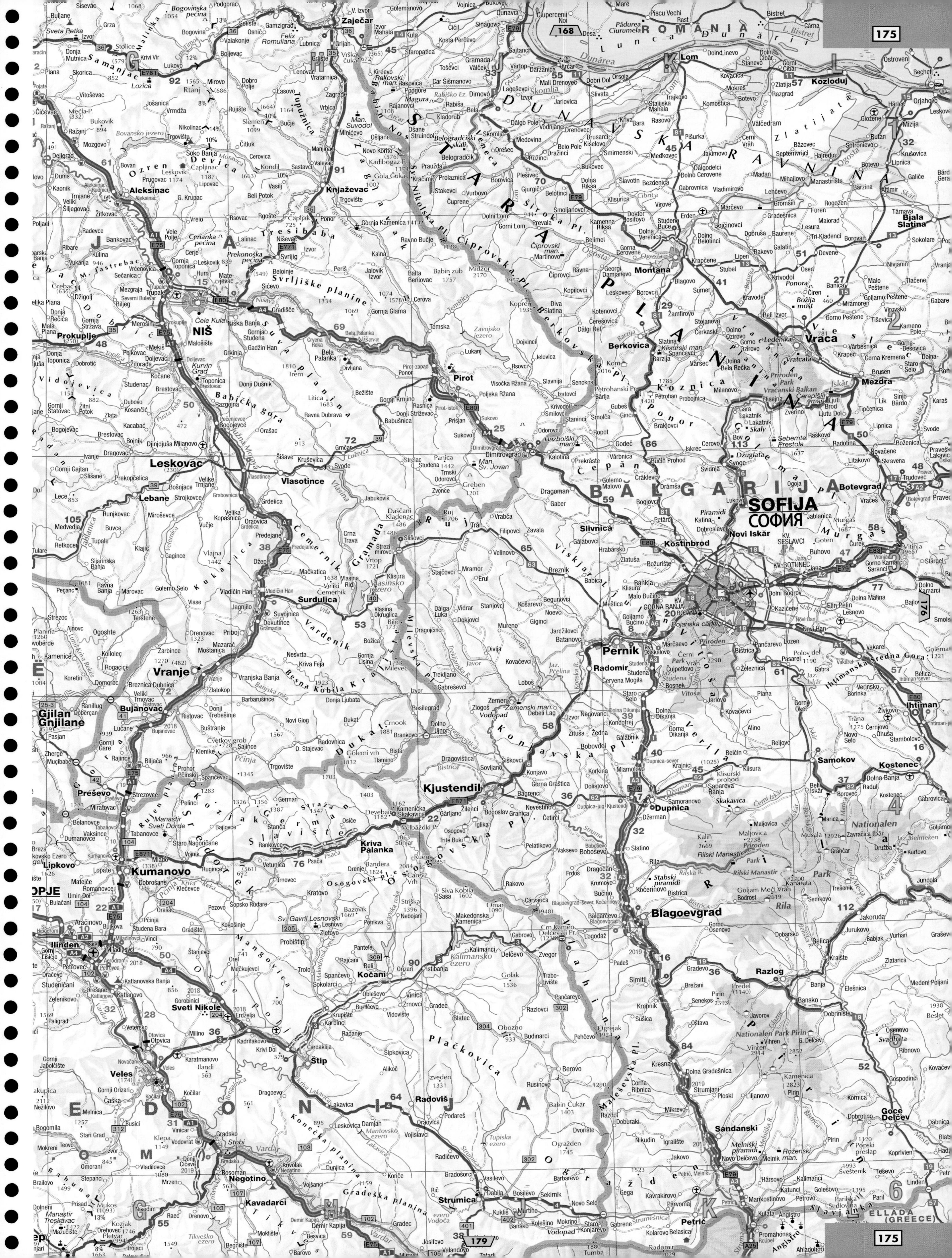

175
ROMANIA
Dunărea
Zaječar
Lom
Kozloduj
Aleksinac
Knjaževac
Montana
Berkovica
Vraca
Mezdra
Niš
Prokuplje
Pirot
Dimitrovgrad
Leskovac
Vlasotince
Lebane
Surdulica
Vranje
BĂLGARIJA
SOFIJA
СОФИЯ
Kostinbrod
Slivnica
Pernik
Radomir
Botevgrad
Ihtiman
Samokov
Kostenec
Dupnica
Kjustendil
Kriva Palanka
Kumanovo
Bujanovac
Preševo
Gjilan
Gnjilane
Blagoevgrad
Razlog
Bansko
Sandanski
Goce Delčev
Petrič
Strumica
Radoviš
Štip
Kočani
Sveti Nikole
Veles
Negotino
Kavadarci
Ilinden
Delčevo
Stara Planina
Rila
Nationalen Park Pirin
Vitoša
ELLÁDA (GREECE)
175

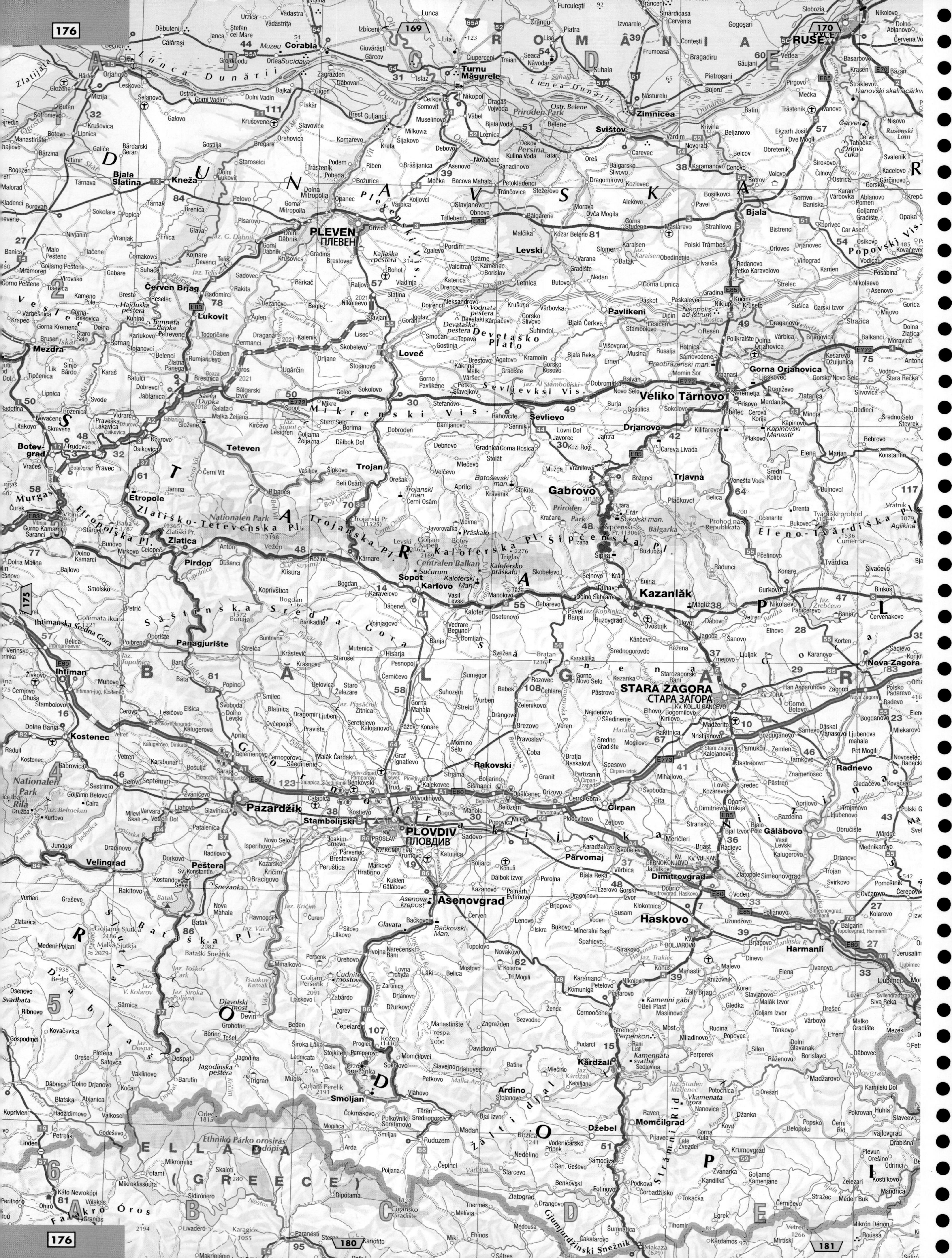

ROMÂNIA
Turnu Măgurele
Zimnicea
RUSE
Corabia
Lunca Dunării
DUNAVSKA
PLEVEN
ПЛЕВЕН
Levski
Svištov
Bjala
Veliko Tărnovo
Gorna Orjahovica
Lovec
Sevlievo
Gabrovo
Trjavna
Drjanovo
Červen Brjag
Lukovit
Teteven
Trojan
Etropole
Zlatica
Pirdop
Botevgrad
Mezdra
Kazanlăk
STARA ZAGORA
СТАРА ЗАГОРА
Nova Zagora
Karlovo
Sopot
Panagjurište
Ihtiman
Kostenec
Pazardžik
PLOVDIV
ПЛОВДИВ
Asenovgrad
Stambolijski
Velingrad
Peštera
Rakovski
Părvomaj
Dimitrovgrad
Haskovo
Harmanli
Čirpan
Gălăbovo
Radnevo
Kărdžali
Momčilgrad
Džebel
Smoljan
Ardino
Dospat
Devin
Rhodopi
ELLÁDA
(GREECE)
Centralen Balkan
Kaloferska Pl.
Trojanska Pl.
Šipčenska Pl.
Zlatiško-Tetevenska Pl.
Sredna Gora
Gornotrakijska
Nizina
Batăška Pl.
Devetaško Plato
Nationalen Park Rila
169
170
175
180
181

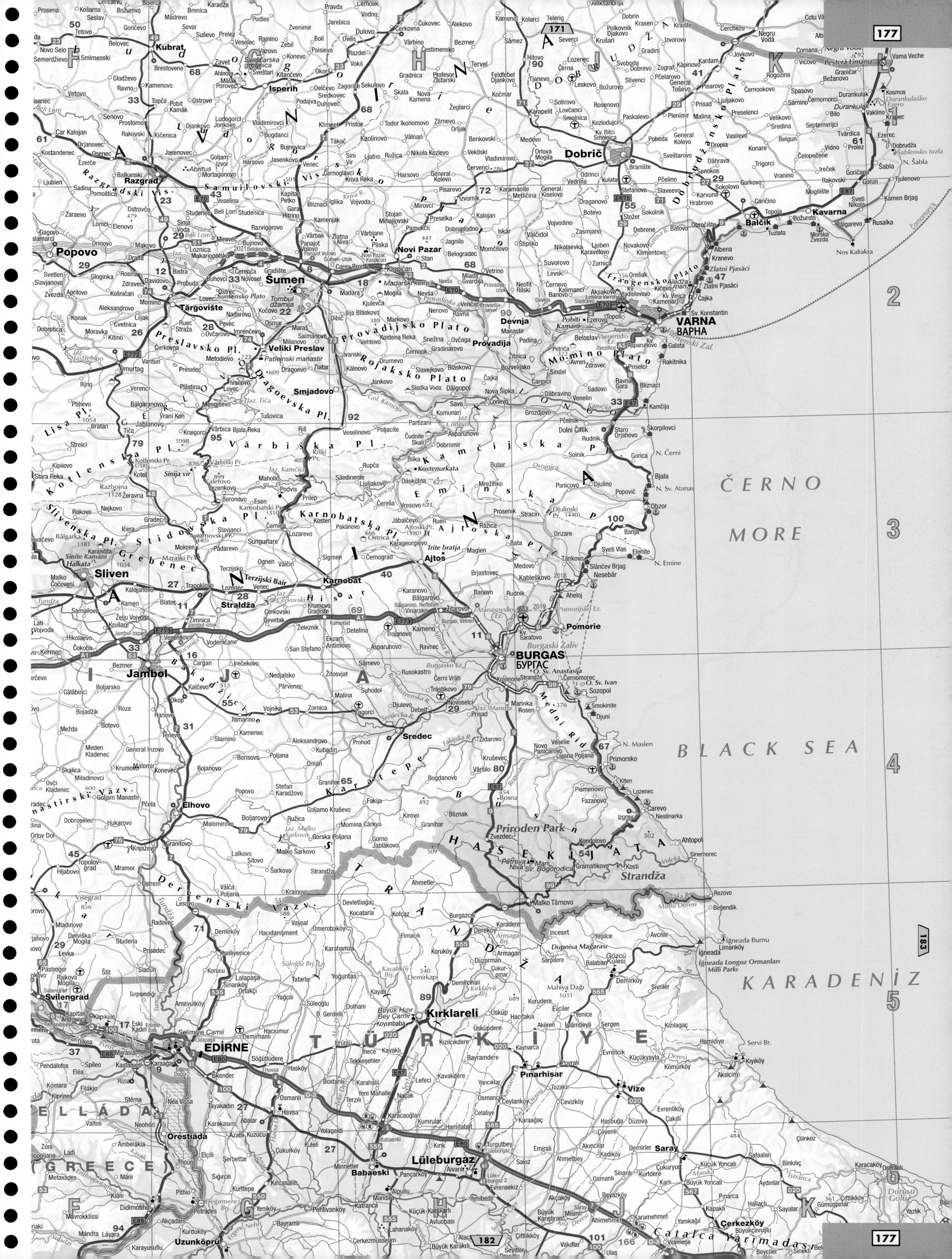

177
Kubrat
Razgrad
Popovo
Isperih
Šumen
Tărgovište
Veliki Preslav
Smjadovo
Novi Pazar
Provadija
Devnja
Dobrič
Balčik
Kavarna
VARNA
ВАРНА
Sliven
Karnobat
Ajtos
Straldža
Jambol
Elhovo
Sredec
BURGAS
БУРГАС
Pomorie
Nesebăr
Sozopol
Primorsko
Carevo
Malko Tărnovo
Strandža
Priroden Park
Kırklareli
EDİRNE
Svilengrad
Orestiáda
Lüleburgaz
Babaeski
Pınarhisar
Vize
Saray
Çerkezköy
Uzunköprü
ČERNO MORE
BLACK SEA
KARADENİZ
ELLÁDA
GREECE
TÜRKİYE
Provadijsko Plato
Rojakско Plato
Frangensko Plato
Dobrudžansko Plato
Preslavska Pl.
Vărbiška Pl.
Kamčijska Pl.
Kotlenska Pl.
Karnobatska Pl.
Ajtoska Pl.
Stidovska Pl.
Grebenec
Dervenstki Vazv.
Burgaski Zaliv
Čatalca Yarımadası
2
3
4
5
6
E70
E87
E773
E772
E80
E85
183
182
177

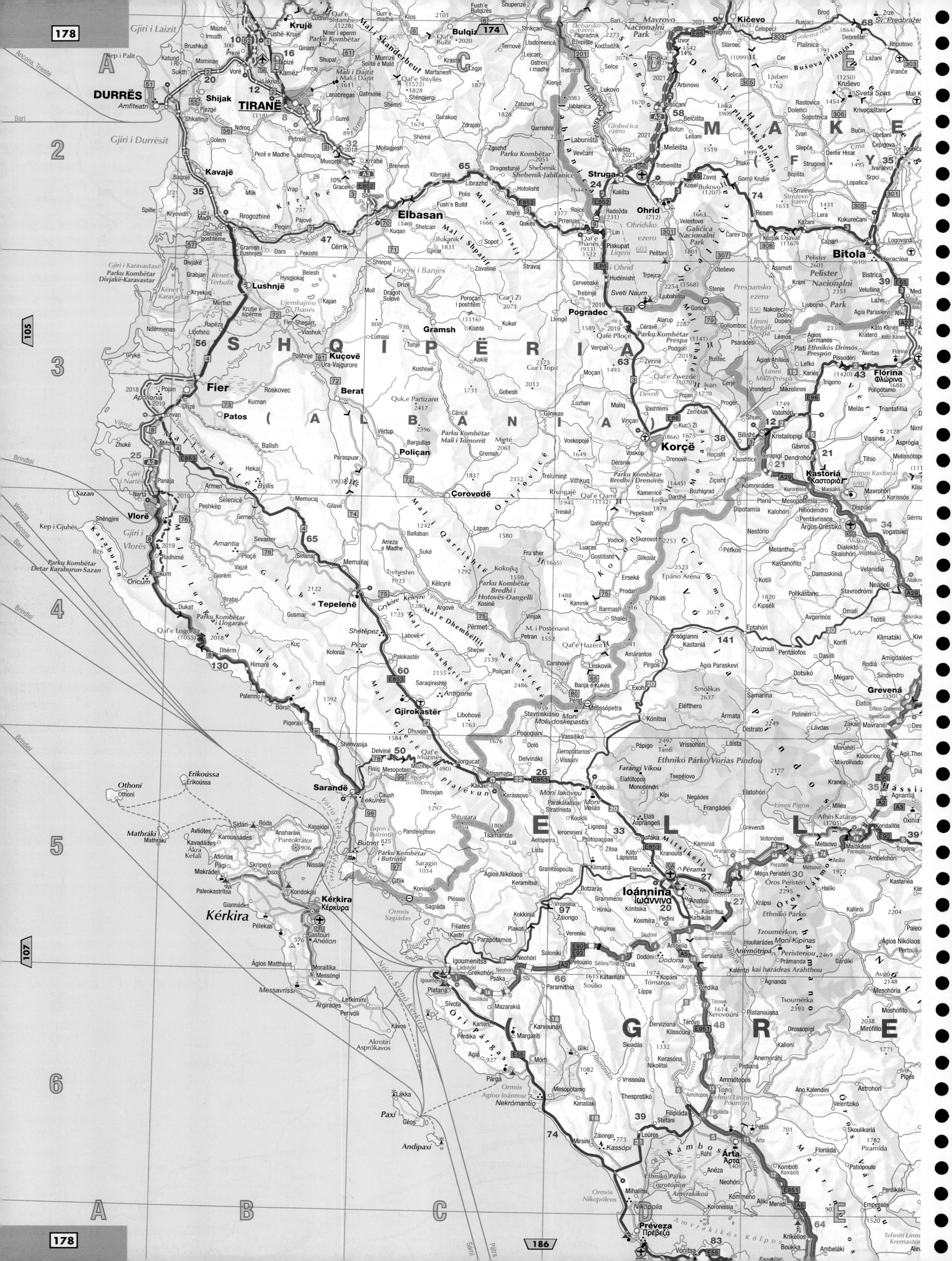

178
DURRËS
TIRANË
Shijak
Kavajë
Elbasan
Lushnjë
Fier
Berat
Patos
Kuçovë
Gramsh
Pogradec
Korçë
Ohrid
Struga
Bitola
Kičevo
Flórina
Φλώρινα
Kastoriá
Καστοριά
Vlorë
Tepelenë
Gjirokastër
Sarandë
Çorovodë
Poliçan
Përmet
Kérkira
Κέρκυρα
Ioánnina
Ιωάννινα
Árta
Άρτα
Préveza
Πρέβεζα
Grevená
SHQIPËRIA
(ALBANIA)
MAKEDONIJA (FYROM)
ELLÁS (GREECE)
Gjiri i Drinit
Gjiri i Durrësit
Gjiri i Vlorës
Ohridsko ezero
Prespansko ezero
Sazan
Othoní
Erikoússa
Mathráki
Paxí
Andipaxí
105
107
A
B
C
D
E
2
3
4
5
6
178
186

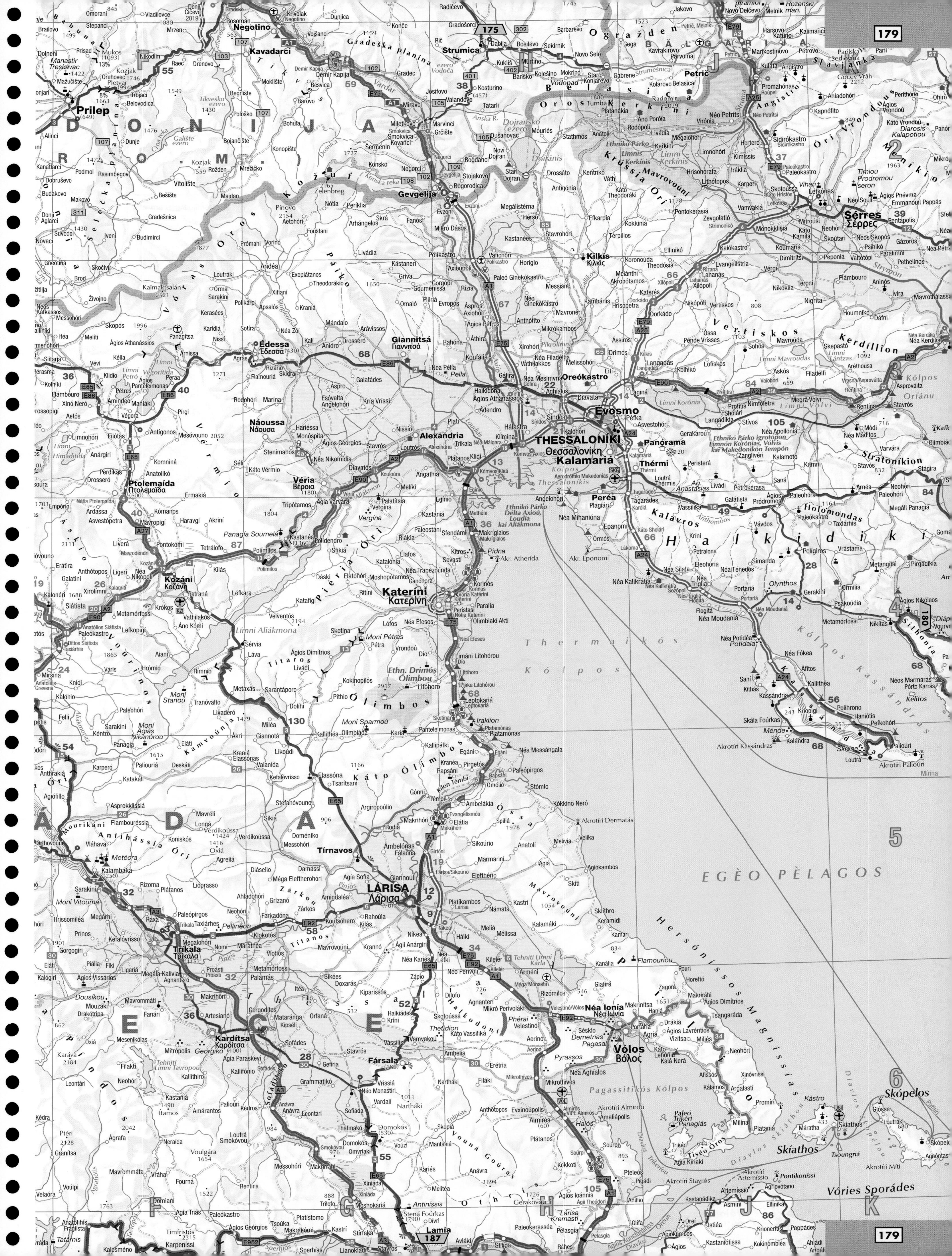
THESSALONÍKI
Θεσσαλονίκη
Kalamariá
Évosmo
Oreókastro
Thérmi
Panórama
Peréa
Kilkís
Κιλκίς
Sérres
Σέρρες
Giannitsá
Γιαννιτσά
Édessa
Έδεσσα
Náoussa
Νάουσα
Véria
Βέροια
Alexándria
Kateríni
Κατερίνη
Kozáni
Κοζάνη
Ptolemaída
Πτολεμαΐδα
LÁRISA
Λάρισα
Tríkala
Τρίκαλα
Kardítsa
Καρδίτσα
Vólos
Βόλος
Néa Ionía
Fársala
Lamía
Tírnavos
Elassóna
Prilep
Kavadarci
Negotino
Gevgelija
Strumica
Petrič
Néa Moudania
Políhrono
Kallithéa
Skópelos
Skiáthos
Vóries Sporádes
EGÈO PÈLAGOS
Thermaikós Kólpos
Pagassitikós Kólpos
Hersónissos Magnissías
Halkidikí
Kassándra
Ólimbos
Káto Ólimbos
Óssa
Vérmio
Vertiskos
Kerdíllion
Belasica
Kožuf
Voúrinos
Ótrhis
Pilio
Meteóra
Kalambáka
Ethnikó Párko Délta Axioú, Loudía kai Aliákmona
Límni Kerkíni
Límni Korónia
Límni Vólvi
Límni Aliákmona
Dojransko ezero
Strymonikós Kólpos
Stratoníkion
Sithonía
Agio Óros
Ágios Nikólaos
E75
E79
E86
E90
E92
E65
A1
A2
A3
A24
A25
175
187
180

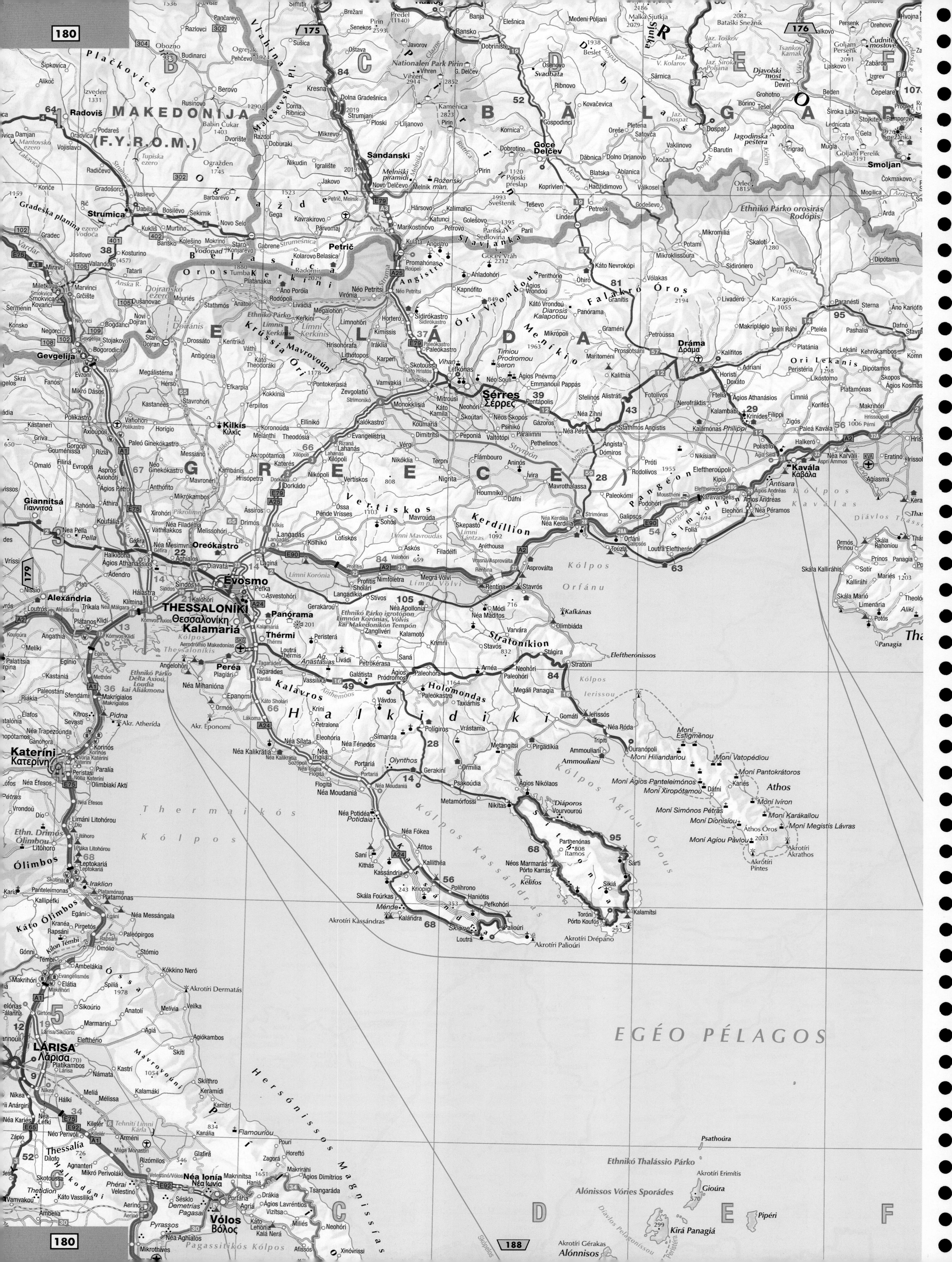180
175
176
MAKEDONIJA
(F.Y.R.O.M.)
Radoviš
Strumica
Gevgelija
Sandanski
Petrič
Goce Delčev
Dospat
Smoljan
Nationalen Park Pirin
Drama
Δράμα
Sérres
Σέρρες
Kilkís
Κιλκίς
Kavála
Καβάλα
Giannitsá
Γιαννιτσά
Évosmo
THESSALONÍKI
Θεσσαλονίκη
Kalamariá
Panórama
Thérmi
Peréa
Oreókastro
GREECE
Halkidikí
Athos
Kateríni
Κατερίνη
Ólimbos
LÁRISA
Λάρισα
Thessalía
Néa Ionía
Νέα Ιωνία
Vólos
Βόλος
Thermaikós Kólpos
Kólpos Orfánu
Kólpos Kassándras
Kólpos Agíou Órous
EGÉO PÉLAGOS
Ethnikó Thalássio Párko
Alónissos Vóries Sporádes
Alónissos
Psathoúra
Gioúra
Pipéri
Kirá Panagiá
Pagassitikós Kólpos
179
188
180

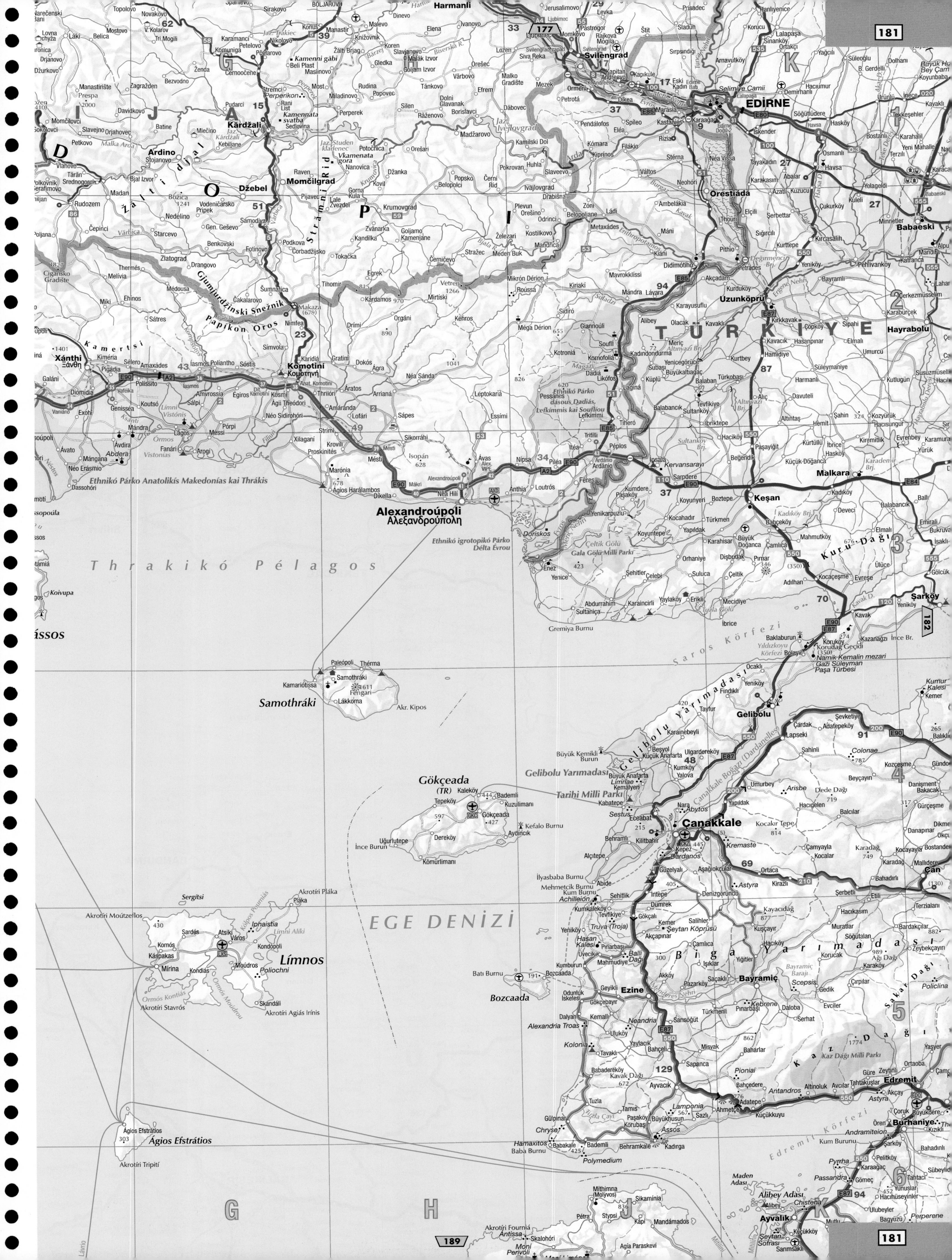
Harmanli
Svilengrad
EDİRNE
Kărdžali
Ardino
Džebel
Momčilgrad
Krumovgrad
Xánthi
Ξάνθη
Komotiní
Κομοτηνή
Orestiáda
Didimótiho
Uzunköprü
Hayrabolu
Babaeski
Malkara
Keşan
Şarköy
Alexandroúpoli
Αλεξανδρούπολη
Ethnikó Párko Anatolikís Makedonías kai Thrákis
Ethnikó igrotopikó Párko Délta Évrou
Ethnikó Párko dásous Dadiás, Lefkimmis kai Soufliou
Thrakikó Pélagos
Saros Körfezi
TÜRKİYE
Samothráki
Gökçeada (TR)
Gelibolu
Gelibolu Yarımadası
Gelibolu Yarımadası Tarihi Milli Parkı
Çanakkale
Çanakkale Boğazı (Dardanelles)
Truva (Troja)
Ezine
Bayramiç
Biga Yarımadası
Bozcaada
EGE DENİZİ
Límnos
Mírina
Ágios Efstrátios
Assos
Kaz Dağı Milli Parkı
Edremit
Burhaniye
Edremit Körfezi
Ayvalık
Alibey Adası
Mithimna (Molyvos)
Gala Gölü Milli Parkı
Kuru Dağı
Enez
Lapseki
Kazdağı
Papikon Oros
Stramni Rid
Gjumjurdžinski Snežnik
Žălti djal
Vetren 1266
E90
E84
E87
E85
E80
182
189
177

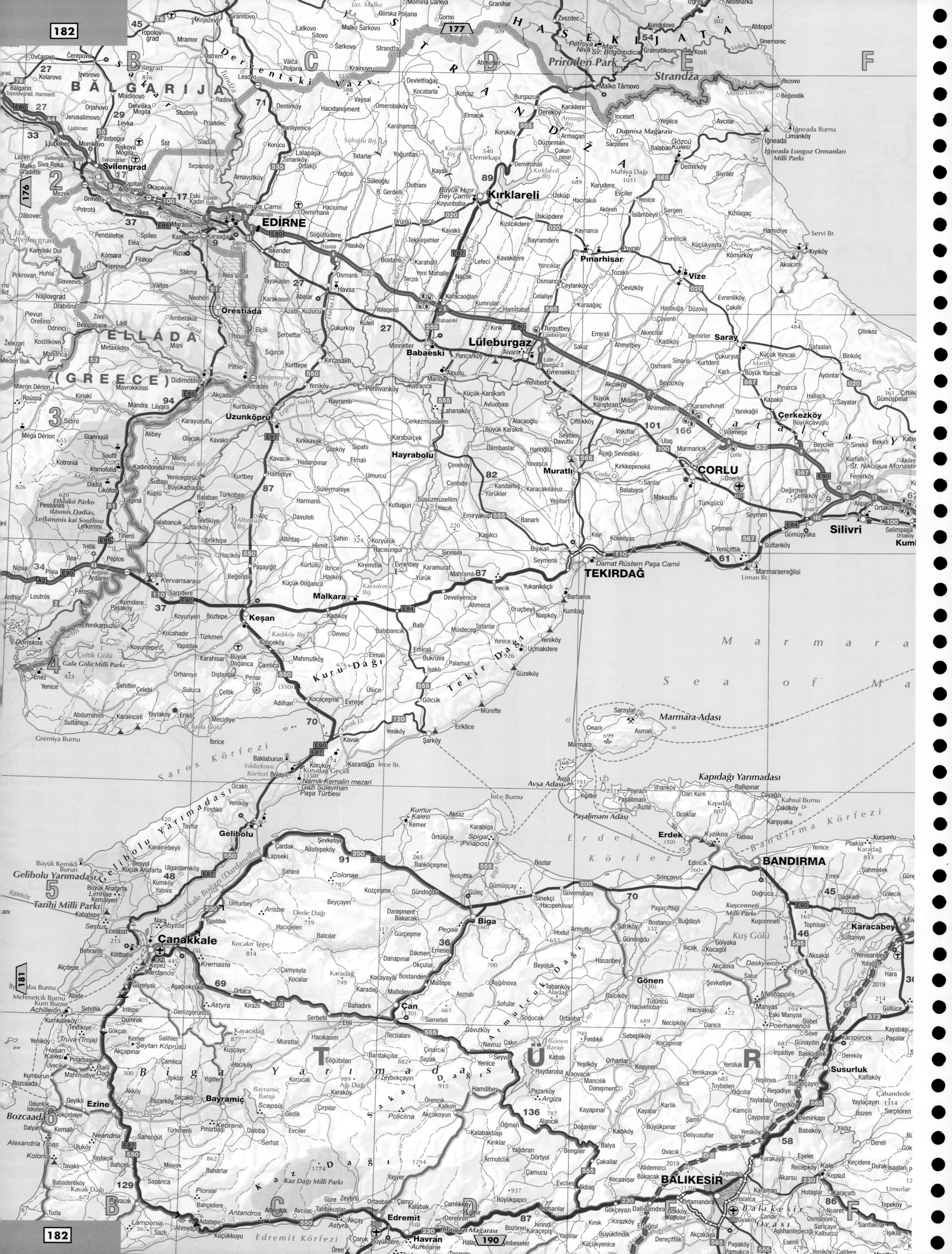
BĂLGARIJA
Svilengrad
Derventski Vazv.
STRANDŽA
HASEKI JATA
Priroden Park Strandža
Malko Tărnovo
EDİRNE
Kırklareli
Pınarhisar
Vize
Saray
Lüleburgaz
Babaeski
Orestiáda
ELLÁDA
(GREECE)
Didimótiho
Uzunköprü
Hayrabolu
Muratlı
Çerkezköy
ÇORLU
Silivri
TEKİRDAĞ
Malkara
Keşan
Kuru Dağı
Tekir Dağı
Şarköy
Saros Körfezi
Marmara Adası
Marmara
Avşa Adası
Kapıdağı Yarımadası
Erdek
Erdek Körfezi
BANDIRMA
Marmara
Sea of Ma
Gelibolu
Gelibolu Yarımadası
Gelibolu Yarımadası Tarihi Milli Parkı
Çanakkale Boğazı (Dardanelles)
Lapseki
Çanakkale
Biga
Karacabey
Kuş Gölü
Gönen
Çan
Ezine
Bozcaada
Bayramiç
Biga Yarımadası
Kaz Dağı
Kaz Dağı Milli Parkı
Edremit
Havran
Edremit Körfezi
BALIKESİR
Balıkesir Ovası
Susurluk
TÜRKİYE

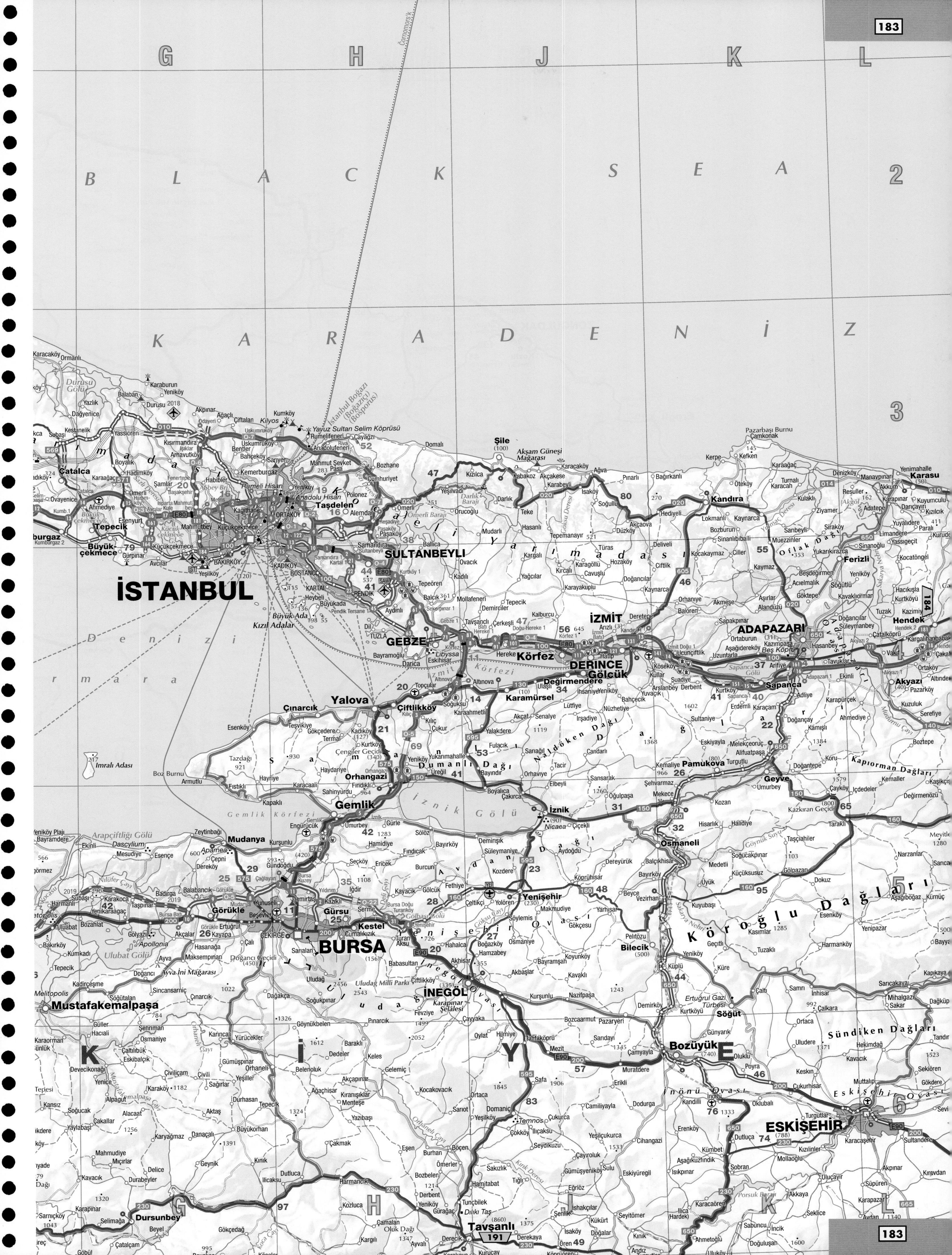
G
H
J
K
L
2
3
4
5
6
B L A C K S E A
K A R A D E N İ Z
İSTANBUL
BURSA
ESKİŞEHİR
Çatalca
Büyükçekmece
Tepecik
Sultanbeyli
Gebze
Yalova
Çınarcık
Gemlik
Mudanya
Orhangazi
İzmit
Derince
Gölcük
Körfez
Karamürsel
Adapazarı
Sapanca
Akyazı
Hendek
Ferizli
Karasu
Kandıra
Şile
Pamukova
Geyve
Osmaneli
İznik
Yenişehir
Bilecik
Söğüt
Bozüyük
İnegöl
Kestel
Gürsu
Görükle
Mustafakemalpaşa
Tavşanlı
Dursunbey
Kızıl Adalar
Büyük Ada
İmralı Adası
İstanbul Boğazı (Boğaziçi) (Bosporus)
Yavuz Sultan Selim Köprüsü
İzmit Körfezi
Gemlik Körfezi
İznik Gölü
Ulubat Gölü
Uludağ
Uludağ Milli Parkı
Samanlı Dağları
Köroğlu Dağları
Sündiken Dağları
Kapıorman Dağları
Naldöken Dağı
Avdan Dağı
Dumanlı Dağı
Sapanca Gölü
Eskişehir Ovası
İnönü Ovası
Yenişehir Ovası
Adapazarı Ovası
Kocaeli Yarımadası
184
191

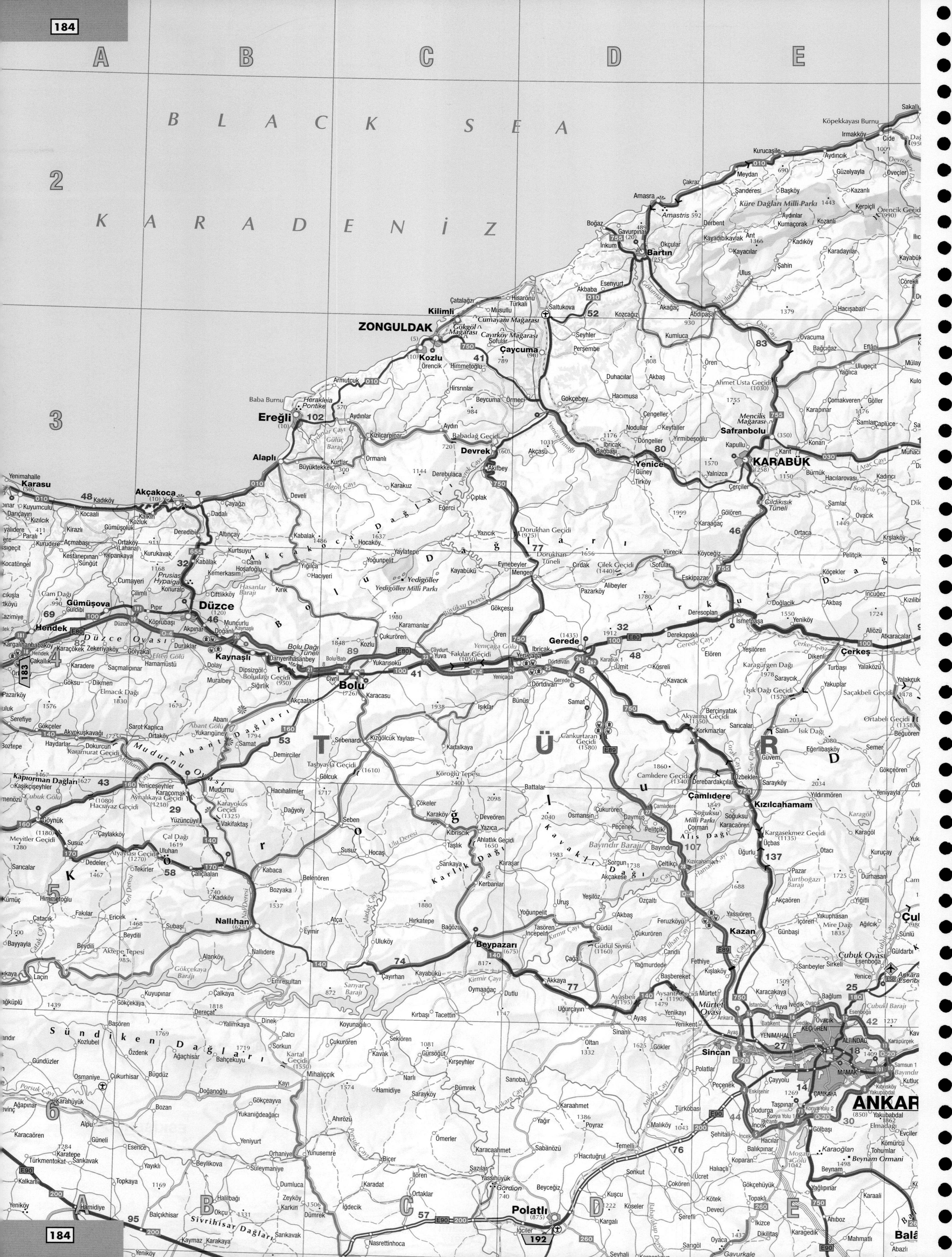
A
B
C
D
E
2
3
4
5
6
BLACK SEA
KARADENİZ
ZONGULDAK
Kilimli
Kozlu
Çaycuma
Ereğli
Alaplı
Devrek
Akçakoca
Karasu
Düzce
Gümüşova
Hendek
Kaynaşlı
Bolu
Gerede
Yeniçağa
Amasra
Bartın
Safranbolu
KARABÜK
Yenice
Eskipazar
Çerkeş
Çamlıdere
Kızılcahamam
Mudurnu
Göynük
Nallıhan
Beypazarı
Kazan
Sincan
ANKARA
Polatlı
Gordion
Yedigöller Milli Parkı
Küre Dağları Milli Parkı
Soğuksu Milli Parkı
Bolu Dağları
Abant Dağları
Akçakoca Dağları
Köroğlu Tepesi
Sündiken Dağları
Sivrihisar Dağları
Düzce Ovası
Mürted Ovası
Çubuk Ovası
TÜRKİYE
Kapıorman Dağları
Sarıyar Barajı
Gökçekaya Barajı
Bayındır Barajı
Mogan Gölü
Abant Gölü
Çubuk Gölü
Karaoğlan
Gölbaşı
Çankaya
Keçiören
Yenimahalle
Mamak
Altındağ

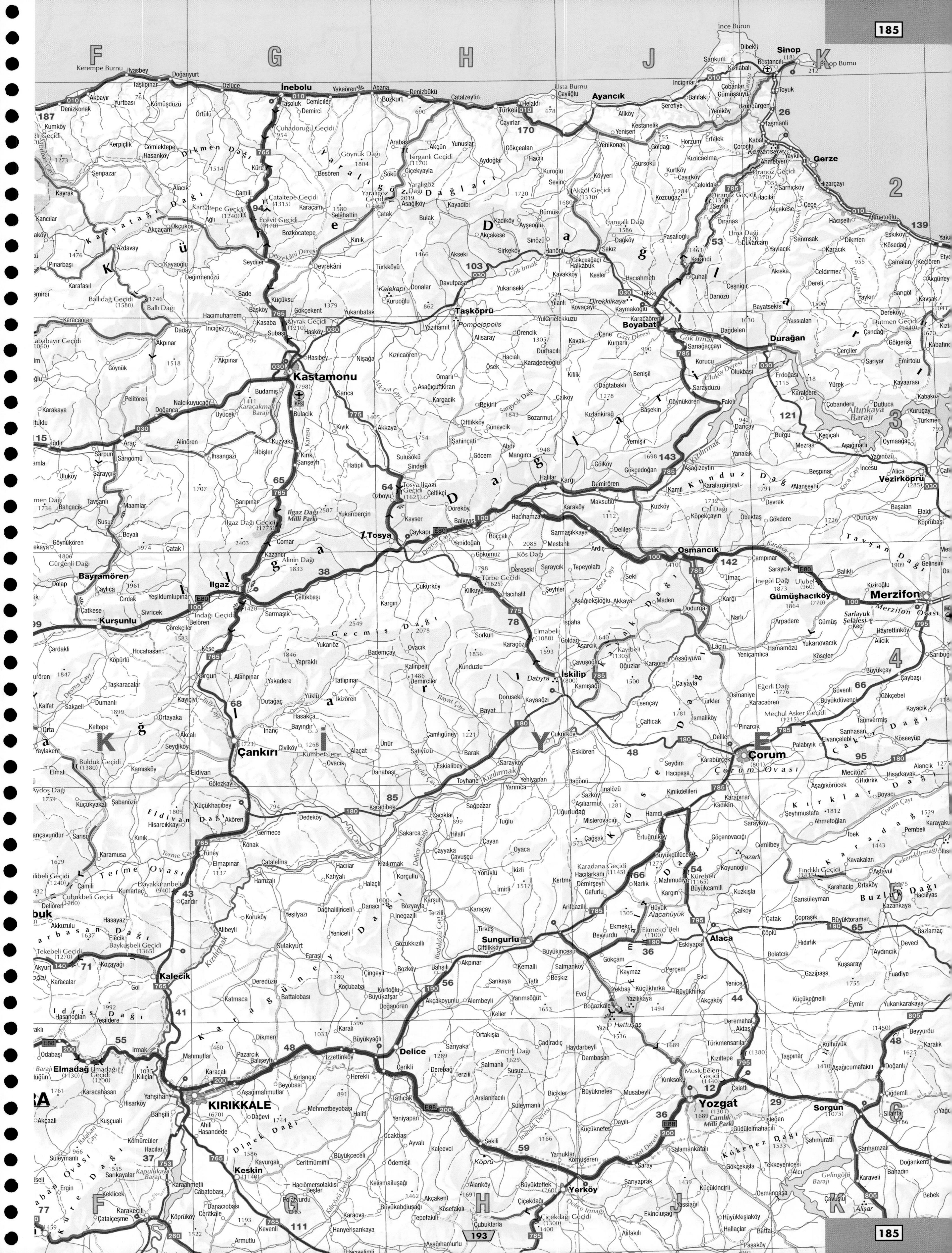
F
G
H
J
K
Sinop
İnebolu
Ayancık
Gerze
Kastamonu
Taşköprü
Boyabat
Durağan
Tosya
Ilgaz
Kurşunlu
Osmancık
Merzifon
Gümüşhacıköy
Vezirköprü
İskilip
Çankırı
Çorum
Sungurlu
Alaca
Kalecik
Delice
KIRIKKALE
Keskin
Yozgat
Sorgun
Yerköy
Elmadağ
Bayramören

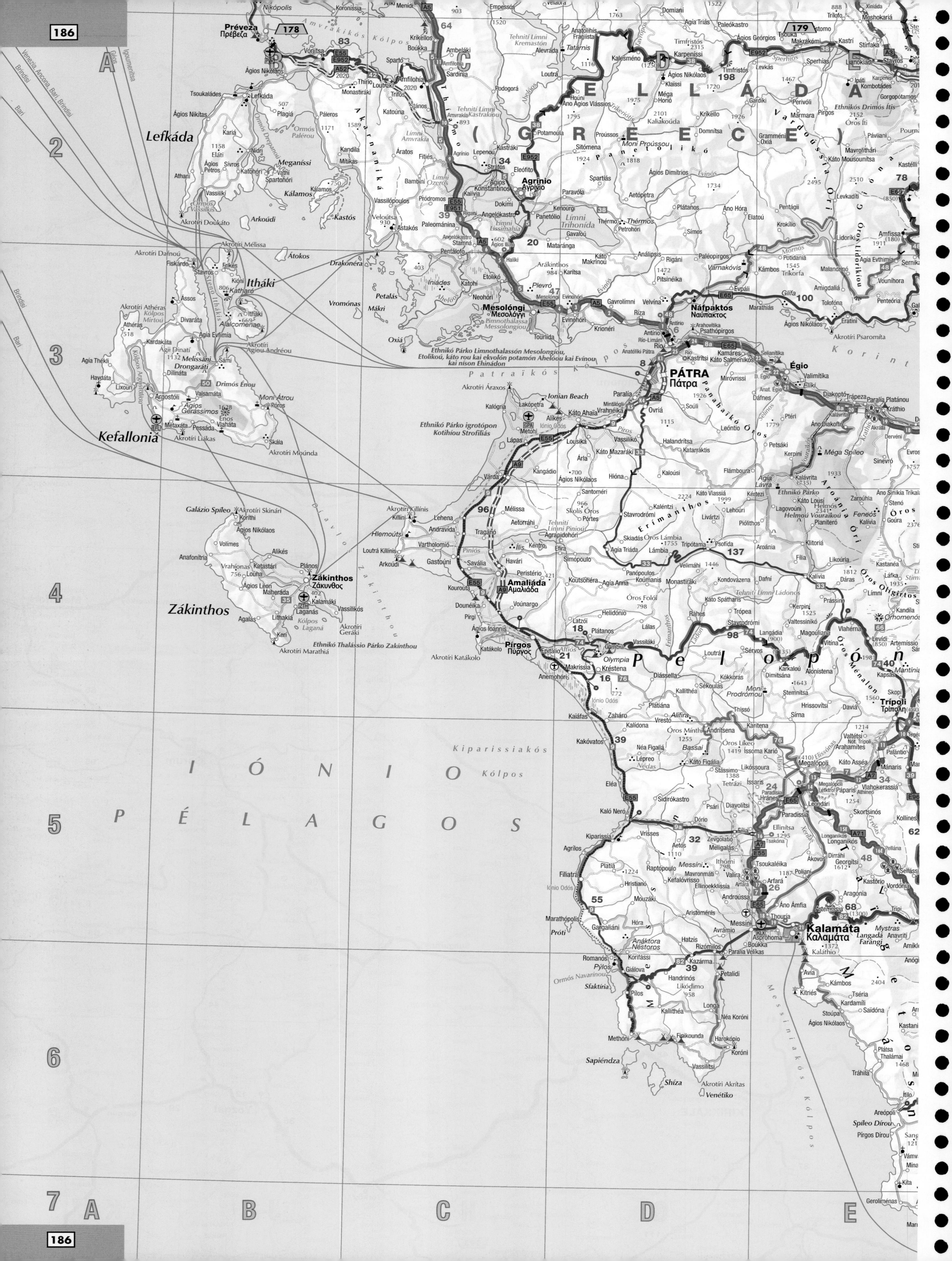
Préveza
Lefkáda
Itháki
Kefalloniá
Zákinthos
Zákinthos
E L L Á D A
(G R E E C E)
Agrínio
Mesolóngi
Náfpaktos
PÁTRA
Pátra
Égio
Amaliáda
Pírgos
Trípoli
Kalamáta
Pílos
Methóni
Koróni
Patraïkós Kólpos
Kiparissiakós Kólpos
Messiniakós Kólpos
I Ó N I O
P É L A G O S
A
B
C
D
E
1
2
3
4
5
6
7

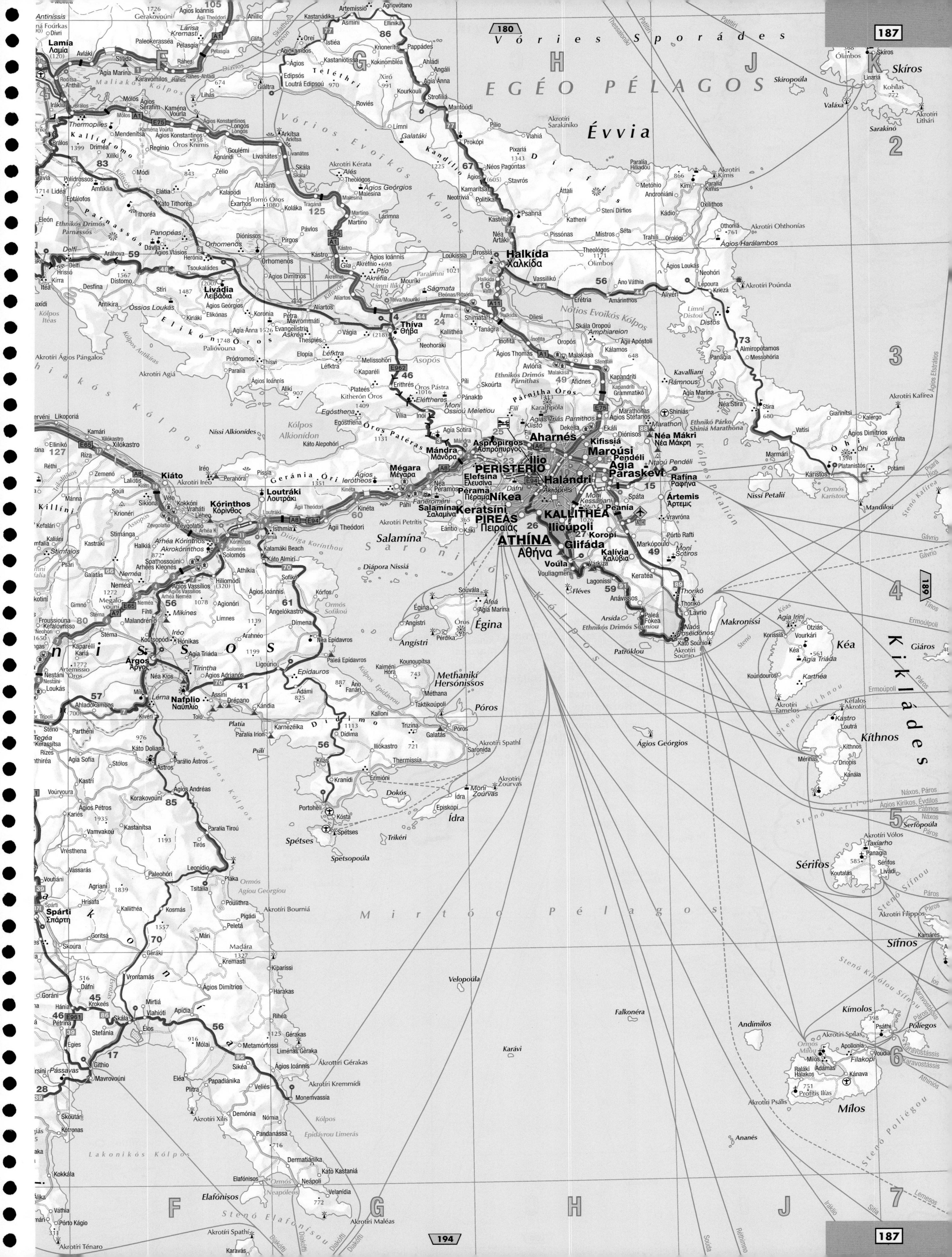
187
180
Vóries Sporádes
EGÉO PÉLAGOS
Évvia
Skíros
Skiropoúla
Lamía
Λαμία
Maliakós Kólpos
Thermopíles
Kallídromo
Parnassós
Delfí
Itéa
Kólpos Itéas
Livadia
Λεβάδεια
Thíva
Θήβα
Halkída
Χαλκίδα
Vórios Evoïkós Kólpos
Nótios Evoïkós Kólpos
Kandíli
Dírfis
Elikónas Óros
Párnitha Óros
Kólpos Alkionídon
Nissí Alkionídes
Kólpos Korinthou
Kiáto
Kórinthos
Κόρινθος
Loutráki
Λουτράκι
Mégara
Μέγαρα
Mándra
Μάνδρα
Elefsína
Ελευσίνα
Aspropirgos
Ασπρόπυργος
Aharnés
PERISTERIO
Ilio
Maroúsi
Halándri
Kifissiá
Agía Paraskeví
Pendéli
Néa Mákri
Νέα Μάκρη
Marathon
Rafína
Ραφήνα
Artemis
Άρτεμις
Peanía
Spáta
Pérama
Πέραμα
Níkea
Keratsíni
PIREAS
Πειραιάς
ATHÍNA
Αθήνα
KALLITHEA
Ilioúpoli
Glifáda
Koropí
Kalívia
Καλύβια
Voúla
Vouliagméni
Salamína
Σαλαμίνα
Saronikós Kólpos
Égina
Angístri
Méthana
Methanikí Hersónissos
Póros
Ídra
Spétses
Spetsopoúla
Dokós
Árgos
Άργος
Nafplio
Ναύπλιο
Argolikós Kólpos
Didimo
Epidauros
Nemea
Mikínes
Tírintha
Lavrio
Sounio
Makronissi
Kéa
Kíthnos
Sérifos
Sífnos
Kímolos
Polígos
Mílos
Andímilos
Falkonéra
Velopoúla
Karávi
Ananés
Mirtóo Pélagos
Kikládes
Giáros
Stira
Káristos
Óhi
Akrotíri Kafíreas
Sparti
Σπάρτη
Lakonikós Kólpos
Monemvassía
Elafónisos
Akrotíri Maléas
Gíthio
Lakonía
194
189
187

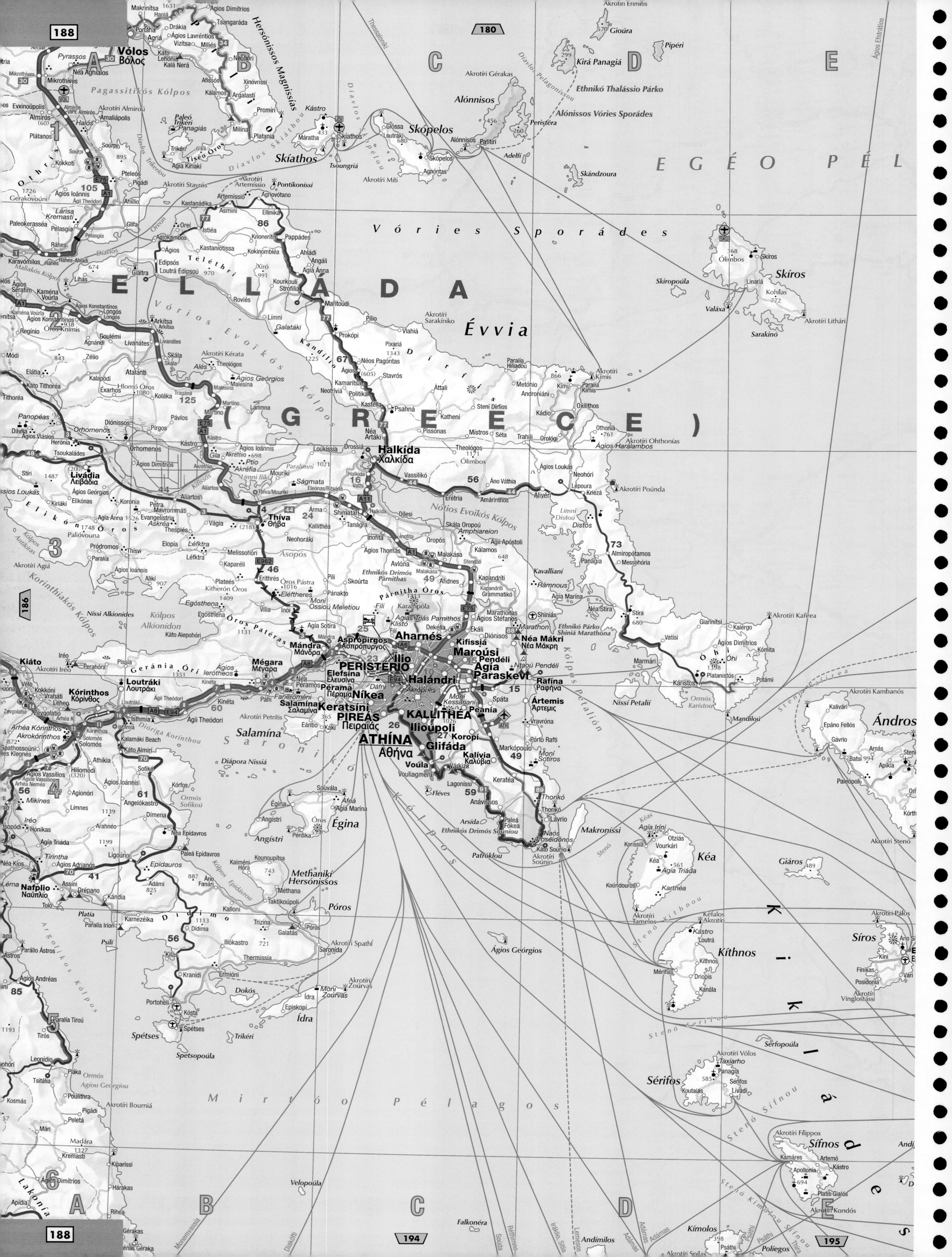

188
180
186
194
195
A
B
C
D
E
1
2
3
4
5
6
ELLÁDA
(GREECE)
Égéo Pélagos
Vóries Sporádes
Évvia
Skíros
Skópelos
Skíathos
Alónnisos
Kirá Panagiá
Gioúra
Pipéri
Skántzoura
Ethnikó Thalássio Párko
Alónissos Vóries Sporádes
Vólos
Βόλος
Pagassitikós Kólpos
Hersónissos Magnissías
Halkída
Χαλκίδα
Lamía
Livádia
Λειβάδια
Thíva
Θήβα
Kórinthos
Κόρινθος
Loutráki
Λουτράκι
Mégara
Μέγαρα
Mándra
Μάνδρα
Aspropírgos
Ασπρόπυργος
Ahamés
Maroúsi
Kifissiá
Ilio
PERISTÉRIO
Elefsína
Ελευσίνα
Pérama
Πέραμα
Níkea
Halándri
Agía Paraskeví
Keratsíni
Salamína
Σαλαμίνα
PIREÁS
Πειραιάς
KALLITHÉA
ATHÍNA
Αθήνα
Ilioúpoli
Glifáda
Voúla
Rafína
Ραφήνα
Artemis
Αρτεμις
Peanía
Kalívia
Καλύβια
Lávrio
Néa Mákri
Νέα Μάκρη
Salamína
Égina
Angístri
Methanikí Hersónissos
Póros
Ídra
Spétses
Spetsopoúla
Dokós
Nafplio
Ναύπλιο
Saronikós Kólpos
Argolikós Kólpos
Mirtóo Pélagos
Korinthiakós Kólpos
Nótios Evoïkós Kólpos
Vórios Evoïkós Kólpos
Kólpos Petalíon
Makronissi
Kéa
Kíthnos
Sérifos
Sífnos
Síros
Ándros
Giáros
Kímolos
Kikládes
Stenó Kíthnou
Stenó Sérifou
Stenó Sífnou
Kárìstos
Marmári
Stíra
Kími
Mantoúdi
Istiéa
Atalánti
Oros Pátéras
Fármos

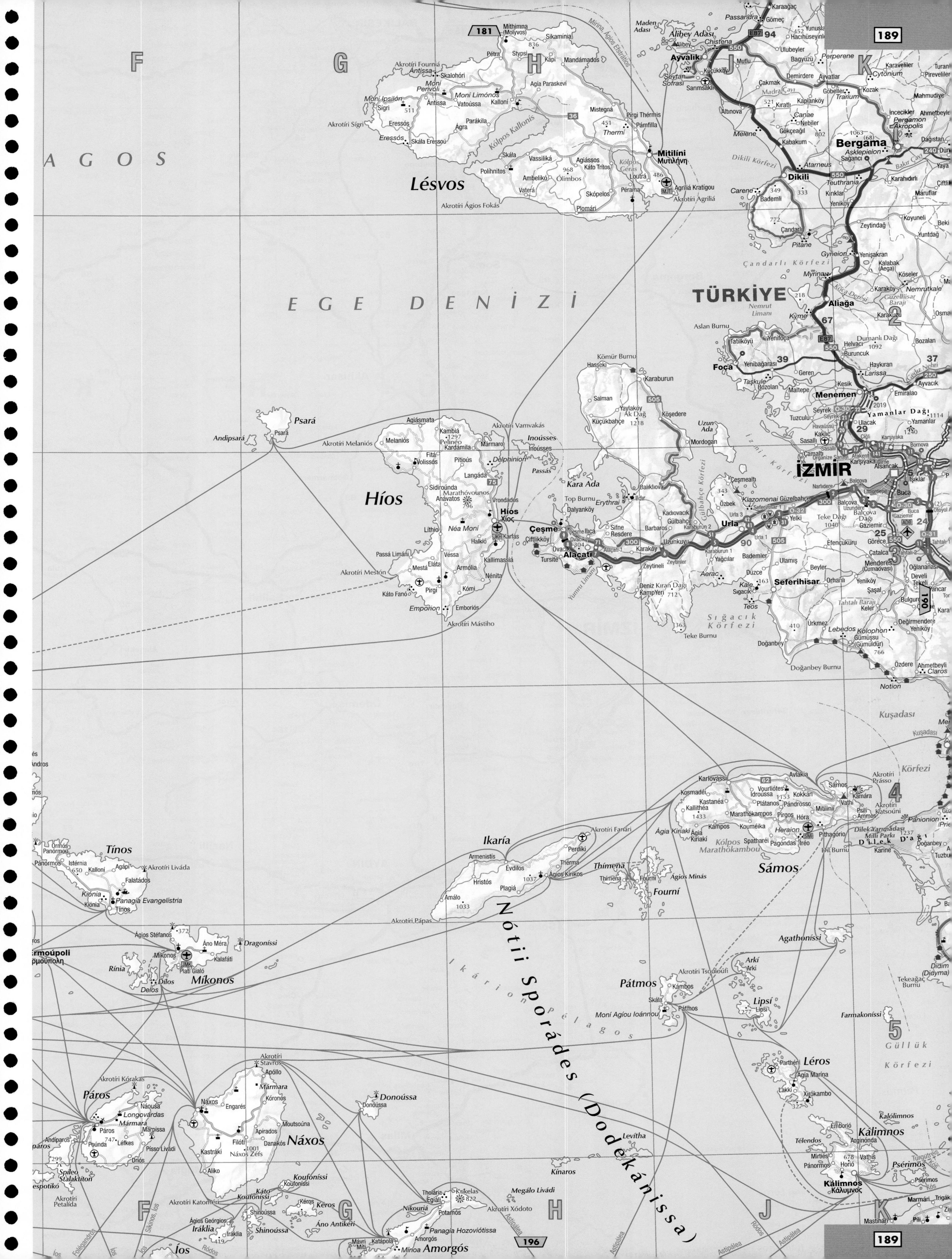
189
F
G
H
J
K
AGOS
Lésvos
Mithimna (Molyvos)
Sikaminia
Pétra
Stypsi
Kápi
Mandamados
Akrotíri Fourniá
Antissa
Skalohóri
Moni Perivoli
Moní Limónos
Agia Paraskeví
Moní Ipsilón
Sigri
Antissa
Vatoússa
Kalloní
Mistegna
Pirgi Thérmis
Pámfilla
Thermi
Akrotíri Sigri
Eressós
Parákila
Ágra
Kólpos Kallonis
Skála Eressoú
Skála
Vassiliká
Agiássos
Káto Trítos
Mitilíni
Μυτιλήνη
Polihnitos
Ambeliko
Ólimbos
Loutrá
Vaterá
Skópelos
Pérama
Agriliá Kratigou
Plomári
Akrotíri Ágios Fokás
Akrotíri Agriliá
Mírina, Ágios Efstrátios
Maden Adası
Alibey Adası
Ayvalık
Küçükköy
Şeytan Sofrası
Sarımsaklı
Bergama
Asklepieion
Pergamon Akropolis
Dikili
Dikili Körfezi
Çandarlı
Pitane
Çandarlı Körfezi
TÜRKİYE
Aliağa
Nemrut Limanı
Aslan Burnu
Foça
Menemen
Yamanlar Dağı
İZMİR
EGE DENİZİ
Psará
Andipsará
Akrotíri Melaniós
Melaniós
Kambiá
Pelineo
Kardámila
Akrotíri Vamvakás
Inoússes
Marmaro
Delphinion
Volissós
Pitioús
Langáda
Passás
Híos
Sidiroúnda
Marathóvounos
Anávatos
Vrondádos
Híos
Χίος
Lithío
Néa Moní
Halkió
Karfas
Passá Limáni
Véssa
Akrotíri Mestón
Mestá
Eláta
Armólia
Kallimassiá
Nénita
Pirgi
Kómi
Káto Faná
Emporion
Emboriós
Akrotíri Mástiho
Kömür Burnu
Hasseki
Karaburun
Salman
Yaylaköy
Ak Dağ
Küçükbahçe
Köşedere
Uzun Ada
Mordogan
İzmir Körfezi
Kara Ada
Top Burnu
Dalyanköy
Erythrai
Ildır
Çeşme
Çiftlikköy
Ovacık
Alaçatı
Tursite
Yumru Limanı
Sifne
Resdere
Barbaros
Gülbahçe Körfezi
Urla
Klazomenai
Güzelbahçe
Balçova
Teke Dağı
Seferihisar
Sığacık Körfezi
Teke Burnu
Teos
Kale
Sığacık
Doğanbey
Doğanbey Burnu
Lebedos
Kolophon
Notion
Claros
Kuşadası
Kuşadası Körfezi
Karlovássi
Samos
Vathí
Sámos
Kólpos Marathókambou
Marathókampos
Pithagório
Heraion
Dilek Yarımadası Milli Parkı
Dilek Dağı
Ikaría
Armenistis
Évdilos
Akrotíri Fanári
Ágios Kírikos
Thérma
Perdíki
Thímena
Fourní
Ágios Minás
Akrotíri Pápas
Nótii Sporádes (Dodekánissa)
Ikário Pélagos
Agathonissi
Arkí
Pátmos
Skála
Kámbos
Akrotíri Tsoúgloúfi
Lipsí
Moní Agíou Ioánnou
Farmakonissi
Léros
Lakki
Ágia Marína
Xirókambo
Kalólimnos
Kálimnos
Télendos
Pothia
Psérimos
Güllük Körfezi
Tinos
Akrotíri Livada
Panagía Evangelístria
Kionia
Ermoúpoli
Ermoúpoli
Rínia
Dilos
Delos
Míkonos
Ágios Stéfanos
Áno Méra
Dragonissi
Kalafáti
Platí Gialó
Páros
Akrotíri Kórakas
Náoussa
Longovárdas
Mármara
Párikia
Lefkes
Pisso Livadi
Drios
Andíparos
Spileo Stalaktíton
Akrotíri Petalida
Náxos
Akrotíri Stavrós
Apóllo
Mármara
Kóronos
Engarés
Apíranthos
Moutsoúna
Filóti
Náxos Zéfs
Danakós
Kastráki
Aliko
Donoússa
Levítha
Kínaros
Koufoníssi
Káto Koufoníssi
Akrotíri Katomeri
Kéros
Shinoússa
Áno Antikéri
Iráklia
Ágios Geórgios
Ios
Amorgós
Katápola
Panagía Hozoviótissa
Nikouriá
Egiáli
Akrotíri Xódoto
Mégalo Livádi
Minoa
196
181
190
189

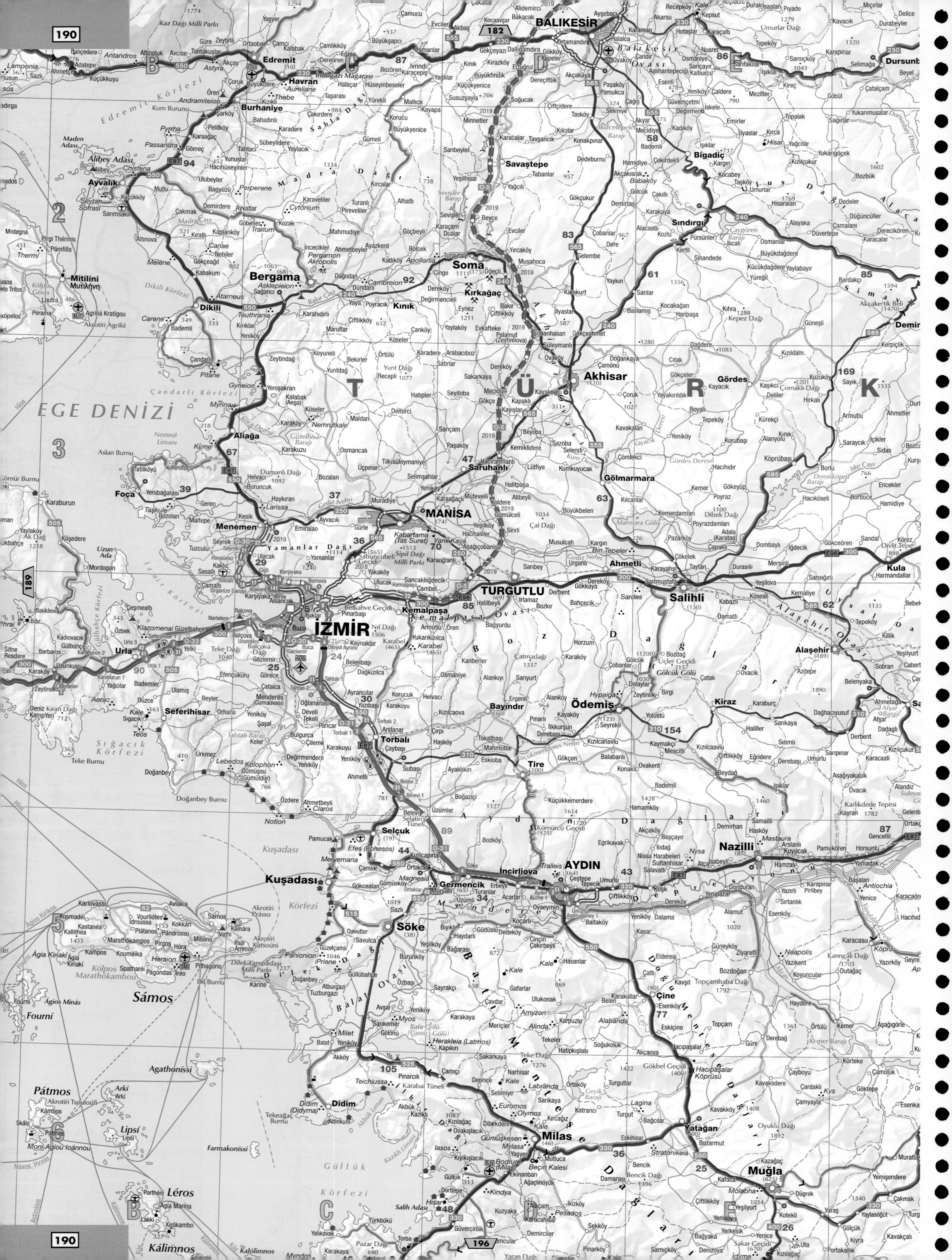

EGE DENİZİ
T Ü R K
BALIKESİR
Edremit
Havran
Burhaniye
Ayvalık
Alibey Adası
Bergama
Dikili
Soma
Kırkağaç
Savaştepe
Sındırgı
Bigadiç
Akhisar
Gördes
Gölmarmara
Aliağa
Foça
Menemen
MANİSA
TURGUTLU
Salihli
Alaşehir
Kula
İZMİR
Kemalpaşa
Urla
Seferihisar
Torbalı
Bayındır
Ödemiş
Kiraz
Tire
Selçuk
Kuşadası
Söke
Germencik
İncirliova
AYDIN
Nazilli
Çine
Milas
Yatağan
Muğla
Didim
Mitilíni
Sámos
Pátmos
Léros
Kálimnos
Fourní
Lipsí
Agathonissi
Kuşadası Körfezi
Güllük Körfezi
Çandarlı Körfezi
İzmir Körfezi
Sığacık Körfezi
Edremit Körfezi
Madra Dağı
Yunt Dağı
Boz Dağları
Aydın Dağları
Menteşe Dağları
Beşparmak Dağı
Dilek Dağı
Ak Dağ
Efes (Ephesos)
Pergamon Akropolis
Milet
Didim (Didyma)
Priene
Bodrum (Milas)
Bafa Gölü
Marmara Gölü
182
189
196

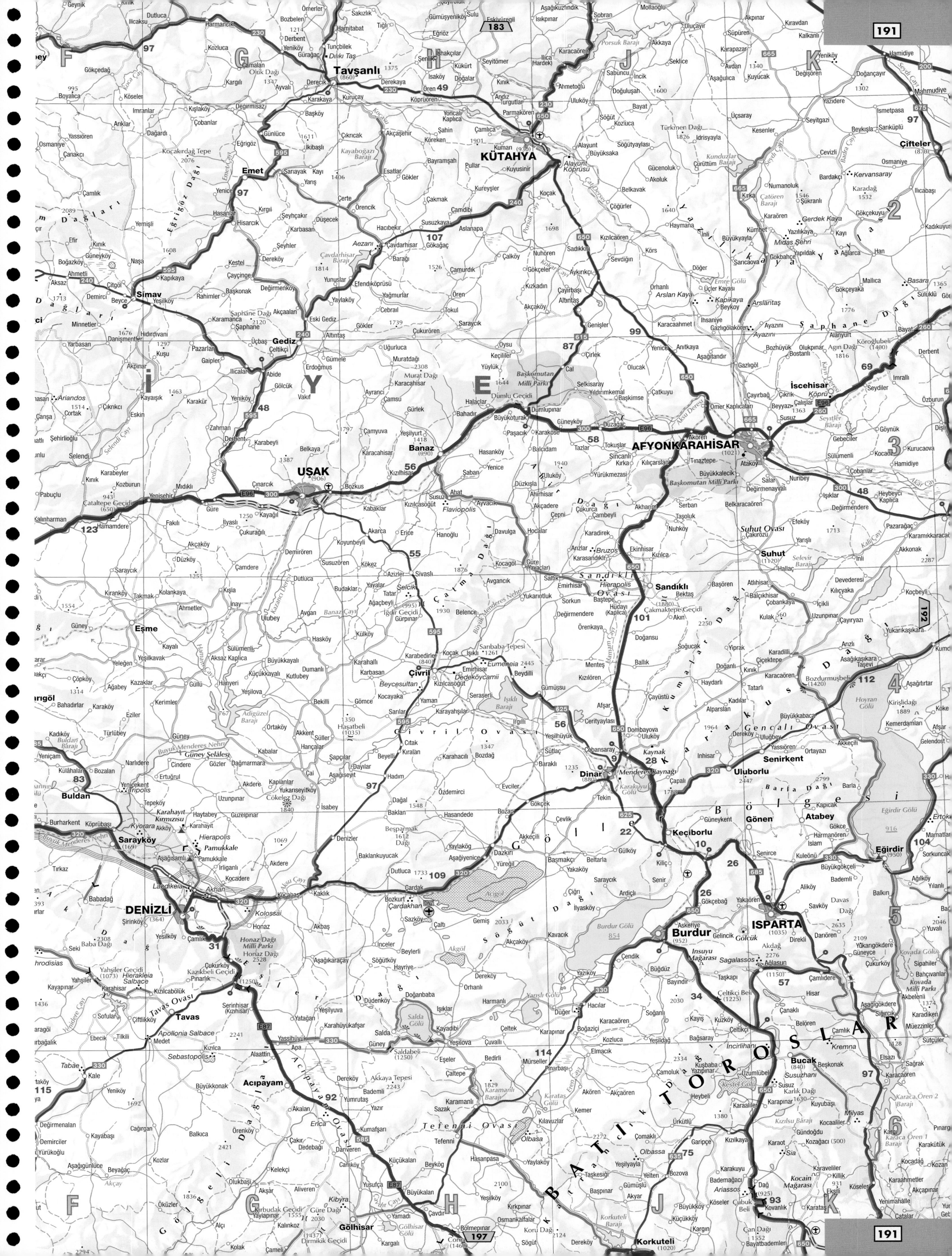
Tavşanlı
KÜTAHYA
Emet
Simav
Gediz
UŞAK
Banaz
AFYONKARAHİSAR
Sandıklı
Suhut
İscehisar
Çifteler
Dinar
Çivril
Eşme
Buldan
Sarayköy
Pamukkale
Hierapolis
DENİZLİ
Honaz
Tavas
Acıpayam
Gölhisar
Burdur
ISPARTA
Eğirdir
Keçiborlu
Gönen
Atabey
Uluborlu
Senirkent
Bucak
Korkuteli
Karataş
Aezani
Başkomutan Milli Parkı
Eğirdir Gölü
Burdur Gölü
Acıgöl
Salda Gölü
Işıklı Barajı
Hoyran Gölü
Honaz Dağı Milli Parkı
Tefenni Ovası
Çivril Ovası
Barla Dağı
Murat Dağı
Şaphane Dağı
Türkmen Dağı
Kemer
Tefenni
Yeşilova
Çardak
Kaynak
Karakuyu Gölü
Menderes Kaynağı
Sagalassos
Ağlasun
Kremna
Çaltı
Kibyra
Dirmil Geçidi
BATI TOROSLAR
İÇ EGE BÖLGESİ
Sandıklı Ovası
Çal
Bozkurt
Hasanpaşa
Yeşilköy
E96
E87
183
197
192

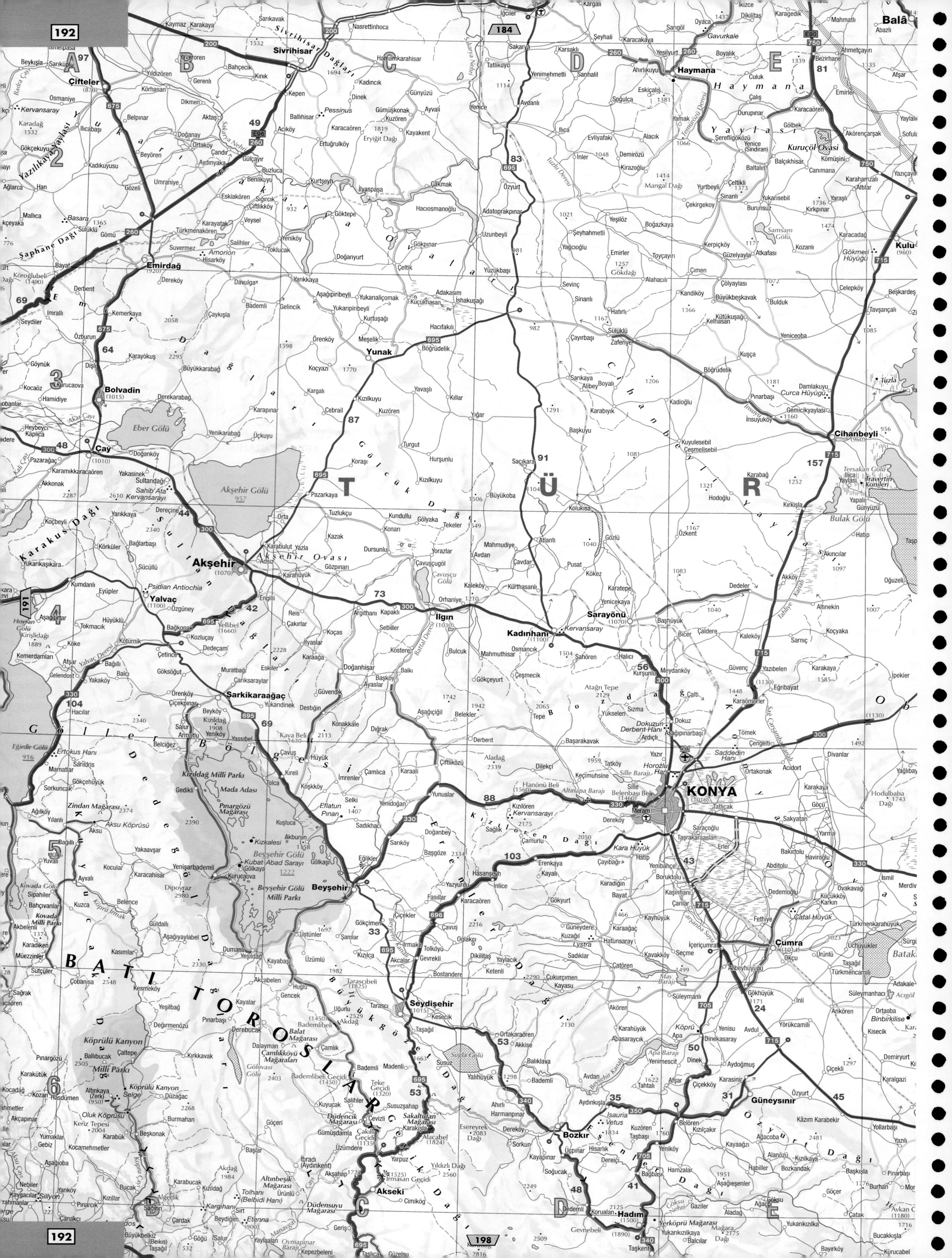

192
184
198
191
Sivrihisar
Sivrihisar Dağları
Haymana
Haymana Yaylası
Bala
Çifteler
Emirdağ
Şaphane Dağı
Yazılıkaya Yaylası
Yukarı Sakarya Ovaları
Emir Dağları
Bolvadin
Eber Gölü
Çay
Akşehir Gölü
Akşehir
Akşehir Ovası
Sultan Dağları
Karakuş Dağı
Yunak
Gölcük Dağı
Cihanbeyli
Cihanbeyli Yaylası
Kulu
Kuruçöl Ovası
Tuzla
Kadınhanı
Sarayönü
Ilgın
Yalvaç
Şarkikaraağaç
Bozdağ
KONYA
Beyşehir
Beyşehir Gölü
Beyşehir Gölü Milli Parkı
Kızıldağ Milli Parkı
Eğirdir Gölü
Gölleri Bölgesi
Dedegöl Dağları
Kızılören Dağı
Erenler Dağı
Seydişehir
Suğla Gölü
Çumra
Çatal Hüyük
Bozkır
Hadım
Akseki
Güneysınır
Köprülü Kanyon
Köprülü Kanyon Milli Parkı
Geyik Dağları
Hodulbaba Dağı
Obruk Yaylası
BATI TOROSLAR
TÜRKIYE
A
B
C
D
E
2
3
4
5
6

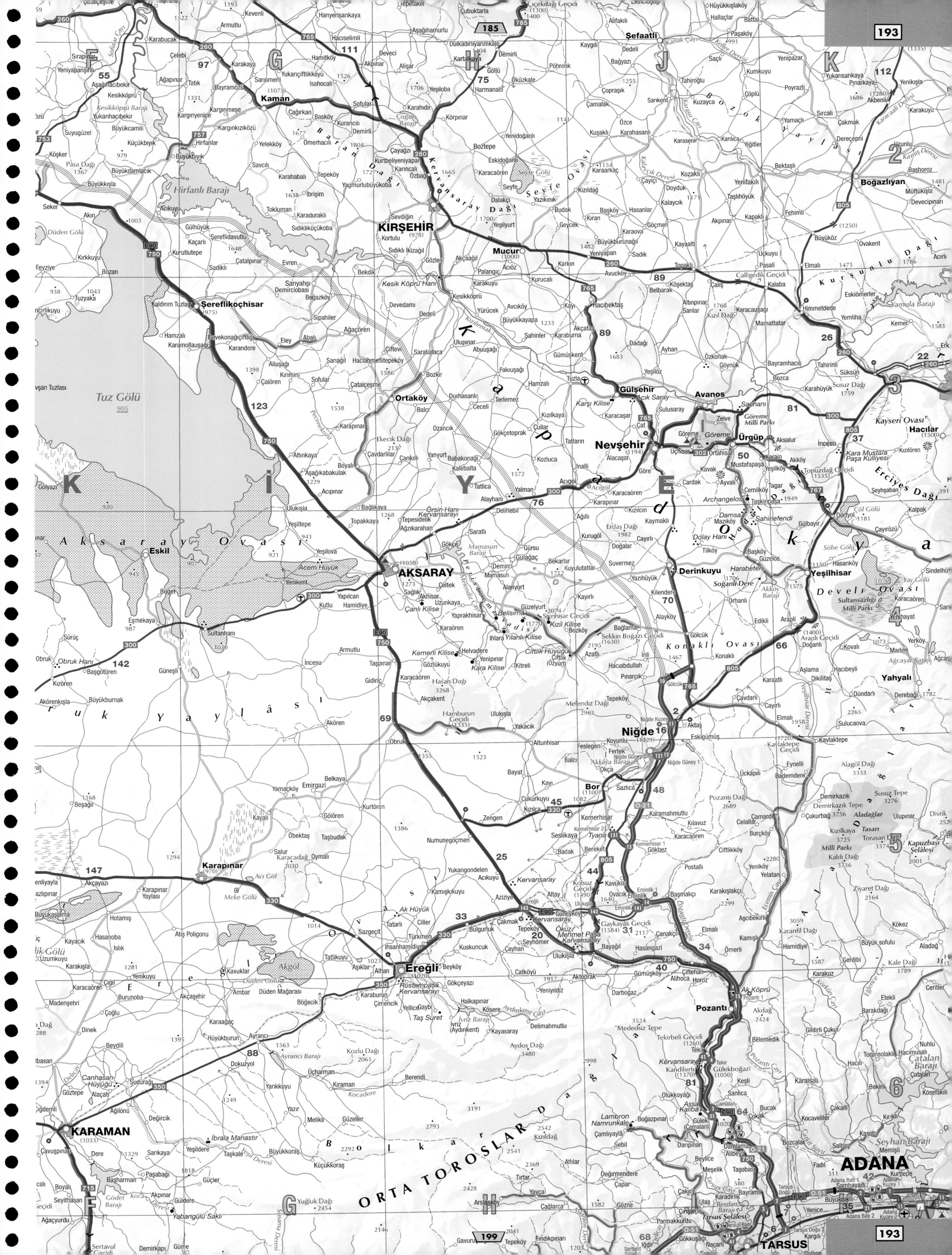
KIRŞEHİR
Kaman
Mucur
Şereflikoçhisar
Tuz Gölü
Hirfanlı Barajı
Seyfe Gölü
Ortaköy
Gülşehir
Avanos
Nevşehir
Ürgüp
Göreme
Göreme Milli Parkı
AKSARAY
Aksaray Ovası
Eskil
Sultanhanı
Derinkuyu
Yeşilhisar
Boğazlıyan
Niğde
Bor
Karapınar
Ereğli
KARAMAN
Pozantı
TARSUS
ADANA
ORTA TOROSLAR
Bolkar Dağları
Aladağlar
Erciyes Dağı
Kapadokya
Bozok Yaylası
Konaklı Ovası
Develi Ovası
Melendiz Dağı
Hasan Dağı
Ihlara Vadisi
Akgöl
Seyhan Barajı
Çatalan Barajı

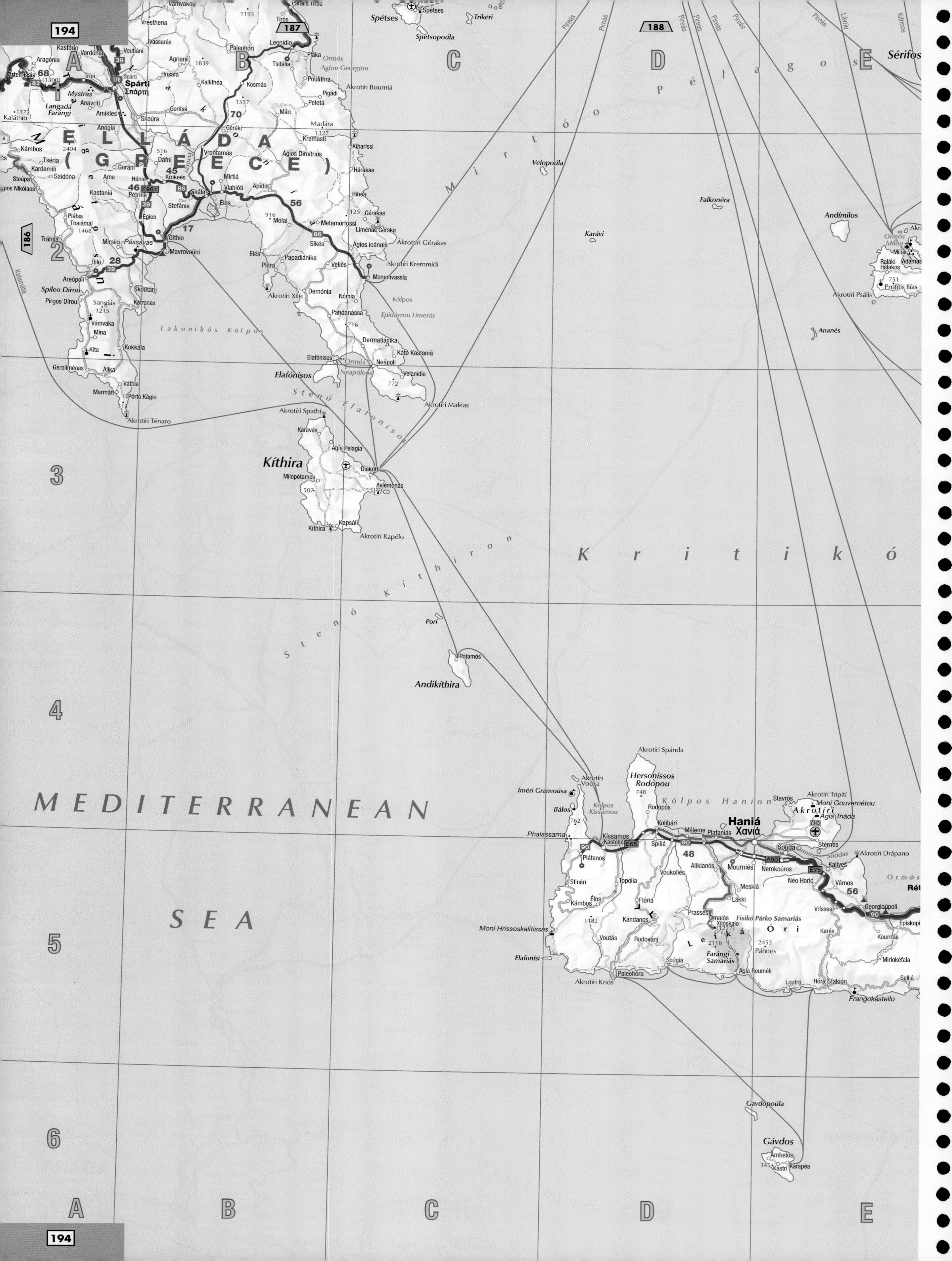
Ellada (Greece)
Spárti
Kíthira
Elafónisos
Andikíthira
Spétses
Sérifos
Andímilos
Velopoúla
Falkonéra
Karávi
Pori
Haniá
Gávdos
Gavdopoúla
Mirtóo Pélagos
Lakonikós Kólpos
Kritikó
Stenó Kíthiron
Stenó Elafonísou
MEDITERRANEAN SEA
Monemvassía
Gíthio
Kólpos Haníon
Kólpos Kíssamou
Lefká Óri
Akrotíri Ténaro
Akrotíri Maléas
Akrotíri Spánda
187
188
186

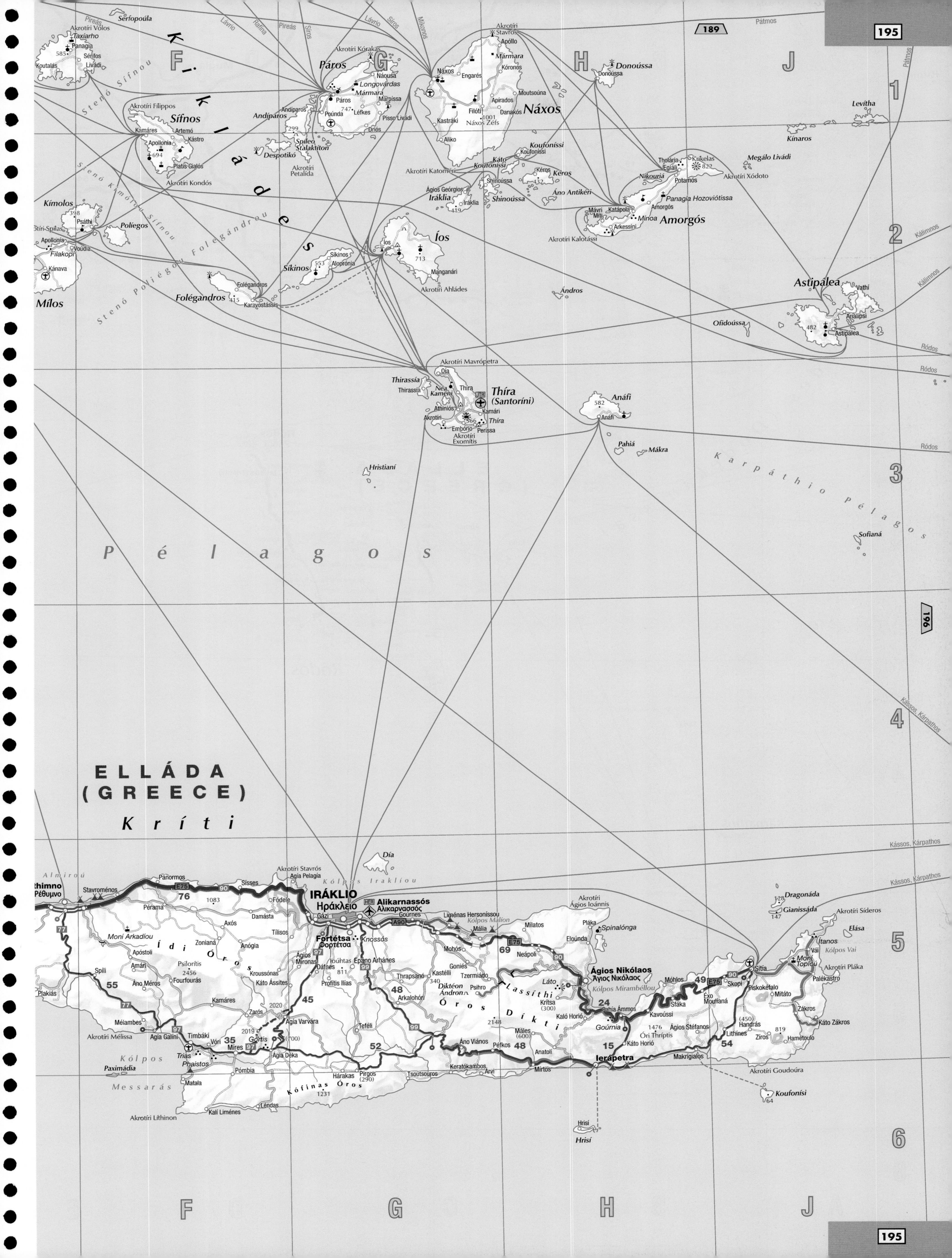

195
189
196
Kikládes
Pélagos
Kárpathio Pélagos
ELLÁDA
(GREECE)
Kríti
Sérifopoúla
Sérifos
Taxiarho
Panagía
Livádi
Koutalas
Akrotíri Vólos
Sténó Sífnou
Sífnos
Akrotíri Filippos
Kamáres
Artemó
Kástro
Apollonía
Platís Gialós
Akrotíri Kondós
Despotikó
Andíparos
Spíleo Stalaktíton
Akrotíri Petalída
Páros
Akrotíri Kórakas
Náousa
Longovárdas
Mármara
Márpissa
Poúnda
Léfkes
Písso Livádi
Dríos
Náxos
Akrotíri Stavrós
Apóllo
Kóronos
Engarés
Moutsoúna
Apíranthos
Filóti
Danakós
Kastráki
Náxos Zéfs
Alikó
Donoússa
Koufoníssi
Káto Koufoníssi
Kéros
Áno Antikéri
Shinoússa
Iráklia
Ágios Geórgios
Akrotíri Katoméri
Amorgós
Tholária
Egiáli
Krikelas
Nikouriá
Potamós
Panagía Hozoviótissa
Katápola
Amorgós
Mínoa
Arkessíni
Mávri Míti
Akrotíri Kalotássi
Akrotíri Xódoto
Megálo Livádi
Levítha
Kínaros
Pátmos
Kálimnos
Ródos
Kímolos
Psáthi
Políegos
Sténó Kímolou Sífnou
Sténó Polyégou Folegándrou
Apollonía
Filakopí
Kánava
Mílos
Folégandros
Karavostássis
Síkinos
Alopronía
Íos
Manganári
Akrotíri Ahládes
Ándros
Ofidoússa
Astipálea
Vathí
Análipsi
Thirassía
Akrotíri Mavrópetra
Oía
Néa Kaméni
Thíra
Thíra (Santoríni)
Athiniós
Akrotíri
Kamári
Emborio
Périssa
Akrotíri Exomítis
Anáfi
Pahiá
Mákra
Hristianí
Sofianá
Kássos, Kárpathos
Día
Almiroú
Réthimno
Ρέθυμνο
Stavroménos
Pánormos
Sísses
Akrotíri Stavrós
Agía Pelagía
Kólpos Irakliou
IRÁKLIO
Ηράκλειο
Alikarnassós
Αλικαρνασσός
Gázi
Gournes
Liménas Hersonissou
Kólpos Malíon
Mália
Akrotíri Ágios Ioánnis
Pláka
Spinalónga
Milatos
Elounda
Neápoli
Ágios Nikólaos
Άγιος Νικόλαος
Kólpos Mirambéllou
Pérama
Moní Arkadíou
Ídi Óros
Axós
Zoniana
Anógia
Damásta
Tílisos
Fódele
Fortétsa
Φορτέτσα
Knossós
Psilorítis
Fourfourás
Spíli
Apóstoli
Amári
Áno Méros
Plakiás
Kroussónas
Káto Ássites
Ágios Mironas
Dáfnes
Profítis Ilías
Epano Arhánes
Thrapsanó
Kastélli
Goniés
Mohós
Tzermiádo
Diktéon Andron
Psihro
Lassíthi
Láto
Kritsa
Óros Díkti
Arkalohóri
Kamáres
Zarós
Agía Varvára
Méiambes
Akrotíri Mélissa
Agía Galíni
Timbáki
Vóri
Míres
Górtis
Agía Déka
Tefeli
Trías
Phaistos
Kólpos Messarás
Paximádia
Mátala
Pómbia
Hárakas
Pírgos
Kófinas Óros
Léndas
Kalí Liménes
Akrotíri Líthinon
Áno Viános
Pefkos
Máles
Anatolí
Kaló Horió
Pahiá Ámmos
Goúrnia
Káto Horió
Ierápetra
Mírtos
Árvi
Keratókambos
Tsoútsouros
Móhlos
Sfáka
Exo Moulianá
Kavoússi
Óri Thriptís
Ágios Stéfanos
Sitía
Skopí
Piskokéfalo
Mitáto
Lithínes
Handrás
Ziros
Makrigialós
Akrotíri Goudoúra
Koufonísi
Hrisí
Dragonáda
Gianissáda
Akrotíri Síderos
Elása
Ítanos
Vái
Kólpos Vái
Moní Toplou
Akrotíri Pláka
Palékastro
Zákros
Káto Zákros
Hametoulo

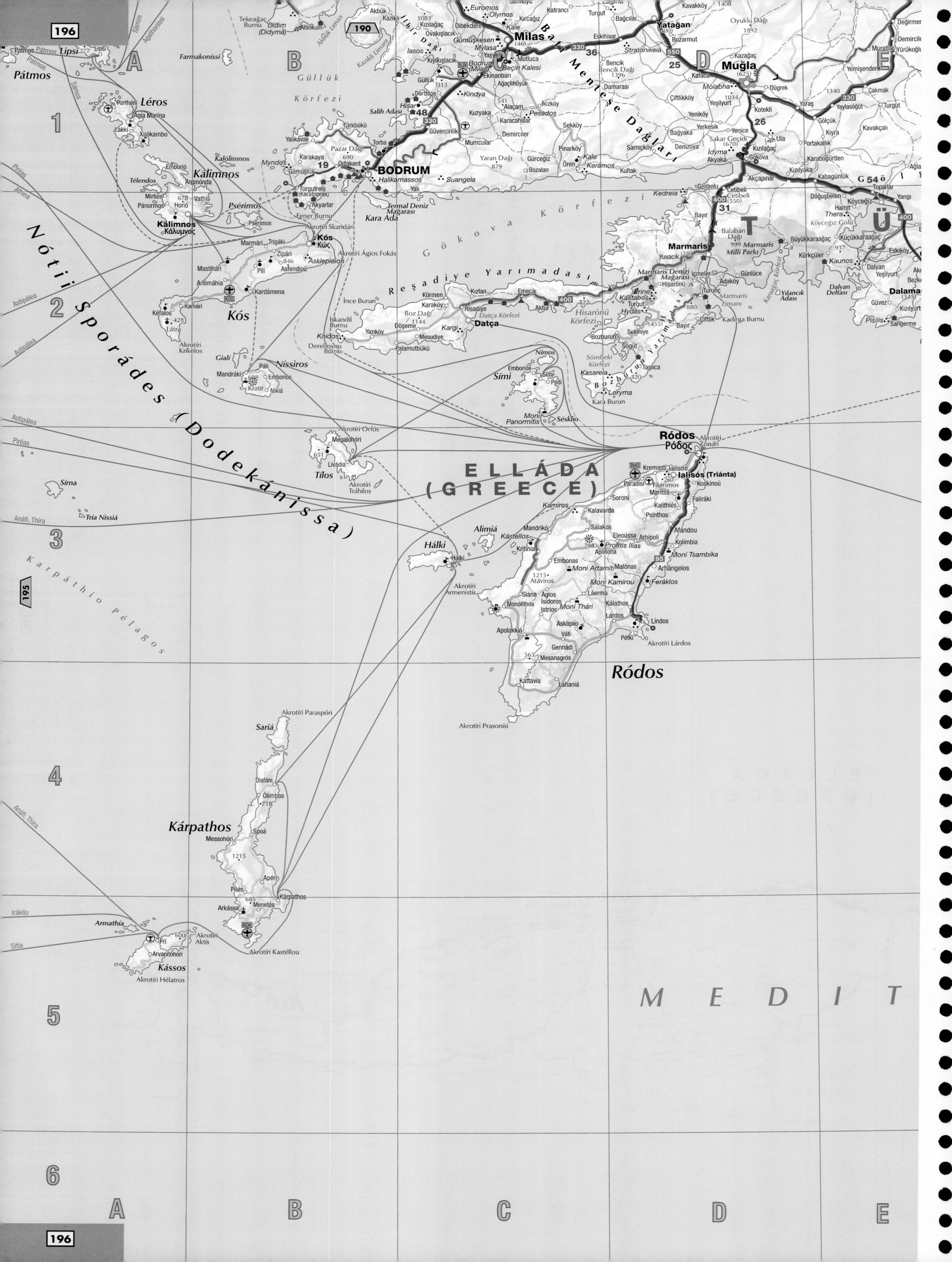
Pátmos
Lipsi
Léros
Kálimnos
Kálimnos
Κάλυμνος
Pserimos
Kós
Κώς
Kós
Nótii Sporádes (Dodekánissa)
Nissiros
Tilos
Sími
Sírna
Tría Nissiá
Kárpathio Pélagos
Alimiá
Hálki
Sariá
Kárpathos
Kássos
Armathia
Akrotíri Kastéllou
Akrotíri Hélatros
Akrotíri Paraspóri
Akrotíri Prasonísi
ELLÁDA (GREECE)
Ródos
Ρόδος
Ródos
Ialisós (Triánta)
Lindos
Kámiros
Moní Tsambika
Profitis Ilias
Moní Kamírou
Moní Thári
Moní Artamíti
Milas
Muğla
Yatağan
BODRUM
Halikarnassos
Güllük Körfezi
Gökova Körfezi
Reşadiye Yarımadası
Datça
Knidos
Marmaris
Marmaris Milli Parkı
Bozburun Yarımadası
Hisarönü Körfezi
Batı Menteşe Dağları
Kaunos
Dalyan
Dalaman
Köyceğiz
Stratonikeia
Didim (Didyma)
Kara Ada
Termal Deniz Mağarası
190
195
MEDIT
A
B
C
D
E
1
2
3
4
5
6

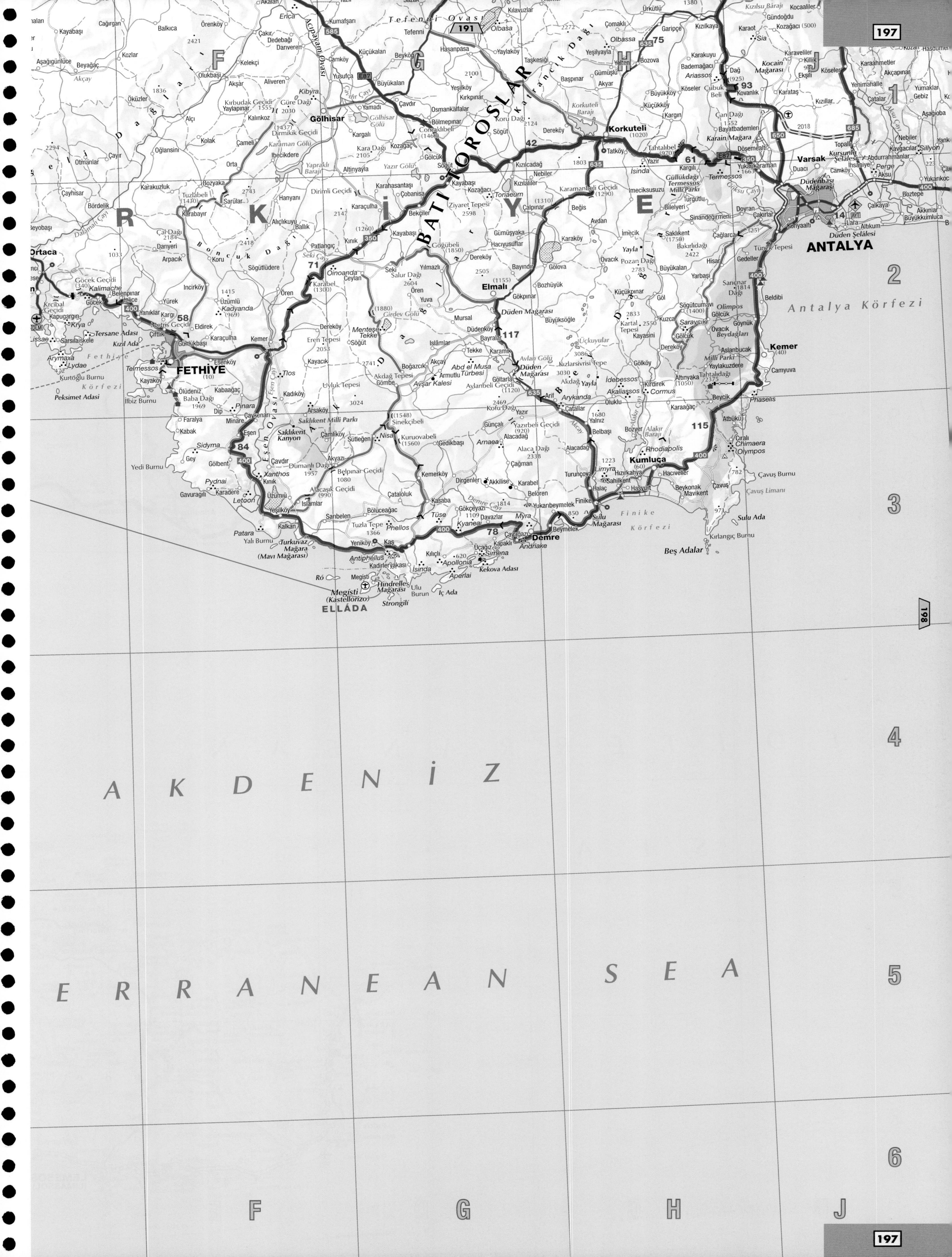

A K D E N İ Z
E R R A N E A N S E A
ANTALYA
FETHİYE
Elmalı
Korkuteli
Kumluca
Demre
Kemer
Varsak
Gölhisar
Finike
Kaş
BATI TOROSLAR
Antalya Körfezi
Finike Körfezi
Fethiye Körfezi
Tefenni Ovası
Düden Mağarası
Saklıkent Milli Parkı
Saklıkent Kanyon
Xanthos
Letoon
Patara
Myra
Olympos
Phaselis
Termessos
Gülükdağı Termessos Milli Parkı
Beş Adalar
Megísti (Kastellórizo)
ELLÁDA
Strongilí
Kekova Adası
Yedi Burnu
Çavuş Burnu
Kırlangıç Burnu
Sulu Ada
F
G
H
J
1
2
3
4
5
6
198

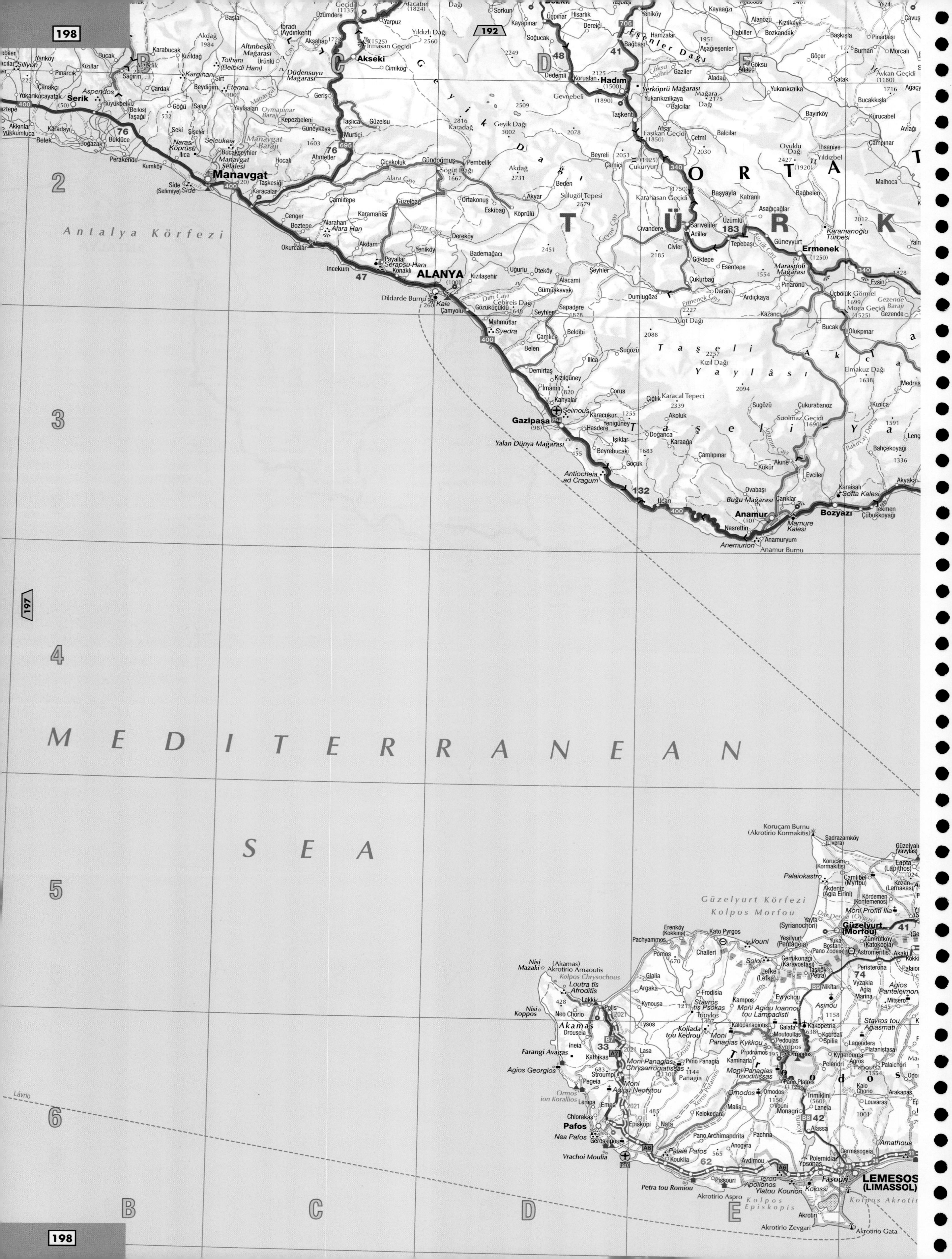
192
197
Manavgat
Side
Serik
Aspendos
Akseki
Hadım
Taşkent
Ermenek
ALANYA
Gazipaşa
Anamur
Bozyazı
Antalya Körfezi
T Ü R K
O R T A T
Geyik Dağları
Taşeli Yaylâsı
M E D I T E R R A N E A N
S E A
Güzelyurt Körfezi
Kolpos Morfou
Güzelyurt (Morfou)
Akamas
Troodos
Pafos
Nea Pafos
LEMESOS (LIMASSOL)
Kolpos Episkopis
Akrotirio Gata
Koruçam Burnu (Akrotirio Kormakitis)
Lávrio
B
C
D
E
2
3
4
5
6

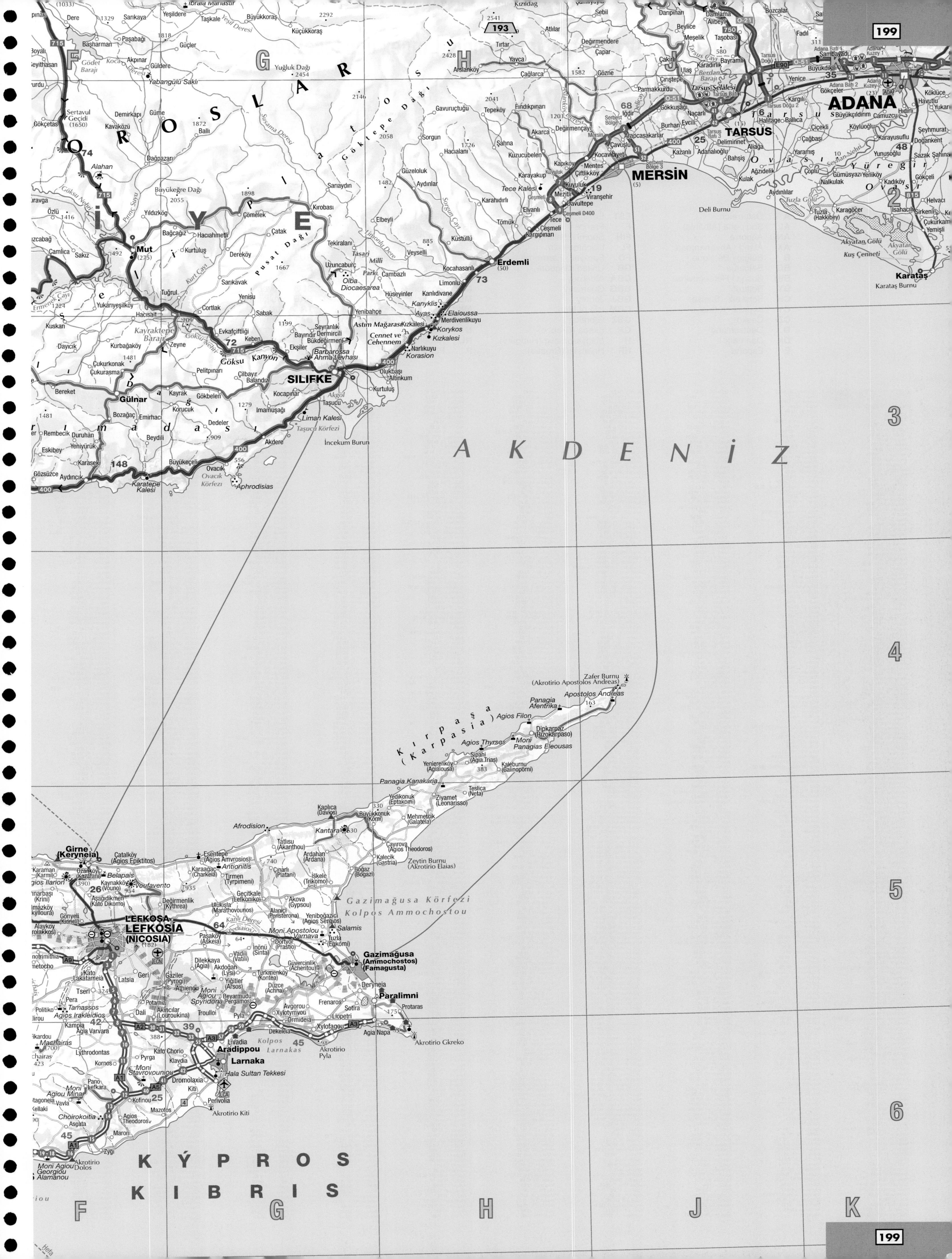

F
G
H
J
K
2
3
4
5
6
199
ADANA
TARSUS
MERSİN
SILIFKE
Erdemli
Mut
Gülnar
Tarsus Şelâlesi
Karataş
Karataş Burnu
Deli Burnu
Akyatan Gölü
Kuş Çenneti
Tuzla Gölü
Yüreğir Ovası
Tarsus Ovası
Göksu Kanyon
Göksu Nehri
Kayraktepe Barajı
Elaioussa
Korykos
Kızkalesi
Narlıkuyu
Korasion
Cennet ve Cehennem
Astım Mağarası
Olba Diocaesarea
Uzuncaburç
Tece Kalesi
Liman Kalesi
Taşucu
Taşucu Körfezi
İncekum Burun
Ovacık Körfezi
Aphrodisias
Karatepe Kalesi
Alahan
Sertavul Geçidi (1650)
Büyükeğre Dağı 2055
Yuğluk Dağı 2454
Göktepe Dağı
Barbarossa Ahmâ Levhası
A K D E N İ Z
Zafer Burnu (Akrotirio Apostolos Andreas)
Apostolos Andreas
Panagia Afentrika
Agios Filon
Dipkarpaz (Rizokarpaso)
Agios Thyrsos
Moni Panagias Eleousas
Kırpaşa (Karpasia)
Yenierenköy (Agialousa)
Sipahi (Agia Trias)
Kaleburnu (Galinoporni)
Panagia Kanakaria
Yedikonuk (Eptakomi)
Ziyamet (Leonarisso)
Teslica (Neta)
Kaplıca (Davlos)
Büyükkonuk (Komi)
Mehmetçik (Galateia)
Afrodision
Kantara
Tatlısu (Akanthou)
Çayırova (Agios Theodoros)
Kalecik (Gastria)
Zeytin Burnu (Akrotirio Elaias)
Girne (Keryneia)
Çatalköy (Agios Epiktitos)
Esentepe (Agios Amvrosios)
Antiphonitis
Belapais
Voufavento
Değirmenlik (Kythrea)
LEFKOŞA LEFKOSIA (NICOSIA)
Gazimağusa Körfezi
Kolpos Ammochostou
Salamis
Moni Apostolou Varnava
Gazimağusa (Ammochostos) (Famagusta)
Deryneia
Paralimni
Protaras
Agia Napa
Akrotirio Gkreko
Kolpos Larnakas
Larnaka
Aradippou
Hala Sultan Tekkesi
Akrotirio Kiti
Akrotirio Pyla
Moni Stavrovouniou
Moni Agiou Minas
Choirokoitia
Moni Spyridona
Agios Irakleidios
Tamassos
Machairas
Moni Agiou Georgiou Alamanou
Akrotirio Dolos
KÝPROS
KIBRIS

Index of place names | Ortsnamenverzeichnis | Index des localités | Navnefortegnelse

①	②	③	④
Aachen	(D)	69	L5

① GB Place name / D Ortsname / F Localité / DK Stednavn
② GB Nation / D Nation / F Nation / DK Folkeslag
③ GB Page number / D Seite / F Numéro de page / DK Sidetal
④ GB Grid reference / D Suchfeld / F Coordonnées / DK Kvadratangivelse

A Österreich	**EST** Eesti	**I** Italia	**PL** Polska
AL Shqipëria (Albania)	**F** France	**IRL** Éire · Ireland	**RKS** Kosovë · Kosovo
AND Andorra	**FIN** Suomi · Finland	**IS** Ísland	**RO** România
AX Åland · Ahvenanmaa	**FL** Liechtenstein	**L** Lëtzebuerg · Luxembourg	**RSM** San Marino
B België · Belgique	**FO** Føroyar · Færøerne	**LT** Lietuva (Lithuania)	**RUS** Rossija
BG Bålgarija	**GB** United Kingdom	**LV** Latvija	**S** Sverige
BIH Bosna i Hercegovina	**GBA** Alderney	**M** Malta	**SK** Slovensko
BY Belarus'	**GBG** Guernsey	**MC** Monaco	**SLO** Slovenija
CH Schweiz · Suisse	**GBJ** Jersey	**MD** Moldova	**SRB** Srbija
CY Kýpros · Kıbrıs	**GBM** Isle of Man	**MK** Makedonija (F.Y.R.O.M.)	**TR** Türkiye
CZ Česko	**GBZ** Gibraltar	**MNE** Crna Gora (Montenegro)	**UA** Ukrajina
D Deutschland	**GR** Elláda (Greece)	**N** Norge	**V** Civitas Vaticana · Città del Vaticano
DK Danmark	**H** Magyarország (Hungary)	**NL** Nederland	
E España	**HR** Hrvatska (Croatia)	**P** Portugal	

A
B
C
D
E
F
G
H
I
J
K
L
M
N
O
P
Q
R
S
T
U
V
W
X
Y
Z

A Sagrada (E) 110 C3
Aşağulıca (TR) 191 J1
Åsaka, Barne- (S) 43 N2
Åsaliseter (N) 24 E8
Asamati (MK) 178 E3
Åsan (N) 24 G5
Åsäng (S) 33 N2
Åsäng (S) 33 P2
Ásar (IS) 17 H7
Åsår (N) 31 L4
Asarcık (TR) 185 J4
Asare (LV) 138 C1
Asarėvičy (BY) 145 M5
Åsarna (S) 32 G2
Asarum (S) 44 F6
Asasp-Arros (F) 114 B1
Asău (RO) 162 C6
Asavec (BY) 145 H3
Asavec (BY) 145 J4
Asavy (BY) 139 L6
Asbach (D) 70 D5
Asbach (D) 90 D3
Asbach-Bäumenheim (D) 80 D3
Åsbacka (S) 33 L5
Åsberget (S) 32 F5
Åsbø (N) 30 C6
Asbo (S) 40 H6
Åsbräcka (S) 43 K2
Åsbro (S) 40 H5
Åsby (S) 43 K4
Asby (S) 44 G3
Ascain (F) 92 A4
Ascea (I) 106 D2
Ascha (D) 81 H3
Aschach an der Donau (A) 81 L4
Aschaffenburg (D) 71 H7
Aschau (A) 81 G6
Aschau im Chiemgau (D) 81 G5
Aschbach Markt (A) 81 M4
Ascheberg (D) 70 E3
Ascheberg (Holstein) (D) 65 N3
Ascheffel (D) 65 M3
Aschendorf (Ems) (D) 64 G5
Aschersleben (D) 72 E2
Aşchileu Mare (RO) 161 G4
Ascholding (D) 88 F2
Asciano (I) 100 F6
Aşcıbekirli (TR) 193 J5
Ascó (E) 121 K1
Asco (F) 96 E4
Ascoli Piceno (I) 103 H2
Ascoli Satriano (I) 104 E3
Ascona (CH) 87 G5
As Corredoiras (E) 110 C2
Ascot (GB) 58 F5
As Cruces (E) 110 C2
Ascu = Asco (F) 96 E4
Åse (N) 20 E2
Åse (N) 38 B2
Åse (N) 39 J3
Åse (S) 33 N2
Åsebyn (S) 40 B4
Åseda (S) 44 G4
Åsele (S) 25 M6
Åselet (S) 22 C6
Åseli (N) 20 D6
Asemanseutu (FIN) 28 D6
Asemanseutu (FIN) 37 M2
Åsen (N) 24 F7
Åsen (N) 30 E3
Åsen (N) 38 D5
Åsen (S) 25 J8
Åsen (S) 32 F5
Åsen (S) 32 F6
Åsen (S) 32 G4
Åsen (S) 33 K2
Asendorf (D) 65 L6
Åsenhöga (S) 43 N4
Asenovgrad (BG) 176 C4
Asenovo (BG) 176 C1
Asenovo (BG) 176 F2
Åsensbruk (S) 40 B5
Asentopalo (FIN) 23 J1
Åsenvoll (N) 31 P2
Åseral (N) 38 F5
Aseri (EST) 36 G6
Åserud (N) 39 P3
Åsettajet (N) 31 P6
Aševo (RUS) 135 J3
Asfáka (GR) 178 D5
Åsfallet (S) 40 H2
Asfeld (F) 77 K3
Asfendioú (GR) 196 B2
Asfordby (GB) 55 L5
Ásgarðsfjall (IS) 16 G5
Åsgårdstrand (N) 39 M4
Asgata (CY) 199 F6
Åsgreina (N) 39 N2
Ash (GB) 59 K5
Åshagen (S) 40 D2
Åshammar (S) 41 L1
Ashbocking (GB) 59 K3
Ashbourne (GB) 58 D1
Ashbourne (IRL) 63 K1
Ashburton (GB) 57 G4
Ashbury (GB) 58 D4
Ashby-de-la-Zouch (GB) 55 K5
Ásheiði (IS) 17 K2
Ashford (GB) 59 J5
Ashford (IRL) 63 K2
Ashford in the Water (GB) 55 J4
Ashill (GB) 58 B6
Ashill (GB) 59 J2
Ashington (GB) 53 M4
Ashkirk (GB) 53 K4
Ashley (GB) 59 H3
Ashton-in-Makerfield (GB) 54 G4
Ashton-under-Lyne (GB) 55 H4
Ashurst (GB) 59 H5
Ashwell (GB) 59 G3
Asiago (I) 88 F6
Asige (S) 43 L5
Asikkala (FIN) 29 J7
Asikkala (FIN) 36 E2
Asikkalan kirkonkylä (FIN) 36 D2
Aşıklar (TR) 193 G5
Asila (FIN) 29 H8
Aşılıarmut (TR) 185 J5
A Silva (E) 110 B2
Asín (E) 114 A3
Asinavka (BY) 139 M4
Asintorf (BY) 139 N4
Asipova (BY) 139 M4
Asipoviči (BY) 9 L3
Asipovičy (BY) 145 J2
Aşırlar (TR) 183 K4
Ask (N) 39 O2
Ask (S) 44 G1
Ask (S) 47 M2
Aska (FIN) 23 J2
Aska (S) 41 M4
Åskagsberg (S) 40 C2
Askainen (FIN) 35 J3
Åskåsen (S) 32 H5
Askeaton (IRL) 62 E3
Askeby (S) 41 J6
Asker (N) 39 M3
Askeriye (TR) 191 J5
Askern (GB) 55 K3
Askersby (S) 40 H4
Askersund (S) 40 G5
Askeryd (S) 44 G3
Askesta (S) 33 N5
Åskilje (S) 26 D5
Åskiljeby (S) 26 D5
Askim (N) 39 O3
Askim (S) 43 J3
Askje (N) 38 C4
Askjum (S) 44 B2
Askland (N) 38 H5
Asklanda (S) 44 B3
Asklipiío (GR) 196 C3
Askø By (DK) 47 H4
Åskogen (S) 22 D5
Askome (S) 43 L4
Asköping (S) 41 K4
Askós (GR) 180 C3
Askøy (N) 30 C7
Askum (S) 43 H2
Askvåg (N) 30 G2
Askvoll (N) 30 C5
Aslakkala (FIN) 19 H5
Aslaksrud (N) 39 L3
Aşlama (TR) 193 K4
Aslanapa (TR) 191 H2
Aslanbucak (TR) 197 H2
Aslestad (N) 38 G4
Aslıhantepeciği (TR) 190 E1
Åsljunga (S) 44 C6
Asma (San Félix) = Asma (San Fix) (E) 110 D3
Asma (San Fix) (E) 110 D3
Asmalı (TR) 182 D5
Asmalı (TR) 182 E4
Åsmandrud (N) 39 L2
Asman-Kasaeva (BY) 139 L6
Åsmansbo (S) 40 H2
Asmíni (GR) 187 G1
Aśmjanka, Muravana- (BY) 137 O5
Åsmon (S) 26 C8
Ásmundarstaðir (IS) 17 L1
Åsmundtorp (S) 47 L2
Åsmundvåg (N) 24 C7
Asmunti (FIN) 23 J5
Asnæs (DK) 47 J2
Åsnes (N) 24 F6
Åsnes (N) 30 C5
As Neves (E) 110 C2
Åsnorrbodarna (S) 33 N3
Asola (I) 99 J2
Ásólfsstaðir (IS) 16 G6
Asolo (I) 88 F6
Ásólsskáli (IS) 16 G7
Asón (E) 112 D2
Asp (DK) 42 C6
Aspa (N) 30 H1
Aspa (S) 41 M5
Aspach (A) 81 J4
Aspach (D) 79 L4
Aspai (E) 110 D2
Aspan (S) 32 H3
Aspang Markt (A) 91 K4
Aspariegos (E) 111 H5
Asparn an der Zaya (A) 91 K2
Asparuhovo (BG) 177 H3
Aspås (S) 25 J8
Aspåsnäset (S) 25 J8
Aspatria (GB) 53 J5
Aspberget (S) 32 C5
Aspe (E) 127 J3
Aspeå (S) 26 D8
Aspeboda (S) 40 H1
Aspenes (N) 20 F3
Aspered (S) 43 M3
Asperen (NL) 69 J3
Asperg (D) 79 L4
Asperö (S) 43 J3
Aspet (F) 114 E1
Aspet (S) 47 O2
Åsphult (S) 44 D7
Aspliden (S) 26 F4
Aspliden (S) 27 H2
Aspnäs (S) 25 K6
Aspnäs (S) 33 O2
Aspnäs (S) 41 M2
Aspnes (N) 25 H6
Aspö (S) 41 M4
Aspö (S) 44 H6
As Pontes de García Rodríguez (E) 110 D2
Asprángeli (GR) 178 D5
Aspres, Les (F) 76 C4
Aspres-sur-Buech (F) 95 G1
Asprières (F) 93 J1
Áspro (GR) 179 G3
Asprógia (GR) 178 E3
Aspróhoma (GR) 186 E5
Asprokklissiá (GR) 179 F5
Asprópirgos (GR) 188 C3
Áspros (GR) 179 H3
Asprovália (GR) 179 K3
Aspsele (S) 26 E7
Assais-les-Jumeaux (F) 82 E3
Assamalla (EST) 131 K2
Assamstadt (D) 79 M3
Assas (F) 94 C3
Assat (F) 92 D4
Asse (B) 69 G5
Asseiceira (P) 116 E4
Asseln (D) 71 G3
Assemini (I) 97 C5
Assen (NL) 64 F6
Assenede (B) 68 F4
Assenois (B) 78 C2
Assens (DK) 42 F5
Assens (DK) 46 E3
Assentoft (DK) 42 F6
Assérac (F) 75 G6
Assergi (I) 103 H3
Assesse (B) 69 J6
Assíni (GR) 188 A4
Ássiros (GR) 179 J3
Assisi (I) 103 F1
Åssjöbo (S) 33 J5
Aßlar (D) 70 F5
Assling (A) 91 H5
Aßling (D) 88 G2
Assmannshausen (D) 70 E7
Asso (I) 87 H6
Asson (F) 114 C1
Ássos (GR) 186 B3
Asso-Veral (E) 92 C5
Assumar (P) 124 E1
Aßweiler (D) 78 G3
Asta (I) 99 J4
Åstadalen (N) 31 P5
Astaffort (F) 92 F2
Astakós (GR) 186 C2
Åståkra (S) 44 E5
Åstan (N) 24 D7
Astaškavičy (BY) 145 L4
Astašyna (BY) 144 D1
Aştavul (TR) 185 K5
Aste (EST) 130 B4
Åsted (DK) 42 F4
Astelarra (E) 113 F2
Asten (NL) 69 K4
Asterholma (AX) 34 H4
Astfeld = Campolasta (I) 88 E4
Asti (I) 98 E3
Astikkala (FIN) 37 N1
Aştileu (RO) 160 E3
Astillero,El (E) 112 D2
Astipálea (GR) 195 J2
Åstol (S) 43 J3
Aston (GB) 55 K4
Aston (GB) 58 B1
Aston Clinton (GB) 58 F4
Astorga (E) 111 G4
Åstorp (S) 44 B6
Astráin (E) 113 H3
Åstrand (S) 40 D2
Åstrandssätern (S) 40 D2
Åsträsk (S) 22 B7
Astrašycki Garadok (BY) 138 G5
Astratovo (RUS) 135 M2
Astravec (BY) 138 C4
Astravskija (BY) 139 N3
Astražanka (BY) 145 J5
Astrazub (RKS) 174 E4
Astrilovo (RUS) 135 M2
Astrohóri (GR) 178 E6
Astromeritis (CY) 198 F5
Ástros (GR) 187 F5
Astrovna (BY) 139 L3
Astrup (DK) 42 E5
Astrup (DK) 46 F3
Astruptunet (N) 30 E4
Astryna (BY) 143 M3
Astudillo (E) 112 C4
Astwood Bank (GB) 58 D3
Asuaju de Sus (RO) 161 G2
Asuma (FIN) 29 H6
Åsundatorp (S) 40 D4
Asūne (LV) 138 G1
Asuni (I) 97 C4
Asunta (FIN) 28 E7
Ásványráró (H) 154 A6
Asvestohóri (GR) 180 C3
Asvestópetra (GR) 179 F4
Ászár (H) 159 H2
Aszófő (H) 158 E4
Atabey (TR) 191 K5
Atajate (E) 128 D4
Ataköy (TR) 191 K3
Atalaia (P) 116 F5
Atalánti (GR) 188 B2
Atalaya, La (E) 127 H4
Atalaya del Cañavate (E) 120 D4
Atalez (BY) 144 E1
Atanzón (E) 119 L2
Ataquines (E) 119 G1
Atarfe (E) 126 C5
Atašiene (LV) 134 B4
Atbükü (TR) 197 H3
Atburgazi (TR) 190 C5
Atça (TR) 184 C5
Atça (TR) 190 E5
Atea (E) 120 E1
Ateaş (RO) 160 D4
Ateca (E) 113 H6
Atei (P) 110 D6
Aţel (RO) 169 G1
Ateleta (I) 103 J4
Atella (I) 104 E4
Atena Lucana (I) 104 E5
Atessa (I) 104 B1
Ath (B) 68 F5
Athaní (GR) 186 B2
Athboy (IRL) 63 J1
Athea (IRL) 62 D4
Athenry (IRL) 62 E2
Athenstedt (D) 71 L3
Athéras (GR) 186 A3
Atherstone (GB) 55 J5
Athesans-Étroitefontaine (F) 86 C2
Athienou (CY) 199 G5
Athies (F) 77 G2
Athíkia (GR) 188 A4
Athína (GR) 187 H4
Athiniós (GR) 195 G3
Áthira (GR) 179 H3
Athis (F) 77 K3
Athis-Val-de-Rouvre (F) 75 L3
Athleague (IRL) 62 F1
Athlone (IRL) 62 G2
Áth na nUrlainn = Urlingford (IRL) 63 G3
Athy (IRL) 61 J6
Atid (RO) 161 L5
Atienza (E) 112 F6
Atina (I) 103 H4
Aţintiş (RO) 161 J5
Atios (E) 110 C1
Atış Poligonu (TR) 193 F5
Atkafası (TR) 192 E2
Atkaracalar (TR) 184 F4
Atla (EST) 130 A4
Atlantı (TR) 192 D4
Atlıhisar (TR) 191 K4
Atlılar (TR) 199 H1
Åtlo (N) 24 E7
Atnbrua (N) 31 N4
Atnikstugan (S) 25 J4
Atnosen (N) 31 O4
Atolina (BY) 138 F6
Åtorp (S) 40 F4
Atostugan (S) 25 J3
Åtran (S) 44 B4
Åträsk (S) 22 D4
Åträsk (S) 27 G4
Atri (I) 103 H2
Atripalda (I) 104 C4
Atsikí (GR) 181 G5
Atspuka (LV) 134 C4
Attadale House (GB) 50 G5
Áttali (GR) 187 H2
Atteln (D) 71 G3
Attendorn (D) 70 E4
Attenkirchen (D) 80 F3
Attersee am Attersee (A) 81 K5
Attert (B) 78 D2
Attichy (F) 77 H3
Attigliano (I) 102 E2
Attignat (F) 85 H4
Attigny (F) 77 L3
Attimis (I) 89 J5
Attleborough (GB) 59 K2
Attlebridge (GB) 59 K2
Attmar (S) 33 N3
Attnang-Puchheim (A) 89 K1
Åttonträsk (S) 26 E6
Attu (FIN) 35 K4
Åtvidaberg (S) 45 J2
Atzara (I) 97 D4
Atzendorf (D) 71 N3
Atzeneta del Maestrat (E) 122 A2
Au (CH) 80 B6
Au (D) 80 F5
Aub (D) 79 N2
Aubagne (F) 95 G4
Aubange (B) 78 D2
Aubel (B) 69 K5
Aubenas (F) 94 D1
Aubenton (F) 77 K2
Aubérive (F) 77 K3
Auberive (F) 77 M6
Aubeterre-sur-Dronne (F) 82 F6
Aubiet (F) 93 F3
Aubignan (F) 94 F2
Aubigné (F) 82 E4
Aubigny-au-Bac (F) 68 E6
Aubigny-en-Artois (F) 68 D6
Aubigny-Les-Clouzeaux (F) 82 C3
Aubigny-sur-Nère (F) 76 F7
Aubin (F) 93 J1
Aubonne (CH) 85 K4
Aubrac (F) 94 A1
Aubure (F) 78 G5
Aubusson (F) 83 K5
Auby (F) 68 E6
Auce (LV) 137 H1
Auch (F) 92 F3
Auchagallon (GB) 52 E3
Auchavan (GB) 51 L6
Auchel (F) 68 C5
Auchencairn (GB) 53 H5
Auchentiber (GB) 52 F3
Auchindroin (GB) 52 E2
Auchinleck (GB) 52 G4
Auchmithie (GB) 53 K1
Auchnagatt (GB) 51 N5
Auchronie (GB) 51 M6
Auchterarder (GB) 53 H2
Auchtermuchty (GB) 53 J2
Auchy-au-Bois (F) 68 C5
Aucloggeen (IRL) 60 E5
Aucun (F) 114 C2
Auddè = Aullène (F) 96 E5
Audenarde = Oudenaarde (B) 68 F5
Audenge (F) 92 B1
Auderville (F) 75 H1
Audeux (F) 86 A3
Audevälja (EST) 130 F2
Audierne (F) 74 B4
Audincourt (F) 78 F7
Auðkúla (IS) 16 F3
Audlem (GB) 55 G5
Audley (GB) 55 H4
Audnedal (N) 38 F6
Auðnir (IS) 17 J3
Audru (EST) 130 F4
Audruicq (F) 59 M6
Auðsstaðir (IS) 16 E5
Audun-le-Roman (F) 78 D3
Audun-le-Tiche (F) 78 D3
Aue (D) 70 F4
Aue (D) 152 C2
Auer = Ora (I) 88 E5
Auerbach (Vogtland) (D) 73 G4
Auerbach in der Oberpfalz (D) 80 F1
Auetal (D) 71 H2
Auf dem Löh (D) 65 K4
Auf der Au (A) 89 K2
Auffach (A) 80 G6
Auffay (F) 76 D2
Aufhausen (D) 152 B6
Aufseß (D) 72 E6
Augan (F) 75 G5
Augasantas (E) 110 C4
Augerans (F) 85 J2
Augerolles (F) 84 E5
Augher (GB) 61 H3
Aughils (IRL) 62 C4
Aughnacloy (GB) 52 B6
Aughrim (IRL) 60 F5
Aughrim (IRL) 63 K3
Augisey (F) 85 J3
Augsburg (D) 80 D4
Augšlīgatne (LV) 133 L3
Augstkalne (LV) 132 G5
Augusta (I) 109 H3
Augustdorf (D) 70 G3
Augustenborg (DK) 46 E4
Augustendorf (D) 65 L5
Augustów (PL) 143 H3
Augustusburg (D) 152 D2
Auho (FIN) 29 H2
Au in der Hallertau (D) 80 F3
Aukan (N) 24 C8
Aukea (S) 21 N6
Aukra (N) 30 F2
Aukrug (D) 46 E5
Aukštadvaris (LT) 143 M1
Aukštelkai (LT) 132 H6
Aukštelkė (LT) 132 G6
Auktsjaure (S) 26 F3
Aulaga, La (E) 128 B2
Auldhame (GB) 53 K2
Aulendorf (D) 79 M6
Aulesti (E) 113 F2
Aulestia = San Andrés de Aulestia (Etxebarría) (E) 113 G2
Auletta (I) 104 D4
Aulla (I) 99 H4
Aullène (F) 96 E5
Aulnay (F) 82 E4
Aulnay-la-Rivière (F) 76 F5
Aulnois (F) 78 D5
Aulnois-sur-Seille (F) 78 E4
Aulnoye-Aymeries (F) 68 F6
Aulon (F) 83 J4
Aulon (F) 93 F4
Aulosen (D) 66 F5
Aulstad (N) 31 N5
Ault (F) 68 A6
Aulum (DK) 42 C6
Aulus-les-Bains (F) 115 F2
Aumale (F) 76 E2
Auma-Weidatal (D) 152 A2
Aumeistari (LV) 131 K5
Aumenau (D) 70 F6
Aumeville-Lestre (F) 75 J1
Aumont (F) 85 J3
Aumont-Aubrac (F) 94 B1
Aumühle (D) 66 C3
Aunay-sur-Odon (F) 75 K2
Aune (I) 88 F5
Aune (N) 25 G5
Aune (N) 25 H6
Auneau-Bleury-St-Symphorien (F) 76 E5
Aunet (N) 24 E6
Aunet (N) 24 E7
Aunet (N) 25 G5
Auneuil (F) 76 E3
Auning (DK) 42 F6
Aunkirchen (D) 90 D2
Aups (F) 95 H3
Aura (FIN) 35 L3
Aurach (D) 80 C2
Aurau (D) 80 E2
Auray (F) 74 F5
Aurdal (N) 31 L6
Aurdalsseter (N) 39 L1
Aure (N) 24 C8
Aurec-sur-Loire (F) 84 F6
Aureil (F) 83 H5
Aurelia (I) 102 D3
Aurel Vlaicu (RO) 161 G6
Aureskoski (FIN) 28 D8
Aurich (Ostfriesland) (D) 64 G5
Aurignac (F) 93 F4
Aurillac (F) 84 B7
Auriol (F) 95 G4
Aurisina, Duino- (I) 164 B3
Aurlandsvangen (N) 30 G6
Auron (F) 98 B4
Auronzo di Cadore (I) 89 G4
Aurora (RO) 171 H6
Auros (F) 92 D2
Auroux (F) 94 C1
Aursfjordgård (N) 18 A5
Aursjøhytta (N) 31 K3
Aurskog (N) 39 O3
Aursmoen (N) 39 O3
Ausa-Corno (I) 89 J6
Ausås (S) 44 B6
Ausejo (E) 113 G4
Ausel (RO) 168 E2
Auşeu (RO) 160 E3
Ausleben (D) 72 E1
Ausonia (I) 103 H5
Außerlienbachalm (A) 90 D4
Außernbrünst (D) 152 E6
Aussois (F) 85 L6
Aussonne (F) 93 G3
Aussurucq (F) 114 B1
Austad (N) 38 F6
Austad (N) 38 G4
Austad (N) 39 L4
Austafjord (N) 24 E5
Austaraland (IS) 17 K2
Austbø (N) 25 G3
Austbygda (N) 39 J2
Austefjord (N) 30 E3
Austevoll (N) 38 B2
Austgulen (N) 30 C6
Austis (I) 97 D3
Austlid fjellstue (N) 31 N5
Austmarka (N) 40 B2
Austnes (N) 20 F3
Austnes (N) 30 E2
Austpollen (N) 20 E3
Austråt (N) 24 D7
Austrheim (N) 30 B6
Austrumdal (N) 38 D5
Auterive (F) 93 G4
Auteuil (F) 76 F3
Autheuil-Authouillet (F) 76 D3
Authon (F) 76 C6
Authon (F) 95 H2
Authon-du-Perche (F) 76 C5
Authon-Ebéon (F) 82 E5
Authon-la-Plaine (F) 76 E5
Autilla del Pino (E) 111 K5
Autio (FIN) 28 E6
Autio (S) 21 N6
Autol (E) 113 G4
Autrans-Méaudre-en-Vercors (F) 85 J6
Autrèche (F) 76 C6
Autretot (F) 76 C2
Autreville (F) 78 D5
Autrey (F) 78 F5
Autrey-lès-Gray (F) 78 C7
Autry (F) 77 L3
Autry-le-Châtel (F) 77 G6
Autti (FIN) 23 K4
Auttoinen (FIN) 35 Q2
Autun (F) 84 F3
Auty (F) 93 G2
Auvere (EST) 37 J6
Auvila (FIN) 29 J8
Auw bei Prüm (D) 69 L6
Auxelles-Bas (F) 78 F6
Auxerre (F) 77 J6
Auxi-le-Château (F) 68 C6
Auxon (F) 77 J5
Auxonne (F) 85 H2
Auzances (F) 83 L4
Auzon (F) 84 D6
Auzouville-sur-Saâne (F) 76 C2
Åva (AX) 34 H4
Availles-Limouzine (F) 83 G4
Avaldsnes (N) 38 B4
Avallon (F) 77 J7
Avan (S) 22 D6
Avan (S) 22 D8
Avan (S) 27 H3
Avanca (P) 116 D2
Avanos (TR) 193 J3
Avant-lès-Ramerupt (F) 77 K5
Avaray (F) 76 E6
Ávas (GR) 181 H3
Avasjö (S) 26 C6
Avasjön = Borgafjäll (S) 25 K5
Ávato (GR) 181 F3
Avaträsk (S) 25 L6
Avaviken (S) 26 E3
Avcıköy (TR) 193 H3
Avcılar (TR) 190 B1
Avdan (TR) 191 J1
Avdan (TR) 192 D4
Avdan (TR) 192 D6
Avdan (TR) 197 H2
Avdanlı (TR) 192 D2
Avdarma (MD) 163 H6
Avdimou (CY) 198 E6
Ávdira (GR) 181 F3
Avdul (TR) 192 E6
Avebury (GB) 57 L3
Åvedal (N) 38 E6
Aveiras de Cima (P) 124 B1
Aveiro (P) 116 D2
Avelar (P) 116 E4
Avelãs de Ambom (P) 118 B2
Aveley (GB) 59 H4
Avelgem (B) 68 E5
Avellanes, les (E) 114 E4
Avellanosa del Páramo (E) 112 D4
Avellino (I) 104 C4
Avenches (CH) 85 M3
Avène (F) 93 L3
Avenida do Marqués de Figueroa (E) 110 C1
Ävensor (FIN) 35 J4
Averbode (B) 69 H4
Avereest (NL) 64 E6
Avereşti (RO) 162 F5
Avernak By (DK) 65 N1
Avernes (F) 76 E3
Avérole (F) 85 M6
Aversa (I) 103 J6
Avesnes-le-Comte (F) 68 D6
Avesnes-lès-Aubert (F) 68 E6
Avesnes-sur-Helpe (F) 68 F6
Avesta (S) 41 K2
Avetrana (I) 105 J5
Avezzano (I) 103 G3
Avgan (TR) 191 G4
Avgancık (TR) 191 H4
Avgerinós (GR) 178 E4
Avgorou (CY) 199 G5
Avià (E) 115 G3
Avía (GR) 186 E6
Aviano (I) 89 H5
Aviemore (GB) 51 K5
Avigliana (I) 98 C2
Avigliano (I) 104 E4
Avigliano Umbro (I) 102 E2
Avignon (F) 94 E3
Avignonet-Lauragais (F) 93 H4
Ávila (E) 119 G2
Avilés (E) 111 H1
Avilley (F) 86 B3
Avinuosta (LT) 138 D2
Avinurme (EST) 131 L3
Avinyó (E) 115 G4
Avinyonet del Penedès (E) 115 G5
Avion (F) 68 D6
Avioth (F) 78 C2
Avis (P) 124 D1
Avize (F) 77 K4
Avižieniai (LT) 137 N4
Avlağı (TR) 198 F2
Avláki (GR) 179 H7
Avlákia (GR) 189 J4
Avlémonas (GR) 194 C3
Avliótes (GR) 178 B5
Avlóna (GR) 187 H3
Avluobası (TR) 182 D3
Avnslev (DK) 46 G3
Avô (P) 116 F3
Avoca (IRL) 63 K3
Avoch (GB) 51 J4
Avola (I) 109 H4
Avonbridge (GB) 53 H3
Avonmouth (GB) 57 J2
Avord (F) 83 L2
Avoriaz (F) 85 L4
Avradsberg (S) 40 E2
Avrămeni (RO) 157 L5
Avrămeşti (RO) 161 L5
Avram Iancu (RO) 160 D4
Avram Iancu (RO) 160 E5
Avram Iancu (RO) 160 F5
Avrámio (GR) 186 D5
Avranches (F) 75 J3
Avratyn (UA) 150 C4
Avren (BG) 177 J2
Avrig (RO) 169 G2
Avrillé (F) 75 K5
Avrillé (F) 82 C4
Avşa (TR) 182 D4
Avşar (TR) 190 C5
Avtovac (BIH) 173 J3
Avucköy (TR) 193 J3
Avvil = Ivalo (FIN) 19 K6
Avvil Mahtte = Ivalon Matti (FIN) 19 H7
Avžže (N) 21 N2
Axams (A) 88 E3
Axat (F) 93 J5
Axberg (S) 40 H4
Axbridge (GB) 58 B5
Axel (NL) 68 F4
Axente Sever (RO) 169 G1
Axintele (RO) 170 D4
Axiohóri (GR) 180 B3
Axioúpoli (GR) 179 H3
Ax-les-Thermes (F) 93 H5
Axmar (S) 33 N5
Axminster (GB) 57 J4
Axós (GR) 195 F5
Axstedt (D) 65 K5
Axvall (S) 40 E6
Ay (F) 77 K3
Aya = Aia (E) 113 G2
Ayaklıkırı (TR) 190 D4
Ayamonte (E) 124 E5
Ayancık (TR) 13 K5
Ayancık (TR) 185 J2
Ayaş (TR) 184 D5
Ayaslar (TR) 192 C4
Ayazını (TR) 191 K2
Ayazkent (TR) 190 C2
Aybastı (TR) 13 L5
Ay-Champagne (F) 77 K3
Aydat (F) 84 C5
Aydın (TR) 184 C3
Aydın (TR) 190 D5
Aydıncık (TR) 13 K7
Aydıncık (TR) 181 H4
Aydıncık (TR) 184 E2
Aydıncık (TR) 185 K5
Aydıncık (TR) 199 F3
Aydınkışla (TR) 192 D6
Aydınlar (TR) 177 K6
Aydınlar (TR) 184 C3
Aydınlar (TR) 184 E2
Aydınlar (TR) 199 H2
Aydınlı (TR) 183 H4
Aydınlılar (TR) 199 J2
Aydınyaka (TR) 192 B2
Aydoğdu (TR) 183 J5
Aydoğlar (TR) 185 H2
Aydoğmuş (TR) 192 E6
Ayen (F) 83 H6
Ayent (CH) 86 D5
Ayer (CH) 86 E5
Ayerbe (E) 114 B3
Ayhan (TR) 193 J3
Ayherre (F) 113 J2
Aying (D) 88 F2
Aykırıkçı (TR) 191 J2
Ayla (FIN) 23 K7
Aylburton (GB) 58 B4
Aylesbury (GB) 58 F4
Aylesham (GB) 59 K5
Ayllón (E) 112 E6
Aylsham (GB) 59 K2
Ayna (E) 127 F2
Aynac (F) 93 H1
Aynho (GB) 57 M2
Ayódar (E) 121 H3
Ayora (E) 127 H1
Ayr (GB) 52 F4
Ayrancı (TR) 191 H3
Ayrancı (TR) 193 G6
Ayrancılar (TR) 190 C4
Ayrens (F) 84 B7
Ayron (F) 82 F3
Ayros-Arbouis (F) 114 C1
Ayşebacı (TR) 182 E6
Ayşeoğlu (TR) 185 H2
Aysgarth (GB) 55 J2
Äyskoski (FIN) 29 G5
Äystö (FIN) 28 B7
Ayton (GB) 55 M2
Aytré (F) 82 C4
Ayuelas (E) 112 E3
Ayva (TR) 183 G5
Ayvacık (TR) 182 B6
Ayvacık (TR) 190 C3
Ayvacık (TR) 191 H3
Ayvalı (TR) 185 H6
Ayvalı (TR) 191 G1
Ayvalı (TR) 192 B5
Ayvalı (TR) 192 C2
Ayvalı (TR) 193 J3
Ayvalık (TR) 181 K6
Ayvatlar (TR) 190 B2
Aywaille (B) 69 K6
Azagador, El (E) 121 F5
Azagra (E) 113 H4
Azaila (E) 113 L6
Azambuja (P) 124 B1
Azanja (SRB) 167 G5
Azannes-et-Soumazannes (F) 78 C3
Azanúy-Alíns (E) 114 D4
Azaruja (P) 124 D2
Azaryčy (BY) 9 L4
Azaryčy (BY) 144 C4
Azaryčy (BY) 145 K4
Azat-le-Ris (F) 83 H4
Azatlı (TR) 177 G6
Azatlı (TR) 193 J4
Azay-le-Ferron (F) 83 H3
Azay-le-Rideau (F) 83 F2
Azay-sur-Thouet (F) 82 E3
Azdamičy (BY) 144 G4
Azdavay (TR) 13 K5
Azdavay (TR) 185 F2
Azdzjacičy (BY) 139 J5
Azé (F) 85 G4
Azeglio (I) 98 D2
Azeiteiros (P) 124 E1
Azenhas do Mar (P) 116 C6
Azerables (F) 83 H4
Azerščyna (BY) 145 M4
Azëry (BY) 139 N4
Azëry (BY) 143 L3
Azina (BY) 139 J2
Azinhaga (P) 116 D5
Azinhal (P) 124 E5
Azinheira dos Barros (P) 124 C3
Azinhoso (P) 111 F6
Azitepe (TR) 190 E4
Aziziye (TR) 193 H5
Azizler (TR) 191 H3
Azjarany (BY) 145 L2
Azjarco (BY) 138 F6
Azjarcy (BY) 144 F2
Azjarnica (BY) 143 N4
Azjarnica (BY) 144 F4
Azjaryšča (BY) 138 G6
Azkoitia (E) 113 G2
Aznalcázar (E) 125 G5
Aznalcóllar (E) 128 B2
Azohía, La (E) 127 H4
Azovo (RUS) 134 F2
Azow (RUS) 13 M3
Azoz (E) 92 A5
Azpeitia (E) 113 G2
Azuaga (E) 125 H3
Azuara (E) 113 K6
Azuel (E) 126 B3
Azuga (RO) 170 B3
Ažuny (BY) 138 F3
Ažuolų Būda (LT) 137 K4
Azuqueca de Henares (E) 119 K2
Azur (F) 92 B3
Azzano Decimo (I) 89 H6
Azzate (I) 87 G6

B

Baabe (D) 47 N5
Baad (A) 87 K3
Baak (NL) 70 B2
Baal (D) 70 B4
Baamonde (E) 110 D2
Baar (CH) 87 G3
Baar (Schwaben) (D) 80 D3
Baarland (NL) 68 F4
Baarle-Nassau (B) 69 H4
Baarlo (NL) 70 B4
Baarn (NL) 69 J2
Baba Ana (RO) 170 C4
Babadag (RO) 171 H4
Babadağ (TR) 191 F5
Babadere (TR) 181 J5
Babaeski (TR) 181 L2
Babaevo (RUS) 7 U6
Babaevo (RUS) 134 F2
Băbăiţa (RO) 169 J5
Babaj-Bokës (RKS) 174 D4
Babaj Boks = Babaj-Bokës (RKS) 174 D4
Babakale (TR) 181 J6
Babakonağı (TR) 193 H3
Babaköy (TR) 182 F6
Babanka (UA) 163 L1
Babarc (H) 166 C1
Babasultan (TR) 183 H5
Babcy (BY) 138 H4
Babčyn (BY) 145 M5
Babčynci (UA) 162 G2
Babek (BG) 176 D4
Babele (RO) 170 A3
Babelsberg (D) 67 J6
Babenhausen (D) 71 G7
Babenhausen (D) 80 C4
Băbeni (RO) 161 G3
Băbeni (RO) 169 G4
Băbeni (RO) 170 D3
Babensham (D) 89 G1
Babiak (PL) 141 L6
Babiak (PL) 142 C2
Babica (BG) 175 J3
Babica (PL) 148 E6
Babići (BIH) 172 F1
Băbiciu (RO) 169 H5
Babięta (PL) 142 E3
Babigoszcz (PL) 140 C3
Babilafuente (E) 118 F2
Babi Les (BY) 139 H5
Babimost (PL) 146 D1
Babina Greda (HR) 166 C3
Babinavičy (BY) 139 N4
Babine (SRB) 173 L3
Babinek (PL) 140 C4
Babiničy (BY) 139 M3
Babiničy (BY) 139 M5
Babino (RUS) 134 E3
Babino Polje (HR) 173 G4
Babirova (BY) 145 J2
Babjak (BG) 175 L5
Bab'jakovo (RUS) 131 O5
Babki (RUS) 135 K5
Babócsa (H) 165 J2
Bábolna (H) 158 E2
Baborów (PL) 147 H5
Baboszewo (PL) 142 C5
Babovičy (BY) 145 N4
Babovo (BG) 170 C6
Babrova (BY) 139 J3
Babrovičy (BY) 138 E5
Babrovičy (BY) 144 C3
Babrovičy (BY) 145 J3
Babrujsk (BY) 9 L3
Babrujsk (BY) 145 K2
Babsk (PL) 148 B2
Babtai (LT) 137 K3
Babuk (BG) 170 E5
Babušnica (SRB) 175 H2
Babyči (UA) 156 C5
Babyči (UA) 156 G1
Babynci (UA) 151 J4
Babynci (UA) 151 L2
Babyne (UA) 157 N2
Babyničy (BY) 139 H3
Babyničy (BY) 144 B2
Bac (GB) 50 E3
Bač (MNE) 174 D3
Bač (SLO) 164 C3
Bač (SRB) 166 D3
Băcani (RO) 162 F6
Bacares (E) 127 F5
Bacău (RO) 162 D5
Baccarat (F) 78 F5
Baccinello (I) 102 C2
Baccon (F) 76 E6
Bačėjkava (BY) 139 K3
Băceşti (RO) 162 E5
Bacėvičy (BY) 145 K2
Bach (A) 87 K3
Bach (F) 93 H2
Bach an der Donau (D) 81 G2
Bacharach (D) 70 E6
Bachellerie, La (F) 83 H6
Bachl (D) 80 F3
Bachmač (UA) 9 N4
Bachmut (UA) 9 P5
Bachórz (PL) 148 F6
Bachtyn (UA) 150 E6
Băcia (RO) 161 F6
Bačina (SRB) 174 F1
Baciu (RO) 161 H4
Baciu (RO) 169 J5
Back (GB) 50 E3
Bäck (S) 27 G6
Bäck (S) 40 F5
Backa (S) 40 D1
Backa (S) 40 E3
Backa (S) 41 P3
Backa (S) 43 J3
Backa (S) 43 J4
Bäckaby (S) 44 F4
Backadammen (S) 40 D1
Bačka Gradište (SRB) 166 F2
Backaland (GB) 51 M1
Bäckan (S) 33 K3
Bačka Palanka (SRB) 166 D3
Backaryd (S) 44 G6
Bäckaskog (S) 44 F6
Bačka Topola (SRB) 159 J6
Backberg (S) 41 L1
Bäckboda (S) 28 A3
Backbodarna (S) 40 H2
Backböle = Pakila (FIN) 36 E3
Backe (S) 26 C7
Bäckebo (S) 45 J5
Bäckefors (S) 40 B5
Bäckegruvan (S) 40 H3
Backen (S) 26 G7
Backen (S) 40 C2
Bäckhammar (S) 40 F4
Bački Breg (SRB) 159 G6
Bački Brestovac (SRB) 166 D2
Bački Gračac (SRB) 166 D2
Bački Jarak (SRB) 166 E3
Bački Monoštor (SRB) 159 G6
Bačkininkai (LT) 138 D3
Bački Petrovac (SRB) 166 E3
Bački Sokolac (SRB) 159 J6
Bäckland (S) 33 O2
Bäcklösen (S) 41 M2
Bäcklund (S) 26 F3
Backnang (D) 80 A3
Bäcknäs (S) 26 F4
Bačko Dobro Polje (SRB) 166 E2
Bačko Novo Selo (SRB) 166 D3
Bačko Petrovo Selo (SRB) 166 F2
Bačkovo (BG) 176 C5
Baćkowice (PL) 148 D4
Bäckseda (S) 44 G4
Bäckvallen (S) 32 D2
Bäckviken (S) 47 L2
Backwell (GB) 58 B5
Băcleş (RO) 168 E5
Bacoli (I) 103 J6
Baconnière, La (F) 75 K4
Baconsthorpe (GB) 59 K2
Bacor-Olivar (E) 126 E4
Bacova Mahala (BG) 176 C1
Bacqueville-en-Caux (F) 76 C2
Bácsalmás (H) 166 D1
Bácsbokod (H) 166 D1
Bácsszentgyörgy (H) 159 H6
Bacup (GB) 55 H3
Bacúrov (SK) 154 E4
Bad (D) 72 C1
Bada (S) 40 D2
Bad Abbach (D) 80 G3
Badacsonytomaj (H) 158 E4
Bad Aibling (D) 88 G2
Badajoz (E) 124 F2
Badak (TR) 193 H5
Badalona (E) 115 H5
Badalucco (I) 98 D5
Badanj (SRB) 174 E2
Badarán (E) 112 F4
Badarne (S) 41 J3
Bad Arolsen (D) 71 H4
Badaroux (F) 94 C1
Bad Aussee (A) 89 K2
Bad Bederkesa (D) 65 K4
Bad Bellingen (D) 86 E2
Bad Belzig (D) 73 H1
Bad Bentheim (D) 70 D2
Badbergen (D) 65 H6
Bad Bergzabern (D) 79 J3
Bad Berka (D) 72 E4
Bad Berleburg (D) 70 F4
Bad Berneck im Fichtelgebirge (D) 72 F5
Bad Bertrich (D) 70 D6
Bad Bevensen (D) 66 D4
Bad Bibra (D) 71 N4
Bad Birnbach (D) 81 J4
Bad Blankenburg (D) 72 E4
Bad Bleiberg (A) 164 B1
Bad Blumau (A) 91 K5
Bad Bocklet (D) 71 K6
Bad Bodenteich (D) 66 D5
Bad Boll (D) 79 M4
Bad Brambach (D) 73 G5
Bad Bramstedt (D) 46 E6
Bad Breisig (D) 70 D5
Bad Brückenau (D) 72 B5
Bad Buchau (D) 79 M5
Badby (GB) 58 E3
Bad Camberg (D) 70 F6
Badcaul (GB) 50 G4
Bad Colberg-Heldburg (D) 72 D5
Baddeckenstedt (D) 72 C1
Badderen (N) 18 E4
Bad Doberan (D) 66 F2
Bad Driburg (D) 71 H3
Bad Düben (D) 73 H2
Bad Dürkheim (D) 79 J3
Bad Dürrenberg (D) 72 G3
Bad Dürrheim (D) 79 K5
Badefols-d'Ans (F) 83 H6
Badefols-sur-Dordogne (F) 93 F1
Bad Eilsen (D) 71 H2
Bad Eisenkappel = Železna Kapla (A) 90 G7
Bad Elster (D) 152 B3
Bademağacı (TR) 191 J6
Bademağacı (TR) 198 D2
Bademçay (TR) 185 G4
Bademdere (TR) 193 K5
Bademler (TR) 189 J3
Bademli (TR) 181 J5
Bademli (TR) 189 J1
Bademli (TR) 190 E2
Bademli (TR) 190 E4
Bademli (TR) 191 H6
Bademli (TR) 192 B3
Bademli (TR) 192 C6
Bademli (TR) 192 D6
Bad Ems (D) 70 E6
Bad Emstal (D) 71 H4
Baden (A) 158 B1
Baden (CH) 79 J7
Baden-Baden (D) 79 J4
Bad Endbach (D) 70 F5
Bad Endorf (D) 89 G2
Badenscoth (GB) 51 N5
Badenstedt (D) 65 L5
Badenweiler (D) 79 H6
Baderna (HR) 164 B4
Bad Essen (D) 70 F2
Bădeuţi (RO) 157 J6
Bad Fallingbostel (D) 65 M6
Bad Feilnbach (D) 88 G2
Bad Fischau (A) 91 K4
Bad Frankenhausen (Kyffhäuser) (D) 72 E3
Bad Fredeburg (D) 70 F4
Bad Freienwalde (Oder) (D) 67 L5
Bad Friedrichshall (D) 79 L3
Bad Fusch (A) 90 C5
Bad Füssing (D) 81 J4
Bad Gams (A) 91 H6
Bad Gandersheim (D) 71 K3
Bad Gastein (A) 89 J3
Bad Gleichenberg (A) 91 J6
Bad Godesberg (D) 70 D5
Bad Gögging (D) 80 F3
Bad Goisern am Hallstättersee (A) 90 E4
Bad Gottleuba-Berggießhübel (D) 152 E2
Bad Griesbach im Rottal (D) 90 D3
Bad Grönenbach (D) 88 C2
Bad Großpertholz (A) 91 G2
Bad Grund (Harz) (D) 72 C2
Bad Hall (A) 89 L1
Bad Harzburg (D) 71 L3
Bad Heilbrunn (D) 88 E2
Bad Herrenalb (D) 79 J4
Bad Hersfeld (D) 72 B4
Bad Hindelang (D) 88 C2
Bad Hofgastein (A) 90 D5
Bad Höhenstadt (D) 152 D7
Bad Homburg vor der Höhe (D) 70 G6
Bad Honnef (D) 70 D5
Bad Hönningen (D) 70 D5
Badia Calavena (I) 99 L1
Badia Gran (E) 123 G4
Badia Polesine (I) 100 F2
Badia Prataglia (I) 101 F5
Badia Tedalda (I) 101 G5
Bad Iburg (D) 70 F2
Bădiceni (MD) 162 G2
Badırga (TR) 183 G5
Bad Ischl (A) 89 K2
Badje-Sohppar = Övre Soppero (S) 18 D7
Bad Karlshafen (D) 72 A2
Bad Kissingen (D) 72 C5
Bad Kleinen (D) 66 E3
Bad Kleinkirchheim (A) 89 K4
Bad Klosterlausnitz (D) 152 A2
Bad Kohlgrub (D) 87 M2
Bad König (D) 79 L2
Bad Königshofen im Grabfeld (D) 72 C5
Bad Kösen (D) 72 F3
Bad Köstritz (D) 72 G4
Bad Kötzting (D) 152 C5
Bądków (PL) 147 L2
Bad Kreuznach (D) 79 H2
Bad Krozingen (D) 79 H6
Bad Laasphe (D) 70 F5
Bad Laer (D) 70 F2
Bad Langensalza (D) 71 L4
Bad Laterns (A) 87 J3
Bad Lauchstädt (D) 72 F3
Bad Lausick (D) 73 H3
Bad Lauterberg im Harz (D) 72 C2
Bad Leonfelden (A) 90 F2
Bad Liebenstein (D) 72 C4
Bad Liebenwerda (D) 73 J2
Bad Liebenzell (D) 79 K4
Bad Lippspringe (D) 71 G3
Badljevina (HR) 165 J3
Bad Lobenstein (D) 72 F5
Badluarach (GB) 50 G4
Bad Marienberg (Westerwald) (D) 70 E5
Bad Mergentheim (D) 80 B2
Bad Mitterndorf (A) 81 K5
Bad Münder am Deister (D) 72 A1
Bad Münster am Stein-Ebernburg (D) 79 H2
Bad Münstereifel (D) 70 C5
Bad Muskau (D) 73 M2
Bad Nauheim (D) 70 G6
Bad Nenndorf (D) 66 A6
Bad Neuenahr-Ahrweiler (D) 70 D5
Bad Neustadt an der Saale (D) 72 C5
Bad Oeynhausen (D) 71 G2
Badolato (I) 107 G5
Badolato Marina (I) 107 G5
Badolatosa (E) 126 A5
Bad Oldesloe (D) 66 C3
Badonviller (F) 78 F4
Bad Orb (D) 72 A5
Badovinci (SRB) 166 D4
Bad Peterstal-Griesbach (D) 79 J5
Bad Pirawarth (A) 91 L3
Bad Pyrmont (D) 71 H3
Bad Radkersburg (A) 165 F1
Bad Ragaz (CH) 87 J3
Bad Rappenau (D) 79 L3
Bad Rehburg (D) 66 A6
Bad Reichenhall (D) 89 H2
Bad Rippoldsau-Schapbach (D) 79 J5
Bad Rodach bei Coburg (D) 72 D5
Bad Rothenfelde (D) 70 F2
Bad Saarow (D) 67 L6
Bad Sachsa (D) 72 D2
Bad Säckingen (D) 79 H6
Bad Salt = Bagni di Salto (I) 88 D4
Bad Salzdetfurth (D) 72 C1
Bad Salzhausen (D) 71 G6
Bad Salzig (D) 70 E6
Bad Salzschlirf (D) 72 B4
Bad Salzuflen (D) 70 G2
Bad Salzungen (D) 72 C4
Bad Sankt Leonhard im Lavanttal (A) 91 G6
Bad Sankt Peter (D) 65 K3
Bad Sassendorf (D) 70 F3
Bad Saulgau (D) 87 J1
Bådsbøl-Ballum (DK) 65 K1
Bad Schallerbach (A) 90 E3
Bad Schandau (D) 73 L4
Bad Schlema (D) 152 C2
Bad Schmiedeberg (D) 73 H2
Bad Schönborn (D) 79 K3
Bad Schussenried (D) 87 J1
Bad Schwalbach (D) 70 F6
Bad Schwartau (D) 46 G6
Bad Segeberg (D) 46 F6
Bad Sobernheim (D) 79 H2
Bad Soden am Taunus (D) 70 G6
Bad Soden-Salmünster (D) 72 A5
Bad Sooden-Allendorf (D) 72 B3
Bad Staffelstein (D) 72 D5
Bad Steben (D) 72 F5
Bad Suderode (D) 72 E2
Bad Sulza (D) 71 N4
Bad Sülze (D) 47 L5
Bad Tabarz (D) 72 D4
Bad Teinach-Zavelstein (D) 79 K4
Bad Tennstedt (D) 71 L4
Bad Tölz (D) 80 F5
Bad Traunstein (A) 91 H3
Badules (E) 121 F1
Bădulești (RO) 169 J4
Bad Urach (D) 79 L5
Bad Vellach (A) 89 M5
Bad Vilbel (D) 70 G6
Bad Vöslau (A) 158 B2
Bad Waldliesborn (D) 70 F3
Bad Waldsee (D) 79 M6
Bad Waltersdorf (A) 91 K5
Bad Wiessee (D) 80 F5
Bad Wildbad im Schwarzwald (D) 79 K4
Bad Wildungen (D) 71 H4
Bad Wilsnack (D) 66 F5
Bad Wimpfen (D) 79 L3
Bad Windsheim (D) 80 C1
Bad Wörishofen (D) 88 D1
Bad Wünnenberg (D) 70 G3
Bad Wurzach (D) 80 B5
Bad Zell (A) 81 M4
Badzeni (BY) 138 F4
Bad Zurzach (CH) 86 F2
Bad Zwesten (D) 71 H4
Bad Zwischenahn (D) 65 J5
Bae Colwyn = Colwyn Bay (GB) 54 E4
Bæir (IS) 16 D2
Bæivašgiedde (N) 18 G5
Bække (DK) 46 D2
Bækmarksbro (DK) 42 B6
Bælum (DK) 42 F5
Baen = Bain-de-Bretagne (F) 75 H5
Baena (E) 126 B4
Bær (IS) 16 E3
Bær (IS) 16 E5
Bærum (N) 39 M3
Baesweiler (D) 69 L5
Baeva (BY) 139 O5
Baevo (RUS) 135 N5
Baevo (RUS) 135 O5
Baeza (E) 126 D4
Bafra (TR) 13 L5
Bagà (E) 115 G3
Băgaciu (RO) 161 J5
Bagaladi (I) 109 J1
Bagamér (H) 160 D3
Bağarası (TR) 190 D5
Bagas (F) 92 D1
Bagaslaviškis (LT) 137 M3
Bagband (D) 65 H5
Bağbaşı (TR) 184 D3
Bağbaşı (TR) 198 D1
Bağbelen (TR) 198 E2
Bağcağız (TR) 199 G2
Bağcığaz (TR) 184 E3
Bağcılar (TR) 190 E6
Bagdanaŭka (BY) 144 D4
Bagdanavičy (BY) 145 N2
Bagdoniškis (LT) 133 M6
Bâgé-le-Châtel (F) 84 F6
Bagenkop (DK) 46 G4
Bages (F) 94 A5
Baggård (S) 26 F7
Baggböle (S) 26 G7
Baggendorf, Wendisch (D) 67 H2
Baggetorp (S) 41 K4
Bagh a Chaister (GB) 50 B6
Bagheria (I) 108 E1
Bağıllı (TR) 192 B4
Bağıllı (TR) 192 B5
Bağırkanlı (TR) 183 K3
Bağkonak (TR) 192 B4
Bağlama (TR) 193 J4
Bağlarbaşı (TR) 192 B4
Bağlıkaya (TR) 193 G3
Baglio Messina (I) 108 C1
Bağlum (TR) 184 E5
Bagn (N) 31 M6
Bagnacavallo (I) 101 F4
Bagnac-sur-Célé (F) 93 J1
Bagnaia (I) 102 E3
Bagnara Calabra (I) 106 E6
Bagnasco (I) 98 E4
Bagnères-de-Bigorre (F) 114 D1
Bagnères-de-Luchon (F) 92 F5
Bagneux-la-Fosse (F) 77 K6
Bagni di Gogna (I) 89 G4
Bagni di Lucca (I) 100 D4
Bagni di Lusnizza (I) 164 A1
Bagni di Masino (I) 87 J5
Bagni di Petriolo (I) 102 C1
Bagni di Salto (I) 88 D4
Bagni di San Giuseppe (I) 89 G4
Bagni di Valgrande (I) 89 G4
Bagni di Vinadio (I) 98 C4
Bagni San Filippo (I) 102 D2
Bagno a Ripoli (I) 100 E5
Bagno di Romagna (I) 101 F5
Bagnoles-de-l'Orne Normandie (F) 75 L3
Bagnoli (I) 103 J6
Bagnoli del Trigno (I) 104 B2
Bagnoli di Sopra (I) 101 F2
Bagnoli Irpino (I) 104 D4
Bagnolo in Piano (I) 100 D3
Bagnolo Mella (I) 87 K7
Bagnols (F) 83 L6
Bagnols-en-Forêt (F) 95 J3
Bagnols-les-Bains (F) 94 C1
Bagnols-sur-Cèze (F) 94 E2
Bagnone (I) 99 H4
Bagnoregio (I) 102 E2
Bagnu, lu (I) 97 C2
Bagny (PL) 143 J3
Bågø By (DK) 46 E3
Bagod (H) 91 L6
Bagojë (AL) 178 A2
Bagolino (I) 87 K6
Bagolyirtás (H) 154 F6
Bagotoji (LT) 137 J4
Bağözü (TR) 184 C5
Bagrationovo (RUS) 142 G2
Bagrationovsk (RUS) 142 D2
Bagrdan (SRB) 167 H5
Bagrenci (BG) 175 J4
Bağsaray (TR) 191 J5
Bagucičy (BY) 145 K5
Báguena (E) 121 F1
Bağurdu (TR) 190 D4
Bagušoŭka (BY) 143 K3
Bağyaka (TR) 196 D1
Bağyazı (TR) 193 J2
Bágyogszovát (H) 158 D2
Bağyüzü (TR) 190 B2
Bahabón de Esgueva (E) 112 D5
Bahačivka (UA) 163 M3
Bahadın (TR) 185 K6
Bahadınlı (TR) 181 L6
Bahadır (TR) 191 H3
Bahadırlar (TR) 191 F4
Bahadırlı (TR) 181 K4
Baharlar (TR) 181 K5
Bahate (UA) 171 H3
Bahatkivci (UA) 157 H3
Bahçecik (TR) 183 J4
Bahçecik (TR) 185 F3
Bahçecik (TR) 190 D4
Bahçecik (TR) 192 B2
Bahçedere (TR) 190 B1
Bahçeköy (TR) 182 C4
Bahçeköy (TR) 183 G3
Bahçekoyağı (TR) 198 F3
Bahçekuyu (TR) 184 B6
Bahçeli (TR) 182 B6
Bahçıvanlar (TR) 192 A5
Bahdany (BY) 149 J2
Bahíllo (E) 111 K4
Bahlingen am Kaiserstuhl (D) 79 H5
Bahmutovo (RUS) 7 T7
Bahna (RO) 162 D5
Bahnea (RO) 161 J5
Báhoň (SK) 154 A5
Bahovycja (UA) 162 D1
Bahratal = Hellendorf (D) 73 K4
Bahrenborstel (D) 65 K6
Bahrynivci (UA) 150 F5
Bahrynivka (UA) 157 J6
Bahşili (TR) 185 F6
Bahşılı (TR) 185 H5
Bahşiş (TR) 199 J2
Bahušėusk (BY) 139 M4
Bahuslaŭka (BY) 149 J2
Baia (RO) 162 C4
Baia (RO) 168 C1
Baia (RO) 171 H4
Baia de Aramă (RO) 168 D4
Baia de Arieş (RO) 161 G5
Baia de Criş (RO) 167 L1
Baia de Fier (RO) 168 F3
Baia delle Zagare (I) 104 F2
Baia Domizia (I) 103 H5
Baia Mare (RO) 161 H2
Baiano (I) 103 K6
Baião (P) 116 E1
Baiardo (I) 98 D5
Baia Sardinia (I) 97 D1
Baia Sprie (RO) 161 H2
Băicoi (RO) 169 K3
Băiculeşti (RO) 169 H3
Baides (E) 120 C1
Baienfurt (D) 79 M6
Baierbach (D) 90 B3
Baiersbronn (D) 79 J4
Baiersdorf (D) 80 E1
Baignes-Sainte-Radegonde (F) 82 E6
Baigneux-les-Juifs (F) 77 L6
Baile Ailein (GB) 50 D3
Băile Amara (RO) 170 E4
Baile an Bhuinneánaigh = Ballybunnion (IRL) 62 C3
Baile an Chaistil = Ballycastle (GB) 61 K1
Baile an Chaistil = Ballycastle (IRL) 60 D3
Baile an Chollaigh = Ballincollig (IRL) 62 E5
Baile an Ghearlánaigh = Castlebellingham (IRL) 61 K4
Baile an Sceilg (IRL) 62 B5
Baile Átha Cliath = Dublin (IRL) 63 K2
Baile Átha Fhirdhia = Ardee (IRL) 61 J4
Baile Átha I = Athy (IRL) 61 J6
Baile Átha Luain = Athlone (IRL) 62 G2
Baile Átha Seanaidh = Ballyshannon (IRL) 60 F3
Baile Átha Troim = Trim (IRL) 63 J1
Baile Basna (RO) 169 G1
Baile Bhlainséir = Blanchardstown (IRL) 61 K5
Baile Brigín = Balbriggan (IRL) 63 K1
Baile Chathail = Charlestown (IRL) 60 E4
Baile Chláir (IRL) 62 E2
Baile Easa Dara = Ballycadare (IRL) 60 E3
Băile Govora (RO) 169 G3
Băile Herculane (RO) 167 K4
Băile Homorod (RO) 161 L5
Baile Locha Riach = Loughrea (IRL) 62 E2
Baile Mhic Andáin = Thomastown (IRL) 63 H3
Baile Mhic Íre (IRL) 62 D5
Baile Mhistéala = Mitchelstown (IRL) 62 F4
Băile Miercurea (RO) 161 H6
Baile Mór (GB) 52 C2
Bailén (E) 126 C3
Baile na Finne (IRL) 60 F2
Baile na gCros = Castlepollard (IRL) 63 H1
Baile na nÁith (IRL) 62 B4
Baile na n Gall (IRL) 62 B4
Baile na nGallóglach = Millford (IRL) 60 G1
Băile Olăneşti (RO) 169 G3
Băile Rodbay (RO) 161 K6
Băileşti (RO) 168 E5
Băile Tuşnad (RO) 170 B1
Baile Uí Mhatháin = Ballymahon (IRL) 63 G1
Bailieborough (IRL) 61 J4
Baillé (F) 75 J4
Bailleau-le-Pin (F) 76 D5
Baillet (F) 92 C1
Bailleul (F) 68 D5
Bailleul-sur-Thérain (F) 76 F3
Bailo (E) 114 B2
Baimaclia (MD) 171 G1
Baiñas (E) 110 A2
Bainbridge (GB) 55 H2
Bain-de-Bretagne (F) 75 H5
Bains (F) 84 E6
Bains-les-Bains (F) 78 E5
Bainton (GB) 55 L3
Bainville-sur-Madon (F) 78 E4
Baio Grande (E) 110 B2
Baiona (E) 110 B4
Bairro da Sapec (P) 124 B3
Bais (F) 75 L4
Băişoara (RO) 161 G4
Baisogala (LT) 137 K2
Baisweil (D) 80 D5
Băiţa (RO) 161 G2
Băiţa (RO) 168 D1
Băiţa de Sub Codru (RO) 161 G2
Báittasjárvi = Paittasjärvi (S) 18 E7
Băiuţ (RO) 161 J2
Baix (F) 94 E1
Baixas (F) 94 A5
Baja (H) 159 G5
Bajánsenye (H) 158 B4
Bajary (BY) 138 E4
Bajary (BY) 138 F4
Bajary (BY) 143 M3
Bajas, Cuevas (E) 128 F3
Bajč (SK) 154 C6
Bajcsa (H) 158 C5
Bajë (RKS) 174 E4
Bajgora = Bajgorë (RKS) 174 F3
Bajgorë (RKS) 174 F3
Bajina Bašta (SRB) 166 E6
Bajišta (MNE) 173 L4
Bajkal (BG) 176 B1
Bajlovce (MK) 175 G4
Bajlovo (BG) 176 A3
Bajmok (SRB) 159 H6
Bajna (H) 158 G2
Bajovo Polje (MNE) 173 J3
Bajrakivka (UA) 151 H5
Bajram Curri (AL) 174 D4
Bajša (SRB) 166 E2
Bak (H) 158 C4
Baka (SK) 154 B6
Bakacak (TR) 181 L4
Bakacak (TR) 190 D1
Bakałarzewo (PL) 136 H5
Bakar (HR) 164 D4
Bakarebo (S) 44 D5
Bakel en Milheeze (NL) 69 K3
Bakewell (GB) 55 J4
Bakino (RUS) 134 G4
Bakır (TR) 190 D2
Bakırköy (TR) 183 F5
Bakırköy (TR) 183 G4
Bakırtolu (TR) 192 E5
Bakka (N) 30 F6
Bakka (N) 39 K3
Bakkafjörður (IS) 17 M2
Bakkaflöt (IS) 16 G4
Bakkagerði (IS) 17 N3
Bakkasel (IS) 17 H4
Bakkasund (N) 38 B2
Bakke (N) 39 O4
Bakkebø (N) 38 D6
Bakkebu (N) 38 H2
Bakkeby (N) 18 C4
Bakkefean = Bakkeveen (NL) 64 E5
Bakkejord (N) 21 H1
Bakken (N) 24 C8
Bakken (N) 25 J6
Bakken (N) 32 B6
Bakkerud (N) 39 K3
Bakketun (N) 25 J3
Bakkeveen (NL) 64 E5
Bakki (IS) 16 F7
Bakki (IS) 16 G3
Baklaburun (TR) 182 C4
Baklan (TR) 191 H5
Baklankuyucak (TR) 191 H5
Bakonybél (H) 158 E3
Bakonycsernye (H) 158 F3
Bakonygyepes (H) 158 E3
Bakonykoppány (H) 158 E3
Bakonysárkány (H) 158 F3
Bakonyszentkirály (H) 158 E3
Bakonyszombathely (H) 158 E3
Bakov nad Jizerou (CZ) 153 G3
Bąków (PL) 147 J4
Bąków (PL) 147 K6
Bąkowa (PL) 148 D3
Baksa (H) 158 F6
Bakša (UA) 163 K2
Baksjöliden (S) 26 E6
Baksjönäset (S) 25 G7
Bakšty (BY) 138 D6
Bakšty (BY) 138 E5
Bakšty (BY) 143 M3
Bakta (SK) 155 G5
Baktåive (S) 26 E3
Baktakék (H) 155 J5
Baktalórántháza (H) 156 B6
Baktsjaur (S) 26 F4
Bakum (D) 65 J6
Bakuny (BY) 143 L5
Bakvattnet (S) 25 J7
Bäl (S) 45 O3
Bala (GB) 54 E5
Băla (RO) 161 J4
Bala (RO) 168 D4
Bala (TR) 13 K6
Balâ (TR) 192 F1
Balaban (MD) 171 H2
Balaban (TR) 183 G3
Balabancık (TR) 183 G5
Bălăbăneşti (RO) 170 F1
Balabanivka (UA) 151 K5
Balabanlı (TR) 182 E3
Balabanlı (TR) 190 D4
Balabanovo (RUS) 7 U7
Bălăceanu (RO) 170 E3
Balaci (RO) 169 H5
Bălăciţa (RO) 168 E5
Balaciu (RO) 170 D4
Balaguer (E) 114 E4
Balahanovo (RUS) 37 N3
Balajčuk (UA) 163 M4
Balaklija (UA) 9 O5
Balallan (GB) 50 D3
Balamutivka (UA) 157 M3
Bălan (RO) 161 G3
Bălan (RO) 162 B5
Balandız (TR) 199 G3
Balanegra (E) 126 E6
Balanivka (UA) 163 J2
Balaruc-les-Bains (F) 94 C4
Bälaryd (S) 44 F3
Bălăşeşti (RO) 170 F1
Balaševičy (BY) 145 J3
Bălăsineşti (MD) 157 L5
Balašivka (UA) 150 D2
Balassagyarmat (H) 159 H1
Balástya (H) 159 K5
Balašy (BY) 138 F4
Balat (TR) 190 C5
Balatina (MD) 162 E3
Balatonakali (H) 158 E4
Balatonalmádi (H) 158 F3
Balatonboglár (H) 158 E4
Balatonföldvár (H) 158 E4
Balatonfüred (H) 158 E4
Balatonfűzfő (H) 158 F3
Balatonkenese (H) 158 F3
Balatonlelle (H) 158 E4
Balatonszabadi (H) 158 F4
Balatonszárszó (H) 158 E4
Balatonszemes (H) 158 E4
Balatonszentgyörgy (H) 158 D4
Balatonudvari (H) 158 E4
Bălăuşeri (RO) 161 K5
Baláže (SK) 154 E4
Balazote (E) 120 D6
Balbacienta (E) 112 E2
Balbeggie (GB) 53 J2
Balbieriškis (LT) 143 K1
Balbigny (F) 84 F5
Balblair (GB) 51 J4
Balboa (E) 110 F3
Balbriggan = Baile Brigín (IRL) 63 K1
Balc (RO) 160 F3
Bălcaciu (RO) 161 J5
Bălcani (RO) 162 D5
Bălcăuţi (RO) 157 K6
Bălceşti (RO) 169 F4
Balcı (TR) 192 B4
Balcı (TR) 193 H3
Balcı (TR) 193 H5
Balcıdam (TR) 191 H3
Balčik (BG) 177 K2
Balcık (TR) 183 H4
Balçıkhisar (TR) 183 J5
Balçıkhisar (TR) 184 B6
Balçıkhisar (TR) 191 K4
Balçıkhisar (TR) 192 E2
Balcıköy (TR) 182 E5
Balcılar (TR) 181 K4
Balcılar (TR) 192 E7
Balcılar (TR) 198 E2
Balcombe (GB) 59 G5
Balçova (TR) 190 B4
Balde (D) 70 F5
Baldellou (E) 114 E4
Baldern (D) 80 C3
Balderschwang (D) 80 C6
Baldichieri d'Asti (I) 98 E3
Baldock (GB) 59 G4
Baldone (I) 100 C3
Baldone (LV) 133 J4
Baldovineşti (RO) 170 F3
Bale (HR) 164 B4
Bâle = Basel (CH) 79 H6
Baleal (P) 116 C5
Bâlea Lac (RO) 169 H2
Baleia (RO) 168 E3
Baleix (F) 92 D4
Baleizão (P) 124 D3
Balej (BG) 167 L5
Balen (B) 69 J4
Băleni (RO) 170 F2
Băleni-Români (RO) 169 K4
Balerma (E) 126 E6
Balerno (GB) 53 J3
Băleşti (RO) 168 E3
Băleşti (RO) 170 E3
Balestrand (N) 30 F5
Balestrate (I) 108 D1
Balewo (PL) 142 A2
Balf (H) 91 L4
Bålforsen (S) 26 E5
Balfour (GB) 51 M1
Balfron (GB) 52 G2
Bälganet (S) 44 G6
Bălgaranovo (BG) 177 F2
Bălgarčevo (BG) 175 K4
Bălgarene (BG) 176 D2
Bălgarevo (BG) 177 K2
Bălgarin (BG) 176 E5
Bălgarka (BG) 170 E5
Bălgarovo (BG) 177 H3
Bălgarski Izvor (BG) 176 B2
Bălgarsko Slivovo (BG) 176 D1
Balge (D) 65 L6
Balgray (GB) 53 K1
Balgudè = Belgodere (F) 96 E3
Bälgviken (S) 41 K4
Balıfaki (TR) 185 J2
Baligród (PL) 156 B3
Balıkesir (TR) 190 D1
Balıklava (TR) 192 D6
Balıklı (TR) 185 K4
Balıklıçeşme (TR) 181 L4
Balıklıdere (TR) 182 F6
Balıklıova (TR) 190 B4
Balıkpınar (TR) 184 E6
Bălileşti (RO) 169 H3
Bălineşti (RO) 157 K6
Bålinge (S) 27 H3
Bålinge (S) 41 M5
Bålinge (S) 41 N3
Bålinge (S) 44 C6
Balingen (D) 79 K5
Balinţ (RO) 160 D6
Balintore (GB) 51 K4
Balışeyh (TR) 185 G6
Balje (D) 65 L4
Baljevac (SRB) 174 E2
Baljvine (BIH) 165 J6
Balk (NL) 64 D6
Balkanci (BG) 176 F2
Balkanski (BG) 177 F1
Balkány (H) 155 K6
Balkastaðir (IS) 16 E4
Balkbrug (NL) 64 E6
Balke (N) 31 O6
Balkıca (TR) 191 G6
Balkırı (TR) 191 K5
Balkıyıs (TR) 185 H3
Balla (IRL) 60 D4
Ballaban (AL) 178 C4
Ballabio (I) 87 H6
Ballachulish (GB) 52 E1
Ballagh (IRL) 62 G3
Ballaghaderreen (IRL) 60 E4
Ballancourt-sur-Essonne (F) 76 F4
Ballangen (N) 20 F4
Ballantrae (GB) 61 N1
Ballao (I) 97 D4
Ballará (IS) 16 D4
Ballasalla (GBM) 54 C2
Bállasluoktta = Ballasviken (S) 20 F8
Ballasviken (S) 20 F8
Ballater (GB) 51 L5
Balle (DK) 42 G6
Ballebro (DK) 46 E4
Bällefors (S) 40 F5
Ballen (DK) 46 G2
Ballenstedt (D) 72 E2
Balleroy-sur-Drôme (F) 75 K2
Ballerup (DK) 47 K2
Ballestero, El (E) 120 D6
Ballesteros de Calatrava (E) 119 J6
Ballı (TR) 181 L3
Ballı (TR) 199 G2
Ballıbucak (TR) 192 B6
Ballıca (TR) 183 H4
Ballıca (TR) 199 K2
Ballickmoyler (IRL) 63 J3
Ballıhisar (TR) 192 C2
Ballık (TR) 191 J4
Ballık (TR) 197 F2
Ballina (IRL) 60 D3
Ballinaby (GB) 52 C3
Ballinafad (IRL) 60 F3
Ballinagar (IRL) 63 H2
Ballinagleragh (IRL) 60 F3
Ballinakill (IRL) 63 H3
Ballinalee (IRL) 60 G4
Ballinamallard (GB) 60 G3
Ballinamore (IRL) 60 G3
Ballinasloe (IRL) 60 F5
Ballincollig (IRL) 62 E5
Ballincurrig (IRL) 62 F5
Ballinderry (IRL) 62 F2
Ballindine (IRL) 62 E1
Ballineen (IRL) 62 E5
Ballingarry (IRL) 62 E4
Ballingarry (IRL) 62 F2
Ballingarry (IRL) 63 G3
Ballingry (GB) 53 J2
Ballingslöv (S) 47 N1
Ballingurteen (IRL) 62 D5
Ballinhassig (IRL) 62 E5
Ballinlough (IRL) 60 E4
Ballinluig (GB) 53 H1
Ballinrobe (IRL) 62 D1
Ballintober (IRL) 60 F4
Ballintogher (IRL) 60 F3
Ballintoy (GB) 61 K1
Ballinure (IRL) 63 G3
Ballıpınar (TR) 182 E4
Ballivor (IRL) 63 J1
Ballobar (E) 114 D4
Balloch (GB) 52 F2
Ballon (IRL) 63 J3
Ballon-Saint-Mars (F) 76 B5
Ballota (E) 111 G1
Ballots (F) 75 J5
Ballsh (AL) 178 B3
Ballstad (N) 20 C4
Ballyagran (IRL) 62 E4
Ballybay (IRL) 61 J3
Ballybofey (IRL) 60 G2
Ballyboghill (IRL) 63 K1
Ballybrittas (IRL) 61 H5
Ballybrophy (IRL) 63 G3
Ballybunnion (IRL) 62 C3
Ballycadare (IRL) 60 E3
Ballycahill (IRL) 62 G3
Ballycarry (GB) 61 L2
Ballycastle (GB) 61 K1
Ballycastle (IRL) 60 D3
Ballyclare (GB) 52 C5
Ballyclogh (IRL) 62 E4
Ballycolla (IRL) 63 H3
Ballyconneely (IRL) 60 B5
Ballyconnell (IRL) 60 G3
Ballycotton (IRL) 62 F5
Ballycroy (IRL) 60 C3
Ballycumber (IRL) 63 G2
Ballydangan (IRL) 60 F5
Ballydavid (IRL) 60 F5
Ballydehob (IRL) 62 D5
Ballyderahan (IRL) 63 G4
Ballydesmond (IRL) 62 D4
Ballyduff (IRL) 62 C4
Ballyduff (IRL) 62 F4
Ballyfarnan (IRL) 60 F3
Ballyforan (IRL) 60 F5
Ballygalley (GB) 52 D5
Ballygar (IRL) 62 F1
Ballygawley (GB) 52 A6
Ballyglass (IRL) 60 D4
Ballygowan (GB) 52 D6
Ballyhack (IRL) 63 J4
Ballyhaise (IRL) 61 H3
Ballyhalbert (GB) 52 E6
Ballyhale (IRL) 63 H4
Ballyhaugh (GB) 52 B1
Ballyhaunis (IRL) 60 E4
Ballyheige (IRL) 62 C4
Ballyhillin (IRL) 60 H1
Ballyhooly (IRL) 62 F4
Ballyjamesduff (IRL) 61 H4
Ballykeeran (IRL) 60 G5
Ballykelly (GB) 52 A4
Ballylanders (IRL) 62 F4
Ballyliffin (IRL) 60 H1
Ballylongford (IRL) 62 D3
Ballylooby (IRL) 62 G4
Ballylynan (IRL) 61 H6
Ballymacarbry (IRL) 63 G4
Ballymaconda (IRL) 62 G5
Ballymacward (IRL) 60 F5
Ballymahon (IRL) 63 G1
Ballymakenny (IRL) 61 K4
Ballymena (GB) 52 C5
Ballymoe (IRL) 62 F1
Ballymoney (GB) 61 J1
Ballymore (IRL) 63 G2
Ballymore Eustace (IRL) 61 J5
Ballymote (IRL) 60 E3
Ballynacally (IRL) 62 D3
Ballynacarrigy (IRL) 63 G1
Ballynacourty (IRL) 63 G4
Ballynagore (IRL) 60 H5
Ballynahinch (GB) 52 D6
Ballynahown (IRL) 60 G5
Ballynamallaght (GB) 61 H2
Ballynamult (IRL) 63 G4
Ballynana = Baile na nÁith (IRL) 62 B4
Ballynoe (IRL) 62 F4
Ballynure (GB) 61 L2
Ballyporeen (IRL) 62 F4
Ballyragget (IRL) 63 H3
Ballyroan (IRL) 61 H6
Ballyronan (GB) 61 J2
Ballyroney (GB) 61 K3
Ballyshannon (IRL) 60 F3
Ballytoohy (IRL) 60 C4
Ballyvaughan (IRL) 62 D2
Ballywalter (GB) 54 B1
Ballyward (GB) 61 K3
Balmacara (GB) 50 F5
Balmaseda (E) 112 E2
Balmazújváros (H) 160 C2
Balme (I) 98 C2
Balme-de-Sillingy, La (F) 86 B6
Balmedie (GB) 51 N5
Balmerino (GB) 53 J2
Balmuccia (I) 86 F6
Balnacoil (GB) 51 J3
Balnafoich (GB) 51 J5
Balnahard (GB) 52 C2
Balnapaling (GB) 51 J4
Balneario de Panticosa (E) 92 D5
Balninkai (LT) 138 B3
Bálojávri = Palojärvi (FIN) 21 N3
Bálojohnjálbmi = Palojoensuu (FIN) 21 N4
Balonav Sjalec (BY) 145 L1
Balören (TR) 183 K4
Balota de Jos (RO) 168 F4
Balotčycy (BY) 144 F3
Baloteşti (RO) 169 L4
Baloty (BY) 149 L1
Baloži (LV) 133 J4
Balquhidder (GB) 52 G2
Balrath (IRL) 63 K1
Balrothery (IRL) 63 K1
Balş (RO) 169 G5
Balşa (RO) 168 E1
Balsa de Ves (E) 121 F5
Balsareny (E) 115 G4
Bal'šavik (BY) 145 N3
Balschwiller (F) 78 G6
Balsfjord (N) 18 B5
Balsiai (LT) 136 G2
Balsicas (E) 127 J4
Balsjö (S) 26 F7
Balsorano Vecchio (I) 103 H4
Balsovo (RUS) 131 N4
Bålsta (S) 41 N3
Balsthal (CH) 86 E3
Balsupiai (LT) 143 J1
Balta (UA) 9 L5
Balta (UA) 163 K3
Balta Albă (RO) 170 E3
Balta Berilovac (SRB) 175 H2
Balta Doamnei (RO) 169 L4
Baltaköy (TR) 190 D5
Baltalın (TR) 192 E2
Baltanás (E) 112 C5
Baltar (E) 110 D5
Baltasound (GB) 49 G2
Bălţăteşti (RO) 162 C4
Bălţaţi (RO) 162 E4
Bălţaţi (RO) 169 H4
Bălteni (RO) 162 F5
Bâlteni (RO) 168 E4
Bălţeşti (RO) 170 C3
Baltezers (LV) 133 J3
Bălţi (MD) 162 F3
Baltiec (RUS) 37 K3
Baltijsk (RUS) 142 B1
Baltimore (IRL) 62 D6
Baltinava (LV) 134 E4
Baltinglass (IRL) 61 J6
Baltoji Vokė (LT) 143 N2
Baltrum (D) 64 G4
Bałucz (PL) 147 L2
Balungstrand (S) 33 K6
Balvan (BG) 176 D2
Bâlvăneşti (RO) 167 L4
Bălvănyos, Băile (RO) 170 B1
Balve (D) 70 E4
Balvi (LV) 134 D3
Balya (TR) 182 E6
Balyn (UA) 150 D6
Balynci (UA) 157 H4
Balze (I) 101 G5
Balzers (FL) 87 J3
Balzhausen (D) 80 C4
Bamberg (D) 72 D6
Bambíni (GR) 186 C2
Bamble (N) 39 L4
Bamburgh (GB) 53 M3
Bamford (GB) 55 J4
Bampton (GB) 57 H4
Bana (H) 158 E2
Baña, A (E) 110 B3
Baña, La (E) 111 F4
Banada (IRL) 60 E3
Banagher (IRL) 62 G2
Banaleg = Bannalec (F) 74 D5
Banarlı (TR) 182 D3
Banatski Brestovac (SRB) 167 G4
Banatski Dvor (SRB) 167 G2
Banatski Karlovac (SRB) 167 H3
Banatski Palanka (SRB) 167 H4
Banatsko Aranđelovo (SRB) 166 F1
Banatsko Veliko Selo (SRB) 159 L6
Banaz (TR) 191 H3
Banbridge (GB) 52 C6
Banbury (GB) 57 M1
Banca (F) 92 B4
Banca (RO) 162 F6
Bancali (I) 97 B2
Banchory (GB) 51 N5
Band (RO) 161 J4
Bandaksli (N) 38 H4
Bandary (BY) 143 L3
Bande (E) 110 D4
Bandeira (E) 110 C3
Ban-de-Laveline (F) 78 G5
Bandholm (DK) 47 H4
Bandırma (TR) 182 E5
Bando (I) 101 F3
Bandol (F) 95 G4
Bandon (IRL) 62 E5
Bandurove (UA) 163 K2
Băneasa (RO) 169 L5
Băneasa (RO) 170 F2
Băneasa (RO) 170 F5
Bañeres (E) 127 J2
Băneşti (RO) 170 B3
Banevo (BG) 177 H3
Bañeza, La (E) 111 H4
Banff (GB) 51 M4
Bångnäs (S) 26 B5
Bangor (F) 74 E6
Bangor (GB) 54 D4
Bangor (GB) 61 L2
Bangor (IRL) 60 C3
Bangor-is-y-coed (GB) 58 B1
Bangsund (N) 24 F6
Bangueses (E) 110 C4
Bănia (RO) 168 C4
Banica (BG) 175 L2
Baničevac (HR) 165 J4
Banići (HR) 173 G4
Banie (PL) 140 C4
Banie Mazurskie (PL) 142 G2
Baniewice (PL) 140 C4
Baniocha (PL) 148 D1
Baniska (BG) 176 E2
Bănişor (RO) 160 F3
Banište (BG) 176 C5
Băniţa (RO) 168 E3
Banja (BG) 175 L5
Banja (BG) 176 B4
Banja (BG) 176 C3
Banja (BG) 176 E3
Banja (BG) 177 J3
Banja (SRB) 166 E6
Banja (SRB) 173 L2
Banja (SRB) 174 E2
Banja = Bajë (RKS) 174 E4
Banja e Kukës (AL) 178 D4
Banja Koviljača (SRB) 166 D4
Banjaloka (SLO) 164 D3
Banja Luka (BIH) 165 J5
Banjani (SRB) 166 E4
Banja Vrućica (BIH) 166 A4
Banje (RKS) 174 E3
Banjevci (HR) 172 C2
Banjica = Llixhë e Pejes (RKS) 174 D3
Banjišta (MK) 174 E5
Banjole (HR) 101 K3
Banjska (RKS) 174 E3
Bankekind (S) 41 J6
Bankeryd (S) 43 O3
Bankfoot (GB) 53 H2
Bankja (BG) 175 K3
Bankovac (SRB) 175 G2
Banloc (RO) 167 H3
Bannalec (F) 74 D5
Bannegon (F) 83 L3
Bannes (F) 77 J4
Bannia (I) 89 H6
Bannivka (UA) 171 H2
Bannockburn (GB) 53 H2
Bañobárez (E) 118 C2
Bañón (E) 114 A6
Banon (F) 95 G2
Baños de Alicún de las Torres (E) 126 D4
Baños de Benasque (E) 92 F5
Baños de Cerrato (E) 111 L5
Baños de Fuente de la Encina (E) 126 C3
Baños de la Encina (E) 126 C3
Baños de Molgas (E) 110 D4
Baños de Montemayor (E) 117 K3
Baños de Río Tobía (E) 112 F4
Baños de Valdearados (E) 112 D5
Bánov (CZ) 154 B4
Bánovce nad Bebravou (SK) 154 C4
Banovci (SLO) 165 G1
Banovići (BIH) 166 C5
Banovići Selo (BIH) 166 B5
Banovo (BG) 177 J2
Bánréve (H) 155 G5
Bansha (IRL) 62 F4
Bansin (D) 47 O6
Banská Bystrica (SK) 154 E4
Banská Štiavnica (SK) 154 D5
Banska Topola (SRB) 167 F2
Banské (SK) 155 K4
Banski Despotovac (SRB) 167 G3
Banski Stanovi (MNE) 173 K3
Bansko (BG) 175 K5
Bansko (MK) 175 J6
Bansko Karađorđevo (SRB) 167 G2
Bansko Novo Selo (SRB) 167 G4
Banteer (IRL) 62 E4
Bantheville (F) 77 M3
Bantry (IRL) 62 D5
Bantzenheim (F) 79 H6
Bañuelos de Bureba (E) 112 E3
Banwell (GB) 57 J3
Banyalbufar (E) 123 G3
Banyliv (UA) 157 H5
Banyliv-Pidhirnyj (UA) 162 A2
Banyoles (E) 115 J3
Banyuls-sur-Mer (F) 93 L6
Banzin (D) 66 D4
Banzkow (D) 66 F3
Baod = Baud (F) 74 E5
Bapaume (F) 68 D6
Bar (F) 93 J2
Bár (H) 166 C1
Bar (MNE) 173 K5
Bar (UA) 150 F5
Bara (RO) 160 D6
Bâra (RO) 162 E4
Bara (S) 47 M2
Barabhas = Barvas (GB) 50 D3
Baraboi (MD) 162 F2
Baracaldo = Barakaldo (E) 112 F2
Barachty (UA) 151 L3
Baracska (H) 159 G3
Baradili (I) 97 C4
Baradziničy (BY) 138 F2
Bărăganul (RO) 170 F4
Barağı (TR) 191 H2
Baragiano (I) 104 E4
Bárago (E) 111 K2
Barahona (E) 113 F6
Bărăitaru (RO) 170 C4
Barajas (E) 120 A3
Barajas de Melo (E) 119 L3
Barajevo (SRB) 167 F4
Barak (TR) 13 M7
Barak (TR) 185 H4
Barakaldo (E) 112 F2
Barakdağı (TR) 193 K6
Baraklı (TR) 183 H6
Baraklı (TR) 191 H4
Baralla (E) 110 E3
Baralla (Neira de Xusá) = Baralla (E) 110 E3
Baran' (BY) 139 M5
Barañáin (E) 92 A5
Baranava (BY) 143 K3
Baranavičy (BY) 144 D2
Báránd (H) 160 C3
Baranda (E) 112 D2
Baranda (SRB) 167 F3
Barane = Barani (RKS) 174 D3
Barani (RKS) 174 D3
Baranivka (UA) 150 F3
Baranivka (UA) 151 J2
Baranjsko Petrovo Selo (HR) 166 B2
Barano d'Ischia (I) 104 A4
Baranove (UA) 163 L5
Baranoviči = Baranavičy (BY) 144 D2
Baranovo (RUS) 135 J1
Baranovo (RUS) 139 O2
Baranów (PL) 148 F2
Baranowo (PL) 140 G6
Baranowo (PL) 142 E4
Barão de São João (P) 124 B5
Baraolt (RO) 169 K1
Baraqueville (F) 93 J2
Baraši (UA) 150 G2
Barásoain (E) 92 A5
Bărăşti (RO) 169 H4
Barava (BY) 138 C6
Baraviki (BY) 145 L3
Baravljany (BY) 138 G5
Baravljany (BY) 139 H5
Baravoe (BY) 144 F1
Baravoe (BY) 144 H5
Baravucha (BY) 139 J2
Baravucha 1ja (Pervaja) (BY) 138 H2
Baravuha 1-ja (BY) 139 J2
Barbacena (P) 117 G6
Barbadillo (E) 117 K2
Barbadillo de Herreros (E) 112 E4
Barbadillo del Mercado (E) 112 E4
Barbadillo del Pez (E) 112 E4
Barbaggio (F) 96 E3
Barbaghju = Barbaggio (F) 96 E3
Barbalimpia (E) 120 D4
Barban (HR) 101 L2
Barbantes (E) 110 C4
Barbara (I) 101 J5
Barbarano Vicentino (I) 99 M2
Barbarevo (MK) 175 J6
Barbaros (TR) 182 D4
Barbaros (TR) 190 A4
Barbarov (BY) 145 K5
Barbarušince (SRB) 175 H4
Barbastro (E) 114 D3
Barbat (HR) 164 D5
Barbate (E) 128 C5
Barbate de Franco = Barbate (E) 128 C5
Bărbătescu (RO) 170 D4
Bărbăteşti (RO) 169 G3
Barbatovac (SRB) 174 F2
Barbâtre (F) 82 A3
Barbazan (F) 114 E1
Barbazan-Debat (F) 92 E4
Barbeitos (E) 110 E2
Bārbele (LV) 133 K5
Barber Booth (GB) 55 J4
Barberino di Mugello (I) 99 L5
Barbezieux-Saint-Hilaire (F) 82 E6
Barbières (F) 85 H7
Barbing (D) 152 B5
Barbizon (F) 77 G5
Bărbo (S) 41 L5
Barboeni (MD) 162 G4
Bárboles (E) 114 A4
Barbonne-Fayel (F) 77 J4
Barbullush (AL) 173 L6
Barbuñales (E) 114 C3
Barby (D) 72 F2
Bårby (S) 45 J5
Barca (E) 113 F6
Bârca (RO) 168 F6
Barca de Alva (P) 118 C1
Barca de la Florida, La (E) 128 C4
Barcaldine (GB) 52 E1
Bărcăneşti (RO) 169 L4
Bărcăneşti (RO) 170 D4
Barcani (RO) 169 L2
Barcarès, le (F) 93 L5
Barcarrota (E) 125 F2
Barcea (RO) 170 E2
Barcellona Pozzo di Gotto (I) 109 H1

Câmpia Turzii (RO) 161 H4
Campi Bisenzio (I) 99 L5
Campiglia Marittima (I) 102 B1
Campiglia, la (I) 102 D2
Campigna (I) 101 F5
Campigny (F) 76 C3
Campili = Longiarù (I) 88 F4
Campillo (E) 111 H5
Campillo, El (E) 125 F4
Campillo, El (E) 126 D3
Campillo, El (E) 126 E3
Campillo de Altobuey (E) 120 E4
Campillo de Arenas (E) 126 C4
Campillo de Deleitosa (E) 118 E4
Campillo de Dueñas (E) 120 E2
Campillo de la Jara, El (E) 119 F4
Campillo de las Doblas (E) 127 G2
Campillo de Llerena (E) 125 H2
Campillos (E) 125 K5
Câmpina (RO) 168 K3
Campinar (TR) 185 J4
Campinar (TR) 198 F2
Câmpineanca (RO) 170 E2
Campione del Garda (I) 88 D6
Campione d'Italia (I) 87 G6
Campisábalos (E) 112 E6
Campo Salentina (I) 107 K2
Campitello Matese (I) 104 B3
Campli (I) 103 H2
Camplongo de Arbás (E) 111 H3
Campo (E) 92 E6
Campo (I) 87 J5
Campo (P) 116 E1
Campo (P) 124 D3
Campo (Blenio) (CH) 87 G4
Campo, Cuevas del (E) 126 E4
Campo Arcis (E) 121 F5
Campobasso (I) 103 K4
Campobecerros (E) 110 E4
Campobello di Licata (I) 108 E3
Campobello di Mazara (I) 108 C2
Campo Catino (I) 103 G4
Campo da Feira (E) 110 D2
Campodarbe (E) 92 E6
Campodarsego (I) 101 F2
Campo de Besteiros (P) 116 E2
Campo de Criptana (E) 120 B5
Campo de la Feira = Campo da Feira (E) 110 D2
Campo dell'Osso (I) 103 G4
Campo de Peñaranda, El (E) 119 F2
Campo de San Pedro (E) 112 D6
Campo di Giove (I) 104 B1
Campodipietra (I) 104 C2
Campodolcino (I) 87 H5
Campodonico (I) 101 H6
Campofelice di Roccella (I) 108 E2
Campofiorito (I) 108 D2
Campoformido (I) 89 J5
Campofranco (I) 108 E2
Campofrío (E) 125 F4
Campohermoso (E) 127 F6
Campolasta (I) 88 E4
Campolattaro (I) 104 C3
Campolieto (I) 104 C2
Campo Ligure (I) 98 F3
Campo Lugar (E) 117 K5
Campo Maior (P) 124 E1
Campomanes (E) 111 H2
Campomarino (I) 107 J2
Campomarino (I) 104 C2
Campomolino (I) 95 K2
Campomorone (I) 98 F3
Campon (I) 89 G5
Campone (I) 89 H5
Campora San Giovanni (I) 106 F4
Campo Real (E) 120 B3
Camporeale (I) 108 D2
Camporgiano (I) 101 G6
Camporgiano (I) 100 C4
Camporrells (E) 114 E4
Camporrobles (E) 121 F4
Campos (E) 123 H4
Camposampiero (I) 101 F1
Camposanto (I) 99 L3
Camposines, les (E) 121 K1
Campotéjar (E) 126 C5
Campotosto (I) 103 G2
Campo Tures (I) 88 F4
Camprodon (E) 115 H3
Campsas (F) 93 G3
Camps-en-Amiénois (F) 76 E2
Câmpu Cetății (RO) 161 L4
Câmpulung (RO) 169 J3
Câmpulung Moldovenesc (RO) 161 M2
Campu Moru, U = Campomoro (F) 96 D5
Câmpuri (RO) 170 D1
Camyu (TR) 191 H3
Camucia (I) 101 F6
Camucu (TR) 182 D6
Camugnano (I) 99 L4
Camurlu (E) 119 K5
Çamurdık (TR) 191 H2
Çamurlu (TR) 192 D5
Çamuzcu (TR) 199 K2
Çamyayla (TR) 181 K4
Çamyayla (TR) 183 J6
Çamyayla (TR) 186 D3
Çamyolu (TR) 198 D2
Çamyuva (TR) 191 H3
Çamyuva (TR) 197 J2
Can (TR) 181 L4
Caña (SK) 155 J4
Canabal (E) 110 D4
Cañada (E) 127 J2
Cañada, La (E) 119 H2
Cañada de Cañepla, La (E) 127 F4
Cañada de la Cruz (E) 127 F3
Cañada del Hoyo (E) 120 E4
Cañada del Rosal (E) 125 J4
Cañada de San Urbano, La (E) 127 F6
Cañada de Verich, La (E) 114 C6
Cañadajuncosa (E) 120 D4
Cañada Vellida (E) 121 G2
Cañadillas (E) 128 F3
Çanakçı (TR) 190 F4
Çanakçı (TR) 191 F2
Çanakçı (TR) 192 B7
Çanakçı (TR) 193 J5
Çanakkale (TR) 182 B5
Canaki (TR) 191 K5
Canal, Sa (E) 122 D5
Canale (I) 98 D3
Canaleja (E) 111 H3
Canalejas del Arroyo (E) 120 C3
Canals (E) 121 G6
Canal San Bovo (I) 88 F5
Cañamares (E) 120 D3
Cañamares (E) 126 E2
Cañamero (E) 118 F5
Canaples (F) 68 C6
Canara (E) 127 G3
Canarios, Los = Fuencaliente de la Palma (E) 129 b4
Canaro (I) 101 F3
Cañart, Cuevas de (E) 121 H2
Canas de Senhorim (P) 116 F2
Cañaveral (E) 120 D4
Cañaveral (E) 117 J4
Cañaveral de León (E) 128 A1
Cañaveras (E) 120 D3
Canazei (I) 88 F5
Cancale (F) 75 H3
Cancarix (E) 127 G3
Cancellara (I) 104 E4
Cancello ed Arnone (I) 103 J5
Canchy (F) 68 B6
Cancienes (E) 111 H1
Cancon (F) 92 F1
Canda, A (E) 110 F4
Çandağ (TR) 185 K3
Çandarlı (E) 110 D2
Candanchú (E) 114 B2
Candasnos (E) 114 D5
Candás (E) 111 H1
Cândeşti (RO) 162 D3
Cândeşti (RO) 170 D3
Candelo (I) 98 E1
Candemil (P) 110 B5
Candemil (P) 110 D6
Candes-Saint-Martin (F) 82 F2
Cândeşti (RO) 162 D5
Cândeşti (RO) 170 D3
Cândeşti-Vale (RO) 169 J3
Candia Lomellina (I) 98 F2
Çandır (TR) 182 F6
Çandır (TR) 185 F5
Çandır (TR) 192 B2
Candlesby (GB) 55 N4
Candlı (TR) 184 D5
Candón (E) 125 F5
Candosa (P) 116 F3
Canedo (E) 110 D2
Canejan (E) 114 E2
Canelli (I) 98 E3
Canena (E) 126 D3
Canencia (E) 119 J2
Canepina (I) 102 E3
Canero (E) 111 G1
Căneşti (RO) 170 D3
Canet (F) 94 B3
Canet de Mar (E) 115 J4
Cañete (E) 120 E3
Cañete de las Torres (E) 126 B4
Cañete la Real (E) 125 J6
Canet lo Roig (E) 122 B1
Canet-Plage (F) 93 L5
Canfanaro = Kanfanar (HR) 164 B4
Canfranc (E) 113 K3
Canfranc-Estación (E) 113 K3
Cangas (E) 110 B4
Cangas (E) 110 E1
Cangas del Narcea (E) 111 F2
Cangas de Onís (E) 112 A2
Cangues d'Onís = Cangas de Onís (E) 112 A2
Canha (P) 124 B2
Canhestros (P) 124 C3
Canhidir (TR) 182 D3
Canicattì (I) 108 E3
Canicattini Bagni (I) 109 H3
Canicosa de la Sierra (E) 112 E5
Canido (E) 110 B4
Caniles (E) 126 E5
Canimana (TR) 192 E2
Canino (I) 102 D3
Canisy (F) 75 J2
Cañiza, A (E) 110 C4
Cañizal (E) 118 F1
Cañizares (E) 120 D2
Canizzo, O (E) 110 E4
Canjáyar (E) 126 E5
Cankaya (TR) 184 E6
Çankılı (TR) 193 K3
Çankırı (TR) 13 K5
Çankırı (TR) 185 G4
Çankıy (TR) 190 C2
Canlia (RO) 170 F5
Canna (I) 105 G5
Cannai (I) 97 B5
Cannara (I) 103 F2
Cannero Riviera (I) 87 G5
Cannes (F) 95 K3
Cannet-des-Maures, le (F) 95 H4
Canneto (I) 106 C6
Canneto sull'Oglio (I) 99 J2
Cannich (GB) 51 H5
Cannigione (I) 97 D1
Canningstown (IRL) 61 H4
Cannington (GB) 58 A5
Cannobio (I) 87 G5
Cannock (GB) 58 C2
Cano (P) 117 F6
Ca' Noghera (I) 101 G1
Canon, Mézidon- (F) 76 A3
Canonbie (GB) 53 K4
Canosa di Puglia (I) 104 F3
Canosa Sannita (I) 103 J3
Canos de Meca, Los (E) 128 B5
Canosio (I) 95 K2
Canourgue, La (F) 94 B2
Ca'n Pastilla (E) 123 G3
Can Picafort (E) 123 H3
Çanqa (TR) 190 F3
Can Salvos (E) 122 D5
Cantagallo (I) 100 E4
Cantalapiedra (E) 119 F1
Cantalejo (E) 112 D6
Cantalice (I) 103 F3
Cantallops (E) 94 A6
Cantalobos (E) 114 C4
Cantalojas (E) 112 E6
Cantalpino (E) 118 F1
Cantalupo in Sabina (I) 103 F3
Cantalupo nel Sannio (I) 103 J4
Cantanhede (P) 116 D3
Cantavieja (E) 121 H2
Cantavir (SRB) 159 J6
Canteiros (E) 110 C1
Canteleu (F) 76 D3
Cantemir (MD) 163 G6
Cantenac (F) 82 D6
Canteras (E) 127 H4
Canterbury (GB) 59 K5
Cantiano (I) 101 H6
Cantillana (E) 125 H4
Cantimpalos (E) 119 H1
Cantinella (I) 107 F3
Cantoira (I) 98 D1
Cantoria (E) 127 F5
Cantù (I) 87 H6
Cañuelas (E) 127 H4
Canvey Island (GB) 59 J4
Cany-Barville (F) 76 C2
Canyelles (E) 115 G5
Canyet de Mar (E) 115 J4
Canyt (UA) 156 G1
Canzo (I) 87 H6
Caol (GB) 50 G6
Caoles (GB) 52 B1
Caorla di Bientina (I) 88 F5
Caorle (I) 101 H1
Caorso (I) 99 H2
Capaccio (I) 106 D2
Capajevka (UA) 163 K2
Capajevka = Kalynove (UA) 151 L5
Çapaklı (TR) 190 E3
Capalbio (I) 102 C3
Çapali (TR) 191 J4
Căpâlna (RO) 168 F2
Căpâlnaş (RO) 160 E6
Căpâlnița (RO) 161 M5
Capannoli (I) 99 K5
Capannori (I) 99 K5
Caparde (BIH) 166 C5
Capareiros (P) 110 B5
Capari (MK) 178 E2
Caparica (P) 124 A2
Caparrosa (P) 116 E2
Caparroso (E) 113 H4
Capbreton (F) 92 B3
Cap-d'Agde, le (F) 94 C4
Capdella, Es (E) 123 F3
Capdenac-Gare (F) 93 J1
Capdepera (E) 123 H3
Capel (GB) 59 G5
Capel Curig (GB) 54 E4
Capelins (Aldeia de Ferreira) (P) 124 E2
Capel'ka (RUS) 7 B6
Capel'ka (RUS) 134 G1
Capella (E) 114 D4
Capellades (E) 115 G4
Capelle, La (F) 77 G1
Capelle, La (F) 78 E1
Capelle, Spring- (NL) 69 J3
Capelle aan de IJssel (NL) 69 H3
Capelle-les-Boulogne, La (F) 68 B5
Capelo (P) 129 b1
Capel Saint Mary (GB) 59 K3
Capel-y-ffin (GB) 58 A4
Capendu (F) 93 K4
Capestang (F) 93 L4
Capestrano (I) 103 H3
Cap-Ferret (F) 92 B1
Capidava (RO) 171 G4
Capileira (E) 126 D6
Capinha (P) 117 G3
Capistrello (I) 103 G4
Capitello (I) 101 F2
Capitignano (I) 103 G2
Capizzi (I) 109 F2
Çapjat (BY) 144 F3
Čapjalinka (BY) 139 N5
Čaplani (MD) 163 K6
Čapleni (RO) 160 F2
Čapleni (UA) 13 K3
Čaplje (BIH) 165 H5
Čapljina (BIH) 173 G3
Capluce (TR) 184 E3
Çaplıgın (RUS) 9 P3
Capodacqua (I) 103 F1
Capodimonte (I) 102 D2
Capo di Ponte (I) 88 C5
Capodistria = Koper (SLO) 101 K1
Capo d'Orlando (I) 109 G1
Capoliveri (I) 102 A2
Capo Rizzuto (I) 107 H5
Caposele (I) 101 H1
Capostrada (I) 100 D5
Capoterra (I) 97 C5
Cappadocia (I) 103 G4
Cappagh White (IRL) 62 F3
Cappamore (IRL) 62 F3
Cappeln (D) 72 C6
Cappel (D) 70 F3
Cap-Pelat (F) 92 E3
Cappeln (Oldenburg) (D) 65 J6
Cappenberg (D) 72 C3
Cappoquin (IRL) 63 G4
Cappotella (I) 104 B2
Capraia = Capraia Isola (I) 100 B6
Capraia Isola (I) 100 B6
Capranica (I) 102 E3
Caprarola (I) 102 E3
Capraropla (I) 102 E3
Caprese Michelangelo (I) 101 F5
Capri (I) 104 B4
Capriana (MD) 163 G4
Capriasca (CH) 87 G5
Capriati a Volturno (I) 103 J5
Capriccioli (I) 97 E1
Caprile (I) 88 F5
Caprino Bergamasco (I) 87 H6
Caprino Veronese (I) 99 K1
Caprionul (RO) 167 K2
Căpruța (RO) 168 C1
Capestang (F) 92 D2
Captieux (F) 92 D2
Capua (I) 104 B3
Capu Codrului (RO) 162 B3
Capu Corbului (RO) 162 B4
Capu di Feno (F) 96 D4
Capu Piscului (RO) 169 J3
Căpuşu Mare (RO) 161 G4
Caputh (D) 67 J6
Capvern-les-Bains (F) 114 D1
Cara (HR) 172 E4
Çara (RO) 161 H4
Carabaña (E) 119 K3
Carabias (E) 112 D6
Caracal (RO) 169 G5
Caracenilla (E) 112 E6
Caracuel (E) 120 C3
Caradeuc (F) 75 G4
Caragele (RO) 170 E4
Caragh Lake (IRL) 62 C4
Caragiu (I) 98 C4
Caraguna (I) 98 E4
Caraman (F) 93 H3
Caramanico Terme (I) 104 B1
Caramulo (P) 116 E2
Cărand (RO) 160 E5
Caranga (E) 111 G2
Caranguejeira (P) 116 D4
Caransebeş (RO) 167 K3
Carantec (F) 74 D3
Caraorman (RO) 171 J3
Carapelle (I) 104 E3
Caracaldo (I) 100 A4
Car Asen (BG) 176 F2
Carasova (RO) 167 J3
Caratelec (RO) 160 F3
Carasy (BY) 138 G2
Carate Brianza (I) 99 G1
Carauta (RO) 168 E5
Caravaca de la Cruz (E) 127 G3
Caravaggio (I) 100 B1
Carbajales de Alba (E) 111 H5
Carbajo (E) 118 B4
Carballal (E) 110 B4
Carballeda de Avia (E) 110 C4
Carballino = Carballiño, O (E) 110 C4
Carballino, O (E) 110 C4
Carballo (E) 110 B2
Carballo (Vilanova) (E) 110 D4
Carbellino (E) 111 G6
Cărbeşti (RO) 168 E4
Carbis Bay (GB) 56 D5
Carbon-Blanc (F) 92 C1
Carbonera de Frentes (E) 113 F5
Carboneras (E) 127 G6
Carboneras de Guadazaón (E) 120 E4
Carbonero el Mayor (E) 119 H1
Carboneros (E) 126 C3
Carbonia (I) 97 C5
Carbonin (I) 88 G4
Carbonne (F) 93 G4
Cărbunari (RO) 168 B4
Carbunyi (BG) 169 L3
Carbury (IRL) 63 J2
Carcaboso (E) 118 D3
Carcabuey (E) 126 B5
Carcaixent (E) 121 H5
Carcaliu (RO) 171 G3
Carcans (F) 82 C6
Carcans-Plage (F) 82 C6
Carção (P) 111 F5
Carcar (E) 113 H4
Carcare (I) 98 E4
Carcassonne (F) 93 J4
Carcastillo (E) 92 B6
Carcea (RO) 168 F5
Carcelén (E) 127 H1
Carcen-Ponson (F) 92 C3
Carchelejo (E) 126 C4
Carčmilyсy (BY) 138 E4
Carcoforo (I) 86 F6
Čarcy (BY) 139 J4
Çardak (TR) 181 K4
Çardak (TR) 191 H5
Çardak (TR) 192 B7
Çardak (TR) 193 J3
Çardaklı (TR) 185 F4
Çardaklı (TR) 190 E6
Čardaklija (MK) 175 H5
Cardaño de Abajo (E) 111 K3
Cardaño de Arriba (E) 112 B3
Cardedeu (E) 115 H4
Cardejón (E) 113 G5
Cardeña (E) 126 B3
Cardenchosa, La (E) 125 H3
Cardenchosa, La (E) 126 D1
Cardenete (E) 120 E4
Cardeñosa (E) 119 G2
Cardeston (GB) 54 G5
Cardeto (I) 109 J1
Cardiff (GB) 58 A5
Cardigan (GB) 56 E1
Cardigos (P) 116 E4
Cardinale (I) 107 F5
Cardo (E) 114 E6
Cardon (RO) 171 K3
Cardona (E) 115 G4
Cardoso de la Sierra, El (E) 119 K1
Cardross (GB) 52 F3
Caredarivka (UA) 163 M3
Carei (RO) 160 E2
Careja (BY) 139 K4
Carennac (F) 83 J7
Carentan-les-Marais (F) 75 J2
Carentoir (F) 75 G5
Careri (I) 109 K1
Carevac (SRB) 168 A4
Careva Livada (BG) 176 D3
Carev Brod (BG) 177 H2
Carevci (BG) 177 J2
Carevdar (HR) 158 C5
Carevdol (BG) 170 D6
Carev Dvor (MK) 178 E2
Carevec (BG) 176 D1
Carevo (BG) 177 J4
Carew (GB) 56 E2
Carezza al Lago (I) 88 F5
Carfizzi (I) 107 G4
Cargan (BG) 177 G4
Cargèse (F) 96 D4
Cargèse = Cargèse (F) 96 D4
Cargiaca (F) 96 E5
Carhaix-Plouguer (F) 74 D4
Caria (P) 118 B3
Cariati (I) 107 G4
Caričino (BG) 177 K2
Caridad, La (E) 111 F1
Carignan (F) 77 M2
Carignano (I) 98 D3
Carişkar (TR) 198 E3
Carışkarayıe (TR) 193 K2
Canılar (TR) 182 E5
Cariñena (E) 113 J6
Carini (I) 108 D1
Carinish (Cairinis) (GB) 50 C4
Carinola (I) 104 A3
Carisio (I) 98 E2
Cărjiţi (RO) 168 D2
Cark (GB) 54 G2
Car Kalojan (BG) 177 F1
Carla-Bayle (F) 115 F1
Carla-de-Roquefort (F) 115 G2
Carlanstown (IRL) 61 J4
Carlat (F) 93 K1
Carlepont (F) 77 H2
Carlet (E) 121 G5
Cărlibaba (RO) 161 L2
Carlingford (IRL) 61 K3
Carlisle (GB) 53 K5
Carloforte (I) 97 B5
Carlogani (RO) 169 G4
Carlota, La (E) 125 K4
Carlow (D) 66 F4
Carlow (IRL) 63 J3
Carlow = Ceatharlach (IRL) 63 H3
Carluke (GB) 52 F4
Carlux (F) 83 H7
Carlyle (GB) 53 K5
Carlsfeld (D) 73 H5
Carlton (GB) 55 K3
Carlton in Lindrick (GB) 55 K4
Carlux (F) 83 H7
Carluke (GB) 53 H3
Carmagnola (I) 98 D3
Carmanova (MD) 163 K4
Carmarthen (GB) 56 F2
Carmaux (F) 93 J2
Carmel (GB) 54 D4
Carmenes (E) 111 H3
Carmignano (I) 100 E5
Carmona (E) 125 H5
Carmzow-Wallmow (D) 140 B4
Carna (IRL) 60 C5
Carnac (F) 74 E5
Carnach (GB) 60 G5
Carnagh (GB) 61 J3
Carnagrazi (BY) 139 H6
Carna Pumpa = Schwarze Pumpe (D) 146 A2
Carnaross (IRL) 61 J4
Carnaučycy (BY) 143 J1
Carnava (BY) 139 H6
Carncastle (GB) 61 L2
Carn Domhnach = Carndonagh (IRL) 61 H1
Carndonagh (IRL) 61 H1
Carnevichy (BY) 139 J5
Carnew (IRL) 63 K3
Carnforth (GB) 54 G2
Carnia Piani (I) 89 J5
Carnica (BY) 139 M5
Carnikava (LV) 133 J3
Carnjany (BY) 149 K2
Carnjavka (BY) 139 J3
Carnlough (GB) 52 C5
Carnon-Plage (F) 94 C3
Carnota (E) 110 A3
Carnoules (F) 95 H4
Carnoustie (GB) 53 K2
Carnteel (GB) 52 B6
Carnwath (GB) 53 H3
Carolei (I) 106 F4
Caroli (SK) 44 B3
Carolina, La (E) 126 C3
Carolinensiel (D) 65 H4
Carolles (F) 75 H3
Carona (I) 87 J5
Carona (I) 109 F1
Caronka (BY) 139 K3
Carosino (I) 107 K2
Carovigno (I) 105 J4
Carovilli (I) 103 J4
Carozero (RUS) 7 V5
Carpaneto Piacentino (I) 99 H3
Carpen (RO) 168 E5
Carpenedolo (I) 99 J2
Carpentras (F) 94 F2
Car Petrovo (BG) 167 L6
Carpi (I) 99 K3
Carpiano (I) 98 G2
Carpignano Salentino (I) 105 K5
Carpignano Sesia (I) 98 E1
Carpin (D) 67 J4
Carpineti (I) 99 J4
Carpineto Romano (I) 103 G4
Carpinheira (P) 116 D3
Carpino (I) 105 D3
Carpinone (I) 104 B2
Carpiquet (F) 76 A3
Carpizna (RO) 161 G4
Carpio, El (E) 125 K4
Carpio de Azaba (E) 117 H2
Carpio de Tajo, El (E) 119 H4
Carquefou (F) 82 C2
Carqueiranne (F) 95 H5
Carradale (GB) 52 E4
Carragosa (P) 111 F5
Carragosa (P) 111 F3
Carraig Airt (IRL) 60 G1
Carraig an Chabhaltaigh = Carrigallen (IRL) 61 J4
Carraig Mhachaire = Carrickmacross (IRL) 61 J4
Carraig na Siúire = Carrick on Suir (IRL) 63 H4
Carraig Uí Leighin = Carrigaline (IRL) 62 F5
Carral (E) 110 C2
Carrapateira (P) 124 B5
Carrara (I) 99 J4
Carrascal (E) 119 K1
Carrasca, La (E) 126 B5
Carrasca, La (E) 126 E2
Carrascal del Obispo (E) 117 J2
Carrascosa (E) 120 D2
Carrascosa de Haro (E) 120 C4
Carrascosa del Campo (E) 120 C3
Carrasqueta (E) 125 K5
Carrazeda de Ansiães (P) 110 E6
Carrazedo de Montenegro (P) 110 E5
Carrbridge (GB) 51 K5
Carregado (P) 116 C6
Carregal do Sal (P) 116 E2
Carreira = Carreira (Miño) (E) 110 C2
Carreira (Miño) (E) 110 C2
Carreña (Cabrales) (E) 112 B2
Carresse-Cassaber (F) 113 K2
Carretera (Gutín de Pallares) (E) 110 D3
Carretera de Pallares (Guntín) = Guntín (E) 110 D3
Carrick (GB) 52 F2
Carrick = An Charraig (IRL) 60 E2
Carrickart = Carraig Airt (IRL) 60 G1
Carrickfergus (GB) 61 L2
Carrick Ho (GB) 49 G5
Carrickmacross (IRL) 61 J4
Carrickmore (GB) 61 H3
Carrick-on-Shannon (IRL) 60 F4
Carrick on Suir (IRL) 63 H4
Carrigaholt (IRL) 62 C3
Carrigahorig (IRL) 62 F2
Carrigaline (IRL) 62 F5
Carrigallen (IRL) 60 G4
Carrigtohill (IRL) 62 F5
Carril (E) 110 B3
Carrio (E) 111 H2
Carrión de Calatrava (E) 126 C1
Carrión de los Céspedes (E) 128 B3
Carrión de los Condes (E) 111 K4
Carrizo de la Ribera (E) 111 H3
Carrizosa (E) 119 L6
Carro (F) 94 F4
Carrodano (I) 100 B4
Carronbridge (GB) 53 H4
Carrouges (F) 76 A4
Carrowdore (GB) 54 A1
Carrowkeel (IRL) 60 G1
Carrowkeel (IRL) 61 H1
Carrowmoreknock (IRL) 60 D5
Carrù (I) 98 D4
Carrutherstown (GB) 53 J4
Carryduff (GB) 52 D5
Carry-le-Rouet (F) 94 F4
Cars, Les (F) 83 H5
Carsac-Aillac (F) 93 G1
Carsaig (GB) 52 D2
Çarşamba (TR) 13 L5
Car Samuil (BG) 170 C6
Carshovë (AL) 178 D4
Car Šišmanovo (BG) 167 L6
Carski Izvor (BG) 176 E2
Carsoli (I) 103 G3
Carsphairn (GB) 52 G4
Carstairs (GB) 53 H3
Cârţa (RO) 162 B5
Cârţa (RO) 169 H2
Cartagena (E) 127 J4
Cártama (E) 126 A6
Cartaojal (E) 126 A5
Cartavičy (BY) 138 D5
Cartaxo (P) 124 B1
Cartaya (E) 124 E5
Cartelle (E) 110 C4
Carteret (F) 75 H2
Carteret, Barneville- (F) 75 H2
Carterton (GB) 57 L2
Cartignac (F) 82 C6
Cartigny (F) 77 H2
Cârţişoara (RO) 169 H2
Cartmel (GB) 54 G2
Cartoceto (I) 101 H5
Cartuja de Aula Dei (E) 114 B4
Carucedo (E) 111 F4
Carukiv (UA) 149 M4
Carvajal (E) 128 E4
Carvalhal (P) 116 C5
Carvalhal (P) 117 G2
Carvalhal (P) 117 G3
Carvalhal Benfeito (P) 116 C5
Carvalhelhos (P) 110 D5
Carvalho (P) 116 E3
Carvalhosa (P) 116 F2
Carvarica (BG) 175 J4
Carvicais (P) 117 H1
Carvin (F) 68 D6
Carvoeiro (P) 124 C5
Casabermeja (E) 128 F4
Casabona (I) 107 G4
Casablanca (E) 125 H5
Casa Blanca (E) 127 H3
Casabona (I) 107 G4
Casa Branca (P) 124 C2
Casa Branca (P) 124 D3
Casacalenda (I) 104 C2
Casacanditella (I) 103 J3
Casa Capitán (E) 127 F1
Casaccia (CH) 87 J5
Casa del Capitán (E) 127 F1
Casa della Marina (I) 97 E5
Casa di Garibaldi (I) 97 E1
Casa Ferrato (I) 97 E5
Casaio (E) 111 F4
Casais de São Lourenço (P) 116 C5
Casa l'Abate (I) 105 K5
Casalappi (I) 102 B1
Casalarreina (E) 112 F3
Casalattico (I) 103 H4
Casalbordino (I) 103 K3
Casalborgone (I) 98 D2
Casalbuono (I) 104 E5
Casalbuttano ed Uniti (I) 100 B2
Casal di Principe (I) 103 J5
Casalecchio di Reno (I) 99 L4
Casaleggio Boiro (I) 98 F3
Casale Monferrato (I) 98 E2
Casaletto Ceredano (I) 100 B2
Casalgrasso (I) 98 D3
Casalincontrada (I) 103 J3
Casalino (I) 98 F2
Casalmaggiore (I) 99 J3
Casalmorano (I) 100 B2
Casalnuovo Monterotaro (I) 104 D2
Casaloldo (I) 100 C2
Casalpusterlengo (I) 99 H2
Casalromano (I) 100 B2
Casalromano (I) 100 C2
Casalvecchio Siculo (I) 106 D7
Casal Velino (I) 106 D2
Casalvieri (I) 103 H4
Casamassima (I) 105 G4
Casamicciola Terme (I) 104 A4
Casamozza (F) 96 E3
Casanova (I) 99 G3
Casanova Lerrone (I) 98 E4
Casa Palacio (E) 127 G4
Casaprota (I) 103 F3
Casarabonela (E) 125 K5
Casarano (I) 107 M2
Casar de Cáceres (E) 117 J4
Casar de Escalona, El (E) 119 G3
Casar de Talamanca, El (E) 120 B2
Casarejos (E) 112 E5
Casares (E) 128 D5
Casariche (E) 125 K5
Casarrubios del Monte (E) 119 H3
Casarsa della Delizia (I) 89 H6
Casas (P) 116 E5
Casas Bajas (E) 121 F3
Casas Bergés (E) 120 E5
Casas de Benítez (E) 120 D5
Casas de Don Pedro (E) 125 J1
Casas de Fernando Alonso (E) 120 D5
Casas de Haro (E) 120 D5
Casas de Juan Núñez (E) 127 G1
Casas de la Peña (E) 120 D5
Casas de Lázaro (E) 120 D6
Casas del Monte (E) 118 D3
Casas de los Pinos (E) 120 D5
Casas del Puerto de Tornavacas (E) 117 K3
Casas del Río (E) 121 F5
Casas de Madrona (E) 121 F6
Casas de Millán (E) 118 D4
Casas de Panes (E) 127 G4
Casas de Ves (E) 121 F5
Casas-Ibáñez (E) 121 F5
Casasimarro (E) 120 D5
Casasola de Arión (E) 111 J5
Casatejada (E) 118 E4
Casavecchia (I) 103 G3
Casaveja (E) 119 G3
Casazza (I) 88 B6
Cascais (P) 116 C6
Cascante (E) 113 H5
Cascante del Río (E) 121 F3
Cascia (I) 103 G2
Casciana Terme (I) 99 K5
Cascina (I) 99 K5
Cascine Vecchie (I) 99 J5
Casciolarele (RO) 170 C5
Casebres (P) 124 C2
Caseda (E) 113 J3
Casei Gerola (I) 98 F2
Căpeiu (RO) 161 H3
Casel (D) 73 L2
Caselle (I) 88 D6
Caselle (I) 98 G3
Caselle (I) 88 F6
Caselle in Pittari (I) 106 E2
Caselle Torinese (I) 98 D2
Casemurate (I) 101 G4
Casenove (I) 103 F2
Caserta (I) 104 B3
Caserta Vecchia (I) 104 B3
Casetas (E) 114 A4
Case Val Viola (I) 88 C5
Casével (P) 124 C4
Casez (I) 87 M5
Cashel (IRL) 62 F2
Cashel Bay (IRL) 62 C2
Cashel Bay (IRL) 60 C5
Cashmoor (GB) 57 K4
Casicas, La (E) 127 F3
Casillas (E) 119 G3
Casimcea (RO) 171 G4
Casimcea (RO) 171 G4
Caşin (RO) 170 D1
Casina (I) 100 D3
Casinos (E) 121 G4
Caşinu Nou (RO) 170 C1
Časiva (HR) 164 D5
Čaška (MK) 175 G5
Caskel (N) 118 G3
Čáslav (CZ) 146 C6
Časlavice (CZ) 153 J5
Časlovsko (CZ) 153 H1
Čašniki (BY) 139 J3
Casnewydd = Newport (GB) 58 B4
Čašniki (BY) 139 K4
Casola (I) 106 D6
Casoja (RO) 160 D5
Casola in Lunigiana (I) 100 C4
Casola Valsenio (I) 100 F4
Casole d'Elsa (I) 99 L6
Casoli (I) 103 J3
Casoria (I) 103 J6
Casoria (I) 104 A3
Casovo (BG) 177 G3
Caspe (E) 114 C5
Cassà de la Selva (E) 115 J4
Cassagnabère-Tournas (F) 93 F4
Cassagnes (F) 93 H1
Cassagnes-Bégonhès (F) 93 K2
Cassano allo Ionio (I) 105 F6
Cassano d'Adda (I) 100 B1
Cassano delle Murge (I) 105 G4
Cassano Spinola (I) 98 F3
Cassel (F) 59 M6
Cassine (I) 98 E3
Cassinelle (I) 98 E3
Cassino (I) 103 H4
Cassis (F) 95 G4
Cassolnovo (I) 98 F2
Cassuéjouls (F) 94 A1
Cast (F) 74 C4
Castà (E) 93 K5
Castà (SK) 91 M3
Castagnaro (I) 100 E2
Castagneto Carducci (I) 100 D6
Castagnito (I) 98 E3
Castagno (I) 100 F4
Castagno, Il (I) 99 K6
Castanet-Tolosan (F) 93 H3
Castanheira de Pêra (P) 116 E3
Castano Primo (I) 98 F1
Castaños, Los (E) 127 F5
Castaños y Trasierra (E) 125 G2
Casteggio (I) 99 G2
Casteição (P) 117 G2
Casteião (E) 113 J5
Castejón del Puente (E) 114 D4
Castejón de Monegros (E) 114 C4
Castejón de Sos (E) 92 E5
Castejón de Valdejasa (E) 114 B4
Castelbajac (F) 93 E4
Castel Baronia (I) 104 D3
Castelbellino (I) 101 H6
Castelbelforte (I) 100 D2
Castelbello-Ciardes (I) 88 D4
Castelbiague (F) 114 E1
Castel Bolognese (I) 101 F4
Castelbuono (I) 109 F2
Castel Castagna (I) 103 H2
Castel d'Aiano (I) 100 E4
Castel d'Ario (I) 100 D2
Casteldarne (I) 88 F4
Castel del Cabra (E) 114 B6
Castel del Giudice (I) 103 J4
Casteldelci (I) 101 G5
Casteldelfino (I) 95 K1
Castel del Monte (I) 103 H3
Castel del Piano (I) 102 D2
Castel del Rio (I) 99 M4
Castel di Casio (I) 100 E4
Castel di Sangro (I) 104 B2
Castel di Tora (I) 103 F3
Castelejo (P) 118 A3
Castelfidardo (I) 101 K6
Castelfiorentino (I) 100 D6
Castelfiorite (E) 114 C4
Castel Focognano (I) 101 F5
Castelforte (I) 103 H5
Castelfranc (F) 93 G1
Castelfranco di Sopra (I) 100 F5
Castelfranco Emilia (I) 100 E3
Castelfranco in Miscano (I) 104 D3
Castelfranco Veneto (I) 88 F6
Castel Frentano (I) 104 B1
Castel Gandolfo (I) 103 F4
Castelginest (F) 93 G3
Castel Giorgio (I) 102 D2
Castel Goffredo (I) 100 C3
Casteljaloux (F) 92 E2
Castel (D) 80 C1
Castell, Es (E) 123 K3
Castella, le (I) 107 H5
Castellabate (I) 106 C2
Castellaftalfo (I) 103 H2
Castellammare del Golfo (I) 108 C1
Castellammare di Stabia (I) 104 B4
Castellamonte (I) 98 D2
Castellana Grotte (I) 105 H4
Castellana Sicula (I) 109 F2
Castellane (F) 95 J3
Castellaneta (I) 105 G4
Castellaneta Marina (I) 105 G5
Castellar (E) 126 D3
Castellarano (I) 99 K3
Castellar de la Frontera (E) 128 D5
Castellar de la Ribera (E) 115 F3
Castellar del Vallès (E) 115 H4
Castellar de n'Hug (E) 115 G3
Castellar de Santiago (E) 126 D2
Castellar de Santisteban (E) 126 D3
Castellarquato (I) 100 B3
Castell'Azzara (I) 102 D2
Castellazzo Bormida (I) 98 F3
Castelldans (E) 114 E5
Castell de Cabres (E) 122 B1
Castell de Castells (E) 122 A5
Castelldefels (E) 115 G5
Castell de Ferro (E) 126 D6
Castelleone (I) 100 B2
Castellfollit de la Roca (E) 115 J3
Castellfollit de Riubregós (E) 115 F4
Castellfort (E) 122 A1
Castelli (I) 103 H3
Castelli = Kaštelir (HR) 164 B4
Castellina in Chianti (I) 99 L6
Castellina Marittima (I) 99 K6
Castell-nedd = Neath (GB) 57 G2
Castellnou (E) 121 H4
Castelló de Farfanya (E) 114 E4
Castelló de la Plana (E) 122 A3
Castelló de Rugat (E) 127 K2
Castelló d'Empúries (E) 115 K3
Castell of Lindsay (GB) 54 A1
Castello di Annone (I) 98 E3
Castello-Molina di Fiemme (I) 88 E5
Castellón de la Plana = Castelló de la Plana (E) 122 A3
Castellón de Rugat = Castelló de Rugat (E) 127 K2
Castellote (E) 114 C6
Castello Tesino (I) 88 F5
Castellserà (E) 114 E4
Castellterçol (E) 115 H4
Castelluccio (I) 103 G1
Castelluccio dei Sauri (I) 104 D3
Castelluccio Inferiore (I) 106 E2
Castell'Umberto (I) 109 G1
Castelluzzo (I) 108 C1
Castel Madama (I) 103 F4
Castel Maggiore (I) 99 L3
Castelmarino (I) 103 J5
Castelmassa (I) 100 D3
Castelmauro (I) 104 C2
Castelmoron-sur-Lot (F) 92 E2
Castelnau-Barbarens (F) 93 F3
Castelnaudary (F) 93 J4
Castelnau-d'Auzan (F) 92 E3
Castelnau-de-Gratecambe (F) 92 F2
Castelnau-de-Lévis (F) 93 J3
Castelnau-de-Mandailles (F) 94 A1
Castelnau-de-Médoc (F) 82 D6
Castelnau-de-Montmiral (F) 93 H3
Castelnau-la-Chapelle (F) 93 G1
Castelnau-Durban (F) 115 F1
Castelnau-Magnoac (F) 93 F4
Castelnau-Montratier-Sainte-Alauzie (F) 93 G2
Castelnau-Picampeau (F) 93 G4
Castelnau-sur-Gupie (F) 92 E1
Castelnou (E) 114 C5
Castelnou (F) 115 J2
Castelnovo di Bassela (E) 115 F3
Castelnovo Bariano (I) 100 E2
Castelnovo di Sotto (I) 100 D3
Castelnovo ne' Monti (I) 99 J4
Castelnuovo Berardenga (I) 99 M6
Castelnuovo Bocca d'Adda (I) 100 B2
Castelnuovo della Daunia (I) 104 D2
Castelnuovo dell'Abate (I) 102 D2
Castelnuovo della Daunia (I) 104 D2
Castelnuovo di Garfagnana (I) 99 J4
Castelnuovo di Val di Cecina (I) 100 D6
Castelnuovo Scrivia (I) 98 F3
Castelo (P) 110 C6
Castelo (P) 116 E2
Castelo Branco (P) 111 F6
Castelo Branco (P) 118 B4
Castelo de Paiva (P) 116 E1
Castelo de Penalva (P) 117 F2
Castelo de Vide (P) 117 G5
Castelo do Neiva (P) 110 B5
Castelões (P) 116 E3
Castelões (P) 116 C2
Castelo Mendo (P) 117 H2
Castelo Rodrigo (P) 117 H2
Castel Porziano (I) 102 E4
Castelraimondo (I) 101 J6
Castel Rigone (I) 101 G6
Castel Ritaldi (I) 103 F2
Castelrotto (I) 88 F4
Castel San Gimignano (I) 99 L6
Castel San Giorgio (I) 104 B4
Castel San Giovanni (I) 99 G2
Castel San Lorenzo (I) 106 D2
Castel San Niccolò (I) 101 F5
Castel San Pietro Terme (I) 99 M4
Castelsantangelo sul Nera (I) 103 G2
Castel Sant'Elia (I) 102 E3
Castelsaraceno (I) 106 E2
Castelsardo (I) 97 C2
Castelsarrasin (F) 93 G2
Castelseras (E) 114 C6
Castelsilano (I) 107 G4
Castelterminì (I) 108 E2
Castelvecchio Subequo (I) 103 H3
Castelvetere in Val Fortore (I) 104 C3
Castelvetrano (I) 108 C2
Castel Viscardo (I) 102 E2
Castel Volturno (I) 104 A3
Castenedolo (I) 87 K7
Castéra-Verduzan (F) 92 E3
Castetpugon (F) 92 D3
Castets (F) 92 B3
Castex (F) 92 E4
Castiadas (I) 97 E5
Castiello de Jaca (E) 92 C5
Castiglioncello (I) 99 K6
Castiglioncello (I) 103 G3
Castiglione d'Adda (I) 99 H2
Castiglione dei Pepoli (I) 99 L4
Castiglione del Lago (I) 101 G6
Castiglione della Pescaia (I) 102 B2
Castiglione delle Stiviere (I) 99 J2
Castiglione di Garfagnana (I) 100 C4
Castiglione di Ravenna (I) 101 G4
Castiglione di Sicilia (I) 109 H2
Castiglione d'Orcia (I) 102 D2
Castiglione Fibocchi (I) 101 F5
Castiglione Fiorentino (I) 101 F6
Castiglione in Teverina (I) 102 E2
Castiglione Messer Marino (I) 104 B2
Castiglione Olona (I) 87 G6
Castiglion Fibocchi (I) 101 F5
Castiglion Fiorentino (I) 101 F6
Castilblanco (E) 118 F5
Castilblanco de los Arroyos (E) 128 C2
Castil de Peones (E) 112 E4
Castilfrío de la Sierra (E) 113 G5
Castilisar (E) 92 B6
Castilleja de la Cuesta (E) 125 G5
Castillejar (E) 126 E4
Castillejo de Iniesta (E) 120 E4
Castillejo de Martín Viejo (E) 117 H2
Castillejo de Mesleón (E) 112 D6
Castillejo de Robledo (E) 112 E5
Castillo de Bayuela (E) 119 G3
Castillo de Castellar (E) 128 D5
Castillo de Garcimuñoz (E) 120 D4
Castillo de las Guardas, El (E) 128 B2
Castillo de Locubín (E) 126 C4
Castillo de Villamalefa (E) 121 H3
Castillon-de-Castets (F) 92 D1
Castillon-en-Couserans (F) 114 F2
Castillon-la-Bataille (F) 92 D1
Castillonnès (F) 92 F1
Castiltierra (E) 112 D6
Castione della Presolana (I) 88 C6
Castions di Strada (I) 89 J6
Castle (SK) 153 M6
Castlebar = Caisleán an Bharraigh (IRL) 60 D4
Castlebay (GB) 50 C6
Castlebellingham (IRL) 61 K4
Castleblayney (IRL) 61 J3
Castlebridge (IRL) 63 K4
Castle Bytham (GB) 55 L5
Castle Caereinion (GB) 58 A2
Castle Cary (GB) 57 K3
Castlecaufield (GB) 52 B5
Castle Combe (GB) 57 K2
Castlecomer (IRL) 63 H3
Castleconnell (IRL) 62 E3
Castlederg (GB) 60 G2
Castlederid (IRL) 61 J6
Castle Donington (GB) 58 E2
Castle Douglas (GB) 53 H5
Castlefinn (IRL) 60 G2
Castleford (GB) 55 K3
Castle Frome (GB) 57 K1
Castlegregory (IRL) 62 B4
Castle Gresley (GB) 55 J5
Castle Hedingham (GB) 59 J4
Castleisland (IRL) 62 D4
Castlemaine (IRL) 62 C4
Castlemartyr (IRL) 62 F5
Castlepollard (IRL) 63 H1
Castlerea (IRL) 60 F4
Castleton (GB) 55 J4
Castletown (GB) 49 B6
Castletown (GBM) 54 C2
Castletown (IRL) 63 H2
Castletownbere (IRL) 62 B5
Castletownroche (IRL) 62 F4
Castletownshend (IRL) 62 D5
Castlewellan (GB) 61 L3
Castrelos (E) 110 B4
Castrillo de Don Juan (E) 112 C5
Castrillo de la Reina (E) 112 E5
Castrillo de la Vega (E) 112 D5
Castrillo de Murcia (E) 112 C4
Castrillo de Sepúlveda (E) 112 D6
Castrillo-Matajudíos (E) 112 C4
Castrillo-Tejeriego (E) 112 C5
Castriz (E) 110 B2
Castro (CH) 87 G5
Castro (E) 110 E2
Castro (I) 107 K2
Castro Caldelas (E) 110 E4
Castro Caldelas (E) 110 D3
Castrobarto (E) 112 E2
Castrocalbón (E) 111 H4
Castrocaro Terme (I) 101 F4
Castrocontrigo (E) 111 G4
Castro Daire (P) 116 F2
Castro de Filabres (E) 127 F5
Castro de Fuentidueña (E) 112 D6
Castro del Rio (E) 125 K3
Castro del Volsci (I) 103 G4
Castro de Rei (E) 110 D3
Castro de Rei (E) 110 E2
Castro de Rei = Castro de Rei (E) 110 D3
Castrofuerte (E) 111 J4
Castrogeriz (E) 112 C4
Castro Laboreiro (P) 110 C4
Castro Marim (P) 124 E5
Castromocho (E) 112 B4
Castromonte (E) 112 A5
Castronuevo (E) 111 H5
Castronuño (E) 111 J6
Castronovo di Sicilia (I) 108 E2
Castropignano (I) 103 K4
Castropodame (E) 111 G3
Castrop-Rauxel (D) 70 D3
Castroreale (I) 109 H1
Castroregio (I) 105 F6
Castros (E) 110 D1
Castro Urdiales (E) 112 E2
Castrov (CZ) 153 H5
Castroverde (E) 110 D2
Castroverde (E) 110 E2
Castroverde de Campos (E) 111 J5
Castroverde de Cerrato (E) 112 C5
Castrovillari (I) 106 F3
Castuera (E) 125 H2
Çat (TR) 193 J3
Cața (RO) 169 J1
Čata (SK) 154 D6
Čatacik (TR) 184 A5
Cataeggio (I) 87 J5
Çatak (TR) 185 F3
Çatak (TR) 185 H5
Çatak (TR) 190 E4
Çatak (TR) 198 E1
Çatak (TR) 199 G2
Çatalağzı (TR) 184 C2
Çatalan (TR) 193 K6
Çatalar (TR) 197 J1
Çatalca (TR) 183 K3
Çatalçam (TR) 190 F1
Çatalçeşme (TR) 185 F6
Çatalçeşme (TR) 193 G3
Catalina (RO) 170 C2
Catalina (RO) 185 G5
Catalina (RO) 170 C2
Çatalköprü (TR) 183 L4
Čatalkőy (TR) 199 F5
Çatallar (TR) 197 H3
Çatalöluk (TR) 197 G3
Çatalpınar (TR) 193 G2
Çatalzeytin (TR) 13 K5
Çatalzeytin (TR) 185 H2
Catane (RO) 168 E6
Catania (I) 109 H2
Catanzaro (I) 107 G5
Catanzaro Marina (I) 107 G5
Catarroja (E) 121 H5
Cățcău (RO) 161 H3
Catelau-Cambrésis, Le (F) 68 F6
Catenanuova (I) 109 G2
Caterham (GB) 59 G5
Cateri (F) 96 E3
Catel, l' = Caten (F) 96 D3
Caterinovca (MD) 163 H2
Catenhangr (F) 96 F4
Cathair na Mart = Westport (IRL) 60 C4
Cati (E) 122 B2
Catl = Cati (E) 122 B2
Čătlașu (RO) 169 L3
Čatići (BIH) 173 H1
Catignano (I) 103 H3
Čătina (RO) 169 L3
Catino, Campo (I) 103 G4
Catignano (I) 103 H3
Çatkese (TR) 185 H4
Çatköy (TR) 193 H5
Çatkuyu (TR) 191 J3
Catoira (E) 110 B3
Čatören (TR) 192 D3
Catral (E) 127 J3
Catrine (GB) 52 G3
Cattenom (F) 78 E3
Catterick Bridge (GB) 53 M6
Catterick Garrison (GB) 53 M6
Cattolica (I) 101 H5
Cattolica Eraclea (I) 108 D3
Catus (F) 93 G1
Căuaș (RO) 160 F2
Caudebec-en-Caux (F) 76 C2
Caudete (E) 127 J2
Caudete de las Fuentes (E) 121 F4
Caudiel (E) 121 G4
Caudrot (F) 92 D1
Caudry (F) 68 E6
Caujac (F) 93 G4
Caulnes (F) 75 G4
Caulonia (I) 107 F6
Caumont (F) 93 F3
Caumont (F) 114 F1
Caumont-sur-Aure (F) 75 K2
Caumont-sur-Durance (F) 94 E3
Caunes-Minervois (F) 93 K4
Cauro (F) 96 D5
Căușeni (MD) 163 J5
Caussade (F) 93 G2
Cauterets (F) 114 D2
Cava (BIH) 166 G4
Cavadinești (RO) 163 J2
Cava d'Aliga (I) 109 G4
Cava de' Tirreni (I) 104 C4
Cavadinești (RO) 170 G1
Cavaglià (I) 98 E2
Cavaillon (F) 94 F3
Cavalaire-sur-Mer (F) 95 J4
Cavaleiro (P) 124 B4
Cavalerie, La (F) 93 L2
Cavalese (I) 88 E5
Cavalieri (I) 103 H3
Cavallermaggiore (I) 95 L1
Cavallino (I) 101 G1
Cavallino (I) 105 K5
Cavan (IRL) 60 H4
Cavarzere (I) 101 G2
Cavazzo (I) 89 H6
Cavdarhisar (TR) 191 H2
Cavdar (TR) 190 D5
Cavdar (TR) 192 D4
Cavdarhisar (TR) 191 H2
Cavdarlı (TR) 183 M4
Cavdarlı (TR) 193 K6
Cavdır (TR) 198 F2
Cave (I) 103 F4
Cave del Predil (I) 89 J5
Caveira (P) 129 a3
Cavernes (F) 94 D3
Cavezzo (I) 100 D3
Cavignac (F) 82 E6
Çavuşköy (TR) 183 L4
Cavo (I) 102 A2
Cavour (I) 98 C3
Cavriago (I) 99 J3
Cavriglia (I) 100 E6
Cavtat (HR) 174 D3
Çavuş (TR) 193 H3
Çavuşçu (TR) 192 C4
Çavuşçugöl (TR) 192 C4
Çavuşköy (TR) 183 J4
Çavuşlu (TR) 185 H5
Çavuşlu (TR) 199 J2
Çavuşoğlu (TR) 184 F3
Cawdor (GB) 51 K4
Cawood (GB) 55 K3
Cawsand (GB) 56 F6
Caxias (P) 116 C6
Caxton (GB) 59 G3
Çay (TR) 192 B3
Çayağazi (TR) 182 E5
Çayağazı (TR) 183 H3
Çayağazi (TR) 184 B3
Çayağazı (TR) 193 H2
Çayan (TR) 185 H5
Çaybaşı (TR) 185 K4
Çaybaşı (TR) 190 C4
Çayboyu (TR) 190 E6
Çayçınge (TR) 191 G2
Çaycuma (TR) 184 D3
Cayeux-sur-Mer (F) 68 B6
Çayhan (TR) 193 H5
Çayhisar (TR) 197 E2
Çayırbağı (TR) 192 D5
Çayiçi (TR) 193 J2
Çayır (TR) 197 E1
Çayırbağı (TR) 191 K3
Çayırbaşı (TR) 191 J2
Çayırbaşı (TR) 192 D3
Çayırhan (TR) 184 C5
Çayırköy (TR) 185 J2
Çayırlar (TR) 185 F4
Çayırlı (TR) 193 J4
Çayırolluk (TR) 183 J6
Çayırova (TR) 183 M5
Çayırözü (TR) 193 K4
Çayıryazı (TR) 191 K4
Çaykışla (TR) 192 B3
Çayköy (TR) 183 K5
Çaylakköy (TR) 184 A5
Caylar, Le (F) 94 B3
Çaylıca (TR) 185 F4
Çaylıca (TR) 185 H2
Caylus (F) 93 H2
Çaypınar (TR) 182 E6
Cayres (F) 94 B1
Çayüstü (TR) 191 J4
Çayyaka (TR) 183 H6
Çayyaka (TR) 185 H5
Çayyolu (TR) 184 E6
Cazalegas (E) 119 G3
Cazalla de la Sierra (E) 125 H4
Cazals (F) 93 H2
Căzănești (MD) 163 H3
Căzănești (RO) 170 E4
Căzănești (RO) 171 G3
Cazaubon (F) 92 E3
Cazaux (F) 92 B1
Cazavet (F) 114 F1
Cazères (F) 93 G4
Cazères-sur-l'Adour (F) 92 D3
Cazes-Mondenard (F) 93 G2
Cazin (BIH) 165 F5
Čazma (HR) 165 H3
Cazorla (E) 126 D4
Cazouls-lès-Béziers (F) 93 L4
Ca' Zuliani (I) 101 G3
Cea (E) 111 K4
Cea (San Cristóbal de Cea) = Cea (San Cristovo de Cea) (E) 110 D4
Cea (San Cristovo de Cea) (E) 110 D4
Ceadea (E) 111 G5
Ceadîr-Lunga (MD) 171 H1
Ceahlău (RO) 162 B4
Ceamurlia de Jos (RO) 171 H4
Ceamurlia de Sus (RO) 171 H4
Ceanannas (IRL) 61 J4
Ceann Toirc = Kanturk (IRL) 62 E4
Ceann Trá (IRL) 62 B4
Ceanu Mare (RO) 161 H4
Ceapach Choinn = Cappoquin (IRL) 63 G4
Ceatalchioi (RO) 171 H3
Ceatharlach (IRL) 63 H3
Ceaucé (F) 75 K4
Cebas (E) 126 E4
Cebolla (E) 119 G4
Cebolleros (E) 112 E3
Cebrail (TR) 191 H2
Cebrail (TR) 192 C3
Cebreros (E) 119 H3
Cebrones del Río (E) 111 H4
Cebrykove (UA) 163 L4
Ceccano (I) 103 G4
Čečava (BIH) 165 J6
Ceccavo (BIH) 165 J6
Čečejovce (SK) 155 J4
Čečeli (TR) 193 H3
Čečel'nyk (UA) 163 J2
Čechanivka (UA) 163 J4
Čechtice (CZ) 153 H4
Čechtín (CZ) 153 J5
Cécina (I) 99 K6
Cecina (SRB) 174 D2
Ceckley (GB) 58 D2
Ceclavín (E) 118 C4
Cecos (E) 111 F2
Čecuni (MNE) 174 C3
Čecylówka (PL) 148 D2
Ceda (BY) 144 F2
Čedasai (LT) 136 B1
Cedeira (E) 110 C1
Cedillo (E) 117 G4
Cedillo del Condado (E) 119 J3
Cedrillas (E) 121 G3
Cedros (P) 129 b1
Cedynia (PL) 67 L5
Cée (E) 110 A3
Cefa (RO) 160 D4
Cefalù (I) 109 F2
Cefn-coed-y-cymmer (GB) 57 H2
Cefn-mawr (GB) 54 F5
Ceggia (I) 89 H6
Cegléd (H) 159 J3
Ceglie Messapica (I) 105 J4
Cegłów (PL) 148 E1
Cegrane (MK) 174 E5
Cehal (RO) 160 F3
Cehăluț (RO) 160 F3
Cehegín (E) 127 G3
Cehei (RO) 161 F3
Čeheriv (BG) 176 D4
Čehnice (CZ) 152 F5
Cehovanka (UA) 163 J5
Cehov (RUS) 142 D1
Cehu Silvaniei (RO) 161 G3
Ceica (RO) 160 E4
Ceikiai (LT) 136 F3
Ceilhes-et-Rocozels (F) 93 L3
Ceillac (F) 95 J1
Ceinewydd = New Quay (GB) 56 F1
Ceinos de Campos (E) 112 A4
Ceintrey (F) 78 E4
Ceira (P) 116 E3
Ceivães (P) 110 C4
Čejč (CZ) 153 J6
Čejkov (SK) 155 K5
Čejkovice (CZ) 91 L2
Čejkovice (CZ) 153 J5
Čekanje (MNE) 173 J5
Čekcyn (PL) 141 K3
Čekerek (TR) 13 L5
Čekirdekli (TR) 190 E2
Čekirge (TR) 183 G2
Čekirge (TR) 183 L5
Čekirgeli (TR) 137 K3
Čekiški (LT) 137 K3
Čeków (PL) 147 J2
Čekšino (RUS) 7 W6
Cela (BIH) 165 F5
Čela (BIH) 165 H5
Čela (P) 110 C4
Celadas, El 121 F3
Celadas (E) 121 F3
Čeladná (CZ) 154 C2
Celákovice (CZ) 153 G1
Celalive (TR) 182 D2
Celalliye (TR) 193 J5
Celano (I) 103 H3
Celanova (E) 110 D4
Čelarevo (SRB) 166 E3
Celaru (RO) 169 G5
Celbridge (IRL) 63 J2
Čelčice (CZ) 153 J6
Čelé (TR) 184 C1
Celebi (TR) 182 B4
Çelebi (TR) 193 G2
Çelebiç (BIH) 172 G3
Çelebiç (BIH) 174 A2
Čelepköy (TR) 183 J3
Čelerina (CH) 88 B4
Čeleştimen (TR) 182 B4
Čelič (BIH) 166 C4
Celico (I) 107 F4
Čelikhan (TR) 13 M6
Čelikovo Polje (BIH) 173 J3
Čelina (CZ) 152 E4
Celinac (BIH) 165 J5
Čelinac Donji (BIH) 165 J5
Celiny (PL) 147 L4
Celja (LV) 135 L1
Celje (SLO) 164 E2
Čelkow (PL) 148 D1
Cella (E) 121 F3
Čelldömölk (H) 91 M5
Celle (D) 66 C6
Celle di Bulgheria (I) 104 D5
Celle-en-Morvan, La (F) 84 F2
Celle-Guénand, La (F) 83 G3
Celle Ligure (I) 98 F4
Cellere (I) 102 D3
Celles (B) 68 E5
Celles (B) 69 J6
Celles (F) 83 F5
Celle-Saint-Avant, La (F) 83 G2
Celles-sur-Belle (F) 82 E4
Celles-sur-Plaine (F) 78 F5
Cellino Attanasio (I) 103 H2
Cellino San Marco (I) 107 J2
Celmaņi (RUS) 7 U4
Celon (F) 83 H3
Čelopeč (BG) 176 D3
Čelopečene (BG) 177 J1
Čelopek (MK) 174 F5
Čelopek (MK) 174 E5
Celorico da Beira (P) 118 B2
Celorico de Basto (P) 110 D6
Celra (E) 115 J3
Çeltek (TR) 191 H5
Çeltek (TR) 185 F4
Çeltik (TR) 192 C2
Çeltikçi (TR) 185 G4
Çeltikçi (TR) 184 D5
Çeltikçi (TR) 191 J5
Çeltikçi (TR) 191 H5
Çeltikçi (TR) 191 J5
Çeltikçi (TR) 191 J5
Çeltikli (TR) 199 L6
Čembra (I) 88 E5
Čemerivci (UA) 150 C5
Čemerno (MNE) 155 K4
Čemerno (MNE) 174 A2
Čemernyci (UA) 156 G2
Čemerovec (BG) 185 G2
Čemilköy (TR) 193 J3
Čemilköy (TR) 193 J3
Čeminac (HR) 166 C2
Cemmaes Road (GB) 54 E5
Čemny Les (BY) 139 D5
Čemorsko (BG) 175 J6
Čemoz (BG) 178 E5
Čemoz Cille Móire = Kilmore Quay (IRL) 56 A1
Cenad (RO) 167 G1
Cenade (RO) 169 G1
Cenaja (E) 127 G3
Cenarro (E) 112 E3
Cencenighe Agordino (I) 88 F5
Čendik (TR) 191 J5
Čene (TR) 185 J3
Čenei (RO) 167 G2
Čenekóy (TR) 182 D3
Čenes de la Vega (E) 126 C5
Čeneselli (I) 99 L2
Čenevieres (F) 93 H2
Čengeller (TR) 184 D3
Čengelli (TR) 192 E4
Čenger (TR) 198 C2
Čengio (I) 98 E4
Čeniceiro (E) 112 F4
Čenicientos (E) 119 H3
Čenizate (E) 120 E5
Čenon (F) 92 D1
Čenovo (BG) 176 E5
Čenovo (BG) 176 E1
Čenserey (F) 84 F2
Čenta (SRB) 167 G5
Čentallo (I) 95 L1
Čentellas (E) 115 H4
Čentenaros, Los (E) 126 E3
Čentenillo, El (E) 126 C3
Čento (I) 100 E3
Čentola (I) 106 D2
Čentovalli (CH) 87 G5
Čenturipe (I) 109 G2
Čepagatti (I) 103 J3
Čepelare (BG) 180 F1
Čepeliivka (UA) 150 D4
Čepigova (MK) 178 E2
Čepikuće (HR) 173 G4
Čepin (HR) 166 C2
Čepinci (BG) 176 C5
Čepleniţa (RO) 162 D4
Čepli (RUS) 135 N6
Čepljuki (BY) 138 G1
Čepni (TR) 185 G3
Čepni (TR) 191 J3
Čepões (P) 117 F1
Čepos (P) 116 F3
Čepovan (SLO) 89 K5
Čepoy (F) 77 G6
Čeprano (I) 103 G4
Čepreni (I) 103 H4
Čeptura de Jos (RO) 170 C3
Čepukai (LT) 138 E2
Čepure (SRB) 167 H6
Čer (MK) 174 F6
Čerabury (BY) 144 H2
Čerahovka (BY) 145 N2
Čeraino (I) 100 D1
Čeralije (HR) 165 K3
Čerami (I) 109 G2
Čeran (F) 92 F3
Čerani (BIH) 166 A4
Čeranica Gora (MNE) 173 K4
Čerano (I) 98 F2
Čerans-Foulletourte (F) 76 A6
Čerasi (I) 107 H5
Čerasuolo (E) 77 G5
Čerasupole (BY) 139 H2
Čerasu (RO) 169 L3
Čerat (RO) 168 F5
Čeravë (AL) 178 D3
Čerbaia (I) 99 L5
Čerbăl (RO) 167 L2
Čerbère (F) 93 L6
Čerca, La (E) 113 E3
Čercadillo (E) 120 C1
Čercal (P) 116 D5
Čercal (P) 124 B4
Čerčany (CZ) 146 B6
Čercedilla (E) 119 J2
Čercemaggiore (I) 104 C3
Čerchiara di Calabria (I) 105 F6
Čerčiler (TR) 184 E3
Čerčiler (TR) 185 K3
Čercs (E) 115 G3
Čercy-la-Tour (F) 84 E3
Čerda (I) 108 E2
Čerdanyola del Vallès (E) 115 H5
Čerdedo (E) 110 C3
Čerdeira (P) 116 E3
Čerdeira (P) 118 B2
Čerdon (F) 76 F6
Čere (LV) 132 F3
Čerea (I) 100 E2
Čerecinos de Campos (E) 111 J5
Čeredell (I) 98 E3
Čereded (F) 98 E3
Čereja (E) 112 F3
Čered (H) 159 J1
Čerekwica (PL) 154 B1
Čeréla-Ronde (F) 83 H2
Čerella (E) 112 F3
Čerenkov (UA) 150 C4
Čerenkov (UA) 151 H3
Čerental (BY) 139 D6
Čerenčiy (RUS) 135 N2
Čerepin (BY) 143 N1
Čerepovec (RUS) 7 U6
Čerepovo (BG) 182 B1
Čerepovo (UA) 151 K5
Čeres (I) 98 C2
Čeresa (I) 98 C2
Čeresa (I) 103 H4
Čeresiura (RO) 160 C3
Čereso (I) 160 E3
Čereşole Reale (I) 86 D7
Čeresova (BG) 175 K2
Čereşova (RO) 161 G3
Čeresova (BG) 176 C4
Čerevacha (UA) 144 B6
Čerević (SRB) 166 E3
Čerevisti (BG) 184 G5
Čerevka (UA) 145 H6
Čerezal (E) 118 D3
Čerezal de Peñahorcada (E) 117 H1
Čerezo de Abajo (E) 112 D6
Čerezo de Riotirón (E) 112 E4
Čerezos, Los (E) 113 G5
Čerfontaine (B) 69 G6
Čergău Mare (RO) 169 F1
Čerhenice (CZ) 146 C5
Čeriale (I) 98 E4
Čerignola (I) 104 E3
Čerikli (TR) 185 H6
Čérilly (F) 84 C3
Čerin (BIH) 173 G3
Čerin (SK) 154 E4
Čerisiers (F) 77 H5
Čerisy-la-Forêt (F) 75 K2
Čerisy-la-Salle (F) 75 J3
Čeritkale (TR) 185 G6
Čeritter (TR) 193 K6
Čeritmümini (TR) 185 G6
Čeritsay (TR) 191 J4
Čerizay (F) 82 D3
Čerizols (F) 114 F1
Čerja (BIH) 165 F4
Čerkassi (RUS) 174 D4
Čerkassy (UA) 150 G1
Čerkasov (RUS) 37 L3
Čerkasy (UA) 150 G1
Čerkes (TR) 13 K5
Čerkeş (TR) 184 E4
Čerkeşli (TR) 183 M4
Čerkezköy (TR) 183 J3
Čerkezmüsellim (TR) 181 L2
Čerkizovo (RUS) 7 V4
Čerkna (SLO) 164 F3
Čerkno (SLO) 164 D3
Čerknica (SLO) 164 E3
Čerkovna (BG) 176 C1
Čerkovište (BG) 170 E6
Čerkovnjak (BG) 176 F4
Čerkovo (BY) 138 G1
Čerkovo (SLO) 165 F1
Čerkwica (PL) 67 N2
Čerler (E) 92 F5
Čerlina (RO) 161 F5
Čermë e poshtëme (AL) 178 B2
Čermei (RO) 160 D4
Čermeno (HR) 174 D4
Čermik (TR) 13 N6
Čermna (SLO) 165 F1
Čermjanki (RUS) 174 D4
Černa (HR) 166 C4
Černa (RO) 170 G1
Černa (RO) 169 E1
Černa (HR) 166 C4
Černa (SLO) 165 F1
Černache do Bonjardim (P) 116 E4
Černadoi (I) 88 F5
Černá Gora (BG) 176 D4
Černá Hora (CZ) 153 H4
Černá Hora (BG) 176 E3
Černaja Rečka (RUS) 37 O4
Černat (RO) 169 M2
Černavodă (RO) 170 G5
Černava (RUS) 9 P3
Černavoda (RO) 171 G4
Černavčyci (BY) 144 C2
Černay (F) 78 G6
Černay-en-Dormois (F) 77 L3
Černay-la-Ville (F) 76 E4
Černčice (CZ) 152 F2
Černcice (CZ) 153 G3
Černé Voda (CZ) 146 C5
Černecovo (RUS) 135 M2
Černeni (RUS) 139 L1
Černegula (I) 106 B2
Černelavci (SLO) 165 G1
Černelica (BG) 170 G2
Černelnica (UA) 150 A6
Černelyca (UA) 150 A6
Černeni = Schwarze Wasser (D) 163 H3
Černeni (I) 98 F2
Černeux (F) 77 H4
Černevo (UA) 149 H6
Černevo (BG) 177 J4
Černevo (RUS) 135 N2
Černevo (RUS) 135 O3
Černica (BG) 177 G3
Černica (RO) 170 C5
Černičevo (BG) 176 E6
Černičevo (BG) 180 F1
Černihiv (UA) 13 H3
Černihiv (UA) 150 F3
Černik (HR) 165 J4
Černik (SK) 154 B5
Černiki (RUS) 181 H1
Černík (BG) 145 K3
Černín (SK) 155 H3
Černin (BY) 145 K3
Černí Osam (BG) 176 C3
Černí Vrah (BG) 176 F3
Černiv (UA) 156 F3
Černivci (UA) 157 J5
Černivci (UA) 162 G1
Černi Vit (BG) 176 B3
Černi Vrah (BG) 175 H1
Černi Vrah (BG) 177 H4
Černjachiv (UA) 151 H3
Černjachiv (UA) 151 H3
Černjahovsk (RUS) 142 F1
Černjatin (UA) 151 H4
Černjatyn (BG) 175 L4
Černobbio (I) 87 H6
Černoglavci (BG) 177 G1
Černogorci (RUS) 163 H6
Černogor (BG) 176 B4
Černogorovo (BG) 177 H3
Černomorec (BG) 177 J4
Černomorski (RUS) 135 L1
Černomorsk (UA) 163 H5
Černomorsk (BG) 177 K1
Černomorec (BG) 177 J4
Černon (F) 77 K4
Černon (F) 85 J4
Černon (F) 95 G2
Černovo (BG) 176 D5
Černovoskovo (BG) 177 H2
Černovkovo (BG) 177 K1
Černovorki (RUS) 163 C3
Černoz (UA) 151 H3
Černoz (BG) 146 A6
Černosin (CZ) 152 C4
Černozemelsk (RUS) 131 O2
Černucy (CZ) 73 L5
Černychovo (RUS) 157 J5
Černovo (UA) 151 H3
Černovice (CZ) 153 G5
Černovo (CZ) 145 H6
Černovka (RUS) 131 O2
Černuc (CZ) 73 L5
Černychivci (UA) 150 B4
Černy-en-Laonnois (F) 77 J3
Černyn (UA) 151 L4
Černyšovo (RUS) 135 N4
Cerollera, La (E) 114 C6
Cerova (SRB) 175 J2
Cerovac (SRB) 167 G5
Cerova Korija (BG) 176 E2
Cerovica (SRB) 175 H1
Cerovlje (HR) 101 L2
Cerovo (BG) 175 K2
Cerovo (BG) 176 B4
Cerovo (SK) 154 E5
Cerpessa (RUS) 135 L4
Cerqueto (I) 102 E2
Cerralbo (E) 118 C2
Cerreto d'Esi (I) 101 H6
Cerreto Guidi (I) 100 D5
Cerreto Sannita (I) 103 K5
Cerrigydrudion (GB) 54 E4
Cërrik (AL) 178 B2
Cerrina Monferrato (I) 98 E2
Cerro al Volturno (I) 103 J4
Cerro de Andévalo, El (E) 125 F4
Cerro Muriano (E) 126 E1
Cerro Veronese (I) 87 M6
Čersk (BY) 149 J2
Čertaldo (I) 100 E5
Čerte (TR) 191 G2
Čerteju de Sus (RO) 161 F6
Čertejul (RO) 170 F1
Čerteze (RO) 156 D6
Čerteze, Huta- (RO) 156 D6
Čertež (SK) 154 E3
Čertižne (SK) 155 K3
Čertov (SK) 154 C3
Červa (P) 110 D6
Červantes = San Román (E) 110 E3
Červara (P) 110 D6
Červarezza (I) 100 C4
Červaro (I) 104 A3
Červatos de la Cueza (E) 112 B4
Červen (BG) 176 C5
Červen (BG) 176 F1
Červen' (BY) 9 L3
Červenaké (AL) 178 D3
Červenakovo (BG) 176 F3
Červena Mogila (BG) 175 K3
Červena Rečice (CZ) 153 H5
Červena Skala (SK) 154 G4
Červená Voda (BG) 169 L6
Červená Voda (CZ) 153 L3
Červen Brjag (BG) 176 B2
Červenci (BG) 177 H1
Červené Janovice (CZ) 146 C6
Červenia (RO) 169 J6
Červený Kameň (SK) 154 C3
Červený Kostelec (CZ) 153 K3
Cervera (E) 115 F4
Cervera (E) 115 G4
Cervera de Buitrago (E) 120 A2
Cervera de la Cañada (E) 113 H6
Cervera del Llano (E) 120 D4
Cervera del Río Alhama (E) 113 H4
Cervera de los Montes (E) 119 G3
Cervera de Maestrat = Cervera de Maestrat (E) 121 J3
Cervera de Maestrat (E) 121 J3
Cervera de Pisuerga (E) 111 K3
Cervere (I) 98 D3
Cerveseina (I) 98 G2
Cerveteri (I) 102 E4
Cervia (I) 101 G4
Cervià = Cervià de les Garrigues (E) 114 E5
Cervià de les Garrigues (E) 114 E5
Cervià de Ter (E) 115 J3
Cervignano del Friuli (I) 89 J6
Cervinara (I) 104 B3
Cervione (F) 96 E4
Cervione = Cervione (F) 96 E4
Cervo (E) 110 E1
Cervo (I) 98 E5
Cervoedy (RUS) 139 L1
Červona Hrebłja = Popova Hreblja (UA) 163 J2
Červona Motovylivka = Motovylivka (UA) 151 L3
Červona Volja (UA) 150 E2
Červone (UA) 151 H4
Červone (UA) 163 K3
Červonoarmijs'k = Pulyny (UA) 151 G3
Červonoarmijs'k = Radyvyliv (UA) 157 H1
Červonoarmijs'ke = Kubej (UA) 171 H2
Červonograd = Červonohrad (UA) 149 K5
Červonohrad (UA) 149 K5
Červonosilka (BY) 151 H5
Červonoslobodymyrivka = Mychajlivka (UA) 163 M4
Červonoznamjanka = Znamjanka (UA) 163 L4
Červonyj (UA) 151 L5
Červonyj Jar (UA) 171 J2
Červonyj Kut = Comyj Kut (UA) 163 L4
Červonyj Orač = Semenivka (UA) 163 L3
Cerzeto (I) 106 F3
Cesana Torinese (I) 85 L7
Cesano (I) 101 J5
Cesano Boscone (I) 87 H7
Cesaro (I) 109 G2
Cesarica (HR) 164 E5
Cesaró (I) 109 G2
Cesarzowice (PL) 146 F3
Česavlja (BY) 144 C2
Česavlja (BY) 143 L3
Česenatico (I) 101 G4
Česiljava (BY) 138 F3
Česis (LV) 133 L3
Česká Bělá (CZ) 153 J4
Česká Kamenice (CZ) 146 A4
Česká Kubice (CZ) 81 H2
Česká Lípa (CZ) 146 B4
Česká Metuje (CZ) 146 E4
Česká Skalice (CZ) 153 K3
Česká Třebová (CZ) 153 K4
České Budějovice (CZ) 81 L3
České Libchavy (CZ) 146 E5
České Velenice (CZ) 153 G6
Český Brod (CZ) 153 G3
Český Dub (CZ) 153 G3
Český Krumlov (CZ) 90 F2
Český Těšín (CZ) 154 D2
Česma (TR) 189 H3
Česmealti (TR) 189 H3
Česme (TR) 189 H3
Česmeciik (TR) 192 D4
Česmedeşi (TR) 193 K6
Česmelı (TR) 183 F2
Česmelisebil (TR) 185 J3
Česnava (BY) 138 E6
Čespedal (E) 118 D2
Čespedosa (E) 117 K2
Čessalto (I) 89 H6
Česse (F) 77 L2
Česselon-sur-Orb (F) 93 L4
Česseford (GB) 53 L2
Česseras (F) 93 K4
Česses (F) 77 G4
Česson (F) 74 F3
Česson-Sévigné (F) 75 H4
Čestepe (TR) 190 D5
Čestimensko (BG) 170 E6
Čestin (CZ) 153 H4
Čestobrodica (SRB) 166 F6
Četa (RO) 160 F4
Četari (RO) 160 D3
Četate (RO) 161 H3
Četate (RO) 168 E2
Četate (RO) 168 E5
Četate de Baltă (RO) 161 J5
Četăţeni (RO) 169 J3
Četibeli (TR) 196 D1
Četina (E) 113 H6
Četina (HR) 172 D2
Četince (TR) 192 B4
Četingrad (HR) 164 F4
Četinje (MNE) 173 J5
Četirci (BG) 175 J4
Četirci (RO) 169 K5
Četmi (TR) 198 E2
Četon (F) 76 C5
Četona (I) 102 D2
Četraro (I) 106 E3
Čeuaşu de Câmpie (RO) 161 K4
Čeuta (E) 128 D6
Čeuti (E) 127 H3
Čeva (I) 98 E4
Čevetjärvi = Sevettijärvi (FIN) 19 L4
Čevico de la Torre (E) 112 C5
Čevico Navero (E) 112 C5
Čevins (F) 95 M1
Čevio (CH) 87 G5
Čevizli (TR) 182 D3
Čevizli (TR) 191 K2
Čevizli (TR) 192 C6
Čevizli (TR) 193 K5
Čevizli (TR) 199 G5
Čevizlik (TR) 191 J5
Čevlik (TR) 184 C5
Čevo (MNE) 173 J4
Čewice (PL) 141 J2
Čewków (PL) 149 G5
Čeyhan (TR) 13 L7
Čeylan (TR) 197 G2
Čeylanköy (TR) 177 H5
Čeyrat (F) 84 B5
Čeyzériat (F) 85 H4
Čézanne, Refuge (F) 85 K7
Čezieni (RO) 169 G5
Chaam (NL) 69 H3
Chabanais (F) 83 G5
Chabanière (F) 85 G5
Chabeuil (F) 85 G7
Chabeuil (F) 95 F1
Chablis (F) 84 F1
Chabówka (PL) 147 L3
Chábľe, Le (CH) 86 D5
Chabris (F) 77 J6
Chabrolche (F) 84 E5
Chabris (F) 83 J2
Chacim (P) 110 F6
Chač'koúcy (BY) 143 L4
Chadzilon (BY) 143 M3
Chaffois (F) 85 K3
Chagey (F) 79 J6
Chagford (GB) 57 G4
Chagny (F) 85 G3
Chailland (F) 75 K4
Chaillé-les-Marais (F) 82 C4
Chailles (F) 76 D6
Chailley (F) 77 J5
Chailly-en-Gâtinais (F) 76 G6
Chailly-sur-Armançon (F) 84 F2
Chaintrix-Bierges (F) 77 K4
Chaise-Dieu, La (F) 84 E6
Chaize-Giraud, La (F) 82 B3
Chaize-le-Vicomte, La (F) 82 C3
Chajew (PL) 147 J2
Chalabre (F) 115 H2
Chalais (F) 82 F6
Chalamera (E) 114 D4
Chalamer'e (BY) 139 L2
Chalamont (F) 85 H5
Chalampé (F) 79 J6
Chalča (UA) 151 M4
Chale (GB) 57 M4
Chalet-du-Gioberney (F) 95 H1
Chalets-de-Laval (F) 85 L6
Chalette-sur-Loing (F) 77 G6
Chalindrey (F) 78 C6
Chalivoy-Milon (F) 83 L3
Challacombe (GB) 57 G3
Challain-la-Potherie (F) 75 J5
Challans (F) 82 B3
Challes-les-Eaux (F) 86 A6
Challock (GB) 59 J5
Challuy (F) 84 D3
Châlmazel-Jeansagnière (F) 84 E5
Chalmazel (F) 84 E5
Chalonnes-sur-Loire (F) 75 K6
Châlons-en-Champagne (F) 77 K4
Châlons-sur-Marne = Châlons-en-Champagne (F) 77 K4
Chalon-sur-Saône (F) 85 G3
Chalopenićy (BY) 139 J4
Chalo-Saint-Mars (F) 76 F5
Chalupki (PL) 147 J6
Chalupy (PL) 141 L1
Châlus (F) 83 G5
Cham (CH) 87 G3
Cham (D) 81 H2
Chamagnieu (F) 85 H5
Chambéret (F) 83 J5
Chambéria (F) 85 J4
Chambéry (F) 85 J6
Chambilly (F) 84 F4
Chamblet (F) 83 L4
Chambley-Bussières (F) 78 D3
Chambly (F) 76 F3
Chambois (F) 75 M3
Chambolle-Musigny (F) 85 G2
Chambon-la-Forêt (F) 76 F6
Chambon-Sainte-Croix (F) 83 J4
Chambon-sur-Lignon, Le (F) 84 F6
Chambon-sur-Voueize (F) 84 B4
Chambord (F) 76 D6
Chamborêt (F) 83 H4
Chambost-Allières (F) 84 G5
Chambray (F) 76 D3
Chambre, la (F) 85 K6
Chamonix-Mont-Blanc (F) 86 C6
Chamonix-sur-Gelon (F) 85 B6
Chamoux-sur-Gelon (F) 85 B6
Chamoy (F) 77 J5
Champagnac-le-Vieux (F) 84 E6
Champagnole (F) 76 B5
Champagne (F) 75 M5
Champagne-en-Valromey (F) 85 J5
Champagne-Mouton (F) 83 F5
Champagne-Saint-Hilaire (F) 83 F4
Champagne-sur-Seine (F) 77 G5
Champdeniers (F) 82 E3
Champagnole (F) 86 A4
Champagnolles (F) 82 D5
Champagny-en-Vanoise (F) 86 C7
Champaubert (F) 77 J4
Champdeniers-Saint-Denis (F) 82 E4
Champdieu (F) 84 F5
Champ-du-Feu (F) 79 H5
Champeaux (F) 77 H4
Champéry (CH) 86 C5
Champigny-sur-Veude (F) 83 F2
Champlitte (F) 78 D5
Champrond-en-Gâtine (F) 76 C5
Champs-sur-Tarentaine-Marchal (F) 84 B6
Champtoceaux (F) 75 J6
Champvans (F) 85 J2
Chamrousse (F) 95 G1
Chanac (F) 94 B2
Chança, A (Cotobade) (E) 110 C4
Chanas (F) 85 G6
Chancelade (F) 83 G6
Chanceaux (F) 85 G2
Chandrexa (Chandrexa de Queixa) (E) 110 E4
Chandrexa de Queixa = Chandrexa (Chandrexa de Queixa) (E) 110 E4
Chaniers (F) 82 D5
Chantada (E) 110 D3
Chantelle (F) 84 D4
Chantonnay (F) 82 C3
Chantrans (F) 85 K2
Chantilly (F) 76 F3
Chaource (F) 77 J6
Chapareillan (F) 85 J6
Chapelle-en-Vercors, La (F) 85 H7
Chapelle-la-Reine, La (F) 76 G5
Chapelle-Royale (F) 76 D5
Chapelle-Saint-Luc, La (F) 77 J5
Chapel-en-le-Frith (GB) 55 J4
Chapelle-sur-Erdre, La (F) 82 C2
Chapelle-Vendômoise, La (F) 76 D6
Chapinería (E) 119 H3
Charavines (F) 85 H6
Charbonnières-les-Bains (F) 85 G5
Charbowo (PL) 141 H5
Charches (E) 126 E5
Chard (GB) 57 J4
Chardstock (GB) 57 J4
Charenton-du-Cher (F) 83 L3
Charité-sur-Loire, La (F) 84 D2
Charkeia (TR) 199 G5
Charlieu (F) 84 F4
Charlbury (GB) 57 M2
Charleroi (B) 69 G6
Charlestown (IRL) 60 E4
Charlestown of Aberlour (GB) 51 L5
Charleval (F) 76 D3
Charleville (IRL) 62 E4
Charleville-Mézières (F) 77 L2
Charlieu (F) 84 F4
Charlottenberg (S) 40 B3
Charlton on Trent (GB) 55 L4
Charly (F) 77 H4
Charmes (F) 78 F5
Charmey (CH) 85 M3
Charmont (F) 77 K4
Charny (F) 77 H6
Charolles (F) 84 F4
Chârost (F) 83 K3
Charras (F) 82 F5
Charroux (F) 83 F4
Charsfield (GB) 68 A2
Charsznica (PL) 148 A5

Chartres (F) 76 E5
Chartre-sur-le-Loir, La (F) 76 C6
Charytancy (BY) 139 K4
Charytonivka (UA) 151 J3
Charzykowy (PL) 141 J3
Châs de Tavares (P) 118 A2
Chassaing, le (F) 83 J6
Chassant (F) 76 D5
Chasseneuil-sur-Bonnieure (F) 83 F5
Chassepierre (B) 78 C2
Chasseradès (F) 94 C1
Chassey-Beaupré (F) 78 C5
Chassigny-Aisey (F) 78 C6
Chassillé (F) 76 A5
Chastanier (F) 94 C1
Chastellux-sur-Cure (F) 84 E2
Châtaigneraie, La (F) 82 D3
Chatain (F) 83 F4
Château-Arnoux (F) 95 H2
Châteaubourg (F) 75 J4
Châteaubriant (F) 75 J5
Château-Chervix (F) 83 H5
Château-Chinon (F) 84 E2
Château-des-Prés (F) 84 A4
Château-d'Oex (CH) 85 M4
Château-d'Oléron, Le (F) 82 C5
Château-du-Loir (F) 76 B6
Châteaudun (F) 76 D5
Châteaufort (F) 76 F4
Château-Garnier (F) 83 F4
Châteaugiron (F) 75 H4
Château-Gontier (F) 75 K5
Château-Landon (F) 77 G5
Château-Larcher (F) 83 F4
Château-la-Vallière (F) 76 B6
Château-l'Evêque (F) 83 G6
Châteaulin (F) 74 C4
Châteaumeillant (F) 83 K3
Châteauneuf (F) 84 F4
Châteauneuf-de-Galaure (F) 85 G6
Châteauneuf-de-Randon (F) 94 C1
Châteauneuf-d'Ille-et-Vilaine (F) 75 H3
Châteauneuf-du-Faou (F) 74 C4
Châteauneuf-du-Pape (F) 94 E2
Châteauneuf-en-Thymerais (F) 76 D4
Châteauneuf-la-Forêt (F) 83 J5
Châteauneuf-le-Rouge (F) 95 G4
Châteauneuf-les-Bains (F) 84 C4
Châteauneuf-sur-Charente (F) 82 E5
Châteauneuf-sur-Cher (F) 83 K3
Châteauneuf-sur-Loire (F) 76 F6
Châteauneuf-sur-Sarthe (F) 75 L5
Châteauneuf-Val-de-Bargis (F) 84 D2
Châteauponsac (F) 83 H4
Château-Porcien (F) 77 K2
Château-Queyras (F) 98 B3
Châteaurenard (F) 95 H2
Châteaurenard (F) 77 G6
Châteaurenard (F) 94 E3
Château-Renault (F) 76 C6
Châteauroux (F) 83 J3
Châteauroux (F) 95 J1
Château-Salins (F) 78 F4
Château-Thierry (F) 77 H3
Châteauvert (F) 95 H4
Châteauvieux (F) 95 J3
Châteauvillain (F) 78 B5
Châtel (F) 86 C5
Châtelaillon-Plage (F) 82 C4
Châtelard, Le (F) 85 K5
Châtelaudren (F) 74 F3
Châtelblanc (F) 85 K3
Châtel-Censoir (F) 77 J6
Châtel-de-Neuvre (F) 84 D4
Châteldon (F) 84 E5
Châtelet (B) 69 H6
Châtelet, Le (F) 84 B3
Châtelet-en-Brie, Le (F) 77 G4
Châtel-Gérard (F) 77 K6
Châtelguyon (F) 84 D5
Châtellerault (F) 83 F3
Châtel-Montagne (F) 84 E4
Châtel-Saint-Denis (CH) 86 C4
Châtel-sur-Moselle (F) 78 E5
Châtelus-le-Marcheix (F) 83 J5
Châtelus-Malvaleix (F) 83 K4
Châtenois (F) 78 D5
Châtenois (F) 79 G5
Châtenois-les-Forges (F) 78 F6
Châtenoy (F) 76 F6
Châtenoy-le-Royal (F) 85 G3
Chatham (GB) 59 J5
Châtillon (F) 85 L4
Châtillon (I) 86 D6
Châtillon-Coligny (F) 77 G6
Châtillon-de-Michaille (F) 85 J4
Châtillon-en-Bazois (F) 84 E2
Châtillon-en-Diois (F) 95 F1
Châtillon-en-Vendelais (F) 75 J4
Châtillon-la-Palud (F) 85 H5
Châtillon-le-Roi (F) 76 F5
Châtillon-sur-Chalaronne (F) 85 G4
Châtillon-sur-Colmont (F) 75 K4
Châtillon-sur-Indre (F) 83 H3
Châtillon-sur-Loire (F) 77 G6
Châtillon-sur-Marne (F) 77 J3
Châtillon-sur-Seine (F) 77 L6
Châtre, La (F) 84 A3
Châtres-sur-Cher (F) 83 J2
Chatteris (GB) 55 N6
Chatton (GB) 53 M3
Chauché (F) 82 C3
Chauchina (E) 126 C5
Chaudes-Aigues (F) 93 L1
Chaudeyrac (F) 94 C1
Chaudfontaine (B) 69 K5
Chaudon-Norante (F) 95 H3
Chaudron-en-Mauges (F) 82 D2
Chauffailles (F) 84 F4
Chauffayer (F) 95 H1
Chauffour-lès-Bailly (F) 77 K5
Chaulnes (F) 77 G2
Chaumard (F) 84 E2
Chaume, la (F) 82 B4
Chaume-les-Baigneux (F) 77 L6
Chaumergy (F) 85 H3
Chaumes-en-Brie (F) 77 G4
Chaumes-en-Retz (F) 82 B2
Chaumont (F) 77 M5
Chaumont-en-Vexin (F) 76 E3
Chaumont-Gistoux (B) 69 H5
Chaumont-Porcien (F) 77 K2
Chaumont-sur-Loire (F) 76 D7
Chaumont-sur-Tharonne (F) 76 E6
Chaunay (F) 82 F4
Chauny (F) 77 H2
Chaus (E) 110 C5
Chaussée-Saint-Victor, La (F) 76 D6
Chaussée-sur-Marne, La (F) 77 L4
Chaussin (F) 85 H3
Chauvé (F) 82 B2
Chauvigny (F) 83 G3
Chaux (F) 78 F6
Chaux-de-Fonds, La (CH) 85 L2
Chavagnac (F) 83 H6
Chavagnes-les-Redoux (F) 82 D3
Chavanat (F) 83 J5
Chavanay (F) 85 G6
Chavanges (F) 77 L4
Chavanoz-sur-Suran (F) 85 H4
Chavashchyna (BY) 139 H5
Chave (E) 110 B3
Chaves (P) 110 E5
Chaves = Chave (E) 110 B3
Chaveyriat (F) 85 H4
Chavornay (CH) 86 C4
Chawston (GB) 55 M6
Chazelles-sur-Lyon (F) 84 F5
Chazé-sur-Argos (F) 75 K5
Chazhyn (UA) 151 H4
Chbany (CZ) 152 D6
Cheadle (GB) 55 H4
Cheadle (GB) 55 J5
Cheb (CZ) 73 G5
Checa (E) 120 E2
Chechło (PL) 147 M5
Chęciny (PL) 148 B4
Chécy (F) 76 F6
Chedburgh (GB) 59 J3
Cheddar (GB) 58 B5
Chedworth (GB) 58 D4
Chef-Boutonne (F) 82 E4
Cheglevici (RO) 167 F1
Chei, Bicaz- (RO) 162 B5
Cheia (RO) 169 K3
Cheia (RO) 171 G4
Cheles (E) 124 E2
Chelford (GB) 55 H4
Chelle-Debat (F) 92 E4
Chełm (PL) 149 H3
Chelmac (RO) 168 B1
Chełmek (PL) 154 E1
Chełmiec (PL) 155 H2
Chełmno (PL) 141 K4
Chełmno (PL) 147 K1
Chelmondiston (GB) 59 K4
Chelmsford (GB) 59 H4
Chełmsko Śląskie (PL) 146 E4
Chełmża (PL) 141 L4
Cheltenham (GB) 58 C4
Chelva (E) 121 G4
Chemazé (F) 75 K5
Chemenot (F) 85 J3
Chémeré-le-Roi (F) 75 L5
Chémery (F) 83 H2
Chémery-Chéhéry (F) 78 B2
Chemillé-en-Anjou (F) 82 D2
Chemillé-sur-Dême (F) 76 C6
Chemilly (F) 84 D4
Chemin (F) 85 H3
Cheminot (F) 78 E4
Chemiré-le-Gaudin (F) 76 A6
Chemnitz (D) 73 H4
Chénac-Saint-Seurin-d'Uzet (F) 82 D5
Chenay (F) 82 E4
Chêne-Bourg (CH) 86 B5
Chênehutte-Trèves-Cunault (F) 82 E2
Chênelette (F) 84 G4
Chêne-Pignier (F) 83 G5
Chênérailles (F) 83 K4
Chenoise (F) 77 H4
Chenonceaux (F) 83 H2
Chenôve (F) 85 H2
Chens-sur-Léman (F) 86 B5
Chenu (F) 76 B6
Cheny (F) 77 J6
Chepoix (F) 76 F2
Chepstow (GB) 57 J2
Chera (E) 121 G4
Cherain (B) 69 K6
Cherasco (I) 98 D3
Cherbonnières (F) 82 E5
Cherbourg-en-Cotentin (F) 75 H1
Cherbourg-Octeville = Cherbourg-en-Cotentin (F) 75 H1
Chereluş (RO) 160 D5
Chérencès-le-Roussel (F) 75 J3
Cheresig (RO) 160 D3
Cherestur (RO) 160 A5
Cheriton (GB) 57 M3
Chéroy (F) 77 G5
Cherrueix (F) 75 H3
Cherson (UA) 153 J3
Chert = Xert (E) 122 B1
Chertsey (GB) 58 G5
Chervens-Châtelars (F) 83 G5
Cherves-Richemont (F) 82 E5
Cherveux (F) 82 E4
Chesham (GB) 58 F4
Cheshunt (GB) 59 G4
Chesley (F) 77 K6
Chesne, Le (F) 78 B2
Chessy (F) 85 G5
Chessy-lès-Prés (F) 77 J5
Cheste (E) 121 G5
Chester (GB) 54 G4
Chesterfield (GB) 55 K4
Chester-le-Street (GB) 53 M5
Chetani (RO) 161 J5
Chetrosu (MD) 162 F2
Chevagnes (F) 84 E3
Chevanceaux (F) 82 E6
Chevanes (F) 77 H6
Chevereşu Mare (RO) 168 A2
Chevigny, Lilbraneum (B) 78 C2
Chevillon (F) 77 M4
Cheviré-le-Rouge (F) 75 L5
Chevrefosse (F) 78 F5
Chew Magna (GB) 58 B5
Chewnica (PL) 141 J2
Chewton Mendip (GB) 57 J3
Chey (F) 82 E4
Cheylade (F) 84 C6
Cheylard, Le (F) 94 D1
Chezal-Benoît (F) 83 K3
Chèze, La (F) 74 F4
Chezelles (F) 83 J3
Chézery-Forens (F) 85 J4
Chialamberto (I) 98 C2
Chiampo (I) 100 E1
Chianale (I) 95 K1
Chianciano Terme (I) 102 D1
Chianni (I) 99 K6
Chiappera (I) 95 J1
Chiaramonte Gulfi (I) 109 G3
Chiaramonti (I) 97 C2
Chiaravalle (I) 101 J5
Chiaravalle Centrale (I) 107 F5
Chiareggio (I) 88 B5
Chiari (I) 100 B1
Chiaromonte (I) 106 F2
Chiassa (I) 101 F5
Chiasso (CH) 87 H6
Chiatona (I) 105 H4
Chiatra (F) 96 E4
Chiavari (I) 100 A4
Chiavenna (I) 87 H5
Chiché (F) 82 E3
Chichester (GB) 58 F6
Chichiş (RO) 169 K2
Chicklade (GB) 57 K3
Chiclana de la Frontera (E) 128 B5
Chiclana de Segura (E) 126 D3
Chiddingfold (GB) 58 F5
Chiddingstone (GB) 59 H5
Chideock (GB) 57 J4
Chieming (D) 89 H2
Chienes (I) 88 F4
Chieri (I) 98 D2
Chiesa (I) 88 E6
Chiesa in Valmalenco (I) 88 B5
Chiesazza (I) 100 F2
Chieşd (RO) 160 F3
Chies d'Alpago (I) 89 G5
Chiesina Uzzanese (I) 100 D5
Chieti (I) 103 J3
Chieuti (I) 172 B6
Chieveley (GB) 57 M3
Chièvres (B) 68 F5
Chigné (F) 75 M5
Chignolo Po (I) 99 G2
Chigy (F) 77 H5
Chiheru de Jos (RO) 161 K4
Chilches = Xilxes (E) 122 A3
Chilham (GB) 59 J5
Chilia Veche (RO) 171 J3
Chiliile (RO) 170 D3
Chilivani (I) 97 C2
Chillarón de Cuenca (E) 120 D3
Chilleurs-aux-Bois (F) 76 F5
Chillingham (GB) 53 M3
Chillón (E) 125 K2
Chilluévar (E) 126 D3
Chiloeches (E) 120 B2
Chimay (B) 69 G6
Chimeneas (E) 126 C5
Chimparra (E) 110 C1
Chinchilla de Monte Aragón (E) 120 E6
Chinchón (E) 119 K3
Chinnor (GB) 58 F4
Chinon (F) 83 F2
Chinteni (RO) 161 H4
Chiochiş (RO) 161 J4
Chioggia (I) 100 G2
Chiojdeni (RO) 169 L3
Chiomonte (I) 85 L6
Chiopeni (RO) 161 L6?
Chiosella Rusa (MD) 171 H1
Chipiona (E) 128 B4
Chippenham (GB) 57 K3
Chippenham (GB) 59 H3
Chipping Campden (GB) 57 L1
Chipping Norton (GB) 58 D4
Chipping Ongar (GB) 59 H4
Chipping Sodbury (GB) 57 M1
Chiprana (E) 114 C5
Chirac (F) 94 B1
Chiraleu (RO) 161 J3
Chirens (F) 85 J6
Chiriet-Lunga (MD) 171 H1
Chirivel (E) 127 F4
Chirk (GB) 58 A2
Chirnogeni (RO) 171 G6
Chirnogi (RO) 170 D5
Chirnside (GB) 53 L3
Chirpăr (RO) 135 P6
Chirsova (MD) 168 H6
Chisa (F) 96 E5
Chiscani (RO) 170 F3
Chiseldon (GB) 57 L2
Chiselet (RO) 170 D5
Chişinău (MD) 163 H4
Chisindia (RO) 160 E5
Chişineu-Criş (RO) 160 D4
Chişlaz (RO) 160 E3
Chissey-en-Morvan (F) 84 F2
Chiştelniţa (MD) 163 H3
Chitcani (MD) 163 K5
Chitignano (I) 101 F5
Chitila (RO) 170 B4
Chitray (F) 83 H3
Chittering (GB) 55 N6
Chiuiești (RO) 161 H3
Chiusa (I) 88 F4
Chiusa, Rifugio (I) 88 F4
Chiusa di Pesio (I) 95 L2
Chiusaforte (I) 89 K5
Chiusa Sclafani (I) 108 D2
Chiusdino (I) 100 E6
Chiusi (I) 102 D1
Chiusi della Verna (I) 101 F5
Chiuza (RO) 161 J3
Chiva (E) 121 G5
Chivasso (I) 98 D2
Chizé (F) 82 E4
Chjatra = Chiatra (F) 96 E4
Chłaba (SK) 159 G2
Chłanów (PL) 149 G4
Chłapowo (PL) 147 G1
Chlebnice (SK) 154 E3
Chlebowo (PL) 140 E6
Chlewiska (PL) 148 C3
Chlibodars'ka (UA) 163 M6
Chlivčany (UA) 149 J5
Chłopiatyn (PL) 149 J5
Chłopice (PL) 149 G6
Chłopków (PL) 149 G4
Chłopowo (PL) 140 F3
Chlorakas (CY) 198 D6
Chludowo (PL) 140 G5
Chlum (CZ) 153 L4
Chlumec (CZ) 152 E2
Chlumec nad Cidlinou (CZ) 146 C5
Chlum u Třeboně (CZ) 153 G6
Chmeleva (UA) 150 A6
Chmelnyc'kyj (UA) 150 D5
Chmeľov (SK) 155 J3
Chmeľová (UA) 157 J1
Chmiel Drugi (PL) 149 G3
Chmielek (PL) 149 G5
Chmieleń (PL) 153 H2
Chmielewo (PL) 141 M3
Chmielnik (PL) 148 C4
Chmielnik (PL) 149 G5
Chmielno (PL) 141 J2
Chmielów (PL) 146 D3
Chmiel'ne (UA) 149 L5
Chmil'nyk (UA) 151 K6
Chmil'nyk (UA) 150 F4
Chobienia (PL) 146 E2
Chocen (CZ) 153 K3
Chochołów (PL) 155 F1
Chocianów (PL) 146 D3
Chociwel (PL) 140 D4
Chocholów (PL) 155 F3
Chocianów (PL) 146 C3
Chocimsk (BY) 9 M3?
Chocz (PL) 148 B2
Chociwel (PL) 140 D4
Chocjuchova (BY) 139 J5
Chocne (UA) 144 G6
Chocz (PL) 147 H2
Choczewo (PL) 141 J1
Chodaki (PL) 147 K2
Chodaky (UA) 151 H2
Chodecz (PL) 141 M6
Chodel (PL) 148 F3
Chodoriv (UA) 150 B3
Chodorkiv (UA) 151 J3
Chodorów (UA) 156 F2
Chodosivka (UA) 151 M3
Chodov (CZ) 152 C3
Chodová Planá (CZ) 73 H6
Chodzież (PL) 140 F5
Chojna (PL) 140 B5
Chojnice (PL) 141 J3
Chojniki (BY) 9 L4
Chojno (PL) 146 G2
Chojnów (PL) 146 D3
Cholderton (GB) 58 D5
Cholet (F) 82 D2
Chollonges (F) 86 A5
Cholovičí (BY) 145 N4
Cholmok (UA) 155 L4
Cholms'ke (UA) 171 J2
Cholodna Balka (UA) 163 M5
Cholojny (UA) 149 N5?
Chomsk (BY) 149 L2
Chomutov (CZ) 152 D2
Chomiaków (CZ) 153 J3?
Chomutov (CZ) 146 A4?
Chomutivka (UA) 151 L4
Chomutov (CZ) 152 D4?
Chomutovka (RO) 148 F4?
Chomutyv (UA) 153 K1
Chomutyv (UA) 164 G1?
Choňkivci (UA) 162 F1
Chorhkovce (SK) 156 B4
Chopyiv (UA) 157 K3
Chorges (F) 95 H1
Chorin (D) 67 K5
Chorn (UA) 150 D3
Chorley (GB) 54 G3
Chorlivka (UA) 151 J4
Chornice (CZ) 153 L4
Chorobriv (UA) 149 K4
Chorochoryn (UA) 149 L4
Chorol (UA) 9 N5
Choroń (PL) 147 L4
Chorošiv (UA) 151 G2
Chorostkiv (UA) 150 B5
Choroszcz (PL) 143 H4
Chorovec' (UA) 150 E3
Chorupan' (UA) 150 B3
Chorzele (PL) 142 D4
Chorzew (PL) 147 K5
Chorzeszów (PL) 147 L2
Chorzów (PL) 147 K5
Chorzów (PL) 154 D1?
Chošebuz = Cottbus (D) 146 A2
Choszczewo (PL) 147 K2
Choszczno (PL) 140 D4
Chotcza (PL) 148 E3
Chotěboř (CZ) 153 J4
Chotel Czerwony (PL) 148 C5
Chotešiv (UA) 149 L2
Chotěšov (CZ) 146 B5
Chotěvice (CZ) 153 J2
Chotiešov (CZ) 152 F4
Chotjačiv (UA) 149 K4
Chotomów (PL) 142 D6
Chotymyr (UA) 157 H4
Chotyń (UA) 149 M5
Chotyn (UA) 150 D2
Chotyn (UA) 162 D1
Chotyněc (PL) 149 J5?
Choustník (CZ) 153 G5
Chouto (P) 116 C5
Chouvigny (F) 84 C4
Chozé, La (F) 77 G6
Chouzy-sur-Cisse (F) 76 D6
Chozas de Canales (E) 119 H3
Chraboły (PL) 143 J5
Chrališčava (BY) 139 L5
Chrast (CZ) 146 D6
Chrást (CZ) 152 D4
Chrastava (CZ) 153 G2
Chřibská (CZ) 146 A4
Chřič (CZ) 73 K6
Christchurch (GB) 58 D6
Christiansfeld (DK) 46 D3
Chrjebja-Nowa Wjes = Kreba-Neudorf (D) 73 M3
Christchurch (GB)?
Chřic (CZ) 153 L5
Chroberz (PL) 148 C5
Chrolyn (UA) 151 M1
Chromin (PL) 148 E2
Chropyně (CZ) 154 A3
Chroščyce (PL) 147 K3?
Chrościce = Crostwitz (D) 73 L3
Chrościna (PL) 146 F2
Chróstnik (PL) 146 E3
Chrostowa (PL) 148 B6
Chrudim (CZ) 146 D6
Chruściechów (PL) 147 L3
Chruślin (PL) 147 M1
Chrzanów (PL) 148 E3
Chrypa's'k (UA) 149 J2
Chryslova (BY) 138 F3
Chrystynivka (UA) 151 K6
Chrzan (PL) 147 H1
Chrzanów (PL) 149 G4
Chrzanów (PL) 154 E1
Chrząstowice (PL) 147 J4
Chrząstowo (PL) 147 G1
Chrzypsko Wielkie (PL) 142 F6
Chrzęsne (PL) 142 F6
Chtelnica (SK) 154 B4
Chucena (E) 128 B3
Chuchelná (CZ) 147 J6
Chuchulivky (BY) 139 K5
Chudleigh (GB) 57 G5
Chudoba (PL) 147 J4
Chulmleigh (GB) 57 G4
Chur (CH) 87 J4
Churáňov (CZ) 152 E5
Churchill (GB) 57 J3
Church Langton (GB) 58 F2
Church Stoke (GB) 58 A2
Church Stretton (GB) 54 G5
Churchtown (GBM) 61 D3
Churchtown (IRL) 56 B1
Churchtown (IRL) 63 J4
Churriana (E) 126 A6
Churwalden (CH) 87 J4
Chust (UA) 161 G1
Chutir (BY) 139 J6
Chutcze (PL) 149 H3
Chvalatice (CZ) 153 J4?
Chvaleč (CZ) 146 E4
Chvorostiv (UA) 149 K3
Chwarszczany (PL) 67 M5
Chwaszczyno (PL) 141 K2
Chybice (PL) 148 D4
Chybie (PL) 147 K6
Chyliń (PL) 147 J3?
Chym, Perin- (SK) 155 J4
Chymčyn (UA) 157 H5
Chyňava (CZ) 152 F3
Chynoř (UA) 144 J5?
Chynorany (SK) 154 C4
Chynov (CZ) 153 G5
Chynów (PL) 148 E1
Chynowa (PL) 147 H2
Chyrów (UA) 156 C2
Chyše (CZ) 73 J5
Chyšky (CZ) 153 H5?
Chyža (UA) 161 G1
Chyżne (PL) 154 F3
Chyżnja (UA) 151 L5
Ciacova (RO) 167 H2
Ciadîr-Lunga = Ceadîr-Lunga (MD) 171 H1
Ciampino (I) 103 F4
Cianciana (I) 108 D2
Ciaño (E) 111 H2
Ciasna (PL) 147 K4
Ciavolo (I) 108 C2
Ciażeń (PL) 147 H1
Cibakháza (H) 159 H4
Ciba (LV) 134 E4
Ciboure (F) 92 A4
Cicagna (I) 99 G4
Čičata (RUS) 135 P6
Ciccano (I) 103 K6
Cicekdagi (TR) 185 H6
Cicekköy (TR) 192 E6
Cicekler (TR) 192 C5
Cicekli (TR) 170 D5
Cicekli (TR) 192 E6
Cicekli (TR) 199 K2
Cicekoluk (TR) 198 D2
Cicekpınar (TR) 192 B4
Ciçekyaka (TR) 191 K4
Ciçekyayla (TR) 185 H2
Cicencie (CZ) 152 E5
Ciceri (RO) 106 D2
Cicevac (SRB) 168 A6
Cichy (PL) 142 A4
Cichobórz (PL) 149 J4
Cichów Mały (PL) 149 H1
Cicil (BG) 191 J5?
Ciciliano (I) 103 G4
Ciclova Română (RO) 168 B3
Čičmany (SK) 154 D4
Cicogna (I) 86 F5
Cicognolo (I) 100 C2
Cidade Nova de Santo André (P) 124 B3
Cide (TR) 13 K5
Cide (TR) 184 E2
Cidones (E) 113 F5
Cidreag (RO) 161 F2
Ciechanów (PL) 142 D5
Ciechanowiec (PL) 143 H5
Ciechanów (PL) 140 E3
Ciechocinek (PL) 141 L5
Ciechocin (PL) 141 L5?
Ciechomin Włościański (PL) 148 E2
Ciecierzyn (PL) 149 G3
Cieklin (PL) 155 J2
Cielądz (PL) 148 B2
Cielcze (PL) 147 K2
Cieletniki (PL) 147 M4
Cieljachany (BY) 144 C3
Ciempozuelos (E) 119 K3
Cienac (MD) 163 H6
Cieniawa (PL) 155 H2
Cienin Kościelny (PL) 147 J1
Cieplewo (PL) 141 K2
Cieplice (PL) 148 F5
Cieplowody (PL) 146 F4
Cierna (SK) 155 L5
Čierna Lehota (SK) 154 C4
Čierna nad Tisou (SK) 157 J1
Čierny Balog (SK) 154 F4
Cierp-Gaud (F) 92 F5
Cierva, La (E) 120 D3
Cieza (E) 127 H3
Cierva = Ziérbena (Abanto y Zierbena) (E) 112 E2
Cieśle (PL) 147 G3
Cieszanów (PL) 149 H5
Cieszków (PL) 147 G3
Cieszyn (PL) 147 H3
Cieszyn (PL) 154 D2
Cieux (F) 83 H5
Cieza (E) 127 H3
Ciężkowice (PL) 155 H2
Cifer (SK) 154 B5
Ciftehan (TR) 193 J5
Cifteler (TR) 193 L2
Ciftevi (TR) 193 H5
Ciftlik (TR) 183 K4
Ciftlik (TR) 193 J5
Ciftlik (TR) 199 J4
Ciftlikköy (TR) 182 D3
Ciftlikköy (TR) 183 F3
Ciftlikköy (TR) 183 H4
Ciftlikköy (TR) 183 K5
Ciftlikköy (TR) 184 B4
Ciftlikköy (TR) 184 E5
Ciftlikköy (TR) 185 H5
Ciftlikköy (TR) 189 H3
Ciftlikköy (TR) 190 D2
Ciftlikköy (TR) 190 E4
Ciftlikköy (TR) 190 F6
Ciftlikköy (TR) 191 H3
Ciftlikköy (TR) 192 B2
Ciftlikköy (TR) 192 G5
Ciftlikköy (TR) 193 K3
Ciftlikköy (TR) 196 D1
Ciftlikköy (TR) 199 J3
Ciftlikköy (TR) 196 F6
Ciftlikköy (TR) 193 F3?
Ciftlikközü (TR) 193 G2
Cifuentes (E) 120 C2
Cig (RO) 160 F2
Cigales (E) 111 K5
Ciganda (TR) 185 J6
Cigdemli (TR) 192 F6
Cigel (SK) 154 D3
Cigli (TR) 193 J2
Cigliano (I) 98 E2
Cigli (TR) 198 E3
Cigoc (HR) 91 J5
Cigunuela (E) 111 H5
Cihačeva (RUS) 135 J3
Cihanbeyli (TR) 13 K6
Cihangazi (TR) 193 J3
Cihavolja (BY) 143 K5
Cihnčiny (BY) 145 L2
Cikat (HR) 164 C5
Cikatové (RKS) 174 E3
Čikatovo = Čikatové (RKS) 174 E3
Čikrnck (TR) 191 H3
Cikrik (TR) 191 J6
Cikrikci (TR) 191 F3
Čikši (LV) 133 L3
Ciladas (S. Romão) (P) 117 G6
Cilbayır (TR) 199 G3
Cildi (LV) 132 D4
Cileme (TR) 189 K3
Ciliau-Aeron (GB) 56 F1
Cilibia (RO) 170 E3
Cilieni (RO) 169 H6
Cilimli (TR) 184 B4
Cilinkoz (TR) 191 J6?
Cilipi (HR) 173 H4
Cill Airne (IRL) 62 D4
Cillamayor (E) 112 C3
Cillas (E) 120 E2
Cill Bheagáin = Kilbeggan (IRL) 60 H5
Cill Chainnigh (IRL) 63 H3
Cill Chaoi = Kilkee (IRL) 62 C3
Cill Charthaigh (IRL) 60 E2
Cill Chiaráin (IRL) 60 C5
Cill Chóca = Kilcock (IRL) 63 J2
Cill Chormaic = Kilcormac (IRL) 60 G5
Cill Chuillin = Kilcullen (IRL) 61 J5
Cill Dalua = Killaloe (IRL) 62 F3
Cill Dara = Kildare (IRL) 63 J2
Cill Dhéagláin = Ashbourne (IRL) 63 K1
Cill Droichid = Celbridge (IRL) 63 J2
Cillero (E) 118 D2?
Ciller (TR) 193 H5
Cillero (E) 117 J2?
Cilleros (E) 118 C3
Cilleruelo de Abajo (E) 112 D5
Cilleruelo de Bezana (E) 112 D3
Cill = Cielje (SLO) 164 E2
Cillín Chaoimhín = Hollywood (IRL) 61 J5
Cill Inion Léinín = Killiney (IRL) 61 K5
Cill Mhantáin = Wicklow (IRL) 61 K6
Cill Mhuirbhigh (IRL) 62 C2
Cill Náile = Killenaule (IRL) 63 G3
Cill Orglan = Killorglin (IRL) 62 C4
Cill Rois = Kilrush (IRL) 62 C3
Cill Rónáin (IRL) 60 C5
Cilnov (BG) 176 E1
Cilycwm (GB) 57 G1
Cimadevilla (E) 111 H1
Cima di Vorno (I) 100 D5
Cimadolmo (I) 89 G6
Cimalmotto (CH) 86 F5
Cimanes de la Vega (E) 111 H4
Cimanes del Tejar (E) 111 H3
Cimaşkovo (BY) 144 F4
Cimbalevcy (BY) 144 E2?
Cimelice (CZ) 81 L2
Cimen (TR) 185 H4
Cimen (TR) 190 C3?
Cimenli (TR) 191 G5?
Cimenlik (TR) 193 H6
Cimkıköy (TR) 198 C1
Ciminna (I) 108 E2
Cimişlia (MD) 163 H5
Cimkavićy (BY) 144 E2
Cimochy (PL) 143 H3
Cimolais (I) 89 G5
Cimoszka (BY) 138 H2
Cimpello (I) 89 H6
Cimpu lui Neag (RO) 168 E3
Cinarcık (TR) 183 G5
Cinarcık (TR) 183 H4
Cinarcık (TR) 191 G3
Cinarlı (CY) 199 G5
Cinarlı (TR) 182 E4
Cincin (TR) 190 D5
Cinco Casas (E) 126 D1
Cinco Olivas (E) 114 B5
Cinctorres (E) 122 A1
Cincu (RO) 161 K6
Cinderford (GB) 57 K2
Cine (TR) 190 E5
Cineral (E) 111 H3
Ciney (B) 69 J6
Cinfães (P) 116 E1
Cinge (TR) 190 C2
Cingöz (TR) 185 G5
Cingoli (I) 101 J6
Cingoli (I) 110 H2?
Cinigiano (I) 102 C2
Ciniseuti (MD) 163 H3
Cinisi (I) 108 D1
Cinn Mhara = Kinvarra (IRL) 60 E5
Cinobaña (SK) 154 F5
Cinovec (CZ) 152 E2
Cinq-Mars-la-Pile (F) 83 F2
Cinquefrondi (I) 106 F6
Cintano (I) 98 D2
Cintegabelle (F) 93 H4
Cintei (RO) 160 D5
Cintrey (F) 78 D6
Cintruénigo (E) 113 H4
Cinzano (I) 98 D2
Ciobănita (RO) 171 G5
Ciobanu (RO) 170 F4
Ciobiškis (LT) 137 M4
Ciocănari (RO) 170 D5
Ciocăneşti (RO) 169 K4
Ciocăneşti (RO) 170 D5
Ciochina (RO) 170 E4
Ciocile (RO) 170 E4
Ciocîlteni (MD) 163 H4
Cioclovina (RO) 168 E2
Cioc Mediu (RO) 163 H6
Cioiănești din Deal (RO) 169 J5
Ciołkowo (PL) 141 M6
Cionn Átha Gad = Kinnegad (IRL) 61 H5
Cionn tSáile = Kinsale (IRL) 62 E5
Ciora (MD) 163 H3
Cioranii de Jos (RO) 170 C4
Ciorăști (RO) 170 E3
Ciorna (MD) 163 H3
Ciorogârla (RO) 170 B5
Ciorogârla (RO) 170 B5?
Ciorteşti (RO) 162 F5?
Ciorogla = Ciorragia (E) 112 E2?
Ciorteşti (RO) 163 G4
Ciortea (RO) 170 E5?
Cipiak (TR) 184 C3
Ciprian Porumbescu (RO) 162 C3
Ciprovci (BG) 175 J2
Cirák (H) 91 M5
Cırakh (TR) 197 H3
Cirat (E) 121 H3
Ciraugui (E) 113 G3
Cîrava (LV) 132 C4
Circeni (LV) 132 D3
Çirdak (TR) 184 C4
Cirella (I) 106 E3
Ciren (BG) 175 L2
Cirencester (GB) 58 D4
Cirençe (TR) 167 L4
Cireşu (RO) 167 L4?
Cirey-sur-Blaise (F) 78 B5
Cirey-sur-Vezouze (F) 78 F4
Cirié (I) 98 D2
Ciriè, Rifugio (I) 85 M6
Cirio (E) 110 E2
Cirişciuki (BY) 145 K4?
Cirişgediği (TR) 193 K6
Cirişte (TR) 193 J7?
Cirkale (LV) 133 K4
Cirkovic (BY) 145 H3?
Cirkulane (SLO) 165 G2
Cirlau (LV) 133 J5
Cirò (I) 107 H4
Cirò Marina (I) 107 H4
Ciron (F) 83 H3
Ciruelos (E) 119 K3
Cirpeşti (MD) 163 K5
Cirpi (TR) 190 C4
Cirpılar (TR) 182 C5
Ciruelos (E) 120 A4
Ciruelos de Coca (E) 112 B6
Cirujı (LV) 134 E3
Ciry-le-Noble (F) 84 F3
Cis (I) 87 L5
Cisac (E) 94 A1?
Cisar (E) 110 D1?
Cisek (PL) 147 J5
Ciserie (TR) 197 G2
Cisiec (PL) 154 E2
Ciskádi (LV) 133 P5
Cisla (E) 119 F2
Cislago (I) 98 F1
Cislău (RO) 170 C2
Cismar (D) 66 B2
Cismon del Grappa (I) 88 F6
Cisna (PL) 156 B3
Cisnădie (RO) 169 G2
Cisnădioara (RO) 169 G2
Cisneros (E) 112 A4
Cisse (F) 83 F3
Ciśniawy (PL) 154 F2
Cisowa (PL) 155 H2?
Cissé (F) 82 F3
Cista (CZ) 73 K5
Cistá (CZ) 146 D4
Cista Mala (HR) 172 C2
Cista Provo (HR) 172 E2
Cisterna di Latina (I) 103 F4
Cisterna (E) 105 H4?
Cisternino (I) 105 H4
Cistierna (E) 111 K3
Cistierna (RUS) 135 N4
Čistye Prudy (RUS) 136 D5
Cisy (PL) 155 J1
Ciszyca Przewozowa (PL) 148 E3
Citak (TR) 190 E3
Citak (TR) 191 H4
Citeaux (F) 85 H2
Citluk (BIH) 172 F4
Citluk (SRB) 174 B6
Citluk (SRB) 175 C4?
Citluk (SRB) 175 H5?
Citolibyy (CZ) 73 K5
Citou (F) 93 K4
Citov (CZ) 146 A5
Cittadella (I) 88 F6
Cittadella del Capo (I) 106 E3
Città della Pieve (I) 102 D2
Città del Vaticano = Vaticana, Civitas (V) 102 E4
Città di Castello (I) 101 G6
Cittaducale (I) 103 G3
Cittanova (I) 106 F6
Cittanova = Novigrad (HR) 164 B4
Cittareale (I) 103 H2
Città Sant'Angelo (I) 103 J2
Cittiglio (I) 87 G6
Ciuc, Miercurea- (RO) 162 B6
Ciuc, Păuleni- (RO) 162 B6
Ciucea (RO) 160 F4
Ciuchici (RO) 168 B4
Ciuciulieni (MD) 163 G4
Ciuciulmi (RO) 171 G1?
Ciucsângeorgiu (RO) 162 B6
Ciucur Mingir (MD) 163 H6
Ciucurova (RO) 171 G4
Ciudad Real (E) 119 J6
Ciudad Rodrigo (E) 117 H2
Ciudanovita (RO) 168 B3
Ciufu (RO) 160 E3
Ciulnita (RO) 170 E4
Ciulnita (RO) 171 E4?
Ciumeghiu (RO) 160 D4
Ciumani (RO) 162 B5?
Ciuperceni (RO) 168 E4
Ciuperceni Noi (RO) 168 D6
Ciurea (RO) 162 F4
Ciurila (RO) 161 H4
Ciuruleasa (RO) 161 G5
Ciusllice (PL) 148 C5
Ciutadella (E) 123 J2
Ciutadilla (E) 115 F4
Ciužiakampis (LT) 138 B5
Civaux (F) 83 G4
Čivaux (F) 83 G4?
Civenna (I) 87 H6
Cividale del Friuli (I) 164 A2
Cividate Mantovano (I) 100 C2
Civikey (TR) 185 G4
Civili (TR) 183 G6
Civilgam (TR) 183 G6
Civitacampomarano (I) 103 K4
Civita Castellana (I) 102 E3
Civitanova Marche (I) 101 K6
Civitas Vaticana (V) 102 E4
Civitavecchia (I) 102 D3
Civitella Casanova (I) 103 H3
Civitella d'Agliano (I) 102 E2
Civitella del Tronto (I) 103 H2
Civitella di Romagna (I) 101 F4
Civitella in Val di Chiana (I) 101 F6
Civitella Marittima (I) 102 C2
Civitella Roveto (I) 103 G4
Civray (F) 83 F4
Civril (TR) 198 E2
Civray (F) 83 F4?
Civril (TR) 184 C4
Civril (TR) 191 J6
Cizer (RO) 160 F3
Cizur Mayor (E) 113 H3
Cjacerki (BY) 138 F2
Cjahcin (BY) 145 H2?
Cjaljakava (BY) 144 F1
Cjaredy (BY) 145 K2
Cjarenicy (BY) 145 K3
Cjarečki (BY) 139 J4
Cjasny (UA) 145 N5
Cjurupyns'k (UA) 13 K3
Ckalava (BY) 145 L4
Ckalava (BY) 145 M3
Ckeynė (BY) 145 M3
Ckla (MNE) 174 B4
Ckyniė (CZ) 81 K3
Clabby (GB) 60 H3
Clachan (GB) 50 E5
Clachan (GB) 52 D3
Clachan (GB) 52 H1
Clachan Mór (GB) 52 B1
Clachan of Glendaruel (GB) 52 E2
Clachtoll (GB) 53 H2
Clackmannan (GB) 53 H2?
Clacton-on-Sea (GB) 59 K4
Cladich (GB) 52 E2
Clady (GB) 60 G3
Claggan (GB) 52 D1
Claim con Osténo (I) 87 H5
Clairac (F) 92 E2
Clairavaux (F) 83 L5
Clairvaux-les-Lacs (F) 85 J3
Clamecy (F) 84 E2
Clamensane (F) 95 H2
Clamerey (F) 84 F2
Clane (IRL) 61 J5
Clans (F) 98 C4
Claonaig (GB) 52 D3
Claonaig (GB) 52 E3?
Clapham (GB) 54 H2
Clara (IRL) 61 K3
Clarach (GB) 54 F6?
Clarbeston Road (GB) 56 E2
Clár Chlainne Mhuiris = Claremorris (IRL) 60 E4
Clarde-Riviere, Saint- (F) 93 G4
Clarecastle (IRL) 62 E3
Clareen (IRL) 60 G5
Claregalway = Baile Chláir (IRL) 62 E2
Claremorris (IRL) 60 E4
Clarholz, Herzebrock- (D) 70 F3
Clarina (IRL) 62 E3
Claro (CH) 87 H5
Clarinbridge (IRL) 62 E2
Clashmore (IRL) 63 G4
Clauby (GB) 61 H4?
Claudy (GB) 61 H2?
Claushitz (D) 71 J2?
Clausthal-Zellerfeld (D) 71 K3
Claut (I) 89 H5
Clautzig (LV) 133 ?
Claverig (GB) 59 H4?
Clavijo (E) 113 G4
Claville (F) 76 D3
Clawdd-newydd (GB) 54 F4
Clawton (GB) 56 F4
Clay Cross (GB) 55 K4
Claydon (GB) 59 K3
Claye-Souilly (F) 77 G4
Clayette, La (F) 84 F4
Cleadale (GB) 50 E6
Cleator Moor (GB) 54 E1
Clécy (F) 75 L3
Clédén-Poher (F) 74 D4
Cléder (F) 74 C3
Cleedownton (GB) 56 G6?
Cleethorpes (GB) 55 M3
Cleeve Hill (GB) 57 K2
Clefmont (F) 78 D5
Clefs-Val-d'Anjou (F) 76 A6
Cléguer (F) 74 E4
Cléguérec (F) 74 E4
Cleja (RO) 162 D6
Clejani (RO) 169 K5
Clelles-en-Trièves (F) 95 G1
Clementes, Los (E) 126 D6
Clemenţeni (RO) 162 E6
Clenze (D) 66 D5
Cleobury Mortimer (GB) 55 H6
Cleobury North (GB) 55 H6
Cléon (F) 76 D3
Cléon-d'Andran (F) 94 E1
Clephanton (GB) 51 K4
Cléré-les-Pins (F) 83 F2
Cléres (F) 76 D2
Cléré-sur-Layon (F) 82 E2
Clérey (F) 77 K5
Clergoux (F) 84 A6
Clermain (F) 85 G4
Clermont (F) 76 F3
Clermont (F) 83 F5
Clermont (F) 113 K1
Clermont (F) 114 F3?
Clermont-Créans (F) 76 A6
Clermont-de-Beauregard (F) 83 G6
Clermont-en-Argonne (F) 77 M3
Clermont-Ferrand (F) 84 D5
Clermont-l'Hérault (F) 94 B3
Cléron (F) 85 K2
Clerval (F) 86 A2
Clervaux (L) 69 L6
Cléry-Saint-André (F) 76 E6
Cles (I) 88 D5
Clevedon (GB) 57 J3
Cleveleys (GB) 54 G3
Cley (F) 68 C5
Clevedon (GB) 58 B5
Clévilliers (F) 76 D4
Clézentaine (F) 78 F5
Clifden (IRL) 60 B5
Cliffe (GB) 59 H5
Clifford (GB) 58 A3
Climăuţi (MD) 162 F2
Clinchamps-sur-Orne (F) 75 L2
Clingen (D) 71 L4
Clion (F) 83 H3
Cliponville (F) 76 C2
Clipston (GB) 58 E2
Clisson (F) 82 C2
Clitheroe (GB) 55 H3
Clocher (GB) 60 H2?
Clogh (GB) 61 K2
Clogh (IRL) 63 H3
Cloghan (IRL) 60 G5
Cloghan (IRL) 61 H2?
Cloghane (IRL) 62 B4
Cloghaneely = An Clochán (IRL) 60 F1?
Clogheen (IRL) 63 G4
Clogher (GB) 61 H3
Clogher (IRL) 60 F4
Clogherhead (IRL) 61 K4
Cloghjordan (IRL) 63 F2
Clogh Mills (GB) 52 C5
Cloghroe (IRL) 62 D5
Clohars-Carnoët (F) 74 D5
Cloich na Coillte = Clonakilty (IRL) 62 D5
Clonakilty (IRL) 62 D5
Clonalvy (IRL) 63 K1
Clonaslee (IRL) 63 H1
Clonbern (IRL) 60 E5
Clonbulloge (IRL) 61 H5
Clondalkin = Cluain Dolcáin (IRL) 63 K2
Clonea (IRL) 63 H4
Clonee (IRL) 61 J5
Clonee (IRL) 63 K2
Cloneen (IRL) 63 G3
Clonegal (IRL) 63 J3
Clones (IRL) 61 H3
Clonfert (IRL) 60 F5
Clonmacnoise (IRL) 62 G2
Clonmany (IRL) 61 H1
Clonmel (IRL) 63 G4
Clonmellon (IRL) 61 H4
Clonmore (IRL) 63 G3
Clonoulty (IRL) 63 G3
Clonroche (IRL) 63 J4
Clontarf (IRL) 63 K2
Clontibret (IRL) 61 J3
Clontuskert (IRL) 60 F5
Clonygowan (IRL) 63 H2
Cloonacool (IRL) 60 E3
Cloonbannin (IRL) 62 D4
Cloonfad (IRL) 62 E3
Cloonlara (IRL) 62 E3
Clophill (GB) 58 G3
Clopotiva (RO) 168 D3
Cloppenburg (D) 65 J6
Closani (RO) 168 D4
Closeburn (GB) 53 J4
Close Clark (GBM) 61 N3
Clough (GB) 61 L3
Cloughton (GB) 55 M1
Clova (GB) 53 J1
Clovelly (GB) 56 F4
Clovelly (GB) 56 F3?
Clovenfords (GB) 53 K3
Cloyes-sur-le-Loir (F) 76 D6
Cloyne (IRL) 62 F5
Cluain Cearbán = Louisburgh (IRL) 60 C4
Cluain Eois = Clones (IRL) 61 H3
Cluain Meala = Clonmel (IRL) 63 G4
Cluer (GB) 50 D4
Clun (GB) 54 G6
Cluis (F) 83 J3
Cluj (RO) 161 H4
Cluj-Napoca (RO) 161 H4
Clumanc (F) 95 H2
Clun (GB) 58 A3
Clunderwen (GB) 56 E2
Clungunford (GB) 54 G6
Cluny (F) 85 G4
Cluny (F) 85 G4?
Clusane (I) 99 H1
Cluses (F) 86 A5
Cluse, La (F) 95 G1
Cluse-et-Mijoux, la (F) 85 K3
Cluses (F) 85 L4
Clusone (I) 88 B6
Clutton (GB) 57 K3
Clydach (GB) 57 G2
Clydebank (GB) 52 G3
Clynnog-fawr (GB) 61 O5
Clyst Saint Mary (GB) 57 H4
Cmarl (RO) 160 E4?
Cmielów (PL) 148 E4
Cminsk Kościelny (PL) 148 C3
Cminy (UA) 144 E4?
Cmjalevičy (BY) 138 H5
Cmolas (PL) 148 E5
Coachford (IRL) 62 E5
Coagh (GB) 52 B5
Coalisland (GB) 52 B5
Coalmimi = Salme (S) 18 C7
Coalville (GB) 55 K5
Coaña (E) 111 F1
Coarnele Caprei (RO) 162 E4
Coaş (RO) 161 H2
Coatbridge (GB) 52 H3
Coat-Méal (F) 74 B3
Coatti (I) 100 E3
Coazze (I) 98 C2
Coba (BG) 176 D4
Coba (E) 110 E4?
Cobadin (RO) 171 G5
Cobanbeyli (TR) 185 K3?
Cobanisa (TR) 190 D2
Cobani (MD) 162 E3
Cobanisa (TR) 192 B6
Cobanisa (TR) 197 G2
Cobankaya (TR) 191 K4
Cobanlar (TR) 185 K3?
Cobanlar (TR) 190 D2
Cobanlar (TR) 190 D4
Cobanlar (TR) 191 G2
Cobanlar (TR) 191 K3
Cobansaray (TR) 191 J4
Cobatillas (E) 127 G3
Cobatillas (E) 127 F4
Cobbel (D) 66 F6
Cóbdar (E) 127 F5
Cobertelada (E) 113 F6
Cobeta (E) 120 D2
Cobh = An Cóbh (IRL) 62 F5
Cobo, El (E) 127 G3?
Cobor (RO) 161 L6
Cobos de Cerrato (E) 112 C4
Cobreces (E) 112 C2
Cobres (E) 110 B4
Coburg (D) 71 L6
Co bussa Veche (MD) 163 J5
Coca (E) 112 B6
Coccaglio (I) 100 B1
Coccanile (I) 101 F3
Cocciu (I) 164 B1
Cocciola (F) 93 G2
Cocconato (I) 98 E2
Cocentaina (E) 127 K2
Cochem (D) 70 D6
Cochirleanca (RO) 170 E3
Cochirleni (RO) 170 G5
Cocieşti (RO) 162 F3?
Cocioc (D) 72 E2
Cociuba Mare (RO) 160 E4
Cockburnspath (GB) 53 L3
Cockerham (GB) 54 G3
Cockenzie and Port Seton (GB) 53 K3
Cockermouth (GB) 54 F1
Cockley Cley (GB) 59 J2
Cocksburg, Dr (NL) 64 B5
Coclois (F) 77 K5
Cocora (RO) 170 B4
Cocoraşti Colt (RO) 170 B4
Cocoraşti Mislii (RO) 169 K3
Cocumont (F) 92 E2
Cocuşteni (RO) 162 F5
Coda (LV) 133 J5
Codevigo (I) 101 G2
Codigoro (I) 101 G3
Codlea (RO) 170 A2
Codo (E) 113 K6
Codogno (I) 99 H2
Codoñera, La (E) 114 C6
Codos (E) 113 J6
Codosera, La (E) 117 G5
Codreni (RO) 170 D5
Codreanca (MD) 163 H3
Codrii Noui (MD) 163 H3
Codru (MD) 163 H5
Codrul Nou (MD) 163 H3
Codsall (GB) 58 C2
Coesfeld (D) 70 D3
Coësmes (F) 75 J5
Cœuvres-et-Valsery (F) 77 H3
Coevorden (NL) 64 F6
Coëx (F) 82 B3
Cofrentes (E) 121 F5
Cogealac (RO) 171 H4
Cogeces del Monte (E) 112 C5
Coggeshall (GB) 59 J4
Coghinas (I) 96 B?
Coglu (TR) 193 K6?
Cognac (F) 82 E5
Cognac-la-Forêt (F) 83 H5
Cogne (I) 98 C1
Cogolin (F) 98 F4
Cogollos (E) 112 D4
Cogollos Vega (E) 126 C5
Cogolludo (E) 120 B2
Cogul, el (E) 114 E5
Cogul, el (E) 114 E5?
Cogun (TR) 183 K6
Coğurler (TR) 191 J2
Cohiniac (F) 74 F4
Cohkkiras = Jukkasjärvi (S) 21 K5
Coignafearn Lodge (GB) 51 J5
Coimbra (P) 116 E3
Coimbrão (P) 116 D4
Coin (E) 128 E4
Coirós = Coirós de Arriba (E) 110 C2
Coirós de Arriba (E) 110 C2
Coja (P) 116 F3
Cojasca (RO) 170 B4
Cojocna (RO) 161 H4
Çoka (SRB) 159 K6
Cokak (TR) 193 H5
Cokelek (TR) 190 E3
Cokeler (TR) 184 C5
Cokeli (TR) 184 E5
Çokelez (SRB) 166 D4
Cokelii (TR) 199 G6
Cokelii (TR) 183 J6
Cokmakovo (BG) 180 F1
Cokoba (BG) 177 F3
Cokören (TR) 191 K6
Col (SLO) 89 L5
Colares (P) 116 A6
Colayrac-Saint-Cirq (F) 92 F2
Cölbe (D) 71 G5
Colbitz (D) 66 E6?
Colbordolo (I) 101 H5
Colbost (GB) 50 D5
Colceag (RO) 170 C4
Colchester (GB) 59 J4
Colchester (GB) 59 J4?
Cold Ashton (GB) 58 C5
Coldingham (GB) 53 L3
Colditz (D) 73 H3
Coldstream (GB) 53 L3
Coleford (GB) 57 K2
Coleraine (GB) 61 J1
Colerne (GB) 57 K3
Colfiorito (I) 103 F1
Colgrave (I) 106 D1?
Coli (I) 100 A3
Colibas (MD) 171 G2
Colibaşi (RO) 169 J4
Colibaşi (RO) 169 H4
Colichet (F) 84 D4?
Colico (I) 87 H6
Coligny (F) 85 H4
Colinas de Trasmonte (E) 111 H4
Colindres (E) 112 E2
Colintraive (GB) 52 E3
Coll = Col (GB) 50 D5?
Colla (I) 98 B5?
Collado Villalba (E) 119 H2
Collagna (I) 100 C4
Collalto Sabino (I) 103 G3
Collancelle, La (F) 84 E2
Collanzo (E) 111 H2
Collarmele (I) 103 H3
Collazzone (I) 102 E2
Coll de Nargó (E) 115 F3
Coll d'en Rabassa (E) 123 G3
Colle (I) 88 D5
Colle (I) 89 H5
Collecchio (I) 99 J3
Colle di Val d'Elsa (I) 99 L6
Colleferro (I) 103 F4
Colle Isarco (I) 88 E4
Collepardo (I) 103 G4
Collepasso (I) 107 K2
Collesalvetti (I) 100 C5
Colle Sannita (I) 104 C3
Colle Santa Lucia (I) 88 F5
Collesano (I) 109 F2
Colletorto (I) 104 C2
Colleville-sur-Mer (F) 75 K2
Collio (I) 88 B6?
Collie (I) 99 G6?
Colli a Volturno (I) 104 B2
Colli di Montebove (I) 103 G3
Collier Law (GB) 53 M5
Colliers (F) 76 C2?
Collieston (GB) 51 M5
Collinée (F) 74 F4
Collingbourne Kingston (GB) 57 L3
Collingham (GB) 55 L4
Collingtree (GB) 58 E3?
Collinstown (IRL) 63 H1
Collio (I) 88 C6
Collioure (F) 93 L5
Collobrières (F) 95 H4
Colloghy (F) 98 D3?
Collon (IRL) 61 J4
Collonges (F) 85 J4
Collonges (F) 96 B5
Colmar (F) 79 G5
Colmars (F) 95 J2
Colmenar (E) 126 B6
Colmenar, El (E) 128 D4
Colmenar de Oreja (E) 119 K3
Colmenar del Arroyo (E) 119 H3
Colmenar Viejo (E) 119 J2
Colnabaichin (GB) 51 K5
Colnbrook (GB) 58 F5
Colobraro (I) 107 F2
Cologna Veneta (I) 99 L2
Cologne (F) 93 F3
Cologne = Köln (D) 71 B1?
Colombes (F) 77 G4
Colombey-les-Belles (F) 78 D4
Colombey-les-Deux-Églises (F) 78 B5
Colombières-sur-Orb (F) 93 L3
Colombres (E) 112 B2
Colombres (Ribadedeva) (E) 112 B2
Colomera (E) 126 C5
Colomers (E) 115 K3
Colonard-Corubert (F) 76 C5
Colondannes (F) 83 J4
Colonesti (RO) 162 E5
Colonesti (RO) 169 K5
Colonesti (RO) 170 E5
Colonia de Sant Jordi (E) 123 G4
Colonia de Sant Pere, Sa (E) 123 H3
Colonia Grande (RO) 169 F5?
Colonia (RO) 160 D3?
Colons (P) 124 C4
Colosterworth (GB) 55 L5
Colova (GB) 50 D4?
Colţi (RO) 170 C3
Colunga (E) 111 J2
Colwich (GB) 58 D2
Colyton (GB) 57 H4
Colyford (GB) 58 A5?
Comacchio (I) 101 G3
Comana (RO) 170 C5
Comandău (RO) 170 C1?
Comănești (RO) 162 C6
Comano (I) 100 C4
Comar (TR) 185 G3
Comares (E) 126 B6
Comarna (RO) 162 F4
Comarnic (RO) 169 K3
Combarro (E) 110 B4
Combarros (E) 111 G3
Combeaufontaine (F) 86 A2
Combe Martin (GB) 56 F3
Comber (GB) 54 A1
Comberton (GB) 59 H3
Combiers (F) 83 F6
Comblain-au-Pont (B) 69 K6
Combles (F) 77 G1
Combloux (F) 86 C6
Combourg (F) 75 H4
Combray, Bény- (F) 76 D5
Combrée (F) 75 J5
Combres (F) 76 D5
Combrit (F) 74 C5
Combronde (F) 84 D5
Comeat (RO) 160 D6
Comeglians (I) 90 C6
Cömelek (TR) 199 G2
Comellico Superiore (I) 90 C6
Comenda (P) 117 F5
Comillas (E) 112 C2
Comines (F) 68 D5
Comişani (RO) 169 K4
Comiso (I) 109 G4
Comisoaia (RO) 170 D3
Cömlekçi (TR) 190 D3
Cömlektepe (TR) 185 F2
Comloşu Mare (RO) 159 L6
Commana (F) 74 D4
Commarin (F) 85 G2
Commentry (F) 84 C4
Commerau bei Klix (D) 146 B3
Commercy (F) 78 D4
Como (I) 87 H6
Comorâşte (RO) 168 B3
Compains (F) 84 C6
Compasscum = Emmer- (NL) 64 G6
Compatsch (CH) 87 K4
Compeix, le (F) 83 J5
Compeyre (F) 94 A2
Compiègne (F) 77 G3
Compolibat (F) 93 J2
Comporta (P) 124 B2
Comporta (P) 124 B3?
Compreignac (F) 83 H5
Comps (F) 95 J3
Comps-sur-Artuby (F) 95 J3
Comrat (MD) 163 H6
Comrie (GB) 52 H2
Comunanza (I) 103 G2
Conan (F) 76 D6
Conca (F) 96 E5
Concabella (E) 115 F4
Conca della Campania (I) 104 A3
Concarneau (F) 74 D5
Conceição (P) 124 C4
Concerviano (I) 103 F3
Concesio (I) 99 J1
Concești (RO) 162 D2
Concha = Concha, La (Valle de Carranza) (E) 112 E2
Concha, La (Valle de Carranza) (E) 112 E2
Conches, Les (F) 82 C4
Conches-en-Ouche (F) 76 C4
Conchy-les-Pots (F) 77 G2
Concise (CH) 86 C4
Conco (I) 88 E6
Concordia sulla Secchia (I) 99 K3
Concots (F) 93 H2
Concressault (F) 77 G7
Condado (E) 111 J2
Condat (F) 84 C6
Condé-en-Brie (F) 77 J3
Condé-en-Normandie (F) 75 K3
Condé-Folie (F) 76 F1
Condeixa-a-Nova (P) 116 E3
Condé-sur-Huisne (F) 76 C5
Condé-sur-l'Escaut (F) 68 F6
Condé-sur-Noireau (F) 75 K3?
Condé-sur-Vesgre (F) 76 E4
Condé-sur-Vire (F) 75 J2
Condino (I) 88 D6
Condom (F) 92 E3
Condove (I) 98 C2
Condrieu (F) 85 G6
Condroz, Barvaux- (B) 69 J6
Conegliano (I) 89 G6
Conesa (E) 115 F4
Conevo (BG) 177 J4
Conflans (F) 85 K6?
Conflans-en-Jarny (F) 78 D3
Conflans-Sainte-Honorine (F) 76 F3
Conflans-sur-Lanterne (F) 78 E6
Confolens (F) 83 G4
Cong (IRL) 60 D5
Congaz (MD) 171 H1
Congleton (GB) 55 H4
Congosto (E) 111 G3
Congosto de Valdavia (E) 111 L3
Congostrina (E) 119 L1
Conil de la Frontera (E) 128 B5
Conisbrough (GB) 55 K4
Coniston (GB) 53 J6?
Conlie (F) 75 M5
Conliege (F) 85 H3?
Conna (IRL) 62 F4
Connah's Quay (GB) 54 F4
Connaux (F) 94 E2
Connel (GB) 52 E2
Connerré (F) 76 C5
Conon Bridge (GB) 51 J4
Conop (RO) 160 B1?
Conoplja (SRB) 159 H6
Conques-en-Rouergue (F) 93 J1
Conques-sur-Orbiel (F) 93 K4
Conquet, Le (F) 74 B4
Conquista (E) 125 K3
Conselice (I) 101 F3
Consell (E) 123 G3
Conselve (I) 101 F2
Consett (GB) 53 M5
Consistorio (Arbo) (E) 110 C4
Constância (P) 116 E5
Constanța (RO) 171 H5
Constanti (E) 115 F5
Constantina (E) 125 H4
Constantin Daicoviciu (RO) 167 K2
Constantin Gabrielescu (RO) 170 F3
Constantinovca (MD) 163 J5
Constanzana (E) 119 G2
Consuegra (E) 120 A5
Consuma (I) 100 E5
Contadero (E) 126 C3
Contamines-Montjoie, les (F) 85 L5
Contaut, le (F) 92 E4
Contay (F) 77 G1
Contessa Entellina (I) 108 D2
Conțești (RO) 169 J6
Conțești (RO) 169 K5
Conteville (F) 76 E2
Conthey (CH) 86 D5
Conti, Rifugio (I) 109 H2
Contienda, La (E) 125 F3
Contigliano (I) 103 F3
Contin (GB) 51 H4
Contis-Plage (F) 92 B2
Contrada (I) 104 C4
Contres (F) 83 H2
Contrexéville (F) 78 D5
Controguerra (I) 103 H2
Contrones (I) 104 D4
Contursi Terme (I) 104 D4
Conty (F) 77 F2
Convento, O (Poio) (E) 110 B4
Conversano (I) 105 H4
Conwy (GB) 54 E4
Cookstown (GB) 61 J2
Cookstown (GB) 61 J3?
Coola (IRL) 60 F4
Coole (F) 77 K4
Coole (IRL) 60 H4
Coombe (GB) 56 F6?
Coombe Bissett (GB) 58 D5
Coonagh (IRL) 62 E3?
Cooraclare (IRL) 62 D3
Cootehill (IRL) 61 H3
Cop (UA) 155 L5
Copa, La (E) 127 G3
Copacel (RO) 160 E4
Copăceni (RO) 168 E6
Copăceni (RO) 170 B6
Copăceni (RO) 162 E6?
Copălău (RO) 162 D3
Copalnic-Mănăștur (RO) 161 H2
Copciac (MD) 171 H2
Copdock (GB) 59 K3
Cope (E) 127 H5
Copertino (I) 107 K2
Çöpköy (TR) 181 K2
Çöpköy (TR) 183 J2
Copley (GB) 55 J1
Çöplü (TR) 193 J2
Çöplü (TR) 193 L5
Copons (E) 115 G4
Copovyći (UA) 151 H2
Copparo (I) 101 F3
Coppathorne (GB) 56 E4
Coppenbrügge (D) 70 J2
Coppet (CH) 86 B5
Copplestone (GB) 57 G4
Coppull (GB) 54 G3
Çopraşık (TR) 185 K5
Çopraşık (TR) 199 J2
Copşa Mică (RO) 169 G1
Coquille, La (F) 83 G5
Çoral (TR) 193 K3
Corabia (RO) 169 G6
Corachar = Coraxá (E) 122 B1
Coraci (I) 107 F4
Cora Droma Rúisc = Carrick-on-Shannon (IRL) 60 F4
Coral, C (E) 112 F2?
Coral, C (I) 112 A2?
Coraini (I) 106 B2?
Coraxá (E) 122 B1
Corazzo (I) 107 F4
Corbadjisko (BG) 176 D6
Corbalán (E) 121 G3
Corbasca (RO) 162 E6
Corbara (I) 102 E3
Corbeanca (RO) 170 B4
Corbeil-Essonnes (F) 76 F4
Corbeilles (F) 77 G5
Corbeny (F) 77 J3
Corbera (E) 121 H5
Corbera d'Ebre (E) 121 J1
Corbie (F) 77 G1
Corbigny (F) 84 E2
Corbii Mari (RO) 169 J4
Corbita (RO) 162 E6
Corbolo (I) 114 E4?
Corbola (I) 101 G2
Corbridge (GB) 53 L5
Corbu (RO) 162 B5
Corbu (RO) 169 H5
Comano?
Corby (GB) 55 L6
Corby Glen (GB) 55 L5
Corcagnano (I) 99 J3
Corcaigh (IRL) 62 F5
Corchiano (I) 102 E3
Corcieux (F) 78 F5
Corcoles (E) 120 C3
Corcoles (E) 119 F5?
Corcolle (F) 85 J3?
Corcova (RO) 168 D4
Corcubión (E) 110 A3
Cordal (E) 110 E2
Cordăreni (RO) 162 F2
Cordemais (F) 82 B2
Cordenons (I) 89 H6
Cordes-sur-Ciel (F) 93 H2
Córdoba (E) 125 K4
Cordobilla de Lácara (E) 125 G1
Cordovado (I) 89 J6
Cordovilla (E) 127 G2
Cordovilla la Real (E) 112 C4
Corduente (E) 120 D2
Cordun (RO) 162 D5
Coreglia Antelminelli (I) 99 K4
Çörekçiler (TR) 185 F4
Corellia (E) 113 H4
Coreses (E) 111 H5
Corestauti (MD) 157 M5
Corfe Castle (GB) 58 C6
Corfinio (I) 104 A1
Corgnac-sur-l'Isle (F) 83 G6
Corgo = Corgo, O (E) 110 E3
Corgo, O (E) 110 E3
Corhampton (GB) 58 E6
Cori (I) 103 F4
Coria (E) 118 C4
Coria del Río (E) 125 G5
Coriano (I) 101 H5
Corigliano Calabro (I) 107 G3
Corinaldo (I) 101 J5
Corips (E) 125 J6
Corjeuti (MD) 162 E2
Cork (IRL) 62 F5
Cork = Corcaigh (IRL) 62 F5
Corlăteni (RO) 162 D3
Corlăţeni (RO) 157 L6
Corlay (F) 74 E4
Corleone (I) 108 D2
Corleto Monforte (I) 106 D2
Corleto Perticara (I) 104 F5
Corlu (TR) 182 E3
Cormaia (RO) 161 J3
Cormainville (F) 76 E5
Corman (TR) 184 D5
Cormatin (F) 85 G3
Cormeilles (F) 76 B3
Corme-Porto (E) 110 B2
Cormery (F) 83 G2
Cormigk (D) 72 F2
Cormons (I) 164 A3
Cormontreuil (F) 77 K3
Cormost (F) 77 K5
Cormoz (F) 85 H4
Corna (UA) 150 C6
Corna (UA) 150 E4
Corna (UA) 161 G1
Corna (UA) 163 J3
Cornae (BY) 138 F3
Cornago (E) 113 G4
Corna Kamjanka (UA) 151 M5
Corna Ribnica (BG) 180 C1
Cornăţel (RO) 168 G1
Cornăţelu (RO) 169 K3
Corna Tysa (UA) 156 F5
Cornau (D) 65 J6
Cornberg (D) 71 J4
Corné (F) 75 L6
Cornea (RO) 168 C3
Cornedo Vicentino (I) 100 E1
Cornellà de Llobregat (E) 115 H5
Cornellà del Terri (E) 115 J3
Cornellana (E) 111 G2
Cornereva (RO) 167 K3
Corneşti (MD) 162 F4
Cornești (RO) 161 H3
Cornești (RO) 170 B4
Cornești (RO) 169 L3?
Cornhill (GB) 53 L3
Corni (RO) 162 D3
Corni (RO) 170 F2
Cornice (I) 100 B4
Corniglio (I) 100 C4
Cornimont (F) 78 F6
Corniolo (I) 101 F5
Corni Oslavy (UA) 156 G5
Cornivka (UA) 162 C2
Cornobyl' (UA) 9 M4
Cornobyl' (UA) 145 M6
Cornohirka (UA) 163 M5
Cornoholovka (UA) 155 M4
Cornokinci (UA) 150 C6
Cornolo (E) 111 F2
Cornomors'k (UA) 163 M6
Cornomors'ke (Krym) 13 K3
Cornomyn (UA) 163 J2
Cornucaka (UA) 151 J4
Cornutychi (UA) 161 G1
Cornudella de Montsant (E) 114 E5
Cornudilla (E) 112 E3
Cornu Luncii (RO) 162 C4
Cornus (F) 93 L3
Cornwood (GB) 56 G5
Corny-sur-Moselle (F) 78 E3
Coroana (RO) 170 F6
Corod (RO) 170 F2
Corodia (I) 103 G1?
Coroieni (RO) 161 H3
Coroisânmartin (RO) 161 K5
Coronada, La (E) 125 H2
Coronada, La (E) 125 J3
Coronil, El (E) 128 C3
Corovodë (AL) 178 C3
Corpach (GB) 50 G6
Corpaci (MD) 162 E2
Corps (F) 95 G1
Corps-Nuds (F) 75 H5
Corral de Almaguer (E) 119 K4
Corral de Calatrava (E) 119 H6
Corralejo (E) 129 d4
Corrales (E) 111 H5
Corrales (E) 124 F5
Corrales, Los (E) 125 K5
Corrales, Los (Los Corrales de Buelna, Los) (E) 112 C2
Corral-Rubio (E) 120 F6
Corrano (F) 96 E5
Corran (GB) 52 E1
Corrany (GBM) 54 C2
Corréggio (I) 99 K3
Correggioverde (I) 99 K3?
Corrèze (F) 83 J6
Corribo (I) 114 B2?
Corridonia (I) 101 K6
Corrieri de Pero (I) 109 H3
Corrie (GB) 52 E3
Corrilo = Mimetiz (E) 112 E2
Corringham, Stanford-le-Hope (GB) 59 H4
Corris (GB) 54 E5
Corrofin (IRL) 60 D6
Corroy (F) 77 J4
Corsavy (F) 93 K6
Corsham (GB) 58 C5
Corsico (I) 100 A2
Corte (F) 96 E4
Cortaillod (CH) 86 C4
Cortak (TR) 191 F3
Cortale (I) 107 F5
Cortanovci (SRB) 166 F3
Cortazar (E) 112 E2
Corte (F) 96 E4
Corte de Peleas (E) 125 F2
Corte Centrale (I) 101 G3
Corteconcepción (E) 128 A2
Corte de Pallás (E) 121 G5
Corte Franca (I) 99 J1
Cortegada (E) 110 B5
Cortegana (E) 125 F4
Cortemaggiore (I) 99 H3
Cortemilia (I) 98 E3
Cortenova (I) 87 H6
Cortes (E) 113 J5
Cortes (E) 121 F5
Cortes de Aragón (E) 114 B6
Cortes de Arenoso (E) 121 H3
Cortes de Baza (E) 126 E4
Cortes de la Frontera (E) 128 D4
Cortes de Pallás (E) 121 G5
Corte Sines (P) 124 D4
Cortiçô (P) 116 F3?
Cortiçô da Serra (P) 117 G2
Cortiglione (I) 98 E3
Cortijada el Pilar (E) 127 F5
Cortijo de Arriba (E) 119 H5
Cortijo de García-Gómez (E) 119 H5?
Cortijo de Tortas (E) 127 F2
Cortijos Nuevos (E) 126 E3
Cortijos Nuevos del Campo (E) 127 F4
Cortina (I) 113 G6
Cortina d'Ampezzo (I) 89 G4
Cortina (E) 103 H2
Cortkiv (UA) 150 B5
Cortona (I) 101 F6
Coruche (P) 116 D6
Coruh (TR) 190 B1
Corum (TR) 190 D3
Corulion (E) 111 F3
Corum (TR) 13 K5
Corum (TR) 185 J4
Coruña, A (E) 110 C2
Coruña del Conde (E) 112 D5
Corund (RO) 161 L5
Corvara (I) 88 F4
Corvara in Badia (I) 88 F4
Corvées-les-Yys, Les (F) 76 D5
Corvera (E) 127 H4
Corvo, Vila do (P) 129 a1
Corvol-l'Orgueilleux (F) 84 D2
Corvoy (IRL) 61 J3
Corwen (GB) 54 F5
Coryton (GB) 59 J4
Cosambeşti (RO) 170 E4
Coşava (RO) 160 E6
Coşbuc (RO) 161 J3
Coscojuela de Sobrarbe (E) 92 E6
Coşeiu (RO) 161 F3
Cosel-Zeishotz (D) 73 K3
Cosenza (I) 106 F4
Coşereni (RO) 170 D4
Coşeşti (RO) 169 H3
Cosići (BIH) 173 F1
Coslada (E) 120 A3
Cosmeşti (RO) 169 J5
Cosmeşti (RO) 162 E6?
Cosmina de Jos (RO) 170 B3
Cosnardière, la (F) 75 H2
Cosne-Cours-sur-Loire (F) 84 C2
Cosne-d'Allier (F) 84 C4
Cosoleto (I) 106 E6
Coşoveni (RO) 168 F5
Cossato (I) 98 E1
Cossaye (F) 84 D3
Cossebaude (D) 73 K4
Cossé-le-Vivien (F) 75 K5
Cossignano (I) 103 H2
Cossonay (CH) 86 C4
Costa (P) 124 B3
Costa, La (E) 128 C5
Costacciaro (I) 101 H6
Costache Negri (RO) 170 F2
Costa da Caparica (P) 116 C6
Costa de Canyamel (E) 123 H3
Costa Molini (I) 88 F4
Costăna (RO) 162 C3
Costana,La (E) 112 C2
Costangalic (MD) 171 G1
Costa Nova (E) 122 B5
Costa Nova (P) 116 D2
Costa Paradiso (I) 97 C1
Costaros (F) 94 C1
Coşteiu (RO) 168 B2
Costeşti (MD) 157 M6
Costeşti (MD) 163 H5
Costeşti (RO) 168 E2
Costeşti (RO) 169 H4
Costeşti (RO) 170 E3
Costeşti din Vale (RO) 169 J4
Costigliole d'Asti (I) 98 E3
Costigliole Saluzzo (I) 95 K1
Costineşti (RO) 171 H6
Costişa (RO) 162 D5
Costuleni (RO) 162 F4
Coşula (RO) 162 D3
Coswig (D) 73 K3
Coswig (Anhalt) (D) 73 G2
Coţatcu (RO) 170 E3
Coteana (RO) 169 G5?
Coteana (RO) 169 G5
Coteau, Le (F) 84 F4
Cotebrook (GB) 54 G4
Côte-Saint-André, La (F) 85 H6
Coteşti (RO) 170 E2
Cotgrave (GB) 55 K5
Cotherstone (GB) 55 J1
Cotî-Chiavari (F) 96 D5
Cotignac (F) 95 H3
Cotignola (I) 101 F4
Cotillas (E) 127 E3
Cotillo, El (E) 129 c4
Cotinière, La (F) 82 C5
Cotiujeni (UA) 162 D2
Cotiujenii Mari (MD) 163 H3
Cotiujenii Mici (MD) 163 H3
Cotmeana (RO) 169 H4
Cotnari (RO) 162 D4
Cotofăneşti (RO) 170 D1
Coţofenii din Dos (RO) 168 F5
Cotronei (I) 107 G4
Cottanello (I) 103 F3
Cottbus (D) 146 A2
Cottenham (GB) 55 N6
Cottens (CH) 85 K3?
Cottered (GB) 59 G4
Cottingham (GB) 55 M3
Cotușca (RO) 157 L5
Cotu Văii (RO) 171 G6
Cotyrkaky (UA) 157 M1
Couarde-sur-Mer, La (F) 82 C4
Coubert (F) 77 G4
Couches (F) 84 G3
Coucieiro (E) 110 A2?
Couço (P) 116 E6
Coucourou (F) 94 C1
Coucy-le-Château-Auffrique (F) 77 H2
Coudekerque-Branche (F) 68 C4
Coudray (F) 75 K5
Coudray-Saint-Germer, Le (F) 76 E3
Coudres (F) 76 D4
Coudures (F) 92 C3
Couëron (F) 82 B2
Couffy-sur-Sarsonne (F) 84 B5
Couflens (F) 93 G5
Couhé (F) 82 F4
Couilly-Pont-aux-Dames (F) 77 G4
Couiza (F) 115 H2
Coulanges-la-Vineuse (F) 77 J6
Coulanges-sur-Yonne (F) 77 J6
Coulans-sur-Gée (F) 75 M4
Coulaures (F) 83 G6
Couledoux (F) 93 F5
Coulevon (F) 78 E6?
Coulimer (F) 76 B4?
Coulommiers (F) 77 H4
Coulon (F) 82 D4
Coulonges-sur-l'Autize (F) 82 D4
Couloumé-Mondebat (F) 92 E3
Coulounieix-Chamiers (F) 83 G6
Coup (F) 82 F2?
Coupar Angus (GB) 53 J1
Coupru (F) 77 H3
Couptrain (F) 75 L4
Courances (F) 77 F5?
Courant (F) 82 D4
Courban (F) 78 B6
Courbiac (F) 93 G2?
Courcelles (F) 86 E1?
Courcelles-Chaussy (F) 78 E3
Courcemont (F) 76 B5
Courchaton (F) 78 F6
Courcheval (F) 98 B2?
Cour-Cheverny (F) 76 D6
Courcôme (F) 82 F5
Courçon (F) 82 D4
Courcy-aux-Loges (F) 76 F5
Cour-et-Buis (F) 85 H6
Courgains (F) 76 C5
Courgenard (F) 76 C5
Courgenay (CH) 85 M2
Courgivaux (F) 77 H4
Courmayeur (I) 85 L5
Courmelles (F) 77 H3
Cournon (F) 77 J3?
Cournonterral (F) 93 K4?
Courmont (F) 94 B4?
Cournon-d'Auvergne (F) 84 D5
Cournonterral (F) 94 C4
Couronne, La (F) 82 F5
Courpalay (F) 77 H4
Courpière (F) 84 E5
Courpignac (F) 82 E6
Courrendlin (CH) 86 D3
Courrières (F) 68 C4?
Cours (F) 84 F4
Cours (F) 93 H1
Coursac (F) 83 G6
Coursan (F) 93 L4
Coursegoules (F) 95 K3
Courseulles-sur-Mer (F) 75 L2
Cours-la-Ville (F) 84 F5?
Cours-sur-Loire, Cosne- (F) 84 C2
Courtalain (F) 76 D5
Courteix (F) 84 B5?
Courtenay (F) 77 H5
Courthézon (F) 94 E2
Courtils (F) 75 J3
Courtine, La (F) 84 B5
Courtisols (F) 77 L4
Courtomer (F) 76 B4
Courtown (IRL) 63 K3
Courtrai = Kortrijk (B) 68 E5
Court-Saint-Étienne (B) 69 H5
Courville-sur-Eure (F) 76 D5
Coussac-Bonneval (F) 83 H6
Coussey (F) 78 D5
Coustellet (F) 94 F3
Coustouges (F) 93 K6
Coutainville, Agon- (F) 75 H2
Coutances (F) 75 J2
Couterne (F) 75 L4
Couterne (F) 75 L3?
Coutras (F) 82 E6
Couture-d'Argenson (F) 82 E5
Couvertoirade, La (F) 94 B3
Couvet (CH) 85 K3
Couvin (B) 69 G6
Couvron-et-Aumencourt (F) 77 J2
Coux-et-Bigaroque-Mouzens (F) 93 F1
Couzon-et-Saint-Front (F) 93 F1
Cova = Coba (E) 110 D4?
Covadonga (E) 112 A2
Covaleda (E) 112 F5
Covanera (E) 112 D3
Covarrubias (E) 112 D4
Covas (E) 110 D1
Covas (P) 110 B5
Covas (P) 116 F2
Covas do Barroso (P) 110 D5
Covasăni (RO) 160 D5
Covasna (RO) 169 L2
Cove (GB) 50 F4
Cove (GB) 52 E3
Covedale (GB) 59 K2?
Covelo (P) 116 F2
Covelo = Covelo, O (E) 110 C4
Covelo, O (E) 110 C4
Coventi (TR) 197 J6?
Coventry (GB) 55 J6
Coverack (GB) 56 D6
Covet (E) 115 F3
Coveta Fumá, La = Coveta Fumada, la (E) 127 K3
Coveta Fumada, la (E) 127 K3
Covilhã (P) 118 A3
Covilhã (P) 116 F3?
Covões (P) 116 D3
Covrik = Tjalurek (S) 18 B8
Covurlui (MD) 163 G5
Cowan (GB) 55 G5?
Cowbridge (GB) 57 H3
Cowdenbeath (GB) 53 J2
Cowes (GB) 57 M4
Cowfold (GB) 58 F6
Cowie (GB) 53 H2
Cowley (GB) 58 C4
Cowshill (GB) 53 L5
Cox (E) 127 J3
Cox (F) 93 G3
Coxwold (GB) 55 K2
Coylton (GB) 52 F4
Cozaclia (MD) 171 H1
Cozăneşti (RO) 161 L3
Cozangic (MD) 163 G5
Cozar (E) 126 D2
Cozes (F) 82 D5
Cozieni (RO) 169 M3
Cozma (RO) 161 K4
Cozmeşti (RO) 162 G5
Cozzano (F) 96 E5
Cozze (I) 105 H3
Cracăoani (RO) 162 C4
Crăciunelu de Jos (RO) 161 H5
Craco (I) 107 F2
Craidorolț (RO) 160 F2
Craiești (RO) 161 J4
Craigavon (GB) 52 C6
Craigellachie (GB) 51 L5
Craighouse (GB) 52 D3
Craignure (GB) 52 D2
Craig-y-nos (GB) 57 G2
Crail (GB) 53 K2
Crail (GB) 53 K2?
Crailsheim (D) 80 C2
Craiova (RO) 168 F5
Craiova (RO) 169 H5?
Crambe (GB) 55 M2?
Cramlington (GB) 53 M4
Cranagh (IRL) 61 H2
Cranborne (GB) 58 D6
Cranbrook (GB) 59 J5
Cranfield (GB) 58 F3
Crângeni (RO) 169 H5
Crângu (RO) 169 J6
Cranleigh (GB) 58 G5
Crans (CH) 86 D5
Crans-Montana (CH) 86 D5
Crans-près-Céligny (CH) 86 B5
Craon (F) 75 K5
Craonne (F) 77 J3
Craponne-sur-Arzon (F) 84 E6
Crarae (GB) 52 E2
Crăsani de Sus (RO) 170 D4
Crasi (RO) 161 J3
Crasna (RO) 160 F3
Crasna (RO) 168 F3
Crasna (RO) 170 C2
Crasnarmeiscoe (MD) 163 G5
Crasnoe (MD) 163 K5
Craster (GB) 53 M4
Crathes (GB) 51 N5
Crathie (GB) 51 L5
Crathorne (GB) 53 N6
Crato (P) 117 F5
Crau, La (F) 95 H4
Cravagliana (I) 86 F6
Cravant-les-Côteaux (F) 83 F2
Cravegga (I) 86 F5
Craven Arms (GB) 54 G6
Crawford (GB) 53 J4
Crawinkel (D) 72 D4
Crawley (GB) 59 G5
Creaca (RO) 161 G3
Creag Ghoraidh = Creagorry (GB) 50 C5
Creagorry (GB) 50 C5
Creag Riabhach = Craig (IRL) 62 F1?
Crean's Cross Roads (IRL) 62 E5
Créateri (GB) 55 L6?
Crecente (E) 110 C4
Crèche, La (F) 82 E4
Crêches-sur-Saône (F) 85 G4
Crécy-en-Ponthieu (F) 68 B6
Crécy-sur-Serre (F) 77 J2
Credenhill (GB) 57 J1
Crediton (GB) 57 G4
Creegh (IRL) 62 D3
Creeslough (IRL) 60 G1
Creetown (GB) 61 O2
Creggan (IRL) 61 K3?
Creggs (IRL) 60 F5
Creggan (GB) 52 A5
Creggan (GB) 61 J2?
Creglingen (D) 79 N3
Creğan (GB) 61 H2?
Creil (F) 76 F3
Crema (I) 100 B2
Cremenes (E) 112 A3
Cremenea (RO) 170 F4?
Cremlingen (D) 71 L2
Cremona (I) 100 B2
Cremyll (GB) 56 F5
Créon (F) 92 D1
Créon-d'Armagnac (F) 92 D3
Crepaja (SRB) 167 G3
Crépey (F) 78 D4
Crépy-en-Valois (F) 77 G3
Cres (HR) 164 C5
Crès, Le (F) 94 C3
Crescentino (I) 98 E2
Crescenzio (CH) 87 H5?
Crespano del Grappa (I) 88 F6
Crespian (F) 94 D3
Crespi d'Adda (I) 99 H1
Crespino (I) 101 F3
Crespino del Lamone (I) 100 F4
Crespos (E) 119 G2
Cressa (I) 86 F6
Cressage (GB) 55 G5
Cressanges (F) 84 D4
Cressensac (F) 83 J6
Crest (F) 94 E1
Crest (F) 94 F1?
Crest (F) 83 J5?
Cresta (CH) 87 J5
Crestet, Le (F) 85 G6
Crestuma (P) 116 E1
Creswell (GB) 55 K4
Crêt de la Neige?
Creteil (F) 76 F4
Cretesti (RO) 162 F5
Cretas (E) 114 D6
Creţeni (RO) 169 J3?
Creţeşti (RO) 170 F4?
Creuil (F) 76 E4
Creußen (D) 72 D5?
Creuzburg (D) 72 C5
Creuzburg (D) 72 C5?
Crevacuore (I) 86 F6
Crevalcore (I) 100 E3
Crevant-Laveine (F) 84 D5
Crévechamps (F) 78 E4
Creveçoeur-le-Grand (F) 76 F2
Crevedia (RO) 170 B4
Crevedia Mare (RO) 169 K5
Crevenicu (RO) 169 K5
Crevillente (E) 127 J3
Crévoux (F) 95 J1
Crewe (GB) 55 H4
Crewkerne (GB) 58 B6
Crialés (E) 112 E3
Crianlarich (GB) 52 G2
Cricău (RO) 168 F1
Criccieth (GB) 54 D5
Crichton (GB) 53 K3
Cricíova (RO) 168 C2
Crickadarn (GB) 58 A3
Crickhowell (GB) 57 H2
Cricklade (GB) 57 L2
Cricov, Gornet- (RO) 170 C3
Cricova (MD) 163 H4
Cricova (MD) 163 H4?
Crieff (GB) 53 H2
Criegoles (F) 76 E3?
Criel-sur-Mer (F) 76 D1
Crikvenica (HR) 164 D4
Crimmitschau (D) 73 G4
Crimmitschau (D) 73 G4?
Crinan (GB) 52 D2
Crinitz (D) 73 K2
Criquetot-l'Esneval (F) 75 M1
Criș (RO) 169 H1
Criș, Chișineu- (RO) 160 D4
Crișan (RO) 171 J3
Crișcior (RO) 168 D1
Crișeni (RO) 160 F3
Crișeni (RO) 161 G3
Crișeni (RO) 161 H3
Crispiano (I) 105 H4
Crissay-sur-Manse (F) 83 F2
Crissolo (I) 95 K1
Criștești (RO) 161 J4
Criștinești (RO) 162 D3
Cristian (RO) 169 G2
Cristian (RO) 169 K2
Cristiana (RO) 170 A2
Cristianos, Los (E) 129 b4
Cristinești (RO) 157 K5
Cristiesti (RO) 162 C4
Cristóbal (E) 118 E3
Cristo del Espíritu Santo (E) 119 H5
Cristolț (RO) 161 G3
Cristur, Reconi (RO) 161 H3
Cristuru Secuiesc (RO) 161 L5
Criț (RO) 169 J1
Criuleni (MD) 163 J4
Crivina (RO) 167 K3
Crivitz (D) 66 F3
Crizbav (RO) 170 A2
Crkvice (MNE) 173 H4
Crkvice (HR) 173 F4
Crkvice (MNE) 173 J4
Crkvine (MNE) 174 B3
Crkvine (SRB) 167 F6
Crljivica (BIH) 165 G6
Crmljan = Cermjan (RKS) 174 D4
Crna Bara (SRB) 166 E4
Crna Bara (SRB) 166 D4
Crna Bara (SRB) 166 D6?
Crnac (HR) 165 K2
Crnac (RKS) 174 E2
Crna Gora (MNE) 174 B2
Crna na Koroškem (SLO) 91 G7
Crna Trava (SRB) 175 H3
Crnča (SRB) 166 D5
Crnči (MNE) 173 G4
Crni Lug (BIH) 165 H6
Crni Lug (HR) 172 E1
Crni Vrh (SLO) 164 D2
Crni Vrh (SLO) 164 B3
Crni Kal (SLO) 164 B3?
Crnjelovo Gornje (BIH) 166 D4
Crnomelj (SLO) 164 E4
Crnook (SRB) 174 D2
Crnoljevo = Carralevë (RKS) 174 E4
Crnomelj (SLO) 164 E3
Crnuce (SLO) 89 M5
Crocetta del Montello (I) 88 G6
Crockernwell (GB) 57 G4
Crockets Town (IRL) 60 D3
Crockford or Ninemile Bar (GB) 53 H4
Crocq (F) 84 B5
Crocy (F) 75 M3
Croë (F) 78 A4
Crodo (I) 86 F5
Croggnaleto (I) 103 G2
Crögnitz (D) 65 H3?
Crois (F) 84 E3?
Croisic, Le (F) 82 A2
Croisilles (F) 68 D6
Croisille-sur-Briance, la (F) 83 J5
Croissanville (F) 75 L3
Croismare (F) 78 F4
Croissant-Marie-Jaffré (F) 74 D4
Croissy-sur-Selle (F) 76 F2
Croisy-sur-Andelle (F) 76 D2
Croix, La (F) 98 G2
Croix-Blanche, la (F) 92 F2
Croix-Chapeau (F) 82 D4
Croix-de-Vie, Saint-Gilles- (F) 82 B3
Croix-Haute, La (F) 95 G1?
Croix-Valmer, La (F) 95 J4
Crolles (F) 85 J6
Cromarty (GB) 51 J4
Cromer (GB) 55 Q6?
Cromer (GB) 59 K2
Cromford (GB) 55 J4
Cromhall (GB) 57 K2
Cromwell (GB) 55 L4?
Crook (GB) 53 M5
Crookedwood (IRL) 63 H1
Crookham (GB) 53 L3
Crookhaven (IRL) 62 C5
Crookstown (IRL) 62 E5
Crookstown (IRL) 63 J2
Croom (IRL) 62 E3
Cropalati (I) 107 G3
Cropani (I) 107 G5

A B C D E F G H I J K L M N O P Q R S T U V W X Y Z

208 Cropani Marina

F

Förby (FIN) 35 L4
Forcall (E) 122 A1
Forcalqueiret (F) 95 H4
Forcalquier (F) 95 H4
Forcarei (E) 110 C3
Forchheim (D) 80 E1
Forchtenberg (D) 79 M3
Ford (GB) 62 K3
Förde (N) 30 D4
Førde (N) 30 E4
Förde (N) 30 E4
Ford (N) 59 H4
Förde (N) 59 M6
Fordingbridge (GB) 57 L4
Fordon (GB) 59 M6
Fordongianus (I) 97 C4
Fordstown (IRL) 63 J1
Fordyce (GB) 51 M4
Fore (N) 20 C7
Fore (N) 30 D3
Forenza (I) 120 D2
Forest (GB) 59 F3
Foresta di Burgos (I) 97 C3
Forest-Montiers (F) 68 B6
Forest-Saint-Julien (F) 95 H1
Forêt-sur-Sèvre, La (F) 82 D3
Forfar (GB) 50 L1
Forges, les (F) 72 C4
Forges-les-Eaux (F) 76 E2
Forio (I) 104 A4
Forkila (E) 44 G6
Forkill (GB) 61 K3
Forland (N) 38 E2
Förlanda (S) 38 F6
Forlì (I) 101 G4
Forlì del Sannio (I) 103 J4
Forlimpopoli (I) 101 G4
Forlitz-Blaukirchen (D) 64 G5
Förlösa (S) 45 J5
Formamba (I) 110 B3
Formazza (I) 86 F5
Formentor (E) 123 H3
Formia (I) 76 E2
Formigine (I) 99 K3
Formigliana (I) 98 E2
Formigmara (I) 101 F3
Forminy (F) 75 K2
Formiguères (F) 93 J2
Formofoss (N) 20 E4
Fornahás (P) 124 C4
Fornbu (N) 39 N3
Fornelli (I) 97 B2
Fornelli (I) 123 K2
Forni Avoltri (I) 89 H4
Forni di Sopra (I) 89 H5
Forni di Sotto (I) 89 H5
Forno (I) 86 F6
Forno Alfone (I) 98 C5
Forno Alpi Graie (I) 98 C2
Fornos de Algodres (P) 118 A2
Fornovo di Taro (I) 100 C3
Förolach (A) 90 D6
Foronda (I) 113 F3
Forøya (UA) 157 K5
Foróstic (RO) 167 J3
Forráskút (H) 159 J5
Forró (H) 155 J5
Fors (GB) 51 K4
Fors (S) 26 E8
Fors (S) 33 M1
Fors (S) 41 K2
Fors (S) 41 L2
Forsa (S) 20 F4
Forsand (N) 38 D5
Forsbacka (S) 22 C7
Forsbacka (S) 34 D3
Forsbacka (S) 41 L1
Forsbodarna (S) 40 G1
Forsby (S) 33 L5
Forsby (N) 37 J7
Forsen (N) 25 J2
Forseng (N) 25 J8
Förset (N) 31 N5
Forshaga (S) 40 D3
Forshälla (S) 43 J2
Forshällan (S) 22 B3
Forsheda (S) 44 D5
Forsinard (S) 51 K3
Förslöv (S) 44 B6
Forsmark (S) 34 B4
Forsmo (N) 25 M8
Forsnäs (S) 25 L6
Forsnes (S) 27 G2
Forsnäs (S) 40 C3
Forsol (N) 18 F2
Forssa (S) 43 K5
Forssjö (S) 41 K5
Forst (Lausitz) (D) 146 B2
Forstråkhed (S) 27 J2
Forsvik (S) 40 F5
Fortanete (E) 122 B1
Fort Augustus (GB) 51 H5
Fort-Bloqué, le (F) 74 E5
Fortézza (I) 89 G5
Fortezza (I) 86 E6
Fort George (GB) 51 J4
Forth (GB) 50 L3
Fortim (F) 124 D5
Fortingall (GB) 52 G1
Port-Mahon-Plage (F) 68 B6
Fortios (P) 124 D3
Fortuna (N) 30 M4
Fortuna (E) 127 F3
Fortuneswell (GB) 58 C6
Fort William (GB) 50 G6
Forus (N) 38 C5
Forua (N) 25 G3
Forxa, A Porqueira (E) 110 D4
Forza d'Agró (I) 106 D7
Fos (F) 114 E2
Fosdinovo (I) 100 C4
Fosnavåg (N) 30 D3
Fosnes (N) 30 G4
Fossesvågen (N) 24 F5
Foss (N) 17 J7
Fossa (I) 103 J3
Fossacésia (I) 103 J3
Fossacesia Marina (I) 103 K3
Fossan (N) 31 M3
Fossan (N) 38 M4
Fossan (N) 95 L1
Fossbakken (N) 21 H3
Fossbakken (N) 31 O3
Fossen (N) 39 M4
Fossen (N) 38 D5
Fosses-la-Ville (B) 69 H6
Fossestua (N) 20 F3
Fossheim (N) 21 K1
Fossheim (N) 17 J3
Fossholl (N) 30 G7
Fossholl (N) 30 D5
Fossli (N) 38 H3
Fossmoi (N) 38 D5
Fossol (N) 101 G2
Fossombrone (I) 101 H4
Fossum (N) 30 D4
Fossum (S) 30 H5
Fos-sur-Mer (F) 94 E4
Foston (GB) 55 L5
Fót (H) 159 H2
Fotheringhay (GB) 58 G2
Fotovo (RO) 176 D6
Fotolivos (GR) 180 B2
Fotwimere (GB) 59 H3
Foxai (E) 110 C2
Foumières (F) 77 F4
Foumeaux (F) 84 F5
Foumet (F) 95 G3
Foumoi (F) 84 F5
Fouras (F) 82 C5
Fourchambault (F) 77 E3
Fourfourás (GR) 195 F5
Fourias, Skála (GR) 180 C4
Fourmies (F) 77 K1
Fournà (N) 179 F6
Foumel (F) 93 H2
Fournels (F) 85 H4
Fournois (F) 85 J4
Foumoi (GR) 189 H4
Fourques (F) 94 E3
Foussais-Payré (F) 82 D3
Foussenol, Le (F) 93 G4
Fouxet Alios (E) ...
Fowant (GB) 57 L3
Fowey (GB) 62 D3
Fowls Wester (GB) 53 H2
Fowlmere (GB) 59 H3
Foxai (E) 110 C3
Foxford (IRL) 62 D3
Foza (I) 88 F6
Foz de Odeleite (P) 124 E5
Foz do Arelho (P) 116 C5
Fozbosa Soprana (I) 98 D4
Fraccano (I) 90 D5
Fracei (GB) 79 C6
Frades de la Sierra (E) 118 E2
Fradixeno (I) 89 M5
Fragagnano (I) 107 H2
Fragg (S) 41 J2
Fragni (E) 118 E7
Fragnalier (E) 32 G4
Frâirac, El (E) 113 K4
Fraize (F) 78 F5
Fråkenvik (S) 27 J5
Fralova (BY) 139 M2
Fram (SLO) 91 J7
Framford (N) 30 E5
Framley (DK) 46 F1
Framlingham (GB) 59 K3
Främlingshem (A) 41 L1
Frammersbach (D) 72 A5
Främmestad (S) 40 C6
Framnes (S) 16 F2
Franca, La (E) 111 H6
Francaltroff (F) 78 F4
Francardo « Francarello (F) 96 K4
Francavilla al Mare (I) 103 J3
Francavilla di Sicilia (I) 106 D7
Francenigo (I) 89 H6
Franceses (I) 129 N4
Francesc (RO) 169 G4
Franchesse (F) 84 D3
Francoforte (I) 109 G3
Francorchamps (B) 70 A6
Franco (I) 112 E6
Francova Lhota (CZ) 154 C3
Francuel (F) 83 H2
Frandefors (S) 43 J4
Frangádes (I) 178 D7
Franfelter (NL) 64 D5
Frankaplats (GB) 56 C6
Frankau (I) 117 G4
Frankenberg (I) 152 D2
Frankenberg (Eder) (D) 71 G4
Frankenberg am Hausruck (A) 89 J1
Frankenfelde (D) 73 J1
Frankenhardt (D) 79 M3
Frankenheim (D) 71 K5
Frankenmarkt (A) 89 J2
Frankenthal (Pfalz) (D) 79 J2
Frankfurt (Oder) (D) 67 M6
Frankfurt am Main (D) 70 G6
Franking (B) 35 H7
Fränninge (S) 44 F7
Fränsta (S) 33 L2
Frante (S) 59 M5
Franti Klový Lázne (CZ) 73 G5
Franzburg (D) 67 J3
Franzensfeste « Fortezza (I) 88 F4
Frascati (I) 103 F4
Frascineto (I) 105 F6
Frasdorf (D) 89 G2
Fraserburgh (GB) 51 N4
Fra'shär (AL) 178 C4
Frásin (RO) 162 B3
Fräsnet (D) 170 D5
Fråsvik (N) 38 C6
Frasne (F) 86 B4
Frasnes-lez-Buissenal (B) 68 F5
Frasso, El (E) 113 J6
Frasso Telesino (I) 103 K5
Fratta (RO) 161 J4
Frättáddi Nei (I) 157 J6
Frättáddi Vechi (RO) 157 J6
Fratres (D) 73 K1
Frättesti (N) 21 J3
Frifelt (DK) 46 D2
Frigento (I) 104 C4
Friis (I) 89 J6
Fritala (FIN) 35 J2
Friska (N) 38 M4
Friinand (N) 38 D4
Frinton-on-Sea (GB) 59 K4
Friockheim (GB) 53 K1
Frosinone (I) 103 H4
Frosta (N) 30 G5
Frostadheim (N) 16 G3
Frosterley (GB) 54 G4
Frøstrup (DK) 46 C3
Frostviken (S) 25 H5
Fróttey-lès-Vesoul (F) 86 B2
Fróttey-sur-Saône (F) ...
Frouard (F) 78 E4
Frøya (N) 20 F3
Fruges (F) 68 C5
Frula (I) 113 L5
Frumoasa (RO) 162 B6
Frumoasa (RO) 167 J2
Frumuşani (RO) 175 G3
Frumuşica (RO) 168 A1
Frunzoaia (RO) 162 D3
Fruntişeni (RO) 168 A4
Frutigen (CH) 86 E4
Fryele (S) 44 D6
Frygnowo (PL) 141 J3
Frykerud (S) 40 C4
Fryksås (S) 32 F5
Frymburk (CZ) 73 K4
Fryšták (CZ) 154 C3
Fryzlant nad Ostravicí (CZ) 154 C2
Frzenburk (CZ) 73 K4

G

Gaal (N) 89 M3
Gaanderen (NL) 69 L3
Gaasterian-Sloten « Gaasterân-Sleat (NL) 64 E4
Gaasterlân-Sleat (NL) 64 E4
Gabaldón (E) 120 E4
Gabarevo (BG) 176 D6
Gaberdu (I) 35 D5
Gaberi (I) 107 H3
Gabiano (I) 98 E3
Gabicce Mare (I) 101 H4
Gabin (PL) 142 G3
Gabino (S) 154 B6
Gabilan (LV) 157 F5
Gabiano (I) 96 E6
Gaborova (BG) 176 A1
Gabrovnica (MK) 175 K1
Gabrovo (BG) 176 D5
Gabrovica (BG) 179 M4
Gabrovo (BG) 176 D5
Gäbsten (D) 45 M4
Gåda (S) 33 K3
Gaceo (E) 113 G3
Gäche (DK) 46 D2
Gádbjerg (DK) 46 D2
Gäddede (S) 25 H5
Gädderás (I) 102 E6
Gader (E) 127 F4
Gädheim (D) 80 E6
Gädmaheim (S) 45 J3
Gadoros (H) 159 K5
Gádor (E) 127 F4
Gadžin Han (SRB) 175 J2
Gaf (PL) 142 G4
Gaflenz (A) 90 F2
Gaggenau (D) 79 K4
Gagliano (I) 108 F3
Gagliano Castelferrato (I) 109 G2
Gadkowice-Gôrne (PL) 148 E2
Gadin (E) 110 H3
Gadoros (H) 159 K5
Gador (E) 127 F4

Gaafanha da Boa Hora (P) 116 D2
Gafarlari (TR) 190 D5
Gafete (P) 117 F5
Gáfferu (TR) 185 J5
Gägelow (D) 47 H6
Gaggio (D) 67 K2
Gäggenau (D) 79 K4
Gaggi (I) 101 G1
Gagino (RO) 161 F2
Gaglio (SRB) 175 G3
Gagliano Castelferrato (I) 111 J4
Gagliano del Capo (I) 105 K6
Gagliato (SRB) 174 F1
Gagliole (I) 101 J5
Gagnef (S) 32 F7
Gagny (F) 76 E4
Gähyelira « Kâpponis (S) 26 G2
Gaianire (I) 89 G6
Gaiberg (I) 101 F3
Gaibova (BG) 162 E6
Gaick Lodge (GB) 51 J6
Gaienhofen (D) 87 G2
Gaigalava (LV) 138 H4
Gaik (I) 117 K5
Gaildorf (D) 79 M4
Gailingen (D) 87 G2
Gailtal (I) 124 D5
Gadola (I) 96 F6
Gaillac (F) 93 H3
Gaillac-Toulza (F) 93 G4
Gaillimh « Galway (IRL) 62 D5
Gaillon (F) 76 D3
Gainago (BY) 139 M3
Gainsborough (GB) 55 L4
Gaiola (I) 96 E6
Gaiole in Chianti (I) 99 L6
Gaipler (TR) 191 G3
Gairloch (GB) 50 H6
Gairmshiel Lodge (GB) 51 L5
Gais (CH) 87 H2
Gaisin (TR) 190 D4
Gaita (I) 118 C5
Gaj (PL) 142 G5
Gaj (SRB) 167 F6
Gaj (SRB) 174 F2
Gajary (SK) 158 E1
Gajdobra (SRB) 174 D4
Gajeva (LV) 134 E5
Gaj, Olawski (PL) 147 G4
Gajik (BY) 139 J3
Gajowniki (PL) 143 J2
Gâjt (MK) 145 O2
Gajdovo (BY) 145 O2
Gakovo (SRB) 159 J6
Gala (I) 118 D5
Galabova, Surdia (RO) 170 E3
Gäläseni (RO) 169 K4
Galaktonovo (BG) 176 F6
Galan (F) 93 F4
Galán (SK) 158 E1
Galanpage (I) 119 H2
Galapagar (E) 119 G3
Galäroža (E) 124 F4
Gala setter (N) 31 O4
Galata (BG) 176 B2
Galatás (GR) 187 K4
Galatás (GR) 189 F6
Galates (I) 121 L3
Galatina (I) 107 J3
Galatista (GR) 180 C4
Galatone (I) 107 J3
Galatro (I) 106 D6
Galaxidi (GR) 186 E5
Galba (LV) 139 K6
Galbally (IRL) 62 F6
Galbena (RO) 162 A4
Gâlbinasi (RO) 175 K2
Galdakao (E) 112 F7
Galdavai (TR) 190 A4
Galdin (E) 113 J1
Galdsstaðir (IS) 32 D3
Gáldvhar (GB) 51 ...
Gales (GR) 195 G5
Galeata (I) 101 F4
Galegos (E) 118 C5
Gâlênesti (RO) 162 B3
Galende (E) 110 E4
Galera (E) 126 E3
Galera, la (E) 122 B1
Galeria (F) 96 J4
Galgagueno (I) 98 F4
Galgamácsa (H) 159 H2
Galgon (F) 92 D2
Galiano (I) 104 D3
Galiano di Lucania (I) 104 ...

Gammelstaden (S) 22 E5
Gammersvik (N) 30 D6
Gammertingen (D) 79 L6
Gamstorp (S) 41 H3
Gamvik (N) 18 E3
Gamvik (N) 18 F2
Gan am Kamp (A) 153 J6
Ganacker (D) 90 C2
Gânara (AL) 178 B4
Gancary (BY) 138 B6
Gandi (E) 121 G4
Gândul (RO) 175 K4
Gandvik (N) 19 M3
Gane (BG) 179 L2
Ganesa (RO) 175 G5
Gang (GR) 178 F3
Gangi (I) 109 G3
Gângurova (RO) 168 F6
Gangkofen (D) 90 B3
Gannay-sur-Loire (F) 84 D3
Gams am Inn (D) 90 B3
Gansdale Head (GB) 56 F4
Garsten (A) 90 F2
Garrucha (E) 127 G4
Garsnäs (S) 44 C7
Garvagh (GB) 52 E5
Garvagh (RL) 60 A4
Garvan (BG) 177 G3
Garvin (E) 124 C4
Garvock (GB) 52 A1
Garwolin (PL) 148 E2
Garyn (BY) 140 C3
Garzyn (PL) 146 F2
Gás (N) 158 F7
Gascò (RO) 168 F6
Gascuña (E) 120 C3
Gåscueña (E) 120 C3
Gäsene (S) 43 J1
Gásene (S) 43 J3
Gáseni (RO) 169 K3
Gåsewaijaur (S) 25 J6
Gäsgelli (RO) 168 F6
Gaspole, El (E) 125 J6
Gasport (PL) 148 E2
Gaspoltshofen (A) 90 ...

Geiselhöring (D) 81 G3
Geiselwind (D) 80 C1
Geisenfeld (D) 80 E3
Geisenhausen (D) 90 B3
Geisingen (D) 79 K5
Geislingen an der Steige (D) 80 B3
Geisfeld (Rhön) (D) 72 B5
Geisteren (D) 76 B4
Geiten (D) 72 C4
Geiten (D) 64 G6
Gekan (CH) 87 G4
Gela (I) 108 F4
Gelbensande (D) 67 K2
Geldelser (E) 120 B3
Gelemovo (BG) 176 D4
Geleen (NL) 70 A4
Gelemo (TR) 196 D2
Gelendost (TR) 191 H4
Gelendžik (RUS) 173 M4
Geligneret (GB) 56 C5
Gelincik (TR) 191 G4
Gelibolu (TR) 181 K4
Gellidin (TR) 196 D2
Gelida (E) 113 G6
Gelinck (TR) 191 J5
Gelnica (SK) 155 G6
Gelnhausen (D) 71 H6
Gelsa (E) 113 L4
Gelse (H) 158 F4
Gelsenkirchen (D) 70 D3
Gelsted (DK) 46 D3
Geltendorf (D) 79 H7
Gelting (D) 65 M2
Gelu (RO) 159 L5
Gembloux (B) 69 H6
Gemeinde Liebenfeld (A) 90 F5
Gemerská Panica (SK) 155 G5
Gemert (NL) 69 K3
Gémini (TR) 194 D3
Gemio (GR) 191 H5
Geminne (F) 78 D4
Gemmenich (B) 70 B5
Gemona del Friuli (I) 89 J5
Gemünd (D) 70 C5
Gemünden (Felda) (D) 71 H5
Gemünden (Wohra) (D) 71 G5
Gemünden am Main (D) 71 J6
Gemzigo, Crosna (RO) 161 J3
Geraci Siculo (I) 109 G3
Gerakarou (GR) 180 C3
Gerakas (GR) 187 J6
Gerakia (I) 121 H6

Gerolzhofen (D) 72 C6
Geroplátanos (GR) 178 C6
Gerovo (RO) 164 D3
Gerrards Cross (GB) 58 F4
Gerri de la Sal (E) 114 F3
Gersau (CH) 87 G4
Gersfeld (Rhön) (D) 72 B5
Gersheim (D) 78 G3
Gersten (D) 64 G6
Gerstetten (D) 80 C3
Gerthofen (D) 80 B4
Getup (TR) 72 C4
Gerwisch (D) 66 F6
Gerze (TR) 13 L5
Gerze (TR) 13 M6
Gescher (D) 69 N3
Geseke (D) 70 G3
Geslau (D) 80 C2
Gespunsart (F) 77 L2
Gessertshausen (D) 80 D4
Gestad (S) 43 K1
Gesten (D) 71 J2
Gesualdo (I) 104 B3
Geszved (S) 116 E1
Getafe (E) 119 H3
Getesjön (S) 33 J3
Geteló (S) 45 L6
Getinge (S) 43 L5
Getiklen (S) 33 J3
Gets, les (F) 86 C5
Getterö (S) 41 L6
Getxo « Getko (E) 112 E7
Geuensee (I) 87 H5
Geveresdorf (D) 65 N1
Geversdorf (D) 65 J4
Gévora del Caudillo (E) 117 H6
Gevsjön (S) 24 G7
Gevrey-Chambertin (F) 85 G2
Gex (F) 86 C3
Gey (TR) 197 F3
Geyikli (TR) 181 K6
Geyre (TR) 190 F4
Geyve (TR) 183 K4
Gezende (TR) 198 F2
Gezir (TR) 198 F3
Gezu (TR) 198 H3
Ghedi (I) 100 D2
Ghelari (RO) 168 D2
Ghencl (RO) 160 F2
Gheorghe Doja (RO) 161 K5
Gheorghe Doja (RO) 175 H4
Gherăesti (RO) 162 D4
Gherghești (RO) 162 F6
Ghergheu (RO) 169 K2
Gherla (RO) 161 K3
Ghernesig (RO) 169 J4
Ghidfalău (RO) 162 D6
Ghidigeni (RO) 170 C1
Ghidigeni (RO) 162 F5
Ghilad (RO) 174 C2
Ghilarza (I) 97 C4
Ghimbav (RO) 169 K4
Ghimeş-Făget (RO) 162 D5
Ghimpati (RO) 175 G3
Ghimpeteni (RO) 169 H6
Ghindari (RO) 162 B5
Ghiroda (RO) 167 H2
Ghisonaccia (F) 96 K4
Ghisoni (F) 96 K4
Giano dell'Umbria (I) 102 F3
Giardinetto Vecchio (I) 104 D3
Giardini-Naxos (I) 109 E6
Giarmata (RO) 167 H2
Giarratana (I) 109 G3
Giarre (I) 109 F3
Giat (F) 84 E4
Giave (I) 97 C3
Giaveno (I) 98 D2
Giazza (I) 100 D1
Gibellina (I) 108 C2
Gibilmanna (I) 109 G3
Gibostad (N) 21 H2
Gideå (S) 26 E8
Gideåbacka (S) 22 C7
Gideå bruk (S) 26 E8
Gidle (PL) 148 B2
Gien (F) 84 C1
Giengen an der Brenz (D) 80 C3
Giera (RO) 174 C2
Gieraltowice (PL) 154 G1
Gieten (NL) 64 F4
Giethoorn (NL) 64 E5
Giers (F) 85 K7
Gietrzwałd (PL) 141 J3
Giewont (PL) ...
Giffaumont-Champaubert (F) 77 L4
Gifhorn (D) 66 B6
Gige (H) 158 F5
Gignac (F) 94 C3
Gignac (F) 95 H4
Gignod (I) 98 D2
Gijón « Xixón (E) 111 J4
Gilau (RO) 161 J3
Gilberdyke (GB) 55 L3
Gilbkan (IS) 15 E5
Gildeskål (N) 24 F2
Gilford (GB) 61 K3
Gillberga (S) 40 C4
Gillenfeld (D) 70 C6
Gilleleje (DK) 39 N7
Gilley (F) 86 C3
Gillhov (S) 32 G2
Gillingham (GB) 59 H5
Gilmu (TR) 191 G5
Gilocourt (F) 76 E3
Gilze (NL) 69 H3
Gimat (TR) 196 C2
Gimåt (TR) 196 D2
Gimigliano (I) 107 F4
Gimo (S) 34 B4
Gimont (F) 93 F3
Gimsøy (N) 20 D4
Gine (CH) 87 G4
Ginasservis (F) 95 G3
Gingin (CH) 86 C5
Gingelom (B) 69 J6
Ginosa (I) 105 H3
Ginosa Marina (I) 105 J3
Gioi (I) 104 C5
Gioia del Colle (I) 105 G3
Gioia Sannitica (I) 104 B3
Gioia Tauro (I) 106 D6
Gioiosa Ionica (I) 107 F6
Gioiosa Marea (I) 109 G1
Giornico (RO) 87 G3
Giovinazzo (I) 105 G2
Gipka (LV) 130 C3
Girftekovo (BG) 176 D5
Girgenti (MT) ...
Girona « Gerona (E) 115 J4
Girtan (RO) 175 K2
Gistel (B) 68 E4
Giswil (CH) 87 G3
Gioba (RO) 168 B5
Gizalki (PL) 147 G2
Gizycko (PL) 135 F5
Gizzeria (I) 106 E5
Gizzeria Lido (I) 106 E5
Gjemnes (N) 30 G4
Gjendesheim (N) 31 H4
Gjermundshamn (N) 38 E3
Gjern (DK) 46 D2
Gjerstad (N) 39 K5
Gjerstad (N) 31 O2
Gjesvær (N) 18 E1
Gjevallen (S) 32 E6
Gjilan « Gnjilane (RKS) 175 H4
Gjinar (AL) 178 C3
Gjøl (DK) 46 D1
Gjøra (N) 31 H3
Gjøvdal (N) 39 J5
Gjøvik (N) 31 M5
Gladbeck (D) 70 D3
Gladenbach (D) 71 F5
Gladhammar (S) 40 H3
Gladstad (N) 24 D4
Glaisdale (GB) 55 K4
Glamis (GB) 53 J1
Glamoč (BIH) 165 H3
Glamsbjerg (DK) 46 D3
Glanberg (A) 90 F3
Glandorf (D) 65 H6
Glane (N) 39 K5
Glanshammar (S) 40 H4
Glan-y-afon (GB) 54 F5
Glarus (CH) 87 H3
Glarus Süd (CH) 87 H3
Glarus Süd (CH) 87 H4
Glashütte (D) 67 H6
Glasson (GB) 54 F2
Glasgow (GB) 50 K3
Glashütte (D) 73 H3
Glashütten (D) 80 E7
Glasinac (BIH) 166 B5
Glastonbury (GB) 57 K3
Glattfelden (CH) 87 G2
Glauburg (D) 71 H6
Glaubitz (D) 67 J7
Glauchau (D) 72 E4
Glava (BG) 176 B5
Glava (S) 40 C4
Glavace (HR) 164 F3
Glavan (BG) 179 M4
Glavatićevo (BIH) 166 B5
Glavice (BIH) 165 J3
Glavinica (BG) 177 G3
Glavnik (RKS) 175 G3
Glažňovo (BG) ...
Glebowo (PL) 140 G2
Gledici (SRB) 174 F3
Gledin (RO) 161 L3
Gleina 211

Ilieni (RO) 169 K2
Ilija Blăskovo (BG) 177 H2
Ilijaš (BIH) 166 B6
Ilijno (MK) 175 G5
Ilini (LV) 132 E3
Ilíno (RUS) 135 M6
Il'inskoe (RUS) 136 H4
Ilio (GR) 187 H3
Iliokastro (GR) 188 B5
Iliospół (GR) 187 H4
Ilijnska Bistrica (SLO) 164 C3
Ilijepił (RO) 162 C3
Ilip (TR) 13 K5
Iliçu (TR) 189 F5
Iljušinc (RUS) 136 H4
Iľkaviły (FIN) 139 L5
Ilkeston (GB) 58 D2
Ilkkurşun (TR) 190 D4
Ilkley (GB) 55 J3
Ilkowice (PL) 148 B5
Iľana (E) 120 C3
Illar (E) 126 E6
Illby = Ilola (FIN) 36 E4
Illertissen (D) 80 C4
Illescas (E) 119 J3
Ille-sur-Têt (F) 93 K5
Illfurth (F) 86 D2
Illhaeusern (F) 79 G5
Illičivs'k = Comomors'k (UA) 163 M6
Illiers-Combray (F) 76 D5
Illiat (F) 75 F4
Illinci (UA) 151 J5
Illinci (UA) 157 H5
Illingen (D) 79 K3
Illjašivka (UA) 163 H4
Ilľjašivka (UA) 163 H4
Illkirch-Graffenstaden (F) 79 H4
Illmanns (A) 153 H6
Illmensee (D) 79 L6
Illmitz (A) 91 L4
Illo (FIN) 35 L4
Illo (FIN) 35 M2
Illois (F) 76 E2
Illora (E) 126 C5
Illot, S' (E) 123 H3
Illugastaðir (IS) 16 F3
Illugastaðir (IS) 17 J3
Illuka (EST) 131 N2
Illvästetra (N) 31 G4
Ilľzach (F) 79 G6
Ilmajoki (FIN) 28 C6
Il Marziano (I) 104 F3
Ilmenau (D) 71 L1
Ilmington (GB) 57 L1
Ilminster (D) 58 B6
Ilmmünster (D) 80 F4
Ilmola (FIN) 35 O2
Ilmolahti (FIN) 28 F6
Ilmoçvija (FIN) 38 F7
Ilmova Gora (RUS) 134 G4
Ilhyçia (UA) 156 D5
Ilok (HR) 166 E3
Ilola (FIN) 36 E4
Ilomantsi (FIN) 29 L6
Ilóren (TR) 189 H4
Ilosjoki (FIN) 28 E5
Ilovĕ (RO) 168 D4
Ilovik (HR) 164 D6
Ilovita (RO) 167 K4
Ilow (PL) 142 C6
Ilowa (F) 146 C3
Ilowo-Osada (PL) 142 C4
Ilsbo (S) 33 N4
Ilsede (D) 71 K2
Ilsenburg (Harz) (D) 71 L3
Ilseng (N) 31 P6
Ilsfeld (D) 79 L3
Ilshofen (D) 80 B2
Il'skij (RUS) 18 H4
Ilskov (FIN) 42 D6
Iltula (FIN) 35 L4
Ilukste (LV) 134 B6
Ilumetsa (EST) 131 M5
Ilva Mare (RO) 161 K3
Ilva Mică (RO) 161 K3
Ilvesjoki (FIN) 35 K2
Ilyaskôy (TR) 191 J5
Ilyasiar (TR) 190 D2
Ilyasiar (TR) 192 E4
Ilyasli (TR) 191 J3
Ilyaspaşa (TR) 192 C2
Iľzaj (AL) 91 J5
Ilze (PL) 148 D3
Ilze (PL) 138 D1
Ilzeskains (LV) 134 H4
Imamli (TR) 198 D3
Imamuşağı (FIN) 199 G3
Imatra (FIN) 37 L2
Imatu (EST) 131 N2
Imavere (EST) 131 J3
Imbradas (LT) 133 N6
Imecik (TR) 197 H2
Imeckdususuzu (TR) 197 H2
Imende (I) 110 B4
Imeri Morozova (RUS) 37 Q5
Imer (I) 88 F5
Imfors (S) 26 C7
Imielin (PL) 164 E1
Iminoñ Fjellstue (N) 39 J2
Imintzillu (F) 113 J3
Imiri (FIN) 28 E6
Imjanin (BY) 149 K1
Imjärvi (BY) 149 L1
Immala (FIN) 37 L2
Immelborn, Barchfeld- (D) 72 C4
Immenhausen (D) 71 K3
Immenreode (D) 71 K3
Immenstaad am Bodensee (D) 87 H2
Immenstadt im Allgäu (D) 88 C2
Immenstedt (D) 64 C6
Immilä (FIN) 36 E2
Immingham (GB) 55 M3
Imminghausen (D) 51 P2
Imón (E) 120 C1
Imotski (HR) 172 F3
Imperia (I) 98 B5
Imphy (F) 84 D3
Implanti (FIN) 7 S5
Implanti (RUS) 37 Q1
Imposta (I) 103 H2
Imprunéta (I) 100 E5
Imrali (FIN) 37 L2
Imranlar (TR) 191 M6
Imrendovo (BG) 177 G2
Imrenler (TR) 192 D5
Imroz = Gökçeada (TR) 181 H4
Ims (N) 38 C5
Imsdalen (N) 31 O4
Imsen (N) 31 O4
Imsland (N) 38 C4
Imt (AL) 88 B3
Instićovo (UA) 156 D5
Insweilor (D) 36 A4
Ina, La (E) 128 B4
Inagh (A) 62 D3
Inalli (TR) 193 J3
Inalözi (TR) 185 G4
Inand (RO) 160 G4
Inari (FIN) 19 K5
Inari (FIN) 19 K5
Inay (FIN) 191 G4
Ince (TR) 123 G3
Ince (TR) 191 G4
Incekara (TR) 184 F3
Incekaya (TR) 198 C2
Inceler (TR) 191 H5
Incepilli (TR) 184 D6
Inceson (TR) 185 M3
Incesu (TR) 185 K3
Incesu (TR) 193 K3
Inch (IRL) 61 K3
Inchcleraigh (IRL) 62 D5
Inchnadamph (GB) 50 H3
Inchture (GB) 53 J2
Inciems (LV) 133 K3
Incira (TR) 191 J1
Incinillas (E) 112 D3
Incipinar (TR) 185 J2
Incirköy (TR) 197 F2
Incirliova (TR) 191 G5
Inciriköy (TR) 190 D5
Incisa in Val d'Arno (I) 99 L5
Incisa Scapaccino (I) 98 E3
Incourt (B) 69 H5
Incugez (TR) 184 E4
Inčukalns (LV) 133 K3
Incy (RUS) 7 W3
Inden (D) 70 B5
Independenza (RO) 170 E5
Independenza (RO) 170 F3
Independenza (RO) 171 G6
Indersdorf, Markt (D) 80 E4
Indevillers (F) 86 E2
India (S) 41 J3
Indira (LV) 134 E3
Indjija (SRB) 167 H2
Indre Arna (N) 30 C7
Indre Billefjord (N) 19 H3
Indre Brenna (N) 19 M2
Indreede (N) 30 G3
Indre Hävik (N) 38 B3
Indrek (LV) 134 D6
Indrelandsnes (N) 30 E4
Indre Leirpollen (N) 19 M1
Indreveg (N) 30 F2
Industrial Estate (GB) 51 O4
Inebolu (TR) 18 H5
Inecik (TR) 181 L2
Inegöl (TR) 183 J6
Ineu (TR) 185 N1
Inežili (TR) 183 J5
Inhel (LV) 134 F6
Inhulec' (UA) 158 D6
Inhulec' (UA) 158 D6
Inkee (FIN) 29 O3
Inkila (FIN) 36 H2
Inkilän (LV) 134 F6
Inkernő (TR) 193 J2
Inkisto (TR) 191 M6
Inkoo (FIN) 36 C4
Inland (RO) 160 G4

J

Jääkdyspohja (FIN) 28 D7
Jaakkopää (FIN) 29 L6
Jaala (FIN) 36 F2
Jaalanka (FIN) 23 L6
Jaala (FIN) 29 K2
Jaalanka (FIN) 29 K2
Jaama (EST) 131 N2
Jaamaa (FIN) 29 M7
Jääskö (FIN) 23 H2
Jabalanac (HR) 164 E6
Jabalera (E) 120 D2
Jabalquinto (E) 126 C2
Jabapusta (H) 158 F4
Jabel (D) 67 H3
Jablanac (HR) 164 E6
Jablanica (BIH) 172 E3
Jablanica (BG) 176 B2
Jablanica (SRB) 175 L3
Jablanica (SRB) 176 B2
Jablanica (MK) 175 H4
Jablanica (BG) 178 D2
Jablanica (SRB) 167 F6
Jablanovac (RO) 169 H4
Jablonec nad Nisou (CZ) 146 C4
Jablonica (SK) 153 G4
Jablonka (PL) 155 G2
Jablonka Kościelna (PL) 142 G5
Jablonkov (CZ) 155 G1
Jablonna (PL) 142 E6
Jablonna (PL) 148 E2
Jablonne v Podještědí (CZ) 73 M4
Jablonov (CZ) 146 D5
Jabłonów (PL) 154 B4
Jablonów Pomorskie (PL) 141 M3
Jablunka (CZ) 155 G1
Jabuka (SRB) 167 H2
Jabugo (E) 125 J5
Jabuka (BIH) 172 B3
Jabukovac (SRB) 168 C3
Jabukovac (SRB) 168 C5
Jabukovik (SRB) 175 K2
Jaca (E) 114 F4
Jaçaba (F) 113 H2
Jaca (E) 121 M1
Jacentów (PL) 148 D3
Jachenau (D) 88 E5
Jachymów (PL) 144 D3
Jáchymov (CZ) 72 E4
Jackaliken (S) 27 G5
Jacob (D) 80 D2
Jacobsdorf (D) 73 M2
Jaderberg (D) 65 J5
Jadów (PL) 148 F1
Jadraque (E) 120 C1
Jægersborg (DK) 47 J7
Jaén (E) 126 C3
Jafari (FIN) 28 E5
Jaffa (E) 121 M1
Jagel (D) 64 D4
Jagenbach (A) 91 P4
Jagerilld (PL) 148 B4
Jagodar (E) 121 M1
Jagel (D) 64 D4
Jaghini (BY) 135 M4
Jagodina (SRB) 167 M5
Jagodkino (RUS) 136 H2
Jagodnjak (HR) 166 C2
Jagodnjak (HR) 166 C2
Jagów (D) 67 K4
Jagstzell (D) 80 A2
Jahkola (FIN) 36 E2
Jahodná (SK) 153 G5
Jahodné (SRB) 167 G3
Jajce (BIH) 172 E1
Jajkowo (PL) 142 B4
Jakabszállás (H) 159 G3
Jakalj (BIH) 172 B3
Jakgbgk (FIN) 35 N3
Jakipgk (FIN) 35 N3
Jakkukylä (FIN) 29 J2
Jakkula (FIN) 35 J1
Jäkkvik (S) 26 C3
Jakobsbyn (FIN) 29 H4
Jakobstad = Pietarsaari (FIN) 28 D5
Jakokoski (FIN) 29 L6
Jakšić (HR) 166 B3
Jakubany (SK) 154 C3
Jakubčovice (CZ) 146 D6
Jakubovice (CZ) 146 D6
Jakubovo (BY) 135 N5
Jakubów (PL) 148 F1
Jakunowo (PL) 142 F3
Jälä (FIN) 28 F6
Jala (LT) 136 E2
Jalasjärvi (FIN) 28 C7

K

Kaakamo (FIN) 22 G5
Kaalasjärvi (FIN) 18 C6
Kaamanen (FIN) 19 K4
Kaamasmukka (FIN) 19 J5
Kaanaa (FIN) 35 K4
Kaanaa (FIN) 36 C1
Kaananmaa (FIN) 29 K7
Kaaresuvanto (FIN) 18 D4
Kaarina (FIN) 35 K4
Kaarlela (FIN) 28 C5
Kaaro (FIN) 28 D6
Kaartilankoski (FIN) 37 H2
Kaavi (FIN) 29 K6
Kaba (H) 160 C2
Kabakça (TR) 182 F5
Kabakçı (TR) 185 K3
Kabakoz (TR) 183 J3
Kabala (EST) 131 J3

Kalana (EST) 130 B3
Kalana (EST) 131 K3
Kalandia (UA) 171 H2
Kalandra (UA) 180 C5
Kala Nera (GR) 180 C6
Kalanti (FIN) 35 J3
Kalapódi (GR) 188 A2
Kalaraš = Călăraşi (MD) 163 G4
Kalarna (S) 33 L2
Kálathos (N) 198 D3
Kalávita (N) 36 C4
Kalavárda (GR) 199 G5
Kalawa = Calau (D) 73 K2
Kalax (N) 28 B7
Kalazalny (BY) 143 M5
Kalbach (D) 71 J6
Kalbe (Milde) (D) 66 E5
Kalce (RUS) 89 L6
Kalčeva (UA) 171 H2
Kaldbak (D) 177 G4
Kaldbak (F) 48 E3
Kaldbakur (IS) 16 F6
Kaldenkirchen (D) 69 L4
Kaldfarnes (N) 20 F2
Kaldhusseter (N) 30 G3
Kaldrm Tuzlası (TR) 193 F3
Kaldvåg (N) 20 E4
Kale (FIN) 191 F6
Kale (TR) 197 G2
Kalebalta (TR) 193 H3
Kaleburnu (CY) 199 H4
Kaleck (TR) 185 F5
Kaleck (TR) 193 J2
Kaleck (TR) 199 H5
Kaleczyn (PL) 142 E3
Kalefeld (D) 72 C2
Kalej (PL) 147 K4
Kaiek (CZ) 73 J4
Kalekovec (RUS) 176 C4
Kalekóy (TR) 192 D4
Kalekóy (TR) 192 E4
Kalen (S) 32 K2
Kälen (S) 33 L3
Kalena (UA) 144 C5
Kalenés (GR) 167 L5
Kalenic (TR) 176 C2
Kalentzi (GR) 178 D5
Kaléro (GR) 187 K3
Kalérgo (GR) 188 D4
Kalesninkai (LT) 143 M2
Kaleti (LV) 132 C5
Kalety (BY) 137 K6
Kaleva (FIN) 191 K4
Kaleva (RUS) 7 S3
Kalfaköy (TR) 182 F6
Kalfat (TR) 185 F4
Kalfholt (IS) 16 F4
Kalho (FIN) 36 E2
Kalhovd (N) 38 H2
Kali (FIN) 191 G3
Kali (HR) 172 B1
Kaliec (UA) 187 F4
Kalisach (UA) 174 D3
Kaličane = Kaliçan (RKS) 174 D3
Kalidona (GR) 186 D5
Kalittos (GR) 180 E2
Kali Limènes (GR) 195 F6
Kalimanci (BG) 175 K6
Kalimanci (TR) 177 J2
Kalimantsi (BG) 180 C4
Kalimash (AL) 174 D4
Kalimnos (GR) 189 J6
Kálimnos (GR) 189 J6
Kalinaika (BY) 145 H3
Kalinga (BY) 199 F3
Kalináovo (SK) 149 H3
Kalinharman (TR) 190 F3
Kalini (UA) 161 H1
Kalinina (BY) 145 N3
Kalinine (UA) 163 J1
Kaliningrad (RUS) 136 C4
Kalinino (RUS) 136 H5
Kalinkavičy (BY) 9 L4
Kalinkovy (BY) 197 F1
Kalinovka (RUS) 173 M3
Kalinovka (TR) 185 F4
Kalinovo (SK) 54 F5
Kalinowa (PL) 147 J2
Kalinówka (PL) 146 H4
Kalinpetti (TR) 185 F6
Kalipki (PL) 141 K3
Kálita (M) 178 G4
Kalisz (PL) 141 J2
Kalisz Pomorski (PL) 140 E4
Kalithéa (GR) 180 D2
Kalithés (GR) 196 D3
Kaliti (SF) 37 N6
Kality (BY) 138 F3
Kalivac (AL) 174 C5
Kalivári (GR) 188 E4
Kalivári (GR) 196 E3
Kalivia (GR) 186 C4
Kalivia (GR) 186 D5
Kalivia (GR) 187 H4
Kalix (S) 22 F5
Kalixfors (S) 22 F5
Kaljord (N) 20 E3
Kaljuha (BY) 138 G5
Kalk (A) 161 J2
Kallaste (EST) 131 M3
Kallbäcken (S) 40 G2
Kallbäcken (S) 45 K4
Kallby (S) 44 C1
Kallebo (S) 44 C1
Kallenhardt (D) 70 F4
Kallersted (S) 43 K3
Kallerstad (S) 44 D6
Kallfall (S) 71 G2
Kallfält (S) 41 J3
Kalli (EST) 130 F3
Kallial (AL) 173 L6
Kallimasia (GR) 189 H5
Kállio (FIN) 36 D6
Kallioaho (FIN) 29 G7
Kalliojärvi (FIN) 29 L3
Kalliokylä (FIN) 29 K4
Kallioniemi (FIN) 29 M6
Kalliosalmi (FIN) 23 J3
Kalliovaara (FIN) 29 L6
Kallipéfi (FIN) 29 L6
Kalljärn (S) 180 F3
Kallirákhi, Skála (GR) 180 F3
Kallisbträz (FIN) 29 J8
Kallithéa (GR) 178 C3
Kállithéa (GR) 180 C4
Kallithéa (GR) 186 D6
Kallithéa (GR) 186 E4
Kallithéa (GR) 187 H4
Kállithéa (GR) 187 H4
Kallithéa (GR) 189 J4
Kallithéa (GR) 199 H4
Kallithiro (GR) 179 F6
Kallmet (AL) 173 L6
Kallmünz (D) 32 H5
Kallo (S) 22 G2
Kallö (FIN) 159 H2
Kallön (S) 72 B4
Kallon (S) 178 E6
Kállon (S) 188 B4
Kalloni (GR) 189 F4
Kalloni (GR) 189 F4
Kalloseml (FIN) 155 K6
Kallsedet (S) 25 G7
Kállsjö (S) 43 L4
Kallsjön (S) 33 M6
Kaltbrunn (CH) 80 F4
Källunga (D) 43 M2
Källvik (S) 45 K5
Källväderen (S) 22 D8
Kamankallio (FIN) 16 F5
Kalmar (S) 45 J5
Kalmari (FIN) 28 F6
Kalmavirta (FIN) 28 F7
Kalmomáki (FIN) 29 J4
Kalmthout (B) 69 G4
Kalna (IS) 16 F5
Kalna (IS) 157 H2
Kalna nad Hronom (SK) 158 G1
Kalnciems (LV) 132 E4
Kální (LV) 132 C3
Kaloboklovšiv (RUS) 13 N3
Kalnica (UA) 155 L3
Kalnici (UA) 130 D6
Kalnovo (BG) 177 H2
Kalo Chorió (CY) 198 F6
Kaló Chorió = Kakó Chorió (CY) 162 D1
Kalocsa (H) 144 C5
Kalodzicy (BY) 138 G7
Kalofer (BG) 176 C3
Kalogír (GR) 179 F6
Kalogria (GR) 186 C3
Kalohóri (GR) 179 F4
Kalohóri (GR) 178 E4
Kalohóri (GR) 179 H3
Kalo Horió (GR) 195 H6
Kalojanovec (BG) 176 E4
Kalojanovo (BG) 177 F2
Kalokastro (GR) 179 J2
Kaloneri (GR) 179 F4
Kaló Neró (GR) 186 C6
Kaloónja (BY) 143 M6
Kalopagadi (GR) 186 C3
Kalotina (BG) 158 E5
Kaloz (H) 158 F4
Kalpáki (GR) 178 C3
Kals am Großglockner (A) 90 C5
Kalsdorf bei Graz (A) 91 H6
Kalsepeseter (N) 31 L4
Kalsvik (N) 30 C4
Kaltanena (LT) 138 C3
Kaltenkirchen (D) 65 M4
Kaltenordheim (D) 72 C4
Kaltenherberg (D) 70 B5
Kaltental (D) 88 E5
Kaltenw (AT) 130 C6
Kalténé (LT) 136 G2
Kaltsila (FIN) 35 M2
Kaluderica (SRB) 167 G4
Kaludjerske Bare (SRB) 173 L2
Kaludjerski (MNE) 174 C3
Kalugerovo (BG) 176 B4
Kaluga (RUS) 9 03
Kalundborg (DK) 46 H2
Kaluge (LV) 138 E1
Kaluszyn (PL) 148 E1
Kaluzskoe (RUS) 136 F4
Kalv (S) 44 C4
Kalvåg (N) 30 B4
Kalvarija (LT) 143 J2
Kalvatn (N) 30 E3
Kalvehave (DK) 47 K4
Kálvelsi (LT) 137 D4
Kalven (N) 18 G2
Kalvene (LV) 132 D4
Kalvene (N) 28 D4
Kandalaika (RUS) 7 T3
Kandamy (TR) 182 D3
Kandanos (GR) 194 D5
Kanari (S) 26 B4
Kandi (RUS) 136 F4
Kandia (LV) 132 F3
Kandel (D) 79 J3
Kandergrund (CH) 80 E2
Kandersteg (CH) 80 E2
Kandle (D) 86 E2
Kanel (BY) 143 L5
Kanepi (EST) 134 D2
Kanestraum (N) 30 J1
Kanevskaya (RUS) 13 M3
Kangal (TR) 193 G2
Kangal (TR) 13 L6
Kangas (N) 27 L6
Kangasala (FIN) 36 B2
Kangaskylä (FIN) 29 H5
Kangaskylä (FIN) 29 J5
Kangaslampi (FIN) 29 27
Kangasniemi (FIN) 29 J5
Kangos (S) 22 F1
Kangosjärvi (FIN) 22 H2
Kanin (PL) 140 G2
Kaniv (UA) 9 M5
Kanjon (BY) 139 M5
Kanjola (FIN) 37 M7
Kanjučh (BY) 145 F5
Kankaanpää (FIN) 35 M2
Kankainen (FIN) 28 G7
Kankari (FIN) 29 H4
Kankava (GR) 188 B6
Kankava (GR) 194 D5
Kannas (FIN) 29 K8
Kannonkoski (FIN) 28 F6
Kannus (FIN) 28 E5
Kannusjärvi (FIN) 37 K1
Kanonji (UA) 163 G2
Kanpezu (GB) 53 H5
Kantala (FIN) 29 J6
Kanti (N) 20 B4
Kántja (FIN) 29 H7
Kantemirovka (RUS) 9 P5
Kanton (FIN) 28 C7
Kantornaya (RUS) 13 M3
Kantors (N) 21 J2
Kantornes (N) 21 J2
Kanturk (IRL) 62 E4
Kanunnikova (RUS) 131 N3
Kany-Barville (F) 68 B4
Kaolinovo (BG) 177 H1
Kaon = Çaurhes (F) 75 G4
Kapaclik (TR) 185 J2
Kapai (FIN) 192 C4
Kapakli (TR) 182 B3
Kapándriti (GR) 188 C3
Kapanli (TR) 183 J3
Kapellen (B) 69 G4
Kapellen (A) 90 F3
Kapellen (Erft) (D) 69 K4
Kapellen-Drusweiler (D) 79 J3
Kapfenberg (A) 90 F3
Kapfenstein (A) 91 H6
Kapidere (TR) 191 K5
Kapildere İstanbul (TR) 13 L6
Kapikaya (TR) 191 G2
Kapikaya (TR) 193 H1
Kapiköy (TR) 185 F4
Kaplice (CZ) 152 D6
Kapljuh (BG) 165 G5
Kaposfő (H) 158 D6
Kaposvár (H) 158 D6
Kapp (N) 31 D6
Kappel (D) 46 M1
Kappel (D) 72 F6
Kappeln (D) 66 B1
Kappelshamn (S) 45 N2
Kappelskär (S) 45 03
Kappi (A) 89 L6
Kaple (H) 172 C2
Kaprije (HR) 172 C1
Kaprun (A) 89 M5
Kapsévity (BY) 139 M5
Kapshagay (RUS) 13 L6
Kapsylan (FIN) 35 L5
Kaptol (HR) 172 D1
Kapciov (RUS) 9 03
Kapuvár (H) 157 H3
Karaaağaç (TR) 181 L2
Karabağlar (TR) 191 H5
Karabağlar (TR) 183 G3
Kápyla (FIN) 27 M6
Kapyl (BY) 139 M5
Karabijük (TR) 185 F5
Karabijük (TR) 192 B6
Karabiga (TR) 181 L5
Karabulak (TR) 185 F4
Karabükü (TR) 185 F6
Karaburun (TR) 176 C4
Karacabey (TR) 182 C6
Karacadağ (TR) 193 G1
Karacakılavuz (TR) 182 A3
Karaçali (TR) 193 F6
Karaçalılı (TR) 193 J5
Karaçam (TR) 191 H6
Karaçam (TR) 192 D4
Karaçam (TR) 183 G5
Karacaören (TR) 191 K2
Karacasu (TR) 191 K6
Karaçoban (TR) 13 L6
Kara-čurek (TR) 182 B5
Kara-čurek (TR) 182 D5
Karadere (TR) 184 A4
Karadere (TR) 185 H5
Karadere (TR) 185 J5
Karadag (TR) 193 G2
Karadibek (TR) 185 H5
Karadiken (TR) 191 K4
Karagöz (TR) 182 C5
Karahallı (TR) 192 A6
Karaağaç (TR) 193 G5
Karalksi (FIN) 17 N5
Karalov (TR) 192 D4
Karatsarvnadet (S) 21 M4
Karamanovo (BG) 176 E2
Karamürsel (TR) 183 F5
Karaman (TR) 192 D5
Karamani (TR) 192 D5
Karanova (TR) 192 D6
Karapelit (BG) 177 H1
Karaman (TR) 192 E4
Karasjok (N) 19 04
Karatmanovo (MK) 175 G5
Karatzadikia (GR) 176 C3
Karaurman (TR) 185 H5
Karbasan (TR) 191 H4
Karby (DK) 46 H2
Karby (S) 45 03
Karcag (H) 159 L3
Karczew (PL) 148 E1
Kardakáta (GR) 186 A3
Karditsa (GR) 179 F5
Kardos (H) 159 L4
Kardzhali (BG) 176 E4
Karesuando (S) 21 M4
Kargali (TR) 185 H5
Kargi (TR) 185 H1
Kargin (TR) 192 D6
Kargowa (PL) 141 G1
Karhula (FIN) 37 K2
Karia (GR) 187 F4
Kariani (GR) 180 B4
Karijoki (FIN) 35 L2
Karine (TR) 191 G5
Kariselki (FIN) 29 J8
Karitaina (GR) 187 G5
Karjalohja (FIN) 35 M4
Karkali (TR) 193 F5
Kärkölä (FIN) 36 E3
Kärksi-Nuia (EST) 133 M1
Karleby (S) 44 B5
Karlino (PL) 140 D4
Karlobag (HR) 164 E5
Karlovac (HR) 164 E3
Karlovasi (GR) 189 H5
Karlovo (BG) 176 C3
Karlovy Vary (CZ) 72 E3
Karlsborg (S) 44 D2
Karlshamn (S) 45 H4
Karlshof (D) 73 H1
Karlskoga (S) 44 D1
Karlskrona (S) 45 H4
Karlsruhe (D) 79 J2
Karlstad (S) 44 C1
Karlstadt (D) 79 K1
Karmanovo (RUS) 9 N2
Karnobat (BG) 177 G3
Karpacz (PL) 152 D2
Karpefss (GR) 196 C6
Karpenisi (GR) 187 F2
Karpuzlu (TR) 191 H5
Karsämáki (FIN) 29 G4
Karsava (LV) 135 G3
Karstädt (D) 66 F5
Kärsämäki (FIN) 29 G4
Karstula (FIN) 28 F6
Kartal (TR) 182 E5
Kartepe (TR) 183 F5
Kartuzy (PL) 141 J1
Karvia (FIN) 28 E7
Kaš (BG) 176 E2
Kašin (RUS) 7 T6
Kasari (EST) 130 E2
Kašin (RUS) 7 T6
Kaşıçelik (TR) 193 G2
Kašira (RUS) 9 03
Kasımlar (TR) 192 C6
Kaskinen (FIN) 35 L2
Kasko (FIN) 35 L2
Kašperské Hory (CZ) 72 F5
Kassándria (GR) 180 C5
Kastamonu (TR) 13 L5
Kastav (HR) 164 D3
Kastéli (GR) 195 G6
Kastellaun (D) 70 C6
Kastoria (GR) 178 D4
Kástro (GR) 187 G3
Kastrosikiá (GR) 186 D2
Katerini (GR) 179 G3
Kato Achaia (GR) 187 F4
Kato Klines (GR) 178 E4
Kato Nevrokopi (GR) 176 C5
Katowice (PL) 148 F5
Katrineholm (S) 44 F1
Kattavia (GR) 199 G6
Katwijk aan Zee (NL) 69 F2
Kaub (D) 70 D6
Kaufbeuren (D) 88 E6
Kaufbeuren (D) 88 E6
Kaukonen (FIN) 22 H3
Kauliranta (FIN) 22 G4
Kaunas (LT) 137 L3
Kaupanger (N) 30 F3
Kaustinen (FIN) 28 E5
Kautokeino (N) 19 L5
Kavajë (AL) 174 B5
Kavala (GR) 180 B4
Kavarna (BG) 177 J1
Kävlinge (S) 47 L3
Kaysersberg (F) 80 C1
Kazanlak (BG) 176 D3
Kazimierz Dolny (PL) 148 G2
Kazincbarcika (H) 149 J4
Kdyně (CZ) 72 F4
Kecel (H) 158 F5
Kecskemét (H) 158 G4
Kefalos (GR) 189 J6
Kehl (D) 79 H3
Kehra (EST) 131 H2
Kehtna (EST) 130 F2
Kekava (LV) 133 G4
Kelheim (D) 88 G2
Kellinghusen (D) 65 M4
Kelmė (LT) 137 H2
Kemalpaşa (TR) 191 H4
Kemi (FIN) 23 H5
Kemijärvi (FIN) 23 K3
Kempele (FIN) 28 G3
Kempten (Allgäu) (D) 88 E6
Kendal (GB) 55 F4
Kenderes (H) 159 K3
Kerava (FIN) 36 F3
Kerč' (UA) 11 Q7
Keri (GR) 186 B4
Kerimäki (FIN) 37 M1
Kerken (D) 69 K4
Kerkrade (NL) 69 L5
Kerpen (D) 69 L5
Kerteminde (DK) 46 G3
Keszthely (H) 158 D4
Ketrzyn (PL) 142 E2
Kettering (GB) 56 F5
Kevelaer (D) 69 K4
Keynsham (GB) 58 E3
Kežmarok (SK) 149 J3
Kidsgrove (GB) 55 G6
Kiel (D) 66 B2
Kielce (PL) 148 F3
Kierspe (D) 70 E4
Kietrz (PL) 153 J3
Kijevo (HR) 172 D1
Kikinda (SRB) 167 F2
Kil (S) 44 C1
Kilafors (S) 40 E2
Kilboghamn (N) 20 C8
Kilbotn (N) 20 F3

A B C D E F G H I J K L M N O P Q R S T U V W X Y Z

Kostomukša (RUS) 7 S4
Kostomukša (RUS) 29 L2
Kostopil (UA) 150 C2
Kostow (RUS) 139 H1
Kostry (PL) 149 G2
Kostrova (RUS) 139 H1
Kostry (PL) 149 G2
Kostrzhivka (UA) 157 J4
Kostrzyn (PL) 141 H6
Kostrzynek (PL) 67 L5
Kostula nad Odrą (PL) 140 C5
Kostula (FIN) 35 M1
Kostveit (N) 38 G8
Kostylivka (UA) 156 F6
Kosuła (FIN) 29 J6
Kosundet (S) 40 F3
Kosy, Borki- (PL) 148 F1
Kosylovo (RUS) 186 B6
Kosyny (UA) 156 B5
Koszalin (PL) 140 F2
Koszarawa (PL) 154 E2
Koszary (PL) 141 L6
Koszęcin (PL) 147 K4
Koszęg (H) 158 C3
Koszewo (PL) 67 M4
Koszyce Wielkie (PL) 148 C6
Kóta (H) 160 D1
Kotajärvi (FIN) 27 M4
Kotajärvi (FIN) 29 L3
Kotala (H) 23 M2
Kotala (FIN) 28 E7
Kotapeä (FIN) 28 F7
Kótek (TR) 184 E6
Koteki (TR) 196 D1
Kotel (BG) 177 F3
Koteli (TR) 184 C3
Kotelevka (RUS) 157 K5
Kotelev (UA) 151 H3
Kotel'va (UA) 9 N4
Kotenovci (BG) 175 K2
Kotezicken (A) 158 B8
Köthel (Kreis Herzogtum Lauenburg) (D) 65 O4
Köthen (Anhalt) (D) 29 H5
Kotkyla (FIN) 35 M1
Kotila (FIN) 23 K7
Kotila (S) 178 E4
Kotla (PL) 150 B2
Kotlary (UA) 151 J2
Kotlina (FIN) 36 G4
Kotka (FIN) 35 M2
Kotki (PL) 148 C4
Kotla (PL) 146 E2
Kotarnia (PL) 147 J5
Kotlenno (HR) 172 E2
Kotlice (PL) 149 J4
Kotlin (PL) 147 H2
Kotlovina (UA) 171 M2
Kotly (RUS) 37 L5
Kotomierz (PL) 141 K4
Kotor (MNE) 173 J5
Kotor Varoš (BIH) 166 A4
Kotorsko (BIH) 166 A4
Kotor Varoš (BIH) 166 A4
Kotovo (RUS) 9 O3
Kotovsk (RUS) 9 Q3
Kotów (PL) 141 H8
Kotovs'k (UA) 151 L4
Kotovs'k = Podi'ls'k (UA) 163 H5
Kotovs'ke = Kuca Baba (UA) 163 M2
Kotowice (PL) 147 L4
Kotowice (PL) 147 H6
Kotraža (SRB) 174 D1
Kótronas (GR) 187 E6
Kotronia (GR) 181 J2
Kötschach-Mauthen (A) 89 J4
Köttkulla (S) 44 D3
Kotmar (D) 152 G4
Köttsjön (S) 26 B8
Kötú (UA) 148 F1
Kotúmle (TR) 192 B4
Koty, Szulborze- (PL) 142 G2
Kötzin (D) 67 G5
Kotzanka (S) 41 K1
Koudekerke (NL) 64 C6
Koudum (NL) 64 C8
Köue (EST) 131 H2
Koufalia (GR) 179 M3
Koúfalis (GR) 180 D5
Koukli (GR) 178 G6
Koumanis (GR) 186 F4
Koumaria (R) 179 J2
Koumikka (GR) 189 J4
Koundouros (GR) 188 D4
Kounice (SLO) 153 G3
Kounoupitsa (GR) 188 B4
Koura (FIN) 28 D6
Kouratil (CY) 198 E6
Kourim (CZ) 153 H3
Kourkouli (GR) 187 G2
Kourofadas (GR) 194 E5
Kousa (FIN) 36 E4
Koutajärvi (FIN) 28 G5
Koutalas (GR) 195 E1
Koutsó (GR) 180 G3
Koutselió (GR) 179 G5
Koutsóthodos (GR) 187 F4
Kouty nad Desnou (CZ) 153 M3
Koúva (UA) 23 K5
Kouveia (FIN) 36 G3
Kovačgorr (PL) 185 J2
Kovačevci (SRB) 167 G5
Kovačevci (BG) 175 K4
Kovačevica (BG) 175 L6
Kovačevica (BG) 178 A5
Kovačevo Polje (BIH) 173 G2
Kovači (BIH) 172 F2
Kovačica (BG) 168 E6
Kovačica (SRB) 166 B3
Kovaczelenska (H) 166 B1
Kovala (N) 24 N3
Kovalki (TR) 135 M6
Kovall (TR) 193 K4
Kovalivka (UA) 151 K5
Kovanci (MK) 180 A2
Kovano (RUS) 37 M4
Kovanka (UA) 144 H6
Kovao (BIH) 173 H1
Kovarce (SK) 154 C5
Kovářov (CZ) 81 L1
Kovarce (SK) 73 J5
Kovbarn (PL) 138 G5
Kovborg (PL) 46 D2
Kovda (RUS) 7 T3
Kovdor (RUS) 7 S2
Kvodozen (RUS) 7 S3
Kovel' (UA) 149 L3
Koveland (N) 39 H6
Kovero (FIN) 30 H8
Kóvágó (H) 181 H1
Kovin (SRB) 167 G4
Kovjok (FIN) 27 J7
Kovrov (RUS) 33 N3
Kovpyta (UA) 145 N6
Kovra (S) 32 G2
Kovern (MNE) 173 L3
Kovlevata (UA) 151 M5
Kowal (PL) 141 J3
Kowalki (PL) 147 J3
Kowale Oleckie (PL) 143 G2
Kowale Pańskie (PL) 147 K2
Kowalewo Pomorskie (PL) 141 L4
Kowalów (PL) 140 C6
Kowandowki (PL) 148 B1
Kowanz (PL) 67 L4
Kowiesy (PL) 142 G6
Kowno (PL) 148 G6
Koxgáz (TR) 184 E4
Köyceğiz (TR) 196 E2
Köyceğiz (TR) 196 E2
Köyhäjoki (FIN) 28 D4
Köyliö (FIN) 35 K2
Köylönsjö (S) 41 J3
Koyuhisar (TR) 185 M2
Koyuhisar (TR) 13 M5
Koyulhisar (TR) 184 C6
Koyunbaba (TR) 184 C5
Koyunbeyli (TR) 192 B2
Koyunceler (TR) 191 G3
Koyunculer (TR) 184 E6
Koyunlu (TR) 189 J5
Koyunlu (TR) 193 J5
Koyunyeri (TR) 182 B4
Koyutepe (TR) 185 J6
Koz (RUS) 23 M5
Kozaçık (TR) 192 E4
Kozağaç (TR) 191 M3
Kozak (TR) 192 C2
Kozakievi (UA) 156 G3
Kozan (TR) 185 K5
Kozan (TR) 199 F4
Kozani (GR) 179 K4
Kozarac (BIH) 165 M4
Kozarac (HR) 165 F4
Kozar Belene (BG) 176 D2
Kozarevec (BG) 176 E4
Kozarska Dubica = Bosanska Dubica (BIH) 165 H4
Kozárovce (SK) 154 D6
Kozarzów (PL) 147 J1
Kozaua (TR) 184 D3

Kozağaç (TR) 185 J2
Kozcağız (TR) 181 L4
Kozelec (TR) 183 J5
Kozeliva (UA) 163 K5
Kozelnik (SK) 154 D4
Kozenki (PL) 145 K4
Kozia Wola (PL) 148 C3
Koziegłowy (HR) 172 F3
Koźce (SRB) 168 B4
Kozice (PL) 153 K2
Koziebrody (PL) 142 B5
Koziegłowy (PL) 147 L5
Koziegłowy (PL) 140 G6
Kozienice (PL) 148 E2
Koz'any (PL) 139 L2
Kozica (SLO) 164 B3
Kozienice (RUS) 186 M6
Koz Hoj (BG) 176 D3
Kozina (SLO) 164 B2
Kozhlovce (PL) 154 C4
Kozlov Bereg (RUS) 131 N3
Kozlovice (CZ) 154 C2
Kózki (PL) 143 J4
Kozłow (PL) 142 C4
Koz'jany (RY) 139 L2
Kozlany (UA) 156 F4
Kozlu (TR) 190 E2
Kozlu (TR) 184 A6
Kozlu (TR) 181 J6
Kozluca (TR) 191 J2
Kozluca (TR) 192 H3
Kozluçay (TR) 184 B6
Kozluk (TR) 185 M4
Kozluk (BIH) 166 B3
Kozluyaka (TR) 192 D4
Kozłubov (RUS) 131 O5
Kozłówka (PL) 150 G4
Kozmacj (UA) 156 G5
Kozmin Wielkopolski (PL) 147 G2
Kozmyn (CZ) 73 K6
Kozolupy (CZ) 152 D4
Kozówka (UA) 157 H3
Kozub (PL) 140 B4
Kozubar (SRB) 166 E4
Kozubszczyzna (PL) 150 F3
Kozuchów (PL) 140 D5
Kozufe (AL) 174 D6
Kozuv (PL) 140 D6
Kozuvák-Parcele (PL) 148 B1
Krasylivka (UA) 145 J6
Krasyliv (UA) 150 E2
Krasylivka (UA) 151 K1
Krasyliv (UA) 150 D2
Krasyliv (UA) 151 M3
Kraszkowice (PL) 147 K3
Kraszewo (PL) 141 N5
Kraterő (PL) 178 E3
Kráthio (GR) 186 E3
Kratovo (MK) 167 M4
Kratovska Stena (SRB) 166 F6
Kratyn (UA) 156 E5
Krauchenwies (D) 79 L5
Kraubath an der Mur (A) 91 G5
Krauschwitz (D) 71 J8
Kravaře (CZ) 154 C2
Kräveník (BG) 176 C3
Kravík (N) 38 B7
Kravaré (CZ) 82 D6
Kravárov (BY) 139 J3
Kráva-Dev (CZ) 152 E3
Kravoder (SRB) 167 G3
Kreba-Neudorf (D) 71 J8
Krečany (SK) 73 M3
Krečelník (D) 71 M8
Kreiensen (D) 67 J4
Kremenčuk (UA) 156 F3
Kremenets (UA) 150 D2
Kremmen (D) 67 E6
Kremnica (SK) 154 D4
Krempachy (PL) 154 F2
Krempe (D) 66 B1
Kremsmünster (A) 81 J8
Krems an der Donau (A) 91 J3
Krems in Kärnten (A) 90 E6
Krepaljin (PL) 154 C5
Kretinga (LT) 132 C6
Kretingalė (LT) 132 C6
Kreuzburg (D) 80 D5
Kreutzbergy (D) 81 K3
Kreuzlingen (CH) 79 L4
Kreuzlingen (CH) 79 L4
Kreuzstetten (A) 91 K2
Kreuznach, Bad (D) 80 B3
Kreva (BY) 134 G3
Krevas (LT) 133 J6
Krhanice (CZ) 81 M1
Krupa (GR) 187 F5
Krupa na Vrbasu (BIH) 165 L4
Krupac (SRB) 167 H5
Krupka (CZ) 152 G2
Krušar (BG) 177 F3
Krušé (BG) 176 D6
Krušedol Prnjavor (SRB) 166 E3
Kruševo (MK) 179 K2
Krušovica (BIH) 172 E5
Krušovljani (UA) 157 H4
Krupac (SRB) 167 K6
Krušovo (MK) 179 J2

Krásné Louky (CZ) 147 H5
Krásno (PL) 154 F2
Krasné (CZ) 153 K5
Krásno (UA) 163 J3
Krasné'ke (UA) 163 L2
Krasnik (PL) 148 F4
Krásnik Dolny ... (UA) 163 J3
Krasno (HR) 172 F3
Krasno (PL) 152 C2
Krasne'ke (RUS) 37 O3
Krasnoarmejsk = Pokrovs'k (UA) 9 N6
Krasnodar (RUS) 13 M4
Krasnoe (RUS) 186 D1
Krasnoe (RUS) 140 G6
Krasno Polje (HR) 164 F5
Krasnogradka (RUS) 131 M1
Krasnoje'lsk (UA) 161 M1
Krasnolesie (PL) 150 G5
Krasno nad Kysucou (SK) 154 D3
Krasnopol (RUS) 143 H2
Krasnopol (UA) 150 K6
Krasnopol (BG) 168 B4
Krasnosel'ci (UA) 163 L3
Krasnoiselc (PL) 142 E4
Krasnosielka (UA) 150 G4
Krasnosilka (UA) 149 L5
Krasnoselsje (PL) 148 F4
Krasnousol'sk (RUS) 142 D2
Krasny Brod (SK) 155 K3
Krasny Bor (RUS) 37 P5
Krasny Bor (RUS) 37 P6
Krasný Bor (RUS) 136 E4
Krasný Holm (RUS) 37 U6
Krásný Les (SK) 155 G5
Krasny Lyman (UA) 9 P5
Krasny Ostrov (RUS) 37 L4
Krasny Sokol (RUS) 37 J2
Krasnyj Les (CZ) 152 G2
Krasojiči (PL) 147 J3
Krason (P) 148 B4
Krासnyk (PL) 155 M3
Krassilya (UA) 145 J6
Krasylivka (UA) 151 K3
Krasylivka (UA) 151 M3
Krasylivka (UA) 151 M2
Krasywa (UA) 147 K3
Krzemeniewo (PL) 146 E4
Krzepice (PL) 147 L3
Krzeszów (UA) 9 N4
Krzeszowo (PL) 150 C4
Kreszowice (PL) 148 B5
Kreszewo (PL) 67 L7
Krzeszyce (PL) 67 N6
Krzewa (UA) 149 G1
Krzyci Wielkie (PL) 155 M3
Krzycko Małe (PL) 146 D3
Krzynowłoga Mała (PL) 149 G3
Krzyszkowice (PL) 147 M3
Krzywcza (PL) 155 M2
Krzywe (PL) 146 F2
Krzywizna (PL) 147 J2
Krzywonoga (PL) 147 H2
Krzywa (PL) 146 E4
Krzyżanowice (PL) 148 D3
Krzyżewo-Jurki (PL) 142 G3
Krzyżowice (PL) 147 H4
Krzyżowa (PL) 146 C4
Krzyżowice (PL) 140 G6
Ksar el-Ksar (D) 79 H2
Ksiaginica (BG) 187 G5
Kumanica (SRB) 174 D2
Kumani (SRB) 166 D2
Kumanova (SRB) 167 L3
Kuman (AL) 174 D5
Kumanite (SRB) 175 K5

Krivi Vir (SRB) 167 J6
Krivodol (BG) 175 K2
Krivogaštani (MK) 174 F6
Krivoklat (CZ) 152 E3
Krivokut (PL) 148 F4
Krivosel' Olciy (UA) 163 J3
Krizanov (CZ) 153 K4
Križance (CZ) 153 H5
Križ (HR) 165 H3
Križani (SK) 152 G2
Križkraj (SLO) 164 A3
Krka (SLO) 164 D3
Krklja (SRB) 167 F4
Krnja pela (MNE) 174 B3
Krnjeuša (BIH) 165 K5
Krnov (CZ) 154 B1
Krnjak (HR) 164 G4
Krnjača (SRB) 174 A4
Krobia (PL) 141 L4
Krokeide (N) 38 B2
Krokek (S) 41 K6
Krivi čyk (RY) 139 K5
Krokeio (N) 25 H3
Kroken (N) 35 J4
Kroken (N) 24 B4
Kroken (N) 30 G5
Kroken (N) 40 E4
Krokvik (N) 30 E3
Krokoviště (CZ) 73 H4
Krokoviště (SK) 31 P5
Krokstein (S) 16 E4
Krokeid (S) 25 J8
Kökskägi (S) 26 G6
Krokolys (LT) 137 M5
Krokstadelva (N) 39 M3
Krokstad (N) 20 E8
Krokstrand (N) 20 E8
Krokvik (N) 39 P3
Krokstorp (S) 45 J5
Krokom (N) 25 K6
Kroken (PL) 141 J5
Krokos (GR) 179 F4
Krokowa (PL) 147 L1
Krokowo (PL) 149 G2
Krolevec (PL) 141 G6
Krolew (UA) 145 M6
Kromerz (CZ) 154 B2
Krumbach (Schwaben) (D) 80 C4
Krummesse (D) 65 O3
Kuç (A) 174 B4
Kuça Baba (UA) 163 M2
Kuçevo (SRB) 168 B2
Kuçova (AL) 174 D4
Kuçukaali (TR) 193 K4
Küçükboğaz (TR) 192 E2
Kücük Bük (A) 80 B6

Kružowa Wyżna (PL) 155 H2
Krýčaj (BY) 9 M3
Krýsovatyn (PL) 150 C1
Krivsglätt (MK) 174 F4
Krivokat (CZ) 152 D2
Kryeku (UA) 162 F2
Kryevdh (UA) 178 B2
Kryzan (UA) 174 D4
Kridanic (CZ) 153 K4
Kližanić (CZ) 153 K6
Klžany (CZ) 153 G2
Kryhivka (UA) 156 G5
Krylivka (UA) 151 J4
Kryloc'k (UA) 156 F5
Krylow (HR) 165 K6
Krylo (PL) 149 K4
Krylovo (RUS) 142 F2
Krylovo (RUS) 142 F2
Krymok (UA) 151 J2
Krymsk (RUS) 13 M4
Kryna (AL) 91 K5
Kukomiharja (FIN) 35 L2
Kryspinów (PL) 147 G3
Kkrystampolle (BY) 144 G1
Krystyna (BY) 144 G3
Krytyliszów (UA) 156 F3
Krytyn-Polje (UA) 157 L4
Krywa (UA) 156 G6
Kryvce (UA) 9 M5
Kryvec'ke (UA) 163 J3
Kryve Ozero (UA) 163 L4
Kryvunka (UA) 151 K5
Kryve Sjalo (BY) 139 L3
Kryvin (UA) 150 E2
Kryvopillja (UA) 156 F6
Kryvoi Rih (UA) 9 N5
Kryvorivnja (UA) 156 F6
Kryvyi Rih (UA) 9 N5
Krzanica (PL) 154 C1
Kroken (SRB) 174 F5

Kubýševe (UA) 13 L3
Kucya (UA) 9 P5
Kučova (TR) 37 O6
Kukaskýla (FIN) 27 N8
Kukaskýla (FIN) 28 F7
Kukey (AL) 174 B3
Kukey (AL) 162 F1
Küçüny (FIN) 27 M7
Kulakkaya (FIN) 29 M1
Kulak (BIH) 166 D3
Kukel (UA) 163 J3
Kukes (AL) 174 D4
Kukey (TR) 189 M4
Kukey (TR) 199 M2
Kukkola (GR) 22 G6
Kukkolanvaara (FIN) 29 M1
Kukkura (FIN) 29 M4
Kukkolan (FIN) 176 C4
Kukolje (FIN) 147 G2
Kukljica (HR) 172 B1
Kuklen (BG) 176 D5
Kukljin (SRB) 167 G6
Kukoš (UA) 9 M4
Kukovo (RUS) 37 P7
Kukur (AL) 174 C5
Kukuj (RUS) 37 M1
Kula (TR) 192 C3
Kula (BIH) 166 A3
Kula (TR) 193 K3
Kula (SRB) 166 C2
Kula (RUS) 37 K6
Kulan (BIH) 173 G3
Kulata (BG) 175 L6
Kulaura (PL) 137 K4
Kulak (UA) 163 L3
Kuldiga (LV) 133 D4
Kulen Vakuf (BIH) 165 K5
Kiurpe (LV) 133 K3
Kulja (RUS) 37 N3
Kulla (BIH) 173 H2
Kullar (UA) 145 N3
Kulen (TR) 184 B6
Kubík (N) 20 E8
Kübek (TR) 185 M4
Kumru (TR) 184 C6
Kukuš- Kushin (RKS) 174 E4
Kunovice (CZ) 154 A3

Kuuksenvaara (FIN) 29 M6
Kuuminainen (FIN) 28 B9
Kusamo (FIN) 23 M7
Kusamo (FIN) 138 A2
Kusa (AL) 162 F1
Kusani (TR) 28 F7
Kusapää (FIN) 23 H1
Kusaka (FIN) 38 G6
Kusaki (FIN) 35 L4
Kusaki (FIN) 36 G3
Kusamo (FIN) 29 E6
Kuusikko (FIN) 27 M6
Kuusiranta (FIN) 23 L7
Kuusjarvi (FIN) 35 M6
Kuusivaara (FIN) 35 M3
Kuusjoki (FIN) 35 L3
Kuusjärvi (FIN) 29 L4
Kuusra (FIN) 28 M7
Kuusnimi (FIN) 30 H1
Kuvaskangas (FIN) 28 B8
Kuvataz (UA) 145 N5
Kuvataz (UA) 145 N5
Kuyucak (TR) 192 G6
Kuyuçukt (TR) 188 F3
Kuyu (TR) 189 K6
Kuyunlu (TR) 185 M6
Kuzlica (UA) 145 N5
Kuzculu (TR) 184 B5
Kuzdere (TR) 191 M2
Kuz'minec (HR) 164 F3
Kuzmino (TR) 192 G6
Kuzmice (SK) 155 H4
Kuzne (RKS) 174 D3
Kuzuculu (TR) 185 K5
Kuzulu (TR) 185 M3
Kuzuören (TR) 193 J2
Kuzuören (TR) 193 H5
Kuzuören (TR) 191 H5
Kürkoy (TR) 189 J4
Kyläinpää (FIN) 28 C4
Kylänlahti (FIN) 29 M5
Kyläsaari (FIN) 28 B9

Kyrmäkosken asema (FIN) 35 N2
Kymäkoski (FIN) 35 N2
Kymbo (S) 43 M2
Kymönkoski (FIN) 28 F7
Kyndby Huse (DK) 47 J2
Kynsperk (CY) 198 E5
Kynsimäe (FIN) 23 M5
Kyöpeli Gjon (SRB) 174 D4
Kyōto (FIN) 36 C3
Kypárissia (CY) 198 E5
Kyprava (LV) 134 B3
Kyrenia (CY) 198 E5
Kyrkolanberget (S) 26 E6
Kyriaki (GR) 187 F3
Kyritz (D) 67 E5
Kyrkäs (S) 40 B2
Kyrkosand (S) 25 N7
Kyrksaeterøra (N) 24 D5
Kyrkbyn (S) 41 L3
Kyösti (FIN) 35 M5
Kyrnasivka (UA) 163 K3
Kyrönjoki (FIN) 39 J4
Kyršäj (FIN) 30 G3
Kyösti (GR) 187 F2
Kyrö (FIN) 35 L4
Kyrö (FIN) 36 H2
Kyśej (CZ) 152 F3
Kysucké Nové Mesto (SK) 154 D3
Kyšenskov (RUS) 7 T8
Kytäjärvi (FIN) 35 M2
Kytlym (UA) 149 L4
Kyyhkylä (FIN) 36 C3
Kyyjärvi (FIN) 28 E5
Kythnos (GR) 188 D5

Column L:
L

Laa an der Thaya (A) 153 K6
Laaben (A) 91 J3
Laaber (D) 80 F2
La Acefuela (E) 125 G6
La Adrada (E) 118 G2
Laage (D) 67 K6
Laagri (EST) 35 P6
Laasi (FIN) 23 L7
Laajakoski (FIN) 22 G2
Laajala (FIN) 28 F6
Laakajärvi (FIN) 29 J4
Laaksola (FIN) 36 F4
Laakso (N) 20 E8
Laanila (EST) 131 M4
Laaslahti (N) 30 D3
La Alberca (E) 118 E3
La Aldea de San Nicolás (E) 129 c5
La Alfahuara (E) 127 J4
La Algaida (E) 128 B3
La Algaba (E) 125 G6
La Almunia de Doña Godina (E) 113 J6
Laamala (FIN) 37 J2
Laanila (FIN) 23 H2
Laanetmetsa (EST) 134 B2
Laane (FIN) 29 J6
La Antilla (E) 124 E5
Laaslahti (FIN) 35 N4
Lapangas (N) 24 D5
Laane (FIN) 29 J6
La Aulaga (E) 125 G6
La Azohía (E) 127 M4
Labacolla (E) 110 C2
La Barca de la Florida (E) 128 C4
La Barre-en-Ouche (F) 76 C4
Labastide-Clairence (F) 92 B4
Labastide-Rouairoux (F) 93 K4
Labastide-Saint-Pierre (F) 93 G3
Labastide-Villefranche (F) 92 B4
Labatan (F) 93 G4
La Baule (F) 75 G6
Labbezanga (RUS) 135 J5
La Bazana (E) 117 K4
La Bazoge (F) 76 D3
Labécéde-Lauragais (F) 93 H3
Labenne (F) 92 B4
Laberget (S) 40 H4
Laberweinting (D) 80 F3
La Bérarde (F) 91 D4
Labin (HR) 164 D4
Labinot-Fushe (AL) 174 C4
La Bisbal del Penedès (E) 115 K4
Labková (UA) 9 L5
La Bóveda de Toro (E) 118 F1
Labod (H) 158 D5
Labord (F) 93 J5
La Bóveda de Toro (E) 118 F1
La Bourboule (F) 83 H6
La Bove (F) 78 E5
La Braña (E) 111 H4
La Bórbolla (E) 112 C2
La Brède (F) 82 D5
Labrit (F) 92 D3
La Broque (F) 79 H5
Labruguière (F) 93 J3
La Bruyère (B) 79 G2
Labrujo (P) 117 D6
La Cabrera (E) 119 H5
La Calahorra (E) 126 G3
La Caletta (I) 123 H5
La Campana (E) 125 H6
Lac (AL) 174 C4
La Canonja (E) 115 K4
La Cañada de Cañepla (E) 127 K4
La Cañada de San Urbano (E) 127 J4
La Cañada de Verich (E) 114 C6
Lacanau (F) 82 C5
Lacanau-Océan (F) 82 C4
La Canourgue (F) 83 M6
La Capelle (F) 78 F4
Laćarak (SRB) 166 D3
La Cardanchosa (E) 118 C5
La Carlota (E) 125 J6
Lacaune (F) 93 K3
La Cavada (E) 112 E2
La Cellera de Ter (E) 115 M2
Lacenas (F) 84 A6
La Cerca (E) 112 E3
Lácháda (CY) 198 E6

La Coruña = A Coruña (E) 110 C2
La Costa (E) 128 C5
La Côte-Saint-André (F) 84 F5
Lacoste (F) 84 E2
Lacoquette-Cadoul (F) 93 H3
La Coveta Fumada (E) 127 K3
La Crau (F) 85 H4
la Croix-Avranchin (F) 75 J3
Lacroix-Barez (F) 93 K1
Lacroix-Saint-Ouen (F) 77 G3
Lacroix (F) 93 G6
La Crosetta (I) 89 H2
La Cuesta (E) 119 J1
La Cumbre (E) 117 K5
Lacunza (E) 113 G3
Ladapeyre (F) 83 H5
Ladbergen (D) 70 E2
Ladce (SK) 154 C3
Lådd (GR) 177 F6
Lade (S) 41 L6
La Ferté-sous-Jouarre (F) 77 J4
la Encimilla (E) 125 H6
Lädemitz (D) 80 D5
Lädersta (S) 40 G5
Lærdalsøyri (N) 30 H2
Lærum (N) 30 H2
La Estación (E) 128 C2
Laeva (EST) 131 M4
Laevejokgedde (N) 19 J4
La Farlède (F) 85 H4
La Fatarella (E) 121 J1
La Felipa (E) 127 G3
La Ferté-sous-Jouarre (F) 77 J4
Lafrançaise (F) 93 G3
La Garde-Freinet (F) 95 H4
La Garganta (E) 111 H5
La Garganta (E) 118 E3
La Garrovilla (E) 117 J6
La Giattola (I) 100 C4
Lagedi (EST) 36 C6
Lagan (S) 43 G6
Lagardell (E) 116 D6
Lagardère (F) 82 E4
Laghy (IRL) 60 F2
Lagiewniki (PL) 147 M3
La Gineta (E) 127 G3
La Gironda (E) 125 H5
Laginá (GR) 179 M4
Lagnieu (F) 84 F5
Lagny-le-Sec (F) 77 G3
Lagny-sur-Marne (F) 77 G4
Lagoa (F) 116 C5
La Gomes (E) 126 C5
Lagoa (P) 124 B4
Lagodekhi (GE) 13 O5
Lagonegro (I) 104 E5
Lagny (IRL) 61 J3
La Granadella (E) 121 J1
La Granja de San Vicente (E) 111 J3
La Granja de Escarp (E) 114 D5
Lagrasse (F) 115 J3
La Gravelle (F) 75 K4
Lágrimas (P) 110 C4
La Guàrdia (E) 119 H4
La Guardia de Jaén (E) 126 E2
La Guarda (E) 126 E2
La Guardia (E) 110 C5
Laguarres (E) 114 D3
Laguardia (E) 113 G4
La Guerche-de-Bretagne (F) 75 K5
La Guerche-sur-l'Aubois (F) 83 J2
Laguna Dalga (E) 111 H4
Laguna del Marquesado (E) 120 E3
Laguna de Negrillos (E) 111 H4
Laguna Rodrigo (E) 118 G2
Lagunilla (E) 118 E3
La Guijarrosa (E) 125 J6
La Hague (F) 75 H1
Lahdenkylä (FIN) 28 F7
Lahanás (GR) 180 A2
Lähte (FIN) 28 E6
La Haye (F) 71 H2
Lähenmäki (FIN) 28 G5
Laheycourt (F) 78 F6
La Herrada (E) 126 C2
La Herrera (E) 127 G3
La Higuera (E) 127 H2
La Higuera de Vargas (E) 117 J6
Lähiniva (FIN) 29 H3
Lahinch (IRL) 61 D8
Lahishyn (BY) 9 K3
Lahnstein (D) 80 B2
Laholm (S) 43 G6
Laholuoma (FIN) 28 C8
Lahome (FIN) 30 H2
Lahovaara (FIN) 29 L4
Lahti (FIN) 36 B3
Lahti (FIN) 35 L5
Lahti (FIN) 36 G4
Lai = Lenzerheide (CH) 88 B4
Laide (IRL) 62 E2
Laiglo (E) 118 F3
Laihia (FIN) 28 C4
Laimbach am Ostrong (A) 91 H3
Laimoluokta (S) 15 H6
Lainach (A) 90 D6
La Iglesuela (E) 118 F3
La Iglesuela del Cid (E) 121 H3
Laingen (D) 79 L3
Lainio (S) 15 J4
La Iruela (E) 126 G2
Laisvall (S) 15 D8
Laitila (FIN) 35 J3
Laíva (GR) 187 H2
Laives (I) 89 H1
Laize-la-Ville (F) 76 C3
Lajosmizse (H) 159 G4
Lákavica (MK) 179 L2
Lakenheath (GB) 59 H4
Lakinsk (RUS) 33 M3
Lakócsa (H) 165 L1
La Codoñera (E) 114 C6
Lacave (F) 93 H1
Lakki (GR) 189 K6
Laknes (S) 16 B9
Lakaluoma (FIN) 28 D7
Laitila (FIN) 35 J3
La Lantejuela (E) 125 H6
Lalapasa (TR) 183 J4
La Laguna (E) 126 D3
Lalić (SRB) 166 C2
Laliótis (GR) 187 E4
La Línea de la Concepción (E) 128 C5
La Loupe (F) 76 E4

Luz = Luz de Tavira (P) 124 D5
Lužaja (I) 120 D2
Lužanka (RUS) 37 K3
Lužane (HR) 165 K4
Lužani (HR) 171 J1
Lužarches (F) 76 F3
Luz de Tavira (P) 124 D5
Luzech (CZ) 146 E6
Luzern (CZ) 93 G2
Lužnad Vltavou (CZ) 146 A5
Luzenec (F) 81 H4
Luzern (D6) 86 F3
Lužianka (P) 124 C4
Lužica (RUS) 131 P3
Luz i Madr (AL) 178 B2
Luzino (RUS) 37 M4
Lužki (RUS) 136 F5
Lužki (RUS) 139 O3
Lužna (LV) 130 A5
Luz-Saint-Sauveur (F) 92 D5
Lužzi (I) 100 D3
Luzzi (I) 107 F4
L'vov = L'viv (UA) 149 K6
Lwówek Śląski (PL) 140 F6
Lwówek Śląski (PL) 146 D3
Lyberget (S) 32 F6
Lybster (GB) 51 L3
Lycevoði (BY) 139 L4
Lychen (D) 87 J4
Lycke (S) 43 J3
Lychkovo (UA) 150 C5
Lyckeby (RUS) 135 O2
Lyckseln (S) 86 E5
Lydd (GB) 59 J6
Lydford (GB) 56 F4
Lydham (GB) 58 D4
Lydd (GB) 58 B4
Lydum (DK) 44 B2
Lye (S) 45 O4
Lyefjell (N) 38 C5
Lygna (S) 31 O7
Lygre (N) 38 C2
Lygumai (LT) 132 H5
Lykinti (FIN) 39 J2
Lykiv (UA) 149 K3
Lykkja (N) 31 K5
Lykkja (N) 31 K5
Lykkebo (N) 30 B4
Lyksborg = Glücksburg (Ostsee) (D) 46 E4
Lyjoti (BY) 138 D4
Lykylä (FIN) 29 J2
Lyman (UA) 171 K2
Lyman's'ke (UA) 151 M4
Lymans'ke (UA) 163 K5
Lyme Regis (GB) 57 J4
Lymington (GB) 58 D6
Lymm (GB) 55 H4
Lympne (GB) 59 J6
Lyndhurst (GB) 57 L4
Lyne (DK) 44 B2
Lyneham (GB) 58 D4
Lyness (GB) 51 L2
Lynešiölna (RUS) 131 N3
Lyngby (DK) 42 B5
Lyngdal (N) 38 F6
Lyngdal (N) 31 K3
Lynge (DK) 47 K2
Lyngen (N) 30 G5
Lyngsa (DK) 42 B5
Lyngseidet (N) 21 K1
Lyngnes (N) 24 F5
Lyngvoll (N) 30 F3
Lynmouth (GB) 57 G3
Lyntupy (BY) 138 F3
Lyny (BY) 139 G4
Łyski (PL) 141 G4
Lyökki (FIN) 34 H3
Lyon (F) 77 H4
Lyonshall (GB) 54 G6
Lypec'ke (UA) 163 K3
Lypivka (UA) 151 K3
Lypiv (UA) 156 G4
Lypne (UA) 150 F4
Lypnyk (UA) 151 G4
Lypnyky (UA) 162 A2
Lypovec' (UA) 151 K5
Lypoven'ke (UA) 163 M2
Lypove (UA) 162 E2
Lysa Góra (PL) 148 B6
Lysá nad Dunajcom (CZ, 155 G3
Lysá nad Labem (CZ) 153 G3
Lysa Polana (PL) 154 E3
Lyšča (RUS) 144 D4
Lyšëčory (BY) 149 J1
Lyse (S) 43 H2
Lyseki (S) 43 H2
Lysedstoline (N) 38 E4
Lysgård (DK) 40 D6
Lysice (CZ) 153 L5
Lysiny (UA) 146 E2
Lysol pod Makýlou (SK) 154 C3
Lysjatči (UA) 150 B6
Lysna (RUS) 139 N2
Lyškava (BY) 143 M5
Łysi (PL) 154 C1
Lyšnivka (UA) 144 E6
Lysnes (CY) 141 L4
Lysosund (N) 24 D7
Lyss (CH) 86 D3
Lyssås (S) 40 B3
Lysthaugen (N) 24 F7
Lystrup (DK) 46 F1
Lystvyn (UA) 145 H6
Lysühol (S) 16 C5
Lysvik (S) 40 D2
Łysyčans'k (UA) 9 P5
Łysychovo (PL) 148 F6
Lytham St Anne's (GB) 54 F3
Lythrodontas (CY) 199 F6
Lyngostaðir (IS) 16 G2
Lytovel (UA) 149 K4
Lyttylä (FIN) 35 J1
Lytvynivka (UA) 151 L2
Lytynka (UA) 150 F5
Lyxaberg (S) 26 E4

M

Maaskeski (FIN) 36 D2
Maakylä (FIN) 36 C3
Maalahti = Malax (FIN) 27 H9
Maalisma (FIN) 27 M4
Maamar (FIN) 185 F3
Maaninka (FIN) 29 L6
Maaninkavaara (FIN) 23 L4
Maanselkä (FIN) 29 J4
Maardu (EST) 35 O6
Maarheeze (N) 69 K4
Maaria (FIN) 35 K3
Maarianhamina = Mariehamn (AX) 34 E4
Maarianvaara (FIN) 29 K6
Maarssen (EST) 131 L4
Maarn (NL) 69 J2
Maarssen (NL) 69 J2
Maasbracht (NL) 70 A4
Maasbull (N) 70 B4
Maaseik (B) 69 K4
Maaseká (FIN) 29 H7
Maaselká (FIN) 29 K6
Maasmechelen (B) 69 K5
Maasslius (NL) 69 K5
Määttälä (FIN) 27 L7
Määttälänvaara (FIN) 23 M4
Maavehmaa (FIN) 35 M4
Maavesi (FIN) 29 J7
Mäbjerg (DK) 42 C6
Macael (E) 127 F6
Mačanet de la Selva (E) 93 K6
Maçanet de la Selva (E) 115 J4
Maçãs (FIN) 174 F6
Mäcesti (MD) 162 F4
Macau (BY) 139 K3
Macaú (RO) 161 G4
Maccagno (I) 87 G6
Macclesfield (GB) 55 H4
Macduff (GB) 50 G3
Mače (HR) 165 G2
Maceda (E) 110 D4
Macedo de Cavaleiros (P) 110 F5
Macerevič (P) 140 F2
Macerá (I) 116 D4
Macep da Sos (RO) 168 F6
Macerej ta Maceivdy (BY) 145 K1
Macharce (PL) 137 J4
Machčiniec (MD) 162 F4
Machčiniec (MD) 162 F4
Macha (DK) 40 C6
Machecoul (F) 74 E3
Machelen (D) 85 H3
Machine (LT) 84 D3
Machnivka (Sauveur) (UA) 151 H4

Machnów Nowy (PL) 148 J5
Machoras, Las (E) 112 D2
Machov (CZ) 146 E5
Machrihanish (GB) 52 D4
Machynlleth (GB) 54 E5
Machynlleth (GB) 57 H1
Maciejowice (PL) 148 E2
Maciejowce (PL) 148 E2
Macieva (BY) 139 L5
Macikowry (BY) 145 K1
Maciuki (LT) 133 K5
Macikovi (SLO) 91 K6
Macias (F) 85 H6
Macodio (I) 87 K7
Macomer (I) 97 C3
Macon (F) 85 G4
Macon (RUS) 13 N4
Macra Leirota (GR) 154 D4
Macu (RUS) 169 J4
Macugnaga (I) 86 E6
Macúčvište (BY) 143 J6
Macure (HR) 172 C1
Macuty (BY) 138 G3
Mad (H) 160 C1
Mäd (SK) 154 B6
Madalena (P) 129 b1
Madan (BG) 175 H3
Madan (BG) 175 K1
Madara (BG) 177 H2
Madaras (H) 166 D1
Mádaró (RO) 160 D4
Mádáráj (RO) 161 J4
Madariaga (E) 113 G2
Madarska (RO) 162 E4
Maddalena Spiaggia (I) 97 D5
Maddaloni (I) 104 B3
Madehira (I) 69 N2
Madenški (P) 116 B4
Mader (TR) 185 J4
Maden (TR) 184 K4
Madeira (F) 81 G6
Madenšehri (TR) 193 F6
Madenuelo (F) 76 D5
Madez (D) 70 G4
Madingley (GB) 55 N6
Madiran (F) 92 D3
Madidwil (CH) 86 E3
Nādo (M) 38 C5
Madladna (LT) 137 N4
Madeira (I) 133 L4
Madocsa (H) 159 G4
Madona (LV) 132 N4
Madonna del Bosco (I) 101 G3
Madonna della Neví, Rifugio (I) 87 J5
Madonna di Baiano (I) 103 F2
Madonna di Campiglio (I) 88 D5
Madonna di Senales (I) 88 D4
Madrange (F) 83 J6
Madre (I) 102 C2
Madrešov (RO) 170 D6
Mádró (I) 119 J3
Madridejos (E) 120 A5
Madrigal de las Altas Torres (E) 119 F1
Madrigal de la Vera (E) 118 F3
Madrigalejo (E) 125 H1
Madrigalejo del Monte (E) 112 D4
Madrigueli (RO) 168 F6
Madrigueras (E) 120 E5
Madroñera (E) 119 H2
Madrofera (F) 117 K5
Madrovič, El (E) 128 A2
Madoñal (RO) 169 G4
Madžarovo (BG) 181 H1
Madžerci (RO) 169 G6
Maella (E) 121 J1
Maella (E) 119 G2
Mael-Pestivien (F) 74 E4
Maenclochog (GB) 56 D1
Maen-Roch (F) 75 J4
Maentenka (FIN) 35 M4
Mientakc (FIN) 35 M3
Maenza (I) 103 G4
Maerdy (GB) 57 H2
Maere (N) 24 F7
Maerrigdaleri (N) 31 L4
Märte (RO) 160 F3
Mäd|berg (D) 70 G4
Maestani (I) 63 L6
Maestu (Arraia Maeztu) (E) 113 G3
Maestu = Maeztu (Arraia Maeztu) (E) 113 G3
Maetaguse (EST) 131 M2
Maëívka (RUS) 142 F1
Maevo (RUS) 135 P4
Maffe (B) 69 J6
Magacela (E) 119 H3
Magagüili (E) 123 G3
Magagnós (E) 113 G6
Magallón (E) 113 J5
Magas (RUS) 190 B5
Magaz de Pisuerga (E) 112 C3
Maj, Shrezé (AL) 174 E5
Majos ts (UA) 163 K4
Majovská (FIN) 22 D3
Magda (RO) 171 M5
Magdalena, La (E) 111 H3
Magdeburg (D) 79 N2
Magdalena (D) 38 E2
Magereir (RO) 65 L6
Magescq (F) 87 G7
Magherafelt (GB) 60 E3
Mages, Les (F) 94 D2
Mägi (RO) 160 E3
Magura (HR) 165 J3
Maggiore (Lago) (I) 86 F6
Maghera (RO) 161 K4
Maghera (GB) 60 E2
Magherberg, Täuti- (RO) 161 G2
Mäghúrus, Sieu- (RO) 161 J3
Maghull-Lydiate (GB) 54 F3
Mäglicy (BY) 145 H4
Magione (I) 101 G6
Magirešti (RO) 169 G3
Mägle-Bourg (F) 83 H5
Magnac-Laval (F) 83 H4
Magnetiserer (N) 29 G7
Magnetsetter (N) 29 J8
Magnor (S) 40 D3

Malälešti (MD) 163 K5
Mälästi (BG) 168 D3
Malälein Brg (RO) 168 E2
Malaja Berastavica (BY) 143 K4
Malaja Tičovo (BY) 139 E2
Malaja Dvfja (UA) 150 F2
Maiden Bradley (GB) 58 C5
Maidenhead (GB) 58 F4
Maiden Newton (GB) 58 B6
Maidesford (GB) 57 M4
Maickuj (BY) 145 K1
Maidla (EST) 131 M4
Malaja Rača (UA) 131 P5
Malaja Svatova (UA) 144 C2
Malaja Uchaloda (BY) 139 J5
Malaja Viša (BY) 135 L4
Malaja Viša (RUS) 7 T6
Malaja Vulha (UA) 144 D6
Maigh Chromtha = Macroom (IRL) 60 F5
Maigh Cuilinn (IRL) 62 E2
Maighean Ratha = Mountrath (IRL) 62 D4
Maigh Nuad = Maynooth (IRL) 63 J2
Maignelay-Montigny (F) 76 G2
Maikammer (D) 79 J3
Mailálín, Malpica (Malpica de Bergantiños = Malpica (E) 110 B2
Malpica de Tajo (E) 119 G4
Malpica de Tajo (E) 118 B4
Malaja Viňadka (BY) 145 O2
Malaja Vulha (UA) 144 D6
Maiko (RUS) 13 N4
Malala Letota (GR) 194 D4
Malamocco (I) 102 E1
Mailag (FIN) 35 N4
Maila Moràvka (CZ) 154 A1
Malasedv (N) 30 H6
Malandréno (GR) 189 H1
Malandréno (GR) 186 E3
Malársec (I) 92 D2
Malaöget (N) 21 H1
Malarás (F) 82 D4
Malausert (F) 93 H6
Malbork (PL) 141 H5
Malíce (CZ) 152 G5
Maldegem (B) 68 C3
Maldon (GB) 59 H4
Maldroni (GR) 194 C5
Maleas = Malešov (CZ) 83 H4
Malechevo (UA) 144 E6
Malecice (F) 77 K4
Maleras (S) 43 O2
Malatesz (E) 41 O2
Mailard (TR) 193 G3
Malatya (TR) 185 J4
Maalesine (I) 88 D6
Maldó (SK) 154 B5
Maleo (I) 87 H3
Maldoniec (PL) 140 E5
Maldon (GB) 59 H4
Malamoèco (I) 102 E1
Mailag (FIN) 35 N4
Mala Morávka (CZ) 154 A1
Malasedv (N) 30 H6

Malopolovice (UA) 151 K4
Malorad (RO) 175 H4
Malosika (UA) 151 G4
Maloš (SRB) 175 G2
Mala Tičovo (BY) 139 E2
Malochavily (RO) 144 C4
Malojaroslavec (RUS) 135 J5
Maldalena de Cáceres (E) 117 H5
Malpartida de la Serena (E) 125 H2
Maisterto (I) 106 F5
Malpas (GB) 54 G4
Malpica (Malpica de Bergantiños = Malpica (E) 110 B2
Malpica de Tajo (E) 119 G4
Malpica de Tajo (E) 118 B4
Maisberg (RUS) 187 H3
Malakásva (GR) 178 E5
Mälák Čardak (BG) 176 C4
Mala Viaduša (BH) 164 F6
Malik Porovec (BG) 177 G1
Malak Preslavec (BG) 176 C6
Malak Izvor (BG) 175 H4
Malakborgo (RO) 170 F3
Maia Lehota (SK) 154 D4
Mailat (MD) 163 M4
Malmesbury (GB) 55 K4
Malmö (S) 42 C5
Malmköping (S) 33 J3
Malmslätt (S) 40 F4
Malnaş Băi (RO) 169 G1
Malnava (LV) 133 K5
Malo (I) 89 G6
Malo les Bains (F) 68 B3
Malobozne (UA) 163 L4
Malojevka (RUS) 144 C2
Maloje Lapino (RUS) 135 L4
Maloje Verevo (RUS) 135 M4
Malojemjakovo (RUS) 144 D4
Malojeroslavec (RUS) 135 J5
Malolázov (PL) 147 H3
Maloe Zrnova (SRB) 166 D5
Maloe Šarkovo (BG) 182 A2
Malovrh (MK) 173 L2
Malowidz (PL) 141 J4
Małszow (RUS) 135 O6
Mälta (GR) 190 E4
Malta (LV) 133 K4
Maltat (F) 85 G3
Maltby (GB) 55 K3
Maltepe (TR) 189 J2
Mãlăieşti (RO) 161 K3
Malumfashi (N) 24 B8
Malung (S) 31 Q6
Malunt (A) 90 D1
Malu cu Flori (RO) 168 B2
Malu Mare (RO) 168 E4
Malu Roşu (RO) 168 G3
Malurenii de Jos (RO) 170 D1
Malurenii de Sus (RO) 170 D1
Maivern (N) 31 K5
Malye Jazy (BY) 135 L4
Mályi (H) 160 B1
Mályinád (H) 158 E6
Maivyk (UA) 163 K3

Mannersdorf am Leithagebirge (A) 91 L4
Mannervaara (FIN) 29 L7
Mannewitz (RUS) 135 O3
Mannheim (D) 73 G4
Mannila (FIN) 35 K2
Mannila (FIN) 35 K3
Mannila (FIN) 35 O3
Mannilä (FIN) 35 K2
Manojlovac (HR) 172 D1
Manolíti (RO) 169 G4
Manole (BG) 176 C4
Manolovo (BG) 176 D4
Manoppello (I) 103 J3
Manosque (F) 95 G3
Manowo (PL) 140 F4
Manresa (E) 115 J2
Manschnow (D) 87 L2
Manston (GB) 58 C5
Mansilla (E) 112 F4
Mansjöbacken (S) 25 F7
Mäns¡ödern (S) 25 G7
Manskivi (FIN) 35 L4
Mansle (F) 82 F3
Manso (F) 96 H4
Mansoniemi (FIN) 35 L1
Manstad (S) 43 G3
Manston (GB) 58 C5
Mantamádos (GR) 188 A2
Manteigas (P) 118 E3
Mantel (D) 80 E2
Mantes-la-Jolie (F) 76 E4
Mantes-la-Ville (F) 76 E4
Mantila (FIN) 27 J8
Mantila (FIN) 35 K1
Mäntlahti (FIN) 36 F4
Mäntoniemi (FIN) 29 H5
Mantova (I) 99 F2
Mänttä (FIN) 28 D7
Mänttyä (FIN) 36 G2
Mäntyharju (FIN) 36 E3
Mäntyjärvi (FIN) 23 K6
Mäntylahti (FIN) 29 J6
Mäntylänmäki (FIN) 29 H5
Mäntyluoto (FIN) 28 B8
Mäntyvaara (FIN) 23 L7
Manturov (RUS) 7 X4
Manuden (GB) 59 G3
Manulla (IRL) 62 E2
Manzac-sur-Vern (F) 83 G5
Manzanares (E) 120 B6
Manzanares el Real (E) 119 G2
Manzaneda (E) 110 F4
Manzaneque (E) 119 G5
Manzanera (E) 121 G3
Manzanilla (E) 124 F4
Manzano (I) 90 E6
Manziana (I) 102 E4
Manzat (F) 85 G5
Manziana (I) 102 E4
Mão (EST) 131 J3
Maón = Mahón (E) 123 K3
Mao (F) 75 J4
Magrsë (AL) 178 B2
Maqueda (E) 119 G4
Mar (I) 110 B5
Marà (I) 97 B2
Maràcàlàt (RO) 160 E5
Maraena (GR) 195 F4
Marajón (F) 82 E5
Marange-Silvange (F) 78 E2
Maranhão (P) 118 C5
Maranna (BY) 138 D5
Maranura (FIN) 27 M4
Maratalle (E) 120 F6
Marateca (P) 124 B1
Marathódamo (GR) 195 K6
Marathea (GR) 195 H2
Marathon (GR) 187 H4
Marathónas (GR) 187 H4

Martres-Tolosane (F) 114 F1
Mårtsbo (S) 32 F5
Martti (FIN) 23 L4
Marttila (FIN) 35 J3
Marttila (FIN) 35 K2
Marttila (FIN) 28 D6
Märtsbackan (FIN) 29 G4
Martti (FIN) 23 L4
Maru (RO) 167 K3
Marufiar (FIN) 189 K1
Marugán (E) 119 H2
Marugáo (I) 105 J9
Marvão (P) 118 D4
Marum (NL) 67 K1
Marusici = Maruščić (HR) 101 K2
Marval (F) 83 G5
Marvão (P) 117 G5
Marvejols (F) 93 H1
Marwik (UA) 162 F3
Märville (F) 78 D3
Marville (F) 78 C3
Marwick (GB) 51 L2
Marxell (D) 79 M2
Marykivka (UA) 157 K2
Marykovka (UA) 150 B5
Maryneavka (UA) 150 A6
Marypol's'ke (UA) 163 M3
Marynivka (UA) 163 M4
Marynopole (UA) 151 H5
Marypol's'ke (UA) 163 L4
Marypol's'ke (UA) 162 B2
Marzabotto (I) 101 F4
Marzamemi (I) 107 G8
Marzaniki (UA) 75 K6
Marzáhna (D) 73 H1
Marzanera (I) 89 J2
Märzängesti (RO) 169 G2
Marzell (D) 87 K2
Marzamemi (I) 107 G8

Mazízeras-en-Gátine (F)
Mazères (F) 92 F4
Mazzo di Valtellina (I) 88 C5
Mcely (CZ) 153 H3
Mdyk (BY) 139 M4
Mealhada (P) 118 B3
Meana Sardo (I) 97 C4
Meaning (IRL) 62 E3
Meare (GB) 57 J4
Mearim (F) 75 H5
Meanus (IRL) 62 F4
Mebby (N) 20 F1

Medby **221**

Medby (N) 20 G2
Meddo (NL) 69 M2
Medebach (D) 70 G4
Medeikiai (LT) 133 K5
Medelín (E) 110 D5
Medellín (E) 117 G3
Medellín (D) 26 E5
Medelim (P) 110 C4
Medemblik (NL) 64 G6
Medembilk (NL) 64 G6
Medena Seliśta (BIH) 174 B3
Meden Buk (BG) 176 F6
Medénec (CZ) 152 D3
Medesano (I) 100 C3
Medet (TR) 191 G5
Medet (TR) 183 K5
Medevi (S) 60 G5
Medgidia (RO) 171 G6
Medgina (LT) 132 H5
Medgyesegyháza (H) 159 M4
Mediana (E) 113 K6
Mediaş (RO) 169 C3
Medicina (I) 100 F4
Medière (F) 78 F7
Medieşu Aurit (RO) 156 D6
Medinaceli (E) 120 D1
Medina de las Torres (E) 125 G3
Medina del Campo (E) 111 K6
Medina de Pomar (E) 112 E3
Medina de Rioseco (E) 112 A5
Medinas, Las Cuevas de los (E) 127 F6
Medina-Sidonia (E) 128 C5
Medinglanda (LT) 128 G5
Medininkai (LT) 137 Q4
Medjarda (E) 115 J3
Medona (E) 115 H5
Medjana (BIH) 37 L3
Medjeda (BIH) 166 C5
Medjedja (BIH) 173 K2
Medjuhana (SRB) 174 F2
Medjuneje (MNE) 174 B3
Medjurječje = Medjureča (BIH) 174 B1
Medkovec (BG) 175 K1
Medle (S) 28 A2
Medni (LV) 134 D3
Mednikalvoro (BG) 176 F4
Medole (I) 100 D2
Medovina (RUS) 175 J1
Medreac (F) 75 G4
Medtern (D) 198 F3
Medskogen (S) 32 D3
Medstugan (S) 25 C7
Medugorje (BIH) 174 B1
Medumm (LV) 134 B6
Meduno (I) 89 H5
Medurječe (BIH) 174 B1
Meduvode (BIH) 167 H5
Meduvrbanja (SRB) 173 K3
Medvećik (SK) 154 B6
Medveja (UA) 157 L5
Medveže (UA) 151 G6
Medvedjegorsk (RUS) 7 T4
Medvida (HR) 172 C1
Medvode (SLO) 164 C2
Medvode (UA) 151 M6
Medyka (PL) 156 C2
Medyn (RUS) 9 Q3
Medynia Głogowska (PL) 156 B1
Medzev (SK) 155 H4
Medzilaborce (SK) 155 K3
Meždititja (MK) 178 E3
Medžitlija (MK) 150 E5
Meeder (D) 71 L6
Meeks (EST) 131 M5
Meerane (D) 73 G4
Meerapalu (EST) 131 M4
Meerbusch (D) 69 M4
Meerdorf (D) 66 C6
Meerhof (D) 71 G3
Meerhout (B) 64 A4
Meerkerk (NL) 69 J3
Meerle (B) 69 H4
Meerlo-Wanssum (NL) 69 L3
Meersburg (D) 79 L6
Meeuwen-Gruitrode (B) 69 K4
Méga Dérion (GR) 18 G2
Méga Eleftherochóri (GR) 179 G5
Méga Horió (GR) 186 D2
Megáli Kalivia (GR) 179 F5
Megáli Panagía (GR) 179 K4
Megálochóri (GR) 186 D2
Megálohóri (GR) 178 E5
Megalópoli (GR) 179 J2
Megalópoli (GR) 186 H3
Méga Peristéri (GR) 178 E5
Megdani (N) 35 G6
Megdani (GR) 178 F9
Mégara (GR) 178 E4
Megeces (E) 112 B6
Megève (F) 85 L4
Meggerdorf (D) 66 A2
Meggethead (GB) 53 J4
Megisti (GR) 197 G3
Megisti (GR) 197 G3
Megra Vöivi (GR) 179 J3
Megruam (N) 31 N5
Megyaszó (H) 155 H3
Mehadia (RO) 168 C4
Mehadica (RO) 167 K3
Mehamn (N) 19 K1
Mehamn (F) 113 J2
Mehedeby (S) 41 M2
Mehikoorma (EST) 131 M4
Mehlingen (D) 70 H3
Mehlis Zeile-(D) 72 D4
Mehmetbeyobagi (TR) 185 G6
Mehmetcik (CY) 199 H5
Mehra (D) 72 F4
Mehren (D) 70 N3
Mehrum (D) 66 C6
Mehriküll (FIN) 27 L6
Mehtäpera (FIN) 28 B4
Mehun-sur-Yèvre (F) 84 B2
Meiania (I) 101 F2
Meidrim (GB) 56 F2
Meigle (GB) 53 J1
Meijel (NL) 70 A4
Meikirch (CH) 86 D3
Meikleour (GB) 53 J1
Meilen (CH) 87 G3
Meilhards (F) 83 J5
Meilhan-en-Médoc (F) 92 H4
Meillerie (F) 85 L6
Meille (F) 84 D3
Meillant (F) 84 D3
Meinberg (D) 71 G3
Meinerzhagen (D) 70 D3
Meinersen (D) 66 D6
Meiningen (D) 72 D4
Meira (E) 110 D2
Meiringen (CH) 86 F4
Meisenheim (D) 70 G3
Meissen (D) 65 N6
Meißner (D) 71 H2
Meitingen (D) 72 B3
Meitzendorf (D) 65 M6
Meiseu (EST) 131 N1

Montbrun-les-Bains (F) 95 F2
Montcabrier (F) 93 G1
Montcaret (F) 92 E1
Montceau-les-Mines (F) 84 F3
Montceaux-lès-Provins (F) 77 H4
Montcenis (F) 84 F3
Montchamp (F) 84 D6
Montchanin (F) 84 F3
Montchevrier (F) 83 J4
Montcornet (F) 77 K2
Montcoy (F) 85 H3
Montcresson (F) 77 G6
Montcuq-en-Quercy-Blanc (F) 93 G2
Montdardier (F) 94 C3
Mont-Dauphin (F) 95 J1
Mont-de-Marsan (F) 92 D3
Montdidier (F) 76 G2
Mont-Dore (F) 84 C5
Monte (E) 110 C1
Monte (E) 111 J2
Monteagudo (E) 113 H5
Monteagudo de las Salinas (E) 120 E4
Monteagudo de las Vicarías (E) 113 G6
Montealegre (E) 112 B5
Montealegre del Castillo (E) 127 H2
Montebello (I) 102 D3
Montebello di Bertona (I) 103 H3
Montebello Ionico (I) 106 E7
Montebello Vicentino (I) 99 L2
Montebelluna (I) 88 G6
Montebibico (I) 103 F2
Montebourg (F) 75 J2
Montebruno (I) 99 G3
Montecalvo in Foglia (I) 101 H5
Montecalvo Irpino (I) 104 D3
Montecarelli (I) 99 L4
Monte-Carlo (MC) 96 A1
Montecarotto (I) 101 J5
Montecassiano (I) 101 J6
Montecastrilli (I) 103 E2
Montecatini Terme (I) 100 D5
Montecatini Val di Cecina (I) 99 K6
Montecchia di Crosara (I) 99 L2
Montecchio (I) 101 H5
Montecchio (I) 102 E2
Montecchio Emilia (I) 99 J3
Montecchio Maggiore (I) 100 E1
Montecelio, Guidonia- (I) 103 F4
Monte Cerignone (I) 101 G5
Montech (F) 93 G3
Montecilfone (I) 104 C2
Monte Claro (P) 117 F4
Montecompatri (I) 103 F4
Montecorto (E) 125 J6
Montecorvino Rovella (I) 104 C4
Montecos (P) 124 B4
Montecosaro (I) 101 K6
Montecreto (I) 100 D4
Monte da Légua (P) 124 D4
Monte da Pedra (P) 117 F5
Monte de Goula (P) 117 F4
Montederramo (E) 110 E4
Montedor (P) 110 B5
Montedoro (I) 108 E3
Monte do Trigo (P) 124 D3
Monte Estremo (F) 96 D4
Montefalco (I) 103 F2
Montefalcone di Val Fortore (I) 104 D3
Montefalcone nel Sannio (I) 103 K4
Montefano (I) 101 J6
Montefelcino (I) 101 H5
Montefiascone (I) 102 E2
Monte Fidalgo (P) 118 A4
Montefiore Conca (I) 101 H5
Montefiore dell'Aso (I) 103 H1
Montefiorino (I) 100 D4
Monteforte Irpino (I) 103 K6
Montefortino (I) 103 G2
Montefrío (E) 126 B5
Montegabbione (I) 102 E2
Montegalda (I) 101 F2
Montegil (E) 125 H5
Montegiordano (I) 105 G5
Montegiordano Marina (I) 107 G2
Montegiorgio (I) 101 K6
Montéglin, Laragne- (F) 95 G2
Monte Gordo (P) 124 E5
Montegranaro (I) 101 K6
Montegrosso Pian Latte (I) 98 D4
Montegrotto Terme (I) 101 F2
Montehermoso (E) 117 J3
Monteils (F) 93 H2
Montejaque (E) 128 D4
Montejícar (E) 126 C4
Montejo de Bricia (E) 112 D3
Montejo de la Sierra (E) 120 A1
Montejo de la Vega de la Serrezuela (E) 112 D5
Montejos del Camino (E) 111 H3
Montelanico (I) 103 G4
Montelavar (P) 116 C6
Montel-de-Gelat (F) 83 L5
Monteleone di Puglia (I) 104 D3
Monteleone di Spoleto (I) 103 F2
Monteleone d'Orvieto (I) 102 E2
Monteleone Rocca Doria (I) 97 C3
Montelepre (I) 108 D1
Montelibretti (I) 103 F3
Montélimar (F) 94 E1
Montella (I) 104 D4
Montellano (E) 125 H6
Montelupo Fiorentino (I) 99 L5
Montemaggiore Belsito (I) 108 E2
Montemagno (I) 98 E3
Montemarano (I) 104 C4
Montemarciano (I) 101 J5
Montemassi (I) 102 C2
Montemayor (E) 111 L5
Montemayor (E) 126 A4
Montemayor, Baños de (E) 117 K3
Montemayor del Río (E) 118 E3
Montemerano (I) 102 C2
Montemesola (I) 105 H4
Montemignaio (I) 100 F5
Montemolín (E) 125 G3
Montemonaco (I) 103 G2
Montemor-o-Novo (P) 124 C2
Montemor-o-Velho (P) 116 D3
Montemurlo (I) 99 L5
Montemurro (I) 106 E2
Montendre (F) 82 E6
Montenegro de Cameros (E) 112 F4
Montenero (I) 99 J6
Montenero di Bisaccia (I) 104 C2
Montenero Sabino (I) 103 F3
Monteneuf (F) 75 G5
Monteoru, Sărata- (RO) 170 D3
Montepastore (I) 100 E4
Montepescali (I) 102 C2
Monte Petrosu (I) 97 E2
Montepiano (I) 100 E4
Monte Porzio (I) 101 J5
Montepulciano (I) 102 D1
Monterchi (I) 101 G6
Monterde de Albarracín (E) 120 F2
Monte Real (P) 116 D4
Montereale (I) 103 G2
Montereau (F) 77 G6
Montereau-Fault-Yonne (F) 77 G5
Monte Redondo (P) 116 D4
Montereggio (I) 99 H4
Monterenzio (I) 100 E4
Monteriggioni (I) 99 L6
Monte Rinaldo (I) 103 H1
Monte Romano (I) 102 D3
Monteroni d'Arbia (I) 100 E6
Monteros, Los (E) 128 E4
Monterosi (I) 102 E3
Monterosso al Mare (I) 99 H4
Monterosso Almo (I) 109 G3
Monterotondo (I) 103 F3
Monterotondo Marittimo (I) 100 D6
Monterroso (E) 110 D3
Monterrubio de la Serena (E) 118 F6
Monterrubio de la Sierra (E) 118 E2
Monterubbiano (I) 103 H1
Montesa (E) 121 G6
Monte Salgueiro (E) 110 C2
Montesalgueiro = Monte Salgueiro (E) 110 C2
Monte San Giovanni (I) 99 L4
Monte San Giovanni in Sabina (I) 103 F3
Monte San Giusto (I) 101 K6
Montesano Salentino (I) 105 K6
Montesano sulla Marcellana (I) 106 E2
Monte San Savino (I) 101 F6
Monte Santa Maria Tiberina (I) 101 G6
Monte Sant'Angelo (I) 104 E2
Montesarchio (I) 103 K5
Montescaglioso (I) 105 G4
Montesclaros (E) 119 G3
Montescudo (I) 101 H5
Montese (I) 99 K4
Montesilvano Marina (I) 103 J2
Montespertoli (I) 100 E5
Montespluga (I) 87 H5
Montesquieu (F) 93 G2
Montesquieu-Avantès (F) 115 F1
Montesquieu-Volvestre (F) 93 G4
Montesquiou (F) 92 E3
Montestruc-sur-Gers (F) 92 F3
Montet, Le (F) 84 D4
Monte Urano (I) 101 K6
Monteu Roero (I) 98 D3
Monteux (F) 94 E2
Montevago (I) 108 C2
Montevarchi (I) 100 F5
Montevecchio (I) 97 C4
Monteverde (I) 104 E4
Monteverdi Marittimo (I) 100 D6
Monte Virgem (P) 117 F6
Montfalcó Murallat (E) 115 F4
Montfaucon (CH) 85 M2
Montfaucon (F) 77 M3
Montfaucon (F) 82 C2
Montfaucon (F) 93 H1
Montfaucon-en-Velay (F) 84 F6
Montferrand-du-Périgord (F) 93 F1
Montferrat (F) 85 J6
Montferrat (F) 95 H3
Montfoort (NL) 69 H2
Montfort (F) 113 K2
Montfort (NL) 70 A4
Montfort-en-Chalosse (F) 92 C3
Montfort-l'Amaury (F) 76 E4
Montfort-le-Gesnois (F) 76 B5
Montfort-sur-Boulzane (F) 115 H2
Montfort-sur-Meu (F) 75 H4
Montfort-sur-Risle (F) 76 C3
Montfranc (F) 93 K3
Montgaillard (F) 93 H3
Montgaillard (F) 114 D1
Mont-Gauthier (B) 69 J6
Montgenèvre (F) 85 L7
Montgibaud (F) 83 H5
Montgiscard (F) 93 H4
Montgomery (GB) 58 A2
Montguyon (F) 82 E6
Mönthal (CH) 86 F2
Montheries (F) 78 B5
Monthermé (F) 77 L2
Monthey (CH) 85 L4
Monthoiron (F) 83 G3
Monthois (F) 77 L3
Monthou-sur-Cher (F) 83 H2
Monthureux-sur-Saône (F) 78 D5
Monti (I) 97 D2
Montiano (E) 112 E2
Montiano (I) 101 G4
Montiano (I) 102 C2
Monticelli d'Ongina (I) 99 H2
Monticelli Ripa d'Oglio (I) 99 J2
Montichiari (I) 100 C2
Monticiano (I) 100 E6
Montiel (E) 126 E2
Montiela, La (E) 125 K4
Montier-en-Der (F) 78 B5
Montieri (I) 100 E6
Montiers-sur-Saulx (F) 78 C4
Montiglio Monferrato (I) 98 E2
Montignac (F) 83 H6
Montignac-Charente (F) 82 F5
Montignac-de-Lauzun (F) 92 E1
Montigny (F) 78 F4
Montigny-le-Gannelon (F) 76 D5
Montigny-Lencoup (F) 77 H5
Montigny-lès-Metz (F) 78 E3
Montigny-le-Tilleul (B) 69 G6
Montigny-sur-Aube (F) 78 B6
Montijo (E) 117 H6
Montijo (P) 124 B2
Montilla (E) 126 A4
Montils, Les (F) 76 D7
Montinho (P) 124 B2
Montivilliers (F) 75 M1
Montjay (F) 95 G2
Montjean (F) 82 F4
Montjean-sur-Loire (F) 75 K6
Montlandon (F) 76 D5
Montlaur (F) 94 A3
Montlaur (F) 115 J1
Montlieu-la-Garde (F) 82 E6
Mont-Louis (F) 93 J5
Montlouis-sur-Loire (F) 83 G2
Montluçon (F) 83 L4
Montluel (F) 85 H5
Montmarault (F) 84 C4
Montmartin-sur-Mer (F) 75 H3
Montmaurin (F) 92 F4
Montmédy (F) 78 C2
Montmélian (F) 85 K5
Montmerle-sur-Saône (F) 85 G4
Montmesa (E) 113 K4
Montmeyan (F) 95 H3
Montmeyran (F) 94 E1
Montmirail (F) 76 C5
Montmirail (F) 77 J4
Montmirey-le-Château (F) 85 J2
Montmoreau-Saint-Cybard (F) 82 F6
Montmorency (F) 76 F4
Montmorillon (F) 83 G4
Montmorin (F) 95 G2
Montmorot (F) 85 J3
Montmort-Lucy (F) 77 J4
Montoggio (I) 98 G3
Montoille (F) 78 E6
Montoir-de-Bretagne (F) 75 G6
Montoire-sur-le-Loir (F) 76 C6
Montoito (P) 124 D2
Montolieu (F) 93 J4
Montón (E) 113 H6
Montone (I) 101 G6
Montopoli in Val d'Arno (I) 99 K5
Montorio al Vomano (I) 103 H2
Montoro (E) 128 F1
Montpaon (F) 93 L3
Montpelhièr = Montpellier (F) 94 C3
Montpellier (F) 94 C3
Montpezat (F) 92 F2
Montpezat-de-Quercy (F) 93 G2
Montpezat-sous-Bauzon (F) 94 D1
Montpon-Ménestérol (F) 82 F6
Montpont-en-Bresse (F) 85 H3
Montpreveyres (CH) 86 C4
Mont-ral (E) 114 F5
Montréal (F) 77 K6
Montréal (F) 92 E3
Montréal (F) 93 J4
Montreal = Mont-ral (E) 114 F5
Montredon-Labessonié (F) 93 J3
Montregard (F) 84 F6
Montréjeau (F) 92 F4
Montrésor (F) 83 H2
Montresta (I) 97 C3
Montret (F) 85 H3
Montreuil (F) 59 L7
Montreuil-Bellay (F) 82 E2
Montreuil-Bonnin (F) 82 F3
Montreuil-Juigné (F) 75 K5
Montreuil-l'Argillé (F) 76 B4
Montreuil-sur-Ille (F) 75 H4
Montreux (CH) 86 C5
Montreux-Château (F) 78 G6
Montrevault-sur-Èvre (F) 82 C2
Montrevel-en-Bresse (F) 85 H4
Montrichard-Val-de-Cher (F) 83 H2
Montricoux (F) 93 H2
Mont-roig del Camp (E) 114 E5
Montrond-les-Bains (F) 84 F5
Montrose (GB) 53 L1
Montroulez = Morlaix (F) 74 D3
Montroy (E) 121 G5
Montrozier (F) 93 K2
Mont-Saint-Aignan (F) 76 D3
Mont-Saint-Jean (F) 84 F2
Mont-Saint-Michel, Le (F) 75 H3
Mont-Saint-Vincent (F) 84 F3
Montsalvy (F) 93 K1
Montsauche-les-Settons (F) 84 F2
Montségur (F) 115 G2
Montségur-sur-Lauzon (F) 94 E2
Montseny (E) 115 H4
Montséret (F) 115 J1
Montsoreau (F) 82 F2
Monts-sur-Guesnes (F) 82 F3
Montsûrs-Saint-Céneré (F) 75 K4
Montsurvent (F) 75 J2
Montuenga (E) 119 G1
Montuenga de Soria (E) 113 G6
Montuïri (E) 123 G3
Monturque (E) 126 A5
Montville (F) 76 D2
Monza (I) 99 G1
Monze (F) 115 H1
Monzón (E) 114 D4
Monzón de Campos (E) 111 L4
Monzone (I) 100 C4
Monzuno (I) 99 L4
Moordorf (D) 64 G5
Moorenweis (D) 80 E4
Moorfields (GB) 61 K2
Moormerland (D) 64 G5
Moorsele (B) 68 E5
Moorslede (B) 68 E5
Moortown (GB) 55 M4
Moorweg (D) 65 H4
Moos (A) 91 G4
Moos (D) 90 C2
Moosbach (D) 81 G1
Moosburg (A) 164 C1
Moosburg an der Isar (D) 80 F4
Moosch (F) 78 G6
Moosdorf (A) 89 H1
Moos in Passeier = Moso in Passiria (I) 87 M4
Mooskirchen (A) 91 H6
Mooste (EST) 131 M4
Moosthenning (D) 152 C6
Mór (H) 158 F3
Mora (E) 119 J4
Mora (P) 116 E6
Mora (S) 32 H5
Mora (S) 41 J2
Morač (BY) 144 E3
Moracz (PL) 140 C3
Móra d'Ebre (E) 121 K1
Mora de Rubielos (E) 121 G3
Moradillo de Roa (E) 112 D5
Moraduccio (I) 99 L4
Morąg (PL) 142 B3
Mórahalom (H) 159 J5
Moraice (MNE) 173 K3
Moraira (E) 122 B5
Morais (P) 111 F6
Moraïtika (GR) 178 B6
Morakovo (MNE) 173 K4
Moral, El (E) 127 F4
Móra la Nova (E) 121 K1
Moral de Calatrava (E) 120 A6
Moraleda de Zafayona (E) 126 C5
Moraleja (E) 117 H3
Moraleja del Vino (E) 111 H6
Moraleja de Sayago (E) 118 D1
Morales de Arcediano (E) 111 G4
Morales de Campos (E) 111 J5
Morales del Vino (E) 111 H6
Morales de Rey (E) 111 H4
Morales de Toro (E) 111 J5
Morales de Valverde (E) 111 H5
Moralina (E) 111 G6
Moralzarzal (E) 119 J2
Morancelle (E) 110 A3
Morăneni (RO) 161 K4
Moräng (S) 22 B6
Morannes-sur-Sarthe-Daumeray (F) 75 L5
Morano Calabro (I) 104 F6
Morano sul Po (I) 98 E2
Morărești (RO) 169 H3
Mörarp (S) 44 B6
Morás (E) 110 E1
Morasverdes (E) 117 J2
Morata de Jalón (E) 113 J6
Morata de Jiloca (E) 113 H6
Morata de Tajuña (E) 120 B3
Moratalla (E) 127 G3
Moratalla (E) 128 D2
Morava (BG) 176 D2
Morava (SLO) 164 D3
Moravče (SLO) 164 D2
Moravec (CZ) 153 K5
Moravica (BG) 176 F2
Moravice (HR) 164 E4
Moravița (RO) 167 H3
Moravka (BG) 177 F2
Morávka (CZ) 154 C2
Moravská Třebová (CZ) 153 L4
Moravské Bránice (CZ) 153 K5
Moravské Budějovice (CZ) 153 J5
Moravské Lieskové (SK) 154 B4
Moravský Beroun (CZ) 154 A2
Moravský Krumlov (CZ) 153 K5
Moravský Písek (CZ) 153 M6
Morawica (PL) 148 C4
Morawin (PL) 147 J2
Morbach (D) 78 G2
Morbegno (I) 87 J5
Mörbisch am See (A) 158 C2
Mörby (S) 45 N3
Morbygget (S) 40 H1
Mörbylånga (S) 45 J5
Morcalı (TR) 198 F1
Morcenx (F) 92 C2
Morciano di Romagna (I) 101 H5
Morcillo (E) 118 D3
Morcone (I) 103 K5
Morcote (CH) 87 G6
Morcott (GB) 58 F2
Morcuera (E) 112 E6
Mordalsvågen (N) 30 F2
Mordano (I) 101 F4
Mordelles (F) 75 H4
Mordoğan (TR) 190 B3
Mordy (PL) 149 G1
Mor'e (RUS) 7 S5
Mor'e (RUS) 37 Q4
Moreanes (P) 124 D4
Morebattle (GB) 53 L3
Morecambe (GB) 54 G2
Moreda (E) 111 H2
Moreda (E) 126 D5
Morée (F) 76 D6
Moreira (P) 110 B6
Moreira (P) 110 C4
Moreira de Geraz do Lima (P) 110 B5
Moreira do Rei (P) 110 C6
Moreiras (E) 110 D4
Moreleigh (GB) 57 G5
Mörel-Filet (CH) 86 F5
Morell, el (E) 115 F5
Morella (E) 122 A1
Moreni (RO) 170 B4
Morera, La (E) 125 F2
Moreras, Las (E) 127 J3
Mores (I) 97 C2
Morestel (F) 85 H5
Moret-Loing-et-Orvanne (F) 77 G5
Moreton (GB) 58 C6
Moretonhampstead (GB) 57 G4
Moreton-in-Marsh (GB) 57 L2
Moretta (I) 95 L1
Moreuil (F) 76 F2
Morez (F) 86 B4
Morfasso (I) 100 B3
Mörfelden-Walldorf (D) 70 G7
Mórfi (GR) 178 C6
Morfjord (N) 20 D4
Morfou = Güzelyurt (TR) 198 F5
Morgårdshammar (S) 40 H2
Morgat (F) 74 B4
Morgedal (N) 38 H3
Morges (CH) 85 K3
Morgex (I) 85 M5
Morgie, le (I) 103 K3
Morgins, Pas de (F) 86 C5
Morgny (F) 76 E3
Morgongåva (S) 41 L3
Morgunovo (RUS) 136 D4
Morhange (F) 78 F4
Morhet (B) 78 D2
Morhovo (RUS) 135 M3
Mori (I) 88 D6
Morialmé (B) 69 H6
Moriani-Plage (F) 96 F4
Møriaunet (N) 24 E7
Mórichida (H) 158 D2
Moricone (I) 103 F3
Morienval (F) 77 G3
Moriles (E) 126 A5
Morillas (E) 112 F3
Morillo de Liena (E) 92 E6
Mořina (CZ) 73 L6
Morina = Morinë (RKS) 174 D4
Morinë (AL) 174 E4
Morinë (RKS) 174 D4
Moringen (D) 72 B2
Morinj, Donji (MNE) 173 J5
Morino (RUS) 135 K2
Moritzburg (D) 73 K3
Morivs'k (UA) 151 M1
Morjärv (S) 27 J2
Mörk (IS) 16 G7
Mörk (IS) 17 H7
Mørk (N) 39 O3
Morka (PL) 146 F1
Morkarla (S) 34 A4
Mørke (DK) 42 F6
Mørkedal (N) 24 C8
Mørken (N) 31 K5
Mörkö (S) 41 N4
Mořkov (CZ) 154 C2
Mørkøv (DK) 47 J2
Morkovice-Slížany (CZ) 153 M5
Mörkret (S) 32 D4
Mørkri (N) 30 H4
Morl (D) 72 F2
Morlaàs (F) 92 D4
Morlac (F) 83 K3
Morla de la Valdería (E) 111 G4
Morlaix (F) 74 D3
Morlanda (S) 39 P6
Morlanne (F) 113 K1
Mörlenbach (D) 79 K2
Morles (D) 72 B4
Morlet (F) 84 G3
Morley (F) 78 C4
Morley (GB) 55 J3
Mörlunda (S) 44 H4
Mormal' (BY) 145 L3
Mormanno (I) 104 E6
Mormant (F) 77 G4
Mormoiron (F) 94 F2
Mormont (B) 69 K6
Mornant (F) 85 G5
Mornas (F) 94 E2
Mornay-Berry (F) 84 C2
Mornay-sur-Allier (F) 84 D3
Mornico al Serio (I) 100 B1
Mörnsheim (D) 80 E3
Moročne (UA) 144 C5
Moroe (IRL) 62 F3
Moroeni (RO) 169 J3
Möron (S) 22 D6
Morón de Almazán (E) 113 G6
Morón de la Frontera (E) 128 D3
Morones, Los (E) 126 D6
Moros (E) 113 H6
Morosaglia (F) 96 E4
Morović (SRB) 166 D3
Morozivka (UA) 151 J4
Morozovo (RUS) 134 F3
Morozzo (I) 98 D4
Morpeth (GB) 53 M4
Morra, La (I) 98 D3
Morre (F) 85 K2
Morro d'Alba (I) 101 J5
Morro Reatino (I) 103 F2
Morrovalle (I) 101 K6
Mörrum (S) 44 F6
Morșa (RO) 162 E4
Morsains (F) 77 J4
Moršansk (RUS) 9 Q3
Morsbach (D) 70 E5
Morschen (D) 71 J4
Mörse (D) 66 D6
Mørset (N) 24 F7
Mörsil (S) 25 H8
Morska Zvezda (BG) 177 K2
Morskoga krog (S) 40 H3
Mörskom = Myrskylä (FIN) 36 E3
Morsleben (D) 71 M2
Morsum (D) 46 B4
Mørsvikbotn (N) 20 E5
Moršyn (UA) 156 E3
Mortagne-au-Perche (F) 76 C4
Mortagne-sur-Gironde (F) 82 D6
Mortagne-sur-Sèvre (F) 82 D3
Mortagonovo (BG) 177 G1
Mortágua (P) 116 E3
Mortain-Bocage (F) 75 K3
Mortara (I) 98 F2
Mortavika (N) 38 C4
Mörtberg (S) 21 L8
Morteau (F) 85 L2
Mörtebo (S) 33 M6
Mortegliano (I) 89 J6
Mortehoe (GB) 56 F3
Mortemart (F) 83 G4
Morteni (RO) 169 J4
Mortensnes (N) 18 F3
Mortensnes (N) 19 M3
Mortimer's Cross (GB) 54 G6
Mörtjärn (S) 26 F4
Mörtnäs (S) 40 B3
Mortnäs (S) 41 O4
Mortop (S) 41 L4
Mortorp (S) 45 J5
Mortrée (F) 75 M3
Mortsel (B) 69 G4
Mörtsjön (S) 25 J7
Morud (DK) 46 F3
Morunglav (RO) 169 G5
Morup (S) 43 K5
Morvah (GB) 56 C5
Morvich (GB) 50 G5
Morville (GB) 55 H5
Morwenstow (GB) 56 E4
Moryń (PL) 140 B5
Moryna (BY) 138 C6
Morzeszczyn (PL) 141 L3
Morzhell = Mordelles (F) 75 H4
Morzine (F) 85 L4
Mos (E) 110 B4
Mos (S) 45 O3
Moșana (MD) 162 F2
Mošanec' (UA) 162 D2
Mosar (BY) 138 F3
Mosar (BY) 139 J3
Mosarski, Luck- (BY) 138 F3
Mosätt (S) 32 G3
Mosbach (D) 79 L3
Mosbjerg (DK) 42 F4
Mosby (N) 42 A2
Moščanycja (UA) 150 D3
Moščenica (HR) 165 G4
Moščenička Draga (HR) 164 C4
Mosciano Sant'Angelo (I) 103 H2
Mościska (PL) 148 D5
Mościsko (PL) 146 F4
Moscovei (MD) 171 G2
Mosėdis (LT) 136 F1
Mösel (A) 90 G6
Mosel (D) 73 G4
Möser (D) 72 F1
Mosfell (IS) 16 E6
Mosfell (IS) 16 F6
Mosfellsbær (IS) 16 E6
Moshófito (GR) 178 E6
Moshokariá (GR) 179 G7
Moshopótamos (GR) 179 G4
Moshult (S) 44 C5
Mosigkau (D) 72 G2
Mosina (PL) 146 F1
Mosiny (PL) 141 H3
Mosjö (S) 26 D8
Mosjö (S) 40 H4
Mosjøen (N) 25 H3
Mosjön (S) 33 L5
Moskenes (N) 20 C5
Mosko (BIH) 173 H4
Moskodalen (N) 21 L1
Moskog (N) 30 D5
Moskorzew (PL) 148 A4
Moskosel (S) 26 F3
Moskuvaara (FIN) 23 J1
Moskva (RUS) 7 U7
Moskvyn (Selo) (UA) 150 D2
Moslavina Podravska (HR) 166 A2
Moșna (RO) 162 F5
Moșna (RO) 169 G1
Mošnica (BY) 138 F6
Moșnița Nouă (RO) 167 H2
Moșoaia (RO) 169 H4
Moso in Passiria (I) 87 M4
Mosonmagyaróvár (H) 158 D2
Mosonszentmiklós (H) 158 D2
Mosonszolnok (H) 91 M4
Mošorin (SRB) 166 F3
Mošovce (SK) 154 D4
Mosqueirão (P) 124 B3
Mosqueruela (E) 121 H3
Moss (N) 39 N4
Mossa (I) 89 K6
Mossala (FIN) 34 H4
Mossat (GB) 51 M5
Mossatråsk (S) 25 M7
Mossblown (GB) 52 F4
Mossbo (S) 33 L5
Mossebo (S) 43 M4
Mosset (F) 93 J5
Mosshult (S) 45 J2
Mossiberg (S) 32 F4
Mössingen (D) 79 L5
Mosstodloch (GB) 51 L4
Mosstorp (S) 40 F5
Most (BG) 176 E5
Most (CZ) 152 E3
Møst (N) 30 H1
Most = Heinersbrück (D) 73 M2
Moštanica (SRB) 175 G3
Mostar (BIH) 173 G3
Moste (SLO) 89 L5
Moste (SLO) 89 M5
Mosteiro (Meis) (E) 110 B3
Mostek (CZ) 153 J3
Moșteni (RO) 169 K5
Moster- (N) 38 B3
Mosterhamn (N) 38 B3
Mostišče (RUS) 134 G5
Mostiště (CZ) 153 K5
Mostki (PL) 148 D4
Mostkowo (PL) 142 C3
Most na Soči (SLO) 89 K5
Móstoles (E) 119 J3
Mostovo (BG) 181 F1
Mostów (PL) 149 G1
Mostowice (PL) 146 E5
Mostowo (PL) 140 F2
Most pri Bratislave (SK) 158 D1
Mosty (PL) 140 C3
Mosty (PL) 149 H2
Mostys'ka (UA) 156 D2
Mosty u Jablunkova (CZ) 154 D2
Mošuriv (UA) 151 L6
Mošuriv (UA) 151 M6
Mosvik (N) 24 F7
Mosyr (UA) 149 K3
Moszczanka (PL) 148 E2
Mota del Cuervo (E) 120 C5
Mota del Marqués (E) 111 J5
Moțăineni (RO) 169 J3
Motal' (BY) 144 C4
Motala (S) 44 G1
Moțăței (RO) 168 E5
Moțca (RO) 162 D4
Mothe-Achard, La (F) 82 B3
Motherwell (GB) 52 H3
Mothe-Saint-Héray, La (F) 82 E4
Motike (BIH) 165 H6
Motilla del Palancar (E) 120 E4
Motilleja (E) 120 E5
Motiș (RO) 169 G1
Motjärnshyttan (S) 40 E3
Motkowice (PL) 148 B4
Motnik (SLO) 164 D2
Motornoe (RUS) 37 O3
Motoseni (RO) 162 E6
Motovun (HR) 101 K2
Motovylivka (UA) 150 F4
Motovylivka (UA) 151 L3
Motril (E) 126 C6
Motru (RO) 168 D4
Motru, Breznița (RO) 168 E4
Motrunky (UA) 150 E4
Motta d'Affermo (I) 106 B7
Motta di Livenza (I) 89 H6
Motta Montecorvino (I) 104 D2
Motta San Giovanni (I) 109 J1
Motte-Chalancon, La (F) 95 F2
Motte-d'Aigues, La (F) 95 F3
Motte-du-Caire, La (F) 95 H2
Motten (D) 72 B5
Mottgers (D) 71 J6
Mottola (I) 105 H4
Möttölanniemi (FIN) 23 L8
Möttönen (FIN) 28 E5
Motyžyn (UA) 151 K3
Mötzing (D) 81 G3
Mötzingen (D) 79 K4
Mou (DK) 42 F5
Mouchamps (F) 82 C3
Mouchan (F) 92 E3
Mouchard (F) 85 J3
Moudon (CH) 85 L3
Moúdros (GR) 181 G5
Mougins (F) 98 B5
Mougon-Thorigné (F) 82 E4
Mouguerre (F) 92 B4
Mouhijärvi (FIN) 35 M1
Mouhu (FIN) 36 G2
Mouilleron-Saint-Germain (F) 82 D3
Moulay (F) 75 K4
Mouliherne (F) 75 M6
Moulinet (F) 98 C5
Moulin-Mage (F) 94 A3
Moulin-Neuf (F) 115 G1
Moulins (F) 84 D3
Moulins, Les (CH) 85 M4
Moulins, les (F) 84 E5
Moulins-Engilbert (F) 84 E3
Moulins-la-Marche (F) 76 B4
Moulismes (F) 83 G4
Moulle (F) 59 M6
Moulton (GB) 58 F3
Mountain Ash (GB) 57 H2
Mountain Cross (GB) 53 J3
Mount Bellew (IRL) 62 F2
Mountbenger (GB) 53 J3
Mountcharles (IRL) 60 F2
Mountfield (GB) 61 H2
Mountmellick (IRL) 63 H2
Mountrath (IRL) 60 H5
Mountshannon (IRL) 60 F6
Moura (P) 124 E3
Mourão (P) 124 E3
Mourens (F) 92 D1
Mourentán (E) 110 C4
Mourenx (F) 92 C4
Mouret, Le (CH) 85 M3
Mouriès (F) 94 E3
Mouriés (GR) 179 H2
Mouriki (GR) 187 G3
Mouriscas (P) 116 E4
Mourmelon-le-Grand (F) 77 K3
Mourmelon-le-Petit (F) 77 K3
Mourniés (GR) 194 D5
Mouromorto (E) 110 D3
Mourujärvi (FIN) 23 L4
Mouscron (B) 68 E5
Mousehole (GB) 56 C5
Moussac (F) 94 D3
Moussey (F) 78 F4
Moustéru (F) 74 E3
Moustey (F) 92 C2
Moustiers-Sainte-Marie (F) 95 H3
Moutchic, le (F) 82 C6
Moutfort (L) 78 E2
Mouthe (F) 85 K3
Mouthoumet (F) 93 K5
Moutier (CH) 86 D3
Moûtiers (F) 86 C7
Moutiers-les-Mauxfaits (F) 82 C4
Moutiers-sous-Argenton (F) 82 E3
Moutiers-sur-le-Lay (F) 82 C3
Moutnice (CZ) 153 L5
Moutoullas (CY) 198 E6
Moutsoúna (GR) 195 H1
Moux (F) 93 K4
Moux-en-Morvan (F) 84 F2
Mouy (F) 76 F3
Mouzáki (GR) 179 F6
Mouzáki (GR) 186 D5
Mouzieys-Teulet (F) 93 J3
Mouzon (F) 77 M2
Movatn (N) 39 N2
Movattnet (S) 26 E7
Movčanivka (UA) 151 J4
Movelier (CH) 86 D3
Movik (N) 38 A2
Movila (RO) 170 F4
Movila Banului (RO) 170 D4
Movila Miresii (RO) 170 F3
Movileni (RO) 162 E4
Movileni (RO) 169 H5
Movileni (RO) 170 E2
Movilița (RO) 170 C4
Movilița (RO) 170 E2
Moville (IRL) 52 A4
Movollen (N) 32 B2
Moy (GB) 52 B6
Moyaux (F) 76 B3
Moy-de-l'Aisne (F) 77 H2
Moyenmoutier (F) 78 F5
Moyenvic (F) 78 F4
Moyeuvre-Grande (F) 78 E3
Möykky (FIN) 28 B7
Möykkylä (FIN) 23 G7
Möykkylänperä (FIN) 29 G3
Moy Lodge (GB) 51 H6
Moylough (IRL) 62 E2
Moynalty (IRL) 61 J4
Moyne (IRL) 60 G4
Moyrazès (F) 93 J2
Moyuela (E) 121 G1
Moyvore (IRL) 63 G1
Mozac (F) 84 D5
Mozăceni (RO) 169 J4
Možaevo (RUS) 135 P4
Možajsk (RUS) 7 U7
Mózar (E) 111 H5
Mozárbez (E) 117 K2
Mozelj (SLO) 164 D3
Mozgovo (SRB) 175 G1
Mozirje (SLO) 164 D2
Mozoncillo (E) 119 H1
Mozuli (RUS) 134 F4
Mozyr' (RUS) 142 E2
Mozyr' = Mazyr (BY) 145 K4
Mozza, Torre (I) 105 K6
Mozzanica (I) 87 J7
Mozzecane (I) 99 K2
Mraclin (HR) 165 G3
Mrągowo (PL) 142 E3
Mrákotín (CZ) 153 H5
Mramor (BG) 175 J3
Mramor (BG) 182 B1
Mramor (RKS) 174 F3
Mramorak (SRB) 167 G4
Mramoren (BG) 175 L2
Mratín (CZ) 152 G3
Mrázov (CZ) 73 H6
Mrčajevci (SRB) 167 G6
Mrežičko (MK) 179 F2
Mrežihko (BG) 177 H3
Mrkalji (BIH) 173 J1
Mrkonjić Grad (BIH) 165 J6
Mrkonjići (BIH) 173 H4
Mrkopalj (HR) 164 D4
Mrmoš (SRB) 174 F1
Mrocza (PL) 141 J4
Mroczeń (PL) 147 H3
Mroczki, Tarnowo- (PL) 142 G5
Mroczno (PL) 142 B4
Mrowino (PL) 140 G5
Mrzen (MK) 175 G6
Mrzezino (PL) 141 K1
Mrzeżyno (PL) 140 D2
Mrzygłód (PL) 155 L2
Msanec' (UA) 150 A4
Mšanec' (UA) 150 B5
Mšanec' (UA) 156 C3
Mścice (PL) 140 F2
Mscioava (BY) 143 L4
Mscislaŭ (BY) 9 M3
Msciž (BY) 139 H4
Mšec (CZ) 152 E3
Mšené-Lázně (CZ) 73 L5
Mšeno (CZ) 152 G3
Mstów (PL) 147 L4
Mszana Dolna (PL) 154 G2
Mszczonów (PL) 148 C2
Mtež (RUS) 134 E1
Muccia (I) 103 G1
Much (D) 70 D5
Muchamiel = Mutxamel (E) 127 K3
Muchariv (UA) 150 E2
Mucharz (PL) 154 F2
Muchavec (BY) 149 J1
Mücheln (Geiseltal) (D) 72 F3
Much Marcle (GB) 57 K2
Muchówka (PL) 155 G2
Much Wenlock (GB) 55 G5
Muči (LV) 132 D3
Mučibaba = Muçibabë (RKS) 175 G4
Muçibabë (RKS) 175 G4
Mucientes (E) 111 K5
Mücka (D) 146 B3
Mücke (D) 71 H5
Mucur (TR) 13 K6
Mucur (TR) 193 H2
Muda (P) 124 B4
Muda, La (I) 88 G5
Mudanya (TR) 183 G5
Mudarlı (TR) 183 J3
Mudarra, La (E) 112 B5
Mudau (D) 79 L2
Müden (Aller) (D) 66 C5
Müden (Mosel) (D) 70 D6
Müden (Örtze) (D) 65 N6
Mudersbach (D) 70 E5
Muel (E) 114 A5
Muela, La (E) 112 F5
Muela, La (E) 114 A4
Muelas de los Caballeros (E) 111 G4
Muelas del Pan (E) 111 H5
Muereasca (RO) 169 G3
Muezerskij (RUS) 7 S4
Müezzinler (TR) 183 K4
Müezzinler (TR) 192 A5
Muff (IRL) 61 H1
Müftükışla (TR) 193 K2
Muga de Sayago (E) 111 G6
Mugardos (E) 110 C2
Muge (P) 124 B1
Mügeln (D) 73 J2
Mügeln (D) 73 J3
Mugeni (RO) 161 L5
Muggendorf (D) 80 E1
Muggensturm (D) 79 J4
Muggia (I) 164 B3
Mugla (BG) 180 E1
Muğla (TR) 196 D1
Mugnano (I) 102 E1
Mugron (F) 92 C3
Muhacir (TR) 184 F3
Muharevo (RUS) 135 K3
Muhi (H) 155 H6
Mühlacker (D) 79 K4
Mühlanger (D) 73 H2
Mühlbach (D) 80 F2
Mühlbach am Hochkönig (A) 81 J6
Mühlbach am Manhartsberg, Hohenwarth- (A) 153 J6
Mühlberg (D) 71 L5
Mühlberg (Elbe) (D) 73 J3
Mühldorf (A) 91 H3
Mühldorf am Inn (D) 90 C3
Mühleck = Costa Molini (I) 88 F4
Mühlen (A) 90 G5
Mühlen = Molini di Tures (I) 88 F4
Mühlen-Eichsen (D) 66 E3
Mühlhausen (D) 80 D1
Mühlhausen (D) 80 E2
Mühlhausen (D) 80 F3
Mühlhausen (D) 81 G3
Mühlhausen (Thüringen) (D) 72 C3
Mühlheim am Main (D) 71 G6
Mühlheim an der Donau (D) 79 K5
Mühlingen (D) 87 H2
Mühlstetten (D) 80 E2
Mühltal (A) 88 E3
Mühltroff (D) 152 A2
Mühltroff, Pausa- (D) 152 A2
Mühlwald = Selva dei Molini (I) 88 F4
Muhola (FIN) 27 M8
Muhola (FIN) 29 J7
Muhos (FIN) 28 F2
Muhovicy (RUS) 37 M5
Muhovo (BG) 176 A4
Muhr (A) 89 K3
Mühring (A) 81 K4
Muides-sur-Loire (F) 76 E6
Muids (F) 76 D3
Muimenta (E) 110 C3
Muineachán (IRL) 61 J3
Muineachán = Monaghan (IRL) 61 J3
Muine Bheag (IRL) 63 J3
Muiños (E) 110 A2
Muirhead (GB) 53 J2
Muirkirk (GB) 52 G3
Muir of Ord (GB) 51 J4
Mujejärvi (FIN) 29 K4
Mukačeve (UA) 155 M5
Mukačevo = Mukačeve (UA) 155 M5
Mukařov (CZ) 73 M6
Mukkajärvi (S) 21 N7
Mukošyn (BY) 149 M2
Mula (E) 127 H3
Mula (N) 25 H2
Mülayim (TR) 184 F3
Mul'čyci (UA) 144 C5
Mulda (Sachsen) (D) 152 D2
Muldenberg (D) 73 G5
Muldenhammer (D) 73 G5
Muldenstein (D) 73 G2
Muldestausee (D) 73 G2
Mulegns (CH) 88 B4
Mules (I) 88 F4
Mulestad (S) 45 J3
Mulfingen (D) 80 B2
Mülhausen = Mulhouse (F) 79 G6
Mülheim an der Mosel (D) 78 G2
Mülheim an der Ruhr (D) 70 C4
Mülheim-Kärlich (D) 70 D6
Mulhouse (F) 79 G6
Múli (FO) 48 E3
Múli (IS) 16 F6
Muljala (FIN) 29 K7
Mulknitz (D) 73 M2
Mulkoila (FIN) 35 P1
Mullach Íde = Malahide (IRL) 61 K5
Mullagh (IRL) 61 J4
Mullagh (IRL) 63 J2
Mullaghmore (IRL) 60 F3
Mullany's Cross (IRL) 60 E3
Müllendorf (A) 158 B2
Müllheim (D) 79 H6
Mullhyttan (S) 40 G4
Mullinahone (IRL) 63 H3
Mullinavat (IRL) 63 H4
Mullingar (IRL) 63 H1
Mullinkylä (FIN) 36 H4
Mullion (GB) 56 D5
Müllrose (D) 146 A1
Mullsjö (S) 26 F7
Mullsjö (S) 43 N3
Mulrany (IRL) 60 C4
Mulsanne (F) 76 B6
Mülsen (D) 73 H4
Mülsen Sankt Jacob (D) 152 C2
Mulseryd (S) 44 D3
Mulsum (D) 66 A3
Multia (FIN) 28 E7
Multyfarnham (IRL) 60 H4
Mülverstedt (D) 71 L4
Mumbles Head (GB) 56 F2
Mumby (GB) 55 N4
Mumcular (TR) 196 C1
Mümliswil (CH) 86 E3
Munakka (FIN) 28 C6
Munalaid (EST) 130 F4
Muñana (E) 119 F2
Munapirtti (FIN) 36 G4
Muncelu Mare (RO) 160 F6
Münchberg (D) 72 F5
Müncheberg (D) 67 L5
Münchehof (D) 71 K3
Münchehofe (D) 73 K1
München (D) 80 F4
Münchenbernsdorf (D) 152 A2
Münchenbuchsee (CH) 86 D3
Münchhausen (D) 70 G5
Münchnerau (D) 80 G3
Münchsmünster (D) 80 F3
Münchsteinach (D) 80 D1
Münchweiler, Glan- (D) 79 G3
Münchweiler an der Alsenz (D) 79 H2
Münchwilen (CH) 79 K7
Muncurlu (TR) 184 B4
Mundaka (E) 113 F2
Mundal (N) 30 F5
Münden = Hann. Münden (D) 71 J4
Munderfing (A) 89 J1
Munderkingen (D) 79 M5
Mundesley (GB) 59 K2
Mundford (GB) 59 J2
Mundheim (N) 38 C2
Mundolsheim (F) 79 H4
Mundraching (D) 88 D2
Munébrega (E) 113 H6
Munera (E) 127 F1
Munga (S) 41 M2
Mungía (E) 112 F2
Muņi (LV) 132 E2
Muniaczkowice (PL) 148 B5
Muñico (E) 119 F2
Muniesa (E) 121 G1
Munka-Ljungby (S) 44 B6
Munkarp (S) 47 M2
Munkaþverá (IS) 17 H3
Munkbyn (S) 33 L3
Munke Bjergby (DK) 47 J2
Munkebo (DK) 46 G3
Munkeby (N) 24 F7
Munkedal (S) 39 P6
Munkelva (N) 19 M4
Munken (N) 24 D7
Munkflohögen (S) 25 J7
Munkfors (S) 40 E3
Munkinvaara (FIN) 29 L5
Munknes (N) 19 M4
Munksund (S) 27 H4
Munktorp (S) 41 K3
Münnerstadt (D) 72 C5
Muñogalindo (E) 119 G2
Muñopedro (E) 119 H2
Muñorrodero (E) 111 L2
Munsala (FIN) 28 C5
Münsing (D) 88 E2
Münsingen (CH) 86 E4
Münsingen (D) 80 A4
Munslow (GB) 54 G6
Munsö (S) 41 N4
Munster (D) 65 N6
Münster (D) 70 E3
Münster (D) 79 K2
Münster (D) 80 D3
Munster (F) 78 G5
Münster = Müstair (CH) 88 C4
Münsterbrock (D) 71 H3
Münster-Geschinen (CH) 86 F5
Münsterlingen (CH) 87 H2
Münstermaifeld (D) 70 D6
Münstertal/Schwarzwald (D) 86 E2
Munsvattnet (S) 25 J6
Muntele Cacovei (RO) 161 G4
Munteni (RO) 170 E2
Munteni-Buzău (RO) 170 D4
Muntenii de Jos (RO) 162 F5
Munți, Rușii- (RO) 161 K4
Münzenberg (D) 71 G6
Münzkirchen (A) 90 E3
Muodoslompolo (S) 18 F8
Muonio (FIN) 18 F8
Muonionalusta (S) 18 F8
Muorjevaara (S) 22 D2
Muotathal (CH) 87 G4
Muotkajärvi (FIN) 21 N4
Muotkavaara (FIN) 18 G8
Mur (SRB) 174 D2
Muradiye (TR) 190 C3
Murafa (UA) 151 G6
Murakeresztúr (H) 165 H2
Murakka (FIN) 28 G8
Muralbey (TR) 184 B4
Muráň (SK) 154 G4
Murane (N) 30 H5
Murano (I) 101 G2
Murat (F) 84 C6
Muratdağı (TR) 191 H3
Muratdere (TR) 183 J6
Muratlar (TR) 182 C6
Muratlar (TR) 190 F6
Muratlı (TR) 182 E3
Murato (F) 96 E3
Muratovac = Bosanski Petrovac (BIH) 165 G5
Murat-sur-Vèbre (F) 94 A3
Muratu = Murato (F) 96 E3
Murau (A) 90 F5
Murava (BY) 143 L5
Muravana-Ašmjanka (BY) 137 O5
Muravera (I) 97 E5
Muravlivka (UA) 171 J2
Muravyšče (UA) 150 B2
Murazzano (I) 98 E4
Murazzo (I) 95 L2
Murça (P) 110 E6
Murça (P) 117 G1
Murchin (D) 47 N6
Murci (I) 102 C2
Murcia (E) 127 H4
Murczyn (PL) 141 J5
Mur-de-Barrez (F) 93 K1
Mûr-de-Bretagne (F) 74 F4
Mur-de-Sologne (F) 83 J2
Mure, La (F) 95 G1
Mureaux, Les (F) 76 E4
Mureck (A) 91 J6
Mürefte (TR) 182 D4
Mureno (BG) 175 J3
Mures (E) 126 C5
Muret (F) 93 G4
Muret, le (F) 92 C2
Muret-le-Château (F) 93 K2
Murgeni (RO) 170 G1
Murgenthal (CH) 86 E3
Murgești (RO) 170 D3
Murgia (E) 112 F3
Murguia = Murgia (E) 112 F3
Murgula = Murqullë (RKS) 174 F2
Muri (CH) 86 D4
Muri (AG) (CH) 86 F3
Murialdo (I) 98 E4
Murias de Paredes (E) 111 G3
Muriedas (E) 112 D2
Murighiol (RO) 171 J3
Murillo de Gállego (E) 92 C6
Murillo de Río Leza (E) 113 G4
Murillo el Fruto (E) 92 B6
Murino (MNE) 174 C3
Muriqan (AL) 174 B4
Murjek (S) 27 G2
Murlaggan (GB) 50 G6
Mürlenbach (D) 70 C6
Murlo (I) 100 E6
Murmansk (RUS) 7 T2
Murnau am Staffelsee (D) 80 E5
Muro (E) 123 H3
Muro (F) 96 D3
Muro (P) 110 B6
Muro de Aguas (E) 113 G4
Muro del Alcoy (E) 127 K2
Murol (F) 84 C5
Murole (FIN) 35 N1
Muro Leccese (I) 107 K2
Muro Lucano (I) 104 D4
Muron (F) 82 D4
Murony (H) 159 M4
Muros (E) 110 A3
Muros (E) 111 G1
Muros de Nalón = Muros (E) 111 G1
Müro Strėvininkai (LT) 137 M4
Murovane (UA) 149 K5
Murovani Kurylivci (UA) 162 F1
Murovano-Ošmjanka (BY) 138 C5
Murowana Goślina (PL) 140 H5
Murqullë (RKS) 174 F2
Murrë (AL) 174 D5
Mürren (CH) 86 E4
Murrhardt (D) 79 M4
Murrisk (IRL) 60 C4
Murrizë (AL) 174 D6
Murroogh (IRL) 60 D5
Murs (F) 95 F3
Mursal (TR) 197 G2
Mursallı (TR) 190 D5
Mürseller (TR) 191 H6
Murska Sobota (SLO) 165 G1
Mursko Središće (HR) 165 G1
Murstetten (A) 91 J3
Murtamo (FIN) 35 J2
Murtas (E) 126 D6
Murten (CH) 85 M3
Murter (HR) 172 C2
Mürtet (TR) 184 E5
Murtiçi (TR) 198 C2
Murtino (MK) 175 J6
Murto (FIN) 27 M5
Murtoi (FIN) 29 L7
Murtoinen (FIN) 29 G7
Murtolahti (FIN) 29 H5
Murtomäki (FIN) 29 H3
Murton (GB) 53 N5
Murtosa (P) 116 D2
Murtovaara (FIN) 23 M5
Murtovaara (FIN) 29 K5
Murum (S) 44 C3
Muruvik (N) 24 E8
Murvica (HR) 172 B1
Murvica (HR) 172 E3
Murviel-lès-Béziers (F) 93 L4
Murvoll (N) 24 E7
Mürzsteg (A) 91 H4
Murzynowo (PL) 142 B5
Mürzzuschlag (A) 91 J4
Musabeyli (TR) 185 J6
Musahoca (TR) 190 D2
Müsch (D) 69 M6
Muschwitz (D) 72 G3
Musculdy (F) 113 K2
Musel-Arnao (E) 111 H1
Muselinovo (BG) 176 C1
Mușenița (RO) 157 J6
Mușetești (RO) 168 E3
Musetrene (N) 31 L4
Musijky (UA) 151 K1
Musina (BG) 176 D2
Musken (N) 20 F5
Muskö (S) 41 O4
Muškovića Rijeka (MNE) 173 L4
Musland (N) 38 C3
Musninkai (LT) 137 M4
Musqetë (AL) 178 B2
Mussalo (FIN) 36 G4
Musselburgh (GB) 53 J3
Musselkanaal (NL) 64 G6
Mussey (F) 77 M4
Mussey-sur-Marne (F) 77 M5
Mussidan (F) 83 F6
Musso (I) 87 H5
Mussomeli (I) 108 E2
Mussy-sur-Seine (F) 77 K6
Mustadfors (S) 40 B5
Mustafakemalpaşa (TR) 183 F5
Mustafapaşa (TR) 193 J3
Müstair (CH) 88 C4
Mustajärvi (FIN) 28 C7
Mustajärvi (FIN) 28 E7
Mustajoki (FIN) 28 C8
Mustalammi (FIN) 28 C7
Mustamaa (FIN) 23 J8
Mustamaa (FIN) 27 K8
Mustapić (SRB) 168 B4
Mustasaari = Korsholm (FIN) 27 H8
Mustavaara (FIN) 23 L6
Mustavaara (FIN) 23 L8
Müstecep (TR) 182 D4
Musteika (LT) 137 L6
Mustér = Disentis (CH) 87 G4
Mustila (FIN) 35 P2
Mustin (D) 66 D3
Mustinlahti (FIN) 29 J6
Mustinsalo (FIN) 29 J7
Mustio = Svartå (FIN) 35 N4
Mustjala (EST) 130 B4
Mustjärvi (FIN) 36 E2
Mustjõe (EST) 131 H2
Mustla (EST) 131 J4
Mustolanmäki (FIN) 29 H6
Mustolanmäki (FIN) 29 J4
Mustolanmutka (FIN) 29 J3
Mustvee (EST) 131 L3
Musulcalı (TR) 190 D3
Musullu (TR) 184 C2
Mušutište = Meshutishtë (RKS) 174 E4
Mušyčy (BY) 138 G5
Muszaki (PL) 142 D4
Muszyna (PL) 155 H3
Muszynka (PL) 155 J3
Mut (TR) 13 K7
Mut (TR) 199 F2
Muta (SLO) 164 E1
Mutala (FIN) 28 D8
Mutalahti (FIN) 29 M7
Mutanj (SRB) 167 F5
Mutějovice (CZ) 152 E3
Mutenica (BG) 176 C3
Mutěnice (CZ) 153 M6
Mütevelli (TR) 190 D3
Muthill (GB) 53 H2
Mutka (FIN) 29 K5
Mutlu (TR) 190 B2
Mutluca (TR) 190 D6
Mutne (SK) 154 E3
Mutovozovo (RUS) 134 H4
Mutriku (E) 113 G2
Muttalıp (TR) 183 L6
Muttenz (CH) 86 E2
Mutters (A) 88 E3
Muttersholtz (F) 79 H5
Mutterstadt (D) 79 J3
Mutxamel (E) 127 K3
Mutzig (F) 79 G4
Mutzschen (D) 73 H3
Muuga (EST) 131 L2
Muukko (FIN) 37 K2
Muuksi (EST) 131 J1
Muurame (FIN) 28 F7
Muuras (FIN) 28 F4
Muurasjärvi (FIN) 27 M7
Muurikkala (FIN) 37 J3
Muurla (FIN) 35 M4
Muurola (FIN) 27 M2
Muurola (FIN) 37 J3
Muuruvesi (FIN) 29 J5
Muxía (E) 110 A2
Muy, Le (F) 98 B6
Mužakow = Bad Muskau (D) 73 M2
Muzga (BG) 176 D3
Muzilheg = Muzillac (F) 74 G5
Muzillac (F) 74 G5
Muzinë (AL) 178 C5
Mužla (SK) 158 G2
Mužlja (SRB) 167 F3
Mybster (GB) 49 B7
Mycevci (UA) 157 L3
Mychajlivka (UA) 150 A3
Mychajlivka (UA) 151 G6
Mychajlivka (UA) 151 H1
Mychajlivka (UA) 151 H5
Mychajlivka (UA) 151 K6
Mychajlivka (UA) 157 L4
Mychajlivka (UA) 157 M3
Mychajlivka (UA) 163 J1
Mychajlivka (UA) 163 M4
Mychajlivka (UA) 171 K2
Mychajlo-Oleksandrivka (UA) 163 M4
Mychajlopil' (UA) 163 L4
Mychalyn (UA) 150 D1
Mychijivka (UA) 150 E2
Myckelberget Vastra (S) 40 E1
Myckelgensjö (S) 26 D7
Myckleby (S) 43 J2
Myckling (S) 33 O3
Mydland (N) 38 D6
Mydroilyn (GB) 56 F1
Myggenäs (S) 43 J2
Myggsjö (S) 32 H4
Myhalky (UA) 151 K2
Myhinpää (FIN) 29 G7
Myhove (UA) 161 L1
Myjava (SK) 154 B4
Mykanów (PL) 147 L4
Mykines (FO) 48 C3
Myking (N) 30 C6
Mykland (N) 30 E4
Mykland (N) 38 H5
Myklebost (N) 30 E2
Myklebostad (N) 20 E5
Myklebostad (N) 30 H2
Myklebust (N) 30 F4
Mykolaivka-Novorosijs'ke (UA) 171 K1
Mykolajiv (UA) 13 J3
Mykolajiv (UA) 149 L5
Mykolajiv (UA) 150 D4
Mykolajiv (UA) 156 E2
Mykolajivka (UA) 150 F1
Mykolajivka (UA) 163 M3
Mykolajivka (UA) 171 L2
Mykulyči (UA) 149 L4
Mykulyčyn (UA) 156 G5
Mykulynci (UA) 150 B5
Mykulynci (UA) 150 G5
Mylenki (RUS) 135 J5
Myljanovyči (UA) 149 K3
Myljatyn (UA) 150 D3
Mylly-Karttu (FIN) 35 L1
Myllykoski (FIN) 27 J8
Myllykoski (FIN) 36 G3
Myllykylä (FIN) 19 J9
Myllykylä (FIN) 28 C6
Myllykylä (FIN) 28 E7
Myllykylä (FIN) 35 N3
Myllykylä (FIN) 36 A4
Myllykylä (FIN) 36 B4
Myllykylä (FIN) 36 E2
Myllykylä (FIN) 36 H3
Myllylä (FIN) 29 J5
Myllylahti (FIN) 29 K1
Myllymaa (FIN) 35 L2
Myllymäki (FIN) 28 E6
Myllyperä (FIN) 28 E7
Mymäs (S) 33 N3
Mynämäki (FIN) 35 J3
Myn'kivci (UA) 150 E6
Myn'kivci (UA) 151 J4
Mynterlä (FIN) 35 O4
Myntilä (FIN) 36 G2
Myon (F) 86 A3
Myöntäjä (FIN) 35 K1
Myra (N) 39 K5
Myran (N) 24 E7
Myrane (N) 38 C5
Mýrar (IS) 16 C3
Mýrar (IS) 16 E4
Mýrar (IS) 16 F3
Mýrar (IS) 17 H7
Myrås (S) 26 D3
Myrdal (N) 30 G6
Myre (N) 20 E2
Myre (N) 20 E3
Myre (S) 26 E8
Myren (S) 40 D2
Myreng (N) 31 L4
Myresjö (S) 44 F4
Myrgrubben (S) 40 C2
Myrhaug (N) 21 J2
Myrhaug (N) 31 P2
Myrheden (S) 26 G3
Myrheden (S) 26 G4
Myrhorod (UA) 9 N5
Mýri (IS) 17 J4
Myrivka (UA) 151 M4
Myrkky (FIN) 28 B7
Myrland (N) 20 C4
Myrland (N) 20 E3
Myrlandshaug (N) 20 G3
Myrmoen (N) 31 Q2
Myrne (UA) 149 L4
Myrne (UA) 150 D2
Myrne (UA) 163 L6
Myrnes (N) 18 E3
Myrnopil'a (UA) 171 J1
Myrohošča-Perša (UA) 150 B3
Myroljubiv (UA) 150 G1
Myroljubivka (UA) 151 H3
Myronivka (UA) 9 M5
Myronivka (UA) 151 M4
Myropil' (UA) 150 F3
Myroslavl' (UA) 150 E3
Myrset (N) 20 F2
Myrskylä (FIN) 36 E3
Myrtou (CY) 198 E5
Myrvik (N) 24 F5
Myrviken (S) 32 G1
Mysailivka (UA) 151 M4
Myščana (UA) 149 J6
Myščiv (UA) 149 K4
Mysen (N) 39 O3
Myshall (IRL) 63 J3
Mysingsborg (S) 33 J4
Myškavičy (BY) 145 L2
Mysłaków (PL) 148 B1
Mysłakowice (PL) 146 D4
Myślakowice (PL) 148 B2
Myślenice (PL) 154 F2
Mysletín (CZ) 153 H5
Myslibořice (CZ) 153 J5
Myślibórz (PL) 67 M5
Myślina (PL) 147 J4
Myslivka (UA) 156 E4
Mysłowice (PL) 147 L5
Mysovka (RUS) 136 E3
Mysubyttseter (N) 30 H4
Mysuseter (N) 31 M4
Mysy (UA) 145 N5
Myšyn (UA) 157 G5
Myszewo (PL) 141 M2
Myszków (PL) 147 L4
Myszyniec (PL) 142 E4
Mytišči (RUS) 7 U7
Mytky (UA) 150 F6
Mýtna (SK) 154 F5
Mýtne Ludany (SK) 158 G1
Mytnycja (UA) 149 M5
Mýto (CZ) 152 E4
Mýto (SK) 154 F4
Myttäälä (FIN) 35 O2
Myza (RUS) 134 F4
Myzove (UA) 149 L3

N

Näälävaara (FIN) 23 M7
Naaldwijk (NL) 69 G3
Naamijoki (FIN) 22 F3
Naantali (FIN) 35 K4
Naapila (FIN) 36 B1
Naapurinvaara (FIN) 29 J3
Naarajärvi (FIN) 29 H7
Naarajoki (FIN) 28 C6
Naarden (NL) 69 J2
Näärinki (FIN) 37 J1
Naarminkylä (FIN) 28 D7
Naartijärvi (S) 27 K3
Naarva (FIN) 29 M5
Naas (IRL) 61 J5
Näätämö (FIN) 19 M4
Näätänmaa (FIN) 29 J7
Nabben (S) 44 H6
Nabburg (D) 152 B5
Naburn (GB) 55 K3
Nača (BY) 143 M2
Naçak (TR) 181 L1
Nacarlı (TR) 193 J7
Na Cealla Beaga = Killybegs (IRL) 60 F2
Načeradec (CZ) 153 G4
Náchod (CZ) 146 E5
Nachrodt-Wiblingwerde (D) 70 E4
Nacimiento (E) 126 E5
Nacka (S) 41 O4
Näckådalen (S) 32 G5
Nackel (D) 67 H5
Nackenheim (D) 79 J2
Nacław (PL) 140 G2
Na Clocha Liatha = Greystones (IRL) 63 K2
Nadaillac (F) 83 H6
Nadalj (SRB) 166 E2
Nadarevo (BG) 177 G2
Nadarzyn (PL) 148 C1
Nadăș (RO) 160 D5
Nadaș (RO) 160 D6
Nádasd (H) 158 C4
Nádasdladány (H) 158 F3
Naddnistrjans'ke (UA) 162 E1
Naddvik (N) 30 H5
Nadela (E) 110 E3
Nådendal = Naantali (FIN) 35 K4
Nadeș (RO) 161 K5
Nadinići (BIH) 173 H3
Nădlac (RO) 167 G1
Nadlymans'ke (UA) 163 L6
Nadma (PL) 142 E6
Nădrag (RO) 168 C2
Nadrične (UA) 157 G2
Nadrične (UA) 163 J6
Nádudvar (H) 159 M3
Nadvirna (UA) 156 G4
Nadvoicy (RUS) 7 T4
Nadynivka (UA) 151 N1
Nadzież (PL) 147 J3
Næfurholt (IS) 16 G7
Năeni (RO) 170 C3
Naensen (D) 72 B2
Nærbø (N) 38 C5
Nærøysteine (N) 24 F5
Nærsnes (N) 39 N3
Næs (DK) 47 K4
Næsby (DK) 47 J2
Næstved (DK) 47 J3
Näfels (CH) 87 H3
Náfpaktos (GR) 186 D3
Nafplio (GR) 187 F4
Nafría la Llana (E) 112 F5
Nagarodavičy (BY) 144 B1
Nagatkino (RUS) 135 M2
Nagel (D) 72 F6
Nagele (NL) 64 D6
Nages (F) 93 K3
Naggen (S) 33 K3
Na Gleannta = Glenties (IRL) 60 F2
Nagłowice (PL) 148 B4
Nagnajów (PL) 148 E4
Nagodzice (PL) 146 F5
Nagold (D) 79 K4
Nago-Torbole (I) 88 D6
Nagu (FIN) 35 J4
Nagueviçy (BY) 144 B2
Nagyacsád (H) 158 D3
Nagyalásony (H) 158 D3
Nagyatád (H) 158 D5
Nagybajom (H) 158 E5
Nagybaracska (H) 166 C1
Nagyberki (H) 165 L2
Nagybörzsöny (H) 154 D6
Nagycenk (H) 158 C2
Nagydobos (H) 160 E1
Nagydorog (H) 158 G4
Nagyecsed (H) 156 B6
Nagyesztergár (H) 158 E3
Nagyfüged (H) 154 G6
Nagyhalász (H) 160 D1
Nagyharsány (H) 158 F6
Nagyigmánd (H) 158 F2
Nagyiván (H) 159 L3
Nagykálló (H) 155 K6
Nagykamarás (H) 159 M5
Nagykanizsa (H) 91 L7
Nagykapornak (H) 91 L6
Nagykáta (H) 159 J3
Nagykereki (H) 160 D3
Nagykölked (H) 158 C3
Nagykónyi (H) 165 L1
Nagykőrös (H) 159 J3
Nagylak (H) 167 G1
Nagylóc (H) 159 J1
Nagymágocs (H) 160 A4
Nagymaros (H) 159 G2
Nagyoroszi (H) 159 H1
Nagypeterd (H) 166 A1
Nagyrábé (H) 160 C3
Nagyszékely (H) 158 G4
Nagyszénás (H) 160 B4
Nagyvázsony (H) 158 E4
Nahačiv (UA) 156 D1
Nahavki (BY) 138 F4
Nahe (D) 65 N4
Nahirne (UA) 171 G3
Nahod (RUS) 135 M3
Nahrendorf (D) 66 D4
Nahtavárri = Nattavaara (S) 21 K7
Nahwinden (D) 71 M5
Naidăs (RO) 167 J4
Naila (D) 72 F5
Naillat (F) 83 J4
Nailloux (F) 93 H4
Nailly (F) 77 H5
Nailsea (GB) 57 J3
Nailsworth (GB) 57 K2
Nain (S) 40 E2
Naintré (F) 83 F3
Naipköy (TR) 182 D4
Naipu (RO) 169 K5
Nairn (GB) 51 K4
Naisey-les-Granges (F) 85 K2
Naisiai (LT) 132 H5
Naisjärv (S) 27 J1
Naitschau (D) 72 G4
Naizin (F) 74 F5
Najac (F) 93 H2
Najdenovo (BG) 176 D4
Nájera (E) 113 F4
Näkkälä (FIN) 18 F6
Nakkeslett (N) 18 B3
Nakkila (FIN) 35 K2
Nakksjø (N) 39 K4
Nakło (PL) 147 J4
Nakło (PL) 147 M4
Nakło nad Notecią (PL) 141 J4
Nakolec (MK) 178 E3
Nakomiady (PL) 142 E2
Nakovo (SRB) 159 L6
Nakskov (DK) 46 H4
Nakvaša (UA) 149 M6
Nalbach (D) 78 F3
Nalbant (RO) 171 H3
Nalcıkuyucağı (TR) 185 G3
Nalda (E) 113 G4
Nälden (S) 25 J8
Nałęczów (PL) 148 F3
Nálepkovo (SK) 155 H4
Nalibaki (BY) 138 D6
Näljänkä (FIN) 23 L6
Nalkulak (TR) 199 K2
Nalles (I) 88 E4
Nallıdere (TR) 184 B5
Nalliers (F) 82 C4
Nallıhan (TR) 184 B5
Nalovardo (S) 26 D3
Nals = Nalles (I) 88 E4
Nalyvajkivka (UA) 151 K3
Nalzen (F) 93 H5
Nalžovské Hory (CZ) 152 E5
Nămăești (RO) 169 J3
Námata (GR) 180 B5
Namborn (D) 78 G2
Nambroca (E) 119 J4
Namdalseid (N) 24 F6
Nämdö (S) 41 P4
Namèche (B) 69 J6
Namen = Namur (B) 69 H6
Náměšť nad Oslavou (CZ) 153 K5
Náměšť na Hané (CZ) 153 M4
Námestovo (SK) 154 E3
Namlos (A) 80 D6
Namnå (N) 40 B1
Nămoloasa (RO) 170 F2
Namoše (RUS) 135 N3
Nämpnes (FIN) 28 B6
Nampont-Saint-Martin (F) 68 B6
Nampteuil-sous-Muret (F) 77 H3
Namsos (N) 24 F6
Namsskogan (N) 25 H5
Namsvassgardan (N) 25 H5
Namur (B) 69 H6
Namyślin (PL) 67 M5
Namysłów (PL) 147 H3
Nana (RO) 170 D5
Nançay (F) 83 K2
Nanclares de la Oca (E) 112 F3
Nancras (F) 82 D5
Nancray (F) 85 K2
Nancy (F) 78 E4
Nandlstadt (D) 80 F3
Nănești (RO) 170 F2
Nangis (F) 77 H4
Nannberga (S) 41 J4
Nannerch (GB) 54 F4
Nanov (RO) 169 J5
Nanovica (BG) 181 H1
Nans-les-Pins (F) 95 G4
Nans-sous-Sainte-Anne (F) 86 B4
Nant (F) 94 B2
Nanterre (F) 76 F4
Nantes (F) 82 B2
Nantes-en-Ratier (F) 85 J7
Nanteuil-le-Haudouin (F) 77 G3
Nantiat (F) 83 H4
Nantmel (GB) 54 F6
Nantua (F) 85 J4
Nantwich (GB) 55 G4
Nant-y-moel (GB) 57 G2
Naours (F) 76 F1
Náousa (GR) 195 G1
Náoussa (GR) 179 G3
Năpădeni (MD) 162 G4
Napadivka (UA) 157 K2
Nåpågard (N) 39 J3
Napajedla (CZ) 153 N5
Napierki (PL) 142 C4
Napiwoda (PL) 142 C4
Napkor (H) 155 K6
Napoca, Cluj- (RO) 161 H4
Napodova (MD) 163 H2
Napola (I) 108 C2
Napoli (I) 104 B4
Napp (N) 20 C4
Năpradea (RO) 161 G3
Napton on the Hill (GB) 58 E3
Náquera (E) 121 H4
När (S) 45 O3
När (S) 45 O4
Nåra (N) 30 B5
Nara (TR) 182 B5
Narač (BY) 138 E4
Narajiv (UA) 156 G2
Narajivka (UA) 151 K6
Naramice (PL) 147 J3
Naran (IRL) 60 F2
Narberth (GB) 56 E2
Narbonne (F) 94 A4
Narbonne-Plage (F) 115 K1
Narborough (GB) 59 J2
Narbuvoll (N) 32 A3
Narcao (I) 97 C5
Narcy (F) 84 D2
Nardo (I) 107 K2
Narew (PL) 143 K5
Narewka (PL) 143 K5
Narfeyri (IS) 16 D4
Närhilä (FIN) 29 G6
Narhisar (TR) 190 D6
Narila (FIN) 29 H7
Narjoki (FIN) 35 J2
Narkaus (FIN) 27 N2
Narken (S) 22 E3
Narlı (TR) 184 C6
Narlı (TR) 185 J4
Narlıdere (TR) 191 F4
Narlıı (TR) 13 L7
Narlık (TR) 185 J5
Närlinge (S) 41 N2
Narni (I) 103 F2
Naro (I) 108 E3
Narodyči (UA) 151 J1
Narol (PL) 149 H5
Naronovo (RUS) 131 O5
Naroulja (BY) 145 L5
Närpes (FIN) 28 B7
Närpiö = Närpes (FIN) 28 B7
Narranco (E) 111 H2
Narros del Castillo (E) 119 F2
Närsäkkälä (FIN) 29 L8
Närsen (S) 40 F2
Narta (AL) 178 A4
Narta (HR) 158 C6
Narteikiai (LT) 137 L1
Närtesalo (FIN) 29 J8
Narthákí (GR) 179 G6
Närtuna (S) 41 O3
Năruja (RO) 170 D2
Nårunga (S) 44 B3
Naruska (FIN) 23 M2
Naruszewo (PL) 142 C5
Narva (EST) 37 K6
Närvä (FIN) 28 F8
Narva (FIN) 35 M2
Närvä = Mertajärvi (S) 18 E7
Narva-Jõesuu (EST) 37 K6
Närvijoki (FIN) 28 B6
Narvik (N) 20 G4
Narvydžiai (LT) 132 D5
Narzanlar (TR) 183 L5
Narzole (I) 98 D3
Näs (AX) 34 F4
Näs (N) 39 K4
Näs (S) 33 M1
Näs (S) 40 G2
Näs (S) 41 J2
Näs (S) 45 N4
Naşa (TR) 191 F2
Nasafjället (S) 20 E8
Näsåker (S) 26 C8
Năsăud (RO) 161 J3
Nasavrky (CZ) 146 D6
Näsberg (S) 27 G2
Näsberg (S) 33 K4
Näsberget Östra (S) 40 E2
Nasbinals (F) 93 L1
Näs bruk (S) 41 K2
Näsby (S) 40 H4
Näsby (S) 41 K3
Näsby (S) 44 G4
Na Sceirí = Skerries (IRL) 63 K1
Nascio (I) 100 A4
Näset (S) 25 K5
Näset (S) 26 C8
Näset (S) 26 F5
Näset (S) 32 J5
Näset (S) 39 P3
Näset (S) 41 J4
Nasevičy (BY) 145 L4
Näsfjällsåsen (S) 32 D5
Nashec (RKS) 174 E4
Näshult (S) 44 G4
Näshulta (S) 41 K4
Našice (HR) 165 L4
Nasiedle (PL) 154 B1
Nasielsk (PL) 142 D5
Näsinge (S) 39 O4
Näske (S) 26 E8
Näskott (S) 25 J8
Näsland (S) 26 F6
Näsmark (S) 26 F7
Naso (I) 109 G1
Nasrettin (TR) 198 E3
Nasrettinhoca (TR) 192 C1
Nassakka (FIN) 23 K4
Nassau (D) 70 E6
Nassenfels (D) 80 E3
Nassenheide (D) 67 J5
Nassereith (A) 88 D3
Nässja (S) 40 G6
Nässja (S) 41 L2
Nässjö (S) 26 C7
Nässjö (S) 44 F3
Naßwald (A) 91 J4
Nastadsæter (N) 24 F6
Nastansjö (S) 25 L5
Nastasiv (UA) 150 B5
Nastaška (UA) 151 L4
Nastätten (D) 70 E6
Nastazin (PL) 67 N3
Nästebacka (S) 40 B4
Nästeln (S) 32 G2
Nästi (FIN) 35 J3
Nastola (FIN) 36 E3
Năsturelu (RO) 176 D1
Näsum (S) 44 F6
Nasutów (PL) 149 G3
Nasva (EST) 130 B4
Nasva (RUS) 135 K4
Näsviken (S) 25 K7
Näsviken (S) 33 M4
Nata (CY) 198 E6
Natalinci (SRB) 167 G5
Natendorf (D) 66 C4
Naters (CH) 86 E5
Natkiškiai (LT) 136 F3
Natland (N) 38 D4
Natolin (PL) 148 D2
Natoye (B) 69 J6
Nätsby (AX) 34 E4
Nattavaara (S) 21 K7
Nattavaara by (S) 22 D3
Natternberg (D) 90 C2
Nattheim (D) 80 C3
Nättraby (S) 44 H6
Nattvatn (N) 19 H4
Naturno (I) 87 M4
Naturns = Naturno (I) 87 M4
Natzungen (D) 71 H3
Natzwiller (F) 79 G5
Naucelle (F) 93 J2
Nauders (A) 88 D4
Naudvaris (LT) 137 J2
Nauen (D) 67 H5
Nauen (N) 39 M4
Naŭgarody (BY) 138 G2
Nauheim (D) 79 J2
Naujamiestis (LT) 137 L2
Naujasis Daugėliškis (LT) 138 D3
Naujas Obelynas (LT) 136 G3
Naujoji Akmenė (LT) 137 H1
Naujoji Ūta (LT) 143 K1
Naukšēni (LV) 131 H5
Naul (IRL) 63 K1
Naulaperä (FIN) 29 H2
Naulavaara (FIN) 29 J4
Naum (S) 44 B2
Naumburg (D) 71 H4
Naumburg (Saale) (D) 72 F3
Naumovščina (RUS) 131 O4
Naundorf (D) 152 D2
Naunhof (D) 73 H3
Naurisniemi (S) 21 M7
Naurisvaara (FIN) 29 M6
Naurod (D) 70 F6
Naurstad (N) 20 D6
Naussac (F) 93 J1
Nausta (S) 21 J8
Naustan (N) 24 E7
Naustbukt (N) 18 A4
Naustdal (N) 30 D4
Nauste (N) 30 J2
Naustermoen (N) 31 N3
Naustvika (N) 31 K3
Nautijaur (S) 22 B3
Nautsi (RUS) 19 M5
Nautsund (N) 30 C5
Nauvo = Nagu (FIN) 35 J4
Nava (E) 111 J2
Navacepeda de Tormes (E) 119 F3
Navacepedilla de Corneja (E) 119 F3
Navacerrada (E) 119 H2
Navacerrada (E) 119 H6
Navachrosty (BY) 139 J5
Navaconcejo (E) 118 E3
Nava de Abajo (E) 127 G2
Nava de Arévalo (E) 119 G2
Nava de Campana (E) 127 G3
Nava de la Asunción (E) 119 H1
Nava del Rey (E) 112 A6
Nava de Ordunte (E) 112 E2
Nava de Ricomalillo, La (E) 119 G4
Nava de Roa (E) 112 D5
Nava de Santiago, La (E) 125 F1
Navadruck (BY) 138 F3
Navagrudak (BY) 144 C1
Navahermosa (E) 119 H4
Navailles-Angos (F) 113 L2
Navajel'nja (BY) 144 C2
Naval (E) 114 D3
Navalacruz (E) 119 G3
Navalagamella (E) 119 H3
Navalcaballo (E) 113 F5
Navalcán (E) 119 F3
Navalcarnero (E) 119 H3
Navalcuervo (E) 125 J3
Navaleno (E) 112 E5
Navalguijo (E) 117 K3
Navalilla (E) 112 D6
Navalmanzano (E) 112 C6
Navalmoral (E) 119 G3
Navalmoral de la Mata (E) 118 E4
Navalmorales, Los (E) 119 G4
Navalón de Arriba (E) 121 G6
Navalonguilla (E) 117 L3
Navalperal de Pinares (E) 119 H2
Navalpotro (E) 120 C2
Navalucillos, Los (E) 119 G4
Navaluenga (E) 119 G3
Navalvillar de Pela (E) 118 F5
Navamorcuende (E) 119 G3
Navan (IRL) 63 J1
Navapolack (BY) 139 J2
Navapol'cy (BY) 144 E2
Navarcles (E) 115 G4
Navardún (E) 114 A2
Navarnäs (S) 32 F5
Navarrenx (F) 113 K2
Navarrés (E) 127 J1
Navarrete (E) 113 F4
Navarrete del Río (E) 121 F2
Navarrevisca (E) 119 G3
Navars = Navàs (E) 115 G4
Navàs (E) 115 G4
Navas, Las (E) 126 B5
Navasa (E) 113 L3
Navascués (E) 114 A2
Navas de Estena (E) 119 G5
Navas de Jorquera (E) 120 E5
Navas de la Concepción, Las (E) 128 D2
Navas del Madroño (E) 117 H4
Navas del Marqués, Las (E) 119 H2
Navas del Rey (E) 119 H3
Navas de Oro (E) 112 C6
Navas de San Antonio (E) 119 H2
Navas de San Juan (E) 126 D3
Navasëlki (BY) 139 J5
Navasëlki (BY) 139 L4
Navasëlki (BY) 139 M6
Navasëlki (BY) 144 D3
Navasëlki (BY) 144 E2
Navasëlki (BY) 145 J4
Navasëlki (BY) 145 L5
Navaselki (BY) 149 K1
Navasfrías (E) 118 C3
Navata (E) 115 J3
Navatalgordo (E) 119 G3
Navatrasierra (E) 119 F4
Nave (P) 117 H3
Nave de Haver (P) 118 C2
Nävekvarn (S) 41 L5
Navelgas (E) 111 F2
Navelli (I) 103 H3
Navelsaker (N) 30 E4
Nävelsjö (S) 44 F4
Nåverdal (N) 31 N2
Näverede (S) 33 J1
Navereż'e (RUS) 135 H3
Näverkärret (S) 41 J3
Naveros, Los (E) 128 C5
Naveros de Pisuerga (E) 112 C4
Näversjön (S) 25 J8
Naverstad (S) 39 P5
Navès (E) 115 G4
Navia (E) 111 F1
Navicello (I) 100 E3
Navilly (F) 85 H3
Navincy (BY) 138 H2
Navis (A) 88 F3
Naviščyna (BY) 139 J6
Navit (N) 18 D4
Naviz (UA) 150 A1
Navlica (BY) 139 H3
Navlja (RUS) 9 N3
Năvodari (RO) 169 J6
Năvodari (RO) 171 H5
Navolok (RUS) 135 M3
Nävragöl (S) 44 H6
Navruz (TR) 182 D6
Nawcz (PL) 141 J1
Nawiady (PL) 142 E3
Nawojowa (PL) 155 H2
Nawra (PL) 141 L4
Nawsie (PL) 148 E6
Na Xemena (E) 122 D4
Náxos (GR) 195 G1
Nay-Bourdettes (F) 114 C1
Nayland (GB) 59 J4
Nayrac, Le (F) 93 K1
Nazarcea (RO) 171 G5
Nazaré (P) 116 C4
Nazarenkove (UA) 157 H4
Nazarje (SLO) 164 D2
Nazelles-Négron (F) 83 G2
Nazifpaşa (TR) 183 J5
Nazilli (TR) 190 E5
Nazimovo (RUS) 134 G2
Nazza (D) 71 K4
Ndërmenas (AL) 178 A3
Ndroq (AL) 178 B2
Néa Aghíalos (GR) 179 H6
Néa Apollonía (GR) 180 C3
Néa Artáki (GR) 187 H2
Néa Éfesos (GR) 180 A4
Néa Epídavros (GR) 188 B4
Néa Figaliá (GR) 186 D5
Néa Filadélfia (GR) 179 H3
Néa Fókea (GR) 180 C4
Neagra Şarului (RO) 161 L3
Neahčil = Näkkälä (FIN) 18 F6
Néa Híli (GR) 181 H3
Néa Ionía (GR) 180 B6
Néa Kalikrátia (GR) 179 J4
Néa Kariés (GR) 180 A5
Néa Karváli (GR) 180 F3
Néa Kerdília (GR) 180 D3
Néa Kíos (GR) 187 F4
Néa Koróni (GR) 186 D6
Neale (IRL) 62 D1
Néa Léfki (GR) 180 A5
Néa Máditos (GR) 179 K3
Néa Mákri (GR) 188 C3
Néa Mesimvría (GR) 180 B3
Néa Messángala (GR) 179 H5
Néa Mihaniόna (GR) 179 H4
Néa Moudaniá (GR) 179 J4
Neamţ, Piatra- (RO) 162 C5
Neamţ, Vânători- (RO) 162 C4
Néa Nikomídia (GR) 179 G3
Néa Nikópoli (GR) 179 F4
Néant-sur-Yve (F) 75 G4
Neap (GB) 49 F3
Néa Pélla (GR) 179 H3
Néa Péramos (GR) 180 E3
Néa Péramos (GR) 188 B4
Néa Pétra (GR) 180 D3
Neápoli (GR) 178 E4
Neápoli (GR) 187 G7
Neápoli (GR) 195 H5
Néa Potidéa (GR) 179 J4
Néa Róda (GR) 180 D4
Néa Sánda (GR) 181 H2
Néa Sílata (GR) 180 C4
Néa Stíra (GR) 188 D3
Néa Ténedos (GR) 180 C4
Neath (GB) 57 G2
Néa Trapezoúnda (GR) 179 H4
Néa Tríglia (GR) 179 J4
Neaua (RO) 161 K5
Neauphle-le-Vieux (F) 76 E4
Néa Víssa (GR) 181 K1
Néa Zíhni (GR) 180 D2
Néa Zoí (GR) 179 G3
Nebel (D) 46 B4
Nebelivka (UA) 163 M1
Nebelycja (UA) 151 K3
Nebiler (TR) 189 J1
Nebiler (TR) 192 A6
Nebiler (TR) 197 H2
Nebljusi (HR) 165 F5
Nebojani (MK) 175 H4
Nebolči (RUS) 7 T6
Nebory (CZ) 154 D2
Nebra (Unstrut) (D) 71 N4
Nebreda (E) 112 D5
Nebrowo Wielkie (PL) 141 L3
Nebyliv (UA) 156 F4
Nechanice (CZ) 153 J3
Nechvalice (CZ) 81 L1
Nechvoroša (UA) 149 K4
Nechvorošč (UA) 151 H4
Nechvorošča (UA) 9 N5
Nečín (CZ) 81 L1
Necipköy (TR) 182 E5
Neckargemünd (D) 79 K3
Neckargerach (D) 79 L3
Neckarsteinach (D) 79 K3
Neckarsulm (D) 79 L3
Neckartenzlingen (D) 79 L4
Neckenmarkt (A) 158 C2
Necpaly (SK) 154 D4
Necșești (RO) 169 J5
Nečtiny (CZ) 73 J6
Necton (GB) 59 J2
Nečujam (HR) 172 D3
Neda (E) 110 C2
Nedajka (BY) 145 M3
Nedal' (BY) 139 H4
Nedalshytta (N) 32 C2
Nedan (BG) 176 D2
Nedančyči (UA) 145 N5
Nedansjö (S) 33 M3
Nedašky (UA) 151 J2
Nedavić (BIH) 173 H3
Nedde (F) 83 J5
Neddemin (D) 67 J3
Neded (SK) 158 E1
Nedelino (BG) 176 D6
Nedelišće (HR) 158 B5
Nederby (DK) 42 D5
Nederhögen (S) 32 G3
Nederkalix (S) 27 K3
Nedervetil (FIN) 27 K7
Nederweert (NL) 69 K4
Nedging Tye (GB) 59 J3
Nedjalsko (BG) 177 G4
Nedlitz (D) 72 F1
Nedlitz (D) 73 G1
Nedoblicy (RUS) 37 L6
Nedožery (SK) 154 D4
Nedre Bäck (S) 22 D7
Nedreberg (N) 32 B5
Nedre Flåsjön (S) 27 H3
Nedre Gärdsjö (S) 33 J6
Nedre Heimdalen (N) 31 L5
Nedre Jervan (N) 24 E8
Nedre Rikeby (FIN) 36 E3
Nedre Saxnäs (S) 26 D4
Nedre Soppero (S) 18 D7
Nedre Tollådal (N) 20 D7
Nedre Tväråselet (S) 27 G3
Nedre Ullerud (S) 40 D3
Nedre Vojakkala (S) 27 K3
Neðri-Ás (IS) 16 G3
Nedstrand (N) 38 C4
Nedvědice (CZ) 153 K5
Nędza (PL) 147 J5
Neede (NL) 69 M2
Needham Market (GB) 59 K3
Neëlovo (RUS) 131 O5
Neeme (EST) 36 D5
Neemisküla (EST) 131 K4
Neerijnen (NL) 69 J3
Neerlage (D) 70 D2
Neermoor (D) 64 G5
Neeroeteren (B) 69 K4
Neerpelt (B) 69 J4
Neerstedt (D) 65 J6
Nees (DK) 42 B6
Neetze (D) 66 D4
Neftegorsk (RUS) 13 M4
Neftenbach (CH) 79 K6
Nefyn (GB) 61 N6
Negádes (GR) 178 D5
Negarélae (BY) 144 F1
Negbina (SRB) 174 C1
Negenborn (D) 72 B2
Negorci (MK) 180 A2
Negoslavci (HR) 166 D3
Negotin (SRB) 167 L5
Negotino (MK) 174 E5
Negotino (MK) 175 H6
Negovanci (BG) 175 J4
Negras, Las (E) 127 F6
Negrași (RO) 169 J4
Negreira (E) 110 B3
Nègrepelisse (F) 93 H2
Negrești (RO) 162 C4
Negrești (RO) 162 E5
Negrești-Oaș (RO) 156 D6
Negri (RO) 162 D5
Négrondes (F) 83 G6
Negru Vodă (RO) 171 G6
Negureni (RO) 170 F5
Neheim-Hüsten (D) 70 E4
Nehoiu (RO) 169 L3
Nehringen (D) 47 L6
Nehvonniemi (FIN) 29 M6
Nehyn (UA) 150 D6
Neiden (N) 19 M4
Neila (E) 112 F4
Neilston (GB) 52 G3
Neindorf (D) 66 D6
Neistenkangas (S) 22 F3
Neitisuanto (S) 18 C9
Neittävä (FIN) 29 G2
Nejdek (CZ) 73 H5
Nejkove (UA) 163 M4
Nejkovo (BG) 177 F3
Nekla (PL) 141 H6
Nekrasove (UA) 151 G5
Nekrašovo (RUS) 135 N4
Nekrasovo (RUS) 136 D4

Nekrasovo 223

Nekrašuny (BY) 138 C4
Nekse = Nexø (DK) 47 O3
Nelas (P) 116 F2
Nelaug (N) 39 J5
Nelidovo (RUS) 7 T7
Nellim (FIN) 19 L6
Nellingen (D) 80 B3
Nelson (GB) 55 H3
Nelypivci (UA) 157 L5
Nemakščiai (LT) 137 H3
Néman (BY) 144 E2
Neman (RUS) 136 G3
Nemanica (BY) 139 J5
Nemanice (CZ) 152 C5
Nemanskoe (RUS) 136 G3
Nembro (I) 87 J6
Nemčice (SK) 154 C4
Němčice nad Hanou (CZ) 153 M5
Nemčiňany (SK) 154 C5
Neméa (GR) 187 F4
Nemenčinė (LT) 138 B4
Nemenikuće (SRB) 167 G5
Nemeño (E) 110 B2
Nemesnádudvar (H) 159 H5
Némethkér (H) 159 G4
Nemėžis (LT) 143 N1
Nemours (F) 77 G5
Nemovyči (UA) 144 E6
Nemška Loka (SLO) 164 E3
Nemšová (SK) 154 C4
Nemteni (MD) 162 G5
Nemti (H) 159 J1
Nemunaitis (LT) 137 L5
Nemunėlio Radviliškis (LT) 133 K5
Nemyr (UA) 149 L4
Nemyrinci (UA) 151 J4
Nemyriv (UA) 9 L5
Nemyriv (UA) 151 H6
Nemyriv (UA) 156 D1
Nemyriv's'ke (UA) 163 K3
Nemyryci (UA) 150 E4
Nemyryntci (UA) 157 K3
Nenagh (IRL) 62 F3
Nenaševo (RUS) 9 P3
Neninice (SK) 159 H1
Nénita (GR) 189 H3
Nen'kovyči (UA) 144 D5
Nennhausen (D) 67 H5
Nenonpelto (FIN) 29 H7
Nenovo (BG) 177 H2
Nenset (N) 39 L4
Nensjö (S) 33 O2
Nentershausen (D) 70 E6
Nentershausen (D) 72 B3
Nenthead (GB) 53 L5
Nenthorn (GB) 53 K3
Nenzing (A) 88 B3
Néo Chorio (CY) 198 D5
Néo Erásmio (GR) 181 F3
Neofit Rilski (BG) 177 J2
Néo Gineikókastro (GR) 180 B3
Neochoráki (GR) 187 G3
Neochóri (GR) 177 F5
Neochóri (GR) 178 C5
Neochóri (GR) 178 E6
Neochóri (GR) 179 E5
Neochóri (GR) 179 F6
Neochóri (GR) 179 K2
Neochóri (GR) 180 D4
Neochóri (GR) 186 C3
Neochóri (GR) 188 D3
Néo Horió (GR) 194 E5
Néo Monastíri (GR) 179 G6
Neoneli (I) 97 C3
Néo Perivóli (GR) 180 B6
Néo Petrítsi (GR) 180 C2
Neoric (HR) 172 E2
Néo Sidirohóri (GR) 181 G2
Néos Kalikrátis (GR) 179 E3
Néos Marmarás (GR) 180 D4
Néo Souli (GR) 179 K2
Néos Pagóntas (GR) 188 C2
Néos Skopós (GR) 179 K2
Neotrivia (GR) 187 H2
Nepi (I) 102 E3
Nepolokivci (UA) 157 J5
Nepomuk (CZ) 152 E5
Neptun (RO) 171 H6
Nérac (F) 92 E2
Neraida (GR) 179 F6
Neratovice (CZ) 152 G3
Nerău (RO) 159 L6
Nerchau (D) 73 H3
Nerdal (N) 20 F4
Nerdal (N) 31 K2
Nerdvika (N) 24 C8
Néré (F) 82 E5
Nereju (RO) 170 D2
Nerenstetten (D) 80 D3
Neresheim (D) 80 C3
Neresnica (SRB) 167 J5
Nereta (LV) 137 N1
Nereto (I) 103 H2
Neretve (HR) 164 C5
Nerežišća (HR) 172 E3
Nergård (N) 31 N3
Neringa (LT) 136 E3
Néris-les-Bains (F) 83 L4
Nerja (E) 126 C4
Nerkoo (FIN) 29 H5
Nerodime e Epërme (RKS) 174 F4
Neroďakis (GR) 180 E2
Nerokoúros (GR) 194 E5
Nerola (I) 103 F3
Néronde (F) 84 F5
Néronnes (F) 84 C3
Nerpio (E) 127 F3
Nersac (F) 82 F5
Nerskogen (N) 31 M2
Nerubajs'ke (UA) 163 M5
Nerušaj (UA) 171 K2
Nerva (E) 125 F4
Nervesa della Battaglia (I) 89 G6
Nervi (I) 98 F4
Nervieux (F) 84 F5
Nes (FO) 48 E3
Nes (IS) 17 J3
Nes (N) 24 E6
Nes (N) 24 D7
Nes (N) 24 E7
Nes (N) 30 D4
Nes (N) 30 E4
Nes (N) 30 G5
Nes (N) 31 M6
Nes (N) 38 D2
Nes (N) 38 F2
Nes (N) 39 K4
Nes (N) 39 L1
Nes (N) 39 M4
Nes (NL) 64 D5
Nesaseter (N) 25 G5
Nesbostjøen (N) 30 C6
Nesbru (N) 39 M3
Nesbyggen (N) 39 M4
Nesbyen (N) 39 K1
Neschwitz (D) 74 A3
Nese (N) 30 C6
Nesebăr (BG) 177 J3
Nešec = Nashec (RKS) 174 E4
Neset (N) 18 D3
Neset (N) 30 C6
Neset (N) 31 N4
Neset (N) 38 H3
Nesflaten (N) 38 E3
Nesgrenda (N) 39 J5
Nesham (N) 38 B3
Nesheim (N) 30 E6
Nesheim (N) 38 C4
Nesholmen (N) 30 D4
Nesjar (IS) 16 E6
Nesjavellir (IS) 16 E6
Nesje (N) 30 B4
Neskaupstaður (IS) 17 N4
Neskot (IS) 16 E2
Nesland (N) 20 C4
Nesland (N) 39 J4
Neslandsvatn (N) 39 K5
Nesle (F) 77 G2
Neslovice (CZ) 153 K5
Nesluša (SK) 154 D3
Nesna (N) 25 H2
Nesoddtangen (N) 39 N3
Nesodden (N) 39 M3
Nesovice (CZ) 153 M5
Nespereira (P) 117 F2
Nesscliffe (GB) 54 G5
Nesseby (N) 19 L3
Nesselwang (D) 87 K2
Nesset (N) 24 C7
Nesslau (CH) 87 H3
Neßmersiel (D) 64 G4
Nesso (I) 87 H6
Nestani (GR) 187 E4
Nestanitiki (BY) 138 D4
Nestavoll (N) 31 M3
Nestenvol (UA) 150 A4
Nesterivka (UA) 151 L6
Nesterov (RUS) 136 H4
Nestil'nanka (RUS) 136 H4
Nestojita (UA) 163 J3
Neston (GB) 54 F4
Nestório (GR) 178 E4
Nesttun (N) 38 B2
Nesukhyiv (BY) 144 C1
Nesvady (SK) 154 C6
Nesvatnstemmen (N) 38 H5
Nesvik (N) 38 D4
Nesvollberget (N) 32 D5
Nesvorta (SRB) 175 H3
Netečynci (UA) 157 M3
Netišyn (UA) 150 D3
Nether Broughton (GB) 55 L5
Nether Langwith (GB) 55 K4
Netherton (GB) 53 J1
Netherton (GB) 53 L4
Netin (CZ) 153 J5
Netolice (CZ) 152 F5
Netphen (D) 70 F5
Netra (D) 71 K4
Netretić (HR) 164 E3
Netro (I) 98 D1
Nettelsee (D) 65 N3
Nettersheim (D) 69 M6
Nettetal (D) 70 B4
Nettlebed (GB) 57 N2
Nettleton (GB) 55 M4
Nettuno (I) 103 F5
Netvořice (CZ) 152 G4
Netzschkau (D) 152 B2
Neualbenreuth (D) 73 G6
Neu-Anspach (D) 70 G6
Neubeckum (D) 70 F3
Neuberend (D) 70 F3
Neuberg an der Mürz (A) 91 J4
Neuborger (D) 64 G6
Neubourg, Le (F) 76 C3
Neubrandenburg (D) 67 J3
Neubruchhausen (D) 65 K6
Neubruck (A) 91 H4
Neubrück (Spree) (D) 67 L6
Neubrunn (D) 79 M2
Neubukow (D) 66 F2
Neubulach (D) 79 K4
Neuburg am Inn (D) 90 D2
Neuburg an der Donau (D) 80 E3
Neuburg an der Kammel (D) 80 C4
Neuburg-Steinhausen (D) 47 J6
Neuburxdorf (D) 73 J3
Neuchâtel (CH) 86 C4
Neu Darchau (D) 66 D4
Neudenau (D) 79 L3
Neudietendorf (D) 72 D4
Neudorf (D) 152 C3
Neudorf (RO) 167 J1
Neudorf, Graben- (D) 79 J3
Neudorf bei Staatz (A) 153 K6
Neudorf im Sausal (A) 91 H6
Neudörfl (A) 158 B2
Neudrossenfeld (D) 71 N6
Neu-Eichenberg (D) 72 B3
Neuenburg (D) 65 H5
Neuenburg (D) 79 K4
Neuenburg = Neuchâtel (CH) 86 C4
Neuenburg am Rhein (D) 79 H6
Neuendeich (D) 65 M4
Neuendettelsau (D) 80 D2
Neuendorf (D) 67 J1
Neuendorf am Damm (D) 66 E5
Neuendorf bei Elmshorn (D) 66 B3
Neuendorf-Sachsenbande (D) 46 D6
Neuenfelde (D) 65 M4
Neuengamme (D) 65 N5
Neuenhagen bei Berlin (D) 67 K5
Neuenhaus (D) 70 C2
Neuenheerse (D) 71 G3
Neuenkirchen (CH) 86 F3
Neuenkirchen (D) 65 K4
Neuenkirchen (D) 65 K5
Neuenkirchen (D) 65 M5
Neuenkirchen (D) 67 J1
Neuenkirchen (D) 70 D2
Neuenkirchen (D) 70 E2
Neuenkirchen (D) 70 F2
Neuenkirchen-Vörden (D) 70 F1
Neuenmarkt (D) 71 N6
Neuenrade (D) 70 E4
Neuensalz (D) 152 B2
Neuenstein (D) 79 M3
Neuental (D) 71 H4
Neuenwalde (D) 65 K4
Neuenweg (D) 86 E2
Neuerburg (D) 78 D2
Neufahrn bei Freising (D) 80 F4
Neufahrn in Niederbayern (D) 152 B6
Neuf-Brisach (F) 79 H5
Neufchâteau (B) 78 C2
Neufchâteau (F) 78 D5
Neufchâtel-en-Bray (F) 76 D2
Neufchâtel-en-Saosnois (F) 76 B5
Neufchâtel-Hardelot (F) 68 B5
Neufchâtel-sur-Aisne (F) 77 K3
Neufeld (D) 46 D6
Neufelden (A) 90 F3
Neuffen (D) 79 L4
Neuf-Marché (F) 76 E3
Neufra (D) 79 L5
Neugattersleben (D) 72 F2
Neugersdorf, Ebersbach- (D) 152 G1
Neugersdorf, Ebersbach- (D) 152 G2
Neuglobsow (D) 67 J4
Neuhardenberg (D) 67 L5
Neuharlingersiel (D) 65 H4
Neuhaus (D) 66 D4
Neuhaus (D) 71 J3
Neuhaus (Oste) (D) 65 L4
Neuhaus am Rennweg (D) 72 E4
Neuhaus an der Pegnitz (D) 80 F1
Neuhäusel (D) 70 E6
Neuhausen/Erzgebirge (D) 73 J4
Neuhausen am Rheinfall (CH) 79 K6
Neuhausen bei Landshut (D) 80 A2
Neuhausen ob Eck (D) 87 G2
Neu Heinde (D) 67 G2
Neuhof (D) 70 F6
Neuhof (D) 71 J6
Neuhof an der Zenn (D) 80 D2
Neuhofen an der Krems (A) 89 L1
Neuillay-les-Bois (F) 83 H3
Neuillé-Pont-Pierre (F) 76 C6
Neuilly-en-Donjon (F) 84 E4
Neuilly-le-Réal (F) 84 D4
Neuilly-l'Évêque (F) 78 C6
Neuilly-Saint-Front (F) 77 H3
Neu-Isenburg (D) 70 G6
Neukalen (D) 67 H3
Neu Kaliß (D) 66 E4
Neukamperfehn (D) 65 H5
Neukieritzsch (D) 73 G3
Neukirch (D) 79 M6
Neukirch/Lausitz (D) 74 A3
Neukirch, Stein- (D) 70 F5
Neukirchen (A) 81 K5
Neukirchen (D) 65 K2
Neukirchen (D) 66 D2
Neukirchen (D) 71 H5
Neukirchen (D) 72 A4
Neukirchen (D) 73 H4
Neukirchen (D) 80 F2
Neukirchen (D) 80 G2
Neukirchen (Altmark) (D) 66 F5
Neukirchen (Erzgebirge) (D) 73 H4
Neukirchen am Großvenediger (A) 90 B5
Neukirchen am Walde (A) 81 K4
Neukirchen an der Enknach (A) 90 D3
Neukirchen beim Heiligen Blut (D) 152 C5
Neukirchen bei Sulzbach-Rosenberg (D) 80 F1
Neukirchen-Vluyn (D) 69 M4
Neukirchen vorm Wald (D) 81 J3
Neukloster (D) 66 F3
Neukloster (D) 66 F3
Neulengbach (A) 91 J3
Neuleiningen (D) 79 J3
Neulikko (FIN) 23 K7
Neulise (F) 84 F5
Neu Lübbenau (D) 73 K1
Neum (BIH) 173 G4
Neumagen-Dhron (D) 78 F2
Neumark (D) 72 E3
Neumark (D) 73 G4
Neumarkt am Wallersee (A) 89 J2
Neumarkt im Hausruckkreis (A) 81 K4
Neumarkt im Tauchental (A) 158 B3
Neumarkt in der Oberpfalz (D) 80 E2
Neumarkt in Steiermark (A) 90 F5
Neumarkt-Sankt Veit (D) 81 H4
Neu Mukran (D) 67 K2
Neumünster (D) 66 B2
Neunburg vorm Wald (D) 81 G2
Neung-sur-Beuvron (F) 76 E6
Neunkirch (CH) 86 F2
Neunkirchen (A) 91 K4
Neunkirchen (D) 70 F5
Neunkirchen (D) 78 G3
Neunkirchen (D) 80 A1
Neunkirchen am Brand (D) 80 E1
Neunkirchen-Seelscheid (D) 70 D5
Neuötting (D) 81 H4
Neupölla (A) 91 H2
Neupré (B) 69 J5
Neuried (D) 79 H5
Neuruppin (D) 67 H5
Neusäß (D) 80 D4
Neusiedl (A) 91 L6
Neusiedl am Sand (D) 72 C6
Neusiedl am See (A) 158 C2
Neusiedl an der Zaya (A) 91 L2
Neusorg (D) 152 A4
Neuss (D) 70 C4
Neussargues-en-Pinatelle (F) 84 C6
Neustadt (D) 66 E5
Neustadt (D) 72 F2
Neustadt (D) 145 G3
Neustadt (Dosse) (D) 67 G5
Neustadt (Hessen) (D) 71 H5
Neustadt, Titisee- (D) 86 F2
Neustadt (Wied) (D) 70 D5
Neustadt am Kulm (D) 80 F1
Neustadt am Main (D) 72 B6
Neustadt am Rennsteig (D) 71 L5
Neustadt am Rübenberge (D) 71 H1
Neustadt an der Aisch (D) 80 D1
Neustadt an der Donau (D) 80 F3
Neustadt an der Orla (D) 72 F4
Neustadt an der Waldnaab (D) 152 B4
Neustadt an der Weinstraße (D) 79 J3
Neustadt bei Coburg (D) 71 N4
Neustadt-Glewe (D) 66 F4
Neustadt in Holstein (D) 66 D2
Neustadt in Sachsen (D) 152 F1
Neustadt-Innermanzing (A) 91 J3
Neustift im Stubaital (A) 88 E3
Neustift an der Lafnitz (A) 91 K5
Neustift im Stubaital (A) 88 E3
Neustrelitz (D) 67 J4
Neutal (A) 158 B2
Neutraubling (D) 152 B6
Neutz-Lettewitz (D) 72 F2
Neu-Ulm (D) 80 C4
Neuvéglise-Chaudes-Aigues (F) 84 C7
Neuve-Lyre, la (F) 76 C4
Neuves-Maisons (F) 78 E4
Neuvic (F) 83 F6
Neuvic (F) 84 B6
Neuville-aux-Bois (F) 76 F5
Neuville-de-Poitou (F) 82 F3
Neuville-en-Tourne-à-Fuy, la (F) 77 K3
Neuville-les-Dames (F) 85 H4
Neuville-lès-Decize (F) 84 D3
Neuville-sur-Saône (F) 85 G5
Neuvilly-en-Argonne (F) 77 M3
Neuvoton (FIN) 36 H3
Neuvy-Bouin (F) 82 E3
Neuvy-le-Roi (F) 76 C6
Neuvy-Pailloux (F) 83 J3
Neuvy-Saint-Sépulchre (F) 83 J3
Neuvy-sur-Barangeon (F) 83 K2
Neuvy-sur-Loire (F) 77 G6
Neuwarft (D) 46 C4
Neuwegersleben (D) 72 E1
Neuwied (D) 70 D6
Neuwilen (CH) 79 L6
Neuwiller-lès-Saverne (F) 79 G4
Neuwittenbek (D) 46 C5
Neu Wulmstorf (D) 66 B4
Neuzelle (D) 73 M1
Neuzina (SRB) 167 G3
Neu Zittau (D) 67 K6
Neva (S) 40 F2
Névache (F) 98 B2
Nevade (SRB) 167 G5
Nevarėnai (LT) 136 G1
Nevelkov (CZ) 152 G4
Nevel' (RUS) 7 R7
Nevel' (RUS) 139 L1
Nevel' (UA) 144 C5
Nevele (B) 68 F4
Neverdal (N) 20 C7
Neverfjord (N) 18 F3
Nevern (GB) 56 E1
Nevernes (N) 25 G4
Nevers (F) 84 D3
Nevers, As (E) 110 C4
Nevers, As (E) 110 C4
Nevesinje (BIH) 173 H3
Nevest (HR) 172 D2
Nevestino (BG) 175 J4
Nevez (F) 74 D5
Nevhody (UA) 151 H1
Neviano degli Arduini (I) 99 J3
Neviges (D) 70 D4
Néville (F) 76 C2
Nevinnomyssk (RUS) 13 N4
Nevir (BY) 149 M2
Nevirkiv (UA) 150 D2
Nevlunghavn, Helgeroa- (N) 39 L5
Nevša (BG) 177 H2
Nevşehir (TR) 13 K6
Nevşehir (TR) 193 J3
Nevskoe (RUS) 143 H1
New Abbey (GB) 53 H5
New Addington (GB) 59 H5
New Alresford (GB) 58 E5
Newark on Trent (GB) 55 L4
Newbald (GB) 55 L3
Newbiggin (GB) 55 H1
Newbiggin-by-the-Sea (GB) 53 M4
Newbliss (IRL) 61 H3
Newborough (GB) 61 O5
Newbridge (IRL) 62 F1
Newbridge = Droichead Nua (IRL) 61 J5
Newbridge-on-Wye (GB) 57 H1
New Buckenham (GB) 59 K3
New Buildings (GB) 60 H2
Newburgh (GB) 51 N5
Newburgh (GB) 53 J2
Newburn (GB) 53 M5
Newbury (GB) 57 M3
Newby Bridge (GB) 54 G2
Newcastle (GB) 54 F6
Newcastle (GB) 61 L3
Newcastle (IRL) 63 G4
Newcastle (IRL) 63 K2
Newcastle Emlyn (GB) 56 F1
Newcastleton (GB) 53 K4
Newcastle-under-Lyme (GB) 58 C1
Newcastle upon Tyne (GB) 53 M5
Newcastle West (IRL) 62 D4
Newchurch (GB) 58 A3
New Cross (GB) 54 D6
New Cumnock (GB) 52 G4
New Deer (GB) 51 N4
Newent (GB) 58 C4
Newgale (GB) 56 D2
New Galloway (GB) 52 G4
Newhaven (GB) 59 H6
New Holland (GB) 55 M3
New Houghton (GB) 59 J2
New Inn (IRL) 61 H4
New Inn (IRL) 62 F2
Newinn (IRL) 63 G4
New Kildimo (IRL) 62 E3
New Luce (GB) 52 F5
Newmachar (GB) 51 N5
Newmains (GB) 53 H3
Newmarket (GB) 59 H3
Newmarket (IRL) 62 E4
Newmarket on Fergus (IRL) 62 E3
New Mills (GB) 54 F5
New Mills (GB) 55 J4
New Milton (GB) 58 D6
Newnham (GB) 58 C4
Newnham Bridge (GB) 55 G6
New Pitsligo (GB) 51 N4
Newport (GB) 52 C4
Newport (GB) 57 M4
Newport (GB) 58 B4
Newport (GB) 58 D6
Newport (GB) 59 H4
Newport (IRL) 60 C4
Newport (IRL) 62 F3
Newport-on-Tay (GB) 53 K2
Newport Pagnell (GB) 58 F3
Newport Trench (IRL) 61 J2
Newquay (GB) 56 D5
New Quay (GB) 56 F1
New Radnor (GB) 58 A3
New Romney (GB) 59 J6
New Ross (IRL) 63 J4
New Rossington (GB) 55 K4
Newry (GB) 61 K3
New Scone (GB) 53 J2
Newton (GB) 50 G3
Newton (GB) 53 G2
Newton (GB) 55 N5
Newton (GB) 57 M3
Newton (GB) 59 J2
Newton (IRL) 63 J3
Newton Abbot (GB) 57 G4
Newton Aycliffe (GB) 55 J1
Newton Ferrers (GB) 56 F5
Newtonferry (GB) 50 B4
Newtongrange (GB) 53 J3
Newtonhill (GB) 51 N5
Newton-le-Willows (GB) 54 G4
Newton Mearns (GB) 52 G3
Newtonmore (GB) 51 J5
Newton-on-Trent (GB) 55 L4
Newton Poppleford (GB) 57 H4
Newton Sandes (IRL) 62 D3
Newton Stewart (GB) 52 F5
Newtown (GB) 54 F5
Newtown (GB) 57 J1
Newtownabbey (GB) 61 L2
Newtownards (GB) 54 A1
Newtownbutler (GB) 60 H3
Newtown-Crommelin (GB) 61 K2
Newtown-Cunningham (IRL) 60 G2
Newtown Forbes (IRL) 60 G4
Newtown Gore (IRL) 60 G3
Newtownhamilton (GB) 61 J3
Newtown Mount Kennedy (IRL) 61 K5
Newtown Saint Boswells (GB) 53 K3
Newtownstewart (GB) 60 H2
New Tredegar (GB) 57 H2
Nexon (F) 83 H5
Nexø (DK) 47 O3
Neyland (GB) 56 E2
Nezavertailovca (MD) 163 K5
Neželovo (MK) 174 F5
Neženovo (RUS) 137 J5
Nezvys'ko (UA) 157 H4
Nezlobna (UA) 157 J5
Nežlyovyči (UA) 151 K3
Nežyn (BY) 145 H3
Nianfors (S) 33 M4
Nibbiano (I) 100 A3
Nibe (DK) 42 E5
Nibles (F) 95 H2
Nica (LV) 132 C5
Nica (AL) 174 C4
Nice (F) 98 C5
Nicgale (LV) 138 D1
Nickelsdorf (A) 91 M4
Nickelsdorf (A) 91 M4
Nicolae Bălcescu (RO) 162 D6
Nicolae Bălcescu (RO) 170 E5
Nicolae Bălcescu (RO) 171 F5
Nicolae Titulescu (RO) 169 H5
Nicolinț (RO) 167 J4
Nicolosi (I) 109 H2
Nicoreşti (RO) 170 E2
Nicosia (I) 109 G2
Nicosia = Lefkosia (CY) 199 F5
Nicotera (I) 106 E5
Nicotera Marina (I) 106 E5
Nicșeni (RO) 157 L6
Niculițel (RO) 171 H4
Niculiței (RO) 171 G3
Nida (LT) 136 D3
Nidau (CH) 86 M2
Nidderau (D) 71 H6
Nide (S) 22 C6
Nidegen (D) 69 L5
Nidri (GR) 186 B2
Nidzica (PL) 142 C4
Niebieszczany (PL) 155 L2
Niebla (E) 125 F5
Niebüll (D) 46 B4
Nieborów (PL) 148 B1
Niebrzydów (PL) 148 E2
Niebüll (D) 46 C4
Nieby (D) 46 E4
Niechanowo (PL) 141 J6
Niechmirów (PL) 147 K3
Niechorze (PL) 140 E6
Niechorze (PL) 67 N2
Niedalino (PL) 140 F2
Niedaltdorf (D) 78 E3
Niedenstein (D) 71 H4
Niederaudorf (D) 80 G5
Niederalteich (D) 81 H3
Niederau (D) 73 K4
Niederaula (D) 71 J5
Niederbipp (CH) 86 E3
Niederbobritzsch (D) 73 J4
Niederbrechen (D) 70 F6
Niederbronn-les-Bains (F) 79 H4
Niederdorf = Villabassa (I) 90 B6
Niedere Börde (D) 71 N1
Niedereisenhausen (D) 70 F5
Niedererns (D) 70 F5
Niedereschach (D) 79 J5
Niederfinow (D) 67 K5
Niederfischbach (D) 70 E5
Niedergründau (D) 71 J3
Niedergründau (D) 71 H6
Niederhaïn, Langenleuba- (D) 73 H4
Niederhaverbeck (D) 65 M5
Niederhofen (D) 71 K3
Niederhone (D) 71 K4
Niederjossa (D) 71 J5
Niederkassel (D) 69 N5
Niederkreuzstetten (A) 91 M3
Niederkrüchten (D) 70 B4
Niedermodeleben (D) 71 N2
Niedermorf (D) 90 B4
Niedermuhlau (A) 90 F4
Niedernhall (D) 79 M3
Niedernhausen (D) 70 G6
Niederndorf (A) 81 G5
Niederoblungen (D) 79 K4
Niederorschel (D) 72 C3
Niederpöllnitz (D) 72 F4
Niederöblarn (A) 90 E5
Niederrotschwind (D) 80 B1
Niederschönenfeld (D) 80 D3
Niedersteinebach (D) 71 G6
Niederstetten (D) 79 M3
Niederstotzingen (D) 80 C4
Niedersulz (A) 153 L7
Niederurnen (CH) 87 H3
Niederwalgern (D) 70 G5
Niederwerrn (D) 71 K6
Niederwiesa (D) 73 H4
Niederwinkling (D) 81 H3
Niederwölz (A) 90 F5
Niederzeuzheim (D) 70 G2
Niederzier (D) 69 L5
Niedrzwica Duża (PL) 148 F3
Niedrzwica Kościelna (PL) 148 F3
Niedźwiada (PL) 149 G2
Niedźwiedź (PL) 155 H2
Niedźwiedzice (PL) 147 H2
Niedźwiedź (PL) 155 H2
Niedzica (PL) 155 G3
Niefern-Öschelbronn (D) 79 K4
Niegosławice (PL) 146 D2
Niegowa (PL) 147 L4
Niegowonice (PL) 147 L5
Niegrzyn (PL) 149 M1
Nieheim (D) 71 H3
Niekłań Mały (PL) 148 C3
Niel (B) 69 G4
Nieledew (PL) 149 J4
Nielisz (PL) 149 H4
Niemce (PL) 149 G3
Niemcza (PL) 146 F4
Niemegk (D) 73 H1
Niemelä (FIN) 18 G9
Niemelä (FIN) 19 K3
Niemelä (FIN) 23 M3
Niemelänkylä (FIN) 27 L6
Niemenkylä (FIN) 28 B6
Niemenkylä (FIN) 28 C8
Niemenkylä (FIN) 35 J2
Niemenkylä (FIN) 36 E3
Niemenmäki (FIN) 29 J4
Niemica (PL) 140 F2
Niemijärvi (FIN) 29 M6
Niemikylä (FIN) 37 J2
Nieminen (FIN) 29 K7
Niemirów (PL) 143 J6
Niemisel (S) 27 J2
Niemisjärvi (FIN) 29 G7
Niemisjärvi (FIN) 29 H6
Niemiskylä (FIN) 29 K3
Niemistenkylä (FIN) 28 G8
Niemitalo (FIN) 23 M4
Niemodlin (PL) 153 N2
Niemojki (PL) 149 G1
Niemysłów (PL) 147 K2
Nienadówka (PL) 148 F5
Nienaszów (PL) 155 K2
Nienborstel (D) 65 M3
Nienburg (Saale) (D) 72 F2
Nienburg (Weser) (D) 65 L6
Niendorf, Grebe- (D) 66 E4
Niendorf (Schönberger Land) (D) 66 D3
Nienhagen (D) 47 J5
Nienstädt (D) 71 H2
Nienstedt am Harz (D) 71 K3
Niepars (D) 67 H2
Niepart (PL) 146 F2
Niepołomice (PL) 155 G1
Nieporęt (PL) 142 E6
Nierodzim (PL) 154 D2
Nieröbro (PL) 143 J3
Nierstein (D) 79 J2
Niesi (FIN) 23 H2
Niesky (D) 73 M3
Niestę (D) 72 B3
Niestetal (D) 71 J4
Niestronno (PL) 141 J5
Nieszkow-Kolonia (PL) 147 M2
Nieświń (PL) 148 B3
Nieszawa (PL) 141 L5
Nietków (PL) 146 C1
Nietos, Los (E) 127 J4
Nieul-l'Espoir (F) 83 F4
Nieul (F) 83 H5
Nieul-le-Dolent (F) 82 B3
Nieul-lès-Saintes (F) 82 D5
Nieul-le-Virouil (F) 82 D6
Nieul-sur-Mer (F) 82 C4
Nieuw-Amsterdam (NL) 64 F6
Nieuwegein (NL) 69 J2
Nieuwendijk (NL) 69 H3
Nieuwe Pekela (NL) 64 F5
Nieuwerkerk aan den IJssel (NL) 69 H3
Nieuwerkerken (B) 69 J5
Nieuweschans (NL) 64 G5
Nieuwe-Tonge (NL) 69 G3
Nieuwerkerke (B) 68 D5
Nieuwkoop (NL) 69 H2
Nieuwleusen (NL) 64 E6
Nieuw Milligen (NL) 69 K2
Nieuwolda (NL) 64 F5
Nieuwpoort (B) 68 D4
Nieuw-Vennep (NL) 69 H2
Nieuw-Vossemeer (NL) 69 G3
Nieves = Neves, As (E) 110 C2
Niewęgłosz (PL) 149 G2
Niewiesze (PL) 147 J5
Niewisch (D) 146 A1
Niezdów (PL) 148 E3
Nieznajowa (PL) 155 J3
Niezamierowice (PL) 148 C3
Niezyn (PL) 140 E2
Nigde (TR) 13 K6
Nigde (TR) 193 J5
Nigran (E) 110 B4
Nigrande (LV) 132 E5
Nigrita (GR) 179 K3
Niharra (E) 119 G2
Nihattula (FIN) 35 O2
Nihtiä (EST) 130 C3
Nihtiä (EST) 130 C3
Niihkaluokta = Nikkaluokta (S) 18 B8
Niinikoski (FIN) 36 E3
Niinikumpu (FIN) 29 J7
Niinilahti (FIN) 28 F4
Niinimaa (FIN) 28 D6
Niinimäki (FIN) 28 G4
Niinimäki (FIN) 29 H4
Niinimäki (FIN) 29 J7
Niinimäki (FIN) 36 H2
Niinisaari (FIN) 37 K2
Niinisalo (FIN) 28 C8
Niinivaara (FIN) 29 J5
Niinivesi (FIN) 29 G6
Niiralа (FIN) 29 L7
Niirokumpu (FIN) 23 L4
Niitsiku (EST) 134 D2
Niittumaa (FIN) 35 J2
Niittylahti (FIN) 29 M8
Niittylahti (FIN) 29 K6
Nijar (E) 127 F6
Nij Beets (NL) 64 E5
Nijeberkoop (NL) 64 D5
Nijemci (HR) 166 D3
Nijkerk (NL) 69 J2
Nijlen (B) 69 H4
Nijmegen (NL) 70 A3
Nijvel = Nivelles (B) 69 G5
Nijverdal (NL) 70 B2
Nikanavičy (BY) 145 M2
Nikaranpera (FIN) 28 F6
Nikea (GR) 180 A5
Nikea (GR) 186 C6
Nikel' (RUS) 7 S2
Nikel' (RUS) 19 N5
Níki (GR) 178 E3
Níki (GR) 196 B2
Nikinci (SRB) 166 E4
Nikisiani (GR) 180 E3
Nikitari (CY) 198 E5
Nikitari (TR) 13 K6
Nikitsch (A) 158 C2
Nikjup (BG) 176 E2
Nikkala (S) 27 K3
Nikkaluokta (S) 18 B8
Nikkaroinen (FIN) 36 E2
Nikkeby (N) 18 G3
Nikodim (MK) 175 G6
Nikokléia (GR) 180 C3
Nikolaevo (BG) 177 J2
Nikolaevo (BG) 176 C2
Nikolaevo (BG) 176 E3
Nikolaevo (BG) 176 E3
Nikola Kozlevo (BG) 177 H1
Nikolićevo (SRB) 167 K6
Nikoliči (HR) 164 E6
Nikolinci (SRB) 175 G1
Nikolinci (SRB) 167 H3
Nikolovo (BG) 178 D6
Nikolovo (BG) 169 L6
Nikolovo (BG) 176 D5
Nikolskoe (RUS) 37 P5
Nikopol (BG) 176 C1
Nikopol' (UA) 9 N5
Nikopol' (UA) 13 K2
Nikopoli (GR) 186 C1
Nikovići (MNE) 173 J3
Niksar (TR) 13 L5
Nikšić (MNE) 173 J4
Nikšić (MNE) 173 J4
Nikudin (BG) 180 C1
Niliivaara (FIN) 23 H1
Nillivaara (S) 21 L6
Nilvo (RUS) 137 H2
Nilsby (S) 40 D3
Nilsiä (FIN) 29 J5
Nilsiansberg (S) 33 L6
Nim (DK) 46 E2
Nimec'ka Mokra (UA) 156 E5
Nimereuca (MD) 163 H2
Nîmes (F) 94 D3
Nimfea (GR) 181 G2
Nimfeo (GR) 178 D3
Nimfeo (GR) 179 J3
Nimigea de Jos (RO) 161 J3
Nimis (I) 89 J5
Nimisenkangas (FIN) 29 J4
Nimisjärvi (FIN) 29 J4
Nimitofte (DK) 42 G6
Nin (HR) 164 E6
Ninemilehouse (IRL) 63 H4
Ninfield (GB) 59 H6
Ninkovo (RUS) 135 J2
Niño, El (E) 127 J3
Ninove (B) 68 G5
Niort (F) 82 E4
Nipen (N) 20 F3
Nipsa (GR) 181 J3
Nirza (LV) 134 E5
Niš (SRB) 175 G2
Nisa (P) 117 F4
Nisanda (TR) 185 J3
Niscemi (I) 109 F3
Nischwitz (D) 73 H3
Nišence (SRB) 174 G2
Nisipitu (RO) 157 H6
Niska = Niesky (D) 73 M3
Nisko (PL) 149 J6
Niskakangas (FIN) 27 L7
Niskia Banja (SRB) 175 H2
Niska (PL) 148 F4
Niskos (FIN) 28 D7
Nisovo (BG) 176 F1
Nispen (NL) 69 H4
Nisporeni = Nisporeni (MD) 162 G4
Nisporeni (MD) 162 G4
Nisporeni = Nisporeni (MD) 162 G4
Nissafors (S) 43 N4
Nissa Hanaberi (TR) 190 E5
Nissaki (GR) 178 B5
Nissedal (N) 39 J4
Nissi (GR) 179 F3
Nissia (GR) 178 H2
Nissum Bredning (DK) 42 D6
Nissumvaara (FIN) 23 M6
Nissia (GR) 180 A3
Nissoria (I) 109 F2
Nissumby (DK) 42 B5
Nisstrode (NL) 69 K3
Nisteroti (RO) 170 D2
Nistru (RO) 160 G1
Nisula (FIN) 28 F6
Nisula (FIN) 29 J7
Nitaure (LV) 133 J5
Nitzhdorf (RO) 168 B2
Niton (GB) 58 E6
Nitra (SK) 154 C5
Nitrianske Pravno (SK) 154 D4
Nitry (F) 77 J6
Nittel (D) 78 E2
Nittenau (D) 152 B5
Nittorp (S) 44 C3
Niúronys (LT) 138 B2
Niva (FIN) 23 J6
Niva (FIN) 23 L1
Niva (FIN) 29 K3
Niva (RUS) 37 O1
Nivala (FIN) 27 L7
Nivankyl' (RUS) 19 N7
Nivankylä (FIN) 23 H3
Nivelles (B) 69 G5
Nivenskoe (RUS) 142 D1
Nivjanin (BG) 176 A2
Nivki (BY) 138 F4
Nivki (BY) 138 G5
Nivki (RUS) 135 L3
Nivnice (CZ) 154 B4
Nivka (PL) 73 M2
Niwiska (PL) 146 C2
Niwiska (PL) 148 E5
Niwiski (PL) 148 F1
Nizbor (CZ) 73 L5
Nizino (RUS) 37 N5
Nizny (PL) 148 D4
Nizip (TR) 13 M7
Nizkabor'e (BY) 139 N2
Nizkavičy (BY) 144 F2
Nizki Harabec (BY) 139 L4
Nižmozero (RUS) 7 V4
Nižná Boca (SK) 154 F4
Nižná Jablonka (SK) 156 B3
Nižná Polianka (SK) 155 J3
Nižná Sitnica (SK) 155 J3
Nižná Slaná (SK) 155 G4
Nižný Hrabovec (SK) 155 K4
Nižný Hrušov (SK) 155 J4
Nižný Mirošov (SK) 155 J3
Nižný Slavkov (SK) 155 H3
Nižný Žipov (SK) 155 K4
Nižný (BY) 144 F2
Nizov'e (RUS) 136 D4
Nizovicy (RUS) 131 N4
Nizy-le-Comte (F) 77 K2
Nižyn (UA) 9 M4
Nizza = Nice (F) 98 C5
Nizza Monferrato (I) 98 E3
Njaceč (BY) 143 N3
Njagnevičy (BY) 144 D1
Njahačeva (BY) 143 N5
Njalbliekevš (S) 25 K3
Njallavārri = Nilivaara (S) 21 L6
Njamojta (BY) 139 J4
Njandoma (RUS) 7 W5
Njarðvík (IS) 16 D7
Njasjata (BY) 145 K2
Njasviž (BY) 144 E2
Njavdán = Näätämö (FIN) 19 M4
Njavve (S) 21 H7
Njegovuđa (MNE) 173 K3
Njellim = Nellim (FIN) 19 L6
Njesmačdo = Neschwitz (D) 146 A3
Njetsavare (S) 21 K7
Njetsavare = Njetsavare (S) 21 K7
Njivice (HR) 164 D4
Njunnás = Nunnanen (FIN) 18 G7
Njuorggán = Nuorgam (FIN) 19 K3
Njurunda (S) 33 N3
Njurundabommen (S) 33 N3
Njutånger (S) 33 N4
Noailles (F) 76 F3
Noáin (E) 92 A5
Noale (I) 101 G1
Noalejo (E) 126 C4
Noarootsi (EST) 130 E2
Noasca (I) 86 D7
Nöbbele (S) 44 G5
Nobber (IRL) 61 J4
Nobel' (UA) 144 C5
Nobitz (D) 73 G4
Noblejas (E) 120 B4
Nocaj (SRB) 166 E4
Noceda (E) 111 G3
Nocedo de Curueño (E) 111 J3
Nocera Inferiore (I) 103 K6
Nocera Terinese (I) 106 F4
Nocera Umbra (I) 103 F1
Noceto (I) 100 C3
Nočevo (RUS) 134 F4
Nochten (D) 73 M3
Noci (I) 105 H4
Nociglia (I) 107 K2
Nocina (E) 112 E2
Noceto (I) 100 C3
Nociünai (LT) 137 L3
Nockenthal, Rödeweiler- (D) 78 G2
Nocrich (RO) 161 J6
Nodar (E) 110 D2
Nodeland (N) 38 G6
Nödinge-Nol (S) 43 K3
Nodre Latkberg (S) 25 M5
Nods (CH) 86 M2
Nodullar (TR) 184 D3
Noepoli (I) 105 F5
Noer (D) 46 F5
Noeux-les-Mines (F) 68 D6
Noevci (BG) 175 J3
Noez (E) 119 H4
Nofuentes (E) 112 E3
Nogais, As (E) 110 E3
Nogales (E) 125 F2
Nogara (I) 99 L2
Nogaredo (I) 88 F5
Nogarejas (E) 111 G4
Nogaro (F) 92 D3
Nogent (F) 77 J3
Nogent (F) 78 C5
Nogent-le-Roi (F) 76 E4
Nogent-le-Rotrou (F) 76 C5
Nogent-sur-Oise (F) 76 F3
Nogent-sur-Seine (F) 77 J5
Nogent-sur-Vernisson (F) 77 G6
Noginsk (RUS) 9 P1
Nogna (F) 85 J3
Nógrádkövesd (H) 154 E6
Nógrádmegyer (H) 159 J1
Nógrádsipek (H) 159 J1
Nógrádszakál (H) 159 J1
Nogueira (E) 110 C4
Nogueira (E) 110 B4
Nogueras, Las (E) 121 F4
Nogueras (E) 92 C4
Nogueroles, Los (E) 126 B4
Noguerueles (E) 121 G4
Nohant-Vic (F) 83 J3
Nohfelden (D) 152 C7
Nohant-Vic (F) 83 J3
Nohèdes (F) 93 J5
Nohfelden (D) 78 G2
Nohn (D) 69 M6
Nohra (D) 71 M5
Noia (E) 110 B3
Noicattaro (I) 105 G3
Noidanpolla (FIN) 21 N4
Noirétable (F) 84 E5
Noirmoutier-en-l'Île (F) 82 A3
Nois (E) 110 E1
Noiseux (B) 69 J6
Nojorid (RO) 160 D3
Nokia (FIN) 28 D9
Nokia (FIN) 36 F1
Nokkosmäenkulma (FIN) 28 C8
Nol (S) 43 K3
Nol, Nödinge- (S) 43 K3
Nola (I) 103 K6
Nolay (F) 85 G3
Nolby (F) 85 B3
Noli (I) 98 E4
Nolimo (FIN) 23 L4
Nolo (FIN) 23 L4
Nolsoy (FO) 48 E3
Nolvik (S) 26 B3
Nolyma (S) 41 M2
No Man's Heath (GB) 54 G4
Nombela (E) 119 H3
Noméceurt (F) 77 M5
Nomeland (N) 38 F4
Nomeny (F) 78 E4
Nomexy (F) 78 E5
Nomi (GR) 179 F5
Nomia (GR) 194 C2
Nomparedes (E) 113 G5
Nompatelize (F) 78 F5
Nonancourt (F) 76 D4
Nonant-le-Pin (F) 76 B4
Nonantola (I) 99 M3
Nonaspe (E) 114 D6
Nonio (I) 87 H5
None (I) 98 D3
Nonnenwiller (D) 78 F2
Nontron (F) 83 G5
Nonza (F) 96 E3
Noó (EST) 131 K4
Noo (EST) 131 N1
Noordbeemster (NL) 69 J2
Noordhorn (NL) 64 E4
Noordwijk aan Zee (NL) 69 G2
Noordwijkerhout (NL) 69 G2
Noordwolde (NL) 64 D5
Nopala (FIN) 36 H3
Nopankylä (FIN) 28 C4
Noppikoski (S) 32 G5
Nopbo (FIN) 36 C3
Nor (S) 33 J2
Nor (S) 40 D2
Nor (S) 40 D4
Nora (N) 31 P2
Nora (S) 33 N1
Nora (S) 33 P2
Nora (S) 40 G2
Nora (S) 41 K5
Norager (DK) 42 E5
Noraguume (I) 97 C3
Noran (S) 40 H2
Norberg (S) 41 J2
Norcia (I) 103 G2
Nordagutu (N) 39 K4
Nordanåker (S) 26 C8
Nordanås (S) 26 D5
Nordanede (S) 33 L2
Nordanholen (S) 33 N3
Nordankäl (S) 26 C7
Nordankäl (S) 26 C8
Nordanså (S) 40 G5
Nordanö (S) 41 K2
Nordansjö (S) 26 C5
Nordansjö (S) 33 M3
Nordanstig (S) 33 M4
Nordausques (F) 59 M6
Nordbakk (N) 25 H5
Nordborg (DK) 65 M1
Nordby (DK) 46 B3
Nordby (DK) 46 G2
Nordby (N) 39 G4
Norddeich (D) 64 G4
Norddorf (D) 46 B4
Norddorf (D) 46 B4
Nordeide (N) 30 D5
Nordeidet (N) 18 D3
Nordeidet (N) 18 D3
Nordelph (GB) 59 H2
Norden (D) 64 G4
Norden (GB) 54 F3
Norden (S) 26 B3
Nordenham (D) 65 K4
Nordenstedt (D) 80 D3
Nordenham (D) 65 K4
Norderåsen (S) 25 J8
Norderhov (N) 39 M2
Nordernay (D) 64 G4
Norderö (S) 32 G1
Norderstapel (D) 46 D5
Norderstedt (D) 65 M4
Nordeste (P) 129 d2
Nordfjordeid (N) 30 C5
Nordfjord (N) 19 N2
Nordfjord (N) 20 E6
Nordfjordbotn (N) 21 J2
Nordfjordeid (N) 30 C4
Nordfold (N) 20 E5
Nordhalben (D) 71 N6
Nordhallen (S) 25 G8
Nordhastedt (D) 65 L3
Nordhausen (D) 71 L3
Nordheim (D) 72 C5
Nordheim (D) 79 L3
Nordheim vor der Rhön (D) 72 C5
Nordholz (D) 65 K4
Nordhorn (D) 69 N2
Nordhugło (N) 38 C3
Nordingrå (S) 26 E9
Nordkirchen (D) 70 E3
Nordkisa (N) 39 G2
Nordkjosbotn (N) 21 J2
Nordland (N) 20 B5
Nordleda (D) 65 K4
Nord-Leirvåg (N) 19 M4
Nord-Lenangen (N) 18 C4
Nordli (N) 25 H4
Nordli (N) 25 H6
Nordlifjellstova (N) 38 F3
Nördlingen (D) 80 C3
Nordmaling (S) 26 F7
Nordmannset (N) 19 H2
Nordmark (S) 40 F3
Nordmela (N) 20 E2
Nordnesøya (N) 20 B7
Nordomsjön (S) 32 E4
Norboyn (FO) 48 E3
Nordrach (D) 79 J5
Nordreisa = Storslett (N) 18 D4
Nordre Løset (N) 31 P5
Nordre Osen (N) 32 B5
Nordre Rasen (N) 31 Q6
Nordrollnes (N) 20 G3
Nordsæter (N) 31 G5
Nordsætern (S) 32 B2
Nord-Sel (N) 31 L4
Nordsinni (N) 31 M6
Nordsjö (S) 33 J4
Nordsjö (S) 33 M4
Nordsjöbruket (S) 40 B3
Nordsjøen (N) 24 F5
Nordsjøna (N) 20 C8
Nordskäl (FO) 48 E3
Nordskjer (N) 24 E6
Nordskot (N) 20 E5
Nordskov (DK) 46 G2
Nord-Statland (N) 24 F5
Nordstedstalseter (N) 30 M4
Nordstemmen (D) 72 B1
Nörd-Stensvattnet (S) 25 L7
Nordstrand (N) 39 M3
Nordstrono (N) 38 B2
Nordstrand (N) 31 N4
Nordtunga (S) 16 E5
Nordvamma (N) 20 C7
Nordvåggen (S) 40 C1
Nordvik (N) 20 G5
Nordvik (N) 24 C8
Nordwalde (D) 70 D2
Nordwohlde (D) 65 K6
Noré (N) 39 K2
Noreña (E) 111 H2
Noresund (N) 39 L2
Noret (S) 40 F1
Norg (NL) 64 E5
Norham (GB) 53 L3
Norheimsund (N) 38 D2
Norholm (DK) 42 E4
Norhyttan (S) 40 G2
Norinkylä (FIN) 28 C6
Norionai (LT) 133 K6
Norkavičy (BY) 138 E3
Norma (I) 103 F4
Normanton (GB) 55 K3
Normanville (F) 76 D3
Normlösa (S) 40 H6
Noros (N) 41 J2
Nornäs (S) 32 E3
Noroy-le-Bourg (F) 86 B2
Norra (S) 22 D7
Norra Amsberg (S) 40 H1
Norra Björke (S) 43 J2
Norra Bredåker (S) 27 H3
Norra Bredsjön (S) 40 H3
Norra Bro (S) 40 H4
Norra Fågelås (S) 40 F6
Norra Finnfall (S) 40 H3
Norra Fjällnäs (S) 25 K3
Norra Flät (S) 33 K5
Norra Hammar (S) 43 N3
Norra Härene (S) 40 D6
Norra Holmnäs (S) 26 F6
Norra Kedum (S) 40 D6
Norraker (S) 26 B6
Norra Klagshamn (S) 47 L2
Norra Kölviken (S) 39 P4
Norra Kvinnestad (S) 43 L3
Norra Ljungsjön (S) 22 D5
Norra Lundby (S) 40 E6
Norra Möckleby (S) 45 K5
Norra Myrbacka (S) 32 H4
Norra Nordsjö (S) 26 E7
Norra Ossjö (S) 44 C6
Norra Rörum (S) 47 N1
Norra Sandby (S) 47 N1
Norra Sandsjö (S) 44 H4
Norra Skärvången (S) 25 J7
Norra Solberga (S) 44 F3
Norra Stensund (S) 25 M3
Norra Sunderbyn (S) 27 H3
Norra Transtrandsätern (S) 40 C1
Norra Ulvsund (S) 25 L4
Norra Unnared (S) 43 N3
Norra Vallgrund (FIN) 27 H8
Norra Vånga (S) 40 D6
Norrbäck (S) 26 D5
Norrbäck (S) 33 H3
Norrbäck (S) 33 M3
Norrberg (S) 25 L4
Norrberg (S) 26 C8
Norrberg (S) 33 M3
Norrbo (S) 33 M5
Norrbo (S) 40 G2
Norrboda (AX) 34 F4
Norrboda (S) 33 J5
Norrboda (S) 34 B4
Norrby (EST) 130 D2
Norrbyberg (S) 27 H3
Norrbyberg (S) 26 E5
Norrbyn (S) 26 F7
Norrdal (S) 33 L4
Norre Aaby (DK) 46 E3
Nørre Aby = Nørre Aaby (DK) 46 E3
Norre Alslev (DK) 47 J4
Norre Arup (DK) 42 C5
Norre Asmindrup (DK) 47 J2
Norre Broby (DK) 46 F3
Norre Felding (DK) 42 C6
Norre Hojrup (DK) 46 F2
Norre Ekedal (S) 41 L2
Norre Kollemorten (DK) 46 D2
Norre Kongerslev (DK) 42 F5
Norre Lyndelse (DK) 46 F3
Norre Lyngby (DK) 42 E4
Norre Lyngvig (DK) 46 B1
Norre Nebel (DK) 46 B2
Norre Snede (DK) 46 D2
Norre Snedstrup (DK) 42 E4
Norre Tvismark (DK) 46 C3
Norre Vilstrup (DK) 46 D2
Norre Vium (DK) 46 C1
Norre Vorupør (DK) 42 B5
Norrfällsviken (S) 26 E9
Norrfjärden (S) 22 D6
Norrfjärden (S) 26 G7
Norrfjärden (S) 33 N3
Norrfors (S) 26 E7
Norrgrässmåsen (S) 33 H4
Norr-Greningen (S) 25 K8
Norrhede (S) 33 H3
Norrhult-Klavreström (S) 44 G4
Norrköping (S) 41 K5
Norrköping (S) 41 J6
Norrlia (S) 33 M4
Norrliden (S) 33 M3
Norr Lövsta (S) 33 N1
Norrmesunda (S) 26 E8
Norrnora (S) 26 G7
Norrnäs (FIN) 28 B6
Norrbo (FIN) 33 G6
Norrsjön (S) 26 F5
Norrsjön (S) 32 E5
Norrskedika (S) 41 M2
Norrsundet (S) 41 K5
Norrsunda (S) 41 K5
Norrsunda (S) 41 N3
Norrsundet (S) 33 M5
Norrtälje (S) 41 N3
Norrtannflo (S) 25 M8
Norrvåge (S) 26 E5
Norrviken (S) 26 D5
Nors (DK) 42 C4
Norsholm (S) 41 J6
Norsjö (S) 26 F5
Norsjövallen (S) 26 F5
Norstelia (N) 31 M3
Nort, Le (F) 83 J6
Nort Ballachulish (GB) 52 E1
Norten-Hardenberg (D) 71 J3
Northallerton (GB) 55 K1
Northampton (GB) 58 F3
North Berwick (GB) 53 K2
North Cave (GB) 55 M3
North Charlton (GB) 53 M4
North Dalton (GB) 55 L3
Northeim (D) 71 J3
North Elmham (GB) 59 J2
North Ferriby (GB) 55 L3
North Grimston (GB) 55 L2
North Hykeham (GB) 55 L4
North Kessock (GB) 51 J4
North Kilworth (GB) 58 F3
Northleach (GB) 58 D4
Northleach (GB) 57 C2
Northop (GB) 54 F4
North Petherton (GB) 58 A5
North Roe (GB) 49 E2
North Shields (GB) 53 N5
North Somercotes (GB) 55 N4
North Tawton (GB) 56 G4
North Thoresby (GB) 55 M4
North Tidworth (GB) 58 D5
North Tolsta = Tolastadh (GB) 50 E3
Northwall (GB) 49 D5
North Walsham (GB) 59 K2
North Weald Bassett (GB) 59 H4
Northwich (GB) 55 H4
Norton (GB) 57 L1
Norton-on-Derwent (GB) 55 L2
Nortorf (D) 46 E5
Nortrup (D) 65 H6
Nort-sur-Erdre (F) 75 H6
Norvasalo (FIN) 19 K7
Nörvenich (D) 69 M5
Norvik (N) 30 G2
Norwich (GB) 59 K2
Norwick (GB) 49 G2
Noryns'k (UA) 145 J6
Nos (N) 30 E4
Nosedole (I) 100 D2
Nosen (N) 31 K6
Noskivci (UA) 150 F6
Noslac (RO) 161 H5
Nosovo (RUS) 134 E3
Noss (N) 20 E2
Noss (N) 31 J6
Nossa Senhora da Boa Fé (P) 124 C2
Nossa Senhora da Graça do Divor (P) 116 F6
Nossa Senhora da Graça dos Degolados (P) 124 E1
Nossa Senhora das Neves (P) 124 D3
Nossa Senhora da Torega (P) 124 C3
Nossa Senhora de Machede (P) 124 D2
Nossebro (S) 44 B2
Nössemark (S) 39 P4
Nossen (D) 152 D1
Nossendorf (D) 47 L6
Nossentiner Hütte (D) 67 G3
Nösslinge (S) 43 L4
Nosykivka (UA) 150 G6
Noszlop (H) 158 D3
Noszvaj (H) 155 G6
Nota (GR) 179 G2
Noto (I) 109 H5
Noto (I) 109 H4
Notodden (N) 39 K3
Notre-Dame-de-Gravenchon (F) 76 C3
Notre-Dame-de-Londres (F) 94 C3
Notre-Dame-de-Monts (F) 82 A3
Nötsch im Gailtal (A) 164 B1
Notset (N) 30 B4
Nøttebäck (S) 44 G4
Notterøy (N) 39 M4
Nottingham (GB) 55 K5
Nöttja (S) 44 D5
Nottuln (D) 70 D3
Notviken (S) 22 E5
Notzing (D) 80 F4
Nouaillé-Maupertuis (F) 83 F3
Nouan-le-Fuzelier (F) 76 F6
Nouans-les-Fontaines (F) 83 H2
Nouart (F) 77 M3
Nouillers, Les (F) 82 D5
Nouni (EST) 131 L4
Nou Săsesc (RO) 169 H1
Nousiainen (FIN) 35 K3
Nousionmäki (FIN) 29 J5
Nousu (FIN) 23 L2
Nouvion (F) 68 B6
Nouvion-en-Thiérache, le (F) 77 J1
Nouzerines (F) 83 J4
Nouzonville (F) 77 L2
Nõva (EST) 130 D3
Nova (H) 158 C4
Novà (I) 89 J5
Nová Baňa (SK) 154 D5
Nova Borova (UA) 151 H2
Nová Bošáca (SK) 154 B4
Nova Breznica (MK) 174 F5
Nova Bukovica (HR) 165 K3
Nová Bystrica (SK) 154 E3
Nová Bystřice (CZ) 91 H1
Novačene (BG) 176 C1
Nová Cerekev (CZ) 153 H5
Nova Černa (BG) 176 F1
Novačevo (BG) 176 F3
Novaci (MK) 178 E2
Novaci (RO) 169 G3
Novaci (SRB) 166 E5
Novaci Strâini (RO) 169 G3
Nová Crnja (SRB) 167 G2
Novadneki (LV) 132 E4
Nová Dubnica (SK) 154 C4
Novaféltria (I) 101 H6
Nova Gorica (SLO) 89 K6
Nova Gradiška (HR) 165 J4
Nova Ivanivka (UA) 171 J2
Novaja Buda (BY) 145 B5
Novaja Čavovka (UA) 144 B5
Novaja Derevnja (RUS) 135 N2
Novaja Dubrova (BY) 144 G3
Novaja Dubrova (BY) 145 J3
Novaja Elča (BY) 145 N5
Novaja Kalitva (RUS) 9 P4
Novaja Ladoga (RUS) 7 S5
Novaja Milča (BY) 145 N4
Novaja Niva (BY) 139 J6
Novaja Pašta (BY) 134 H6
Novaja Ropša (RUS) 37 N5
Novaja Ruda (BY) 143 L3
Novaja Ruda (UA) 144 B6
Novaja Rudnja (BY) 145 K5
Novaja Usiča (RUS) 135 N4
Novaja Usman' (RUS) 9 P4
Novaja Vēska (BY) 138 C4
Novajadziarny (RUS) 7 P3
Nova Kachovka (UA) 13 K3
Nova Kamena (BG) 177 H1
Novakovo (BG) 176 D5
Novakovo (BG) 177 G2
Nová Lehota (SK) 154 B4
Novales (E) 114 C3
Novalesa (I) 85 M6
Nova Levante (I) 88 E5
Novalja (HR) 164 D5
Nová L'ubovňa (SK) 155 G3
Novalukomł (BY) 139 K4
Nova Mahala (BG) 176 B5
Nová Paka (CZ) 146 D5
Nova Pazova (SRB) 166 F4
Nová Pec (CZ) 90 E2
Nova Ponente (I) 88 E5
Nova Popina (BG) 170 D5
Novara (I) 87 G7
Nova Rača (UA) 145 K6
Nova Rača (HR) 165 J3
Novara di Sicilia (I) 109 H1
Nova Reguengo Pequeno (P) 124 B4
Nová Říše (CZ) 153 J5
Nová Sedlica (SK) 155 M3
Nova Šipka (BG) 177 J2
Nová Siri Stazione (I) 107 G2
Nova Synjavka (UA) 150 F4
Nova Topola (BIH) 165 J4
Nova Ušycja (UA) 157 L4
Nova Ušycja (UA) 150 E6
Nová Varoš (SRB) 174 C2
Nova Vas (SLO) 164 D3
Nová Včelnice (CZ) 153 H5
Nová Ves (CZ) 81 H1
Nova Vyžva (UA) 149 K3
Nova Zadova (UA) 162 B2
Nova Zagora (BG) 176 F3
Novéant-sur-Moselle (F) 78 E3
Novegļia (I) 100 B4
Nové Hamry (CZ) 73 H5
Nové Heřminovy (CZ) 153 M3
Nové Hrady (CZ) 153 H6
Nové Hrady (CZ) 146 E6
Novela (E) 121 H6
Novelda del Guadiana (E) 117 H6
Novellara (F) 100 C4
Novellara (I) 100 D3
Nové Město nad Metují (CZ) 153 K3
Nové Město na Moravě (CZ) 153 K4
Nové Město nad Váhom (SK) 154 B4
Nové Město pod Smrkem (CZ) 153 H2
Nové Mesto (UA) 156 D4
Noventa Vicentina (I) 99 M2
Noves (F) 94 E3
Nové Sady (SK) 154 C5
Nové Sady (SK) 160 D5
Nove Sedlo (CZ) 152 D3
Nové Strašecí (CZ) 152 E3
Nove Syrovatky (UA) 151 M6
Nove Syrovatky (UA) 151 M6
Nove Selo (RUS) 177 G3
Nové Veselí (CZ) 153 J4
Nové Zámky (SK) 154 C6
Novgorod (RUS) 7 S6
Novgorodka (RUS) 134 G3
Novgorod (BG) 176 E1
Novhorod-Sivers'kyj (UA) 9 M4
Novi Bečej (SRB) 166 F2
Novi Belokorovyči = Novi Bilokorovyči (UA) 150 G1
Novi Bilokorovyči (UA) 150 G1
Novi Čakovci (HR) 166 D3
Novi Červo (BG) 176 D3
Novi Dojran (MK) 179 H2
Novi Dojran (MK) 179 H2
Novigrad (HR) 164 F6
Novigrad (HR) 164 H2
Novigrad (HR) 164 F6
Novigrad Podravski (HR) 165 H2
Novi Han (BG) 175 L3
Novi Iskăr (BG) 175 K3
Novi Jarylovyči (BY) 145 O4
Novi Jurjan (BY) 145 O4
Novi Kaplani (UA) 171 J1
Novi Karlovci (SRB) 166 F3
Novi Kneževac (SRB) 166 F1
Novi Kozarci (SRB) 167 G2
Novi Ligure (I) 98 F3
Novillars (F) 85 K2
Novillas (E) 113 G5
Noville (B) 69 K6
Novi Marof (HR) 165 H2
Novion-Porcien (F) 77 K2
Novi Pazar (BG) 177 H2
Novi Pazar (SRB) 174 E3
Novi Šad (SRB) 166 F3
Novi Šeher (BIH) 165 L5
Novi Slankamen (SRB) 166 F3
Novi Strilyšča (UA) 156 F3
Novi Travnik (BIH) 173 G1
Novi Trojany (UA) 171 H2
Novi Varvs'k (UA) 151 J2
Novi Vinodolski (HR) 164 D4
Novi Žednik (SRB) 159 J6
Novo (RUS) 135 J6
Novoajdar (UA) 9 P5
Novoaleksandrovsk (RUS) 13 N3
Novoarchanhel's'k (UA) 9 M5
Novoazovs'k (UA) 13 M3
Novobeograd (SRB) 166 F4
Novoberdë (RKS) 174 F3
Novobohdanivka (UA) 9 M5
Novobohdanivka (UA) 13 K2
Novobranove (RUS) 134 D4
Novo Brdo = Novobërdë (RKS) 174 F3
Novočerkassk (RUS) 13 N3
Novo Delčevo (BG) 179 J1
Novodnistrovs'k (UA) 162 E1
Novo Doroslovo (SRB) 166 E2
Novo Drahovo (SRB) 159 J6
Novoe (RUS) 135 J4
Novoe Kirsino (RUS) 131 N4
Novo Gorado (BY) 134 F2
Novoelyzavetivka (UA) 163 L4
Novoe Nikolskoe (RUS) 134 G3
Novo Goražde (BIH) 165 L3
Novogeorgijivka (UA) 163 M4
Novo Goražde = Ustiprača (BIH) 173 K2
Novograd-Volynskij = Novohrad-Volyns'kyj (UA) 150 F2
Novogrudino (BIH) 155 J6
Novohovanskij (RUS) 135 J4
Novohrad-Volyns'kyj (UA) 150 F2
Novohuchyns'k (UA) 151 H3
Novojavorovs'ke (UA) 149 J6
Novokarbivka (UA) 163 L3
Novokonstjantynivka (UA) 150 F5
Novo Konto (SRB) 175 H1
Novolabun' (UA) 157 M1
Novoli (I) 107 K3
Novomalyn (UA) 150 C3
Novo mesto (SLO) 164 E3
Novo Miloševo (SRB) 166 F2
Novomoskovsk (RUS) 9 P3
Novomoskovs'k (UA) 9 N5
Novomoskovsk (RUS) 142 C1
Novonikraskova (UA) 171 H3
Novooleksandrivka (UA) 163 K4
Novooleksandrivka (UA) 163 L3
Novooleksijivka (UA) 13 K3
Novoozerjanka (UA) 163 M4
Novo Paničarovo (BG) 177 J4
Novopavlivka (UA) 163 M3
Novopil' (UA) 151 G3
Novopol' (UA) 163 K2
Novo Poljance = Poliaci i Vjetër (RKS) 174 E3
Novopolock = Navapolack (BY) 139 J2
Novopskov (UA) 9 P5
Novorossijsk (RUS) 13 L4
Novorževe (RUS) 7 R7
Novoržev (RUS) 134 H3
Novošachtinsk (RUS) 9 P5
Novosamarka (UA) 163 K3
Novosedly nad Nežárkou (CZ) 153 G5
Novosel (BG) 177 G2
Novoselec (BG) 177 H3
Novoselë (RKS) 174 D3
Novo Selo (MK) 174 D3
Novoselci (RUS) 131 O3
Novoselci (RUS) 134 G1
Novoselec (BG) 176 F4
Novoselivka (UA) 150 B2
Novoselivka (UA) 150 D4
Novoselivka (UA) 163 H3
Novoselivka (UA) 163 L4
Novoselivka (UA) 163 M3
Novoselivka (UA) 171 J2
Novoselka (UA) 163 M2
Novoselo (RKS) 174 D3
Novo Selo (BG) 168 D5
Novo Selo (BG) 169 L6
Novo Selo (BG) 176 E3
Novo Selo (BG) 176 F4
Novo Selo (BIH) 166 A3
Novo Selo (MK) 175 J6
Novo Selo (MK) 178 F2
Novo Selo (SRB) 166 D4
Novo Selo (SRB) 167 H5
Novo Selo (SRB) 174 E4
Novo Selo = Novoselë (RKS) 174 D3
Novoselovo (RUS) 141 O2
Novoselyci (RUS) 131 M6
Novoselycja (UA) 156 D4
Novoselycja (UA) 157 K5
Novoselycja (UA) 157 M3
Novoselycja (UA) 161 M1
Novoselycja (UA) 162 D2
Novoselycja (UA) 163 L2
Novosemeniivka (UA) 163 K2
Novosil' (RUS) 9 O3
Novosilky (UA) 150 B2
Novosilky (UA) 150 C3
Novosilky (UA) 151 M2
Novosilky (UA) 162 D3
Novosil's'ke (RUS) 9 P4
Novosokolniki (RUS) 135 K5
Novostroevo (RUS) 142 F2
Novosvitivka (UA) 163 M4
Novoukrainka (UA) 9 M5
Novoukrajinka (UA) 162 D2
Novoukrainka (UA) 163 L5
Novovasylivka (UA) 163 M3
Novovelyka (UA) 155 H4
Novovolyns'k (UA) 149 K4
Novovolyns'k = Novovolyns'k (UA) 149 K4
Novozybkov (RUS) 9 M4
Novožukiv (UA) 150 B2
Novo Zvečevo (HR) 165 K3
Novozybkov (RUS) 9 M4
Novska (HR) 165 H4
Nový Bor (CZ) 152 G2
Nový Bydžov (CZ) 153 H3
Novycja (UA) 156 F4
Nový Dvůr (BY) 144 D4
Nový Dvůr (BY) 144 D4
Nový Dvůr (BY) 145 L2
Nový Dvůr (CZ) 146 D6
Novye Anenny = Anenii Noi (MD) 163 J5
Nový Hrozenkov (CZ) 154 C3
Nový Jičín (CZ) 154 C2
Nový Kyiv (UA) 9 M4
Nový Izborsk (RUS) 134 E2
Novyja Dzjaniaviči (BY) 139 K5
Novyja Kruki (BY) 138 G2
Novyja Maksimavičy (BY) 145 K1
Novyja Valosavičy (BY) 139 J4
Novy Buh (UA) 9 N5
Nový Bydžov (CZ) 153 J3
Novy Čornokal' (UA) 150 D2
Nový Jičín (CZ) 154 C2
Nový Kalyniv (UA) 156 D2
Nový Mašocer (RUS) 7 T4
Nový Poseick (RUS) 134 F3
Novy Rozdil (UA) 156 F3
Novy Svit (UA) 13 K4
Nový Knín (CZ) 152 F4
Nový Pahost (BY) 138 F3
Nový Rychnov (CZ) 153 H5
Nový Tekov (SK) 158 G1
Nowa Bogacica (PL) 148 C5
Nowa Dęba (PL) 148 E5
Nowa Karczma (PL) 141 K2
Nowa Ruda (CZ) 153 L2
Nowa Sarzyna (PL) 148 G5
Nowa Słupia (PL) 148 D4
Nowa Sól (PL) 146 D2
Nowa Wieś (PL) 140 F5
Nowa Wieś (PL) 140 G5
Nowa Wieś (PL) 141 J5
Nowa Wieś (PL) 146 F5
Nowa Wieś Ełcka (PL) 142 G3
Nowa Wieś Królewska (PL) 141 H1
Nowa Wieś Lęborska (PL) 141 J1
Nowa Wieś Legnicka (PL) 146 E3
Nowa Wieś Wielka (PL) 141 J6
Nowa Wieś Zachodnia (PL) 142 E4
Nowa Wola (PL) 146 E2
Nowe (PL) 141 L4
Nowe Brusno (PL) 149 H5
Nowe Brzesko (PL) 155 G1
Nowe Czarnowo (PL) 140 B4
Nowe Dwory (PL) 140 F5
Nowe Holowczyce (PL) 149 J1
Nowe Jaroszowice (PL) 146 D3
Nowe Miasteczko (PL) 146 D2
Nowe Miasto (PL) 142 D5
Nowe Miasto Lubawskie (PL) 142 B4
Nowe Miasto nad Pilicą (PL) 148 C2
Nowe Miasto nad Wartą (PL) 147 G1
Nowe Opole (PL) 148 F1
Nowe Piekuty (PL) 143 H5
Nowe Rutki (PL) 143 H3
Nowe Skalmierzyce (PL) 147 H2
Nowe Warpno (PL) 140 B3
Nowe Worowo (PL) 140 F3
Nowica (PL) 136 B5
Nowinka (PL) 137 H6
Nowiny Wielkie (PL) 140 D5
Nowogard (PL) 67 N3
Nowogród (PL) 142 F4
Nowogród Bobrzański (PL) 146 C2
Nowogrodziec (PL) 146 C3
Nowosielce (PL) 156 B2
Nowosiółki (PL) 143 K4
Nowosiółki (PL) 149 J4
Nowosiółky (PL) 149 J4
Nowotaniec (PL) 155 L2
Nowy Duninów (PL) 142 B6
Nowy Dwór (PL) 143 K3
Nowy Dwór (PL) 147 H3
Nowy Dwór Gdański (PL) 141 M2
Nowy Dwór Mazowiecki (PL) 142 D6
Nowy Dzików (PL) 149 J6
Nowy Folwark (PL) 147 L3
Nowy Korczyn (PL) 148 C5
Nowy Kościół (PL) 146 D3
Nowy Łupków (PL) 155 L3
Nowy Staw (PL) 141 M2
Nowy Sącz (PL) 155 H2
Nowy Targ (PL) 154 G3
Nowy Tomyśl (PL) 146 E1
Nowy Wiec (PL) 141 J3
Nowy Wiśnicz (PL) 148 B6
Nowy Żmigród (PL) 155 K2
Noyal (F) 74 G4
Noyal-Pontivy (F) 74 F4
Noyal-sur-Vilaine (F) 75 H4
Noyalo (F) 74 F5
Noyant (F) 75 K5
Noyant-Villages (F) 75 M5
Noyelles-sur-Mer (F) 68 B6
Noyen-sur-Sarthe (F) 75 L5
Noyers (F) 77 K6
Noyers-Saint-Martin (F) 76 F2
Noyers-sur-Jabron (F) 95 G2
Noyon (F) 77 H2
Nozay (F) 75 H5
Nožarevo (BG) 170 D5
Nozdrzec (PL) 155 L2
Nožičko (BIH) 165 J4
Nozières (F) 83 J1
Nuaillé-d'Aunis (F) 82 D4
Nuarbe (E) 113 G2
Nuasjärvi (FIN) 23 J5
Nubbensieter (N) 32 A4
Nubbel (D) 66 B1
Nubl (N) 65 B1
Nuccio (I) 106 D1
Nucet (RO) 160 E5
Nucet (RO) 169 K4
Nucetto (I) 98 E4
Nuci (RO) 170 C4
Nucia, la (E) 122 D5
Nucice (CZ) 73 L5
Nucşoara (RO) 169 H3
Nudyže (UA) 149 J3
Nuel-Les-Aubiers (F) 82 E3
Nuenen (NL) 69 K4
Nueno (E) 113 J4
Nueva (E) 112 E1
Nueva Andalucía (E) 128 E5
Nueva Carteya (E) 126 B3
Nueva Jarilla (E) 125 H5
Nuévalos (E) 113 H6
Nuevo Baztán (E) 120 B3
Nuevo Guadiaro (E) 128 D5
Nuevo Riaño (E) 111 K3
Nuez de Arriba, La (E) 112 D3
Nuffaru (RO) 171 K3
Nufenen (CH) 87 H4
Nuhkıy (TR) 191 J3
Nuhören (TR) 191 H2
Nuijamaa (FIN) 37 L3
Nuijamaa (FIN) 37 L3
Nuits-Saint-Georges (F) 85 G2
Nujno (UA) 149 L2
Nukari (FIN) 36 C3
Nukarinkulma (FIN) 35 L1
Nukši (LV) 134 E5
Nuksujärvi (S) 22 E1
Nule (I) 97 D3
Nules (E) 122 A3
Nulvi (I) 97 C2
Numana (I) 101 K5
Numanoluk (TR) 191 K2
Numansdorp (NL) 69 G3
Numão (P) 117 G1
Nümbrecht (D) 70 E5
Nummela (FIN) 36 B4
Nummelan (FIN) 35 M3
Nummenkylä (FIN) 36 B4
Nummi (FIN) 36 A4
Nummijärvi (FIN) 28 C7
Nummikoski (FIN) 28 C7
Nummi nen (FIN) 36 D3
Numunagöjmen (TR) 193 H5
Nünchritz (D) 73 J3
Nuneaton (GB) 58 E2
Nunkirchen (D) 78 F3
Nunnanlahti (FIN) 29 K5
Nunnanen (FIN) 18 G7
Nunney (GB) 57 K3
Nunnykirk (GB) 53 M4
Nunspeet (NL) 69 K2
Nuntaşi (RO) 171 H4
Nunton (GB) 50 C5
Nuojua (FIN) 29 G2
Nuoksujärvi (S) 22 E3
Nuolijärvi (FIN) 29 J4
Nuoramoinen (FIN) 36 E2
Nuorgam (FIN) 19 K3
Nuoritta (FIN) 23 J6
Nuoro (I) 97 D3
Nuorpiniemi (FIN) 19 H4
Nupsdalstunga (IS) 16 F4
Nupsfjalla (IS) 17 K1
Nupur (IS) 16 C3
Nupur (IS) 17 K2
Nur (PL) 142 G5
Nuragus (I) 97 D4
Nurallao (I) 97 D4
Nuraminis (I) 97 D5
Nuret-le-Ferron (F) 83 H3
Nuribey (TR) 191 K3
Nurkankylä (FIN) 36 F3
Nurmaa (RUS) 37 Q5
Nurmas (FIN) 36 G2
Nurmes (FIN) 29 K4
Nurmesperä (FIN) 27 M7
Nurmijärvi (FIN) 29 L4
Nurmijärvi (FIN) 36 B4
Nurmiranta (FIN) 29 K4
Nurmo (FIN) 28 C6
Nürnberg (D) 80 E2
Nurri (I) 97 D4
Nurste (EST) 130 B3
Nürtingen (D) 79 L4
Nurzec (PL) 143 J6
Nurzec-Stacja (PL) 143 J6
Nus (I) 86 D6
Nusco (I) 104 C5
Nuşeni (RO) 161 J3
Nusenna (I) 99 M6
Nușfalău (RO) 160 F3
Nusnäs (S) 40 F1
Nuşfalău (RO) 160 F3
Nusse (D) 66 D4
Nusplingen (D) 79 K5
Nusret (TR) 190 E1
Nußbach (A) 89 H4
Nußdorf am Attersee (A) 90 E4
Nußdorf am Inn (D) 80 G5
Nusse (D) 66 D3
Nustar (HR) 166 C3
Nüsttal (D) 72 B4
Nuth (NL) 70 A5
Nuthem (N) 39 J3
Nuthe-Urstromtal (D) 73 J1
Nuttuperä (FIN) 28 F4
Nuukavaara (FIN) 23 K5
Nuuksio (FIN) 36 C4
Nuupas (FIN) 27 N2
Nuutajärvi (FIN) 35 M2
Nuutilla (FIN) 36 F3
Nuutilanmäki (FIN) 29 H8
Nuvella = Novella (F) 96 E3
Nuvolento (I) 100 C1
Nuvsvåg (N) 18 E3
Nuvvus = Nuvvus (FIN) 19 J4
Nuvvus (FIN) 19 J4
Nuxis (I) 97 C5
Nuzéjouls (F) 93 G1
Nüzhetiye (TR) 183 J4
Ny (S) 40 B3
Nya Bastuselet (S) 26 E4
Nyadal (S) 33 O2
Nyåker (S) 26 D7
Nyåker (S) 26 F7
Nyåker (S) 33 K4
Nyåkersätern (S) 26 F6
Nyång (S) 41 K1
Nyárlörinc (H) 159 J4
Nyasvol (N) 38 E3
Nybakk (N) 39 O2
Nybble (S) 40 F4
Nybergsund (N) 32 C5
Nybo (S) 33 J3
Nyboda (S) 32 B3
Nybodarna (S) 33 K6
Nybodvallen (S) 33 L4
Nyborg (DK) 46 F3
Nyboliden (S) 40 E2
Nyboslk (DK) 46 B3
Nyborg (DK) 46 G3
Nyborg (N) 19 L3
Nyborg (S) 27 K3
Nybro (S) 44 H5
Nybrostrand (S) 47 N3
Nybyen (SRB) 51 L2
Nyby (FIN) 28 B6
Nyby (N) 19 H3
Nyby (S) 25 K8
Nybygget (S) 41 J4
Nybyn (S) 22 D4
Nybyn (S) 33 J4
Nydala (S) 44 E4
Nydek (CZ) 154 D2
Nye (S) 44 G4
Nyékládháza (H) 155 H6
Nyergesújfalu (H) 158 G2
Nyfaboden (S) 33 H5
Nyfors (S) 27 G4
Nyfors (S) 40 H3
Nygård (N) 21 G4
Nygård (N) 30 E6
Nygård (N) 26 G4
Nygård (S) 40 A5
Nygård (S) 41 M4
Nygården (S) 25 L5
Nygården (S) 40 H3
Nyhammar (S) 40 G2
Nyhammar (S) 40 H2
Nyhamn (S) 26 B6
Nyhamnsläge (S) 47 L1
Nyhem (S) 33 K2
Ny Hesselager (DK) 46 G3
Nyhöfn (IS) 17 K3
Nyhusetra (N) 31 N4
Nyhyttan (S) 40 H4
Nyírábrány (H) 160 E2
Nyíracsád (H) 160 E2
Nyírád (H) 158 D3
Nyíradony (H) 160 D2
Nyírbátor (H) 160 E2
Nyírbéltek (H) 160 E2
Nyírbogát (H) 155 L6
Nyírbogdány (H) 155 K5
Nyíregyháza (H) 155 K6
Nyíregyháza (H) 155 L6
Nyírkarász (H) 160 E1
Nyírkáta (H) 156 B6
Nyírlugos (H) 160 E2
Nyírmada (H) 160 E1
Nyírmeggyes (H) 160 E1
Nyírtelek (H) 160 D1
Nyírtura (H) 160 D1
Nykälä (FIN) 29 G7
Nykarleby (FIN) 27 J7
Nykarleby = Uusikaarlepyy (FIN) 27 J7
Nyker (DK) 47 N3
Nykil (S) 44 G1
Nykirke (N) 31 N6
Nykirke (N) 39 M4
Nykløbing (DK) 42 D5
Nykøbing Falster (DK) 47 J4
Nykøbing Mors (DK) 42 C5
Nykøbing Sjælland (DK) 47 J2
Nykøbing Strandhuse (DK) 66 F1
Nykroppa (S) 40 G3
Nykvarn (S) 41 L4
Nykvarn (S) 41 M5
Nyköping (S) 41 L5
Nykyrka (S) 40 G6
Nyland (N) 20 E3
Nyland (S) 33 M2
Nyland (S) 25 H3
Nyland (S) 26 D3
Nyland (S) 26 D4
Nyland (S) 26 E8
Nyland (S) 33 N1
Nyland (S) 33 O1
Nyland (S) 33 P1
Nylinden (S) 26 D3
Nyliden (S) 33 M1
Nymindegab (DK) 46 B2
Nymo (N) 18 C3
Nymoen (N) 25 H5
Nymoen (N) 31 N6
Nymoen (N) 39 J3
Nymolla (S) 47 P1
Nymyhra (N) 32 G1
Nynäshamn (S) 41 M5
Nyneset (N) 25 G6
Nyon (CH) 86 B5
Nyons (F) 95 G2
Nyöarn (N) 24 H6
Nyørn (N) 31 M5
Nýrčany (CZ) 152 D4
Nyrud (N) 19 M6
Nysa (PL) 146 G6
Nysa Kłodzka (PL) 147 G5
Nysäter (S) 40 C4
Nysäter (S) 33 M2
Nysätern (S) 33 M5
Nyséla Dubečnja (UA) 151 M2
Nyše (UA) 157 H2
Nysel' (S) 40 G4
Nysether (N) 31 J3
Nyskote (N) 20 F4
Nysetra (N) 31 L2
Nysetra (S) 32 C4
Nysetertekken (N) 31 M3
Nysetrene (N) 31 L4
Nysjö (S) 33 M5
Nyskoga (S) 40 D2
Nyskogsvallen (S) 32 F2
Nyskolla (N) 31 M2
Nysted (DK) 47 J4
Nystad = Uusikaupunki (FIN) 34 H3
Nysted (DK) 66 F1
Nysteen (N) 30 E5
Nystrand (S) 27 G3
Nystuen (N) 31 H6
Nysund (N) 40 F4
Nyträsk (S) 26 F5
Nytrøa (N) 31 M4
Nyttjorp (S) 26 D7
Nyttorp (S) 40 G3
Nytuba (FIN) 28 F6
Nyvallen (S) 33 M3
Nyvoe's'k (UA) 150 E3
Nyvollen (N) 25 H5
Nyvoll (N) 18 F3
Nyvollen (N) 24 F7
Nyvollen (N) 31 M3
Nyvycy (UA) 149 L5
Nyystölö (FIN) 36 D2
Nyžankovyči (UA) 156 C2
Nyžne Vysoc'ke (UA) 156 D3
Nyžni Haji (UA) 156 E3
Nyžnij Bystryj (UA) 156 E5
Nyžni Jalovec' (UA) 157 G6
Nyžni Synivy (UA) 162 C2
Nyžni Vorota (UA) 156 D4
Nyžnja Rožanka (UA) 156 E4
Nyžnje Selyšče (UA) 161 G1

O

O (Avión) Igrexario (E) 110 C4
O (Tomiño) Seixo (E) 110 B5
Oaivoš (N) 18 E5
Oakamoor (GB) 58 D1
Oakengates-Donnington (GB) 58 C2
Oakham (GB) 58 F2
Oak Hill (GB) 57 J3
Oakley (GB) 58 E2
Oakley (GB) 57 M2
Oallolukta = Ållolukta (S) 21 J6
O Amenal (E) 110 C3
Oancea (RO) 171 G2
Oandu (EST) 131 M2
Oanes (N) 38 D5
Oarda (RO) 168 F1
Oarta de Jos (RO) 161 G3
Oaș, Călinești- (RO) 156 D6
Oaș, Negrești- (RO) 156 D6
Oba (TR) 139 K3
Obal' (BY) 139 L2
Obal' (BY) 139 M3
Oban (GB) 52 E2
Obaniv (UA) 156 C2
Obarok (H) 158 G3
Obârșia-Cloșani (RO) 167 L3
Obârșia (RO) 169 G6
Obbola (S) 26 G7
Obdach (A) 89 M3
Obecnice (CZ) 152 E4
Obedinenie (BG) 176 E2
Obejo (E) 128 E1
Obektası (TR) 185 J3
Obektaş (TR) 193 G5
Obeliai (LT) 133 M6
Obenheim (F) 79 H5
Oberalfeld (D) 80 E1
Oberammergau (D) 87 M2
Oberasbach (D) 80 D2
Oberaula (D) 72 A4
Oberaurach (D) 80 C1
Oberbergen (D) 79 H5
Oberbruch (D) 69 M5
Oberdrauburg (A) 90 C5
Ober Buchhorn (D) 81 G4
Oberderdingen (D) 79 K3
Oberdiessbach (CH) 86 E4
Oberdorf (D) 80 F4
Oberdorf im Burgenland (A) 91 K5
Oberdrauburg (A) 89 H4
Oberelsbach (D) 72 B5
Oberems (CH) 86 E5
Oberentfelden (CH) 86 F3
Obere Palfau (A) 91 G4
Oberes Gailtal (D) 80 E3
Oberfellabrunn (A) 153 K6
Oberfrohna, Limbach- (D) 152 C2
Obergeis (D) 72 B4
Obergloßhof (D) 79 H5
Obergrafenhain (D) 73 H4
Obergünzburg (D) 87 M1
Obergurgl (A) 88 D4
Oberhaching (D) 88 F1
Oberhambrechten (D) 79 J5
Oberharz am Brocken (D) 71 L3
Oberhaslach (F) 79 G4
Oberhausen (D) 70 C4
Oberhergheim (F) 79 G6
Oberhof (D) 72 C5
Oberhofen (D) 70 F4
Oberhollabrunn (D) 71 C4
Oberiaichlsberg (A) 90 E4
Oberkail (D) 70 C6
Oberkappel (A) 90 E2
Oberkirch (D) 79 J4
Oberkirch (D) 79 J5
Oberkirchen (D) 78 G2
Oberkochen (D) 80 C3
Oberkotzau (D) 152 A3
Oberkrich (A) 88 C3
Oberlahnstein (D) 70 D5
Oberleichtersbach (D) 72 B5
Oberlindhart (D) 152 B6
Oberlungwitz (D) 73 H4
Obermaiselstein (D) 87 L3
Obermarchtal (D) 79 M5
Obermaßfeld-Grimmenthal (D) 71 K5
Obermeitingen (D) 80 D5
Obermichelbach (D) 79 J2
Obermoschel (D) 79 H2
Obermühlhausen (D) 88 D2
Obermünchen (D) 80 F3
Obernberg am Brenner (A) 88 E3
Obernberg am Inn (A) 90 D3
Obernburg am Main (D) 79 L2
Oberndorf (D) 65 L4
Oberndorf (D) 79 K5
Oberndorf an der Melk (A) 91 J3
Oberndorf bei Salzburg (A) 81 H5
Obernfeld (D) 72 C3
Obernheim (D) 79 K5
Obernkirchen (D) 71 H2
Obernzell (D) 81 K3
Oberpfrimm (D) 80 C2
Oberpöring (D) 81 G3
Oberpurkla (D) 80 F5
Oberpullendorf (A) 158 C2
Oberrieden (D) 87 L1
Oberrohrbach (CH) 86 E3
Oberrot (A) 81 J6
Oberrot (D) 79 M3
Oberrüti (CH) 86 G3
Obersalzbach (A) 81 J5
Obersalzberg (D) 81 J5
Oberschleißheim (D) 80 F4
Oberschwappach (D) 80 C1
Obersdorf (D) 88 C4
Obersontheim (D) 79 M3
Obersdorf (D) 72 E6
Obersdorf (D) 87 L3
Oberstadt (D) 72 D5
Oberstaufen (D) 87 K2
Obersteinebach (D) 70 E5
Oberstenfeld (D) 79 L3
Oberstein, Idar- (D) 79 G2
Obersteinbach (F) 79 H4
Oberstorf (D) 80 E2
Oberstdorf (D) 87 L3
Obersulm (D) 79 L3
Obertal (A) 88 E3
Obertauern (A) 89 L3
Obertaufkirchen (D) 90 B3
Obertilliach (A) 88 G4
Obertraubling (D) 81 G2
Obertrum (A) 89 J2
Obertrum am See (A) 89 J2
Oberuckersee (D) 67 K4
Oberursel (D) 70 G6
Obervellach (A) 89 J4
Oberviechtach (D) 152 C4
Obervieschtach (D) 81 G1
Obervellach (A) 89 J4
Oberwart (A) 158 B3
Oberwarthe (D) 152 C7
Oberwiesenthal (D) 73 H5
Oberwil (CH) 86 E3
Oberwölz (A) 90 F5
Oberwölz Stadt (A) 90 F5
Obrabiach (D) 80 E5
Obzor (BG) 177 J3
Obrzycko (PL) 140 G5
Obudovac (BIH) 166 C6
Obrenovac (SRB) 166 F6
Obretenik (BG) 176 E1
Obrež (SRB) 166 F5
Obrež (SRB) 167 H6
O'Briensbridge (IRL) 62 E3
Obrigheim (D) 79 L3

Obříství (CZ) 146 A5
Obrocz (PL) 149 H4
Obrośyne (UA) 149 H4
Obrov (SLO) 164 C3
Obrovac (HR) 172 C1
Obrovac (SRB) 166 D3
Obrovac Sinjski (HR) 172 E2
Obrani (MK) 138 D3
Obrtiči (BIH) 166 C6
Obrubište (BIH) 176 E4
Obruk (MK) 155 H3
Obruk (TR) 193 F6
Obruk (TR) 193 H4
Obrzycko (PL) 140 G6
Obuchiv (UA) 151 M3
Obydcovy (UA) 151 K2
Obudovac (BIH) 166 C4
Obuhovo (RUS) 135 O5
Obychody (UA) 151 H1
Obzor (BG) 177 J3
Obżyle (PL) 140 G3
O Cádabo (Baleira) (E) 110 E2
O Cádavo (Baleira) = Cádabo (Baleira), O
  (E) 110 E2
O Cadramón (E) 110 E2
Očakovo (TR) 185 G6
Očakiv (UA) 13 J3
Očaklar (TR) 192 B5
Očarlı (TR) 182 C5
Ocaña (E) 110 E4
Ocaña (E) 96 D5
O Carizo (E) 110 E4
O Carballino (E) 110 C3
O Castillo (Salvaterra de Miño) = Salvaterra
  do Miño (E) 110 C4
Occhiobello (I) 99 M3
Occimiano (I) 98 F2
Ocomante (BG) 176 E3
Ocenego (I) 102 D2
Očeretnja (UA) 151 J5
Očeretuvata (UA) 163 G2
Oče Zagradska = Hoçé e Qytetit (RKS)
  174 B4
Ochaby (PL) 147 K6
Ochagavía (E) 114 A2
Ochey-Thuilley (F) 78 D4
Ochla (PL) 146 C2
Ochmativ (UA) 151 L5
Ochodze (PL) 147 H4
Ochojec (PL) 147 K6
Ocholt (D) 65 H5
Ochota (PL) 148 G1
Ochotivka (UA) 151 G4
Ochotnica Dolna (PL) 155 G2
Ochotnica Górna (PL) 153 L5
Ochoz u Brna (CZ) 153 H4
Ochsenfurt (D) 79 N2
Ochsenhausen (D) 88 A4
Ochsenwerder (D) 66 C4
Ochtendung (D) 70 D6
Ochtyrka (UA) N4
Ocieka (PL) 155 K1
Ocislovo (PL) 148 C4
Ockbrook (GB) 55 K5
Ockelbächen (S) 33 H6
Ockerö (S) 43 J3
Ockholm (D) 65 K2
Ocklla (D) 73 J3
Ockon (GB) 52 D1
Ocłova (SK) 154 E4
O Corvelo (E) 110 C4
Ocrkavlje (BIH) 173 J2
Ocsa (FIN) 159 H3
Ocsö (H) 160 A4
Ocsak (RO) 160 F4
Ocolis (RO) 161 G5
Ocón (E) 113 G4
Ocova (SK) 154 E4
Oč (S) 32 H1
Oda (S) 43 M3
Odabaşı (TR) 185 F6
Odáile (RO) 170 D3
Odâkres (S) 47 L1
Odalsverk (N) 40 A2
Odame (BG) 176 C2
Odda (N) 38 E2
Odden (N) 20 K1
Odden (N) 31 N2
Oddense (DK) 42 C5
Odder (DK) 46 F2
Oddi (IS) 16 F7
Oddsta (DK) 49 G2
Odeborg (S) 43 J1
Odeby (S) 40 H4
Odecerre (F) 89 B5
Odechowiec (PL) 148 D3
Odelfte (D) 124 E5
Odemira (P) 129 D5
Odemira (TR) 190 C4
Odemiş (TR) 185 F3
Odena (E) 115 G4
Odensala (S) 41 K4
Odensbacken (S) 41 J4
Odensjö (S) 43 M3
Odensjö (S) 44 D5
Odensvi (S) 41 J3
Odensvi (S) 45 J3
Oderberg (D) 67 L5
Oderljunga (S) 47 J2
Odermheim am Glan (D) 79 H2
Odersberg (D) 146 B4
Odesa (I) 13 J3
Ödesa (S) 80 B4
Odeshög (S) 47 H1
O Destierro (E) 110 E2
Odesos (BG) 161 G2
Ödestugu (S) 43 M2
Odiham (GB) 58 F5
Odivelre (P) 124 C3
Odivelas (P) 128 D6
Odjaci (SRB) 165 M3
Ödkarby (AX) 34 G4
Odnes (N) 31 N6
Odobeşti (RO) 170 E2
Odobeşti (RO) 147 H2
Ödolo (I) 99 J1
Odön (S) 32 H6
Odónak Iskelesi (TR) 181 G5
Odoom (GB) 64 F6
Odorec (RO) 161 F3
Odorhei Secuiesc (RO) 161 L5
Odorci (CY) 198 B5
Odranci (SLO) 165 G1
Odrinci (BG) 170 F6
Odrinci (Z) 148 C3
Odry (PL) 141 K3
Ödrzywół (PL) 148 D2
Oddoš (S) 40 B5
Østad (DK) 46 B2
Ostad (BIH) 173 H2
Odžak (BIH) 166 B3
Odžak (MNE) 173 K3
Odžak (MNE) 173 K3
Debielaska (LV) 103 H4
Oechesen (D) 72 C4
Oedeem (D) 68 E4
Oederquart (D) 65 L4
Oefelt (N) 70 A3
Oegstgeest (D) 69 G2
Deiras (P) 73 J2
Deira (D) 116 C6
Deisig (D) 70 F3
Deisnitz (D) 72 G5
Deisnitz (Erzgebirge) (D) 152 C2
Dencia (E) 110 F3
Denele Mari (RO) 169 G3
Densingen (CH) 84 D3
Oerel (D) 65 L3
Oer-Erkenschwick (D) 70 D3
Derlenbach (D) 71 K6
Derlinghausen (D) 70 F2
Derel (D) 68 B1
Derzen (D) 65 N5
Oestenreden (D) 70 F3
Oest Prätt Pämänten (RO) 169 H3
Oettingen in Bayern (D) 80 D3
Destrich-Winkel (D) 70 F6
Oettingen (D) 79 N2
Oetzen (D) 66 D4
Oeuf-en-Ternois (F) 63 J2
Oeversee (D) 65 F3
Oever (Den) (N) 64 C6
Oeversee (D) 65 L2
Ofena (I) 103 H3
Offagna (I) 101 J3
Offenbach am Main (D) 71 G6
Offenbach an der Queich (D) 79 J3
Offenberg (D) 81 H2
Offenburg (D) 79 H5
Offenberg (S) 33 L4
Offida (I) 101 K3
Offne (S) 25 J8
Ofterdingen (D) 79 L5
Ogardy (PL) 140 E5

Ogbourne Saint George (GB) 57 L3
Ögenbargen (D) 65 H4
Opesta (S) 41 L3
Oggebbio (I) 84 E2
Oggestorp (S) 44 E3
Oglaianco (UA) 132 H5
Oglaic (TR) 192 C5
Oglananas (TR) 190 C4
Oglansli (TR) 197 F1
Oglastro Cilento (I) 106 D2
Ogledi (BiH) 166 D6
Oglen (TR) 182 D6
Oglin (TR) 182 D6
Ognern (N) 21 K1
Ogny-au-Sea (GB) 57 G3
Ogmore Vale (GB) 57 G2
Ogna (S) 38 C5
Ogno (S) 177 G3
Ogrnanovo (BG) 170 F6
Ognyanovo (RUS) 135 M5
Ogonki (UA) 151 H3
Ogorelo (RUS) 135 M5
Ogori (PL) 142 F2
Ogorodyn (RUS) 135 O1
Ogoshte = Ogoshte (RKS) 175 G3
Ogosto (S) 161 J6
Ögra (LV) 133 K4
Ogrezeni (RO) 170 B5
Ogrodniki (PL) 142 D6
Ogrodzieniec (PL) 147 M5
Ogrosen (D) 73 L2
O Grove (E) 110 B4
Ogulin (HR) 164 E5
Oğuzeler (TR) 189 J4
Oğuzlar (TR) 185 J4
Ohaba (RO) 168 F1
Ohaba Lungă (RO) 160 D6
Ohanes (E) 126 E5
Ohcejohka = Utsjoki (FIN) 19 K4
Ohepalu (EST) 36 E6
Ohey (B) 69 J6
Ohey (GR) 176 A6
Ohiba (N) 38 C3
Ohl (D) 70 D4
Ohlendorf (D) 72 C1
Ohljadiv (UA) 149 L5
Ohrenheim (D) 80 G3
Ohrika (UA) 150 B5
Ohrnsvåg (N) 38 C3
Ohř (D) 56 B4
Oiartzun (E) 113 K2
Oia (E) 110 B5
Olen (GR) 69 H4
Oienga (HR) 129 B7
Oilgate (IRL) 63 A4
Oimbra (E) 110 E5
Oinaala (FIN) 36 B3
Oinasjärvi (FIN) 35 N3
Oinasmäki (FIN) 36 C5
Oion, Oyón (E) 113 G3
Oiron (F) 82 E3
Oirschot (NL) 69 J3
Oirterwijk (NL) 69 J3
Oisquerc (F) 76 D3
Oisterwijk (NL) 69 J3
Oisu (EST) 131 J4
Oişemont (F) 76 E2
Oisseau (F) 75 K4
Oiteni (UA) 151 K2
Oitti (FIN) 36 D3
Oittila (FIN) 28 F8
Oituz (RO) 170 D1
Oja (S) 47 N3
Oja (FIN) 23 M4
Oji (S) 115 J3
Ox (S) 44 F5
Oja (S) 45 N4
Ojaby (S) 44 F5
Ojakkala (FIN) 35 O4
Ojakylä (FIN) 23 J7
Ojakylä (FIN) 23 J4
Ojakylä (FIN) 28 F4
Ojala (FIN) 27 K8
Ojaka (FIN) 23 L2
Ojaperä (FIN) 27 K8
Ojalankulma (FIN) 35 O3
Ojanperä (FIN) 29 G6
Ojdogskoy (S) 32 G4
Ojing (S) 25 K7
Ojasoo (EST) 131 H2
Ojców (PL) 147 M5
Ojen (E) 128 E4
Ojebyn (S) 23 G6
Ojen (E) 128 E4
Ojdorvik (N) 31 N2
Ojos Negros (E) 120 F2
Ojuels (UA) 147 H2
Ojuelos, Los (E) 125 J3
Ojuelos Altos (E) 125 J3
Oyvallberget (S) 32 E4
Ojvasslan (S) 32 E4
Okaniai (LT) 137 L3
Okalevo (RUS) 141 M4
Okanykylä (FIN) 36 C2
Okana (LV) 124 E2
Okamy (H) 160 A6
Okcjul (TR) 193 J5
Okçu (TR) 185 F2
Okçukuy (TR) 185 F2
Okçular (TR) 182 D2
Okcukova (UA) 149 N4
Okkampohjan (GB) 64 F4
Oker (D) 71 K3
Okkelberg (N) 24 F7
Okkenhaug (N) 24 F7
Oklaj (HR) 172 D2
Okletac (SRB) 173 L1
Okkjuka (HR) 172 D1
Okkjanani (FIN) 23 J3
Ökna (S) 44 G4
Okna nåtten (S) 41 K4
Okny (UA) 163 J3
Okol (AL) 174 B4
Okoli (AL) 174 B4
Okol (PL) 148 E3
Okonek (PL) 140 E4
Okonin (PL) 141 J4
Okolo (S) 43 L4
Okons'k (UA) 144 C6
Okonin (PL) 141 K4
Okorici (BG) 177 G3
Okoriši, Ottendorf (D) 73 K3
Okov (S) 153 J5
Okrouhlá (CZ) 153 H4
Okrouhlice (CZ) 153 M4
Okruglica (UA) 164 E4
Ølme (S) 40 F5
Olmeda de la Cuesta (E) 120 D3
Olmeda del Rey (E) 120 D4
Ølmet (S) 43 L4
Ølmos (S) 29 G4
O, Nedrstaz (S) 32 E6
Ölme (S) 43 J4
Olnehy (Z) 148 C6
Olmsana (FIN) 23 L7
Ohlola (FIN) 23 L7
Olofsbo (S) 43 J5
Olofstorp (S) 43 K3
Olofström (S) 44 E6
Olomberga (I) 113 L7
Olomouc (CZ) 153 H4
Olocrue (HR) 172 D1
Olocuy (PL) 148 F3
Olsnik (PL) 147 F1
Olszak (TR) 198 C1
Olszy (BIH) 173 H1
Olsztyn (PL) 148 E3
Olsztyn (PL) 141 K4
Olkusz (PL) 147 M5
Olszanka (PL) 149 J2
Olszana (UA) 149 L6
Olszanica (PL) 149 H6
Olszany (PL) 147 F4
Olszowa (PL) 149 J3
Olszowa Wola (PL) 148 C2
Olteny (Z) 148 F4
Olszyny (PL) 142 E4
Olszyna (PL) 146 C3
Olszyna (PL) 141 K4
Olsztynek (PL) 141 L4
Olszyna (PL) 146 D5
Olszyny (PL) 146 B2

Oldebroek (NL) 69 K2
Oldeide (N) 30 C4
Oldekerk (NL) 64 E5
Oldemarkt (NL) 69 K2
Oldenal (N) 30 F4
Oldenbarg (D) 65 J5
Oldenburg in Holstein (D) 66 D2
Oldendorf (D) 72 F2
Oldendorf (D) 72 F2
Oldendorf an der Göhrde (D) 66 D4
Oldlansiri (TR) 197 F1
Ollastro Cilento (I) 106 D2
Olderdalen (N) 21 K1
Olderen (N) 16 G3
Oldersum (D) 64 G5
Oldervik (N) 18 B4
Oldervik (N) 17 G3
Oldham (GB) 55 J3
Oldhamstocks (GB) 53 L3
Old Hurst (GB) 59 G3
Oldisleben (D) 71 M4
Old Leake (GB) 58 C5
Oldmeldrum (GB) 51 N5
Old Radnor (GB) 57 G6
Olea (N) 66 B4
Olejów (PL) 149 L5
Olecko (PL) 136 H5
Oleggio (I) 98 F1
Oleiros (E) 110 D4
Omagh (GB) 61 H2
Omali (HR) 178 E4
Omalo (BG) 161 H2
Omalos (GR) 194 D5
Omarak (BG) 177 G4
Omarčevo (BG) 176 F4
Omarn (BiH) 165 H6
Omassa (FIN) 23 L1
Omboly (H) 160 A2
Ombrée-d'Anjou (F) 75 J5
Omereiro (E) 110 D2
Omeath (IRL) 63 A3
Omedu (EST) 131 M3
Omegna (I) 98 F6
Omenain (FIN) 29 J4
Omerhacik (TR) 193 G2
Omer Kaplıcaları (TR) 191 J3
Omerkoy (TR) 182 H6
Omerli (TR) 184 A4
Omerli (TR) 195 E6
Omencadayı (TR) 182 C2
Omessa (F) 96 E4
Omlynci (UA) 151 J6
Omhofter (N) 38 E3
Omis (HR) 172 E3
Omisalj (HR) 164 D4
Ommedal (N) 30 D4
Ommen (NL) 69 L1
Omnes (N) 39 J4
Omne (S) 26 B5
Omoljica (SRB) 179 H5
Omolica (SRB) 167 G4
Ona (N) 30 F2
Oncala, Val (E) 110 E4
Onano (I) 100 E6
Oncesti (PL) 149 E6
Onda (E) 121 J6
Ondara (E) 121 G4
Ondarra (I) 113 J3
Ondic (HR) 164 F6
Olias del Rey (E) 119 J4
Olib (HR) 164 D5
Oliena (I) 97 D3
Olette (F) 114 B6
Olevsk (UA) 150 E4
Onderga (RUS) 162 D5
Onda (I) 121 J6
Ondres (F) 88 F6
Onega (RUS) 11 B1
Oneglia (I) 98 D3
Onedra (RUS) 151 J6
Oneszti (RO) 170 D1
Onezamos (FIN) 35 O4
Onega (RUS) 162 E2
Önerler (TR) 182 E3
Onesse-et-Laharie (F) 92 B2
Onex (CH) 85 K4
Oneska (UA) 149 M6
Oni (GE) 11 H6
Onía (GR) 187 L7
Onkaineni (FIN) 36 F2
Onkijoki (FIN) 35 N3
Önkoy (FIN) 36 D3
Onkkaala (FIN) 35 O3
Onnadingen (D) 84 G4
Onnela (S) 32 G4
Onolala (FIN) 23 L7
Onolhals (S) 29 G4
Onset (FIN) 36 E2
Onstmettingen (D) 79 L5
Ontinyent (E) 121 G5
Ontojoki (FIN) 29 J6
Ontur (E) 120 E6
Olchov (HR) 171 K5
Oonga (EST) 130 D3
Ondo (LV) 131 J4
Ontinent (E) 121 G6
Ontojoki (FIN) 29 J6
Oondza (UA) 151 H3
Oongi (EST) 130 D2
Onziévena (F) 64 E4
Oostbur (NL) 68 D4
Oostende = Oostende (B) 68 B3
Oostende (B) 68 B3
Oosterbeek-Bad (D) 68 D4
Oosterhout (NL) 69 H3
Oosterzee (NL) 64 D6
Oosterzele (B) 68 B4
Oostham (B) 69 J3
Oostkapelle (NL) 68 D4
Oostkamp (B) 68 B3
Oostmalle (B) 69 G3
Oostrum (NL) 69 K3
Oost-Vlieland (NL) 64 D5
Oostvoorne (NL) 68 E3
Ootmarsum (NL) 70 C2
Opaka (BG) 176 F2
Opalej (BG) 176 F4
Opalenica (PL) 146 D1
Opálenica (SRB) 174 F1
Opalin (UA) 148 G2
Oparany (CZ) 152 F4
Oparty (CZ) 153 H6
Opava (CZ) 153 J4
Opatija (HR) 164 D4
Opatovac (HR) 166 B2
Opatov (CZ) 153 J4
Opatov (CZ) 153 H5
Opatovac (HR) 166 B2
Opatovice nad Labem (CZ) 153 J3
Opatów (PL) 148 D4
Opatów (PL) 147 J3
Opatówek (PL) 147 J2
Opatowiec (PL) 148 C4
Opava (CZ) 147 H6
Ope (S) 32 G3
Ophasselt (B) 68 B4
Ophovva (PL) 147 M5
Opi (I) 103 H5
Opishny (UA) 151 N4
Opisseni (FIN) 28 F6
Opočka (RUS) 135 J5
Opočno (CZ) 153 H2
Opoka (PL) 148 E4
Opoka Duża (PL) 148 D4
Opola (PL) 147 K3
Opolany (H) 73 J2
Opole (PL) 147 J4
Opole Lubelskie (PL) 148 E4
Opolno-Zdrój (PL) 152 G2
Oponowo (S) 42 D5
Oppedal (N) 30 D6
Oppeby (S) 42 H1
Oppegard (N) 31 N4
Oppelo (N) 30 F4
Oppeano (I) 99 K2
Oppenau (D) 79 J5
Oppenberg (A) 159 H5
Oppenheim (D) 70 F6
Oppenweiler (D) 80 A2
Oppenweiler-Rietenau (D) 80 A2
Oppewein (D) 64 F5
Oppstry (N) 40 B5
Oppenwehe (D) 64 F6
Oppido Lucano (I) 104 F6
Oppido Mamertina (I) 107 H5
Oppland (N) 38 D2
Oppurg (D) 72 B4

Olszyna (PL) 153 H1
Olszyny (PL) 155 J2
Olt, Drăgănești-Olt (RO) 169 H5
Oltan (TR) 184 D6
Oltania (TR) 189 J6
Olten (CH) 36 B3
Öltenj (RO) 169 J5
Olteni (RO) 169 J5
Oltenia (RO) 170 D5
Olteni (RO) 170 F5
Oltmannsfehn (D) 65 H5
Olto e Colle (I) 88 B6
Oltu (BY) 149 J2
Oltu (TR) 185 F6
Oltulan (BY) 64 G5
Olukbaşı (TR) 185 K3
Olukman (TR) 191 G3
Olukköy (TR) 199 H3
Olukoyağı (TR) 193 J6
Olukova (TR) 197 H3
Olula del Rio (E) 127 F5
Olune (E) 115 G3
Olvega (E) 113 J4
Olvera (E) 125 J6
Olvera (E) 125 J6
Olym (FIN) 35 H1
Olyka (UA) 151 H4
Oiyzarka (UA) 151 K2
Olza (PL) 147 K6
Olzheim (D) 70 B5
Omali (HR) 178 E4
Omuraki (BG) 177 G6
Omutnina (FIN) 29 J7
Onjaki (RUS) 151 J5
Onuria (RUS) 161 J3
Omuta (BIH) 166 D6
Onuta (BiH) 166 D6
Onalan (TR) 191 G5
Orani (I) 97 D3
Oranienbaum-Wörlitz (D) 73 G2
Oranienburg (D) 67 J6
Oranmore (IRL) 60 D6
Orašac (BiH) 165 K1
Orašac (MK) 173 H4
Orašje (BiH) 166 B2
Orašje (BY) 143 M3
Orašani (MNE) 173 J5
Orahovica (BiH) 173 G2
Orajärvi (FIN) 18 H8
Orakylä (FIN) 19 J6
Orani (I) 97 D3
Oranli (TR) 182 H5
Oranmore (IRL) 60 D6
Orašac (SRB) 179 G6
Orašje (BY) 143 M3
Orašje (BiH) 166 B2
Orange (F) 95 G2
Orani (I) 97 D3
Orash (RO) 170 D6
Orba (I) 122 A5
Orbais-l'Abbaye (F) 77 H4
Orbanija (MK) 172 F4
Orbassano (I) 98 C2
Örbäcken (S) 41 K2
Örbäck (S) 40 D6
Örberga (S) 47 H1
Orbetello (I) 100 F6
Orbetello Scalo (I) 100 F6
Örbottyan (H) 159 H2
Orbrieg (P) 83 J2
Ordruf (D) 72 A4
Orce (E) 127 F4
Örby (S) 43 J4
Orby (DK) 46 F2
Orby (DK) 42 E6
Örby (S) 41 L2
Orbyhus (S) 41 K2
Orce (E) 127 F4
Orcelles (UA) 149 L4
Orchomos (GR) 187 G6
Orchamps (F) 84 B1
Orchamps-Vennes (F) 84 C1
Orchies (F) 68 C5
Orchomenós (GR) 187 G6
Orchowo (PL) 147 H1
Orcières (F) 95 M1
Orcival (F) 83 M6
Orco Feglino (I) 98 E3
Ordăcioiu (RO) 170 A5
Ordejon de Arriba o San Juan (E) 112 C3
Orden (I) 98 D1
Orders (GB) 53 K2
Ordes (E) 110 C3
Ordheim (D) 80 C1
Ordona (I) 104 D4
Ordu (TR) 11 G5
Ordua (E) 112 F3
Orebić (HR) 172 F4
Örebro (S) 41 J4
Orechovno (RUS) 135 H5
Oredez (RUS) 135 G3
Orehova (UA) 163 G2
Orehovica (MK) 175 H5
Orehovo (RUS) 135 H4
Oreja (E) 119 G4
Orellana la Vieja (E) 118 E6
Orellana la Sierra o Orellanita (E) 125 J1
Öreman (S) 26 E5
Ören (TR) 185 G3
Ören (TR) 184 D4
Ören (TR) 190 D4
Ören (TR) 190 D5
Ören (TR) 191 H2
Oren (TR) 191 J6
Ören (TR) 196 C1
Oren (TR) 191 H6
Orsbäck (S) 26 F7
Orenburg (D) 80 B4
Orencik (TR) 184 D4
Orencik (TR) 191 H4
Orenhaus (D) 80 B4
Orenköy (TR) 182 C3
Örenler (TR) 190 E2
Ørenler (TR) 191 G6
Orenyayla (TR) 191 H3
Orense = Ourense (E) 110 D4
Orentano (I) 99 J6
Oreokastro (GR) 175 H7
Orešak (BG) 176 D2
Orešec (MK) 175 H5
Oresmaux (F) 76 F2
Orešnica (BG) 177 K4
Orešnik (BG) 176 D4
Orestiada (GR) 181 G3
Oreye (B) 69 H6
Orford (GB) 59 J4
Orgal (TR) 182 D3
Orgañà (E) 114 F3
Organyà (E) 114 F3
Organós (GR) 186 F5
Orgaz (E) 119 J4
Orgelet (F) 84 B3
Örgeyaylası (TR) 192 A6
Orgères-en-Beauce (F) 76 E4
Orgibet (F) 114 C3
Orgiva (E) 126 D5
Orglandes (F) 75 J2
Orgoglio (MD) 163 H4
Orgon (F) 95 G3
Orgosolo (I) 97 D3
Orgovány (H) 159 H4
Ořechov (CZ) 153 H4
Oria (I) 105 H6
Oria (E) 127 F5
Orihuela (E) 127 G3
Orihuela del Tremedal (E) 120 E2
Orikhiv (UA) 13 L2
Orikum (AL) 178 B3
Ørik (N) 30 D4
Orimattila (FIN) 36 E3
Orimlahti (FIN) 35 H2
Orinbyn (FIN) 23 M6
Orini (GR) 176 A6
Orino (I) 98 F6
Orino (I) 98 F6

Orini (FIN) 35 M2
Oriniemi (RO) 162 E6
Oriniemi (FIN) 35 O1
Orini (GR) 107 H5
Oriolo (I) 107 H5
Oriolo Romano (I) 102 E3
Oriovac (HR) 165 K4
Oripää (FIN) 35 L3
Orisberg (FIN) 28 E6
Orissa (FIN) 173 G3
Orisaare (EST) 130 D3
Oriszentpéter (H) 158 B4
Ørje (N) 31 N7
Orkanger (N) 24 B7
Orizare (BG) 177 J3
Orizovo (BG) 176 D4
Örkelljunga (S) 47 J2
Orkendorf (D) 72 C1
Örken (S) 43 L5
Orkonbasi (TR) 193 J6
Orla (BY) 143 J5
Orla (PL) 142 F6
Orla (BY) 143 J5
Orlane = Orlan (RKS) 174 F3
Örlenbach (D) 71 H6
Orle (PL) 141 H3
Orléans (F) 76 E5
Orlec (HR) 164 D5
Orlea (RO) 169 H6
Orlik (RUS) 135 N1
Ørnik (AL) 174 C6
Orlino (BG) 161 F4
Orljava o de Sus (RO) 168 E2
Orlová (CZ) 147 K6
Orlovac (BG) 177 F4
Orlovka (RUS) 135 N3
Örlovo (RUS) 141 O2
Orlik (RUS) 135 N3
Orly (F) 76 F4
Orljane (BG) 176 D2
Orljakovo (BG) 176 E3
Orljane (BG) 161 E3
Orlyak (BG) 177 J1
Ormož (SLO) 164 F2
Ormelle (I) 98 D1
Ormos (GR) 188 E4
Ormos (GR) 189 J4
Ormos Korinthou (GR) 187 H6
Ormos Panormou (GR) 189 F4
Ormos Prinou (GR) 180 E4
Ornäs (S) 40 H3
Ørnes (N) 17 O2
Örna (PL) 189 G5
Ornans (F) 89 J4
Orneta (PL) 141 L3
Ørnhøj (DK) 46 C1
Orneta (PL) 141 L3
Ornö (S) 41 L4
Orňava (SK) 154 A3
Oropos (GR) 187 H6
Oropa (I) 98 E1
Orosei (I) 97 D3
Oroszlány (H) 159 G2
Orotell (I) 97 D3
Orsha (BY) 10 E5
Orsay (F) 76 F4
Orsova (RO) 168 E3
Orsk (RUS) 11 N5
Ørslev (DK) 48 E3
Ørslev (DK) 42 E6
Orsmaal-Gussenhoven (B) 69 J5
Ørsnes (N) 30 F2
Orsomarso (I) 106 F3
Orşova (RO) 168 E3
Ørsta (N) 30 E3
Ørsted (DK) 43 G5
Örstorp (S) 43 M3
Örsund (S) 33 H5
Orta (I) 98 F6
Orta di Atella (I) 106 C1
Orta Nova (I) 104 E4
Ortaca (TR) 196 D2
Ortaca (TR) 191 G5
Ortakent (TR) 190 C4
Ortakent (TR) 191 H5
Ortakent (TR) 184 A4
Ortaklar (TR) 185 F3
Ortaklar (TR) 192 B5
Ortaköy (TR) 182 C5
Ortaköy (TR) 185 G4
Ortaköy (TR) 185 H6
Ortaköy (TR) 193 H2
Ortaköy (TR) 185 H2
Ortaköy (TR) 189 J6
Ortaca (TR) 191 G6
Orta San Giulio (I) 98 F6
Ortaoba (TR) 184 E4
Ortatepe (TR) 193 F6
Ortauk (UA) 149 G4
Orte (I) 102 E2
Orteşti (RO) 170 E2
Ortenberg (D) 79 J5
Ortenberg (D) 71 H5
Ortenburg (D) 81 J2
Orterer Krolewski Pierwszy (D) 149 G4
Orthez (F) 113 M1
Ortigosa (E) 113 G4
Ortigueira (E) 110 E1
Ortilla (E) 114 B4
Ortnevik (N) 30 E5
Orto (I) 97 D4
Ortoki (BIH) 173 G2
Ortona (I) 103 J4
Ortover (RO) 160 D1
Ortucchio (I) 103 H5
Orturli (TR) 191 K5
Ortürli (TR) 192 C3
Orubica (HR) 165 K4
Oruç (TR) 182 E6
Orune (I) 97 D3
Oružjano (SRB) 174 E2
Orval (DK) 42 G5
Orvault (F) 81 H3
Orvelte (NL) 64 E6
Orvenmäki (FIN) 28 F7
Orvieto (I) 100 G6
Orvilliers-Saint-Julien (F) 77 H4
Orvinio (I) 102 F3
Oryaktan (TR) 192 B6
Ory (PL) 147 K5
Orzechowo (PL) 147 H1
Orzechówka (PL) 149 H6
Orzechowo (PL) 141 L3
Orzesze (PL) 147 K5
Orzinuovi (I) 99 G2
Orzrmy (PL) 141 M4
Orzola (E) 125 D6
Orzyny (PL) 141 L4
Orzysz (PL) 142 D4
Os (N) 25 G5
Os (N) 24 F4
Osada, Czyżew- (PL) 142 G5
Osada, Kuczbork- (PL) 141 L5

Orió (S) 45 H2
Orion (SB) 53 K6
Orissare (EST) 130 D3
Orita (PL) 120 E3
Orjaku (EST) 130 D2
Orianta (PL) 159 G5
Ořechov (CZ) 153 J4
Oreland (N) 24 D7
Ørrin (N) 24 F4
Ørsten (N) 30 E3
Örträsk (S) 26 E6
Orvala (S) 33 J3
Os (N) 24 E5
Osbeveren (D) 70 D3
Ørsbirk (D) 46 E2
Orta (F) 185 G2
Osbakk (N) 17 N6
Osby (S) 44 E6
Osecina (SRB) 166 E5
Osek (CZ) 152 D2
Oskamen (SE) 175 K5
Oskarström (S) 43 K4
Osilo (I) 97 C2
Osing (FIN) 36 C5
Osny (F) 76 F3
Osova (I) 98 D5
Osten (D) 65 L4
Österby (S) 40 H6
Ösaterby (S) 32 G5
Österbybruk (S) 41 N2
Östersund (S) 32 G3
Osterholz-Scharmbeck (D) 65 K5
Osternienburg (D) 73 G2
Osterode am Harz (D) 71 K3
Österode (S) 26 F5
Osterwald (D) 64 F6
Osterwieck (D) 72 D2
Ostia Antica (I) 102 E4
Ostiano (I) 99 J2
Ostiglia (I) 99 L2
Ostrach (D) 88 A3
Ostra Ed (S) 45 K3
Östra Ed (S) 45 K3
Östra Flakaträsk (S) 27 K2
Östra Flytte (S) 45 K3
Östra Grevie (S) 47 H4
Östraha (HR) 172 D1
Ostra Ljungby (S) 47 H3
Östramark (S) 41 K3
Ostra Merasjärvi (S) 19 J8
Östra Skrukby (S) 44 F1
Östra Vemmenhög (S) 47 J4
Östra Torp (S) 41 L4
Ostrau (D) 72 E3
Ostrhauderfehn (D) 64 G5
Osterfeld (D) 72 E3
Ostritz (D) 153 G1
Ostroda (PL) 141 L4
Ostrożany (PL) 142 F5
Ostróg (UA) 151 G4
Ostroh (UA) 151 G4
Ostróda (PL) 141 L4
Ostrołęka (PL) 142 C4
Ostromer (CZ) 153 H2
Ostrov (CZ) 152 D2
Ostrov (RO) 170 E5
Ostrov (RO) 169 L4
Ostrov (RUS) 135 H4
Ostrov (BG) 176 C1
Ostrov (RO) 170 F4
Ostroveni (RO) 169 G6
Ostrovno (BY) 143 M2
Ostrovica (SRB) 175 G2
Ostrovul (RO) 168 D3
Ostrów (PL) 155 K1
Ostrówek (PL) 148 C3
Ostrówek (PL) 148 E3
Ostrów Lubelski (PL) 142 F6
Ostrów Mazowiecka (PL) 142 E5
Ostrówek (PL) 147 L3
Ostrowiec (PL) 140 D4
Ostrowiec Świętokrzyski (PL) 148 D4
Ostrowite (PL) 147 K1
Ostrowite (PL) 141 H5
Ostrów Wielkopolski (PL) 147 H2
Ostrowy nad Okszą (PL) 147 M4
Ostrowy (PL) 148 G1
Ostrowy (PL) 141 L4
Ostrożany (PL) 142 F5
Ostroszowice (PL) 146 F5
Ostróżnica (PL) 147 J4
Ostrv (CZ) 153 H5
Ostuni (I) 105 H5
Osula (EST) 131 M6
Osuna (E) 125 K4
Osuschy (UA) 151 J2
Osvjata (RUS) 135 J6
Oswaldkirk (GB) 55 L2
Oswestry (GB) 57 G4
Oswetim (PL) 147 L5
Oszczów (PL) 149 H3
Oszelno (PL) 147 K4
Oszki (PL) 148 F3
Oszmiany (BY) 137 M5

Östanskär (S) 33 N2
Ostapy (UA) 151 G2
Östavall (S) 32 G1
Östavik (FIN) 34 F7
Ostbevern (D) 70 E2
Östbjörka (S) 40 G2
Östbro (S) 32 B1
Ostby (N) 25 J5
Ostby (S) 32 G2
Osted (DK) 47 J2
Oster Bjerregrav (DK) 42 E5
Osterbo (N) 30 G6
Oster Højst (DK) 46 F4
Oster (TR) 190 D4
Östergötland (S) 41 L2
Osterbruch (D) 65 L3
Østerbyen (D) 42 D3
Øster-Åkarp (S) 26 G6
Oster Assels (DK) 42 C5
Öster Bjerregrav (DK) 42 E6
Österby (S) 43 K3
Österbymo (S) 44 G2
Österbybruk (S) 41 N2
Öster-Ålden (S) 26 G4
Östergötland (S) 41 L2
Osternienburg (D) 73 G2
Ostenfeld (D) 65 K2
Österforse (S) 33 H1
Österhaninge (S) 41 L4
Østerild (DK) 42 C4
Osterhofen (D) 81 H2
Osterholz-Scharmbeck (D) 65 K5
Osterode am Harz (D) 71 K3
Osterröd (S) 65 M6
Osterwieck (D) 72 D2
Ostby (S) 32 G1
Ostrach (D) 88 A3
Ostrogen (D) 71 K2
Ostheim vor der Rhön (D) 71 K6
Ostiano (I) 99 J2
Ostiglia (I) 99 L2
Ostmarsch (D) 64 F6
Ostmannheim (D) 79 H6
Ostrau (D) 72 E3
Ostranda (RUS) 135 M4
Ostra Nye (S) 44 F3
Osterode (S) 26 F5
Osterwald (D) 64 F6
Osterwieck (D) 72 D2
Ostheim (D) 79 K1
Östhammar (S) 41 N2
Osbark (N) 17 N6
Osterburg (Altmark) (D) 66 F6
Osterburken (D) 80 B2
Ostercappeln (D) 70 F2
Ostereistedt (D) 65 L5
Osterfeld (D) 72 E3
Osterhever (D) 65 J2
Osterhofen (D) 81 H2
Osterholz-Scharmbeck (D) 65 K5
Osterrode am Harz (D) 71 K3
Osterwick (D) 70 D2
Osterwieck (D) 72 D2
Ostheim (D) 79 K1
Östhammar (S) 41 N2
Osthausen-Wülfershausen (D) 72 A4
Ostiano (I) 99 J2
Ostiglia (I) 99 L2
Ostiano (I) 99 J2
Ostra (I) 101 J2
Ostra Vaccia (I) 101 J2
Ostrach (D) 88 A3
Ostramondra (D) 72 B3
Ostrau (D) 72 E3

Osula (E) 125 J5
Osvallen (S) 32 D2
Osvärmany (D) 138 H1
Osvhirany (D) 142 E3
Os Verdiales (E) 110 C2
Oswestry (GB) 57 G4
Osztyko (PL) 147 J3
Oszczów (PL) 149 H3
Otava (FIN) 35 J3
Otelfingen (CH) 84 F3
Oteo (E) 112 F3
Oter de Herreros (E) 119 H2
Otero de las Dueñas (E) 111 H3
Oterstad (S) 43 J4
Otes (S) 26 E7
Otey (FIN) 29 H6
Otegn (MK) 178 D7
Oteşani (RO) 169 G3
Oterber (D) 26 G6
Otepää (EST) 131 L5
Oteřemy (FIN) 23 L7
Oteriarde (FIN) 23 L7
Oterma (FIN) 23 L4
Oteşti (RO) 169 H4
Otesivka (UA) 163 K2
Otheim (D) 65 N4
Othni (GR) 178 A5
Othonoi (GR) 187 J2
Oti (S) 26 E4
Otışani (RO) 170 F2
Otivar (E) 126 C5
Otkryta (RUS) 151 G6
Otmuchów (PL) 147 G4
Otman (TR) 197 E1
Otmanice (PL) 147 J2
Otnes (N) 31 M4
Otočac (HR) 164 E6
Otočec (SLO) 164 E3
Otok (HR) 172 D2
Otok (HR) 172 F2
Otok (HR) 166 B2
Otoka (BIH) 165 H4
Otorowo (PL) 146 D1
Otovica (MK) 175 G5
Otranto (I) 105 L6
Otrokovice (CZ) 153 J5
Otslav (RUS) 151 K5
Otta (N) 31 M4
Ottana (I) 97 D3
Ottaviano (I) 106 C1
Ottavarpet (S) 26 E3
Ottenbüren (D) 87 H5
Ottenby (S) 45 K6
Ottenhöfen im Schwarzwald (D) 79 J5
Ottensheim (A) 90 C1
Ottenstein (D) 72 C2
Otter (D) 65 M5
Otterbach (D) 79 H2
Otterberg (D) 70 F6
Otterbach (D) 79 H2
Otterfing (D) 88 E3
Otterndorf (D) 65 K4
Otterø (N) 31 L6
Otteröy (S) 24 E5
Otterswick (D) 64 G4
Otterup (DK) 46 E3
Otterville (F) 76 E3
Otterwisch (D) 72 F3
Ottnang am Hausruck (A) 89 K1
Ottobeuren (D) 87 J4
Ottobrunn (D) 88 E2
Ottonträsk (S) 26 F6
Ottraw (GB) 50 G4
Ottrott (F) 79 J5
Ottveny (H) 158 E2
Ouanne (F) 77 H5
Ouchas (GB) 59 G2
Oud-Beijerland (NL) 69 G3
Oud-Gastel (NL) 69 G3
Ouddorp (NL) 64 D6
Oudekerk (NL) 64 D6
Oude Pekela (NL) 64 G5
Ouder-Amstel (NL) 69 H2
Oudesluis (NL) 64 C6
Oudewater (NL) 69 H2
Oud Gastel (NL) 64 D5
Ouges (F) 84 A2
Ouhei (N) 31 K5
Ougney (F) 84 B2
Ouistreham (F) 75 L2
Oulainen (FIN) 23 J6
Oulanka (FIN) 27 L1
Oulart (IRL) 63 B4
Ouletta (F) 96 E4
Oulains (GB) 50 G4
Oulches (F) 82 F3
Oulchy-le-Château (F) 77 H3
Oulainen (FIN) 23 J6
Oulu (FIN) 23 K5
Oulujoki (FIN) 23 L5
Oulunsalo (FIN) 23 J5
Oundle (GB) 58 D3
Ouranoupoli (GR) 180 D5
Ourém (P) 116 D3
Ourense (E) 110 D4
Ourville-en-Caux (F) 76 D2
Ousse (F) 92 D4
Outakoski (FIN) 19 J4
Outeiro (P) 111 G5
Outeiro da Cabeça (P) 116 C5
Outeiro de Rei (E) 110 E3
Outes (E) 110 B3
Outines (F) 77 K4
Outomuro (E) 110 C4
Outrup (DK) 46 B3
Outwell (GB) 58 E3
Ouville-le-Marche (F) 76 E2
Ouzouer-le-Marché (F) 76 E5
Ouzouer-sur-Loire (F) 76 F5
Ouzouer-sur-Trézée (F) 77 G5

Ovčarovo (BG) 177 G2
Ovelgönne (D) 65 J5
Ovčl Kladenec (BG) 177 F4
Qveçler (TR) 184 E2
Oved (E) 47 N2
Overa (UA) 149 N4
Overammer (D) 71 J2
Överbo (S) 33 J3
Overesjö (S) 43 J3
Överhörnäs (S) 26 E6
Overjenstad (D) 71 G2
Overborg (S) 32 G3
Överby (S) 33 J3
Överby (S) 34 G5
Överby (S) 34 D5
Överby (S) 39 D5
Övergran (S) 41 K4
Överhmi (S) 41 M4
Overhaanen (S) 41 M3
Överänäset (N) 30 G2
Överhogdal (S) 32 G2
Övre Ardal (N) 30 H5
Överberg (S) 32 G3
Övermark (FIN) 28 C6
Övermö (S) 33 J3
Överön (S) 26 E6
Övertällje (S) 41 K4
Övre Bole (S) 23 J6
Övre Eide (N) 30 F2
Övre Jervik (N) 18 A2
Övre Jordet (N) 31 M4
Övre Kilen (N) 31 N5
Överlida (S) 43 K4
Övre Ringdal (N) 30 F4
Överlänna (S) 44 B4
Övermark (FIN) 28 C6
Övermo (S) 40 G2
Överö (AX) 34 G5
Övre Rendal (N) 31 M4
Övre Rindal (N) 24 B8
Övre Ramse (S) 44 E5
Övre Sätra (S) 33 H6
Övre Soppero (S) 18 F7
Övre Tväråselet (S) 22 G5
Övre Vojakkala (S) 22 G3
Övre Ä (N) 24 B7
Övsjö (S) 32 F2
Övtrup (DK) 46 B3
Ovčarovo (BG) 177 G2
Ovar (P) 116 D1
Övre Ullern (DK) 47 J4
Övre Espedal (N) 38 D4
Ovre Gärdsjö (S) 33 J6
Ox-Vestersjö (S) 41 M5
Övre Jervan (N) 24 D7
Övrerängen (S) 33 H2
Oxby (DK) 46 B3
Oxel (GB) 55 H4
Oxford (GB) 58 A4
Oxie (S) 47 H4
Oxilithos (GR) 187 J2
Oxnead (GB) 59 H2
Oxsjön (S) 33 H2
Oxton (GB) 53 K3
Oyace (I) 84 D6
Oyam (TR) 193 H5
Oyardıbı (TR) 192 B6
Øye (N) 31 L5
Øye (N) 30 E3
Øye (N) 24 B6
Øyer (N) 31 M5
Øyeren (N) 31 N5
Oygarden (N) 30 E4
Oykel Bridge (GB) 50 F3
Oymaağaç (TR) 184 E4
Oymalı (TR) 192 D5
Oymalı (TR) 195 F4
Oymapınar (TR) 196 B1
Øymark (N) 31 N7
Oynak (TR) 195 F5
Øyon (N) 30 G3
Oysayla (TR) 192 A6
Oyóndarri (E) 113 G3
Øysletta (N) 24 F3
Øystese (N) 30 E6
Øyulvstad (N) 30 F5
Øyungen (N) 24 D6
Oyuntepe (TR) 189 J3
Øyvatn (N) 38 F3
Ozalj (HR) 164 E4
Ożanna (PL) 149 G5
Ozarów (PL) 148 E4
Ozarów (PL) 148 C2
Ozarów Mazowiecki (PL) 148 C1
Özbek (TR) 185 E2
Özbel (TR) 192 C5
Özburun (TR) 193 G3
Ozd (H) 160 A2
Özdemirci (TR) 191 H4
Özdenek (TR) 184 B6
Ozga (UA) 149 M6
Ozierany (PL) 149 H1
Özhöyük (TR) 193 J5
Ozieri (I) 97 D2
Ozimek (PL) 147 K4
Ozimica (BIH) 166 B5
Oziersk (RUS) 141 M2
Oziora (PL) 148 E4
Ozoir-la-Ferrière (F) 76 F4
Ozolnieki (LV) 133 J4
Ozoli (LV) 132 G4
Ozora (H) 159 F4
Ozorków (PL) 147 L2
Ozourt (F) 92 B4
Ozren (BIH) 173 K1
Özükini (TR) 193 F2
Ozun (RO) 170 C1
Ozzano dell'Emilia (I) 99 M4

A B C D E F G H I J K L M N O P Q R S T U V W

Reichenau an der Rax (A) 91 J4
Reichenau im Mühlkreis (A) 90 F3
Reichenbach (CH) 88 E4
Reichenbach (D) 79 H6
Reichenbach (D) 79 K2
Reichenbach/Oberlausitz (D) 146 B3
Reichenbach im Vogtland (D) 152 B2
Reichenbach-Reichenau (D) 73 K3
Reichenberg (D) 67 L5
Reichenhofen (D) 90 C3
Reichenhofen (D) 90 B5
Reichenhofen (D) 80 B3
Reichenberg (D) 67 K5
Reichertshausen (D) 80 F4
Reichertsheim (D) 80 B3
Reichertshofen (D) 80 E3
Reichmannsdorf (D) 71 M5
Reichshof (D) 70 E6
Reichshoffen (F) 79 H4
Reichstädt (D) 73 K4
Reiden (CH) 86 E3
Reidenbach (CH) 86 D4
Reiff (D) 50 G3
Reifferscheid (D) 70 B6
Reigada, La (E) 111 F2
Reignac (F) 92 D6
Reignier (F) 85 K4
Reigoldswil (H) 86 E2
Reila (FIN) 32 K6
Reilm (F) 77 K3
Reimüller (A) 90 G5
Rein (N) 34 D7
Reina (E) 105 H4
Reinach (AG) (CH) 86 F3
Reinbek (D) 54 N4
Reinberg-Litschau (A) 153 H6
Rein dalsaeter (N) 30 A5
Reine (N) 20 C5
Reinfeld (Holstein) (D) 66 C3
Reinfjellet (N) 25 J2
Reinhardsh (N) 18 D3
Reinhardtsgrimma (D) 72 B3
Reinhardtsgrimma (D) 73 K4
Reininge (F) 86 D2
Reinøya (N) 31 L6
Reinosa (E) 112 C2
Reinsdorf (D) 72 B2
Reinsfeld (D) 78 F2
Reinsliseter (N) 31 N3
Reinsnos (N) 38 B3
Reinstadt (D) 71 M5
Reinsvoll (N) 31 O6
Reinthal (A) 153 L6
Reira (TR) 192 C4
Reisbach (D) 90 C2
Reisdorf (D) 78 E2
Reischach (D) 90 C5
Reisjärvi (FIN) 27 L7
Reiskirchen (D) 71 G5
Reistad (N) 20 E3
Reistad (N) 39 M3
Reitan (N) 32 A2
Reitano (I) 106 B7
Reitdorf (A) 81 J6
Reit im Winkl (D) 81 G5
Reitkalli (FIN) 36 H3
Reittiu (FIN) 29 H5
Reitzengeschwenda (D) 71 N5
Reizenstein (D) 152 D2
Reja (N) 151 N3
Rejowa (SK) 155 G4
Rejowiec (PL) 149 H3
Rejowiec Fabryczny (PL) 149 H3
Reka (C) 154 D2
Rekawice (RUS) 165 J5
Rekeland (N) 38 D6
Reken (D) 69 N3
Rekijoki (FIN) 35 N4
Rekivaara (FIN) 29 L7
Rekovac (I) 147 M2
Rekova (I) 114 S4
Rekovac (SRB) 167 N8
Rejkov (PL) 153 L2
Rekowo Lipborskie (PL) 141 J1
Reksa (N) 24 D7
Reksnes (N) 30 D4
Rekszowice (PL) 147 L4
Rekta (BY) 145 N2
Rekuby (FIN) 35 L5
Relki (N) 21 H1
Relecq-Kerhuon, Le (F) 74 C4
Reliquias (P) 104 D4
Relijovo (BG) 175 K4
Rellanos (E) 111 F2
Relleu (E) 123 G7
Relleu (E) 127 K2
Rellingen (D) 66 B3
Rélmagen (D) 70 D6
Rémalard-en-Perche (F) 76 C5
Remanzacco (I) 164 A2
Rembeck (TR) 192 B3
Rembeccourt-aux-Pots (F) 77 M4
Remblinghausen (D) 70 F4
Remeda-Teichel (D) 71 M5
Remelo (D) 65 H6
Remeskylä (FIN) 29 G4
Remeta (RO) 160 D2
Remeta (RO) 161 L4
Remeta Chicurului (RO) 161 H2
Remeta Mare (RO) 168 A2
Remedo (N) 160 F4
Remezovci (UA) 152 G2
Remeln (D) 71 N5
Rémilly (F) 78 E3
Remeremont (F) 78 F6
Remich (L) 78 E3
Remmem (S) 36 E7
Remmen (S) 32 K3
Remmes (S) 36 G2
Remolinos (E) 114 A4
Remoncourt (F) 95 H2
Remouchamps (B) 79 K6
Remoulins (F) 94 E3
Rempstone (GB) 58 E2
Rempston (D) 74 F4
Rementod (D) 70 D4
Remsfeld (D) 72 A3
Remagne (F) 74 F5
Remuzat (F) 95 H7
Rena (N) 31 P5
Renac (F) 84 E4
Renaison (F) 84 F4
Renas (S) 25 K7
Renales (E) 120 C2
Renazé (F) 75 J5
Rencinii (LV) 131 H5
Renchen (D) 79 J4
Renda (LV) 132 E3
Rende (I) 109 G5
Renedo (E) 111 K5
Renedo (E) 112 C2
Renedo de Valderaduey (E) 111 K3
Renfree (GB) 52 G3
Rengshausen (D) 72 B3
Rengsjö (S) 33 M5
Renholmen (S) 22 D6
Reni (UA) 173 L5
Renielias (E) 113 G5
Reningelst (B) 68 D5
Renkenberge (D) 64 G6
Renko (FIN) 36 D3
Renkomäki (FIN) 36 G3
Renmark (S) 36 H2
Renmaz (CH) 86 C5
Rennbu (N) 31 M2
Rennerod (D) 70 F5
Rennertshofen (D) 80 E3
Rennes (F) 75 H4
Rennes-les-Bains (F) 93 J5
Renningen (D) 79 K4
Renoras (N) 30 B3
Renovica (BIH) 173 J2
Renqushausen (D) 79 H5
Renström (S) 22 C5
Renrij (S) 25 L4
Rensjön (S) 21 L8
Rensø (S) 22 K8
Reńska Wieś (PL) 147 J5
Renström (S) 26 G5
Renth (E) 130 F2
Rentería = Errentería (E) 113 H2
Rentilä (S) 28 G4
Rentina (GR) 179 K3
Rentina (GR) 179 H5
Renviken (S) 26 E3
Renwez (F) 71 H5
Renzow (D) 66 E3
Repbäcken (S) 40 H1
Repcelak (H) 158 C3
Repedea (RO) 156 F6
Repel (F) 78 D5
Rep'evka (RUS) 37 M4
Repojoki (FIN) 14 G6
Reposi (RUS) 37 M4
Repojoki (FIN) 28 B7
Repooki (FIN) 19 F7
Reppen (D) 67 G2
Reppenstedt (D) 66 D4
Reppe, Le (F) 85 J4
Represa del Condado (E) 111 J3
Repstad (N) 38 D6
Repovesi (N) 162 E2
Repvåg (N) 15 H2
Requejo (E) 111 H4
Requeixo (E) 121 K2
Requista (F) 93 K2
Regadyie (TR) 191 K8
Regadiye (TR) 182 F6

Resana (I) 88 F6
Resanovci (BIH) 165 G6
Resavica (SRB) 167 J5
Reschen = Resia (I) 87 L4
Resdere (TR) 189 H3
Resele (S) 25 M8
Reselec (BG) 176 B2
Resell (N) 31 M1
Resen (BG) 176 B2
Resen (MK) 178 E2
Resenbro (DK) 46 E1
Resenje (N) 91 N6
Résjajrni (HR) 165 J4
Rešetry (RUS) 133 G4
Resia (I) 87 L4
Rešita (RO) 168 B3
Resutta (I) 88 A3
Reskyem (N) 39 K4
Resku (L) 140 D3
Resku (L) 174 D5
Reškuténai (LT) 138 D3
Resmo (S) 45 J5
Resnik (SRB) 167 F4
Resö (S) 39 G5
Respenda de la Peña (E) 111 K3
Resovo (SI) 71 J1
Ressons-sur-Matz (F) 77 G2
Restelica = Restelicë (RKS) 174 E5
Rester = Reters (F) 75 J5
Reston (GB) 53 L3
Restöd (S) 43 J2
Resuler (TR) 183 L3
Resuttaro (I) 109 F2
Reszel (PL) 136 E5
Retamal (E) 125 H2
Retamoso (E) 127 F6
Retamoso (E) 119 G4
Retascón (E) 121 F1
Retaud (F) 82 D5
Reteag (RO) 161 J3
Retelo (SLO) 93 H4
Retford (GB) 55 L4
Retgendorf (D) 66 F3
Retherm (Aller) (D) 66 A5
Rethi (AR) 187 E3
Rethimno (GR) 186 D5
Rettousse (F) 93 H4
Retie (B) 69 J4
Retiers (F) 75 J5
Retiro (E) 110 E5
Retkoz (CZ) 73 M6
Retlefsdorf (D) 72 C4
Retníi (GR) 52 B6
Retormond (D) 69 G6
Retortillo de Soria (E) 112 F6
Retournac (F) 84 F6
Retsag (H) 154 F6
Retschow (D) 47 J5
Rétszilas (H) 158 G4
Rettenbach, Markt (D) 87 K2
Rettenberg (D) 90 D2
Rettenegg (A) 91 J5
Rettenschöss (A) 89 L6
Rettert (A) 80 D6
Reuden (Anhalt) (D) 73 G1
Reudnitz (D) 152 B2
Reugny (F) 76 C7
Reugny (F) 83 L4
Reuilly (F) 83 K4
Reuland (B) 69 L6
Reusel (NL) 69 H4
Reuskula (RUS) 29 L8
Reutel (MD) 162 F3
Reutenbach Stüvenhagen (D) 67 H3
Reuth (D) 152 A3
Reith bei Erbendorf (D) 72 G6
Reutte (A) 80 D6
Reuver (NL) 69 L4
Revda (RUS) 7 T2
Revel (F) 93 J4
Revel (F) 95 J2
Reveléo (I) 95 K1
Rèselajärvi (FIN) 35 H3
Revere (I) 98 C3
Revesjö (S) 44 C4
Revest-du-Bion (F) 95 G2
Revfülöp (H) 158 E4
Revholmen (N) 39 K4
Reviga (RO) 170 E4
Revigny (F) 85 J3
Revigny-sur-Ornain (F) 77 L4
Revilla, La (E) 112 C2
Revin (F) 77 L2
Revingse-Lago (I) 89 G6
Révkanyvár (H) 155 H5
Revna (S) 38 C2
Revničov (CZ) 73 L6
Revonsula (FIN) 29 K6
Revonlahti (FIN) 22 G7
Revonoja (FIN) 29 K4
Rexbo (S) 40 H1
Reyðarbarður (IS) 16 F7
Reydon (GB) 59 L3
Reyhanli (TR) 23 L7
Reykholt (IS) 16 E5
Reykhólar (IS) 16 E4
Reynés (IS) 16 F3
Reyniyaiar (IS) 16 E3
Reyrevieux (F) 85 G3
Réjuilyholt (IS) 16 E5
Rīmajõkuna = Reppjoki (FIN) 19 H7
Rézbanya (F) 77 M3
Rezé (F) 82 B2
Rézekne (LV) 134 D4
Rezina (MD) 163 H3
Rezovo (BG) 177 K4
Řezé (F) 82 B2
Rezzato (I) 90 G4
Rgotina (SRB) 175 H1
Rhade (D) 65 L5
Rhade (D) 69 N3
Rhayader (GB) 57 G1
Rhauderfehn (D) 65 H5
Rhaunen (D) 79 G2
Rhayador (GB) 57 H1
Rhédon (F) 75 J5
Rheda-Wiedenbrück (D) 70 F3
Rheden (NL) 70 B2
Rheinau (D) 79 H4
Rheinau (D) 79 N4
Rheinbach (D) 70 D6
Rheinberg (D) 69 M3
Rheinböllen (D) 79 G2
Rheinbrohl (D) 70 D5
Rheinfelden (D) 70 D5
Rheindahlen (D) 34 H2
Rheineck (D) 70 D6
Rhéneck (CH) 79 M7
Rheinfelden (Baden) (D) 86 E2
Rheinhausen (D) 69 M4
Rheinhausen (D) 79 J4
Rheinsberg (D) 67 H4
Rheinstetten (D) 79 J4
Rheinzabern (D) 79 J3
Rhémes-Notre-Dame (I) 98 C1
Rhenen (NL) 69 K3
Rheurdt (D) 70 B4
Rhiconich (GB) 50 H3
Rhinau (F) 79 H5
Rhinow (D) 67 G5
Rho (I) 98 D3
Rhode (E) 123 L8
Rhondda (GB) 57 G3
Rhoslan (GB) 54 D5
Rhoslanerchrugog (GB) 54 F4
Rhostyllen (GB) 54 F4
Rhos-y-gwaliau (GB) 54 E5
Rhu (GB) 52 F2
Rhyl (GB) 54 E3
Rhynern (D) 70 E3
Riace (I) 107 F6
Riace Marina (I) 107 G6
Riala (E) 123 F4
Riáklea (GR) 186 E3
Rial (Soutomaior) (E) 110 B4
Rialp (E) 122 E5
Rialb de Noguera = Rialp (E) 93 G6
Riaño (E) 111 K2
Riala, La (E) 119 H2
Rians (F) 95 G4
Riantec (F) 74 F6
Riaza (E) 112 E6
Rībadeo (E) 111 G1
Riba de Saelices (E) 120 D2
Ribadesella (E) 112 A2

Rimbsö (S) 33 L5
Rimili (LT) 138 D2
Rimini Torplice (SLO) 164 E2
Rimsting (D) 81 G6
Rincón (E) 127 G5
Rincón de la Victoria (E) 126 B6
Rincón de Soto (E) 113 N3
Rindal (N) 31 K1
Rindsetter (N) 31 K4
Rindby Strand (DK) 46 B3
Rindskedal (N) 31 N5
Rindal (N) 31 N5
Rindsetter (N) 31 K1
Ringe (DK) 47 D6
Rinøy (N) 75 L4
Ringaskiddy (IRL) 62 F5
Ringe (IRL) 46 F3
Ringan (GR) 186 F4
Ringebu (N) 31 N6
Ringelai (D) 71 M4
Ringe (N) 43 K4
Ringkøbing (DK) 46 B1
Ringleben (D) 71 M4
Ringe (N) 30 C1
Ringsted (DK) 47 K3
Ringvassøy (N) 15 J2
Ringville (IRL) 62 G2
Ringwood (GB) 57 H4
Rinkaby (S) 44 E7
Rinkeröde (D) 70 E3
Rinmo (GR) 170 G5
Rinnau = Rennes (F) 75 H4
Rintala (FIN) 35 H2
Rinteln (D) 71 H2
Rinyaszentkirály (FIN) 165 K2
Río (GR) 186 D3
Riobianco (I) 88 E4
Riocavado (I) 103 O4
Riccione (I) 101 H6
Rioccono (I) 101 H6
Río de Moinhos (P) 124 E2
Río de Onor (P) 103 H2
Río de Trueba (E) 112 D2
Rodeva (E) 121 F3
Riofreddo (I) 90 E7
Riofrío (E) 111 K6
Riofrío (E) 119 G2
Río Frío (P) 104 C5
Riofrío de Aliste (E) 111 G5
Riofrío del Llano (E) 120 C1
Riojuan = Rioán (E) 110 E2
Riola di Vergato (I) 99 L4
Riolobregal (E) 105 H4
Riolo Terme (I) 101 F4
Riomaggiore (I) 98 F4
Rión (F) 85 M2
Río Maior (P) 116 D5
Rió Marina (I) 100 B5
Rión de Arriba (E) 117 J3
Ric Marina (I) 92 D3
Río Mau (P) 110 B5
Roč (HR) 91 N8
Roca de Sierra, La (E) 105 F3
Roca del Vallès, la (E) 115 H4
Rocafort de Queralt (E) 115 H5
Rocamadour (F) 93 H1
Roccabascerana (I) 104 C3
Roccacasale (I) 98 D2
Roccacasale (I) 106 D2
Roccada'Cri (I) 105 G6
Rocca di Cambio (I) 103 G3
Rocca di Mezzo (I) 103 H3
Rocca di Neto (I) 107 G4
Rocca di Papa (I) 103 H4
Roccaforte del Greco (I) 109 J1
Roccafranca (I) 98 B3
Roccagiorgia (I) 100 A4
Roccagloriosa (I) 103 H1
Rocca Imperiale (I) 105 G6
Rocca Imperiale Marina (I) 105 G6
Roccalbegna (I) 102 E2
Roccalumera (I) 106 D7
Roccamonfina (I) 104 A3
Roccamorice (I) 103 J3
Roccanova (I) 106 F1
Roccapalumba (I) 108 F2
Roccaporena (I) 103 G4
Rocca San Casciano (I) 101 F4
Rocca Santo Stefano (I) 103 H4
Rocca Sinibalda (I) 103 H3
Roccasecca (I) 104 A3
Roccastrada (I) 100 E1
Roccavigne (I) 98 D2
Roccavione (I) 96 E2
Rocca Villoresi (F) 75 H4
Rocroi (F) 77 L2
Rodacherfrido (P) 117 H6
Roda de Andalucía, La (E) 125 N4
Roda de Bara (E) 115 G6
Roda de Ter (E) 115 H4
Rodach (D) 71 L5
Rödach (DK) 42 D5
Rodakino (GR) 186 C6
Rodalquilar (E) 127 F6
Rodar (AL) 174 D3

Rodonya (E) 115 F5
Rodópoli (GR) 179 J2
Rodovár-Audru (EST) 130 E6
Rodovar (RUS) 133 J2
Rodován (EST) 130 E6
Rodzone (D) 72 F6
Rodonë (TR) 185 F5
Roghudi (Riotorto) (I) 110 E2
Rodigas = Rodrigas (Riotorto) (E) 110 E2
Rodigliello, el (E) 127 H3
Rodingersdorf (A) 91 J3
Rodna (RO) 161 J3
Roguno (RO) 161 N3

Runnskogen **229**

Runovo (RUS) 135 J5
Runskij (RUS) 135 O3
Runsten (S) 45 K5
Runtuna (S) 41 M5
Ruohola (FIN) 23 H5
Ruokkee (FIN) 37 N1
Ruokojärvi (FIN) 22 G2
Ruokojärvi (FIN) 29 K8
Ruokojärvi (S) 21 N7
Ruokolahti (FIN) 37 L2
Ruokolanranta (FIN) 29 K2
Ruokoniemi (FIN) 29 J8
Ruokotaipale (FIN) 37 J2
Ruokto (S) 22 B2
Ruolahti (FIN) 36 D1
Ruomi (FIN) 37 J2
Ruoms (F) 94 D2
Ruona (FIN) 23 J4
Ruona (FIN) 28 D6
Ruona (FIN) 35 J2
Ruonlahti (FIN) 35 L4
Ruopsa (FIN) 23 K3
Ruorasmäki (FIN) 36 F1
Ruosniemi (FIN) 35 J1
Ruotanen (FIN) 28 G4
Ruotanmäki (FIN) 29 G5
Ruotsalo (FIN) 28 D4
Ruotsinkylä (FIN) 36 F3
Ruotsinpyhtää (FIN) 36 F3
Ruottisenharju (FIN) 23 K6
Ruovesi (FIN) 28 E8
Rupa (SLO) 164 C4
Rupča (BG) 177 H3
Rupci (BG) 167 L6
Rupe (HR) 172 C2
Rupea (RO) 169 J1
Rupingrande (I) 164 B3
Rupit (E) 115 H3
Rupniów (PL) 155 G2
Ruppersdorf (D) 71 N5
Ruppertenrod (D) 71 H5
Ruppertshütten (D) 71 J6
Ruppichteroth (D) 70 D5
Ruppovaara (FIN) 29 L7
Ruprechtshofen (A) 91 H3
Rupt-sur-Moselle (F) 78 F6
Rus (RO) 161 H3
Rusaky (UA) 151 K1
Rusalja (BG) 176 D2
Rusalka (BG) 177 L2
Rusånes (N) 20 E7
Rusava (UA) 163 G2
Rusazia = Rosazia (F) 96 D4
Rusbend (D) 71 H2
Rusca Montană (RO) 168 C2
Ruscova (RO) 156 F6
Rusdal (N) 38 D5
Ruse (BG) 170 B6
Ruše (SLO) 164 F1
Rusele (S) 26 E5
Ruseni (MD) 157 M5
Rușețu (RO) 170 E4
Ruševo (HR) 165 L4
Rusfors (S) 26 E5
Rush (IRL) 63 K1
Rushden (GB) 55 L6
Rusi (FIN) 28 G8
Ruși (RO) 161 J6
Rusiec (PL) 147 K3
Rușii-Munți (RO) 161 K4
Rusinovo (MK) 180 B1
Rusinów (PL) 146 D2
Rusinów (PL) 148 C3
Rusiny (BY) 138 E3
Rusjaci (MK) 174 F6
Rus'ka (UA) 157 H6
Rus'ka (UA) 163 M5
Rus'ka, Rava- (UA) 149 J5
Ruskae Sjalo (BY) 138 E4
Ruská Poruba (SK) 155 K3
Ruskeala (FIN) 28 G8
Ruskeala (RUS) 29 L8
Ruskela (FIN) 36 C4
Ruski Bród (PL) 148 C3
Ruski Krstur (SRB) 166 D2
Ruskila (FIN) 29 J6
Ruskington (GB) 58 G1
Rusko (FIN) 35 K3
Rusko (PL) 140 F2
Rusko (PL) 147 G2
Rus'koivanivka (UA) 163 K6
Rusko Selo (SRB) 167 G2
Ruskov (SK) 155 J4
Ruskselе (S) 26 E5
Ruskträsk (S) 26 E5
Ruskulava (LV) 134 E4
Ruskulla (FIN) 35 L4
Ruský Hrabovec (SK) 156 B4
Ruský Potok (SK) 156 B3
Rusnė (LT) 136 E3
Rusokastro (BG) 177 H4
Rusovce (SK) 158 D1
Rußbach am Pass Gschütt (A) 89 J2
Rüsselsheim am Main (D) 70 F7
Russeluft (N) 18 F3
Russelv (N) 18 C4
Russenes (N) 19 H3
Russey, Le (F) 85 L2
Russhaugen (N) 20 F4
Russi (I) 101 G4
Russkoe (RUS) 136 C4
Russów (PL) 147 J2
Rust (A) 158 C2
Rust (D) 79 H5
Rust (N) 31 M5
Rustan (N) 39 M3
Rustand (N) 39 K2
Rustefjelbma (N) 19 L3
Rusteikiai (LT) 138 D2
Rusteseter (N) 31 K3
Rusti (N) 31 L4
Rustoy (N) 30 F4
Rustrel (F) 95 F3
Ruswil (CH) 86 F3
Ruszki (PL) 148 B1
Ruszów (PL) 146 C3
Rutakoski (FIN) 29 G7
Rutalahti (FIN) 28 F7
Rutalahti (FIN) 36 E2
Rutava (FIN) 35 L2
Rute (E) 126 B5
Rute (S) 45 O3
Rütenbrock (D) 64 G6
Rüthen (D) 70 F4
Ruthin (GB) 54 F4
Ruthwell (GB) 53 J5
Rüti (ZH) (CH) 87 G3
Rutigliano (I) 105 H3
Rutki-Kossaki (PL) 143 G4
Rutledal (N) 30 C5
Rutoši (SRB) 174 C1
Rutsgården (S) 40 B3
Rutten (NL) 64 D6
Rutvik (S) 22 E5
Ruuhijärvi (FIN) 22 G3
Ruuhijärvi (FIN) 36 F2
Ruuhimäki (FIN) 28 G7
Ruukki (FIN) 27 M5
Ruukki (FIN) 35 N4
Ruunaa (FIN) 29 L5
Ruurlo (NL) 70 B2
Ruusmäe (EST) 133 P2
Ruutana (FIN) 29 G4
Ruutana (FIN) 35 O1
Ruuvaoja (FIN) 23 L1
Ruvalivka (UA) 151 L5
Ruvaslahti (FIN) 29 K6
Ruvo di Puglia (I) 105 F3
Ruynes-en-Margeride (F) 84 D6
Ruza (RUS) 7 U7
Ružany (BY) 143 M5
Ružić (HR) 172 D2
Ružica (BG) 177 G4
Ružica (BG) 177 H1
Ružinci (BG) 175 J1
Ružomberok (SK) 154 E3
Ruzsa (H) 159 J5
Ružyn (UA) 151 J4
Rvenicy (RUS) 135 P3
Rvy (RUS) 135 K2
Ry (DK) 46 E1
Ryan (S) 32 E6
Rybačij (RUS) 136 D3
Rybačij (RUS) 142 B1
Rybaki (PL) 148 E3
Rybaľče (UA) 171 K2
Rybany (SK) 154 C4
Ryberg (N) 38 H2
Rybiczyzna (PL) 148 D3
Rybinsk (RUS) 7 V6
Rybitví (CZ) 153 J3
Rybjažėvičy (BY) 144 E1
Rybnica (BY) 143 L3
Rybnica = Ribnița (MD) 163 J3
Rybníček (CZ) 153 H5
Rybník (CZ) 81 H1
Rybnik (PL) 154 D1
Rybniště (CZ) 152 G2
Rybotycze (PL) 155 M2
Rycerka Górna (PL) 154 E3
Rychaľs'ke (UA) 150 F2
Rychliki (PL) 141 N3
Rychłocice (PL) 147 K3
Rychnov (CZ) 153 L4
Rychnov nad Kněžnou (CZ) 153 K3
Rychnowo (PL) 141 O3
Rychta (UA) 162 C1
Rychtal (PL) 147 H3
Rychvald (CZ) 147 J6
Rychwał (PL) 147 J1
Ryczeń (PL) 146 F2
Ryczywół (PL) 140 G5
Ryczywół (PL) 148 D2
Ryd (S) 44 D3
Ryd (S) 44 F3
Ryd (S) 44 F6
Ryda (S) 44 B2
Rydaholm (S) 44 E5
Rydal (S) 43 L3
Rydamlja (BY) 139 L4
Rydboholm (S) 44 B3
Ryde (DK) 47 H4
Ryde (GB) 58 E6
Rydebäck (S) 47 L2
Rydet (S) 43 K4
Rydland (N) 38 B3
Rydöbruk (S) 43 M5
Rydomyľ (UA) 150 B4
Rydsgård (S) 47 N3
Rydsnäs (S) 44 G3
Rydułtowy (PL) 154 C1
Rydzyna (PL) 146 F2
Rye (DK) 47 J2
Rye (GB) 59 J6
Rye (N) 24 E8
Ryet (N) 20 D6
Ryfoss (N) 31 K5
Rygge (N) 20 D3
Rygge (N) 39 N4
Rygge (S) 33 K4
Ryggesbo (S) 33 K4
Ryglice (PL) 148 D6
Rygnestad (N) 38 G4
Rygozy (RUS) 134 H4
Ryhälä (FIN) 37 K1
Ryhälänmäki (FIN) 29 H4
Ryhall (GB) 58 G2
Ryhill (GB) 55 K3
Ryjewo (PL) 141 L3
Rykene (N) 39 J6
Ryki (PL) 148 E2
Rykšino (RUS) 135 J5
Rykšino (RUS) 135 J6
Rylane Cross (IRL) 62 E5
Ryliškiai (LT) 137 L5
Ryłowice (PL) 148 E4
Ryl'sk (RUS) 9 N4
Rylsk Duży (PL) 148 B2
Rymači (UA) 149 J3
Rymanów (PL) 155 K2
Rymarivka (UA) 163 J4
Rýmařov (CZ) 147 G6
Rymašy (BY) 144 E2
Rymättylä (FIN) 35 J4
Rymnäsbodarna (S) 32 G5
Ryn (PL) 136 F6
Ryn (PL) 141 N3
Rynarcice (PL) 146 E3
Rynarzewo (PL) 141 J4
Ryomgård (DK) 42 G6
Ryönä (FIN) 29 J6
Ryönänjoki (FIN) 29 G4
Rypefjord (N) 18 F2
Ryphusseter (N) 31 M3
Rypin (PL) 142 A4
Ryšavka (UA) 151 G2
Rysjedalsvika (N) 30 C5
Ryslinge (DK) 46 G3
Ryssa (S) 32 G6
Ryssby (S) 43 O5
Ryssby (S) 45 J5
Ryssefjell (N) 30 J6
Rysstad (N) 38 G4
Rystad (S) 41 J6
Rysum (D) 64 G5
Ryszewo (PL) 141 J5
Rytel (PL) 141 J3
Rytilahti (FIN) 23 K3
Rytinki (FIN) 23 K5
Rytky (FIN) 29 G5
Ryto (RUS) 135 N2
Rytro (PL) 155 H3
Rytterne (S) 41 K4
Ryttylä (FIN) 35 P3
Rytwiany (PL) 148 D4
Rywałd (PL) 141 M4
Rywałdzik (PL) 141 M4
Ryžanivka (UA) 151 M5
Ryžany (UA) 151 H2
Ryžavka (UA) 163 L1
Ryžikovo (RUS) 139 O4
Ryzyne (UA) 151 M5
Rząśnik (PL) 142 E5
Rząśnik (PL) 153 J1
Ržavcy (BY) 139 M5
Ržavynci (UA) 162 C1
Rzecin (PL) 140 F5
Rzeczenica (PL) 141 H3
Rzeczyca (PL) 146 F3
Rzeczyca (PL) 148 B2
Rzeczyca Ziemiańska (PL) 148 F4
Rzęgnowo (PL) 142 D4
Rzejowice (PL) 147 M3
Rzemień (PL) 148 E5
Rzepedź (PL) 156 B3
Rzepiennik Strzyżewski (PL) 155 J2
Rzepin (PL) 67 M6
Rzeszotary (PL) 146 E3
Rzeszów (PL) 155 L1
Ržev (RUS) 7 T7
Rževskoe (RUS) 136 F3
Rzewnowo (PL) 140 C3
Rzgów (PL) 147 J1
Rzgów (PL) 147 L2
Rzozów (PL) 148 A6
Rzuchów (PL) 149 G5
Rzuchów (PL) 154 C1
Rzuców (PL) 148 C3
Rzyki (PL) 154 E2

S

Saá (E) 110 E3
Saakoski (FIN) 28 F8
Sääksjärvi (FIN) 28 C9
Sääksjärvi (FIN) 28 D5
Sääksjärvi (FIN) 35 N2
Sääksjärvi (FIN) 36 D3
Sääkskoski (FIN) 35 K2
Sääksmäki (FIN) 35 O2
Saal (D) 67 G2
Saalahti (FIN) 28 F8
Saal an der Donau (D) 80 F3
Saal an der Saale (D) 72 C5
Saalbach-Hinterglemm (A) 81 H6
Saalburg-Ebersdorf (D) 72 F4
Saales (F) 78 G5
Saalfeld (D) 71 M5
Saalfelden am Steinernen Meer (A) 81 H6
Saamainen (FIN) 29 H6
Saananmaja (FIN) 18 C5
Saanen (CH) 86 D5
Saanenmöser (CH) 86 D4
Säänjärvi (FIN) 37 J2
Saapaskylä (FIN) 35 Q3
Saarakivi (FIN) 19 J4
Saaramaa (FIN) 36 H3
Saarbrücken (D) 78 F3
Saarburg (D) 78 F2
Sääre (EST) 130 B5
Saaren kirkonkylä (FIN) 37 N1
Saarenkylä (FIN) 23 H3
Saarenmaa (FIN) 35 J2
Säärenperä (FIN) 23 G7
Saarepeedi (EST) 131 J4
Saaresmäki (FIN) 29 G3
Saargemünd = Sarreguemines (F) 78 G3
Saari (FIN) 36 D3
Saari (FIN) 37 N1
Saariharju (FIN) 23 K5
Saarijärvi (FIN) 28 F6
Saarijärvi (FIN) 35 K1
Saari-Kämä (FIN) 27 N2
Saarikas (FIN) 28 G6
Saarikoski (FIN) 21 L3
Saarikoski (FIN) 27 M3
Saarikoski (FIN) 28 F2
Saarikoski (FIN) 35 J1
Saarikylä (FIN) 23 M6
Saarikylät (FIN) 35 O2
Saarilampi (FIN) 28 G7
Saario (FIN) 29 L7
Saaripudas (FIN) 22 F2
Saariselkä (FIN) 19 K7
Saarivaara (FIN) 29 K2
Saarivaara (FIN) 29 K6
Saarivaara (FIN) 29 L7
Saarlouis (D) 78 F3
Saarmäki (FIN) 29 J4
Saarmund (D) 67 J6
Saaroinen (FIN) 29 L7
Saarwellingen (D) 78 F3
Saas-Almagell (CH) 86 E5
Saas-Balen (CH) 86 E5
Saas-Fee (CH) 86 E5
Saas-Grund (CH) 86 E5
Saas im Prättigau (CH) 87 J4
Sääskilahti (FIN) 23 K4
Sääskiniemi (FIN) 29 J5
Sääskjärvi (FIN) 36 F3
Saatse (EST) 134 E2
Saba, Santa (I) 106 E6
Šabac (SRB) 166 E4
Sabadell (E) 115 H4
Sabak (TR) 199 G3
Sabali (BY) 139 K4
Şaban (TR) 191 H3
Şabangia (RO) 171 H4
Šabanovo (RUS) 135 K3
Sabanözü (TR) 13 K5
Sabanözü (TR) 184 D6
Şabanözü (TR) 185 F5
Šabany (RUS) 131 O6
Săbăoani (RO) 162 D4
Sabarat (F) 115 F1
Sabarigo (E) 110 B4
Sabatynivka (UA) 163 L2
Sabaudia (I) 103 G5
Sabbioneta (I) 100 C2
Šabeľnyky (UA) 163 L4
Sabero (E) 112 A3
Sabile (LV) 132 F3
Sabiñánigo (E) 113 L3
Sabinar, El (E) 113 J4
Sabinar, El (E) 127 F3
Sabinares (E) 120 C6
Sabinov (SK) 155 J3
Sabiote (E) 126 D3
Šabla (BG) 177 L1
Sables-d'Olonne, Les (F) 82 B3
Sables-d'Or-les-Pins (F) 75 G3
Sablières (F) 94 D1
Šabo (UA) 171 L1
Sabóia (P) 124 C5
Såböle (S) 25 H8
Saborsko (HR) 164 E5
Sabres (F) 92 C2
Sabro (DK) 46 F1
Sabrosa (P) 110 D6
Sabugal (P) 117 G3
Sabuncu (TR) 191 J1
Säby (S) 41 K3
Säby (S) 44 F3
Šabyn'ki (BY) 139 J5
Šaca (SK) 155 J4
Sa Cabaneta (E) 123 G3
Săcădat (RO) 160 E3
Săcădate (RO) 169 G2
Săcălășeni (RO) 161 H2
Săcălaz (RO) 159 M6
Sa Calobra (E) 123 G3
Sa Canal (E) 122 D5
Sacañet (E) 121 G4
Săcășeni (RO) 160 F3
Sacavém (P) 124 A2
Sacecorbo (E) 120 D2
Saceda (E) 111 F4
Sacedón (E) 120 C3
Săcel (RO) 161 J2
Săcel (RO) 161 K5
Săcele (RO) 170 B2
Săcele (RO) 171 H5
Săcelu (RO) 168 F3
Săceni (RO) 169 J5
Saceruela (E) 126 A2
Sachans'ke (UA) 163 L4
Saché (F) 83 G2
Sachrang (D) 90 B4
Sachseln (CH) 86 F4
Sachsenberg (D) 71 G4
Sachsenbrunn (D) 72 D5
Sachsenburg (A) 90 D6
Sachsenhagen (D) 66 A6
Sachsenhausen (D) 71 H4
Sachsenheim (D) 79 L4
Sachsenkam (D) 88 F2
Saçıkara (TR) 192 D3
Sacilava (BY) 139 K3
Sacile (I) 89 H6
Šack (BY) 144 G2
Šack (RUS) 9 Q3
Šac'k (UA) 149 J3
Saçklı (TR) 182 C6
Saclay (F) 76 F4
Saçlı (TR) 193 J2
Saçmalıpınar (TR) 184 A4
Sacoias (P) 111 F5
Sa Colònia de Sant Pere (E) 123 H3
Sacos (Santa María) (E) 110 C3
Sacoșu Mare (RO) 167 J2
Sacoșu Turcesc (RO) 168 A2
Sacramenia (E) 112 D6
Sacu (RO) 167 K2
Sacudello (I) 89 H6
Săcueni (RO) 160 E3
Săcuieu (RO) 160 F4
Sačurov (SK) 155 K4
Sacy-le-Grand (F) 76 G3
Sačyvljany (BY) 144 B2
Sada (Miño) (E) 110 C2
Sádaba (E) 113 J4
Sadaclia (MD) 163 H6
Sadala (EST) 131 L3
Saddell (GB) 52 D3
Sade (TR) 185 G2
Sadelkow (D) 67 J3
Sadenbeck (D) 67 G4
Sadhora (UA) 162 B2
Sadîc (MD) 163 H6
Sădievo (BG) 176 F3
Sadık (TR) 193 J2
Sadıkhacı (TR) 192 C5
Sadıkkırı (TR) 191 J2
Sadıklar (TR) 192 D5
Sadıklı (TR) 193 G2
Sadillac (F) 92 E1
Sadina (BG) 177 F2
Sadiv (UA) 149 L4
Sadki (PL) 141 H4
Sadków (PL) 148 D4
Sadków (PL) 153 L1
Sadkowa Góra (PL) 148 D5
Sadkowice (PL) 148 C2
Sadłowo (PL) 142 B4
Sadova (MD) 163 G4
Sadova (RO) 162 A3
Sadova (RO) 169 F6
Sadove (UA) 150 D2
Sadove (UA) 151 J3
Sadovec (BG) 176 B2
Sadovo (BG) 176 C4
Sadovo (BG) 177 J2
Sadovoe (RUS) 142 F2
Sadovoe (RUS) 143 G1
Sadów (PL) 147 K4
Sadowne (PL) 142 F5
Sadrazamköy (TR) 198 E5
Sadská (CZ) 153 G3
Sadu (RO) 169 G2
Sadukula (EST) 131 K3
Sadurki (PL) 148 F3
Sädvaluspen (S) 20 F8
Sädvvaluspe = Sädvaluspen (S) 20 F8
Sadzarzewice (PL) 73 M2
Sadžavka (UA) 157 G4
Sæbø (N) 30 E3
Sæbø (N) 30 G7
Sæból (IS) 16 C2
Sæbovik (N) 38 C3
Sæby (DK) 42 G4
Sæby (DK) 47 H2
Sæd (DK) 46 C4
Sædder (DK) 47 K3
Săedinenie (BG) 176 C4
Săedinenie (BG) 176 D4
Săedinenie (BG) 177 H3
Sægrov (N) 30 E4
Sæle (N) 30 E5
Saelices (E) 120 C4
Saelices de Mayorga (E) 111 J4
Sæluhús (IS) 16 D3
Sælwig (DK) 46 G2
Saerbeck (D) 70 E2
Særløse (DK) 47 J2
Særslev (DK) 46 F2
Şaeș (RO) 169 H1
Sæter (N) 30 F2
Sæter (N) 32 B3
Sætervik (N) 24 E6
Sætra (N) 20 G2
Sætre (N) 31 P5
Sætre (N) 39 N3
Saeul (L) 78 D2
Sævareid (N) 38 C2
Sævarþland (IS) 17 L2
Sævråsvåg (N) 30 C6
Safa (TR) 183 J6
Safaalan (TR) 177 K6
Safara (P) 124 E3
Säffle (S) 40 C4
Saffré (F) 75 H5
Saffron Walden (GB) 59 H3
Safien Platz (CH) 87 H4
Safonovo (RUS) 7 T7
Safonovo (RUS) 135 L6
Safranbolu (TR) 184 E3
Säfsnäs (S) 40 F2
Safurdão (P) 118 B2
Săg (RO) 160 F3
Şag (RO) 167 H2
Sagadi (EST) 131 K1
Săgagea (RO) 161 G5
Sagaidac (MD) 163 H5
Sagallos (E) 111 G5
Sağancı (TR) 189 K1
Sagard (D) 67 K1
Sagatun (S) 25 L6
Săgeata (RO) 170 D3
Sågen (S) 40 F2
Saggart (IRL) 63 K2
Saggrenda (N) 39 L3
Sagiáda (GR) 178 C5
Sağırın (TR) 198 B1
Sağırlar (TR) 183 G6
Sağırlar (TR) 190 E2
Sağlık (TR) 192 D5
Sağlık (TR) 193 H4
Sågmyra (S) 33 J6
Sagna (RO) 162 E5
Sagne, La (CH) 85 L2
Sagone (F) 96 D4
Sağpazar (TR) 185 H5
Sagra (E) 122 A5
Sagrada, A (E) 110 C3
Sağrak (TR) 192 A6
Sagres (P) 124 B5
Şagu (RO) 167 H1
Sagunt (E) 121 H4
Sagunto = Sagunt (E) 121 H4
Sagvåg (N) 38 B3
Ságvár (H) 158 F4
Sagvollen (N) 39 N2
Saha (EST) 36 C6
Saha (FIN) 36 E3
Sahagún (E) 112 A4
Sahalahti (FIN) 28 E9
Sahankylä (FIN) 28 C7
Saharna Nouă (MD) 163 H3
Săhateni (RO) 170 D3
Sahilkent (TR) 197 H3
Şahin (TR) 181 K2
Şahin (TR) 184 E2
Şahin (TR) 191 H2
Şahinağa (TR) 199 K2
Şahinçati (TR) 185 H3
Şahinler (TR) 193 H3
Şahinli (TR) 182 C5
Şahinyurdu (TR) 183 H5
Sahlis, Kohren- (D) 152 C1
Şahmelek (TR) 182 F5
Şahmuratlı (TR) 185 K6
Şahna (TR) 199 H2
Şahören (TR) 192 D4
Sahorre (F) 93 J5
Šahovskaja (RUS) 7 U7
Sahrajärvi (FIN) 28 F7
Sahryń (PL) 149 J4
Sahuco, El (E) 127 F4
Šahy (SK) 159 G1
Săi (RO) 161 G2
Saiano, Rodengo- (I) 99 J1
Saïdóna (GR) 186 E6
Saignelégier (CH) 86 C3
Saija (FIN) 23 L2
Säijä (FIN) 35 N2
Saikari (FIN) 29 G6
Saikkola (FIN) 37 K2
Saillagouse (F) 93 J6
Saillans (F) 95 F1
Sail-les-Bains (F) 84 E4
Saimaanharju (FIN) 37 K2
Saimbeyli (TR) 13 L6
Säimen (FIN) 29 K7
Sainovina (SRB) 173 L2
Sains-en-Amiénois (F) 76 F2
Sains-Richaumont (F) 77 J2
Saint-Affrique (F) 94 A3
Saint-Agnan (F) 83 H6
Saint-Agnan-en-Vercors (F) 85 H7
Saint-Agnant (F) 82 D5
Saint Agnes (GB) 56 D5
Saint-Agrève (F) 84 F6
Saint-Aignan (F) 83 H2
Saint-Aignan-des-Noyers (F) 84 C3
Saint-Aignan-sur-Roë (F) 75 J5
Saint-Aigulin (F) 82 E6
Saint-Albain (F) 85 G4
Saint-Alban (F) 74 F3
Saint Albans (GB) 59 G4
Saint-Alban-sur-Limagnole (F) 94 B1
Saint-Allouestre (F) 74 F5
Saint-Alyre-d'Arlanc (F) 84 E6
Saint-Alyre-ès-Montagne (F) 84 C6
Saint-Amand-en-Puisaye (F) 77 H6
Saint-Amand-les-Eaux (F) 68 E6
Saint-Amand-Longpré (F) 76 D6
Saint-Amand-Montrond (F) 83 L3
Saint-Amand-sur-Fion (F) 77 L4
Saint-Amand-sur-Sèvre (F) 82 D3
Saint-Amans (F) 94 B1
Saint-Amans-des-Cots (F) 93 K1
Saint-Amans-Soult (F) 93 J4
Saint-Amant-Roche-Savine (F) 84 E5
Saint-Amarin (F) 78 G6
Saint-Ambroix (F) 94 D2
Saint-Amour (F) 85 H4
Saint-Andiol (F) 94 E3
Saint-André-de-Corcy (F) 85 G5
Saint-André-de-Cubzac (F) 82 E7
Saint-André-de-l'Eure (F) 76 D4
Saint-André-de-Sangonis (F) 94 C3
Saint-André-de-Valborgne (F) 94 C2
Saint-André-le-Bouchoux (F) 85 H4
Saint-André-les-Alpes (F) 95 J3
Saint-André-les-Vergers (F) 77 K5
Saint Andrews (GB) 53 K2
Saint Andrews Major (GB) 57 H3
Saint-Angeau (F) 83 F5
Saint-Angel (F) 83 K5
Saint Anne (GBA) 75 G1
Saint-Anthème (F) 84 E5
Saint-Antoine (F) 96 E4
Saint-Antoine-de-Ficalba (F) 93 F2
Saint-Antoine-l'Abbaye (F) 85 H6
Saint-Antoine-sur-l'Isle (F) 82 F6
Saint-Antonin-Noble-Val (F) 93 H2
Saint-Août (F) 83 J3
Saint-Aquilin (F) 83 F6
Saint-Armel (F) 74 F5
Saint-Arnoult-en-Yvelines (F) 76 E4
Saint Arvans (GB) 58 B4
Saint Asaph (GB) 54 F4
Saint-Astier (F) 83 G6
Saint-Auban (F) 95 J3
Saint-Auban-sur-l'Ouvèze (F) 95 F2
Saint-Aubin (F) 85 G3
Saint-Aubin (F) 85 H2
Saint-Aubin (F) 92 C3
Saint-Aubin (GBJ) 75 G2
Saint-Aubin-d'Aubigné (F) 75 H4
Saint-Aubin-de-Blaye (F) 82 D6
Saint-Aubin-des-Châteaux (F) 75 J5
Saint-Aubin-du-Cormier (F) 75 J4
Saint-Aubin FR (CH) 85 L3
Saint-Aubin-la-Plaine (F) 82 C3
Saint-Aubin-Sauges (CH) 86 C4
Saint-Aubin-sur-Aire (F) 78 C4
Saint-Aubin-sur-Loire (F) 84 E3
Saint-Aubin-sur-Mer (F) 75 L2
Saint-Augustin (F) 82 C5
Saint-Augustin (F) 83 J6
Saint-Augustin-des-Bois (F) 75 K6
Saint-Aulaye-Puymangou (F) 82 F6
Saint Austell (GB) 56 E5
Saint-Avé (F) 74 F5
Saint-Aventin (F) 92 F5
Saint-Avit (F) 83 L5
Saint-Avold (F) 78 F3
Saint-Aygulf (F) 98 B6
Saint-Bard (F) 84 B5
Saint-Barthélemy (F) 77 H4
Saint-Barthélemy-de-Bellegarde (F) 82 F6
Saint-Baudel (F) 83 K3
Saint-Bauzille-de-Montmel (F) 94 C3
Saint-Bauzille-de-Putois (F) 94 C3
Saint-Béat (F) 114 E2
Saint-Beauzély (F) 94 A2
Saint Bees (GB) 53 H6
Saint-Benin-d'Azy (F) 84 D2
Saint-Benoist-sur-Vanne (F) 77 J5
Saint-Benoît (F) 83 F3
Saint-Benoît (F) 115 H1
Saint-Benoît-des-Ondes (F) 75 H3
Saint-Benoît-du-Sault (F) 83 H4
Saint-Benoît-en-Woëvre (F) 78 D4
Saint-Benoît-la-Chipotte (F) 78 F5
Saint-Benoît-sur-Loire (F) 76 F6
Saint-Béron (F) 85 J6
Saint-Berthevin (F) 75 K4
Saint Bertrand-de-Comminges (F) 114 E1
Saint-Blaise (CH) 85 L2
Saint Blazey (GB) 56 E5
Saint-Blimont (F) 68 B6
Saint-Blin-Semilly (F) 78 C5
Saint-Bomer (F) 76 C5
Saint-Bonnet-de-Bellac (F) 83 G4
Saint-Bonnet-de-Joux (F) 84 F4
Saint-Bonnet-de-Rochefort (F) 84 D4
Saint-Bonnet-en-Champsaur (F) 95 H1
Saint-Bonnet-le-Courreau (F) 84 E5
Saint-Bonnet-le-Froid (F) 84 F6
Saint-Bonnet-près-Bort (F) 84 B5
Saint-Bonnet-sur-Gironde (F) 82 D6
Saint Boswells (GB) 53 K3
Saint-Branchs (F) 83 G2
Saint-Bresson (F) 86 C2
Saint-Brevin-les-Pins (F) 82 A2
Saint-Briac-sur-Mer (F) 75 G3
Saint Briavels (GB) 57 J2
Saint-Brice (F) 92 D1
Saint-Brice-en-Coglès (F) 75 J4
Saint-Brieuc (F) 74 F3
Saint-Bris-des-Bois (F) 82 E5
Saint-Bris-le-Vineux (F) 77 J6
Saint-Brisson (F) 84 F2
Saint-Broladre (F) 75 H3
Saint-Calais (F) 76 C6
Saint-Cannat (F) 95 F3
Saint-Caradec (F) 74 F4
Saint-Cast-le-Guildo (F) 75 G3
Saint-Céneri-le-Gérei (F) 76 A5
Saint-Céré (F) 93 H1
Saint-Cergue (CH) 86 B5
Saint-Cernin (F) 84 B6
Saint-Cernin-de-l'Herm (F) 93 G1
Saint-Cézaire-sur-Siagne (F) 98 B5
Saint-Chamant (F) 83 J6
Saint-Chamas (F) 94 F3
Saint-Chamond (F) 84 G6
Saint-Chaptes (F) 94 D3
Saint-Chély-d'Apcher (F) 94 B1
Saint-Chély-d'Aubrac (F) 94 A1
Saint-Chinian (F) 94 A4
Saint-Christol (F) 95 F2
Saint-Christol-lès-Alès (F) 94 D2
Saint-Christoly-Médoc (F) 82 D6
Saint-Christophe-des-Bois (F) 75 J4
Saint-Christophe-du-Ligneron (F) 82 B3
Saint-Christophe-en-Bazelle (F) 83 J2
Saint-Christophe-en-Brionnais (F) 84 F4
Saint-Christophe-en-Oisans (F) 85 K7
Saint-Christophe-Vallon (F) 93 J2
Saint-Ciers-Champagne (F) 82 E6
Saint-Ciers-du-Taillon (F) 82 D6
Saint-Ciers-sur-Gironde (F) 82 D6
Saint-Cirgues-de-Jordanne (F) 83 L6
Saint-Cirgues-en-Montagne (F) 94 D1
Saint-Cirq-Lapopie (F) 93 H2
Saint-Cirq-Madelon (F) 93 G1
Saint-Clair-sur-Epte (F) 76 E3
Saint-Clar (F) 93 F3
Saint-Clarde-Riviere (F) 93 G4
Saint-Claud (F) 83 F5
Saint-Claude (F) 85 J4
Saint Clears (GB) 56 E2
Saint-Clément (F) 78 F4
Saint-Clément-des-Baleines (F) 82 B4
Saint-Clément-sur-Durance (F) 95 J1
Saint-Clet (F) 74 E3
Saint-Cloud-en-Dunois (F) 76 D5
Saint-Colomban (F) 82 B2
Saint-Colomban-des-Villards (F) 85 K6
Saint Columb Major (GB) 56 E5
Saint Columb Minor (GB) 56 D5
Saint Combs (GB) 51 O4
Saint-Côme-d'Olt (F) 94 A1
Saint-Constant-Fournoulès (F) 93 J1
Saint-Cosme-en-Vairais (F) 76 B5
Saint-Coulomb (F) 75 H3
Saint-Crépin (F) 82 D4
Saint-Crépin (F) 95 J1
Saint-Crépin-de-Richemont (F) 83 G6
Saint-Crépin-Ibouvillers (F) 76 F3
Saint-Cricq-Chalosse (F) 113 K1
Saint-Cybardeaux (F) 82 E5
Saint-Cyprien (F) 93 G1
Saint-Cyprien (F) 93 G2
Saint-Cyprien-Plage (F) 93 L5
Saint-Cyprien-sur-Dourdou (F) 93 J1
Saint-Cyr-en-Bourg (F) 82 E2
Saint-Cyr-en-Talmondais (F) 82 C4
Saint-Cyr-en-Val (F) 76 E6
Saint-Cyr-le-Chatoux (F) 84 G4
Saint-Cyr-l'École (F) 76 F4
Saint-Cyr-sur-Loire (F) 83 G2
Saint-Cyr-sur-Mer (F) 95 G4
Saint-Cyr-sur-Morin (F) 77 H4
Saint-Dalmas-de-Tende (F) 95 L2
Saint-Dalmas-le-Selvage (F) 98 B4
Saint David's (GB) 63 M5
Saint-Denis (F) 76 F4
Saint-Denis-d'Anjou (F) 75 L5
Saint-Denis-de-Gastines (F) 75 K4
Saint-Denis-de-Jouhet (F) 83 J3
Saint-Denis-de-Pile (F) 82 E7
Saint-Denis-d'Oléron (F) 82 C4
Saint-Denis-d'Orques (F) 75 L4
Saint-Denis-en-Margeride (F) 94 B1
Saint-Denis-la-Chevasse (F) 82 C3
Saint-Denis-les-Ponts (F) 76 D5
Saint-Denis-sur-Sarthon (F) 76 A5
Saint-Denoual (F) 75 G3
Saint-Derrien (F) 74 C3
Saint-Désiré (F) 84 B4
Saint-Didier-en-Velay (F) 84 F6
Saint-Didier-sur-Doulon (F) 84 E6
Saint-Dié (F) 78 F5
Saint-Dier-d'Auvergne (F) 84 D5
Saint-Disdier (F) 95 G1
Saint-Divy (F) 74 C4
Saint-Dizier (F) 78 B4
Saint-Dizier-Leyrenne (F) 83 J4
Saint Dogmaels (GB) 56 E1
Saint-Domineuc (F) 75 H4
Saint-Donat-sur-l'Herbasse (F) 85 G6
Saint-Doulchard (F) 84 B2
Sainte-Alvère-Saint-Laurent-Les-Bâtons (F) 83 G7
Sainte-Anne (F) 76 C4
Sainte-Anne-d'Auray (F) 74 F5
Sainte-Bazeille (F) 92 E1
Sainte-Catherine (F) 83 F5
Sainte-Cécile (F) 84 G4
Sainte-Cécile-les-Vignes (F) 94 E2
Sainte-Cérotte (F) 76 C6
Sainte-Colombe (F) 85 K3
Sainte-Croix (CH) 86 C4
Sainte-Croix (F) 85 H3
Sainte-Croix (F) 95 F1
Sainte-Croix-du-Mont (F) 92 D1
Sainte-Croix-en-Plaine (F) 86 D1
Sainte-Croix-Hague (F) 75 H1
Sainte-Croix-Volvestre (F) 93 G4
Sainte-Enimie (F) 94 B2
Sainte-Eulalie-en-Born (F) 92 B2
Sainte-Feyre (F) 83 J4
Sainte-Florence (F) 82 C3
Sainte-Fortunade (F) 83 J6
Sainte-Foy-de-Montgommery (F) 75 M3
Sainte-Foy-la-Grande (F) 92 E1
Sainte-Foy-l'Argentière (F) 84 F5
Sainte-Foy-Tarentaise (F) 98 B1
Sainte-Gauburge-Sainte-Colombe (F) 76 B4
Sainte-Geneviève (F) 76 F3
Sainte-Geneviève-des-Bois (F) 76 F4
Sainte-Geneviève-sur-Argence (F) 93 K1
Sainte-Hélène (F) 82 D7
Sainte-Hermine (F) 82 C3
Sainte-Jalle (F) 95 F2
Sainte-Juliette-sur-Viaur (F) 93 K2
Saint-Elix-le-Château (F) 93 G4
Saint-Elix-Theux (F) 92 E4
Saint-Ellier-du-Maine (F) 75 J4
Saint-Eloy (F) 74 C4
Saint-Eloy-de-Gy (F) 84 B2
Saint-Eloy-les-Mines (F) 84 C4
Saint-Eloy-les-Tuileries (F) 83 H6
Sainte-Lucie-de-Porto-Vecchio (F) 96 E5
Sainte-Lucie-de-Tallano (F) 96 E5
Sainte-Madeleine (F) 95 L2
Sainte-Marie-aux-Mines (F) 78 G5
Sainte-Marie-de-Campan (F) 92 E5
Sainte-Marie-du-Mont (F) 75 J2
Sainte-Marie-Plage (F) 93 L5
Sainte-Marie-sur-Ouche (F) 85 G2
Sainte-Maure-de-Peyriac (F) 92 E2
Sainte-Maure-de-Touraine (F) 83 G2
Sainte-Maxime (F) 95 J4
Sainte-Menehould (F) 78 B3
Sainte-Mère (F) 92 F2
Sainte-Mère-Église (F) 75 J2
Saint-Emiland (F) 84 F3
Saint-Emilion (F) 92 D1
Sainte-Montaine (F) 76 F7
Saint-Ennemond (F) 84 D3
Sainteny (F) 75 J2
Sainte-Orse (F) 83 H6
Saint-Epain (F) 83 G2
Sainte-Pazanne (F) 82 B2
Saint-Erme-Outre-et-Ramecourt (F) 77 J2
Saintes (F) 82 D5
Sainte-Sabine-Born (F) 93 F1
Sainte-Scolasse-sur-Sarthe (F) 76 B4
Sainte-Sévère (F) 82 E5
Sainte-Sévère-sur-Indre (F) 83 K4
Sainte-Sigolène (F) 84 F6
Saintes-Maries-de-la-Mer (F) 94 D4
Sainte-Soulle (F) 82 C4
Saint-Esteben (F) 113 J2
Saint-Estèphe (F) 82 D6
Saint-Estève (F) 94 A5
Sainte Suzanne (F) 115 F1
Sainte-Suzanne-et-Chammes (F) 75 L4
Sainte-Thorette (F) 84 B2
Saint-Étienne (F) 84 F6
Saint-Étienne-de-Baïgorry (F) 113 J2
Saint-Étienne-de-Cuines (F) 85 K6
Saint-Étienne-de-Fursac (F) 83 J4
Saint-Étienne-de-Lugdarès (F) 94 C1
Saint-Étienne-de-Mer-Morte (F) 82 B3
Saint-Étienne-de-Montluc (F) 82 B2
Saint-Étienne-de-Saint-Geoirs (F) 85 H6
Saint-Étienne-de-Tinée (F) 98 B4
Saint-Étienne-du-Bois (F) 85 H4
Saint-Étienne-du-Grès (F) 94 E3
Saint-Étienne-du-Rouvray (F) 76 D3
Saint-Étienne-en-Dévoluy (F) 95 G1
Saint-Étienne-les-Orgues (F) 95 G2
Saint-Étienne-lès-Remiremont (F) 78 F5
Sainte-Trinité (F) 96 E5
Saint-Evarzec (F) 74 C5
Saint-Fargeau (F) 77 H6
Saint-Félicien (F) 85 G6
Saint-Félix (F) 82 D4
Saint-Félix (F) 82 F6
Saint-Félix-de-Sorgues (F) 94 A3
Saint-Félix-Lauragais (F) 93 H4
Saint-Ferréol (F) 93 F4
Saint-Fiacre (F) 74 E4
Saintfield (GB) 52 D6
Saint Fillans (GB) 52 G2
Saint-Firmin (F) 95 H1
Saint-Florent (F) 76 F6
Saint-Florent (F) 96 E3
Saint-Florent-des-Bois (F) 82 C3
Saint-Florentin (F) 77 J5
Saint-Florent-le-Vieil (F) 75 J6
Saint-Florent-sur-Cher (F) 84 B3
Saint-Floret (F) 84 D5
Saint-Flour (F) 84 D6
Saint-Flovier (F) 83 H3
Saint-Folquin (F) 59 M6
Saint-Fort-sur-Gironde (F) 82 D6
Saint-Fort-sur-le-Né (F) 82 E5
Saint-Fraigne (F) 82 E5
Saint-François (F) 85 K6
Saint-Front (F) 84 F7
Saint-Fulgent (F) 82 C3
Saint-Galmier (F) 84 F5
Saint-Gatien-des-Bois (F) 75 M2
Saint-Gaudens (F) 114 E1
Saint-Gaudéric (F) 115 G1
Saint-Gaultier (F) 83 H3
Saint-Gein (F) 92 D3
Saint-Gély-du-Fesc (F) 94 C3
Saint-Genès-Champespe (F) 84 C6
Saint-Gengoux-le-National (F) 85 G3
Saint-Geniès (F) 83 H7
Saint-Geniez-d'Olt-et-d'Aubrac (F) 94 A2
Saint-Genis-de-Saintonge (F) 82 D6
Saint-Genis-des-Fontaines (F) 94 A5
Saint-Genis-d'Hiersac (F) 82 F5
Saint-Genis-Pouilly (F) 85 K4
Saint-Genou (F) 83 H3
Saint-George (CH) 86 B4
Saint-Georges-d'Aurac (F) 84 E6
Saint-Georges-de-Didonne (F) 82 D5
Saint-Georges-de-Montaigu (F) 82 C3
Saint-Georges-de-Noisné (F) 82 E4
Saint-Georges-de-Reneins (F) 85 G4
Saint-Georges-d'Oléron (F) 82 C5
Saint-Georges-du-Bois (F) 75 M5
Saint-Georges-du-Vièvre (F) 76 C3
Saint-Georges-lès-Baillargeaux (F) 83 F3
Saint-Georges-les-Landes (F) 83 H4
Saint-Georges-Nigremont (F) 84 B5
Saint-Georges-sur-Baulche (F) 77 J6
Saint-Georges-sur-Eure (F) 76 D5
Saint-Georges-sur-Loire (F) 75 K6
Saint-Georges-sur-Meuse (B) 69 J5
Saint-Geours-de-Maremne (F) 92 B3
Saint-Gérand-le-Puy (F) 84 E4
Saint-Gérard (B) 69 H6
Saint-Germain (F) 86 C2
Saint-Germain-Beaupré (F) 83 J4
Saint-Germain-de-Calberte (F) 94 C2
Saint-Germain-de-Confolens (F) 83 G4
Saint-Germain-de-Joux (F) 85 J4
Saint-Germain-de-la-Coudre (F) 76 C5
Saint-Germain-des-Fossés (F) 84 D4
Saint-Germain-des-Prés (F) 77 G6
Saint-Germain-du-Bois (F) 85 H3
Saint-Germain-du-Plain (F) 85 G3
Saint-Germain-du-Puch (F) 92 D1
Saint-Germain-du-Puy (F) 84 B2
Saint-Germain-du-Salembre (F) 83 F6
Saint-Germain-du-Teil (F) 93 L2
Saint-Germain-en-Laye (F) 76 F4
Saint-Germain-la-Campagne (F) 76 B3
Saint-Germain-Laval (F) 84 F5
Saint-Germain-Lembron (F) 84 D6
Saint-Germain-lès-Arlay (F) 85 J3
Saint-Germain-les-Belles (F) 83 H5
Saint-Germain-Lespinasse (F) 84 E4
Saint-Germain-l'Herm (F) 84 E6
Saint-Germain-sur-Ay (F) 75 H2
Saint Germans (GB) 56 F5
Saint-Germé (F) 92 D3
Saint-Germer-de-Fly (F) 76 E3
Saint-Germier (F) 82 E4
Saint-Gervais-d'Auvergne (F) 84 C4
Saint-Gervais-les-Bains (F) 85 L5
Saint-Gervais-sur-Mare (F) 93 L3
Saint-Géry (F) 83 F7
Saint-Géry-Vers (F) 93 H2
Saint-Geyrac (F) 83 G6
Saint-Gildas (F) 74 F4
Saint-Gildas-de-Rhuys (F) 74 F5
Saint-Gildas-des-Bois (F) 75 G5
Saint-Gilles (F) 94 D3
Saint-Gilles-Croix-de-Vie (F) 82 B3
Saint-Gilles-du-Mené (F) 74 F4
Saint-Gilles-Pligeaux (F) 74 E4
Saint-Gingolph (F) 86 C5
Saint-Girons (F) 93 G5
Saint-Girons-en-Marensin (F) 92 B3
Saint-Girons-Plage (F) 92 B3
Saint-Glen (F) 74 F4
Saint-Gobain (F) 77 H2
Saint-Gravé (F) 75 G5
Saint-Guen (F) 74 F4
Saint-Guénolé (F) 74 C5
Saint-Guilhem-le-Désert (F) 94 C3
Saint-Haon (F) 94 C1
Saint Helens (GB) 54 G4
Saint Helens (GB) 58 E6
Saint Helier (GBJ) 75 G2
Saint-Herblain (F) 82 B2
Saint-Hilaire (F) 115 H1
Saint-Hilaire, Talmont- (F) 82 B4
Saint-Hilaire-Bonneval (F) 83 H5
Saint-Hilaire-de-Brens (F) 85 H5
Saint-Hilaire-des-Loges (F) 82 D4
Saint-Hilaire-de-Villefranche (F) 82 D5
Saint-Hilaire-de-Voust (F) 82 D3
Saint-Hilaire-du-Harcouët (F) 75 J3
Saint-Hilaire-Fontaine (F) 84 E3
Saint-Hilaire-la-Palud (F) 82 D4
Saint-Hilaire-la-Treille (F) 83 H4
Saint-Hilaire-le-Vouhis (F) 82 C3
Saint-Hippolyte (F) 79 G5
Saint-Hippolyte (F) 82 D5
Saint-Hippolyte (F) 83 H2
Saint-Hippolyte (F) 86 C3
Saint-Hippolyte-du-Fort (F) 94 C3
Saint-Honoré-les-Bains (F) 84 E3
Saint-Hubert (B) 69 J6
Saint-Hubert (F) 76 B6
Saint-Illide (F) 84 B6
Saint-Imier (CH) 85 L2
Saint-Inglevert (F) 59 L6
Saint Ive (GB) 56 F5
Saint Ives (GB) 56 D5
Saint Ives (GB) 59 G3
Saint-Jacques (I) 86 E6
Saint-Jacques-des-Blats (F) 84 C6
Saint-James (F) 75 J3
Saint-Jean-Brévelay (F) 74 F5
Saint-Jean-d'Angély (F) 82 D5
Saint-Jean-d'Angle (F) 82 D5
Saint-Jean-d'Arvey (F) 85 K5
Saint-Jean-d'Assé (F) 75 M4
Saint-Jean-d'Aulps (F) 85 L4
Saint-Jean-de-Barrou (F) 94 A5
Saint-Jean-de-Blaignac (F) 92 D1
Saint-Jean-de-Bournay (F) 85 H5
Saint-Jean-de-Côle (F) 83 G6
Saint-Jean-de-Daye (F) 75 J2
Saint-Jean-de-Duras (F) 92 E1
Saint-Jean-de-Liversay (F) 82 D4
Saint-Jean-de-Losne (F) 85 H2
Saint-Jean-de-Luz (F) 92 A4
Saint-Jean-de-Marsacq (F) 113 J1
Saint-Jean-de-Maruéjols-et-Avéjan (F) 94 D2
Saint-Jean-de-Maurienne (F) 85 K6
Saint-Jean-de-Monts (F) 82 A3
Saint-Jean-de-Sauves (F) 82 F3
Saint-Jean-de-Sixt (F) 86 B6
Saint-Jean-d'Illac (F) 92 C1
Saint-Jean-d'Ormont (F) 78 F5
Saint-Jean-du-Bruel (F) 94 B2
Saint-Jean-du-Doigt (F) 74 D3
Saint-Jean-du-Gard (F) 94 C2
Saint-Jean-en-Royans (F) 85 H6
Saint-Jean-la-Rivière (F) 95 K3
Saint-Jean-le-Centenier (F) 94 E1
Saint-Jean-le-Thomas (F) 75 H3
Saint-Jean-le-Vieux (F) 85 H4
Saint-Jean-le-Vieux (F) 113 J2
Saint-Jean-Ligoure (F) 83 H5
Saint-Jeannet (F) 95 K3
Saint-Jean-Pied-de-Port (F) 113 J2
Saint-Jean-Poutge (F) 92 E3
Saint-Jean-Soleymieux (F) 84 F5
Saint-Jean-sur-Erve (F) 75 L4
Saint-Jean-sur-Reyssouze (F) 85 J6
Saint-Jeoire (F) 86 B5
Saint-Jeure-d'Ay (F) 85 G6
Saint-Joachim (F) 75 G6
Saint John's (GBM) 61 N3
Saint John's Chapel (GB) 53 L5
Saint Johnstown (IRL) 60 H2
Saint John's Town of Dalry (GB) 52 G4
Saint-Jores (F) 75 J2
Saint-Jory (F) 93 G3
Saint-Jouin-Bruneval (F) 75 M1
Saint-Jouin-de-Marnes (F) 82 E3
Saint-Jouvent (F) 83 H5
Saint-Juéry (F) 93 J3
Saint Julian's (M) 109 F6
Saint-Julien (F) 85 H4
Saint-Julien (F) 93 G4
Saint-Julien-Chapteuil (F) 84 F6
Saint-Julien-de-Civry (F) 84 F4
Saint-Julien-des-Landes (F) 82 B3
Saint-Julien-de-Vouvantes (F) 75 J5
Saint-Julien-du-Sault (F) 77 H5
Saint-Julien-en-Beauchêne (F) 95 G1
Saint-Julien-en-Born (F) 92 B2
Saint-Julien-en-Genevois (F) 86 B5
Saint-Julien-en-Quint (F) 95 F1
Saint-Julien-l'Ars (F) 83 G3
Saint-Julien-la-Vêtre (F) 84 E5
Saint-Julien-le-Faucon (F) 75 M2
Saint-Julien-lès-Metz (F) 78 E3
Saint-Julien-sur-Reyssouze (F) 85 H4
Saint-Junien (F) 83 G5
Saint-Just (F) 94 E2
Saint Just (GB) 56 C5
Saint-Just-en-Chausée (F) 76 F2
Saint-Just-en-Chevalet (F) 84 E5
Saint-Justin (F) 92 D3
Saint-Just-Luzac (F) 82 C5
Saint-Just-Malmont (F) 84 F6
Saint-Just-Saint-Rambert (F) 84 F5
Saint Keverne (GB) 56 D5
Saint Kew Highway (GB) 56 E4
Saint-Lambert-du-Lattay (F) 75 K6
Saint-Laon (F) 82 E3
Saint-Lary (F) 92 F3
Saint-Lary-Soulan (F) 114 D2
Saint-Lattier (F) 85 H6
Saint-Laurent (F) 93 F4
Saint-Laurent-d'Aigouze (F) 94 D3
Saint-Laurent-de-Cerdans (F) 93 K6
Saint-Laurent-de-Chamousset (F) 84 F5
Saint-Laurent-de-la-Cabrerisse (F) 115 J1
Saint-Laurent-de-la-Plaine (F) 75 K6
Saint-Laurent-de-la-Prée (F) 82 C5
Saint-Laurent-de-la-Salanque (F) 94 A5
Saint-Laurent-de-Mure (F) 85 H5
Saint-Laurent-de-Neste (F) 114 D1
Saint-Laurent-des-Autels (F) 82 C2
Saint-Laurent-des-Bois (F) 76 D6
Saint-Laurent-des-Hommes (F) 83 F6
Saint-Laurent-du-Bois (F) 92 D1
Saint-Laurent-du-Pape (F) 94 E1
Saint-Laurent-du-Pont (F) 85 J6
Saint-Laurent-en-Caux (F) 76 C2
Saint-Laurent-en-Gâtines (F) 76 C6
Saint-Laurent-en-Grandvaux (F) 86 A4
Saint-Laurent-la-Vallée (F) 93 G1
Saint-Laurent-la-Vernède (F) 94 D2
Saint-Laurent-les-Bains (F) 94 C1
Saint-Laurent-Médoc (F) 82 D6
Saint-Laurent-sur-Gorre (F) 83 G5
Saint-Laurent-sur-Manoire (F) 83 G6
Saint-Laurent-sur-Mer (F) 75 K2
Saint-Léger (B) 78 D2
Saint-Léger-en-Yvelines (F) 76 E4
Saint-Léger-Magnazeix (F) 83 H4
Saint-Léger-sous-Beuvray (F) 84 F3
Saint-Léger-sur-Dheune (F) 85 G3
Saint-Léon (F) 84 E4
Saint-Léonard-de-Noblat (F) 83 J5
Saint-Léon-sur-Vézère (F) 83 H6
Saint-Lizier (F) 93 G5
Saint-Lizier (F) 114 F1
Saint-Lô (F) 75 J2
Saint-Lô-d'Ourville (F) 75 H2
Saint-Loubès (F) 92 D1
Saint-Louis (F) 86 E2
Saint-Louis-de-Montferrand (F) 82 D7
Saint-Louis-et-Parahou (F) 93 J5
Saint-Loup-de-la-Salle (F) 85 G3
Saint-Loup-du-Dorat (F) 75 L5
Saint-Loup-Hors (F) 75 K2
Saint-Loup-Lamaire (F) 82 E3
Saint-Loup-sur-Semouse (F) 78 E6
Saint-Lunaire (F) 75 G3
Saint-Lyphard (F) 75 G6
Saint-Lys (F) 93 G4
Saint-Macaire (F) 92 D1
Saint-Macaire-en-Mauges (F) 82 C2
Saint-Maclou (F) 76 B3
Saint-Magne (F) 92 C1
Saint-Maigrin (F) 82 E6
Saint-Maixant (F) 83 K5
Saint-Maixent-l'École (F) 82 E4
Saint-Malo (F) 75 G3
Saint-Malo-de-Beignon (F) 75 G5
Saint-Malo-des-Trois-Fontaines (F) 74 G4
Saint-Malô-du-Bois (F) 82 D3
Saint-Malo-en-Donziois (F) 84 D2
Saint-Mamert (F) 84 G4
Saint-Mamert-du-Gard (F) 94 D3
Saint-Mamet-la-Salvetat (F) 93 J1
Saint-Mandrier-sur-Mer (F) 95 G4
Saint-Marcel-de-Careinet (F) 94 D2
Saint-Marcellin (F) 85 H6
Saint-Marcet (F) 114 E1
Saint-Marc-sur-Seine (F) 77 L6
Saint-Mard-de-Reno (F) 76 C4
Saint-Mards-en-Othe (F) 77 J5
Saint-Mard-sur-le-Mont (F) 77 L4
Saint Margaret's at Cliffe (GB) 68 A4
Saint Margaret's Hope (GB) 49 C6
Saint-Mars-des-Pres (F) 82 C3
Saint-Mars-d'Outillé (F) 76 B6
Saint-Mars-du-Désert (F) 75 J6
Saint-Mars-la-Jaille (F) 75 J5
Saint-Martial (F) 94 D1
Saint-Martial-de-Valette (F) 83 G5
Saint-Martial-sur-Isop (F) 83 G4
Saint Martin (GBG) 74 F2
Saint-Martin-aux-Buneaux (F) 76 C2
Saint-Martin-d'Ablois (F) 77 J3
Saint-Martin-d'Ardèche (F) 94 E2
Saint-Martin-d'Auxigny (F) 84 B2
Saint-Martin-de-Belleville (F) 85 L6
Saint-Martin-de-Boscherville (F) 76 C3
Saint-Martin-de-Bossenay (F) 77 J5
Saint-Martin-de-Bréhal (F) 75 H3
Saint-Martin-de-Crau (F) 94 E3
Saint-Martin-de-la-Lieue (F) 76 B3
Saint-Martin-de-Lamps (F) 83 J3
Saint-Martin-de-la-Place (F) 75 L6
Saint-Martin-de-Londres (F) 94 C3
Saint-Martin-d'Entraunes (F) 95 J2
Saint-Martin-de-Queyrières (F) 98 B3
Saint-Martin-de-Ré (F) 82 C4
Saint-Martin-des-Besaces (F) 75 K2
Saint-Martin-de-Seignanx (F) 113 J1
Saint-Martin-des-Faux (F) 93 K2
Saint-Martin-des-Puits (F) 115 J1
Saint-Martin-d'Estréaux (F) 84 E4
Saint-Martin-d'Estréaux (F) 84 G5
Saint-Martin-de-Valmas (F) 84 F7
Saint-Martin-d'Oney (F) 92 C3
Saint-Martin-d'Ordon (F) 77 H5
Saint-Martin-d'Oydes (F) 115 F1
Saint-Martin-du-Fouilloux (F) 82 E3
Saint-Martin-du-Frêne (F) 85 J4
Saint-Martin-en-Campagne (F) 76 D2
Saint-Martin-l'Ars (F) 83 G4
Saint-Martin-le-Gaillard (F) 76 D2
Saint-Martin-Lestra (F) 84 F5
Saint-Martin-le-Vieux (F) 83 H5
Saint-Martin-lez-Tatinghem (F) 59 M6
Saint-Martin-l'Heureux (F) 77 K3
Saint-Martin-Osmonville (F) 76 D2
Saint-Martin-sur-Ouanne (F) 77 H6
Saint-Martin-Valmeroux (F) 84 B6
Saint-Martin-Vésubie (F) 98 C4
Saint-Martory (F) 93 F4
Saint Mary's (GB) 49 C6
Saint-Mathieu (F) 83 G5
Saint-Mathieu-de-Tréviers (F) 94 C3
Saint-Mathurin-sur-Loire (F) 75 L6
Saint-Matré (F) 93 G2
Saint-Maulvis (F) 76 E2
Saint-Maur (F) 76 E2
Saint-Maurice (CH) 85 M4
Saint-Maurice-de-Lignon (F) 84 F6
Saint-Maurice-des-Lions (F) 83 G5
Saint-Maurice-lès-Charencey (F) 76 C4
Saint-Maurice-près-Pionsat (F) 83 L4
Saint-Maurice-sur-Aveyron (F) 77 G6
Saint-Maurice-sur-Moselle (F) 86 C2
Saint-Maurin (F) 93 F2
Saint Mawes (GB) 56 D5
Saint-Max (F) 78 E4
Saint-Maximin-la-Sainte-Baume (F) 95 G4
Saint-Maxire (F) 82 E4
Saint-Méard-de-Drône (F) 83 F6
Saint-Méard-de-Gurçon (F) 92 E1
Saint-Médard-de-Guizières (F) 82 E6
Saint-Médard-de-Presque (F) 93 H1
Saint-Médard-en-Jalles (F) 92 C1
Saint-Médart (F) 82 E5
Saint-Méen-le-Grand (F) 75 G4
Saint-Meille (F) 92 E2
Saint-Menges (F) 78 B2
Saint-Menoux (F) 84 D3
Saint-Mesmin (F) 77 J5
Saint-Mesmin (F) 82 D3
Saint-Michel (F) 77 K2
Saint-Michel (F) 92 E4
Saint-Michel (F) 114 F1
Saint-Michel-Chef-Chef (F) 82 A2
Saint-Michel-de-Castelnau (F) 92 D2
Saint-Michel-de-Double (F) 83 F6
Saint-Michel-de-Maurienne (F) 85 K6
Saint-Michel-en-Brenne (F) 83 H3
Saint-Michel-en-Grève (F) 74 D3
Saint-Michel-en-l'Herm (F) 82 C4
Saint-Michel-l'Observatoire (F) 95 G3
Saint-Michel-Mont-Mercure (F) 82 D3
Saint-Mihiel (F) 78 D4
Saint-Mitre-les-Remparts (F) 94 F4
Saint Monance (GB) 53 K2
Saint Mullin's (IRL) 63 J4
Saint-Nabord (F) 78 F5
Saint-Nauphary (F) 93 G3
Saint-Nazaire (F) 82 A2
Saint-Nazaire-le-Désert (F) 95 F1
Saint-Nectaire (F) 84 D5
Saint Neot (GB) 56 E5
Saint-Nic (F) 74 C4
Saint Nicholas (GB) 57 H3
Saint-Nicodème (F) 74 E4
Saint-Nicolas (B) 69 K5
Saint-Nicolas = Sint-Niklaas (B) 68 G4
Saint-Nicolas-de-la-Grave (F) 93 G2
Saint-Nicolas-de-Port (F) 78 E4
Saint-Nicolas-des-Motets (F) 76 D6
Saint-Nicolas-du-Pélem (F) 74 E4
Saint-Omer (F) 68 C5
Saint-Omer-en-Chaussée (F) 76 F2
Saint-Ost (F) 92 E4
Saint-Ouen-de-Thouberville (F) 76 C3
Saint-Ouen-du-Breuil (F) 76 D2
Saint-Ovin (F) 75 J3
Saint-Pair-sur-Mer (F) 75 H3
Saint-Palais (F) 113 J2
Saint-Palais-sur-Mer (F) 82 C5
Saint-Pal-de-Mons (F) 84 F6
Saint-Pal-de-Senouire (F) 84 E6
Saint-Papoul (F) 93 J4
Saint-Pardoux (F) 82 E3
Saint-Pardoux (F) 83 H4
Saint-Pardoux-la-Rivière (F) 83 G6
Saint-Parize-le-Châtel (F) 84 D3
Saint-Pastour (F) 92 F2
Saint-Paterne-Racan (F) 76 B6
Saint-Paul (F) 83 H5
Saint-Paul (F) 95 J1
Saint-Paul (F) 95 K3
Saint-Paul-Cap-de-Joux (F) 93 H3
Saint-Paul-de-Fenouillet (F) 115 H2
Saint-Paul-de-Jarrat (F) 115 G2
Saint-Paul-des-Landes (F) 83 K7
Saint-Paul-de-Varax (F) 85 H4
Saint-Paul-d'Oueil (F) 92 F5
Saint-Paul-en-Forêt (F) 95 J3
Saint-Paul-et-Valmalle (F) 94 C3
Saint-Paulien (F) 84 E6
Saint-Paul-le-Gaultier (F) 76 A5
Saint-Paul-le-Jeune (F) 94 D2
Saint-Paul-lès-Dax (F) 92 B3
Saint Paul's Walden (GB) 59 G4
Saint-Paul-Trois-Châteaux (F) 94 E2
Saint-Pé-de-Bigorre (F) 114 C1
Saint-Pée-sur-Nivelle (F) 92 A4
Saint-Péran (F) 75 G4
Saint-Péravy-la-Colombe (F) 76 E5
Saint-Péray (F) 85 G7
Saint-Perdon (F) 92 C3
Saint-Père (F) 84 C2
Saint-Père-en-Retz (F) 82 A2
Saint-Peter (GBJ) 75 G2
Saint Peter Port (GBG) 74 F2
Saint-Pey-d'Armens (F) 92 D1
Saint-Philbert-de-Grand-Lieu (F) 82 B2
Saint-Pierre (I) 86 D6
Saint-Pierre-à-Champ (F) 82 E2
Saint-Pierre-d'Albigny (F) 85 K5
Saint-Pierre-de-Chartreuse (F) 85 J6
Saint-Pierre-de-Chignac (F) 83 G6
Saint-Pierre-de-Jards (F) 84 A2
Saint-Pierre-de-Maille (F) 83 G3
Saint-Pierre-d'Entremont (F) 75 K3
Saint-Pierre-de-Plesguen (F) 75 H4
Saint-Pierre-des-Corps (F) 83 G2
Saint-Pierre-des-Nids (F) 76 A5
Saint-Pierre-de-Trivisy (F) 93 J3
Saint-Pierre-d'Oléron (F) 82 C5
Saint-Pierre-du-Chemin (F) 82 D3
Saint-Pierre-du-Vauvray (F) 76 D3
Saint-Pierre-Église (F) 75 J1
Saint-Pierre-en-Auge (F) 75 M2
Saint-Pierre-en-Port (F) 76 B2
Saint-Pierre-le-Moûtier (F) 84 D3
Saint-Pierre-Montlimart (F) 82 C2
Saint-Pierre-Quiberon (F) 74 E5
Saint-Pierre-sur-Dives (F) 76 A3
Saint-Pierre-sur-Mer (F) 93 L4
Saint-Pierre-sur-Orthe (F) 75 L4
Saint-Pierre-Toirac (F) 93 H1
Saint-Pierreville (F) 94 D1
Saint-Plancard (F) 92 F4
Saint-Pois (F) 75 J3
Saint-Poix (F) 75 J5
Saint-Pol-de-Léon (F) 74 D3
Saint-Polgues (F) 84 E5
Saint-Pol-sur-Mer (F) 59 M5
Saint-Pol-sur-Ternoise (F) 68 C6
Saint-Polycarpe (F) 115 H1
Saint-Pompont (F) 93 G1
Saint-Poncy (F) 84 D6
Saint-Pons-de-Thomières (F) 93 K4
Saint-Porchaire (F) 82 D5
Saint-Pourçain-sur-Sioule (F) 84 D4
Saint-Priest-des-Champs (F) 84 C5
Saint-Priest-sous-Aixe (F) 83 H5
Saint-Priest-Taurion (F) 83 H5
Saint-Privat (F) 83 K6
Saint-Privat-la-Montagne (F) 78 E3
Saint-Prouant (F) 82 D3
Saint-Puy (F) 92 E3
Saint-Quay-Portrieux (F) 74 F3
Saint-Quentin (F) 77 H2
Saint-Quentin-en-Tourmont (F) 68 B6
Saint-Quentin-la-Poterie (F) 94 D2
Saint-Quentin-les-Anges (F) 75 K5
Saint-Quentin-sur-Indrois (F) 83 H2
Saint-Quentin-sur-Isère (F) 85 J6
Saint-Quirin (F) 78 G4
Saint-Rambert-d'Albon (F) 85 G6
Saint-Raphaël (F) 98 B6
Saint-Remèze (F) 94 E2
Saint-Rémy (F) 82 F7
Saint-Rémy (F) 85 G3
Saint-Rémy-Blanzy (F) 77 H3
Saint-Rémy-de-Chaudes-Aigues (F) 93 L1
Saint-Rémy-de-Provence (F) 94 E3
Saint-Rémy-du-Plain (F) 75 H4
Saint-Rémy-en-Bouzemont-Saint-Genest-et-Isson (F) 78 B4
Saint-Rémy-en-Montmorillon (F) 83 G4
Saint-Rémy-en-Rollat (F) 84 D4
Saint-Rémy-sur-Avre (F) 76 D4
Saint-Rémy-sur-Durolle (F) 84 E5
Saint-Renan (F) 74 B4
Saint-Révérien (F) 84 E2
Saint-Rhémy-en-Bosses (I) 86 D6
Saint-Riquier (F) 68 B6
Saint-Rivoal (F) 74 C4
Saint-Romain (F) 83 F4
Saint-Romain-de-Colbosc (F) 76 B2
Saint-Romain-le-Puy (F) 84 F5
Saint-Rome-de-Cernon (F) 94 A2
Saint-Rome-de-Tarn (F) 94 A2
Saint-Saëns (F) 76 D2
Saint-Salvy-de-la-Balme (F) 93 J3
Saint Sampson (GBG) 74 F2
Saint-Samson-la-Poterie (F) 76 E2
Saint-Sardos (F) 93 G3
Saint-Satur (F) 84 C2
Saint-Saturnin (F) 83 K3
Saint-Saturnin (F) 84 D5
Saint-Saturnin-de-Lenne (F) 93 L2
Saint-Saturnin-lès-Apt (F) 95 F3
Saint-Saud-Lacoussière (F) 83 G5
Saint-Saulge (F) 84 E2
Saint-Sauvant (F) 82 E5
Saint-Sauvant (F) 82 F4
Saint-Sauves-d'Auvergne (F) 83 L5
Saint-Sauveur (F) 74 C4
Saint-Sauveur (F) 82 A3
Saint-Sauveur (F) 82 E3
Saint-Sauveur (F) 86 B2
Saint-Sauveur-de-Montagut (F) 94 E1
Saint-Sauveur-en-Puisaye (F) 77 H6
Saint-Sauveur-en-Rue (F) 84 F6
Saint-Sauveur-Lendelin (F) 75 J2
Saint-Sauveur-le-Vicomte (F) 75 H2
Saint-Sauveur-sur-Tinée (F) 98 C4
Saint-Savin (F) 82 E6
Saint-Savin (F) 83 G3
Saint-Savinien (F) 82 D5
Saint-Sébastien-sur-Loire (F) 82 B2
Saint-Secondin (F) 83 F4
Saint-Séglin (F) 75 G5
Saint-Seine (F) 84 E3
Saint-Seine-en-Bâche (F) 85 H2
Saint-Seine-l'Abbaye (F) 77 L7
Saint-Senoch (F) 83 G2
Saint-Sernin-sur-Rance (F) 93 K3
Saint-Servan-sur-Mer (F) 75 G3
Saint-Seurin-de-Cadourne (F) 82 D6
Saint-Sever (F) 92 C3
Saint-Sever-Calvados (F) 75 J3
Saint-Sever-de-Rustin (F) 92 E4
Saint-Séverin (F) 83 F6
Saint-Sorlin-d'Arves (F) 85 K6
Saint-Sornin (F) 83 F5
Saint-Sornin-Leulac (F) 83 H4
Saint-Soupplets (F) 77 G3
Saint-Sulpice (F) 93 H1
Saint-Sulpice (F) 93 H3
Saint-Sulpice-de-Favières (F) 76 F4
Saint-Sulpice-Laurière (F) 83 H4
Saint-Sulpice-les-Champs (F) 83 K5
Saint-Sulpice-sur-Lèze (F) 93 G4
Saint-Sylvain (F) 75 L2
Saint-Symphorien (F) 92 D2
Saint-Symphorien-de-Lay (F) 84 F5
Saint-Symphorien-d'Ozon (F) 85 G5
Saint-Symphorien-sur-Coise (F) 84 F5
Saint-Thégonnec (F) 74 D3
Saint-Thibault (F) 84 F2
Saint-Thibéry (F) 94 B4
Saint-Thurien (F) 74 D5
Saint-Trivier-de-Courtes (F) 85 H4
Saint-Trivier-sur-Moignans (F) 85 G4
Saint-Trojan-les-Bains (F) 82 C5
Saint-Trond = Sint-Truiden (B) 69 J5
Saint-Tropez (F) 95 J4
Saint-Urcize (F) 93 L1
Saint-Ursanne (CH) 86 D3
Saint-Vaast-la-Hougue (F) 75 J1
Saint-Valérien (F) 77 H5
Saint-Valery-en-Caux (F) 76 C2
Saint-Valery-sur-Somme (F) 68 B6
Saint-Vallier (F) 84 F3
Saint-Vallier (F) 85 G6
Saint-Vallier-de-Thiey (F) 98 B5
Saint-Varent (F) 82 E3
Saint-Vaury (F) 83 J4
Saint-Venant (F) 68 D5
Saint-Véran (F) 95 J1
Saint-Viâtre (F) 76 E6
Saint-Victor (F) 83 L4
Saint-Victor-de-Chrétienville (F) 76 C3
Saint-Victor-et-Melvieu (F) 94 A2
Saint-Victor-l'Abbaye (F) 76 D2
Saint-Vigor-des-Mézerets (F) 75 K3
Saint-Vigor-le-Grand (F) 75 K2
Saint-Vincent-Bragny (F) 84 F3
Saint-Vincent-de-Connezac (F) 83 F6
Saint-Vincent-de-Reins (F) 84 F4
Saint-Vincent-de-Tyrosse (F) 113 J1
Saint-Vincent-du-Lorouër (F) 76 B6
Saint-Vincent-la-Châtre (F) 82 E4
Saint-Vincent-Sterlanges (F) 82 C3
Saint-Vincent-sur-Jabron (F) 95 G2
Saint-Vincent-sur-Oust (F) 75 G5
Saint-Vit (F) 85 J2
Saint-Vith (B) 69 L6
Saint-Vivien-de-Médoc (F) 82 C6
Saint-Vran (F) 75 G4
Saint-Vulbas (F) 85 H5
Saint-Wandrille-Rançon (F) 76 C2
Saint-Yaguen (F) 92 C3
Saint-Yorre (F) 84 D4
Saint-Yrieix-la-Perche (F) 83 H5
Saint-Yvy (F) 74 D5
Saint-Yzans-de-Médoc (F) 82 D6
Saint-Zacharie (F) 95 G4
Sainville (F) 76 E5
Sairakkala (FIN) 36 D2
Sairiala (FIN) 35 P2
Sairinen (FIN) 35 J3
Saissac (F) 93 J4
Saittarova (S) 22 E2
Saizerais (F) 78 E4
Sajach (A) 91 J6
Sajaniemi (FIN) 35 O3
Şajince (SRB) 175 H4
Šajkaš (SRB) 166 F3
Sajólád (H) 160 B1
Sajópüspöki (H) 155 G5
Sajószentpéter (H) 155 H5
Sajóvámos (H) 160 B1
Såjvis (S) 27 K3
Saka (LV) 132 C4
Sakaevi (TR) 185 F4
Säkäjärvi (FIN) 37 J3
Sakališča (BY) 134 G6
Sakallı (TR) 184 F2
Sakalova (BY) 138 G3
Sakalova (BY) 143 N4
Sakalovičy (BY) 139 K5
Sakar (TR) 183 L5
Sakarca (TR) 185 H5
Sakarkaya (TR) 190 D3
Sakarkaya (TR) 190 D6
Sakarya (TR) 192 D1
Sakarya = Adapazarı (TR) 183 K4
Šakiai (LT) 137 J4
Säkinmäki (FIN) 29 G7
Sakız (TR) 177 H6
Sakız (TR) 185 J2
Sakız (TR) 199 F2
Sakızlık (TR) 183 J6
Säkkilä (FIN) 23 M4
Saklıkent (TR) 197 H2
Sakovičy (BY) 138 G4
Sakovščina (BY) 138 D5
Sakowczyk (PL) 155 L3
Sakrishei (N) 20 D8
Saksala (FIN) 35 K3
Saksala (FIN) 36 E4
Sakseid (N) 38 B3
Saksild (DK) 46 F2
Sakskøbing (DK) 47 J4
Saksum (N) 31 N5
Saksun (FO) 48 D3
Saku (EST) 130 G2
Šakule (SRB) 167 F3
Šakvietis (LT) 136 G3
Saky (Krym) 13 K3
Sakyatan (TR) 192 E5
Säkylä (FIN) 35 K2
Šakyna (LT) 137 J1
Sal (S) 40 C6
Sala (I) 101 G4
Sala (S) 41 L3
Šaľa (SK) 158 E1
Sala Baganza (I) 99 J3
Sălacea (RO) 160 E3
Salacgrīva (LV) 133 J2
Sala Consilina (I) 104 E5
Saladamm (S) 41 L3
Salaguba (BY) 144 G5
Salahmi (FIN) 29 G4
Salahovo (RUS) 139 K1
Salakas (LT) 138 D2
Sálakos (GR) 196 C3
Salakovac (SRB) 167 H4
Salamajärvi (FIN) 27 L8
Salamanca (E) 117 K2
Salamankafalı (TR) 185 J6
Salamína (GR) 187 G4
Salamy (BY) 145 N2
Salance (BY) 145 M3
Salandra (I) 105 F4
Salanky (UA) 156 C5
Salantai (LT) 136 F1
Salar (E) 126 B5
Salar (TR) 191 K3
Sălard (RO) 160 E3
Sălard (RO) 161 L4
Salardú (E) 93 F5
Salas (E) 111 G2
Salaš (SRB) 168 C5
Salas, Las (E) 112 A3
Salas Altas (E) 114 D3
Salasco (I) 98 E2
Salas de Bureba (E) 112 E3
Salas de los Infantes (E) 112 E4
Salàs de Pallars (E) 114 E3
Salaši (UA) 156 D1
Salaspils (LV) 133 J4
Sălașu de Sus (RO) 168 D2
Sălățig (RO) 161 G3
Sălătrucu (RO) 169 H3
Salavatlı (TR) 190 E5
Salbantone = Salmantón (E) 112 E2
Salbaş (TR) 199 K1
Salbertrand (I) 98 B2
Salbo (S) 40 G3
Sälboda (S) 40 C3
Salbohed (S) 41 K3
Salboro (I) 101 F2
Sal-Breizh = Sel-de-Bretagne, Le (F) 75 H5
Salbris (F) 83 K2
Salbrovad (DK) 46 E3
Salbu (N) 30 C5
Salce (E) 111 K2
Salcea (RO) 162 C3
Salcedo (E) 111 H2
Salcia (RO) 170 C3
Salcia Tudor (RO) 170 E3
Șălciile (RO) 170 C4
Šalčininkai (LT) 138 B5
Šalčininkėliai (LT) 138 B5
Sălcioara (RO) 170 D4
Sălciua de Jos (RO) 161 G5
Salcombe (GB) 57 G5
Sălcuța (MD) 163 J5
Salda (TR) 191 H5
Saldaña (E) 111 K3
Säldebråten (S) 40 D3
Saldes (E) 115 G3
Saldus (LV) 132 E4
Sale (GB) 55 H4
Sale (I) 98 F3
Saleby (S) 40 D6
Salem (D) 79 L6
Salem (S) 41 N4
Salemi (I) 108 C2
Salen (GB) 52 D1
Salen (N) 24 F5
Sälen (S) 32 E5
Saler, el (E) 121 H5
Salérans (F) 95 G2
Salernes (F) 95 H3
Salerno (I) 104 C4
Salers (F) 84 B6
Salettes (F) 94 C1
Salford (GB) 55 H4
S'Algar (E) 123 K3
Salgótarján (H) 159 J1
Salgueiro do Campo (P) 118 A4
Sali (HR) 172 B2
Salica (I) 107 H4
Salice (F) 96 D4
Salice Salentino (I) 105 J5
Salice Terme (I) 98 G3
Saliente Alto (E) 127 F4
Salientes (E) 111 G3
Salies-de-Béarn (F) 113 K2
Salies-du-Salat (F) 93 F4
Salignac-Eyvignes (F) 83 H7
Saligny (RO) 171 G5
Saligny-sur-Roudon (F) 84 E4
Salihler (TR) 182 B6
Salihler (TR) 192 B2
Salihler (TR) 192 C6
Salihli (TR) 190 E4
Salihorsk (BY) 144 G3
Salillas (E) 114 C4
Salin (TR) 184 E4
Salinas (E) 111 H1
Salinas (E) 127 J2
Salinas de Pinilla (E) 120 C6
Salinas de Pisuerga (E) 112 C3
Salinas de Sin (E) 92 E5
Salin-de-Giraud (F) 94 E4
Salindres (F) 94 D2
Saline (F) 75 L2
Saline di Volterra (I) 99 K6
Salines, ses (E) 123 H4
Salinge (S) 41 M3
Sälinkää (FIN) 36 D3
Salins-d'Hyères, les (F) 95 H4
Salins-les-Bains (F) 86 A4
Salir (P) 124 C5
Salir do Porto (P) 116 C5
Salisbury (GB) 58 D5
Săliște (RO) 161 H6
Săliștea (RO) 161 G6
Săliștea de Sus (RO) 161 J2
Salka (SK) 154 D6
Salkola (FIN) 35 N3
Saľkove (UA) 163 K2
Salla (A) 91 G5
Salla (EST) 131 K3
Salla (FIN) 23 L3
Sallahn (D) 66 D4
Sallanches (F) 86 C6
Sallent (E) 115 G4
Sallent de Gállego (E) 113 L3
Sälleryd (S) 44 H6
Salles (F) 92 C1
Salles (F) 93 J2
Salles-Courbatiès (F) 93 J2
Salles-Curan (F) 94 A2
Salles-sur-l'Hers (F) 93 H4
Salles-sur-Verdon, Les (F) 95 H3
Sallgast (D) 73 K2
Sällinkylä (FIN) 28 E7
Sallins (IRL) 63 J2
Sällsjö (S) 25 H8
Sällstorp (S) 43 K4
Salmaise (F) 77 L7
Salman (TR) 189 H2
Salmanköy (TR) 185 J5
Salmanlı (TR) 185 H6
Salmanovo (BG) 177 G2
Salmanskirchen (D) 81 G4
Salmantón (E) 112 E2
Salme (EST) 130 B4
Salme (S) 18 C7
Salmenkylä (FIN) 29 G7
Salmenkylä (FIN) 29 J5
Salmentaka (FIN) 35 O2
Salmerón (E) 120 D2
Salmi (FIN) 35 M2
Salmi (FIN) 36 H3
Salmi (RUS) 7 S5
Salmiech (F) 93 K2
Salmijärvi (FIN) 23 K6
Saľmijarvi (RUS) 19 N5
Salminen (FIN) 29 H6
Salmis (S) 22 F5
Salmivaara (FIN) 22 F1
Salmivaara (FIN) 23 L3
Salmoral (E) 119 F2
Saľnycja (UA) 150 G4
Salo (E) 115 G4
Salo (FIN) 35 M4
Salo (FIN) 36 E2
Salò (I) 99 K1
Salobral, El (E) 120 E6
Salobreña (E) 126 C6
Saločiai (LT) 137 L1
Saloinen (FIN) 22 G7
Saloinen (FIN) 36 C3
Salo-Issakka (FIN) 37 L2
Salokunta (FIN) 28 E8
Salokylä (FIN) 29 K6
Salokylä (FIN) 29 L5
Salon (F) 77 K4
Salon-de-Provence (F) 94 F3
Saloníki (GR) 178 D5
Saloníki = Thessaloníki (GR) 179 H3
Salonkylä (FIN) 27 K7
Salonpää (FIN) 29 K7
Salonta (RO) 160 D4
Salorino (E) 118 B5
Salornay-sur-Guye (F) 84 G3
Salorno (I) 88 E5
Salou (E) 115 F5
Salouël (F) 76 F2
Šalovci (SLO) 158 B4
Sálpi (GR) 181 G2
Salsadella = Salzedella, La (E) 122 B2
Salsån (S) 32 H2
Salsbruket (N) 24 F5
Salses (F) 94 A5
Sălsig (RO) 161 G2
Šal'sk (RUS) 13 N3
Šal'skij (RUS) 7 U5
Salsomaggiore Terme (I) 99 H3
Salt (E) 115 J4
Saltador, El (E) 127 G5
Saltanova (BY) 145 M4
Saltarö (S) 34 C6
Saltash (GB) 56 F5
Saltbæk (DK) 46 H2
Saltburn-by-the-Sea (GB) 53 O5
Saltcoats (GB) 52 F3
Saltfleet (GB) 55 N4
Saltık (TR) 191 J4
Salto (P) 110 D5
Saltö (S) 39 O5
Saltoluoktafjällstation (S) 21 H6
Salton (GB) 55 L2
Saltrød (N) 39 J6
Saltsjöbaden (S) 41 O4
Saltuklu (TR) 184 F3
Saltukova (TR) 184 D2
Saltum (DK) 42 E4
Saltvik (AX) 34 F4
Saltvik (IS) 17 J3
Saltvik (S) 45 K4
Saltvikhamn (N) 24 E7
Saluböle (S) 26 F8
Saludecio (I) 101 H5
Saludes de Castroponce (E) 111 H4
Saluggia (I) 98 E2
Salungen (S) 40 C3
Salur (TR) 182 E5
Salur (TR) 192 B4
Salur (TR) 192 B7
Salur (TR) 193 G5
Salurn = Salorno (I) 88 E5
Salussola (I) 86 F7
Salute di Livenza, la (I) 89 H6
Saluzzo (I) 95 L1
Salva (RO) 161 J3
Salvacañete (E) 120 E3
Salvada (P) 124 D4
Salvador de Zapardiel (E) 119 G1
Salvagnac (F) 93 H3
Salvaleón (E) 125 F2
Salvaterra de Magos (P) 124 B1
Salvaterra do Extremo (P) 117 H4
Salvaterra do Miño (E) 110 C4
Salvatierra (E) 113 G3
Salvatierra de Escá (E) 114 A2
Salvatierra de los Barros (E) 125 F3
Salve (I) 105 K6
Salvetat-Peyralès, La (F) 93 J2
Salvetat-sur-Agout, La (F) 93 K3
Salviac (F) 93 G1
Salvore = Savudrija (HR) 164 B4
Salwayash (GB) 58 B6
Salza di Pinerolo (I) 98 C3
Salzano (I) 101 G1
Salzatal (D) 72 F2
Salzberg (D) 71 J5
Salzbergen (D) 70 D2
Salzburg (A) 89 J2
Salzedella, La (E) 122 B2
Salzgitter (D) 72 C1
Salzhausen (D) 66 C4
Salzhemmendorf (D) 72 B1
Salzkotten (D) 70 G3
Salzmünde (D) 72 F2
Salzwedel (D) 66 E5
Salzweg (D) 90 D2
Šama (E) 111 H2
Šamac (BIH) 166 B3
Samachvalavičy (BY) 138 G6
Samadet (F) 92 D3
Samadrexhë (RKS) 174 F3
Samaila (SRB) 174 E1
Samailli (TR) 190 E4
Samala (GB) 50 C4
Şamalia (MD) 163 G6
Şamandağ (TR) 13 L7
Şamandıra (TR) 183 H4
Sámano (E) 112 E2
Samaravičy (BY) 143 M4
Samarína (GR) 178 E4
Samarinești (RO) 168 E4
Samary (BY) 149 L2
Samassi (I) 97 C5
Samat (TR) 184 B4
Samat (TR) 184 D4
Samatan (F) 93 F4
Samatzai (I) 97 D5
Sambade (P) 110 F6
Sâmbăta (RO) 160 E4
Sâmbăta, Stațiunea (RO) 169 H2
Sâmbăta de Jos (RO) 161 K6
Sâmbăta de Sus (RO) 169 H2
Şambayadı (TR) 199 K1
Sambir (UA) 156 D2
Samboal (E) 112 C6
Samborowo (PL) 141 N3
Sambreville (B) 69 H6
Sambron (SK) 155 H3
Sambuc, le (F) 94 E3
Sambuca di Sicilia (I) 108 D2
Sambuca Pistoiese (I) 100 E4
Sâmburești (RO) 169 G4
Samčyky (UA) 157 M2
Samedan (CH) 87 J4
Sameniv (UA) 157 K2
Samer (F) 68 B5
Sames (E) 112 A2
Sameteli (TR) 182 D5
Samhorodok (UA) 151 H4
Samhorodok (UA) 151 K4
Sámi (GR) 186 B3
Şamlar (TR) 183 G3
Şamlar (TR) 184 E3
Şamlar (TR) 184 E3
Şamlı (TR) 182 E6
Sammakko (S) 22 D3
Sammakkola (FIN) 29 J4
Sammakkovaara (FIN) 29 K6
Sammaljärvi (FIN) 37 K2
Sammaljoki (FIN) 35 M2
Såmmarlappastugan (S) 20 G6
Sammatti (FIN) 28 D7
Sammatti (FIN) 35 N4
Sammi (FIN) 35 K1
Sammichele di Bari (I) 105 G4
Samnaun (CH) 87 K4
Samo (I) 109 K1
Samobor (HR) 164 F3
Samodiva (BG) 176 D6
Samodreža = Samadrexhë (RKS) 174 F3
Samoëns (F) 86 C5
Samões (P) 110 E6
Samokleski (PL) 148 F3
Samokleski Małe (PL) 141 J4
Samokov (BG) 175 L4
Samokov (MK) 174 F5
Samolukovo (RUS) 135 K4
Samolva (RUS) 131 N4
Samora Correira (P) 116 D6
Şamoranovo (BG) 175 K4
Šamorín (SK) 158 D1
Samos (E) 110 E3
Sámos (GR) 189 J4
Samoš (SRB) 167 G3
Samothráki (GR) 181 H4
Samovodene (BG) 176 E2
Samper de Calanda (E) 113 L6
Sampeyre (I) 95 K1
Sampieri (I) 109 G4
Sampigny (F) 78 D4
Samprizón (E) 110 C3
Sampu (FIN) 35 L2
Samrı (TR) 183 K5
Samson (F) 86 A3
Samsonów (PL) 148 C4
Şamșud (RO) 161 F3
Samsun (TR) 13 L5
Samtens (D) 47 M5
Samuel (P) 116 D3
Samugheo (I) 97 C4
Samuilovo (BG) 177 F3
Samujlikovo (RUS) 131 O3
Samuliha (RUS) 135 J3
Saná (GR) 180 C3
San Abbondio (CH) 87 G5
Sanadinovo (BG) 176 C1
San Adrián (E) 113 H4
San Agustín de Guadalix (E) 120 A2
Sanaigmore (GB) 52 C3
Sânandrei (RO) 159 M6
San Andrés (E) 113 F4
San Andrés de Aulestia (Etxebarría) (E) 113 G2
San Andrés de la Regla (E) 111 K3
San Andrés del Rey (E) 120 C2
San Andrés de San Pedro (E) 113 G5
San Andrés y Sauces (E) 129 b4
San Antonino (E) 111 G2
San Antoniño (Barro) (E) 110 B3
San Antonio del Fontanar (E) 125 J5
San Antonio de Requena (E) 121 F4
Sanary-sur-Mer (F) 95 G4
San Asensio (E) 112 F4
Sănătăuca (MD) 163 H2
Sanaüja (E) 115 F4
San Bartolomé de las Abiertas (E) 119 G4
San Bartolomé de la Torre (E) 124 E5
San Bartolomé de Pinares (E) 119 G2
San Bartolomé de Rueda (E) 111 J3
San Bartolomé de Tirajana (E) 129 c5
San Bartolomeo al Mare (I) 98 E5
San Bartolomeo in Galdo (I) 104 D3
San Bartolomeo Valmara (I) 87 G5
San Basilio (I) 105 G4
San Benedetto (I) 100 B4
San Benedetto dei Marsi (I) 103 H3
San Benedetto del Tronto (I) 103 H2
San Benedetto in Alpe (I) 101 F5
San Benedetto Po (I) 99 K2
San Benedetto Val di Sambro (I) 99 L4
San Benito (E) 126 A2
San Benito de la Contienda (E) 124 E2
San Bernardino (CH) 87 H5
San Besso, Rifugio (I) 98 D1
San Biagio di Callalta (I) 89 G6
San Biagio Platani (I) 108 E2
San Blas (E) 121 F3
San Bonifacio (I) 100 E2
San Buono (I) 103 K4
San Cadurniño = Avenida do Marqués de Figueroa (E) 110 C1
Sancaklıiğdecik (TR) 190 D4
San Calixto (E) 125 J4
San Candido (I) 90 B6
San Carlo (CH) 87 G5
San Carlo (I) 101 G4
San Carlo (I) 108 D2
San Carlos del Valle (E) 119 K6
San Casciano dei Bagni (I) 102 D2
San Casciano in Val di Pesa (I) 99 L5
San Cassiano (I) 88 F4
San Cassiano (I) 101 F4
San Cataldo (I) 105 K5
San Cataldo (I) 109 E3
San Cebrián de Campos (E) 111 K4
San Cebrián de Mazote (E) 112 A5
Sâncel (RO) 161 H5
Sancergues (F) 84 C2
Sancerre (F) 84 C2
San Cesario di Lecce (I) 107 K2
Sancey-le-Grand (F) 85 L2
Sancheville (F) 76 E5
Sanchidrián (E) 119 G2
San Chirico Nuovo (I) 104 F4
San Chirico Raparo (I) 104 F5
Sancho Abarca (E) 113 J5
Sanchón de la Ribera (E) 117 J1
Sanchonuño (E) 112 C6
Sanchotello (E) 117 K3
San Cibrao (E) 110 E1
San Cipirello (I) 108 D2
San Ciprián (E) 111 F4
San Ciprián = San Cibrao (E) 110 E1
San Cipriano Picentino (I) 104 C4
San Clemente (E) 120 D5
San Clemente (E) 126 E4
San Clemente (I) 100 E4
San Clemente, Cuevas de (E) 112 D4
Sancoins (F) 84 C3
San Colombano al Lambro (I) 99 G2
San Cosme (Barreiros) (E) 110 E1
San Costanzo (I) 101 J5
Sâncrăieni (RO) 162 B6
Sâncraiu (RO) 161 F4
San Cristóbal de Entreviñas (E) 111 H4
San Cristóbal de La Laguna (E) 129 b4
San Cristóbal de la Vega (E) 119 G1
San Cristóbal de los Mochuelos (E) 117 J2
Sancti Petri (E) 128 B5
Sancti-Spíritus (E) 117 J2
Sancti-Spíritus (E) 119 F6
Sand (A) 81 L5
Sand (D) 79 J4
Sand (N) 20 C4
Sand (N) 38 D3
Sand (N) 39 O2
Sand (N) 39 O3
Sand (N) 39 P2
Sanda (AX) 34 G4
Sanda (N) 39 K4
Sanda (S) 41 O2
Sandal (TR) 190 F3
San Damiano d'Asti (I) 98 E3
San Damiano Macra (I) 95 K2
Sandane (N) 30 E4
San Daniele del Friuli (I) 89 J5
San Daniele Po (I) 99 J2
Sandanski (BG) 180 C1
Sandar (IS) 16 F4
Sandared (S) 44 B3
Sandarne (S) 33 N5
Sandau (Elbe) (D) 66 G5
Sandavágur (FO) 48 D3
Sandbach (GB) 55 H4
Sandbäckshult (S) 45 J4
Sandbakk (N) 20 E5
Sandberg (D) 71 K6
Sandbol (S) 40 C5
Sandbrekka (IS) 17 M3
Sandbu (N) 39 J2
Sandbukt (N) 18 D4
Sandby (DK) 46 H4
Sandby (S) 41 N2
Sande (D) 65 J5
Sande (D) 70 G3
Sande (N) 30 C3
Sande (N) 30 D5
Sande (N) 30 E5
Sande (N) 30 F4
Sande (N) 39 M3
Sande, Enge- (D) 46 C4
Sandefjord (N) 39 M4
Sandeggen (N) 21 J1
Sandeid (N) 38 C3
Sandem (N) 39 P3
San Demetrio Corone (I) 107 F3
San Demetrio ne' Vestini (I) 103 H3
Sanden (N) 39 J3
Sandersdorf-Brehna (D) 73 G2
Sandersleben (D) 71 N3
Sanderstølen (N) 31 L6
Sandfellshagi (IS) 17 K2
Sandfors (S) 22 C7
Sandgerði (IS) 16 D6
Sandhamn (S) 41 P4
Sandhead (GB) 52 F5
Sandhem (S) 44 D3
Sandhult (S) 44 B3
Sandiás (E) 110 D4
Sandıklı (TR) 191 J4
Sandillon (F) 76 F6
Sandim (P) 110 E5
Sandín (E) 111 G4
Sand in Taufers = Campo Tures (I) 88 F4
Sandl (A) 152 G6
Sandla (EST) 130 C4
Sandland (N) 18 D3
Sandnäset (S) 32 H2
Sandnes (N) 30 C6
Sandnes (N) 31 J2
Sandnes (N) 38 C5
Sandnes (N) 39 K4
Sandnes (N) 39 K5
Sandnesbotn (N) 20 F5
Sandneshamn (N) 21 H1
Sandnessjøen (N) 25 G2
Sandö (AX) 34 F4
Sando (E) 117 J2
Sandö (S) 33 O2
San Domenico (I) 86 F5
Sandomierz (PL) 148 E4
Sândominic (RO) 162 B5
Sandon (GB) 55 H5
Sandön (S) 27 J3
San Donaci (I) 105 J5
San Donà di Piave (I) 89 H6
San Donato (I) 102 C2
San Donato di Ninea (I) 106 F3
San Donato Val di Comino (I) 103 H4
Sandørenget (N) 25 J3
Sándorfalva (H) 159 K5
San Dorligo della Valle (I) 164 B3
Sandoval de la Reina (E) 112 C3
Sandown (GB) 58 E6
Sandøy (N) 30 F2
Sandøy (N) 30 G1
Sandøysund (N) 39 M4
Sandra (RO) 160 B6
Şandrigo (I) 99 M1
Šandrovac (HR) 158 D6
Sandrovo (BG) 169 L6
Sandsbråten (N) 39 L2
Sandsele (S) 26 D4
Sandsjö (S) 26 D4
Sandsjö (S) 26 D6
Sandsjö (S) 32 H4
Sandsjön (S) 40 F3
Sandsjönäs (S) 26 D4
Sandslån (S) 33 O1
Sandsnes (N) 39 O2
Sandsøy (N) 20 F3
Sandstad (N) 24 D7
Sandstad (N) 39 Q2
Sandstedt (D) 65 K5
Sandtorg (N) 20 F3
Sandträsk (S) 22 D4
Sandudden (S) 22 E4
Sânduleni (RO) 162 D6
Sândulești (RO) 161 H4
Sandum (N) 39 L2
Sandur (FO) 48 E4
Sandur (IS) 17 J3
Sandvad (S) 41 J4
Sandvarp (S) 33 P2
Sandvatn (N) 38 E6
Sandve (N) 38 B4
Sandved (DK) 47 J3
Sandvid (N) 25 H3
Sandvig (DK) 47 K3
Sandvig (DK) 47 N3
Sandvík (FO) 48 E4
Sandvík (IS) 17 J3
Sandvik (N) 18 A4
Sandvik (N) 20 D6
Sandvik (N) 20 F3
Sandvik (N) 25 G3
Sandvik (N) 30 C3
Sandvik (N) 32 B5
Sandvik (S) 33 L4
Sandvik (S) 43 M4
Sandvik (S) 44 G2
Sandvik (S) 45 K4
Sandvika (N) 39 N3
Sandvika (S) 24 G7
Sandvika fjellstue (N) 24 G7
Sandvikdal (N) 38 E6
Sandviken (S) 25 H7
Sandviken (S) 32 F3
Sandviken (S) 41 L1
Sandviken (S) 41 N4
Sandvikhamn (N) 38 B2
Sandviki (N) 30 G5
Sandvikvåg (N) 38 B3
Sandwich (GB) 68 A4
Sandwick (GB) 49 F4
Sandy (GB) 59 G3
Sandygate (GBM) 52 F6
San Elia (I) 97 D5
Sanem (L) 78 D2
San Emiliano (E) 111 G3
San Esteban (E) 111 F2
San Esteban (E) 111 G1
San Esteban = Santo Estevo (E) 110 D2
San Esteban de Gormaz (E) 112 E5
San Esteban de Litera (E) 114 D4
San Esteban del Molar (E) 111 H5
San Esteban del Valle (E) 119 G3
San Esteban de Nogales (E) 111 H4
San Esteban de Valdueza (E) 111 F3
San Fele (I) 104 E4
San Felice Circeo (I) 103 G5
San Felices de los Gallegos (E) 117 H2
San Felice sul Panaro (I) 99 L3
San Feliz de Torío (E) 111 H3
San Ferdinando (I) 106 E6
San Ferdinando di Puglia (I) 104 F3
San Fernando (E) 128 B5
San Fernando de Henares (E) 120 A3
San Fili (I) 106 F4
San Filippo e Giacomo (I) 108 C2
Sanfins do Douro (P) 110 D6
San Fiurenzu = Saint-Florent (F) 96 E3
San Francesco (I) 89 H5
San Francisco de Olivenza (E) 118 B6
San Fratello (I) 109 G1
Sanfront (I) 95 K1
Sånga (S) 26 D8
Sangalhos (P) 116 E3
Sangarcía (E) 119 H2
Sangarrén (E) 113 L4
Sángas (GR) 187 E4
Sangaste (EST) 134 B2
Sangatte (F) 59 L6
San Gavino Monreale (I) 97 C4
San Gemini (I) 103 F2
San Genesio Atesino (I) 88 E4

230 Runovo

San Genesio ed Uniti (I) 99 G2
Sângeorgiu de Mureş (RO) 161 K4
Sângeorgiu de Pădure (RO) 161 K5
Sângeorz-Băi (RO) 161 K3
Sânger (RO) 161 J4
Sangerhausen (D) 72 E3
San Germano Chisone (I) 98 C3
San Germano Vercellese (I) 98 E2
Săngeru (RO) 170 C3
San Giacomo (I) 88 F4
San Gillio (I) 98 D2
San Gimignano (I) 99 L6
San Ginesio (I) 103 G1
Sangineto Lido (I) 106 E3
Sanginjoki (FIN) 28 G2
Sanginkylä (FIN) 29 G2
San Giobbe (I) 99 L3
San Giorgio (I) 109 G1
San Giorgio Albanese (I) 107 F3
San Giorgio a Liri (I) 103 H5
San Giorgio Canavese (I) 98 D2
San Giorgio della Richinvelda (I) 89 H5
San Giorgio del Sannio (I) 104 C3
San Giorgio di Lomellina (I) 98 F2
San Giorgio di Nogaro (I) 89 J6
San Giorgio di Piano (I) 99 L3
San Giorgio in Bosco (I) 101 F1
San Giorgio Ionico (I) 107 H2
San Giorgio la Molara (I) 104 C3
San Giorgio Lucano (I) 107 F2
San Giorgio Piacentino (I) 99 H3
San Giovanni (I) 89 H5
San Giovanni Bianco (I) 87 J6
San Giovanni d'Asso (I) 100 F6
San Giovanni di Sinis (I) 97 B4
San Giovanni Incarico (I) 103 H4
San Giovanni in Croce (I) 100 C2
San Giovanni in Fiore (I) 107 G4
San Giovanni in Galilea (I) 101 G5
San Giovanni in Marignano (I) 101 H5
San Giovanni in Persiceto (I) 99 L3
San Giovanni la Punta (I) 109 H2
San Giovanni Rotondo (I) 104 E2
San Giovanni Suergiu (I) 97 C5
San Giovanni Teatino (I) 103 J3
San Giovanni Valdarno (I) 100 F5
Sangis (S) 27 K3
San Giuliano (I) 101 G2
San Giuliano Nuovo (I) 98 F3
San Giuliano Terme (I) 99 J5
San Giuseppe Vesuviano (I) 103 K6
San Giustino (I) 101 G5
San Godenzo (I) 100 F5
Sangonera La Verde (E) 127 H4
San Gregorio (I) 109 J1
San Gregorio da Sassola (I) 103 F4
San Gregorio Magno (I) 104 D4
Sangrūda (LT) 143 J2
Sångshyttan (S) 40 F3
Sangüesa (E) 92 B5
Sanguinet (F) 92 B2
Sanguinetto (I) 99 L2
Šani (BY) 143 L5
Saní (GR) 180 C4
Sanica (BIH) 165 H5
San Ildefonso o La Granja (E) 119 H2
Sanilhac (F) 83 G6
San Isidro de Níjar (E) 127 F6
Sanislău (RO) 160 E2
Sanitz (D) 67 G2
San Javier (E) 127 J4
San Jorge = Sant Jordi del Maestrat (E) 122 B1
San José (E) 127 F6
San José de la Rábita (E) 126 B5
San José de la Rinconada (E) 125 H5
San José del Valle (E) 128 C4
San Juan (E) 112 D4
San Juan d'Alacant (E) 127 K3
San Juan de Alicante = San Juan d'Alacant (E) 127 K3
San Juan de Aznalfarache (E) 128 B3
San Juan de la Encinilla (E) 119 G2
San Juan de la Nava (E) 119 G3
San Juan de los Terreros (E) 127 G5
San Juan del Puerto (E) 125 F5
San Juan de Nieva (E) 111 H1
San Juan de Plan (E) 92 E5
San Justo de la Vega (E) 111 G4
Sankikangas (FIN) 23 M5
Sankola (FIN) 36 C2
Sankt Andrä (A) 89 G3
Sankt Andrä (A) 91 G6
Sankt Andrä = Sant'Andrea in Monte (I) 88 F4
Sankt Andrä-Wördern (A) 91 K3
Sankt Andreasberg (D) 72 D2
Sankt Anna (S) 41 L6
Sankt Anna am Aigen (A) 91 J6
Sankt Anton am Arlberg (A) 87 K3
Sankt Anton an der Jeßnitz (A) 91 H4
Sankt Anton im Montafon (A) 88 B3
Sankt Augustin (D) 70 D5
Sankt Barbara im Mürztal (A) 91 J4
Sankt Blasien (D) 86 F2
Sankt Christina in Gröden = Santa Cristina Valgardena (I) 88 F4
Sankt Christoph am Arlberg (A) 87 K3
Sankt Englmar (D) 90 C1
Sankt Gallen (A) 90 G4
Sankt Gallen (CH) 79 L7
Sankt Gallenkirch (A) 88 B3
Sankt Georgen am Fillmannsbach (A) 89 J1
Sankt Georgen am Längsee (A) 89 L4
Sankt Georgen am Reith (A) 91 G4
Sankt Georgen an der Gusen (A) 81 L4
Sankt Georgen an der Stiefing (A) 91 J6
Sankt Georgen bei Salzburg (A) 89 H1
Sankt Georgen im Attergau (A) 90 D4
Sankt Georgen im Lavanttal (A) 91 G6
Sankt Georgen im Schwarzwald (D) 79 J5
Sankt Georgen ob Judenburg (A) 90 F5
Sankt Gertraud = Santa Gertrude (I) 87 L5
Sankt Gilgen (A) 90 D4
Sankt Goar (D) 70 E6
Sankt Goarshausen (D) 70 E6
Sankt Heinrich (D) 80 E5
Sankt Ingbert (D) 78 G3
Sankt Jacob, Mülsen (D) 152 C2
Sankt Jakob = San Giacomo (I) 88 F4
Sankt Jakob bei Mixnitz (A) 91 H5
Sankt Jakob im Lesachtal (A) 89 H4
Sankt Jakob im Rosental (A) 164 C1
Sankt Jakob im Rosental = Šentjakob v Rožu (A) 164 C1
Sankt Jakob in Defereggen (A) 89 G4
Sankt Johann am Tauern (A) 81 L6
Sankt Johann am Walde (A) 89 J1
Sankt Johann im Pongau (A) 81 J6
Sankt Johann in Tirol (A) 81 G5
Sankt Kanzian am Klopeiner See (A) 90 G6
Sankt Kassian = San Cassiano (I) 88 F4
Sankt Katharein, Tragöß- (A) 91 H5
Sankt Katharinen (D) 70 D5
Sankt Lambrecht (A) 89 L3
Sankt Leonhard (A) 89 L4
Sankt Leonhard am Forst (A) 91 H3
Sankt Leonhard an der Saualpe (A) 89 M4
Sankt Leonhard im Pitztal (A) 88 D3
Sankt Leonhard in Passeier = San Leonardo in Passiria (I) 88 E4
Sankt Lorenzen = San Lorenzo di Sebato (I) 88 F4
Sankt Lorenzen im Lesachtal (A) 89 H4
Sankt Magdalena = Santa Maddalena (I) 88 F4
Sankt Magdalena = Santa Maddalena (I) 90 B6
Sankt Marein bei Graz (A) 91 J5
Sankt Marein im Mürztal (A) 91 H5
Sankt Margareten im Rosental (A) 164 C1
Sankt Margarethen (D) 46 D6
Sankt Margarethen an der Raab (A) 91 J5
Sankt Margarethen im Burgenland (A) 91 L4
Sankt Margarethen im Lavanttal (A) 91 G6
Sankt Märgen (D) 86 F1
Sankt Margrethen (CH) 80 B6
Sankt Marien (A) 90 F3
Sankt Marienkirchen bei Schärding (A) 81 J4
Sankt Martin (A) 81 J6
Sankt Martin (A) 91 G2
Sankt Martin (CH) 87 H4
Sankt Martin im Innkreis (A) 90 D3
Sankt Martin im Sulmtal (A) 91 H6
Sankt Michael (A) 91 H3
Sankt Michael im Burgenland (A) 91 K5
Sankt Michael im Lungau (A) 89 K3
Sankt Michael in Obersteiermark (A) 91 H5
Sankt Michaelisdonn (D) 46 D6
Sankt Michel = Mikkeli (FIN) 36 H1
Sankt Moritz (CH) 88 B5
Sankt Niklaus (CH) 86 E5
Sankt Nikola an der Donau (A) 91 G3
Sankt Nikolai im Sölktal (A) 81 L6
Sankt Olav (N) 31 P6
Sankt Olof (S) 47 O2
Sankt Oswald (A) 89 K4
Sankt Oswald bei Freistadt (A) 90 G2
Sankt Oswald bei Plankenwarth (A) 91 H5
Sankt Oswald in Freiland (A) 91 H6
Sankt Oswald-Möderbrugg (A) 90 G5
Sankt Oswald ob Eibiswald (A) 91 H6
Sankt Oswald-Riedlhütte (D) 81 J3
Sankt Pankraz = San Pancrazio (I) 87 M4
Sankt Pauli (D) 65 M4
Sankt Paul im Lavanttal (A) 91 G6
Sankt Peter = San Pietro (I) 88 G3
Sankt Peter, Westerndorf (D) 80 G5
Sankt Peter am Kammersberg (A) 89 L3
Sankt Peter am Ottersbach (A) 91 J6
Sankt-Peterburg (RUS) 7 S5
Sankt-Peterburg (RUS) 37 O5
Sankt Peter im Lavanttal (A) 89 M3
Sankt Peter in der Au (A) 89 M1
Sankt Peter-Ording (D) 46 C5
Sankt Peter-Pagig (CH) 88 B4
Sankt Peterzell (CH) 87 H3
Sankt Pölten (A) 91 J3
Sankt Radegund bei Graz (A) 91 H5
Sankt Ruprecht an der Raab (A) 91 J5
Sankt Salvator (A) 90 F6
Sankt Sigfrid (S) 45 J5
Sankt Sigmund im Sellrain (A) 87 M3
Sankt Stefan (A) 91 G6
Sankt Stefan an der Gail (A) 164 B1
Sankt Stefan im Rosental (A) 91 J6
Sankt Stefan ob Stainz (A) 91 H6
Sankt Thomas am Blasenstein (A) 81 M4
Sankt Ulrich = Ortisei (I) 88 F4
Sankt Ulrich am Pillersee (A) 81 H5
Sankt Urban (A) 90 F6
Sankt Valentin (A) 90 G3
Sankt Valentin auf der Haide = San Valentino alla Muta (I) 87 L4
Sankt Veit, Neumarkt- (D) 81 H4
Sankt Veit an der Glan (A) 90 F6
Sankt Veit im Mühlkreis (A) 81 L4
Sankt Veit in Defereggen (A) 89 G4
Sankt-Vith = Saint-Vith (B) 69 L6
Sankt Wendel (D) 78 G3
Sankt Willibald (A) 90 E3
Sankt Wolfgang (A) 90 G5
Sankt Wolfgang (D) 80 G4
Sankt Wolfgang im Salzkammergut (A) 89 J2
San Lazzaro di Savena (I) 99 L4
San Leo (I) 101 G5
San Leonardo de Siete Fuentes (I) 97 C3
San Leonardo de Yagüe (E) 112 E5
San Leonardo in Passiria (I) 88 E4
San Leone (I) 108 E3
Sanlıca (TR) 193 J6
Şanlıurfa = Urfa (TR) 13 M7
San Lorenzo (E) 119 H2
San Lorenzo al Mare (I) 98 D5
San Lorenzo a Merse (I) 100 E6
San Lorenzo Bellizzi (I) 105 F6
San Lorenzo de Calatrava (E) 126 C3
San Lorenzo de la Parrilla (E) 120 D4
San Lorenzo di Sebato (I) 88 F4
San Lorenzo in Campo (I) 101 H5
San Lorenzo Nuovo (I) 102 D2
San Lovrenzo = Lovreč (HR) 101 K2
San Luca (I) 109 K1
Sanlúcar de Barrameda (E) 125 G6
Sanlúcar de Guadiana (E) 124 E5
Sanlúcar la Mayor (E) 125 G5
San Lucido (I) 106 F4
San Lugano (I) 88 E5
San Luis de Sabinillas (E) 128 D5
Sanluri (I) 97 C4
San Mamés (E) 112 F2
San Marcello Pistoiese (I) 99 K4
San Marco (I) 104 C5
San Marco Argentano (I) 106 F3
San Marco dei Cavoti (I) 104 C3
San Marco in Lamis (I) 104 E2
San Marco la Catola (I) 104 D2
San Marcos (E) 110 C3
San Marcos, Cuevas de (E) 128 F3
San Marino (RSM) 101 G5
San Martín (E) 118 C1
Sânmartin (RO) 160 C5
Sânmartin (RO) 160 D3
Sânmărtin (RO) 161 J3
Sânmartin (RO) 162 B6
San Martín = San Martíno (Neira de Rei) (E) 110 E3
San Martín de Boniches (E) 120 E4
San Martín de Castañeda (E) 111 F4
San Martín de la Vega (E) 120 A3
San Martín de los Herreros (E) 111 K3
San Martín del Pedroso (E) 111 F5
San Martín del Pimpollar (E) 119 F3
San Martín de Montalbán (E) 119 H4
San Martín de Oscos (Samartín) (E) 110 F2
San Martín de Pusa (E) 119 G4
San Martín de Trevejo (E) 118 C3
San Martín de Unx (E) 92 A5
San Martín de Valdeiglesias (E) 119 H3
San Martín de Valderaduey (E) 111 J5
San Martino (I) 98 F4
San Martíno (Neira de Rei) (E) 110 E3
San Martino al Cimino (I) 102 E3
San Martino dall'Argine (I) 99 K2
San Martiño de Cambre = Cambre (E) 110 C2
San Martino di Campagna (I) 89 H5
San Martino di Castrozza (I) 88 F5
San Martino di Venezze (I) 101 F2
San Martino o el Tesorillo (E) 128 D5
San Martino in Colle (I) 102 E1
San Martín Sarroca = Sant Martí Sarroca (E) 115 G5
San Mateo de Gállego (E) 114 B4
San Mateu = Sant Mateu (E) 122 B2
San Maurizio (I) 98 E1
San Maurizio Canavese (I) 98 D2
San Mauro Castelverde (I) 109 F2
San Mauro Forte (I) 105 F5
San Mauro Marchesato (I) 107 G4
San Menaio (I) 172 C6
San Michele (I) 103 F5
San Michele all'Adige (I) 87 M5
San Michele al Tagliamento (I) 89 H6
San Michele di Ganzaria (I) 109 F3
San Michele Extra (I) 99 L2
San Michele Mondovì (I) 98 D4
San Michele Salentino (I) 105 J4
Sânmiclăuş (RO) 161 J5
San Miguel de Bernúy (E) 112 D6
San Miguel del Arroyo (E) 111 L6
San Miguel de las Dueñas (E) 111 F3
San Miguel de Salinas (E) 127 J4
Sânmihaiu Almaşului (RO) 161 G3
Sânmihaiu de Cîmpie (RO) 161 J4
San Millán de la Cogolla (E) 112 F4
San Millán de San Zadornil (E) 112 E3
San Millao (E) 110 D5
San Miniato (I) 100 D5
Sanmsak (TR) 185 K2
San Muñoz (E) 118 D2
Sannahed (S) 40 H4
Sannainen (FIN) 36 E4
Sannäs = Sannainen (FIN) 36 E4
Sannazzaro de'Burgondi (I) 98 F2
San Nazzaro Val Cavargna (I) 87 H5
Sanne (S) 25 J9
Sanne (S) 39 P5
Sannerud (S) 40 A4
Sannicandro di Bari (I) 105 G4
San Nicandro Garganico (I) 172 C6
San Nicola da Crissa (I) 107 F5
San Nicola dell'Alto (I) 107 G4
San Nicola di Tremiti (I) 104 E1
San Nicola l'Arena (I) 108 E1
San Nicolás, La Aldea de (E) 129 c5
San Nicolás del Puerto (E) 128 C1
San Nicolás de Tolentino = La Aldea de San Nicolás (E) 129 c5
Sânnicolau Mare (RO) 167 G1
San Nicolò (I) 101 F3
San Nicolò d'Arcidano (I) 97 C4
San Nicolò Gerrei (I) 97 D5
Sannidal (N) 39 K5
Sanniki (PL) 142 B6
Sänningstjärn (S) 33 M3
Sänningsvallen (S) 33 K3
Sanok (PL) 155 L2
Sanovo (BG) 176 E3
San Pablo = Sant Pau (E) 122 A2
San Pablo de los Montes (E) 119 H4
San Pablo o Buceite (E) 128 D5
San Pancrazio (I) 87 M4
San Pancrazio Salentino (I) 105 J5
San Pantaleo (I) 97 D1
San Pantaleón de Losa (E) 112 E3
San Paolo (I) 99 J2
San Paolo (I) 109 H4
San Paolo Cervo (I) 98 E1
San Paolo di Civitate (I) 104 D2
San Pedro (E) 112 D2
San Pedro (E) 120 D6
San Pedro Alcántara (E) 128 E5
San Pedro Cansoles (E) 112 B3
San Pedro de Ceque (E) 111 G4
San Pedro del Arroyo (E) 119 G2
San Pedro de las Dueñas (E) 112 A4
San Pedro de Latarce (E) 111 J5
San Pedro del Pinatar (E) 127 J4
San Pedro del Romeral (E) 112 D2
San Pedro del Valle (E) 117 K1
San Pedro de Mérida (E) 117 J6
San Pedro de Ribas = Sant Pere de Ribes (E) 115 G5
San Pedro de Riudevitlles = Sant Pere de Riudebitlles (E) 115 G5
San Pedro de Valderaduey (E) 112 B4
San Pedro Manrique (E) 113 G4
San Pedro Palmiches (E) 120 D3
San Pelaio = San Pelayo (E) 112 F2
San Pelayo (E) 112 F2
San Pellegrino Terme (I) 87 J6
Sânpetru (RO) 170 B2
Sânpetru de Câmpie (RO) 161 J4
Sânpetru Mare (RO) 167 G1
San Piero a Sieve (I) 99 L5
San Piero in Bagno (I) 101 F5
San Piero Patti (I) 109 G1
San Pietro (I) 87 H5
San Pietro (I) 88 G3
San Pietro (I) 106 D5
San Pietro al Natisone (I) 164 A2
San Pietro di Cadore (I) 90 C6
San Pietro in Bevagna (I) 105 J5
San Pietro in Cariano (I) 100 D1
San Pietro in Casale (I) 100 E3
San Pietro in Gu (I) 101 F1
San Pietro in Palazzi (I) 99 K6
San Pietro in Vincoli (I) 101 G4
San Pietro in Volta (I) 101 G2
San Pietro Vara (I) 99 H4
San Pietro Vernotico (I) 105 J5
San Polo d'Enza (I) 99 J3
San Priamo (I) 97 E5
Sanquhar (GB) 53 H4
San Quintín de Mediona = Sant Quintí de Mediona (E) 115 G5
San Quirico (I) 100 D5
San Quirico d'Orcia (I) 102 D1
San Rafael (E) 119 H2
San Rafael del Río = Sant Rafael del Maestrat (E) 122 B1
Sanremo (I) 98 D5
San Remo = Sanremo (I) 98 D5
San Rocco Cadarese (I) 86 F5
San Román (E) 110 E3
San Román (E) 112 D2
San Román de Hornija (E) 111 J6
San Román de la Cuba (E) 112 B4
San Román de los Montes (E) 119 G3
San Román el Antiguo (E) 111 H4
San Roque (E) 128 D5
San Roque (Coristanco) (E) 110 B2
San Sadurní de Noya = Sant Sadurní d'Anoia (E) 115 G5
San Sadurniño = Avenida do Marqués de Figueroa (E) 110 C1
Sansais (F) 82 D4
San Salvador de Cantamuda (E) 111 L3
San Salvatore (I) 97 B4
San Salvatore (I) 100 C2
San Salvatore Monferrato (I) 98 F3
San Salvatore Telesino (I) 103 J5
San Salvo (I) 104 C1
San Salvo Marina (I) 104 C1
Sansarak (TR) 183 J5
San Sebastián (E) 111 L2
San Sebastián, Donostia / (E) 113 H2
San Sebastián de La Gomera (E) 129 b4
San Sebastián de los Ballesteros (E) 125 K4
San Sebastián de los Reyes (E) 120 A2
San Sebastiano Curone (I) 99 G3
San Secondo Parmense (I) 100 C3
Sansepolcro (I) 101 G5
San Severino Lucano (I) 106 F2
San Severino Marche (I) 101 J6
San Severo (I) 104 D2
San Silvestre de Guzmán (E) 124 E5
Sânsimion (RO) 162 B6
Sanski Most (BIH) 165 H5
San Sosti (I) 106 F3
San Sperate (I) 97 D5
San Stefano (BG) 177 G3
Sanț (RO) 161 K3
Santa Agnès de Corona (E) 122 D4
Santa Amalia (E) 125 G1
Santa Ana (E) 120 E6
Santa Ana (E) 126 C5
Santa Ana (E) 127 F2
Santa Bárbara (E) 112 C4
Santa Bárbara (E) 120 F5
Santa Bàrbara (E) 121 J2
Santa Bárbara (E) 127 G5
Santa Bárbara de Casa (E) 124 E4
Santa Bárbara de Nexe (P) 124 D5
Santa Bárbara de Padrões (P) 124 D4
Santa Brígida (E) 128 F1
Santacara (E) 92 A6
Santa Catarina da Fonte do Bispo (P) 124 D5
Santa Catarina da Serra (P) 116 D4
Santa Caterina (I) 88 E4
Santa Caterina dello Ionio (I) 107 G5
Santa Caterina dello Ionio-Marina (I) 107 G5
Santa Caterina di Pittinuri (I) 97 B3
Santa Caterina Valfurva (I) 88 C5
Santa Caterina Villarmosa (I) 109 F2
Santa Cecilia del Alcor (E) 111 K5
Santa Clara-a-Velha (P) 124 C4
Santa Clara de Louredo (P) 124 D4
Santa Coloma de Farners (E) 115 J4
Santa Coloma de Queralt (E) 115 F4
Santa Colomba (E) 110 F2
Santa Colomba de Somoza (E) 111 G4
Santa Comba (E) 110 B2
Santa Comba Dão (P) 116 E3
Santa Cristina de la Polvorosa (E) 111 H5
Santa Cristina Valgardena (I) 88 F4
Santa Croce (I) 164 B3
Santa Croce Camerina (I) 109 G4
Santa Croce di Magliano (I) 104 D2
Santa Croce sull'Arno (I) 99 K5
Santa Croya de Tera (E) 111 H5
Santa Cruz (E) 126 A4
Santa Cruz (P) 116 C5
Santa Cruz (P) 124 D5
Santa Cruz da Graciosa (P) 129 b1
Santa Cruz da Trapa (P) 116 E2
Santa Cruz de Alhalma o del Comercio (E) 126 C5
Santa Cruz de Campezo (E) 113 G3
Santa Cruz de Grío (E) 113 J6
Santa Cruz de la Palma (E) 129 b4
Santa Cruz de la Serós (E) 92 C5
Santa Cruz de la Zarza (E) 120 B4
Santa Cruz de Llanera (E) 111 H2
Santa Cruz del Retamar (E) 119 H3
Santa Cruz de Moya (E) 121 F4
Santa Cruz de Mudela (E) 126 D2
Santa Cruz de Tenerife (E) 129 b4
Santa Cruz de Yanguas (E) 113 G4
Santadi (I) 97 C5
Santa Domenica Talao (I) 104 E6
Santa Domenica Vittoria (I) 106 C7
Sant'Adriano (I) 101 F4
Santa Elena (E) 126 C3
Santa Elena de Emera = Santa Elena de Emerando (E) 112 F2
Santa Elena de Emerando (E) 112 F2
Santa Elisabetta (I) 108 E3
Santaella (E) 125 K4
Santa Engracia (E) 113 J5
Santa Espina, La (E) 112 A5
Santa Eufemia (E) 110 D4
Santa Eufemia (E) 125 K2
Santa Eufémia (P) 117 G2
Santa Eufemia Lamezia (I) 106 F5
Santa Eugènia (E) 123 G3
Santa Eugenia (Ribeira) = Santa Uxia (Ribeira) (E) 110 B3
Santa Eugènia de Berga (E) 115 H4
Santa Eulalia (E) 111 J2
Santa Eulalia (E) 121 F2
Santa Eulália (P) 124 E1
Santa Eulalia de Gállego (E) 114 B3
Santa Eulalia de Oscos (Santalla d'Ozcos) (E) 110 E2
Santa Eulàlia de Riuprimer (E) 115 H4
Santa Eulalia de Tineo (E) 111 G2
Santa Eulària des Riu (E) 122 E5
Santa Fé (E) 126 C5
Santa Fiora (I) 102 D2
Santa Gadea (E) 112 D3
Santa Gadea del Cid (E) 112 E3
Sant'Agata (I) 106 E6
Sant'Agata de'Goti (I) 103 K5
Sant'Agata di Esaro (I) 106 E3
Sant'Agata di Militello (I) 109 G1
Sant'Agata di Puglia (I) 104 D3
Sant'Agata Feltria (I) 101 G5
Sant'Agata sui Due Golfi (I) 103 J6
Santa Gertrude (I) 87 L5
Santa Gertrudis de Fruitera (E) 122 D5
Santa Giuletta (I) 99 G2
Santa Giulia (I) 101 G3
Santa Giusta (I) 97 C4
Santa Giustina (I) 88 G5
Sant'Agostino (I) 99 L3
Sant Agustí de Lluçanès (E) 115 H3
Sant Agustí des Vedrà (E) 122 D5
Santahamina (FIN) 35 Q4
Santaika (LT) 143 K2
Santa Isabel (E) 114 B4
Sant'Alberto (I) 101 G3
Sant-Albin-an-Hiliber = Saint-Aubin-du-Cormier (F) 75 J4
Sant-Albin-Elvinieg = Saint-Aubin-d'Aubigné (F) 75 H4
Santalha (P) 110 E5
Santa Liestra y San Quílez (E) 114 D3
Sant Altoni de Calonge (E) 115 K4
Santa Lucia (I) 97 E2
Santa Lucía (Moraña) (E) 110 B3
Santa Lucia del Mela (I) 109 H1
Santa Lucia di Portivechju = Sainte-Lucie-de-Porto-Vecchio (F) 96 E5
Santa Luzia (P) 124 C4
Santa Maddalena (I) 88 F4
Santa Maddalena (I) 90 B6
Santa Magdalena de Polpís (E) 121 J3
Santa Magdalena de Pulpis = Santa Magdalena de Polpís (E) 121 J3
Santa Mare (RO) 162 E3
Santa Margalida (E) 123 H3
Santa Margarida da Serra (P) 124 B3
Santa Margarida de Montbui (E) 115 G4
Santa Margarida do Sado (P) 124 C3
Santa Margherita (I) 97 C6
Santa Margherita di Belice (I) 108 D2
Santa Margherita Ligure (I) 99 G4
Santa María (E) 92 C6
Santa Maria, el Pla de (E) 115 F5
Santa Maria al Bagno (I) 107 K2
Santa Maria a Monte (I) 99 K5
Santa Maria Capua Vetere (I) 104 B3
Santa Maria da Feira (P) 116 D2
Santa María de Arzua = Arzúa (E) 110 C3
Santa María de Corcó (E) 115 H3
Santa María de Getxo (E) 112 E2
Santa Maria degli Angeli (I) 103 F1
Santa María de Huerta (E) 113 G6
Santa Maria dei Sabbioni (I) 99 H2
Santa María del Águila (E) 126 E6
Santa María de las Hoyas (E) 112 E5
Santa María de la Vega (E) 111 H4
Santa María del Berrocal (E) 118 F2
Santa Maria del Camí (E) 123 G3
Santa María del Campo (E) 112 D4
Santa María del Campo Rus (E) 120 D4
Santa Maria del Cedro (I) 106 E3
Santa María del Espino (E) 120 D2
Santa Maria della Versa (I) 100 A3
Santa María de los Caballeros (E) 118 F3
Santa María del Páramo (E) 111 H4
Santa Maria del Taro (I) 100 A4
Santa María de Mave (E) 112 C3
Santa María de Nava la Zapatera u Hoya de Santa María (E) 128 B1
Santa María de Nieva (E) 127 G5
Santa María de Redondo (E) 111 L3
Santa María de Riaza (E) 112 E6
Santa María de Trassierra (E) 125 K4
Santa Maria di Licodia (I) 109 G2
Santa María la Real de Nieva (E) 119 H1
Santa Maria Maggiore (I) 86 F5
Santa Maria Navarrese (I) 97 E4
Santa Maria Nuova (I) 101 J6
Sântămăria-Orlea (RO) 168 D2
Santa Maria Rezzonico (I) 87 H5
Santa Maria Val Mustair (CH) 87 K4
Santa Marina (E) 111 H2
Santa Marina (I) 109 H1
Santa Marina del Rey (E) 111 H3
Santa Marina del Sil (E) 111 F3
Santa Marina Salina (I) 106 C5
Santa Marinella (I) 102 D3
Santa Marta (E) 125 F2
Santa Marta (E) 127 F1
Santa Marta de Magasca (E) 118 D4
Santa Marta de Penaguião (P) 110 D6
Santa Marta de Tormes (E) 118 E2
Santana (E) 111 K3
Santana (P) 124 A3
Santana (P) 129 b2
Sântana (RO) 160 D5
Santana da Serra (P) 124 C4
Sântana de Mureş (RO) 161 K4
Sant'Anatolia di Narco (I) 103 F2
Santander (E) 112 D2
Sant'Andrea Apostolo dello Ionio (I) 107 G5
Sant'Andrea Bagni (I) 100 C3
Sant'Andrea Frius (I) 97 D5
Sant'Andrea in Monte (I) 88 F4
Sântandrei (RO) 160 D3
Sant Andreu de Llavaneres (E) 115 H4
Sant'Angelo (I) 101 G1
Sant'Angelo (I) 104 A4
Sant'Angelo (I) 106 F5
Sant'Angelo a Fasanella (I) 106 D2
Sant'Angelo d'Alife (I) 103 J5
Sant'Angelo dei Lombardi (I) 104 D4
Sant'Angelo di Brolo (I) 109 G1
Sant'Angelo in Lizzola (I) 101 H5
Sant'Angelo in Pontano (I) 103 G1
Sant'Angelo in Vado (I) 101 G5
Sant'Angelo Lodigiano (I) 99 G2
Santa Ninfa (I) 108 C2
Sant'Anna (I) 109 K1
Sant'Anna Arresi (I) 97 C5
Sant'Anna di Valdieri (I) 98 C4
Sant'Anna Pelago (I) 100 D4
Sant'Antioco (I) 97 B5
Sant'Antioco di Bisarcio (I) 97 C2
Sant'Antone = Saint-Antoine (F) 96 E4
Sant Antoni Abat = Sant Antoni de Portmany (E) 122 D5
Sant Antoni de Llombai (E) 121 G5
Sant Antoni de Portmany (E) 122 D5
Sant'Antonino di Susa (I) 98 C2
Sant'Antonio (I) 101 F3
Sant'Antonio di Gallura (I) 97 D2
Sant'Antonio di Santadi (I) 97 B4
Santanyí (E) 123 H4
Santa Olaja de la Acción (E) 112 A3
Santa Olaja de la Vega (E) 111 K3
Santa Olalla (E) 119 H3
Santa Olalla del Cala (E) 128 B2
Santa Pau (E) 115 J3
Santa Pola (E) 127 J3
Santa Ponça (E) 123 F3
Santar (P) 116 F2
Sant'Arcangelo (I) 105 F5
Santarcangelo di Romagna (I) 101 G4
Santarém (P) 116 D5
Sant'Arsenio (I) 106 D2
Santa Saba (I) 106 E6
Santa Sabina (I) 105 J4
Santa-Severa (F) 96 E3
Santa Severa (I) 102 D3
Santa Severina (I) 107 G4
Santaskylä (FIN) 28 C8
Santas Martas (E) 111 J4
Santa Sofia (I) 101 F5
Santa Sofia (P) 124 C2
Santa Susana (P) 124 C3
Santa Susanna (E) 115 G4
Santa Suvera = Santa-Severa (F) 96 E3
Santa Teresa di Gallura (I) 97 D1
Santa Teresa di Riva (I) 106 D7
Santău (RO) 160 F2
Santăul Mare (RO) 160 D3
Santa Uxia (Ribeira) (E) 110 B3
Santa Valha (P) 110 E5
Santa Venere (I) 104 E6
Santa Venerina (I) 109 H2
Santa Vitória (P) 124 C4
Santa Vittoria (I) 99 K3
Santa Vittoria d'Alba (I) 98 D3
Santa Vittoria in Matenano (I) 103 G1
Sant Boi de Llobregat (E) 115 H5
Sant-Brieg = Saint-Brieuc (F) 74 F3
Sant-Brizh-Gougleiz = Saint-Brice-en-Coglès (F) 75 J4
Sant Carles de la Ràpita (E) 122 C1
Sant Carles de Peralta (E) 122 E4
Sant Celoni (E) 115 H4
Sant Climenç (E) 115 F4
Sant Climent (E) 123 K3
Sant Climent Sescebes (E) 94 A6
Sant Cugat del Vallès (E) 115 H5
Santed (E) 120 E1
Sant'Egidio alla Vibrata (I) 103 H2
Sant'Elia a Pianisi (I) 104 C2
Santelices (E) 112 D2
Sant Elm (E) 123 F3
San Telmo (E) 124 F4
Sant'Elpidio a Mare (I) 101 K6
Sante Marie (I) 103 G3
Santenay (F) 76 D6
San Teodoro (I) 97 E2
Santeramo in Colle (I) 105 G4
Santervás de Campos (E) 112 A4
Santervás de la Vega (E) 111 K3
Santes Creus (E) 115 F5
Santesteban (E) 92 A4
Santeuil (F) 76 E5
Sant Feliu de Codines (E) 115 H4
Sant Feliu de Guíxols (E) 115 K4
Sant Feliu de Pallerols (E) 115 J3
Sant Feliu Sasserra (E) 115 H4
Sant Francesc de Formentera (E) 122 D5
Sant Francesc de ses Salines (E) 122 D5
Sant Gregori (E) 115 J4
Sant Guim de Freixenet (E) 115 F4
Santhià (I) 98 E2
Sant Hilari Sacalm (E) 115 J4
Sant Hipòlit de Voltregà (E) 115 H3
Santiago da Guarda (P) 116 E4
Santiago de Alcántara (E) 117 G4
Santiago de Calatrava (E) 126 B4
Santiago de Castroverde = Castroverde (E) 110 E2
Santiago de Compostela (E) 110 B3
Santiago de la Espada (E) 126 E3
Santiago de la Puebla (E) 118 F2
Santiago de la Ribera (E) 127 J4
Santiago del Campo (E) 117 J4
Santiago del Teide (E) 129 b4
Santiago do Cacém (P) 124 B3
Santiago do Escoural (P) 124 C2
Santiago Maior (Aldeia das Pias) (P) 124 E2
Santibáñez de Ayllón (E) 112 E6
Santibáñez de Béjar (E) 117 K3
Santibáñez de la Peña (E) 111 K3
Santibáñez de la Sierra (E) 118 E2
Santibáñez de Murias (E) 111 H2
Santibáñez de Vidriales (E) 111 G4
Sant'Ilario d'Enza (I) 99 J3
Santillán (E) 112 A2
Santillana (E) 112 C2
Sântimbru (RO) 168 F1
Santiorxo (E) 110 D4
Santiponce (E) 128 B3
Sant'Ippolito (I) 101 H5
Santiscal, El (E) 128 C4
Santisteban del Puerto (E) 126 D3
Santiuste de San Juan Bautista (E) 119 G1
Sant Jaume d'Enveja (E) 121 K2
Sant Joan (E) 123 H3
Sant Joan de Labritja (E) 122 E4
Sant Joan de les Abadesses (E) 115 H3
Sant Joan de Penyagolosa (E) 121 H3
Sant Joan de Vilatorrada (E) 115 G4
Sant Joan les Fonts (E) 115 J3
Sant Jordi = Platja Es Pirat (E) 122 D5
Sant Jordi del Maestrat (E) 122 B1
Sant Josep de sa Talaia (E) 122 D5
Sant Llorenç de Morunys (E) 115 G3
Sant Llorenç d'es Cardassar (E) 123 H3
Sant Llorenç Savall (E) 115 H4
Sant Lluís (E) 123 K3
Sant-Maloù = Saint-Malo (F) 75 G3
Sant Martí de Llémena (E) 115 J3
Sant Martí de Maldà = Sant Martí de Riucorb (E) 114 F4
Sant Martí de Riucorb (E) 114 F4
Sant Martí de Tous (E) 115 G4
Sant Martí Sarroca (E) 115 G5
Sant Mateu (E) 122 B2
Sant Mateu d'Aubarca (E) 122 D4
Sant Maurici (E) 114 F2
Sant Miquel de Balansat (E) 122 D4
Santo Aleixo (P) 117 G6
Santo Aleixo da Restauração (P) 124 E3
Santo Amador (P) 124 E3
Santo André (P) 124 B3
Santo André das Tojeiras (P) 117 F4
Santo António (São Jorge) (P) 129 b1
Santo Domingo de la Calzada (E) 112 F4
Santo Domingo de Moya (E) 121 F4
Santo Domingo de Silos (E) 112 E5
Santo Estêvão (P) 116 D6
Santo Estêvão (P) 124 D5
Santo Estevo (E) 110 D2
Santo Isidro de Pegões (P) 124 B2
Santok (PL) 140 D5
Santomera (E) 127 H3
Santoméri (GR) 186 D4
Sant'Omobono Terme (I) 87 J6
Santoña (E) 112 E2
Santo Pietro (I) 109 F3
Santo-Pietro-di-Tenda = Santu Petru di Tenda (F) 96 E3
Santorcaz (E) 119 K3
Sant'Oreste (I) 103 F3
Santoríni = Thíra (GR) 195 G3
Santos, Los (E) 117 K2
Santos de Maimona, Los (E) 125 G3
Santo Spirito (I) 105 G3
Santo Stefano Belbo (I) 98 E3
Santo Stefano d'Aveto (I) 100 A3
Santo Stefano di Cadore (I) 89 H4
Santo Stefano di Camastra (I) 109 F1
Santo Stefano di Magra (I) 100 B4
Santo Stefano in Aspromonte (I) 109 J1
Santo Stefano Lodigiano (I) 99 H2
Santo Stefano Quisquina (I) 108 D2
Santo Stefano Udinese (I) 89 J6
Santo Stino di Livenza (I) 89 H6
Santo Tirso (P) 110 C6
Santo Tomé (E) 126 D3
Santo Tomé de Rozados (E) 118 E2
Santo Tomé Lourenzá = Lourenzá (San Tomé) (E) 110 E2
Santovenia (E) 111 H5
Sant Pau (E) 122 A2
Sant Pau de Seguries (E) 115 H3
Santpedor (E) 115 G4
Sant Pere de Ribes (E) 115 G5
Sant Pere de Riudebitlles (E) 115 G5
Sant Pere de Torelló (E) 115 H3
Sant Pere Pescador (E) 115 K3
Sant Pol de Mar (E) 115 J4
Santpoort (NL) 69 H2
Sant Quintí de Mediona (E) 115 G5
Sant Quirze de Besora (E) 115 H3
Sant Rafael del Maestrat (E) 122 B1
Sant Rafel de Forca (E) 122 D5
Sant Ramon (E) 115 F4
Sant Sadurní d'Anoia (E) 115 G5
Sant Salvador de Guardiola (E) 115 G4
Sant-Tegoneg = Saint-Thégonnec (F) 74 D3
Sant-Teve = Saint-Avé (F) 74 F5
Santtio (FIN) 34 H3
Sant Tomàs (E) 123 K3
Santu Lussurgiu (I) 97 C3
Santu Petru di Tenda (F) 96 E3
Sant'Urbano (I) 103 F3
Santurde (E) 112 F4
Sant Vicenç de Castellet (E) 115 G4
Sant Vicenç dels Horts (E) 115 H5
Sant-Yann-Brevele = Saint-Jean-Brévelay (F) 74 F5
San Valentino alla Muta (I) 87 L4
San Valentino in Abruzzo Citeriore (I) 103 H3
San Venanzo (I) 102 E2
Sanvensa (F) 93 J2
San Vicente (E) 110 E4
San Vicente (A Baña) = Baña, A (E) 110 B3
San Vicente de Alcántara (E) 117 G5
San Vicente de Barakaldo = Barakaldo (E) 112 F2
San Vicente de la Barquera (E) 111 L2
San Vicente de la Sonsierra (E) 112 F3
San Vicente del Raspeig (E) 127 J3
San Vicente dels Horts = Sant Vicenç dels Horts (E) 115 H5
San Vicente do Mar (E) 110 B4
Sanvicenti = Svetvinčenat (HR) 164 B4
San Vincenzo (I) 102 B1
San Vincenzo Valle Roveto (I) 103 H4
San Vitero (E) 111 G5
San Vito (I) 97 E5
San Vito al Tagliamento (I) 89 H6
San Vito Chietino (I) 103 J3
San Vito dei Normanni (I) 105 J4
San Vito di Cadore (I) 89 G5
San Vito lo Capo (I) 108 C1
San Vito Romano (I) 103 F4
San Vito sullo Ionio (I) 107 F5
San Vittore del Lazio (I) 104 A3
San Vittore delle Chiuse (I) 101 H6
Sanxay (F) 82 F4
Sanxenxo (E) 110 B4
Sanxenxo (Sangenjo) = Sanxenxo (E) 110 B4
Sanza (I) 104 E5
Sanzeno (I) 87 M5
San Zenone al Lambro (I) 100 A2
Sânzieni (RO) 169 L1
Sanzoles (E) 111 H6
São Barnabé (P) 124 C5
São Bartolomeu da Serra (P) 124 B3
São Bartolomeu de Messines (P) 124 C5
São Bartolomeu dos Galegos (P) 116 C5
São Bento (P) 116 D4
São Bento da Porta Aberta (P) 110 B5
São Bento do Cortiço (P) 117 F6
São Brás da Regedoura (P) 124 C3
São Brás de Alportel (P) 124 D5
São Cipriano (P) 116 F1
São Cosmado (P) 117 F1
São Cristóvão (P) 124 C3
São Domingos (P) 116 E4
São Domingos (P) 124 B4
São Facundo (P) 116 E5
São Francisco da Serra (P) 124 B3
São Geraldo (P) 124 C2
São Jacinto (P) 116 D2
São Joaninho (P) 116 E3
São João da Corveira (P) 110 E5
São João da Madeira (P) 116 E2
São João da Pesqueira (P) 117 G1
São João da Ribeira (P) 116 D5
São João de Negrilhos (P) 124 C4
São João de Tarouca (P) 117 F2
São João do Campo (P) 116 D3
São João do Monte (P) 116 E2
São João dos Caldeireiros (P) 124 D4
São Jorge (P) 116 D2
São Jorge (P) 116 D4
São Jorge da Beira (P) 117 F3
São José das Matas (P) 116 F4
São José de Lamarosa (P) 124 C1
São Lourenço (P) 124 A2
São Lourenço de Mamporcão (P) 118 A6
São Luís (P) 124 B4
São Mamede de Ribatua (P) 110 E6
São Manços (P) 124 D3
São Marcos da Ataboeira (P) 124 D4
São Marcos da Serra (P) 124 C5
São Martinho da Cortiça (P) 116 E3
São Martinho das Amoreiras (P) 124 C4
São Martinho de Angueira (P) 111 G5
São Martinho de Antas (P) 110 D6
São Martinho do Porto (P) 116 C4
São Mateus (P) 129 b1
São Matias (P) 117 F4
São Matias (P) 124 D3
São Miguel de Acha (P) 118 B3
São Miguel de Machede (P) 124 D2
São Miguel do Outeiro (P) 116 E2
São Miguel do Pinheiro (P) 124 D4
Saône (F) 85 K2
São Pedro (P) 110 E6
São Pedro da Cadeira (P) 116 C5
São Pedro da Gafanhoeira (P) 124 C2
São Pedro da Torre (P) 110 B5
São Pedro de Muel (P) 116 C4
São Pedro de Serracenos (P) 111 F5
São Pedro de Solis (P) 124 D5
São Pedro de Tomar (P) 116 E4
São Pedro do Esteval (P) 116 F4
São Pedro do Sul (P) 116 E2
São Roque (P) 110 B5
São Roque do Pico (P) 129 b1
São Salvador da Aramenha (P) 118 B5
São Sebastião (P) 129 c1
São Sebastião dos Carros (P) 124 D4
São Teotónio (P) 124 B4
Saou (F) 94 F1
São Vicente (P) 110 E5
São Vicente (P) 129 b2
São Vicente da Beira (P) 118 A3
Sap (SK) 154 B6
Sapadere (TR) 198 D2
Sapakpınar (TR) 183 K4
Sapanca (TR) 182 B6
Sapanca (TR) 183 K4
Sapaniv (UA) 157 J1
Săpânţa (RO) 156 E6
Sapareva Banja (BG) 175 K4
Şapçılar (TR) 191 G4
Sapčycy (BY) 145 M2
Sapërnoe (RUS) 37 N3
Sápes (GR) 181 H2
Saphane (TR) 191 G2
Sapiãos (P) 110 D5
Säpilä (FIN) 35 K2
Sapine (SRB) 167 H4
Šapinka (RUS) 135 J3
Sapjalevičy (BY) 139 L5
Šapkino (RUS) 134 H4
Šapkino (RUS) 135 M4
Săpoca (RO) 170 D3
Sapockin (BY) 143 K3
Saponara (I) 109 H1
Sappada (I) 89 H4
Sappee (FIN) 35 P2
Sappee (FIN) 36 C1
Sappemeer, Hoogezand- (NL) 64 F5
Sappen (N) 21 L1
Sappetsele (S) 26 D4
Sappu (FIN) 29 J7
Sapri (I) 106 E2
Sapsoperä (FIN) 29 J3
Sara (FIN) 28 C7
Saraby (N) 18 F3
Saracena (I) 106 F3
Saracoğlu (TR) 192 E5
Saračyna (BY) 139 J3
Sarafovo, Kvartal (BG) 177 J3
Sarai (RUS) 9 Q3
Saraiķi (LV) 132 C4
Säräisniemi (FIN) 29 G3
Saraiu (RO) 171 G4
Saraj (MK) 174 F5
Saraja (BG) 176 B4
Sarajärvi (FIN) 23 K5
Sarajärvi (FIN) 37 M1
Sarajevo (BIH) 166 B6
Sarakiní (GR) 179 F3
Sarakiní (GR) 179 F4
Sarakiní (GR) 179 F5
Saralıalaca (TR) 193 H3
Saramo (FIN) 29 K4
Saramon (F) 93 F3
Saran (F) 76 E6
Sarančany (BY) 138 D3
Saranci (BG) 176 A3
Sáránd (H) 160 D3
Sarandë (AL) 178 B5
Saranovo (SRB) 167 G5
Saranskoe (RUS) 136 E4
Sarantáporo (GR) 179 G4
Saraorci (SRB) 167 H5
Sarapanivka (UA) 163 H2
Sarapiniškės (LT) 143 M2
Sa Ràpita (E) 123 G4
Šarapovo (RUS) 135 N5
Saraqinishtë (AL) 178 C4
Sarasa (E) 113 H3
Şarasău (RO) 156 E6
Sarašova (BY) 143 L5
Sarata (UA) 13 H3
Sarata (UA) 171 K1
Sărata-Monteoru (RO) 170 D3
Sărata Noua (MD) 162 F4
Sărata Yalbenă (MD) 163 H5
Sărăţel (RO) 161 J3
Sărăţeni (RO) 161 L4
Saratlı (TR) 193 H4
Saratovskoe (RUS) 136 G4
Saray (TR) 177 J6
Saray (TR) 185 J6
Saraycık (TR) 184 E4
Saraycık (TR) 185 F3
Saraycık (TR) 185 H4
Saraycık (TR) 185 K4
Saraycık (TR) 190 F3
Saraycık (TR) 191 F3
Saraycık (TR) 191 H2
Saraycık (TR) 191 J5
Saraydüzü (TR) 185 J3
Sarayköy (TR) 184 C6
Sarayköy (TR) 184 E4
Sarayköy (TR) 185 H4
Sarayköy (TR) 185 J5
Sarayköy (TR) 191 F5
Saraylar (TR) 182 E4
Sarayönü (TR) 192 D4
Šarbanovac (SRB) 167 K6
Sărbenii de Jos (RO) 169 J5
Sârbi (RO) 160 E3
Sarbia (PL) 140 G5
Sarbinowo (PL) 67 M5
Sarbinowo (PL) 140 E2
Sárbogárd (H) 158 G4
Sarby Dolne (PL) 153 M2
Sarche (I) 87 L5
Sardañola del Vallés = Cerdanyola del Vallès (E) 115 H5
Sardara (I) 97 C4
Şardés (GR) 181 G5
Sardice (CZ) 153 M6
Sardínia (GR) 186 C2
Sardoal (P) 116 E4
Sare (F) 92 A4
Šare (SRB) 174 D2
s'Arenal (E) 123 G3
Šarengrad (HR) 166 D3
Šarenik (SRB) 174 D1
Sarentino (I) 88 E4
Särestad (S) 40 C6
Särevere (EST) 131 H3
Sargans (CH) 88 A3
Sargentes de la Lora (E) 112 D3
Sargé-sur-Braye (F) 76 C6
Sárggavárre = Sarkavare (S) 21 K7
Şărhat (H) 166 C1
Šarhorod (UA) 162 G1
Sarıağaçayı (TR) 185 J3
Sarıağıl (TR) 183 J4
Sarıağıl (TR) 193 G3
Sariai (LT) 138 D3
Sarıalan (TR) 183 H5
Sarıayak (TR) 191 G2
Sarıaydın (TR) 199 G2
Sarıbelen (TR) 197 F3
Sarıbey (TR) 190 D3
Sarıbeyler (TR) 184 E5
Sarıbeyler (TR) 190 D2
Sarıbeyli (TR) 183 K3
Sarıbuğday (TR) 185 K4
Sarıca (TR) 185 G3
Sarıca (TR) 193 K4
Sarıcakaya (TR) 183 L5
Sarıcalar (TR) 183 L5
Sarıcalar (TR) 184 E4
Sarıçam (TR) 190 D3
Sarıcaova (TR) 191 K2
Sarıçayır (TR) 190 E1
Sarichioi (RO) 171 H4
Sarıdayı (TR) 183 J6
Sarıderesi (TR) 184 E2
Sari-d'Orcino (F) 96 D4
Sariego (E) 111 H2
Sarıfakılar (TR) 190 E1
Sarıgerme (TR) 196 E2
Sarighiol de Deal (RO) 171 H4
Sarıgöl (TR) 185 K2
Sarıgöl (TR) 190 F4
Sarıgöl (TR) 192 D1
Sarıgömü (TR) 185 F3
Sarıhalil (TR) 192 D2
Sarıhamzalı (TR) 185 K6
Sarıhasan (TR) 185 K4
Sarıidris (TR) 192 B5
Sarıkavak (TR) 184 A6
Sarıkavak (TR) 192 B1
Sarıkavak (TR) 199 G2
Sarıkaya (TR) 13 L6
Sarıkaya (TR) 184 C5
Sarıkaya (TR) 185 H5
Sarıkaya (TR) 190 D6
Sarıkaya (TR) 190 E4
Sarıkaya (TR) 192 D3
Sarıkaya (TR) 199 F1
Sarıkayalar (TR) 185 F6
Sarıkemer (TR) 190 C5
Sarıköy (TR) 182 E5
Sarıköy (TR) 192 C5
Sarıkum (TR) 185 J1
Sarıküplü (TR) 192 A2
Sarılar (TR) 190 D2
Sarılar (TR) 191 H4
Sarılar (TR) 193 J3
Sările (RO) 170 D2
Sarımsaklı (TR) 190 B2
Sarinasuf (RO) 171 J3
Sariñena (E) 114 C4
Sarıoba (TR) 184 D6
Sarıömerli (TR) 193 G2
Sarıot (TR) 183 H6
Sarıpınar (TR) 185 G3
Sarıpınar (TR) 190 E4
Sárisáp (H) 158 G2
Sarışeyh (TR) 185 G3
Sarısığırlı (TR) 190 E3
Sarısöğüt (TR) 182 B6
Šarišské Čierne (SK) 155 J3
Šarišské Michaľany (SK) 155 J3
Šarišský Štiavnik (SK) 155 K3
Sarısu (TR) 185 F5
Sarısüleyman (TR) 185 K5
Sarıveliler (TR) 198 E2
Sarıyahşı (TR) 193 G3
Sarıyaka (TR) 185 H6
Sarıyaprak (TR) 185 J6
Sarıyar (TR) 185 K3
Sarıyer (TR) 183 H3
Sarıyurt (TR) 190 D4
Sar'ja (BY) 134 E6
Sarjankylä (FIN) 28 F4
Sårjåsjaurestugan (S) 20 F6
Sarkad (H) 160 C4
Sarkadkeresztúr (H) 160 C4
Sarkamäki (FIN) 29 J7
Šarkamen (SRB) 168 C5
Šarkaŭščyna (BY) 138 F3
Sarkavare (S) 21 K7
Särkela (FIN) 23 L2
Särkelä (FIN) 23 L5
Sárkeresztes (H) 158 F3
Sárkeresztúr (H) 158 G3
Särkijärvi (FIN) 18 F8
Särkijärvi (FIN) 27 M3
Särkijärvi (FIN) 29 H2
Särkijärvi (FIN) 29 K3
Särkijärvi (FIN) 36 E2
Şarkikaraağaç (TR) 192 B4
Särkikorpi (FIN) 29 K5
Särkilahti (FIN) 36 E1
Särkilahti (FIN) 37 M1
Särkiluoma (FIN) 23 M4
Särkimäki (FIN) 29 G7
Särkimo (FIN) 28 C5
Särkiniemi (FIN) 29 H6
Särkisalmi (FIN) 29 K8
Särkisalo (FIN) 28 G6
Särkisalo (FIN) 35 L4
Şarkışla (TR) 13 L6
Särkkä (FIN) 29 J5
Šarkovo (BG) 182 C1
Şarköy (TR) 181 K6
Şarköy (TR) 181 L3
Sarlat-la-Canéda (F) 93 G1
Sarliac-sur-l'Isle (F) 83 G6
Sărmaş (RO) 161 L4
Sărmăşag (RO) 160 F3
Sărmăşel Gară (RO) 161 J4
Sarmaşık (TR) 185 G4
Sarmaşıkkaya (TR) 185 J3
Sărmaşu (RO) 161 J4
Sármellék (H) 91 M6
Sarmijärvi (FIN) 19 L6
Sarmingstein (A) 91 G3
Sarmizegetusa (RO) 168 D2
Särna (S) 32 E4
Sarnadas de Ródão (P) 117 F4
Sarnaki (PL) 143 H6
Sarnano (I) 103 G1
Sārnate (LV) 132 C3
Sarnen (CH) 86 F4
Sarnesfield (GB) 57 J1
Sărnevo (BG) 176 E4
Sărnevo (BG) 177 H4
Sărnez (BG) 170 E6
Sarnia Zwola (PL) 148 D4
Sarnıç (TR) 192 E4
Sărnica (BG) 176 B5
Sarnıçköy (TR) 185 K2
Sarnıçköy (TR) 190 E1
Sarnıçköy (TR) 196 D1
Sarnico (I) 88 B6
Sărnino (BG) 177 K1
Sarno (I) 103 K6
Sarnonico (I) 87 M5
Sarnovyči (UA) 151 H1
Sarnow (D) 67 K3
Sarnów (PL) 148 E5
Sarnowa (PL) 146 F2
Sarnówek Duży (PL) 148 D3
Sarnowo (PL) 141 O4
Särnstugan (S) 32 E4
Sarntal = Sarentino (I) 88 E4
Sarny (UA) 144 E6
Sarny (UA) 151 K6
Sarö (S) 43 J3
Sa Roca Llisa (E) 122 D5
Sarone (I) 89 G6
Saronída (GR) 188 B5
Saronno (I) 98 G1
Şaroş (RO) 161 K5
Sárosd (H) 158 G3
Sárospatak (H) 155 K5
Şarot Kaplıca (TR) 184 A4
Šarovce (SK) 158 G1
Sarpdere (TR) 182 B4
Sarpdere (TR) 182 E2
Sărpovo (BG) 170 E5
Sarpsborg, Fredrikstad- (N) 39 N4
Sarpsborg, Fredrikstad- (N) 39 O4
Sarpun (TR) 185 F3
Sarracín (E) 112 D4
Sarral (E) 115 F5
Sarralbe (F) 78 G3
Sarrance (F) 114 B1
Sarrancolin (F) 92 E5
Sarras (F) 85 G6
Sarraz, La (CH) 86 C4
Sarreal = Sarral (E) 115 F5
Sarreaus (E) 110 D4
Sarrebourg (F) 78 G4
Sarreguemines (F) 78 G3
Sárrétudvari (H) 159 M3
Sarre-Union (F) 78 G4
Sarria (E) 110 E3
Sarrià de Ter (E) 115 J3
Sarrians (F) 94 E2
Sarrión (E) 121 G3
Sarroca = Sarroca de Lleida (E) 114 E5
Sarroca de Bellera (E) 93 F6
Sarroca de Lleida (E) 114 E5
Sarroch (I) 97 D5
Sarrola-Carcopino (F) 96 D4
Sarron (F) 113 L1
Sarrula Carcupinu = Sarrola-Carcopino (F) 96 D4
Šarscin (BY) 145 O3
Sarsılaiskelesi (TR) 197 E2
Sarsina (I) 101 G5
Sarstedt (D) 71 J2
Šarstova (BY) 134 H6
Sárszentlőrinc (H) 158 G4
Sart (B) 70 A5
Sartaguda (E) 113 G4
Sartè = Sartène (F) 96 D5
Sarteano (I) 102 D2
Sartène (F) 96 D5
Sárti (GR) 180 D4
Sartilly-Baie-Bocage (F) 75 J3
Sartininkai (LT) 136 F3
Sartirana Lomellina (I) 98 F2
Sartmustafa (TR) 190 E4
Šartovo (RUS) 134 E1
Sart-Saint-Laurent (B) 69 H6
Saru (EST) 134 C2
Sarud (H) 159 L2
Şaru Dornei (RO) 161 L3
Saruhanlı (TR) 190 D3
Sarülar (TR) 197 F2
Sarule (I) 97 D3
Sărulești (RO) 170 D3
Sărulești (RO) 170 D5
Sárvár (H) 158 C3
Sarvela (FIN) 28 C7
Sarvijoki (FIN) 28 B6
Sarvikas (FIN) 28 D6
Sarvikotamaa (FIN) 19 K7
Sarvikumpu (FIN) 29 K7
Sarvilahti = Sarvlax (FIN) 36 F4
Sarviluoma (FIN) 28 C7
Sarvinki (FIN) 29 L6
Sarvisalo = Sarvsalö (FIN) 36 E4
Sarvisé (E) 114 C2
Sarvisvaara (S) 21 L7
Sarvlax (FIN) 36 F4
Sarvsalö (FIN) 36 E4
Särvsjön (S) 32 E2
Sarzana (I) 100 B4
Sarzbüttel (D) 46 D5
Sarzeau (F) 74 F5
Sarzedas (P) 117 F4
Sarzedo (P) 117 F1
Şarzhav = Sarzeau (F) 74 F5
Saš (HR) 165 H4
Sasa (MK) 175 J4
Sása (SK) 154 E5
Sasa del Abadiado (E) 114 C3
Şaşal (TR) 189 K3
Şaşallı (TR) 189 J3
Sasamón (E) 112 C4
Săşăuş (RO) 161 K6
Sa Savina (E) 122 D5
Sasbach (D) 79 J4
Sasbach am Kaiserstuhl (D) 79 H5
Sasbachwalden (D) 79 J4
Sasca-Română (RO) 168 B4
Saschiz (RO) 161 K5
Săsciori (RO) 161 H6
Sascuț (RO) 170 E1
Sásd (H) 165 L2
Sase (BIH) 166 D6
Sase (BIH) 173 K1
Sasi (FIN) 35 M1
Sąsiadka (PL) 149 G4
Šasina (BIH) 165 H5
Šašinci (SRB) 166 E4
Sasiv (UA) 157 G2
Sasnava (LT) 143 J1
Sasnavka (BY) 139 M3
Sasnovy Bor (BY) 134 G6
Sasnovy Bor (BY) 145 L3
Sasovo (RUS) 9 Q3
Sassalbo (I) 100 C4
Sassali (FIN) 23 H2
Sassari (I) 97 C2
Sassello (I) 98 E4
Sassenage (F) 85 J6
Sassenberg (D) 70 F3
Sassenburg (D) 66 D5
Sassenheim (NL) 69 H2
Sassen-Trantow (D) 47 M5
Sassetta (I) 100 D6
Sassnitz (D) 67 K1
Saßnitz = Sassnitz (D) 67 K1
Sasso (I) 102 E3
Sassocorvaro (I) 101 G5
Sassoferrato (I) 101 H6
Sassoleone (I) 100 E4
Sasso Marconi (I) 100 E4
Sassuolo (I) 99 K3
Sástago (E) 113 L6
Sastavci (SRB) 175 H1
Sas van Gent (NL) 68 F4
Sašy (BY) 139 K3
Såtåhaugen (N) 31 O2
Sataniv (UA) 157 K3
Sátão (P) 117 F2
Satchinez (RO) 159 M6
Šateikiai (LT) 132 D6
Säter (S) 40 E6
Säter (S) 41 J2
Säterbo (S) 41 J4
Saterland (D) 65 H5
Šatės (LT) 136 F1
Sāti (LV) 132 F4
Sätila (S) 43 K3
Satillieu (F) 84 G6
Satırlar (TR) 190 C3
Satıyüzü (TR) 185 H4
Sătmărel (RO) 160 F2
Satnica Đakovačka (HR) 166 B3
Sątopy (PL) 136 E5
Sátoraljaújhely (H) 155 K5
Satovča (BG) 176 A5
Satow (D) 47 J6
Sätra (S) 41 J2
Sätrabrunn (S) 41 K3
Sátres (GR) 181 G2
Satriano di Lucania (I) 104 E4
Satrup (D) 46 E4
Šatry (RUS) 135 O5
Sattajärvi (FIN) 22 G4
Sattajärvi (S) 21 N6
Sattanen (FIN) 23 J1
Satteins (A) 87 J3
Sattel (CH) 87 G3
Satteldorf (D) 80 C2
Sattendorf (A) 164 B1
Satter (S) 22 D3
Sättna (S) 33 N3
Sattvik (N) 18 F4
Satul Nou (MD) 163 H5
Satulung (RO) 161 G2
Satu Mare (RO) 156 C6
Satu Mare (RO) 157 J6
Satu Nou (RO) 170 F5
Satu Nou (RO) 171 G5
Saturn (RO) 171 H6
Saturnia (I) 102 D2
Satyjiv (UA) 150 B2
Sauar (N) 39 K3
Saubach (D) 71 N4
Saubusse (F) 113 J1
Saucats (F) 92 C1
Sauceda, La (E) 128 C4
Saucejo, El (E) 125 J5
Saucelle (E) 118 C1
Sauclières (F) 94 B3
Sauda (N) 38 D3
Sauðafell (IS) 16 E4
Sauðanes (IS) 17 L2
Sauðárkrókur (IS) 16 G3
Saudasjøen (N) 38 D3
Sauðlauksdalur (IS) 16 B3
Saue (EST) 35 P6
Saue (N) 30 E6
Sauensiek (D) 66 B4
Sauerlach (D) 80 F5
Sauga (EST) 130 G4
Saughtree (GB) 53 K4
Saugnacq-et-Muret (F) 92 C2
Saugon (F) 82 D6
Saugos (LT) 136 E3
Saugues (F) 84 E7
Sauguis-Saint-Etienne (F) 114 B1
Saugykla (LT) 137 M4
Sauherad (N) 39 K4
Saujon (F) 82 D5
Saukėnai (LT) 137 H2
Saukko (FIN) 29 J4
Saukkojärvi (FIN) 27 N2
Saukkola (FIN) 28 F7
Saukkola (FIN) 36 A4
Saukkoriipi (FIN) 22 G3
Saukonkylä (FIN) 27 K9
Saukonperä (FIN) 35 M1
Saukonsaari (FIN) 37 L1
Saukotas (LT) 137 J2
Saul (GB) 57 K2
Sauland (N) 39 J3
Saulburg (D) 152 C6
Saulce, La (F) 95 G2
Saulce-sur-Rhône (F) 94 E1
Sauldorf (D) 87 H2
Saule (LV) 131 J5
Saules (F) 85 K2
Sauleskalns (LV) 133 N4
Saulgé (F) 83 G4
Saulgond (F) 83 G5
Saulgrub (D) 87 M2
Saulheim (D) 79 J2
Şăulia (RO) 161 J4
Sauliai (LT) 137 N4
Saulieu (F) 84 F2
Saulkalne (LV) 133 J4
Saulkrasti (LV) 133 J3
Saulnay (F) 83 H3
Saulnot (F) 78 F6
Sault (F) 95 F2
Sault-de-Navailles (F) 113 K1
Saulx (F) 86 B2
Saulxures-sur-Moselotte (F) 86 C2
Saulzais-le-Potier (F) 83 K3
Saumeray (F) 76 D5
Saumos (F) 92 C1
Saumur (F) 82 E2
Saunajärvi (FIN) 29 K4
Saunakylä (FIN) 27 L8
Saunakylä (FIN) 28 C7
Saunavaara (FIN) 23 K2
Saundersfoot (GB) 56 E2
Saunton (GB) 56 F3
Sauqueville (F) 76 D2
Saurat (F) 93 H5
Saurbær (IS) 16 C4
Saurbær (IS) 16 E6
Saurbær (IS) 17 H4
Saurieši (LV) 133 J4
Sauris (I) 90 C7
Saury (RUS) 139 O3
Sausses (F) 98 B4
Saussy (F) 78 B7
Sausvatn (N) 25 G4
Sauvagère, La (F) 75 L3
Sauvamäki (FIN) 29 G7
Sauve (F) 94 C3
Sauve, La (F) 92 D1
Sauvere (EST) 130 B4
Sauvetat-de-Savères, La (F) 93 F2
Sauveterre-de-Béarn (F) 113 K2
Sauveterre-de-Guyenne (F) 92 D1
Sauveterre-de-Rouergue (F) 93 J2
Sauveterre-la-Lémance (F) 93 G1
Sauvo (FIN) 35 L4
Saux (F) 93 G2
Sauxillanges (F) 84 D5
Sauze, Le (F) 95 H2
Sauze, Le (F) 95 J2
Sauze d'Oulx (I) 98 B2
Sauzet (F) 93 G2
Sauzet (F) 94 E1
Sauzé-Vaussais (F) 82 F4
Sauzon (F) 74 E6
Sava (BG) 177 H2
Sava (BY) 139 N5
Sava (I) 105 J5
Săvădisla (RO) 161 G4
Savalberget (N) 31 O3
Savalen (N) 31 O3
Savália (GR) 186 C4
Savaloja (FIN) 27 M5
Savani (BY) 144 E2
Savar (HR) 172 B1
Sävar (S) 26 G7
Săvârşin (RO) 168 C1
Sävast (S) 22 D5
Savaştepe (TR) 190 D2
Savčanki (BY) 139 M3
Savci (SLO) 91 K7
Savcılı (TR) 193 G2
Savčyn (UA) 149 K5
Savčyne (UA) 163 H2
Sávdijári = Skaulo (S) 22 D2
Säve (S) 43 J3
Sävedalen (S) 43 K3
Saveenkylä (FIN) 28 C6
Savelletri (I) 105 H4
Savelli (I) 103 G2
Savelli (I) 107 G4
Savenaho (FIN) 28 G8
Savenay (F) 75 H6
Săveni (RO) 157 L6
Săveni (RO) 170 F4
Saverdun (F) 93 H4
Savères (F) 93 G4
Saverkeit (FIN) 34 H4
Saverna (EST) 134 C1
Saverne (F) 79 G4
Savero (FIN) 36 G3
Sävi (FIN) 35 L1
Säviä (FIN) 29 G5
Saviaho (FIN) 29 J4
Savičy (BY) 145 K4
Savigliano (I) 95 L1
Savignano Irpino (I) 104 D3
Savignano sul Rubicone (I) 101 G4
Savigné-l'Évêque (F) 76 B5
Savigné-sous-le-Lude (F) 75 M5
Savigny-en-Sancerre (F) 84 C2
Savigny-sur-Braye (F) 76 C6
Savigny-sur-Orge (F) 76 F4
Savijärvi (FIN) 29 K4
Savijoki (FIN) 36 E3
Savikylä (FIN) 29 J4
Savilahti (FIN) 37 L2
sa Vileta (E) 123 G3
Savimäki (FIN) 29 G4
Savina, Sa (E) 122 D5
Saviñán (E) 113 H6
Savines-le-Lac (F) 95 H1
Săvineşti (RO) 162 C5
Saviniemi (FIN) 23 K8
Saviniemi (FIN) 35 N3
Savino Polje (MNE) 174 C2
Savino Selo (SRB) 166 E2
Savinovščina (RUS) 131 O2
Savinskij (RUS) 7 W4
Savio (FIN) 28 G7
Savio (I) 101 G4
Saviore dell'Adamello (I) 87 K5
Saviselkä (FIN) 28 G3
Savitaipale (FIN) 37 J2
Šävja (S) 41 N3
Savjarničy (BY) 139 K6
Şavköy (TR) 191 K5
Šavnik (MNE) 173 K4
Savo (FIN) 36 A2
Savognin (CH) 87 J4
Savoľščina (RUS) 37 M5
Sávoly (H) 165 J1
Savona (I) 98 E4
Savonkylä (FIN) 28 D5
Savonlahti (FIN) 29 G7
Savonlinna (FIN) 37 L1
Savonranta (FIN) 29 K7
Savosťe (BY) 139 N3
Savoulx (I) 85 L6
Savran' (UA) 163 L2
Sävsjö (S) 44 F4
Sävsjön (S) 26 F5
Sävsjön (S) 40 G3
Sävsjöström (S) 44 G5
Sävtorp (S) 40 C2
Savudrija (HR) 164 B4
Savukoski (FIN) 23 L2
Savulca (TR) 190 C5
Savyn (UA) 151 M2
Savynci (UA) 151 M4
Savynci (UA) 163 J2
Sawbridge Worth (GB) 59 H4
Sawin (PL) 149 H3
Sawley (GB) 55 H3
Sawrey (GB) 54 G2
Sawston (GB) 59 H3
Sax (E) 127 J2
Saxån (S) 40 F3
Saxängen (S) 41 L4
Saxby (EST) 130 D2
Saxby = Saksala (FIN) 36 E4
Saxdalen (S) 40 G2
Saxemara (S) 44 G6
Saxhyttan (S) 40 F3
Saxhyttan (S) 40 H2
Saxilby (GB) 55 L4
Saxmundham (GB) 68 A2
Saxnäs (S) 25 K5
Saxtead Green (GB) 68 A2
Saxthorpe (GB) 59 K2
Saxtorp (S) 47 L2
Saxvallbygget (S) 32 E3
Saxvallen (S) 25 G7
Sayalar (TR) 182 F3
Sayatón (E) 120 C3
Sayda (D) 73 J4
Säyhtee (FIN) 36 F3
Sayık (TR) 190 F3
Säynäja (FIN) 23 M4
Säynätsalo (FIN) 28 F7
Säyneinen (FIN) 29 J5
Säynejärvi (FIN) 29 L8
Säynelahti (FIN) 29 J7
Sayrakçı (TR) 190 D5
Säytsjärvi (FIN) 19 K5
Sazak (TR) 182 D6
Sazak (TR) 191 H6
Sazak (TR) 199 K2
Sázava (CZ) 153 J4
Sazgeçit (TR) 193 G5
Sazılar (TR) 184 C6
Sažino (RUS) 135 J2
Sazköy (TR) 185 J5
Sazköy (TR) 191 H5
Sazlı (TR) 190 A1
Sazlı (TR) 190 C5
Sazlıca (TR) 193 J5
Sazlıpınar (TR) 193 F5
Şazoba (TR) 190 D3
Ščadryn (BY) 145 L3
Scăeni, Boldeşti- (RO) 170 C3
Scaër (F) 74 D4
Scăeşti (RO) 168 F5
Scafa (I) 103 H3
Scalasaig (GB) 52 C2
Scalby (GB) 55 M2
Scalea (I) 104 E6
Scaletta Zanclea (I) 109 H1
Scalloway (GB) 49 F3
Scamblesby (GB) 55 M4
Scampton (GB) 55 L4
Scandiano (I) 99 K3
Scandicci (I) 100 E5
Scandolara Ravara (I) 100 C2
Scandolaro (I) 103 F2
Ščanec (BY) 143 L3
Ščanernja (BY) 139 J2
Scanno (I) 104 A2
Scano di Montiferro (I) 97 C3
Scansano (I) 102 C2
Scânteia (RO) 162 F5
Scânteia (RO) 170 E4
Scânteieşti (RO) 170 G2
Scanzano Jonico (I) 105 G5
Scar (GB) 49 C5
Scarborough (GB) 55 M2
Ščarby (BY) 138 G3
Ščarčova (BY) 143 L6
Scardovari (I) 101 G3
Scardroy (GB) 50 H4
Scarfskerry (GB) 51 L2
Scarinish (GB) 52 B2
Scario (I) 104 D5
Scărişoara (RO) 160 F5
Scarlino (I) 102 B2
Scarperia (I) 100 E5
Scarriff (IRL) 60 E6
Scartaglin (IRL) 62 D4
Scarva (GB) 61 K3
Scastlyva (UA) 151 H5
Scauri (I) 103 H5
Scauri (I) 108 A4
Sceaux (F) 76 F4
Sceaux-d'Anjou (F) 75 K5
Ščegly (RUS) 142 G1
Ščekino (RUS) 9 P3
Ščekyčyn (UA) 150 D2
Ščenica-Bobani (BIH) 173 H4
Ščepan Polje (MNE) 173 J3
Ščepčino (RUS) 135 J5
Ščerbanka (UA) 163 L5
Ščerbašynci (UA) 151 M5
Ščerkava (BY) 138 B6
Scerni (I) 104 C1
Scešycy (BY) 138 F4
Scey-sur-Saône-et-Saint-Albin (F) 86 A2
Ščėžar (BY) 139 N6
Schaafheim (D) 79 L2
Schaan (FL) 87 J3
Schadeleben (D) 71 M3
Schaffhausen (CH) 79 K6
Schafflund (D) 65 L2
Schafstädt (D) 72 F3
Schafstedt (D) 66 A2
Schäftlarn (D) 88 E2
Schagen (NL) 64 B6
Schagerbrug (NL) 64 B6
Schaijk (NL) 69 K3
Schalchen (A) 89 J1
Schale (D) 70 E2
Schalkau (D) 71 M6
Schalkenmehren (D) 70 C6
Schalksmühle (D) 70 E4
Schallstadt (D) 86 E2
Schambach (D) 80 D3
S-chanf (CH) 88 B4
Schangnau (CH) 86 E4
Schänis (CH) 87 H3
Schaprode (D) 67 J1
Scharbeutz (D) 46 G5
Schärding (A) 90 D3
Scharendijke (NL) 68 F3
S-charl (CH) 87 K4
Scharmbeck, Osterholz- (D) 65 K5
Scharnebeck (D) 65 O5
Scharnitz (A) 80 E6
Scharnstein Markt (A) 89 K2
Scharrel (Oldenburg) (D) 65 H5
Scharsterland = Skarsterlân (NL) 64 D6
Schauenburg (D) 72 A3
Schauenstein (D) 72 F5
Scheden (D) 71 J4
Scheemda (NL) 64 F5
Scheeßel (D) 66 A4
Scheffau (D) 89 J2
Schefflenz (D) 79 L3
Scheggia (I) 101 H6
Scheggino (I) 103 F2
Şcheia (RO) 162 C3
Şcheia (RO) 162 F5
Scheibbs (A) 91 H3
Scheibenberg (D) 152 C2
Scheidegg (D) 88 B2
Scheidingen (D) 70 E3
Scheifling (A) 89 L3
Scheinfeld (D) 80 C1
Schela (RO) 168 E3
Schela (RO) 169 J5
Schela (RO) 170 F3
Schelklingen (D) 79 M5
Schellerten (D) 72 C1
Schellinkhout (NL) 64 C6
Schemmerhofen (D) 80 B4
Schenefeld (D) 66 A2
Schenefeld (D) 66 B3
Schengen (L) 78 E3
Schenklengsfeld (D) 71 J5
Scheppach, Jettingen- (D) 80 C4
Scherfede (D) 71 H3
Schermbeck (D) 69 M3
Scherpenheuvel (B) 69 H5
Scherpenisse (NL) 68 G3
Scherpenzeel (NL) 69 J2
Scheßlitz (D) 71 M7
Scheuring (D) 80 D4
Scheveningen (NL) 69 G2
Schiavi di Abruzzo (I) 104 B2
Schiavon (I) 88 F6
Schidnycja (UA) 156 D3
Schiedam (NL) 69 G3
Schieder-Schwalenberg (D) 71 H3
Schieranco (I) 86 F5
Schierke (D) 72 D2
Schierling (D) 80 G3
Schiermonnikoog = Skiermûntseach (NL) 64 E5
Schiers (CH) 87 J4
Schiffdorf (D) 65 K4
Schifferstadt (D) 79 J3
Schifflange (L) 78 E2
Schiffweiler (D) 78 G3
Schijndel (NL) 69 J3
Schildau (D) 73 H3
Schildau, Belgern- (D) 73 J3
Schilde (B) 69 H4
Schildow (D) 67 J5
Schildthurn (D) 90 C3
Schillerslage (D) 66 B6
Schillingsfürst (D) 80 C2
Schilpario (I) 87 K5
Schiltach (D) 79 J5
Schiltigheim (F) 79 H4
Schimborn (D) 71 H6
Schimm (D) 66 F3
Schinteieşti (RO) 167 L4
Schinznach-Dorf (CH) 79 J7
Schio (I) 88 E6
Schipkau (D) 73 K2
Schirgiswalde-Kirschau (D) 146 A3
Schirmeck (F) 78 G5
Schirmitz (D) 80 G1
Schirnding (D) 152 B3
Schitu (RO) 170 B5
Schitu Duca (RO) 162 F4
Schitu Goleşti (RO) 169 J3
Schkeuditz (D) 73 G3
Schkölen (D) 72 F3
Schköna (D) 73 H2
Schkopau (D) 72 F3
Schladen-Werla (D) 72 D1
Schladming (A) 81 K6
Schlagsdorf (D) 66 D3
Schlaitz (D) 73 G2
Schlanders = Silandro (I) 88 D4
Schlangen (D) 71 G3
Schlarigna = Celerina (CH) 88 B4
Schlaubetal (D) 146 A1
Schleching (D) 81 G5
Schledehausen (D) 70 F2
Schleiden (D) 69 L5
Schleife (D) 146 B2
Schleithal (F) 79 J4
Schleitheim (CH) 86 F2
Schleiz (D) 72 F4
Schlepzig (D) 73 K1
Schlesen (D) 46 F5
Schleswig (D) 66 B1
Schlettau (D) 73 H4
Schleusegrund (D) 71 L5
Schleusingen (D) 71 L5
Schlieben (D) 73 J2
Schliengen (D) 86 E2
Schlierbach (A) 89 L2
Schlierbach (D) 71 H5
Schlieren (CH) 86 F3
Schliersee (D) 88 F2
Schlitz (D) 72 B4
Schloß Holte-Stukenbrock (D) 70 G3
Schloß Neuhaus (D) 70 G3
Schloßvippach (D) 72 E3
Schlotheim (D) 72 D3
Schluchsee (D) 79 J6
Schlüchtern (D) 72 B5
Schluderbach = Carbonin (I) 90 B6
Schluderns = Sluderno (I) 88 D4
Schlüsselburg (D) 71 H2
Schlüsselfeld (D) 80 D1
Schlüttsiel (D) 46 C4
Schmalfeld (D) 46 E6
Schmalförden (D) 65 K6
Schmalkalden (D) 72 C4
Schmallenberg (D) 70 F4
Schmatzin (D) 47 N6
Schmelz (D) 78 F3
Schmidgaden (D) 80 G2
Schmidmühlen (D) 80 F2
Schmidt (D) 70 B5
Schmidtheim (D) 69 M6
Schmiedeberg (D) 152 E2
Schmiedefeld am Rennsteig (D) 72 D4
Schmilau (D) 66 D3
Schmirn (A) 88 F3
Schmitten (CH) 86 D4
Schmittlotheim (D) 71 G4
Schmölau (D) 66 D5
Schmölln (D) 73 G4
Schmölln (D) 140 B4
Schnackenburg (D) 66 F4
Schnaitsee (D) 89 G1
Schnaittach (D) 80 E1
Schnaittenbach (D) 80 G1
Schnals = Senales (I) 88 D4
Schneeberg (D) 152 C2
Schneegattern (A) 89 J1
Schneeren (D) 66 A5
Schnega (D) 66 D5
Schneizlreuth (D) 89 H2
Schnelldorf (D) 80 C2
Schnepfau (A) 80 B6
Schneverdingen (D) 66 B4
Schöder (A) 90 F5
Schœnau (F) 79 H5
Schöftland (CH) 86 F3
Scholen (D) 65 K6
Schollene (D) 67 G5
Schöllkrippen (D) 71 H6
Schöllnach (D) 152 D6
Schömberg (D) 79 K4
Schömberg (D) 79 K5
Schönach (D) 81 G3
Schönach, Herdwangen- (D) 79 L6
Schonach im Schwarzwald (D) 79 J5
Schönau (D) 79 K3
Schönau (D) 152 C7
Schönau = Belprato (I) 87 M4
Schönau am Königssee (D) 81 H5
Schönau an der Brend (D) 71 K6
Schönau im Schwarzwald (D) 79 H6
Schönbeck (D) 67 K3
Schönberg (B) 70 B6
Schönberg (D) 66 C3
Schönberg (D) 66 D3
Schönberg (D) 81 J3
Schönberg (Holstein) (D) 65 N3
Schönberg am Kamp (A) 153 J6
Schönbühl, Urtenen- (CH) 86 E3
Schönburg (D) 72 F3
Schondorf am Ammersee (D) 88 E1
Schönebeck (D) 67 G4
Schönebeck (Elbe) (D) 72 F1
Schöneck (D) 71 G6
Schöneck (Vogtland) (D) 73 G5
Schönecken (D) 69 L6
Schönefeld (D) 67 J6
Schöneiche bei Berlin (D) 67 K6
Schönenberg-Kübelberg (D) 79 G3
Schönermark (D) 67 J4
Schönermark (D) 67 K4
Schönermark (D) 140 B4
Schönewalde (D) 73 J2
Schönfeld (A) 91 H2
Schönfeld (D) 73 K3
Schönfels (D) 73 G4
Schongau (D) 88 D2
Schöngleina (D) 72 F4
Schöngrabern (A) 91 K2
Schönhagen (D) 66 C1
Schönhagen (D) 71 J3
Schönhausen (Elbe) (D) 66 G5
Schönheide (D) 73 H4
Schöningen (D) 72 D1
Schöninghsdorf (D) 64 G6
Schönkirchen (D) 66 C2
Schönsee (D) 81 H1
Schöntal (D) 79 M3
Schönthal (D) 81 H2
Schonungen (D) 72 C5
Schönwald (D) 72 G5
Schönwalde (D) 67 J5
Schönwalde (D) 73 K2
Schönwalde am Bungsberg (D) 66 D2
Schönwalde-Glien (D) 67 J5
Schönwald im Schwarzwald (D) 79 J5
Schoondijke (NL) 68 F4
Schoonebeek (NL) 64 F6
Schoonhoven (NL) 69 H3
Schoonloo (NL) 64 F6
Schoonoord (NL) 64 F6
Schoorl (NL) 64 B6
Schopfheim (D) 79 H6
Schöpfigitter (A) 91 J3
Schopfloch (D) 79 K5
Schopfloch (D) 80 C2
Schöppenstedt (D) 72 D1
Schoppernau (A) 80 C6
Schöppingen (D) 70 D2
Schorfheide (D) 67 K5
Schörfling am Attersee (A) 90 E4
Schorndorf (D) 79 M4
Schortens (D) 65 H4
Schoten (B) 69 G4
Schotten (D) 71 H5
Schötz (CH) 86 E3
Schramberg (D) 79 J5
Schraplau (D) 71 N4
Schrecken (A) 80 B6
Schrecksbach (D) 71 H5
Schrems (A) 153 H6
Schrems bei Frohnleiten (A) 91 H5
Schrick (A) 153 L6
Schriesheim (D) 79 K3
Schrobenhausen (D) 80 E3
Schröcken (A) 87 K3
Schrozberg (D) 80 B2
Schruns (A) 87 J3
Schuby (D) 66 A1
Schuddebeurs (NL) 68 F3
Schuld (D) 69 M6
Schulenberg im Oberharz (D) 71 K3
Schulenburg (Leine) (D) 72 B1
Schuls = Scuol (CH) 88 C4
Schulzendorf (D) 67 J4
Schulzendorf (D) 67 K6
Schüpfen (CH) 86 D3
Schüpfheim (CH) 86 F4
Schüttdamm (D) 65 L4
Schuttertal (D) 79 H5
Schutterwald (D) 79 H5
Schüttorf (D) 70 D2
Schützen am Gebirge (A) 158 C2
Schwaan (D) 47 K6
Schwabach (D) 80 E2
Schwabbach (D) 79 L3
Schwaben, Markt (D) 80 F4
Schwabhausen (D) 80 E4
Schwabhausen bei Landsberg (D) 80 D4
Schwäbisch Gmünd (D) 80 B3
Schwäbisch Hall (D) 79 M3
Schwabmünchen (D) 80 D4
Schwabstedt (D) 65 L3
Schwadorf (A) 158 C1
Schwaförden (D) 65 K6
Schwagstorf (D) 70 E1
Schwaiganger (D) 80 E5
Schwaigern (D) 79 L3
Schwaikheim (D) 79 L4
Schwaim (D) 90 D3
Schwalbach (Saar) (D) 78 F3
Schwalenberg, Schieder- (D) 71 H3
Schwalmstadt (D) 71 H5
Schwalmtal (D) 69 L4
Schwalmtal (D) 71 H5
Schwanau (D) 79 H5
Schwanberg (A) 91 H6
Schwanden (CH) 87 H3
Schwandorf (D) 80 G2
Schwanebeck (D) 71 M3
Schwanenstadt (A) 89 K1
Schwanewede (D) 65 K5
Schwaney (D) 71 G3
Schwangau (D) 87 L2
Schwanheide (D) 66 D4
Schwante (D) 67 J5
Schwarme (D) 65 L6
Schwarmstedt (D) 66 B5
Schwarz (D) 67 H4
Schwarza (D) 71 L5
Schwarzach (D) 79 J4
Schwarzach (D) 81 H3
Schwarzach bei Nabburg (D) 152 B5
Schwarzach im Pongau (A) 81 J6
Schwarzautal (A) 91 J6
Schwarzbach (D) 72 B4
Schwarzburg (D) 71 M5
Schwarzenau (A) 91 H2
Schwarzenbach (D) 73 G6
Schwarzenbach (D) 152 A4
Schwarzenbach am Wald (D) 72 F5
Schwarzenbach an der Saale (D) 152 A3
Schwarzenbek (D) 66 C4
Schwarzenberg/Erzgebirge (D) 73 H4
Schwarzenberg im Mühlkreis (A) 152 E6
Schwarzenborn (D) 72 A4
Schwarzenburg (CH) 86 D4
Schwarzenegg (CH) 86 E4
Schwarzenfeld (D) 80 G2
Schwarze Pumpe (D) 146 A2
Schwarzhausen (D) 72 C4
Schwarzheide/Niederlausitz (D) 73 K3
Schwarzhofen (D) 81 G2
Schwarzsee (CH) 86 D4
Schwaz (A) 80 F6
Schwebenried (D) 72 C5
Schwebheim (D) 71 K7
Schwechat (A) 158 B1
Schwedt/Oder (D) 140 B4
Schwei (D) 65 J5
Schweiburg (D) 65 J5
Schweich (D) 78 F2
Schweiggers (A) 91 H2
Schweighouse-sur-Moder (F) 79 H4
Schweinfurt (D) 72 C5
Schweinitz (D) 73 J2
Schweinrich (D) 67 H4
Schweinsberg (D) 71 G5
Schweitenkirchen (D) 80 F3
Schwelm (D) 70 D4
Schwemsal (D) 73 H2
Schwend (D) 80 F2
Schwenden (CH) 86 D4
Schwendi (D) 80 B4
Schwendt (A) 81 G5
Schwenningen (D) 79 K5
Schwenningen (D) 80 D3
Schwenningen, Villingen- (D) 79 K5
Schwentinental (D) 65 N3
Schwepnitz (D) 73 K3
Schwerfen (D) 70 C5
Schwerin (D) 66 E3
Schwertberg (A) 90 G3
Schwerte (D) 70 E4
Schwerting (A) 81 H5
Schwesing (D) 46 D5
Schwetzingen (D) 79 K3
Schwieberdingen (D) 79 L4
Schwielochsee (D) 146 A1
Schwiesau (D) 66 E5
Schwindkirchen (D) 90 B3
Schwinkendorf (D) 67 H3
Schwörstadt (D) 79 H6
Schwülper (D) 66 C6
Schwyz (CH) 87 G3
Sciacca (I) 108 D2
Sciale Frattarolo (I) 104 E2
Scianica (I) 88 C5
Sciara (I) 108 E2
Scicli (I) 109 G4
Şciez (F) 86 B5
Ščigry (RUS) 9 O4
Scilla (I) 106 E6
Şcillé (F) 82 D3
Ścinawa (PL) 146 E3
Ścinawa Mała (PL) 153 N3
Ścinawka Dolna (PL) 153 L3
Ścinawka Średnia (PL) 153 K2
Ščit (BIH) 173 G2
Scleddau (GB) 63 N5
Scoarța (RO) 168 E3
Scobinţi (RO) 162 D4
Scoglitti (I) 109 F4
Ščokatava (BY) 139 N5
Scole (GB) 59 K3
Ščomyslica (BY) 138 F6
Sconser (GB) 50 E5
Scopello (I) 86 F6
Scopello (I) 108 C1
Scoppito (I) 103 G3
Scordia (I) 109 G3
Scoreni (MD) 163 H4
Scorniceşti (RO) 169 H4
Scorrano (I) 107 K2
Ščorsivka = Bilošyci (UA) 151 H2
Scorţaru Nou (RO) 170 F3
Scorţaru Vechi (RO) 170 F3
Scorţeni (RO) 162 D5
Scorţeni (RO) 170 B3
Scorţoasa (RO) 170 D3
Scorzè (I) 101 G1
Scotch Corner (GB) 53 M6
Scotter (GB) 55 L4
Scourie (GB) 50 G3
Scoury (F) 83 H3
Scrabbi (IRL) 60 G4
Scrabster (GB) 49 A6
Scremerston (GB) 53 M3
Scrignac (F) 74 D4
Scrioaştea (RO) 169 H5
Scriob (IRL) 62 C2
Ščuč'e (RUS) 135 O6
Ščuč'ja Gora (RUS) 134 H2
Ščučyn (BY) 143 M3
Ščuki (BY) 138 F5
Ščukino (RUS) 134 H4
Sculeni (RO) 162 F4
Scunthorpe (GB) 55 L3
Scuol (CH) 88 C4
Scurcola Marsicana (I) 103 G3
Ščurivci (UA) 157 L1
Ščurovyči (UA) 149 M5
Scurteşti (RO) 170 D3
Scurtu Mare (RO) 169 J5
Scutelnici (RO) 170 D4
Ščyrec' (UA) 156 E2
Ščytkavičy (BY) 144 G2
Ščytyns'ka Volja (BY) 149 L2
Seaca de Padure (RO) 168 E5
Seaford (GB) 59 H6
Seaham (GB) 53 N5
Seamer (GB) 55 M2
Seamill (GB) 52 F3
Sea Palling (GB) 59 L2
Seara (P) 110 B5
Seascale (GB) 53 J6
Seaton (GB) 58 A6
Seaton Delaval (GB) 53 M4
Seave Green (GB) 53 N6
Sebbersund (DK) 42 E5
Šebečevo (SRB) 174 D2
Šebekino (RUS) 9 O4
Seben (TR) 184 C5
Sebenardı (TR) 184 C4
Sebepliköy (TR) 182 E6
Sebeş (RO) 161 H6
Šebetov (CZ) 153 L4
Sebež (RUS) 7 R7
Sebež (RUS) 134 F5
Sebil (TR) 199 J1
Sebiller (TR) 192 C4
Şebinkarahisar (TR) 13 M5
Sebiş (RO) 160 E5
Sebnitz (D) 146 A4
Seboncourt (F) 77 H2
Seborga (I) 95 L3
Sebranice (CZ) 153 K4
Sebta = Ceuta (E) 128 D6
Sebuzín (CZ) 152 F2
Seč (CZ) 81 K1
Seč (CZ) 146 D6
Seca, La (E) 111 K6
Sečanica (SRB) 175 G2
Sečanj (SRB) 167 G3
Seča Reka (SRB) 173 L1
Secăria (RO) 170 B3
Secaş (RO) 160 D6
Seccagrande (I) 108 D3
Sece (LV) 133 L4
Secemin (PL) 148 A4
Séchault (F) 78 B3
Secinaro (I) 103 H3
Secjanec (BY) 134 H6
Seckau (A) 91 G5
Seckington (GB) 55 J5
Seçköy (TR) 183 H5
Seclin (F) 68 E5
Seçme (TR) 192 E5
Secondigny (F) 82 E3
Sečovce (SK) 155 K4
Sečovlje (SLO) 164 B4
Sečovská Polianka (SK) 155 K4
Secu (RO) 167 J3
Secu (RO) 168 E5
Secugnago (I) 100 B2
Secui (RO) 168 F5
Secuieni (RO) 161 K5
Secuita, la (E) 115 F5
Secuiu (RO) 169 L2
Secusigiu (RO) 167 G1
Secymin Polski (PL) 142 C6
Seda (LT) 136 G1
Seda (LV) 133 M2
Sedan (F) 78 B2
Sedano (E) 112 D3
Sedas (P) 124 D4
Sedbergh (GB) 55 G2
Sedča (BY) 144 G1
Seddin (D) 67 J6
Sedegliano (I) 89 H5
Sedella (E) 126 B6
Séderon (F) 95 G2
Sedgeberrow (GB) 57 L1
Sedgefield (GB) 55 K1
Sedgley (GB) 58 C2
Sedico (I) 88 G5
Sedilo (I) 97 C3
Sedini (I) 97 C2
Sedlare = Shalë (RKS) 174 E4
Sedlarica (HR) 158 D6
Sedlčany (CZ) 81 L1
Sedlec-Prčice (CZ) 152 G4
Sedlice (CZ) 152 E5
Sedlice (SK) 155 J4
Sedliská (SK) 155 K4
Sedlitz (D) 73 L2
Sedlóvina (BG) 181 G1
Sedmihorky (CZ) 153 H2
Sedriano (I) 87 G7
Sedrina (I) 87 J6
Sedring (DK) 42 F5
Sedrun (CH) 87 G4
Šeduva (LT) 137 K2
Sędziszów (PL) 148 B4
Sędziszów Małopolski (PL) 155 K1
See (A) 88 C3
Seebauer (A) 90 D5
Seeboden am Millstätter See (A) 89 J4
Seebruck, Seeon- (D) 81 G5
Seebs (A) 91 H2
Seeburg (D) 72 F3
Seeburg (D) 80 A4
Seedorf (D) 66 C2
Seefeld (D) 65 J5
Seefeld (D) 88 E1
Seefeld in Tirol (A) 80 E6
Seehausen (D) 65 K5
Seehausen (D) 72 E1
Seehausen (D) 73 H2
Seehausen (Altmark) (D) 66 F5
Seeheim-Jugenheim (D) 79 K2
Seekirchen am Wallersee (A) 81 J5
Seeland (D) 72 E2
Seelbach (D) 79 H5

Seelbach 231

Steinhude (D) 66 A6
Steinigtwolmsdorf (D) 152 F1
Steinkjer (N) 24 F6
Steinland (N) 20 E3
Steinløysa (N) 30 H2
Steinnes (N) 18 B3
Stein-Neukirch (D) 70 F5
Steinsasen (N) 39 M2
Steinsbøle (N) 39 J2
Steinsdal (N) 24 D7
Steinsdorf (D) 73 M1
Steinset (N) 30 D5
Steinshamn (N) 30 E2
Steinsholt (N) 39 L4
Steinsland (N) 20 F3
Steinsland (N) 25 H1
Steinsland (N) 30 D6
Steinsmýri (IS) 17 H7
Steins-øynes (N) 24 B8
Steins-øy-Sund (N) 24 C8
Steinstølen (N) 39 J1
Steinsund (N) 18 B4
Steinsvik (N) 30 D3
Steinvåg (N) 19 L1
Steinvollen (N) 18 B3
Steinwiesen (D) 72 E5
Steiro (N) 25 H2
Steißlingen (D) 87 G2
Stejărişu (RO) 169 H1
Stejaru (RO) 171 H4
Stejeriş (RO) 161 H5
Stekene (B) 68 G4
Stekenjåkk (S) 25 J4
Steklin (PL) 141 L5
Steklino (RUS) 135 O4
Stekljannyj (RUS) 37 O4
Steknica (PL) 141 J1
Stellata (I) 100 E3
Stelle (D) 65 N5
Stellendam (NL) 68 G3
Stelle-Wittenwurth (D) 65 L3
Stelmužė (LT) 133 N6
Stelnica (RO) 170 F5
Stelpe (LV) 133 K4
Stelvio (I) 87 L4
Stemnitsa (GR) 186 E4
Stemwede (D) 70 F2
Stenabäck (S) 26 F5
Stenåsa (S) 45 K5
Stenåsen (S) 40 E3
Stenay (F) 77 M3
Stenberga (S) 44 G4
Stenbjerg (DK) 42 B5
Stenbo (S) 45 J4
Stenbrohult (S) 43 O5
Stenbyn (S) 40 C4
Stendal (D) 66 F5
Stende (LV) 132 F3
Stenderup (DK) 46 C2
Stene (N) 31 M1
Steneby (S) 40 B5
Stenestad (S) 47 M1
Stengårdshult (S) 44 D3
Stengelsrud (N) 39 L3
Stenhamra (S) 41 N4
Steni Dirfios (GR) 187 H2
Steniés (GR) 188 E4
Stenímahos (GR) 179 G3
Steninge (S) 43 L5
Stenjatyn (UA) 149 K4
Stenje (MK) 178 D3
Stenkullen (S) 43 K3
Stenkumla (S) 45 N3
Stenkyrka (S) 39 P6
Stenlille (DK) 47 J2
Stenløse (DK) 47 K2
Stennäs (S) 26 E7
Stenness (GB) 49 E3
Stenó (GR) 186 E4
Stenó (GR) 187 E5
Stěnovice (CZ) 81 J1
Stensån (S) 33 J3
Stensåsen (N) 31 Q2
Stensby (N) 32 B4
Stensdals stugorna (S) 32 D1
Stensele (S) 25 M4
Stensjö (S) 25 L8
Stensjö (S) 33 L2
Stensjö by (S) 45 J4
Stensjön (S) 40 C3
Stensjön (S) 44 F3
Stensnäs = Kiviniemi (FIN) 36 G4
Stenstorp (S) 40 E6
Stenstrup (DK) 46 G3
Stenstugu (S) 45 O3
Stensund (S) 25 M4
Stensund (S) 26 E2
Stensund (S) 26 E4
Stensund (S) 26 E5
Stensved (DK) 47 K4
Stensyr (S) 43 J1
Stenträsk (S) 22 B4
Stenträsk (S) 22 B6
Stenudden (S) 26 D1
Stenungsund (S) 43 J2
Stenvad (DK) 42 G6
Stenviksstrand (S) 25 L7
Stenžaryči (UA) 149 K4
Steòrnabhagh = Stornoway (GB) 50 E3
Stepan' (UA) 150 C1
Stepanci (MK) 175 G6
Stepanhorod (UA) 144 D5
Stepanivka (UA) 163 K1
Stepan'kino (RUS) 135 J3
Štěpánov (CZ) 153 M4
Stepanovićevo (SRB) 166 E3
Štěpánov nad Svratkou (CZ) 153 K4
Stepenitz (D) 66 G4
Stephanskirchen (D) 90 B4
Stepnica (PL) 140 C3
Stepojevac (SRB) 166 F4
Stepov (MNE) 174 B4
Stepove (UA) 163 L5
Stepping (DK) 46 D3
Step-Soci (MD) 163 H4
Stępuchowo (PL) 141 H5
Sterdyń (PL) 142 G5
Sterevnevo (RUS) 135 L6
Sterkrade (D) 70 C3
Sterławki Wielkie (PL) 136 F5
Sterley (D) 66 D3
Stern = La Villa (I) 88 F4
Stérna (GR) 177 F5
Sterna (GR) 180 F2
Stérna (GR) 187 F4
Sterna (HR) 164 B4
Sterna = Šterna (HR) 164 B4
Sternberg (D) 66 F3
Šternberk (CZ) 153 M4
Sternebeck-Harnekop (D) 67 K5
Stérnes (GR) 194 E4
Sterringi (N) 31 K4
Sterup (D) 65 M2
Sterzing = Vipiteno (I) 88 E4
Stestrup (DK) 47 J2
Stešyna (UA) 151 K1
Stęszew (PL) 146 F1
Štěti (CZ) 146 A5
Stetten am kalten Markt (D) 79 L5
Stettfeld (D) 71 L7
Stěučen' = Stauceni (MD) 163 H4
Steutz (D) 72 G2
Stevenage (GB) 59 G4
Stevenson (GB) 52 F3
Stevrek (BG) 176 F3
Stewarton (GB) 52 D4
Stewarton (GB) 52 F3
Stewartstown (GB) 61 J2
Stewkley (GB) 58 F4
Steyerberg (D) 65 L6
Steyr (A) 89 L1
Steyregg (A) 81 L4
Stezerovo (BG) 176 D1
Stężyca (PL) 146 F2
Stężyca (PL) 148 E2
Stia (I) 101 F5
Štiavnické Bane (SK) 154 D5
Stibanken (DK) 47 H4
Stibb Cross (GB) 56 F4
Stichtse Vecht (NL) 69 J2
Stickhausen (D) 65 H5
Stična (SLO) 164 D3
Stiens (NL) 64 D5
Stift Griffen (A) 89 M4
Stige (DK) 46 F3
Stigen (N) 32 C5
Stigen (S) 43 K1
Stigliano (I) 106 F2
Stigniţa (RO) 168 E5
Stigsbo (S) 41 K2
Stigsjö (S) 33 O2
Stigtomta (S) 41 L5
Stijena (BIH) 165 G5
Stiklestad (N) 24 F7
Stikli (LV) 132 E3
Stilfs = Stelvio (I) 87 L4
Stilida (GR) 179 H7
Stilling (DK) 46 E1
Stillinge Strand (DK) 46 H3
Stilo (I) 107 F6
Stil's'ke (UA) 156 F2
Stimánga (GR) 187 F4
Stimfalia (GR) 187 E4
Stimigliano (I) 103 F3
Štimlje = Shtime (RKS) 174 F4
Stimpfach (D) 80 C2
Stinica (HR) 164 D5
Stintino (I) 97 B2
Stio (I) 106 D2
Štip (MK) 175 H5
Štipoklasy (CZ) 153 H4
Stipsko (BG) 177 J2
Stira (GR) 188 D3
Stirfaka (GR) 179 G7
Stiri (GR) 187 F3
Stiring-Wendel (F) 78 F3
Stirling (GB) 53 H2
Štit (BG) 177 F5
Štitar (SRB) 166 E4
Stithians (GB) 56 D5
Štitkovo (SRB) 174 C2
Štítná nad Vláří (CZ) 154 B3
Štítnik (SK) 155 G4
Štíty (CZ) 146 F6
Stiubieni (RO) 157 L6
Stiuca (RO) 167 J2
Stivan (HR) 164 C5
Stivica (HR) 165 K4
Stivos (GR) 179 J3
Stižok (UA) 157 J1
Stjärnfors (S) 40 H3
Stjärnhov (S) 41 M4
Stjärnorp (S) 44 H1
Stjärnsund (S) 41 K2
Stjärnvik (S) 41 J3
Stjern (N) 24 E6
Stjørdalshalsen (N) 24 E8
Stø (N) 20 E2
Støa (N) 24 F6
Støa (N) 31 N2
Støa (N) 32 D5
Stobnica (PL) 140 G5
Stobno (PL) 141 J3
Stoby (S) 47 N1
Stobychva (UA) 144 B6
Stochov (CZ) 73 K5
Stocka (S) 33 N4
Stöckach (D) 72 D5
Stockach (D) 87 H2
Stöckalp (CH) 86 F4
Stockamöllan (S) 47 M2
Stockaryd (S) 44 F4
Stockbridge (GB) 57 M3
Stockbriggs (GB) 53 H3
Stöcke (S) 26 G7
Stockelsdorf (D) 46 G6
Stockenchurch (GB) 58 F4
Stockerau (A) 91 K3
Stockhausen (D) 72 A4
Stockheim (D) 72 E5
Stockholm (S) 34 B6
Stockport (GB) 55 H4
Stocksbo (S) 33 K4
Stocksbo (S) 33 L6
Stocksbridge (GB) 55 J4
Stöckse (D) 66 A5
Stocksee (D) 66 C2
Stöcksjö (S) 26 G7
Stockstadt am Main (D) 71 H7
Stockton-on-Tees (GB) 55 K1
Stockvik (S) 33 N3
Stoczek (PL) 142 F5
Stoczek Klasztorny (PL) 136 D5
Stoczek Łukowski (PL) 148 E2
Stoczki (PL) 147 K2
Stod (CZ) 81 J1
Stöð (IS) 17 N5
Stod (N) 24 F6
Stöde (S) 33 M3
Stødi (N) 20 E7
Stødle (N) 38 C3
Stodoły (PL) 148 E4
Stöðvarfjörður (IS) 17 N5
Stoeneşti (RO) 169 G5
Stoeneşti (RO) 169 J3
Stoeneşti (RO) 170 B5
Stoetze (D) 66 D4
Støfring (N) 30 E5
Stoholm (DK) 42 D6
Stoicăneşti (RO) 169 H5
Stoina (RO) 168 F4
Stojakovo (MK) 179 H2
Stojaniv (UA) 149 L5
Stojan Mihajlovski (BG) 177 H2
Stojanovci (BG) 176 B2
Stojanovo (BG) 175 K2
Stojanovo (BG) 176 C2
Stojanovo (BG) 181 G1
Stojdraga (HR) 164 F3
Stojkite (BG) 180 F1
Stojnci (SLO) 165 F2
Stoke Ash (GB) 59 K3
Stoke Bruerne (GB) 58 F3
Stoke-by-Nayland (GB) 59 J4
Stoke Ferry (GB) 59 J2
Stoke Fleming (GB) 57 G5
Stoke Goldington (GB) 58 F3
Stokenham (GB) 57 G5
Stoke-on-Trent (GB) 58 C1
Stokesley (GB) 53 N6
Stokite (BG) 176 D3
Stokka (N) 25 G3
Stokkasjøen (N) 25 G3
Stokke (N) 39 M4
Stokkeland (N) 42 A2
Stokkemarke (DK) 47 H4
Stokkseyri (IS) 16 E7
Stokksund (N) 24 E6
Stokksund (N) 30 D3
Stokkvågen (N) 20 C8
Stokmarknes (N) 20 D3
Štoky (CZ) 153 J4
Stolac (BIH) 173 G3
Stolät (BG) 176 C3
Stolberg (Harz) (D) 72 D2
Stolberg (Rheinland) (D) 70 B5
Stolbovo (RUS) 135 K6
Stolec (PL) 146 F4
Stølen (N) 31 M5
Stolerova (LV) 134 E5
Stolice (SRB) 166 D5
Stolin (BY) 144 E5
Stollberg (Erzgebirge) (D) 152 C2
Stöllet (S) 40 D2
Stollhamm (D) 65 J4
Stolniceni (RO) 169 G3
Stolnici (RO) 169 H4
Stolno (PL) 141 L4
Stólos (GR) 187 F5
Stolpe (D) 66 F4
Stolpe (D) 67 L5
Stolpen (D) 152 F1
Stølsvang (N) 31 M2
Stolypino (RUS) 134 H3
Stolzenau (D) 71 H1
Stolzenhain (D) 73 J2
Stómio (GR) 179 H5
Stommeln (D) 69 M4
Stömne (S) 40 C4
Stomorska (HR) 172 D3
Stompetoren (NL) 64 B6
Ston (HR) 173 G4
Stonařov (CZ) 153 J5
Stonava (CZ) 154 D2
Stone (GB) 55 H5
Stonehaugh (GB) 53 L4
Stonehaven (GB) 51 N6
Stonehouse (GB) 52 H3
Stonehouse (GB) 57 K2
Stoney Cross (GB) 58 D6
Stöng (IS) 16 G6
Stongfjorden (N) 30 C5
Stonglandet (N) 20 G2
Stonndalen (N) 30 G6
Stonne (F) 78 B2
Stønnesbotn (N) 21 G2
Stonybreck (GB) 49 E4
Stöpafors (S) 40 D3
Stopanja (SRB) 174 F1
Stöpen (S) 40 E6
Stoperce (SLO) 164 F2
Stopnica (PL) 148 C5
Storå (S) 40 H3
Stora Åby (S) 44 F2
Stora Blåsjön (S) 25 J5
Storaborg (IS) 16 F6
Stora Forsa (S) 40 H5
Stóra-Giljá (IS) 16 F3
Stora Herrestad (S) 47 N3
Stórahof (IS) 16 F6
Stora Höga (S) 43 J2
Stora Levene (S) 44 B2
Stora Malm (S) 41 K5
Stóra-Melfell (IS) 16 G6
Stora Mellby (S) 44 B2
Stora Mellösa (S) 41 J4
Stora rör (S) 45 K5
Storås (N) 24 D8
Stóra-Sandfell (IS) 17 M4
Storåsen (S) 25 J7
Storåsen (S) 33 L3
Stora Sten (S) 40 G2
Stora Stensjön (S) 25 H7
Storbäck (S) 26 B5
Storbacka (FIN) 27 K8
Storbacken (S) 21 K8
Storbäcken (S) 32 D4
Storberg (S) 26 E3
Storberget (N) 32 B6
Storberget (S) 22 D3
Storberget (S) 25 M5
Storborgaren (S) 26 E7
Storbränna (S) 25 J7
Storbrännan (S) 26 G5
Storbron (S) 32 D5
Storbudal (N) 31 O2
Storbudalsetra (N) 31 O2
Storbukt (N) 19 M4
Storby (AX) 34 E4
Stord (N) 38 C3
Stordal (N) 24 F6
Stordal (N) 24 F8
Stordal (N) 30 F3
Stordalfjellstove (N) 30 D6
Stordalselv (N) 18 B5
Štore (SLO) 164 E2
Store Brevik, Son- (N) 39 N3
Storebro (S) 44 H3
Store Brøndum (DK) 42 F5
Storebru (N) 30 D4
Store Ebberup (DK) 47 J3
Storefjell (N) 31 K6
Støregarden (N) 31 P5
Storehaug (N) 30 D5
Store Heddinge (DK) 47 K3
Storeidet (N) 20 E5
Storekorsnes (N) 18 F3
Store Kvalfjord (N) 18 E3
Storel (N) 18 E2
Storelvavoll (N) 32 B2
Stor-Elvdal (N) 31 P4
Store Merløse (DK) 47 J2
Store Molvik (N) 19 L2
Støren (N) 24 E8
Storeng (N) 18 D4
Storenga (N) 20 E7
Storerikvollen (N) 32 B1
Store-Rørebæk (DK) 42 E5
Storeskar (N) 31 J6
Store Sommarøy (N) 21 H1
Store Standal (N) 30 E3
Storestølen (N) 30 H6
Store Taskeby (N) 18 C4
Storfall (S) 26 F7
Stor-Finnforsen (S) 26 C7
Storfjäten (S) 32 E3
Storfjellseter (N) 31 O4
Storfjord (N) 18 B5
Storfors (S) 40 F3
Storforshei (N) 20 D8
Storgård (FIN) 35 L5
Storhågna (S) 32 G3
Storhallaren (N) 24 C7
Stor-Hallen (S) 32 G2
Storhögen (S) 25 K8
Storholiseter (N) 31 L5
Storholmsjön (S) 25 J7
Stóriás (IS) 16 E5
Stóridalur (IS) 16 G4
Stóridalur (IS) 16 G7
Stóri-Laugardalur (IS) 16 C3
Stórinúpur (IS) 16 F6
Štorje (SLO) 164 B3
Storjord (N) 20 E7
Storkåge (S) 27 G5
Storkow (D) 140 B4
Storkow (Mark) (D) 67 K6
Storkyan (S) 40 E1
Stor-Laxjön (S) 33 N2
Storli (N) 38 D3
Storlia (N) 31 L2
Storlien (S) 24 G8
Stormark (S) 27 G5
Stormi (FIN) 35 M2
Storms (S) 45 N5
Stormyren (S) 26 D3
Stormyrsätern (S) 32 D6
Størna (N) 24 D7
Stornara (I) 104 E3
Stornarella (I) 104 E3
Stornäs (S) 25 K4
Storndorf (D) 71 H5
Stornes (N) 20 F3
Storneset (N) 21 H2
Storneshamn (N) 18 D4
Stornoway = Steòrnabhagh (GB) 50 E3
Storo (I) 88 D6
Storobăneasa (RO) 169 J6
Storoddan (N) 24 D8
Storön (S) 22 F5
Storøy vollen (N) 31 O2
Storoživ (UA) 150 E2
Storožynec' (UA) 157 J5
Storridge (GB) 57 K1
Storrington (GB) 58 G6
Storrøsta (N) 31 O3
Storsandsjö (S) 26 F6
Storsätern (S) 32 C3
Storsävarträsk (S) 22 B8
Storsele (S) 25 L5
Storsjö (S) 26 D7
Storsjö (S) 32 E2
Storsjön (S) 33 M5
Storslett (N) 18 D4
Storsletta (N) 18 C4
Storstein (N) 18 C3
Storsteinnes (N) 18 B5
Storsund (S) 22 C5
Storsveden (S) 33 N3
Storsvedjan (S) 22 E4
Stortorgnes (N) 24 G3
Stortorp (S) 40 H4
Storträsk (S) 26 G4
Storträskbyn (S) 22 D6
Storulvåns fjällstation (S) 32 C1
Storuman (S) 25 M4
Stórutjarnir (IS) 17 J3
Storvallen (S) 24 G8
Stor-Vasselnäs (S) 32 G5
Storvik (S) 41 L1
Storvika (N) 24 E6
Storvollen (N) 31 M3
Storvollen (N) 31 N3
Storvollseter (N) 31 K3
Storvorde (DK) 42 F4
Storvreta (S) 41 N3
Štós (SK) 155 H4
Stößen (D) 72 F3
Stössing (A) 91 J3
Stotfold (GB) 59 G3
Stötten am Auerberg (D) 87 L2
Stotternheim (D) 72 E3
Stotzing (A) 91 L4
Stoŭbcy (BY) 144 E2
Stouby (DK) 46 E2
Stoughton (GB) 58 F6
Stoumont (B) 69 K6
Stoúpa (GR) 186 E6
Stourbridge (GB) 55 H6
Stourport-on-Severn (GB) 55 H6
Stovpec' (UA) 150 B3
Støvring (DK) 42 E5
Støvset (N) 20 D6
Stow (GB) 53 K3
Stowięcino (PL) 141 H1
Stowmarket (GB) 59 J3
Stow-on-the-Wold (GB) 58 D4
Stożec (CZ) 152 E6
Stožer (BG) 177 J2
Stozer (MNE) 173 L3
Stožer Mračaj (BIH) 173 F2
Strà (I) 101 G2
Straach (D) 73 H2
Strabane (GB) 60 H2
Strabyčovo (UA) 155 M5
Strachan (GB) 51 M5
Strachomino (PL) 140 E2
Strachotice (CZ) 153 K6
Strachówka (PL) 142 F6
Strachur (GB) 52 E2
Stracia (I) 106 E7
Stracin (BG) 177 J3
Strackholt (D) 65 H5
Strada in Chianti (I) 100 E5
Strådalen (S) 32 E3
Stradbally (IRL) 61 H5
Stradbally (IRL) 63 H4
Stradbroke (GB) 59 K3
Stradella (I) 99 G2
Stradishall (GB) 59 J3
Stradone (IRL) 61 H4
Stradouň (CZ) 146 E6
Stradsett (GB) 59 H2
Stradunia (PL) 147 J5
Straduny (PL) 142 G3
Stradzečy (BY) 149 J2
Straelen (D) 69 L4
Stræte (N) 20 F3
Strætkvern (N) 32 B6
Stragari (SRB) 167 G5
Strahilovo (BG) 176 E2
Straid (IRL) 60 D4
Straimont (B) 78 C2
Straiton (GB) 52 F4
Straja (RO) 161 M2
Strakonice (CZ) 81 K2
Straky (CZ) 153 G3
Straldža (BG) 177 G3
Stralendorf (D) 66 E3
Stralendorf (D) 66 F4
Straličava (BY) 145 L5
Stralki (BY) 134 F6
Stralsund (D) 47 M5
Štramberk (CZ) 154 C2
Strambino (I) 98 D2
Stramproy (NL) 69 K4
Strâmtura (RO) 161 J2
Strand (N) 20 D7
Strand (N) 20 E3
Strand (N) 31 M5
Strand (N) 31 P5
Strand (S) 41 J2
Stranda (N) 19 H2
Stranda (N) 20 E3
Stranda (N) 30 F3
Stranda (N) 31 N5
Strandarkirkja (IS) 16 E7
Strandasmyrvallen (S) 32 G4
Strandbro (S) 40 H2
Strandby (DK) 42 D5
Strandby (DK) 42 F4
Strandebarm (N) 38 D2
Strandhill (IRL) 60 E3
Strandhöfn (IS) 17 M3
Strandlykkia (N) 39 O1
Strandrak (N) 39 J4
Strandval (N) 24 F5
Strandvik (N) 38 C2
Strandža (BG) 177 J4
Strandža (BG) 182 C1
Strangford (GB) 54 A2
Strängnäs (S) 41 M4
Strängsered (S) 43 N3
Strångsjö (S) 41 K5
Strångsund (S) 32 J2
Stráni (CZ) 154 B4
Stranice (SLO) 164 E2
Stranocum (GB) 61 K1
Stranorlar (IRL) 60 G2
Stranraer (GB) 61 M2
Stransko (BG) 176 E4
Străoane (RO) 170 E2
Strasatti (I) 108 C2
Strasbourg (F) 79 H4
Strasburg (Uckermark) (D) 67 K3
Străşeni (MD) 163 H4
Strašeny = Străşeni (MD) 163 H4
Strašice (CZ) 152 E4
Strašín (CZ) 81 K2
Stråsjö (S) 33 K3
Straškov- Vodochody (CZ) 73 L5
Strašnicy (RUS) 135 J2
Stråssa (S) 40 H3
Straßberg (D) 71 M3
Straßburg (A) 90 F6
Straßburg = Strasbourg (F) 79 H4
Straßengel, Judendorf- (A) 91 H5
Straß im Straßertale (A) 91 J3
Strass im Zillertal (A) 80 F6
Straßkirchen (D) 152 C6
Straßlach-Dingharting (D) 88 F1
Straßwalchen (A) 81 J5
Straszów (PL) 146 B2
Straszydle (PL) 156 A2
Straszyn (PL) 141 L2
Stratford (IRL) 61 J6
Stratford-upon-Avon (GB) 57 L1
Strathaven (GB) 52 G3
Strathblane (GB) 52 G3
Strathcarron (GB) 50 G5
Strath Kanaird (GB) 50 G4
Strathpeffer (GB) 51 H4
Strathyre (GB) 52 G2
Stratinista (GR) 178 C5
Stratinska (BIH) 165 H5
Stratóni (GR) 180 D3
Strátos (GR) 186 C2
Stratton (GB) 56 E4
Straubing (D) 152 C6
Straufhain (D) 72 D5
Straum (N) 25 H3
Straumbu (N) 31 N4
Straume (N) 30 D4
Straume (N) 30 D6
Straume (N) 39 K4
Straumen (N) 20 D6
Straumen (N) 20 E6
Straumen (N) 20 F3
Straumen (N) 20 G3
Straumen (N) 21 H2
Straumen (N) 24 C8
Straumen (N) 24 F5
Straumen (N) 24 F7
Straumen (N) 25 H2
Straumfjord (N) 20 E5
Straumfjordnes (N) 18 D4
Straumgjerde (N) 30 F3
Straumshamn (N) 30 E3
Straumsjøen (N) 20 D3
Straumsli (N) 21 J2
Straumsnes (N) 20 D3
Straumsnes (N) 20 E6
Straumsnes (N) 20 G2
Straumsnes (N) 20 G3
Straumsnes (N) 20 G4
Straumsnes (N) 30 C7
Straumsvik (IS) 16 D6
Straupe (LV) 133 K3
Straupitz (D) 73 L2
Strausberg (D) 67 K5
Straußfurt (D) 71 L4
Stravaj (AL) 178 C3
Strawczynek (PL) 148 B4
Stráž (CZ) 81 H1
Straža (BG) 177 G2
Straža (SLO) 164 E3
Straža (SRB) 167 H4
Stráže, Šaštín- (SK) 91 M2
Stražec (BG) 176 E6
Stražica (BG) 176 E2
Strážkovice (CZ) 90 G2
Stráž nad Nežárkou (CZ) 153 G5
Strážnice (CZ) 153 M6
Strážný (CZ) 81 K3
Strážov (CZ) 152 D5
Stráž pod Ralskem (CZ) 73 M4
Strážske (SK) 155 K4
Štrba (SK) 154 G3
Štrbské pleso (SK) 154 G3
Streatham (GB) 59 G5
Streatley (GB) 58 E4
Strechivci (UA) 150 D5
Strečno (SK) 154 D3
Streda nad Bodrogom (SK) 155 K5
Street (GB) 57 J3
Strehaia (RO) 168 E4
Strehla (D) 73 J3
Strei (RO) 161 F6
Streisângeorgiu (RO) 168 E2
Streitberg (D) 80 E1
Strejeşti (RO) 169 G4
Strejnicu (RO) 170 B4
Strekov (SK) 154 C6
Strelac (SRB) 175 H3
Strelča (BG) 176 B3
Strelci (BG) 176 C4
Strelci (BG) 176 D5
Strelci (BG) 177 F3
Strel'covo (RUS) 37 M3
Strel'čynci (UA) 151 H6
Strelec (BG) 176 E2
Strėliškiai (LT) 132 D5
Strelkovo (BG) 170 E6
Strellci i Epërm (RKS) 174 D3
Streller (DK) 46 C2
Strel'na (RUS) 37 O5
Strelníky (SK) 154 E4
Strem (A) 158 B3
Stremilče (UA) 149 M5
Stremţ (RO) 161 H5
Stremutka (RUS) 131 O5
Stremyhorod (UA) 151 H2
Strenči (LV) 133 M2
Strendene (N) 25 H4
Strendur (FO) 48 E3
Strengberg (A) 90 G3
Strengelvåg (N) 20 E3
Strengen (A) 88 C3
Strengen (N) 39 K4
Strengereid (N) 42 C1
Strenggjerdet (N) 25 G2
Strèn'ki (BY) 145 L2
Streptiv (UA) 156 F1
Stresa (I) 87 G6
Strèšen' = Străşeni (MD) 163 H4
Strèšin (BY) 145 M3
Stretham (GB) 55 N6
Stretivka (UA) 151 M3
Stretti (I) 89 H6
Stretton (GB) 55 L5
Strettura (I) 103 F2
Streufdorf (D) 72 D5
Strezimirovci (SRB) 175 H3
Strežino (RUS) 135 N4
Strezovce (RKS) 175 G4
Strezovce (SRB) 175 G3
Strib (DK) 46 E2
Striberg (S) 40 G3
Stříbro (CZ) 152 D4
Strichen (GB) 51 N4
Stridholm (S) 27 H4
Striesow, Dissen- (D) 73 L2
Strigleben (D) 66 F4
Strigno (I) 88 F5
Strigova (HR) 91 K7
Strihovce (SK) 156 B4
Strijen (NL) 69 H3
Strikçan (AL) 174 D6
Strilec'kyj Kut (UA) 157 J5
Strilki (UA) 156 C3
Strilsk (UA) 144 E6
Strimasund (S) 25 J2
Strimi (GR) 181 H3
Strimmelen (N) 19 L3
Strinda (N) 20 E5
Stripeikiai (LT) 138 C3
Stripuny (BY) 138 D5
Střítež (CZ) 153 K5
Striževo (BIH) 173 G2
Strizivojna (HR) 166 B3
Strjama (BG) 176 C4
Strjukove (UA) 163 M4
Strmac (HR) 165 J4
Strmec = Novi Cerkev (SLO) 164 E2
Strmica (HR) 172 D1
Strmilov (CZ) 153 H5
Strmovo (SRB) 173 L1
Strö (S) 43 M1
Strobl (A) 81 J5
Ströbohög (S) 41 J3
Strøby (DK) 47 K3
Strøby Egede (DK) 47 K3
Strodi (LV) 138 F1
Stroenie (RUS) 37 P6
Stroeşti (RO) 168 F3
Strofiliá (GR) 187 G2
Ströhen (D) 65 K6
Strohkirchen (D) 66 E4
Stroieşti (RO) 162 C3
Strojec (PL) 147 K3
Strojkovce (SRB) 175 G3
Strojne (UA) 156 D4
Strokestown (IRL) 60 F4
Strokiv (UA) 151 K4
Strokkur (IS) 16 F6
Strøm (N) 24 C7
Ström (S) 25 J3
Ström (S) 26 F6
Ström (S) 40 B4
Strömåker (S) 26 C5
Strömåker (S) 26 E7
Strömås (S) 33 O2
Strömbacka (S) 33 M4
Stromberg (D) 70 F3
Stromberg (D) 79 H2
Stromboli (I) 106 D5
Strömby (S) 44 H6
Stromeferry (GB) 50 F5
Strömfors (S) 26 G4
Strömfors (S) 26 G5
Strömfors = Ruotsinpyhtää (FIN) 36 F3
Stromiec (PL) 148 D2
Strömma (AX) 34 E4
Strömma (FIN) 35 L4
Strömma (S) 41 P4
Strömnäs (S) 26 C5
Strömnäs (S) 26 C7
Stromness (GB) 49 B6
Strømsått (N) 39 L2
Strömsbäck (S) 26 G7
Strömsberg (S) 41 N2
Strömsbruk (S) 33 N4
Strömsdal (S) 40 G2
Strömsfors (S) 41 K5
Strömsholm (S) 41 K4
Strømsik (N) 20 C7
Strømsmo (N) 21 H3
Strömsnäs (S) 21 M8
Strömsnäs (S) 33 K1
Strömsnäsbruk (S) 43 N5
Strömstad (S) 39 O5
Strömsund (S) 25 K7
Strömsund (S) 26 C4
Strona (I) 86 F6
Stronachlachar (GB) 52 F2
Stroncone (I) 103 F3
Strongoli (I) 107 H4
Stronie Śląskie (PL) 153 L3
Stronsdorf (A) 153 K6
Strońsko (PL) 147 K2
Strontian (GB) 52 D1
Stropkov (SK) 155 K3
Stroppiana (I) 98 E2
Stroppo (I) 95 K1
Stroud (GB) 58 C4
Stroumpi (CY) 198 D6
Strovja (MK) 174 F5
Stróża (PL) 154 F2
Stróże (PL) 155 H2
Štrpce = Shtërpcë (RKS) 174 F4
Štrpci (SRB) 174 B1
Struckum (D) 65 K2
Strudnica (BY) 143 M4
Struer (DK) 42 C6
Strueth (F) 78 G6
Strug (MNE) 174 B3
Struga (MK) 178 D2
Struga (UA) 144 E5
Strugovo (MK) 178 E2
Struha (UA) 157 M4
Struindol (BG) 175 J1
Struki (BY) 138 G4
Strullendorf (D) 72 D6
Strumen' (BY) 145 N2
Strumica (MK) 175 J6
Strumień (PL) 147 K6
Strumjani (BG) 180 C1
Strumkivka (UA) 155 L4
Strumok (UA) 171 J2
Strunga (RO) 162 D4
Strunguri (RO) 168 F2
Strupčice (CZ) 73 K5
Strupina (PL) 146 F3
Strupin Mały (PL) 149 J3
Strupļi (LV) 133 O4
Strusiv (UA) 150 B5
Struth (D) 71 K4
Strutyn' (UA) 156 F4
Strutynka (UA) 163 L2
Struvenhütten (D) 65 N4
Struy (GB) 51 H5
Strūžāni (LV) 134 D4
Stružec (HR) 165 H3
Strużka (PL) 73 N2
Strybež (UA) 150 G3
Strycksele (S) 26 F6
Stryeŭka (BY) 143 L3
Strygi (BY) 139 M4
Strygin' (BY) 143 N5
Stryi (BY) 143 L6
Stryj (UA) 156 E3
Stryjno Drugie (PL) 149 G3
Stryków (PL) 147 M2
Strykowo (PL) 146 F1
Stryn (N) 30 F4
Stryno By (DK) 65 O2
Stryszawa (PL) 154 F2
Stryžava (BY) 139 K3
Stryživka (UA) 151 J3
Strzakły (PL) 149 G2
Strzałków (PL) 147 L3
Strzałkowo (PL) 141 J6
Strzebielino (PL) 141 K1
Strzegocin (PL) 142 D5
Strzegom (PL) 146 E4
Strzegowo (PL) 142 C5
Strzelbiń (PL) 147 K4
Strzelce (PL) 141 M6
Strzelce Dolne (PL) 141 K4
Strzelce Krajeńskie (PL) 140 E5
Strzelce Opolskie (PL) 147 J4
Strzelce Wielkie (PL) 147 L3
Strzelin (PL) 153 M2
Strzelno (PL) 141 K5
Strzemiele (PL) 140 E3
Strzepcz (PL) 141 K2
Strzeszkowice Duże (PL) 148 F3
Strzyboga (PL) 148 B2
Strzyżew (PL) 147 H2
Strzyżewice (PL) 148 F3
Strzyżów (PL) 148 E6
Strzyżów (PL) 149 K4
Strzyżowice (PL) 147 L5
Stua (N) 39 M3
Stubal (SRB) 174 E1
Stubbekøbing (DK) 47 K4
Stubben (D) 65 N4
Stubbendorf (D) 47 L6
Stubel (BG) 175 K2
Stuben am Arlberg (A) 87 K3
Stubenberg (A) 91 J5
Stubica (SRB) 168 A6
Stubičke Toplice (HR) 165 F3
Stubik (SRB) 168 C5
Stubline (SRB) 166 F4
Stubno (PL) 149 G6
Stuböen (N) 30 J2
Stuchów (PL) 67 N3
Studánka (CZ) 152 C4
Studena (BG) 175 K3
Studena (BG) 177 F5
Studená (CZ) 153 H5
Studena (SRB) 175 J3
Studena (UA) 163 H2
Studena Bara (MK) 175 G4
Studenac (SRB) 175 G2
Studençanë (RKS) 174 E4
Studenčane = Studençanë (RKS) 174 E4
Studenci (HR) 164 E5
Studenci (HR) 172 F2
Studenec (BG) 177 G2
Studenec (CZ) 153 J2
Studenica (BG) 177 G2
Studeničani (MK) 175 G5
Studénka (CZ) 154 C2
Studeno Buče (BG) 175 K2
Studënoe (RUS) 37 N3
Studenycja (UA) 151 H3
Studenzen (A) 91 J5
Studienka (SK) 91 M2
Studina (RO) 169 G6
Studland (GB) 58 D6
Studley (GB) 58 D3
Studnica (PL) 146 E3
Studsviken (S) 26 E7
Studzeniki (BY) 143 L5
Studzënka (BY) 139 H6
Studzianna (PL) 148 B2
Studzienice (PL) 141 J2
Studzieniec (PL) 142 B6
Studzienki (PL) 141 J4
Studzionka (PL) 147 K6
Studzjanica (BY) 138 F4
Stuer (D) 67 G4
Stugsund (S) 33 N5
Stugubacken (S) 33 L5
Stuguflåten (N) 30 J3
Stuguliseter (N) 31 N3
Stugun (S) 33 K1
Stuguvattentjälen (S) 25 L7
Stuguvollenmoen (N) 32 B2
Stuhlfelden (A) 81 G6
Stühlingen (D) 86 F2
Stuhr (D) 65 K5
Stukany (BY) 138 G3
Stukenbrock, Schloß Holte- (D) 70 G3
Stulgiai (LT) 136 H3
Stul'hi (BY) 138 C5
Stul'hi (BY) 143 L4
Stülpe (D) 73 J1
Stulpicani (RO) 162 B4
Stumbriškis (LT) 133 K6
Stumlia (N) 31 N5
Stumsnäs (S) 32 H6
Stun' (UA) 149 K3
Stuoramjargga (N) 21 N2
Stupany (RUS) 134 E3
Stupari (BIH) 166 C5
Stupava (SK) 91 M3
Stupina (RO) 171 G4
Stupna (BIH) 165 J6
Stupnik (HR) 164 F3
Stupnycja (UA) 156 D3
Stuposiany (PL) 155 M3
Stuppach (D) 80 B2
Stupstad (N) 38 G6
Sturefors (S) 41 J6
Sturevågen (N) 30 B6
Stūri (LV) 132 F4
Sturkö (S) 44 H6
Šturlić (BIH) 164 F4
Sturluflöt (IS) 17 L5
Sturminster Newton (GB) 57 K4
Štúrovo (SK) 154 D6
Sturry (GB) 59 K5
Sturton by Stow (GB) 55 L4
Sturzelbronn (F) 79 H3
Sturzeşti (MD) 162 F3
Stusshyttan (S) 41 K2
Stutensee (D) 79 J3
Stuttgart (D) 79 L4
Stützerbach (D) 72 D4
Stuv (S) 43 K4
Stuvetra (N) 38 H3
Stužycja (UA) 155 M3
Stvolny (CZ) 152 D3
Štvrtok na Ostrove (SK) 158 D1
Stwolno (PL) 146 F2
Stybbersmark (S) 26 E8
Styggberget (S) 33 L3
Styggbo (S) 33 K5
Stykkishólmur (IS) 16 D4
Styków (PL) 148 D4
Stypsi (GR) 181 J6
Stypułów (PL) 146 D2
Styri (N) 39 O2
Styrkesvik (N) 20 E5
Styrnäs (S) 33 O1
Styrsö (S) 43 J3
Su (E) 115 G4
Suances (E) 112 C2
Suare (F) 96 D4
Suatu (RO) 161 H4
Subačius (LT) 133 K6
Subačius (LT) 137 M2
Subaşı (TR) 182 B3
Subaşı (TR) 183 F3
Subaşı (TR) 183 G5
Subaşı (TR) 184 B5
Subaşı (TR) 185 G3
Subaşı (TR) 190 C4
Subate (LV) 138 C1
Subbiano (I) 101 F5
Subcetaţe (RO) 161 L4
Subcetate (RO) 168 D2
Sübeylidere (TR) 181 L6
Subiaco (I) 103 G4
Šubino (RUS) 135 N2
Šubířov (CZ) 153 L4
Subivka (UA) 151 M4
Subkowy (PL) 141 L2
Sublaines (F) 83 G2
Subotica (SRB) 166 E1
Subotica Podravska (HR) 165 H2
Subotište (SRB) 166 E4
Subotniki (BY) 138 C5
Sučany (SK) 154 E3
Suceava (RO) 162 C3
Sucé-sur-Erdre (F) 75 H6
Suceviţa (RO) 162 B3
Suchá (CZ) 146 D5
Sucha (PL) 147 H1
Sucha (PL) 148 E3
Sucha Beskidzka (PL) 154 F2
Suchá Hora (SK) 154 F3
Sucha Koszalińska (PL) 140 F2
Suchań (PL) 140 D4
Suchary (BY) 139 N6
Suchaverch'e (BY) 138 G2
Suchdol nad Lužnicí (CZ) 153 G6
Suchdol nad Odrou (CZ) 154 B2
Suchedniów (PL) 148 C3
Suchodoly (UA) 149 K4
Suchohrdly (CZ) 153 K6
Sucholisy (UA) 151 L4
Suchomasty (CZ) 73 L6
Suchorze (PL) 141 H2
Suchovoija (UA) 157 H1
Suchowola (PL) 143 J3
Suchowola (PL) 148 D4
Suchowola (PL) 149 G2
Suchowola (PL) 149 H4
Suchożebry (PL) 148 F1
Süchteln (D) 69 L4
Suchyj Jar (UA) 151 L5
Suchyj Tašlyk (UA) 163 M2
Suchy Las (PL) 140 G6
Sucin (BY) 145 H2
Sucina (E) 127 J4
Sücüllü (TR) 192 B4
Sućuraj (HR) 172 F3
Sudak (Krym) 13 K4
Sudargas (LT) 136 H3
Súðavík (IS) 16 D2
Südbrookmerland (D) 64 G5
Sudbury (GB) 58 D2
Sudbury (GB) 59 J3
Sudče (UA) 144 C5
Suddesjaur (S) 26 F3
Süden (D) 46 C5
Süderbrarup (D) 66 B1
Suderburg (D) 65 N6
Süderhafen (D) 46 C5
Süderhastedt (D) 65 L3
Süderlügum (D) 46 C4
Süderzollhaus (D) 66 A1
Südharz (D) 71 L3
Sudice (CZ) 154 C1
Sudislavl' (RUS) 7 W6
Sudiste (EST) 133 M1
Sudiţi (RO) 170 F4
Sudjávárri = Suijavaara (S) 18 E7
Südliches Anhalt (D) 72 F2
Südlohn (D) 70 C3
Sudniki (BY) 138 F5
Sudnozero (RUS) 23 N7
Sudoměřice (CZ) 81 M1
Sudoměřice (CZ) 152 G5
Sudova Vyšnja (UA) 156 D2
Sudovec (HR) 158 B5
Suduraği (TR) 193 F6
Suðureyri (IS) 16 C2
Sudwalde (D) 65 K6
Sudylkiv (UA) 157 M1
Sudža (RUS) 9 O4
Sudzilavičy (BY) 143 N6
Sueca (E) 121 H5
Suelli (I) 97 D4
Sueros de Cepeda (E) 111 G3
Suèvres (F) 76 D6
Suffersheim (D) 80 E3
Şugag (RO) 168 F2
Sugères (F) 84 D5
Suginčiai (LT) 137 O3
Sugözü (TR) 198 D3
Sugözü (TR) 198 E3
Suha (BIH) 165 L6
Suhače (BG) 176 B2
Suhaia (RO) 176 D1
Suhaja Niva (RUS) 135 P2
Suharekë (RKS) 174 E4
Suhary (BY) 143 L3
Suhindol (BG) 176 D2
Suhiniči (RUS) 9 O3
Suhiničy (BY) 143 L4
Suhl (D) 72 D4
Sühlen (D) 66 C3
Suhlendorf (D) 66 D5
Suhlovo (RUS) 135 J2
Suhmura (FIN) 29 K7
Suhodol (BG) 170 D6
Suhodol (BG) 177 H4
Suhodol (RUS) 138 C5
Suhodoľe (RUS) 37 O3
Suho Polje (BIH) 166 D4
Suhopolje (HR) 165 K3
Suhozem (BG) 176 C4
Suhr (CH) 86 F3
Suhut (TR) 191 K3
Šuica (BIH) 172 F2
Şuici (RO) 169 H3
Suigu (EST) 130 G3
Suijavaara (S) 18 E7
Suikka (FIN) 37 K2
Suilly-la-Tour (F) 84 D2
Suinula (FIN) 28 E8
Suinula (FIN) 36 B1
Suippes (F) 77 L3
Suislepa (EST) 131 J4
Sujemci (UA) 150 F3
Šujstamo (RUS) 29 M8
Sukajvoda (UA) 151 K6
Sukë (AL) 178 C4
Šukeva (FIN) 29 H4
Šukioniai (LT) 132 H6
Šukionys (LT) 137 M1
Sukkozero (RUS) 7 T4
Sukošan (HR) 172 B1
Sükösd (H) 159 G5
Sukovo (SRB) 175 J2
Sukow (D) 66 F3
Sükow (D) 66 F4
Suków (PL) 148 C4
Şükranlı (TR) 191 K2
Süksün (TR) 193 K3
Sukth (AL) 174 B6
Sul (N) 24 G7
Šula (MNE) 173 K3
Šula (N) 24 C7
Šuľa (SK) 154 E5
Sulaghju, U = Solaro (F) 96 E5
Sulakyurt (TR) 185 G5
Sulåmo (N) 24 F7
Suldalseid (N) 38 D3
Suldalsosen (N) 38 D3
Suldalsosen (N) 38 E3
Sulden = Solda (I) 87 L4
Suldrup (DK) 42 E5
Sulechów (PL) 146 D1
Sulęcin (PL) 67 N6
Sulęcinek (PL) 147 G1
Sulęczyno (PL) 141 J2
Sulejów (PL) 148 A3
Sulejów (PL) 148 E4
Sulejówek (PL) 148 D1
Süleoğlu (TR) 182 C2
Suleskard (N) 38 E4
Sulesund (N) 30 E3
Şuletea (RO) 162 F6
Süleymanbey (TR) 183 K4
Süleymanhacı (TR) 192 F6
Süleymaniye (TR) 182 C3
Süleymaniye (TR) 183 J5
Süleymaniye (TR) 184 B6
Süleymanlı (TR) 185 F6
Süleymanlı (TR) 185 H6
Süleymanlı (TR) 190 D3
Süleymanlı (TR) 192 E6
Sülfeld (D) 66 C3
Sulgen (CH) 87 H2
Sulgrave (GB) 57 M1
Sulheim (N) 31 J4
Sulibórz (PL) 140 E4
Suličava (BY) 149 M1
Sulików (PL) 73 N3
Sulina (RO) 171 K3
Sulingen (D) 65 K6
Sulisławice (PL) 148 D4
Sulistrowice (PL) 146 F4
Suliszewice (PL) 140 E3
Suliţa (RO) 162 D3
Suliţa, Moldova- (RO) 161 L2
Sulitjelma (N) 20 F6
Šuljaky (UA) 151 K5
Suljatyči (UA) 156 F3
Sulkava (FIN) 29 G5
Sulkava (FIN) 36 D3
Sulkava (FIN) 37 K1
Sulkavanjärvi (FIN) 28 G5
Sulkavanjärvi (FIN) 29 G5
Sulkavankylä (FIN) 28 D7
Süller (TR) 191 G4
Sully (F) 84 F2
Sully-sur-Loire (F) 76 F6
Sulmierzyce (PL) 147 H2
Sulmierzyce (PL) 147 L3
Sulmona (I) 104 A1
Sułoszowa (PL) 147 M5
Súľov (SK) 154 D3
Sułów (PL) 147 G3
Sułów (PL) 148 F4
Sułów (PL) 149 G4
Sulseter (N) 31 M4
Sulsted (DK) 42 E4
Sultana (RO) 170 D5
Sultanbeyli (TR) 183 H4
Sultançayırı (TR) 182 F6
Sultandağı (TR) 192 B3
Sultandere (TR) 183 L6
Sultanhanı (TR) 13 K6
Sultanhisar (TR) 190 E5
Sultaniça (TR) 181 J3
Sultaniye (TR) 182 F5
Sultaniye (TR) 183 K4
Sultanköy (TR) 182 B3
Sultanköy (TR) 182 E3
Sülte (D) 66 E3
Sulu (TR) 183 J6
Suluca (TR) 182 B4
Sulucaova (TR) 193 K4
Sülüklü (TR) 192 A2
Sülüklü (TR) 192 D3
Sülümenli (TR) 191 G4
Sülümenli (TR) 191 K3
Sulusaray (TR) 13 L5
Sulusaray (TR) 193 J3
Sulusökü (TR) 185 H3
Sulva = Solf (FIN) 27 H8
Sulvik (S) 40 B3
Sulviken (S) 25 H7
Sülysáp (H) 159 J3
Sulz am Neckar (D) 79 K5
Sulzbach am Inn (D) 90 D3
Sulzbach am Main (D) 79 L2
Sulzbach an der Donau (D) 152 B5
Sulzbach an der Murr (D) 80 A2
Sulzbach-Laufen (D) 79 M4
Sulzbach-Rosenberg (D) 80 F1
Sulzdorf an der Lederhecke (D) 71 L6
Sülze (D) 65 N6
Sulzemoos (D) 80 E4
Sulzfeld (im Grabfeld) (D) 71 K6
Sulzheim (D) 72 C6
Sulz im Weinviertel (A) 153 L6
Sulz im Wienerwald (A) 158 B1
Sumacàrcer (E) 127 J1
Šumartin (HR) 172 E3
Šumavské Hoštice (CZ) 152 E5
Sumba (FO) 48 E5
Šume (SRB) 174 D1
Sümeg (H) 158 D4
Šumegor (BG) 176 C4
Šumen (BG) 177 G2
Šumenci (BG) 170 D6
Šumer (BG) 175 K2
Šumiac (SK) 154 G4
Sumiainen (FIN) 28 G6
Šumijany (UA) 157 G3
Šumilina (BY) 139 L3
Šumilovo (RUS) 139 O2
Sumiswald (CH) 86 E3
Šumivka (UA) 163 J2
Summa (FIN) 36 H3
Summer Bridge (GB) 55 J2
Summerhill (IRL) 61 J5
Šumná (CZ) 153 J6
Šumnatica (BG) 181 G2
Šumperk (CZ) 146 F6
Šumsa (FIN) 29 K3
Šums'k (UA) 157 K1
Šumskas (LT) 138 C4
Šumskij Posad (RUS) 7 U4
Sumstad (N) 24 E6
Sumukka (FIN) 29 K5
Sumundshytta (N) 31 P3
Sumy (UA) 9 N4
Sunākste (LV) 133 L5
Sünching (D) 81 G3
Şuncuiuş (RO) 160 F4
Sund (AX) 34 F4
Sund (N) 25 G2
Sund (N) 38 B2
Sund (S) 26 E8
Sund (S) 33 K3
Sund (S) 34 B4
Sund (S) 39 P4
Sund (S) 44 G3
Sundals-Ryr (S) 43 K1
Sundborn (S) 41 J1
Sundby (DK) 42 C5
Sundby (DK) 47 J4
Sundby (FIN) 27 J7
Sundby (N) 40 A2
Sundby (S) 40 F4
Sundby (S) 41 L4
Sundby (S) 41 M4
Sundbyberg (S) 41 N4
Sundbyfoss (N) 39 M3
Sunde bru (N) 39 K5
Sunderland (GB) 53 N5
Sundern (Sauerland) (D) 70 F4
Sundet (N) 24 E6
Sundet (N) 39 M4
Sundet (S) 25 G7
Sundet (S) 26 C6
Sunde-Valen (N) 38 C3
Sundginge (S) 40 B4
Sundhultsbrunn (S) 44 F3
Sundnes (N) 38 C3
Sundö (S) 26 F6
Sundom (FIN) 27 H8
Sundom (S) 27 J3
Sundøy (N) 25 G3
Sundre (S) 45 N5
Sunds (DK) 46 D1
Sundsbø (N) 30 F2
Sundsby (N) 24 C8
Sundsbyn (S) 39 P4
Sundsfjord (N) 20 D7
Sundsjö (S) 32 J2
Sundsjöåsen (S) 32 J1
Sundsjön (S) 40 E3
Sundsli (N) 38 H4
Sundsnäs (S) 27 H2
Sundstabyn (S) 40 A4
Sundsvall (S) 33 N3
Sundvollen (N) 39 M2
Sungurlare (BG) 177 G3
Sungurlu (TR) 13 K5
Sungurlu (TR) 185 H5
Sünğüt (TR) 184 A4
Suni (I) 97 C3
Šunja (HR) 165 H4
Šun'ky (UA) 157 K1
Sünlü (TR) 184 F5
Sünlük (TR) 182 F6
Sunnan (N) 24 F6
Sunnanå (S) 26 F6
Sunnanhed (S) 33 J5
Sunnansjö (S) 26 F6
Sunnansjö (S) 26 F7
Sunnansjö (S) 33 M2
Sunnansjö (S) 40 G2
Sunnås (S) 33 M2
Sunnäs (S) 33 N5
Sunndal (N) 30 D4
Sunndal (N) 38 D2
Sunndalen (N) 30 G4
Sunndalsøra (N) 31 K2
Sunndalsseter (N) 30 G4
Sunne (S) 25 J8
Sunne (S) 40 D3
Sunnemo (S) 40 E3
Sunnerå (S) 33 K2
Sunnersberg (S) 43 M1
Sunnervik (S) 40 D5
Sunnet (S) 32 F4
Sunnfjordtunet (N) 30 D5
Sunnudalur (IS) 17 M3
Šunskai (LT) 143 J1
Suntaži (LV) 133 K4
Sünzhausen (D) 80 F3
Suo-Antilla (FIN) 37 J3
Suobbat (S) 21 L8
Suodenniemi (FIN) 35 L1
Suodnjo (N) 18 F5
Suojala (FIN) 29 K3
Suojanperä (FIN) 19 L5
Suojarvi (RUS) 7 S5
Suojoki (FIN) 28 B7
Suolahti (FIN) 28 F6
Suolijärvi (FIN) 23 L6
Suolijoki (FIN) 27 M2
Suolipera (FIN) 23 L6
Suoločielgi = Saariselkä (FIN) 19 K7
Suolovuobme (N) 21 N1
Suomela (FIN) 35 O4
Suomenkylä (FIN) 36 H2
Suomenniemi (FIN) 36 H2
Suomijärvi (FIN) 28 C7
Suomusjärvi (FIN) 35 N4
Suomussalmi (FIN) 23 L7
Suonenjoki (FIN) 29 H6
Suonsalmi (FIN) 29 G8
Suontaka (FIN) 35 J3
Suontee (FIN) 29 H7
Suopelto (FIN) 28 F9
Suorajärvi (FIN) 23 M4
Suorrva = Suorva (S) 21 H5
Suorsa (FIN) 23 K4
Suorva (S) 21 H5
Suošjavrre (N) 18 G5
Suotaalanmaa (FIN) 35 L2
Suotuperä (FIN) 28 F3
Suovaara (FIN) 29 J3
Suovaara (FIN) 29 K6
Suovanlahti (FIN) 28 G5
Šuparka (UA) 162 B1
Šupeniv (BY) 139 L5
Superbagnères (F) 92 F5
Superga (I) 98 D2
Super-Sauze (F) 95 J2
Supetar (HR) 172 E3
Supetarska Draga (HR) 164 D5
Suphella (N) 30 F5
Supino (I) 103 G4
Suplac (RO) 161 K5
Suplacu de Barcău (RO) 160 F3
Suplai (RO) 161 J3
Supraneny (BY) 138 D4
Supraśl (PL) 143 J4
Supska (SRB) 167 H5
Süpüren (TR) 191 J1
Supuru de Jos (RO) 160 F3
Suradówek (PL) 141 M5
Surahammar (S) 41 K3
Suraia (RO) 170 E2
Şura Mare (RO) 161 J6
Şura Mică (RO) 161 J6
Suramščyna (BY) 138 G2
Šurany (SK) 158 F1
Suraž (BY) 139 N3
Suraż (PL) 143 H5
Suraž (UA) 157 K1
Surbo (I) 105 K5
Surch = Zurich (NL) 64 C5
Surčin (SRB) 166 F4
Surd (H) 165 H2
Surdegis (LT) 137 M2
Surdeşti (RO) 161 H2
Surdila-Găiseanca (RO) 170 E3
Surdila-Greci (RO) 170 E3
Surduc (RO) 161 G3
Surducu Mic (RO) 167 K2
Surduk (SRB) 166 F3
Surdulica (SRB) 175 H3
Surean (RO) 168 F2
Surgères (F) 82 D4
Sürgüç (TR) 192 F5
Surhuisterveen (NL) 64 E5
Surhústerfean = Surhuisterveen (NL) 64 E5
Súria (E) 115 G4
Surier (I) 85 M5
Surin (F) 83 F4
Suris (F) 83 G5
Surju (EST) 130 G4
Surka (N) 39 N2
Surliden (S) 26 E4
Surmin (PL) 147 H3
Surnadalsøra (N) 24 C9
Suroide (D) 65 M6
Šúrovce (SK) 154 B5
Surowe (PL) 142 E4
Surroj (AL) 174 D4
Sursee (CH) 86 F3
Surtainville (F) 75 H2
Surte (S) 43 K3
Suruç (TR) 13 M7
Sürüç (TR) 193 F4
Survie (F) 76 B4
Surviliškis (LT) 137 L3
Surwold (D) 65 H6
Sury-ès-Bois (F) 84 C2
Sury-le-Comtal (F) 84 F5
Suryty (PL) 136 D5
Surzur (F) 74 F5
Sus (F) 92 C4
Susa (I) 85 M6
Susak (HR) 164 C5
Susam (BG) 176 D5
Susana, A (E) 110 C3
Şuşani (RO) 169 G4
Šušanino (RUS) 37 O6
Šušara (SRB) 167 H4
Šušary (RUS) 37 O5
Suščany (UA) 144 G6
Suščevo (RUS) 135 J3
Susch (CH) 87 K4
Susegana (I) 89 G6
Suşehri (TR) 13 M5
Susek (SRB) 166 E3
Süsel (D) 46 G5
Suseľnica (RUS) 135 K3
Suseni (RO) 169 H4
Suševo (BG) 170 D6
Susholuč'čja (UA) 151 L2
Sušica (BG) 176 E2
Sušica (MK) 175 K5
Sušice (CZ) 152 E5
Susikas (FIN) 36 A3
Sušino (RUS) 37 N2
Sus'k (UA) 150 A2
Sus'k (UA) 150 C2
Suškava (BY) 138 G4
Suškivka (UA) 163 L1
Sušky (UA) 151 G2
Susleni (MD) 163 H4
Šūsninkai (LT) 137 J5
Šušnjevica (HR) 101 L2
Suspiro del Moro (E) 126 C5
Süßen (D) 80 B3
Susteren (NL) 70 A4
Sustinente (I) 99 L2
Susurluk (TR) 182 F6
Susuz (TR) 184 A5
Susuz (TR) 184 C5
Susuz (TR) 185 F3
Susuz (TR) 185 H6
Susuz (TR) 191 H3
Susuz (TR) 191 K3
Susuz (TR) 191 K6
Susuz (TR) 192 C6
Susuzkaya (TR) 191 H2
Susuzmüsellim (TR) 181 L2
Susuzören (TR) 191 G3
Susuzşahap (TR) 192 C6
Susuzyayla (TR) 190 D1
Susz (PL) 142 A3
Şuszec (PL) 154 D1
Šutai (LT) 138 D3
Šutaky (UA) 162 F1
Šutavičy (BY) 138 D5
Sütçüler (TR) 192 A5
Suteşti (RO) 169 G4
Şuţeşti (RO) 170 E3
Šutina (BIH) 173 F2
Sutivan (HR) 172 D3
Sutjeska Cyrjecka (SRB) 167 G3
Sütlaç (TR) 191 H4
Sütleğen (TR) 197 G3
Sutme (S) 25 J5
Sutoki (BY) 138 H5
Sutoki (RUS) 134 H5
Sutoki (RUS) 139 O4
Sutomore (MNE) 173 K5
Sutri (I) 102 E3
Sutterhöjden (S) 40 E3
Sutterton (GB) 59 G2
Sutton (GB) 55 N6
Sutton (GB) 59 G5
Sutton Bridge (GB) 55 N5
Sutton Coldfield (GB) 58 D2
Sutton in Ashfield (GB) 55 K4
Sutton on Sea (GB) 55 N4
Sutton-on-the-Forest (GB) 55 K2
Sutton Saint James (GB) 55 N5
Sutton Scotney (GB) 57 M3
Sutton-under-Whitestonecliffe (GB) 55 K2
Sutysky (UA) 151 G5
Suuraho (FIN) 29 J6
Suure-Jaani (EST) 131 H3
Suurejõe (EST) 131 H3
Suuremõisa (EST) 130 C3
Suure-Usenitsa (EST) 131 N5
Suurikylä (FIN) 37 N1
Suurimäki (FIN) 29 H5
Suurlahti (FIN) 37 J2
Suurmäki (FIN) 29 J6
Suur-Miehikkälä (FIN) 37 J3
Suurpea (EST) 131 J1
Suur-Saimaa (FIN) 37 K2
Suur-Selänpää (FIN) 36 G2
Suutarinkylä (FIN) 23 H7
Suutarinkylä (FIN) 23 J8
Suutarla (FIN) 35 L3
Suvainiškis (LT) 137 N1
Suvanto (FIN) 23 K2
Suva Reka = Suharekë (RKS) 174 E4
Suvereto (I) 102 B1
Suvermez (TR) 192 B2
Suvermez (TR) 193 J4
Suvi Do (SRB) 168 B5
Suvi Do (SRB) 174 D2
Suvidy (BY) 145 M5
Suviekas (LT) 133 N6
Suvodol (MK) 179 F2
Suvojnica (SRB) 175 H3
Suvorove (UA) 171 H2
Suvorovo (BG) 177 J2
Suvorovo = Ştefan Vodă (MD) 163 K5
Suwałki (PL) 137 H5
Suyugüzel (TR) 193 F2
Suze-la-Rousse (F) 94 E2
Suze-sur-Sarthe, La (F) 75 M5
Suzette (F) 94 F2
Sužionys (LT) 137 O4
Suzzara (I) 99 K3
Sva (S) 40 H6
Svabensverk (S) 33 K5
Svadhall (S) 41 J4
Sværdborg (DK) 47 J3
Sværen (N) 30 E5
Svaipavalle (S) 25 L2
Svalbarð (IS) 17 L2
Svalbarðseyri (IS) 17 H3
Svalenik (BG) 176 F1
Svålestad (N) 38 D5
Svaljava (UA) 156 C4
Svallerup (DK) 46 H2
Svalöv (S) 47 M2
Svalsjö (S) 44 G2
Svalvogar (IS) 16 C3
Svanabyn (S) 26 C6
Svaneke (DK) 47 O3
Svanesund (S) 43 J2
Svängsta (S) 44 F6
Svanhals (S) 40 G6
Svanhult (S) 40 G5
Svaningen (S) 25 K6
Svannäs (S) 25 L5
Svannäs (S) 26 E2
Svanön (S) 33 O2
Svanøy (N) 30 C4
Svansele (S) 22 B7
Svansele (S) 25 K5
Svanskog (S) 40 C4
Svanstein (S) 22 F3
Svanträsk (S) 22 B6
Svappavaara (S) 22 D1
Svapušča (RUS) 135 P3
Svärdsjö (S) 33 K6
Svare (N) 31 L4
Svarinci (LV) 138 G1
Svarstad (N) 39 L4
Svartå (FIN) 35 N4
Svartå (S) 40 G4
Svärta (S) 41 M5
Svartárkot (IS) 17 J4
Svartåsen (N) 21 H2
Svartbäck = Purola (FIN) 36 G4
Svartberget (S) 21 N8
Svartbyn (S) 27 J2
Svarte (S) 47 N3
Svarteborg (S) 43 J1
Svartehallen (S) 43 J2
Svarthyttan (S) 40 H2
Svärtinge (S) 41 K5
Svartisdalen (N) 20 D8
Svartlå (S) 27 H2
Svartliden (S) 26 E5
Svartnäs (S) 33 L6
Svartnes (N) 18 B5
Svartnes (N) 20 D6
Svartöstaden (S) 27 J3
Svartrå (S) 43 L4
Svarttorp (S) 44 E3
Svartvik (N) 19 G1
Svartvik (S) 33 N3
Svarycevyči (UA) 144 D5
Svaryn' (BY) 149 M2
Svatki (BY) 138 F4
Svatoborice (CZ) 153 M6
Svatove (UA) 9 P5
Svatsum (N) 31 M5
Svätý Jur (SK) 91 M3
Svätý Peter (SK) 154 C6
Svea (N) 30 F5
Svebølle (DK) 47 H2
Svedala (S) 47 M2
Svedasai (LT) 137 N2
Svederník (SK) 154 D3
Svedje (S) 25 J8
Svedje (S) 26 E7
Svedje (S) 26 E8
Svedje (S) 33 N3
Svedjorna (S) 33 L5
Švedlár (SK) 155 H4
Švedy (BY) 138 E5
Sveg (S) 32 G3
Sveggesundet (N) 24 B8
Šveicarija (LT) 137 L3
Sveinatunga (IS) 16 E5
Sveindal (N) 38 F6
Sveingardsbotn (N) 30 H6
Sveio (N) 38 B3
Svejbæk (DK) 46 E1
Šveklino (RUS) 134 F3
Švekšna (LT) 136 F2
Svelgen (N) 30 C4
Svelvik (N) 39 M3
Svenarum (S) 44 E4
Švenčionėliai (LT) 138 D3
Švenčionys (LT) 138 D3
Švenčiuliškiai (LT) 137 L3
Svendborg (DK) 46 G3
Svene (N) 39 L3
Sveneby (S) 40 E5
Svenes (N) 38 H5
Svenljunga (S) 43 M4
Svenneby (N) 39 P2
Svenneby (S) 43 H1
Svennebyseter (N) 31 Q6
Svennevad (S) 40 H4
Svensby (N) 21 J1
Svensbyn (S) 27 H4
Svenskby = Ruotsinkylä (FIN) 36 F3
Svensköp (S) 47 N2
Svensnäs (S) 40 H3
Svenstavik (S) 32 G2
Svenstrup (DK) 42 E5
Svenstrup (DK) 46 H3
Švente (LV) 134 B6
Šventininkai (LT) 143 N1
Šventoji (LT) 136 E1
Šventorp (S) 40 F6
Švermov (CZ) 152 F3
Sveštari (BG) 177 G1
Sveštarovo (BG) 177 J1
Sveta Ana = Tenja (HR) 166 C2
Sveta Marija (HR) 165 H2
Sveta Nedelja (HR) 164 F3
Světe (LV) 132 H4
Sveti Đurađ (HR) 166 B2
Sveti Filip i Jakov (HR) 172 B2
Sveti Ivan Žabno (HR) 158 C6
Sveti Ivan Zelina (HR) 158 B6
Sveti Juraj (HR) 164 D5
Sveti Jurij (SLO) 91 K6
Sveti Jurij ob Pesnici = Jurski Vrh (SLO) 164 F1
Sveti Konstantin (BG) 176 B4
Sveti Konstantin (BG) 177 J2
Sveti Nikola (BG) 177 K2
Sveti Nikola (MNE) 173 K6
Sveti Nikole (MK) 175 G5
Sveti Petar na moru (HR) 172 B2
Sveti Petar u šumi (HR) 164 B4
Sveti Rok (HR) 164 F6
Sveti Stefan (MNE) 173 J5
Sveti Tannflo (S) 26 C8
Sveti Vlas (BG) 177 J3
Svetlahorsk (BY) 9 L3
Světlá nad Sázavou (CZ) 153 H4
Svetlen (BG) 177 F2
Svetlice (SK) 156 B3
Svetlina (BG) 177 F4
Svetlodolins'ke (UA) 171 K1
Svetloe (RUS) 142 C1
Svetlogorsk (RUS) 136 C4
Svetlogorsk = Svietlahorsk (BY) 145 L3
Svetlyj (RUS) 19 L6
Svetlyj (RUS) 141 O1
Svetogorsk (RUS) 37 L2
Svetozar Miletić (SRB) 159 H6
Svetvinčenat (HR) 164 B4
Svežen (BG) 176 D3
Sviby (EST) 130 D3
Svidník (SK) 155 K3
Svidnja (BG) 175 K3
Svietlahorsk (BY) 145 L3
Svignaskarð (IS) 16 E5
Švihov (CZ) 81 J2
Svihus (N) 38 C5
Svilajnac (SRB) 167 H5
Svilengrad (BG) 182 B2
Svínadalur (IS) 17 K3
Svínafell (IS) 17 L6
Svínarnes (IS) 16 G6
Svínavatn (IS) 16 F3
Svineng (N) 19 H5
Svines (N) 25 G3
Svinesund (S) 39 O4
Svingvoll (N) 31 N5
Svinhult (S) 44 G3
Svinica (SK) 155 J4
Sviniţa (RO) 167 K4
Svinná (SK) 154 C4
Svinndal (N) 39 O4
Svinnegarn (S) 41 M3
Svinninge (DK) 47 H2
Svinninge (S) 34 B6
Svinø (DK) 47 J3
Svinø = Svínoy (FO) 48 F3
Svínoy (FO) 48 F3
Svinvik (N) 24 C8
Svir (BY) 138 D4
Svirany (BY) 138 E4
Svirkančiai (LT) 136 H1
Svirkovo (BG) 176 E4
Svirneve (UA) 163 L2
Svirž (UA) 156 F2
Sviščaki (SLO) 164 C3
Sviščova (BY) 143 K6
Svislač (BY) 143 L4
Svislač (BY) 145 J2
Svištov (BG) 176 D1
Svit (SK) 155 G3
Svitanok (UA) 157 G3
Svitava (BIH) 173 G3
Svitavy (CZ) 153 K4
Svitjaz' (UA) 149 J3
Svjača (BY) 139 K3
Svjacica (BY) 144 D3
Svjadica (BY) 139 J4
Svjatoslav (UA) 156 D3
Svoboda (BG) 176 B4
Svoboda (BG) 176 D4
Svoboda (BG) 177 J1
Svoboda (RUS) 142 F1
Svoboda nad Úpou (CZ) 146 D4
Svobodné Heřmanice (CZ) 147 H6
Svobodnoe (RUS) 37 M2
Svobodyšče (UA) 151 G3
Svode (BG) 176 A2
Svođe (SRB) 175 H3
Svodín (SK) 158 G2
Svodna (BIH) 165 H4
Svoge (BG) 175 K3
Svogerslev (DK) 47 K2
Svojetín (CZ) 152 E3
Svoňa (BY) 138 H2
Svolvær (N) 20 D4
Svor (CZ) 152 G2
Svork-land (N) 24 D8
Svorkmo (N) 24 D8
Svortemyr (N) 30 D5
Svortevik (N) 30 C4
Svortland (N) 38 B3
Svratouch (CZ) 153 K4
Svrčinovec (SK) 154 D3
Svrljig (SRB) 175 H2
Svržno (CZ) 81 H1
Svukuriset (N) 31 R3
Svullrya (N) 40 B2
Svynaryn (UA) 149 L4
Swadlincote (GB) 55 J5
Swaffham (GB) 59 J2
Swainshill (GB) 57 J1
Swalmen (NL) 69 L4
Swanage (GB) 57 L4
Swanley (GB) 59 H5
Swansea (GB) 56 G2
Swanton Novers (GB) 59 K2
Swarland Estate (GB) 53 M4
Swarożyn (PL) 141 L2
Swarzędz (PL) 141 H6
Swaton (GB) 55 M5
Świątniki Górne (PL) 148 A6
Świbie (PL) 147 K4
Świderki (PL) 148 F2
Świdnica (PL) 146 C2
Świdnica (PL) 146 E4
Świdnik (PL) 149 G3
Świdry (PL) 148 F2
Świdwin (PL) 140 E3
Świebodzice (PL) 146 E4
Świebodzin (PL) 146 D1
Święcica (PL) 148 D4
Świecie (PL) 141 K4
Święciechowa (PL) 146 F2
Świecko (PL) 67 M6
Świedziebnia (PL) 142 B4
Świekatowo (PL) 141 K4
Świeradów-Zdrój (PL) 153 H2
Świerczów (PL) 147 H4
Świerczyna (PL) 146 F2
Świerki Górne (PL) 146 E4
Świerklaniec (PL) 147 K5
Świerklany Górne (PL) 154 D1
Świerzawa (PL) 153 J1
Świerże (PL) 149 J3
Świerzno (PL) 67 M3
Świeszyno (PL) 140 F2
Święta (PL) 140 C3
Święta Anna (PL) 147 M4
Świętajno (PL) 142 E3
Święta Katarzyna (PL) 148 C4
Święta Lipka (PL) 142 E2
Święte (PL) 149 G6
Świętno (PL) 146 E1
Świętoszów (PL) 146 C3
Świętów Polski (PL) 147 G5
Święty Gaj (PL) 142 A3
Swifterbant (NL) 64 D6
Świlcza (PL) 155 K1
Swindon (GB) 57 L2
Swinefleet (GB) 55 L3
Swineshead (GB) 59 G2
Swinford (IRL) 60 E4
Świniary (PL) 142 D4
Świnice Warckie (PL) 147 K1
Świniokierz Włościański (PL) 148 A2
Świnoujście (PL) 47 O6
Swinton (GB) 53 L3
Swisttal (D) 70 C5
Swobnica (PL) 140 C4
Swords = Sord (IRL) 63 K2
Swornegacie (PL) 141 H3
Swory (PL) 149 G1
Swyre (GB) 58 B6
Sybena (UA) 157 K2
Sybene (UA) 151 L2
Syberia (PL) 141 N4
Syčevičy (BY) 138 F5
Syčevka (RUS) 7 T7
Sycewice (PL) 140 G2
Syčkava (BY) 145 K2
Syców (PL) 147 H3
Sydänmaa (FIN) 28 C8
Sydänmaa (FIN) 28 D6
Sydänmaa (FIN) 29 H7
Sydänmaa (FIN) 35 J2
Sydänmaankylä (FIN) 27 N7
Syðir-Reykir (IS) 16 F6
Sydlangeland (DK) 46 G4
Sydlivci (UA) 150 C5
Sydmo (FIN) 35 K4
Sydorivka (UA) 151 M5
Sydorovyči (UA) 151 K2
Syðra-Áland (IS) 17 L2
Syðradalur (FO) 48 E3
Syðribrú (IS) 16 F6
Sydrivik (IS) 17 J7
Syðrugøta (FO) 48 E3
Sygnefest (N) 30 C5
Syhaja Dalina (BY) 143 L4
Sykäräinen (FIN) 28 E4
Syke (D) 65 K6
Sykkylven (N) 30 F3
Sylda (D) 72 E2
Sylin (BY) 143 N6
Sylivka (UA) 163 L4
Sylling (N) 39 M3
Syl'ne (UA) 149 K3
Syl'ne (UA) 150 B2
Sylstationen Sylarna (S) 32 C1
Sylt (D) 65 J2
Sylte (N) 30 D3
Sylte (N) 30 G2
Sylte (N) 30 G3
Sylte (N) 31 M4
Syltevikmyra (N) 19 N2
Sylvänä (FIN) 35 M3
Symbister (GB) 49 F3
Symkove (UA) 163 L3
Symoneli (BY) 138 C4
Symony (UA) 150 F2
Syndicat, le (F) 78 F5
Synel'nykove (UA) 9 O5
Synes (N) 30 E2
Synevyr (UA) 156 E5
Synevyrs'ka Poljana (UA) 156 E4
Syniv (UA) 150 D2
Synjak (UA) 156 C4
Synjava (UA) 151 L4
Synjuchyn Brid (UA) 163 M2
Synkaŭcy (BY) 143 M3
Synki (BY) 139 K5
Syn'ky (UA) 163 L2
Synnerby (S) 40 D6
Synod Inn (GB) 56 F1
Synove (UA) 149 L3
Synžerej = Sîngerei (MD) 162 G3
Syötekylä (FIN) 23 K5
Sypilavičy (BY) 144 H3
Syra (N) 31 P5
Syraji (UA) 151 N2
Syrau (D) 72 G4
Syri (FIN) 28 E4
Syrjä (FIN) 29 J7
Syrjajeve (UA) 163 L4
Syrjäntaka = Tuulos (FIN) 36 C2
Syrke (UA) 171 L2
Syrkovicy (RUS) 37 M6
Syrkovo (RUS) 135 J3
Syrmež (BY) 138 E4
Syrmivka (UA) 151 J4
Syroka Balka (UA) 163 L5
Syroke (UA) 9 N5
Syrokyj Luh (UA) 156 E5
Syrovary (UA) 157 H2
Syrovatki (BY) 138 D4
Syrove (UA) 163 L3
Syrstad (N) 31 M1
Syrynia (PL) 154 C1
Syščycy (BY) 9 L3
Syščycy (BY) 144 G2
Syšlivči (UA) 155 L4
Sysmä (FIN) 28 F9
Sysmänsärkkä (FIN) 29 M6
Sysoevo (RUS) 135 J3
Sysova (RUS) 135 K3
Sysslebäck (S) 32 D6
Syston (GB) 55 K5
Sytkivci (UA) 151 J6
Sytnjaky (UA) 151 K3
Sytnycja (UA) 150 B1
Sytovyči (UA) 149 M3
Syväjärvi (FIN) 23 H2
Syvälahti (FIN) 28 F6
Syvänniemi (FIN) 29 H6
Syvänsi (FIN) 29 H7
Syvärinpää (FIN) 29 H5
Syväsmäki (FIN) 36 G1
Syvde (N) 30 D3
Syvdsnes (N) 30 D3
Syvinki (FIN) 28 E7
Syvsten (DK) 42 F4
Syyspohja (FIN) 37 L2
Szabadbattyán (H) 158 F3
Szabadszállás (H) 159 H4
Szabás (H) 158 D5
Szachy (PL) 149 G2
Szadek (PL) 147 K2
Szadki (PL) 142 E5
Szadkowice (PL) 148 B3
Szaflary (PL) 154 G3
Szajol (H) 159 K3
Szakcs (H) 165 L1
Szakmár (H) 159 H4
Szákszend (H) 158 F2
Szalafő (H) 158 B4
Szalánta (H) 158 F6
Szalejów Górny (PL) 146 F5
Szalkszentmárton (H) 159 H4
Szalonna (H) 155 H5
Szamocin (PL) 141 H4
Szamotuły (PL) 140 G5
Szanda (H) 154 E6
Szandaszőlős (H) 159 K3
Szank (H) 159 J4
Szany (H) 158 D3
Szápár (H) 158 F3
Szarbków (PL) 148 C4
Szárföld (H) 91 M4
Szarvas (H) 159 L4
Szarvaskő (H) 155 G6
Szatmárcseke (H) 160 F1
Szatymaz (H) 159 K5
Százhalombatta (H) 159 G3
Szczaniec (PL) 146 D1
Szczawa (PL) 155 G2
Szczawnica (PL) 155 G3
Szczawno-Zdrój (PL) 153 K2
Szczebrzeszyn (PL) 149 G4
Szczecin (PL) 140 C4
Szczecinek (PL) 140 G3
Szczecno (PL) 148 C4
Szczejkowice (PL) 154 D1
Szczekociny (PL) 148 A4
Szczepańcowa (PL) 155 K2
Szczepankowo (PL) 142 F4
Szczepanów (PL) 146 F3
Szczepanowice (PL) 148 B5
Szczepocice Rządowe (PL) 147 L3
Szczerbice (PL) 154 C1
Szczerców (PL) 147 L3
Szczucin (PL) 148 D5
Szczuczki Czwarte (PL) 148 F3
Szczuczyn (PL) 142 G3
Szczurkowo (PL) 142 D2
Szczurowa (PL) 155 H1
Szczyrk (PL) 154 E2
Szczytna (PL) 153 K3
Szczytniki (PL) 67 N3
Szczytniki (PL) 147 J2
Szczytno (PL) 142 D3
Szécsény (H) 159 J1
Szederkény (H) 158 F6
Szedres (H) 158 G5
Szeged (H) 159 K5
Szeghalom (H) 159 M3
Szegvár (H) 159 K4
Székely (H) 160 D1
Székesfehérvár (H) 158 F3
Székkutas (H) 159 L4
Szekszárd (H) 158 G5
Szeleste (H) 158 C3
Szelevény (H) 159 K4
Szellő (H) 166 B1
Szemere (H) 155 J5
Szemud (PL) 141 K2
Szendehely (H) 154 E6
Szendrő (H) 155 H5
Szenna (H) 165 K2
Szenta (H) 165 J2
Szentbalázs (H) 165 K2
Szentendre (H) 159 H2
Szentes (H) 159 K4
Szentgotthárd (H) 158 B4
Szentgyörgyvölgy (H) 158 B4
Szentlászló (H) 166 A1
Szentliszló (H) 165 H1
Szentlőrinc (H) 166 A1
Szentmártonkáta (H) 159 J3
Széphalom (H) 155 K5
Szepietowo-Stacja (PL) 143 H5
Szerencs (H) 159 M1
Szerzyny (PL) 155 J2
Szestno (PL) 136 E6
Szewnia Górna (PL) 149 H4
Szigetszentmiklós (H) 159 H3
Szigetvár (H) 166 A1
Szigliget (H) 158 D4
Szikáncs (H) 160 A5
Szikszó (H) 160 B1
Szil (H) 158 D2
Szilsárkány (H) 158 D2
Szilvágy (H) 91 L6
Szilvásvárad (H) 160 A1
Szin (H) 155 H4
Szirák (H) 154 F6
Szkaradowo (PL) 147 G2
Szklarnia (PL) 148 F4
Szklarska Poręba (PL) 146 D4
Szklary Dolne (PL) 146 E3
Szklary Górne (PL) 146 E3
Szkodna (PL) 148 E6
Szlachta (PL) 141 K3
Szlichtyngowa (PL) 146 E2
Szob (H) 159 G2
Szőcsénypuszta (H) 165 J1
Szokolya (H) 154 E6
Szolnok (H) 159 K3
Szombathely (H) 158 C3
Szonów (PL) 147 H5
Szostaki (PL) 143 G4
Szóstka (PL) 149 G2
Szpetal Górny (PL) 141 M5
Szpica (PL) 149 H3
Szprotawa (PL) 146 D2
Szprotawka (PL) 146 D2
Szreniawa (PL) 148 A5
Szreńsk (PL) 142 C4
Sztabin (PL) 143 J3
Sztum (PL) 141 M3
Sztutowo (PL) 141 M2
Sztynort Duży (PL) 142 F2
Szubin (PL) 141 J4
Szúcs (H) 159 K1
Szűcsi (H) 154 F6
Szufranowa (PL) 148 E6
Szulborze-Koty (PL) 142 G5
Szulok (H) 158 E5
Szumanie (PL) 142 B5
Szumowo (PL) 142 G5
Szwagrów (PL) 148 D5
Szwarszowice (PL) 148 D4
Szwecja (PL) 140 G4
Szybowice (PL) 147 G5
Szydłów (PL) 148 C4
Szydłowiec (PL) 148 C3
Szydłówka (PL) 149 G1
Szymany (PL) 142 D4
Szymbark (PL) 142 A3
Szymbark (PL) 155 J2
Szymiszów (PL) 147 J4
Szymki (PL) 143 K5
Szymonka (PL) 136 F6
Szynkielów (PL) 147 K3
Szypliszki (PL) 143 J2
Szyszków (PL) 149 G5

T

Taagepera (EST) 131 J5
Taalintehdas = Dalsbruk (FIN) 35 L4
Taapajärvi (FIN) 22 G2
Taarstedt (D) 66 B1
Taasia (FIN) 36 F3
Taastrup (DK) 47 K2
Taattola (FIN) 29 J3
Taavetti (FIN) 37 J3
Taavetti = Luumäki (FIN) 37 J3
Tab (H) 158 F4
Tabačka (BG) 176 E1
Tåbäcken (S) 40 F4
Tabaky (UA) 171 H2
Tabalt (RO) 168 B1
Tabanera de Cerrato (E) 112 C4
Tabanera la Luenga (E) 119 H1
Tabanköy (TR) 182 D5
Tabanlar (TR) 190 D2
Tabanovac (SRB) 167 H5
Tabanovce (MK) 175 G4
Tabaqueros (E) 120 F5
Tábara (E) 111 H5
Tabăra (MD) 163 H4
Tabariškės (LT) 137 O5
Tabaza (E) 111 H1
Taberg (S) 43 O3
Tabernas (E) 127 F5
Tabernes = Tavernes de la Valldigna (E) 127 K1
Taberno (E) 127 F5
Tabivere (EST) 131 L3
Tablate (E) 126 C6
Tablier, le (F) 82 C3
Tablones, Los (E) 126 D6
Taboada (E) 110 D3
Taboadela (E) 110 D4
Tabód (H) 158 G5
Tábor (CZ) 81 M2
Tábua (P) 116 E3
Tabuaço (P) 117 F1
Tabuenca (E) 113 H5
Tabuyo del Monte (E) 111 G4
Täby (S) 34 B6
Täby (S) 45 J1
Tăcău (RO) 170 F4
Taceno (I) 87 H5
Tacettin (TR) 184 C5
Tacherting (D) 89 H1
Tachoires (F) 92 F4
Tachov (CZ) 152 C4
Tacir (TR) 183 J4
Tackåsen (S) 32 J4
Tackskog = Takkula (FIN) 36 C4
Tăcuta (RO) 162 F5
Tacuz (MD) 163 J5
Taczanów II (PL) 147 H2
Tadaiķi (LV) 132 C4
Tadan' (UA) 156 F1
Tadcaster (GB) 55 K3
Tadley (GB) 58 E5
Tadulina (BY) 138 G5
Taebla (EST) 130 E3
Tæbring (DK) 42 C5
Tælavåg (N) 38 A2
Taevaskoja (EST) 134 D1
Tafalla (E) 92 A5
Tafers (CH) 86 D4
Tafjord (N) 30 G3
Täftea (S) 26 E8
Täfteå (S) 26 G7
Taftesund (N) 30 E2
Taga (RO) 161 J4
Taganrog (RUS) 13 M3
Tagar (TR) 193 J3
Tagarádes (GR) 179 J4
Tagaranna (EST) 130 B3
Tagarp (S) 47 L2
Tagavere (EST) 130 C3
Taggia (I) 98 D5
Taghmon (IRL) 63 J4
Tagliacozzo (I) 103 G3
Taglio di Po (I) 101 G2
Tagnière, La (F) 84 F3
Tagoat (IRL) 63 K4
Tagsdorf (F) 86 D2
Tågsjöberg (S) 25 L7
Tagula-1 (EST) 134 B2
Tahačyn (UA) 149 L3
Tahal (E) 127 F5
Tahirinli (TR) 193 K3
Tahiroğlu (TR) 193 J2
Tahitótfalu (H) 159 H2
Tahivilla (E) 128 C5
Tahkoranta (FIN) 29 H7
Tahta (RUS) 13 N3
Tahtacı (TR) 181 K6
Tahtaköprü (TR) 183 J6
Tahtakuşlar (TR) 190 B1
Tahtalı (TR) 192 D6
Tähtelä (FIN) 23 J2
Tähtelä = Täkter (FIN) 35 O4
Taibeart = Tarbert (IRL) 62 D3
Taibique (E) 129 b5
Taíde (P) 110 C5
Taikkokylä (FIN) 29 G6
Tailfingen (D) 79 L5
Taillant (F) 82 D5
Taillebois (F) 75 L3
Taillebourg (F) 82 D5
Tailovo (RUS) 134 E2
Taimoniemi (FIN) 27 M8
Tain (GB) 51 J4
Tainionkoski (FIN) 37 L2
Tain-l'Hermitage (F) 85 G6
Taintrux (F) 78 F5
Taio (I) 87 M5
Taipale (FIN) 23 H5
Taipale (FIN) 29 G5
Taipale (FIN) 29 H5
Taipale (FIN) 36 E1
Taipaleenharju (FIN) 23 J6

234 Steinhude

Taipaleensuu (S) 18 F8
Taipalsaari (FIN) 37 K2
Taipas (Caldelas) (P) 110 C6
Tai'f Bull (GB) 57 K2
Taiskirchen im Innkreis (A) 81 K4
Taivalkoski (FIN) 23 L5
Taivalmaa (FIN) 35 M2
Taivassalo (FIN) 28 D6
Taivassalo (FIN) 28 J3
Taizé (F) 85 D3
Taizé (F) 111 G2
Taize-Aizie (F) 83 F4
Taizon (F) 82 E2
Taja (E) 111 G2
Tajkury (UA) 150 C2
Taja (UA) 150 F2
Tajmanara (E) 145 M2
Tajov (SK) 174 E5
Tajov (SK) 154 E4
Takåt (BG) 177 H1
Takås (H) 158 D3
Takamaa (FIN) 28 D8
Takamaa (FIN) 36 G3
Takaryśki (BY) 138 D5
Takeley (GB) 59 H4
Takene (S) 46 D4
Takkula (FIN) 36 C4
Takkulankulma (FIN) 35 K3
Takle (N) 30 C5
Takmak (TR) 191 F4
Takovo (SRB) 166 F6
Taktaharkany (H) 159 M1
Taktaszada (H) 159 J3
Tal (BG) 177 H4

Tässi (LV) 132 C4
Tannière, la (F) 75 K4
Tanning (N) 23 H6
Tannisby (DK) 42 F3
Tåno (S) 43 D4
Tannroda (D) 72 F4
Tannsjön (S) 26 B7
Tannremmy (P) 185 K4
Tanovo (PL) 162 E6
Tansor (GB) 58 G3
Tantonville (F) 78 E5
Tantow (D) 67 L4
Tantula (FIN) 35 P3
Tanum (S) 39 M5
Tanumshede (S) 39 O5
Tanus (F) 93 J2
Tanvald (CZ) 153 H2
Tanyeri (TR) 185 K2
Taole = Taulé (F) 74 D3
Taormina (I) 109 H2
Taouté (IRL) 55 J6
Tapa (EST) 131 J2
Tapadia (Rio Casarego (E) 110 F1
Tápiócsüce (H) 159 J3
Tápiógyörgye (H) 159 J3
Tápionmeim (FIN) 23 K3
Tápioszele (H) 159 J3
Tápioszőlős (H) 159 J3
Tapizel (AL) 174 C6
Tastgory (I) 44 B6
Tapolca (H) 158 D4
Tapsony (H) 165 J2
Tapu (RO) 169 G1
Tar (HR) 101 K2

Terichel (D) 72 E4
Terjan = Tartano (I) 88 E4
Techwollmannsdorf (D) 152 B2
Teichwollmarsdorf, Mohlsdorf- (D) 152 B2
Tegebyen (N) 39 O2
Teignmouth (GB) 57 G4
Teguise (E) 16 E4
Teijo (S) 35 L4
Tel, La (F) 94 E1
Taskövi (TR) 190 D2
Taskövi (TR) 185 P5
Taskövi (TR) 198 H5
Tajlanar (TR) 185 F1
Tajghöyük (TR) 193 J2
Tajicik (TR) 190 D1
Taşpınar (TR) 185 F1
Tarperi (TR) 185 K2
Tajil (TR) 186 C2
Tasörem (TR) 184 D5
Tasör (TR) 35 M7
Tapanküla (FIN) 33 H4
Tasovice (CZ) 153 K5
Tejeda y Segoyuela (E) 118 D2

Teijerina (E) 112 A3
Teke (H) 183 J3
Tekeler (TR) 190 D5
Tekeli (TR) 189 H2
Tekenje (H) 91 M6
Tekerdj (SRB) 168 C4
Tekeit (TR) 190 J1
Tekenye (H) 91 M6
Tekirdağ (TR) 188 E7
Tekirler (TR) 184 B6
Tekke (TR) 185 J2
Tekovské (SK) 154 E4
Teksali (MK) 175 G6
Teksali (MK) 163 M3
Tejna (RUS) 134 F4
Tekirova (TR) 193 J4
Tejca (BG) 177 H5

Teijerina (E) 112 A3
Theologos (GR) 188 C3
Théoule-sur-Mer (F) 95 K4
Thermis (GR) 181 H3
Thérmis (GR) 176 D6
Thérmon (GR) 179 J3
Thermo (GR) 181 M1
Terme de Brennero (I) 88 B4
Terme di Lurisia (I) 98 D4
Terme di Sardara (I) 97 C4
Terme di Valderi (I) 97 C4
Terme sulla Strada del Vino (I) 88 E5
Termeno (I) 88 E4
Termini Imerese (I) 108 E2
Termoli (I) 103 F3
Termoli (I) 172 A6
Ternaard (NL) 63 G1
Terneuzen (NL) 63 H1
Ternivka (UA) 157 L2
Ternopil (UA) 149 G2
Ternes, Les (F) 84 D7
Ternhill (GB) 55 G3
Ternuka (I) 103 G5
Teno (E) 16 B2
Tensfeld (D) 67 G3

Tietelsen (D) 71 H3
Tietjerksteradeel = Tytsjerksteradiel (NL) 63 G1
Tifeğti (RO) 170 E2
Tiftauges (F) 82 E2
Tiğanaş (RO) 167 L5
Tiğaneşti (RO) 169 J6
Titchmarsh (GB) 58 G3
Titisee (D) 80 C3
Titta (RO) 170 A3
Titova Korenica (I)
Titz (D) 69 L4
Tiukka = Tjöck (FIN) 28 B7
Tiurajärvi (FIN) 22 D3
Tivat (MNE) 173 J5
Tivenys (E) 121 K1
Tiverton (GB) 57 G3
Tivoli (I) 102 E6
Tivriz (UA) 156 D3
Tizzano Val di Parma (I) 87 H5

Titova Mitrovica = Mitrovicë (RKS) 174 E3
Titov Drvar = Drvar (BIH) 165 G6
Titov Užice = Užice (SRB) 166 E6
Titovo Velenje = Velenje (SLO) 164 E2
Titran (N) 24 C7
Tittling (D) 90 D2
Titova (FIN) 23 K6
Titova (FIN) 29 M7
Titova (C) 125 K6
Tiurari (FIN) 23 H3
Tiurajärvi (FIN) 41 J5
Tiva (FIN) 23 L4

Tolmin (SLO) 89 K5
Tolminske Ravne (SLO) 89 K5
Tolna (H) 159 G5
Tolnanémedi (H) 158 F4
Tolo (GR) 180 D3
Tolob (E) 50 C3
Tolochin (BY) 135 J2
Tolofana (GR) 186 E3
Tolosa (E) 119 O1
Tolosa (P) 116 F3
Tolosanmäki (FIN) 29 L7
Titosa (P) 125 K6
Tolosa (P) 117 F5

Tonja (I) 119 K2
Toriki (RUS) 37 O5
Torla (E) 108 F5
Torlana (F) 159 G5
Tolmarieed (m) 158 F4
Torma (FIN) 28 E6
Torna (E) 159 P3
Torkamäki (UA) 24 C9
Torkandiz (S) 31 L3
Torkelsbo (S) 33 L4
Torkkala (FIN) 35 L3
Torkkala (FIN) 35 L3
Törmälä (FIN) 29 J3
Törmänen (FIN) 19 K6
Törmänen (FIN) 29 J4
Törmänen (FIN) 29 H2
Törmäs (FIN) 23 M6
Törmäsjärvi (FIN) 22 F2
Tormestorp (S) 47 N1
Torna (E) 94 D2
Tornada (P) 116 C5
Tornio (FIN) 18 A7
Tornos (E) 120 D3
Torroella de Montgrí (E) 122 A3

Torrico 235

Torri del Benaco (I) 99 K1
Torridon (GB) 50 F4
Torriglia (I) 99 G3
Torrijas (E) 121 G3
Torrijos (E) 119 H4
Torrin (GB) 50 E5
Torring (DK) 46 D2
Torring (N) 24 F6
Torrita di Siena (I) 101 F6
Torrita Tiberina (I) 107 F6
Torrivaara (S) 21 L7
Tórtoli (DK) 46 F2
Torrony (N) 35 N3
Torrcal (P) 124 B3
Torroella de Fluvià (E) 115 K3
Torroella de Montgrí (E) 115 K3
Torrox (E) 110 D4
Torrox-Costa (E) 126 C6
Torsåker (S) 41 M5
Torsåker (S) 82 F5
Torsåker (S) 33 O1
Torsåker (S) 41 K1
Torslanda (FIN) 37 M2
Torsås (S) 45 J6
Torsborg (S) 32 G2
Torsby (S) 31 J6
Torsby (S) 40 C2
Torsby (S) 45 O5
Torsby (S) 43 J3
Torsdalsdammen (N) 38 G4
Torsebro (S) 47 O1
Torserud (S) 40 D4
Torsetlia (N) 39 H2
Torsfjärden (S) 25 J6
Torshälla (S) 41 K4
Torshavn (DK) 48 E3
Torshälla (S) 41 L2
Torshov (N) 38 F3
Torsholma (AX) 34 H4
Torshov (N) 39 O3
Torsken (N) 24 D8
Torskbäcken (S) 40 F3
Tors'ke (UA) 147 G6
Torsken (N) 20 G2
Torskinge (S) 43 N4
Torslunda (DK) 46 H4
Torsö (S) 42 B6
Tòrsmo (S) 32 H5
Torsø (S) 40 E5
Torsted (DK) 46 B1
Torstensbo (N) 30 B7
Torstrup (DK) 46 B2
Torsvåg (N) 19 B3
Tórtel (H) 159 J3
Tortima (I) 88 F6
Tortinmäki (FIN) 35 K3
Tòrtola (E) 120 D4
Tortolas de Henares (E) 120 B2
Tórtoles de Esgueva (E) 112 C5
Tortolì (I) 97 E4
Tortona (I) 98 F3
Tortoreto (I) 103 H2
Tortoreto Lido (I) 103 H2
Tortorici (I) 106 G1
Tortosa (E) 121 K2
Tortosendo (P) 118 A3
Tortuera (E) 120 F2
Tortuna (S) 41 L3
Tòrtuna (E) 113 N5
Torul (TR) 13 N7
Torun (PL) 141 L4
Torunskialti (TR) 193 K6
Tõrva (S) 43 M5
Tõrva (EST) 131 J1 G5
Tòrvaianica (I) 102 E4
Torvenkylä (FIN) 28 D3
Torver (GB) 53 J6
Tórvik (N) 24 C9
Tørvik (N) 30 F2
Torvikbukt (N) 24 B9
Torviskas (S) 26 D4
Torvinen (FIN) 22 C3
Torvola (I) 126 D6
Torvøya (FIN) 36 C2
Torvund (N) 30 D5
Torysa (SK) 155 H3
Torżek (RUS) 7 T7
Tòrzym (PL) 67 N6
Torsevån (N) 25 G4
Toscaig (GB) 50 F5
Toscanella (I) 101 F4
Toscolano-Maderno (I) 99 K1
Toŝčicà (Y) 87 L3
Tòseera (A) 87 L3
Toser, Le (F) 86 D4
Tosno (RUS) 7 S6
Tosno (RUS) 37 P5
Tossa (S) 37 K2
Tossa de Mar (E) 115 J4
Tossavanlahti (FIN) 28 G5
Tossås (F) 92 B3
Tostanå (EST) 130 E4
Tostared (S) 43 K4
Tòstarup (F) 62 F3
Tòsterup (F) 63 P6
Tòssjö (S) 32 G5
Tostedt (D) 57 O7
Tòstra (S) 33 N6
Totalis (S) 25 H6
Totana (E) 127 G4
Totebo (S) 45 J3
Tòtkomlós (H) 159 L5
Tótmanok (I) 151 M2
Tòtkomlós (H) 159 L5
Totland (GB) 57 L4
Totleáivvi (N) 20 G2
Tótszentmárton (H) 151 J4
Totton (GB) 57 L4
Tòtvazony (H) 158 E3
Toucy (F) 88 B3
Touça (F) 118 B1
Touches-de-Périgny, Les (F) 82 E5
Toucy (F) 77 H6
Touët-sur-Var (F) 98 C5
Touffailles (F) 93 G2
Touguinha (P) 110 B6
Tòukkiwe, la (B) 57 J2
Toul (F) 78 H4
Toulat (FIN) 28 G5
Toulon (F) 95 G4
Toulon-sur-Arroux (F) 84 F3
Toulouges (F) 93 J3
Toulouse (F) 93 G3
Toulx-Sainte-Croix (F) 83 K4
Tounan (RUS) 7 W2
Tourah (FIN) 164 E4
Touques (F) 75 M2
Touquet-Paris-Plage, Le (F) 73 G4
Tour-Blanche-Cercles, La (F) 83 F6
Tourcoing (F) 68 E5
Tour-d'Aigues, La (F) 95 G3
Tour-d'Auvergne, La (F) 83 L5
Tour-de-Faure (F) 93 H2
Tour-de-Scay, la (F) 88 B5
Tour-du-Parc, Le (F) 74 F5
Tour-du-Pin, La (F) 85 H6
Tour-Fondue, La (F) 95 J4
Tourlàn (F) 110 A2
Touraville (F) 75 H1
Tourelle (B) 68 E5
Tournaig (GB) 50 F4
Tournan-en-Brie (F) 77 G4
Tournay (F) 93 F3
Tournefeuri-sur-la-Horn (F) 59 M6
Tournoisis (F) 76 F2
Tournon-d'Agenais (F) 93 G2
Tournon-Saint-Martin (F) 83 G3
Tournon-sur-Rhône (F) 85 G6
Tournus (F) 85 G3
Touro (P) 117 F2
Touroumë-au-Perche (F) 76 C4
Tourrette-Levens (F) 95 K3
Tours (F) 76 C4
Tours-en-Savoie (F) 98 A1
Tours-en-Vimeu (F) 76 F6
Tourteron (F) 78 B3
Tourtoirac (F) 83 H6
Tourula (FIN) 35 L3
Tourville-la-Rivière (F) 75 G4
Tourville-sur-Sienne (F) 75 H2
Toury (F) 76 F5
Touson (F) 79 F6
Toulancourt (F) 76 B3
Touvet, Le (F) 85 J6
Touvois (F) 82 B3
Touzac (F) 93 G2
Toužim (CZ) 153 G2
Tovačov (CZ) 153 M5

A B C D E F G H I J K L M N O P Q R S T U V W X Y Z

Vesnovo (RUS) 136 G4
Vesoul (F) 86 B2
Vespolate (I) 98 F2
Véssa (GR) 189 H3
Vesseaux (F) 94 D1
Vessem (NL) 69 J4
Vessige (S) 43 L5
Vestad (N) 30 G2
Vestbjerg (DK) 42 E4
Vestby (N) 39 N3
Vestbygd (N) 20 E4
Vestbygd (N) 38 E6
Vestdafalseyri (IS) 17 M4
Vester (DK) 46 C3
Vesterbølle (DK) 42 D5
Vesterborg (DK) 47 H4
Vester Bregninge (DK) 46 F4
Vesterby (DK) 46 E2
Vesterby (DK) 46 F2
Vester Egesborg (DK) 47 J3
Vesterelv (N) 19 L3
Vester Gammelby (DK) 65 K1
Vester Grønning (DK) 42 D5
Vester Hæsinge (DK) 46 F3
Vester Hassing (DK) 42 F4
Vester Hjermitslev (DK) 42 E4
Vester Hornum (DK) 42 D5
Vesterli (N) 20 E6
Vesterlund (DK) 46 D2
Vester Nebel (DK) 46 D2
Vesterø Havn (DK) 42 G4
Vester Skørringe (DK) 47 H4
Vester Sottrup (DK) 46 E4
Vestertana (N) 19 K3
Vester Tørslev (DK) 42 E5
Vester-Vandet (DK) 42 C4
Vester Velling (DK) 42 E6
Vestervig (DK) 42 B5
Vestfossen (N) 39 L3
Vesti (FIN) 35 L4
Vestiena (LV) 133 M4
Vestlax (FIN) 35 L4
Vestmanhavn = Vestmanna (FO) 48 D3
Vestmanna (FO) 48 D3
Vestmannaeyjar (IS) 16 F8
Vestmarka (N) 40 A3
Vestnes (N) 30 G2
Vestone (I) 87 K6
Vestpollen (N) 20 D4
Vestre (Ås) (N) 31 O6
Vestre Åmøy (N) 38 C4
Vestre Jakobselv (N) 19 M3
Vestre Kile (N) 38 G4
Vestre Vallesverd (N) 42 B2
Vesturbotn (IS) 16 C3
Vesturhópshólar (IS) 16 F3
Vestvågan (N) 25 G3
Vestvik (N) 24 E7
Vesunti (FIN) 35 L1
Veszprém (H) 158 E3
Veszprémvarsány (H) 158 E3
Vésztő (H) 160 C4
Vetaherrado (E) 128 C3
Vețca (RO) 161 K5
Vețel (RO) 160 F6
Veteli (FIN) 28 D5
Veteren (N) 39 L2
Veterja (RUS) 131 N4
Veternik (SRB) 166 E3
Vetersko (MK) 175 G5
Vétheuil (F) 76 E3
Vetiş (RO) 156 C6
Vetla (EST) 131 H2
Vetlanda (S) 44 G4
Vetleifsholt (IS) 16 F7
Vetly (BY) 149 M2
Vetoški (RUS) 135 M4
Vetovo (BG) 177 F1
Vetovo (HR) 165 K4
Vētraine (LV) 131 M6
Vetralla (I) 102 E3
Vetren (BG) 170 E5
Vetren (BG) 176 B4
Vetren (BG) 176 E3
Vetren Dol (BG) 176 B4
Vetrino (BG) 177 H2
Vetrişoaia (RO) 163 G6
Větrný Jeníkov (CZ) 153 H5
Vetschau (Spreewald) (D) 73 L2
Vetsikko (FIN) 19 K4
Vettaland (N) 38 C5
Vettasjärvi (S) 21 L6
Vetterud (N) 39 P2
Vetti (N) 30 H5
Vettin (D) 66 G4
Vetto (I) 99 J4
Vettweiß (D) 69 M5
Vetulonia (I) 102 B2
Vetunica (SRB) 175 H4
Vetvenik (RUS) 131 N3
Veules-les-Roses (F) 76 C2
Veulettes-sur-Mer (F) 76 C2
Veum (N) 38 H4
Veurdre, le (F) 84 D3
Veurne = Furnes (B) 68 D4
Vevang (N) 30 G2
Vevčani (MK) 178 D2
Veverská Bítýška (CZ) 153 K5
Vevey (CH) 85 L4
Vévi (GR) 179 F3
Vevring (N) 30 C4
Vex (CH) 86 D5
Vexala (FIN) 28 C5
Vexin-sur-Epte (F) 76 E3
Veynes (F) 95 G1
Veyrier-du-Lac (F) 85 K5
Veysel (TR) 192 B2
Veyselli (TR) 199 H2
Věž (CZ) 153 H4
Vėžaičiai (LT) 132 C6
Vézaponin (F) 77 H3
Vezdemarbán (E) 111 J5
Vézelay (F) 77 J7
Vézelise (F) 78 E5
Vézelois (F) 86 C2
Vezels-Roussy (F) 93 K1
Vezendiu (RO) 160 E2
Vezenkovo (BG) 177 G3
Vézénobres (F) 94 D2
Vézilly (F) 77 J3
Vezins (F) 82 D2
Vézins-de-Lévézou (F) 94 A2
Vėžionys (LT) 143 M2
Vezirhan (TR) 183 K5
Vezirköprü (TR) 185 K3
Vežycja (BY) 144 F5
Vezza d'Oglio (I) 87 K5
Vezzani (F) 96 E4
Vezzano (I) 87 M5
Vezzano sul Crostolo (I) 99 K3
Vezzola (I) 100 D3
Vi (S) 33 N3
Via (S) 33 N4
Viadana (I) 99 K3
Viagrande (I) 109 H2
Vialas (F) 94 C2
Viam (F) 83 J5
Viana (E) 113 G3
Viana do Alentejo (P) 124 D3
Viana do Bolo (E) 110 E4
Viana do Castelo (P) 110 B5
Vianden (L) 78 E2
Viane (F) 93 K3
Vianen (NL) 69 J3
Viaño Pequeno (Trazo) (E) 110 B2
Viaño Pequeño (Trazo) = Viaño Pequeno (Trazo) (E) 110 B2
Vianos (E) 127 E2
Vianta (FIN) 29 H5
Viantie (FIN) 23 G5
Viareggio (I) 100 C5
Viarmes (F) 76 F3
Vias (F) 94 B4
Viașiu (RO) 168 D5
Viasvesi (FIN) 35 J2
Viatodos (P) 110 B6
Viator (E) 127 F6
Vibal, Le (F) 93 K2
Vibberbo (S) 41 J2
Vibble (S) 45 N3
Vibbyn (S) 22 D5
Viblemo (N) 38 F6
Viborg (DK) 42 D6
Vibo Valentia (I) 106 F5
Vibo Valentia Marina (I) 106 F5
Vibrac (F) 82 E5
Vibraye (F) 76 C5
Viby (DK) 47 K2
Viby (S) 40 G4
Viby (S) 47 O1
Vic' (BY) 145 L5
Vic (E) 115 H4
Viča (SRB) 174 D1
Vicálvaro (E) 120 A3
Vicari (I) 108 E2
Vicchio (I) 99 L5
Vicdessos (F) 115 F2
Vicebsk (BY) 7 S7
Vicebsk (BY) 139 M3
Vicedo (E) 110 D1
Vic-en-Bigorre (F) 92 E4
Vicenza (I) 100 F1
Vic-Fezensac (F) 92 E3
Vi'chovec' (UA) 151 M5
Vichy (F) 84 D4
Vicién (E) 113 L4
Viciomaggio (I) 101 F6
Vickan (S) 43 K4
Vickleby (S) 45 J5
Vic-le-Comte (F) 84 D5
Vico (F) 96 D4
Vico del Gargano (I) 172 C6
Vico Equense (I) 103 J6
Vicoforte (I) 98 D4
Vicopisano (I) 100 D5
Vicosoprano (CH) 87 J5
Vicovaro (I) 103 F3
Vičovo (BG) 171 G6
Vicovu de Jos (RO) 157 J6
Vicovu de Sus (RO) 157 J6
Vicq-sur-Nahon (F) 83 J2
Vicques (CH) 86 D3
Vic-sur-Aisne (F) 77 H3
Vic-sur-Cère (F) 83 L7
Victoria (M) 109 F5
Victoria (RO) 162 F4
Victoria (RO) 169 H2
Victoria (RO) 170 F4
Victoria, La (E) 125 K4
Vicu = Vico (F) 96 D4
Vičyni (UA) 149 L4
Vid, La (E) 112 E5
Vid (Narona) (HR) 173 G3
Vidago (P) 110 D5
Vidais (P) 116 C5
Vidamlja (BY) 143 K6
Vidanes (E) 112 A3
Vidángoz (E) 114 A2
Viðareiði (FO) 48 E3
Vidauban (F) 95 H4
Vidbo (S) 41 O3
Viddal (N) 30 F3
Viddalba (I) 97 C2
Vide (P) 117 F3
Videbæk (DK) 46 C1
Videle (RO) 169 K5
Videm (SLO) 89 M6
Videm = Videm ob Ščavnici (SLO) 165 G1
Videm ob Ščavnici (SLO) 165 G1
Videm pri Ptuju (SLO) 165 F2
Videniškiai (LT) 137 N3
Videseter (N) 30 G4
Vidhareidhi = Viðareiði (FO) 48 E3
Vidice (CZ) 81 H1
Víðidalstunga (IS) 16 F4
Víðidalur (IS) 17 L3
Vidigueira (P) 124 D3
Vidigulfo (I) 100 A2
Víðiker (IS) 17 J4
Vidima (BG) 176 C3
Vídimýri (IS) 16 G3
Vidin (BG) 167 L6
Víðirhóll (IS) 17 K3
Vidiškiai (LT) 137 M3
Vidlin (GB) 49 F3
Vidly (CZ) 147 G5
Vidnava (CZ) 153 M3
Vidno (BG) 177 K1
Vidoky (BY) 138 H2
Vidoni (RUS) 135 J1
Vidonín (CZ) 153 K5
Vidor (I) 88 G6
Vidou (F) 92 E4
Vidovište (MK) 175 H5
Vidra (RO) 161 F5
Vidra (RO) 169 L5
Vidra (RO) 170 D2
Vidrar (BG) 175 J3
Vidrare (BG) 176 B3
Vidreres (E) 115 J4
Vidriži (LV) 133 K3
Vidsel (S) 22 C5
Vidsodis (LT) 132 F6
Viduklė (LT) 137 H3
Vidutinė (LT) 138 D3
Viðvík (IS) 16 G3
Vidža (RUS) 135 M2
Vidzy (BY) 138 E3
Viechtach (D) 81 H2
Viečiūnai (LT) 143 L2
Viedås = Vietas (S) 21 H6
Viehbrock (D) 66 A4
Viehhofen (A) 81 H6
Vieille-Brioude (F) 84 D6
Vieillevigne (F) 82 C3
Vieils-Maisons (F) 77 H4
Vieira de Leiria (P) 116 D4
Vieira do Minho (P) 110 C5
Vieki (FIN) 29 K5
Viekšniai (LT) 136 H1
Vielank (D) 66 E4
Vielha e Mijaran (E) 114 E2
Viella-Mitg Arán = Vielha e Mijaran (E) 114 E2
Vielle-Aure (F) 114 D2
Vielle-Soubiran (F) 92 D2
Vielmur-sur-Agout (F) 93 J3
Vielsalm (B) 70 A6
Vieluft (N) 18 F3
Vienenburg (D) 72 D2
Vienne (F) 85 G5
Viens (F) 95 G3
Viensuu (FIN) 29 K5
Vierchnjadzvinsk (BY) 134 E6
Viereck (D) 140 B3
Vieremä (FIN) 29 G4
Viereth-Trunstadt (D) 72 D6
Vierhouten (NL) 69 K2
Vieritz (D) 67 G5
Vierlinden (D) 67 L5
Vierlingsbeek (NL) 69 L3
Viernheim (D) 79 K2
Vierraden (D) 140 B4
Viersen (D) 70 B4
Viersla (N) 38 F2
Vierumäki (FIN) 36 E2
Vierville-sur-Mer (F) 75 K2
Vierzon (F) 83 K2
Viesāti (LV) 132 F4
Vieselbach (D) 71 M5
Viesimo (FIN) 29 L7
Viešintos (LT) 138 A2
Viesīte (LV) 133 M5
Viessoix (F) 75 K3
Vieste (I) 172 D6
Viešvėnai (LT) 132 E6
Viešvilė (LT) 136 G3
Vietas (S) 21 H6
Vietmannsdorf (D) 67 K4
Vietri di Potenza (I) 104 E4
Vietri sul Mare (I) 104 C4
Vietryna (BY) 139 H3
Vietze (D) 66 E4
Vieux-Boucau-les-Bains (F) 92 B3
Vievis (LT) 137 M4
Vieyes (I) 98 C1
Vif (F) 85 J6
Viffort (F) 77 H4
Vig (AL) 173 L6
Vig (DK) 47 J2
Vigan, Le (F) 94 C3
Viganj (HR) 172 F4
Vīganti (LV) 138 E1
Vigarano Mainarda (I) 99 M3
Vigasio (I) 100 D2
Vigdalsmo (N) 24 E8
Vigdel (N) 38 C5
Vigeland (N) 38 F6
Vigeland (N) 42 C2
Vigeois (F) 83 J6
Vigevano (I) 98 F2
Vigge (S) 32 G2
Vigge (S) 33 M3
Viggianello (I) 104 F6
Viggiano (I) 106 E2
Viggja (N) 24 E8
Vigľaš (SK) 154 E4
Vigmostad (N) 38 F6
Vignacourt (F) 76 F1
Vignale Monferrato (I) 98 E2
Vignanello (I) 102 E3
Vignats (F) 76 A4
Vignes, Les (F) 94 B2
Vigneulles-lès-Hattonchâtel (F) 78 D4
Vigneux-de-Bretagne (F) 75 H6
Vigneux-Hocquet (F) 77 J2
Vignola (I) 99 L4
Vignola Mare (I) 97 D1
Vignole (I) 88 G5
Vignolles (F) 82 E5
Vignory (F) 77 M5
Vignoux-sous-les-Aix (F) 84 B2
Vignoux-sur-Barangeon (F) 83 K2
Vigny (F) 76 E3
Vigo (E) 110 B4
Vigone (I) 98 C3
Vigonza (I) 101 F2
Vigo Rendena (I) 88 D5
Vigrestad (N) 38 C5
Vigsnæs (DK) 47 J4
Vigsø (DK) 42 C4
Viguzzolo (I) 98 F3
Vigy (F) 78 E3
Vihajärvi (FIN) 23 K7
Vihanninkylä (FIN) 28 E6
Vihantasalmi (FIN) 36 G2
Vihanti (FIN) 23 G8
Vihari (FIN) 29 K4
Vihavuosi (FIN) 36 C2
Viherlahti (FIN) 34 H3
Vihiers (F) 82 D2
Vihren (BG) 175 K5
Vihrišče (RUS) 135 K4
Vihtajärvi (FIN) 29 G6
Vihtalahti (FIN) 28 F7
Vihtari (FIN) 29 K7
Vihtasuo (FIN) 29 K5
Vihtavuori (FIN) 28 F7
Vihteljärvi (FIN) 28 C8
Vihti (FIN) 36 B4
Vihtiälä (FIN) 35 M2
Vihtijärvi (FIN) 35 P3
Vihu (FIN) 28 C8
Vihula (EST) 131 K1
Viiala (FIN) 35 N2
Viianki (FIN) 23 N7
Viiksimo (FIN) 29 L3
Viile (RO) 170 F5
Viile Satu Mare (RO) 161 F2
Viimsi (EST) 130 G1
Viinijärvi (FIN) 29 K6
Viinikkala (FIN) 29 G5
Viinistu (EST) 131 J1
Viiratsi (EST) 131 J4
Viirilä (FIN) 36 F3
Viirinkylä (FIN) 23 J4
Viisarimäki (FIN) 28 G7
Viişoara (MD) 162 E2
Viişoara (RO) 160 E3
Viişoara (RO) 162 C5
Viişoara (RO) 162 D2
Viişoara (RO) 162 F6
Viişoara (RO) 171 G5
Viitaila (FIN) 36 D2
Viitajärvi (FIN) 28 F5
Viitakoski (FIN) 29 L4
Viitakylä (FIN) 28 G6
Viitala (FIN) 28 D6
Viitala (FIN) 29 L4
Viitamäki (FIN) 29 G4
Viitaniemi (FIN) 29 J5
Viitapohja (FIN) 35 O1
Viitasaari (FIN) 27 M8
Viitataival (FIN) 29 H6
Viitavaara (FIN) 29 J3
Viitavaara (FIN) 29 K2
Viitna (EST) 36 F6
Viivikonna (EST) 37 J6
Vijciems (LV) 133 M2
Vijtivci (UA) 150 D5
Vijtivci (UA) 150 F4
Vik (N) 24 F5
Vik (N) 24 G4
Vik (N) 30 F2
Vik (N) 30 F5
Vik (N) 39 K3
Vika (FIN) 23 J3
Vika (N) 24 F7
Vika (N) 31 Q2
Vika (N) 32 B4
Vika (S) 41 J1
Vikajärvi (FIN) 23 J3
Vikan (N) 24 C8
Vikane (N) 39 N4
Vikanes (N) 30 D6
Vikarbodrna (S) 33 O3
Vikarbyn (S) 32 J6
Víkarbyrgi (FO) 48 E5
Vikartovce (SK) 155 G4
Vika Sörda (S) 32 G6
Vikatunet (N) 38 D4
Vikbyn (S) 41 K2
Vike (N) 30 J2
Vike (N) 38 E2
Vike (S) 33 M2
Vikebukt (N) 30 G2
Vikedal (N) 38 C3
Vikeid (N) 20 E3
Viken (S) 25 H5
Viken (S) 25 J9
Viken (S) 32 J3
Viken (S) 33 K3
Viken (S) 40 F3
Viken (S) 47 L1
Viker (N) 31 P6
Viker (S) 40 A4
Viker (S) 40 G4
Vikersund (N) 39 L3
Vikesá (N) 38 D5
Vikevåg (N) 38 C4
Vikholmen (N) 25 G2
Viki (EST) 130 B4
Viki (N) 38 F4
Vík í Mýrdal (IS) 17 G8
Víkingavatn (IS) 17 K2
Vikingstad (S) 44 G2
Vikjorda (N) 20 D4
Vikmanshyttan (S) 41 J2
Vikna (N) 24 E5
Vikno (UA) 162 B1
Vikoč (BIH) 173 J3
Vikran (N) 18 A4
Vikran (N) 20 F3
Viksberg (S) 41 J3
Viksdalen (N) 30 E5
Viksfjord, Lauve- (N) 39 M4
Viksjö (S) 33 N2
Viksjöfors (S) 33 K5
Viksmon (S) 33 N1
Viksøy (N) 38 B2
Viksøyri (N) 30 F5
Viksta (S) 41 N2
Vikstøl (N) 38 H2
Vikstraum (N) 24 C7
Viksvatn (N) 24 E6
Viktorivka (UA) 163 L4
Viktring (A) 164 C1
Víkur (IS) 16 F2
Vila Baleira = Porto Santo (P) 129 b2
Vilaboa (E) 110 E2
Vila Boa (P) 110 B5
Vila Boim (P) 117 G6
Vilachá (E) 110 E4
Vila Chã (P) 110 B6
Vila Chã (P) 116 E3
Vila Chão do Marão (P) 110 C6
Vilacoba (E) 110 C2
Vila Cortês da Serra (P) 118 A2
Vila Cova a Coelheira (P) 117 F2
Vila Cova da Lixa (P) 110 C6
Viladamat (E) 115 K3
Vila da Praia da Vitória (P) 129 c1
Vila de Cruces (E) 110 C3
Vila de Cucujães (P) 116 D2
Vila de Frades (P) 124 D3
Vila de Punhe (P) 110 B5
Vila de Rei (P) 116 E4
Vila do Bispo (P) 124 B5
Vila do Conde (P) 110 B6
Vila do Corvo (P) 129 a1
Vilafamés (E) 122 A2
Vilafant (E) 115 J3
Vila Fernando (P) 117 G3
Vila Fernando (P) 117 G6
Vila Flor (P) 110 E6
Vilaframil (E) 110 E2
Vila Franca das Naves (P) 117 G2
Vilafranca de Bonany (E) 123 H3
Vilafranca del Maestrat (E) 121 H3
Vilafranca del Penedès (E) 115 G5
Vila Franca de Xira (P) 116 D6
Vila Franca do Campo (P) 129 d2
Vilafrio (E) 110 D3
Vilagarcía de Arousa (E) 110 B3
Vilainiai (LT) 137 L3
Vila Joiosa, La (E) 122 A5
Vilajuïga (E) 115 K3
Viļaka (LV) 134 E3
Vilalba (E) 110 D2
Vilalba dels Arcs (E) 121 J1
Vilaller (E) 93 F6
Vilamaior da Boullosa (E) 110 D5
Vilamarxant (E) 121 G4
Vilamoura (P) 124 C5
Viļāni (LV) 133 O4
Vila Nogueira de Azeitão = São Lourenço (P) 124 A2
Vilanova (E) 110 B4
Vilanova (E) 110 E4
Vilanova (E) 111 F4
Vila Nova (P) 110 E5
Vilanova (Lourenzá) (E) 110 E2
Vila Nova da Baronia (P) 124 C3
Vila Nova da Barquinha (P) 116 E5
Vilanova de Arousa (E) 110 B3
Vilanova de Bellpuig (E) 114 E4
Vila Nova de Cacela (P) 124 D5
Vila Nova de Cerveira (P) 110 B5
Vila Nova de Famalicão (P) 110 B6
Vila Nova de Foz Côa (P) 118 B1
Vila Nova de Gaia (P) 116 D1
Vilanova del Camí (E) 115 G4
Vilanova de Meià (E) 114 F4
Vila Nova de Milfontes (P) 124 B4
Vila Nova de Ourém = Ourém (P) 116 D4
Vila Nova de Paiva (P) 117 F2
Vila Nova de Poiares (P) 116 E3
Vilanova de Sau (E) 115 H4
Vila Nova do Ceira (P) 116 E3
Vila Nova do Corvo = Corvo, Vila do (P) 129 a1
Vilanova i la Geltrú (E) 115 G5
Vilaosende (E) 110 E2
Vilapedre (E) 110 D2
Vilapedre (San Miguel) (E) 110 E3
Vila Pouca de Aguiar (P) 110 D6
Vila Praia de Âncora (P) 110 B5
Vilar (E) 110 C3
Vilar (P) 116 C5
Vilarandelo (P) 110 E5
Vilarbacú (E) 110 E3
Vilarbarú = Vilarbacú (E) 110 E3
Vilar da Veiga (P) 110 C5
Vilar de Barrio (E) 110 D4
Vilar de Donas (E) 110 D3
Vilar de Ossos (P) 110 E5
Vilar de Santos (E) 110 D4
Vilardevós (E) 110 E5
Vila-real (E) 122 A3
Vila Real (P) 110 D6
Vila Real de Santo António (P) 124 E5
Vilarello (E) 110 D3
Vilar Formoso (P) 118 C2
Vilarinho (P) 110 B6
Vilarinho (P) 116 E3
Vilarinho da Castanheira (P) 117 G1
Vilarinho das Azenhas (P) 110 E6
Vilarinho do Bairro (P) 116 D3
Vilariño de Conso (E) 110 E4
Vilariño Frío (E) 110 D4
Vilar Maior (P) 117 H3
Vila-rodona (E) 115 F5
Vilarouco (P) 117 G1
Vilar Torpim (P) 117 H2
Vila Ruiva (P) 124 D3
Vilasantar = Ru (E) 110 C2
Vilas de Turbón (E) 92 F6
Vila Seca (P) 110 B6
Vila Seca (P) 116 E3
Vilaseca = Vila-seca de Solcina (E) 115 F5
Vila-seca de Solcina (E) 115 F5
Vilassar de Dalt (E) 115 H4
Vilassar de Mar (E) 115 H4
Vila Velha de Ródão (P) 117 F4
Vilavella, La (E) 122 A3
Vila Verde (P) 110 C5
Vila Verde da Raia (P) 110 E5
Vila Verde de Ficalho (P) 124 E4
Vila Viçosa (P) 117 G6
Vilaza (E) 110 E5
Vilce (LV) 132 H5
Vilcele (MD) 163 G6
Vil'cha (UA) 150 F3
Vilches (E) 126 C3
Vil'chivci (UA) 161 H1
Vil'chove (UA) 163 L2
Vil'chuvatka (UA) 9 O4
Vilčycy (BY) 139 M6
Vildbjerg (DK) 46 C1
Vilë (AL) 174 C4
Vilela (E) 110 D3
Vilella Baja = Vilella Baixa, la (E) 114 E5
Vilémov (CZ) 153 J4
Vilers (E) 115 J4
Vileta, sa (E) 123 G3
Vilhelmina (S) 25 L5
Vilia (GR) 187 G3
Viliejka (BY) 138 E5
Vilija (UA) 150 C3
Viljakkala (FIN) 35 M1
Viljandi (EST) 131 J4
Viljanemi (FIN) 36 E3
Viljevo (HR) 165 L3
Viljolahti (FIN) 29 J7
Vilkaviškis (LT) 143 J1
Vilkene (LV) 130 G5
Vilkiautinis (LT) 143 L2
Vilkija (LT) 137 K3
Vilkjärvi (FIN) 37 J3
Vilkyškiai (LT) 136 G3
Villa (I) 88 G5
Villa, La (I) 88 F4
Villabáñez (E) 112 B5
Villa Bartolomea (I) 99 L2
Villabáscones (E) 112 D2
Villa Basilica (I) 100 D5
Villabassa (I) 90 B6
Villablanca (E) 124 E5
Villablino (E) 111 G3
Villabona (E) 111 H2
Villabona (E) 113 G2
Villabrágima (E) 112 A5
Villabruna (I) 88 F5
Villabuena del Puente (E) 111 J6
Villacañas (E) 119 K4
Villacarriedo (E) 112 D2
Villacarrillo (E) 126 D3
Villa Castelli (I) 105 H4
Villacastín (E) 119 H2
Villach (A) 164 B1
Villacidro (I) 97 C5
Villaciervos (E) 113 F5
Villacintor (E) 112 A4
Villaconejos (E) 119 K3
Villaconejos de Trabaque (E) 120 D3
Villada (E) 111 K4
Villadangos del Páramo (E) 111 H3
Villa de Don Fadrique, La (E) 120 B4
Villa del Conte (I) 101 F1
Villa del Prado (E) 119 H3
Villa del Rey (E) 117 H4
Villa del Río (E) 126 B4
Villa di Chiavenna (I) 87 H5
Villadiego (E) 112 C3
Villadose (I) 101 F2
Villadossola (I) 86 F5
Villaeles de Valdavia (E) 111 K3
Villaescusa de Haro (E) 120 C4
Villaescusa la Sombría (E) 112 E4
Villaespesa (E) 121 F3
Villa Estense (I) 101 F2
Villaesteres, Los (E) 111 J5
Villafáfila (E) 111 H5
Villafalletto (I) 95 L1
Villaflores (E) 119 F1
Villafontana (I) 99 L2
Villafranca (E) 113 H4
Villafranca d'Asti (I) 98 E3
Villafranca de Córdoba (E) 126 A4
Villafranca de Ebro (E) 113 K5
Villafranca del Bierzo (E) 111 F3
Villafranca del Campo (E) 121 F2
Villafranca del Cid = Vilafranca del Maestrat (E) 121 H3
Villafranca de los Barros (E) 125 G2
Villafranca de los Caballeros (E) 119 K5
Villafranca del Panadés = Vilafranca del Penedès (E) 115 G5
Villafranca di Forlì (I) 101 G4
Villafranca di Verona (I) 99 K2
Villafranca in Lunigiana (I) 99 H4
Villafranca-Montes de Oca (E) 112 E4
Villafranca Padovana (I) 101 F2
Villafranca Piemonte (I) 95 L1
Villafranca Tirrena (I) 106 D6
Villafranco del Guadalquivir (E) 128 B3
Villafrati (I) 108 D2
Villafrechos (E) 111 J5
Villafruela (E) 112 D5
Villagarcía de Campos (E) 111 J5
Villagarcía de la Torre (E) 125 G3
Villagarcía del Llano (E) 120 E5
Villa Garibaldi (I) 100 D2
Villa Garzoni (I) 100 D5
Villaggio Mancuso (I) 107 G4
Villagómez la Nueva (E) 112 A4
Villagonzalo (E) 117 J6
Villagrains (F) 92 C1
Villagrande (I) 103 G3
Villagrande Strisaili (I) 97 E4
Villa Grazia di Carini (I) 108 D1
Villaharta (E) 125 K3
Villähde (FIN) 36 E3
Villahermosa (E) 126 E2
Villahermosa del Río (E) 121 H3
Villaherreros (E) 111 L4
Villahizán (E) 112 D4
Villahoz (E) 112 D4
Villainclán (E) 111 F1
Villaines-en-Duesmois (F) 77 L6
Villaines-la-Juhel (F) 75 L4
Villajimena (E) 111 L4
Villa Joyosa = Vila Joiosa, La (E) 122 A5
Villala (FIN) 29 K7
Villala (FIN) 37 K3
Villalago (I) 104 A2
Villalangua (E) 92 C6
Villalba (I) 108 E2
Villalba = Vilalba (E) 110 D2
Villalba de Calatrava (E) 126 C2
Villalba del Alcor (E) 128 B3
Villalba de la Sierra (E) 120 D3
Villalba de los Alcores (E) 111 K5
Villalba de los Arcos = Vilalba dels Arcs (E) 121 J1
Villalba de los Barros (E) 125 F2
Villalba de los Morales (E) 121 F2
Villalba del Rey (E) 120 C3
Villalba de Rioja (E) 112 F3
Villalbilla de Burgos (E) 112 D4
Villalcampo (E) 111 G5
Villalcázar de Sirga (E) 112 B4
Villalebrín (E) 111 K4
Villalegre (E) 111 H1
Villalengua (E) 113 H6
Villalgordo del Júcar (E) 120 D5
Villalgordo del Marquesado (E) 120 C4
Villa Literno (I) 104 B3
Villalmanzo (E) 112 D4
Villalobar de Rioja (E) 112 F4
Villalobos (E) 111 J5
Villalón de Campos (E) 112 A4
Villalonga (E) 121 H6
Villalpando (E) 111 J5
Villalpando, Castillo de o Torres Secas (E) 114 B3
Villalpardo (E) 120 E5
Villalquite (E) 111 J3
Villalta (I) 101 F1
Villalube (E) 111 H5
Villaluenga de la Sagra (E) 119 J3
Villaluenga del Rosario (E) 128 D4
Villalumbroso (E) 112 B4
Villálvaro (E) 112 E5
Villalvernia (I) 98 F3
Villamalea (E) 120 E5
Villamañán (E) 111 H4
Villamanín (E) 111 H3
Villamanrique (E) 126 D2
Villamanrique de la Condesa (E) 128 B3
Villamanta (E) 119 H3
Villamar (I) 97 C4
Villamarco (E) 111 J4
Villamartín (E) 125 H6
Villamartín de Campos (E) 112 B4
Villamartín de Don Sancho (E) 112 A3
Villamartín del Sil (E) 111 F3
Villamassargia (I) 97 C5
Villamayor (E) 111 J2
Villamayor (E) 114 B4
Villamayor (E) 118 E1
Villamayor de Calatrava (E) 119 H6
Villamayor de Campos (E) 111 J5
Villamayor de Santiago (E) 120 C4
Villamayor de Treviño (E) 112 C4
Villamblard (F) 83 G6
Villambrán de Cea (E) 112 B4
Villameca (E) 111 G3
Villamediana (E) 112 C4
Villamejil (E) 111 G3
Villamesías (E) 117 K5
Villaminaya (E) 119 J4
Villa Minozzo (I) 99 J4
Villamo (FIN) 28 B7
Villamontán de la Valduerna (E) 111 H4
Villamor de los Escuderos (E) 111 H6
Villamuelas (E) 119 J4
Villamuera de la Cueza (E) 111 K4
Villamuriel de Campos (E) 111 J5
Villamuriel de Cerrato (E) 111 K5
Villanasur-Río de Oca (E) 112 E4
Villandraut (F) 92 D2
Villandry (F) 83 G2
Villaño (E) 112 E3
Villanova (I) 101 F4
Villanova (I) 105 J4
Villanova d'Asti (I) 98 D3
Villanova del Battista (I) 104 D3
Villanovafranca (I) 97 C4
Villanova Marchesana (I) 101 F3
Villanova Mondovì (I) 98 D4
Villanova Monferrato (I) 98 E2
Villanova Monteleone (I) 97 B2
Villanova sull'Arda (I) 100 C2
Villanova Truschedu (I) 97 C4
Villanova Tulo (I) 97 D4
Villanovilla (E) 113 L3
Villanterio (I) 99 G2
Villanubla (E) 111 K5
Villanueva de Alcardete (E) 119 K4
Villanueva de Alcorón (E) 120 D2
Villanueva de Algaidas (E) 128 F3
Villanueva de Araquil (E) 113 H3
Villanueva de Argaño (E) 112 D4
Villanueva de Bogas (E) 120 A4
Villanueva de Cameros (E) 113 F4
Villanueva de Cauche (E) 128 F4
Villanueva de Córdoba (E) 126 A3
Villanueva de Duero (E) 111 K5
Villanueva de Gállego (E) 114 B4
Villanueva de Gumiel (E) 112 D5
Villanueva de Huerva (E) 114 A5
Villanueva de la Cañada (E) 119 H3
Villanueva del Aceral (E) 119 G1
Villanueva de la Concepción (E) 126 A6
Villanueva de la Fuente (E) 126 E2
Villanueva de la Jara (E) 120 E5
Villanueva de la Nía (E) 112 C3
Villanueva de la Peña (E) 112 C2
Villanueva de la Reina (E) 126 C3
Villanueva del Arzobispo (E) 126 D3
Villanueva de las Cruces (E) 124 E4
Villanueva de la Serena (E) 117 K6
Villanueva de la Sierra (E) 118 D3
Villanueva de las Torres (E) 126 D4
Villanueva de la Vera (E) 118 F3
Villanueva del Campo (E) 111 J5
Villanueva del Duque (E) 125 J3
Villanueva del Fresno (E) 124 E3
Villanueva de los Castillejos (E) 124 E4
Villanueva de los Infantes (E) 126 D2
Villanueva del Rey (E) 125 J3
Villanueva del Río y Mina (E) 128 C2
Villanueva del Trabuco (E) 126 B5
Villanueva de Oscos (E) 110 F2
Villanueva de San Carlos (E) 126 C2
Villanueva de San Juan (E) 128 D3
Villanueva de Sijena (E) 114 C4
Villanueva de Tapia (E) 126 B5
Villanueva y Geltrú = Vilanova i la Geltrú (E) 115 G5
Villanuño de Valdavia (E) 112 B3
Villány (H) 158 F6
Villapalacios (E) 126 E2
Villapeceñil (E) 112 A4
Villapiana (I) 105 F6
Villapiana Lido (I) 107 F3
Villa Potenza (I) 101 J6
Villapourçon (F) 84 E3
Villapriolo (I) 109 F2
Villaproviano (E) 111 K4
Villaputzu (I) 97 E5
Villaquejida (E) 111 H4
Villaquilambre (E) 111 H3
Villaquirán de los Infantes (E) 112 C4
Villar (E) 128 D2
Villaralbo (E) 111 H6
Villaralto (E) 125 K3
Villarcayo (E) 112 D3
Villarcazo (E) 111 J2
Villar-d'Arène (F) 85 K6
Villard-Bonnet (F) 85 J6
Villard-d'Abas, le (F) 95 J2
Villard-de-Lans (F) 85 J6
Villar de Arnedo, El (E) 113 G4
Villardebelle (F) 115 H1
Villar de Cañas (E) 120 C4
Villar de Chinchilla (E) 120 E6
Villar de Ciervo (E) 117 H2
Villardeciervos (E) 111 G5
Villar de Corneja (E) 118 F3
Villar de Domingo García (E) 120 D3
Villardefrades (E) 111 J5
Villar de Huergo (E) 111 J2
Villar de la Encina (E) 120 C4
Villar del Arzobispo (E) 121 G4
Villar del Buey (E) 111 G6
Villar del Cobo (E) 120 E3
Villar del Humo (E) 120 E4
Villar de los Navarros (E) 114 A5
Villar del Pedroso (E) 119 F4
Villar del Rey (E) 125 F1
Villar del Río (E) 113 G4
Villar del Salz (E) 120 E2
Villar del Saz de Navalón (E) 120 D3
Villar de Mazarife (E) 111 H4
Villar de Olalla (E) 120 D3
Villar de Olmos (E) 121 F4
Villar de Peralonso (E) 118 D1
Villardiegua de la Ribera (E) 111 G5
Villardompardo (E) 126 B4
Villard-sur-Doron (F) 86 C6
Villarejo de Fuentes (E) 120 C4
Villarejo de Montalbán (E) 119 G4
Villarejo de Salvanés (E) 120 B3
Villarejo-Periesteban (E) 120 D4
Villarente (E) 111 J3
Villares, Los (E) 126 B5
Villares, Los (E) 126 C4
Villares del Saz (E) 120 C4
Villaretto (I) 85 M6
Villargordo (E) 126 C4
Villargordo del Cabriel (E) 120 F4
Villaricos (E) 127 G5
Villarino (E) 111 G6
Villarino del Sil (E) 111 G3
Villarluengo (E) 121 G2
Villarmayor (E) 117 K1
Villarosa (I) 109 F2
Villarquemado (E) 121 F2
Villarramiel (E) 111 K4
Villarrasa (E) 125 F5
Villarreal (E) 124 E2
Villarreal = Vila-real (E) 122 A3
Villarrín de Campos (E) 111 H5
Villarroañe (E) 111 H4
Villarrobledo (E) 120 C5
Villarrodrigo (E) 126 E3
Villarrodrigo de la Vega (E) 112 B4
Villarroquel (E) 111 H3
Villarroya de la Sierra (E) 113 H6
Villarroya de los Pinares (E) 121 G2
Villarrubia (E) 125 K4
Villarrubia de los Ojos (E) 120 A5
Villarrubia de Santiago (E) 119 K4
Villarrubio (E) 120 C4
Villars (F) 76 E5
Villars (F) 83 G6
Villars-Burquin (CH) 85 L3
Villars-les-Dombes (F) 85 H4
Villars-sur-Ollon (CH) 85 M4
Villars-sur-Var (F) 98 C5
Villarta (E) 120 E5
Villarta de los Montes (E) 119 G5
Villarta de San Juan (E) 119 K5
Villasalto (I) 97 D5
Villasana de Mena (E) 112 E2
Villasandino (E) 112 C4
Villa San Giovanni (I) 109 J1
Villa Santa Maria (I) 103 J4
Villa Santina (I) 89 H5
Villasarracino (E) 112 B4
Villasavary (F) 93 J4
Villasayas (E) 113 F6
Villaseca (E) 112 F3
Villaseca de Laciana (E) 111 G3
Villaseco (E) 111 H6
Villaseco de los Gamitos (E) 118 D1
Villaseco de los Reyes (E) 117 J1
Villasequilla de Yepes (E) 119 J4
Villasimius (I) 97 E5
Villasor (I) 97 C5
Villasrubias (E) 118 C3
Villastar (E) 121 F3
Villastellone (I) 98 D3
Villatalla (I) 98 D5
Villatobas (E) 120 B4
Villatoro (E) 119 F2
Villatoya (E) 121 F5
Villatuerta (E) 113 H3
Villaurbana (I) 97 C4
Villaute (E) 112 D3
Villava (E) 92 A5
Villavallelonga (I) 103 H4
Villavaquerín (E) 111 L5
Villa Vela (I) 109 H4
Villaverde de Guadalimar (E) 127 E3
Villaverde de Íscar (E) 112 B6
Villaverde del Monte (E) 112 D4
Villaverde del Río (E) 128 C2
Villaverde de Medina (E) 112 A6
Villaverde de Pontones (E) 112 D2
Villaverde y Pasaconsol (E) 120 D4
Villaverla (I) 99 L1
Villaviciosa (E) 111 J2
Villaviciosa de Córdoba (E) 128 D1
Villaviciosa de Odón (E) 119 J3
Villavieja = Vilavella, La (E) 122 A3
Villavieja de Yeltes (E) 118 D2
Villaviudas (E) 112 C5
Villayón (E) 111 F2
Villchovjec' (UA) 157 M4
Villé (F) 79 G5
Ville-aux-Clercs, La (F) 76 D6
Villebaudon (F) 75 J3
Villebois-Lavelette (F) 83 F6
Villebon (F) 76 D5
Villebrumier (F) 93 G3
Villecerf (F) 77 G5
Villecomtal (F) 93 K1
Villecomtal-sur-Arros (F) 92 E4
Villecroze (F) 95 H3
Villedaigne (F) 94 A4
Villedieu (F) 77 K6
Villedieu, La (F) 94 C1
Villedieu-du-Clain, La (F) 83 F4
Ville-Dieu-du-Temple, La (F) 93 G2
Villedieu-en-Fontenette, la (F) 78 E6
Villedieu-les-Poêles-Rouffigny (F) 75 J3
Villedieu-sur-Indre (F) 83 J3
Villefagnan (F) 82 F4
Villefort (F) 94 C2
Villefranche (I) 86 D6
Villefranche-d'Albigeois (F) 93 J3
Villefranche-d'Allier (F) 84 C4
Villefranche-de-Conflent (F) 115 H2
Villefranche-de-Lauragais (F) 93 H4
Villefranche-de-Lonchat (F) 82 F7
Villefranche-de-Panat (F) 93 K2
Villefranche-de-Rouergue (F) 93 J2
Villefranche-du-Périgord (F) 93 G1
Villefranche-sur-Cher (F) 83 J2
Villefranche-sur-Mer (F) 98 C5
Villefranche-sur-Saône (F) 85 G5
Villegenon (F) 84 C2
Villegongis (F) 83 J3
Villel (E) 121 F3
Villelaure (F) 95 F3
Villel de Mesa (E) 120 E1
Villemade (F) 93 G2
Villemaur-sur-Vanne (F) 77 J5
Villemeux-sur-Eure (F) 76 D4
Villemontais (F) 84 E5
Villemorien (F) 77 K5
Villemur-sur-Tarn (F) 93 H3
Villena (E) 127 J2
Villenauxe-la-Grande (F) 77 J4
Villenave (F) 92 C3
Villenave-d'Ornon (F) 92 C1
Villeneuve (CH) 85 L4
Villeneuve (F) 82 B3
Villeneuve (F) 82 D6
Villeneuve (F) 93 F5
Villeneuve (F) 93 J2
Villeneuve-d'Allier (F) 84 D6
Villeneuve-de-Berg (F) 94 E1
Villeneuve-de-Marsan (F) 92 D3
Villeneuve-d'Olmes (F) 115 G2
Villeneuve-la-Comtesse (F) 82 D4
Villeneuve-la-Guyard (F) 77 H5
Villeneuve-l'Archevêque (F) 77 J5
Villeneuve-le-Comte (F) 77 G4
Villeneuve-lès-Avignon (F) 94 E3
Villeneuve-lès-Béziers (F) 94 B4
Villeneuve-sur-Allier (F) 84 D3
Villeneuve-sur-Cher (F) 84 B2
Villeneuve-sur-Lot (F) 93 F2
Villeneuve-sur-Vère (F) 93 J2
Villeneuve-sur-Yonne (F) 77 H5
Villentrois (F) 83 H2
Villepinte (F) 93 J4
Villequier (F) 76 C2
Villeréal (F) 93 F1
Villerest (F) 84 F5
Villerías de Campos (E) 111 K5
Villerouge-Termenès (F) 115 J1
Villers-aux-Bois (F) 77 J4
Villers-Bocage (F) 68 C7
Villers-Bocage (F) 75 K2
Villers-Bretonneux (F) 76 G2
Villers-Carbonnel (F) 77 G2
Villers-Cotterêts (F) 77 H3
Villersexel (F) 86 B2
Villers-Farlay (F) 85 J2
Villers-la-Ville (B) 69 H5
Villers-le-Gambon (B) 69 H6
Villers-le-Lac (F) 85 L2
Villers-lès-Nancy (F) 78 E4
Villers-sur-Mer (F) 75 M2
Villers-sur-Meuse (F) 78 C3
Villerupt (F) 78 D3
Villerville (F) 75 M2
Villeseneux (F) 77 K4
Villesèque (F) 93 G2
Ville-sur-Illon (F) 78 E5
Ville-sur-Terre (F) 78 B5
Ville-sur-Tourbe (F) 78 B3
Villetelle, La (F) 84 B5
Villetta Barrea (I) 104 A2
Villeurbanne (F) 85 G5
Villeveyrac (F) 94 C4
Villevocance (F) 84 G6
Villiers (F) 83 H3
Villiers-Charlemagne (F) 75 K5
Villiers-en-Bois (F) 82 E4
Villiers-en-Plaine (F) 82 D4
Villiers-Saint-Benoît (F) 77 H6
Villiers-Saint-Georges (F) 77 H4
Villiers-sur-Loir (F) 76 C6
Villikkala (FIN) 36 F3
Villikkala (FIN) 36 G3
Villingaholt (IS) 16 F7
Villinganes (IS) 16 G4
Villingen-Schwenningen (D) 79 J5
Villingsberg (S) 40 G4
Villmanstrand = Lappeenranta (FIN) 37 K2
Villmar (D) 70 F6
Villmergen (CH) 86 F3
Villnöß = Funes (I) 88 F4
Villodrigo (E) 112 C4
Villoldo (E) 112 B4
Villora (E) 120 E4
Villorba (I) 89 G6
Villoria (E) 118 F2
Villorobe (E) 112 E4
Villoruela (E) 118 F1
Villotta (I) 89 H6
Villstad (S) 44 C4
Villtungla (S) 41 J4
Villvattnet (S) 26 G5
Vilminore di Scalve (I) 88 C5
Vil'ne (UA) 171 L1
Vilnes (N) 30 B5
Vilnius (LT) 137 N4
Viloria (E) 113 G3
Vilosell, el (E) 114 E5
Vilov (CZ) 152 D5
Vilovo (SRB) 166 F3
Vilppula (FIN) 28 E7
Vilpulka (LV) 133 L2
Vils (A) 87 L2
Vil'šanka (UA) 163 H2
Vil'šanka (UA) 163 M2
Vil'šany (UA) 156 E5
Vil'šanycja (UA) 151 M4
Vil'šanycja (UA) 157 G4
Vilsbiburg (D) 81 G4
Vilseck (D) 80 F1
Vilsen, Bruchhausen- (D) 65 L6
Vilsheim (D) 80 G4
Vilshofen (D) 80 F2
Vilshofen (D) 81 J3
Vilshult (S) 44 E6
Vil's'k (UA) 151 H3
Vil'ška (UA) 151 K3
Vilskekleva (S) 44 C2
Vilsund-Vest (DK) 42 C5
Vil'šynky (UA) 155 M4
Vilters-Wangs (CH) 87 H3
Viluksela (FIN) 35 M3
Vilūnai (LT) 137 L4
Vilusi (MNE) 173 J4
Vilvestre (E) 118 C1
Vilviestre del Pinar (E) 112 E5
Vilvoorde (B) 69 G5
Vilzēni (LV) 130 H5
Vima Mică (RO) 161 H3
Vimbodí (E) 114 F5
Vimeiro (P) 116 C5
Vimercate (I) 99 G1
Vimianzo (E) 110 A2
Vimieiro (P) 124 D2
Vimioso (P) 111 F5
Vimmerby (S) 44 H3
Vimoutiers (F) 76 B4
Vimpeli (FIN) 28 D5
Vimperk (CZ) 81 K2
Vinac (BIH) 165 J6
Vinaceite (E) 114 B5
Vinadio (I) 95 K2
Vinaixa (E) 114 E5
Vinaròs (E) 122 B2
Vinarovo (BG) 168 D5
Vinaroz = Vinaròs (E) 122 B2
Vinarsko (BG) 177 H3
Vinäs (S) 32 H6
Viñas, Las (E) 126 D5
Vinători (RO) 162 D4
Vinători (RO) 170 E2
Vinay (F) 85 H6
Vinça (F) 115 J2
Vinča (SRB) 167 G4
Vinçan (AL) 178 D3
Vincelles (F) 77 J6
Vinchiaturo (I) 103 K5
Vinci (I) 100 D5
Vinci (MK) 175 G5
Vind (DK) 42 C6
Vindáshlíð (IS) 16 E6
Vindblæs (DK) 42 D5
Vindbyholt (DK) 47 K3
Vindeby (DK) 46 G3
Vindedalen (N) 30 G5
Vindeikiai (LT) 137 M3
Vindelgransele (S) 26 E4
Vindelkroken (S) 25 K2
Vindeln (S) 26 F6
Vinderei (RO) 170 F1
Vinderslev (DK) 42 D6
Vinderup (DK) 42 C6
Vindheimar (IS) 16 E7
Vindhella (N) 30 H5
Vindinge (DK) 47 K2
Vindsvik (N) 38 D4
Vinebre (E) 114 E5
Vinets (F) 77 K4
Vinga (RO) 167 H1
Vingåker (S) 41 J4
Vingelen (N) 31 O3
Vingnes (N) 31 N5
Vingrau (F) 115 J2
Vingsand (N) 24 E6
Vingstad (N) 21 J2
Vinhais (P) 110 E5
Vinica (MK) 175 J5
Vinica (SK) 159 H1
Vinica (SLO) 164 E4
Vinicar (MK) 175 G5
Viniegra de Abajo (E) 112 F4
Viniśće (HR) 172 D3
Vinjak (AL) 178 C4
Vinjall (AL) 174 D5
Vinje (N) 30 F6
Vinje (N) 38 G3
Vinjeøra (N) 24 C8
Vinjestøtta (N) 31 O4
Vinjoll (AL) 174 C5
Vinkara (FIN) 29 L5
Vinkel (DK) 42 D6
Vinkeveen (NL) 69 H2
Vin'kivci (UA) 157 M3
Vinkkilä (FIN) 35 J3
Vinköl (S) 40 D6
Vinkovci (HR) 166 C3
Vinliden (S) 26 D5
Vinnari (FIN) 35 K2
Vinne (N) 24 F7
Vinné (SK) 155 K4
Vinni (EST) 131 K2
Vinnica = Vinnycja (UA) 151 G5
Vinnicy (RUS) 7 U5
Vinninga (S) 40 D6
Vinnycja (UA) 9 L5
Vinnycja (UA) 151 G5
Vinnykivci (UA) 150 F5
Vinograd (BG) 176 E2
Viñón (E) 111 K2
Vinön (S) 41 J4
Vinon-sur-Verdon (F) 95 G3
Vinor (S) 45 P3
Vinromà, Les Coves de (E) 121 J3
Vinsa (S) 21 M7
Vinslöv (S) 47 N1
Vinsternes (N) 24 C8
Vinstra (N) 31 M4
Vintala (FIN) 35 K3
Vintermossen (S) 40 G3
Vintervollen (N) 19 N4
Vintilă Vodă (RO) 170 D3
Vintjärn (S) 33 L6
Vintl = Vandoies (I) 88 F4
Vintrosa (S) 40 G4
Vintu de Jos (RO) 161 G6
Viñuela (E) 126 B6
Viñuela de Sayago (E) 111 H6
Viñuelas (E) 119 K2
Vinuesa (E) 112 F5
Vinzaglio (I) 98 F2
Vinzelberg (D) 66 F5
Viöl (D) 66 A1
Viola (I) 98 D4
Violay (F) 84 F5
Viols-le-Fort (F) 94 C3
Vion (F) 85 G6
Vionnaz (CH) 86 C5
Viozene (I) 98 D4
Vipava (SLO) 89 K6
Vipereşti (RO) 170 C3
Vipiteno (I) 88 E4
Viplaix (F) 84 B4
Vipperød (DK) 47 J2
Vipperow (D) 67 H4
Vir (BIH) 172 F2
Vír (CZ) 153 K4
Vir (HR) 164 E6
Vir (MNE) 173 J4
Vira (HR) 172 D3
Vira (Gambarogno) (CH) 87 G5
Virala (FIN) 35 P3
Virandozero (RUS) 7 U4
Viranşehir (TR) 13 M7
Viranşehir (TR) 199 J2
Viravlja (BY) 139 L2
Virbalis (LT) 143 H1
Virböle = Viirilä (FIN) 36 F3
Vircava (LV) 132 H4
Virda (RUS) 29 L4
Vireda (S) 44 F3
Virenoja (FIN) 36 E3
Vire Normandie (F) 75 K3
Vireši (LV) 131 K6
Virestad (S) 44 E5
Vireux-Wallerand (F) 69 H6
Virgem, Monte (P) 117 F6
Virgen (A) 89 G3
Virgen de la Cabeza (E) 126 B3
Virgen de la Vega (E) 121 G3
Virginia (IRL) 61 H4
Virieu-le-Grand (F) 85 H6
Virje (HR) 165 J2
Virkby = Virkkala (FIN) 36 A4
Virkkala (FIN) 36 A4
Virkkula (FIN) 23 M4
Virkkunen (FIN) 23 K5
Virklund (DK) 46 E1
Virksund (DK) 42 D5
Virmaanpää (FIN) 29 H6
Virmaila (FIN) 36 D2
Virmutjoki (FIN) 37 L2
Virneburg (D) 70 D6
Virojoki (FIN) 37 J3
Virolahden kirkonkylä (FIN) 37 J3
Vironchaux (F) 68 B6
Virónia (GR) 180 C2
Virove (BG) 175 K1
Virovitica (HR) 158 D6
Virovsko (BG) 176 A2
Virpazar (MNE) 173 K5
Virpe (LV) 130 B6
Virrankylä (FIN) 23 L4
Virrat (FIN) 28 D7
Virring (DK) 42 F6
Virsbo (S) 41 K3
Virserum (S) 44 H4
Viršužiglis (LT) 137 L4
Virtaa (FIN) 36 E2
Virtaniemi (FIN) 19 L6
Virtasalmi (FIN) 29 H7
Virton (B) 78 D2
Virtsu (EST) 130 E3
Virttaa (FIN) 35 L3
Viru-Jaagupi (EST) 131 K2
Viru-Nigula (EST) 36 G6
Virville (F) 76 B2
Viry (F) 86 B5
Vis (HR) 172 D3
Viš (MNE) 173 K4
Visag (RO) 167 J2
Visaginas (LT) 134 B6
Visaille, La (I) 85 L5
Višakio Rūda (LT) 137 J4
Visan (F) 94 E2
Vişani (RO) 170 E3
Visbek (D) 65 J6
Visby (DK) 42 B5
Visby (S) 45 N3
Visé (B) 69 K5
Višegrad (BIH) 173 K2
Visegrád (H) 159 G2
Višegrad Banja (BIH) 166 D6
Viserba (I) 101 H4
Viseu (P) 116 F2
Vişeu de Jos (RO) 161 J2
Vişeu de Sus (RO) 161 J2
Visiedo (E) 121 F2
Vişina (RO) 169 J4
Vişineşti (RO) 170 B3
Visingsö (S) 43 O2
Viška (UA) 155 M4
Viskafors (S) 44 B3
Viskan (S) 33 L3
Viskedal (N) 30 E5
Viski (LV) 138 E1
Visland (N) 38 E5
Vislanda (S) 44 E5
Višlevo (RUS) 134 H3
Višļi (LV) 132 E3
Visnes (N) 38 B4
Višneva (BY) 138 D5
Višněvcy (BY) 138 F4
Višnevka (RUS) 37 M4
Višnevo (BY) 138 E4
Vişniovca (MD) 163 G6
Višnja Gora (SLO) 89 M6
Višnjan (HR) 101 K2
Višnjevac (HR) 166 C2
Višnjica (SRB) 167 G4
Višnjića Do (MNE) 173 J3
Višnjićevo (SRB) 166 D4
Višňová (CZ) 73 N4
Višňové (CZ) 91 K2
Visnum (S) 40 F4
Visnumskil (S) 40 F4
Viso, El (E) 125 K3
Visoca (MD) 162 F2
Visočka Ržana (SRB) 175 J2
Viso del Alcor, El (E) 128 C3
Viso del Marqués (E) 126 C2
Visoka (SRB) 174 C1
Visoko (BIH) 166 B6
Visoko (SLO) 164 C2
Visone (I) 98 F3
Višovgrad (BG) 176 D2
Visp (CH) 86 E5
Vispvallen (S) 32 E2
Viss (H) 155 K5
Vissani (GR) 178 D5
Vissefjärda (S) 44 H5
Visselhövede (D) 66 B5
Visseltofta (S) 44 D6
Vissenbjerg (DK) 46 F3
Vissinéa (GR) 178 E3
Visso (I) 103 G2
Vissoie (CH) 86 E5
Vistabella (E) 114 A5
Vistabella del Maestrat (E) 121 H3
Vistabella del Maestrazgo = Vistabella del Maestrat (E) 121 H3
Vistasstugorna (S) 21 H4
Vistheden (S) 22 C5
Visthus (N) 25 G3
Vistino (RUS) 37 K5
Vistorp (S) 43 N2
Vištytis (LT) 143 H2
Visuvesi (FIN) 28 D7
Vita (I) 108 C2
Vitåfors (S) 27 J3
Vitănești (RO) 169 J5
Vitanje (SLO) 164 E2
Vitanovac (SRB) 167 G6
Vitanovac (SRB) 174 E1
Vitanovac (SRB) 174 F2
Vitanvaara (FIN) 23 K5
Vitaperä (FIN) 23 K6
Viťaz (SK) 155 H4
Vitberget (S) 26 G3
Vitebsk = Vicebsk (BY) 139 M3
Vitemölla (S) 47 O2
Viterbo (I) 102 E3
Vitez (BIH) 173 G1
Vithkuq (AL) 178 D3
Viti (EST) 36 B6
Viti (RKS) 174 F4
Vitigudino (E) 117 J1
Vitina (BIH) 173 F3
Vitína (GR) 186 E4
Vitina = Viti (RKS) 174 F4
Vītiņi (LV) 137 H1
Vitino (RUS) 37 N5
Vitis (A) 153 H6
Vitkovo (SRB) 174 F2
Vitkov Wigstadl (CZ) 154 B2
Vitkovyči (UA) 150 D1
Vitolište (MK) 179 F2
Vitomirica = Vitumirusë (RKS) 174 D3
Vitonice (CZ) 153 K6
Vitorchiano (I) 102 E3
Vitoria-Gasteiz (E) 113 F3
Vitoševac (SRB) 175 G1
Vitovlje (BIH) 165 K6
Vitrac (F) 93 G1
Vitrac-Saint-Vincent (F) 83 G5
Vitré (F) 75 J4
Vitrey-sur-Mance (F) 78 D6
Vitrolles (F) 95 F4
Vitrolles (F) 95 G3
Vitry-aux-Loges (F) 76 F6
Vitry-en-Artois (F) 68 D6
Vitry-le-Croisé (F) 77 L5
Vitry-le-François (F) 77 L4
Vitry-sur-Seine (F) 76 F4
Vitsakumpu (FIN) 23 H1
Vitsikkopalo (FIN) 18 F8
Vitt (D) 67 J1
Vittajoki (FIN) 23 K7
Vittangi (S) 22 D1
Vittaryd (S) 43 N5
Vitte (D) 67 J1
Vitteaux (F) 84 G2
Vittel (F) 78 D5
Vittiko (FIN) 23 L3
Vittinge (S) 41 M3
Vittjärn (S) 40 C2
Vittjärv (S) 27 H3
Vittoria (I) 109 G4
Vittorio Veneto (I) 89 G6
Vittorp (S) 41 K4
Vittsjö (S) 43 N6
Vitulano (I) 103 K5
Vitumirusë (RKS) 174 D3
Vituniči (BY) 138 G4
Vitvattnet (S) 27 K2
Vitzenburg (D) 71 N4
Vitzlj (UA) 156 C4
Vitznau (CH) 86 F3
Viù (I) 98 C2
Viuf (DK) 46 D2
Viuhkola (FIN) 36 H2
Viul (N) 39 M2
Viuruniemi (FIN) 29 J6
Vivar del Cid (E) 112 D4
Vivares (E) 125 H1
Vivario (F) 96 E4
Vivariu = Vivario (F) 96 E4
Vivaro (I) 89 H5
Vivastbo (S) 41 L2
Vive (DK) 42 F5
Viveda (E) 112 C2
Viveiro (E) 110 D1
Viveiró (E) 110 D2
Vivel del Río Martín (E) 114 B6
Vivelstadsvea (N) 31 P5
Viver (E) 121 G4
Viverols (F) 84 E6
Viveros (E) 120 C6
Vivestad (N) 39 M4
Viviers (F) 94 E2
Vivier-sur-Mer, Le (F) 75 H3
Vivild (DK) 42 F6
Vivljunga (S) 44 D5
Vivonne (F) 83 F4
Vivsja (UA) 157 H3
Vivsja (UA) 157 K3
Vivsjanyky (UA) 151 H5
Vivungi (S) 21 M5
Vivunperä (FIN) 27 M8
Vivy (F) 75 L6
Vix (F) 82 D4
Vizcaínos (E) 112 E4
Vize (TR) 177 J5
Vizić (SRB) 166 D3
Vizille (F) 85 J6
Vižinada (HR) 101 K2
Viziru (RO) 170 F3
Vizítsa (GR) 180 C6
Vizovice (CZ) 154 B3
Vizsoly (H) 155 J5
Vizvár (H) 158 D5
Vizzavona (F) 96 E4
Vizzini (I) 109 G3
Vjalikae Sjalo (BY) 138 G3
Vjalikae Vosava (BY) 139 J5
Vjalikaja Berastavica (BY) 143 L4
Vjalikaja Maščanica (BY) 139 L6
Vjalikaja Mažėjkava (BY) 143 M3
Vjalikaryta (BY) 149 K2
Vjalikie Čučavičy (BY) 144 E3
Vjalikie Dofcy (BY) 139 H3
Vjalikija Ejsmanty (BY) 143 L4
Vjalikija Lětcy (BY) 139 L3
Vjalikija Lipavičy (BY) 139 K4
Vjalikija Stajki (BY) 139 L3
Vjaliki Sjalo (BY) 138 E6
Vjaliki Vjazok (BY) 139 K5
Vjaljacičy (BY) 139 J5
Vjarchove (BY) 139 K4
Vjarchovičy (BY) 143 K6
Vjarėčča (BY) 139 M2
Vjaréjcy (BY) 145 J2
Vjarhi (BY) 143 L6
Vjarhovity (BY) 143 J6
Vjarhučina (BY) 144 H3
Vjartsilja (RUS) 7 S5
Vjartsilja (RUS) 29 L7
Vjarzjki (BY) 143 L4
Vjaseja (BY) 144 G2
Vjašovka (BY) 139 K4
Vjatčyn (BY) 145 H4
Vjazavnica (BY) 145 J2
Vjaz'e (BY) 145 J2
V'jazivka (UA) 151 H1
Vjaz'ma (BY) 145 L2
Vjazovec (UA) 150 C4
Vjazovoe (RUS) 135 L4
Vjazyn' (BY) 138 F5
Vjetrenik (BIH) 166 C6
VjR'ma (RUS) 7 T7
Vlaardingen (NL) 69 G3
Vlachovice (CZ) 154 B3
Vlachovo (SK) 155 G4
Vlachovo Březí (CZ) 81 K2
Vlad (AL) 174 D4
Vlădeni (RO) 162 D3
Vlădeni (RO) 162 E4
Vlădeni (RO) 170 B4
Vlădeni (RO) 170 F4
Vlădeşti (RO) 169 G3
Vlădeşti (RO) 169 H3
Vlădeşti (RO) 171 G2
Vladičin Han (SRB) 175 H3
Vlădila (RO) 169 G5
Vladilovce (MK) 179 F1
Vladimir (MNE) 174 B4
Vladimir (RO) 168 F4
Vladimir (Andreesti) (RO) 168 F4
Vladimirci (SRB) 166 E4
Vladimirec (RUS) 134 H3
Vladimirescu (RO) 167 H1
Vladimirovac (SRB) 167 G3
Vladimirovci (BG) 177 G1
Vladimirovka (RUS) 37 O3
Vladimirovo (BG) 175 K1
Vladimirovo (BG) 177 J1
Vladimirskij (RUS) 37 O5
Vladimirskoe (RUS) 7 T7
Vladinja (BG) 176 C2
Vladislav (CZ) 153 J5
Vlad Tepeș (RO) 170 E5
Vlăduleni (RO) 169 G5
Vladyčen' (UA) 171 H2
Vladyčna (UA) 162 C2
Vladyčnoe (RUS) 7 V6
Vladyslavka (UA) 151 M4
Vlagtwedde (NL) 64 G5
Vlaháta (GR) 186 B3
Vlahava (GR) 179 F5
Vlahérna (GR) 186 E4
Vlahiá (GR) 188 C2
Vlahii (RO) 170 F5
Vlahióti (GR) 187 F6
Vlăhita (RO) 161 M5
Vlahnë (AL) 174 D4
Vlahokerassiá (GR) 186 E5
Vlahović (HR) 165 G4
Vlahovići (BIH) 173 H3
Vlahovo (BG) 181 F1
Vlajkovac (SRB) 167 H3
Vlajkovci (SRB) 174 E2
Vlajnovići (SRB) 166 D5
Vlaka (HR) 172 D3
Vlakča (SRB) 167 G5
Vlaole (SRB) 168 B5
Vlasatice (CZ) 91 K2
Vlase (SRB) 175 G3
Vlasenica (BIH) 173 J1
Vlashuk (AL) 178 B3
Vlašići (HR) 164 E6
Vlašim (CZ) 153 G4
Vlașin (RO) 170 B5
Vlasina Okruglica (SRB) 175 H3
Vlasina Rid (SRB) 175 H3
Vlăsinești (RO) 157 L6
Vlaška (SRB) 167 G5
Vlaški Do (SRB) 167 H5
Vlaško Polje (MNE) 174 C3
Vlasotince (SRB) 175 H3
Vlatten (D) 69 M5
Vlazovo (RUS) 134 G3
Vlčany (SK) 158 E1
Vlčice (CZ) 153 J2
Vlčnov (CZ) 154 B3
Vledder (NL) 64 E6
Vlesno (RUS) 134 F4
Vleuten (NL) 69 J2
Vlijmen (NL) 69 J3
Vlissingen (NL) 68 F4
Vlkava (CZ) 153 G3
Vlkolínec (SK) 154 E3
Vlohós (GR) 179 G5
Vlönkylä (FIN) 35 L4
Vlorë (AL) 178 A4
Vlotho (D) 71 G2
Vluyn, Neukirchen- (D) 69 M4
Vnorovy (CZ) 153 M6
Vnučki (RUS) 135 N4
Vnučkove (UA) 156 E5
Vo (I) 101 F2
Vobarno (I) 99 K1
Vochabni (BY) 138 F4
Voćin (HR) 165 K3
Vöcklabruck (A) 89 K1
Vöcklamarkt (A) 89 J1
Voden (BG) 176 D5
Voden (BG) 176 E4
Vodeničane (BG) 177 G3
Vodeničarsko (BG) 176 D6
Voderady (SK) 154 B5
Vodica (BG) 176 F2
Vodica (BIH) 172 F1
Vodicë (AL) 178 D4
Vodice (HR) 101 L2
Vodice (HR) 172 C2
Vodinci (HR) 166 C3
Vodjanyky (UA) 151 M5
Vodná (CZ) 73 H5
Vodna (SRB) 168 B5
Vodňany (CZ) 152 F5
Vodnjan (HR) 164 B5
Vodnjanci (BG) 175 J1
Vodno (BG) 176 F2
Vodnyky (UA) 156 F2
Vodobeg (RUS) 134 H4
Vodokrty (CZ) 81 J1
Vodotyn (UA) 151 J3
Vodovrat (MK) 175 G5
Vodskov (DK) 42 F4
Vodycja (UA) 161 H1
Voe (GB) 49 F3
Voel (DK) 46 E1
Voer (DK) 42 F5
Voerde (Niederrhein) (D) 69 M3
Voerendaal (NL) 70 A5
Voerladegård (DK) 46 E1
Voersá (DK) 42 F4
Vœuil-et-Giget (F) 82 F5
Vogar (IS) 16 D7
Vogatsikó (GR) 178 E4
Vogelsberg (D) 71 M4
Vögelsen (D) 65 N5
Voghenza (I) 101 F3
Voghera (I) 98 G3
Vognill (N) 31 M2
Vognsild (DK) 42 D5
Vogogna (I) 86 F5
Vogošća (BIH) 166 B6
Vogt (D) 80 B5
Vogtareuth (D) 90 B4
Vogtei (D) 72 C3
Vogüé (F) 94 D1
Vohburg an der Donau (D) 80 F3
Vohenstrauß (D) 81 G1
Vöhl (D) 71 G4
Võhma (EST) 130 B3
Võhma (EST) 131 J3
Võhmuta (EST) 131 J2
Vohonovo (RUS) 37 N5
Vöhrenbach (D) 79 J5
Vöhringen (D) 79 K5
Vöhringen (D) 80 C4
Vöhrum (D) 66 C6
Vohtoga (RUS) 7 W6
Voiakkala (FIN) 22 G5
Voicești (RO) 169 G4
Void-Vacon (F) 78 D4
Voikkaa (FIN) 36 G3
Voikoski (FIN) 36 G2
Voila (RO) 161 K6
Voilemont (F) 77 L3
Voilovo (RUS) 135 M6
Voiluoto (FIN) 34 H2
Voina (RO) 169 J3
Voineasa (RO) 169 F3
Voinești (RO) 169 J3
Voinsalmi (FIN) 29 J7
Voiron (F) 85 J6
Voismaut (A) 91 J4
Võiste (EST) 130 F4
Voiteg (RO) 167 H3
Voiteur (F) 85 J3
Voitoinen (FIN) 35 K2
Voitsberg (A) 91 H5
Voitsdorf (A) 89 L1
Võivaku (EST) 131 J4
Voivodeni (RO) 161 K4
Vojakkala (FIN) 36 B3
Vojany (SK) 155 K4
Vojens (DK) 46 D3
Vojislavci (MK) 180 A1
Vojka (SRB) 166 F4
Vojlovica (SRB) 167 G4
Vojmån (S) 26 C5
Vojnić (HR) 164 F4
Vojnica (BG) 167 L6
Vojnica (RUS) 7 S3
Vojnica (RUS) 23 N6
Vojnidenjaty (BY) 138 D4
Vojnik (MK) 175 G4
Vojnik (SLO) 164 E2
Vojnika (BG) 177 G4
Vojnjagovo (BG) 176 C3
Vojnův Městec (CZ) 153 J4
Vojnyčeve (UA) 163 K4
Vojnyliv (UA) 156 F3
Vojšanci (MK) 175 H6
Vojska (SRB) 167 H5
Vojskaja (BY) 143 K6
Vojskovicy (RUS) 37 N5
Vojstom (BY) 138 E4
Vojtanov (CZ) 73 G5
Vojtivci (UA) 151 H5
Vojtjajaurekapell (S) 25 K3
Vojtkavičy (BY) 143 M4
Vojutyči (UA) 156 D2
Vojvoda (BG) 177 H2
Vojvoda Stepa (SRB) 167 G2
Vojvodino (BG) 177 J2
Vojvodinovo (BG) 176 C4
Voka (EST) 37 J6
Vokana (BY) 139 J4
Vokil (BG) 170 E6
Voknavolok (RUS) 7 S4
Voknavolok (RUS) 29 L2
Voksa (N) 30 C3
Vokslev (DK) 42 E5
Vólakas (GR) 176 B6
Volary (CZ) 90 E2
Voľberavičy (BY) 138 G4
Volbu (N) 31 L5
Volčja Draga (SLO) 89 K6
Volda (N) 30 E3
Voldby (DK) 42 G6
Voldby (DK) 46 E1
Volden (N) 31 O2
Volders (A) 88 F3
Volduchy (CZ) 152 E4
Voldum (DK) 42 F6
Volendam (NL) 69 J2
Volenice (CZ) 81 K2
Volenseter (N) 31 M5
Volesy = Valjasy (BY) 139 H1
Volgoverhov'e (RUS) 135 O3
Volgovo (RUS) 37 N5
Volgsele (S) 26 C5
Volhov (RUS) 7 S6
Volímes (GR) 186 B4
Volintiri (MD) 163 K6
Volissós (GR) 189 G3
Volja (BY) 143 L6
Volja Baranec'ka (UA) 156 D2
Volja-Blaživs'ka (UA) 156 D3
Voljice (BIH) 173 G2
Voľka (BY) 144 C3
Voľka (BY) 144 D3
Voľka-1-ja (BY) 144 E4
Volkach (D) 72 C6
Volkenschwand (D) 80 F3
Völkermarkt (A) 90 G6
Volketswil (CH) 87 G3
Völklingen (D) 78 F3
Volkmarsen (D) 71 H4
Volkošiv (UA) 150 D2
Volkovija (MK) 174 E5
Volkovija (MK) 174 F5
Volkovo (BY) 139 N4
Volkovynci (UA) 150 F5
Volkringhausen (D) 70 E4
Voll (N) 30 G2
Voll (N) 31 O6
Voll (N) 39 L4
Volleberg (N) 42 A2
Vollen (N) 18 A4
Vollen (N) 31 N3
Völlenerfehn (D) 64 G5
Vollenhove (NL) 64 D6
Vollersode (D) 65 K5
Vollerup (DK) 65 L2
Völlinghausen (D) 70 F4
Vollnes (N) 30 D3
Vollom (N) 30 C6
Vollrathsruhe (D) 67 G3
Vollseter (N) 30 F3
Vollseter (N) 31 M4
Vollum (N) 31 N4
Volma (BY) 138 G6
Volmunster (F) 79 G3
Voľnja (UA) 151 J3
Volnovacha (UA) 9 N5
Voločaevka (RUS) 37 N4
Voločys'k (UA) 150 C4
Volodarka (UA) 151 K4
Volodars'k-Volynskyj = Chorošiv (UA) 151 G2
Voloder (HR) 165 H3
Volodymyrec' (UA) 144 D6
Volodymyrivka (UA) 163 M3
Volodymyr-Volyns'kyj (UA) 149 K4
Vologda (RUS) 7 W6
Voloiac (RO) 168 E4
Volojarvi (RUS) 37 P4
Volok (RUS) 135 M4
Voloka (UA) 157 J5
Volokolamsk (RUS) 7 U7
Volokovoe (RUS) 135 L4
Vólos (GR) 180 B6
Vološča (UA) 156 E2
Volosivci (UA) 157 M2
Volosjanka (UA) 156 C4
Volosjanka (UA) 156 D4
Vološky (UA) 149 L3
Volosovo (RUS) 7 R6
Volot (RUS) 135 L2
Volovăț (RO) 157 J6
Volovec' (UA) 156 D4
Volovo (BG) 176 E1
Volovo (RUS) 9 P4
Volpago del Montello (I) 88 G6
Volpriehausen (D) 71 J3
Vöis (A) 88 E3
Völs am Schlern = Fiè allo Sciliar (I) 88 E4
Volsemenhusen (D) 46 D6
Volsted (DK) 42 E5
Voltaggio (I) 98 F3
Volta Mantovana (I) 99 K2
Voltana (I) 101 F3
Volterra (I) 99 K6
Voltlage (D) 70 E2
Voltri (I) 98 F4
Voltti (FIN) 27 J8
Volturara Irpina (I) 104 C4
Volturino (I) 104 D3
Voluja (SRB) 167 J5
Volujac (SRB) 166 E4
Volum (N) 32 C5
Voluntari (RO) 169 L5
Volvera (I) 98 D3
Volvic (F) 84 D5
Volx (F) 95 G3
Volyсja (BY) 144 B5
Volycja (UA) 149 J5
Volycja (UA) 151 J3
Volycja (UA) 151 K3
Volycja-Druha (UA) 157 L2
Volyně (CZ) 152 E5
Volyns'kyj, Novohrad- (UA) 150 F2
Volynskyj, Volodars'k- (UA) 151 G2
Volyns'kyj, Volodymyr- (UA) 149 K4
Volyšovo (RUS) 135 J2
Vomúlastaðir (IS) 16 F7
Vonêche (B) 69 H6
Vonešta Voda (BG) 176 E3
Vónitsa (GR) 178 D7
Vonnas (F) 85 G4
Võnnu (EST) 131 M4
Vönöck (H) 91 M5
Vooobu (EST) 131 H2
Vööpsu (EST) 134 E1
Voorburg (NL) 69 G2
Voorschoten (NL) 69 G2
Voorthuizen (NL) 69 K2
Vopnafjörður (IS) 17 M3
Vopša (RUS) 37 O5
Vörå (FIN) 28 C5
Voran' (BY) 139 J3
Voranava (BY) 138 B5
Vorau (A) 91 J5
Vorbasse (DK) 46 D2
Vorchdorf (A) 89 K2
Vorde (DK) 42 D5
Vorden (NL) 70 B2
Vörden, Neuenkirchen- (D) 70 F1
Vorderkaser = Casera di Fuori (I) 88 D4
Vorderlanersbach (A) 88 F3
Vorderriß (D) 80 E5
Vorderstoder (A) 81 L5
Vordingborg (DK) 47 J3
Vordónia (GR) 194 A1
Vorë (AL) 174 C6
Voreppe (F) 85 J6
Vorey (F) 84 E6
Vorhelm (D) 70 E3
Vóri (GR) 195 F5
Vorinó (GR) 179 G2
Vormsele (S) 26 E5
Vormstad (N) 24 D8
Vormsund (N) 39 O2
Vormträsk (S) 26 E5
Vorna (FIN) 23 H8
Vorniceni (RO) 157 L6
Vorob'i (RUS) 135 M5
Vorobino (RUS) 135 H1
Vorobjove (UA) 163 L4
Vorobleviči (UA) 156 E3
Vorochta (UA) 156 G5
Vorona (RO) 162 D3
Voroncovo (RUS) 134 G3
Vorone (UA) 151 L5
Voronež (RUS) 9 P4
Voroniči (BY) 138 E4
Voronjaky (UA) 157 G2
Voronkiv (UA) 151 M3
Voronkova Niva (RUS) 134 H3
Voronovo (RUS) 135 M1
Voronovycja (UA) 151 H5
Voronzovo (RUS) 135 P6
Voropajiv (UA) 151 M2
Voropajivka (UA) 151 L2
Vorošilovo (RUS) 135 O4
Vorotkovo (RUS) 135 J5
Voroźba (UA) 9 N4
Vorring (DK) 42 E5
Vorselaar (B) 69 H4
Vorsfelde (D) 66 D6
Vorsivka (UA) 151 J2
Vorst (D) 70 B4
Vorța (RO) 167 L1
Võru (EST) 133 P2
Vorwerk (D) 65 L5
Vorzel' (UA) 151 L2
Vosa (BY) 149 K2
Vosava (BY) 138 G4
Vosava (BY) 145 J2
Vosavcy (BY) 149 M1
Vosiliškis (LT) 137 K2
Voskop (AL) 178 D3
Voskopojë (AL) 178 D3
Voșlăbeni (RO) 162 B5
Voss (N) 30 E6
Vostrav (BY) 144 C3
Vostrav (UA) 144 D5
Vostrava (BY) 138 H3
Vostrava (BY) 143 N4
Võsu (EST) 131 J1
Votice (CZ) 81 M1
Votolino (RUS) 135 P2
Votonóssi (GR) 178 E5
Vou (F) 83 G2
Voŭčyn (BY) 143 J6
Voúdia (GR) 195 E2
Voué (F) 77 K5
Vougy (F) 84 F4
Vougy (F) 85 K4
Vouhé (F) 82 D4
Vouillé (F) 82 F3
Vouillé-les-Marais (F) 82 D4
Vouillon (F) 83 J3
Voukoliés (GR) 194 D5
Voúla (GR) 188 C4
Vouliagméni (GR) 188 C4
Voúlpi (GR) 179 F6
Voulte-sur-Rhône, La (F) 94 E1
Voulx (F) 77 G5
Voúnargo (GR) 186 C4
Vouneuil-sous-Biard (F) 83 F3
Vouneuil-sur-Vienne (F) 83 G3
Vouni (CY) 198 E6
Vounihora (GR) 186 E3
Vouno = Kaynakköy (CY) 199 F5
Voŭpa (BY) 143 L4
Vourkári (GR) 188 D4
Vourliótes (GR) 190 B5
Voúrvoura (GR) 187 E5
Vourvouroú (GR) 180 D4
Voussac (F) 84 D4
Voutás (GR) 194 D5
Voutenay-sur-Cure (F) 77 J6
Voutiáni (GR) 187 E5
Vouvant (F) 82 D3
Vouvry (CH) 85 L4
Vouzailles (F) 82 F3
Vouzela (P) 116 E2
Vouzeron (F) 83 K2
Voúzi (GR) 179 G6
Vouziers (F) 78 B3
Vouzon (F) 76 F6
Vovčans'k (UA) 9 O4
Vovče (UA) 156 C3
Vovčkiv (UA) 151 K1
Vovčkovci (UA) 157 H5
Vovčok (UA) 151 N1
Voves (F) 76 E5
Vovkavščyna (BY) 138 F2
Vovkovyj (UA) 150 A3
Vowchurch (GB) 57 J1
Voxna (S) 33 K5
Voxnabruk (S) 33 J5
Voxtorp (S) 43 O4
Voxtorp (S) 45 J5
Vöyri = Vörå (FIN) 28 C5
Vožega (RUS) 7 W5
Vozera (BY) 144 F1
Vozgjaljancy (BY) 138 E3
Vozilići (HR) 101 L2
Voznesenka (UA) 171 J1
Voznesens'k (UA) 9 M5
Voznice (CZ) 152 F4
Voznyči (UA) 145 H5
Vozroždenie (RUS) 37 L3
Vozsijats'ke (UA) 9 M5
Vozuča (BIH) 166 B5
Vožyna (BY) 145 J1
Vrå (DK) 42 E4
Vrå (S) 44 C5
Vrabča (BG) 175 J3
Vráble (SK) 154 C5
Vraca (BG) 175 L2
Vračeš (BG) 175 L3
Vračev Gaj (SRB) 168 A4
Vraćevšnica (SRB) 167 G5
Vracov (CZ) 153 M6
Vrådal (N) 39 H4
Vradijivka (UA) 163 M3
Vráha (GR) 179 F6
Vraháti (GR) 187 F4
Vrahnéika (GR) 186 D3
Vraie-Croix, La (F) 74 F5
Vrakún (SK) 154 B6
Vråliosen (N) 38 H4
Vrana (HR) 164 C5
Vrana (HR) 172 C2
Vranče (MK) 174 F6
Vrâncioaia (RO) 170 D2
Vranduk (BIH) 166 A5
Vrångfall (S) 45 J3
Vrångö (S) 43 J3
Vrani (RO) 168 B3
Vranić (SRB) 166 F4
Vranići (BIH) 173 J2
Vrani Kon (BG) 177 G2
Vranilovci (BG) 176 D3
Vranino (BG) 177 K1
Vranja (HR) 101 L2
Vranjak (BG) 176 A2
Vranjak (BIH) 165 L5
Vranje (SRB) 175 G3
Vranjina (MNE) 173 K5
Vranjit (AL) 174 D5
Vranjska (BIH) 173 H3
Vranjska Banja (SRB) 175 H3
Vrankunge (S) 44 F5
Vranov (CZ) 152 C5
Vranovice (CZ) 91 L2
Vranov nad Dyjí (CZ) 153 J6
Vranov nad Topľou (SK) 155 K4
Vranovo (SRB) 167 G4
Vransko (SLO) 164 D2
Vrap (AL) 178 B2
Vrapčići (BIH) 173 G3
Vrapčište (MK) 174 E5
Vrástama (GR) 179 K4
Vratarnica (SRB) 168 C6
Vratimov (CZ) 154 C2
Vrátna (SK) 154 E3
Vratna (SRB) 167 K5
Vratnica (MK) 174 F4
Vrăv (BG) 167 L5
Vravróna (GR) 187 J4
Vražogrnac (SRB) 167 K6
Vrba (MNE) 174 B2
Vrbanj (HR) 172 E3
Vrbanja (BIH) 165 J5
Vrbanja (HR) 166 C4
Vrbanjci (BIH) 165 J5
Vrbanje (MNE) 173 J4
Vrbanovec (HR) 165 H2
Vrbas (SRB) 166 E2
Vrbaška (BIH) 165 J4
Vrbeštica = Verbeshticë (RKS) 174 E4
Vrbica (SRB) 175 H1
Vrbka (CZ) 153 H4
Vrbnica = Vërmicë (RKS) 174 E4
Vrbnik (HR) 164 D4
Vrbno pod Pradědem (CZ) 147 G5
Vrboska (HR) 172 E3
Vrbov (SK) 155 G3
Vrbovce (SK) 154 A4
Vrbové (SK) 154 B4
Vrbovec (HR) 158 B6
Vrbovsko (HR) 164 E4
Vrčenovica (SRB) 175 G2
Vrchlabí (CZ) 153 J2
Vrchotovy Janovice (CZ) 152 G4
Vrčin (SRB) 167 G4
Vrdnik (SRB) 166 E3
Vrdy (CZ) 146 C6
Vrebac (HR) 164 E5
Vrecourt (F) 78 D5
Vreden (D) 69 M2
Vrees (D) 65 H6
Vrela = Vrelë (RKS) 174 D3
Vrelë (RKS) 174 D3
Vrelo (SRB) 166 F5
Vrelo (SRB) 175 G2
Vrelo Koreničko (HR) 164 F5
Vremski Britof (SLO) 164 C3
Vrena (S) 41 L5
Vrengen (N) 39 M4
Vreoci (SRB) 166 F5
Vresovo (BG) 177 H3
Vresse-sur-Semois (B) 77 L2
Vrésthena (GR) 187 E5
Vrestó (GR) 186 D4
Vreta (FIN) 35 L4
Vretstorp (S) 40 G4
Vrev (RUS) 134 G3
Vrgada (HR) 172 C2
Vrginmost = Gvozd (HR) 164 F4
Vrgorac (HR) 173 F3
Vrh (HR) 164 D4
Vrhnika (SLO) 89 L6
Vrhovine (HR) 164 E5
Vrhpolje (BIH) 165 H5
Vrhpolje (SRB) 173 K1
Vrhprača (BIH) 173 J2
Vridsted (DK) 42 D6
Vries (NL) 64 F5
Vriezenveensewijk, Westerhaar- (NL) 70 C2
Vrigne-au-Bois (F) 78 B2
Vrigstad (S) 44 E4
Vrin (CH) 87 H4
Vrinners (DK) 46 F1
Vrísses (GR) 186 D5
Vrísses (GR) 194 E5
Vrissiá (GR) 179 G6
Vrissohóri (GR) 178 D5
Vrissoúla (GR) 178 D6
Vrlika (HR) 172 D2
Vrmdža (SRB) 175 G1
Vrnčani (SRB) 166 F6
Vrnjačka Banja (SRB) 174 E1
Vrnograč (BIH) 165 F4
Vron (F) 68 B6
Vrondádos (GR) 189 H3
Vronderó (GR) 178 E3
Vrondoú (GR) 179 G4
Vrontamás (GR) 187 F6
Vroomshoop (NL) 70 C2
Vrossina (GR) 178 D5
Vrpile (HR) 164 F5
Vrpolje (HR) 166 B3
Vrpolje (HR) 172 D2
Vrrith (SRB) 174 D4
Vršac (SRB) 167 H3
Vršani (BIH) 166 D4
Vrsar (HR) 164 B4
Vršatské Podhradie (SK) 154 C3
Vrsi (HR) 164 E6
Vrtoče (BIH) 165 G5
Vrubllvka (UA) 150 F3
Vruda (RUS) 37 M6
Vrulja (MNE) 173 K3
Vrulje (HR) 172 B2
Vrutice (CZ) 146 A4
Vrútky (SK) 154 D3
Vrutok (MK) 174 E5
Všestary (CZ) 153 J3
Všetaty (CZ) 152 G3
Vsetín (CZ) 154 B3
Vsevoložsk (RUS) 37 P4
Vsini (RUS) 134 H1
Vsteselovo (RUS) 135 L5
Vuarrens (CH) 85 L3
Vuča (MNE) 174 D3
Vučiniće (SRB) 174 D2
Vučitrn = Vushtri (RKS) 174 E3
Vučje (SRB) 175 G3
Vučkovica (SRB) 167 G6
Vue (F) 82 B2
Vught (NL) 69 J3
Vugly (BY) 144 C3
Vugly (BY) 145 M5
Vujetinci (SRB) 167 G6
Vujinovača (SRB) 173 L1
Vuka (HR) 166 C3
Vukanja (SRB) 175 G2
Vukël (AL) 173 L5
Vukova Gorica (HR) 164 E4
Vukovar (HR) 166 D3
Vukovići (MNE) 174 B4
Vuku (N) 24 F7
Vulcan (RO) 168 E3
Vulcan (RO) 169 J2
Vulcana-Băi (RO) 169 J3
Vulcana-Pandele (RO) 169 J3
Vulcănești (MD) 171 G2
Vuľka (BY) 144 D4
Vuľka Abrovskaja (BY) 144 B3
Vulkan, Kvartal (BG) 176 E4
Vulpeni (RO) 168 F5
Vulpești (RO) 169 H4
Vultureni (RO) 161 H4
Vultureni (RO) 162 E6
Vulturești (RO) 162 C3
Vulturești (RO) 162 F5
Vulturești (RO) 169 G4
Vulturu (RO) 170 E2
Vulturu (RO) 171 G4
Vuoggatjålme (S) 20 F7
Vuohčču = Vuotso (FIN) 19 K7
Vuohijärvi (FIN) 36 G2
Vuohiniemi (FIN) 36 B3
Vuohtomäki (FIN) 28 G4
Vuojalahti (FIN) 29 G8
Vuojärvi (FIN) 23 J2
Vuojat stugorna (S) 21 H7
Vuokatti (FIN) 29 J3
Vuoksenniska (FIN) 37 L2
Vuolenkoski (FIN) 36 F2
Vuolijoki (FIN) 29 G3
Vuolijoki (FIN) 35 O2
Vuolleriebme = Vuollerim (S) 21 K8
Vuollerim (S) 21 K8
Vuomajärvi (S) 22 F4
Vuomatakka (N) 18 D5
Vuonisjärvi (FIN) 29 L5
Vuonislahti (FIN) 29 L5
Vuontisjärvi (FIN) 18 G7
Vuontispirtti (FIN) 18 G7
Vuorenkylä (FIN) 36 E1
Vuorenmaa (FIN) 29 H8
Vuorenmaa (FIN) 35 L2
Vuoreslahti (FIN) 29 H3
Vuorijärvi (FIN) 28 C7
Vuorijarvi (RUS) 23 N3
Vuorilahti (FIN) 27 M9
Vuorimäki (FIN) 28 D6
Vuorimäki (FIN) 29 H4
Vuoriniemi (FIN) 37 M1
Vuorz = Waltensburg (CH) 87 H4
Vuosaari (FIN) 35 Q4
Vuosanka (FIN) 23 M8
Vuoskojaure (S) 18 C7
Vuosnainen (FIN) 34 H3
Vuostimo (FIN) 23 K3
Vuotinainen (FIN) 35 O3
Vuotlahti (FIN) 29 J5
Vuotso (FIN) 19 K7
Vuottas (S) 21 L8
Vuottesjávri = Vuontisjärvi (FIN) 18 G7
Vuottolahti (FIN) 29 H3
Vuotunki (FIN) 23 M4
Vuovdaguoika = Outakoski (FIN) 19 H4
Vurben (BG) 176 C4
Vurbovo (BG) 175 J1
Vurhari (BG) 175 L5
Vurpăr (RO) 161 J6
Vusanje (MNE) 174 C3
Vusav (BY) 145 J5
Vusce (BY) 139 M5
Vushtri (RKS) 174 E3
Vuško (UA) 151 G5

Zabalac' (BY) 137 M6
Zabalacce (BY) 139 M6
Zabalacce (BY) 139 N6
Zabalacce (BY) 145 L2
Zabalat' (BY) 144 G3
Žabalj (SRB) 166 F3
Zabalocce (BY) 138 F4
Zabalocce (BY) 139 H6
Zabalocce (BY) 139 J4
Zabalocce (BY) 139 L5
Zabalocce (BY) 139 L6
Zabalocce (BY) 145 J3
Zabaloccie (BY) 145 N3
Zabar (H) 154 G5
Zabărdo (BG) 180 F1
Žabari (SRB) 167 H5
Zabaro-Davydivka (UA) 150 E2
Zabartowo (PL) 141 J4
Zabašavičy (BY) 139 J5
Zabeile (BY) 139 L3
Zabelsdorf (D) 67 J4
Zabel'sko (RUS) 131 O4
Zaberfeld (D) 79 K3
Žabica (BIH) 173 H4
Zabiče (SLO) 164 C3
Zábiedovo (SK) 154 F3
Zabiele (PL) 142 F4
Zabierzów (PL) 154 F1
Zabiločyja (UA) 151 J3
Žabinec (RUS) 134 H2
Žabinka (BY) 149 K1
Zabirja (UA) 151 L3
Ząbki (PL) 142 E6
Ząbkowice Śląskie (PL) 153 L2
Zablaće (SRB) 167 F6
Žabljak (MNE) 173 K3
Žabljak (MNE) 173 K5
Zabłudów (PL) 143 J4
Żabnica (PL) 154 E2
Żabno (PL) 155 H1
Zabok (HR) 165 F2
Žabokreky nad Nitrou (SK) 154 C4
Žabokryč (UA) 163 J2
Žabokryčka (UA) 163 J2
Zabolotci (UA) 149 K4
Zabolotci (UA) 157 G1
Zabolotiv (UA) 157 H5
Zabolottja (UA) 149 K2
Zabolottja (UA) 161 F2
Zaborcy (BY) 138 G4
Zabor'e (BY) 139 J4
Zabor'e (RUS) 135 O4
Zabor'e (RUS) 138 G4
Zaboroľ (UA) 149 M4
Zaboroľ (UA) 150 C2
Zaborów (PL) 148 C1
Zaborów (PL) 155 H1
Zaborowice (PL) 146 F2
Zaborowo (PL) 147 G1
Zabory (RUS) 135 O6
Żabów (PL) 140 C4
Żabowo (PL) 67 N3
Zăbrani (RO) 167 J1
Zabrđe (BIH) 166 C4
Zabrđe (MNE) 173 K3
Zabrđe (SRB) 174 B1
Zabrdje = Zabrđe (MNE) 173 K3
Zabrdje = Zabrđe (SRB) 174 B1
Zabrega (SRB) 168 A4
Zábřeh (CZ) 146 F6
Žabren (SRB) 174 D2
Zabrez'e (BY) 138 D5
Zăbriceni (MD) 162 E2
Zabrnie (PL) 148 D5
Zabrnie Dolne (PL) 148 E4
Zabrnjica (SRB) 174 B1
Zabroddze (BY) 139 M5
Zabrowo (PL) 142 A3
Zabrze (PL) 147 K5
Zabrzeg (PL) 147 K6
Zabrzeż (PL) 155 G2
Zabujannja (UA) 151 K2
Zabužžja (UA) 149 J3
Zabzuni (AL) 178 C2
Zacharivka (UA) 163 K4
Zacharivka (UA) 163 M3
Zacharni (BY) 138 G2
Zacharzew (PL) 147 H2
Zacharzowice (PL) 147 K5
Záchlumí (CZ) 152 C4
Žacléř (CZ) 146 D4
Začysce (BY) 139 J5
Žadany (UA) 151 J5
Zadar (HR) 172 B1
Zădăreni (RO) 167 H1
Zadariv (UA) 157 H3
Žadeikoniai (LT) 137 L1
Žaden (UA) 144 E5
Zaderijivka (UA) 145 N5
Zadežža (BY) 134 F6
Zádielske Dvorníky (SK) 155 H4
Žaďky (UA) 151 H2
Zador'e (RUS) 135 O6
Žadricy (RUS) 134 H4
Zadub'e (BY) 144 D3
Zadub'e (BY) 145 N2
Zadubenne (BY) 138 F4
Zadubrivci (UA) 162 A1
Zadubrov'e (BY) 139 N3
Zadunaivka (UA) 171 J2
Žadvainiai (LT) 136 F2
Zadyby (UA) 149 L3
Zadzetuni (BY) 139 N3
Zadzim (PL) 147 K2
Zadzveja (BY) 144 D2
Zaesse (BY) 139 J4
Zafarraya (E) 126 B6
Zaferiye (TR) 192 D3
Zafferana Etnea (I) 109 H2
Zafirovo (BG) 170 D6
Zafra (E) 125 G3
Zafra de Záncara (E) 120 C4
Zafrilla (E) 120 E3
Žaga (SLO) 164 A2
Zagacce (BY) 145 L1
Zagajica (SRB) 167 H4
Żagań (PL) 146 C2
Zagăr (RO) 161 K5
Zagaradna (BY) 139 N3
Zagarane (BY) 139 M2
Žagarė (LT) 132 G5
Žagarinė (LT) 137 N5
Zagarise (I) 107 G5
Zagarolo (I) 103 F4
Zaglav (HR) 172 B2
Zaglavak (SRB) 166 E6
Zaglavica (BIH) 165 G6
Zagłobień (PL) 155 K1
Zagnańsk (PL) 148 C4
Zagon (RO) 170 C2
Zagoni (BIH) 166 D4
Zagorá (GR) 180 C6
Zagora (MNE) 173 J5
Zagora (MNE) 173 K4
Zagorci (BG) 176 E4
Zagorci (BG) 177 H4
Zagorica (SLO) 164 D3
Zagoriče (BG) 177 H1
Zagorje ob Savi (SLO) 164 E2
Zagórnik (PL) 149 J4
Zagorów (PL) 147 H1
Zagórsko (PL) 148 D5
Zagorskoe (RUS) 136 F4
Zagórz (PL) 155 L2
Zagórze (PL) 154 E1
Zagórze Śląskie (PL) 146 E4
Zagra (E) 126 B5
Zagra (RO) 161 J3
Zagrad (MNE) 174 C3
Zagrađe (SRB) 167 K5
Zagrađe (SRB) 168 C6
Zagradje (SRB) 167 F5
Zagražden (BG) 176 C1
Zagražden (BG) 181 F1
Zagreb (HR) 165 F3
Zagrilla (E) 126 B5
Zagriv'e (RUS) 131 N2
Zagrivje (RUS) 134 E4
Zagrodno (PL) 146 D3
Žagubica (SRB) 168 B5
Zagumienie (PL) 149 H2
Zagvozd (HR) 172 F3
Zagwiździe (PL) 147 H4
Zahajki (PL) 149 G2
Zahaľci (UA) 151 K2
Zahara (E) 125 J6
Zahara de los Atunes (E) 128 C5
Zaharničy (BY) 139 J2
Zaháro (GR) 186 D4
Zahattja (UA) 156 C5
Zahinci (UA) 157 M3
Zahínos (E) 125 F3
Zahir'a (UA) 156 F3
Zahirja (UA) 150 A4
Zahman (TR) 191 G3
Zahna-Elster (D) 73 H2
Zahnitkiv (UA) 163 H2
Zahodskoe (RUS) 37 M4
Zahody (RUS) 134 E3
Zahody (RUS) 134 F1
Zahon'e (RUS) 135 K2
Záhony (H) 155 L5
Záhor (SK) 155 L4
Zahor'e (BY) 139 J3
Zahor'e (BY) 139 K2
Záhoří (CZ) 81 L2
Záhorská Ves (SK) 91 L3
Zahrádky (CZ) 152 G2
Zahrensdorf (D) 66 D4
Zahrisht (AL) 174 D4
Zăicani (MD) 157 M6
Zaidín (E) 114 D4
Žaiginys (LT) 137 J3
Zailov'e (RUS) 135 O5
Zaim (MD) 163 J5
Zainingen (D) 79 M5
Zaisertshofen (D) 80 D4
Zaistovec (HR) 158 B5
Zajača (SRB) 166 D5
Zajačkivka (UA) 163 K1
Zajączki Bankowe (PL) 147 J2
Zajączków (PL) 148 B4
Zajamnjae (BY) 144 E1
Zajas (MK) 174 E5
Zajcevo (RUS) 7 S6
Zajcevo (RUS) 37 M2
Zajcevo (RUS) 142 D2
Zaječar (SRB) 167 K6
Zaječov (CZ) 152 E4
Zajezierze (PL) 142 B3
Zajezierze (PL) 148 E2
Zajkava (BY) 139 N2
Zajkovo (RUS) 135 M4
Žakai (LT) 136 G3
Zakaľnoe (BY) 144 G3
Zákamenné (SK) 154 E3
Zákány (H) 165 H2
Zákányszék (H) 159 J5
Zákas (GR) 178 E4
Zákinthos (GR) 186 B4
Zakliczyn (PL) 148 C6
Zaklików (PL) 148 F4
Zaklin'e (RUS) 131 O3
Zaklin'e (RUS) 135 J2
Zaklopača (BIH) 173 K1
Zakopane (PL) 154 F3
Zákopčie (SK) 154 D3
Zakroczym (PL) 142 D6
Zákros (GR) 195 J5
Zakrzew (PL) 148 C3
Zakrzewo (PL) 141 H4
Zakrzewo (PL) 141 L5
Zakrzów (PL) 147 J5
Zakrzów (PL) 149 G3
Zakrzów (PL) 154 F2
Zakrzówek-Osada (PL) 148 F4
Zakucce (BY) 145 K1
Zakupne (UA) 157 K3
Zákupy (CZ) 152 G2
Zalabaksa (H) 91 L6
Zalabér (H) 91 M6
Zalaceeva (BY) 143 M4
Zalacsány (H) 91 M6
Zalaegerszeg (H) 91 L6
Zalaháshágy (H) 158 C4
Zalahtov'e (RUS) 131 N4
Zalakaros (H) 165 J1
Zalakomár (H) 165 J1
Zalakoppány (H) 91 M6
Zalalövő (H) 91 L6
Zalamea de la Serena (E) 125 H2
Zalamea la Real (E) 125 F4
Žalany (CZ) 73 K4
Zalas (PL) 154 F1
Zalasowa (PL) 148 D6
Zalaszabar (H) 91 M6
Zalaszántó (H) 158 D4
Zalaszentbalázs (H) 165 H1
Zalaszentgrót (H) 91 M6
Zalaszentlászló (H) 91 M6
Zalatárnok (H) 158 C4
Zalatuha (BY) 145 L4
Zalău (RO) 161 G3
Zalaudvarnok (H) 91 M6
Zalav'ja (UA) 144 F6
Załazy (PL) 148 E3
Zalazzja (BY) 149 M2
Zaldibar (E) 113 F2
Žalec (SLO) 164 E2
Żalęcino (PL) 67 N4
Załęcze (PL) 146 F2
Zalenieki (LV) 132 H4
Zales'e (BY) 138 E5
Zales'e (RUS) 135 J2
Zales'e (RUS) 136 F4
Zales'e (UA) 149 J3
Zalesie (PL) 149 H1
Zalesie Śląskie (PL) 147 J5
Zalesse (BY) 138 G3
Zalesse (BY) 139 J2
Zalesse (BY) 139 K3
Zalesse (BY) 145 N3
Zaleszany (PL) 143 K5
Zaleszany (PL) 148 E4
Zalewo (PL) 141 N3
Zalha (RO) 161 H3
Zalisci (UA) 150 B4
Zalisci (UA) 150 D6
Zališčyky (UA) 162 B1
Zalissja (UA) 151 J1
Zalivnoe (RUS) 136 D4
Zalizci (UA) 150 A4
Zaliznyčne (UA) 163 L4
Zaljadynne (BY) 144 B5
Zalla = Mimetiz (E) 112 E2
Zall i Dardhës (AL) 174 D5
Zall i Gjogjesh (AL) 174 D5
Zallkuq (RKS) 174 E3
Zalnoc (RO) 160 F3
Zalog (SLO) 89 M5
Zalogovac (SRB) 174 F1
Zálongo (GR) 178 D5
Zálongo (GR) 178 D6
Zalosem'e (RUS) 134 F5
Zaloseme (RUS) 134 F5
Založci = Zalizci (UA) 150 A4
Žalpiai (LT) 137 H3
Zaltbommel (NL) 69 J3
Žălti Brjag (BG) 176 E5
Žaludok (BY) 143 M3
Záluží (CZ) 73 K4
Zalužne (UA) 150 F3
Zalužža (BY) 144 E2
Zalužža (BY) 144 H2
Zalužža (BY) 145 H2
Zalužžja (UA) 157 L1
Zalve (LV) 133 L5
Zalyšany (UA) 151 K1
Zalyvanščyna (UA) 151 H4
Zam (RO) 168 C1
Zamačulle (BY) 139 L6
Zamárdi (H) 158 E4
Zamarte (PL) 141 H3
Zamascjany (BY) 143 M3
Zamašša I (BY) 139 H3
Zamastočča (BY) 138 G4
Zamastočča (BY) 139 M3
Žamberk (CZ) 153 K3
Zambra (E) 128 F3
Zambrana (E) 112 F3
Zâmbreasca (RO) 169 H5
Zambrów (PL) 142 G5
Zambrzyce (PL) 154 F2
Zambujeira do Mar (P) 124 B4
Zamch (PL) 149 H5
Zamechiv (UA) 150 E6
Zamfirovo (BG) 175 K2
Zamočok (UA) 156 E1
Zamogiľe (RUS) 131 N3
Zámoly (H) 158 F3
Zamora (E) 111 H6
Zamość (PL) 149 H4
Zamosce (BY) 144 G2
Zamosce (BY) 145 L4
Zamoš'e (RUS) 134 G2
Zamoški (RUS) 135 K2
Zamošša (BY) 138 F3
Zamošša (BY) 139 H5
Zamošša (BY) 139 L4
Zamošša (BY) 145 H5
Zamosťe (RUS) 37 O3
Zamostea (RO) 157 K6
Zamostja (UA) 162 A2
Zamostoč'e (RUS) 134 H2
Zams (A) 87 L3
Zamšany (BY) 149 K2
Zamšany (UA) 149 L2
Zámutov (SK) 155 K4
Zamyslovyči (UA) 150 F1
Žandov (CZ) 146 A4
Zandt, 't (NL) 64 F5
Zandvoort (NL) 69 H2
Zănești (RO) 162 D5
Zangenstein (D) 81 G2
Zanglivéri (GR) 180 C3
Zaniemyśl (PL) 147 G1
Zaniże (PL) 149 J4
Zănoaga (RO) 169 G5
Zante (LV) 132 F4
Zaorejas (E) 120 D2
Zaostrog (HR) 172 F3
Zaostrov'e (RUS) 37 O3
Zaovine (SRB) 166 D6
Zaozer'e (RUS) 139 O3
Zaozernoe (RUS) 142 F2
Zapadynci (UA) 150 E4
Zapałów (PL) 156 C1
Zapasiški (BY) 134 E6
Zapfendorf (D) 71 L6
Zapillja (UA) 149 J3
Zápio (GR) 180 A6
Zapod (AL) 174 E4
Zăpodeni (RO) 162 F5
Zapole (PL) 147 K3
Zapole (PL) 148 E5
Zapol'e (RUS) 7 R6
Zapol'e (RUS) 37 N6
Zapoľe (RUS) 135 L3
Zapolie (BY) 139 L6
Zapoljarnyj (RUS) 19 N5
Zapolle (BY) 139 N2
Zapolle (BY) 143 L4
Zapolle (BY) 144 C2
Zapolle (BY) 145 L2
Zaporižžja (UA) 9 O5
Zaporožskoe (RUS) 7 S5
Zaporožskoe (RUS) 37 P3
Zapovednoe (RUS) 136 E3
Zapponeta (I) 104 E3
Zaprešić (HR) 164 F3
Zaprosse (BY) 144 F4
Zaprudka (UA) 151 K2
Zaprudne (UA) 151 M4
Zaprudynci (UA) 151 J4
Zapuntel (HR) 164 D6
Zaputki (BY) 139 K5
Zapyškis (LT) 137 K4
Zapytiv (UA) 149 K6
Zara (TR) 13 M6
Zarabkovičy (BY) 144 D2
Zaraevo (BG) 177 F2
Zaragoza (E) 114 B4
Zarajsk (RUS) 9 P3
Zărand (RO) 160 D5
Zarańsko (PL) 140 E3
Zarasai (LT) 138 D2
Zaratán (E) 112 B5
Zarautz (E) 113 G2
Zarbince (SRB) 175 G3
Zarcilla de Ramos (E) 127 G4
Zaręba Górna (PL) 146 C3
Zaręby Kościelne (PL) 142 G5
Zaréčča (BY) 138 G5
Zaréčča (BY) 139 L2
Zarèčča (BY) 139 L5
Zareč'e (RUS) 134 H2
Zareč'e (RUS) 134 H5
Zarec'e (RUS) 136 D4
Zarečensk (RUS) 7 S3
Zaréčka (BY) 149 M1
Žarėnai (LT) 132 E6
Zarenthien (D) 66 D4
Zaričanka (UA) 150 C6
Zariččja (UA) 145 J6
Zariččja (UA) 149 L3
Zariččja (UA) 156 G4
Zaričevo (UA) 155 M4
Zarične (UA) 144 D5
Żarki (PL) 147 L4
Žarki (RUS) 135 J4
Zárkos (GR) 179 G5
Žarkovskij (RUS) 135 O6
Zărnești (RO) 169 J2
Zărnevo (BG) 177 H1
Zarnik (BG) 170 F6
Žarnovica (SK) 154 D5
Żarnów (PL) 148 B3
Żarnowiec (PL) 141 K1
Żarnowiec (PL) 148 A5
Żarnówka (PL) 154 F2
Zarnsdorf (A) 91 H3
Zarodišči (RUS) 134 G5
Zaroevo (RUS) 135 P3
Zaroj (BY) 144 C2
Zaronica (BG) 176 C5
Zaronova (BY) 139 L3
Zarós (GR) 195 F5
Zaroúhla (GR) 186 E4
Žarovnica (HR) 165 G2
Zarów (PL) 146 E4
Zarožje (SRB) 173 L1
Zarpen (D) 65 O4
Zarrendorf (D) 67 J2
Zarrentin am Schaalsee (D) 66 D3
Zarren-Werken (B) 68 D4
Zarszyn (PL) 155 L2
Zarubanae (BY) 145 J5
Zarubynci (UA) 151 J3
Zaruč'e (RUS) 131 P3
Zarudaŭe (BY) 143 L4
Zaruddja (UA) 151 K2
Zarudnia (PL) 149 J3
Zarvanci (UA) 151 G5
Žary (BY) 139 J3
Żary (PL) 146 C2
Žary (RUS) 135 K4
Zarza, La (E) 112 B6
Zarza-Capilla (E) 119 F6
Zarza da Alange (E) 117 J6
Zarza de Granadilla (E) 118 D3
Zarza de Pumareda, La (E) 117 H1
Zarza de Tajo (E) 119 K3
Zarzadilla de Totana (E) 127 G4
Zarza la Mayor (E) 117 H4
Zarzecze (PL) 147 L3
Zarzecze (PL) 155 J2
Zarzosa (E) 113 G4
Zarzuela (E) 120 D3
Zarzuela del Monte (E) 119 H2
Zarzuela del Pinar (E) 112 C6
Żarzyn (PL) 140 D6
Zas (E) 110 B2
Zás = Zas (E) 110 B2
Zasa (LV) 133 M5
Zasavica (SRB) 166 E4
Zašeek (RUS) 7 S3
Zaseki (RUS) 134 G1
Zaselica (RUS) 135 N4
Zasiadki (PL) 149 G1
Zasieki (PL) 73 M2
Zasincy (BY) 145 J5
Zasitino (RUS) 134 F5
Zaskarki (BY) 139 J3
Žaškiv (UA) 151 L5
Zaskoviči (BY) 138 E5
Žaskovyči (UA) 149 K4
Zaslav'e (BY) 138 F5
Žasliai (LT) 137 M4
Zaslonava (BY) 139 J4
Zasmjano (BG) 177 J2
Zásmuky (CZ) 146 C6
Zasów (PL) 155 J1
Zaspa (BY) 145 N4
Zastávka (CZ) 153 K5
Zastavna (UA) 162 B1
Zastavne (UA) 149 K4
Zastavne (UA) 149 K6
Zastawa, Adamowo- (PL) 143 J6
Zastražišće (HR) 172 E3
Zastronie (PL) 148 C3
Zasulle (BY) 144 E1
Zasvir (BY) 138 D4
Žatec (CZ) 152 E3
Zatesy (BY) 139 N4
Zatoka (UA) 171 L1
Zaton (HR) 172 C2
Zaton (MNE) 174 C2
Zatonie (PL) 146 D2
Zatonje (SRB) 168 A4
Zator (PL) 147 L6
Zator (PL) 148 B2
Zatory (PL) 142 E5
Zaturci (UA) 149 L4
Zatyššja (UA) 163 K4
Zaube (LV) 133 L4
Zauchseehaus (A) 89 J3
Zauchwitz (D) 73 J1
Zau de Câmpie (RO) 161 J4
Zauliče (BY) 138 F3
Zaumsko (SRB) 174 C2
Zaunhof (A) 87 L3
Žaury (BY) 139 L3
Zauzan (RO) 160 F3
Závada pod Čiernym vrchom (SK) 154 C4
Zavadiv (UA) 156 D1
Závadka (SK) 155 L4
Zavadka (UA) 156 D3
Zavadka (UA) 156 F3
Zavala (BG) 175 J3
Zavala (BIH) 173 G4
Zavala (HR) 172 E3
Zavalatica (HR) 172 E4
Zavalinë (AL) 178 C3
Zavaliv (UA) 157 H3
Zavalje (BIH) 164 F5
Zavallja (UA) 163 L2
Zavar (SK) 154 B5
Zavattarello (I) 100 A3
Zaveľcy (BY) 138 D4
Zaventem (B) 69 G5
Zavernjajka (RUS) 134 G4
Zavet (BG) 177 G1
Zavetnoe (RUS) 37 N2
Zavidčycy (BY) 144 D4
Zavidovići (BIH) 165 L6
Zavišyna (BY) 138 G5
Zav"jazanci (UA) 156 D2
Zavlaka (SRB) 166 D5
Zăvoaia (RO) 170 E4
Závod (SK) 91 M2
Zavodivka (UA) 163 M4
Zavodnje (SLO) 164 E2
Zăvoi (RO) 167 K2
Zavoj (MK) 178 D2
Zavoľša (BY) 139 N4
Zavolžsk (RUS) 7 W6
Zavračica (BG) 175 L4
Zavucce (BY) 138 H3
Zavydiv (UA) 149 L4
Zawada (PL) 141 M6
Zawada (PL) 146 D2
Zawada (PL) 148 B6
Zawada (PL) 149 H4
Zawady-Kolonia (PL) 147 K3
Zawadzkie (PL) 147 J4
Zawichost (PL) 148 E4
Zawidów (PL) 153 H1
Zawiercie (PL) 147 L5
Zawiść (PL) 147 H4
Zawodzie (PL) 147 M2
Zawoja (PL) 154 F2
Zawonia (PL) 147 G3
Zažėvičy (BY) 144 G3
Zázrivá (SK) 154 E3
Zazymja (UA) 151 M2
Žbandaj (HR) 164 B4
Žbany (RUS) 139 J1
Zbaraž (UA) 157 J2
Zbarzewo (PL) 146 E2
Zbąszyń (PL) 146 D1
Zbąszynek (PL) 146 D1
Zbečno (CZ) 73 K5
Zbehy (SK) 154 C5
Zberki (PL) 147 G1
Zbiersk (PL) 147 J2
Zbiroh (CZ) 73 K6
Zblewo (PL) 141 K3
Zbljany (BY) 144 B1
Zboj (SK) 156 B3
Zbójna (PL) 142 F4
Zbójno (PL) 141 M4
Zbojstica (SRB) 166 E6
Zboriv (UA) 157 H2
Zborov (SK) 155 J3
Zborovice (CZ) 153 M5
Zborów (PL) 148 C5
Zborowice (PL) 155 H2
Zborowskie (PL) 147 K4
Zbrachlin (PL) 141 K4
Zbraslav (CZ) 146 A6
Zbraslavice (CZ) 153 H4
Zbryž (UA) 150 C6
Zbucz (PL) 143 J5
Zbuczyn Poduchowny (PL) 148 F1
Zburaž (BY) 149 J2
Zbýšov (CZ) 153 H4
Zbytowa (PL) 147 G3
Ždala (HR) 165 J2
Ždaňa (SK) 155 J4
Ždanavičy (BY) 139 N5
Ždánice (CZ) 153 M5
Ždanivka = Vijtivci (UA) 150 F4
Ždanovičy (BY) 138 F6
Žd'ár (CZ) 152 D3
Žd'ár (CZ) 153 H2
Žd'árec (CZ) 153 K5
Žd'árná (CZ) 153 L5
Žd'ár nad Sázavou (CZ) 153 J4
Zděchov (CZ) 154 C3
Zdechovice (CZ) 153 H3
Ždėheli (BY) 138 E3
Zdenci (HR) 166 A2
Ždenijevo (UA) 156 C4
Ždiar (SK) 155 G3
Zdiby (CZ) 146 A5
Zdice (CZ) 73 K6
Zdíkovec (CZ) 81 K2
Ždírec nad Doubravou (CZ) 153 J4
Zdobnice (CZ) 146 E5
Zdolbuniv (UA) 150 C2
Zdomyšel' (UA) 149 K2
Zdounky (CZ) 153 M5
Zdovbycja (UA) 150 C3
Zdrajsh (AL) 178 C2
Ždralovi (HR) 158 C6
Zdravec (BG) 177 F2
Zdravec (BG) 177 J2
Zdravinje (SRB) 174 F2
Ždrelo (SRB) 168 B5
Zdrój, Lądek (PL) 146 F5
Zdrój, Świeradów- (PL) 153 H2
Zdudzičy (BY) 145 L3
Zdunje (MK) 174 F5
Zduńska Wola (PL) 147 K2
Zduny (PL) 147 G2
Zduny (PL) 148 A1
Zdżary (PL) 148 B2
Zdżary (PL) 155 J1
Ździary (PL) 148 F4
Zdziechów (PL) 148 C3
Zdziechowice (PL) 148 F4
Zdzieszowice (PL) 147 J5
Zdziłowice (PL) 149 G4
Zdzitava (BY) 143 N6
Žebětín (CZ) 153 K5
Zebil (BG) 170 D6
Zebil (RO) 171 H4
Zębowice (PL) 147 J4
Žebrák (CZ) 73 K6
Žebráky (CZ) 152 C4
Zebreira (P) 117 G4
Zebrene (LV) 132 F4
Zeče (SLO) 164 E2
Zečevo Rogozničko (HR) 172 C2
Zechin (D) 140 B5
Zechlin, Flecken (D) 67 H4
Zechlinerhütte (D) 67 H4
Zeddam (NL) 69 L3
Zedelgem (B) 68 E4
Zederhaus (A) 89 K3
Žedna (BG) 175 J4
Żednia (PL) 143 J4
Žedricy (RUS) 135 H3
Zeebrugge (B) 68 E4
Zeeland (NL) 69 K3
Zeetze (D) 66 D4
Zeewolde (NL) 69 K2
Zegama (E) 113 G3
Zegerscappel (F) 59 M6
Żegiestów-Zdrój (PL) 155 H3
Žeglarci (BG) 177 H1
Zeglingen (CH) 86 E3
Żegocina (PL) 155 G2
Žegra = Zhergë (RKS) 175 F4
Zegrze Południowe (PL) 142 E6
Zegrze Pomorskie (PL) 140 F2
Žegulja (BIH) 173 H3
Zehdenick (D) 67 J5
Zehlendorf (D) 67 J5
Zehna (D) 66 G3
Žehra (SK) 155 H4
Zehren (D) 73 J3
Zehrental (D) 66 F5
Žehuň (CZ) 153 H3
Žehušice (CZ) 146 C6
Zeil am Main (D) 72 D5
Zeilarn (D) 90 C3
Zeilfeld (D) 71 L6
Žeimelis (LT) 133 J5
Žeimiai (LT) 132 G6
Žeimiai (LT) 137 L3
Zeiningen (CH) 79 H6
Zeinisjochhaus (A) 87 K4
Zeisholz, Cosel- (D) 73 K3
Zeist (NL) 69 J2
Zeithain (D) 73 J3
Zeitlarn (D) 80 G2
Zeitlofs (D) 71 J6
Zeitz (D) 72 G3
Žejane (HR) 164 C4
Żejtun (M) 109 G6
Zekeriyaköy (TR) 184 A4
Żelazna (PL) 141 J1
Żelazna (PL) 147 G4
Żelazna (PL) 148 B2
Żelazna Góra (PL) 141 O2
Żelazno (PL) 153 L3
Żelazowa Wola (PL) 148 B1
Želdeč (UA) 156 F1
Zele (B) 68 G4
Želeč (CZ) 152 G5
Želechlinek (PL) 148 B2
Żelechów (PL) 148 C1
Żelechów (PL) 148 E2
Zelena (UA) 157 L5
Zelenaja Rošča (RUS) 37 M4
Zelená Lhota (CZ) 152 D5
Zelenče (UA) 150 D6
Zelencovo (RUS) 142 F1
Zelenčukskaja (RUS) 13 N4
Zelene (UA) 144 D5
Zelene (UA) 150 A5
Zelengora (BIH) 173 J3
Zeleni Jadar (BIH) 173 K1
Zelenik (SRB) 168 B4
Zelenika (MNE) 173 J5
Zelenikovo (BG) 176 D4
Zelenikovo (MK) 175 G5
Zeleni Kurylivci (UA) 162 E1
Zelen'kovo (RUS) 135 O5
Zelen'ky (UA) 151 M4
Zelenoborskij (RUS) 7 T3
Zelenogirs'ke (UA) 163 L3
Zelenogorsk (RUS) 7 R5
Zelenogorsk (RUS) 37 N4
Zelenogradsk (RUS) 136 C4
Zelenycja (UA) 151 G2
Zelenyj Mys (UA) 151 L1
Želetava (CZ) 153 J5
Železari (BG) 176 E6
Železná Breznica (SK) 154 E4
Železna Kapla = Bad Eisenkappel (A) 90 G7
Železna Kapla-Bela = Eisenkappel-Vellach (A) 90 G7
Železná Ruda (CZ) 81 J2
Železné (SK) 154 E4
Železnica (BG) 175 K3
Železnice (CZ) 153 H3
Železnik (BG) 177 G3
Železnik (SRB) 166 F4
Železniki (SLO) 89 L5
Železno (RUS) 135 J3
Železnodorožnyj (RUS) 142 E2
Železný Brod (CZ) 153 H2
Zelhem (NL) 70 B2
Zelichów (PL) 148 C5
Želiezovce (SK) 158 G1
Želino (MK) 174 F5
Zélio (GR) 188 A2
Żelisławiec (PL) 67 M4
Żelistrzewo (PL) 141 K1
Želiv (CZ) 153 H4
Želivec (CZ) 73 M6
Żelizna (PL) 149 G2
Željezno Polje (BIH) 166 A5
Željuša (BIH) 173 G3
Želju Vojvoda (BG) 177 F3
Zelki (PL) 142 G3
Żelkowo (PL) 141 H1
Zell (D) 80 E3
Zell (D) 81 G2
Zell (LU) (CH) 86 E3
Zell (Mosel) (D) 70 D6
Zella-Mehlis (D) 72 D4
Zell am Harmersbach (D) 79 J5
Zell am Moos (A) 90 D4
Zell am See (A) 81 H6
Zell am Ziller (A) 88 F3
Zell an der Pram (A) 81 K4
Zellerfeld, Clausthal- (D) 71 K3
Zellerndorf (A) 91 J2
Zell im Fichtelgebirge (D) 72 F5
Zell im Wiesental (D) 79 H6
Zellingen (D) 72 B6
Zell-Pfarre (A) 90 F7
Želno (RUS) 135 N4
Želovce (SK) 159 H1
Zelovo (HR) 172 E2
Zelów (PL) 147 L3
Zeltingen-Rachtig (D) 70 D7
Zeltiņi (LV) 134 C3
Zeltweg (A) 89 M3
Želudivka (UA) 145 K6
Zèľva (BY) 143 M4
Želva (LT) 138 B3
Zelve (TR) 193 J3
Zelzate (B) 68 F4
Žemaičių Kalvarija (LT) 136 G1
Žemaičių Naumiestis (LT) 136 F3
Zemaitėliai (LT) 138 B4
Žemalė (LT) 132 E5
Žemberovce (SK) 154 D5
Zemblak (AL) 178 D3
Zemcy (RUS) 135 O5
Zeme (I) 98 F2
Zeměchy (CZ) 152 E3
Zemen (BG) 175 J4
Zemendorf (A) 158 B2
Zemenó (GR) 187 F3
Zemeș (RO) 162 C5
Zemianska Oľča (SK) 154 B6
Zemīte (LV) 132 F4
Zemitz (D) 47 N6
Zemlen (BG) 176 E4
Zemné (SK) 154 C6
Zempin (D) 140 A2
Zemplénagárd (H) 155 L5
Zemplínska Teplica (SK) 155 K4
Zemun (SRB) 167 F4
Zenda (BG) 176 D5
Zendek (PL) 147 L5
Zengen (TR) 193 H5
Zenica (BIH) 166 A5
Zeniowska (PL) 155 H3
Zen'kavičy (BY) 144 F2
Zenna (I) 87 G5
Zennor (GB) 56 C5
Zentene (LV) 132 F3
Zenyškivči (UA) 157 M3
Žepa (BIH) 166 D6
Žepče (BIH) 165 L6
Żerań Duży (PL) 142 E4
Žeravna (BG) 177 F3
Zerbst/Anhalt (D) 72 G2
Zerčanicy (BY) 139 H3
Žerdenivka (UA) 163 J1
Žerdja (UA) 150 C6
Zerebino (RUS) 134 F4
Žerebkove (UA) 163 K3
Žerebky (UA) 151 G4
Zerevci (UA) 150 G1
Zerf (D) 78 F2
Zeri (I) 100 B4
Zerind (RO) 160 D4
Zerk = Altınkaya (TR) 192 B6
Żerków (PL) 147 H1
Zerkowice (PL) 147 M4
Zermatt (CH) 86 E5
Zernez (CH) 87 K4
Zernien (D) 66 D4
Żerniki (PL) 141 J5
Żerniki (PL) 149 J5
Zernitz-Lohm (D) 67 G5
Zernograd (RUS) 13 N3
Zernsdorf (D) 67 K6
Zero Branco (I) 101 G1
Żerocin (PL) 149 G2
Zerpenschleuse (D) 67 K5
Zerqan (AL) 178 C1
Zerrenthin (D) 140 B4
Zestoa (E) 113 G2
Žetale (SLO) 164 F2
Zetea (RO) 161 L5
Zetel (D) 65 H5
Zetjovo (BG) 176 D4
Zeuchfeld (D) 72 F3
Zeulenroda-Triebes (D) 152 A2
Zeuthen (D) 67 K6
Žėvan' (BY) 139 N5
Ževeď (UA) 145 N6
Zeven (D) 65 L5
Zevenaar (NL) 69 L3
Zevenbergen (NL) 69 H3
Zeverovìči (RUS) 139 O4
Zevgolatió (GR) 179 J2
Zevgolatió (GR) 186 D5
Zevgolatió (GR) 188 A4
Zevio (I) 100 E2
Zeybekçayırı (TR) 181 L5
Zeyköy (TR) 184 B6
Zeyne (TR) 199 G3
Zeytinbağı (TR) 183 G5
Zeytindağ (TR) 189 K2
Zeytinler (TR) 190 A4
Zeytinli (TR) 190 B1
Zeytinlik (TR) 190 E4
Zeytinliova (TR) 190 D2
Zezulin (PL) 149 G3
Zgalevo (BG) 176 C2
Zgierz (PL) 147 L2
Žgilevo (RUS) 134 H3
Zglinna Duża (PL) 148 B2
Zgłobice (PL) 148 C6
Zgniłocha (PL) 142 D3
Zgnornje-Gorje (SLO) 164 C2
Zgornje Jezersko (SLO) 164 C2
Zgornji Duplek (SLO) 164 F1
Zgorzelec (PL) 73 N3
Zgozhd (AL) 178 C2
Zgurița (MD) 162 G2
Zhergë (RKS) 175 F4
Zhorany (UA) 149 J3
Zhubi (RKS) 174 D4
Zhukë (AL) 178 A3
Zhur (RKS) 174 E4
Ziamet (TR) 199 H5
Ziano di Fiemme (I) 88 F5
Žiar nad Hronom (SK) 154 D4
Zibalai (LT) 138 A3
Zibello (I) 100 C2
Zibolky (UA) 156 F1
Žibuliai (LT) 137 K3
Zicavo (F) 96 E5
Zicavu = Zicavo (F) 96 E5
Žiče (SLO) 164 E2
Zichow (D) 140 B4
Ziçisht (AL) 178 D3
Zickhusen (D) 66 E3
Zidani Most (SLO) 164 E2
Zidarovo (BG) 177 H4
Židikai (LT) 132 E5
Židilov Bor (RUS) 131 O5
Židlochovice (CZ) 153 L5
Židovicy (RUS) 135 H2
Ziduri (RO) 170 E3
Ziębice (PL) 153 M2
Zięby (PL) 136 C5
Ziegelroda (D) 71 M4
Ziegendorf (D) 66 F4
Ziegenhain (D) 71 H5
Ziegenrück (D) 72 F4
Zielenice (PL) 148 B5
Zieleniec (PL) 153 K3
Zieleniewo (PL) 140 E2
Zieleniewo (PL) 140 E4
Zielona (PL) 142 B4
Zielona (PL) 147 M4
Zielona Góra (PL) 146 D2
Zielonczyn (PL) 140 C3
Zielonka (PL) 142 E6
Zielonka (PL) 148 F5
Ziembin (BY) 139 H5
Ziemetshausen (D) 80 D4
Ziemupe (LV) 132 C4
Ziérbena (Abanto y Ziérbena) (E) 112 E2
Zierenberg (D) 71 H4
Zierikzee (NL) 68 F3
Ziersdorf (A) 91 J2
Zierzow (D) 66 F4
Ziesar (D) 67 G6
Ziesendorf (D) 47 K6
Ziethen (D) 47 N6
Zieuwent (NL) 69 M2
Žiežmariai (LT) 137 L4
Žigljan (HR) 164 D5
Zigós (GR) 180 E2
Zīguri (LV) 134 E3
Žihárec (SK) 158 E1
Žihle (CZ) 73 J5
Zijaçë (RKS) 174 E2
Zijemlje (BIH) 173 G3
Zilaiskalns (LV) 133 L2
Zīlāni (LV) 133 M4
Zīle (LV) 133 N2
Zile (TR) 13 L5
Žilenci (BG) 175 J4
Zili (RUS) 134 E4
Žilina (SK) 154 D3
Žilino (RUS) 131 P3
Žilino (RUS) 136 F4
Zillis-Reischen (CH) 87 H4
Zilly (D) 72 D2
Ziltendorf (D) 73 M1
Zilupe (LV) 134 F5
Zimadi (RUS) 134 G3
Zimandu-Nou (RO) 160 C5
Zimány (H) 165 K2
Zimbor (RO) 161 G3
Zimbru (RO) 160 E5
Zimbru (RO) 170 D5
Zimin (PL) 147 G1
Zimmernsupra (D) 72 D4
Zimna Brzeźnica (PL) 146 D2
Zimnica (BG) 177 G3
Zimnicea (RO) 176 D1
Zinal (CH) 86 E5
Zinasco Nuovo (I) 98 F2
Zincirlikuyu (TR) 13 K6
Zincirlikuyu (TR) 192 F3
Žindaičiai (LT) 137 H3
Zingsheim (D) 70 C5
Zingst (D) 67 H2
Zinkgruvan (S) 40 H5
Zin'kiv (UA) 150 E5
Zinna, Kloster (D) 73 J1
Zinnik = Soignies (B) 68 G5
Zinnowitz (D) 47 N5
Zinnwald-Georgenfeld (D) 73 K4
Zinswiller, Oberbronn- (F) 79 H4
Zinzenzell (D) 81 H2
Žiobiškis (LT) 138 B1
Zipári (GR) 196 B2
Ziras (LV) 132 D3
Zirc (H) 158 E3
Žirče (SRB) 174 D2
Zirchow (D) 140 B3
Žiri (SLO) 164 C2
Žirje (HR) 172 C2
Zirl (A) 88 E3
Zirndorf (D) 80 D2
Zîrnești (MD) 171 G1
Zirņi (LV) 132 E4
Zíros (GR) 195 J5
Žirovnica (MK) 174 E5
Žirovnica (SRB) 167 H5
Žirovnice (CZ) 153 H5
Zistersdorf (A) 91 L2
Žitara vas = Sittersdorf (A) 164 D1
Žitarovo (BG) 177 H3
Žitište (SRB) 167 G3
Žitkovac (SRB) 175 G1
Žitkovo (RUS) 37 M3
Žitnica (BG) 176 C4
Žitnica (BG) 177 J2
Žitni Potok (SRB) 175 G2
Žitomir = Žytomyr (UA) 151 H3
Žitorađa (SRB) 175 G2
Žitosvjat (BG) 177 G4
Zitsa (GR) 178 D5
Zittau (D) 153 G2
Žituša (BG) 175 J4
Živinice (BIH) 166 C5
Živkovci (SRB) 167 F5
Živkovo (BG) 175 L4
Živogošće (HR) 172 F3
Živojno (MK) 179 F3
Ziyamer (TR) 183 K3
Ziyaretli (TR) 190 E5
Zizers (CH) 87 J4
Žižica (RUS) 135 M5
Žižicy (RUS) 139 O3
Žizlino (RUS) 135 L2
Zjabki (BY) 139 H2
Zjabki (BY) 139 H3
Zjalënka (BY) 139 J2
Zjaleny Bor (BY) 139 H5
Zjalëny Moh (BY) 145 J5
Zjalëny Vostrav (BY) 139 J4
Zjal'ki (BY) 7 R7
Zjaľki (BY) 139 H2
Zjaťkivci (UA) 163 J1
Zjum = Zym (RKS) 174 E4
Złaków Borowy (PL) 148 A1
Zlarin (HR) 172 C2
Zlata (SRB) 175 G2
Zlatá Baňa (SK) 155 J4
Zlatá Koruna (CZ) 152 F6
Zlatar (BG) 177 G2
Zlatar (HR) 165 G2
Zlatar Bistrica (HR) 165 G2
Zlatari (SRB) 174 F2
Zlatarica (BG) 175 L5
Zlatarica (BG) 176 E2
Zlaté Hory (CZ) 147 G5
Zlaté Klasy (SK) 154 A5
Zlaté Moravce (SK) 154 C5
Zlatibor (SRB) 173 L2
Zlatica (BG) 176 B3
Zlatija (BG) 168 F6
Zlati Vojvoda (BG) 177 F3
Zlatna (RO) 168 E1
Zlatna Greda (HR) 166 C2
Zlatná na Ostrove (SK) 154 B6
Zlatna Niva (BG) 177 H2
Zlatna Panega (BG) 176 B2
Zlatni Pjasăci (BG) 177 K2
Zlatograd (BG) 176 D6
Zlatoklas (BG) 170 E6
Zlatokop (SRB) 175 G3
Zlatopole (BG) 176 E4
Zlatovo (SRB) 168 A5
Zlatuša (BG) 175 K3
Zławieś Wielka (PL) 141 K4
Zlazne (UA) 150 C2
Žlebič (SLO) 164 D3
Žleby (CZ) 146 C6
Zlēkas (LV) 132 D3
Zletovo (MK) 175 H5
Žlibinai (LT) 132 E6
Zliechov (SK) 154 C4
Zlín (CZ) 154 B3
Zliv (CZ) 152 F5
Žljebovi (BIH) 166 C6
Żłobek (PL) 155 M3
Žlobin (BY) 9 L3
Žlobin (BY) 145 M3
Zlobin (HR) 164 D4
Zlobyči (UA) 151 H2
Złochowice (PL) 147 K4
Złocieniec (PL) 140 F3
Złoczew (PL) 147 K3
Zlogoš (BG) 175 J4
Złojec (PL) 149 H4
Zlokućane = Zallkuq (RKS) 174 E3
Zlomnae (BY) 145 M3
Zlonice (CZ) 73 L5
Zlosela (BIH) 172 F2
Zlostup (MNE) 173 J4
Zlot (SRB) 167 J5
Złota (PL) 148 C5
Złotniki Lubańskie (PL) 153 H1
Złotoria (PL) 141 L5
Złotoryja (PL) 146 D3
Złotów (PL) 141 H4
Złotów (PL) 147 G3
Złoty Potok (PL) 147 L4
Złoty Stok (PL) 146 F5
Žlutice (CZ) 152 D3
Zmajevac (HR) 159 G6
Zmajevo (SRB) 166 E3
Žman (HR) 172 B2
Zmejovo (BG) 176 E4
Žmerynka (UA) 9 L5
Žmerynka (UA) 150 G5
Zmiennica (PL) 156 A2
Zmievka (RUS) 9 O3
Żmigród (PL) 146 F3
Zmijiv (UA) 9 O5
Žminj = Gimino (HR) 164 B4
Zminjak (SRB) 166 D4
Žmurnae (BY) 145 H5
Znamenka (BY) 138 G5
Znamenosec (BG) 176 E4
Znamensk (RUS) 142 E1
Znamenskoe (RUS) 9 O3
Znamenta (RUS) 131 O4
Znamjanka (UA) 163 L4
Znam'janka Druha (UA) 9 M5
Żnin (PL) 141 J5
Znojmo (CZ) 91 K2
Znosyči (UA) 150 D1
Zoagli (I) 99 G4
Zöbern (A) 91 K4
Zöblitz (D) 152 D2
Zocca (I) 99 K4
Žodino = Žodzina (BY) 139 H5
Žodiški (BY) 138 D4
Žodzina (BY) 139 H5
Zoersel (B) 69 H4
Zoetermeer (NL) 69 G2
Zofingen (CH) 86 E3
Zogaj (AL) 174 B4
Zogaj (AL) 174 D4
Zogno (I) 87 J6
Zograf (BG) 177 J1
Zohor (SK) 91 L3
Zoio (P) 110 F5
Zoița (RO) 170 E3
Zola Predosa (I) 99 L4
Żoliborz (PL) 142 D6
Żółkiewka (PL) 149 G4
Zölkow (D) 66 F3
Zollikofen (CH) 86 D4
Zollikon (CH) 87 G3
Zolling (D) 80 F4
Zoľnja (UA) 150 F1
Žolobky (UA) 157 J1
Žolobne (UA) 150 E3
Zoločiv (UA) 157 G2
Zolote (UA) 144 D5
Zolotievca (MD) 163 J5
Zolotkovyči (UA) 156 D2
Zolotnyky (UA) 150 A5
Zolotolyn (UA) 150 C1
Zolotonoša (UA) 9 M5
Zolotyj Potik (UA) 157 H4
Zolt (RO) 168 C2
Żółtnica (PL) 140 G3
Żołynia (PL) 156 B1
Zomba (H) 158 G5
Zonguldak (TR) 184 C3
Zonhoven (B) 69 J5
Zóni (GR) 177 F6
Zonianá (GR) 195 F5
Zons (D) 69 M4
Zonza (F) 96 E5
Zoppè di Cadore (I) 89 G5
Zora, Kvartal (BG) 176 E4
Żórawina (PL) 153 M2
Zörbig (D) 72 G2
Zorge (D) 71 L3
Zorita (E) 118 E5
Zorita de la Loma (E) 112 A4
Zorita del Maestrazgo = Sorita (E) 121 H2
Zorja (UA) 171 K2
Zorleni (RO) 162 F6
Zorlențu Mare (RO) 168 B3
Žornaŭka (BY) 139 J6
Zorneding (D) 88 F1
Zornica (BG) 177 G4
Zornica (BG) 177 J2
Zornotza = Amorebieta-Etxano (E) 113 F2
Žornyšče (UA) 151 J5
Zorokiv (UA) 151 H3
Żory (PL) 154 D1
Zoryčy (BY) 139 J5
Zosin (PL) 148 F2
Zosin (PL) 149 K4
Zosna (LV) 134 D5
Zossen (D) 73 J1
Zotes del Páramo (E) 111 H4
Zottegem (B) 68 F5
Zoutkamp (NL) 64 E5
Zoutleeuw (B) 69 J5
Zoúzouli (GR) 178 E4
Žovkva (UA) 156 E1
Žovkyni (UA) 144 D6
Žovnino (BY) 138 H2
Žovtancy (UA) 149 K6
Žovten' (UA) 13 J3
Zovten (UA) 157 G3
Žovtneve = Blahodatne (UA) 149 K4
Žovtneve = Kalynivka (UA) 150 E1
Žovtneve = Karakurt (UA) 171 H2
Žovtneve = Kvitneve (UA) 151 K4
Žovtneve = Myroljubiv (UA) 150 G1
Žovtyj Jar (UA) 171 K2
Zoziv (UA) 151 J5
Zozulinci (UA) 150 G4
Zozulynci (UA) 151 H4
Zrajky (UA) 151 K5
Zrenjanin (SRB) 167 F3
Zrmanja-Velo (HR) 172 D1
Zrnovci (MK) 175 H5
Žrnovnica (HR) 172 E2
Zruč nad Sázavou (CZ) 153 H4
Zrze (MK) 178 E1
Zrze = Xërxë (RKS) 174 E4
Zsadány (H) 160 C4
Zsámbék (H) 158 G2
Zsámbok (H) 159 J2
Zsana (H) 159 J5
Zschopau (D) 152 D2
Zschoppach (D) 73 H3
Zschornewitz (D) 73 G2
Zschortau (D) 73 G3
Zsórifürdő (H) 160 A2
Zsurk (H) 156 B5
Zuazo de Cuartango (E) 112 F3
Žub = Zhubi (RKS) 174 D4
Zubaki (BY) 139 N4
Zubarėvičy (BY) 145 J3
Zubava (BY) 139 M5
Zubcov (RUS) 7 T7
Zuberec (SK) 154 F3
Zubia (E) 126 C5
Zubialde (Zeberio) (E) 112 F2
Zubiaur (E) 112 F2
Zubiaur (Orozco) = Zubiaur (Orozko) (E) 112 F2
Zubiaur (Orozko) (E) 112 F2
Zubići (BIH) 173 G1
Zubieta (E) 113 H2
Zubin Potok (RKS) 174 E3
Zubiri (E) 92 A5
Zubkovyči (UA) 150 F1
Zubné (SK) 156 B3
Zubornička = Kleinsaubernitz (D) 146 B3
Zubowice (PL) 149 J4
Zubrec' (UA) 157 H4
Žubrovyči (UA) 150 F1
Zubry (BY) 139 N5
Zubrynka (UA) 151 G2
Zubrzyca Górna (PL) 154 F2
Zubrzyce (PL) 154 B1
Žuč (SRB) 174 F2
Zucaina (E) 121 H3
Zuchau (D) 72 F2
Zuchwil (CH) 86 E3
Zudaire (E) 113 G3
Zudar (D) 67 J2
Zudiviarte (E) 112 E2
Zuera (E) 114 B4
Zufía (E) 113 G3
Zufre (E) 128 B2
Zug (CH) 87 G3
Zuglio (I) 90 D7
Zuheros (E) 126 B4
Zui (RUS) 135 N3
Zuid-Beijerland (NL) 69 G3
Zuidhorn (NL) 64 E5
Zuidlaren (NL) 64 F5
Zuidwolde (NL) 64 E6
Zújar (E) 126 E4
Žukiv (UA) 150 D3
Žukiv (UA) 157 H4
Žukotky (UA) 145 O5
Žukovka (RUS) 9 N3
Žukovo (RUS) 135 N4
Żuków (PL) 146 E2
Żuków (PL) 149 H2
Żukowice (PL) 155 J1
Żukowo (PL) 141 K2
Žukyn (UA) 151 M2
Žuleva (BY) 135 H6
Żulin (PL) 149 H3
Žulin (UA) 156 E3
Žuljana (HR) 173 F4
Žulová (CZ) 153 M3
Zülpich (D) 69 M5
Zumaia (E) 113 G2
Zumárraga (E) 113 G2
Zumiè (I) 88 D6
Zümrütköy (TR) 198 F5
Zundert (NL) 69 H4
Zungoli (I) 104 D3
Zungri (I) 106 E5
Žunjeviće (SRB) 174 D2
Zunzarren (E) 92 B5
Zuoz (CH) 87 J4
Župa (HR) 172 F3
Županja (HR) 166 C3
Županjac (SRB) 166 F5
Županjevac (SRB) 174 F1
Zupče (RKS) 174 E3
Zupčići (BIH) 174 A1
Župrany (BY) 138 D5
Žur = Zhur (RKS) 174 E4
Žuravlivka (UA) 150 F5
Žuravlivka (UA) 163 H1
Žuravlycha (UA) 151 L5
Žuravno (UA) 156 F3
Žuravnyky (UA) 149 L5
Žuravok (BY) 139 K6
Žuravyči (UA) 150 B2
Żuraw (PL) 147 L4
Żurawica (PL) 156 C2
Zurgena (E) 127 F5
Zürich (CH) 87 G3
Zurich (NL) 64 C5
Zuriza (E) 92 C5
Zurndorf (A) 91 M4
Żuromin (PL) 141 N4
Żurominek (PL) 142 C4
Žuroŭka (BY) 139 K6
Zurow (D) 66 F3
Żurrieq (M) 109 F6
Zürs (A) 87 K3
Žurževyči (UA) 144 G6
Žurzynci (UA) 151 M5
Zusamzell (D) 80 D4
Züschen (D) 70 G4
Züschen (D) 71 H4
Zusmarshausen (D) 80 D4
Züsow (D) 47 J6
Züssow (D) 47 N6
Žuta Lokva (HR) 164 E5
Zutendaal (B) 69 K5
Zutphen (NL) 70 B2
Žužeľ (UA) 150 F2
Zuzela (PL) 142 G5
Žužemberk (SLO) 164 D3
Zuzwil (CH) 79 L7
Žvan (MK) 178 E2
Žvan (UA) 162 E1
Zvănari (BG) 170 C6
Zvănarka (BG) 176 E6
Žvanec (BY) 145 M2
Žvanec' (UA) 162 C1
Zvăničevo (BG) 176 B4
Zvečan (RKS) 174 E3
Zveçan = Zvečan (RKS) 174 E3
Zvečka (SRB) 166 F4
Zvegor (MK) 175 J5
Zvejniekciems (LV) 133 J3
Zvenimir (BG) 170 D6
Zvenyhorodka (UA) 9 M5
Zvenyhorodka (UA) 151 M5
Zverino (BG) 175 L2
Zvezda (BG) 177 F2
Zvezdec (BG) 182 D1
Zvezdel (BG) 176 E6
Zvezdivka (UA) 150 C2
Zvíkovské Podhradí (CZ) 81 L2
Zvinkove (UA) 156 B5
Žvirče (SLO) 164 D3
Zvirgzde (LV) 133 J4
Zvirinë (AL) 178 D3
Zvole (CZ) 153 K5
Zvolen (SK) 154 E4
Zvoleněves (CZ) 73 L5
Zvolenská Slatina (SK) 154 E4
Zvonce (SRB) 175 J3
Zvony (RUS) 134 G4
Zvoriștea (RO) 157 K6
Zvornik (BIH) 166 D5
Zvynjač (UA) 157 J3
Zvynjače (UA) 149 L4
Žvyrka (UA) 149 K5
Zwaagwesteinde = De Westerein (NL) 64 E5
Zwanenburg (NL) 69 H2
Zwardoń (PL) 154 D2
Zwaring, Dobl- (A) 91 H6
Zwartsluis (NL) 64 E6
Zweeloo (NL) 64 F6
Zweibrücken (D) 79 G3
Zweifall (D) 69 L5
Zweisimmen (CH) 86 D4
Zwenkau (D) 73 G3
Zwentendorf an der Donau (A) 91 J3
Zwethau, Großtreben- (D) 73 J2
Zwettl (A) 91 H2
Zwettl an der Rodl (A) 81 L4
Zwevezele (B) 68 E4
Zwiartów (PL) 149 J4
Zwickau (D) 73 G4
Zwiefalten (D) 79 L5
Zwierzno (PL) 142 A2
Zwierzyn (PL) 140 E5
Zwierzyniec (PL) 149 G4
Zwiesel (D) 81 J2
Zwieselstein (A) 87 M4
Zwijndrecht (B) 69 G4
Zwillbrock (D) 69 M2
Zwinge (D) 72 C2
Zwingenberg (D) 79 K2
Zwingendorf (A) 153 K6
Zwischenwasser = Longega (I) 88 F4
Zwochau (D) 73 G3
Zwoleń (PL) 148 E3
Zwolle (NL) 69 L1
Zwönitz (D) 152 C2
Żychlin (PL) 147 M1
Życiny (PL) 148 D4
Žyc'kava (BY) 139 J5
Žydačiv (UA) 156 F3
Żydowo (PL) 140 G2
Žydyčyn (UA) 150 A2
Žygaičiai (LT) 136 G3
Zygi (CY) 199 F6
Żygląd (PL) 141 L4
Žyguli (BY) 138 G2
Žylin-Brod (BY) 144 G2
Žylow = Sielow (D) 146 A2
Zym (RKS) 174 E4
Zymne (UA) 149 K4
Żyraków (PL) 155 J1
Żyrardów (PL) 148 B1
Žyrovicy (BY) 144 B2
Žyryči (UA) 149 K2
Żyrzyn (PL) 148 F3
Žytkavičy (BY) 9 L4
Žytkavičy (BY) 144 G4
Żytkiejmy (PL) 143 H2
Žytlin (BY) 144 B3
Żytniów (PL) 147 K3
Żytno (PL) 147 M4
Žytnyky (UA) 151 L5
Žytomlja (BY) 143 L3
Žytomyr (UA) 9 L4
Žytomyr (UA) 151 H3
Žyvačiv (UA) 157 H4
Żywiec (PL) 154 E2
Żywocice (PL) 147 H5